The Norton Anthology
of American Literature

SIXTH EDITION

VOLUME A

Literature to 1820

VOLUME A

Literature to 1700 • FRANKLIN
American Literature 1700–1820 • GURA • MURPHY
Native American Literatures • KRUPAT

VOLUME B

American Literature 1820–1865 • PARKER • KRUPAT

VOLUME C

American Literature 1865–1914 • GOTTESMAN • KRUPAT

VOLUME D

American Literature between the Wars, 1914–1945
BAYM • HOLLAND

VOLUME E

American Prose since 1945 • KLINKOWITZ • PRITCHARD
American Poetry since 1945 • WALLACE • KALSTONE

Wayne Franklin
NORTHEASTERN UNIVERSITY

Ronald Gottesman
UNIVERSITY OF SOUTHERN CALIFORNIA

Philip F. Gura
UNIVERSITY OF NORTH CAROLINA, CHAPEL HILL

Laurence B. Holland
LATE OF THE JOHNS HOPKINS UNIVERSITY

David Kalstone
LATE OF RUTGERS, THE STATE UNIVERSITY OF NEW JERSEY

Jerome Klinkowitz
UNIVERSITY OF NORTHERN IOWA

Arnold Krupat
SARAH LAWRENCE COLLEGE

Francis Murphy
EMERITUS, SMITH COLLEGE

Hershel Parker
EMERITUS, UNIVERSITY OF DELAWARE

William H. Pritchard
EMERITUS, AMHERST COLLEGE

Patricia B. Wallace
VASSAR COLLEGE

The Norton Anthology
of American Literature

SIXTH EDITION

Nina Baym, *General Editor*

SWANLUND CHAIR AND CENTER FOR
ADVANCED STUDY PROFESSOR OF ENGLISH
JUBILEE PROFESSOR OF LIBERAL ARTS AND SCIENCES
UNIVERSITY OF ILLINOIS AT URBANA-CHAMPAIGN

VOLUME A

Literature to 1820

W • W • NORTON & COMPANY • *New York* • *London*

Editor: Julia Reidhead
Developmental Editor: Marian Johnson
Manuscript Editors: Candace Levy, Anne Hellman, Carol Flechner
Assistant Editor: Brian Baker
Production Manager: Diane O'Connor
Permissions Manager: Nancy Rodwan
Permissions Clearing: Margaret Gorenstein
Text Design: Antonina Krass
Art Research: Neil Ryder Hoos

The text of this book is composed in Fairfield Medium
with the display set in Bernhard Modern.
Composition by Binghamton Valley Composition.
Manufacturing by R. R. Donnelley & Sons.

ISBN 0-393-97898-2 (pbk.)

W. W. Norton & Company, Inc., 500 Fifth Avenue, New York, NY 10110
www.wwnorton.com

W. W. Norton & Company Ltd., Castle House, 75/76 Wells Street, London W1T 3QT

0

Contents

American Literature 1700–1820   425

Preface to the Sixth Edition

In this first edition of *The Norton Anthology of American Literature* to appear in the twenty-first century, we respond to numerous requests for a more flexible, more portable format by introducing five individual volumes in two slipcased packages corresponding to the former Volumes 1 and 2. This new format accommodates the many instructors who use the anthology in a two-semester survey, but also opens up possibilities for mixing and matching the five volumes for a variety of courses organized by period or topic.

As with earlier editions, the editors have worked closely with teachers who assign the book and, through these teachers, with the students who use it. From the anthology's inception, three goals have been paramount: first, to present a variety of works rich and substantial enough to enable teachers to build their own courses according to their own ideals (thus, teachers are offered more authors and more selections than they will probably choose to teach); second, to make the anthology self-sufficient by featuring many works in their entirety and longer selections so that individual authors can be covered in depth; and third, to balance traditional interests with developing critical concerns. This commitment to balance has been evident from the first edition of 1979, where, in response to teachers who found that the traditional canon was insufficiently representative of American literary history, we included Anne Bradstreet, Mary Rowlandson, Sarah Kemble Knight, Phillis Wheatley, Margaret Fuller, Harriet Beecher Stowe, Frederick Douglass, Sarah Orne Jewett, Kate Chopin, Mary E. Wilkins Freeman, Booker T. Washington, Charles Chesnutt, Edith Wharton, W. E. B. Du Bois, and many others. Yet we did not shortchange writers like Franklin, Emerson, Thoreau, Hawthorne, Poe, Melville, Hemingway, Fitzgerald, or Faulkner, whom teachers then and now would not think of doing without.

That the "untraditional" authors listed above have now become part of the American literary canon shows that canons are not fixed, but emerge and change. At the same time, teachers over the last thirty years have seen a striking expansion in the extent and diversity of the authors they are expected and want to teach. In endeavoring to ensure that our inclusions—extensive as they are—do not outrun what might conceivably be of use in the classroom, we have always revised our selections in response to detailed suggestions from many teachers. For this Sixth Edition, we have drawn on the careful commentary of 111 reviewers. We are delighted with the new materials we bring to this Sixth Edition, which take several forms:

Volume A
Under the new rubric *Literature to 1700*, for the opening section, we incorporate Native American and explorer materials with settler literature up

through the Salem witchcraft episode. This configuration corresponds to the new emphasis in early American literary studies on the Atlantic Rim, on the multiethnicity of the early colonies, and on the position of Puritan New England as a key but not the only determinant in early American writing. The multilingual, multiethnic colonies are stressed in the expanded period introduction and in the travel writings and biographical narratives of newly included authors Garcilaso de la Vega, Jacob Steendam, Adriaen Van der Donck, and Francis Pastorious. The much-assigned cluster of Native American trickster tales has been expanded with a tale from the Sioux tradition. Also included are additional writings by Samuel de Champlain and Samuel Sewall and Cotton Mather's sensationalist accounts of criminal trials from *Pillars of Salt*.

American Literature 1700–1820 In this section, newly edited by Philip F. Gura, University of North Carolina at Chapel Hill, we distinguish the eighteenth century as a period of consolidation and development in an emergent American literature. Newly included to better convey the range of genres and writers that found readers in early America are voices, free and slave, from the Atlantic Rim: the plantation owner James Grainger and the slaves Briton Hammon and the anonymous author of "The Speech of Moses Bon Sàam." Also new are the poet Annis Boudinot Stockton, the novelist Charles Brockden Brown, and the playwright Royall Tyler, represented by his comedy *The Contrast*.

Volume B

American Literature 1820–1865 broadens our geographical scope by introducing two new California writers, Louise Amelia Smith Clappe and Bayard Taylor. Clappe's "Dame Shirley" letters, among the earliest classics for students of western American literature, constitute a vivid report from the gold mines. Taylor, the era's best-known and most prolific travel writer, depicts in our selection the early days of San Francisco. The esteemed poet Emma Lazarus is newly included with poems, most famously "The New Colossus," that gave a highly cultured voice to Jewish American identity. New selections by Poe, Stowe, and Douglass—three chapters of whose later autobiography, *My Bondage and My Freedom*, have been added—deepen the representation of these central figures.

Volume C

As a convenience to some instructors, Volume C: *American Literature 1865–1914* opens with the selections by Walt Whitman and Emily Dickinson that are included in Volume B. Sarah Morgan Bryan Piatt, increasingly recognized as a major woman poet in the era, is newly represented, as are fiction writers Constance Fenimore Woolson, Abraham Cahan, and Sui Sin Far. These three writers extend this period's regional and ethnic representation, while demonstrating anew the capacious possibilities of American realism.

Volume D

American Literature between the Wars, 1914–1945, now includes two important longer works of fiction by American women—Nella Larsen's *Quicksand*, a tragedy of African American identity, and Katherine Anne Porter's beautifully written novella of romance in a time of war, *Pale Horse, Pale Rider*, both presented here in their entirety—as well as chapters from John Steinbeck's *The Grapes of Wrath*. Short fiction, too, is strengthened with two stories by Willa Cather, "The Sculptor's Funeral" and "Neighbour Rosicky"; the addition of a second story by F. Scott Fitzgerald, the 1922 *Metropolitan Magazine* version of "Winter Dreams"; and two new fiction writers, the Native American writer D'arcy McNickle and the Filipino American Carlos Bulosan. *Trifles*, Susan Glaspell's teachable short play, is newly included.

Volume E

American Prose since 1945 strengthens the anthology's offerings by Latino and Latina writers with the addition of Rudolfo A. Anaya's short story "The Christmas Play," selections from Gloria Anzaldúa's influential work of theory, *Borderlands/La Frontera*, and short fiction by Judith Ortiz Cofer. Strengthening the anthology's rich offerings in modern American drama is Pulitzer Prize-winner Suzan-Lori Parks's *The America Play*. Ralph Ellison's searing story "Cadillac Flambé," excised from the posthumously published *Juneteenth*, Donald Barthelme's "The Balloon," and a dazzling, poignant set piece from Richard Powers's *Galatea 2.2* enrich the representation of recent fiction.

American Poetry since 1945 newly anthologizes work by five important poets: United States Poet Laureate Billy Collins, Stanley Kunitz, Charles Wright, Charles Simic, and Jorie Graham. Frank O'Hara's poems have been reselected, and recent work by Robert Creeley, Galway Kinnell, W. S. Merwin, and Rita Dove is newly anthologized.

The student Web site to accompany the anthology (www.wwnorton.com/naal), by Bruce Michelson, offers timelines, outlines of the period introductions, over 400 annotated links, author resource pages for 160 writers in the anthology, searchable "Explorations" that provide questions and research projects, and, a new feature, self-grading quizzes. *Teaching with* The Norton Anthology of American Literature: *A Guide for Instructors*, by Bruce Michelson and Marjorie Pryse, is a lively, practical resource for questions to motivate close reading and discussion, as well as concise teaching notes for individual periods, authors, and works; model exam questions and essay topics; and reading lists for a wide variety of courses using the anthology.

As in past editions, editorial features—period introductions, headnotes, and annotation—are designed to be concise yet full and to give students the information needed without imposing an interpretation. In the Sixth Edition, much of this editorial material has been revised in response to new scholarship. Several period introductions have been entirely or substantially rewritten, and a number of headnotes have been tightened or rewritten to be more useful to students. The Selected Bibliographies have been thoroughly updated. The Sixth Edition retains two editorial features that help students place their reading in historical and cultural context—a Texts/Contexts timeline following each period introduction and a map on the front endpaper of each volume—and adds to these a third feature to help students consider the relationships among writers within a given period: a chronological chart, located on the back endpaper, showing the lifespans of many of the writers anthologized.

Our policy has been to reprint each text in the form that accords, as far as it is possible to determine, to the intention of its author. There is one exception: we have modernized most spellings and (very sparingly) the punctuation in the sections *Literature to 1700* and *American Literature 1700–1820* on the principle that archaic spellings and typography pose unnecessary problems for beginning students. We have used square brackets to indicate titles supplied by the editors for the convenience of students. Whenever a portion of a text has been omitted, we have indicated that omission with three asterisks.

The editors of this anthology were selected on the basis of their expertness in their individual area. We note with pleasure the addition to the editorial team of Philip F. Gura, William S. Newman Distinguished Professor of American Literature and Culture and Adjunct Professor of Religious Studies at the University of North Carolina at Chapel Hill. He succeeds Francis Murphy as period editor of *American Literature 1700–1820*. Each editor was given ultimate responsibility for his or her period, but all collaborated in the final enterprise. Arnold Krupat edited Native American Literatures in Volumes A and B and the oratory, songs, and chants, Eastman, Oskison, and Black Elk selections in Volumes C and D. Ronald Gottesman prepared the texts and introductions for Abraham Lincoln and Frederick Douglass; and Nina Baym prepared the texts and introductions for Harriet Beecher Stowe and Harriet Jacobs.

We take this opportunity to thank the hundreds of teachers throughout the country who have answered our questions. Those teachers who prepared detailed critiques, or who offered special help in preparing texts, are listed under Acknowledgments, on a separate page. The editors would like to express appreciation for their assistance to Kenneth L. Baughman, Brad Campbell, Samuel L. Gladden, Vince Gotera, Tim Gustafson, Katrina Huffman, Julie Huffman-Klinkowitz, Julie Husband, Judith Kicinski, Daniel Lane, Maurice Lee, David Wei Li, Brenda Lin, Allison McCabe, Anne Myles, James O'Loughlin, Steven Olsen-Smith, Julian Rice, Todd Richardson, Heddy Richter, Monica Rodriguez, Jacob Schoenly, Beth Shube, Alan Shucard, Jesse Swan, John Swope, Karen Tracey, Catherine Waitinas, Jennie Wang, Rachel Watson, and Thomas Wolfe. We also thank the many people at Norton who contributed to the Sixth Edition: Julia Reidhead, who supervised the Sixth Edition; Marian Johnson, development editor; Candace Levy, Anne Hellman, and Carol Flechner, manuscript editors; Brian Baker, who prepared timelines and maps; Eileen Connell, Web site editor; Diane O'Connor, production manager; Toni Krass, designer; Neil Ryder Hoos, art researcher; Nancy Rodwan, permissions manager; and Margaret Gorenstein, who cleared permissions. We also wish to acknowledge our debt to the late George P. Brockway, former president and chairman at Norton, who invented this anthology, and to M. H. Abrams, Norton's advisor on English texts. All have helped us to create an anthology that, more than ever, is testimony to the continuing richness of American literary traditions.

Nina Baym

Acknowledgments

Michel Aaij (University of Alabama), Alan Ainsworth (Houston Community College), David Allen (University College of the Fraser Valley), Robert Allen Alexander Jr. (Nicholls State University), Scott Andrews (California State University, Northridge), Scott Ash (Nassau Community College), Diana Badur (Black Hawk College), Donald Bahr (Arizona State University), Ellen Barker (Georgia Perimeter College), Don Barkin (Yale University), Jonathan N. Barron (University of Southern Mississippi), Craig Bartholomus (Penn Valley College), Laura Behling (Gustavus Adolphus College), Alfred Bendixen (California State University), Denny Berthiaume (Foothill College), Philip Biedler (University of Alabama), Stanley S. Blair (Monmouth University), Nancy J. Brown (Lourdes College), William F. Browne (Brooklyn College), Lisa D. Chavez (Albion College), Colin Clarke (George Washington University), Sheila Coghill (Minnesota State University, Moorhead), Marc Conner (Washington and Lee University), Nancy Cook (University of Rhode Island), John Cosenza (St. John's University), Elana Crane (Miami University), Robert Croft (Gainesville College), Dianne M. Daily (Northern Virginia Community College), Robin G. Daniel (Broward Community College), Michel de Benedictis (Miami-Dade Community College), William J. De-Saegher (Point Loma Nazarene University), L. C. DiCicco (University of London), Brian Diemert (Brescia College), Mary Lynn Dodson (Amarillo College), Sam Dodson (Tarleton State University), Paul Downes (University of Toronto), Gregory Eiselein (Kansas State University), Julie Ellison (University of Michigan), Sharon Felton (Belmont University), Paul Ferlazzo (Northern Arizona University), Marie Foley (Santa Barbara City College), Dean Flower (Smith College), Brian Folker (Central Connecticut State University), Lee Foreman (Edison College), Robert Forman, Andrew Furman (Florida Atlantic University), Ronald Gervais (San Diego State University), Leonard S. Goldberg (Gettysburg College), Henry Golemba (Wayne State University), Lisa Gordis (Barnard College), Richard Grande (Pennsylvania State University), Timothy Gray (College of Staten Island, CUNY), James Green (Arizona State University), Loren C. Gruber (Missouri Valley College), Peter L. Hays (University of California, Davis), Roy Hill (Westark College), Carl S. Horner (Flagler College), Ronald Hurlburt (St. Johns River Community College), Mark Johnson (Missouri State University), AnaLouise Keating (Aquinas College), J. Gerald Kennedy (Louisiana State University), Elizabeth Rodriguez Kessler (California State University at Northridge), David Ketterer (Concordia University), Elizabeth Lamont (Lincoln Memorial University), Philip J. Landon (University of Maryland, Baltimore County), Genevieve Later (University College of the Cariboo), Bruce Levy (Southern Methodist University), Margrit D. Loomis (University of Louisiana at Monroe), Ginny Brown Machann (Blinn College), Veronica Makowsky (University of Connecticut), Saundra Rose Maley (George Washington University), Joseph Malof (University of Texas, Austin), Jean Carwile Masteller (Whitman College), Richard N. Masteller (Whitman College), Philip Mayfield (Fullerton College), David McDowell (Anne Arundel Community College), Ken McLean (Bishop's University), Philip Milner (St. Francis Xavier University, Antigonish, Nova Scotia), Madonne Minter (Texas Tech University), Margaret P. Murray (Western Connecticut State University), Jacqueline O'Connor (University of St. Thomas), James Obertino (Central Missouri State University), Jean Pfaelzer (University of Delaware), Bruce H. Price (McLean Hospital), Larus Reed (Virginia State University), Charles James Reuse (Minnesota State University Moorhead), Eliza Richards (Boston University), Susan Rieke (Saint Mary College), Becky Roberts, Jane Rose (Purdue University), Sherry L. Rosenthal (Community College of South Nevada), Richard E. Rosol (Central Connecticut State University), Michael Runyan (Saddleback College), David Rota (University of Missouri, St. Louis), Jack Ryan (Gettysburg College), Mary Segall (Quinnipiac College), Robert Seltzer (Nova University), Dorothy U. Seyler (Northern Virginia Community College, Annandale), David Shawn (Endicott College), David Shields (The Citadel), Conrad Sienkiewicz, Father Joseph Stefanelli, S.J., Jeffrey Steele (University of Wisconsin, Madison), Gary Storhoff (University of Connecticut, Stamford), Kathleen Thornton (University of Albany), Trysh Travis (Southern Methodist University), John Trimble (University of Texas, Austin), Michael Trussler (University of Regina), Mary Katherine Wainwright (Manatee Community College), Michael Warner (Rutgers University), John Wenke (Salisbury State University), Jill Knight Weinberger (Central Connecticut State University), Susan P. Willens (George Washington University), Ann Winters (Westark College), James N. Wise (University of Missouri, Rolla), Lisa Wittmeyer (Park University), Margaret J. Yonce (Augusta State University).

The Norton Anthology
of American Literature

SIXTH EDITION

VOLUME A

Literature to 1820

Literature to 1700

THE MARVELS OF SPAIN—AND AMERICA

In 1494 a man who had crossed the Atlantic in a large ship returned home to amaze those whom he had left behind with tales of a new world full of "marvels." None of those who listened to him had accomplished anything remotely like this. None had heard of this other world, let alone seen it, and none could begin to comprehend what its discovery might mean for their own familiar universe. As they listened with rapt attention, the voyager told of things undreamed of, plants and animals and most of all strange peoples whose uncanny customs, costumes, and beliefs astonished all who heard him.

The man in question might have been Christopher Columbus or any of the dozens of Europeans who accompanied him on his first voyage, but he was not. In fact, this teller of tales did join in that voyage, but had not sailed from Palos, Spain, with the other men on August 6, 1492, and had not been with them when, at two in the morning of October 12, they sighted the Bahamian island they named San Salvador. Twice he crossed the Atlantic with Columbus, but in reverse: first to Spain from the Indies and then back again. We do not know his original name, but we know that he was a Taino Indian from the Bahamas, one of seven natives whom Columbus seized and took to Spain. There he was baptized and renamed Diego Colón, after the son of Columbus himself. (Colón was the Spanish version of the family's name.) Of the other natives, all of whom were similarly rechristened, one remained in Spain, where he died within a few years. Four others died of sickness on the passage back to America with Columbus and Colón. Colón and the sixth man escaped the same fate only "by a hair's breadth," as the fleet's physician, Diego Alvarez Chanca, wrote in his important letter on the second voyage. Returned to the Caribbean, the two served as translators for the much larger party of Spaniards, perhaps fifteen hundred strong, who arrived in seventeen ships early in November 1493. Colón himself already had seen service as an intermediary during the first voyage.

Of the two men, only Colón is reported by the historian Andrés Bernáldez, who knew Columbus and used the mariner's own lost account of the second voyage, to have regaled the other natives with tales of "the things which he had seen in Castile and the marvels of Spain, . . . the great cities and fortresses and churches, . . . the people and horses and animals, . . . the great nobility and wealth of the sovereigns and great lords, . . . the kinds of food, . . . the festivals and tournaments [and] bull-fighting." Perhaps the other man had died by this point in the second voyage. Perhaps Columbus singled out Colón for special mention because Colón had learned Castilian well enough to speak it and had shown himself to be an intelligent man and a good guide. He was to accompany Columbus on the whole of this voyage, which lasted three years.

The story of Colón catches in miniature the extraordinary changes that were to occur as natives of the Old World encountered natives of the New for the first time in recorded history. His story reminds us first that discovery was mutual rather than one sided. To be sure, far more Europeans voyaged to America than Americans to Europe, and they sent home thousands of reports and letters detailing what they saw and did in the New World. Because many of these European travelers came to America to stay, however, the Indians soon had a colonial imitation of Europe developing before their eyes, complete with fortresses, churches, horses, new foods (on the second voyage, Columbus brought wheat, melons, onions, radishes, salad greens, grapevines, sugar cane, and various fruit trees), and much else that Colón in 1493 could have found only in Europe. Over time the natives of America could discover Europe encroaching on their villages and fields as the imported European landscape vied with their own. Europe was present in the textiles on the colonists' bodies, in the tools in their hands (for both of which the American Indians traded), and in the institutions of the church and state (slavery being the most obvious example) that had begun to reshape the identities and reorganize the lives of Native American peoples. In such concrete terms a new world was being created in the West Indies. It was not the new world Columbus himself was speaking of near the end of his life when he wrote in 1500 to the Spanish sovereigns Ferdinand and Isabella that he had "brought under [their] dominion . . . another world, whereby Spain, which was called poor, is now most rich." The new world that mattered was not just an expanse of space previously unknown to Europeans; it was a genuinely new set of social relationships that would evolve over the next centuries as Europe and the Americas continued to interact. With the European introduction of African slaves early in the sixteenth century, the terms of this new world became much more complex. The cultural and social relations of Americans took their origin in a great mixing of peoples from the whole Atlantic basin during the first century and a half after 1492.

Discovery began with wonder—that of Colón's listeners on his return in 1494 and that of Columbus as he descanted on the green beauty of the islands—evoking a mood that has remained strong in American writing ever since: he saw "trees of a thousand kinds" on San Salvador in November 1492, trees that seemed to "touch the sky . . . as green and as lovely as they are in Spain in May." But beyond that transcendent moment, discovery entailed a many-sided process of influence and exchange that ultimately produced the hybrid cultural universe of the Atlantic world, of which the English colonies were one small part. Much of this universe came through struggle rather than cooperation. Each people used its own traditions or elements recently borrowed from others to endure or conquer or outwit its opposite numbers, and violence often swallowed up the primal wonder glimpsed in the earliest documents. With gunpowder and steel, Europeans had the technological edge in warfare, and it would seem that—despite centuries of propaganda to the contrary—they took violence more seriously than did the American Indians. The natives at first found the scale of European warfare appalling. In New England, the colonists' native allies against the Pequot tribe in 1637 complained that the English manner of fighting, as soldier John Underhill noted in his *Newes from America* (1638), "[was] too furious, and slay[ed] too many men." The natives were quick to adopt European weapons and tactics, however, applying them to their own disputes and to their disputes with the Europeans. The ferocity of what Europeans have called the "Indian wars" was the violent recoil in the face of violence from interlopers who threatened the very life of the native peoples.

Almost literally from 1492, native peoples began to die in large numbers, if not from war then from enslavement, brutal mistreatment, despair, or disease. One of the more insidious forms of "exchange" involved the transfer to the American Indians of the microbes to which Europeans had become inured but to which the Indians had virtually no resistance. Nothing better displays the isolation of the continents and the drama of encounter that began in 1492 than the epidemic disasters that smallpox, measles, typhus, and other Old World maladies unleashed on the Native Americans. Whole populations plummeted as such diseases, combined with the other severe stresses placed on the natives, spread throughout the Caribbean and then on the mainland of Central and South America. The institutional disease of slavery further decimated the native peoples. It is widely agreed that the original population of the island of Hispaniola (estimated at anywhere from one hundred thousand to eight million in 1492) plunged once the Spanish took over the island, partly through disease and partly through the abuses of the *encomienda* system of virtual enslavement. In the face of this sudden decline in available native labor, Spain introduced African slavery into Hispaniola as early as 1501. By the middle of the sixteenth century the native population had been so completely displaced by African slaves that the Spanish historian Antonio de Herrera called the island "an effigy or an image of Ethiopia itself." Thus the destruction of one people was accompanied by the displacement and enslavement of another. By that point, the naive "wonder" of discovery was all but unrecoverable.

It would be inaccurate to picture the Indians, however, as merely victims, suffering decline. The natives made shrewd use of the European presence in America to forward their own aims, as Colón reminds us. In 1519 the disaffected natives in the Aztec Empire clearly threw their lot in with Cortés because they saw in him a chance to settle the score with their overlord Montezuma, which they assuredly did. In New England, the Pequot War of 1637 saw a similar alignment on the English side of tribes such as the Narragansetts and the Mohegans, who had grievances with the fierce Pequots, interlopers in the region. Under ordinary circumstances, as among the Iroquois in the Northeast, European technology and the European market were seized on as a means of consolidating advantages gained before the arrival of the colonists. The Iroquois had begun to organize their famous League of the Five Nations before European settlement, but they solidified their earlier victories over other native peoples by forging canny alliances with the Dutch and then the English in New York. In the Southeast, remnant peoples banded together in the early eighteenth century to create the Catawba, a new political group that constructed what one historian has called a "new world" for itself. No longer known by a bewildering diversity of names, the former Nassaw and Suttirie and Charra and Succa peoples banded together with several others in an attempt to deal more effectively with the encroaching Euro-Americans of Charleston and the Low Country. This hardly was a case of diminishment or reduction. Even as fewer and fewer of the original millions remained, they showed themselves resourceful in resisting, transforming, and exploiting the exotic cultures the Europeans were imposing on their original landscape.

NATIVE AMERICAN ORAL LITERATURE

When Columbus sailed from Europe in 1492, he left behind him a number of relatively centralized nation-states with largely agricultural economies. Europeans spoke some two or three dozen languages, most of them closely related; and they were generally Christian in religious belief and worldview, although many groups had had contact—and conflict—with adherents of Judaism and Islam. A written alphabet had been used by Europeans to preserve and communicate information for many centuries and Gutenberg's invention of moveable type in the mid-1400s had shown the way to a mechanical means of "writing"; by 1492, Europe was on its way to becoming a print culture.

By contrast, in 1492 in North America, native people spoke hundreds of languages, belonging to entirely different linguistic families (e.g., Athapascan, Uto-Aztecan, Chinookan, Siouan, and Algonquian) and structured their cultures in extraordinarily diverse economic and political forms. In the Great Basin of the West, small, loosely organized bands of Utes eked out a bare subsistence by hunting and gathering, while the sedentary Pueblo peoples of the Southwest and the Iroquoians of the Northeast had both highly developed agricultural economies and complex modes of political organization. In spite of some common features, religious and mythological beliefs were also diverse. Among North American peoples alone, eight different types of creation stories have been documented, with wide variations among them. All of these differ substantially from the creation stories of Judaism, Christianity, and Islam.

Also unlike European cultures, North American peoples did not use a written alphabet. Theirs were oral cultures, relying on the spoken word—whether chanted, sung, or presented in lengthy narratives—and the memory of those words to preserve important cultural information. The term *literature* comes from the Latin *littera,* "letter." Native American literatures were not, until long after the arrival of the Europeans, written "littera-tures." Indeed, as the phrase *oral literature* might appear to be a contradiction in terms, some have chosen to call the expressions of the oral tradition *orature*.

These expressions were, like the languages, political economies, and religious beliefs of Native American peoples, extremely various. Europeans in 1492 could name the tragedy, the comedy, the epic, the ode, and a variety of lyric forms as types of literature. In Native America there were almost surely (*almost,* because we have no actual records that predate 1492) such things as Kwakiutl winter ceremonies, Winnebago trickster tale cycles, Apache jokes, Hopi personal naming and grievance chants, Yaqui deer songs, Yuman dream songs, Piman shamanic chants, Iroquois condolence rituals, Navajo curing and blessing chants, and Chippewa songs of the Great Medicine Society, to name only some of the types of Native American verbal expression.

That there are many such types is unquestionable, but are these literary types? This question would not make sense to traditional native peoples, who do not have a category of language use corresponding to our category of literature. From a Western perspective, however, the types of native verbal expression could only be considered as literature after that late-eighteenth- and early-nineteenth-century revolution in European consciousness known as Romanticism. In that period the concept of literature shifted away from being defined by the *medium* of expression (all language preserved in *letters*) to the *kind* of expression (those texts that emphasized the imaginative and emotional possibilities of language). With this shift in the meaning of *literature*, many Native American verbal types could quite comfortably be considered literary.

We read these forms on the page, but it bears repeating that traditional Native American literatures originate as *oral* performances. They are offered to audiences as dramatic events in time, language for the ear, rather than objects in space for the eye. And in performance, a pause, a quickening of pace or a sudden retardation, a gesture, or a lowering of the voice affects meaning. Not surprisingly, scholars differ about the best way to transfer performance to the page. Some have opted for a stylized typography where type size and arrangement seek to convey something of the feeling of what an actual performance might have been like. Others, acknowledging that black marks on a white page cannot reproduce a living voice, have left it to the reader to imagine these words in performance.

This matter of translating the words effectively is controversial. When we know that the original performance used archaic and unfamiliar terms, should we use archaic and unfamiliar terms in the translation, even though they may appear stiff and old-fashioned on the page? What would the contemporary reader think of the following excerpt from J. N. B. Hewitt's rendition of the Iroquois creation story: "Through the crafty machinations of the Fire Dragon of the White Body, the consuming jealousy of the aged presiding chief was kindled against his young spouse." Should we instead opt for the nonstandard English, the Red English, or Reservation English as it has been called, of native collaborators in the translation process—even if it may strike some readers not as lively and colloquial but illiterate? Here are a few lines from a contemporary translation in Red English of a folktale from the Northwest: "He told the chief: 'Yes, I remember, I thought of it, I have a worker[,] a boy, and I asked him [to come] but no, he didn't want to leave his work and his eatings.' " Of course, if we translate these texts into standard, or "literary," English, we may have substantially misrepresented verbal expression that, in the original, would surely strike us as strange. Consider the following translation:

> You
> have been
> falling
> falling
> Have you
> fallen
> from the top
> of the salmon-
> berry bushes
> falling
> falling

This is attractive by contemporary standards, but, for the sake of aesthetics, it gives up a good deal of fidelity to the original, which never appeared on the page.

While the question of how best to translate Native American verbal expression must remain open, reading the words of native oral literature conveys some sense of indigenous literary expression as it may have been before the coming of the Europeans.

VOYAGES OF DISCOVERY

Columbus was still making voyages to America (1492–93; 1493–96; 1498; and 1502–04) as other Europeans, following his example, found their way to the West Indies. Giovanni Caboto (known as John Cabot to the English for whom he sailed) and his fellow Italian Amerigo Vespucci both crossed the ocean before 1500, as did the Portuguese native Pedro Cabral. After that date the voyagers became too many to track. Unlike the Viking invasion of five hundred years before, which had established modest coastal settlements in North America that Native Americans soon wiped out, this second European wave quickly gathered momentum and extended itself far to the north and south of the Caribbean basin that Columbus explored. Cabot was near the mouth of the St. Lawrence in Canada the year before Vespucci found that of the Amazon, nearly five thousand miles away in South America. Soon the Europeans were establishing colonies everywhere. The first colonists lingered on the Caribbean island of Hispaniola following the departure of Columbus in 1493. Although that small settlement of La Navidad was soon destroyed in a clash with Taino natives under the cacique Caonabo of Maguana, the massive second voyage in 1493 came equipped to stay, and from that point on Spain and Europe generally maintained an aggressive presence in the West Indies. The constant battles along vague frontiers with native Americans added fuel to the dissension and political in-fighting among the settlers themselves, whose riots and mutinies nearly ruined settlement after settlement. John Smith's experience during the first Jamestown voyage of 1607 provides probably the most famous example from Anglo-America. Arrested and nearly executed (probably for offending his "betters," something he had the habit of doing) en route to America in 1607, Smith was released in Virginia when the colony's sealed instructions were opened, revealing that this apparently modest soldier had been named to the prestigious governing council even before the ships had left England. Columbus himself became the focus of fierce competitions among greedy settlers and officials in Hispaniola by the time of his third voyage and, stripped of his property and powers by a royal official maddened by the uproar, went back to Spain in chains in 1500.

Europe continued to expand in the New World amid the disorder within settlement walls and the great violence outside. Columbus found the mainland of South America in 1498 and Central America in 1502, by which time John Cabot and the Portuguese Corte-Real brothers, Gaspar and Miguel, had been down the coast of North America from Labrador to the Chesapeake, and Cabral and Vespucci had covered the east coast of South America from the Orinoco River in present-day Venezuela to well south of the Río de la Plata on the border of present-day Uruguay and Argentina. Between 1515 and the 1520s, Spain, under the reign of Charles V, aggressively reached out over the Gulf of Mexico, toward the Yucatán peninsula and Mexico and Florida and the Isthmus of Panama, then sent expeditions into the heart of North America from the 1520s to the 1540s, covering a vast region stretching from Florida to the Gulf of California and north as far as Kansas and the Tennessee River. At the same time, other Spanish explorers and conquistadors spread out over South America, especially its west coast, where in imitation of Cortés's Conquest of Mexico a decade earlier Juan Pizarro overcame the Incan Empire, recently beset with violent civil war. In that same period, the Portuguese established their first permanent settlements in Brazil, and the French explorer Jacques Cartier sailed into the Gulf of St. Lawrence, then up its chief river as far as the site of the future Montreal. Within fifty years of 1492, then, the east coasts of much of both continents had been explored, and many of their major regions had been traversed; the most spectacular of their peoples, the Aztecs and the Incas, had been conquered; and Europe had settled in for a long stay.

Spain under Ferdinand and Isabella and their grandson Charles V took the most aggressively expansive role in America. Other European nations, most conspicuously France and England, were more self-absorbed, awakening slowly to what was happening across the sea. Their first explorers enjoyed bad luck and inconsistent support. John and Sebastian Cabot had sailed for English merchants and the monarchs Henry VII and Henry VIII, but the first Cabot was lost on his voyage in 1498, and the second kept his interest in America alive only by entering the service of the Spanish Crown after 1512. A return to his adopted homeland of England and a royal pension from Edward VI came to him only in the 1540s, by which point he had committed himself to the search for an eastward route to China via the seas north of Russia. In France, Cartier enjoyed early support from Francis I, but his failure to find gold and other riches in the St. Lawrence valley and his dispute with the nobleman Roberval, whom the king appointed to command Cartier's third voyage in 1541, led to profound disenchantment in France. Fishermen from both nations continued to harvest the fabulous riches of the shoals off North America and summered on the shore, drying their catch. But not until the 1570s for England and the beginning of the next century for France, as a new generation of adventurers arose and a period of commercial expansion set in, did broad public support and governmental sanction combine to stir lasting curiosity and investment. A series of luckless North American voyages by the English under Martin Frobisher, Humphrey Gilbert, and then Walter Ralegh ended in the tragedy of the "Lost Colony" of Roanoke Island in the 1580s. For another twenty years few English explorers made serious new efforts, although the press bubbled with publications regarding the New World, particularly the works of Richard Hakluyt the younger, whose great collections gathered the fugitive records of English, and indeed European, expansion overseas. Hakluyt's masterwork, *The Principall Navigations* (1598–1600), brought the literary productions of countless European mariners to the attention of a public newly stirred by what Shakespeare soon was to call this "brave new world" of Euro-America. Hakluyt notwithstanding, only in 1606 did a second Virginia colony set forth, and this one faltered grievously at the start with a shipwreck on Bermuda (which was to inspire Shakespeare's *The Tempest*), riots at Jamestown, near starvation, and violent encounters. By 1603 French interest had revived under the direction of a group of explorers and expansionists, Samuel de Champlain most significantly, who hoped for profit from the New World and, even more, a route through it to the fabled riches of Asia. Seasoned from his voyages to Spanish America, Champlain picked up where Cartier had left off sixty years earlier, founded permanent settlements in the St. Lawrence valley, and through his agents and followers pushed French exploration as far west as Lake Superior at a time when the English were still struggling in Virginia and New England settlement had just begun at Plymouth.

LITERARY CONSEQUENCES OF 1492

The period of European exploration in the New World produced a surprisingly large and intriguing body of literature. While many manuscripts were archived and out of reach until the nineteenth century, a number of texts found their way into print and were widely dispersed, thanks to the establishment of printing in the half century before 1492. Shortly after Columbus's return to Spain in early 1493, there appeared in print his letter to the court official Luis de Santangel, narrating the voyage and lushly describing the perpetual spring Columbus had found in the West Indies the previous autumn. From the appearance of that letter on, the printing press and the European expansion into America were reciprocal parts of a single engine. Without the ready dispersal of texts rich with imagery that stirred individual imagination and national ambition in regard to the West Indies, Europe's movement westward would have been blunted and perhaps thwarted. The sword of conquest found in the pen, and in the printing press, an indispensable ally.

The great mass of early American writings came from the hands of Europeans rather than the native peoples of the New World. Important exceptions happily exist. The natives had a lively oral culture that valued memory over mechanics as a means of preserving texts, although among some groups such as the Aztecs written traditions existed (in North America these records included shellwork belts and painted animal hides, tepees, and shields) and many more groups used visual records in subtle and sophisticated ways. Such cataclysms as the Conquest of Mexico produced not only the Spanish narratives of Cortés, Bernal Díaz del Castillo, and others but also native responses, many of which perished with those who knew them. Those that survived in original native characters or in transliterated form have inestimable ethnographic and literary value. For instance, anonymous native writers working in the Nahuatl language of the Aztecs in 1528—significantly, they used the Roman alphabet introduced by the Spanish—lamented the fall of their capital to Cortés in the following lines:

> Broken spears lie in the roads;
> we have torn our hair in our grief.
> The houses are roofless now, and their walls
> are red with blood.

No one reading these four lines will easily glorify the Conquest of Mexico or of the Americas more generally. The story of the transoceanic encounter, however, ceases to be a matter of easy contrasts once one reads widely in the texts on either side. Although Europeans committed atrocities in the New World, often they did so as a result of blundering and miscommunication rather than cool, deliberate policy. In fact, the split between policy and action goes to the heart of the infant Atlantic world of the sixteenth century and is mirrored in and influenced by the character of the writing that survives from the period. The great distance separating the hemispheres made the coordination of intention and performance extremely difficult. The authorities at home lacked the knowledge to form prudent or practical policy; as a result many texts written by explorers or colonists were intended as "briefs" meant to inform or influence policy decisions made at a distance. To cite a simple example, Columbus himself wrote a point-by-point description of his second voyage in 1495, addressed to Ferdinand and Isabella in a series of "items" to which the specific responses of the sovereigns were added by a court scribe. More complexly, Cortés sought to justify his patently illegal invasion of Mexico in 1519 by sending several long letters to Charles V defending his actions and promising lavish returns if his conquest could proceed.

Most documents sent from America to the European powers reveal such generally political intentions. Europe responded by issuing directives aimed at controlling events across the sea. Even when good policies were articulated in Europe, however, applying them in the New World entailed further problems. By the time instructions arrived in Hispaniola, Mexico, Jamestown, or Quebec, new events in the colony might have rendered them pointless. Distance made control both crucial and difficult. Whereas formal authority typically resided in Europe, power as an informal fact of life and experience and circumstance belonged to America, to those who could seize and use it or who acquired it by virtue of what they did rather than the official investitures they bore. Mutiny became so pervasive a fact or fear in America precisely because individuals and groups had, morally and geographically, great latitude in the thinly populated colonial enclaves. If writing served in this fluid, ambiguous universe as a means to influence official policy at home, it also emerged as a means of justifying actions (as with Cortés) that violated or ignored European directives.

Early American writing had, though, a third and more compelling purpose as a literature of witness. That we know so much about the European devastation of the West Indies comes from the fact that some Europeans responded powerfully to that devastation in writing. Although no one typifies this mood better than Bartolomé de las Casas, who assailed Spain's ruthless destruction of whole peoples in America, it is the rare European document that does not reveal the bloody truths of Europe's colonial dreams. Starting on the Columbian voyages themselves and flowering in the Spanish West Indies, especially in the 1540s and 1550s when debates about the mistreatment of the natives earnestly moved the clerics and government officials at home, the New World inspired an outpouring of written expression. Not all the literature of witness speaks to specific issues of policy, or particular public debates, but in many of the texts one senses a critical eye, a point of view not likely to be swayed by the slogans of empire or faith or even wealth. Writers such as Diaz del Castillo, the chronicler of Cortés, and England's John Smith came from the underclass of their native countries, where but for the opportunities represented by America they might well have spent their days in silence. As a result, their writing could be subversive, even mutinous, achieving its greatest depth when it captured a vision of America as more than a dependent province of the Old World, rather as a place where much that was genuinely new might be learned.

PILGRIM AND PURITAN

The establishment of Plymouth Plantation on the south shore of Massachusetts in 1620 brought to North America a new kind of English settler. The founders of the colony (later called Pilgrims by their leader and historian William Bradford) shared with their allies, the Puritans, a wish to purify Christian belief and practice. Whereas the Puritans initially were willing to work within the confines of the established Church of England, the Pilgrims thought it so corrupt that they wished to separate themselves from it completely. While still in England, they set up their own secret congregation in the village of Scrooby in Nottinghamshire. Often subject to persecution and imprisonment, the Scrooby Separatists (as they were also called) saw little chance for remaining true to their faith as long as they remained in England. In 1608, five years after Queen Elizabeth had been succeeded by James Stuart, an enemy of all such reformers, the Scrooby congregation left England and settled in The Netherlands, where, William Bradford tells us, they saw "fair and beautiful cities"—but, as foreigners, they were confronted by the "grisly face of poverty." Isolated by their language and unable to farm, they took up trades like weaving, Bradford's choice, that promised a living. Eventually, fearing that they might lose their religious identity as their children were swallowed up in Dutch culture, they petitioned for the right to settle in the vast American territories of England's Virginia Company. Backed by English investors, the venture was commercial as well as religious in nature. Among the hundred people on the *Mayflower* there were almost three times as many secular settlers as Separatists. This initial group, set down on the raw Massachusetts shore in November 1620, made hasty arrangements to face the winter. The colonists were helped over this "starving time" by their own fortitude and the essential aid of the nearby Wampanoag Indians and their leader, Massasoit. From these "small beginnings," as Bradford was eager to declare, grew a community of mythical import to the later nation.

Much larger at the start was the well-financed effort that brought a contingent of Puritans under John Winthrop to Massachusetts Bay, not far north of Plymouth, in 1630. Although these settlers initially expressed no overt intention to sever their ties with the Church of England, and they are generally regarded as nonseparating dissenters, the distance they put between themselves and that church's hierarchy was eloquent testimony of a different purpose. On other issues, they shared with the Pilgrims the same basic beliefs: both agreed with Martin Luther that no pope or bishop had a right to impose any law on a Christian without consent and both accepted John Calvin's view that God freely chose (or "elected") those he would save and those he would damn eternally. By 1691, when a new charter subsumed Plymouth as an independent colony under Massachusetts Bay, the Pilgrims and Puritans had merged in all but memory.

Too much can be made of the Calvinist doctrine of election; those who have not read the actual Puritan sermons often come away from secondary sources with the mistaken notion that Puritans talked about nothing but damnation. Puritans did indeed hold that God had chosen, before their birth, those whom he wished to save; but it does not follow that Puritans considered most of us to be born damned. Puritans argued that Adam broke the "Covenant of Works" (the promise God made to Adam that he was immortal and could live in Paradise forever as long as he obeyed God's commandments) when he disobeyed and ate of the tree of knowledge of good and evil, thereby bringing sin and death into the world. Their central doctrine, however, was the new "Covenant of Grace," a binding agreement that Christ made with all people who believed in him and that he sealed with his Crucifixion, promising them eternal life. Puritans thus addressed themselves not to the hopelessly unregenerate but to the indifferent, and they addressed the heart more often than the mind, always distinguishing between "historical" or rational understanding and heartfelt "saving faith." There is more joy in Puritan life and thought than we often credit, and this joy is the direct result of meditation on the doctrine of Christ's redeeming power. Edward Taylor is not alone in making his rapturous litany of Christ's attributes: "He is altogether lovely in everything, lovely in His person, lovely in His natures, lovely in His properties, lovely in His offices, lovely in His titles, lovely in His practice, lovely in His purchases and lovely in His relations." All of Taylor's art is a meditation on the miraculous gift of the Incarnation, and in this respect his sensibility is typically Puritan. Anne Bradstreet, who is remarkably frank about confessing her religious doubts, told her children that it was "upon this rock Christ Jesus" that she built her faith.

Not surprisingly, the Puritans held to the strictest requirements regarding communion, or, as they preferred to call it, the Lord's Supper. It was the more important of the two sacraments they recognized (baptism being the other), and they guarded it with a zeal that set them apart from all other dissenters. In the beginning communion was regarded as a sign of election, to be taken only by those who had become church members by standing before their minister and elders and giving an account of their conversion. This insistence on challenging their members made these New England churches more rigorous than any others and confirmed the feeling that they were a special few. Thus when John Winthrop addressed the immigrants to the Bay Colony aboard the flagship *Arbella* in 1630, he told them that the eyes of the world were on them and that they would be an example for all, a "city upon a hill." Like William Bradford for the Pilgrims, Winthrop in his history of the Puritans wished to record the actualization of that dream.

WRITING IN TONGUES

While the New England colonies have conventionally been regarded as the centerpiece of early American literature, the first North American settlements had been founded elsewhere years, even decades, earlier. St. Augustine, Jamestown, Santa Fe, Albany, and New York, for instance, are all older than Boston. More important, English was not the only language in which early North American texts were written. Indeed, it was a tardy arrival in America, and its eventual emergence as the dominant language of classic American literature hardly was inevitable. To some extent, the large initial immigration to Boston in the 1630s, the high articulation of Puritan cultural ideals, and the early establishment of a college and a printing press in Cambridge all gave New England a substantial edge. Later political events would make English a useful lingua franca for the colonies at large and, in time, the literary medium of choice.

Before 1700, however, and often long after it, other languages remained actively in use not only for mundane purposes but also as expressive vehicles. Particularly beyond the vague borders of the English colonial world (the shifting lines between French Canada and New England and the southern colonies and Spanish Florida, for example), those other languages were completely dominant. Even within the limits of the eventual thirteen colonies, however, large enclaves of speakers of other languages existed, especially in the middle colonies. Among the noteworthy settlers of New Netherland, for instance, were Belgian Walloons, near neighbors of the Dutch in Europe but speakers of a radically different language. The mix of "foreigners" in Albany, begun as a fur trade post by Netherlander merchants on the upper Hudson, made it a minority Dutch town, its population made up of settlers of Scandinavian, French, Portuguese, English, Irish, Scots, German, African, and West Indian derivation—even people from Spain, then the enemy of the Netherlanders, and from faraway Croatia. For two centuries after New Netherland was conquered by the English in 1664 and renamed New York, Dutch and other languages were widely used there in public and private life before eventually dying out. Similar linguistic transformations, with the social and personal losses they bring, occurred in other English-controlled regions that would eventually form the United States. In Pennsylvania, where large groups of Protestants from continental Europe were welcomed by William Penn, German in particular remains a vital language to this day, although the friction between German communities there and "the English" reminds us that language is a ground of contest between ethnic groups, not just of self-expression within each. In fact, the first item printed in Pennsylvania, although it issued from the press established by an immigrant Englishman, was in German, and the largest book printed in any of the colonies before the Revolution was in the same language. When we read American history backward, looking for early precedents of national institutions, practices, and values, we are likely to miss the radical linguistic and cultural diversity of the colonial world. Readers of the colonial record need to attend to the many tongues through which the colonists articulated their experiences, vision, and values. It is to this end that translated selections from works as various as those written by Samuel de Champlain, Garcilaso de la Vega, Jacob Steendam, and Francis Daniel Pastorius—originally composed in French, Spanish, Dutch, and German, respectively—are included along with English texts to represent the first full century of North American writing. Part of the usefulness of such a broad survey is the insight it offers into the themes, forms, and concerns shared by many peoples involved in the cultural and territorial expansion of European peoples at the time.

AMERICAN LITERATURE IN 1700

Along the eastern seaboard by 1700, most of the colonies that were to unite in seeking independence from Britain toward the end of the eighteenth century had been founded—Georgia was to follow in the 1730s. As Britain sought to consolidate and unify its overseas possessions, the map began to resemble that of 1776, and English had already emerged as a powerful inter-colonial tool. But up and down the coast, a surprising variety of peoples was in evidence, most of whom had become accustomed to the transatlantic or local publication of their writings. At the end of the first full century of European colonization, the printing press was active in many areas, from Cambridge and Boston to New York, Philadelphia, and Annapolis. From 1696 to 1700, to be sure, only about 250 separate items were issued in all these places combined. Although this is a small number compared to the output of the printers of London at the time, it must be remembered that printing was established in the American colonies *before* it was allowed in most of England, where restrictive laws, the last of them repealed as late as 1693, had long confined printing to four locations: London, York, Oxford, and Cambridge. In this regard, if only because of the isolation of the American provinces by the ocean, they ventured into the modern world earlier than their provincial English counterparts.

The literary situation in America three centuries ago is suggested by a brief examination of the products of the presses then in operation. Among those 250 items published at the century's end was a whole library of texts by the most prolific colonial author, Cotton Mather. In this period, he published more than three dozen titles, including such things as his account of the "tearful decade" (1688–98) of warfare between New England and New France and the latter's Indian allies, which incorporated his famous narrative of the bloody escape of Hannah Dustan from her captors. Mather also published several biographies of New England's founding ministers and penned treatises on the proper behavior of servants toward their masters, on the "well-ordered family," and on the spiritual risks run by seamen. He also issued a warning against "impostors pretending to be ministers." And he wrote *Pillars of Salt,* a venture into criminal biography that had religious origins but that also reflected the importance of an emergent popular (as opposed to elite) literary culture on both sides of the Atlantic.

Despite their tendency to mirror the self-regarding aspect of Puritan thought, even Mather's works remind us that America in 1700 was opening outward. In the *Magnalia Christi Americana,* published just after the start of the new century, Mather himself told an anecdote that conveys the change at hand. A newly trained minister who had journeyed north from Massachu-setts Bay to Maine was preaching to a group of hardened fishermen. He was urging his listeners not to "contradict the main end of Planting this Wilder-ness," the service of God and God's purposes, when a member of the make-shift gathering had the effrontery to contradict *him*: "Sir, you are mistaken, you think you are Preaching to the People at the Bay; our main end was to catch Fish." Even in New England, Mather suggests, main ends differed profoundly from place to place and from community to community. Else-where, the rich array of purposes was reflected in the diverse items issued by American printers at the time when Mather's *Magnalia* was just appearing (this large book was first published in London, not in Boston, it might be noted). There was a pair of texts, for instance, dealing with the Native Amer-icans of New York that suggest how colonialism was altered by the drive toward cross-cultural interaction. One reported on a conference held in 1696 between the governor of that "province," as all the colonies were then being

called, and the "Five . . . Nations of Indians," the Iroquois, a dynamic confederacy of peoples who had long controlled much of New York's territory
and exacted tribute from far distant native peoples as well. This was a kind
of text that proliferated throughout New York's colonial era, when the governor and his agents made regular visits to the important Iroquois capital at
Onondaga to listen to the concerns of these English allies. The second text
concerning native peoples in New York also reflected this unique cross-
cultural pattern. In the 1690s, when the French and English empires were
coming into serious conflict in America, native peoples were frequently swept
up in the fray. The "Propositions Made by the Five Nations of Indians" to
New York's governor in 1698 accordingly entreated him to protect the Iroquois from harassment by New France's Indian allies, who were moving
eastward into Iroquoia and fiercely raiding the villages there.

Such texts, reaching across the boundaries between the Indian nations
and colonial powers, catch the diplomatic tone of cross-cultural relations in
the Midatlantic region. The complexity of the political culture in early America is borne out in other texts of the era as well, such as *God's Protecting
Providence* (1699), Philadelphian Jonathan Dickinson's much reprinted
account of his shipwreck and Indian captivity in Spanish Florida, which
combined piety, adventure, and exoticism. Similarly exotic was *Barbarian
Cruelties* (1700), which told of European captives in North Africa, an area
of the globe that was long to be the focus of Westerners' anxieties and, in
the post-Revolutionary era, an American war or two. But such adventurous
narratives were not all sited in exotic and distant locales. Some, like the
seemingly mundane textbook in the English language written by Francis
Daniel Pastorius and aimed not only at young Americans but also (as the
author's own Germanic-sounding English suggested) at "those who from foreign countries and nations come to settle amongst us," suggest less dramatic
but still important cross-cultural concerns. Religion, a dominant theme in
the American press in 1700, was itself linked to strong social issues, as was
demonstrated by Daniel Gould's account of the execution of Quaker dissenters in Boston fifty years earlier, a work that appeared in New York in
1700. The printer of Gould's book, in fact, also issued a pair of dissenting
tracts by Quaker and Salem merchant Thomas Maule, including one called
New England's Persecutors Mauled with Their Own Weapons. Maule's name
became famous to later generations of readers through Nathaniel Hawthorne's none too accurate association of it with the curse dooming the Pyn-
cheon family in his Salem novel *The House of the Seven Gables*. Finally,
rounding out the century, came *The Selling of Joseph* by Samuel Sewall,
among the earliest antislavery tracts written and published in America and
thus a work of growing importance in the future. Although the published
items from this half decade of the seventeenth century also comprised almanacs and governmental publications, such items contributed as well to the
establishment of print culture and, ultimately, of literary traditions in British
America. It was to be the almanac, one recalls, that helped make Benjamin
Franklin's fortune as a printer, and it was Franklin who converted that everyday form into a vehicle of rare wit and sturdy English.

LITERATURE TO 1700

TEXTS	CONTEXTS
Peoples indigenous to the Americas orally perform and transmit a variety of "literary" genres that include, among others, speeches, songs, and stories	
	1000–1300 Anasazi communities inhabit southwestern regions.
	1492 Christopher Columbus arrives in the Bahamas • between 4 and 7 million Native Americans estimated in present-day United States, including Alaska
1493 Columbus, "**Letter to Luis de Santangel Regarding the First Voyage**"	
	1500 Native American populations begin to be ravaged by European diseases
	1514 Bartolomé de las Casas petitions Spanish crown to treat Native American peoples like other human (subject) populations
	1519–21 Cortés conquers Aztecs in Mexico
	1526 Spanish explorers bring first African slaves to South Carolina
	1539 First printing press in the Americas set up in Mexico City • Hernando de Soto invades Florida
1542 Álvar Núñez Cabeza de Vaca, *The Relation of Álvar Núñez Cabeza de Vaca*	
1552 Bartolomé de las Casas, *The Very Brief Relation of the Devastation of the Indies*	
	1558–1603 Reign of Elizabeth I
c. 1568 Bernal Díaz del Castillo composes *The True History of the Conquest of New Spain* (pub. 1632)	
	1584 Walter Ralegh lands on "island" of Roanoke; names it "Virginia" for Queen Elizabeth
1588 Thomas Harriot, *A Brief and True Report of the New Found Land of Virginia*	
	1603–13 Samuel de Champlain explores the St. Lawrence River; founds Québec
1605 Garcilaso de la Vega, *The Florida of the Inca*	

Boldface titles indicate works in the anthology.

TEXTS	CONTEXTS
	1607 Jamestown is established in Virginia • Powhatan confederacy prevents colonists from starving; teaches them to plant tobacco
1613 Samuel de Champlain, *The Voyages of Sieur de Champlain*	
	1619 Twenty Africans arrive in Jamestown on a Dutch vessel as indentured servants
	1620 *Mayflower* drops anchor in Plymouth Harbor
	1621 First Thanksgiving, at Plymouth
1624 John Smith, *The General History of Virginia, New England, and the Summer Isles*	
1630 John Winthrop delivers his sermon *A Model of Christian Charity* (pub. 1838)	1630–43 Immigration of English Puritans to Massachusetts Bay
1630–50 William Bradford writes *Of Plymouth Plantation* (pub. 1856)	
1637 Thomas Morton, *New England Canaan*	1637 Pequot War
	1638 Anne Hutchinson banished from Bay Colony for challenging Puritan beliefs.
1643 Roger Williams, *A Key into the Language of America*	
1650 Anne Bradstreet, *The Tenth Muse*	
1655 Adriaen Van der Donck, *A Description of New Netherland*	
1661 Jacob Steendam, "The Praise of New Netherland"	
1662 Michael Wigglesworth, *The Day of Doom*	
1673–1729 Samuel Sewall keeps his *Diary* (pub. 1878–82)	
	1675–78 King Philip's War destroys power of Native American tribes in New England
	1681 William Penn founds Pennsylvania
1682 Mary Rowlandson's *Narrative of the Captivity and Restoration*	
1682–1725 Edward Taylor continues his *Preparatory Meditations* (pub. 1939, 1960)	
1684 Francis Daniel Pastorius, *Positive Information from America*	
	1692 Salem witch trials
1702 Cotton Mather, *Magnalia Christi Americana*	

STORIES OF THE BEGINNING OF THE WORLD

Stories about the creation of the world tell people who they are by telling them where they come from. Native American creation stories, although never written down or gathered into a bible, serve for native cultures in much the same way as the Book of Genesis serves for the Judeo-Christian world: they posit a general cultural outlook and offer perspectives on what life is and how to understand it. All native peoples have stories of the earliest times; reprinted here are three, one from the Iroquois of the Northeast and two from the Akimel O'odham or Pima of the Southwest. These peoples encountered European explorers, missionaries, and colonists very early in the period of contact, and information and conjecture about the Iroquois and the Pima appear in European texts that go back almost four hundred years. But these early records offer only bare sketches of what native people said, sang, chanted, and narrated; and of course, North American Indians did not themselves write down their stories.

It was not until the mid- to late nineteenth century that Euro-Americans developed the linguistic skills and cultural understanding necessary to translate and transcribe native American creation stories in a manner that begins to do justice to them. It was also not until then that native people collaborated extensively in recording the myths and legends of their people. In the Southwest, the army doctor Washington Matthews began to work on the Navajo *Night Chant* and *Mountain Chant* in the 1880s, while Frank Hamilton Cushing, employed by the Bureau of American Ethnology, had installed himself among the Zuni and begun to record their legends in 1879. J. W. Fewkes, after the turn of the century, and J. W. Lloyd, somewhat later, both worked with the Pima man Thin Leather to record stories of the earliest times. Among the Iroquois, David Cusick, a Tuscarora (the Tuscarora joined the Iroquois Confederacy early in the eighteenth century), had begun to document the legends of his people as early as 1825. He was followed by the distinguished Tuscarora anthropologist J. N. B. Hewitt shortly after the turn of the century.

THE IROQUOIS CREATION STORY

The people known collectively as the Iroquois were made up of the Mohawk, Seneca, Oneida, Onondaga, and Cayuga nations. Joined in the early eighteenth century by the Tuscarora of North Carolina, the Five Nations became the Six Nations. The original Five Nations occupied lands that ranged from the area northeast of lakes Ontario and Erie around the St. Lawrence and Ottawa rivers, then south of the lakes, and eastward almost to the Hudson River. Named Iroquois by the French (the Dutch and English called all these peoples Mohawk, Maqua, or Seneca), the Six Nations called themselves People of the Longhouse (*Haudenosaunee* in Seneca, *Kanosoni* in Mohawk), in reference to their primary type of dwelling. Iroquois longhouses were some twenty feet wide and from forty to two hundred feet long, accommodating several families who shared cooking fires. The largest towns of the Iroquois contained as many as two thousand people.

Warfare was an important element of Iroquois life. According to Iroquois legend, in response to the terrible consequences of ongoing wars, a man named Hiawatha founded the League, or Confederacy, of the Five Nations. Having lost all of his daughters in war, Hiawatha, in a rage of grief and despair, went by himself into the forest. There he encountered a supernatural being named Deganawidah, the Peacemaker, perhaps a reincarnation of the Good Twin of the Iroquois creation story. Deganawidah comforted Hiawatha and taught him Rituals of Condolence that were to be the core of a new creed, the Good News of Peace and Power. Thus the cultural ideal of peace was established. While war continued as a central reality of Iroquois life, there were now ritual means of comforting the bereaved—and an ongoing hope for more lasting peace.

Of special note is the importance of women in Iroquois life. Women owned the property and took responsibility for major decisions of social life (indeed, society is referred to as "she"), attending to agricultural duties in the clearings while the men hunted in the woods or warred against traditional enemies such as the Huron to the north. The principal male figure in an Iroquois child's life was not the father but the mother's brother, and the image of mother-dominated families is established strongly in the creation legend. In the version printed here males are entirely absent at the beginning of the tale, appearing neither as husbands nor as fathers. Indeed, stories of fatherless boys who become heroes are common in Iroquois folk history.

The Iroquois creation myth exists in some twenty-five versions, the earliest of which was taken down by the Frenchman Gabriel Sagard in 1623 from the Huron. Other early accounts derive from the Mohawk and the Seneca. There is, however, no actual transcription and translation of an Iroquois cosmogonic myth—a narrative of the establishment of the world—until that of David Cusick, a Tuscarora, in the nineteenth century.

Little is known about Cusick. He was born in Madison County, New York, before 1800, when his family moved to the lands granted the Tuscarora by the Seneca and Oneida in Niagara County, New York. Most likely, he attended a mission school where he learned to read and write English. He died in 1840. Cusick's Tuscarora version shares many elements with the creation stories of other members of the Iroquois League; indeed, it has surely been influenced by them. But it also omits much material that other versions include.

Other accounts begin with a man and a woman who live together in the sky world on opposite sides of a fire. Although these two do not sleep together, the woman finds herself pregnant and eventually gives birth to a daughter. The man falls ill and dies, and the daughter grieves intensely for him. When the young woman is grown, her father's spirit instructs her to make a difficult journey to a place where she will meet the man destined to become her husband. When at last she finds this man, he too is ill, but the young woman cures him. The two marry but do not sleep together; nonetheless, as had happened to her mother, she becomes pregnant. It is at this point that Cusick picks up the story of the woman who "would have the twin born." Other versions continue past the point where Cusick's terminates. Some tell, for example, of a toad that hoards water long enough to cause a flood.

Cusick's English, as the phrase quoted above makes clear, is not standard. Aware of that, he noted in the preface to his work that he found himself "so small educated that it was impossible for me to compose the work without much difficulty." His style is a curious combination of an Indian-inflected English and what the Euro-American culture of the period would have defined as polite literary style. We have selected Cusick's version of the Iroquois creation story because it is early, because it is by a native person (Cusick was the first native American to record on his own the founding myths of his own people), and because it is fairly accessible to the contemporary reader.

The Iroquois Creation Story[1]

A Tale of the Foundation of the Great Island, Now North America;—
the Two Infants Born, and the Creation of the Universe

Among the ancients there were two worlds in existence. The lower world was in great darkness;—the possession of the great monster; but the upper world was inhabited by mankind; and there was a woman conceived[2] and would have the twin born. When her travail drew near, and her situation seemed to produce a great distress on her mind, and she was induced by some of her relations to lay herself on a mattress which was prepared, so as to gain refreshments to her wearied body; but while she was asleep the very place sunk down towards the dark world.[3] The monsters[4] of the great water were alarmed at her appearance of descending to the lower world; in consequence all the species of the creatures were immediately collected into where it was expected she would fall. When the monsters were assembled, and they made consultation, one of them was appointed in haste to search the great deep, in order to procure some earth, if it could be obtained; accordingly the monster descends, which succeeds, and returns to the place. Another requisition was presented, who would be capable to secure the woman from the terrors of the great water, but none was able to comply except a large turtle came forward and made proposal to them to endure her lasting weight, which was accepted. The woman was yet descending from a great distance. The turtle executes upon the spot, and a small quantity of earth was varnished on the back part of the turtle. The woman alights on the seat prepared, and she receives a satisfaction.[5] While holding her, the turtle increased every moment and became a considerable island of earth, and apparently covered with small bushes. The woman remained in a state of unlimited darkness, and she was overtaken by her travail to which she was subject. While she was in the limits of distress one of the infants in her womb was moved by an evil opinion and he was determined to pass out under the side of the parent's arm, and the other infant in vain endeavoured to prevent his design.[6] The woman was in a painful condition during the time of their disputes, and the infants entered the dark world by compulsion, and their parent expired in a few moments. They had the power of sustenance without a nurse, and remained in the dark regions. After a time the turtle increased to a great Island and the infants were grown up, and one of them possessed with a gentle disposition, and named ENIGORIO, i.e. the good mind. The other youth possessed an insolence of character, and was named ENI-

---

1. The text is from *Sketches of the Ancient History of the Six Nations* (1827).
2. The woman who conceives is, in most Iroquois accounts of the creation, the second generation of sky women to become pregnant without sexual activity. "Mankind": i.e., humans rather than "monsters"—undefined creatures of a time before the world as we know it was established—although these humans have powers quite different from those humans usually possess.
3. Other versions have Sky Woman either being pushed out of the upper world or accidentally falling.
4. In other versions the monsters are a variety of

familiar animals. Cusick conveys the mysterious and dangerous state of affairs in the as-yet-unformed universe.
5. I.e., she lands safely, without harm.
6. Other versions of the story have Sky Woman give birth to a daughter, who again becomes supernaturally pregnant (perhaps by the spirit of the turtle), and it is *she* who conceives the twins. The twins argue even in the womb, the Evil Twin deciding not to be born in the normal way but to burst through his mother's side, which leads to her death. The theme of rival twins is widespread in the Americas.

GONHAHETGEA, i.e. the bad mind.[7] The good mind was not contented to remain in a dark situation, and he was anxious to create a great light in the dark world; but the bad mind was desirous that the world should remain in a natural state. The good mind determines to prosecute his designs, and therefore commences the work of creation. At first he took the parent's head, (the deceased) of which he created an orb, and established it in the centre of the firmament, and it became of a very superior nature to bestow light to the new world, (now the sun) and again he took the remnant of the body and formed another orb, which was inferior to the light (now moon). In the orb a cloud of legs appeared to prove it was the body of the good mind, (parent). The former was to give light to the day and the latter to the night; and he also created numerous spots of light, (now stars): these were to regulate the days, nights, seasons, years, etc. Whenever the light extended to the dark world the monsters were displeased and immediately concealed themselves in the deep places, lest they should be discovered by some human beings. The good mind continued the works of creation, and he formed numerous creeks and rivers on the Great Island, and then created numerous species of animals of the smallest and the greatest, to inhabit the forests, and fishes of all kinds to inhabit the waters. When he had made the universe he was in doubt respecting some being to possess the Great Island; and he formed two images of the dust of the ground in his own likeness, male and female, and by his breathing into their nostrils he gave them the living souls, and named them EA-GWE-HOWE, i.e., a real people;[8] and he gave the Great Island all the animals of game for their maintenance and he appointed thunder to water the earth by frequent rains, agreeable of the nature of the system; after this the Island became fruitful and vegetation afforded the animals subsistence. The bad mind, while his brother was making the universe, went throughout the Island and made numerous high mountains and falls of water, and great steeps, and also creates various reptiles which would be injurious to mankind; but the good mind restored the Island to its former condition. The bad mind proceeded further in his motives and he made two images of clay in the form of mankind; but while he was giving them existence they became apes;[9] and when he had not the power to create mankind he was envious against his brother; and again he made two of clay. The good mind discovered his brothers contrivances, and aided in giving them living souls, (it is said these had the most knowledge of good and evil). The good mind now accomplishes the works of creation, notwithstanding the imaginations of the bad mind were continually evil; and he attempted to enclose all the animals of game in the earth, so as to deprive them from mankind; but the good mind released them from confinement, (the animals were dispersed, and traces of them were made on the rocks near the cave where it

7. More commonly, the Good Twin is called Tharonhiawagon (Sky-Grasper, Creator, or Upholder of the Heavens), and the Evil Twin is named Tawiscaron (Evil-Minded, Flint, Ice, Patron of Winter, and other disasters). Cusick's Enigorio is a rough translation of the Tuscarora word for "good minded" into Mohawk, and his Enigonhahetgea is an equally rough translation into Seneca, Onondaga, or Cayuga of the Tuscarora word for "bad minded." Cusick has probably changed the Tuscarora words best known to him into these other Iroquois languages, because they were considered to be more prestigious than Tuscarora, the Tus-

caroras only recently having joined the Iroquois Confederacy.
8. Humans. "EA-GWE-HOWE": Tuscarora term used by speakers of all the languages of the Six Nations; today, it simply means Indian, or Indians.
9. Cusick may have seen an ape or a depiction of apes (there are no apes native to the New World) and decided to name them as the creatures made by the Evil Twin in contrast to the humans made by the Good Twin. John Buck and Chief John Gibson, in their later renditions of the Iroquois creation narrative, also refer to apes at this point in the narrative.

was closed). The good mind experiences that his brother was at variance with the works of creation, and feels not disposed to favor any of his proceedings, but gives admonitions of his future state. Afterwards the good mind requested his brother to accompany him, as he was proposed to inspect the game, etc., but when a short distance from their moninal[1] [*sic*] residence, the bad mind became so unmanly that he could not conduct his brother any more.[2] The bad mind offered a challenge to his brother and resolved that who gains the victory should govern the universe; and appointed a day to meet the contest. The good mind was willing to submit to the offer, and he enters the reconciliation with his brother; which he falsely mentions that by whipping with flags would destroy his temporal life;[3] and he earnestly solicits his brother also to notice the instrument of death, which he manifestly relates by the use of deer horns, beating his body he would expire. On the day appointed the engagement commenced, which lasted for two days: after pulling up the trees and mountains as the track of a terrible whirlwind, at last the good mind gained the victory by using the horns, as mentioned the instrument of death, which he succeeded in deceiving his brother and he crushed him in the earth; and the last words uttered from the bad mind were, that he would have equal power over the souls of mankind after death; and he sinks down to eternal doom, and became the Evil Spirit.[4] After this tumult the good mind repaired to the battle ground, and then visited the people and retires from the earth.[5]

1827

1. Cusick perhaps means *nominal*, their named or designated residence.
2. I.e., the Evil Twin became so rude and obnoxious that the Good Twin could not lead ("conduct") his brother to the appointed place any longer.
3. The Good Twin tells his brother that he can be killed by being beaten with corn stalks, rushes, reeds, or cattails. Cusick calls this a deception;

other accounts treat it as a confession of weakness. Below, the Evil Twin admits that he would die if beaten with the antlers of deer.
4. This may reflect an awareness of the Christian belief in the devil as the evil spirit, ruler over the lower depths.
5. Other versions go on to say that the Good Twin teaches the people how to grow corn and how to keep from harm by means of prayer and ritual.

PIMA STORIES OF THE BEGINNING OF THE WORLD

The Akimel O'odham, or Pima, live along the Gila and Salt Rivers in the desert of central Arizona and are close relations of the Tohono O'odham (formerly known as the Papago), who occupy lands in the mostly riverless desert to the south of them. Farming close to the rivers, the Akimel O'odham grew corn and beans, gathered wild plants, and hunted small game. Late in the sixteenth century, they encountered the Spanish, who named them "Pima" sometime around 1600. Because of their remoteness from Spanish and Mexican centers of power, the Pima were not immediately subjected to strong European influence. In 1694 Spanish missionaries were sent out to convert them. Today, like many native peoples, most Pima are Christian, although their Christianity both includes and exists alongside traditional beliefs and practices.

The first Pima mythological narrative to be recorded dates from a 1694 journal account written by the Spaniard Juan Manje; Pedro Font, another Spaniard, also recorded a Pima story in 1775. These stories concern the ancestors of the Pima, the

Hohokam (meaning, roughly, the "finished ones" or "those who are gone"). Of great importance to the Pima, the narratives offer an account of how the cultural practices of everyday Pima life came to be established. But these earliest stories do not tell of the creation of the world, of the origins of things, or the actions of the most distant ancestors. Such tales were not recorded until the turn of the twentieth century.

At the Pan-American Fair in Buffalo, New York, in July 1901, J. W. Lloyd met a man named Edward H. Wood, a full-blood Pima, who told him that his greatest dream was to preserve the ancient legends and tales of his people. Wood's grand-uncle, Thin Leather, was a *see-nee-yaw-kum*, a recognized master who knew all the ancient stories. Thin Leather, as Wood told Lloyd, had no successor and feared that with his death the stories would be lost to his people and to the world. Wood persuaded Lloyd to go to the Southwest and work with him and his uncle to record the stories in English. In 1903 Lloyd traveled to Sacaton, Arizona, where he met Thin Leather and, with Wood acting as interpreter, recorded a number of his tales. Lloyd published the results of his work with Wood and Thin Leather privately in 1911, as *Aw-aw-tam, Indian Nights, Being the Myths and Legends of the Pimas of Arizona*. The title refers to the fact that these stories were traditionally told over a period of four nights.

Although the *Story of the Creation* was not narrated until the twentieth century, it is little influenced by the origin story in Genesis, which, however, Thin Leather probably knew. The important animals and vegetation, the chief protagonists, and their personalities and actions are all specific to Pima culture.

Thin Leather's story of the great flood here follows the creation story. Flood stories are among the fifteen pre-Columbian tale types cataloged in Mexico, Central America, and the American Southwest. Although Thin Leather may have heard the stories of Genesis, his Pima version shows no particular European influence. The flood story is important as a foundational narrative in that it tells not of creation but of re-creation, of the reestablishment or rebirth of the divine, natural, and social orders. In addition, the Pima flood story tells or, rather, *specifies* the location of the "middle of the earth," the navel of the universe, the center of all the world—where the Pima, like other Southwestern peoples, believe themselves to dwell.

The texts are from *Aw-aw-tam, Indian Nights, Being the Myths and Legends of the Pimas of Arizona* (1911).

The Story of the Creation[1]

In the beginning there was no earth, no water—nothing. There was only a Person, *Juh-wert-a-Mah-kai* (The Doctor of the Earth).[2]

He just floated, for there was no place for him to stand upon. There was no sun, no light, and he just floated about in the darkness, which was Darkness itself.

He wandered around in the nowhere till he thought he had wandered enough. Then he rubbed on his breast and rubbed out *moah-haht-tack*, that is perspiration, or greasy earth. This he rubbed out on the palm of his hand and held out. It tipped over three times, but the fourth time[3] it staid straight in the middle of the air and there it remains now as the world.

The first bush he created was the greasewood bush.[4]

1. The editor is indebted to Donald Bahr for his help with the annotation of the Pima selections.
2. This title is equivalent to respectfully calling Juhwertamahkai a medicine person, or shaman, with great powers, although his powers seem, in a Western sense, to be godlike.
3. This is the first of several actions that must be

attempted four times before it is achieved [adapted from Lloyd's note]. Four is the pattern number of the Pima, as it is of a great many native peoples; it corresponds to the importance of three and seven as pattern numbers in Western cultures.
4. "The local touch in making the greasewood bush the first vegetation is very strong" [Lloyd's

And he made ants, little tiny ants, to live on that bush, on its gum which comes out of its stem.

But these little ants did not do any good, so he created white ants, and these worked and enlarged the earth; and they kept on increasing it, larger and larger, until at last it was big enough for himself to rest on.

Then he created a Person. He made him out of his eye, out of the shadow of his eyes, to assist him, to be like him, and to help him in creating trees and human beings and everything that was to be on the earth.

The name of this being was *Noo-ee* (the Buzzard).[5]

Nooee was given all power, but he did not do the work he was created for. He did not care to help Juhwertamahkai, but let him go by himself.

And so the Doctor of the Earth himself created the mountains and everything that has seed and is good to eat. For if he had created human beings first they would have had nothing to live on.

But after making Nooee and before making the mountains and seed for food, Juhwertamahkai made the sun.

In order to make the sun he first made water, and this he placed in a hollow vessel, like an earthen dish (*hwas-hah-ah*) to harden into something like ice. And this hardened ball he placed in the sky. First he placed it in the North, but it did not work; then he placed it in the West, but it did not work; then he placed it in the South, but it did not work; then he placed it in the East and there it worked as he wanted it to.

And the moon he made in the same way and tried in the same places, with the same results.

But when he made the stars he took the water in his mouth and spurted it up into the sky. But the first night his stars did not give light enough. So he took the Doctor-stone[6] (diamond), the *tone-dum-haw-teh*, and smashed it up, and took the pieces and threw them into the sky to mix with the water in the stars, and then there was light enough.

Juhwertamahkai's Song of Creation

Juhwertamahkai made the world—
Come and see it and make it useful!
He made it round—
Come and see it and make it useful!

And now Juhwertamahkai, rubbed again on his breast, and from the substance he obtained there made two little dolls, and these he laid on the earth. And they were human beings, man and woman.

And now for a time the people increased till they filled the earth. For the first parents were perfect, and there was no sickness and no death. But when the earth was full, then there was nothing to eat, so they killed and ate each other.

But Juhwertamahkai did not like the way his people acted, to kill and eat each other, and so he let the sky fall to kill them. But when the sky dropped

note]. Greasewood bushes are abundant in the Pima homelands.
5. He is a person and also a buzzard, which, in the earliest times, is not a contradiction or paradox.

6. I.e., it is a particularly powerful stone. Lloyd's interpreter called it a diamond, but as diamonds are uncommon in North America, this is probably a quartz crystal.

he, himself, took a staff and broke a hole thru, thru which he and Nooee emerged and escaped, leaving behind them all the people dead.

And Juhwertamahkai, being now on the top of this fallen sky, again made a man and a woman, in the same way as before. But this man and woman became grey when old, and their children became grey still younger, and their children became grey younger still, and so on till the babies were grey in their cradles.

And Juhwertamahkai, who had made a new earth and sky, just as there had been before, did not like his people becoming grey in their cradles, so he let the sky fall on them again, and again made a hole and escaped, with Nooee, as before.

And Juhwertamahkai, on top of this second sky, again made a new heaven and a new earth, just as he had done before, and new people.

But these new people made a vice of smoking. Before human beings had never smoked till they were old, but now they smoked younger, and each generation still younger, till the infants wanted to smoke in their cradles.

And Juhwertamahkai did not like this, and let the sky fall again, and created everything new again in the same way, and this time he created the earth as it is now.

But at first the whole slope of the world was westward,[7] and tho there were peaks rising from this slope there were no true valleys, and all the water that fell ran away and there was no water for the people to drink. So Juhwertamahkai sent Nooee to fly around among the mountains, and over the earth, to cut valleys with his wings, so that the water could be caught and distributed and there might be enough for the people to drink.

Now the sun was male and the moon was female and they met once a month. And the moon became a mother and went to a mountain called *Tahs-my-et-tahn Toe-ahk* (sun striking mountain) and there was born her baby. But she had duties to attend to, to turn around and give light, so she made a place for the child by tramping down the weedy bushes and there left it. And the child, having no milk, was nourished on the earth.

And this child was the coyote,[8] and as he grew, he went out to walk and in his walk came to the house of Juhwertamahkai and Nooee, where they lived.

And when he came there Juhwertamahkai knew him and called him *Toe-hahvs*,[9] because he was laid on the weedy bushes of that name.

But now out of the North came another powerful personage, who has two names, *See-ur-huh* and *Ee-ee-toy*.[1]

Now Seeurhuh means older brother, and when this personage came to Juhwertamahkai, Nooee and Toehahvs he called them his younger brothers.

7. A specifically local element of the Pima story, as both the Gila and the Salt rivers, important to the Pima, flow westward [adapted from Lloyd's note].
8. It is appropriate that the night-prowling coyote is born of the moon, and there is a symmetry in having the buzzard serve as Juhwertamahkai's agent of the sky and the coyote as his agent of the earth [adapted from Lloyd's note].
9. Or Tohawes; brittlebush, a common plant in Pima country.
1. The name either means "drink it all up" or, according to present-day Pimas, just sounds like the word that means "drink it all up," i.e., it is not translatable. This character is "the most active and mysterious personality in Piman mythology. Out of the North, apparently self-existent, but little inferior in power to Juhwertamahkai, and claiming greater age, he appears, by pure 'bluff,' and persistent push and wheedling, to have induced the really more powerful, but good-natured and rather lazy Juhwertamahkai to give over most of the real work and government of the world to him" [Lloyd's note].

But they claimed to have been here first, and to be older than he, and there was a dispute between them. But finally, because he insisted so strongly, and just to please him, they let him be called older brother.

1911

The Story of the Flood

Now Seeurhuh was very powerful, like Juhwerta Mahkai, and as he took up his residence with them, as one of them, he did many wonderful things which pleased Juhwerta Mahkai, who liked to watch him.

And after doing many marvelous things he, too, made a man.

And to this man whom he had made, Seeurhuh (whose other name was Ee-ee-toy) gave a bow & arrows, and guarded his arm against the bow string by a piece of wild-cat skin, and pierced his ears & made ear-rings for him, like turquoises to look at, from the leaves of the weed called *quah-wool*.[1] And this man was the most beautiful man yet made.

And Ee-ee-toy told this young man, who was just of marriageable age, to look around and see if he could find any young girl in the villages that would suit him and, if he found her, to see her relatives and see if they were willing he should marry her.

And the beautiful young man did this, and found a girl that pleased him, and told her family of his wish, and they accepted him, and he married her.

And the names of both these are now forgotten and unknown.

And when they were married Ee-ee-toy, foreseeing what would happen, went & gathered the gum of the greasewood tree.[2]

✻   ✻   ✻

Now there was a doctor who lived down toward the sunset whose name was Vahk-lohv Mahkai, or South Doctor, who had a beautiful daughter. And when his daughter heard of this young man and what had happened to his wives she was afraid and cried every day. And when her father saw her crying he asked her what was the matter? was she sick? And when she had told him what she was afraid of, for every one knew and was talking of this thing, he said yes, he knew it was true, but she ought not to be afraid, for there was happiness for a woman in marriage and the mothering of children.

And it took many years for the young man to marry all these wives, and have all these children, and all this time Ee-ee-toy was busy making a great vessel of the gum he had gathered from the grease bushes, a sort of olla[3] which could be closed up, which would keep back water. And while he was making this he talked over the reasons for it with Juhwerta Mahkai, Nooee, and Toehahvs,[4] that it was because there was a great flood coming.

1. This is actually a shrub that produces edible fruit, known today as the squawberry.
2. A plant that is common in central Arizona. Here, Lloyd has omitted the details of the young man's "marrying" many women in succession and their delivery of a great many children in a very short time as well as Juhwertamahkai and Ee-ee-toy's sense that these unnatural proceedings will lead to "convulsions" in nature and a flood that will "cover the world." Lloyd does not translate this part of the story because it contains "far too much plainness of circumstantial detail for popular reading."
3. A large earthenware jar (Spanish).
4. The coyote. Nooee is the buzzard (see "The Story of the Creation," p. 24).

And several birds heard them talking thus—the woodpecker, *Hick-o-vick;* the humming-bird, *Vee-pis-mahl;* a little bird named *Gee-ee-sop,* and another called *Quota-veech.*[5]

Eeeetoy said he would escape the flood by getting into the vessel he was making from the gum of the grease bushes or *ser-quoy.*

And Juhwerta Mahkai said he would get into his staff, or walking stick, and float about.

And Toehahvs said he would get into a canetube.

And the little birds said the water would not reach the sky, so they would fly up there and hang on by their bills till it was over.

And Nooee, the buzzard, the powerful, said he did not care if the flood did reach the sky, for he could find a way to break thru.

Now Ee-ee-toy was envious, and anxious to get ahead of Juhwerta Mahkai and get more fame for his wonderful deeds, but Juhwerta Mahkai, though really the strongest, was generous and from kindness and for relationship sake let Ee-ee-toy have the best of it.

And the young girl, the doctor's daughter, kept on crying, fearing the young man, feeling him ever coming nearer, and her father kept on reassuring her, telling her it would be all right, but at last, out of pity for her fears & tears, he told her to go and get him the little tuft of the finest thorns on the top of the white cactus, the *haht-sahn-kahm,*[6] and bring to him.

And her father took the cactus-tuft which she had brought him, and took hair from her head and wound about one end of it, and told her if she would wear this it would protect her. And she consented and wore the cactus-tuft.

And he told her to treat the young man right, when he came, & make him broth of corn. And if the young man should eat all the broth, then their plan would fail, but if he left any broth she was to eat that up and then their plan would succeed.

And he told her to be sure and have a bow and arrows above the door of the *kee,*[7] so that he could take care of the young man.

And after her father had told her this, on that very evening the young man came, and the girl received him kindly, and took his bows & arrows, and put them over the door of the kee, as her father had told her, and made the young man broth of corn and gave it to him to eat.

And he ate only part of it and what was left she ate herself.

And before this her father had told her: "If the young man is wounded by the thorns you wear, in that moment he will become a woman and a mother and you will become a young man."

And in the night all this came to be, even so, and by day-break the child was crying.

And the old woman ran in and said: *"Mossay!"* which means an old woman's grandchild from a daughter.

And the daughter, that had been, said: "It is not your *moss,* it is your *cah-um-maht,*" that is an old woman's grandchild from a son.

And then the old man ran in and said: *"Bah-ahm-ah-dah!"* that is an old man's grandchild from a daughter, but his daughter said: "It is not your *bah-*

---

5. A black phoebe. *"Gee-ee-sop":* a thrasher [adapted from Lloyd's note].
6. The cholla or "jumping" cactus, which has par- ticularly sharp and stiff needles.
7. House or dwelling.

ahm-maht, but it is your *voss-ahm-maht,*" which is an old man's grandchild from a son.[8]

And early in the morning this young man (that had been, but who was now a woman & a mother) made a *wawl-kote,* a carrier, or cradle, for the baby and took the trail back home.

And Juhwerta Mahkai told his neighbors of what was coming, this young man who had changed into a woman and a mother and was bringing a baby born from himself, and that when he arrived wonderful things would happen & springs would gush forth from under every tree and on every mountain.

And the young man-woman came back and by the time of his return Ee-ee-toy had finished his vessel and had placed therein seeds & everything that is in the world.

And the young man-woman, when he came to his old home, placed his baby in the bushes and left it, going in without it, but Ee-ee-toy turned around and looked at him and knew him, for he did not wear a woman's dress, and said to him: "Where is my Bahahmmaht? Bring it to me. I want to see it. It is a joy for an old man to see his grandchild.

I have sat here in my house and watched your going, and all that has happened you, and foreseen some one would send you back in shame, although I did not like to think there was anyone more powerful than I. But never mind, he who has beaten us will see what will happen."

And when the young man-woman went to get his baby, Ee-ee-toy got into his vessel, and built a fire on the hearth he had placed therein; and sealed it up.

And the young man-woman found his baby crying, and the tears from it were all over the ground, around. And when he stooped over to pick up his child he turned into a sand-snipe, and the baby turned into a little teeter-snipe.[9]

Juhwertamahkai's Song before the Flood

My poor people,
Who will see,
Who will see
This water which will moisten the earth!

And then that came true which Juhwerta Mahkai had said, that water would gush out from under every tree & on every mountain; and the people when they saw it, and knew that a flood was coming, ran to Juhwerta Mahkai; and he took his staff and made a hole in the earth and let all those thru who had come to him, but the rest were drowned.

Then Juhwerta Mahkai got into his walking stick & floated, and Toehahvs

8. There is a good deal of wordplay here as various kinship terms are tried out to determine just where this child belongs in the structure of the extended family. The young man's turning into a woman and giving birth to a child continues the theme of aberrations in marriage and childbearing summarized by Lloyd earlier (see n. 2, p. 27). Social interactions and responsibilities are determined by kinship ties, and the story tells of a time when important matters such as these were unsettled and strange. Thus the flood will be necessary to wipe away this earlier, chaotic world and allow a new and more appropriate order to be established.
9. The snipe is a small bird. This is perhaps their only chance to escape destruction in the flood.

got into his tube of cane and floated, but Ee-ee-toy's vessel was heavy & big and remained until the flood was much deeper before it could float.

And the people who were left out fled to the mountains; to the mountains called *Gah-kote-kih* (Superstition Mts.)[1] for they were living in the plains between Gahkotekih and Cheoffskawmack (Tall Gray Mountain.)

And there was a powerful man among these people, a doctor (mahkai), who set a mark on the mountain side and said the water would not rise above it.

And the people believed him and camped just beyond the mark; but the water came on and they had to go higher. And this happened four times.[2]

And the mahkai did this to help his people, and also used power to raise the mountain, but at last he saw all was to be a failure. And he called the people and asked them all to come close together, and he took his doctor-stone[3] (*mah-kai-haw-teh*) which is called Tonedumhawteh or Stone-of-Light, and held it in the palm of his hand and struck it hard with his other hand, and it thundered so loud that all the people were frightened and they were all turned into stone.

The Song of Superstition Mountains

We are destroyed!
By my stone we are destroyed!
We are rightly turned into stone.

And the little birds, the woodpecker, Hickovick; the humming-bird, Vee-pismahl; the little bird named Ge-ee-sop, and the other called Quotaveech, all flew up to the sky and hung on by their bills, but Nooee still floated in the air and intended to keep on the wing unless the floods reached the heavens.

But Juhwerta Mahkai, Ee-ee-toy and Toehahvs floated around on the water and drifted to the west and did not know where they were.

And the flood rose higher until it reached the woodpecker's tail, and you can see the marks to this day.

And Quotaveech was cold and cried so loud that the other birds pulled off their feathers and built him a nest up there so he could keep warm. And when Quotaveech was warm he quit crying.

And then the little birds sang, for they had power to make the water go down by singing, and as they sang the waters gradually receded.

But the others still floated around.

When the land began to appear Juhwerta Mahkai and Toehahvs got out, but Ee-ee-toy had to wait for his house to warm up, for he had built a fire to warm his vessel enough for him to unseal it.

When it was warm enough he unsealed it, but when he looked out he saw the water still running & he got back and sealed himself in again.

And after waiting a while he unsealed his vessel again, and seeing dry land enough he got out.

1. In central Arizona, just east of Phoenix; the mountains derive their name from this story.
2. The terraces of cliffs in the Superstition Mountains are said to mark the successive pausing places of the people, and the clusters of rocks on the top to represent their petrified forms [adapted from Lloyd's note].
3. I.e., a particularly powerful stone; probably a quartz crystal.

And Juhwerta Mahkai went south and Toehahvs went west, and Ee-ee-toy went northward. And as they did not know where they were they missed each other, and passed each other unseen, but afterward saw each other's tracks, and then turned back and shouted, but wandered from the track, and again passed unseen. And this happened four times.

And the fourth time Juhwerta Mahkai and Ee-ee-toy met, but Toehahvs had passed already.

And when they met, Ee-ee-toy said to Juhwerta Mahkai "My younger brother!" but Juhwerta Mahkai greeted him as younger brother & claimed to have come out first. Then Ee-ee-toy said again: "I came out first and you can see the water marks on my body." But Juhwerta Mahkai replied: "I came out first and also have the water marks on my person to prove it."

But Ee-ee-toy so insisted that he was the eldest that Juhwerta Mahkai, just to please him, gave him his way and let him be considered the elder.

And then they turned westward and yelled to find Toehahvs, for they remembered to have seen his tracks, and they kept on yelling till he heard them. And when Toehahvs saw them he called them his younger brothers, and they called him younger brother. And this dispute continued till Ee-ee-toy again got the best of it and, although really the younger brother[,] was admitted by the others to be Seeurhuh, or the elder.

And the birds came down from the sky and again there was a dispute about the relationship, but Ee-ee-toy again got the best of them all.[4]

But Quotaveech staid up in the sky because he had a comfortable nest there, and they called him *Vee-ick-koss-kum Mahkai,* the Feather-Nest Doctor.

And they wanted to find the middle, the navel[5] of the earth, and they sent Veeppismahl, the humming bird, to the west, and Hickovick, the woodpecker, to the east, and all the others stood and waited for them at the starting place. And Veepismahl & Hickovick were to go as far as they could, to the edge of the world, and then return to find the middle of the earth by their meeting. But Hickovick flew a little faster and got there first, and so when they met they found it was not the middle, and they parted & started again, but this time they changed places and Hickovick went westward and Veepismahl went east.

And this time Veepismahl was the faster, and Hickovick was late, and the judges thought their place of meeting was a little east of the center so they all went a little way west. Ee-ee-toy, Juhwerta Mahkai and Toehahvs stood there and sent the birds out once more, and this time Hickovick went eastward again, and Veepismahl went west. And Hickovick flew faster and arrived there first. And they said: "This is not the middle. It is a little way west yet."

And so they moved a little way, and again the birds were sent forth, and this time Hickovick went west and Veepismahl went east. And when the birds returned they met where the others stood and all cried "This is the *Hick,* the Navel of the World!"

And they stood there because there was no dry place yet for them to sit

---

4. These disputes among the gods and then the birds are probably meant to be comic, although they contribute to the serious business of the reorganization of the world based on proper kinship ties.

5. The Pima believe they live in "the middle, the navel," of the world. In this narration, the middle of the world is not specified at the time of creation but only at the time of re-creation, here, after the flood.

down upon; and Ee-ee-toy rubbed upon his breast and took from his bosom the smallest ants, the *O-auf-taw-ton,* and threw them upon the ground, and they worked there and threw up little hills; and this earth was dry. And so they sat down.

Ee-ee-toy's Song When He Made the World Serpents

I know what to do;
I am going to move the water
both ways.

But the water was still running in the valleys, and Ee-ee-toy took a hair from his head & made it into a snake—*Vuck-vahmuht.*⁶ And with this snake he pushed the waters south, but the head of the snake was left lying to the west and his tail to the east.

But there was more water, and Ee-ee-toy took another hair from his head and made another snake, and with this snake pushed the rest of the water north. And the head of this snake was left to the east and his tail to the west. So the head of each snake was left lying with the tail of the other.

And the snake that has his tail to the east, in the morning will shake up his tail to start the morning wind to wake the people and tell them to think of their dreams.

And the snake that has his tail to the west, in the evening will shake up his tail to start the cool wind to tell the people it is time to go in and make the fires & be comfortable.

And they said: "We will make dolls, but we will not let each other see them until they are finished."

And Ee-ee-toy sat facing the west, and Toehahvs facing the south, and Juhwerta Mahkai facing the east.

And the earth was still damp and they took clay and began to make dolls. And Ee-ee-toy made the best. But Juhwerta Mahkai did not make good ones, because he remembered some of his people had escaped the flood thru a hole in the earth, and he intended to visit them and he did not want to make anything better than they were to take the place of them. And Toehahvs made the poorest of all.

Then Ee-ee-toy asked them if they were ready, and they all said yes, and then they turned about and showed each other the dolls they had made.

And Ee-ee-toy asked Juhwerta Mahkai why he had made such queer dolls. "This one," he said, "is not right, for you have made him without any sitting-down parts, and how can he get rid of the waste of what he eats?"

But Juhwerta Mahkai said: "He will not need to eat, he can just smell the smell of what is cooked."

Then Ee-ee-toy asked again: "Why did you make this doll with only one leg—how can he run?" But Juhwerta Mahkai replied: "He will not need to run; he can just hop around."

Then Ee-ee-toy asked Toehahvs why he had made a doll with webs between his fingers and toes—"How can he point directions?" But Toehahvs said he had made these dolls so for good purpose, for if anybody gave them small seeds they would not slip between their fingers, and they could use the webs for dippers to drink with.

6. I.e., red snake.

And Ee-ee-toy held up his dolls and said: "These are the best of all, and I want you to make more like them." And he took Toehahv's dolls and threw them into the water and they became ducks & beavers. And he took Juhwerta Mahkai's dolls and threw them away and they all broke to pieces and were nothing.

And Juhwerta Mahkai was angry at this and began to sink into the ground; and took his stick and hooked it into the sky and pulled the sky down while he was sinking. But Ee-ee-toy spread his hand over his dolls, and held up the sky, and seeing that Juhwerta Mahkai was sinking into the earth he sprang and tried to hold him & cried, "Man, what are you doing! Are you going to leave me and my people here alone?"

But Juhwerta Mahkai slipped through his hands, leaving in them only the waste & excretion of his skin. And that is how there is sickness & death among us.[7]

And Ee-ee-toy, when Juhwerta Mahkai escaped him, went around swinging his hands & saying: "I never thought all this impurity would come upon my people!" and the swinging of his hands scattered disease over all the earth. And he washed himself in a pool or pond and the impurities remaining in the water are the source of the malarias and all the diseases of dampness.

And Ee-ee-toy and Toehahvs built a house for their dolls a little way off, and Ee-ee-toy sent Toehahvs to listen if they were yet talking. And the *Aw-up,* (the Apaches) were the first ones that talked. And Ee-ee-toy said: "I never meant to have those Apaches talk first, I would rather have had the *Aw-aw-tam,*[8] the Good People, speak first."

But he said: "It is all right. I will give them strength, that they stand the cold & all hardships."

And all the different people that they had made talked, one after the other, but the Awawtam talked last.

And they all took to playing together, and in their play they kicked each other as the Maricopas[9] do in sport to this day; but the Apaches got angry and said: "We will leave you and go into the mountains and eat what we can get, but we will dream good dreams and be just as happy as you with all your good things to eat."

And some of the people took up their residence on the Gila, and some went west to the Rio Colorado. And those who builded vahahkkees, or houses out of adobe and stones, lived in the valley of the Gila, between the mountains which are there now.

1911

---

7. In "The Story of the Creation" (p. 24) Juhwer-tamahkai's bodily products (e.g., perspiration) were used for creating, not destroying.
8. The Pima term for themselves (currently spelled "O'odham"). A more accurate translation is simply "people" or "us," as distinct from animals and from other groups of people. The Pima and Apache were traditional enemies.
9. Traditional allies of the Pima.

CHRISTOPHER COLUMBUS
1451–1506

Born into a family of wool workers near the once supreme Mediterranean port of Genoa, Christopher Columbus turned to the sea as a young man; developed a plan to find a commercially viable Atlantic route to Asia; and in 1492 won the support of the Spanish monarchs, Ferdinand and Isabella, for this "enterprise of the Indies." His series of four voyages between 1492 and 1504 produced a brief moment of wonder followed by a long series of disasters and disenchantments. Apparently friendly relations with the Taino Indians on the island of Hispaniola in 1492 turned sour as the settlers Columbus left behind demanded gold and sexual partners from their hosts; on his return there in 1494, none of the Europeans were alive. A new settlement established on the island following this discovery fell into such disorder during the absence of Columbus in Cuba and Jamaica that in 1496 he was forced to return to Spain to clear his name of politically motivated charges made against him by other Europeans in the Indies. A third voyage, begun in 1498, took him for the first time to the South American mainland; the lushness of nature there made him believe himself near Paradise, but that illusion vanished when, on his return to Hispaniola, he encountered Spanish settlers there in open rebellion against his authority. Able to reach a truce only at the expense of the Taino Indians, who were to be virtually enslaved by the rebels, Columbus soon found himself under arrest, sent in chains to Spain in 1500 to answer yet more charges. His last voyage, intended to recoup his tarnished reputation, resulted in a long period of suffering in Panama and shipwreck in Jamaica, and these outer woes were accompanied by nearly delusional periods as Columbus underwent a virtual breakdown. Rescued at last from this extremity, he returned to Europe, where soon afterward he died. The West Indies, as his discoveries were called, remained disordered and bloody.

Several documents regarding the four voyages survive from Columbus's hand. The supposed *Journal* of his first voyage is actually a summary prepared by the cleric and reformer Bartolomé de las Casas. A letter sent by Columbus to Luis de Santangel, a royal official and an early supporter of his venture, provides a more authentic account and served as the basis for the first printed description of America, issued in 1493 in Spain and widely translated and reprinted across Europe. A memorandum regarding the second voyage, intended by Columbus for the Spanish monarchs (whose responses to each point also survive), offers useful insights into the emerging ambiguities and problems of the colony on Hispaniola. For the third and fourth voyages, three letters from Columbus, two sent to the Crown and one to a woman of the Spanish court, detail his deepening worldly and spiritual troubles.

The texts are from *Select Documents Illustrating the Four Voyages of Columbus*, translated and edited by Cecil Jane (1930–33).

From Letter to Luis de Santangel[1] Regarding the First Voyage

[At sea, February 15, 1493]

Sir,

As I know that you will be pleased at the great victory with which Our Lord has crowned my voyage, I write this to you, from which you will learn

1. A former merchant and a court official since 1478 who had supported Columbus's proposal to the Spanish Crown and had helped secure financing for the first voyage.

how in thirty-three days, I passed from the Canary Islands to the Indies with the fleet which the most illustrious king and queen our sovereigns gave to me. And there I found very many islands filled with people innumerable, and of them all I have taken possession for their highnesses, by proclamation made and with the royal standard unfurled, and no opposition was offered to me. To the first island which I found I gave the name *San Salvador,*[2] in remembrance of the Divine Majesty, Who has marvelously bestowed all this; the Indians call it "Guanahani." To the second I gave the name *Isla de Santa María de Concepción;* to the third, *Fernandina;* to the fourth, *Isabella;* to the fifth, *Isla Juana,*[3] and so to each one I gave a new name.

When I reached Juana I followed its coast to the westward, and I found it to be so extensive that I thought that it must be the mainland, the province of Catayo.[4] And since there were neither towns nor villages on the seashore, but only small hamlets, with the people of which I could not have speech because they all fled immediately, I went forward on the same course, thinking that I should not fail to find great cities and towns. And at the end of many leagues, seeing that there was no change and that the coast was bearing me northwards, which I wished to avoid since winter was already beginning and I proposed to make from it to the south, and as moreover the wind was carrying me forward, I determined not to wait for a change in the weather and retraced my path as far as a certain harbor known to me. And from that point I sent two men inland to learn if there were a king or great cities. They traveled three days' journey and found an infinity of small hamlets and people without number, but nothing of importance. For this reason they returned.

I understood sufficiently from other Indians, whom I had already taken, that this land was nothing but an island. And therefore I followed its coast eastwards for one hundred and seven leagues to the point where it ended. And from that cape I saw another island distant eighteen leagues from the former, to the east, to which I at once gave the name "Española."[5] And I went there and followed its northern coast, as I had in the case of Juana, to the eastward for one hundred and eighty-eight great leagues in a straight line. This island and all the others are very fertile to a limitless degree, and this island is extremely so. In it there are many harbors on the coast of the sea, beyond comparison with others which I know in Christendom, and many rivers, good and large, which is marvelous. Its lands are high, and there are in it very many sierras and very lofty mountains, beyond comparison with the island of Tenerife.[6] All are most beautiful, of a thousand shapes, and all are accessible and filled with trees of a thousand kinds and tall, and they seem to touch the sky. And I am told that they never lose their foliage, as I can understand, for I saw them as green and as lovely as they are in Spain in May, and some of them were flowering, some bearing fruit, and some in another stage, according to their nature. And the nightingale was singing and other birds of a thousand kinds in the month of November there where I went. There are six or eight kinds of palm, which are a wonder to behold on account of their beautiful variety, but so are the other trees and fruits

2. The precise identity of the Bahamian island Columbus named San Salvador is not known today, although many theories have been put forward.
3. Of these four islands, only the identity of Juana (Cuba) is today certain.
4. I.e., China (or "Cathay").
5. I.e., Hispaniola, where the countries of Haiti and the Dominican Republic are located.
6. The largest of the Canary Islands.

and plants. In it are marvelous pine groves, and there are very large tracts of cultivatable lands, and there is honey,[7] and there are birds of many kinds and fruits in great diversity. In the interior are mines of metals, and the population is without number. Española is a marvel.

1493

From Letter to Ferdinand and Isabella Regarding the Fourth Voyage[1]

[Jamaica, July 7, 1503]

*   *   *

Of Española, Paria,[2] and the other lands, I never think without weeping. I believed that their example would have been to the profit of others; on the contrary, they are in an exhausted state; although they are not dead, the infirmity is incurable or very extensive; let him who brought them to this state come now with the remedy if he can or if he knows it; in destruction, everyone is an adept. It was always the custom to give thanks and promotion to him who imperiled his person. It is not just that he who has been so hostile to this undertaking should enjoy its fruits or that his children should. Those who left the Indies, flying from toils and speaking evil of the matter and of me, have returned with official employment.[3] So it has now been ordained in the case of Veragua.[4] It is an ill example and without profit for the business and for justice in the world.

The fear of this, with other sufficient reasons, which I saw clearly, led me to pray your highnesses before I went to discover these islands and Terra Firma, that you would leave them to me to govern in your royal name. It pleased you; it was a privilege and agreement, and under seal and oath, and you granted me the title of viceroy and admiral and governor general of all. And you fixed the boundary, a hundred leagues beyond the Azores and the Cape Verde Islands, by a line passing from pole to pole, and you gave me wide power over this and over all that I might further discover. The document states this very fully.

The other most important matter, which calls aloud for redress, remains inexplicable to this moment. Seven years I was at your royal court, where all to whom this undertaking was mentioned, unanimously declared it to be a delusion. Now all, down to the very tailors, seek permission to make discoveries. It can be believed that they go forth to plunder, and it is granted to them to do so, so that they greatly prejudice my honor and do very great damage to the enterprise. It is well to give to God that which is His due and

7. The honeybee, presumably the source of the honey found on the island, is not native to the Western Hemisphere. Nor is the nightingale, mentioned above.
1. Written on Jamaica in 1503, this letter was hand-carried from there to Hispaniola by Diego Mendez.
2. Paria was the mainland region of what is now Venezuela, near the island of Trinidad. Columbus,

who had first landed in South America ("Terra Firma," as he terms it later) in 1498, argued that the terrestrial paradise lay nearby.
3. Although it appears that Columbus has specific personal enemies in mind, it is not clear who he means.
4. I.e., Panama, where Columbus was shipwrecked earlier in this voyage.

to Caesar that which belongs to him. This is a just sentiment and based on justice.

The lands which here obey Your Highnesses are more extensive and richer than all other Christian lands. After I, by the divine will, had placed them under your royal and exalted lordship, and was on the point of securing a very great revenue, suddenly, while I was waiting for ships to come to your high presence with victory and with great news of gold, being very secure and joyful, I was made a prisoner and with my two brothers was thrown into a ship, laden with fetters, stripped to the skin, very ill-treated, and without being tried or condemned. Who will believe that a poor foreigner could in such a place rise against Your Highnesses, without cause, and without the support of some other prince, and being alone among your vassals and natural subjects, and having all my children at your royal court?

I came to serve at the age of twenty-eight years, and now I have not a hair on my body that is not gray, and my body is infirm, and whatever remained to me from those years of service has been spent and taken away from me and sold, and from my brothers, down to my very coat, without my being heard or seen, to my great dishonor. It must be believed that this was not done by your royal command. The restitution of my honor, the reparation of my losses, and the punishment of him who did this, will spread abroad the fame of your royal nobility. The same punishment is due to him who robbed me of the pearls, and to him who infringed my rights as admiral.[5] Very great will be your merit, fame without parallel will be yours, if you do this, and there will remain in Spain a glorious memory of Your Highnesses, as grateful and just princes.

The pure devotion which I have ever borne to the service of Your Highnesses, and the unmerited wrong that I have suffered, will not permit me to remain silent, although I would fain do so; I pray Your Highnesses to pardon me. I am so ruined as I have said; hitherto I have wept for others; now, Heaven have mercy upon me, and may the earth weep for me. Of worldly goods, I have not even a blanca[6] for an offering in spiritual things. Here in the Indies I have become careless of the prescribed forms of religion. Alone in my trouble, sick, in daily expectation of death, and encompassed about by a million savages, full of cruelty and our foes, and so separated from the holy Sacraments of Holy Church, my soul will be forgotten if it here leaves my body. Weep for me, whoever has charity, truth, and justice.

I did not sail upon this voyage to gain honor or wealth; this is certain, for already all hope of that was dead. I came to Your Highnesses with true devotion and with ready zeal, and I do not lie. I humbly pray Your Highnesses that if it please God to bring me forth from this place, that you will be pleased to permit me to go to Rome and to other places of pilgrimage. May the Holy Trinity preserve your life and high estate, and grant you increase of prosperity.

Done in the Indies in the island of Jamaica, on the seventh of July, in the year one thousand five hundred and three.

1505

---

5. The reference is to Alonso de Ojeda (c. 1468– c. 1516), who had taken pearls (part of what was reserved to Columbus under his agreement with the Spanish Crown) from Paria to Española.
6. A small Spanish coin.

BARTOLOMÉ DE LAS CASAS
1474–1566

Early modern Europe's most eloquent apologist for Native American rights, Bartolomé de las Casas first heard of the new "discoveries" as a student in Seville in 1493, when Columbus triumphantly entered that Spanish city. All his life, Casas recalled how Columbus brought with him "seven Indians who had survived the voyage," and "beautiful green parrots, . . . masks made of precious stones and fishbone, . . . sizable samples of very fine gold, and many other things never before seen in Spain." Although Casas later called the seizure of those seven Taino Indians on the island of Guanahaní "the first injustice committed in the Indies," in the Spain of 1493, neither Casas nor anyone else had time to reflect on the moral implications of the pageant taking place before their eyes.

Going to Hispaniola himself in 1502 as a member of a new royal governor's party, Casas soon was participating eagerly in the exploitation of the natives. In his great *History of the Indies*, he was to write of his moral blindness in this period, noting that he "went about his concerns like the others, sending his share of Indians to work fields and gold mines, taking advantage of them as much as he could." Later, after becoming a priest, he grew convinced that such behavior was contrary to Christian teachings and he soon was urging all masters to renounce the slave system (or *encomienda*), as he himself had done. In 1515 Casas took the case to Spain, where the government appointed him "protector of the Indians" and gave him permission to found a peaceful, exemplary colony on the Venezuelan coast. One of his remedies for Indian suffering was a proposal to import Africans to the Indies to replace the enslaved Indians. Soon, however, Casas repented of this suggestion, for (as he wrote in *History of the Indies*) "black slavery was as unjust as Indian slavery, and was no remedy at all." His new venture failed, however, and as Casas withdrew into monastic seclusion on Hispaniola between 1522 and 1529, brutal new conquests in Guatemala, Nicaragua, and Peru buried the promise of his Venezuelan project ever deeper.

Only in the 1530s, when Casas returned to political activity, did his arguments have widespread effect. In 1537 Pope Paul III forbade all further enslavements; in 1542, Emperor Charles V followed suit in the New Laws of the Indies, which gave Native Americans full protection of the courts, forbidding their enslavement on any grounds. "We order and command that henceforth," ran one clause, "for no cause whatsoever, whether of war, rebellion, ransom, or in any other manner, can any Indian be made a slave."

Such victories were bittersweet. As bishop of Chiapas, Mexico, from 1544 to 1547, Casas sought to enforce the new laws, but riots there and broad resistance throughout the Spanish colonies made it clear that his goals would not easily be achieved. Disillusioned by Charles V's revocation, in the face of pressure from the settlers, of key features of the 1542 code, Casas returned in 1547 to Spain, where he spent the last twenty years of his life writing about his long crusade in the West Indies.

Of his writings, the most important in his own era was *The Very Brief Relation of the Devastation of the Indies*, first published in 1552 but based on oral arguments used by Casas a decade earlier to persuade a special royal commission to frame the new code of 1542. It details with such chilling effect the destruction visited on Native Americans by conquistador and colonizer in pursuit of wealth that in his own time Casas was widely accused of treason and even endured charges of heresy, partly because the quick translation of his *Relation* into several other languages provided Spain's enemies with ample evidence of his country's sins in America—a point Protestant nations such as The Netherlands and England especially wished to make. Ironically, the later Protestant "Black Legend" of Spain's devastation of the West Indies derives from the polemical exposé of the Catholic priest Bartolomé de las

Casas, an exposé he intended as a call to Spain's future reform rather than as a denunciation of its past.

From The Very Brief Relation of the Devastation of the Indies[1]

From Hispaniola

This was the first land in the New World to be destroyed and depopulated by the Christians, and here they began their subjection of the women and children, taking them away from the Indians to use them and ill use them, eating the food they provided with their sweat and toil. The Spaniards did not content themselves with what the Indians gave them of their own free will, according to their ability, which was always too little to satisfy enormous appetites, for a Christian eats and consumes in one day an amount of food that would suffice to feed three houses inhabited by ten Indians for one month. And they committed other acts of force and violence and oppression which made the Indians realize that these men had not come from Heaven.[2] And some of the Indians concealed their foods while others concealed their wives and children and still others fled to the mountains to avoid the terrible transactions of the Christians.

And the Christians attacked them with buffets and beatings, until finally they laid hands on the nobles of the villages. Then they behaved with such temerity and shamelessness that the most powerful ruler of the islands had to see his own wife raped by a Christian officer.

From that time onward the Indians began to seek ways to throw the Christians out of their lands. They took up arms, but their weapons were very weak and of little service in offense and still less in defense. (Because of this, the wars of the Indians against each other are little more than games played by children.) And the Christians, with their horses and swords and pikes began to carry out massacres and strange cruelties against them. They attacked the towns and spared neither the children nor the aged nor pregnant women nor women in childbed, not only stabbing them and dismembering them but cutting them to pieces as if dealing with sheep in the slaughter house. They laid bets as to who, with one stroke of the sword, could split a man in two or could cut off his head or spill out his entrails with a single stroke of the pike. They took infants from their mothers' breasts, snatching them by the legs and pitching them headfirst against the crags or snatched them by the arms and threw them into the rivers, roaring with laughter and saying as the babies fell into the water, "Boil there, you offspring of the devil!" Other infants they put to the sword along with their mothers and anyone else who happened to be nearby. They made some low wide gallows on which the hanged victim's feet almost touched the ground, stringing up their victims in lots of thirteen, in memory of Our Redeemer and His twelve Apostles, then set burning wood at their feet and thus burned them alive. To others they attached straw or wrapped their whole bodies in straw and set them afire. With still others, all those they wanted to capture alive, they cut off

1. The text comes from *The Devastation of the Indies: A Brief Account*, translated by Herma Briffault (1974).
2. Columbus and other early European voyagers reported that native peoples took them to be gods who had come from the heavens. See Thomas Harriot's *A Brief and True Report* (p. 81) for a good example.

their hands and hung them round the victim's neck, saying "Go now, carry the message," meaning, Take the news to the Indians who have fled to the mountains. They usually dealt with the chieftains and nobles in the following way: they made a grid of rods which they placed on forked sticks, then lashed the victims to the grid and lighted a smoldering fire underneath, so that little by little, as those captives screamed in despair and torment, their souls would leave them.

I once saw this, when there were four or five nobles lashed on grids and burning; I seem even to recall that there were two or three pairs of grids where others were burning, and because they uttered such loud screams that they disturbed the captain's sleep, he ordered them to be strangled. And the constable, who was worse than an executioner, did not want to obey that order (and I know the name of that constable and know his relatives in Seville), but instead put a stick over the victim's tongues, so they could not make a sound, and he stirred up the fire, but not too much, so that they roasted slowly, as he liked. I saw all these things I have described, and countless others.

And because all the people who could do so fled to the mountains to escape these inhuman, ruthless, and ferocious acts, the Spanish captains, enemies of the human race, pursued them with the fierce dogs they kept which attacked the Indians, tearing them to pieces and devouring them. And because on few and far between occasions, the Indians justifiably killed some Christians, the Spaniards made a rule among themselves that for every Christian slain by the Indians, they would slay a hundred Indians.

From *The Coast of Pearls, Paria, and the Island of Trinidad*

[The Spaniards] have brought to the island of Hispaniola and the island of San Juan[3] more than two million souls taken captive, and have sent them to do hard labor in the mines, labors that caused many of them to die. And it is a great sorrow and heartbreak to see this coastal land which was so flourishing, now a depopulated desert.

This is truth that can be verified, for no more do they bring ships loaded with Indians that have been thus attacked and captured as I have related. No more do they cast overboard into the sea the third part of the numerous Indians they stow on their vessels, these dead being added to those they have killed in their native lands, the captives crowded into the holds of their ships, without food or water, or with very little, so as not to deprive the Spanish tyrants who call themselves ship owners and who carry enough food for themselves on their voyages of attack. And for the pitiful Indians who died of hunger and thirst, there is no remedy but to cast them into the sea. And verily, as a Spaniard told me, their ships in these regions could voyage without compass or chart, merely by following for the distance between the Lucayos Islands[4] and Hispaniola, which is sixty or seventy leagues, the trace of those Indian corpses floating in the sea, corpses that had been cast overboard by earlier ships.

Afterward, when they disembark on the island of Hispaniola, it is heartbreaking to see those naked Indians, heartbreaking for anyone with a vestige

---

3. I.e., Puerto Rico.   4. I.e., the Bahamas.

of piety, the famished state they are in, fainting and falling down, weak from hunger, men, women, old people, and children.

Then, like sheep, they are sorted out into flocks of ten or twenty persons, separating fathers from sons, wives from husbands, and the Spaniards draw lots, the ship owners carrying off their share, the best flock, to compensate them for the moneys they have invested in their fleet of two or three ships, the ruffian tyrants getting their share of captives who will be house slaves, and when in this *"repartimiento"*[5] a tyrant gets an old person or an invalid, he says, "Why do you give me this one? To bury him? And this sick one, do you give him to me to make him well?" See by such remarks in what esteem the Spaniards hold the Indians and judge if they are accomplishing the divine concepts of love for our fellow man, as laid down by the prophets.

The tyranny exercised by the Spaniards against the Indians in the work of pearl fishing is one of the most cruel that can be imagined. There is no life as infernal and desperate in this century that can be compared with it, although the mining of gold is a dangerous and burdensome way of life. The pearl fishers dive into the sea at a depth of five fathoms, and do this from sunrise to sunset, and remain for many minutes without breathing, tearing the oysters out of their rocky beds where the pearls are formed. They come to the surface with a netted bag of these oysters where a Spanish torturer is waiting in a canoe or skiff, and if the pearl diver shows signs of wanting to rest, he is showered with blows, his hair is pulled, and he is thrown back into the water, obliged to continue the hard work of tearing out the oysters and bringing them again to the surface.

The food given the pearl divers is codfish, not very nourishing, and the bread made of maize, the bread of the Indies. At night the pearl divers are chained so they cannot escape.

Often a pearl diver does not return to the surface, for these waters are infested with man-eating sharks of two kinds, both vicious marine animals that can kill, eat, and swallow a whole man.

In this harvesting of pearls let us again consider whether the Spaniards preserve the divine concepts of love for their fellow men, when they place the bodies of the Indians in such mortal danger, and their souls, too, for these pearl divers perish without the holy sacraments. And it is solely because of the Spaniards' greed for gold that they force the Indians to lead such a life, often a brief life, for it is impossible to continue for long diving into the cold water and holding the breath for minutes at a time, repeating this hour after hour, day after day; the continual cold penetrates them, constricts the chest, and they die spitting blood, or weakened by diarrhea.

The hair of these pearl divers, naturally black, is as if burnished by the saltpeter in the water, and hangs down their backs making them look like sea dogs or monsters of another species. And in this extraordinary labor, or, better put, in this infernal labor, the Lucayan Indians are finally consumed, as are captive Indians from other provinces. And all of them were publicly sold for one hundred and fifty castellanos,[6] these Indians who had lived happily on their islands until the Spaniards came, although such a thing was

---

5. Distribution (Spanish). Attempts were made, by royal decree in 1503, to require that the masters of the American Indians convert them to Christianity and serve as trustees for their property, but the *repartimiento* ceased to be anything more than a slave-holding system.

6. A Spanish gold coin bearing the arms of Castile.

against the law. But the unjust judges did nothing to stop it. For all the Indians of these islands are known to be great swimmers.[7]

1542–46   1552

7. I.e., the physical abilities of the Caribbean natives as pearl divers were so extraordinary that the Spanish judges overlooked their mistreatment.

BERNAL DÍAZ DEL CASTILLO
1492–1584

Bernal Díaz del Castillo, born in the town of Medina del Campo in the Spanish province of Castile in the momentous year 1492, went to the West Indies as a young man and remained there, except for two brief returns to Spain, for the rest of his long life. His first American voyage came in 1514, in the company of the future explorer Hernando de Soto and under the command of Pedrárias Dávila, who was sent to replace his son-in-law Vasco Nuñez del Balboa as governor of Darien, a colony in what is now Panama. Eventually, the political turmoil of Darien (where Dávila was later to arrest Balboa on flimsy charges of treason and execute him) disillusioned young Díaz, who along with several companions sailed to Cuba, then under the rule of his own kinsman Diego Velázquez. From there, in 1517 and 1518, Díaz went out with two brief expeditions to Yucatán and Florida before joining Hernán Cortés in the Conquest of Mexico (1519–21).

Because he marched as a mere foot soldier when the army moved inland from Vera Cruz to conquer and later reconquer Tenochtitlán (Mexico City), Díaz knew the grim story in vivid detail. Many years later, the lone survivor of all the conquistadors, living in modest circumstances on a small land grant in Guatemala, he at last undertook to put on paper what he could recall. The tale was the only thing, he said, that he had to leave his children and grandchildren: "I am now an old man, over eighty-four years of age, and have lost both sight and hearing; and unfortunately I have gained no wealth to leave to my children and descendants, except this true story, which is a most remarkable one, as my readers will presently see."

Among the remarkable features of *The True History of the Conquest of New Spain* is the fact that Díaz seems never to have regretted the violence that flooded Mexico with Aztec blood or the subsequent enslavement of the natives there. He had the ordinary soldier's gift, however, for telling what he had seen without dwelling on the official justifications for all the violence and suffering he was party to. As a consequence, his prose catches with rough power this extraordinary meeting of two civilizations as they vied for control of Mexico. During the last siege of the city, for several days he watched across the battle lines as the Aztecs executed captive Spaniards— "their chests struck open and their palpitating hearts drawn out"—and he found his own courage weakened. "I came to fear death more than ever in the past. Before I went into battle, a sort of horror and gloom would seize my heart and I would [urinate] once or twice and commend myself to God, and His blessed Mother."

Such experiences changed Díaz profoundly. Late in his account of the fall of the city, he confessed that even now, more than sixty years later, he could never sleep through the night: "Some may ask when we slept [during the Conquest], and what our beds are like. They were nothing but a little straw and a mat, and anyone who had a curtain put it underneath him. We slept in our armour and sandals with our weapons close beside us. . . . I grew so accustomed to sleeping [this way] that after the conquest of New Spain I kept the habit of sleeping in my clothes and without a bed. . . . Even [now] when I go to the villages of my *encomienda* I do not take a bed, or if I sometimes do, it is not because I want it, but because some gentlemen are travelling with me, and I do not want them to think I do not possess a good bed. But I always lie down fully dressed. What is more, I can only sleep for a short time at night. I have to get up and look at the sky and stars and walk about for a bit in the dew." The passage is especially suggestive, but in some ways it is typical of the artless power of the whole long narrative. Few writers of the age of Conquest told such concrete tales, full of the sights and sounds, beauties and horrors that resulted from Europe's expansion into the New World.

From The True History of the Conquest of New Spain[1]

[GIFTS PRESENTED TO CORTÉS]

About this time[2] many Indians came from the towns of which these two great servants of Montezuma were governors, some of them bringing gold and jewels of little value, or fowls, to exchange with us for green beads, clear glass beads, and other articles. In this way we kept ourselves fed, for almost all the soldiers had brought goods for barter, and we had learnt in Grijalva's[3] time that beads were a good thing to bring.

Six or seven days passed in this way. Then one morning Tendile[4] returned with more than a hundred Indian porters, and accompanied by a great Mexican chief, who in face, features, and body was very like our Captain. The great Montezuma had chosen him on purpose. For it is said when Tendile showed him the portrait of Cortés all the princes present exclaimed that one of their number, Quintalbor, looked exactly like him; and it was Quintalbor who now accompanied Tendile. On account of this resemblance we in the camp called them "our Cortés" and "the other Cortés."

To return to my story, when these people arrived before our Captain they kissed the earth and perfumed him and all the soldiers near him with incense that they had brought in earthenware braziers. Cortés received them kindly and seated them beside him. The prince Quintalbor, who bore the presents and had been appointed joint spokesman with Tendile, welcomed us to the country and after a long speech ordered them to be brought forward. The various objects were placed on mats, which they call *petates,* on which were spread other cotton cloths. The first was a disk in the shape of the sun, as big as a cartwheel and made of very fine gold. It was a marvelous thing engraved with many sorts of figures and, as those who afterward weighed it reported, was worth more than ten thousand pesos. There was another larger disk of brightly shining silver in the shape of the moon, with other figures on it, and this was worth a great deal for it was very heavy. Quintalbor also brought back the helmet[5] full of small grains of gold, just as they come from the mines and worth three thousand pesos.

The gold in the helmet was worth more than twenty thousand pesos to us,

1. The text is from *The Conquest of New Spain,* translated by J. M. Cohen (1963).
2. I.e., April 1519, when Cortés had arrived in the vicinity of the future Vera Cruz and the port of San Juan de Ulua on the Gulf Coast of Mexico but had not yet ventured far inland.
3. Juan de Grijalva (1489?–1527) had led an expedition along the coast of Yucatán in 1518, of which Díaz had been a member.

4. Or Teuhtlilli; a Mexican leader—or cacique, as the Spanish called such a leader—who conveyed messages and gifts from Cortés to Montezuma. He first approached the Spaniards at their camp on Easter Sunday 1519, three days after their landing.
5. Cortés sent Tendile to Mexico City with this helmet, requesting that it be sent back filled with gold. Díaz reports that the gilded helmet, which belonged to an ordinary soldier, was rusty.

because it proved to us that there were good mines in the country. Next came twenty golden ducks, of fine workmanship and very realistic, some ornaments in the shape of their native dogs, many others in the shapes of tigers, lions, and monkeys, ten necklaces of very fine workmanship, some pendants, twelve arrows and a strung bow, and two rods like staffs of justice twenty inches long, all modeled in fine gold. Next they brought crests of gold, plumes of rich green feathers, silver crests, some fans of the same material, models of deer in hollow gold, and many other things that I cannot remember, since all this was very long ago; and after this came thirty loads of beautiful cotton cloth of various patterns, decorated with feathers of many colors, and so many other things that I cannot attempt to describe them.

When the presents had been displayed these great *Caciques* Quintalbor and Tendile asked Cortés to accept them with the same grace as Montezuma had shown in sending them, and to divide them among the *Teules*[6] and men who accompanied him. Cortés accepted the gifts with delight, whereupon the ambassadors told him that they wished to repeat the message with which Montezuma had charged them. First, that he was pleased such valiant men as he had heard we were should come to his country—for he knew what we had done at Tabasco[7]—and that he would much like to see our great Emperor, who was such a mighty prince that his fame had reached him even from the distant lands whence we came. Second, that he would send the Emperor a present of precious stones, and serve us in any way he could during our stay in that port. But as for a meeting, he told us not to think of it, for it was not necessary; and he put forward many objections.

Cortés thanked them with a good countenance, and with many flattering protestations gave each governor two holland[8] shirts, some blue glass beads, and other things, and begged them to go back as his ambassadors to Mexico and inform their lord, the great Montezuma, that since we had crossed so many seas and journeyed from such distant lands solely to see and speak with him in person, our great King and lord would got give us a good reception if we were to return without doing so. Wherever their king might be, said Cortés, we should like to go and visit him and carry out his commands.

* * *

[THE APPROACH TO TENOCHTITLÁN]

Next morning,[9] we came to a broad causeway and continued our march toward Iztapalapa.[1] And when we saw all those cities and villages built in the water, and other great towns on dry land, and that straight and level causeway leading to Mexico, we were astounded. These great towns and *cues*[2] and buildings rising from the water, all made of stone, seemed like an unchanged vision from the tale of Amadis.[3] Indeed, some of our soldiers asked whether it was not all a dream. It is not surprising therefore that I should write in

6. Gods (Nahuatl); i.e., the Mexicans apparently assumed that at least some of the Cortés party were of divine origin.
7. Cortés had arrived at the mouth of the Tabasco River, south of the future Vera Cruz on the Gulf Coast of Mexico, in late March. The year before, Grijalva had found the Maya there friendly, but Díaz reports that in 1519 they attacked Cortés, who lost a shoe in the mud; Díaz received an arrow wound in the thigh.
8. Linen.

9. According to Díaz, this was November 7, 1519.
1. An Aztec town located on a peninsula jutting into Lake Texcoco south of the island capital of Tenochtitlán. The causeway led north across two smaller lakes to the peninsula; other causeways led from Iztapalapa to the capital on Lake Texcoco.
2. Temples (Nahuatl).
3. The medieval romance of the warrior Amadis, based on French originals, survives in the 15th-century version by García de Montalvo.

this vein. It was all so wonderful that I do not know how to describe this first glimpse of things never heard of, seen or dreamed of before.

When we arrived near Iztapalapa we beheld the splendor of the other *Caciques* who came out to meet us, the lord of that city whose name was Cuitlahuac, and the lord of Culuacan,[4] both of them close relations of Montezuma. And when we entered the city of Iztapalapa, the sight of the palaces in which they lodged us! They were very spacious and well built, of magnificent stone, cedar wood, and the wood of other sweet-smelling trees, with great rooms and courts, which were a wonderful sight, and all covered with awnings of woven cotton.

When we had taken a good look at all this, we went to the orchard and garden, which was a marvelous place both to see and walk in. I was never tired of noticing the diversity of trees and the various scents given off by each, and the paths choked with roses and other flowers, and the many local fruit-trees and rose-bushes, and the pond of fresh water. Another remarkable thing was that large canoes could come into the garden from the lake, through a channel they had cut, and their crews did not have to disembark. Everything was shining with lime[5] and decorated with different kinds of stonework and paintings which were a marvel to gaze on. Then there were birds of many breeds and varieties which came to the pond. I say again that I stood looking at it, and thought that no land like it would ever be discovered in the whole world, because at that time Peru was neither known nor thought of. But today all that I then saw is overthrown and destroyed; nothing is left standing.

The *Caciques* of that town and of Coyoacan[6] brought us a present of gold worth more than two thousand pesos; and Cortés thanked them heartily for it, and he showed them great kindness, telling them through our interpreters something about our holy faith, and declaring to them the great power of our lord the Emperor. But there were too many conversations for me to describe them all.

Early next day we left Iztapalapa with a large escort of these great *Caciques*, and followed the causeway, which is eight yards wide and goes so straight to the city of Mexico that I do not think it curves at all. Wide though it was, it was so crowded with people that there was hardly room for them all. Some were going to Mexico and others coming away, besides those who had come out to see us, and we could hardly get through the crowds that were there. For the towers and the *cues* were full, and they came in canoes from all parts of the lake. No wonder, since they had never seen horses or men like us before!

With such wonderful sights to gaze on we did not know what to say, or if this was real that we saw before our eyes. On the land side there were great cities, and on the lake many more. The lake was crowded with canoes. At intervals along the causeway there were many bridges, and before us was the great city of Mexico. As for us, we were scarcely four hundred strong, and we well remembered the words and warnings of the people of Huexotzinco and Tlascala and Tlamanalco,[7] and the many other warnings we had received

4. Cuitlahuac and Culuacan were cities to the south of Tenochtitlán.
5. I.e., whitewash.
6. A city west of Iztapalapa and due south of Tenochtitlán selected by Cortés as his headquarters during the second siege of the capital in 1520.

7. The peoples in question all had differences with Montezuma. Tlascala (or Tlaxcala), for instance, was an independent state east of Mexico City and supplied much support for Cortés in his battles with the Aztecs. The Aztecs told Cortés they could conquer Tlaxcala anytime they wished, but left it

to beware of entering the city of Mexico, since they would kill us as soon as they had us inside. Let the interested reader consider whether there is not much to ponder in this narrative of mine. What men in all the world have shown such daring? But let us go on.

We marched along our causeway to a point where another small causeway branches off to another city called Coyoacan, and there, beside some tower-like buildings, which were their shrines, we were met by many more *Caciques* and dignitaries in very rich cloaks. The different chieftains wore different brilliant liveries, and the causeways were full of them. Montezuma had sent these great *Caciques* in advance to receive us, and as soon as they came before Cortés they told him in their language that we were welcome, and as a sign of peace they touched the ground with their hands and kissed it.

There we halted for some time while Cacamatzin, the lord of Texcoco, and the lords of Iztapalapa, Tacuba,[8] and Coyoacan went ahead to meet the great Montezuma, who approached in a rich litter, accompanied by other great lords and feudal *Caciques* who owned vassals. When we came near to Mexico, at a place where there were some other small towers, the great Montezuma descended from his litter, and these other great *Caciques* supported him beneath a marvelously rich canopy of green feathers, decorated with gold work, silver, pearls, and *chalchihuites*,[9] which hung from a sort of border. It was a marvelous sight. The great Montezuma was magnificently clad, in their fashion, and wore sandals of a kind for which their name is *cotaras*, the soles of which are of gold and the upper parts ornamented with precious stones. And the four lords who supported him were richly clad also in garments that seem to have been kept ready for them on the road so that they could accompany their master. For they had not worn clothes like this when they came out to receive us. There were four other great *Caciques* who carried the canopy above their heads, and many more lords who walked before the great Montezuma, sweeping the ground on which he was to tread, and laying down cloaks so that his feet should not touch the earth. Not one of these chieftains dared to look him in the face. All kept their eyes lowered most reverently except those four lords, his nephews, who were supporting him.

When Cortés saw, heard, and was told that the great Montezuma was approaching, he dismounted from his horse, and when he came near to Montezuma each bowed deeply to the other. Montezuma welcomed our Captain, and Cortés, speaking through Doña Marina,[1] answered by wishing him very good health. Cortés, I think, offered Montezuma his right hand, but Montezuma refused it and extended his own. Then Cortés brought out a necklace which he had been holding. It was made of those elaborately worked and colored glass beads called *margaritas*, of which I have spoken, and was strung on a gold cord and dipped in musk to give it a good odor. This he hung round the great Montezuma's neck, and as he did so attempted to embrace him. But the great princes who stood round Montezuma grasped Cortés' arm to prevent him, for they considered this an indignity.

Then Cortés told Montezuma that it rejoiced his heart to have seen such

free so that they could use it as a training ground for Aztec warriors and a handy source of sacrificial victims.
8. A city west of Tenochtitlán. Texcoco is a city on the lake of that name, east of Tenochtitlán.
9. The Aztec goddess of freshwater bodies. Because her name translates as "She Who Wears

a Jade Skirt," Díaz seems to be using it here as a term for jade stones.
1. A native woman of high caste who was disowned by her mother and stepfather in favor of Marina's half-brother. Cortés made crucial use of her as an interpreter and a negotiator.

a great prince, and that he took his coming in person to receive him and the repeated favors he had done him as a high honor. After this Montezuma made him another complimentary speech, and ordered two of his nephews who were supporting him, the lords of Texcoco and Coyoacan, to go with us and show us our quarters. Montezuma returned to the city with the other two kinsmen of his escort, the lords of Cuitlahuac and Tacuba; and all those grand companies of *Caciques* and dignitaries who had come with him returned also in his train. And as they accompanied their lord we observed them marching with their eyes downcast so that they should not see him, and keeping close to the wall as they followed him with great reverence. Thus space was made for us to enter the streets of Mexico without being pressed by the crowd.

Who could now count the multitude of men, women, and boys in the streets, on the roof-tops and in canoes on the waterways, who had come out to see us? It was a wonderful sight and, as I write, it all comes before my eyes as if it had happened only yesterday.

They led us to our quarters, which were in some large houses capable of accommodating us all and had formerly belonged to the great Montezuma's father, who was called Axayacatl. Here Montezuma now kept the great shrines of his gods, and a secret chamber containing gold bars and jewels. This was the treasure he had inherited from his father, which he never touched. Perhaps their reason for lodging us here was that, since they called us *Teules* and considered us as such, they wished to have us near their idols. In any case they took us to this place, where there were many great halls, and a dais hung with the cloth of their country for our Captain, and matting beds with canopies over them for each of us.

On our arrival we entered the large court, where the great Montezuma was awaiting our Captain. Taking him by the hand, the prince led him to his apartment in the hall where he was to lodge, which was very richly furnished in their manner. Montezuma had ready for him a very rich necklace, made of golden crabs, a marvelous piece of work, which he hung round Cortés's neck. His captains were greatly astonished at this sign of honor.

After this ceremony, for which Cortés thanked him through our interpreters, Montezuma said: "Malinche, you and your brothers are in your own house. Rest awhile." He then returned to his palace, which was not far off.

We divided our lodgings by companies, and placed our artillery in a convenient spot. Then the order we were to keep was clearly explained to us, and we were warned to be very much on the alert, both the horsemen and the rest of us soldiers. We then ate a sumptuous dinner which they had prepared for us in their native style.

So, with luck on our side, we boldly entered the city of Tenochtitlán or Mexico on 8 November in the year of our Lord 1519.

* * *

[CORTÉS IN DIFFICULTIES]

There was never a time when we were not subject to surprises so dangerous that but for God's help they would have cost us our lives.[2] No sooner had we

2. Díaz is writing here of a complex period in the history of the Cortés invasion. In the winter that followed his entrance into Tenochtitlán, Cortés had taken Montezuma hostage under the pretense of protecting him and thus had effective control of the city and much surrounding territory. Cortés

set up the image of Our Lady on the altar, and said mass, than Huichilobos and Tezcatlipoca seem to have spoken to their *papas*,[3] telling them that they intended to leave their country, since they were so ill-treated by the *Teules*. They said that they did not wish to stay where these figures and the cross had been placed, nor would they stay unless we were killed. This, they said, was their answer, and the *papas* need expect no other, but must convey to it Montezuma and all his captains, so that they might at once attack us and kill us. Their gods also observed that they had seen us break up the gold that was once kept in their honor and forge it into ingots, and warned the Mexicans that not only had we imprisoned five great *Caciques* but were now making ourselves masters of their country. They recited many more of our misdeeds in order to incite their people to war.

Wishing us to hear what his gods had said, Montezuma sent Orteguilla[4] to our Captain with the message that he wished to speak to him on very serious business. The page said that Montezuma was very sad and agitated, and that on the previous night and during much of the day many *papas* and important captains had been with him, holding secret discussions which he could not overhear.

On receiving this message Cortés hurried to the palace where Montezuma was, taking with him Cristóbal de Olid, the captain of the guard, and four other captains, also Doña Marina and Jerónimo de Aguilar.[5] All paid great respect to the great Montezuma, who addressed them in these words: "My lord Malinche and captains, I am indeed distressed at the answer which our *Teules* have given to our *papas*, to me, and to all my captains. They have commanded us to make war on you and kill you and drive you back across the sea. I have reflected on this command, and think it would be best that you should at once leave this city before you are attacked, and leave no one behind. This, my lord Malinche, you must certainly do, for it is in your own interest. Otherwise you will be killed. Remember that your lives are at stake."

Cortés and our captains were distressed and even somewhat alarmed; which was not surprising, for the news was so sudden and Montezuma was so insistent that our lives were in the greatest and immediate danger. The matter was clearly urgent. Cortés replied by thanking him for the warning, and saying that at the moment he was troubled by two things: that he had no ships in which to depart, since he had ordered those in which we came to be broken up, and that Montezuma would have to accompany us so that our great emperor might see him. He begged him as a favor therefore to restrain his *papas* and captains until three ships could be built in the sand-dunes. This course, he argued, would be to their advantage, for if they began a war they would all be killed. And to show that he really meant to build these ships without delay, he asked Montezuma to tell his carpenters to go with two of our soldiers who were expert shipbuilders, and cut wood near the coast.

---

began a search for gold mines, built a flotilla to sail on the city's lakes, and ordered the removal of the native idols from the temples. His control of the country was far from complete, however; and as troubles emerged among the Aztec ruling class and the priests by the following spring, a party of Spanish soldiers under Pánfilo de Narváez landed near Villa Rica (Vera Cruz) with the intent of arresting Cortés on orders from Diego Velázquez.
3. Priests. Huichilobos is the Aztec god of war. Tezcatlipoca is the god of creation.
4. A young Aztec who served as page for Cortés.
5. Shipwrecked on the Yucatán coast in 1511, he had been ransomed from the Maya by Cortés. His expertise in the Mayan language made him of vital assistance during the invasion.

On hearing Cortés say that he would have to come with us and visit the Emperor, Montezuma was even sadder than before. He said he would let us have the carpenters, and urged Cortés to hurry up and not waste time in talk but get to work. In the meantime he promised to tell his *papas* and captains not to foment disturbances in the city, and to see that Huichilobos was appeased with sacrifices, though not of human lives. After this excited conversation Cortés and our captain took their leave of Montezuma and we were all left in great anxiety wondering when the fighting would begin.

Cortés immediately sent for Martin López, the ship's carpenter, and Andrés Nuñez,[6] and the Indian carpenters whom Montezuma had lent us, and after some discussion about the size of the three vessels to be built, he ordered López to start work at once and get them ready. For all that was necessary in the way of iron and blacksmith's tackle, tow, caulkers, and tar was to be found at Villa Rica. So they set out and cut the wood near the coast, and after making calculations and templates hastily began to build the ships.

Meanwhile we in Mexico went about in great depression, fearing that at any moment we might be attacked. Our Tlascalan auxiliaries and Doña Marina told Cortés that this was imminent, and the page Orteguilla was always in tears. We all kept on the alert and placed a strong guard on Montezuma. I say that we were on the alert, but I do not have to repeat this so often, since we never took off our armor, gorgets, or leggings by night or day. Some may ask when we slept, and what our beds were like. They were nothing but a little straw and a mat, and anyone who had a curtain put it underneath him. We slept in our armor and sandals with our weapons close beside us. The horses stood saddled and bridled all day, and everything was so fully prepared that at a call to arms we were already at our posts, and waiting. We posted sentinels every night, and every soldier did his guard-duty. There is something else I would say, though I do not like to boast: I grew so accustomed to going about armed and sleeping in the way I have described that after the conquest of New Spain I kept the habit of sleeping in my clothes and without a bed. I slept better that way than on a mattress.

Even when I go to the villages of my *encomienda*[7] I do not take a bed or, if I sometimes do, it is not because I want it, but because some gentlemen are traveling with me, and I do not wish them to think I do not possess a good bed. But I always lie down fully dressed. What is more, I can only sleep for a short time at night. I have to get up and look at the sky and stars and walk about for a bit in the dew; and this without putting a cap or a handkerchief on my head. I am so used to it that, thank God, it does me no harm. I have said all this so that my readers shall know how we, the true conquistadors, lived, and how accustomed we became to our arms and to keeping watch.

* * *

One day when our Captain went to make his usual state visit on Montezuma, he noticed, after the usual civilities, that Montezuma appeared more

6. An expert shipbuilder often put to work on such projects during the Conquest.
7. A grant of Native Americans (with their lands) supposedly to encourage their conversion to Chris-

tianity. In practice, the *encomienda* system degenerated into slavery. Díaz's *encomienda* was located in Guatemala.

cheerful and happy. He asked him how it was, and Montezuma replied that his health was better. But when Cortés paid him a second visit on the same day the prince was afraid that he had learnt about Narváez' ships. So to get the advantage of our Captain and to avoid suspicion, he said: "Lord Malinche, just a moment ago some messengers came to tell me that eighteen or more ships with a great many men and horses have arrived at the port where you disembarked. They brought me a picture of it all painted on cloths; and seeing you visiting me for a second time today I thought you had come to bring me the same news, for now you will not need to build ships. But you have told me nothing about it. So I have been annoyed with you, on the one hand, for keeping me in ignorance, and delighted, on the other hand, at the arrival of your brothers. For now you can all return to Spain without more discussion."

When Cortés heard about the ships and saw the painting on the cloth, he rejoiced greatly. "Thank God, who provides for us at the right time," he said. And we soldiers were so pleased that we could not keep quiet. The horsemen rode skirmishing round, and musket shots were fired. But Cortés grew very thoughtful, for he knew quite well that the fleet had been sent against him and us by the Governor Diego Velázquez. Being a wise man, he told us soldiers and captains what he felt, and by great gifts of gold and promises to make us rich persuaded us to stand by him. He did not yet know who was in command of the fleet, but we were highly delighted with the news, and with the gold he had given us by way of gratuity, since it came from his own property and not from what should have fallen to our share. Our Lord Jesus Christ was indeed sending us help and assistance.

* * *

[THE DESTRUCTION OF TENOCHTITLÁN]

* * *

Just then many companies of Mexicans came down the causeway, wounding us all, including the horsemen. Sandoval[8] too received a stone full in the face. But Pedro de Alvarado and some other horsemen went to his assistance. As so many bands were coming on, and only I and twenty soldiers were opposing them, Sandoval ordered us to retire gradually in order to save the horses; and because we did not retire as quickly as he wished he turned on us furiously and said: "Do you want me and all my horsemen to be killed because of you? For my sake, Bernal Díaz, my friend, please fall back!" Then Sandoval received another wound, and so did his horse. By this time we had got our allies off the causeway; and facing the enemy and never turning our

---

8. A cavalry officer and close associate of Cortés's. Cortés returned to the coast to meet Narváez in the spring of 1520, leaving half his men under the command of Pedro de Alvarado in the Aztec capital. After decisively defeating Narváez and convincing his army to join his cause, Cortés hurried back to Tenochtitlán, enlisting many native allies en route. Badly managed by Alvarado, affairs were in deep confusion when Cortés arrived late in June. Montezuma, now a captive of the invaders set up as a figurehead, was forced to plead for calm, only to be struck down by stones hurled by his people. He soon died, either from the resulting injuries or from stab wounds of uncertain but probably Spanish origin. Cortés was forced to flee the city shortly thereafter, in a long bloody retreat during what became known as *la noche triste*, or the night of sorrow. He was able to regroup again and eventually attacked the following winter. This account of the slow but finally devastating Spanish victory, which was secured in August 1521, begins here with the chilling tale of how some five dozen Spanish captives were sacrificed earlier that summer as their companions, barely escaping over a causeway, looked back in horror at the temple of the war god.

backs, we gradually retired, forming a kind of dam to hold up their advance. Some of our crossbowmen and musketeers shot while others were loading, the horsemen made charges, and Pedro Moreno[9] loaded and fired his cannon. Yet despite the number of Mexicans that were swept away by his shot we could not keep them at bay. On the contrary, they continued to pursue us, in the belief that they would carry us off that night to be sacrificed.

When we had retired almost to our quarters, across a great opening full of water, their arrows, darts, and stones could no longer reach us. Sandoval, Francisco de Lugo, and Andrés de Tápia[1] were standing with Pedro de Alvarado, each one telling his story and discussing Cortés's orders, when the dismal drum of Huichilobos sounded again, accompanied by conches, horns, and trumpet-like instruments. It was a terrifying sound, and when we looked at the tall *cue* from which it came we saw our comrades who had been captured in Cortés's defeat being dragged up the steps to be sacrificed. When they had hauled them up to a small platform in front of the shrine where they kept their accursed idols we saw them put plumes on the heads of many of them; and then they made them dance with a sort of fan in front of Huichilobos. Then after they had danced the *papas* laid them down on their backs on some narrow stones of sacrifice and, cutting open their chests, drew out their palpitating hearts which they offered to the idols before them. Then they kicked the bodies down the steps, and the Indian butchers who were waiting below cut off their arms and legs and flayed their faces, which they afterward prepared like glove leather, with their beards on, and kept for their drunken festivals. Then they ate their flesh with a sauce of peppers and tomatoes. They sacrificed all our men in this way, eating their legs and arms, offering their hearts and blood to their idols as I have said, and throwing their trunks and entrails to the lions and tigers and serpents and snakes that they kept in the wild-beast houses I have described in an earlier chapter.

On seeing these atrocities, all of us in our camp said to one another: "Thank God they did not carry me off to be sacrificed!" My readers must remember that though we were not far off we could do nothing to help, and could only pray God to guard us from such a death. Then at the very moment of the sacrifice, great bands of Mexicans suddenly fell upon us and kept us busy on all sides. We could find no way of holding them. "Look!" they shouted, "that is the way you will all die, as our gods have many times promised us," and the threats they shouted at our Tlascalan allies were so cruel and so frightening that they lost their spirit. The Mexicans threw them roasted legs of Indians and the arms of our soldiers with cries of: "Eat the flesh of these *Teules* and of your brothers, for we are glutted with it. You can stuff yourselves on our leavings. Now see these houses you have pulled down. We shall make you build them again, much finer, with white stone and fine masonry. So go on helping the *Teules*. You will see them all sacrificed."

Guatemoc[2] did something more after his victory. He sent the hands and feet of our soldiers, and the skin of their faces, and the heads of the horses that had been killed, to all the towns of our allies and friends and their relations, with the message that as more than half of us were dead and he

---

9. An artillery officer.
1. A soldier who also wrote an account of the Conquest.
2. A young Aztec chieftain who had led the

repulse of Cortés the year before; he had become the Lord of Mexico and now was making heroic efforts to defeat Cortés for good. Cortés executed him in 1524.

would soon finish off the rest, they had better break their alliance with us and come to Mexico, because if they did not desert us quickly he would come and destroy them.

The Mexicans went on attacking us by day and night; and we all kept guard together, Gonzalo de Sandoval, Pedro de Alvarado, and all the other captains included. So although great bands of warriors came by night, we were able to repel them. Both by day and night half the horsemen remained in Tacuba[3] and the other half on the causeway. But this was not all the harm we suffered. The enemy returned and reopened all the channels that we had blocked since we had first advanced along the causeway, and built even stronger barricades than before. Then our friends from the cities on the lake who had recently allied themselves to us and were coming to help us with their canoes decided that they had "come for wool but gone away shorn." For many of them lost their lives and many went home wounded, and more than half their canoes were destroyed. But even so they did not help the Mexicans any more, for they loathed them. They stood aside, however, and watched events.

*   *   *

Guatemoc and his captains thanked Cortés for this assurance.[4] Then Cortés asked after his wife and the other great ladies, wives of other captains, whom he knew to have come with the prince; and Guatemoc himself answered that he had begged Gonzalo de Sandoval and García Holguin[5] to leave them in their canoes while he came to learn Malinche's orders. Cortés at once sent for them, and ordered that they should be given of the best we had in the camp to eat. Then, as it was late and it was beginning to rain, he arranged for them to be sent to Coyoacan and, taking Guatemoc, his family, and household, and many other chieftains with him, he ordered Pedro de Alvarado, Gonzalo de Sandoval, and the other captains each to go to his own camp and quarters. We went to Tacuba, Sandoval to Tepeaquilla,[6] and Cortés himself to Coyoacan. Guatemoc and his captains were captured on the evening of 13 August 1521. Thanks be to Our Lord Jesus Christ and Our Lady the Virgin Mary, His Blessed Mother.

It rained and thundered that evening, and the lightning flashed, and up to midnight heavier rain fell than usual. After Guatemoc's capture all we soldiers became as deaf as if all the bells in a belfry had been ringing and had then suddenly stopped. I say this because during the whole ninety-three days[7] of our siege of the capital, Mexican captains were yelling and shouting night and day, mustering the bands of warriors who were to fight on the causeway, and calling to the men in the canoes who were to attack the launches and struggle with us on the bridges and build barricades, or to those who were driving in piles, and deepening and widening the channels and bridges, and building breastworks, or to those who were making javelins and arrows, or to the women shaping rounded stones for their slings. Then there was the unceasing sound of their accursed drums and trumpets, and their melancholy kettledrums in the shrines and on their temple towers. Both day

3. A city west of Tenochtitlán.
4. Díaz has just told how, with Tenochtitlán in the hands of the Spanish, Cortés assured the captured Guatemoc that the latter would continue to rule over Mexico.

5. A Spanish sea captain responsible for the capture of Guatemoc.
6. A city north of Tenochtitlán.
7. An exaggerated figure.

and night the din was so great that we could hardly hear one another speak. But after Guatemoc's capture, all the shouting and the other noises ceased, which is why I have made the comparison with a belfry.

Guatemoc was very delicate, both in body and features. His face was long but cheerful, and when his eyes dwelt on you they seemed more grave than gentle, and did not waver. He was twenty-six, and his complexion was rather lighter than the brown of most Indians. They said he was a nephew of Montezuma, the son of one of his sisters; and he was married to one of Montezuma's daughters, a young and beautiful woman.

*　　*　　*

Now to speak of the dead bodies and heads that were in the houses where Guatemoc had taken refuge. I solemnly swear that all the houses and stockades in the lake were full of heads and corpses. I do not know how to describe it but it was the same in the streets and courts of Tlatelolco. We could not walk without treading on the bodies and heads of dead Indians. I have read about the destruction of Jerusalem, but I do not think the mortality was greater there than here in Mexico, where most of the warriors who had crowded in from all the provinces and subject towns had died. As I have said, the dry land and the stockades were piled with corpses. Indeed, the stench was so bad that no one could endure it, and for that reason each of us captains returned to his camp after Guatemoc's capture; even Cortés was ill from the odors which assailed his nostrils and from headache during those days in Tlatelolco.

The soldiers in the launches came off best and gained most spoil, because they were able to go to the houses in certain quarters of the lake where they knew there was cloth, gold, and treasure. They also searched the reed-beds in which the Mexicans had hidden their property when we were assaulting some quarter or group of houses. Under cover of chasing the canoes that were bringing in food and water, they would sometimes capture some chieftains fleeing to the mainland to take refuge in the towns of their neighbors the Otomis,[8] and would rob them of everything they had. We soldiers, on the other hand, who were fighting on the causeways and on land, gained no profit, but plenty of arrows and lance-thrusts and wounds from darts and stones. For when we captured houses, the inhabitants had already carried off any property they possessed, since we could not go through the water without first blocking the gaps and bridges. Therefore, as I said when speaking of Cortés's search for sailors to go in the launches, they were better off than we who fought on land. This was clearly proved when Cortés demanded Montezuma's treasure from Guatemoc and his captains. They told him that the men in the launches had stolen most of it.

As there was such a stench in the city, Guatemoc asked Cortés's permission for all the Mexican forces who remained there to go out to the neighboring towns, and they were promptly told to do so. For three whole days and nights they never ceased streaming out, and all three causeways were crowded with men, women, and children so thin, sallow, dirty, and stinking that it was pitiful to see them. Once the city was free from them Cortés went out to inspect it. We found the houses full of corpses, and some poor Mex-

8. One of the constituent peoples of Tlaxcala, neighbors, but not allies, of the Aztecs.

icans still in them who could not move away. Their excretions were the sort of filth that thin swine pass which have been fed on nothing but grass. The city looked as if it had been plowed up. The roots of any edible greenery had been dug out, boiled, and eaten, and they had even cooked the bark of some of the trees. There was no fresh water to be found; all of it was brackish. I must also remark that the Mexicans did not eat the flesh of their own people, only that of our men and our Tlascalan allies whom they had captured. There had been no live births for a long time, because they had suffered so much from hunger and thirst and continual fighting.

Cortés ordered a banquet to be held in Coyoacan to celebrate the capture of the city, and got plenty of wine for the purpose from a ship that had just come from Spain to Villa Rica, also some pigs that had been brought to him from Cuba. He invited all of us captains and soldiers whom he thought worthy of consideration, from all three camps. But when we came to the banquet there were not enough seats or tables for even a third of the invited guests. Consequently there was much disorder. So many discreditable things occurred, indeed, that it would have been better if the banquet had never been held.

Now that our daily and nightly battles with the Mexicans are far away in the past, for which I give great thanks to God who delivered me from them, there is one thing that I wish to relate, which happened to me after seeing the death by sacrifice of the sixty-two soldiers who were carried off alive. What I am going to say may seem to some to arise from my lack of any great inclination for battle. But, on the contrary, anyone will see on reflection that it was due rather to the excessive daring with which I had to risk my life in the thickest of the fighting. For great courage was at that time required of a soldier. I must say that when I saw my comrades dragged up each day to the altar, and their chests struck open and their palpitating hearts drawn out, and when I saw the arms and legs of these sixty-two men cut off and eaten, I feared that one day or another they would do the same to me. Twice already they had laid hands on me to drag me off, but it pleased God that I should escape from their clutches. When I remembered their hideous deaths, and the proverb that the little pitcher goes many times to the fountain, and so on, I came to fear death more than ever in the past. Before I went into battle, a sort of horror and gloom would seize my heart, and I would make water once or twice and commend myself to God and His blessed Mother. It was always like this before battle, but my fear quickly left me.

It must seem very strange to my readers that I should have suffered from this unaccustomed terror. For I had taken part in many battles, from the time when I made the voyage of discovery with Francisco Hernández de Córdoba till the defeat of our army on the causeway under Alvarado. But up to that time when I saw the cruel deaths inflicted on our comrades before our very eyes, I had never felt such fear as I did in these last battles. Let those experienced in soldiering, who have been at times in great peril of death, say whether my fear is to be attributed to faint-heartedness or to excessive valor. For, as I have said, my own opinion is that having to thrust myself when fighting into such dangerous positions, I was bound to fear death more at that time than at others. Besides, I was not always in good health. I was many times severely wounded, and for this reason was not able to go on all the expeditions. Still, the hardships and risks of death to which

I was personally exposed were not insignificant, either before the capture of Mexico or afterward.

The first orders Cortés gave to Guatemoc were that the conduits from Chapultepec[9] should be repaired and restored to their former condition, so that the water could flow again into the city; that the streets should be cleared of the bodies and heads of the dead, which should be buried, so that the city should be left clean and free from any stench; that all bridges and causeways should be thoroughly restored to their former condition, and the palaces and houses rebuilt so as to be fit for habitation within two months. He marked out the parts in which the Indians were to settle, and those which were to be left clear for us.

Guatemoc and his captains complained to Cortés that many of our men had carried off the daughters and wives of chieftains, and begged him as a favor that they should be sent back. Cortés answered that it would be difficult to take them from their present masters, but they might seek them out and bring them before him, and he would see whether they had become Christians or preferred to go home with their fathers and husbands, in which case he would order them to be given up. So he gave the Mexicans permission to search in all three camps, and issued an order that any soldier who had an Indian woman should surrender her at once if she of her own free will wished to return home. Many chieftains searched from house to house and persevered until they found them. But there were many women who did not wish to go with their fathers or mothers or husbands, but preferred to remain with the soldiers with whom they were living. Some hid themselves, others said they did not wish to return to idolatry, and yet others were already pregnant. So they did not bring back more than three, who by Cortés's express command were handed over to them.

Everyone was agreed that all the gold and silver and jewels in Mexico should be collected together. But this seems to have amounted to very little. For there was a report that Guatemoc had thrown all the rest into the lake four days before we captured him, and that the Tlascalans and the people of Huexotzingo and Cholula[1] and all the rest of our allies who had taken part in the war, also the *Teules* themselves who went about in the launches, had stolen their share. The officers of the Royal Treasury publicly proclaimed therefore that Guatemoc had hidden the treasure, and that Cortés was delighted since he would not have to give it up but could keep it all for himself. For this reason these officers decided to torture Guatemoc and his cousin the lord of Tacuba, who was his great favorite. Cortés and some of the rest of us were very much distressed that they should torture a prince like Guatemoc for greed of gold. Thorough inquiries about the treasure had been made, and all Guatemoc's stewards had said that there was no more than the king's officials already had, which amounted to three hundred and eighty thousand gold pesos, and had been melted and cast into bars, and mulcted of the royal fifth and another fifth for Cortés. On finding that the sum was so little, Cortés' enemies among the Conquistadors, and Narváez' men who distrusted him, told the treasurer Julián de Alderete that they suspected him of opposing the arrest and torture of Guatemoc and his captains

9. A town on the site of a fine spring southwest of Mexico City. Water flowed from it via an aqueduct to the capital.

1. Independent states to the east of Mexico City, near Tlaxcala.

only because he wanted to keep the gold for himself. So, to avoid making any accusations against Cortés, who could not prevent their action, they tortured Guatemoc and the lord of Tacuba by burning their feet with oil, and extorted the confession that four days before they had thrown the gold into the lake, together with the cannon and muskets they had captured from us when they drove us out of Mexico. The place Guatemoc indicated was the palace in which he had lived, where there was a large pond, from which we fished up a great golden sun like the one that Montezuma had given us, and many jewels and articles of small value which belonged to Guatemoc himself. The lord of Tacuba said that in his house at Tacuba, about twelve miles away, he had some gold objects, and that if we would take him there he would tell us where they were buried and give them to us. Pedro de Alvarado and six soldiers, myself among them, took him there. But when we arrived he said he had only told us this story in the hopes of dying on the road, and invited us to kill him, for he possessed neither gold nor jewels. So we returned empty-handed. The truth is that Montezuma's treasure-chamber, of which Guatemoc took possession at his death, did not contain many jewels or golden ornaments, because all the best had been extracted to form the magnificent offering that we had sent to His Majesty, which was worth twice as much as the fifth deducted for him and Cortés's own fifth as well. This we sent to the Emperor by Alonso de Avila, who had just returned from the island of Santo Domingo.

We captains and soldiers were all somewhat sad when we saw how little gold there was and how poor and mean our shares would be. The Mercedarian friar,[2] Pedro de Alvarado, Cristóbal de Olid, and other captains told Cortés that since there was so little gold, the entire share that would fall to us ought to be divided among those who were maimed and lame and blind, or had lost an eye or their hearing, and others who were crippled or had pains in their stomachs, or had been burnt by the powder, or were suffering from pains in their sides. They said that it was only right that it should all be given to them, and that the rest of us who were more or less sound ought to approve. After due consideration they repeated this to Cortés, believing that he would increase our shares, for there was a strong suspicion that he had hidden all the gold away and ordered Guatemoc to say he had none.

Cortés replied that he would see we came out all right, and would take measures to that effect. As we were all anxious to see what our share would be, we were in a hurry for the accounts to be issued. After making the calculation, they told us a horseman would receive eighty pesos, and a crossbowman, musketeer, or shield-bearer fifty or sixty—I do not remember which—and when we heard this figure not a single soldier was willing to accept his share.

While Cortés was at Coyoacan, he lodged in a palace with whitewashed walls on which it was easy to write with charcoal and ink; and every morning malicious remarks appeared, some in verse and some in prose, in the manner of lampoons. One said the sun, moon, and stars, and earth and sea followed their courses, and if they ever deviated from the plane for which they were created, soon reverted to their original place. So it would be with Cortés's

2. The Mercedarian order, or the Order of Our Lady of Mercies, was founded in Barcelona early in the 13th century.

ambition for command. He would soon return to his original condition. Another said that he had dealt us a worse defeat than he had given to Mexico, and that we ought to call ourselves not the victors of New Spain but the victims of Hernán Cortés. Another said he had not been content with a general's share but had taken a king's, not counting other profits; and yet another: "My soul is very sad and will be till that day when Cortés gives us back the gold he's hidden away." It was also remarked that Diego Velázquez had spent his whole fortune and discovered all the northern coast as far as Panuco, and then Cortés had come to enjoy the benefit and rebelliously taken both the land and the treasure. And other words were written up too, unfit to record in this story.

When Cortés came out of his quarters of a morning he would read these lampoons. Their style was elegant, the verses well rhymed, and each couplet not only had point but ended with a sharp reproof that was not so naive as I may have suggested. As Cortés himself was something of a poet, he prided himself on composing answers, which tended to praise his own great deeds and belittle those of Diego Velázquez, Grijalva, and Francisco Hernández de Córdoba. In fact, he too wrote some good verses which were much to the point. But the couplets and sentences they scrawled up became every day more scurrilous, until in the end Cortés wrote: "A blank wall is a fool's writing paper." And next morning someone added: "A wise man's too, who knows the truth, as His Majesty will do very soon!" Knowing who was responsible for this (a certain Tirado, a friend of Diego Velázquez and some others who wished to make their defiance clear) Cortés flew into a rage and publicly proclaimed that they must write up no more libels or he would punish the shameless villains.

Many of us were in debt to one another. Some owed fifty or sixty pesos for crossbows, and others fifty for a sword. Everything we had bought was equally dear. A certain surgeon called Maestre Juan, who tended some bad wounds, charged excessive prices for his cures, and so did a sort of quack by the name of Murcia, who was an apothecary and barber and also treated wounds, and there were thirty other tricks and swindles for which payment was demanded out of our shares. The remedy that Cortés provided was to appoint two trustworthy persons who knew the prices of goods and could value anything that we had bought on credit. An order went out that whatever price was placed on our purchases or the surgeons' cures must be accepted, and that if we had no money, our creditors must wait two years for payment. And I must say that in the end, in compensation for slaves sold by auction, the remaining gold all fell to the King's officials.

When Cortés found that many of the soldiers were still insolently demanding larger shares, and saying that he had stolen everything for himself, and begging him to lend them money, he decided to free himself from their clutches and send them to settle in any province that seemed to him suitable.

* * *

When the news spread through all these distant provinces that Mexico was destroyed their *Caciques* and lords could not believe it. However, they sent chieftains to congratulate Cortés on his victories and yield themselves as vassals to His Majesty, and to see if the city of Mexico, which they had so dreaded, was really razed to the ground. They all carried great presents of gold to Cortés, and even brought their small children to show them Mexico, pointing it out to them in much the same way that we would say: "Here stood Troy."

But let us leave this topic for another that richly deserves explanation. Many interested readers have asked me why the true Conquistadors who won New Spain and the great and strong city of Mexico did not stay to settle, but went on to other provinces. I think this question is justified, and I will give them an answer. Learning from Montezuma's account-books the names of the places which sent him tributes of gold, and where the mines and chocolate and cotton-cloths were to be found, we decided to go to these places; and our resolve was strengthened when we saw so eminent a captain and so close a friend of Cortés as Gonzalo de Sandoval leaving Mexico, and when we realized that there were no gold or mines or cotton in the towns around Mexico, only a lot of maize and the *maguey*[3] plantations from which they obtained their wine. For this reason we thought of it as a poor land, and went off to colonize other provinces. But we were thoroughly deceived.

I remember that when I went to ask Cortés for leave to go with Sandoval he said to me: "On my conscience, Señor Bernal Díaz del Castillo, you are making a mistake. I wish you would stay here with me. But as you want to go with your friend Sandoval, go and good luck to you. I shall always consider your wishes, but I know very well that you will be sorry you left."

1568?   1632

3. An agave plant used by the Aztecs as the source of *pulque*, a fermented drink that in turn is the source of mescal.

ÁLVAR NÚÑEZ CABEZA DE VACA
c. 1490–1558

Among those who may have witnessed the disgrace of Columbus as he passed in chains through Cadiz in 1498 was a boy from the nearby village of Jerez de la Frontera. Álvar Núñez Cabeza de Vaca was the son of the village alderman, grandson of the conqueror of the Guanache people of Grand Canary Island, and a descendant on his mother's side from a hero of the wars against the Moors who was given the family name "Cabeza de Vaca" (or "cow's head") when he used a cow's skull to mark a strategic route through an unguarded mountain pass. Mindful of this family heritage, as a young man Cabeza de Vaca went off to the wars in Italy (he later was to say that the American Indians of Texas were as shrewd in battle "as if they had been reared in Italy in continual feuds"), then fought in Spain itself before, in 1527, he sailed on Panfilo de Narváez's Florida expedition as *aquacil mayor* (provost marshal) and treasurer.

The expedition endured many disasters. Narváez, an impetuous, self-centered man and a poor leader, first took his six hundred men to Hispaniola, where a quarter of them deserted, and then to Cuba, where two of the six ships were lost in a hurricane.

Ten months after leaving Spain the expedition landed in the vicinity of Sarasota Bay, on Florida's west coast. Against Cabeza de Vaca's advice, Narváez sent the ships farther along the shore in search of a rumored port where his army might rejoin them, but the ships were never seen again. Effectually stranded, Narváez took possession of Florida while the inhabitants of Sarasota Bay (probably Calusa Indians) made "many signs and threats [that] left little doubt that they were bidding us to go." Soon the expedition, reduced to eating its horses, sought to escape other groups of Florida Indians, from the Timucuan of the Suwannee River area to the Apalachees of the Panhandle, by building clumsy "barges" and retreating to the sea. Narváez took the best oarsmen in his own craft and left the other barges behind him as they neared Mobile Bay; when he pulled away from the others he told them, with false magnanimity, that "it was no longer a time when one should command another"—that is, every man for himself! With that, Narváez and his crew disappeared, apparently lost at sea.

The other rafts passed the mouth of what must have been the Mississippi, and finally wrecked on Galveston Island, now Texas, in November 1528. Here began a further whittling away of the survivors and a time of extraordinary struggles for Cabeza de Vaca and the three men who survived with him: the Spaniards Andrés Dorantes and Alonso del Castillo Maldonado, and Dorantes's black slave, Estevánico, a native of the Moroccan town of Azemmor. The itinerary of Cabeza de Vaca's North American odyssey was long and involved. Alone or with drifting groups of other survivors, he spent his first two years on the Texas coast as a prisoner and slave of the Han and Capoque clans of the Karankawa Indians and then gradually progressed north and west, gaining status and power among the Caddos, Atakapas, Coahuiltecans, and other natives from his activities as a merchant and especially his skill as a healer. By 1535, he reached present-day New Mexico, where he encountered the Jumanos and Conchos, then headed southwest into Mexico as the leader of a vast crowd of Pimas and Opatas who, revering him, followed him from village to village.

The heady mood of the journey dissipated the following March, however, when the wanderers encountered a party of Spanish slave hunters under Diego de Alcaraz in western Mexico. Seeing the terror of his American Indian escorts at these "Christian slavers," as he acerbically called them, Cabeza de Vaca became openly critical of Alcaraz, who arrested him, sent him south, and seized as slaves the six hundred natives in his company. From Mexico City, where he agitated against the cruel (and strictly illegal) activities of the likes of Alcaraz, Cabeza de Vaca went to Spain in 1537, intent on making similar representations to Emperor Charles V. Allowed to lead an expedition back to the New World himself, Cabeza de Vaca hoped to enact an enlightened American Indian policy, but his Río de la Plata colonists, profiting from the old injustices, removed him forcibly from office and sent him in chains back to Spain in 1545. After long delays in settling the dispute, in 1551 he was exiled to modern Algeria and forbidden to return to America.

During the three years he spent in Spain before his departure for Río de la Plata in 1540, Cabeza de Vaca completed his first narrative of the Narváez expedition. It was published in Spain in 1542; a corrected and expanded version that includes the story of his later American experience appeared in 1555. Addressed to Charles V, the 1542 account sought to justify his conclusions regarding Spanish policy and behavior in America as well as to argue for renewed explorations and settlement in the regions he had traversed (several later Spanish expeditions, including those of Coronado and de Soto, clearly drew on Cabeza de Vaca's arguments and knowledge). More important, however, *The Relation of Álvar Núñez Cabeza de Vaca* sought to recount (with remarkable understatement) his sufferings and many brushes with death and to explore his complex feelings regarding the Native Americans and his own countrymen's dealings with them.

From The Relation of Álvar Núñez Cabeza de Vaca[1]

[DEDICATION]

Sacred Caesarian Catholic Majesty:

Among all the princes who have reigned, I know of none who has enjoyed the universal esteem of Your Majesty[2] at this day, when strangers vie in approbation with those motivated by religion and loyalty.

Although everyone wants what advantage may be gained from ambition and action, we see everywhere great inequalities of fortune, brought about not by conduct but by accident, and not through anybody's fault but as the will of God. Thus the deeds of one far exceed his expectation, while another can show no higher proof of purpose than his fruitless effort, and even the effort may go unnoticed.

I can say for myself that I undertook the march abroad, on royal authorization, with a firm trust that my service would be as evident and distinguished as my ancestors', and that I would not need to speak to be counted among those Your Majesty honors for diligence and fidelity in affairs of state. But my counsel and constancy availed nothing toward those objectives we set out to gain, in your interests, for our sins. In fact, no other of the many armed expeditions into those parts has found itself in such dire straits as ours, or come to so futile and fatal a conclusion.

My only remaining duty is to transmit what I saw and heard in the nine years I wandered lost and miserable over many remote lands. I hope in some measure to convey to Your Majesty not merely a report of positions and distances, flora and fauna, but of the customs of the numerous, barbarous people I talked with and dwelt among, as well as any other matters I could hear of or observe. My hope of going out from among those nations was always small; nevertheless, I made a point of remembering all the particulars, so that should God our Lord eventually please to bring me where I am now, I might testify to my exertion in the royal behalf.

Since this narrative, in my opinion, is of no trivial value for those who go in your name to subdue those countries and bring them to a knowledge of the true faith and true Lord and bring them under the imperial dominion, I have written very exactly. Novel or, for some persons, difficult to believe though the things narrated may be, I assure you they can be accepted without hesitation as strictly factual. Better than to exaggerate, I have minimized all things; it is enough to say that the relation is offered Your Majesty for truth.

I beg that it may be received as homage, since it is the most one could bring who returned thence naked.

* * *

[THE MALHADO WAY OF LIFE]

The people[3] we came to know there are tall and well-built. Their only weapons are bows and arrows, which they use with great dexterity. The men

---

1. The text is based on *Adventures in the Unknown Interior of America*, edited and translated by Cyclone Covey (1961).
2. Emperor Charles V (1500–1558), grandson

and successor of Ferdinand and Isabella.
3. The Capoques and Hans of coastal Texas, near today's Galveston Island, which Cabeza de Vaca calls *Malhado*, or the Island of Doom.

bore through one of their nipples, some both, and insert a joint of cane two and a half palms long by two fingers thick. They also bore their lower lip and wear a piece of cane in it half a finger in diameter.

Their women toil incessantly.

From October to the end of February every year, which is the season these Indians live on the island, they subsist on the roots I have mentioned,[4] which the women get from under water in November and December. Only in these two months, too, do they take fish in their cane weirs. When the fish is consumed, the roots furnish the one staple. At the end of February the islanders go into other parts to seek sustenance, for then the root is beginning to grow and is not edible.

These people love their offspring more than any in the world and treat them very mildly.

If a son dies, the whole village joins the parents and kindred in weeping. The parents set off the wails each day before dawn, again at noon, and at sunset, for one year. The funeral rites occur when the year of mourning is up. Following these rites, the survivors wash off the smoke stain of the ceremony in a symbolic purgation. All the dead are lamented this way except the aged, who merit no regrets. The dead are buried, except medicine-men, who are cremated. Everybody in the village dances and makes merry while the pyre of a medicine-man kindles, and until his bones become powder. A year later, when his rites are celebrated, the entire village again participating, this powder is presented in water for the relatives to drink.

Each man has an acknowledged wife, except the medicine-men, who may have two or three wives apiece. The several wives live together in perfect amity.

When a daughter marries, she must take everything her husband kills in hunting or catches in fishing to the house of her father, without daring to eat or to withhold any part of it, and the husband gets provided by female carrier from his father-in-law's house. Neither the bride's father nor mother may enter the son-in-law's house after the marriage, nor he theirs; and this holds for the children of the respective couples. If a man and his in-laws should chance to be walking so they would meet, they turn silently aside from each other and go a crossbow-shot out of their way, averting their glance to the ground. The woman, however, is free to fraternize with the parents and relatives of her husband. These marriage customs prevail for more than fifty leagues inland from the island.

At a house where a son or brother may die, no one goes out for food for three months, the neighbors and other relatives providing what is eaten. Because of this custom, which the Indians literally would not break to save their lives, great hunger reigned in most houses while we resided there, it being a time of repeated deaths. Those who sought food worked hard, but they could get little in that severe season. That is why Indians who kept me left the island by canoe for oyster bays on the main.

Three months out of every year they eat nothing but oysters and drink very bad water. Wood is scarce; mosquitoes, plentiful. The houses are made of mats; their floors consist of masses of oyster shells. The natives sleep on these shells—in animal skins, those who happen to own such.

4. I.e., "certain roots which taste like nuts, mostly grubbed from [under] the water with great labor."

Many a time I would have to go three days without eating, as would the natives. I thought it impossible that life could be so prolonged in such protracted hunger; though afterwards I found myself in yet greater want, as shall be seen.

The Indians who had Alonso del Castillo, Andrés Dorantes, and the others of their barge who remained alive, spoke a different dialect and claimed a different descent from these I lived among. They frequented the opposite shore of the main to eat oysters, staying till the first of April, then returning.

The distance to the main is two leagues at the widest part of the channel. The island itself, which supports the two tribes commodiously, is half a league wide by five long.

The inhabitants of all these parts go naked, except that the women cover some part of their persons with a wool that grows on trees,[5] and damsels dress in deerskin.

The people are generous to each other with what little they have. There is no chief. All belonging to the same lineage keep together. They speak two languages: Capoque and Han.

They have a strange custom when acquaintances meet or occasionally visit, of weeping for half an hour before they speak. This over, the one who is visited rises and gives his visitor all he has. The latter accepts it and, after a while, carries it away, often without a word. They have other strange customs, but I have told the principal and most remarkable of them.

In April [1529] we went to the seashore and ate blackberries all month, a time of [dance ceremonies] and *fiestas* among the Indians.

* * *

[OUR LIFE AMONG THE AVAVARES AND ARBADAOS]

All the Indians of this region[6] are ignorant of time, either by the sun or moon; nor do they reckon by the month or year. They understand the seasons in terms of the ripening of fruits, the dying of fish, and the position of stars, in which dating they are adept.

The Avavares always treated us well. We lived as free agents, dug our own food, and lugged our loads of wood and water. The houses and our diet were like those of the nation we had just come from, but the Avavares suffer yet greater want, having no corn, acorns, or pecans. We always went naked like them and covered ourselves at night with deerskins.

Six of the eight months we dwelled with these people we endured acute hunger; for fish are not found where they are either. At the end of the eight months, when the prickly pears were just beginning to ripen again [mid-June 1535], I traveled with the Negro[7]—unknown to our hosts—to others a day's journey farther on: the Maliacones.[8] When three days had passed, I sent Estevánico to fetch Castillo and Dorantes.

When they got there, the four of us set out with the Maliacones, who were going to find the small fruit of certain trees which they subsist on for ten or twelve days while the prickly pears are maturing. They joined another tribe,

5. I.e., Spanish moss.
6. At this point in his story, having escaped from his captivity among the Capoques and Hans, Cabeza de Vaca is among the Avavares and Arbadaos in inland Texas.
7. Estevánico, a Moorish slave from the west coast of Morocco.
8. Neighbors of the Avavares and Arbadaos.

the Arbadaos, who astonished us by their weak, emaciated, swollen condition.

We told the Maliacones with whom we had come that we wanted to stop with these Arbadaos. The Maliacones despondently returned the way they came, leaving us alone in the brushland near the Arbadao houses. The observing Arbadaos talked among themselves and came up to us in a body. Four of them took each of us by the hand and led us to their dwellings.

Among them we underwent fiercer hunger than among the Avavares. We ate not more than two handfuls of prickly pears a day, and they were still so green and milky they burned our mouths. In our lack of water, eating brought great thirst. At nearly the end of our endurance we bought two dogs for some nets, with other things, and a skin I used for cover.

I have already said that we went naked through all this country; not being accustomed to going so, we shed our skins twice a year like snakes. The sun and air raised great, painful sores on our chests and shoulders, and our heavy loads caused the cords to cut our arms. The region is so broken and so overgrown that often, when we gathered wood, blood flowed from us in many places where the thorns and shrubs tore our flesh. At times, when my turn came to get wood and I had collected it at heavy cost in blood, I could neither drag nor bear it out. My only solace in these labors was to think of the sufferings of our Redeemer, Jesus Christ, and the blood He shed for me. How much worse must have been his torment from the thorns than mine here!

I bartered with these Indians in combs I made for them and in bows, arrows, and nets. We made mats, which are what their houses consist of and for which they feel a keen necessity. Although they know how to make them, they prefer to devote their full time to finding food; when they do not, they get too pinched with hunger.

Some days the Indians would set me to scraping and softening skins. These were my days of greatest prosperity in that place. I would scrape thoroughly enough to sustain myself two or three days on the scraps. When it happened that these or any people we had left behind gave us a piece of meat, we ate it raw. Had we put it to roast, the first native who came along would have filched it. Not only did we think it better not to risk this, we were in such a condition that roasted meat would have given us pain. We could digest it more easily raw.

Such was our life there, where we earned our meager subsistence by trade in items which were the work of our own hands.

[PUSHING ON]

Eating the dogs seemed to give us strength enough to go forward; so commending ourselves to the guidance of God our Lord, we took leave of our hosts, who pointed out the way to others nearby who spoke their language.

Rain caught us. We traveled the day in the wet and got lost. At last, we made for an extensive scrub wood stretch, where we stopped and pulled prickly pear pads, which we cooked overnight in a hot oven we made. By morning they were ready.

After eating, we put ourselves again in the hands of God and set forth. We located the path we had lost and, after passing another scrub wood stretch, saw houses. Two women who were walking in the "forest" with some boys fled deep into it in fright to call their men, when they noticed us heading for the houses. The men arrived and hid behind trees to look at us. We called to them, and they came up very timidly. After some conversation, they told us their food was very scarce and that many houses of their people stood close by, to which they would conduct us.

At nightfall we came to a village of fifty dwellings. The residents looked at us in astonishment and fear. When they grew somewhat accustomed to our appearance, they felt our faces and bodies and then their own, comparing.

We stayed in that place overnight. In the morning the Indians brought us their sick, beseeching our blessing. They shared with us what they had to eat—prickly pear pads and the green fruit roasted. Because they did this with kindness and good will, gladly foregoing food to give us some, we tarried here several days.

Other Indians came from beyond in that interval and, when they were about to depart, we told our hosts we wanted to go with them. Our hosts felt quite uneasy at this and pressed us warmly to stay. In the midst of their weeping we left them.

[CUSTOMS OF THAT REGION]

From the Island of Doom to this land, all the Indians we saw have the custom of not sleeping with their wives from the time they are discovered pregnant to two years after giving birth. Children are suckled until they are twelve, when they are old enough to find their own support. We asked why they thus prolonged the nursing period, and they said that the poverty of the land frequently meant—as we witnessed—going two or three days without eating, sometimes four; if children were not allowed to suckle in seasons of scarcity, those who did not famish would be weaklings.

Anyone who chances to fall sick on a foraging trip and cannot keep up with the rest is left to die, unless he be a son or brother; him they will help, even to carrying on their back.

It is common among them all to leave their wives when there is disagreement, and directly reconnect with whomever they please. This is the course of men who are childless. Those who have children never abandon their wives.

When Indian men get into an argument in their villages, they fist-fight until exhausted, then separate. Sometimes the women will go between and part them, but men never interfere. No matter what the disaffection, they do not resort to bows and arrows. After a fight, the disputants take their houses (and families) and go live apart from each other in the scrub wood until they have cooled off; then they return and from that moment are friends as if nothing had happened. No intermediary is needed to mend their friendship.

In case the quarrelers are single men, they repair to some neighboring people (instead of the scrub wood), who, even if enemies, welcome them warmly and give so largely of what they have that when the quarrelers' animosity subsides, they return to their home village rich.

✢   ✢   ✢

[THE LONG SWING-AROUND]

After the two days of indecision,[9] we concluded that our destiny lay toward the sunset and so took the trail north only as far as we had to in order to reach the westward one, and then swung down until eventually we came out at the South Sea. The seventeen *jornadas*[1] of hunger the Cow People warned us of, and which proved to be just as bad as they said, could not deter us.

During this desert ascent by the river, the Indians gave us many cowhides, but we passed up their *chacan*[2] in favor of about a handful of deer tallow a day, which we had long since learned to save for such times of famine.

After seventeen *jornadas* we forded the very wide, chest-deep, southern flowing river and traveled another seventeen.

One day as the sun went down out on the plains between massive mountains, we came upon people who for a third of the year eat nothing but powdered straw and, that being the season we passed through, we had to eat it ourselves until at last, at the end of the seventeen *jornadas,* we got to the people of permanent houses[3] who had plenty of corn.

They gave us a great quantity of corn, cornmeal, calabashes, beans, and cotton blankets, all of which we loaded onto the guides who had led us here, and they went back the happiest people on earth. We gave many thanks to God our Lord for bringing us to this land of abundance.

Some of the houses here are made of earth, the rest of cane mats. We marched more than a hundred leagues through continuously inhabited country of such domiciles, where corn and beans remained plentiful. The people gave us innumerable deerhide and cotton blankets, the latter better than those of New Spain, beads made of coral from the South Sea, fine turquoises from the north—in fact, everything they had, including a special gift to me of five emerald arrowheads such as they use in their singing and dancing. These looked quite valuable. I asked where they came from. They said from lofty mountains to the north, where there were towns of great population and great houses, and that the arrowheads had been purchased with feather bushes and parrot plumes.

Among this people, women are better treated than in any part of the Indies we had come through. They wear knee-length cotton shirts and, over them, half-sleeved skirts of scraped deerskin that reach to the ground and that are laced together in front with leather strips. The women soap this outer garment with a certain root which cleanses well and keeps the deerskin becoming. And they wear shoes.

All the people, sick and well, came to us in an attitude of urgency to be touched and blessed; only with great labor did we get through them all. Speaking of labor, there were many times that women accompanying us gave birth to babies and, as soon as they were born, the mothers would bring them to us for our touch and blessing.

These Indians ever stayed with us until they safely delivered us to others.

---

9. Tarrying in the Río Grande valley among the Cow People (so-called by the Spaniards because they hunted buffalo), Cabeza de Vaca's party was reluctant to leave the hospitality and easy living experienced there.
1. Roughly the distance covered in a day's journey, or between stops on a longer trip. The "seventeen *jornadas* of hunger" may refer to the infamous "Journey of Death," the ninety-mile stretch separating the Cow People from the Pueblo Indians of New Mexico.
2. Juniper berries, much used by Suma Indians.
3. These house-dwelling Opata Indians lived in the region of Sonora, in northwestern Mexico.

They were all convinced that we came from Heaven. (Anything that is new to them or beyond their comprehension is explained as coming from Heaven.) We Christians traveled all day without food, eating only at night— and then so little as to astonish our escort. We never felt tired, being so inured to hardship, which increased our enormous influence over them. To maintain this authority the better, we seldom talked with them directly, but made the Negro [Estevánico] our intermediary. He was constantly in conversation, finding out about routes, towns, and other matters we wished to know.

We passed from one strange tongue to another, but God our Lord always enabled each new people to understand us and we them. You would have thought, from the questions and answers in signs, that they spoke our language and we theirs. We did know six Indian languages, but could not always avail ourselves of them; there are a thousand dialectical differences.

Through all these nations, the people who were at war quickly made up so they could come meet us with everything they possessed. Thus we left all the land in peace. And we taught all the people by signs, which they understood, that in Heaven was a Man we called God, who had created the heavens and the earth; that all good came from Him and that we worshiped and obeyed Him and called him our Lord; and that if they would do the same, all would be well with them. They apprehended so readily that, if we had had enough command of their language to make ourselves perfectly understood, we would have left them all Christians.

We told them what we could and, from then on, at sunrise, they would raise their arms to the sky with a glad cry, then run their hands down the length of their bodies. They repeated this ritual at sunset.

They are a substantial people with a capacity for unlimited development.

[THE TOWN OF HEARTS]

In the town where the emeralds were presented us, the people gave Dorantes over 600 opened deer hearts, which they always kept in great supply for food. So we called this place the Town of Hearts. It is the gateway to many provinces on the South Sea, and whoever seeks them without entering here will surely be lost.

The timid, surly Indians of the coast, grow no corn; they eat powdered rushes, straw, and fish, which they catch from rafts, having no canoes. The women cover themselves somewhat, with grass and straw.

We think that near the coast, along the line of those permanent towns we came through, must be more than a thousand leagues of settled, productive land, where three crops a year of corn and beans are sown.

Deer in that belt are of three kinds, one of which are as big as yearling steers in Castile.

The houses are of the kind called *bahíos* in the West Indies.

These people get poison from a certain tree which is about the size of our apple trees. All they have to do is pick the fruit and wet the arrow with it or, if there be no fruit, break a twig and the milk will do as well. The tree is so deadly that, if deer or other animals drink where its bruised leaves have been steeped, they will burst.

We stayed in the Town of Hearts three days.

[THE BUCKLE AND THE HORSESHOE NAIL]

A few days farther on we came to another town where rain was falling so heavily that we could not cross the swollen river and had to wait fifteen days.

In this time Castillo happened to see an Indian wearing around his neck a little sword-belt buckle with a horseshoe nail stitched to it.

He took the amulet, and we asked the Indian what it was. He said it came from Heaven. But who had brought it? He and the Indians with him said that some bearded men like us had come to that river from Heaven, with horses, lances, and swords, and had lanced two natives.

Casually we inquired what had become of those men. They had gone to sea, said the Indians. They had put their lances into the water, got into the water themselves, and finally were seen moving on top of the water into the sunset.

We gave many thanks to God our Lord. Having almost despaired of finding Christians again, we could hardly restrain our excitement. Yet we anxiously suspected that these men were explorers who had merely made a flying visit on their voyage of discovery. But having at last some exact information to go on, we quickened our pace and, as we went, heard more and more of Christians. We told the natives we were going after those men to order them to stop killing, enslaving, and dispossessing the Indians; which made our friends very glad.

We hastened through a vast territory, which we found vacant, the inhabitants having fled to the mountains in fear of Christians. With heavy hearts we looked out over the lavishly watered, fertile, and beautiful land, now abandoned and burned and the people thin and weak, scattering or hiding in fright. Not having planted, they were reduced to eating roots and bark; and we shared their famine the whole way. Those who did receive us could provide hardly anything. They themselves looked as if they would willingly die. They brought us blankets they had concealed from the other Christians and told us how the latter had come through razing the towns and carrying off half the men and all the women and boys; those who had escaped were wandering about as fugitives. We found the survivors too alarmed to stay anywhere very long, unable or unwilling to till, preferring death to a repetition of their recent horror. While they seemed delighted with our company, we grew apprehensive that the Indians resisting farther on at the frontier would avenge themselves on us.

When we got there, however, they received us with the same awe and respect the others had—even more, which amazed us. Clearly, to bring all these people to Christianity and subjection to Your Imperial Majesty, they must be won by kindness, the only certain way.

They took us to a village on the crest of a range of mountains; it was a difficult ascent. The many people who had taken refuge there from the Christians received us well, giving us all they had: over 2,000 backloads of corn, which we distributed to the distressed, pathetic beings who had guided us to that place.

Next day, we despatched four heralds through the country, according to our custom, to call together all the rest of the Indians at a town three *jornadas* distant. We set out, ourselves, the day after that, with all who had congregated on the mountain top.

All along the way we could see the tracks of the Christians and traces of their camps. We met our messengers at noon. They had been unable to contact any Indians, who roved the woods out of sight, eluding the Christians. The night before, our heralds had spied on the Christians from behind trees and seen them marching many Indians in chains.

This intelligence terrified our escort, some of whom ran to spread the news that the Christians were coming, and many more would have followed if we had not managed to forbid them and to palliate their fright. We had with us Indians from a hundred leagues back whom we could not at this time discharge with the recompense due them.

For further reassurance to our escort, we held up where we were for the night. The following day we slept on the trail at the end of the *jornada*. The day after that, our heralds guided us to the place they had watched the Christians. We got there that afternoon and saw at once they had told the truth. We noted by the stakes the horses had been tied to that the men were mounted.

* * *

[THE FIRST CONFRONTATION]

When we saw for certain that we were drawing near the Christians, we gave thanks to God our Lord for choosing to bring us out of such a melancholy and wretched captivity. The joy we felt can only be conjectured in terms of the time, the suffering, and the peril we had endured in that land.

The evening of the day we reached the recent campsite, I tried hard to get Castillo or Dorantes to hurry on three days, unencumbered, after the Christians who were now circling back into the area we had assured protection. They both reacted negatively, excusing themselves for weariness, though younger and more athletic than I; but they being unwilling, I took the Negro and eleven Indians next morning to track the Christians. We went ten leagues, past three villages where they had slept.

The day after that, I overtook four of them on their horses. They were dumbfounded at the sight of me, strangely undressed and in company with Indians. They just stood staring for a long time, not thinking to hail me or come closer to ask questions.

"Take me to your captain," I at last requested; and we went together half a league to a place where we found their captain, Diego de Alcaraz.

When we had talked awhile, he confessed to me that he was completely undone, having been unable to catch any Indians in a long time; he did not know which way to turn; his men were getting too hungry and exhausted. I told him of Castillo and Dorantes ten leagues away with an escorting multitude. He immediately dispatched three of his horsemen to them, along with fifty of his Indian allies. The Negro went, too, as a guide; I stayed behind.

I asked the Christians to furnish me a certificate of the year, month, and day I arrived here, and the manner of my coming; which they did.[4] From this river to the Christian town, Sant Miguel[5] within the government of the recently created province of New Galicia, is a distance of thirty leagues.

4. It was probably March 1536.
5. I.e., Culiacán, the northernmost Spanish set- tlement in Mexico at that time, located in Sinaloa near the mouth of the Gulf of California.

[THE FALLING-OUT WITH OUR COUNTRYMEN]

After five days, Andrés Dorantes and Alonso del Castillo arrived with those who had gone for them; and they brought more than 600 natives of the vicinity whom the Indians who had been escorting us drew out of the woods and took to the mounted Christians, who thereupon dismissed their own escort.

When they arrived, Alcaraz begged us to order the villagers of this river out of the woods in the same way to get us food. It would be unnecessary to command them to bring food, if they came at all; for the Indians were always diligent to bring us all they could.

We sent our heralds to call them, and presently there came 600 Indians with all the corn they possessed. They brought it in clay-sealed earthen pots which had been buried. They also brought whatever else they had; but we wished only a meal, so gave the rest to the Christians to divide among themselves.

After this we had a hot argument with them, for they meant to make slaves of the Indians in our train. We got so angry that we went off forgetting the many Turkish-shaped bows, the many pouches, and the five emerald arrowheads, etc., which we thus lost. And to think we had given these Christians a supply of cowhides and other things that our retainers had carried a long distance!

It proved difficult to persuade our escorting Indians to go back to their homes, to feel apprehensive no longer, and to plant their corn. But they did not want to do anything until they had first delivered us into the hands of other Indians, as custom bound them. They feared they would die if they returned without fulfiling this obligation whereas, with us, they said they feared neither Christians nor lances.

This sentiment roused our countrymen's jealousy. Alcaraz bade his interpreter tell the Indians that we were members of his race who had been long lost; that his group were the lords of the land who must be obeyed and served, while we were inconsequential. The Indians paid no attention to this. Conferring among themselves, they replied that the Christians lied: We had come from the sunrise, they from the sunset; we healed the sick, they killed the sound; we came naked and barefoot, they clothed, horsed, and lanced; we coveted nothing but gave whatever we were given, while they robbed whomever they found and bestowed nothing on anyone.

*　*　*

To the last I could not convince the Indians that we were of the same people as the Christian slavers. Only with the greatest effort were we able to induce them to go back home. We ordered them to fear no more, reestablish their towns, and farm.

Already the countryside had grown rank from neglect. This is, no doubt, the most prolific land in all these Indies. It produces three crops a year; the trees bear a great variety of fruit; and beautiful rivers and brimming springs abound throughout. There are gold- and silver-bearing ores. The people are well disposed, serving such Christians as are their friends with great good will. They are comely, much more so than the Mexicans. This land, in short, lacks nothing to be regarded as blest.

When the Indians took their leave of us they said they would do as we commanded and rebuild their towns, if the Christians let them. And I solemnly swear that if they have not done so it is the fault of the Christians.

After we had dismissed the Indians in peace and thanked them for their toil in our behalf, the Christians subtly sent us on our way in the charge of an *alcalde* named Cebreros, attended by two horsemen.[6] They took us through forests and wastes so we would not communicate with the natives and would neither see nor learn of their crafty scheme afoot. Thus we often misjudge the motives of men; we thought we had effected the Indians' liberty, when the Christians were but poising to pounce.

* * *

c. 1536–40   1542

6. I.e., they were, in effect, under arrest.

GARCILASO DE LA VEGA
1539–1616

With his origins equally in the culture of Spain and that of the Incas who were conquered by Francisco Pizarro, the historian Garcilaso de la Vega well might be seen as the first distinctively American writer. Child of a conquistador and the Inca princess Chimpu Ocllo, he was baptized Gómez Suárez de Figueroa in April of 1539 in Cuzco, Peru's old imperial capital. His mother, whose family and culture he memorialized in *Royal Commentaries of the Incas and General History of Peru* (1609–17), was the granddaughter of an Incan emperor; her family dynasty, already riven by internal violence, was brought to an end by Pizarro's conquest. Like many Inca survivors, Chimpu Ocllo was converted to Catholicism, taking the name Isabel Suárez and uniting with one of Pizarro's followers, Sebastián Garcilaso de la Vega. A veteran of the Spanish imperial service in Mexico and Guatemala, he was descended on both sides from knights who had achieved fame in the Spanish wars against the Moors.

To signify his mixed ancestry, Gómez Suarez de Figeroa proudly called himself Garcilaso de la Vega, "El Inca." He drew his character, his values, and his literary inspiration from the crossing of cultures and families that he himself represented. The *Royal Commentaries* tells how he questioned his mother's family about the Inca kings and "the old times," learning stories that had been preserved in the *quipu*, an archive composed of knotted strings whose intricacies recorded key data. He also heard stories from the conquistadors in his father's circle. After he moved to Spain as a young man in 1560, he wove this diverse lore into the *Royal Commentaries* and *The Florida of the Inca*, his account of Hernando de Soto's ill-fated expedition of 1539–43. Well educated in Peru but denied full recognition as the son of a conqueror, the *mestizo* author saw himself as a defender of native American character and intellect against Old World prejudice. Although he never returned to Peru, while in Spain he circulated among and corresponded with "Americans," among them veterans of the de Soto expedition, who provided him with the narratives that he shaped into *The Florida of the Inca*.

The *Florida of the Inca* interweaves several historical accounts—a genealogy of the author's ancestor, the knight Garcí Pérez de Vargas, as well as tales of encounter relayed by members of the Narváez and de Soto expeditions to the Florida peninsula and north and west into the continent. It was completed by 1596, when the author was fifty-seven, and was published in Lisbon in 1605. The selection printed here is a quasi-independent narrative, derived from Alonso de Carmona, recounting the misfortunes of Juan Ortiz, a Spanish soldier taken prisoner by the Florida chief Hirrihigua during the Narváez expedition (in which Cabeza de Vaca also took part). Saved from execution by a young Indian woman—an episode long predating John Smith's fabled rescue by Pocahontas—Ortiz endured his own array of troubles in Florida while Cabeza de Vaca and his three colleagues labored westward. When finally liberated, he provided de Soto with a skilled interpreter until he took sick and died at the new expedition's winter camp near present-day Fort Smith, Arkansas, in 1541–42.

From The Florida of the Inca[1]

Book II, Part I

CHAPTER II. CONCERNING THE TORTURES THAT A CACIQUE INFLICTED UPON A SPANIARD, HIS SLAVE

The cacique Hirrihigua ordered the four Spaniards to be guarded securely so that on the occasion of their deaths he might hold a solemn festival, which according to his heathen custom he expected to celebrate within a few days.[2] When the time came he ordered that they be brought forth naked to the plaza and be shot with arrows one at a time like wild beasts, running them from one side to the other; and that too many arrows were not to be shot at the same time, in order that they should die more slowly, and their torment be greater, and the Indians' celebration and enjoyment longer and more festive. Thus they dealt with three of the Spaniards, the cacique deriving great satisfaction and pleasure from seeing them run in all directions, seeking help and nowhere finding succor, but only death. When they wished to bring out the fourth, who was a youth scarcely eighteen years of age, a native of Sevilla named Juan Ortiz, the cacique's wife came out accompanied by her three young daughters. Facing her husband, she said to him that she begged him to be content with the three Spaniards killed and pardon that youth, because neither he nor his companions had been to blame for the evil their predecessors had done, for they had not come with Pánfilo de Narváez; and that the boy especially deserved to be pardoned, for his youth absolved him of blame and called for mercy; and that it would be enough for him to remain as a slave and not be killed so cruelly without his having committed any crime.

In order to satisfy his wife and daughters, the cacique granted Juan Ortiz his life for the time, though afterward it was so sad and bitter that often he envied his three dead companions, because the continuous and unceasing labor of carrying wood and water was so great and his food and sleep so scanty, the daily cuffings, buffetings and lashes so cruel, besides the other

1. The text is based on the translation prepared by Charmion Shelby in the 1930s and first published in *The De Soto Chronicles: The Expedition of Hernando de Soto* (1993), ed. Lawrence A. Clayton, Vernon James Knight Jr., and Edward C. Moore. The selection is from the second book, first part of *The Florida of the Inca*.
2. The de Soto expedition landed on the west coast of Florida late in the spring of 1539, perhaps in or near Tampa Bay. Hirrihigua (called Oçita or Ucita in other accounts) was a *cacique*, or leader of a village in that vicinity.

torments that they inflicted upon him at the time of their special festivals, that often, if he had not been a Christian, he would have taken death by his own hands as a remedy. Thus it was that, aside from the daily torment, for his own pastime the cacique ordered on many festival days that Juan Ortiz run all day without stopping (from dawn to dark) in a large plaza that was in the pueblo, where they had shot his companions to death with arrows. The cacique himself would come out to see him run, and with him would come his nobles armed with their bows and arrows in order to shoot him if he ceased running. Juan Ortiz would begin his race at sunrise and would not pause on one side or the other of the plaza until sunset, which was the time that they set for him. And when the cacique would go to eat he would leave his nobles to watch him, so that, if he should cease running, they might kill him. At the end of the day he was left in the sad state that may be imagined, stretched on the ground, more dead than alive. The pity of the wife and daughters of the cacique succored him on these days, because they took him immediately, clothed him, and did him other kindnesses whereby they saved his life. It would have been better to take it away, in order to free him from those excessive hardships. Seeing that so many and such continuous tortures were not sufficient to kill Juan Ortiz, and the hatred that he bore him increasing hourly, the cacique, in order to put an end to him, commanded on one of his feast days that a great fire be built in the middle of the plaza, and when he saw a large bed of coals formed, he ordered it tended and a wooden framework be placed over it in the form of a gridiron, one yard above the ground, and that they put Juan Ortiz upon it in order to roast him alive.

This was done, and here the poor Spaniard remained for some time stretched on one side, fastened to the frame. At the cries that the poor unfortunate gave in the midst of the fire, the wife and daughters of the cacique came, and begging the husband and even reproaching his cruelty, they took him from the fire, already half roasted, having blisters on that side as large as half-oranges, some of them broken and bleeding freely, so that it was pitiful to see him. The cacique allowed it because they were women for whom he cared so much, and perhaps he did it also in order to have someone upon whom to visit his wrath in the future and to show his desire for vengeance, because he would have someone to excite it, and though [this was] very little in proportion to his desires, still he could amuse himself with that little. Thus he said many times that he regretted having killed the three Spaniards so quickly. The women carried Juan Ortiz to their house, and moved by pity at seeing him in that state, they treated him with juices of herbs (the Indians, both men and women, since they have no physicians, are great herbalists). Time and again they repented having saved him from death on the first occasion, because of seeing how slowly and with what cruel tortures they were killing him day by day. After many days Juan Ortiz was cured, though large scars from the burns still remained.

In order not to see him thus, and to free himself from the bother that his wife and daughters gave him with their entreaties, and so that he [Juan Ortiz] might not become lazy, the cacique directed that he be exercised in another punishment, less severe than the past ones. This was that he guard day and night the dead bodies of the inhabitants of that pueblo, which were deposited in the country in a forest at a distance from the settlements, at a place set apart for them. They were placed above ground in wooden chests that served as sepulchers, without hinges or any other security for the cover than some boards placed over them, with stones or timbers on top. Because of the poor protection these chests afforded for the bodies of the dead, they were carried away by the lions [i.e., panthers], of which there are many in that country, much to the grief and anger of the Indians. The cacique ordered Juan Ortiz to guard this place carefully so that the lions should not carry off any body or part of it, protesting and vowing that, if they did so, he would infallibly be roasted to death. For guarding them he gave him four darts to throw at the lions or at other wild beasts that might approach the chests. Juan Ortiz, giving thanks to God for having rid him of the continued presence of the cacique Hirrihigua, his master, went to guard the dead, hoping to have a better life with them than with the living. He guarded them with all care, chiefly at night, because then there was greater danger. It happened that, on one of the nights when he was thus watching, he fell asleep toward dawn, unable to resist his drowsiness, for at this hour it usually attacks most strongly those who are watching. Just at this time a lion came and, knocking off the covers of one of the chests, dragged out the body of a child, which had been thrown into it two days before, and carried it off. Juan Ortiz heard the noise that the covers made in falling, and as he hurried to the chest and failed to find the child's body therein, he considered himself lost; but with all his anxiety and dismay he did not cease hunting for the lion, so that, if he should find him, he might recover the body or die in the attempt. On the other hand he trusted to our Lord to give him strength to die on the following day, confessing and calling upon His name, for he knew that as soon as daylight came the Indians must visit the chests, and not finding the child's body, they would burn him alive. Walking through the forest from one side to another, in fear of death, he came to a wide path that passed through the center of it, and following it for a time with the intention of fleeing, though it was impossible to escape, he heard in the woods not far from where he was walking a noise as of a dog that is gnawing bones. Listening carefully, he made sure of it, and suspecting that it might be the lion that was eating the child, he felt his way very carefully through the underbrush, approaching the place where he heard the noise. By the light of the moon, which was shining, though not very brightly, he saw near him the lion, which was eating the child at its pleasure. Calling upon God and taking courage, Juan Ortiz threw a dart at it, and though he could not then see the shot that he had made, because of the underbrush, yet he felt that it had not been bad because his hand was left "salty," as the hunters say when they feel that they have made a good shot against wild beasts at night. With this very slender hope, and also because he had not heard the lion leave the place where he had shot at him, he waited for morning, commending himself to our Lord, that he might succor him in that necessity.

CHAPTER III. THE HARD LIFE OF THE CAPTIVE CHRISTIAN CONTINUES, AND HOW HE FLED FROM HIS MASTER

With the light of day Juan Ortiz verified the good shot that he had made by guess that night, for he saw the lion dead, the entrails and the center of the heart transfixed (as was found later when they opened it), a thing that he himself, though he saw it, could not believe. With a satisfaction and joy that may be better imagined than told, he dragged it by one foot, not pulling out the dart, so that his master might see it just as he had found it, having first gathered up and taken back to the chest the fragments of the child's body that he found uneaten. The cacique and all those in his pueblo wondered greatly at this deed, for in that land it is held generally to be a miraculous thing for a man to kill a lion, and thus they treat him who succeeds in killing one with great veneration and respect. And because this is such a fierce animal, he who kills it ought to be esteemed everywhere, especially if he does so without a shot from a crossbow or harquebus,[3] as Juan Ortiz did. Although it is true that the lions of La Florida, México, and El Pérú are not so large or so fierce as those of Africa, still they are lions, and the name is enough; and even if the popular proverb may say that they are not as fierce as they are painted, those who have been near them say that they are as much fiercer than their descriptions, as there is difference between the real and the imagined.

With this good fortune on the part of Juan Ortiz, the wife and daughters of the cacique took more spirit and courage to intercede for him, that he might be pardoned entirely and made use of in honorable employments worthy of his strength and valor. For a few days thereafter Hirrihigua treated his slave better, both in the esteem and favor he accorded him in his pueblo and house, and in referring to the heroic deed that they in their vain religion so esteem and honor that they regard it as sacred and more than human. However (and this was the injury that he could not pardon), every time he remembered that they [the Spaniards] had thrown his mother to the dogs and left her to be eaten by them, and when he went to blow his nose and could not find his nostrils, the devil possessed him to avenge himself on Juan Ortiz, as if he had cut them off; and inasmuch as he always carried the offense before his eyes, with the memory of it his ire, rancor, and desire to take vengeance increased from day to day. Though he restrained these passions for some time, being able to resist them no longer, he said one day to his wife and daughters that it was impossible for him to allow that Christian to remain alive because his life was very odious and abominable to him; that every time he saw him past injuries were revived and he was offended anew. Therefore he commanded them that they were in no manner to intercede for him further unless they desired to participate in the same rage and anger, and that in order to finish finally with that Spaniard he had determined that on a certain feast day (which was soon to be celebrated) he was to be shot to death with arrows as his companions had been, notwithstanding his bravery, for as an enemy he should be rather abhorred than esteemed. The wife and daughters of the cacique, because they saw him enraged and understood that no intercession would be effective, and also because it seemed to them that it was too much to importune and so displease the master for the sake of the slave, did not dare say a word in opposition to him. Rather with feminine astuteness they came to tell him that this would be a good thing to do because it was his pleasure. But the eldest of the daughters, in order to further her plan and make it succeed, a few days before the celebration secretly notified Juan Ortiz of her father's determination against him, and

3. An early matchlock gun.

that neither she nor her sisters nor her mother would avail or could do anything with the father, he having imposed silence upon them and threatened them if they should break it.

Desiring to encourage the Spaniard, she added to this sad notice others contrary to it and said to him: "So that you may not distrust me, nor despair of your life, nor fear that I will not do all that I can to save it, if you are a man and have courage to flee, I will favor and help you so that you may escape and reach safety. Tonight at a certain hour and in a certain place you will find an Indian to whom I entrust your safety and my own. He will guide you to a bridge that is two leagues from here; upon reaching it, you will order him not to pass beyond but to return to the pueblo before dawn so that they may not miss him, and my own daring and his may not become known, so that evil may not befall him and me for having done you a good turn. Six leagues[4] beyond the bridge is a pueblo whose lord wishes me well and desires to marry me; his name is Mucoço. Tell him on my behalf that I send you to him so that he may succor and favor you, as he ought to do. I know that he will do all he can for you, as you will see. Commend yourself to your God, for I can do no more for you." Juan Ortiz threw himself at her feet in acknowledgment of the mercy and favor that she was conferring and had always conferred upon him, and he at once made ready to travel on the following night. At the hour appointed, after the members of the cacique's household were asleep, he set out in search of the promised guide and left the pueblo with him without anyone hearing them. Upon reaching the bridge, he told the Indian to return at once very cautiously to his house, having first learned from him that there was no chance of his losing the road as far as the pueblo of Mucoço.

CHAPTER IV. OF THE MAGNANIMITY OF THE CURACA OR CACIQUE MUCOÇO, TO WHOM THE CAPTIVE COMMENDED HIMSELF

Juan Ortiz, as a man who was fleeing, reached the place before dawn but, for fear of causing a disturbance, did not dare enter it. When it was day he saw two Indians come out from the pueblo along the same road that he was taking. They attempted to shoot him with their bows and arrows, as they always go armed with these weapons. Juan Ortiz, who also had them, put an arrow in his bow to defend himself from them and also to attack them. How potent is a little favor, especially if it be from a lady! For we see that shortly before he did not know where to hide himself, being in fear of death; now he dared give it [death] to others with his own hand, simply because of having been favored by a pretty, discreet and generous girl, whose favor exceeds all other human gifts. With which, having recovered spirit and strength and even pride, he told them that he was not an enemy but that he was coming with a message from a lady for the lord of that place.

Hearing this, the Indians did not shoot him but returned with him to the pueblo and notified the cacique that the slave of Hirrihigua was there with a message for him. Mucoço or Mocoço—for it is the same—informed of this, went out to the plaza to receive the message Juan Ortiz was bringing to him.

4. Fifteen to twenty miles, depending on which contemporary definition of league was intended.

After having saluted him as best he could after the manner of the Indians themselves, Juan Ortiz told him briefly of the martyrdom his master had imposed upon him, as evidence of which he showed on his body the scars of the burns, blows and wounds they had given him, and how now finally his lord was determined to kill him in order to celebrate and solemnize with his death such and such a feast day, which he expected to hold soon. He told how the wife and daughters of the cacique, his master, though they had often saved his life, did not now dare to speak in his favor because of the lord's having forbidden it under penalty of his anger; and how the eldest daughter of his lord, desiring that he should not die, as the last and best remedy had ordered and encouraged him to flee and, giving him a guide, had set him on his way to his pueblo and house. In her name he presented himself before him, whom he supplicated by the love that he had for her to receive him under his protection, and as a thing commended by her to favor him, as he ought to do. Mucoço received him affably and heard him with pity at learning of the abuses and torments that he had experienced, which were plainly shown by the scars on his body, for, dressed after the manner of the Indians of the country, he wore only a loincloth.

Alonso de Carmona[5] tells at this point, in addition to what we have said, that he embraced him and kissed him on the face as a sign of peace.

He [the cacique] replied that he was welcome and told him to try to forget the fears of his past life; that in his company and house he would have a very different and opposite existence; that for the sake of serving the person who had sent him, and for him who had come to his person and house for succor, he would do all he could, as he would see by future actions; and that he might be certain that while he lived no one would be allowed to molest him.

All that this good cacique said in favor of Juan Ortiz he performed, and indeed much more than he promised, for he immediately made him his steward and kept him constantly with him, day and night, doing him much honor, more particularly after he learned that he had killed the lion with the dart. In short, he treated him like a well-beloved brother (for there are brothers who love one another like water and fire), and although Hirri-higua, suspecting that he had gone to Mocoço for protection, asked for him many times, Mucoço always made an excuse for not giving him up, saying finally, among other things, that since he had come to his house to let him be, and that he was so odious that he [Hirrihigua] had lost very lit-tle in losing such a slave. He made the same reply to another cacique, his brother-in-law, named Urribarracuxi, through whom Hirrihigua made the request. Seeing that his messages were of no effect, he went personally to ask him, and in his presence Mococo replied the same as in his absence, adding other angry words, and told him that since he was his brother-in-law it was unjust to order him to do a thing against his reputation and honor; that he would not be doing his duty if he should turn over to his own enemy an unfortunate who had come to him for refuge, so that the Hirrihigua might sacrifice and kill him like a wild beast for his own enter-tainment and pastime.

Mococo defended Juan Ortiz from these two caciques, who asked for him

5. One of the men from whom Garcilaso de la Vega gathered stories of the de Soto expedition in Spain.

so urgently and insistently, with such generosity that he was willing to forgo (as he did) the marriage he affectionately desired to make with the daughter of Hirrihigua, and the relationship and friendship of the father-in-law, rather than return the slave to him who asked for him in order to kill him. Mococo kept the latter constantly with him, much esteemed and well treated, until Governor Hernando de Soto entered La Florida.

Juan Ortiz was among those Indians for ten years, one and a half in the power of Hirrihigua and the rest with the good Mococo. Though a barbarian, he dealt with this Christian in quite another manner than those most famous men of the Triumvirate who at Layno, a place near Bologna, made that never sufficiently condemned proscription and agreement to give and exchange their relatives, friends, and defenders for enemies and adversaries. And he did much better than other Christian princes who later have committed here other acts as abominable and worse than that one, considering the innocence of those given up, the rank of some of them, and the faith that their betrayers should have had and kept with them; considering also that the former were heathen and the latter prided themselves on the Christian name and religion. These latter, breaking the laws and statutes of their kingdoms and not respecting their own position and rank, they being kings and great princes, and disregarding their sworn and promised word (a thing unworthy of such names), simply for the purpose of avenging their own anger, delivered up those who had not offended them in order to obtain the offenders, exchanging the innocent for the guilty, as both ancient and modern historians will testify. But we shall leave them, so as not to offend powerful ears and distress the pious.

It suffices to describe the magnanimity of a heathen so that faithful princes may be forced to imitate and excel him if they can, not in his heathenism, as do some who are unworthy of that name, but in virtue and similar noble qualities, to which they are more obligated because of their higher estate. Certainly, considering well the circumstances of the courageous action of this Indian, and seeing by whom and against whom it was performed, and the amount that he was willing to put aside and lose, going even against his own affection and desires in refusing the succor and favor demanded and promised by him, it will be seen that it arose from a most generous and heroic mind, which did not deserve to have been born and to live amidst the barbarous heathendom of that country. But God and human nature often produce such spirits in such uncultivated and sterile deserts for the greater humiliation and shame of those who are born and reared in lands that are fertile and abound in all good doctrine, sciences, and the Christian religion.

CHAPTER V. THE GOVERNOR[6] SENDS FOR JUAN ORTIZ

The governor heard this account, which we have given, of the life of Juan Ortiz, although in a confused form, in the pueblo of the cacique Hirrihigua, where we have left him at present; and he had heard it before, more briefly, in La Havana from one of the four Indians whom we said that the account-

---

6. I.e., Hernando de Soto.

ant, Juan de Añasco,[7] had seized when he was sent to explore the coast of La Florida, and who happened to be a subject of this cacique. When this Indian mentioned Juan Ortiz in the account that he gave in La Havana, leaving off the name Juan, because he did not know it, he said Ortiz, and as to the poor speech of the Indian was added the worse understanding of the good interpreters who stated what he was trying to say, and as all the listeners had for their chief purpose going to seek gold, on hearing the Indian say "Orotiz," without waiting for further statements on his part they thought that he was plainly saying that in his country there was much *oro*, or gold, and they congratulated themselves and rejoiced merely at hearing it mentioned, although with such a different significance and sense.

But when the governor ascertained that Juan Ortiz was in the power of the cacique Mucoço, he thought it would be well to send for him, alike in order to deliver him from the power of the Indians and because he was in need of a speaker and interpreter upon whom he could depend. He therefore chose a gentleman from Sevilla named Baltasar de Gallegos,[8] who was serving as *alguacil mayor* of the fleet and the army—who because of his great virtue, strength and valor deserved to be general of a greater army than that one—and told him to take sixty lancers with him and go to Mucoço, and tell him on his behalf how gratified were he and all the Spaniards who accompanied him by the honor and favors he had shown to Juan Ortiz, and how much he desired that he might have an opportunity of requiting them. At present he begged that he give him [Juan Ortiz] to him [de Soto], for he needed him for very important matters, and he asked when it would be convenient for him to make him a visit, as it would give him great pleasure to know and have him for a friend. In accordance with the orders given him, Baltasar de Gallegos left the camp with the sixty lancers and an Indian guide.

The cacique Mucoço, on the other hand, having learned of the coming of the governor Hernando de Soto with such a force of men and horses, and that he had landed so near his own country, and fearing that he might do him some harm there, desired very prudently and advisedly to avert the evil that might come to him. In order to do so, he summoned Juan Ortiz and said to him: "You must know, brother, that in the pueblo of your good friend Hirrihigua there is a Spanish captain with a thousand fighting men and many horses, who are coming to conquer this country. You well know what I have done for you, and how in order to save your life and not deliver you to him who held you as a slave and desired to kill you, I chose rather to fall into disgrace with all my relatives and neighbors than to do what they asked me against you. Now a time and occasion has come in which you can repay me for the good reception, entertainment and friendship I have accorded you, though I never did it with the expectation of any reward, but since events have happened thus it will be wise not to lose what is offered us.

"Go to the Spanish general and on your behalf and my own beg him that, in return for the service that I have done him and his whole nation

---

7. Sent to reconnoiter the Florida coast while the de Soto expedition lingered in Cuba the year before, he brought back four native captives to serve as guides and interpreters.

8. A kinsman of Cabeza de Vaca who served the expedition as provost marshal, or head of the military police.

through you (since I would do the same for any of them), he be pleased not to do me harm in this small land that I have, and that he deign to receive me into his friendship and service; that from this time forth I offer him my person, house and estate to be placed under his guardianship and protection; and so that you may be escorted as becomes both you and me, I send with you fifty nobles of my household, and you will protect them and me as our friendship obligates you to do."

Juan Ortiz, rejoicing at the good news and inwardly giving thanks to God for it, replied to Mucoço that he was much pleased that a time and occasion had arisen in which to repay the kindness and benefits that he had done him, not only in saving his life, but also in the many favors, and the esteem and honor he had received from his great virtue and courtesy. He would give a very full account and report of all this to the Spanish captain and all his people, so that he might concede to and reward him with that which he asked of them now in his name, and in what might come up in the future. He was very confident that the general on his part would do what he asked, for the Spanish nation prided itself upon being a people grateful for favors received, and thus certainly he could confidently hope to obtain that which he sent to ask of the governor. The fifty Indians whom the cacique had ordered to prepare came at once, and with Juan Ortiz they took the public road that goes from one pueblo to the other; and they set out on the same day that Baltasar de Gallegos left the camp to find him [Ortiz].

It happened that, after the Spaniards had marched more than three leagues along the wide and straight highway that went to the pueblo of Mucoço, the Indian who guided them, thinking that it was not a good thing to behave so loyally toward people who were coming to subjugate them and take away their lands and freedom, and who long before had shown themselves to be declared enemies—though up to the present they had not received injuries of which they could complain from that army—changed his plan in guiding them and took the first footpath he saw that led into the highway. After following it a short distance, he left it, as it was not straight, and thus he led them most of the day without a road and lost, drawing them always in an arc toward the seacoast with the design of coming upon some swamp, creek, or bay in which to drown them, if possible. The Castilians did not discover the deception of the Indian, since they were not acquainted with the country, until one of them saw, through the trees of an open forest through which they were marching, the topsails of the ships they had left and saw that they were very near the coast, of which fact he advised Captain Baltasar de Gallegos. The latter, seeing the guide's iniquity, threatened him with death, making a gesture of throwing a lance at him. Fearing that they would kill him, the Indian indicated with signs and such words as he could that they should return to the highway, but that it was necessary to retrace all their route that lay off the road, and thus they returned by the same way to seek it.[9]

1605

9. In subsequent chapters, de la Vega explains how Ortiz escaped further dangers before arriving at de Soto's camp, where a great celebration was held.

THOMAS HARRIOT
1560–1621

An Oxford graduate who had entered Sir Walter Ralegh's employment in the early 1580s, Thomas Harriot probably trained the members of Ralegh's first Roanoke expedition in navigational skills and may have accompanied Arthur Barlowe when the expedition left England in the spring of 1584. He certainly went on the second voyage, in 1585, and as a naturalist collaborating with the painter John White passed much of the time between their arrival in April 1585 and July of the following year studying and collecting (the two spent that fall and winter, for instance, with an exploring party farther north in the Chesapeake). In the process, Harriot must have compiled substantial notebooks. These do not survive, but we have a glimpse of them in his descriptive work, *A Brief and True Report of the New Found Land of Virginia* (1588), which gives much information about the flora and fauna as well as about the American Indians, from whom Harriot, having been taught their language (perhaps by Wanchese, a Roanoke Indian who returned with Barlowe to England in 1584), learned a great deal.

While Harriot and White were surveying the landscape, the infant colony—planted on Roanoke, an island off what is now North Carolina—was struggling with political unrest. Ralegh's commander-in-chief, the hot-headed Sir Richard Grenville, bullied the native Americans and alienated his own people, while his successor after he left for England in August 1585, Ralph Lane, also dealt poorly with the Roanoke Indians and other nearby native groups. Relations deteriorated, despite the fact that Chief Wingina's people gave much aid to the colonists. Exasperated, the chief began to withhold crucial food supplies from the English, who were told by other Native Americans that he was plotting their annihilation. After nightfall on June 1, 1586, Lane led a preemptive attack on Dasemunkepeuc, Wingina's mainland village. Wounded while asleep, Wingina escaped but was chased down in the woods, killed, and beheaded.

Few of these increasingly serious events are mentioned by Harriot in his *Brief and True Report*. Harriot does glance at Lane's "fierce" dealings with Wingina's people, and he does give ample evidence that diseases imported by the English had already begun to decimate the Native Americans. Had Harriot's own purpose as a writer been less descriptive and propagandistic (apparently he wrote at Ralegh's direction as a new colony was being readied under John White's command), this history of England's first Virginia colony might have been more candid. Harriot's narrative does not acknowledge the disorderly end of the first colony, most of whose survivors were rescued from Roanoke Island by Sir Francis Drake during a severe storm in June 1586. When Grenville returned with reinforcements and supplies later that summer, he found the compound abandoned. Grenville left behind a handful of men (some of them perished there, some went off in a boat but were never seen again) when he departed on what was to prove a long, circuitous return to England.

Harriot did not see his optimistic text through the press until 1588. By that point, a new group of colonists under White's command had left England and sailed for Roanoke, and White had hastily returned to England for more supplies. The great naval encounter between England and the Spanish Armada in 1588 disrupted almost all English shipping, leaving White unable to return to America as quickly as he wished; he was forced to abandon his colonists, whose disappearance from Roanoke Island has never been adequately explained. Ironically, Harriot's propaganda came forth after the fate of the "Lost Colony" had been all but sealed.

From A Brief and True Report of the New Found Land of Virginia

From Of the Nature and Manners of the People[1]

[In] respect of troubling our inhabiting and planting [the natives] are not to be feared,[2] but * * * shall have cause both to fear and love us, that shall inhabit with them.

They are a people clothed with loose mantles made of deerskins, and aprons of the same round about their middles, all else naked, of such a difference of statures only as we in England,[3] having no edge tools or weapons of iron or steel to offend us with (neither know they how to make any). Those weapons that they have are only bows made of witch hazel, and arrows of reeds, [and] flat-edged truncheons[4] also of wood, about a yard long. Neither have they anything to defend themselves [with] but targets made of bark, and some armor made of sticks wickered[5] together with thread.

Their towns are but small, and near the seacoast but few, some containing but ten or twelve houses, some twenty. The greatest that we have seen has been out of thirty houses. If they be walled, it is only done with bark of trees made fast to stakes, or else with poles only fixed upright, and close, one by another.[6]

Their houses are made of small poles, made fast at the tops in round form, after the manner as is used in many arbors[7] in our gardens in England. In most towns [they are] covered with bark, and in some with artificial mats made of long rushes,[8] from the tops of the houses down to the ground. The length of them is commonly double to the breadth. In some places they are but twelve and sixteen yards long, and in other some[9] we have seen [them] of four and twenty.

In some places of the country, one only[1] town belongs to the government of a Wiroans or chief Lord, in other some two or three, in some six, eight, and more. The greatest Wiroans that yet we had been dealing with, had but eighteen towns in his government, and [was] able to make[2] not above seven or eight hundred fighting men at the most. The language of every government is different from any other, and the further they are distant, the greater is the difference.

Their manner of wars amongst themselves is either by sudden surprising one another, most commonly about the dawning of the day, or moonlight, or else by ambushes, or some subtle devices. Set battles are very rare, except it falls out[3] where there are many trees, where either part may have some hope of defense, after the delivery of every arrow, in leaping behind some [tree] or other.

If there fall out any wars between us and them, what their fight[ing] is likely to be (we having advantages against them so many manner of ways, as

1. The text is from Richard Hakluyt, *The Principall Navigations, Voyages, Traffiques & Discoveries of the English Nation*, vol. 8 (1904). "Manners": customs, practices.
2. I.e., they will not resist English settlement.
3. Varying in height much as the English do.
4. Heavy clubs.
5. Woven. "Targets": small shields.
6. I.e., with palisade fences.
7. Small, open shelters.
8. Artfully made from reeds.
9. I.e., in other places.
1. Single, solitary.
2. Recruit, call on.
3. Happens.

by our discipline, our strange weapons and [other devices], especially ordinance great and small), it may easily be imagined. By the experience we have had in some places, the turning up of their heels against us in running away was their best defense.[4]

In respect of us, they are a poor people, and for want of skill and judgment in the knowledge and use of our things,[5] do esteem our trifles before things of greater value. Notwithstanding [this,] in their proper manner[6] (considering the want of such means as we have), they seem very ingenious, for although they have no such tools, nor any such crafts, sciences, and arts as we, yet in those things they do, they show excellence of wit. And by how much they upon due consideration shall find our manner of knowledges and crafts to exceed theirs in perfection, and speed for doing or execution, by so much the more is it probable that they should desire our friendship and love, and have the greater respect for pleasing and obeying us. Whereby may be hoped, if means of good government be used, that they may in short time be brought to civility, and the embracing of true religion.

Some religion they have already, which although it is far from the truth, yet being as it is, there is hope it may be easier and sooner reformed.

They believe that there are many gods, which they call Mantoac, but of different sorts and degrees, one only chief and great God, who has been from all eternity. Who (as they affirm) when he purposed to make the world, made first other gods of a principal order to be as means and instruments to be used in the creation and government to follow, and afterwards [made] the sun, moon, and stars as petty gods. * * * First (they say) were made waters, out of which by the gods was made all diversity of creatures that are visible or invisible.

For mankind they say a woman was made first, who by the working of one of the gods, conceived and brought forth children. And in such sort they say they had their beginning. But how many years or ages have passed since, they say they can make no relation,[7] having no letters or other such means as we to keep records of the particularities of times past, but only tradition from father to son.

They think that all the gods are of human shape, and therefore they represent them by images in the forms of men, which they call Kewasowok (one alone is called Kewas).[8] Them they place in houses appropriate, or temples, which they call Machicomuck, where they worship, pray, sing, and make many times [an] offering unto them. In some Machicomuck we have seen but one Kewas, in some two, and in other some three. The common sort think them to be also gods.[9]

4. Perhaps an obscure reference to Roanoke governor Ralph Lane's (1530–1603) surprise attack on Chief Wingina. After he was attacked in his village, Wingina indeed ran away; he was tracked down, shot in the back, and then beheaded.
5. I.e., European weapons, tools, and so forth. "In respect of": by comparison with. "Want": lack.
6. I.e., within the limits of their own culture and technology.
7. Narration.
8. In the 1590 edition of Harriot's text, which was published on the Continent and contained engravings taken from the watercolors of John White (c. 1545–c. 1593), one such idol is shown. The accompanying text explains, in part: "The people of this country have an Idol, which they call Kiwasa (it is carved of wood; in length, four foot), whose head is like the heads of the people of Florida. The face is of flesh color, the breast white, the rest is all black, the thighs are also spotted with white. He hath a chain around his neck of white beads, between which are other round beads of copper which they esteem more than gold or silver."
9. This comment about the commoner's confusion of the image or icon with the god it represented would be of particular importance to a Protestant English audience, because there was a strong iconoclastic element in English religious thought.

They believe also [in] the immortality of the soul, that after this life as soon as the soul is departed from the body, according to the works it hath done, it is either carried to heaven the habitacle[1] of gods, there to enjoy perpetual bliss and happiness, or else to a great pit or hole, which they think to be in the furthest parts of their part of the world toward the sunset, there to burn continually—[that] place they call Popogusso.

For the confirmation of this opinion, they told me two stories, of two men that had been lately dead and revived again. The one [incident] happened but [a] few years before our coming into the country [to] a wicked man, who having [died and been] buried, the next day the earth of the grave being seen to move, [he] was taken up again. [He] made declaration where his soul had been, that is to say, very near entering into Popogusso, had not one of the gods saved him, and [given] him leave to return again, and teach his friends what they should do to avoid that terrible place of torment. The other [incident] happened in the same year we were there, but in a town that was sixty miles from us, and it was told [to] me for strange news, that one being dead, buried, and taken up again [like] the first, showed that although his body had lain dead in the grave, yet his soul was alive and had traveled far in a long broad way, on both sides whereof grew most delicate and pleasant trees, bearing more rare and excellent fruits than ever he had seen before, or was able to express. And at length [he] came to most brave and fair[2] houses, near which he met his father, [who] had been dead before, who gave him great charge to go back again, and show his friends what good they were to do to enjoy the pleasures of that place, which when he had done he should afterwards come again.

What subtlety soever [there may] be in the Wiroances and priests, this opinion works so much [effect] in many of the common and simple sort of people, that it makes them have great respect to their Governors, and also great care what they do, to avoid torment after death, and to enjoy bliss, although notwithstanding [this fact], there is punishment ordained for malefactors, [such] as stealers, whoremongers, and other sorts of wicked doers, some punished with death, some with forfeitures, some with beating, according to the greatness[3] of the facts.

And this is the sum of their religion, which I learned by having special familiarity with some of their priests, wherein they were not so sure grounded,[4] nor gave such credit to their traditions and stories, but through conversing with us they were brought into great doubts of their own [faith], and no small admiration of ours, [so that there was] earnest desire in many, to learn more than we had means, for want of perfect utterance in their language, to express.

Most things they saw with us—[such] as mathematical instruments; sea compasses; the virtue of the load-stone in drawing iron; a perspective glass[5] whereby were shown many strange sights; burning glasses; wild fireworks; guns; hooks; writing and reading; spring-clocks that seem to go of themselves; and many other things that we had—were so strange unto them, and so far exceeded their capacities to comprehend the reason and means how they should be made and done, that they thought they were rather the works

1. Dwelling place.
2. Splendid, well-built.
3. I.e., seriousness.

4. I.e., secure.
5. A device that produced distorted views of the world. "Load-stone": magnet.

of gods than of men, or at the [least] they had been given and taught [to] us [by] the gods. Which made many of them to have such [an] opinion of us, that if they knew not the truth of God and Religion already, it was rather to be had from us whom God so specially loved, than from a people that were so simple, as they found themselves to be in comparison [with] us. Whereupon greater credit was given unto that [which] we spoke of, concerning such matters.

Many times and in every town where I came, according as I was able, I made declaration of the contents of the Bible, [namely,] that therein was set forth the true and only God, and his mighty works, that therein was contained the true doctrine of salvation through Christ, with many particularities of Miracles and chief points of Religion, as I was able then to utter, and thought fit for the time. And although I told them the book materially and of itself was not of any such virtue, as I thought they did conceive, but only the doctrine therein contained; yet would many be glad to touch it, to embrace it, to kiss it, to hold it to their breasts and heads, and stroke over all their body with it, to show their hungry desire of that knowledge which was spoken of.

The Wiroans with whom we dwelled, called Wingina, and many of his people would be glad many times to be with us at our Prayers, and many times would call upon us both in his own town [and] in others whither he sometimes accompanied us, to pray and sing Psalms, hoping thereby to be partaker of the same effects which we by that means also expected.

Twice this Wiroans was so grievously sick that he was like to die, and as he lay languishing (doubting of any help [from] his own priests and thinking he was in such danger for offending us and thereby our God), sent for some of us to pray and be a means to our God, [so] that it would please Him either that he might live, or after death dwell with Him in bliss, [and] so likewise were the requests of many others in the like case.

[At] a time also when their corn began to wither by reason of a drought which happened extraordinarily,[6] fearing that it had come to pass [because] in something they had displeased us, many would come to us and desire us to pray to our God of England, that he would preserve their corn, promising that when it was ripe we also should be partakers of the fruit.

There could at no time happen any strange sickness, losses, hurts, or any other cross[7] unto them, but that they would impute to us the cause or means thereof, for offending or not pleasing us. One other rare and strange accident, leaving others, will I mention before I end, which moved the whole country that either knew or heard of us, to [hold] us in wonderful admiration.[8]

There was no town where we had any subtle device practiced against us (we leaving it unpunished or not revenged because we sought by all means possible to win them by gentleness) but that within a few days after our departure from every such town, the people began to die very fast, and many in short space, in some towns about twenty, in some forty, and in one six score, which in truth was very many in respect of their numbers. This happened in no place that we could learn, but where we had been, where they

6. I.e., the drought was extraordinarily severe.
7. Accident.

8. I.e., in awe. "Leaving": passing over.

used some practice against us, and after such time.[9] The disease also was so strange, that they neither knew what it was, nor how to cure it, [for] the like by report of the oldest men in the country never [had] happened before, time out of mind (a thing especially observed by us, as also by the natural inhabitants themselves). Insomuch that when some of the inhabitants which were our friends, and especially the Wiroans Wingina, had observed such effects in four or five towns [following] their wicked practices, they were persuaded that it was the work of God through our means, and that we by him might kill and slay whom we would without weapons, and not [have to] come near them. And thereupon when it had happened that they had understanding that any of their enemies had abused us in our journeys (hearing that we had wrought no revenge with our weapons, and fearing upon some cause the matter should so rest), [they] did come and entreat us that we would be a means to our God that they as others that had dealt ill with us might in like sort die, alleging how much it would be for our credit and profit (as also theirs) and hoping furthermore that we would do so much at their request [out] of the friendship we professed them.[1]

[We, however, argued that these requests] were ungodly, affirming that our God would not subject himself to any such prayers and requests of men; that indeed all things have been and were to be done according to his good pleasure as he had ordained; and that we, to show ourselves his true servants, ought rather to make petition for the contrary, [namely], that they with them[2] might live together with us, be made partakers of His truth, and serve Him in righteousness.

But, notwithstanding [our disavowals], * * * because the effect fell out so suddenly and shortly afterwards according to their desires,[3] they thought nevertheless [that] it came to pass by our means, and that we in using such speeches [with] them, did but dissemble the matter; and therefore [they] came unto us to give us thanks in their manner, [because] although we satisfied them not in promise,[4] yet in deeds and effect we had fulfilled their desires.

This marvelous accident[5] [produced] in all the country [such] strange opinions of us, that some people could not tell whether to think us gods or men, and the rather because that all the space of their sickness, there was no man of ours known to die, or [be] especially sick. They noted also that we had no women amongst us, [and] that we did [not] care for any of theirs.

Some therefore were of [the] opinion that we were not born of women, and therefore not mortal, but that we were men of an old generation many years past, then risen again to immortality.

Some would likewise seem to prophecy that there were more of our generation yet to come [to this land] to kill theirs and take their places, as some thought the purpose was, [judging] by that which was already done. Those

9. I.e., it happened after the English had left.
1. Neither Harriot nor the Native Americans understood the accidental exchange of disease that was beginning to devastate the local population with European pathogens. That the ill effects were thought to be limited to villages in which some dispute had arisen between the two groups gave the American Indians the impression that the English were taking revenge. This pattern in the outbreaks has, however, a simpler explanation: the greater intimacy that may well have preceded and even produced the disagreements was one precondition for the spread of infection. Despite their confusion, Wingina's people seized on the usefulness of "English" sickness for their own political disputes with other Indian groups.
2. I.e., both Wingina's people and their enemies.
3. I.e., the enemies for whose suffering they petitioned the English soon were visited with illness.
4. I.e., the English had not vowed to punish Wingina's enemies.
5. Occurrence, incident.

that were immediately to come after us they imagined to be in the air, yet invisible and without bodies, and [imagined] that they by our entreaty and for the love of us, did make the people to die in [the way] they did, by shooting invisible bullets into them.

To confirm this opinion, their physicians (to excuse their ignorance in curing the disease)[6] would not be ashamed to * * * make the simple people believe that the strings of blood they sucked out of the sick bodies, were the strings wherewith the invisible bullets were tied and cast.[7] Some also thought that we shot them ourselves out of our pieces, from the place where we dwelled, and killed the people in any [such] town that had offended us, as we listed,[8] how far distant from us soever it was. And [others] said that it was the special work of God for our sakes, as we ourselves have cause in some sort to think no less. * * * Their opinions I have set down the more at large, that it may appear unto you that there is good hope they may be brought through discreet dealing and government[9] to the embracing of the truth, and consequently to honor, obey, fear, and love us.

And although some of our company towards the end of the year showed themselves too fierce in slaying some of the people in some towns, upon causes that on our part might easily enough have been borne * * * by carefulness of ourselves [there is] nothing at all to be feared.[1]

1588

6. I.e., to find an excuse for their own failure to cure the illness.
7. Shot, thrown. The "strings" of blood may have been partly coagulated strands produced by the unknown illness.
8. Wished.
9. I.e., direction, control. "At large": at such length.

1. Here Harriot hints at the brutal behavior of Ralph Lane, who as governor of the infant colony reacted to rumors of a Roanoke Indian plot against the English by attacking the village of Dasemunkepeuc. By the time Harriot published his *Relation* in 1588, Wingina (one of "some of the people in some towns" whom Lane had killed) had been dead for two years.

SAMUEL DE CHAMPLAIN
c. 1570–1635

Samuel de Champlain was born into a seafaring family around 1570 near La Rochelle on the Atlantic coast of France. More than any other Frenchman of the time, he deepened his country's interest in America and planted that interest solidly in American soil. He had crossed the Atlantic six times already by 1603, when, as "geographer royal" under the command of François Pont-Gravé, he sailed up the St. Lawrence River as far as the future site of Montreal, where the expedition took on valuable furs before returning to France. Early in 1604, Champlain published his official report, *Des Sauvages*, illustrated with his own maps, and in April returned to America under the command of the Sieur de Monts, a Protestant merchant who was a native of Champlain's own region. On this voyage, the Frenchmen explored the coasts of what would become New England and the Maritime Provinces of Canada; and on their next, in 1608, they returned up the St. Lawrence, where Champlain founded Quebec City.

Even as Champlain was spending much of his time shuttling back and forth across the Atlantic, crossing it eighteen times between 1610 and 1633, he remained committed to the survival of Quebec City and thus of New France. Under his guidance, the French made bold claims to much of North America at a time when the English, with the exception of their small and frail coastal settlement in Virginia, had barely arrived. Champlain himself explored as far inland as Georgian Bay on Lake Huron, while Étienne Brulé, under Champlain's direction, traveled as far as Lake Superior in the very year the Pilgrims settled at Plymouth, an area explored and mapped by Champlain fifteen years earlier.

These wide-ranging activities led Champlain to intimate contact with many native Americans. He established strong ties with the Montagnais, near Quebec City, with the Algonkians upriver, and ultimately with the Hurons, who occupied the land around Georgian Bay. In sustaining his friendship with these peoples (such as it was: Champlain long complained that no American Indian would guide him as far into the continent as he wished to go), he encountered and fought their own feared enemies, the Iroquois, with whom the French were to be long in conflict.

Like his English contemporary John Smith, Champlain assiduously recorded his experiences, leaving a large body of works that were mostly published in his own day, from *Des Sauvages* (1603) to *Les Voyages* (1613), *Voyages et Descouvertures* (1619), and the last and largest of his works, *Les Voyages de la Nouvelle France* (1632). Because he kept detailed journals of his explorations and of affairs in the French settlements where he lived, Champlain's narratives offer a great deal of information about colonial experience but also about native American culture and life, particularly in the case of the Hurons, to whom a good part of *Voyages et Descouvertures* is devoted. Champlain's 1613 book, from which the first selection reprinted here derives, offers a valuable perspective on the cultural and economic life of the Massachusetts and Cape Cod Indians before the arrival of permanent European settlement (and disease). He describes an agricultural region, thickly settled, rather than the vacant "wilderness" (awaiting the impress of European order) that the English settlers in this region tended to find, especially as they later sought to justify their presence on the land. The different basis of French and English colonial economies, which were sustained by fur trade and agriculture, respectively, helps account for this difference of view, since the French fur traders relied on the American Indians while English and Indian farmers came into competition.

In his 1619 book, Champlain published the first literary fruit of his deeper westward explorations of the continent in the period from 1613 to 1618. It includes the account, reprinted here, of the young French scout Étienne Brulé's experiences during the fall and winter of 1615–16, when he lived—part of the time as a guest of the Susquehanna Indians, part of it as an Iroquois captive—in the forests of New York and Pennsylvania. Brulé, born in Champigny, France, around 1592, had come to New France in 1608 with Champlain, who sent him among the Indians to learn their language and culture. As noted, Brulé later traveled deep into the continent; in 1629, as it happened, he betrayed Champlain and France by helping the English in a short-lived takeover of Quebec.

Part personal history, part propaganda, part communal record, Champlain's works were widely read and consulted during his lifetime. They accorded him a place in the history of New France that he has never lost.

From The Voyages of Sieur de Champlain[1]

From *Chapter VIII*

CONTINUATION OF THE EXPLORATION OF THE COAST OF THE
ALMOUCHIQUOIS, AND WHAT OF NOTE WE THERE OBSERVED.

The next day we doubled Cape St. Louis,[2] so named by the Sieur de Monts,
a moderately low shore in latitude 42° 45'. That day we made two leagues
along a sandy coast, and saw as we passed a number of wigwams and gardens.
The wind coming ahead, we entered a little bay to await suitable weather for
continuing our route. Two or three canoes approached us on their way back
from fishing for cod and other fish, which are plentiful thereabouts. These
they catch with hooks made of a piece of wood, to which they attach a bone
shaped like a harpoon, which they fasten very securely for fear lest it come
out. The whole thing has the form of a little crook. The line which is attached
to it is made of tree-bark. They gave me one of them, which I took as a
curiosity. In this the bone was attached with hemp, which in my opinion is
like that of France. They informed me that they gathered this plant in their
country without cultivating it, indicating its height as about four to five feet.
The said canoe returned to shore to notify the people in the settlement, who
made signal-smokes for us; and we perceived eighteen or twenty Indians who
came down to the beach and began to dance. Our canoe went ashore to give
them some trifles, with which they were much pleased. Some of them came
out to beg us to enter their river. We raised anchor to do so, but were unable
to get in because the tide was out and the water too shallow; and were obliged
to anchor at the entrance. I went on shore, where I saw many more Indians,
who received us very kindly. I went to explore the river, but saw only an arm
of the sea which extends some little distance into the country, which is
partially cleared. Here it becomes only a brook, which cannot float boats
except at high tide. The bay is about a league in circumference. On one side
of the entrance is a kind of island covered with trees, especially pines, and
it adjoins some sand-dunes which are fairly extensive: on the other side the
land is rather high. Within the said bay are two islets, which cannot be seen
unless one is inside, and round about them the sea recedes almost completely
at low tide. This place is very conspicuous from the sea, inasmuch as the
coast is very low except the cape at the entrance to this bay, which we named
Cape St. Louis harbor.[3] It is distant from the said cape two leagues, and from
Island Cape ten. It lies in approximately the same latitude as Cape St. Louis.

On the nineteenth of the month we set out from this place. Coasting
toward the south we made four to five leagues, and passed close to a rock
which lies on a level with the surface of the water. Continuing our route, we
caught sight of some land which we took to be islands, but when nearer

---

1. The text is derived from *The Works of Samuel
de Champlain*, edited by Henry P. Biggar, vol. 1
(1922). Champlain recorded these observations of
the landscape and peoples of the Massachusetts
coast from Gloucester to the southern shore of
Cape Cod, during two leisurely voyages in 1605
and 1606. "Sieur": sir, sire; Champlain, of common birth, assumed this honorific title on his own,
and only after he had become an accomplished
author.
2. Champlain's party rounded Cape St. Louis
(modern Brant Point), just north of what became
Plymouth Harbor, Massachusetts, on July 18,
1605. The Almouchiquois were inhabitants of this
region.
3. Plymouth Harbor.

perceived that it was mainland, which continued to the north-north-west of us, and that it was the cape of a large bay[4] more than eighteen to nineteen leagues in circumference. We had run so far into this bay that we had to stand on the other tack to double the cape we had seen, which we named the White Cape, because there were sands and dunes which presented this appearance. The favorable wind was of great service here; for otherwise we should have been in danger of being driven upon the coast. This bay is very clear, provided one does not approach the shore nearer than a good league, there being no islands or rocks except the one I have mentioned, which is near a river that extends some distance inland and which we named Ste. Suzanne of the White Cape. From here to cape St. Louis the distance is ten leagues. The White Cape is a point of sand which bends southward some six leagues. This coast has fairly high sand-banks which are very conspicuous from the sea, where soundings are found of thirty, forty and fifty fathoms nearly fifteen or eighteen leagues from land, until one comes to ten fathoms in approaching the shore, which is very clear. There is a great extent of open country along the shore before one enters the woods, which are very delightful and pleasant to the eye. We cast anchor off shore and saw some Indians, toward whom four of our party advanced. Making their way along the sandy beach, they perceived as it were a bay with wigwams bordering it all around. When they were about a league and a half from us an Indian came toward them dancing all over (as they reported to us). He had come down from the high shore, but returned shortly after to give notice of our arrival to those in his settlement.

The next day, the twentieth of the month, we went to the place which our men had discovered, and found it to be a very dangerous port on account of the shoals and sand-banks, where we saw breakers on every side. It was almost low tide when we entered, and there were only four feet of water in the north passage; at high tide there are two fathoms. When we were inside, we saw that this place was rather large, being about three to four leagues in circumference, with all around it little houses about which each owner had as much land as was necessary for his support. A little river enters it which is very pretty; at low tide it has some three and a half feet of water. There are also two or three brooks bordered with meadows. The place would be very fine if only the harbor were good. I took an observation, and found the latitude 42°; and the magnetic variation 18° 40'. There came to us from all sides, dancing, a number of Indians, both men and women. We named this place Malle-barre harbor.[5]

On the next day, the twenty-first of the month, the Sieur de Monts resolved to go and inspect their settlement, and nine or ten of us accompanied him with our arms; the remainder stayed behind to guard the pinnace. We went about a league along shore. Before reaching their wigwams we entered a field planted with Indian corn in the manner I have already described. The corn was in flower, and some five and a half feet in height. There was some less advanced, which they sow later. We saw an abundance of Brazilian beans, many edible squashes of various sizes, tobacco, and roots which they cultivate, the latter having the taste of artichoke. The woods are full of oaks, nut-

4. Cape Cod and Cape Cod Bay.
5. Modern Nauset Harbor, on the Atlantic side of Cape Cod.

trees, and very fine cypresses, which are of reddish color and have a very pleasant smell. There were also several fields not cultivated, for the reason that the Indians let them lie fallow. When they wish to plant them they set fire to the weeds and then dig up the field with their wooden spades. Their wigwams are round, and covered with heavy thatch made of reeds. In the middle of the roof is an opening, about a foot and a half wide, through which issues the smoke of their fire. We asked them if they had their permanent residence in this place, and whether there was much snow; but we could not find this out very well since we did not understand their language, although they attempted to explain by signs, taking up sand in their hand, then spreading it on the ground, and indicating that the snow was the same color as our collars and fell to the depth of a foot. Others indicated that it was less, giving us also to understand that the harbor never froze over; but we were unable to ascertain whether the snow lasted a long time. I consider, however, that this country is temperate and the winter not severe.[6] During the time we were there it blew a gale from the north-east which lasted four days, with the sky so overcast that the sun was hardly visible at all. It was very cold, so that we were obliged to put on our greatcoats which we had entirely laid aside. However, I believe this was exceptional, just as often happens in other localities out of season.

On the twenty-third of the said month of July, four or five sailors having gone ashore with some large kettles to fetch fresh water from among the sand-hills at a distance from our pinnace, certain Indians, being desirous to possess some of these kettles,[7] watched for the time when our men went there, and snatched one by force out of the hands of a sailor who had filled his the first and who had no weapons. One of his companions, starting to run after the Indian, quickly returned, being unable to catch him, inasmuch as the latter was a swifter runner than himself. The other Indians, when they saw our sailors running toward our pinnace and shouting to us to discharge some musket-shots at the Indians who were in considerable numbers, took to flight. At that time there were a few Indians on board our pinnace who threw themselves into the sea, and we were able to seize only one of them. Those on shore who had taken to flight, seeing the others swimming, turned back straight to the sailor from whom they had taken the kettle and shot several arrows at him from behind and brought him down. Perceiving his condition, they at once rushed upon him and despatched him with their knives. Meantime we made haste to go on shore, and fired muskets from our pinnace. Mine exploded in my hands and nearly killed me. The Indians, hearing this fusillade, again took to flight, and redoubled their speed when they saw that we had landed, being frightened on seeing us run after them. There was no likelihood of catching them; for they are as swift-footed as horses. The dead man[8] was brought in, and some hours later was buried. Meanwhile we kept our prisoner bound hand and foot on board our pinnace, fearing lest he should escape. The Sieur de Monts determined to let him go,

6. Because this part of North America lay far south of the latitude of France and England, many early voyagers assumed it would have a mild climate. After visiting this landscape, however, William Bradford wrote, "They that know the winters of that country know them to be sharp and violent and subject to cruel and fierce storms, dangerous to travel to known places, much more to search an unknown coast."
7. Kettles made of iron and other metals were to be much sought after by Northeast Indian groups who traded their furs for European goods. "Pinnace": a small sailing vessel.
8. A carpenter from the town of St. Malo.

feeling persuaded he was not to blame and knew nothing of what had occurred, as was the case also with those who were at the time on board and alongside our pinnace. A few hours later some Indians came toward us, making excuses by signs and outward show that it was not they who had done this evil deed but others farther off in the interior. We were unwilling to do them harm, although it was in our power to avenge ourselves.

*   *   *

From *Chapter XIII*

THE SIEUR DE POUTRINCOURT SETS OUT FROM PORT ROYAL TO MAKE DISCOVERIES. EVERYTHING WE SAW AND THAT HAPPENED AS FAR AS MALLEBARRE.

*   *   *

Continuing our route we went to Island Cape,[9] where we were delayed a little by bad weather and fog, and where we did not see much probability of spending the night, inasmuch as the place was not suitable for this purpose. Whilst we were in this predicament I remembered that when following this coast with the Sieur de Monts, I had noted on my map at a league's distance a place which appeared suitable for vessels, into which we had not entered because, at the time we were passing, the wind was favorable for holding on our course. This place lay behind us, on which account I said to the Sieur de Poutrincourt that we must stand in for a point which was then visible, where was situated the place in question which seemed to me suitable for passing the night. We proceeded to anchor at the entrance, and the next day went inside.[1]

The Sieur de Poutrincourt landed with eight or ten of our company. We saw some very fine grapes which were ripe, Brazilian peas, pumpkins, squashes, and some good roots with a flavor like that of chards, which the Indians cultivate. They presented us with a number of these in exchange for other little trifles which we gave them. They had already completed their harvest. We saw two hundred Indians in this place, which is pleasant enough; and here are many nut-trees, cypresses, sassafras, oaks, ashes, and beeches, which are very fine. The chief of this place, who is called Quiouhamenec, came to see us with another chief, a neighbor of his named Cohouepech, whom we entertained. Onemechin, chief of Saco,[2] also came to see us there, and we gave him a coat, which he did not keep long, but presented to another because, being uncomfortable in it, he could not adapt himself to it. At this place we also saw an Indian who wounded himself so badly in the foot, and lost so much blood, that he fainted. A number of other Indians gathered about him, and sang for some time before touching him. Afterward they made certain motions with their feet and hands, and shook his head; then while they breathed upon him, he came to. Our surgeon dressed his injuries, and afterward he was able to go off in good spirits.

The next day, as we were caulking our shallop,[3] the Sieur de Poutrincourt

---

9. Cape Ann, north of Boston. Champlain writes in this chapter of a voyage undertaken in the fall of 1606, under the Sieur de Poutrincourt, head of the French settlement of Port-Royal, Nova Scotia.

1. Gloucester Harbor, on the south shore of Cape Ann.
2. A river in Maine.
3. A small vessel useful in coastal explorations.

caught sight in the woods of a great many Indians, who with the intention of doing us some injury were on their way toward a little brook in the strait at the causeway leading to the mainland, where some of our men were washing their clothes. As I was walking along the causeway these Indians caught sight of me, and in order to put a good face upon the matter, since they saw clearly that I at the same time had discovered them, they began to shout and to dance; then they came toward me with their bows, arrows, quivers, and other arms. And inasmuch as there was a meadow between them and me, I made a sign to them to dance again, which they did in a circle, putting all their arms in the center. They had hardly begun when they espied in the woods the Sieur de Poutrincourt with eight musketeers, which astonished them. Nevertheless they did not fail to complete their dance, but when it was finished, they withdrew in all directions, being apprehensive lest some bad turn should be done to them. However, we said nothing to them, and showed them only evidences of good will. Then we returned to our shallop to launch it and to take our departure. They begged us to remain a day longer, saying that more than two thousand men would come to see us; but as we could not afford to lose time we were unwilling to delay any longer. I believe that their plan was to surprise us. Some of the land is cleared, and they were constantly clearing more, in the following fashion. They cut down the trees at a height of three feet from the ground; then they burn the branches upon the trunk, and sow their corn between the fallen timber; and in course of time they take out the roots. There are also fine meadows for supporting numbers of cattle. This port is very beautiful and a good one, with water enough for vessels, and shelter behind the islands. It lies in latitude 43°, and we have named it the Beautiful Port.

On the last day of September we departed from the Beautiful Port, and passed Cape St. Louis; and we sailed all night to reach the White Cape. The next morning, an hour before daylight, we found ourselves in the White Bay to leeward of White Cape, in eight feet of water, at a distance of a league from the land. Here we cast anchor in order not to approach closer before daylight, and in order to see how we stood regarding the tide. Meanwhile we sent our shallop to make soundings, and they did not find more than eight feet of water, so that it was necessary to determine, while awaiting daylight, what we should do. The water fell to five feet, and our pinnace sometimes touched upon the sand, without, however, being injured or doing herself any damage; for the sea was calm; and we had not more than three feet of water under us, when the tide began to come in, which gave us great encouragement.

When day dawned we descried to leeward a very low sandy coast off which we lay. We sent the boat to make soundings in the direction of a tract of upland which is somewhat elevated, and where we judged there was much water; and in fact we found there seven fathoms. We went there and cast anchor, and at once prepared the shallop with nine or ten men to go on shore and examine a place where we judged there was a good, safe harbor, in which we might find safety should the wind become stronger. Having explored it, we entered with two, three, and four fathoms of water. When we were inside, we found five and six. There were plenty of oysters, of very good quality, which we had not hitherto seen; and we named the port Oyster Harbor.[4] It

4. Either Barnstable Harbor or Wellfleet Harbor, the major inlets on the inner shore of Cape Cod.

is in latitude 42°. There came to us three canoes of Indians. That day the wind was favorable, and for this reason we weighed anchor to go to White Cape, distant from this place five leagues north a quarter north-east, and we doubled it.

The following day, the second of October, we arrived off Mallebarre, where we remained some time on account of the bad weather we experienced. During this time the Sieur de Poutrincourt, accompanied by twelve to fifteen men, paid a visit to the port in the shallop. There came to meet him some 150 Indians, singing and dancing, in accordance with their custom. After having viewed this place we returned to our vessel, and, the wind coming fair, made sail along the coast, steering south.

Chapter XIV

CONTINUATION OF THE ABOVE-MENTIONED DISCOVERIES; AND WHAT OF NOTE WAS OBSERVED DURING THESE.

When we were some six leagues from Mallebarre, we cast anchor near the shore because the wind was not favorable. Along this coast we observed smoke which the Indians were making; and this made us decide to go and visit them. For this purpose the shallop was got ready; but when we were near the shore, which is sandy, we were unable to land, as the swell was too great. The Indians, seeing this, launched a canoe; and eight or nine of them came out to us, singing and indicating by signs the joy it gave them to see us; and they showed us that lower down was a port where we could place our pinnace in safety.

Being unable to land, the shallop came back to the pinnace, and the Indians, who had been kindly treated, returned to the shore.

The next day, the wind being fair, we continued our course to the [south] five leagues, and we had no sooner gone this far than we found three and four fathoms of water at a distance of a league and a half from the shore. And going a little farther, the depth suddenly lessened to a fathom and a half and two fathoms, which made us apprehensive, since the sea was breaking everywhere, and we could perceive no passage along which we could return upon our course; for the wind was altogether against us.

So it came about that, being caught among the breakers and sand-banks, we had to run at haphazard where one judged there was water enough for our pinnace, which drew but at the most four feet. We kept on among these breakers until we found four feet and a half. Finally by God's favor we succeeded in passing over a sandy point which projects about three leagues into the sea to the south-south-east, making a very dangerous place. Doubling this cape, which we named Reef Cape,[5] and which is twelve or thirteen leagues from Mallebarre, we anchored in two and a half fathoms of water, inasmuch as we found ourselves surrounded on all sides by breakers and shoals, save only in certain places where the sea was not breaking very much. We sent the shallop to seek out a channel in order that we might go to a place which we concluded was the one indicated to us by the Indians. We also believed there was a river there where we could lie in safety.

5. Some part of the group of dangerous shoals and reefs lying off Monomoy Point, Cape Cod's "elbow." It was here, in 1620, that the *Mayflower* was forced to turn back from its intended route to the Hudson River, ultimately leaving William Bradford and the other Pilgrims at Plymouth.

When our shallop reached the place, our men landed and inspected the locality, after which they came back with an Indian whom they brought with them. They informed us that at high tide we could enter, and it was resolved to do so. We at once weighed anchor and, under the guidance of the Indian, who acted as our pilot, proceeded to anchor in a roadstead[6] in front of the port, in six fathoms of water and good bottom; for we could not go inside because night had overtaken us.

The next day men were sent to place buoys upon the extremity of a sand-bank which lies at the harbor's mouth; then at high tide we entered the place with two fathoms of water. Once inside we gave praise to God for bringing us to a place of safety. Our rudder had broken and been mended with ropes, and we feared lest in the midst of these shallows and strong tides it should break again, which would have resulted in our destruction. Inside this harbor there is but one fathom of water, and at high tide two fathoms. Toward the east lies a bay which doubles to the north some three leagues, and therein is an island and two other little coves, which give beauty to the landscape. Here there is much cleared land and many little hills, whereon the Indians cultivate corn and other grains on which they live. Here are likewise very fine vines, plenty of nut-trees, oaks, cypresses, and a few pines. All the inhabitants of this place are much given to agriculture, and lay up a store of Indian corn for the winter, which they preserve in the following manner.

In the sand on the slope of the hills they dig holes some five to six feet deep more or less, and place their corn and other grains in large grass sacks, which they throw into the said holes, and cover them with sand to a depth of three or four feet above the surface of the ground. They take away this grain according to their needs, and it is preserved as well as it would be in our granaries.[7]

At this place we saw some five to six hundred Indians who were all naked except for their privy parts, which they cover with a little piece of deer or sealskin. The women are the same, and, like the men, cover their parts with skins or leaves. Both men and women wear their hair neatly combed and braided in various ways, after the fashion of the Indians at Saco, and are well-proportioned in body, with olive-colored skins. They adorn themselves with feathers, wampum beads, and other knick-knacks, which they arrange very neatly after the manner of embroidery. Their arms consist of bows, arrows, and clubs. They are not so much great hunters as good fishermen and tillers of the soil.

Regarding their polity, government, and religious belief, we were unable to form a judgment, and I believe that in this they do not differ from our Souriquois[8] and Canadians, who worship neither moon nor sun nor any other thing, and pray no more than the beasts. They have indeed among them certain persons who, they say, have communication with the devil, and in these they have great faith. These persons tell them all that is to happen, in which for the most part they lie. Sometimes they succeed in hitting it right,

---

6. An exposed anchoring place; the party evidently had rounded Monomoy Point and was about to enter modern Stage Harbor, which Champlain later names "Misfortune Harbor."

7. William Bradford notes that the Pilgrims dug up some of these caches during their exploration of Cape Cod fifteen years later.

8. The Micmac, who then inhabited Nova Scotia.

and in telling them things similar to what actually happens. This is why they have faith in these persons, as if they were prophets, although they are naught but scamps who inveigle them, as the Egyptians and gypsies do the simple village folk. They have chiefs whom they obey in regard to matters of warfare but not in anything else. These chiefs work, and assume no higher rank than their companions. Each possesses only sufficient land for his own support.

Their lodges are separated from one another according to the extent of land that each is able to occupy. They are lofty, circular, and covered with matting made of grass or husks of Indian corn. Their only furniture consists of a bed or two raised one foot from the floor, and made of a number of saplings laid one against the other, whereon they place a reed-mat, in the Spanish manner (which is a kind of thick mattress two or three fingers in depth), and upon this they sleep. They have a great many fleas in summer, even in the fields. One day when we were out walking, we attracted such a number of them that we were obliged to change our clothes.

All the harbors, bays, and coasts from Saco onward are filled with every kind of fish like those we have near our settlements, and in such abundance that I can guarantee there was never a day or a night during which we did not see and hear more than a thousand porpoises passing alongside our pinnace and chasing the smaller fry. Here are likewise plenty of shellfish of several kinds, and especially oysters. Game birds are very plentiful.

This would prove a very good site for laying and constructing the foundations of a state, if the harbor were a little deeper and the entrance safer than it is.

Before leaving port our rudder was repaired, and we made bread from flour we had brought for our subsistence when our biscuit gave out. Meanwhile we sent the shallop with five or six men and an Indian to see whether they could find a passage more suitable for leaving than that by which we had entered.

When they had gone five or six leagues, and we were close inshore, the Indian took to flight. He gave those in the shallop to understand that he was afraid lest he should be carried off to other Indians farther south who are enemies of his tribe. Upon their return they reported that as far as they had gone, there were at least three fathoms of water, and that farther on there were neither shoals nor reefs.

We accordingly made haste to repair our pinnace and to provide bread for fifteen days. Meanwhile the Sieur de Poutrincourt, accompanied by ten or twelve musketeers, visited all the surrounding country, which is very fine, as I have already stated. Here and there we saw a good number of small lodges.

Some eight or nine days later, on the Sieur de Poutrincourt's going out walking as he had done before, we observed that the Indians were taking down their wigwams and were sending into the woods their wives, children and provisions, and other necessaries of life. This made us suspect some evil design, and that they wished to attack our people who were working on shore, where they remained every night to guard whatever could not be taken on board in the evening except with much labor. This proved to be quite true; for they had resolved among themselves that, when all their goods were in safety, they would surprise the men on shore as best they could, and would carry off everything these men had there. But if perchance they found them on their guard, they would come with signs of friendship, as they were accustomed to do, laying aside their bows and arrows.

Now in view of what the Sieur de Poutrincourt had seen, and of the mode of procedure he had been told they observed when they wished to do a bad turn, we passed among their wigwams where were a number of women, to whom we gave bracelets and rings, in order to keep them quiet and from becoming afraid of us, while to the majority of the prominent and older men we gave axes, knives, and other articles of which they stood in need. This pleased them much, repaying for all by dances, gambols, and speeches, which latter we did not in the least understand. We went about everywhere without their having the boldness to say anything to us. It amused us greatly to see them look so innocent as they made themselves appear.

We came back very quietly to our pinnace, accompanied by a few Indians. On the way we met with several small troops who were gradually collecting together, fully armed, and were much surprised to see us so far inland, little thinking that we had just made a tour of from four to five leagues through their country. When passing near us they trembled for fear lest we should harm them, which it was in our power to do; but we did nothing, although we were aware of their evil intentions. On reaching the spot where our men were at work, the Sieur de Poutrincourt asked if all things were in readiness to oppose the designs of these rascals.

He gave orders for every one on shore to be taken on board: which was done, except that the man who was making the bread remained behind to finish a baking, and two other men with him. They were told that the Indians had some evil design, and that they should make haste in order to come on board in the evening, as it was known that the Indians only put their plans into execution at night or at daybreak, which is the hour for making surprises in most of their schemes.

The evening having come, the Sieur de Poutrincourt ordered the shallop to be sent ashore to fetch the men who were left. This was done as soon as the tide would permit, and those on shore were told that they must embark for the reason already given them. This they refused to do despite the remonstrances made to them on the risks they were running and the disobedience they were showing to their chief. To these they paid no attention, except a servant of the Sieur de Poutrincourt, who came aboard; but two others disembarked from the boat and went off to the three on shore, who remained to eat some biscuits made at the same time as the bread. Since these were unwilling to do what they were told, the shallop returned alongside, but without informing the Sieur de Poutrincourt, who was asleep, and who believed they were all on board the vessel.

The next morning, the fifteenth of October, the Indians did not fail to come and see in what state were our men, whom they found asleep, except one who was before the fire. Seeing them in this condition, the Indians, to the number of four hundred, came quietly over a little hill, and shot such a salvo of arrows at them as to give them no chance of recovery before they were struck dead. Fleeing as fast as they could toward our pinnace, and crying out, "Help, help, they are killing us," some of them fell dead in the water, while the rest were all pierced with arrows, of whom one died a short time afterward.[9] These Indians made a desperate row, with war-whoops which it was terrible to hear.

At this noise, and that of our men, the sentinel on our vessel cried out, "To arms; they are killing our men." Thereupon each quickly seized his weapons, and at the same time some fifteen or sixteen of us embarked in the shallop to go ashore. But being unable to land on account of a sand-bank which lay between us and the shore, we jumped into the water and waded from this bank to the mainland, a distance of a musket-shot. As soon as we reached it, the Indians, seeing us within bowshot, fled inland. To pursue them was useless, for they are wonderfully swift. All we could do was to carry off the dead bodies and bury them near a cross which had been set up the day before, and then to look about to see whether we could catch sight of any Indians; but in this we wasted our time. Realising this we returned. Three hours later they reappeared on the shore. We discharged several shots at them from our little brass cannon; and whenever they heard the report, they threw themselves flat on the ground to avoid the charge. In derision of us they pulled down the cross, and dug up the bodies, which displeased us greatly, and made us go after them a second time;[1] but they fled as they had done before. We again set up the cross, and reinterred the bodies, which they had scattered here and there among the heaths, where they had kindled a fire to burn them. We returned without having accomplished more than before, seeing clearly that there was hardly any chance of taking vengeance for this blow, and that we must postpone the matter until it should please God.

On the sixteenth of the month we set out from Misfortune harbor, so named by us on account of the misfortune which happened to us there. This place is in latitude 41° 20', and distant some twelve or thirteen leagues from Mallebarre.

1613

From The Voyages and Discoveries[1]

From The Voyage of 1618

[ACCOUNT OF ÉTIENNE BRULÉ]

*   *   *

And on the following fifth of July I left Quebec, accompanied by the Sieur de La Mothe, to proceed to the said Three Rivers,[2] both to trade and to see

9. Of the five Frenchmen ashore, the single one who escaped death, Jean Du Val, was executed in Quebec in 1608 for conspiring against Champlain. Marc Lescarbot (c. 1570–c. 1603), a lawyer and writer who accompanied this expedition, wrote that the mutinous shore party was led by a young braggart (probably of noble background) who resented the fact that he had been denied alcohol on the ship. He was found dead on shore, Lescarbot wrote, "his face on the ground, having a little dog upon his back, both of them shot together, and pierced through with one and the selfsame arrow."
1. Lescarbot added that these Nauset Indians turned their backs to those on the ship and "cast sand with their two hands together betwixt their buttocks in derision, howling like wolves."
1. The text is from The Works of Samuel de Champlain, edited by Henry P. Biggar, vol. 3 (1929).
2. Or Trois Riveres; a settlement on the St. Lawrence between Quebec City and Montreal. Nicolas de la Mothe, who joined Champlain for this expedition in France, had been taken by the English and spent time as a prisoner in Virginia before being returned to Europe. He came back to America, Champlain writes earlier, because of "an increased desire" to see Canada again.

the savages, and we arrived in the evening off Sainte Croix, a place on the way so called, where we caught sight of a shallop coming straight towards us, on board of which were some men from the Sieurs du Pont, des Chesnes,[3] and certain other clerks and agents of the merchants. They begged me to despatch the said shallop quickly and to send it to Quebec to fetch some goods still left there, and said that a great number of savages had come down intending to go on the war-path.

This news pleased us greatly, and to meet their wishes, on the morning of the next day I quitted my long-boat and embarked in a shallop in order to reach the savages quicker, and the other which came from Three Rivers continued its course to Quebec. And we made such progress by rowing that we reached that place on the seventh of July about three o'clock in the afternoon, and upon our arrival I landed. Then all the savages of my acquaintance and with whom in their own country I had become intimate, were awaiting me with impatience and came to meet me and as though very pleased and happy to see me again, embracing me one after the other with demonstrations of great joy, as on my part I likewise did the same to them. So we passed the afternoon and remainder of the day in this rejoicing until the following day when the said savages held a council together to learn if I would again assist them in their wars against their enemies, as I had done in the past and as I had promised them: by which enemies they are cruelly troubled and harassed.

And meanwhile on our side we consulted together to determine what we should do in the matter of the murder of those two poor men,[4] so that justice might be done and in that way they should be taught to do nothing [like it] in future.

As to the help asked for by the savages, to make war on their enemies, I replied to them that my inclination had not changed nor was my courage less; but that what prevented me from assisting them was that last year when the chance and opportunity presented itself, they had failed me at need, in that they had promised me to return with a good number of warriors but had not done so, which was the cause of my withdrawing without producing much result. That nevertheless this must be taken into consideration, but for the present it was proper to determine what action should be taken on the murder of those two poor men, and that satisfaction must be made for it. Then [on my] quitting their council as if in wrath and anger over the matter, they offered to kill the criminals and to set about doing so at once, if we agreed to it, well recognising themselves the heinousness of that crime; to which nevertheless we would not consent, but postponing any assistance to them till another time, and requiring them to come down to us again next year with a good number of men. Meanwhile I was to beg the King to help us with men, money and supplies in order to assist them and enable them to enjoy the rest they hoped for and victory over their enemies, whereat they were well pleased. Upon this we parted, although they held two or three meetings on this subject, which cost us several hours of time. Two or three days after my arrival at that place, they began to make merry and to dance,

3. Commander of one of the ships in the fleet that returned Champlain to Canada in 1618.
4. Some two years earlier, a pair of settlers from Quebec who went hunting were murdered in the woods by "two vicious young men of the Montaignais," as Champlain had reported.

and to hold several great feasts on the expectation of the coming war expedition wherein I was to assist them.

Thereupon I represented to the said Sieur du Pont my views regarding this murder, of which it was fitting to make a more urgent case. That unless this were done the savages might feel free not only to do the same again, but even something worse: for I knew them to be people governed by example; that they might accuse the French of lacking courage; that if no further mention of it were made, they would judge that we were in fear and terror of them, and that if we let them off so easily they would become more insolent, bold and unbearable, and ready to engage in more serious and deadly designs. Moreover that the other savage tribes which have heard or will hear of this deed and that it remained unavenged or avenged by a few gifts and presents, as is their custom, might boast that to kill a man is no great matter, since the French make so little account of seeing their comrades killed by their neighbours that they eat and drink with them, who walk and converse familiarly with our people, as may be seen.

But also, on the other hand, realising that the savage folk are without reason, difficult of approach, easily estranged, and very quick to take vengeance, should we urge them to do justice, there would be no security for those of us who may be preparing to make explorations among them. This is why, all things considered, we decided to settle this matter amicably, and to pass things over quietly, letting them trade in peace with the clerks and agents of the merchants and with the others who were charged therewith.

Now there was with them a man named Etienne Brulé,[5] one of our interpreters, who had lived with them for the last eight years, both as a pastime and to see the country and learn their language and mode of life, and it was he whom I had sent and engaged to go towards the Onondagas at Carantoüan,[6] in order to bring back with him the five hundred warriors they had promised to send us to assist us in the war we were engaged in against their enemies, whereof mention is made in the narrative of my preceding book. I sent for this man, to wit, Etienne Brulé, and speaking with him I asked him why he had not brought the reinforcement of the five hundred men and the reason of his delay, and why he had given me no account of it. Then he told me the reason, of which it will not be out of place to give an account, he being more to be pitied than blamed, on account of the mishaps that befell him on this mission.

He began by telling me that after he had taken leave of me to go on his journey and execute his commission, he set out with the twelve savages I had given him as guides and to form an escort on account of the dangers through which he had to pass, and they made such progress that they reached the said town of Carantoüan, but not without running risks, inasmuch as they had to pass through the country and territory of their enemies, and to avoid any evil plot they sought a more secure path by traversing woods, forests and dense and difficult thickets, and by marshy swamps, frightful and

5. Frenchman (c. 1592–1632) who arrived in New France in 1608 with Champlain and was sent to learn the languages and cultures of the native peoples.
6. A village near the present site of Waverly, New York. The "Onondagas" were actually Conestoga or Susquehanna Indians who inhabited the country south of the Iroquois in present-day New York and Pennsylvania.

unfrequented places and wastes, all to avoid the danger of an encounter with their enemies.

And in spite of this great precaution the said Brulé and his savage companions, in traversing a plain, nevertheless met with some hostile savages returning to their village, who were surprised and defeated by our savages, four of the enemy being killed at once and two taken prisoner, whom Brulé and his companions brought along to the said town of Carantoüan, where they were received by the inhabitants of that place very affectionately and with gladness and good cheer, to the accompaniment of dances and feasts wherewith they are in the habit of feasting and honoring strangers.

Some days passed in this friendly reception, and after Brulé had told them his message and made them understand the purpose of his journey, the savages of the said place assembled in council to deliberate and decide on sending the five hundred warriors asked for by the said Brulé.

After the council had been held and the decision taken to send them, orders were given to assemble, make ready and arm them, that they might set out and come to join us, and meet us encamped before the fort and village of our enemies, which was only three short days' journey from Carantoüan, which said village [Carantoüan] is garrisoned with more than eight hundred warriors, and well fortified in the manner of those described above, with high and strong palisades, firmly tied and joined together, and their dwellings of similar construction.

When this decision had thus been reached by the inhabitants of Carantoüan, to send the five hundred men, these were a very long time in getting ready, although urged by Brulé to make haste, who pointed out to them that if they delayed further, they would no longer find us at the place fixed, and in fact they were only able to reach it two days after our departure from that place, which we were constrained to abandon, being too weak and worn out by the inclemency of the weather. This made Brulé and the reinforcement of the said five hundred men he had brought retire and return on their tracks to their village of Carantoüan, where on their return the said Brulé was forced to remain and to pass the remainder of the autumn and all the winter, waiting for company and escort to return. And while awaiting this opportunity he employed himself in exploring the country, visiting the tribes and territories near that place, and making his way along a river which discharges on the coast of Florida,[7] where there are many powerful and warlike tribes which make war one upon another. The climate there is very mild, and there are great numbers of animals and game, but to reach and explore these regions one must have much patience on account of the difficulties in passing through most of its wastes.

And he continued his route along the said river to the sea, past islands and the coasts near them, which are inhabited by several tribes and numerous savage peoples, who nevertheless are well disposed and love the French nation above all others. But as for those who are acquainted with the Dutch, they complain much of them, because the latter treat them too harshly. Among other things he observed is that the winter there is very mild, and

---

7. Refers to the southern parts of the continent then (i.e., in 1618) claimed by Spain. "A river": the Susquehanna, which discharges into the sea via the Chesapeake Bay.

that it very seldom snows, and that even when it does snow, it is not a foot in depth and melts on reaching the ground.

And after he had explored the country and seen what was remarkable, he returned to the village of Carantoüan, in order to find some companions with whom to return to our settlement. And after some stay at the said Carantoüan, five or six of the savages decided to make the journey with the said Brulé, but on their way they met with a great band of their enemies, who attacked the said Brulé and his companions so fiercely that they scattered and separated them from one another, so that they could not come together again. Brulé indeed, who had made off in the hope of escaping, got so separated from the others that he could no longer retrace his steps nor find the trail or any sign so as to effect his retreat in any direction whatever, and thus he continued to wander through the woods and forests for some days without eating and almost despairing of his life from pressure of hunger. At last he came by chance upon a little path which he determined to follow no matter where it might lead, were it towards the enemy or not, preferring to place himself in their hands through the trust he had in God, than to die alone so miserably; moreover he knew how to speak their language, and this might bring some advantage to him.

Now he had not proceeded far when he discovered three savages, laden with fish, who were returning to their village. He made haste to run after them to join them, and coming near them he began to call to them as is their custom, at which call they turned round and, in fear and apprehension, prepared to flee and leave their burden, but Brulé, speaking to them, reassured them and made them lay down their bows and arrows in token of peace, as likewise Brulé on his side laid down his arms, although he himself was very weak and feeble on account of not having eaten for three or four days. And on coming up with them, after having made them hear his mishap and the wretched state to which he was reduced, they smoked together, as is their custom when they and their acquaintances visit one another.

They seemed to have pity and compassion on him, offering him every assistance; they even brought him to their village where they entertained him and gave him something to eat. But as soon as the people of this place heard of it, to wit, that an Adoresetoüy had arrived, for so they call the French, which name is equivalent to saying "iron men," they came crowding in great numbers to see the said Brulé, whom they took and brought to the lodge of one of the principal chiefs, where he was questioned. They asked him who he was, whence he came, what cause had driven and led him to this place and how he had got lost, and further whether he were not one of the French nation which was making war on them? Thereupon he made reply that he belonged to another better nation that was desirous only of their acquaintance and friendship, which they refused to believe, and rushed upon him, and tore out his nails with their teeth, burned him with red-hot firebrands, plucked out his beard hair by hair, contrary nevertheless to the wish of their chief. And in this emergency one of the savages spied an *Agnus Dei*[8] which he had hung about his neck, and on seeing it, asked what he had thus hang-

---

8. A figure of the "lamb of God" worn as a holy necklace.

ing at his neck, and tried to seize it and tear it off, but the said Brulé said to him (in a resolute voice): "If you take it and put me to death, you shall see that immediately afterwards you and all your house will die suddenly"; to which the savage paid no attention, but pursuing his evil purpose tried to seize the *Agnus Dei* and tear it from him; and all together were prepared to put him to death, after first making him suffer many pains and tortures which are usually practised by them upon their enemies. But God who had mercy on him would not permit it, but in His providence caused the sky which had been clear and fine suddenly to become overcast and to be filled with thick heavy clouds, which ended in thunder and lightning so violent and continuous as to be something strange and awful. This storm so frightened the savages, because it was unusual to them, and also because they had never known the like, that it distracted them and made them forget their wicked intentions with regard to Brulé, their prisoner, and they left and forsook him, yet without unbinding him, not daring to approach him. This gave the sufferer an opportunity to use gentle words to them, calling to them and representing the harm they were doing to him without any reason, making them understand how angry our God was with them for having thus ill-treated him.

Then the chief approached the said Brulé, unbound him and brought him into his lodge, where he cleaned and doctored his wounds. After this, there were no dances and feasts or rejoicings to which Brulé was not summoned, and after having spent some time with these savages, he determined to withdraw to our quarters and settlement.

And taking leave of them he promised them to make them friends with the French and their enemies, and to make them swear friendship for one another, and said that with this object he would return to them as soon as he could. On his departure they conducted him four days' journey from their village, whence he came to the country and village of the Atinouaentans[9] which I had already visited, and there the said Brulé remained some time. Then resuming his journey to us he passed along the Freshwater Sea[1] and went by boat along its shores some ten days along the north shore where also I had passed when going to make war, and the said Brulé would have proceeded farther to explore the lie of these regions as I had given him instructions, had it not been for a rumour of war preparations among them which caused him to hold this plan in reserve to another time. And he promised me to pursue and carry it out in a short time, with God's aid, and to guide me thither in order to get more ample and detailed knowledge of it. After he had told me his story I gave him hopes that his services would be recognised, and encouraged him to keep to this good intention until our return, when we should more and more have the means of doing something wherewith he would be pleased. This is indeed the whole account and narrative of his journey after he left me to go on these explorations, which pleased me from the hope of succeeding better by this means in continuing and forwarding these.

And with this object he took leave of me to return to the savage peoples whose acquaintance and kinship he had gained in his travels and explora-

9. The "bear people," one of the four clans of the Huron Indians.

1. Lake Huron.

tions; and I begged him to continue them until next year when I would return with a good number of men, both to reward him for his labours and also to assist the savages, his friends, in their wars as in the past.[2]

* * *

1619

2. Brulé eventually traveled as far as the west end of Lake Superior.

JOHN SMITH
1580–1631

Under the patent granted to Sir Walter Ralegh by Queen Elizabeth I in 1584, the English undertook their first serious effort at colonization in Virginia. By 1590 this attempt, in the vicinity of Roanoke, had ended in disaster. When the English renewed their involvement in America in the 1600s, they replaced the older heroic model of exploration and colonization with a more corporate one. Under this new model, the single controlling figure of Ralegh's era was replaced by larger companies of investors (often merchants), who had more capital to support costly expansion overseas. In fact, King James I split the vaguely defined region of Virginia, which ran from Florida to Canada, into two more manageable parts, giving the direction of each to separate but related groups of investors who together composed the Virginia Company. The southern part (including the area now known as the state of Virginia) came under the care of the company's members from London, while the northern part (from which New England was to be developed) fell to members in the West Country towns of Bristol, Plymouth, and Exeter. Although the so-called First Charter was succeeded by new ones in 1609 and 1612, its broad base of formalized support set the standard for English colonial practice over the next hundred years. As a compromise between large-scale governmental action and isolated individual effort, the format of the colonial "company" proved both useful and enduring.

The push toward corporate structures did not mean that interesting individuals disappeared. Indeed, one of the most colorful of all the Englishmen ever involved in America, the legendary Captain John Smith, proved by his crucial role in the establishment and continuance of the new colony at Jamestown that success in such ventures still required individual initiative and commitment. Few people had more pertinent preparation to reteach the English this old lesson. When named by the London partners to the ruling council (that is, the local governing committee) for the Virginia colony sent out in late December 1606, John Smith brought rich experience to his charge. His early life was deceptively sedate: born into a farmer's family in Lincolnshire, he was apprenticed at fifteen to a shopkeeper near his home. But tales of exploration, piracy, and military adventure already had stirred his imagination. In 1593 he may have tried to join a punitive expedition Sir Francis Drake was thought to be readying against England's enemy Spain, although his father apparently intervened. Shortly after his father's death in 1596, the fiery sixteen-year-old managed to have his indenture to the shopkeeper canceled and went to The Netherlands as a volunteer soldier to fight for the Dutch in their long war of independence from Philip II.

Following his tour of duty in The Netherlands, he saw action in the Mediterranean on a privateer, winning a good share of the prize money when a Venetian galley was captured. Smith next joined the Austrian army in its continuing war (1593–1606) against the Turks, and while in the Austrian service, he fought valiantly in Hungary and was promoted to a captaincy. Eventually, after defeating and beheading a succession of three Turkish officers in single combat in Rumania (his coat of arms, awarded later, showed the three severed heads), Smith was wounded in battle, taken prisoner, and sold into slavery to a Turk. Smith was passed from place to place until, held prisoner on the Black Sea, he murdered his master and fled back to Rumania via Russia and Poland, returning to England in the winter of 1604–05.

Many of these details come to us only through Smith's own at times garbled narratives, most of them penned long after the events. But when the Jamestown backers encountered him as they readied their expedition, he must have had the air of someone deeply experienced in the skills that the quasi-military venture would require. Smith's military background (and temperament), however, also carried liabilities in that age when warfare was brutal and soldiers were far from professional: he sometimes used force unnecessarily, and his hard-to-control temper and stubborn self-reliance made him an often troublesome companion. Already on the voyage over, Smith ran afoul of those in charge, was placed under arrest while the fleet was near the Canary Islands in February 1607, and was threatened with execution in the West Indies the following month. By June 10, some weeks after the arrival in Virginia and the opening of the heretofore secret list of the council members (not revealed sooner so as to prevent difficulties on shipboard), Smith had been given a reprieve and was sworn in to his seat on the council. From then until his final departure for England in October 1609, he was in the middle of the tumultuous colony's affairs. Smith survived the grim period of sickness in 1607 and missed the bleaker "starving time" that came shortly after his departure, but during his years there, he was always at the epicenter of the various political earthquakes that rocked early Virginia.

Placed in charge of its supplies in the fall of 1607, he was elected president of the council—in effect, the colony's governor—the following year, after a series of wide-ranging explorations that made him the most knowledgeable of the settlers regarding the new land. The explorations also led to his imprisonment at the hands of Powhatan, overlord of the Chesapeake Bay Indians, from whom he claimed (much later) that the king's young daughter Pocahontas rescued him. Whatever the role Pocahontas played, what Smith took to be his impending execution may have been nothing more than a harmless adoption ceremony inducting him into Powhatan's tribe. In this episode as in others, Smith's volatile and unpredictable relations with the Native Americans were characteristic. Also characteristic was the fact that as a writer Smith milked the story of his rescue by Pocahontas. Although he failed to have the lasting influence on Virginia's affairs that he sought, in recasting that story fifteen years after the fact he found the immortality that otherwise eluded him. How easily we forget that on his return to Jamestown from Powhatan's village he was charged with the loss of two soldiers and would have been hanged had a fleet with much-needed supplies not arrived from England. Or that when he left Virginia in 1609 (never to return), it was because he had been severely injured when his gunpowder bag mysteriously exploded in his lap while he napped on the deck of an exploring vessel.

Smith and his works form an important bridge between the first two permanent English colonies in North America. The first of his publications, *A True Relation of Such Occurrences and Accidents of Note as Hath Happened in Virginia* (1608), was a badly edited version of a letter he had sent back from the colony without intending that it be published. It was followed by a work to which many colonists including Smith contributed, *A Map of Virginia, with a Description of the Country* . . . [and] *The Proceedings of those Colonies* (sic) (1612). Some years later, Smith enlarged this book by adding more texts by other hands, expanding his own prose, and extending its geographical range and chronological coverage. More its editor than its author, Smith published the resulting *General History of Virginia, New England, and the Summer Isles* (that is, Bermuda) in 1624. This book demonstrated the later reach of Smith's American ambitions beyond Virginia proper, for his knowledge of New

England was based on a voyage he made there in 1614 and on his continuing involvement with the region—which in fact he, not the Puritans, named. During his life, Smith published more works on New England than on Virginia (*A Description of New England*, 1616; *New England's Trials*, 1620 and 1622; and *Advertisements for the Inexperienced Planters of New England, or Anywhere*, 1631). But for some unfortunate setbacks (bad weather several times forced him to abandon other voyages for New England), he might well have become more famous for this second aspect of his American career than for the first. An energetic promoter of the potential of this new region for English settlers, Smith offered the Pilgrims his services as guide for their voyage in 1620, but they chose instead to put Smith's helpful books in the hands of the more temperate Myles Standish. From that point on Smith's America was not the geographical realm about which he had entertained such bright hopes at the century's start but rather the verbal domain he continued to explore in his later writings. When he closed the Virginia part of his *General History* by writing "Thus far have I travelled in this Wilderness of Virginia," he was revealing how much like a country of his mind Virginia had become. Long gone from that still-struggling colony by then, he had internalized it so well that he helped to make it a permanent part of the English—and the Anglo-American—imagination.

The texts are from *The Complete Works of Captain John Smith*, edited by Philip L. Barbour (1986).

From General History of Virginia, New England, and the Summer Isles[1]

From *The Third Book*.

FROM CHAPTER 2. WHAT HAPPENED TILL THE FIRST SUPPLY

Being thus left to our fortunes, it fortuned that within ten days,[2] scarce ten amongst us could either go or well stand, such extreme weakness and sickness oppressed us. And thereat none need marvel if they consider the cause and reason which was this: While the ships stayed, our allowance was somewhat bettered by a daily proportion of biscuit which the sailors would pilfer to sell, give, or exchange with us for money, sassafras,[3] furs, or love. But when they departed, there remained neither tavern, beer-house, nor place of relief but the common kettle.[4] Had we been as free from all sins as [we were free from] gluttony and drunkenness we might have been canonized for saints, but our President would never have been admitted for engrossing to his private, oatmeal, sack, oil, aqua vitae, beef, eggs, or what not but the kettle;[5] that indeed he allowed equally to be distributed, and that was half a

---

1. The Bermuda Islands. The Third Book is titled "The Proceedings and Accidents of the English Colony in Virginia" and is derived from Smith's Virginia book of 1612. The bulk of this chapter, which opens with an account of the sickness whose dire results were chronicled by George Percy, may have been written by John Smith himself, although at its publication in 1612 it was credited solely to Thomas Studley, chief storekeeper of the colony. In 1624, Smith added to Studley's signature at the end of this section of the text not only his own initials but also the names of Robert Fenton and Edward Harrington as part authors. According to Percy, Studley died early in the first year, on August 28, 1607, four days after Harrington, so neither could have written much of what is in part

attributed to them. Of Robert Fenton nothing is known.
2. By the end of June 1607, after Captain Christopher Newport (d. 1617) left to fetch new supplies from England. "Fortuned": happened.
3. The bark of the sassafras tree, sold for its supposed medicinal qualities, was a valuable commodity in London.
4. The communal resources.
5. I.e., President Edward Maria Wingfield (c. 1560–1613), a man of high connections in England, would not have been canonized as a saint because he diverted many supplies (everything except the contents of the common kettle) for his own use, including sack (wine) and aqua vitae (brandy).

pint of wheat and as much barley boiled with water for a man a day, and this, having fried some twenty-six weeks in the ship's hold, contained as many worms as grains so that we might truly call it rather so much bran than corn; our drink was water,[6] our lodgings castles in the air.

With this lodging and diet, our extreme toil in bearing and planting palisades so strained and bruised us and our continual labor in the extremity of the heat had so weakened us, as were cause sufficient to have made us as miserable in our native country or any other place in the world.

From May to September, those that escaped lived upon sturgeon and sea crabs. Fifty in this time we buried; the rest seeing the President's[7] projects to escape these miseries in our pinnace by flight (who all this time had neither felt want nor sickness) so moved our dead spirits as we deposed him and established Ratcliffe in his place (Gosnold being dead), Kendall deposed. Smith newly recovered, Martin[8] and Ratcliffe were by his care preserved and relieved, and the most of the soldiers recovered with the skillful diligence of Master Thomas Wotton our surgeon general.

But now was all our provision spent, the sturgeon gone, all helps abandoned, each hour expecting the fury of the savages, when God, the patron of all good endeavors, in that desperate extremity so changed the hearts of the savages that they brought such plenty of their fruits and provision as no man wanted.[9]

And now where some affirmed it was ill done of the Council to send forth men so badly provided, this incontradictable reason will show them plainly they are too ill advised to nourish such ill conceits: First, the fault of our going was our own; what could be thought fitting or necessary we had, but what we should find, or want, or where we should be, we were all ignorant and supposing to make our passage in two months, with victual to live and the advantage of the spring to work; we were at sea five months where we both spent our victual and lost the opportunity of the time and season to plant, by the unskillful presumption of our ignorant transporters that understood not at all what they undertook.

Such actions have ever since the world's beginning been subject to such accidents, and everything of worth is found full of difficulties, but nothing [is] so difficult as to establish a commonwealth so far remote from men and means and where men's minds are so untoward[1] as neither do well themselves nor suffer others. But to proceed.

The new President and Martin, being little beloved, of weak judgment in dangers, and less industry in peace, committed the managing of all things abroad[2] to Captain Smith, who, by his own example, good words, and fair promises, set some to mow, others to bind thatch, some to build houses, others to thatch them, himself always bearing the greatest task for his own

---

6. It was more customary to drink wine or beer. "Corn": grain.
7. I.e., Wingfield.
8. Captain John Martin (c. 1567–1632?) was a colonist best known for his contentiousness. "Captain John Ratcliffe" was an alias of John Sicklemore, master of one of the vessels on the voyage over and a member of the local council. The most enigmatic figure in Jamestown, he was elected president of the council in September 1607, but

later fell out with Smith. Captain Bartholomew Gosnold (c. 1572–1607), who had explored New England before the first Jamestown voyage, probably had been responsible for Smith's recruitment to the venture. Captain George Kendall (d. 1607) was executed for mutiny later in the year.
9. I.e., was in want.
1. Intractable.
2. I.e., outside the palisade.

share, so that in short time he provided most of them lodgings, neglecting any for himself.

This done, seeing the savages' superfluity begin to decrease, [Smith] (with some of his workmen) shipped himself in the shallop to search the country for trade. The want of[3] the language, knowledge to manage his boat without sails, the want of a sufficient power (knowing the multitude of the savages), apparel for his men, and other necessaries, were infinite impediments yet no discouragement.

Being but six or seven in company he went down the river to Kecoughtan[4] where at first they scorned him as a famished man and would in derision offer him a handful of corn, a piece of bread for their swords and muskets, and such like proportions also for their apparel. But seeing by trade and courtesy there was nothing to be had, he made bold to try such conclusions as necessity enforced; though contrary to his commission, [he] let fly[5] his muskets, ran his boat on shore; whereat they all fled into the woods.

So marching towards their houses, they might see great heaps of corn; much ado he had to restrain his hungry soldiers from present taking of it, expecting as it happened that the savages would assault them, as not long after they did with a most hideous noise. Sixty or seventy of them, some black, some red, some white, some particolored, came in a square order,[6] singing and dancing out of the woods with their Okee (which was an idol made of skins, stuffed with moss, all painted and hung with chains and copper) borne before them, and in this manner, being well armed with clubs, targets, bows, and arrows, they charged the English that so kindly[7] received them with their muskets loaded with pistol shot that down fell their god, and divers lay sprawling on the ground; the rest fled again to the woods and ere long sent one of their Quiyoughkasoucks[8] to offer peace and redeem their Okee.

Smith told them if only six of them would come unarmed and load his boat, he would not only be their friend but restore them their Okee and give them beads, copper, and hatchets besides, which on both sides was to their contents[9] performed, and then they brought him venison, turkeys, wild fowl, bread, and what they had, singing and dancing in sign of friendship till they departed.

In his return he discovered the town and country of Warraskoyack.[1]

> Thus God unboundless by His power,
> Made them thus kind, would us devour.

Smith, perceiving (notwithstanding their late misery) not any regarded but from hand to mouth,[2] (the company being well recovered) caused the pinnace to be provided with things fitting to get provision for the year following,

---

3. Inability to speak. "Shallop": an open boat.
4. A village near the mouth of the James River whose inhabitants, the Kecoughtans, were members of the Powhatan Confederacy.
5. Fired.
6. Formation. "Particolored": i.e., painted for the battle.
7. In such a way. "Targets": small shields.
8. Smith elsewhere defines this term as referring to the "petty gods" of the Algonquian-speaking peoples, but here it may be used to mean priests. "Divers": several.
9. I.e., in mutual contentment.
1. A village on the south side of the James River near the mouth of the modern Pagan River, approximately opposite Smithfield.
2. I.e., none of the settlers, despite their recent sufferings, gave any thought to gathering a store of provision for the future.

but in the interim he made three or four journeys and discovered the people of Chickahominy,[3] yet what he carefully provided the rest carelessly spent.

Wingfield and Kendall, living in disgrace * * * strengthened themselves with the sailors and other confederates to regain their former credit and authority, or at least such means aboard the pinnace (being fitted to sail as Smith had appointed for trade), to alter her course and to go for England.

Smith, unexpectedly returning, had the plot discovered to him, much trouble he had to prevent it, till with store of saker[4] and musket shot he forced them [to] stay or sink in the river: which action cost the life of Captain Kendall.

These brawls are so disgustful, as some will say they were better forgotten, yet all men of good judgment will conclude it were better their baseness should be manifest to the world, than the business bear the scorn and shame of their excused disorders.[5]

The President and Captain Archer[6] not long after intended also to have abandoned the country, which project also was curbed and suppressed by Smith.

The Spaniard never more greedily desired gold than he victual, nor his soldiers more to abandon the country than he to keep it. But [he found] plenty of corn in the river of Chickahominy, where hundreds of savages in divers places stood with baskets expecting his coming.

And now the winter approaching, the rivers became so covered with swans, geese, ducks, and cranes that we daily feasted with good bread, Virginia peas, pumpkins, and putchamins, fish, fowl, and divers sort of wild beasts as fast as we could eat them, so that none of our tuftaffety humorists[7] desired to go for England.

But our comedies never endured long without a tragedy, some idle exceptions[8] being muttered against Captain Smith for not discovering the head of Chickahominy river and [he being] taxed by the Council to be too slow in so worthy an attempt. The next voyage he proceeded so far that with much labor by cutting of trees asunder he made his passage, but when his barge could pass no farther, he left her in a broad bay out of danger of shot, commanding none should go ashore till his return; himself with two English and two savages went up higher in a canoe, but he was not long absent but his men went ashore, whose want of government gave both occasion and opportunity to the savages to surprise one George Cassen whom they slew and much failed not to have cut off the boat and all the rest.[9]

Smith little dreaming of that accident, being got to the marshes at the river's head twenty miles in the desert,[1] had his two men slain (as is supposed) sleeping by the canoe, while himself by fowling sought them victual, who finding he was beset with 200 savages, two of them he slew, still defending

3. The region along the Chickahominy River, which empties into the James River a short distance west of Jamestown.
4. Shot for a small cannon used in sieges and on shipboard. "Discovered": revealed.
5. I.e., it is necessary to rehearse the troubles to lay the blame on the responsible individuals (Wingfield and Kendall), rather than let the whole "business" of the colony suffer ill repute.
6. Gabriel Archer (c. 1575–1609?) had been an associate of Bartholomew Gosnold before the Jamestown voyage. Having gone back to England in 1608 as a confirmed opponent of Smith, he showed up in Virginia again the following year to head an anti-Smith faction but died during the starving time the next winter. Ratcliffe (Sicklemore) was still president.
7. Self-indulgent persons who might be given to wearing lace. "Putchamins": persimmons.
8. Objections.
9. I.e., only through fault of their own did they fail to wipe out Cassen's whole party. "Government": discipline.
1. Wilderness.

himself with the aid of a savage his guide, whom he bound to his arm with his garters and used him as a buckler,[2] yet he was shot in his thigh a little, and had many arrows that stuck in his clothes but no great hurt, till at last they took him prisoner.

When this news came to Jamestown, much was their sorrow for his loss, few expecting what ensued.

Six or seven weeks those barbarians kept him prisoner, many strange triumphs and conjurations they made of him, yet he so demeaned[3] himself amongst them, as he not only diverted them from surprising the fort, but procured his own liberty, and got himself and his company such estimation amongst them, that those savages admired him more than their own Quiyoughkasoucks.

The manner how they used and delivered him is as followeth:

The savages having drawn from George Cassen whither Captain Smith was gone, prosecuting that opportunity they followed him with 300 bowmen, conducted by the King of Pamunkey, who in divisions searching the turnings of the river found Robinson and Emry[4] by the fireside; those they shot full of arrows and slew. Then finding the Captain, as is said, that used the savage that was his guide as his shield (three of them being slain and divers others so galled[5]), all the rest would not come near him. Thinking thus to have returned to his boat, regarding them, as he marched, more than his way, [he] slipped up to the middle in an oozy creek and his savage with him, yet dared they not come to him till being near dead with cold he threw away his arms. Then according to their composition[6] they drew him forth and led him to the fire where his men were slain. Diligently they chafed his benumbed limbs.

He demanding for their captain, they showed him Opechancanough,[7] King of Pamunkey, to whom he gave a round ivory double compass dial. Much they marveled at the playing of the fly[8] and needle, which they could see so plainly and yet not touch it because of the glass that covered them. But when he demonstrated by that globe-like jewel the roundness of the earth and skies, the sphere of the sun, moon, and stars, and how the sun did chase the night round about the world continually, the greatness of the land and sea, the diversity of nations, variety of complexions, and how we were to them antipodes[9] and many other such like matters, they all stood as amazed with admiration.

Notwithstanding, within an hour after, they tied him to a tree, and as many as could stand about him prepared to shoot him, but the King holding up the compass in his hand, they all laid down their bows and arrows and in a triumphant manner led him to Orapaks[1] where he was after their manner kindly feasted and well used.

Their order in conducting him was thus: Drawing themselves all in file,

2. Shield. "Garters": laces used for tying clothing.
3. Behaved.
4. The two men mentioned above as having been killed while they slept. Thomas Emry was a carpenter. John Robinson was a "gentleman."
5. Wounded.
6. Agreement for surrender.
7. Powhatan's younger half-brother and Smith's

captor, Opechancanough (d. 1644) was to lead the Indian Confederacy's attack on the colonists in 1622 and as late as 1644 attempted one last time to expel them from the country.
8. Compass card.
9. On the opposite side of the globe.
1. A village located farther inland, later the residence of Powhatan.

the King in the midst had all their pieces and swords borne before him. Captain Smith was led after him by three great savages holding him fast by each arm, and on each side six went in file with their arrows nocked.[2] But arriving at the town (which was but only thirty or forty hunting houses made of mats, which they remove as they please, as we our tents), all the women and children staring to behold him, the soldiers first all in file performed the form of a bissom[3] so well as could be, and on each flank, officers as sergeants to see them keep their orders. A good time they continued this exercise and then cast themselves in a ring, dancing in such several postures and singing and yelling out such hellish notes and screeches; being strangely painted, every one [had] his quiver of arrows and at his back a club, on his arm a fox or an otter's skin or some such matter for his vambrace, their heads and shoulders painted red with oil and pocones mingled together, which scarlet-like color made an exceeding handsome show, his bow in his hand and the skin of a bird with her wings abroad,[4] dried, tied on his head, a piece of copper, a white shell, a long feather with a small rattle growing at the tails of their snakes tied to it, or some such like toy. All this while, Smith and the King stood in the midst, guarded as before is said, and after three dances they all departed. Smith they conducted to a long house where thirty or forty tall fellows did guard him, and ere long more bread and venison was brought him than would have served twenty men. I think his stomach at that time was not very good; what he left they put in baskets and tied over his head. About midnight they set the meat again before him; all this time not one of them would eat a bit with him, till the next morning they brought him as much more, and then did they eat all the old and reserved the new as they had done the other, which made him think they would fat him to eat him. Yet in this desperate estate, to defend him from the cold, one Maocassater brought him his gown in requital[5] of some beads and toys Smith had given him at his first arrival in Virginia.

Two days after, a man would have slain him (but that the guard prevented it) for the death of his son, to whom they conducted him to recover the poor man then breathing his last. Smith told them that at Jamestown he had a water would do it, if they would let him fetch it, but they would not permit that, but made all the preparations they could to assault Jamestown, craving his advice, and for recompence he should have life, liberty, land, and women. In part of a table book[6] he wrote his mind to them at the fort, what was intended, how they should follow that direction to affright the messengers, and without fail send him such things as he wrote for. And an inventory with them. The difficulty and danger, he told the savages, of the mines, great guns, and other engines[7] exceedingly affrighted them, yet according to his request they went to Jamestown in as bitter weather as could be of frost and snow, and within three days returned with an answer.

But when they came to Jamestown, seeing men sally out as he had told them they would, they fled, yet in the night they came again to the same

2. Notched; i.e., with their arrows fitted on the bowstring ready to use.
3. From an Italian term denoting a snakelike formation.
4. Outspread. "Vambrace": forearm protection.

"Pocones": a dye of vegetative origin.
5. Payment.
6. A notebook.
7. Weaponry.

place where he had told them they should receive an answer and such things as he had promised them, which they found accordingly, and with which they returned with no small expedition to the wonder of them all that heard it, that he could either divine[8] or the paper could speak.

Then they led him to the Youghtanunds, the Mattapanients, the Piankatanks, the Nantaughtacunds, and Onawmanients[9] upon the rivers of Rappahannock and Potomac, over all those rivers and back again by divers other several nations[1] to the King's habitation at Pamunkey where they entertained him with most strange and fearful conjurations:[2]

> As if near led to hell
> Amongst the devils to dwell.

Not long after, early in a morning, a great fire was made in a long-house and a mat spread on the one side as on the other; on the one they caused him to sit, and all the guard went out of the house, and presently came skipping in a great grim fellow all painted over with coal[3] mingled with oil, and many snakes' and weasels' skins stuffed with moss, and all their tails tied together so as they met on the crown of his head in a tassel, and round about the tassel was as a coronet of feathers, the skins hanging round about his head, back, and shoulders and in a manner covered his face, with a hellish voice, and a rattle in his hand. With most strange gestures and passions be began his invocation and environed[4] the fire with a circle of meal; which done, three more such like devils came rushing in with the like antic tricks, painted half black, half red, but all their eyes were painted white and some red strokes like mustaches along their cheeks. Round about him those fiends danced a pretty while, and then came in three more as ugly as the rest, with red eyes and white strokes over their black faces. At last they all sat down right against him, three of them on the one hand of the chief priest and three on the other. Then all with their rattles began a song; which ended, the chief priest laid down five wheat corns;[5] then straining his arms and hands with such violence that he sweat and his veins swelled, he began a short oration;[6] at the conclusion they all gave a short groan and then laid down three grains more. After that, began their song again, and then another oration, ever laying down so many corns as before till they had twice encircled the fire; that done, they took a bunch of little sticks prepared for that purpose, continuing still their devotion, and at the end of every song and oration they laid down a stick betwixt the divisions of corn. Till night, neither he nor they did either eat or drink, and then they feasted merrily with the best provisions they could make. Three days they used this ceremony; the meaning whereof, they told him, was to know if he intended them well or no. The circle of meal signified their country, the circles of corn the bounds of the sea, and the sticks his country. They imagined the world to be flat and round, like a trencher,[7] and they in the midst.

After this they brought him a bag of gunpowder, which they carefully

---

8. Perform magic. "Expedition": speed.
9. These groups were part of the confederacy that was under the rule of Powhatan.
1. Other Algonquian-speaking groups.
2. Incantations; but the following couplet Smith derived from a translation of Seneca published by

Bishop Martin Fotherby in his *Atheomastix* (1622).
3. I.e., charcoal.
4. Encircled.
5. I.e., five kernels of Indian corn.
6. Prayer.
7. A flat wood dish.

preserved till the next spring, to plant as they did their corn, because they would be acquainted with the nature of that seed.

Opitchapam, the King's brother,[8] invited him to his house, where, with as many platters of bread, fowl, and wild beasts as did environ him, he bid him welcome, but not any of them would eat a bit with him but put up all the remainder in baskets.

At his return to Opechancanough's, all the King's women and their children flocked about him for their parts,[9] as a due by custom, to be merry with such fragments:

> But his waking mind in hideous dreams did
>   oft see wondrous shapes,
> Of bodies strange, and huge in growth, and
>   of stupendous makes.[1]

At last they brought him to Werowocomoco,[2] where was Powhatan, their Emperor. Here more than two hundred of those grim courtiers stood wondering at him, as [if] he had been a monster, till Powhatan and his train had put themselves in their greatest braveries.[3] Before a fire upon a seat like a bedstead, he sat covered with a great robe made of raccoon skins and all the tails hanging by. On either hand did sit a young wench of sixteen or eighteen years and along on each side [of] the house, two rows of men and behind them as many women, with all their heads and shoulders painted red, many of their heads bedecked with the white down of birds, but every one with something, and a great chain of white beads about their necks.

At his entrance before the King, all the people gave a great shout. The Queen of Appomattoc[4] was appointed to bring him water to wash his hands, and another brought him a bunch of feathers, instead of a towel, to dry them; having feasted him after their best barbarous manner they could, a long consultation was held, but the conclusion was, two great stones were brought before Powhatan; then as many as could, laid hands on him, dragged him to them, and thereon laid his head and being ready with their clubs to beat out his brains, Pocahontas,[5] the King's dearest daughter, when no entreaty could prevail, got his head in her arms and laid her own upon his to save him from death, whereat the Emperor was contented he should live to make him hatchets, and her bells, beads, and copper, for they thought him as well of all occupations as themselves.[6] For the King himself will make his own robes, shoes, bows, arrows, pots; plant, hunt, or do anything so well as the rest.

> They say he bore a pleasant show,
> But sure his heart was sad.
> For who can pleasant be, and rest,
> That lives in fear and dread:

8. Actually the chief's half-brother; he succeeded Powhatan in 1618.
9. Gifts.
1. From a translation of Lucretius by Fotherby.
2. Powhatan's village on the north shore of the York River, almost due north of Jamestown.
3. Finery; i.e., costumes.
4. Opossunoquonuske was the weroansqua, or leader, of a small village (Appamatuck) near the future site of Petersburg, Virginia. In 1610, she was killed by the English in retaliation for the deaths of fourteen settlers.
5. Daughter of Powhatan (c. 1591–1617), she was mentioned in Smith's earlier versions of his captivity narrative, but first emerged as its heroine only in the History, which was published seven years after her death in England.
6. I.e., they thought him as variously skilled as themselves.

And having life suspected, doth
It still suspected lead.[7]

Two days after, Powhatan, having disguised himself in the most fearfulest manner he could, caused Captain Smith to be brought forth to a great house in the woods and there upon a mat by the fire to be left alone. Not long after, from behind a mat that divided the house, was made the most dolefulest noise he ever heard; then Powhatan more like a devil than a man, with some two hundred more as black as himself, came unto him and told him now they were friends, and presently he should go to Jamestown to send him two great guns and a grindstone for which he would give him the country of Capahowasic and forever esteem him as his son Nantaquoud.[8]

So to Jamestown with twelve guides Powhatan sent him. That night they quartered in the woods, he still expecting (as he had done all this long time of his imprisonment) every hour to be put to one death or other, for all their feasting. But almighty God (by His divine providence) had mollified the hearts of those stern barbarians with compassion. The next morning betimes they came to the fort, where Smith having used the savages with what kindness he could, he showed Rawhunt, Powhatan's trusty servant, two demi-culverins[9] and a millstone to carry [to] Powhatan; they found them somewhat too heavy, but when they did see him discharge them, being loaded with stones, among the boughs of a great tree loaded with icicles, the ice and branches came so tumbling down that the poor savages ran away half dead with fear. But at last we regained some conference with them and gave them such toys and sent to Powhatan, his women, and children such presents as gave them in general full content.

Now in Jamestown they were all in combustion, the strongest preparing once more to run away with the pinnace; which, with the hazard of his life, with saker falcon[1] and musket shot, Smith forced now the third time to stay or sink.

Some, no better than they should be, had plotted with the President the next day to have him put to death by the Levitical law,[2] for the lives of Robinson and Emry; pretending the fault was his that had led them to their ends; but he quickly took such order with such lawyers that he laid them by the heels till he sent some of them prisoners for England.

Now every once in four or five days, Pocahontas with her attendants brought him so much provision that saved many of their lives, that else for all this had starved with hunger.

Thus from numb death our good God sent relief,
The sweet assuager of all other grief.[3]

His relation of the plenty he had seen, especially at Werowocomoco, and of the state and bounty of Powhatan (which till that time was unknown), so

---

7. Derived from a translation of Euripides by Fotherby.
8. I.e., Powhatan would esteem him as highly as his own son Nantaquoud. Capahowasic was along the York River near where Smith was held prisoner.
9. Large cannons.
1. Small falcon.

2. "And he that killeth any man shall surely be put to death" (Leviticus 24.17).
3. Apparently the first line is Smith's own, based on Fotherby, but the second is borrowed directly from Fotherby's translation from a quotation of Euripides found in Plutarch.

revived their dead spirits (especially the love of Pocahontas)[4] as all men's fear was abandoned.

Thus you may see what difficulties still crossed any good endeavor; and the good success of the business being thus oft brought to the very period of destruction; yet you see by what strange means God hath still delivered it.

* * *

From *The Fourth Book*

[SMITH'S FAREWELL TO VIRGINIA]

Thus far I have traveled in this Wilderness of Virginia, not being ignorant for all my pains this discourse will be wrested, tossed and turned as many ways as there is leaves;[5] that I have written too much of some, too little of others, and many such like objections. To such I must answer, in the Company's name I was requesed to do it,[6] if any have concealed their approved experiences from my knowledge, they must excuse me: as for every fatherless or stolen relation,[7] or whole volumes of sophisticated rehearsals, I leave them to the charge of them that desire them. I thank God I never undertook anything yet [for which] any could tax me of carelessness or dishonesty, and what[8] is he to whom I am indebted or troublesome? Ah! were these my accusers but to change cases and places with me [for] but two years, or till they had done but so much as I, it may be they would judge more charitably of my imperfections. But here I must leave all to the trial of time, both myself, Virginia's preparations, proceedings and good events, praying to that great God the protector of all goodness to send them as good success as the goodness of the action[9] and country deserveth, and my heart desireth.

1624

From A Description of New England

Who can desire more content, that hath small means; or but only his merit to advance his fortune, than to tread, and plant that ground he hath purchased by the hazard of his life? If he have but the taste of virtue, and magnanimity,[1] what to such a mind can be more pleasant, than planting and building a foundation for his posterity, got from the rude earth, by God's blessing and his own industry, without prejudice[2] to any? If he have any grain of faith or zeal in religion, what can he do less hurtful to any; or more agreeable to God, than to seek to convert those poor savages to know Christ, and humanity, whose labors with discretion will triple requite thy charge and

---

4. I.e., the evident affection of Pocahontas for Smith and the English was instrumental in reviving the colonists' spirits.
5. Pages.
6. Smith was not requested to write the whole *General History* by the Virginia Company, so it is not clear what his reference is here. Possibly the discourse to which he refers is the brief summary of recommendations for the "reformation" of Vir-

ginia that ends The Fourth Book and that he drew up at the request of the royal commissioners charged with effecting that reformation.
7. I.e., anonymous or "fugitive" narratives. "Approved": proven.
8. Who; i.e., he has been a burden to nobody.
9. Venture. "Events": results.
1. Greatness of spirit.
2. Harm.

pains? What so truly suits with honor and honesty, as the discovering things unknown? erecting townes, peopling countries, informing the ignorant, reforming things unjust, teaching virtue; and gain[ing] to our native mother country a kingdom to attend her; find[ing] employment for those that are idle, because they know not what to do: so far from wronging any, as to cause posterity to remember thee; and remembering thee, ever honor that remembrance with praise?

* * *

Then, who would live at home idly (or think in himself any worth to live) only to eat, drink, and sleep, and so die? Or by consuming that carelessly, [which] his friends got worthily? Or by using that miserably, [which] maintained virtue honestly? Or, for being descended nobly, pine with the vain vaunt of great kindred, in penury?[3] Or (to maintain a silly show of bravery) toil out thy heart, soul, and time, basely, by shifts,[4] tricks, cards, and dice? Or by relating news of others' actions, shark[5] here or there for a dinner, or supper; deceive thy friends, by fair promises, and dissimulation, in borrowing where thou never intendest to pay; offend the laws, surfeit with excess, burden thy country, abuse thyself, despair in want, and then cozen[6] thy kindred, yea even thine own brother, and wish thy parents' death (I will not say damnation) to have their estates? though thou seest what honors, and rewards, the world yet hath for them will seek them and worthily deserve them.

* * *

Let this move you to embrace employment, for those whose educations, spirits, and judgments, want but your purses; not only to prevent such accustomed dangers, but also to gain more thereby than you have. And you fathers that are either so foolishly fond, or so miserably covetous, or so wilfully ignorant, or so negligently careless, as that you will rather maintain your children in idle wantonness, till they grow your masters; or become so basely unkind, as they wish nothing but your deaths; so that both sorts grow dissolute: and although you would wish them anywhere to escape the gallows, and ease your cares; though they spend you here one, two, or three hundred pound a year; you would grudge to give half so much in adventure with them, to obtain an estate, which in a small time but with a little assistance of your providence,[7] might be better than your own. But if an angel should tell you, that any place yet unknown can afford such fortunes; you would not believe him, no more than Columbus was believed there was any such land as is now the well-known abounding America; much less such large regions as are yet unknown, as well in America, as in Africa, and Asia, and Terra Incognita; where were courses for gentlemen (and them that would be so reputed) more suiting their qualities, than begging from their Prince's generous disposition, the labors of his subjects, and the very marrow of his maintenance.

I have not been so ill bred, but I have tasted of plenty and pleasure, as well as want and misery: nor doth necessity yet, or occasion of discontent, force me to these endeavors: nor am I ignorant what small thank I shall have for my pains; or that many would have the world imagine them to be of great

3. I.e., live in poverty while claiming great ancestors.
4. Expedients. "Bravery": fine appearances.

5. Sponge.
6. Deceive. "Excess": overindulgence.
7. Provision.

judgment, that can but blemish these my designs, by their witty objections and detractions: yet (I hope) my reasons with my deeds, will so prevail with some, that I shall not want[8] employment in these affairs, to make the most blind see his own senselesness, and incredulity; hoping that gain will make them affect that, which religion, charity, and the common good cannot. It were but a poor device in me, to deceive myself; much more the king, and state, my friends, and country, with these inducements: which, seeing his Majesty hath given permission, I wish all sorts of worthy, honest, industrious spirits, would understand: and if they desire any further satisfaction, I will do my best to give it: Not to persuade them to go only;[9] but go with them: Not leave them there; but live with them there. I will not say, but by ill providing and undue managing, such courses may be taken, may make us miserable enough:[1] But if I may have the execution of what I have projected; if they want to eat, let them eat or never digest me.[2] If I perform what I say, I desire but that reward out of the gains may suit my pains, quality, and condition. And if I abuse you with my tongue, take my head for satisfaction. If any dislike at the year's end, defraying their charge,[3] by my consent they should freely return. I fear not want of company sufficient, were it but known what I know of those countries; and by the proof of that wealth I hope yearly to return, if God please to bless me from such accidents, as are beyond my power in reason to prevent: For, I am not so simple, to think, that ever any other motive than wealth, will ever erect there a Commonwealth; or draw company from their ease and humors at home, to stay in New England to effect my purposes. And lest any should think the toil might be insupportable, though these things may be had by labor, and diligence: I assure myself there are [those] who delight extremely in vain pleasure, that take much more pains in England, to enjoy it, than I should do here to gain wealth sufficient: and yet I think they should not have half such sweet content: for, our pleasure here is still gains; in England, charges and loss. Here nature and liberty afford us that freely, which in England we want, or it costs us dearly. What pleasure can be more, than (being tired with any occasion a-shore)[4] in planting vines, fruits, or herbs, in contriving their own grounds, to the pleasure of their own minds, their fields, gardens, orchards, buildings, ships, and other works, etc., to recreate themselves before their own doors, in their own boats upon the sea, where man, woman and child, with a small hook and line, by angling, may take diverse sorts of excellent fish, at their pleasures? And is it not pretty sport, to pull up two pence, six pence, and twelve pence, as fast as you can haul and veer[5] a line? He is a very bad fisher [who] cannot kill in one day with his hook and line, one, two, or three hundred cods: which dressed and dried, if they be sold there for ten shillings the hundred (though in England they will give more then twenty); may not both the servant, the master, and merchant, be well content with this gain? If a man work but three days in seven, he may get more than he can spend, unless he will be excessive. Now that carpenter, mason, gardener, tailor, smith, sailor, forgers,[6] or what other, may they not make this a pretty recreation though they

8. Lack.
9. Alone.
1. I.e., he won't promise that even with bad management they'll succeed.
2. I.e., or never read Smith's works.

3. I.e., once they have paid the cost of their support for the year.
4. Some casual occurrence.
5. I.e., fish.
6. I.e., ironworkers.

fish but an hour in a day, to take more than they eat in a week: or if they will not eat it, because there is so much better choice; yet sell it, or change it, with the fishermen, or merchants, for anything they want. And what sport doth yield a more pleasing content, and less hurt or charge than angling with a hook, and crossing the sweet air from isle to isle, over the silent streams of a calm sea, wherein the most curious may find pleasure, profit, and content. Thus, though all men be not fishers: yet all men, whatsoever, may in other matters do as well. For necessity doth in these cases so rule a Commonwealth, and each in their several functions, as their labors in their qualities may be as profitable, because there is a necessary mutual use of all.

For Gentlemen, what exercise should more delight them, than ranging daily those unknown parts, using fowling and fishing, for hunting and hawking? and yet you shall see the wild hawks give you some pleasure, in seeing them stoop[7] (six or seven after one another) an hour or two together, at the schools of fish in the fair harbors, as those ashore at a fowl; and never trouble nor torment yourselves, with watching, mewing, feeding, and attending them: nor kill horse and man with running and crying, See you not a hawk?[8] For hunting also: the woods, lakes, and rivers, afford not only chase sufficient, for any that delights in that kind of toil, or pleasure; but such beasts to hunt, that besides the delicacy of their bodies for food, their skins are so rich, as may well recompence thy daily labor, with a captain's pay.

For laborers, if those that sow hemp, rape,[9] turnips, parsnips, carrots, cabbage, and such like; give twenty, thirty, forty, fifty shillings yearly for an acre of ground, and meat, drink, and wages to use it, and yet grow rich: when better, or at least as good ground, may be had and cost nothing but labor; it seems strange to me, any such should there grow poor.

My purpose is not to persuade children [to go] from their parents; men from their wives; nor servants from their masters: only, such as with free consent may be spared: But that each parish, or village, in city, or country, that will but apparel their fatherless children, of thirteen or fourteen years of age, or young married people, that have small wealth to live on; here by their labor may live exceedingly well: provided always that first there be a sufficient power to command them, houses to receive them, means to defend them, and meet provisions for them; for, any place may be overlain:[1] and it is most necessary to have a fortress (ere this grow to practice) and sufficient masters (as, carpenters, masons, fishers, fowlers, gardeners, husbandmen, sawyers, smiths, spinsters, tailors, weavers, and such like) to take ten, twelve, or twenty, or as there is occasion, for apprentices. The masters by this may quickly grow rich; these may learn their trades themselves, to do the like; to a general and an incredible benefit, for king, and country, master, and servant.

1616

---

7. Swoop down.
8. Smith contrasts the delight of watching wild hawks hunt their prey in America with the tedious care that keepers of trained hawks in England must give their birds—as when such birds fly away and must be hunted for all over the countryside.
9. I.e., the rape plant.
1. Overcome.

From New England's Trials[1]

Here I must entreate a little your favors to digress. They did not kill the English because they were Christians,[2] but for their weapons and commodities, that were rare novelties; but now they fear we may beat them out of their dens, which lions and tigers would not admit but by force. But must this be an argument for an Englishman,[3] or discourage any either in Virginia or New England? No: for I have tried them both. For Virginia, I kept that country with thirty-eight, and had not[4] to eat but what we had from the savages. When I had ten men able to go abroad, our commonwealth was very strong: with such a number I ranged that unknown country fourteen weeks; I had but eighteen to subdue them all, with which great army I stayed six weeks before their greatest king's habitations, till they had gathered together all the power they could; and yet the Dutchmen sent at a needless excessive charge did help Powhatan how to betray me.[5]

* * *

For wronging a soldier but the value of a penny, I have caused Powhatan [to] send his own men to Jamestown to receive their punishment at my discretion. It is true in our greatest extremity they shot me, slew three of my men, and by the folly of them that fled took me prisoner; yet God made Pocahontas the king's daughter the means to deliver me: and thereby taught me to know their treacheries to preserve the rest. It was also my chance in single combat to take the king of Paspahegh[6] prisoner, and by keeping him, [I] forced his subjects to work in chains, till I made all the country pay contribution, having little else whereon to live.

Twice in this time I was their president,[7] and none can say in all that time I had a man slain: but for keeping them in that fear I was much blamed both there and here: yet I left 500 behind me that through their confidence in six months came most to confusion, as you may read at large in the description of Virginia.[8] When I went first to those desperate designs, it cost me many a forgotten pound to hire men to go; and procrastination caused more [to] run away than went. But after the ice was broken, came many brave voluntaries: notwithstanding since I came from thence, the honorable Company have been humble suitors to his Majesty to get vagabonds and condemned men to go thither; nay so much scorned was the name of Virginia, some did

---

1. I.e., tests or experiments, not sufferings.
2. Smith here is speaking of the massacre of settlers in Virginia in March 1622, news of which reached New England sometime in May of that year. In mustering support for settlement in New England, he obviously had to take into account the dampening effect of events in Virginia.
3. I.e., such events are not strong enough to dissuade an Englishman. "Admit": allow.
4. Nothing. "With thirty-eight": i.e., he protected or secured Virginia by means of a very modest force.
5. Several "Dutch" (probably German) skilled workers had been shipped to Virginia in 1608. Sent to build a house for Powhatan, they hinted to him that they would take his side against the English, and soon were plotting against Smith and the col-

ony. Arrested by the English and brought back to Jamestown for execution, they were saved when a new ship arrived from England, bringing fresh supplies and important new instructions for President Smith and Virginia's governing council.
6. Paspahegh was the Algonquian name for the region around Jamestown. Smith took its chief, Wowinchopunck, prisoner in 1609. An engraving in the 1st edition of the *General History* shows this episode.
7. Smith was president of the Virginia council for only a single term; editors generally assume that he here means "twice during the time I was their president these things happened," although the passage may have been garbled.
8. I.e., Smith's first book, which contains a section so titled. "Confidence": i.e., overconfidence.

choose to be hanged ere they would go thither, and were: yet for all the worst of spite, detraction and discouragement, and this lamentable massacre, there is more honest men now suitors to go, than ever hath been constrained knaves; and it is not unknown to most men of understanding, how happy many of those calumniators do think themselves, that they might be admitted, and yet pay for their passage to go now to Virginia: and had I but means to transport as many as would go, I might have choice of 10,000 that would gladly be in any of those new places, which were so basely condemned by ungrateful base minds.

To range this country of New England in like manner I had but eight, as is said, and amongst their brute[9] conditions I met many of their silly encounters, and without any hurt, God be thanked; when your West country men were many of them wounded and much tormented with the savages that assaulted their ship, as they did say themselves, in the first year I was there 1614, and though Master Hunt then master with me did most basely in stealing some savages from that coast to sell, when he was directed to have gone for Spain.[1] * * * I speak not this out of vainglory, as it may be some gleaners,[2] or some was never there may censure me, but to let all men be assured by those examples, what those savages are that thus strangely do murder and betray our countrymen. But to the purpose.

What is already written of the healthfulness of the air, the richness of the soil, the goodness of the woods, the abundance of fruits, fish, and fowl in their season, they still affirm that have been there now near two years, and at one draught[3] they have taken 1000 basses, and in one night twelve hogsheads of herring. They are building a strong fort, they hope shortly to finish, in the interim they are well provided: their number is about a hundred persons, all in health, and well near sixty acres of ground well planted with corn, besides their gardens well replenished with useful fruits; and if their adventurers would but furnish them with necessaries for fishing, their wants would quickly be supplied.[4] To supply them this sixteen of October is going the *Paragon* with sixty-seven persons, and all this is done by private men's purses. And to conclude in their own words, should they write of all plenties they have found, they think they should not be believed.

* * *

Thus you may see plainly the yearly success from New England (by Virginia)[5] which hath been so costly to this kingdom and so dear to me, which either to see perish or but bleed, pardon me though it passionate me beyond the bounds of modesty, to have been sufficiently able to foresee it, and had neither power nor means how to prevent it. By that acquaintance I have with them, I may call them my children, for they have been my wife, my hawks,

---

9. Tough.
1. Smith here refers to the tough going among earlier English voyagers to New England, especially Sir Ferdinando Gorges (1568–1647), a backer of Smith, and Thomas Hunt, who had been with Smith on the latter's 1614 voyage to the region. Hunt had stirred up much trouble with the local American Indians by kidnapping more than twenty of them, including the Native American Tisquantum (called "Squanto" by the Pilgrims) to sell into slavery in Spain.

2. Those who pick through events in search of bits of scandal.
3. A single haul of the fish net.
4. Here Smith speaks of the Plymouth settlers. "Adventurers": the investors who backed the Pilgrim venture.
5. I.e., by Virginia's example; Plymouth had barely been settled, but the longer experience of the English in Virginia (with all its faults) could be used to suggest the probable course of events in New England.

my hounds, my cards, my dice, and in total my best content, as indifferent to my heart as my left hand to my right;[6] and notwithstanding all those miracles of disasters have crossed both them and me, yet were there not one Englishman remaining (as God be thanked there is some thousands) I would yet begin again with as small means as I did at the first; not for that I have any secret encouragement from any I protest, more than lamentable experiences: for all their discoveries I can yet hear of, are but pigs of my own sow;[7] nor more strange to me than to hear one tell me he hath gone from Billingsgate and discovered Greenwich, Gravesend, Tilbury, Queenborough, Leigh and Margate, which to those did never hear of them, though they dwell in England, might be made seem some rare secrets and great countries unknown, except the relations of Master Dirmer.[8]

* * *

What here I have written by relation, if it be not right, I humbly entreat your pardons, but I have not spared any diligence to learn the truth of them that have been actors or sharers in those voyages: in some particulars they might deceive me, but in the substances they could not, for few could tell me anything, except where they fished: but seeing all those [that] have lived there, do confirm more than I have written, I doubt not but all those testimonies with these new-begun examples of plantation, will move both city and country freely to adventure with me and my partners more than promises, seeing I have from his Majesty letters pattent, such honest, free and large conditions assured me from his commissioners, as I hope will satisfy any honest understanding.

1622

6. I.e., as equally dear to me as one hand or the other.
7. The offspring of Smith's deeds; i.e., the accomplishments of others would not have been possible had he not gone before.
8. These are all well-known places in England. Smith's point is that once he had led the way into America, the English who followed him had

accomplished nothing truly bold. The exception was Master Thomas Dermer (d. 1621), who had accompanied Smith to New England in 1614, had spent two years in Newfoundland (1616–18), and had returned to New England in 1619—in the process acquiring more knowledge about the region than Smith.

NATIVE AMERICAN TRICKSTER TALES

Trickster is the term generally used to describe a mythic character who appears in the oral tales of the peoples of Native America. A wandering, excessive, bawdy, gluttonous, and obscene figure—usually male but able to alter his sex whenever necessary—ready to copulate with his own daughter or daughter-in-law or to send his penis swimming across rivers in search of sexual adventure, trickster is selfish, amoral, foolish, and destructive, a threat to order everywhere. Yet trickster is also a culture hero and transformer whose actions, in the earliest times—the time of myth when the earth was yet "soft" and incompletely formed—helped give to the world just that order which humans would historically come to know.

Wakjankaga, the Winnebago trickster, for example, not only is "the Foolish One" but also, as in one of the stories reprinted here, is Kunuga, First Son of Ma'una, the

Earthmaker, sent to instruct or destroy monsters who would be harmful to the people (a mission he foolishly forgets). Iktomi, the Sioux trickster, is also among the first beings created, and in the story printed here he surprisingly does aid the people. It is trickster, too, who, in a Clatsop Chinook tale, establishes the taboos that humans will need to observe if fishing is to be engaged in successfully. In still other stories, trickster is the one who steals fire for the benefit of humankind and who introduces death into the world so that human beings may truly know the value of life. Even in the case of those stories that are broadly comic or bawdy, trickster tales have the power associated with the sacred. Traditional native peoples, in the past and in the present, believe that the stories have real effects in the world; thus they often restrict their narration to the winter, the time between the first killing frost and the first thunderstorm, a period when the earth is still.

The term *trickster*, it should be said, has no equivalent in any native language. Rather, the trickster figure is called Coyote in California, Oregon, the inland plateau, the Great Basin, the Southwest, and the southern plains; Rabbit or Hare in the Southeast; Spider in the northern plains; Raven in the Arctic and sub-Arctic; and Jay or Wolverine in parts of Canada. All of these are names for animals: is the trickster, then, an animal? The answer is a definite yes and no. As Barre Toelken (whose transcription and translation of a Navajo Coyote tale is reprinted here) puts it, for the Navajo:

> There is no possible distinction between Ma'i, the *animal* we recognize as a coyote in the fields, and Ma'i the personification of Coyote power in all coyotes, and Ma'i the *character* (trickster, creator, and buffoon) in legends and tales, and Ma'i, the symbolic character of *disorder* in the myths. Ma'i is not a composite but a complex; a Navajo would see no reason to distinguish separate aspects.

Indeed, in the age of myth the distinction between animals and humans was not nearly so great as we find it today. Paiute Coyote stories, for example, begin, *Sumu onosu numeka nan quane ynas*, "Once long ago when we were all the same." Thus when visualizing Coyote or Rabbit, Bear or Raven, it is entirely appropriate to see them as appearing more or less in the animal shapes with which we are familiar. This is not the case with Iktomi, who, although his name is translated as Spider, does not have the shape of a spider. (And how to visualize Wakjankaga; Manabush of the Great Lakes area; or Gluskabe, a trickster figure from Maine, is much less clear.)

Trickster tales are among the most ancient elements of native American cultures, and they have survived because they have over the years provided both great pleasure and important instruction. In some degree, *any* listener (or, as here, any reader) may enjoy and learn from them. As the Winnebago storyteller Felix White Sr. has phrased it, "The story character, he does so many unthought of things in there that it causes the listener to start thinking, 'Why does he do that?' It's a process of making somebody exercise his mind to think." But the kind of "thinking" a listener must do to learn and even to enjoy is culturally prepared thinking; the listener must be aware, that is, of whether "the story character" is behaving in a manner that his culture views with approval or disapproval. Thus, although some trickster stories do have an etiological element—so *that's why* coyotes have yellow eyes!—many native American audiences do not take them to show the way in which specific actions have served as causes for specific effects. Rather, a more usual response is to understand that it is because Coyote or Rabbit or Raven violated cultural norms that sickness or calamity ensued— or that trickster wound up in some comical mess. Awareness of the cultural norms that provide the unspoken context for each of these tales thus is important for understanding the moral lessons that they teach, as it also increases one's enjoyment of them. (Not all cultures find the same things funny.)

The stories printed here are a varied lot: they come from the Winnebago of the Great Lakes, the Lakota of the Plains, the Muskogean Koasati of the Southeast, the Okanogan and Clatsop Chinook of the Northwest, and the Navajo of the Southwest. They also vary in their appearance on the page. From the end of the nineteenth century to just past the middle of the twentieth century, those who wrote down Native American narratives, influenced by German-American anthropologist Franz Boas's commitment to linguistic accuracy, presented their transcriptions and translations in highly literal prose. (Mourning Dove's choice of prose seems to have come from the straightforward assumption that *stories* imply prose.) Since that time, however, following the pioneering work of the anthropologists and linguists Dell Hymes and Dennis Tedlock, many "mythographers"—transcribers and translators of oral story-telling—have opted for verse forms that attempt to convey the dramatic structure and even the performative dynamics of oral narration, which may include the pace, volume, and pitch of the narrator's voice as well as the audience's response. In one instance, we present the same tale as told by one narrator around 1910 and by another around 1977. Thus the reader can see how the "same" tale may actually differ, traditional and original elements both shaping an actual oral performance (as, indeed, the gender and historical circumstances of the two narrators may also inflect their performances).

Although the editors of this anthology have not been able to contact relatives of the earliest storytellers, they have specifically requested and been granted permission to reprint these stories from surviving family members of Bel Abbey, Ella C. Deloria, Mourning Dove, Felix White Sr., and Hugh Yellowman.

A word of warning before proceeding: trickster figures are found throughout the world; and although there are undoubtedly similarities among them, it is wise to be cautious before venturing cross-cultural generalizations. In addition, the term *trickster* has become fashionable in some contemporary fiction and criticism, in which it has been used to signify virtually anything disruptive or unconventional. Whatever interest this development may have, it is best to think of it separately from the culture-specific traditional tricksters and their tales.

WINNEBAGO

A Siouan-speaking people who came to their homelands at the western end of what is now Green Bay, Wisconsin, from some more southeasterly location perhaps a thousand years ago, the Winnebago lived by hunting large and small game; by fishing; by planting corn, squash, and beans; and by gathering wild rice and berries. Winnebago culture is rich in trickster tales, with stories not only of Wakjankaga, the "Foolish One," but of Hare the trickster as well.

The stories reprinted here come from *The Trickster: A Study in American Indian Mythology* (1956), a collection of forty-nine Winnebago trickster stories edited by anthropologist Paul Radin. Radin, a student of Franz Boas, had begun collecting stories about Wakjankaga as early as 1912; and the manner in which they came into English on the page is of some interest. Radin himself did not hear any of the tales narrated, nor did he know the identity of the narrator. Rather, a Winnebago consultant of Radin's named Sam Blowsnake persuaded "an older individual," as Radin notes, to tell the stories to him in the Winnebago language. Blowsnake wrote them down; and then Radin, Blowsnake, and another Winnebago man, Oliver LaMere, collaborated on the translation into English, which Radin, consistent with Boasian practice, published in quite literal prose.

It was Radin's stated belief that "the identity of the narrator . . . is not really of great importance"; and, it is safe to assume, the dynamics of the stories' actual performance (about which he knew nothing) would also have seemed to him "not really of great importance." But critical opinion has changed considerably. Today it is widely recognized that the storyteller's individuality very much affects the tale and the way in which it is told—and that the way in which it is told affects the way in which it is understood. Thus we supplement the seven tales from Radin's *Trickster* with material from a contemporary Winnebago storyteller, Felix White Sr. His *Introduction to Wakjankaga* serves as a preface to several trickster tales he narrated in the Winnebago language in 1983. The transcription and translation were prepared by Kathleen Danker and White himself. The format in which Danker presents the story on the page is much indebted to the work of Dell Hymes and Dennis Tedlock.

Felix White Sr.'s Introduction to Wakjankaga

Stories about Wakjankaga

Ah—
Wakjankaga,
the stories they used to tell about him,
those,
to begin with—   5

Ah—
I will do them.

About four,[1]
perhaps.
This evening,   10
I will tell them.

His Name

Yes, yes!
and—

Wakjankaga,
Wakjankaga,
they used to call him.   5

When It Was All New.[2]

As I said in whiteman's talk,
this is how it was—
Ma'una (The Earthmaker)—

The sons he made,   10
that's who he was:
he was kununa (the first son).

People,
those who walk on two legs,[3]

---

1. Perhaps a reference to the pattern number frequently found in Native American stories. Trickster, as we shall see, is the first son of Ma'una, the Earthmaker—who, however, has four more sons, five in all.
2. In the earliest, mythic, or sacred time.
3. I.e., humans, not animal people; in particular, Winnebago people.

when, on earth,   15
they were going through difficulties—

That's what happened,
somehow, then,
that's what happened—

Bad things,   20
big things—

Because they[4] were playing rough
with the people,
so it was—

Ma'una,   25
it was because he saw them—

He made for himself a person, and,
when he sent him to the earth,
that's what happened—

He was called Wakjankaga.   30

Until that time
he was called, then,
Kunuga (First Son),
he was called, though.

On arriving,   35
well,
something wakjanka (foolish),
because he did it[5]—

So it was
Wakjankaga (the Foolish One) he was called.   40

He brought the name on himself.

His Duties

Yes,
When It Was All New—

When he arrived here,
it was in order to watch over this earth,
that's what, then, he should have done—   5

Those that were playing rough with people,
this is how it was—

---

4. Unspecified evil beings.
5. The foolish thing he did—forgetting to kill the

evil beings if they could not be taught not to hurt
the people—will be described a bit later on.

He was supposed to kill them.

Then again—

Good—   10
if they would do anything at all good,
he was to teach them things, too.

Not teachable—
if they weren't,
well,   15
he was supposed to kill them;
that's how it was—

He came to do it, maybe.[6]

His Folly and His Travels

Yes,
When It Was All New,
when he arrived here,
it happened like this—

The people,   5
because he saw them, then—

These who walk on two legs,
because he was fascinated by them, then,
he started to tease them, maybe.

Again,   10
because he acted like that,
well—

Whatever he was doing, too—

He forgot about it, and
then all over the earth   15
he went traveling.[7]

His Longing

Yes,
finally, he would arrive someplace, and
then—

Yes and
then—   5

---

6. Like the phrase often translated "it is said" in other tales, "maybe" indicates that the narrator has no personal or direct knowledge of these things. It is not meant to introduce the possibility of any doubt.

7. This tendency to travel or wander over the earth is common to all tricksters.

The Winnebagoes,
again it was to them
he would start to go back, then—

People,
people,   10
because he longed for them.

From The Winnebago Trickster Cycle

19

As [Trickster] continued his aimless wandering unexpectedly, much to his surprise, he met a little fox. "Well, my younger brother, here you are! You are travelling, aren't you?" "Yes, yes, here I am!" answered the little fox. "The world is going to be a difficult place to live in and I am trying to find some clean place in which to dwell. That is what I am looking for." "Oh, oh, my younger brother, what you have said is very true. I, too, was thinking of the very same thing. I have always wanted to have a companion, so let us live together." Trickster consented, and so they went on to look for a place in which to dwell.

As they ran along they encountered a jay. "Well, well, my younger brother, what are you doing?" asked Trickster. "Older brother, I am looking for a place to live in because the world is soon going to be a difficult place in which to dwell."

"We are looking for the very same thing. When I heard my younger brother speaking of this I envied him very much. So let us live together, for we also are hunting for such a place." Thus spoke Trickster.

Then they went on together and soon they came across a *hetcgeniga* (nit). "Well, well, my younger brother, what are you doing?" they asked. "Older brothers, I am looking for a pleasant place to live in," the bird answered. "Younger brother, we are travelling about looking for the same thing. When I heard these others saying that they wanted to live together as companions I liked it. Let us, therefore, live together," said Trickster.

They were all agreed and soon they came to a place where the river forked and where there was a lovely piece of land with red oaks growing upon it. It was indeed a beautiful place. This, they agreed, was a delightful place to live in, and so they stopped there and built themselves a lodge.

In the fall, when everything was ripe, they had, of course, all they wanted to eat. However, winter soon approached and not long after it began, a deep snow fell. The situation of the four now became indeed very difficult. They had nothing to eat and they were getting quite hungry. Then Trickster spoke, "Younger brothers, it is going to be very difficult. However, if we do the thing I am about to suggest, it will be good. So, at least, I think." "All right, if it is indeed something good that our older brother means we certainly will do it, for otherwise some of us will starve to death. What is it that we should do that is good and by which we can get something to eat?" "Listen. There is a village yonder, where they are enjoying great blessings. The chief has a son who is killing many animals. He is not married yet but is thinking of it. Let us go over there. I will disguise myself as a woman and marry him. Thus we can live in peace until spring comes." "Good!" they ejaculated. All were will-ing and delighted to participate.

20

Trickster now took an elk's liver and made a vulva from it. Then he took some elk's kidneys and made breasts from them. Finally he put on a woman's dress. In this dress his friends enclosed him very firmly. The dresses he was using were those that the women who had taken him for a raccoon had given him.[1] He now stood there transformed into a very pretty woman indeed. Then he let the fox have intercourse with him and make him pregnant,[2] then the jaybird and, finally, the nit. After that he proceeded toward the village.

Now, at the end of the village, lived an old woman[3] and she immediately addressed him, saying, "My granddaughter, what is your purpose in travelling around like this? Certainly it is with some object in view that you are trav-elling!" Then the old woman went outside and shouted, "Ho! Ho! There is someone here who has come to court the chief's son."[4] This, at least, is what the old woman seemed to be saying. Then the chief said to his daughters, "Ho! This clearly is what this woman wants and is the reason for her coming; so, my daughters, go and bring your sister-in-law here." Then they went after her. She certainly was a very handsome woman. The chief's son liked her very much. Immediately they prepared dried corn for her and they boiled slit bear-ribs.[5] That was why Trickster was getting married, of course. When this food was ready they put it in a dish, cooled it, and placed it in front of Trickster. He devoured it at once.[6] There she (Trickster) remained.

Not long after Trickster became pregnant.[7] The chief's son was very happy about the fact that he was to become a father. Not long after that Trickster gave birth to a boy. Then again he became pregnant and gave birth to another boy. Finally for the third time he became pregnant and gave birth to a third boy.

21

The last child cried as soon as it was born and nothing could stop it.[8] The crying became very serious and so it was decided to send for an old woman who had the reputation for being able to pacify children. She came, but she, likewise, could not pacify him. Finally the little child cried out and sang:

"If I only could play with a little piece of white cloud!"

They went in search of a shaman, for it was the chief's son who was asking for this and, consequently, no matter what the cost, it had to be obtained. He had asked for a piece of white cloud, and a piece of white cloud, accord-

---

1. In an earlier story of the cycle.
2. It is no problem at all for the male trickster to become pregnant and later to give birth.
3. This is a parody of the conventional type of Winnebago folktale which always has an old woman living at the end of the village [adapted from Radin's note].
4. This paragraph describes things being done in an inappropriate manner, e.g., the son should be doing the courting not the other way around, nor

would a chief permit his son to marry a stranger.
5. This is the proper food for a "bridal" meal [Radin's note].
6. It is completely against Winnebago etiquette to eat in this fashion [Radin's note].
7. Remember that trickster was already pregnant by fox, jay, and nit.
8. It is not usual for Winnebago children to cry. Continuous crying implied something serious and had to be interpreted [Radin's note].

ingly, they tried to obtain. But how could they obtain a piece of white cloud? All tried very hard and, finally, they made it snow. Then, when the snow was quite deep, they gave him a piece of snow to play with and he stopped crying.

After a while he again cried out and sang:

"If I could only play with a piece of blue sky!"

Then they tried to obtain a piece of blue sky for him. Very hard they tried, but were not able to obtain any. In the spring of the year, however, they gave him a piece of blue grass and he stopped crying.

After a while he began to cry again. This time he asked for some blue (green) leaves. Then the fourth time he asked for some roasting ears. They gave him green leaves and roasting ears of corn and he stopped crying.

One day later, as they were steaming corn, the chief's wife teased her sister-in-law.[9] She chased her around the pit where they were steaming corn. Finally, the chief's son's wife (Trickster) jumped over the pit and she dropped something very rotten. The people shouted at her, "It is Trickster!" The men were all ashamed, especially the chief's son. The animals who had been with Trickster, the fox, the jaybird and the nit, all of them now ran away.[1]

22

Trickster also ran away. Suddenly he said to himself, "Well, why am I doing all this? It is about time that I went back to the woman to whom I am really married. Kunu must be a pretty big boy by this time." Thus spoke Trickster. Then he went across the lake to the woman to whom he was really married. When he got there he found, much to his surprise, that the boy that had been born to him was indeed quite grown up. The chief was very happy when Trickster came home. "My son-in-law has come home," he ejaculated. He was very happy indeed. Trickster hunted game for his child and killed very many animals. There he stayed a long time until his child had become a grown-up man. Then, when he saw that his child was able to take care of himself, he said, "Well, it is about time for me to start travelling again for my boy is quite grown up now.[2] I will go around the earth and visit people for I am tired of staying here. I used to wander around the world in peace. Here I am just giving myself a lot of trouble."

23

As he went wandering around aimlessly he suddenly heard someone speaking. He listened very carefully and it seemed to say, "He who chews me will defecate; he will defecate!"[3] That was what it was saying. "Well, why is this

9. By our reckoning she would be her daughter-in-law, but "sister-in-law" is used because, as Radin explains, if trickster had married into the chief's family without changing sex, he would have been the chief's wife's son-in-law and joking between son-in-law and mother-in-law "is simply unthinkable," a very powerful taboo. Joking and teasing between sisters-in-law, however, is a common practice.
1. The three friends run away because the taboos that trickster's disguise has caused to be broken— in general, making a mockery of the chief's family; in particular, causing the chief's son to have engaged in homosexual acts—are very serious. Even trickster himself, in the next segment of the cycle, runs away, soberly questioning his actions rather than merely laughing.
2. Again the reverse of what is appropriate: it is the young man who should venture out into the world [adapted from Radin's note].
3. The tale of the talking "laxative bulb" is widespread throughout Native American cultures. Apart from its entertainment value as gross, scatological humor, it teaches a number of lessons, such as: do not be gullible and do not think yourself superior to natural forces.

person talking in this manner?" said Trickster. So he walked in the direction from which he had heard the speaking and again he heard, quite near him, someone saying: "He who chews me, he will defecate; he will defecate!" This is what was said. "Well, why does this person talk in such fashion?" said Trickster. Then he walked to the other side. So he continued walking along. Then right at his very side, a voice seemed to say, "He who chews me, he will defecate; he will defecate!" "Well, I wonder who it is who is speaking. I know very well that if I chew it, I will not defecate." But he kept looking around for the speaker and finally discovered, much to his astonishment, that it was a bulb on a bush. The bulb it was that was speaking. So he seized it, put it in his mouth, chewed it, and then swallowed it. He did just this and then went on.

"Well, where is the bulb gone that talked so much? Why, indeed, should I defecate? When I feel like defecating, then I shall defecate, no sooner. How could such an object make me defecate!" Thus spoke Trickster. Even as he spoke, however, he began to break wind. "Well this, I suppose, is what it meant. Yet the bulb said I would defecate, and I am merely expelling gas. In any case I am a great man even if I do expel a little gas!" Thus he spoke. As he was talking he again broke wind. This time it was really quite strong. "Well, what a foolish one I am. This is why I am called Foolish One, Trickster." Now he began to break wind again and again. "So this is why the bulb spoke as it did, I suppose." Once more he broke wind. This time it was very loud and his rectum began to smart. "Well, it surely is a great thing!" Then he broke wind again, this time with so much force, that he was propelled forward. "Well, well, it may even make me give another push, but it won't make me defecate," so he exclaimed defiantly. The next time he broke wind, the hind part of his body was raised up by the force of the explosion and he landed on his knees and hands. "Well, go ahead and do it again! Go ahead and do it again!" Then, again, he broke wind. This time the force of the expulsion sent him far up in the air and he landed on the ground, on his stomach. The next time he broke wind, he had to hang on to a log, so high was he thrown. However, he raised himself up and, after a while, landed on the ground, the log on top of him. He was almost killed by the fall. The next time he broke wind, he had to hold on to a tree that stood near by. It was a poplar and he held on with all his might yet, nevertheless, even then, his feet flopped up in the air. Again, and for the second time, he held on to it when he broke wind and yet he pulled the tree up by the roots. To protect himself, the next time, he went on until he came to a large tree, a large oak tree. Around this he put both his arms. Yet, when he broke wind, he was swung up and his toes struck against the tree. However, he held on.

After that he ran to a place where people were living. When he got there, he shouted, "Say, hurry up and take your lodge down, for a big warparty is upon you and you will surely be killed! Come let us get away!" He scared them all so much that they quickly took down their lodge, piled it on Trickster, and then got on him themselves.[4] They likewise placed all the little dogs they had on top of Trickster. Just then he began to break wind again and the force of the expulsion scattered the things on top of him in all directions.

4. These things are contrary to what is appropriate: one does not destroy a lodge that would serve as protection, nor is one expected to run from the enemy.

They fell far apart from one another. Separated, the people were standing about and shouting to one another; and the dogs, scattered here and there, howled at one another. There stood Trickster laughing at them till he ached.

Now he proceeded onward. He seemed to have gotten over his troubles. "Well, this bulb did a lot of talking," he said to himself, "yet it could not make me defecate." But even as he spoke he began to have the desire to defecate, just a very little. "Well, I suppose this is what it meant. It certainly bragged a good deal, however." As he spoke he defecated again. "Well, what a braggart it was! I suppose this is why it said this." As he spoke these last words, he began to defecate a good deal. After a while, as he was sitting down, his body would touch the excrement. Thereupon he got on top of a log and sat down there but, even then, he touched the excrement. Finally, he climbed up a log that was leaning against a tree. However, his body still touched the excrement, so he went up higher. Even then, however, he touched it so he climbed still higher up. Higher and higher he had to go. Nor was he able to stop defecating. Now he was on top of the tree. It was small and quite uncomfortable. Moreover, the excrement began to come up to him.

24

Even on the limb on which he was sitting he began to defecate. So he tried a different position. Since the limb, however, was very slippery he fell right down into the excrement. Down he fell, down into the dung. In fact he disappeared in it, and it was only with very great difficulty that he was able to get out of it. His raccoon-skin blanket was covered with filth, and he came out dragging it after him. The pack he was carrying on his back was covered with dung, as was also the box containing his penis.[5] The box he emptied and then placed it on his back again.

25

Then, still blinded by the filth, he started to run. He could not see anything. As he ran he knocked against a tree. The old man[6] cried out in pain. He reached out and felt the tree and sang:

"Tree, what kind of a tree are you? Tell me something about yourself!"

And the tree answered, "What kind of a tree do you think I am? I am an oak tree. I am the forked oak tree that used to stand in the middle of the valley. I am that one," it said. "Oh, my, is it possible that there might be some water around here?" Trickster asked. The tree answered, "Go straight on." This is what it told him. As he went along he bumped up against another tree. He was knocked backwards by the collision. Again he sang:

"Tree, what kind of a tree are you? Tell me something about yourself!"

"What kind of a tree do you think I am? The red oak tree that used to stand at the edge of the valley, I am that one." "Oh, my, is it possible that there is water around here?" asked Trickster. Then the tree answered and said, "Keep straight on," and so he went again. Soon he knocked against another tree. He spoke to the tree and sang:

5. That trickster carries his penis in a box was established in earlier stories. It is this box that he washes at the end of the next section of the story.

6. The term "old man," instead of First-born, is occasionally applied to Trickster [Radin's note].

"Tree, what kind of a tree are you? Tell me something about yourself!"

"What kind of a tree do you think I am? The slippery elm tree that used to stand in the midst of the others, I am that one." Then Trickster asked, "Oh, my, is it possible that there would be some water near here?" And the tree answered and said, "Keep right on." On he went and soon he bumped into another tree and he touched it and sang:

"Tree, what kind of a tree are you? Tell me something about yourself!"

"What kind of a tree do you think I am? I am the basswood tree that used to stand on the edge of the water. That is the one I am." "Oh, my, it is good," said Trickster. So there in the water he jumped and lay. He washed himself thoroughly.

It is said that the old man almost died that time, for it was only with the greatest difficulty that he found the water. If the trees had not spoken to him he certainly would have died. Finally, after a long time and only after great exertions, did he clean himself, for the dung had been on him a long time and had dried. After he had cleansed himself he washed his raccoon-skin blanket and his box.

SIOUX

Speakers of Nakota, Dakota, and Lakota make up the seven native nations known most commonly as the Sioux (from a French corruption of the Ojibwe word for "enemy"!). Occupying territories ranging from Minnesota to the Badlands of South Dakota, the Plains-dwelling Sioux created the horse and buffalo culture that long provided the image of "Indians" in the American imagination. From the eighteenth century until the end of the twentieth century, the Sioux wore eagle feather war bonnets; bore their lances against enemy warriors (Crow and Ojibwe, traditionally); and hunted the buffalo that supplied them with food, lodging (the tipi), tools, and implements (horn spoons, bone awls, bags), and weapons (bow strings). The Sioux, along with their Cheyenne allies, defeated Custer's Seventh Cavalry at the Battle of the Little Big Horn in 1876. And the Sioux Sitting Bull and Crazy Horse, great warriors and great visionaries, were among the best known Native Americans in their day.

It has been suggested that hunting societies tend to emphasize the transformer or culture maker dimension of their trickster figures more than the bawdy bungler dimension more common to the trickster stories of agriculturalists. Although Iktomi, the trickster of the Sioux, does appear in stories in which he copulates with his mother-in-law or his own daughters and behaves in ways that encourage laughter at his foolishness, there is not only a serious but, indeed, a dangerous aspect to him as well.

The eminent Chief Red Cloud said that "*Iktomi* was *wakan* [powerful, holy] for evil," and Old Horse explained that one reason the Sioux set their lodges up in a circle was so "that each lodge would be towards the door of every other lodge. Then if *Iktomi* came into a lodge, everyone would know it." A knowledgeable contemporary critic affirms that, "while Trickster or Coyote figures are often understood sympathetically as resourceful survivors in many tribal traditions, the Lakota trickster, Iktomi, is consistently portrayed as a powerful enemy of human welfare."

One of the very first beings to be created, Iktomi, for all his mischievousness, is said to have invented language, named the animals, and discovered colors. His name is usually translated as Spider, and he is often thought of as spider-*like*. But unlike other tricksters with animal names—Raven, Rabbit, Coyote—all of whom have the form of the creature whose name is their name, Iktomi does not have the form of a spider. Some have said that "Iktomi was of the size of an ordinary man." Sioux consultants at the turn of the twentieth century told the Pine Ridge physician James Walker that Iktomi's "body was big and round like a bug. His legs and arms were slim like a bug's. His hands and feet were large and long and very powerful." Others, however, described him as "a little one. His body is like a fat bug." Meanwhile, it is well accepted that Iktomi can make himself invisible or take any shape at all—even that of the coyote.

This formidable figure appears in the first story of Ella Cara Deloria's *Dakota Texts* (1932), unusually performing a good rather than an evil deed. Deloria (1889–1971), whose Dakota name was Anpetu Wašté (Beautiful Day), studied at Oberlin College and received a bachelor of science degree from Columbia Teachers College in 1915. In 1927, she was invited by anthropologist Franz Boas of Columbia to help with work on Sioux-language texts. *Dakota Texts* was her first book; and it remains, as the contemporary Lakota scholar Agnes Picotte notes, "the starting place for any study of Sioux dialects, mythology or folklore."

Deloria did not attribute individual tales to the individual storytellers with whom she worked, either because they had a traditional reluctance to put themselves forward or because they preferred to remain anonymous before a white audience. Deloria wrote the stories down in Dakota as she remembered having heard them. She numbered each of the Dakota thought units or sentences and then provided a literal word-for-word translation ("1. And so / Iktomi / into yonder direction / at random / to travel he was going, / they say.") for the first sixteen of her book's sixty-four tales and a "free translation" with corresponding sentence numbers for all of them. This system was consistent with Boas's commitment to accuracy and literalness.

The selection printed here, Deloria's first tale, is "Ikto Conquers Iya, the Eater." Having looked briefly at Ikto, the trickster, let us consider his adversary, Iya. Although Ikto and Iya briefly argue about who is the elder—an important matter for all kin-based societies—Iya was, indeed, created after Ikto, and he is perhaps the chief of all evil beings. Short Feather noted that he is "a bad spirit [who] does harm to everything" and, according to Red Cloud, "Iya inflicts headaches and paralysis." A giant with fetid breath, slow in movement, and dull witted, Iya is nonetheless very dangerous and has an insatiable appetite, leading him, as the story here indicates, to try to eat all the people he encounters. Had Ikto not defeated Iya, he might still be eating people up.

The text is Deloria's free translation. Her sentence numbering and her notes have been omitted, except when indicated, and her unparagraphed text has been broken into paragraphs.

Ikto Conquers Iya, the Eater[1]

Iktomi was wandering off in a certain direction, walking along at random. Just as he reached the hill-top, Iya, the eater, also reached it, coming up from the other side; so Ikto was much frightened and, "Ah! So it is on a day like this that I am to die, is it?" he thought suddenly. He took some earth and polished his thigh vigorously[2] and said, "Well, well, well, my younger

---

1. The editor is indebted to Julian Rice for his help with the annotations of this story.
2. Warriors sometimes rubbed consecrated earth on themselves before going into battle (not necessarily on their thighs). Ikto's action is comical because, although he thinks he may indeed die this day, he has none of the traditional warrior's virtues.

brother,[3]—or is he my elder brother?—*Has!* [Damn it!] which of us is the elder anyway?

But each time Iya took in his breath he jerked Ikto towards him, with such force that he staggered; he therefore was much frightened and said, "Now, now, my younger brother—or my elder,—stand farther off, can't you? I too have something I can do; I can pull you towards me if I care to!" he said.

But Iya did not reply; so then, once more, "Come now, my younger brother,—or is he my elder brother?—*Has!* Which of us is the elder, anyway? . . . Well, when were you born?"[4] Ikto asked.

Iya answered, "Why I was born when this earth and this sky were created." Ikto clamped his palm over his mouth, surprised.[5] "So? Well, you fool, I made the earth and the sky myself! Oh, of course, now as I recall it, there was a bit of leavings, after I had finished making the earth and sky, which I didn't know what to do with; I therefore rolled it into a wad and tossed it aside. And you grew from that! There isn't any doubt now. I am the elder!" he said. "Now then little brother, what errand are you on?"

And Iya said, "Over in this direction there is a tribal camp, and I am going there. I shall eat the people, for they are mine." "Well, of all things! Funny, isn't it? Yet what else can you expect with brothers? Why, little brother, that is just the people I am going to; and we shall travel together!" Ikto told Iya. They were now travelling, but Iya could not manage his weight, and they were obliged, therefore, to stop often; but they were now stopping for the night near the encampment.

When Iya slept, Ikto ventured to look into his body through his mouth, and saw there all the tribes that Iya had eaten in the past, living on in contentment in their respective tribal circles. Inside Iya they were living and having their being in exactly the same fashion as when they lived on earth. Races and *haka* and *pai 'yakapi* games[6] were in progress. Yonder, on the other hand, a game of Dakota ball was being played with great skill; while, in another direction, could be seen a group of *Miwatani*-Society dancers performing their dance around the circle. Meanwhile, successful hunters were returning with game; and also the White-Pack Strap[7] group were going along, dancing. Another thing else [*sic*] was that women were taking food to the council tipi, and there the old men of the tribe foregathered, with much feasting and the recounting of past glories. Taken all in all, the sight presented a picture of the good old days when the people lived;[8] such Ikto saw inside Iya's body.

3. Iktomi always calls everyone his younger brother. In social kinship, when a man seems to have more younger brothers than any other relations, they say he is like Ikto [Deloria's note].

4. The confusion is comic but also of considerable importance, because the answer to the question "Who is the older brother?" determines how people address and behave toward one another.

5. A common Dakota gesture to indicate surprise, real or pretended [Deloria's note].

6. Deloria notes that the *haka* and *pai'yakapi* "are two Dakota group games." The first, also known as the elk game, involves the attempt to catch a ring of sinew about four inches in diameter, at one or another point on a three to four foot stick. The second, extremely popular, involved rolling a large hoop before which wands, or specially prepared long sticks, were thrown, with the intent of anticipating where the hoop might fall.

7. Deloria notes only that "*wi'c'i ska'* means a white pack strap, and so I have translated it that way." Rice adds, "Since [the White-Pack Strap group] were dancing at the same time as the *Miwatani*, they were probably another warrior or chief's society."

8. Deloria published her book the same year as John Neihardt published *Black Elk Speaks* (1932), near the end of a period in which Sioux culture had been under extreme pressure. Several of Deloria's consultants would have remembered well "the good old days when the people lived." Here—as no doubt elsewhere—is the way in which "timeless," "ancient" "myths" serve not merely to preserve the past but to comment on the present.

Very much frightened, Ikto tried to think out a way to capture the Iya. And when he woke, this is what Ikto said to him, "All appearances to the contrary notwithstanding, there must be something that you fear?"—"Yes; the sound of rattles, and drums, the hooting of owls, and the shouts of men—all these I fear," Iya admitted.

So, then, "Well, of all things! Just what you would expect, though, of brothers! Why, little brother, those are exactly what I too fear!" Ikto said. He added, "I'd suggest you stay here, little brother, while I go ahead. I will select the center tipi, and mark it with a cross, and then I shall return. Then we two can go together, and, starting at either end, we shall progress towards the center tipi, eating the people as we go. And he who arrives first at that center tipi shall have the right to eat his opponent, as his reward for winning." And Iya thought that a good idea.

So Ikto ran hard and soon he arrived shouting, at the tribal camp. "Hear ye, everybody! I have something to tell you, so listen! I have just deceived a very supernaturally powerful Iya, and I have come. And when I questioned him, he admitted that he feared certain things: rattles, and drums, and the hooting of owls, and the shouting of men. So make haste!" he said.

"Moreover, while he slept I looked into his mouth, and inside his body there actually live great tribes of people. Tipis with tops painted blue, and some painted black,[9]—many painted tipis I saw," he said. So immediately the people prepared in frantic haste, and followed Ikto out.

At a little distance away, hidden by a hill, they stopped, and allowed Ikto to proceed alone, and after he had disappeared downhill, and it seemed time he had reached Iya, they charged forth, making all those noises that Iya feared.

Iya jumped up and sat with his head turning nervously from side to side, as if someone pulled it about; but they soon surrounded and clubbed him to death. They tore open his body; and then for one entire day, great tribes of people crawled out of Iya, moving their camps, and settled by groups in the many pleasant bends of the river; and soon they built their fires for cooking the evening meal, and no matter where one looked, one could see the camp-fires, sparkling like stars, and it was a beautiful sight.[1]

Now, if Iya had not been destroyed in just that way, he would undoubtedly still be eating people up, White people and all. Iya was killed and that is why the entire country is now so full of people that it is impossible to find any open spaces anymore. From that time on, the expansion of peoples began in earnest, they say. Now that was one time at least that Ikto must be given credit; he did do a great service to people, and merits thanks for it.[2] And from then on, who knows where Ikto went next?[3]

That is all.

---

9. If the upper third of a tipi was painted black or blue, it usually indicated that important men lived there. Obviously Iya's voraciousness would seriously deplete the Dakota world.

1. Another description of the good old days and, again, one that likely refers not only to the long, long ago of the age of myth but to a time still fresh in the memories of some of Deloria's older consultants.

2. "Rarely does Ikto get such thorough praise as here" [Deloria's note]. And yet there seems to be at least a bit of mixed emotion: White people also were spared as a result of Iya's demise, and "the expansion of peoples" that left almost no "open spaces" almost surely refers to the tremendous influx of whites onto traditionally Sioux lands.

3. Many tales end like this [Deloria's note].

KOASATI

Koasati is the name for a branch of the Muskogean language group and also for the five hundred to a thousand people of southwestern Louisiana and eastern Texas who speak it today. Rabbit, *Cokfi*, is the Koasati trickster, and stories about him, generally told by older men and women considered to have a special talent for narration, may be related in any season, not only in winter. So long as the events in a traditional tale occur in prescribed order, narrators have considerable leeway in what they wish to embellish, condense, or even omit. As elsewhere throughout indigenous America, these trickster stories are understood by the audience to illustrate and reaffirm, through positive or negative examples, culturally appropriate behavior. For the Koasati, as also for the Okanogan, trickster tales *are* taken as explaining the origins of some feature of the natural world.

Anthropologist John R. Swanton recorded nearly fifty narratives from two Koasati people in 1910, one of whom was Selin Williams (1841–1917). Her narration of the story type referred to as "The Bungling Host" appears here in a retranslation of Swanton's material by anthropologist and linguist Geoffrey Kimball. Kimball has been collecting stories from Koasati speakers in Louisiana since 1977. The version of "The Bungling Host" story told by Bel Abbey (1916–1992) is from a tape recording Kimball made in 1977. The translation is Kimball's, with the assistance of the narrator.

It is Kimball's supposition that the versions differ so greatly in their length because this is a tale Abbey especially liked (he seems particularly interested in Bear), whereas it was not one of Williams's favorites. Other of her recorded stories are much richer in detail, and she probably agreed to tell this one chiefly because Swanton urged her to tell him all the stories she knew.

The Bungling Host

by Bel Abbey   *by Selin Williams*

SCENE I: BEAR INVITES RABBIT TO DINNER

by Bel Abbey	by Selin Williams
1a Now, Bear used to dwell somewhere,	Bear and Rabbit were friends 1 with each other, so it is said.
b and he and Rabbit used to visit each other, so it is said.	Then, 2a
2 Thereupon,	Bear spoke, b
3 "Visit me later!" he said,	"Go and visit me later," he said 3
4 "Visit me later!" he said to Rabbit.[1]	and went.
5 Thereupon,	
6 "I was about to visit you," said Rabbit to Bear.	

SCENE II: BEAR FEEDS RABBIT WITH HIMSELF

7a Thereupon,	Rabbit went and arrived over 4
b he went over there to visit him,	there,
c and after the two of them were sitting,	And Bear, having sliced himself 5a up the middle,

---

1. Abbey's interest in Bear is indicated by his elaboration of Bear's thought.

d he had nothing to give to
    him to eat;

took out some fat,   b
and fried it, and it is said   c
    that

e "What *am* I going to feed
    him?" he thought,

    Rabbit ate it.

f and then he knew.

8a Well, because Bear was fat,

b he pulled out his stomach,

c and picking up a knife,

d and cutting off a piece,

e cooked it,

f and fed Rabbit with it, so
    it is said.[2]

9a Thereupon,

b Rabbit really sat and watched,
    so it is said.

SCENE III: RABBIT INVITES BEAR TO DINNER

10a Thereupon,

b having merely just visited him,
    he returned home.

Thereupon,   6a
  Rabbit spoke,   b
"You too go over to my place 7
    later!" he said.

11 "You too go over to my place
    later!" he said.

12 "You too go over to my place
    later!" he said,

13 And Bear went to visit Rabbit,
    so it is said.

14a Well, he went over to visit
    Rabbit,

b and after he sat down. . . .

15a Now, Bear's house was the
    inside of a hollow tree,

b the two of them sat dwelling
    in the hollow tree,

c and after the two of them
    dwelt there,

d he went over to Rabbit's
    dwelling place.

16a Rabbit dwelt within a little grass
    dwelling;

b within that was his dwelling,
    so it is said.

17 Over there the two of them sat.

SCENE IV: RABBIT INJURES HIMSELF IMITATING BEAR

18 Rabbit spoke,

19a "Please sit down! I shall cook!"
    he said,

b and after the two of them
    stayed there,

Bear having arrived over there 8
    to visit him

Rabbit sliced himself up the 9a
    middle

    and there was nothing there. b

---

2. Bear can cut away a piece of himself without being hurt not only because he is fat but because—as the audience would know—he has magic power that allows him to do this.

20a He himself did what he had
    seen,
  b   he picked up a knife and cut
      out a piece,
  c   he cut his stomach, so it is
      said.
21a Now he himself being scrawny
    and lean,
  b   he injured himself cutting him-
      self,
  c   "Help me! Help me! I need
      help!" he said.
22 Bear ran over.
23 "What is it?"
24 "I am injured. It is the case that
   I have cut myself," he said.
25 Thereupon,
26a "I intend to look for a doctor,
    then," Bear said,
  b   and it is said that he ran out.
27a The other lay on the ground,
  b   he had cut his stomach.

Bear having sliced himself up   10
    the middle again fried it and
    they ate.[3]
Afterwards,   11a
    Rabbit was about to die.[4]   b

SCENE V: VULTURE IS ENCOUNTERED[5]

28a Thereupon,
  b   after he had run a ways,
  c   he caught sight of him sitting
      on a branch,
  d   he caught sight of Vulture
      sitting on a branch,
  e   he asked questions of
        him, so it is said.
29 Thereupon,
30 After he said, "I need help."
31 "What is it that you want?"
32 "I am looking for a doctor."
33 "Why do you want to look for
   help?"
34a "It is the case that my friend
      Rabbit is injured," he said.
  b   "It is the case that Rabbit is
      injured,

He was laying on the ground,   12
And they[6] went around looking   13
    for a doctor,
And they sent for Vulture.   14

3. Kimball notes that this is a "major stylistic flaw" because Bear's preparation of another meal is inconsistent with the main concern of this scene, Rabbit's serious injury. This may be an indication of Williams's general lack of interest in this particular story.
4. Rabbit, a typical trickster, misunderstands who he is and what he can do: not only that Bear is fat while Rabbit is lean but that Bear's immunity to harm results from special power that Rabbit does not possess.

5. Although Vulture was once considered a legitimate doctor, with genuine power to heal, by the time these tales were told this was no longer the case. For both Williams and Abbey, Vulture is a fraud. It is Hymes's belief that scenes V through VII in both versions actually come from "The Sham Doctor," another type of story widespread in Native American cultures.
6. Williams's error; Rabbit is lying on the ground and only Bear is looking for the doctor.

c   it is the case that he has
         suffered a knife
           wound," he said.

35a "If you tell me about it, I will
       perhaps help him,

b   and it is the case that I will
       doctor him," he said.

SCENE: VI: VULTURE "DOCTORS" RABBIT

36 After they arrived over there,

37 Thereupon,

38 "Where is he lying?" he said.

39 "He lies over here," he said.

40 Thereupon,

41a "What are you doing?

b   What do you want?" he said.

42a "Fence in his house perhaps!

b   Would that it be encircled!" he
     said

43a "Look for palmetto leaves,

b   Fence it all in and make a
     house encircling it!"

44a "Enough now!

b   Go out!

c   He will follow you upon my
     doctoring him," he said.

45a Thereupon, well,

b   Vulture made Rabbit cry out,
     so it is said.

46a When Rabbit cried out,

b   Bear said, "Why is he making a
     sound?"

47 "It is nothing. He does not want
     the medicine from me," he
     said.

48 Thereupon,

49 "Why is it that he doesn't want
     it?" he said.

50a "It is the case that he doesn't
     want me to give him my
     medicine,

b   and he made noise," he said.

51 Thereupon,

52 "What else do you need?" he
     said.

53 Then,

54a "Nothing.

Vulture spoke, 15

"You all are to close me up in 16a
   his house with him,

   and there are to be no cracks, b
     no one can look at me,[7] c
      only so can I doctor him," d
   he said.

They closed him up with him. 17

And then, for a time, Rabbit 18
   cried out, and then it
   ceased.

"Why is it?" they said. 19

"It is nothing! He is really afraid 20
   of the medicine," he said.

Then, 21

"Open ye the door for me!" he 22
   said.

They opened it for him, 23a

   and he flew over there and b
     perched on a branch.

---

7. Williams's interest in Vulture encourages her to elaborate here. Although Vulture has his own reasons for not wanting anyone to watch him work his medicine, the details given in both versions may also reflect the practice of legitimate medicine persons who insisted on secrecy.

b I am about to finish doctoring
    him.
c But now he is good.
d Now it is the case that he is
    good," he said.
e And flying up went and
    perched on a tree
    branch.

SCENE VII: VULTURE IS ASSAULTED

55a Thereupon,

b after Bear went in and saw it,

c that he had eaten Rabbit all
    up,

d that he had eaten up his flesh,

e that he had thrown down
    nothing but bones,

f Bear became extremely
    angry,

g he took out the knife that
    he carried,

h and he threw it over-
    hand at Vulture.

56a After he threw it at him,

b it went through his beak,

c it pierced his beak,

d it went through his beak,
    and he took it,

e he took the knife and
    threw it away, so it is
    said.

They went and saw Rabbit, 24

And it is said that he had laid 25
    down nothing but bones.

Thereupon, 26a

they loathed vulture and shot b
    at him,

They shot and hit and made it 27
    pass through only his beak.

Vulture spoke, 28

"Oh! I will like a nose-ring," he 29
    said.

SCENE VIII: THE RESULT OF BEAR'S ACTION[8]

57a He would have killed him,

b he missed,

c and it is said that he pierced
    his beak.

58a Thereupon,

b he was pierce-beaked,

c it is the case that Bear
    pierced it on him;

d it seems he carried it as his
    possession unceasingly,
    it is said that they carried
    it all the time.

59 Just like that, any kind of bird is
    pierce-beaked.

---

8. Williams ends with Vulture pleased with his
meal, his safe escape, and his pierced beak. She
does not, in this telling, add the etiological or
explanatory feature generally expected by the
Koasati—that birds ever since have had pierced
beaks—as does Abbey.

60 Just so it is said that they are
       pierced.
61 Just so much [is what I know of
       this].
62 *Finis!*

MOURNING DOVE
c. 1888–1936

Christine Quintasket, Humishuma or Mourning Dove, had family among the inland Columbia River tribes: the Lake Indians, the Thompson River Indians, the Okanogan, and the Colville. She believed that her paternal grandfather was Irish, although tribal rolls list her father as a fullblood. Mourning Dove claimed to have been born in the spring of 1888, but documents exist that give her birthdate as 1882, 1886, and 1887. It is not now possible to know whether Mourning Dove's memory or one of the written records is more accurate.

Mourning Dove's formal education consisted of fewer than three years at Catholic boarding school in Washington State and another three years at the government-run Fort Spokane School for Indians. From 1904 to 1908, she worked as matron at the Fort Shaw Indian School in Montana in exchange for the opportunity to take classes. In 1909, she married Hector McLeod, a Flathead Indian. The marriage was not a success, and in 1919 she married a Wenatchee man, Fred Galler, with whom she worked as a migrant laborer.

Mourning Dove had earlier decided she wanted to be a novelist, and somewhere between 1912 and 1914 she managed to complete the manuscript of *Cogewea* (1927), one of the first novels published by a Native American woman. Although the manuscript of *Cogewea* does not seem to have survived, the published novel is unquestionably very different from Mourning Dove's original version, having been substantially edited and expanded by Lucullus Virgil McWhorter, a white businessman and passionate advocate for native rights whom Mourning Dove met in 1914. McWhorter not only worked with her on *Cogewea* but encouraged her to collect what she called her "folklores," that is, the traditions, myths, and legends of her people. She eventually wrote and then typed for McWhorter thirty-eight of these, calling the collection *Okanogan Sweat House*.

It had taken substantial efforts on McWhorter's part over more than a decade to interest a publisher in *Cogewea,* but with *Okanogan Sweat House,* he had no success. Thus it was that in 1929 McWhorter invited Heister Dean Guie, a young newspaperman from Yakima, Washington, to look at the manuscript with an eye toward reworking it further for publication. This Guie did with a vengeance. Convinced that the book's best market was "young adults," Guie substantially revised the manuscript as a whole, cut eleven stories, and added illustrations. The book was published as *Coyote Stories* in 1933.

In the late 1920s and early 1930s, Mourning Dove became an activist for native rights, speaking out against abuses at the Colville Reservation of north-central Washington (she was an enrolled member of the Colville tribe). In 1930 she helped form the Colville Indian Association. She continued to write, working on what would eventually be published as *Mourning Dove: A Salishan Autobiography* (1990). The first woman ever to be elected to the Colville Tribal Council (in 1935), she died of illness brought on by exhaustion the following year.

In 1976, Mourning Dove's original collection of thirty-eight stories, which Mc-

Whorter and Guie had transformed into *Coyote Stories,* appeared under the title *Tales of the Okanogans,* its text drawn from the typescript Mourning Dove had prepared for McWhorter (and which he had only lightly edited). The text printed here goes one step back, to Mourning Dove's handwritten manuscripts. Mourning Dove's original version of "Owlwoman and Coyote" appears here for the first time as transcribed by Alanna Kathleen Brown, with the permission of the Holland Library of Washington State University. Material in brackets has been added by the editor.

Owlwoman and Coyote[1]

Chipmunk was a little girl and lived with her aged grandmother, and she had a special ol-la-la bush[2] that she went [to] each day to see how many ripe berries she could find, and she would climb on the tree and count them one by one as she ate them saying. "One berry is ripe, two berries is ripe, three berries is ripe."

One day while she was on her tree counting the berries and eating them as she picked them without putting any berries in her basket which hung at her side, [she] made out of [the] hoof of a deer[,] She heard heavy footsteps below her, and she saw the Owlwoman[3] with her great big basket on her back filled with many small children that she had stolen away from their parents, and ate them as she grew hungry. She has the habit of going from one camp to another to steal children, and she was the fear of all children and parents, because she was the Owl eating woman.

This appearance frightened Chipmunk very much, but she knew that the Owlwoman couldn't reach her up the tree. So the big woman coaxed her to come down the bush. Saying.

"Your father wants you.["] Chipmunk answered. "Ha ha, I have no father, he died long ago." Then the Owlwoman lied.

"Your mother wants you." Chipmunk sasied[4] back. "My mother died long ago." Owlwoman still lied more.

"Your aunt wants you home.["] "Ha, ha, my aunt never lived."

"Then your uncle wants you. Chipmunk answered, "ha ha, I never had an uncle." Owlwoman coaxed then further.

"Your grandfather wants you." Chipmunk answered back. "Ha ha, my grandfather died before I was born." Then the Owlwoman said. ["]Your grandmother wants you home." Chipmunk then said, "I will not come down the tree unless you hide your eyes"[.] At this the Owlwoman made a pretence at hiding her eyes with her hands, putting them only slightly over them, but Chipmunk was not easily fooled, and told her that she still could see her big eyes blinking. And told her that she will not go down the tree unless she hide all her eyes.[5] Owlwoman then hid all her eyes only leaving a small space to still see Chipmunk come down the tree.

Chipmunk jumped from the top of the tree over the Owlwoman[.] The

1. *Tales of the Okanogans* calls this story "Coyote kills Owl-Woman," and H. D. Guie's edition titles it "Chipmunk and Owl-Woman." The title of Mourning Dove's novel, *Cogewea,* is taken from the Okanogan word for "chipmunk."
2. Mourning Dove apparently means "ooh la la," a French exclamation she probably picked up from time spent in Canada, to refer to the serviceberry bush, or *see'-ah,* whose fruit was much prized by the Okanogans.
3. In "Chipmunk and Owl-Woman," she is called *Snee'-nah,* the desirable bush and the evil creature associated perhaps by their similar-sounding names.
4. Responded in a sassy manner.
5. I.e., hide her eyes completely.

Owlwoman tried to catch her, but only scratched her back leaving the finger marks with her sharp claws deep into Chipmunks back, which she still carries to this day.[6]

Running to her grandmother Chipmunk tried to talk, but she was so frightened that all she could say was "Sing-naw [7] sing-naw"[.] The old grandmother misunderstanding her with her deafened ears, Asked her if she has stepped on a sliver, or a thorn and all the answer she would give would be, "Sing-naw sing-naw.["] At last the old grandmother understood her. She took Chipmunk and tried to hide her in her pillow, but, she runned around inside so much with fear, that she was easily seen through. She put her in the berry basket, but she was to[o] noisy, and she tried to hide her in the soup, and she nearly drowned. At last Meadow Lark flew on a tree close by, and sang,

"Two little oyster shells,[8] put her in". Than the oldwoman put chipmunk between the two oyster shells, and she was well hidden[.] The oldwoman took her necklace from around her neck and gave it to Meadow Lark so as not to tell where Chipmunk was, because she knew that Meadow Lark was a tattler. Than Meadow Lark flew away.

The Oldwoman followed Chipmunk's tracks till it came to the grandmother's typee [tipi], and going in she asked.

["]Where is the hunted child that I am tracking.?" The grandmother denied she knew. At this denial the mean Owlwoman started to look about for Chipmunk, she looked in the pillow and in the basket, and in the soup, and at last she gave up hope, when Meadow Lark flew back to the tree, and sang.

"I will tell you, if you pay me. I will tell you, if you pay me, where she is, she is." Owlwoman went outside the typee and threw her a yellow vest. And Meadow Lark the tattler, sang. "Two little oyster shells, put her out. Two little oyster shells put her out" as she flew away with the necklace and yellow vest, she earned for tattling on Chipmunk.

With all the begging of the oldwoman Chipmunk was taken out of the oyster shell, and cut openned with the sharp claw of Owlwoman, and taking only her heart out, she swallowed it saying. "Yum-yum-yum[.] It is so good, little girl's heart, are the best." Than the Owlwoman left with her big basket full of little children. The aged grandmother cried for some time, than she heard the song of Meadow Lark.

"Put a berry for a heart, put a berry for a heart". At this the old grandmother putting a half-ripe red ol-la-la berry in the breast of Chipmunk she sewed up her breast and stepped over, when Chipmunk jumped up alive.[9]

The Owlwoman had not gone far when she met the notorious Coyote, who told her that he just loved to eat all bad little children, and that he thought if the two of them traveled together that they would have much success getting children. At this suggestion the Owlwoman consented, thinking that they would overcome all the monsters of the earth, because she knew the trickery of Coyote, and his evil powers. They then went on traveling together. They had not gone far when the Owlwoman grew hungry, Coyote suggested that they stop and make a big bonfire and roast the children, which would

6. For the Okanogan, as for the Koasati, the etiological or explanatory element here, as at the end of the story, is considered important and to be taken literally.
7. Owl.
8. Trade items obtained by the inland Okanogan from peoples living near the Pacific Ocean.
9. Stepping over the dead is often a way of bringing them back to life in myth stories, e.g., Fox will sometimes step over Coyote to revitalize him.

tast[e] much better than eating them alive. To this the Owlwoman compliment Coyote for his wisdom, while Coyote flattered her. Coyote then told
her to let all the children out of the basket, so that the children could do the
work while they overseen the work themselves. The children gathered much
pitchwood by Coyote's orders, piling it high in one pile. When the Owlwoman
was out of hearing Coyote told the children to gather the wood with the most
pitch, and to gather the solid pitch in plenty. If they wished to go back to
their parents. This the children gathered in better spirits. At last they set the
big pile of wood afire. Coyote then told the owlwoman that to make the feast
as it should be proper she should have her face blackened with charcoal and
to make the charcoal stick, she should put pitch on her face, this she did,
and also coyote and all the children. He pitched her arms with its many
bracelets and covered them with charcoal. Then they danced around the fire
singing and shouting for the roast feast, while they waited for the coals to
grow hot. Coyote told her that the pitch wood would spoil the meat, when
she grew anxious to roast the children. Coyote said to her, let the children
all get sticks and we will pretend that we are dancing the Sun-dance, and
then we will roast the children afterwards, to this the owlwoman was flattered. Coyote told the children to get all forked sticks, and they did, To this
the Owlwoman wanted to know why, and Coyote told her so that they can
use the sticks to turn the roasting children over with them.

It was not long when the Owlwoman began to grow tired with the dancing,
but still Coyote insisted that the coals were not ready, and they danced some
more flattering her on her knowledge of dancing, she dance till he seen that
she was staggering, and he fell against her purposely at which she fell, and
he only laughed, and he danced harder, and went around the fire a few more
times, when he fell against her on the prentence [pretense] that he was
staggering, which knocked her into the blazing pitch wood fire. Her pitch
covered face and arms blazed instantly. Coyote told the children to help him
with all their forked sticks to keep her in the fire, at which they gladly did,
at last she was burnt to death. Roasted like the many children that she ate.

Coyote then sent all the children back home, after Owlwoman's eyes
bursted and from there flew a small little owl to light the tree where it hooted
its night call. Coyote then told the bird that in the future, the owlwoman's
remains will be only a thing to scare a bad child into sleep, because it will
only travel by night, because it is blind in daylight, and only can see in
darkness. Because its eyes are burnt out with the pitch. So it is to this day,
Indian children are still afraid of the Owlwoman.

CLATSOP CHINOOK

The Clatsop people are Lower Chinookans living at the mouth of the Columbia River
on what is now the Oregon side. They subsisted by hunting deer, elk, bear, and smaller
game; but they also depended, during the hard winter months, on salmon preserved
from catches made in the spring and fall. It was in the winter that the Chinook, like
many native peoples, told myth stories, Coyote tales among them.

Anthropologist Franz Boas visited Washington and Oregon in the summers of 1890 and 1891 to study the languages of the area. Upon learning that some of the Lower Chinookan dialects were spoken by only a few people, Boas traveled first to Clatsop County, Oregon, then to Bay Center, Pacific County, Washington, where he met Charles Cultee and his wife, Catherine, the last remaining speakers of Chinook.

Boas's concerns were linguistic, and he took down the stories Cultee told him not for their literary interest but, rather, for their lexical and grammatical interest. Thus, as Boas wrote in his introduction to *Chinook Texts* (1894), his translations are such that "the form of the Chinook sentences has been preserved as nearly as possible."

William Bright, using a combination of the translation and transcription techniques pioneered by Dell Hymes and Dennis Tedlock, reworked Boas's literal prose translation into a verse format that derives its dramatic structure from linguistic features of the original language. Bright's poetic "adaptation" of Boas appears on the left side of the page. In several places where Bright cut and summarized the original, passages of Boas's prose are included, on the right, for comparison.

Coyote Establishes Fishing Taboos

Coyote was coming,
   he came to Got'at.

Now there was big surf,
  right away he went up to the spruce trees.

Now Coyote was afraid,   5
  he might get washed away,
  he stayed a long time at Got'at.
He took sand,
  he threw it in that surf.
"It will be a prairie,[1]   10
  it will not be surf.
"Generations to come will walk on this prairie."
Now Clatsop became a prairie,
  that surf became a prairie.

Now a creek came into being at Niakhaqshe.   15
He went,
  Coyote made a house at Niakhaqshe,
  he stood at the creek mouth of Niakhaqshe.
He speared two silverside salmon,
  he speared a steelhead,   20
  he speared a fall salmon.
He threw away that steelhead,
  he threw away that fall salmon.
"The creek is too small.
"I don't like its steelhead,   25
  I don't like its fall salmon.
"The creek is too small.
"It will be a bad omen,

---

1. "On the northwest coast, 'prairie' refers to a level grassy place surrounded by woods" [Bright's note]. This is a clear instance of Coyote preparing the world for the people to come.

when a fall salmon is caught here,
   a person will die.   30
"Likewise a steelhead,
   when a female steelhead is caught,
   a woman will die,
   when a male steelhead is caught,
   a man will die.   35
"So it will be for the steelhead,
   so it will be for the fall salmon."[2]

Now he picked up only those silversides,
   he went home.
Right away he cut them up,   40
   right away he steamed them,
   he ate them.
Day came,
   he took his spear,
   he went and stood at the creek mouth of Niakhaqshe.   45
He saw nothing,
   the floodtide set in,
   he went home.
Again daylight came,
   again he went,   50
   he went and stood there.
Again he saw nothing,
   he got angry,
   he went home.
He took a shit,   55
   he said to his shit,
   "Tell me,
   why have those silversides disappeared?"[3]

"Oh, you have no sense,
   you bandylegs!   60
"When silversides are caught,
   when they are first caught,
   they must not be cut up.
"They must be split along the back,
   then they are roasted,   65
   they are not steamed.
"When they go upriver to the creeks,
   then they are steamed."

Coyote went home. On the next day he went again and speared three.[4] He went home and made

2. These things he knows on his own, with no assistance, and he establishes the taboos. Below, the taboos seem already to be established and Coyote has to learn to abide by them, as the people will also have to do.
3. On one hand, this is a bawdy example of Coyote's foolishness; only trickster would consult his shit for advice! On the other hand, it is likely a satire on the shamanic practice of calling on spirit helpers.
4. The number three appears several times, as the number ten—twice five—is repeated later. The usual Northwest Coast pattern number is five; the three's may reflect Christian influence. Mourning Dove, who would have heard her people's Coyote stories around this time, also uses three as well as five. Here Coyote finds himself at fault in regard to taboos established *before* his arrival.

three spits. He roasted each salmon on a spit. He had three salmon and three spits. On the next day he went again and stood at the mouth of the creek. He did not see anything until the flood tide set in. Then he became angry and went home. He defecated. He spoke and asked his excrements: "Why have these silver-side salmon disappeared!" His excrements said to him: "I told you, you with your bandy legs, when the first silver-side salmon are killed spits must be made, one for the head, one for the back, one for the roe, one for the body. The gills must be burnt." "Yes," said Coyote. On the next day he went again. He killed again three silver-side salmon. When he arrived at home he cut them all and made many spits. He roasted them all separately. The spits of the breast, body, head, back, and roe were at separate places. Coyote roasted them. On the next morning he went again. He speared ten silver-side salmon. Coyote was very glad. He came home and split part of the fish. The other part he left and went to sleep. On the next morning he roasted the rest. Then he went again and stood at the mouth of the river. He did not see anything before the flood tide set in. He went home. On the next morning he went again, but again he did not see anything. He went home angry. He defecated and asked his excrements: "Why have these silver-side salmon disappeared!" His excrements scolded him: "When the first silver-side salmon are killed, they are not left raw. All must be roasted. When many are caught, they must all be roasted before you go to sleep." On the next morning Coyote went and stood at the mouth of the river. He speared ten.

Now he made spits,
 he made many spits.

70

Now he stayed awake,
  he roasted all he had caught.
Now he observed the taboos,
  the taboos of the silversides,
  when they first arrive at Niakhaqshe.   75
Then he stayed there,
  Coyote said,
  "So the people will do.
"If a corpse-handler eats silversides,
  right away they will disappear.   80
"If a murderer eats silversides,
  right away they will disappear.
"So also a menstruating girl,
  so also a menstruating woman."

Now he came this way. At some distance he met a number of women who were digging roots. He asked them: "What are you doing?" "We are digging gamass."[5] "How can you dig gamass at Clatsop? You shall dig [a root species?] and thistle [?] roots in this country. No gamass will be dug here." Now they gathered [a root of some kind] and thistle [?] roots. He left these women and spoiled that land. He transformed the gamass into small onions.

Then he came to Clatsop. It was the spring of the year. Then he met his younger brother the snake. He said to him: "Let us make nets." The snake replied: "As you wish." Now they bought material for twine, and paid the frog and the newt[6] to spin it. Now Coyote cleaned all the material for twine while the snake was crawling about. Then the frog and the newt spun it. Then Coyote said to his younger brother: "Clean it, clean it. You crawl about all day." Thus he spoke to the snake. Coyote continued: "You shall make one side of the net, I make the other." Coyote finished his twine and said to the snake: "Quick! quick! you let me wait. Make your net." The snake

---

5. Camass or camas (in Nootka, *chamas*, "sweet"); a lilylike plant with sweet, edible bulbs, which was an important supplementary food source in much of northwestern America. In this instance, Coyote acts as spoiler and perhaps explains why wild onion but not camas was plentiful at Clatsop.

6. Apparently female, because they do women's work.

replied: "You let me wait." Thus he spoke to Coyote. Now, Coyote made his net. He finished it all. The two women made the ropes, Coyote made the net buoys; while the snake crawled about. Coyote said: "Make your net buoys; you let me wait." Thus he said to the snake. The snake replied: "Make haste! you let me wait." Coyote finished his net buoys. Then he went to look for stones, and the snake accompanied him. They went for stones to Tongue point. The snake crawled about among the stones, while Coyote carried them down. They went home. After they reached home Coyote went to gather spruce roots. The snake accompanied him. Coyote dug up the ground and the snake crawled about at the same place. They went home. Coyote split the spruce roots. "Go on; work," he spoke to the snake; "you let me wait." The snake replied: "Quick, quick; work! you let me wait." Now Coyote tied his net to the buoys and laid it down flat on a large mat. Then he tied it to the buoys. The snake crawled about at the same place. Coyote finished his net and hung it up outside. Early the next morning he stepped out of the house, and there hung already the net of the snake. "Oh, brother," he said, "you got the better of me." Coyote was ashamed. The snake had won over him. Coyote said: "When a person makes a net, he shall get tired before he finishes it. It would not be well if he would not get tired." The snake said to him: "I told you that you would let me wait."

It got day. Then they went to catch salmon in their net. They laid the net and caught two in it. Coyote jumped over the net. Now they intended to catch more salmon, but the flood-tide set in. They had caught only two before the flood-tide set in. Now they went home. Coyote said that he was

hungry, and he split the salmon at
once. They roasted them. When they
were done they ate. The frog and the
newt were their cousins. The next
morning they went fishing with their
net. The newt looked after the rope,
the snake stood at the upper end of
the net, Coyote at the lower end.
They intended to catch salmon, but
they did not get anything until the
flood-tide set in. They went home.

Coyote was angry,   85
  he took a shit,
  he consulted his shit,
  he said, "You lied to me!"

"You bandylegs!
When people catch salmon,   90
  they mustn't jump over the net,
  you don't step across your net.

When the first salmon are caught,
  then they're cut up in the afternoon."

✻   ✻   ✻

[On following days, Coyote again catches nothing. He learns about other taboos he
has broken and, finally, he is able to catch fish again. But then he moves from Clatsop
to another site. He catches a few fish on the first day, but nothing on the second day.
His shit tells him, "Oh Coyote, you fool! Do you think it's the same here as at Clatsop?" Finally Coyote learns all the taboos, and he says:][7]

"So the people will do.   95
They will not catch salmon
  if they are murderers,
  corpse-handlers,
  menstruating girls,
  menstruating women,   100
  widowed people.
Those are all the taboos,
  for the generations to come."

7. The Cultee-Boas text contains a lengthy section that repeats a good deal of what has come before;
the summary is Bright's. Repetition was important to teach or reaffirm certain lessons to a listening audience.

NAVAJO

An Athapascan-speaking people whose language is closely related to that of Canadian and Alaskan tribes, the Navajo migrated to the Southwest from a northerly point around five hundred years ago. Once settled in the Southwest, the Navajo learned farming and weaving from the long-settled Pueblo peoples, acquired livestock from the Spanish in the seventeenth century, and developed silver-working skills from contact with Mexicans in the nineteenth century. The Navajo are today the most populous tribe in the United States.

Adopted into the Yellowman family in the 1950s, Barre Toelken recorded Hugh Yellowman's performance of "Coyote, Skunk, and the Prairie Dogs" on a winter visit to the family in 1966. Toelken first published a translation in prose; but impressed, like many others, by the ethnopoetic work of Hymes and Tedlock, he retranslated the story with the help of Orville Tacheeni Scott, a Navajo and a graduate student at the University of Oregon, and published it again, this time in verse format. Listening to the tape of Yellowman's narration with Scott, Toelken heard many things he had missed before—words such as *jiní*, a possible linguistic marker of line breaks whose meaning, "it is said," a phrase that often occurs in myth narratives, conveys to the audience the fact that the narrator believes what he or she tells to be true, although the storyteller has not actually witnessed these things.

The text is Toelken's most recent version of Yellowman's "Coyote, Skunk, and the Prairie Dogs." The 1981 retranslation provides the fullest information that the printed page can give of what Yellowman's actual narration was like, indicating not only audience response but also the dynamics of Yellowman's performance style, such as his use of the untranslatable Navajo intensifier *hááhgóóshįį*; pauses; and shifts in pace, tone, and volume. The apparatus necessary to convey all this information, however, makes for a much less readable page than the later version—which retains notation for audience response.

Coyote, Skunk, and the Prairie Dogs

Ma'ii was trotting along like he's always done.

At a place—I don't know where it is—called Where the Wood Floats Out,
    he was walking along, it is said.

Then, in an open area, it is said,
    he was walking along in the midst of many prairie dogs.   5

The prairie dogs were cursing him, it is said;
    they were all crowding together, yelling at him.

He went along farther into their midst, and
    then he walked along still farther.

He got angry, and soon he began to feel hostile.   10

After a while it was midday.

He wanted a cloud to appear
    (his reason was that he was starting to hate those prairie dogs);

so he thought about rain.[1]
[*quiet laughter*]

Then a cloud appeared, it is said;   15
"If it would only rain on me," he said.[2]
And that's what happened, it is said.

"If only there could be rain in my footprints."
And that's what happened, it is said.
"If only water would ooze up between my toes   20
   as I walk along," he said.

Then everything happened as he said, it is said.

"If only the water would come up to my knees," he said.
And that's what happened.
"If only the water would be up to my back   25
   so that only my ears would be out of the water."

"If I could only float," he said.
Then, as he was starting to float:
"There where the prairie dogs are,
   if I could only land over there," he said.   30
[*quiet laughter*]

He came to rest in the midst of the prairie dog town, it is said.

Someplace in the *diz*—
[*quiet laughter*]
   (*diz* is the name of a plant that grows in clumps)—
he landed, hung up in that clump, it is said.

And there he was lying after the rain.   35
And then Golizhii[3] was running by to fetch water.
   (Ma'ii was pretending to be dead.)
Then Golizhii was running past him.

Ma'ii called out to him, it is said.
"Come here," he said, and Golizhii came over, it is said.   40

"Shiłna'ash,"[4] Ma'ii said.
[*suppressed giggles*]
"Do something for me: tell those small animals,
'The hated one has died and has washed up
   where the prairie dogs are';
   tell them that, shilna'ash.   45

1. The Navajo associate prairie dogs with rain, according to ideas of wholeness, i.e., what lives below ground in relation to what comes from the sky. A good deal of the early part of the story is associated with water, something scarce and precious in the Southwest.
2. An exaggerated nasal tone for Coyote's speech is a standard feature of performance, and Yellow-man used it throughout his narration.
3. Skunk. The one who squirts (sprays or urinates) upward (Navajo).
4. One who walks with me (Navajo, literal trans.). Implies "trust, kinship, and interdependence," according to Toelken; here, ironic, given Coyote's intention to use Skunk and trick him.

'He's already got maggots,' you tell them," he said.

"Slendergrass it is called—shake that slendergrass
    so those crooked seeds fall off.
In my crotch, in my nose, in the back part of my mouth,
    scatter some around; then put some inside my ears," he said.   50
" 'He's got maggots,' you tell them.
'The hated one has been washed out.' "
[*quiet laughter*]

"Make four⁵ clubs and put them under me,
    where I can get them.
'We'll dance over him.   55
We're all going to meet over there,' you tell them," he said.

"This is how to do it," he said.
"Get them to make a circle,
    and when they're dancing around me, tell them,
'Hit Ma'ii in the ribs.'   60
But be careful not to hit me too hard!
'Slowly, gently, like this,' you tell them," he said.
[*laughter*]

This is what happened.
Golizhii ran home and gave out the word to the prairie dogs,
    it is said:
"The hated one is washed out."   65

There were rabbits and other animals
    and even ground squirrels.
Those animals that are food for Ma'ii were gathered together;
now they were dancing, it is said, at that meeting.

First Golizhii said, "It's true! It's true!   70
Let's have one of you fast runners run over there to find out."

Then Jackrabbit ran there and ran back saying,
"It's true!"
    it is said.
[*quiet giggling*]

Then Cottontail ran, and "It's true!" he said,   75
    running back, it is said.

Then Prairie Dog ran, and, they say, "It's true!" he said,
    running back, it is said.

At that time there was a big gathering.
They were dancing, it is said.   80

5. The familiar pattern number.

Whatever song they were singing, I don't know.
"The hated one is dead," they were saying;
   the club is beside him; they were hitting him in the ribs, it is said.

Then they continued with what they were doing,
   and more and more people[6] came.   85
Then that evil Golizhii remembered Ma'ii's plan:
"When you are all dancing,
while you are looking up, while you are saying, you say, 'Dance in
   that manner,' you tell them while you're in charge there,
   shiłna'ash," he had said.   90

Then they were dancing.
Then: "Waay, waay up there something is moving by overhead,"
   Golizhii said to them.

Then, when they were all looking up,
Golizhii urinated upward   95
   so that his urine fell in their eyes.
[open laughter]

The animals were rubbing his urine from their eyes.
"Oh, so 'the one who is hated is dead,' is he?" Ma'ii said,
   jumping up.
[laughter]

He grabbed the clubs from under him.   100
[laughter]

He used the clubs on them.
[laughter]
They were all clubbed to death.
[laughter]

Then: "Let us cook them by burying them in a fire pit,
   shiłna'ash," Ma'ii said.
"Dig right here," he said.   105
And he dug a trench, Golizhii did.

After he dug that ditch, he built a fire.
He put the food into the pit.
Then Ma'ii thought of something new.

"Let's have a footrace, shiłna'ash.   110
Whoever comes back first,
   this will be his," he said.[7]
[light laughter]
"No," Golizhii said, but Ma'ii won the argument.

6. These are all animal people. Toelken noted that the words used for Coyote's toes or feet are not the words for the paws or toes of an animal.

7. Competition for food is strongly disapproved of by the Navajo.

"I can't run fast," Golizhii said.
"I'll give you a head start;   115
while I stay here, you start loping," Ma'ii said.

While Ma'ii pretended to be busy with something,
Golizhii started to run;
then, just over the hill he ran and hid in an abandoned hole.

In a little while Ma'ii suddenly spurted away   120
    toward that mountain.

He had tied a torch to his tail,
    and the smoke was pouring out behind him as he ran.[8]
[laughter]

While he was running over there,
Golizhii ran back, it is said,   125
    there where he had buried the food.
He dug them up and took them up into the rocks, it is said.
Four little prairie dogs he reburied;
    then he was sitting back up there, it is said.
Ma'ii ran back, it is said,   130
[light laughter]
    back to the place where the prairie dogs were buried.
He leaped over it.
[laughter]

"Whew!" he said.
[extended loud laughter]

"Shiłna'ash—I wonder how far back he's plodding along,
    Mr. His Urine," he said.   135
[loud laughter]

Sighing, he lay down,
    pretended to lie down, in the shade.
Then he jumped up and leaped over to the cooking pit.
[laughter]

He thrust a pointed object into the ground
    and grabbed the tail of the first prairie dog, it is said.   140
Only the tail came loose.
[light laughter]

"Oh no! the fire has gotten to the tail," he said.
[loud laughter]

So he grabbed the stick and thrust it into the ground again;
    a little prairie dog he dug up, it is said.

---

8. Coyote running off with a torch tied to his tail presents a hilarious picture. He is so infatuated with himself that he cannot possibly notice Skunk on his way to trick the trickster.

"I'm not going to eat this," he said,   145
    and he flung it away toward the east.[9]
[*light laughter*]

He thrust it into the ground again;
    a little prairie dog he dug up.
"I'm not going to eat this," he said,
    and he flung it away toward the south.   150
[*light laughter*]

He thrust it into the ground again;
    a little prairie dog he dug up.
"I'm not going to eat this," he said,
    and he flung it away toward the west.

He thrust it into the ground again;   155
    a little prairie dog he dug up.
"I'm not going to eat this," he said,
    and he flung it away toward the north.

He thrust repeatedly in many places, it is said,
    and couldn't find any more.   160
Nothing, it is said.
There weren't any, it is said.

He got frustrated; he walked around in circles.
So he went around, and he picked up those little prairie dogs
    he had thrown away.   165
Then he picked up every little bit and ate it all.
[*soft laughter*]

Then he started to follow Golizhii's tracks, it is said,
    but he couldn't pick up the trail.
[*quiet laughter*]
He kept following the tracks, back and forth,
    to where the rock meets the sand.   170
(He didn't bother to look up.)

Golizhii dropped a bone, and Ma'ii looked up, it is said.
It dropped at his feet.
[*quiet laughter*]

"Shiłna'ash, share some meat with me again."[1]
[*laughter*]

"Certainly not," Golizhii said to him, it is said.   175
Ma'ii was begging but to no avail, it is said.
Golizhii kept dropping bones down to him.

9. Throwing food away is something not to be done; eventually, the hungry Coyote will have to retrieve and eat what he has foolishly disdained.

1. Toelken pointed out that "begging for food is contemptible" to the Navajo "and brings laughter." Coyote has throughout taught the audience how *not* to behave.

Ma'ii chewed the bones, it is said.
[*laughter*]

That's how it happened, it is said.

WILLIAM BRADFORD
1590–1657

William Bradford epitomizes the spirit of determination and self-sacrifice that seems to us characteristic of our first "Pilgrims," a word Bradford himself used to describe the community of believers who sailed from Southampton, England, on the *Mayflower* and settled in Plymouth, Massachusetts, in 1620. For Bradford, as well as for the other members of this community, the decision to settle at Plymouth was the last step in a long march of exile from England, and the hardships they suffered in the new land were tempered with the knowledge that they were in a place they had chosen for themselves, where they were safe from persecution. Shortly after their arrival Bradford was elected governor. His duties involved more than that title might imply today: he was chief judge and jury, superintended agriculture and trade, and made allotments of land. It would be hard to imagine a historian better prepared to write the history of this colony.

Bradford's own life provides a model of the life of the community as a whole. He was born in Yorkshire, in the town of Austerfield, of parents who were modestly well off. Bradford's father died when he was an infant. His mother remarried in 1593, and he was brought up by his paternal grandparents and uncles. He did not receive a university education; instead, he was taught the arts of farming. When he was only twelve or thirteen, he heard the sermons of the Nonconformist minister Richard Clyfton, who preached in a neighboring parish; these sermons changed Bradford's life. For Clyfton was the religious guide of a small community of believers who met at the house of William Brewster in Scrooby, Nottinghamshire, and it was with this group, in 1606, that Bradford wished to be identified. Much against the opposition of uncles and grandparents, he left home and joined them. They were known as "Separatists," because unlike the majority of Puritans, they saw no hope of reforming the Church of England from within. They wished to follow Calvin's model and to set up "particular" churches, each one founded on a formal covenant, entered into by those who professed their faith and swore to the covenant. Their model was the Old Testament covenant God made with Adam and that Christ renewed. In their covenanted churches God offered himself as a contractual partner to each believer; it was a contract freely initiated but perpetually binding. They were not sympathetic to the idea of a national church. Separating was, however, by English law an act of treason, and many believers paid a high price for their dreams of purity. Sick of the hidden life that the Church of England forced on them, the Scrooby community took up residence in The Netherlands. Bradford joined them in 1609 and there learned to be a weaver. When he came into his inheritance he went into business for himself.

Living in a foreign land was not easy, and eventually the Scrooby community petitioned for a grant of land in the New World. Their original grant was for land in the Virginia territory, but high seas prevented them from reaching those shores and they settled at Plymouth, Massachusetts, instead. In the second book of Bradford's history he describes the signing of the Mayflower Compact, a civil covenant designed to allow the temporal state to serve the godly citizen. It was the first of a number of plantation covenants designed to protect the rights of citizens beyond the reach of established governments.

Bradford was a self-educated man, deeply committed to the Puritan cause. In his ecclesiastical history of New England, Cotton Mather describes him as "a person for study as well as action; and hence notwithstanding the difficulties which he passed in his youth, he attained unto a notable skill in languages. . . . But the Hebrew he most of all studied, because, he said, he would see with his own eyes the ancient oracles of God in their native beauty. . . . The crown of all his life was his holy, prayerful, watchful and fruitful walk with God, wherein he was exemplary." Bradford served as governor for all but five of the remaining years of his life.

The manuscript of Bradford's *History,* although known to early historians, disappeared from Boston after the Revolution. The first book (through chapter IX) had been copied into the Plymouth church records and was thus preserved, but the second book was assumed lost. The manuscript was found in the residence of the bishop of London and published for the first time in 1856. In 1897 it was returned to this country by ecclesiastical decree and was deposited in the State House in Boston.

From Of Plymouth Plantation[1]

From *Book I*

FROM CHAPTER I. [THE SEPARATIST INTERPRETATION OF THE REFORMATION IN ENGLAND, 1550–1607]

* * * When as by the travail and diligence of some godly and zealous preachers, and God's blessing on their labors, as in other places of the land, so in the North parts,[2] many became enlightened by the Word of God and had their ignorance and sins discovered[3] unto them, and began by His grace to reform their lives and make conscience of their ways; the work of God was no sooner manifest in them but presently they were both scoffed and scorned by the profane[4] multitude; and the ministers urged with the yoke of subscription,[5] or else must be silenced. And the poor people were so vexed with apparitors and pursuivants and the commissary courts,[6] as truly their affliction was not small. Which, notwithstanding, they bore sundry years with much patience, till they were occasioned by the continuance and increase of these troubles, and other means which the Lord raised up in those days, to see further into things by the light of the Word of God. How not only these base and beggarly ceremonies were unlawful, but also that the lordly and tyrannous power of the prelates ought not to be submitted unto; which thus, contrary to the freedom of the gospel, would load and burden men's consciences and by their compulsive power make a profane mixture of persons and things in the worship of God. And that their offices and callings, courts and canons, etc. were unlawful and antichristian; being such as have no warrant in the Word of God, but the same that were used in popery and still retained. Of which a famous author thus writeth in his Dutch commentaries, at the coming of King James into England:

1. The text is from *Of Plymouth Plantation,* edited by Samuel Eliot Morison (1953).
2. I.e., of England and Scotland.
3. Revealed.
4. Unholy.

5. I.e., to subscribe to the tenets of the Church of England. "Urged": threatened.
6. I.e., vexed with officers and summoners of the Church of England and the court of a bishop's jurisdiction.

The new king (saith he) found there established the reformed religion according to the reformed religion of King Edward VI, retaining or keeping still the spiritual state of the bishops, etc. after the old manner, much varying and differing from the reformed churches in Scotland, France and the Netherlands, Emden, Geneva, etc., whose reformation is cut, or shapen much nearer the first Christian churches, as it was used in the Apostles' times.[7]

So many, therefore, of these professors as saw the evil of these things in these parts, and whose hearts the Lord had touched with heavenly zeal for His truth, they shook off this yoke of antichristian bondage, and as the Lord's free people joined themselves (by a covenant[8] of the Lord) into a church estate, in the fellowship of the gospel, to walk in all His ways made known, or to be made known unto them, according to their best endeavors, whatsoever it should cost them, the Lord assisting them. And that it cost them something this ensuing history will declare.

These people became two distinct bodies or churches, and in regard of distance of place did congregate severally; for they were of sundry towns and villages, some in Nottinghamshire, some of Lincolnshire, and some of Yorkshire where they border nearest together. In one of these churches (besides others of note) was Mr. John Smith, a man of able gifts and a good preacher, who afterwards was chosen their pastor. But these afterwards falling into some errors in the Low Countries,[9] there (for the most part) buried themselves and their names.

But in this other church (which must be the subject of our discourse) besides other worthy men, was Mr. Richard Clyfton, a grave and reverend preacher, who by his pains and diligence had done much good, and under God had been a means of the conversion of many. And also that famous and worthy man Mr. John Robinson, who afterwards was their pastor for many years, till the Lord took him away by death. Also Mr. William Brewster[1] a reverend man, who afterwards was chosen an elder of the church and lived with them till old age.

But after these things they could not long continue in any peaceable condition, but were hunted and persecuted on every side, so as their former afflictions were but as flea-bitings in comparison of these which now came upon them. For some were taken and clapped up in prison, others had their houses beset and watched night and day, and hardly escaped their hands; and the most were fain to flee and leave their houses and habitations, and the means of their livelihood.

Yet these and many other sharper things which afterward befell them, were no other than they looked for, and therefore were the better prepared to bear them by the assistance of God's grace and Spirit.

7. From Emanuel van Meteren's *General History of the Netherlands* (1608). King James (1566–1625) ascended the throne in 1603. Most Puritans preferred the model of the Calvinist system in Geneva or the Church of Scotland, which replaced a hierarchy of archbishops, bishops, and priests with a national assembly and a parish presbytery consisting of ministers and elders. King Edward VI reigned from 1547 to 1553.
8. A solemn agreement between the members of a church to act together in harmony with the precepts of the Gospel. "Professors": believers.
9. The Netherlands. John Smith was a Cambridge University graduate who seceded from the Church of England in 1605.
1. A church leader of the Pilgrims in both Leyden and Plymouth (1576–1644). Richard Clyfton and John Robinson, Cambridge University graduates, were Separatists.

Yet seeing themselves thus molested, and that there was no hope of their continuance there, by a joint consent they resolved to go into the Low Countries, where they heard was freedom of religion for all men; as also how sundry from London and other parts of the land had been exiled and persecuted for the same cause, and were gone thither, and lived at Amsterdam and in other places of the land. So after they had continued together about a year, and kept their meetings every Sabbath in one place or other, exercising the worship of God amongst themselves, notwithstanding all the diligence and malice of their adversaries, they seeing they could no longer continue in that condition, they resolved to get over into Holland as they could. Which was in the year 1607 and 1608; of which more at large in the next chapter.

CHAPTER IV. SHOWING THE REASONS AND CAUSES OF THEIR REMOVAL

After they had lived in this city about some eleven or twelve years (which is the more observable being the whole time of that famous truce between that state and the Spaniards)[2] and sundry of them were taken away by death and many others began to be well stricken in years (the grave mistress of Experience having taught them many things), those prudent governors with sundry of the sagest members began both deeply to apprehend their present dangers and wisely to foresee the future and think of timely remedy. In the agitation of their thoughts, and much discourse of things hereabout, at length they began to incline to this conclusion: of removal to some other place. Not out of any newfangledness or other such like giddy humor by which men are oftentimes transported to their great hurt and danger, but for sundry weighty and solid reasons, some of the chief of which I will here briefly touch.

And first, they saw and found by experience the hardness of the place and country to be such as few in comparison would come to them, and fewer that would bide it out and continue with them. For many that came to them, and many more that desired to be with them, could not endure that great labor and hard fare, with other inconveniences which they underwent and were contented with. But though they loved their persons, approved their cause and honored their sufferings, yet they left them as it were weeping, as Orpah did her mother-in-law Naomi, or as those Romans did Cato[3] in Utica who desired to be excused and borne with, though they could not all be Catos. For many, though they desired to enjoy the ordinances of God in their purity and the liberty of the gospel with them, yet (alas) they admitted of bondage with danger of conscience, rather than to endure these hardships. Yea, some preferred and chose the prisons in England rather than this liberty in Holland with these afflictions. But it was thought that if a better and easier place of living could be had, it would draw many and take away these discouragements. Yea, their pastor would often say that many of those who both wrote and preached now against them, if they were in a place where they might have liberty and live comfortably, they would then practice as they did.

2. The struggle for independence by provinces of The Netherlands against Spain was interrupted by a twelve-year truce on March 30, 1609; that truce was now coming to a close. "This city": Leyden.
3. Roman statesman of unbending integrity who committed suicide in 46 B.C.E. when Julius Caesar's cause triumphed. Orpah was the sister-in-law of Ruth: "And they lifted up their voice, and wept again: and Orpah kissed her mother in law; but Ruth clave unto her" (Ruth 1.14).

Secondly. They saw that though the people generally bore all these difficulties very cheerfully and with a resolute courage, being in the best and strength of their years; yet old age began to steal on many of them; and their great and continual labors, with other crosses and sorrows, hastened in before the time. So as it was not only probably thought, but apparently seen, that within a few years more they would be in danger to scatter, by necessities pressing them, or sink under their burdens, or both. And therefore according to the divine proverb, that a wise man seeth the plague when it cometh, and hideth himself, Proverbs xxii.3, so they like skillful and beaten soldiers were fearful either to be entrapped or surrounded by their enemies so as they should neither be able to fight nor fly. And therefore thought it better to dislodge betimes to some place of better advantage and less danger, if any such could be found.

Thirdly. As necessity was a taskmaster over them so they were forced to be such, not only to their servants but in a sort to their dearest children, the which as it did not a little wound the tender hearts of many a loving father and mother, so it produced likewise sundry sad and sorrowful effects. For many of their children that were of best dispositions and gracious inclinations, having learned to bear the yoke in their youth[4] and willing to bear part of their parents' burden, were oftentimes so oppressed with their heavy labors that though their minds were free and willing, yet their bodies bowed under the weight of the same, and became decrepit in their early youth, the vigor of nature being consumed in the very bud as it were. But that which was more lamentable, and of all sorrows most heavy to be borne, was that many of their children, by these occasions and the great licentiousness of youth in that country,[5] and the manifold temptations of the place, were drawn away by evil examples into extravagant and dangerous courses, getting the reins off their necks and departing from their parents. Some became soldiers, others took upon them far voyages by sea, and others some worse courses tending to dissoluteness and the danger of their souls, to the great grief of their parents and dishonor of God. So that they saw their posterity would be in danger to degenerate and be corrupted.

Lastly (and which was not least), a great hope and inward zeal they had of laying some good foundation, or at least to make some way thereunto, for the propagating and advancing the gospel of the kingdom of Christ in those remote parts of the world; yea, though they should be but even as stepping-stones unto others for the performing of so great a work.

These and some other like reasons moved them to undertake this resolution of their removal; the which they afterward prosecuted with so great difficulties, as by the sequel will appear.

The place they had thoughts on was some of those vast and unpeopled countries of America, which are fruitful and fit for habitation, being devoid of all civil inhabitants, where there are only savage and brutish men which range up and down, little otherwise than the wild beasts of the same. This proposition being made public and coming to the scanning of all, it raised many variable opinions amongst men and caused many fears and doubts amongst themselves. Some, from their reasons and hopes conceived, labored

---

4. "It is good for a man that he bear the yoke in his youth" (Lamentations 3.27).
5. Morison notes that the Dutch did not keep the Sabbath Day in the strict sense that the English Puritans did.

to stir up and encourage the rest to undertake and prosecute the same; others again, out of their fears, objected against it and sought to divert from it; alleging many things, and those neither unreasonable nor unprobable; as that it was a great design and subject to many unconceivable perils and dangers; as, besides the casualties of the sea (which none can be freed from), the length of the voyage was such as the weak bodies of women and other persons worn out with age and travail (as many of them were) could never be able to endure. And yet if they should, the miseries of the land which they should be exposed unto, would be too hard to be borne and likely, some or all of them together, to consume and utterly to ruinate them. For there they should be liable to famine and nakedness and the want, in a manner, of all things. The change of air, diet and drinking of water would infect their bodies with sore sicknesses and grievous diseases. And also those which should escape or overcome these difficulties should yet be in continual danger of the savage people, who are cruel, barbarous and most treacherous, being most furious in their rage and merciless where they overcome; not being content only to kill and take away life, but delight to torment men in the most bloody manner that may be; flaying some alive with the shells of fishes, cutting off the members and joints of others by piecemeal and broiling on the coals, eat the collops[6] of their flesh in their sight whilst they live, with other cruelties horrible to be related.

And surely it could not be thought but the very hearing of these things could not but move the very bowels of men to grate within them and make the weak to quake and tremble. It was further objected that it would require greater sums of money to furnish such a voyage and to fit them with necessaries, than their consumed estates would amount to; and yet they must as well look to be seconded with supplies as presently to be transported. Also many precedents of ill success and lamentable miseries befallen others in the like designs were easy to be found, and not forgotten to be alleged; besides their own experience, in their former troubles and hardships in their removal into Holland, and how hard a thing it was for them to live in that strange place, though it was a neighbor country and a civil and rich commonwealth.

It was answered, that all great and honorable actions are accompanied with great difficulties and must be both enterprised and overcome with answerable courages. It was granted the dangers were great, but not desperate. The difficulties were many, but not invincible. For though there were many of them likely, yet they were not certain. It might be sundry of the things feared might never befall; others by provident care and the use of good means might in a great measure be prevented; and all of them, through the help of God, by fortitude and patience, might either be borne or overcome. True it was that such attempts were not to be made and undertaken without good ground and reason, not rashly or lightly as many have done for curiosity or hope of gain, etc. But their condition was not ordinary, their ends were good and honorable, their calling lawful and urgent; and therefore they might expect the blessing of God in their proceeding. Yea, though they should lose their lives in this action, yet might they have comfort in the same and their endeavors would be honorable. They lived here but as men in exile

6. Slices, portions.

and in a poor condition, and as great miseries might possibly befall them in this place; for the twelve years of truce were now out and there was nothing but beating of drums and preparing for war, the events whereof are always uncertain. The Spaniard might prove as cruel as the savages of America, and the famine and pestilence as sore here as there, and their liberty less to look out for remedy.

After many other particular things answered and alleged on both sides, it was fully concluded by the major part to put this design in execution and to prosecute it by the best means they could.

FROM CHAPTER VII. OF THEIR DEPARTURE FROM LEYDEN, AND OTHER THINGS THEREABOUT; WITH THEIR ARRIVAL AT SOUTHAMPTON, WHERE THEY ALL MET TOGETHER AND TOOK IN THEIR PROVISIONS

[MR. ROBINSON'S LETTER]

At length, after much travel and these debates, all things were got ready and provided. A small ship[7] was bought and fitted in Holland, which was intended as to serve to help to transport them, so to stay in the country and attend upon fishing and such other affairs as might be for the good and benefit of the colony when they came there. Another was hired at London, of burthen about 9 score,[8] and all other things got in readiness. So being ready to depart, they had a day of solemn humiliation, their pastor taking his text from Ezra viii.21: "And there at the river, by Ahava, I proclaimed a fast, that we might humble ourselves before our God, and seek of him a right way for us, and for our children, and for all our substance." Upon which he spent a good part of the day very profitably and suitable to their present occasion; the rest of the time was spent in pouring out prayers to the Lord with great fervency, mixed with abundance of tears. And the time being come that they must depart, they were accompanied with most of their brethren out of the city, unto a town sundry miles off called Delftshaven, where the ship lay ready to receive them. So they left that goodly and pleasant city which had been their resting place near twelve years; but they knew they were pilgrims,[9] and looked not much on those things, but lift up their eyes to the heavens, their dearest country, and quieted their spirits.

When they came to the place they found the ship and all things ready, and such of their friends could not come with them followed after them, and sundry also came from Amsterdam to see them shipped and to take their leave of them. That night was spent with little sleep by the most, but with friendly entertainment and Christian discourse and other real expressions of true Christian love. The next day (the wind being fair) they went aboard and their friends with them, where truly doleful was the sight of that sad and mournful parting, to see what sighs and sobs and prayers did sound amongst

7. "Of some 60 tun" [Bradford's note]. The Pilgrims left Amsterdam for Leyden because of disagreements "with the church that was there before them." They decided to leave The Netherlands for reasons Bradford cites in chapter 4 of book I: economic hardship, the availability of inexpensive land for farming, the fear that their children were becoming Hollanders rather than English, and the advancement of the Gospel.

8. The *Mayflower*, a ship weighing 180 tons.
9. "Hebrews xi.31–16" [Bradford's note]. "These all died in faith, not having received the promises, but having seen them afar off, and were persuaded of them and embraced them, and confessed that they were strangers and pilgrims on the earth." It was this passage that caused the *Mayflower* company to be known as Pilgrims.

them, what tears did gush from every eye, and pithy speeches pierced each heart; that sundry of the Dutch strangers that stood on the quay as spectators could not refrain from tears. Yet comfortable and sweet it was to see such lively and true expressions of dear and unfeigned love. But the tide, which stays for no man, calling them away that were thus loath to depart, their reverend pastor falling down on his knees (and they all with him) with watery cheeks commended them with most fervent prayers to the Lord and His blessing. And then with mutual embraces and many tears they took their leaves of one another, which proved to be the last leave to many of them.

* * *

At their parting Mr. Robinson writ a letter to the whole company; which though it hath already been printed;[1] yet I thought good here likewise to insert it. As also a brief letter writ at the same time to Mr. Carver,[2] in which the tender love and godly care of a true pastor appears.

MY DEAR BROTHER, I received enclosed in your last letter the note of information, which I shall carefully keep and make use of as there shall be occasion. I have a true feeling of your perplexity of mind and toil of body, but I hope that you who have always been able so plentifully to administer comfort unto others in their trials, are so well furnished for yourself, as that far greater difficulties than you have yet undergone (though I conceive them to have been great enough) cannot oppress you; though they press you, as the Apostle speaks.[3] The spirit of a man (sustained by the Spirit of God) will sustain his infirmity; I doubt not so will yours.[4] And the better much when you shall enjoy the presence and help of so many godly and wise brethren, for the bearing of the part of your burthen, who also will not admit into their hearts the least thought of suspicion of any the least negligence, at last presumption, to have been in you, whatsoever they think in others.

Now what shall I say or write unto you and your good wife my loving sister?[5] Even only this: I desire, and always shall unto you from the Lord, as unto my own soul. And assure yourself that my heart is with you, and that I will not forslow[6] my bodily coming at the first opportunity. I have written a large letter to the whole, and am sorry I shall not rather speak than write to them; and the more, considering the want of a preacher, which I shall also make some spur to my hastening after you. I do ever commend my best affection unto you, which if I thought you made any doubt of, I would express in more and the same more ample and full words.

And the Lord in whom you trust and whom you serve ever in this business and journey, guide you with His hand, protect you with His wing, and show

1. In *Mourt's Relation* (1622), an account of the first year of the plantation at Plymouth taken from the journals of Edward Winslow and William Bradford and brought to London for publication by Bradford's brother-in-law, George Mourt. Morison places the letters that follow in his appendix; we have restored them to their original position in the manuscript.
2. John Carver (c. 1576–1621) was the first governor of the colony.
3. "For we would not, brethren, have you ignorant of our trouble which came to us in Asia, that we were pressed out of measure, above strength, insomuch that we despaired even of life" (2 Corinthians 1.8); "And when Silas and Timotheus were come from Macedonia, Paul was pressed in the spirit, and testified to the Jews that Jesus was Christ" (Acts 18.5).
4. "Counsel is mine, and sound wisdom: I am understanding; I have strength" (Proverbs 8.14).
5. Mrs. Carver (d. 1621) was John Robinson's sister.
6. Delay.

you and us His salvation in the end, and bring us in the meanwhile together in this place desired, if such be His good will, for His Christ's sake. Amen.

Yours, etc.

July 27, 1620 JOHN ROBINSON

This was the last letter that Mr. Carver lived to see from him. The other follows:

LOVING AND CHRISTIAN FRIENDS, I do heartily and in the Lord salute you all as being they with whom I am present in my best affection, and most earnest longings after you. Though I be constrained for a while to be bodily absent from you. I say constrained, God knowing how willingly and much rather than otherwise, I would have borne my part with you in this first brunt, were I not by strong necessity held back for the present. Make account of me in the meanwhile as of a man divided in myself with great pain, and as (natural bonds set aside) having my better part with you. And though I doubt not but in your godly wisdoms you both foresee and resolve upon that which concernth your present state and condition, both severally and jointly, yet have I thought it but my duty to add some further spur of provocation unto them who run already; if not because you need it, yet because I owe it in love and duty. And first, as we are daily to renew our repentance with our God, especially for our sins known, and generally for our unknown trespasses; so doth the Lord call us in a singular manner upon occasions of such difficulty and danger as lieth upon you, to a both more narrow search and careful reformation of your ways in His sight; lest He, calling to remembrance our sins forgotten by us or unrepented of, take advantage against us, and in judgment leave us for the same to be swallowed up in one danger or other. Whereas, on the contrary, sin being taken away by earnest repentance and the pardon thereof from the Lord, sealed up unto a man's conscience by His Spirit, great shall be his security and peace in all dangers, sweet his comforts in all distresses, with happy deliverance from all evil, whether in life or in death.

Now, next after this heavenly peace with God and our own consciences, we are carefully to provide for peace with all men what in us lieth, especially with our associates. And for that, watchfulness must be had that we neither at all in ourselves do give, no, nor easily take offense being given by others. Woe be unto the world for offenses, for though it be necessary (considering the malice of Satan and man's corruption) that offenses come, yet woe unto the man, or woman either, by whom the offense cometh, saith Christ, Matthew xviii.7. And if offenses in the unseasonable use of things, in themselves indifferent, be more to be feared than death itself (as the Apostle teacheth, I Corinthians ix.15) how much more in things simply evil, in which neither honor of God nor love of man is thought worthy to be regarded. Neither yet is it sufficient that we keep ourselves by the grace of God from giving offense, except withal we be armed against the taking of them when they be given by others. For how unperfect and lame is the work of grace in that person who wants charity to cover a multitude of offenses, as the Scriptures speak![7]

Neither are you to be exhorted to this grace only upon the common

7. "And above all things have fervent charity among yourselves: for charity shall cover the multitude of sins" (1 Peter 4.8).

grounds of Christianity, which are, that persons ready to take offense either want[8] charity to cover offenses, or wisdom duly to weigh human frailty; or lastly, are gross, though close hypocrites as Christ our Lord teacheth (Matthew vii.1, 2, 3), as indeed in my own experience few or none have been found which sooner give offense than such as easily take it. Neither have they ever proved sound and profitable members in societies, which have nourished this touchy humor.

But besides these, there are divers motives provoking you above others to great care and conscience this way: As first, you are many of you strangers, as to the persons so to the infirmities one of another, and so stand in need of more watchfulness this way, lest when such things fall out in men and women as you suspected not, you be inordinately affected with them; which doth require at your hands much wisdom and charity for the covering and preventing of incident offenses that way. And, lastly, your intended course of civil community will minister continual occasion of offense, and will be as fuel for that fire, except you diligently quench it with brotherly forebearance. And if taking of offense causelessly or easily at men's doings be so carefully to be avoided, how much more heed is to be taken that we take not offense at God Himself, which yet we certainly do so for as we do murmur at His providence in our crosses, or bear impatiently such afflictions as wherewith He pleaseth to visit us. Store up, therefore, patience against that evil day, without which we take offense at the Lord Himself in His holy and just works.

A fourth thing there is carefully to be provided for, to wit, that with your common employments you join common affections truly bent upon the general good, avoiding as a deadly plague of your both common and special comfort all retiredness of mind for proper advantage, and all singularly affected any manner of way. Let every man repress in himself and the whole body in each person, as so many rebels against the common good, all private respects of men's selves, not sorting with the general coveniency. And as men are careful not to have a new house shaken with any violence before it be well settled and the parts firmly knit, so be you, I beseech you, brethren, much more careful that the house of God, which you are and are to be, be not shaken with unnecessary novelties or other oppositions at the first settling thereof.

Lastly, whereas you are become a body politic, using amongst yourselves civil government, and are not furnished with any persons of special eminency above the rest, to be chosen by you into office of government; let your wisdom and godliness appear, not only in choosing such persons as do entirely love and will promote the common good, but also in yielding unto them all due honor and obedience in their lawful administrations, not beholding in them the ordinariness of their persons, but God's ordinance for your good; not being like the foolish multitude who more honor the gay coat than either the virtuous mind of the man, or glorious ordinance of the Lord. But you know better things, and that the image of the Lord's power and authority which the magistrate beareth,[9] is honorable, in how mean persons soever. And this

8. Lack.
9. "For he is the minister of God to thee for good. But if thou do that which is evil, be afraid; for he beareth not the sword in vain: for he is the minister of God, a revenger to execute wrath upon him that doeth evil" (Romans 13.4). Morison notes that this passage "is sometimes said to have inspired the drafting of the Mayflower Compact."

duty you both may the more willingly and ought the more conscionably to perform, because you are at least for the present to have only them for your ordinary governors, which yourselves shall make choice of for that work.

Sundry other things of importance I could put you in mind of, and of those before mentioned in more words, but I will not so far wrong your godly minds as to think you heedless of these things, there being also divers among you so well able to admonish both themselves and others of what concerneth them. These few things, therefore, and the same in few words, I do earnestly commend unto your care and conscience, joining therewith my daily incessant prayers unto the Lord, that He who hath made the heavens and the earth, the sea and all rivers of waters, and whose providence is over all His works, especially over all His dear children for good, would so guide and guard you in your ways, as inwardly by His Spirit, so outwardly by the hand of His power, as that both you and we also, for and with you, may have after matter of praising His name all the days of your and our lives. Fare you well in Him whom you trust, and in whom I rest.

An unfeigned wellwiller of your happy success in this hopeful voyage,

JOHN ROBINSON

This letter, though large, yet being so fruitful in itself and suitable to their occasion, I thought meet to insert in this place.

All things being now ready, and every business dispatched, the company was called together and this letter read amongst them, which had good acceptation with all, and after fruit with many. Then they ordered and distributed their company for either ship, as they conceived for the best; and chose a Governor and two or three assistants for each ship, to order the people by the way, and see to the disposing of their provisions and such like affairs. All which was not only with the liking of the masters of the ships but according to their desires. Which being done, they set sail from thence about the 5th of August. But what befell them further upon the coast of England will appear in the next chapter.

CHAPTER IX. OF THEIR VOYAGE AND HOW THEY PASSED THE SEA; AND OF
THEIR SAFE ARRIVAL AT CAPE COD

September 6. These troubles[1] being blown over, and now all being compact together in one ship, they put to sea again with a prosperous wind, which continued divers days together, which was some encouragement unto them; yet, according to the usual manner, many were afflicted with seasickness. And I may not omit here a special work of God's providence. There was a proud and very profane young man, one of the seamen, of a lusty,[2] able body, which made him the more haughty; he would always be condemning the poor people in their sickness and cursing them daily with grievous execrations; and did not let[3] to tell them that he hoped to help to cast half of them overboard before they came to their journey's end, and to make merry with what they had; and if he were by any gently reproved, he would curse and

1. Some of the Scrooby community originally sailed from Delftshaven about August 1, 1620, on board the *Speedwell*, but it proved unseaworthy and it was necessary to transfer everything to the *Mayflower*.
2. Strong, energetic.
3. Hesitate.

swear most bitterly. But it pleased God before they came half seas over, to smite this young man with a grievous disease, of which he died in a desperate manner, and so was himself the first that was thrown overboard. Thus his curses light on his own head, and it was an astonishment to all his fellows for they noted it to be the just hand of God upon him.

After they had enjoyed fair winds and weather for a season, they were encountered many times with cross winds and met with many fierce storms with which the ship was shroudly[4] shaken, and her upper works made very leaky; and one of the main beams in the midships was bowed and cracked, which put them in some fear that the ship could not be able to perform the voyage. So some of the chief of the company, perceiving the mariners to fear the sufficiency of the ship as appeared by their mutterings, they entered into serious consultation with the master and other officers of the ship, to consider in time of the danger, and rather to return than to cast themselves into a desperate and inevitable peril. And truly there was great distraction and difference of opinion amongst the mariners themselves; fain would they do what could be done for their wages' sake (being now near half the seas over) and on the other hand they were loath to hazard their lives too desperately. But in examining of all opinions, the master and others affirmed they knew the ship to be strong and firm under water; and for the buckling of the main beam, there was a great iron screw the passengers brought out of Holland, which would raise the beam into his place; the which being done, the carpenter and master affirmed that with a post put under it, set firm in the lower deck and otherways bound, he would make it sufficient. And as for the decks and upper works, they would caulk them as well as they could, and though with the working of the ship they would not long keep staunch,[5] yet there would otherwise be no great danger, if they did not overpress her with sails. So they committed themselves to the will of God and resolved to proceed.

In sundry of these storms the winds were so fierce and the seas so high, as they could not bear a knot of sail, but were forced to hull[6] for divers days together. And in one of them, as they thus lay at hull in a mighty storm, a lusty young man called John Howland, coming upon some occasion above the gratings was, with a seele[7] of the ship, thrown into sea; but it pleased God that he caught hold of the topsail halyards which hung overboard and ran out at length. Yet he held his hold (though he was sundry fathoms under water) till he was hauled up by the same rope to the brim of the water, and then with a boat hook and other means got into the ship again and his life saved. And though he was something ill with it, yet he lived many years after and became a profitable member both in church and commonwealth. In all this voyage there died but one of the passengers, which was William Butten, a youth, servant to Samuel Fuller, when they drew near the coast.

But to omit other things (that I may be brief) after long beating at sea they fell with that land which is called Cape Cod; the which being made and certainly known to be it, they were not a little joyful. After some deliberation had amongst themselves and with the master of the ship, they tacked about and resolved to stand for the southward (the wind and weather being fair) to find some place about Hudson's River for their habitation. But after they

4. Shrewdly, in its original sense of wickedly.
5. Watertight.
6. Drift with the wind under short sail.
7. Roll.

had sailed that course about half the day, they fell amongst dangerous shoals and roaring breakers, and they were so far entangled therewith as they conceived themselves in great danger; and the wind shrinking upon them withal, they resolved to bear up again for the Cape and thought themselves happy to get out of those dangers before night overtook them, as by God's good providence they did. And the next day they got into the Cape Harbor[8] where they rid in safety.

A word or two by the way of this cape. It was thus first named by Captain Gosnold and his company, Anno[9] 1602, and after by Captain Smith was called Cape James; but it retains the former name amongst seamen. Also, that point which first showed those dangerous shoals unto them they called Point Care, and Tucker's Terror; but the French and Dutch to this day call it Malabar[1] by reason of those perilous shoals and the losses they have suffered there.

Being thus arrived in a good harbor, and brought safe to land, they fell upon their knees and blessed the God of Heaven who had brought them over the vast and furious ocean, and delivered them from all the perils and miseries thereof, again to set their feet on the firm and stable earth, their proper element. And no marvel if they were thus joyful, seeing wise Seneca was so affected with sailing a few miles on the coast of his own Italy, as he affirmed, that he had rather remain twenty years on his way by land than pass by sea to any place in a short time, so tedious and dreadful was the same unto him.[2]

But here I cannot but stay and make a pause, and stand half amazed at this poor people's present condition; and so I think will the reader, too, when he well considers the same. Being thus passed the vast ocean, and a sea of troubles before in their preparation (as may be remembered by that which went before), they had now no friends to welcome them nor inns to entertain or refresh their weatherbeaten bodies; no houses or much less towns to repair to, to seek for succor. It is recorded in Scripture as a mercy to the Apostle and his shipwrecked company, that the barbarians showed them no small kindness in refreshing them,[3] but these savage barbarians, when they met with them (as after will appear) were readier to fill their sides full of arrows than otherwise. And for the season it was winter, and they that know the winters of that country know them to be sharp and violent, and subject to cruel and fierce storms, dangerous to travel to known places, much more to search an unknown coast. Besides, what could they see but a hideous and desolate wilderness, full of wild beasts and wild men—and what multitudes there might be of them they knew not. Neither could they, as it were, go up to the top of Pisgah[4] to view from this wilderness a more goodly country to feed their hopes; for which way soever they turned their eyes (save upward to the heavens) they could have little solace or content in respect of any outward objects. For summer being done, all things stand upon them with a weatherbeaten face, and the whole country, full of woods and thickets, rep-

8. Cape Harbor is now Provincetown Harbor; they arrived on November 11, 1620, the journey from England having taken sixty-five days.
9. In the year (Latin).
1. The prefix *mal* means "bad"; the reference here is to the dangerous sandbars.
2. Bradford notes that this remark may be found in the *Moral Epistles to Lucilius*, line 5, of the Roman Stoic philosopher (4? B.C.E.–65 C.E.).

3. "And when they were escaped, then they knew that the island was called Melita. And the barbarous people showed us no little kindness: for they kindled a fire, and received us every one, because of the present rain, and because of the cold" (Acts 28.1–2).
4. Mountain from which Moses saw the Promised Land (Deuteronomy 34.1–4).

resented a wild and savage hue. If they looked behind them, there was the mighty ocean which they had passed and was now as a main bar and gulf to separate them from all the civil parts of the world. If it be said they had a ship to succor them, it is true; but what heard they daily from the master and company? But that with speed they should look out a place (with their shallop)[5] where they would be, at some near distance; for the season was such as he would not stir from thence till a safe harbor was discovered by them, where they would be, and he might go without danger; and that victuals consumed apace but he must and would keep sufficient for themselves and their return. Yea, it was muttered by some that if they got not a place in time, they would turn them and their goods ashore and leave them. Let it also be considered what weak hopes of supply and succor they left behind them, that might bear up their minds in this sad condition and trials they were under; and they could not but be very small. It is true, indeed, the affections and love of their brethren at Leyden[6] was cordial and entire toward them, but they had little power to help them or themselves; and how the case stood between them and the merchants at their coming away hath already been declared.

What could now sustain them but the Spirit of God and His grace? May not and ought not the children of these fathers rightly say "Our fathers were Englishmen which came over this great ocean, and were ready to perish in this wilderness; but they cried unto the Lord, and He heard their voice and looked on their adversity,"[7] etc. "Let them therefore praise the Lord, because He is good: and His mercies endure forever." "Yea, let them which have been redeemed of the Lord, show how He hath delivered them from the hand of the oppressor. When they wandered in the desert wilderness out of the way, and found no city to dwell in, both hungry and thirsty, their soul was overwhelmed in them. Let them confess before the Lord His loving kindness and His wonderful works before the sons of men."[8]

FROM CHAPTER X. SHOWING HOW THEY SOUGHT OUT A PLACE OF HABITATION; AND WHAT BEFELL THEM THEREABOUT

Being thus arrived at Cape Cod the 11th of November, and necessity calling them to look out a place for habitation (as well as the master's and mariners' importunity); they having brought a large shallop with them out of England, stowed in quarters in the ship, they now got her out and set their carpenters to work to trim her up; but being much bruised and shattered in the ship with foul weather, they saw she would be long in mending. Whereupon a few of them tendered themselves to go by land and discover those nearest places, whilst the shallop was in mending; and the rather because as they went into that harbor there seemed to be an opening some two or three leagues off, which the master judged to be a river.[9] It was

5. Small boat fitted with one or more masts.
6. In The Netherlands, where a substantial number of Separatists remained.
7. "And the Egyptians evil entreated us, and afflicted us, and laid upon us hard bondage: And when we cried unto the Lord God of our fathers, the Lord heard our voice, and looked on our affliction, and our labor and our oppression: And the Lord brought us forth out of Egypt with a mighty hand" (Deuteronomy 26.6–8).
8. "O give thanks unto the Lord, for he is good: for his mercy endureth for ever. Let the redeemed of the Lord say so, whom he hath redeemed from the hand of the enemy; And gathered them out of the lands, from the east, and from the west, from the north, and from the south" (Psalm 107.1–5).
9. Morison observes that "Looking south from Provincetown Harbor where the Pilgrims were, the high land near Plymouth looks like an island on clear days, suggesting that there is a river or arm of the sea between it and Cape Cod."

conceived there might be some danger in the attempt, yet seeing them resolute, they were permitted to go, being sixteen of them well armed under the conduct of Captain Standish,[1] having such instructions given them as was thought meet.

They set forth the 15th of November; and when they had marched about the space of a mile by the seaside, they espied five or six persons with a dog coming towards them, who were savages; but they fled from them and ran up into the woods, and the English followed them, partly to see if they could speak with them, and partly to discover if there might not be more of them lying in ambush. But the Indians seeing themselves thus followed, they again forsook the woods and ran away on the sands as hard[2] as they could, so as they could not come near them but followed them by the track of their feet sundry miles and saw that they had come the same way. So, night coming on, they made their rendezvous and set out their sentinels, and rested in quiet that night; and the next morning followed their track till they had headed a great creek and so left the sands, and turned another way into the woods. But they still followed them by guess, hoping to find their dwellings; but they soon lost both them and themselves, falling into such thickets as were ready to tear their clothes and armor in pieces; but were most distressed for want of drink. But at length they found water and refreshed themselves, being the first New England water they drunk of, and was now in their great thirst as pleasant unto them as wine or beer had been in foretimes.

Afterwards they directed their course to come to the other shore, for they knew it was a neck of land they were to cross over, and so at length got to the seaside and marched to this supposed river, and by the way found a pond[3] of clear fresh water, and shortly after a good quantity of clear ground where the Indians had formerly set corn, and some of their graves. And proceeding further they saw new stubble where corn had been set the same year; also they found where lately a house had been, where some planks and a great kettle was remaining, and heaps of sand newly paddled with their hands. Which, they digging up, found in them divers fair Indian baskets filled with corn, and some in ears, fair and good, of divers colors, which seemed to them a very goodly sight (having never seen any such before). This was near the place of that supposed river they came to seek, unto which they went and found it to open itself into two arms with a high cliff of sand in the entrance[4] but more like to be creeks of salt water than any fresh, for aught they saw; and that there was good harborage for their shallop, leaving it further to be discovered by their shallop, when she was ready. So, their time limited them being expired, they returned to the ship lest they should be in fear of their safety; and took with them part of the corn and buried up the rest. And so, like the men from Eshcol, carried with them of the fruits of the land and showed their brethren;[5] of which, and their return, they were marvelously glad and their hearts encouraged.

After this, the shallop being got ready, they set out again for the better discovery of this place, and the master of the ship desired to go himself. So

1. Myles Standish (1584?–1656) was a professional soldier who had fought in The Netherlands; he was not a Pilgrim.
2. Fast.
3. The pond from which Pond Village, Truro, Massachusetts, gets its name.

4. A salt creek known as Pamet River.
5. In Numbers 13.23–26, Moses' scouts, after searching the wilderness for forty days, brought back clusters of grapes, which they found near the brook that they called "Eshcol."

there went some thirty men but found it to be no harbor for ships but only for boats. There was also found two of their houses covered with mats, and sundry of their implements in them, but the people were run away and could not be seen.[6] Also there was found more of their corn and of their beans of various colors; the corn and beans they brought away, purposing to give them full satisfaction when they should meet with any of them as, about some six months afterward they did, to their good content.

And here is to be noted a special providence of God, and a great mercy to this poor people, that here they got seed to plant them corn the next year, or else they might have starved, for they had none nor any likelihood to get any till the season had been past, as the sequel did manifest. Neither is it likely they had had this, if the first voyage had not been made, for the ground was now all covered with snow and hard frozen; but the Lord is never wanting unto His in their greatest needs; let His holy name have all the praise.

The month of November being spent in these affairs, and much foul weather falling in, the 6th of December they sent out their shallop again with ten of their principal men and some seamen, upon further discovery, intending to circulate that deep bay of Cape Cod. The weather was very cold and it froze so hard as the spray of the sea lighting on their coats, they were as if they had been glazed. Yet that night betimes they got down into the bottom of the bay, and as they drew near the shore[7] they saw some ten or twelve Indians very busy about something. They landed about a league or two from them, and had much ado to put ashore anywhere—it lay so full of flats. Being landed, it grew late and they made themselves a barricado with logs and boughs as well as they could in the time, and set out their sentinel and betook them to rest, and saw the smoke of the fire the savages made that night. When morning was come they divided their company, some to coast along the shore in the boat, and the rest marched through the woods to see the land, if any fit place might be for their dwelling. They came also to the place where they saw the Indians the night before, and found they had been cutting up a great fish like a grampus,[8] being some two inches thick of fat like a hog, some pieces whereof they had left by the way. And the shallop found two more of these fishes dead on the sands, a thing usual after storms in that place, by reason of the great flats of sand that lie off.

So they ranged up and down all that day, but found no people, nor any place they liked. When the sun grew low, they hasted out of the woods to meet with their shallop, to whom they made signs to come to them into a creek[9] hard by, the which they did at high water; of which they were very glad, for they had not seen each other all that day since the morning. So they made them a barricado as usually they did every night, with logs, stakes and thick pine boughs, the height of a man, leaving it open to leeward, partly to shelter them from the cold and wind (making their fire in the middle and lying round about it) and partly to defend them from any sudden assaults of the savages, if they should surround them; so being very weary, they betook them to rest. But about midnight they heard a hideous and great cry, and their sentinel called "Arm! arm!" So they bestirred them and stood to their

6. Descendants of these Nauset Indians may still be found today at Mashpee on Cape Cod.
7. Somewhere near Eastham, Massachusetts.

8. Probably a blackfish (*Globicephala melæna*).
9. The mouth of Herring River in Eastham.

arms and shot off a couple of muskets, and then the noise ceased. They concluded it was a company of wolves or such like wild beasts, for one of the seamen told them he had often heard such a noise in Newfoundland.

So they rested till about five of the clock in the morning; for the tide, and their purpose to go from thence, made them be stirring betimes. So after prayer they prepared for breakfast, and it being day dawning it was thought best to be carrying things down to the boat. But some said it was not best to carry the arms down, others said they would be the readier, for they had lapped them up in their coats from the dew; but some three or four would not carry theirs till they went themselves. Yet as it fell out, the water being not high enough, they laid them down on the bank side and came up to breakfast.

But presently, all on the sudden, they heard a great and strange cry, which they knew to be the same voices they heard in the night, though they varied their notes; and one of their company being abroad came running in and cried, "Men, Indians! Indians!" And withal, their arrows came flying amongst them. Their men ran with all speed to recover their arms, as by the good providence of God they did. In the meantime, of those that were there ready, two muskets were discharged at them, and two more stood ready in the entrance of their rendezvous but were commanded not to shoot till they could take full aim at them. And the other two charged again with all speed, for there were only four had arms there, and defended the barricado, which was first assaulted. The cry of the Indians was dreadful, especially when they saw the men run out of the rendezvous toward the shallop to recover their arms, the Indians wheeling about upon them. But some running out with coats of mail on, and cutlasses in their hands, they soon got their arms and let fly amongst them and quickly stopped their violence. Yet there was a lusty man, and no less valiant, stood behind a tree within half a musket shot, and let his arrows fly at them; he was seen [to] shoot three arrows, which were all avoided. He stood three shots of a musket, till one taking full aim at him and made the bark or splinters of the tree fly about his ears, after which he gave an extraordinary shriek and away they went, all of them. They[1] left some to keep the shallop and followed them about a quarter of a mile and shouted once or twice, and shot off two or three pieces, and so returned. This they did that they might conceive that they were not afraid of them or any way discouraged.

Thus it pleased God to vanquish their enemies and give them deliverance; and by His special providence so to dispose that not any one of them were either hurt or hit, though their arrows came close by them and on every side [of] them; and sundry of their coats, which hung up in the barricado, were shot through and through. Afterwards they gave God solemn thanks and praise for their deliverance, and gathered up a bundle of their arrows and sent them into England afterward by the master of the ship, and called that place the First Encounter.

From hence they departed and coasted all along but discerned no place likely for harbor; and therefore hasted to a place that their pilot (one Mr. Coppin who had been in the country before) did assure them was a good harbor, which he had been in, and they might fetch it before night; of which they were glad for it began to be foul weather.

---

1. I.e., the English.

After some hours' sailing it began to snow and rain, and about the middle of the afternoon the wind increased and the sea became very rough, and they broke their rudder, and it was as much as two men could do to steer her with a couple of oars. But their pilot bade them be of good cheer for he saw the harbor; but the storm increasing, and night drawing on, they bore what sail they could to get in, while they could see. But herewith they broke their mast in three pieces and their sail fell overboard in a very grown sea, so as they had like to have been cast away. Yet by God's mercy they recovered themselves, and having the flood[2] with them, struck into the harbor. But when it came to, the pilot was deceived in the place, and said the Lord be merciful unto them for his eyes never saw that place before; and he and the master's mate would have run her ashore in a cove full of breakers before the wind. But a lusty seaman which steered bade those which rowed, if they were men, about with her or else they were all cast away; the which they did with speed. So he bid them be of good cheer and row lustily, for there was a fair sound before them, and he doubted not but they should find one place or other where they might ride in safety. And though it was very dark and rained sore, yet in the end they got under the lee of a small island and remained there all that night in safety. But they knew not this to be an island till morning, but were divided in their minds; some would keep the boat for fear they might be amongst the Indians, others were so wet and cold they could not endure but got ashore, and with much ado got fire (all things being so wet); and the rest were glad to come to them, for after midnight, the wind shifted to the northwest and it froze hard.

But though this had been a day and night of much trouble and danger unto them, yet God gave them a morning of comfort and refreshing (as usually He doth to His children) for the next day was a fair, sunshining day, and they found themselves to be on an island secure from the Indians, where they might dry their stuff, fix their pieces[3] and rest themselves; and gave God thanks for His mercies in their manifold deliverances. And this being the last day of the week, they prepared there to keep the Sabbath.

On Monday they sounded the harbor and found it fit for shipping, and marched into the land and found divers cornfields and little running brooks, a place (as they supposed) fit for situation.[4] At least it was the best they could find, and the season and their present necessity made them glad to accept of it. So they returned to their ship again with this news to the rest of their people, which did much comfort their hearts.

On the 15th of December they weighed anchor to go to the place they had discovered, and came within two leagues of it, but were fain to bear up again; but the 16th day, the wind came fair, and they arrived safe in this harbor. And afterwards took better view of the place, and resolved where to pitch their dwelling; and the 25th day began to erect the first house for common use to receive them and their goods.

2. I.e., the flood tide.
3. Armaments.
4. Morison notes that this is "the only contemporary authority for the 'Landing of the Pilgrims at Plymouth Rock' on December 21, 1620" (New Style). "Sounded": measured the depth of.

Book II

FROM CHAPTER XI.[1] THE REMAINDER OF ANNO 1620

[THE MAYFLOWER COMPACT]

I shall a little return back, and begin with a combination[2] made by them before they came ashore; being the first foundation of their government in this place. Occasioned partly by the discontented and mutinous speeches that some of the strangers[3] amongst them had let fall from them in the ship: That when they came ashore they would use their own liberty, for none had power to command them, the patent they had being for Virginia and not for New England, which belonged to another government, with which the Virginia Company had nothing to do. And partly that such an act by them done, this their condition considered, might be as firm as any patent,[4] and in some respects more sure. The form was as followeth:

IN THE NAME OF GOD, AMEN.

We whose names are underwritten, the loyal subjects of our dread Sovereign Lord King James, by the Grace of God of Great Britain, France, and Ireland King, Defender of the Faith, etc.

Having undertaken, for the Glory of God and advancement of the Christian Faith and Honor of our King and Country, a Voyage to plant the First Colony in the Northern Parts of Virginia, do by these presents solemnly and mutually in the presence of God and one of another, Covenant and Combine ourselves together into a Civil Body Politic, for our better ordering and preservation and furtherance of the ends aforesaid; and by virtue hereof to enact, constitute and frame such just and equal Laws, Ordinances, Acts, Constitutions and Offices, from time to time, as shall be thought most meet and convenient for the general good of the Colony, unto which we promise all due submission and obedience. In witness whereof we have hereunder subscribed our names at Cape Cod, the 11th of November, in the year of the reign of our Sovereign Lord King James, of England, France and Ireland the eighteenth, and of Scotland the fifty-fourth. Anno Domini[5] 1620.

After this they chose, or rather confirmed, Mr. John Carver[6] (a man godly and well approved amongst them) their Governor for that year. And after they had provided a place for their goods, or common store (which were long in unlading[7] for want of boats, foulness of the winter weather and sickness of divers) and begun some small cottages for their habitation; as time would admit, they met and consulted of laws and orders, both for their civil and military government as the necessity of their condition did require, still adding there unto as urgent occasion in several times, and as cases did require.

In these hard and difficult beginnings they found some discontents and

1. Bradford numbered only the first ten chapters of his manuscript.
2. A form of union, a joining together.
3. Puritans called themselves "saints" and those outside their church "strangers." Many of those who came to Plymouth with them were not church members but adventurers looking forward to business success and making new lives in the New World.

4. A document signed by a sovereign granting privileges to those named in it.
5. In the year of the Lord (Latin).
6. Carver, like Bradford, was an original member of the group who went to Holland and, like Bradford, a tradesman. Bradford was elected governor after Carver's death.
7. Unloading.

murmurings arise amongst some, and mutinous speeches and carriages in other; but they were soon quelled and overcome by the wisdom, patience, and just and equal carriage of things, by the Governor and better part, which clave[8] faithfully together in the main.

[THE STARVING TIME]

But that which was most sad and lamentable was, that in two or three months' time half of their company died, especially in January and February, being the depth of winter, and wanting houses and other comforts; being infected with the scurvy and other diseases which this long voyage and their inaccommodate condition had brought upon them. So as there died some times two or three of a day in the foresaid time, that of 100 and odd persons, scarce fifty remained. And of these, in the time of most distress, there was but six or seven persons who to their great commendations, be it spoken, spared no pains night nor day, but with abundance of toil and hazard of their own health, fetched them wood, made them fires, dressed them meat, made their beds, washed their loathsome clothes, clothed and unclothed them. In a word, did all the homely[9] and necessary offices for them which dainty and queasy stomachs cannot endure to hear named; and all this willingly and cheerfully, without any grudging in the least, showing herein their true love unto their friends and brethren; a rare example and worthy to be remembered. Two of these seven were Mr. William Brewster, their reverend Elder, and Myles Standish, their Captain and military commander, unto whom myself and many others were much beholden in our low and sick condition. And yet the Lord so upheld these persons as in this general calamity they were not at all infected either with sickness or lameness. And what I have said of these I may say of many others who died in this general visitation, and others yet living; that whilst they had health, yea, or any strength continuing, they were not wanting[1] to any that had need of them. And I doubt not but their recompense is with the Lord.

But I may not here pass by another remarkable passage not to be forgotten. As this calamity fell among the passengers that were to be left here to plant, and were hasted ashore and made to drink water that the seamen might have the more beer, and one[2] in his sickness desiring but a small can of beer, it was answered that if he were their own father he should have none. The disease began to fall amongst them also, so as almost half of their company died before they went away, and many of their officers and lustiest men, as the boatswain, gunner, three quartermasters, the cook and others. At which the Master was something strucken and sent to the sick ashore and told the Governor he should send for beer for them that had need of it, though he drunk water homeward bound.

But now amongst his company there was far another kind of carriage in this misery than amongst the passengers. For they that before had been boon companions in drinking and jollity in the time of their health and welfare, began now to desert one another in this calamity, saying they would not hazard their lives for them, they should be infected by coming to help them

8. Past tense of *cleave*.
9. Intimate.
1. Lacking in attention.

2. Which was this author himself [Bradford's note].

in their cabins; and so, after they came to lie by it, would do little or nothing for them but, "if they died, let them die." But such of the passengers as were yet aboard showed them what mercy they could, which made some of their hearts relent, as the boatswain (and some others) who was a proud young man and would often curse and scoff at the passengers. But when he grew weak, they had compassion on him and helped him; then he confessed he did not deserve it at their hands, he had abused them in word and deed. "Oh!" (saith he) "you, I now see, show your love like Christians indeed one to another, but we let one another lie and die like dogs." Another lay cursing his wife, saying if it had not been for her he had never come this unlucky voyage, and anon cursing his fellows, saying he had done this and that for some of them; he had spent so much and so much amongst them, and they were now weary of him and did not help him, having need. Another gave his companion all he had, if he died, to help him in his weakness; he went and got a little spice and made him a mess of meat once or twice. And because he died not so soon as he expected, he went amongst his fellows and swore the rogue would cozen[3] him, he would see him choked before he made him any more meat; and yet the poor fellow died before morning.

[INDIAN RELATIONS]

All this while the Indians came skulking about them, and would sometimes show themselves aloof off, but when any approached near them, they would run away; and once they stole away their tools where they had been at work and were gone to dinner. But about the 16th of March, a certain Indian came boldly amongst them and spoke to them in broken English, which they could well understand but marveled at it.[4] At length they understood by discourse with him, that he was not of these parts, but belonged to the eastern parts where some English ships came to fish, with whom he was acquainted and could name sundry of them by their names, amongst whom he had got his language. He became profitable to them in acquainting them with many things concerning the state of the country in the east parts where he lived, which was afterwards profitable unto them; as also of the people here, of their names, number and strength, of their situation and distance from this place, and who was chief amongst them. His name was Samoset. He told them also of another Indian whose name was Squanto, a native of this place, who had been in England and could speak better English than himself.

Being, after some time of entertainment and gifts dismissed, a while after he came again, and five more with him, and they brought again all the tools that were stolen away before, and made way for the coming of their great Sachem, called Massasoit. Who, about four or five days after, came with the chief of his friends and other attendance, with the aforesaid Squanto. With whom, after friendly entertainment and some gifts given him, they made a peace with him (which hath now continued this 24 years)[5] in these terms:

1. That neither he nor any of his should injure or do hurt to any of their people.

3. Cheat.
4. Samoset was an Algonquin sagamore of Pemaquid Point, Maine, a region much frequented by English fishermen. He probably shipped with Captain Dermer from Monhegan to Cape Cod shortly before the Pilgrims landed and worked his way overland to Plymouth [Morison's note].
5. Morison notes that this passage "dates Bradford's writing of this chapter not earlier than 1644."

2. That if any of his did hurt to any of theirs, he should send the offender, that they might punish him.

3. That if anything were taken away from any of theirs, he should cause it to be restored; and they should do the like to his.

4. If any did unjustly war against him, they would aid him; if any did war against them, he should aid them.

5. He should send to his neighbors confederates to certify them of this, that they might not wrong them, but might be likewise comprised in the conditions of peace.

6. That when their men came to them, they should leave their bows and arrows behind them.

After these things he returned to his place called Sowams, some 40 miles from this place, but Squanto continued with them and was their interpreter and was a special instrument sent of God for their good beyond their expectation. He directed them how to set their corn, where to take fish, and to procure other commodities, and was also their pilot to bring them to unknown places for their profit, and never left them till he died. He was a native of this place, and scarce any left alive besides himself. He was carried away with divers others by one Hunt, a master of a ship, who thought to sell them for slaves in Spain. But he got away for England and was entertained by a merchant in London, and employed to Newfoundland and other parts, and lastly brought hither into these parts by one Mr. Dermer, a gentleman employed by Sir Ferdinando Gorges and others for discovery and other designs in these parts. Of whom I shall say something, because it is mentioned in a book set forth Anno 1622 by the President and Council for New England,[6] that he made the peace between the savages of these parts and the English, of which this plantation, as it is intimated, had the benefit; but what a peace it was may appear by what befell him and his men.

This Mr. Dermer was here the same year that these people came, as appears by a relation written by him and given me by a friend, bearing date June 30, Anno 1620. And they came in November following, so there was but four months difference. In which relation to his honored friend, he hath these passages of this very place:

I will first begin (saith he) with that place from whence Squanto or Tisquantum, was taken away; which in Captain Smith's map[7] is called Plymouth; and I would that Plymouth had the like commodities. I would that the first plantation might here be seated, if there come to the number of 50 persons, or upward. Otherwise, Charlton,[8] because there the savages are less to be feared. The Pocanockets,[9] which live to the west of Plymouth, bear an inveterate malice to the English, and are of more strength than all the savages from thence to Penobscot. Their desire of revenge was occasioned by an Englishman, who having many of them on board, made a greater slaughter with their murderers[1] and small shot when as (they say) they offered no injury on their parts. Whether they

6. Bradford is referring to Sir Ferdinando Gorges (c. 1566–1647), whose *A Briefe Relation of the Discovery and Plantation of New England* was published in 1622.
7. Captain John Smith (1580–1631) published his *Description of New England* in 1616, following his 1614 voyage. Tisquantum is Squanto's Indian name.
8. Near the mouth of the Charles River.
9. Identical to the Wampanoags, the tribe of Massasoit. Samoset was an Algonquin.
1. Small cannons.

were English or no it may be doubted; yet they believe they were, for the French have so possessed them. For which cause Squanto cannot deny but they would have killed me when I was at Namasket, had he not entreated hard for me.

The soil of the borders of this great bay may be compared to most of the plantations which I have seen in Virginia. The land is of divers sorts, for Patuxet is a hardy but strong soil; Nauset and Satucket are for the most part a blackish and deep mould much like that where groweth the best tobacco in Virginia.[2] In the bottom of that great bay is store of cod and bass or mullet, etc. But above all he commends Pocanocket for the richest soil, and much open ground fit for English grain, etc.

Massachusetts is about nine leagues from Plymouth, and situated in the midst between both, is full of islands and peninsulas, very fertile for the most part.

With sundry such relations which I forbear to transcribe, being now better known than they were to him.

He was taken prisoner by the Indians at Manamoyick,[3] a place not far from hence, now well known. He gave them what they demanded for his liberty, but when they had got what they desired, they kept him still, and endeavored to kill his men. But he was freed by seizing on some of them and kept them bound till they gave him a canoe's load of corn. Of which, see *Purchas*, lib. 9, fol. 1778.[4] But this was Anno 1619.

After the writing of the former relation, he came to the Isle of Capawack[5] (which lies south of this place in the way to Virginia) and the aforesaid Squanto with him, where he going ashore amongst the Indians to trade, as he used to do, was betrayed and assaulted by them, and all his men slain, but one that kept the boat. But himself got aboard very sore wounded, and they had cut off his head upon the cuddy of the boat, had not the man rescued him with a sword. And so they got away and made shift to get into Virginia where he died, whether of his wounds or the diseases of the country, or both together, is uncertain. By all which it may appear how far these people were from peace, and with what danger this plantation was begun, save as the powerful hand of the Lord did protect them.

These things were partly the reason why they[6] kept aloof and were so long before they came to the English. Another reason as after themselves made known was how about three years before, a French ship was cast away at Cape Cod, but the men got ashore and saved their lives, and much of their victuals and other goods. But after the Indians heard of it, they gathered together from these parts and never left watching and dogging them till they got advantage and killed them all but three or four which they kept, and sent from one sachem to another to make sport with, and used them worse than

2. Morison notes that Dermer's description of the soil of Cape Cod would not accurately describe the soil today. Patuxet ("at the little falls") was the Indian name for the site of Plymouth. Nauset, named for the Indian tribe, was near present-day Eastham. Satucket ("near the mouth of the stream") was a Nauset village close to the town of Brewster.
3. Or Monomoit, once a harbor near Pleasant Bay in contemporary Orleans and Harwich.
4. Samuel Purchas (1577–1626) was an English clergyman and compiler of travel literature, famous for his publication of the papers of Richard Hakluyt (c. 1552–1616) in four volumes in 1625. Bradford's reference is to volume 4, book 9, p. 1778 of *Purchase His Pilgrimes*. "Lib.": abbreviation for *liber*, or "book" (Latin). "Fol.": abbreviation for *folio*, or "sheet" (Latin).
5. Martha's Vineyard.
6. The Indians.

slaves. Of which the aforesaid Mr. Dermer redeemed two of them; and they conceived this ship[7] was now come to revenge it.

Also, as after was made known, before they came to the English to make friendship, they got all the Powachs[8] of the country, for three days together in a horrid and devilish manner, to curse and execrate them with their conjurations, which assembly and service they held in a dark and dismal swamp.

But to return. The spring now approaching, it pleased God the mortality began to cease amongst them, and the sick and lame recovered apace, which put as [it] were new life into them, though they had borne their sad affliction with much patience and contentedness as I think any people could do. But it was the Lord which upheld them, and had beforehand prepared them; many having long borne the yoke, yea from their youth. Many other smaller matters I omit, sundry of them having been already published in a journal made by one of the company,[9] and some other passages of journeys and relations already published, to which I refer those that are willing to know them more particularly.

And being now come to the 25th of March, I shall begin the year 1621.

FROM CHAPTER XII. ANNO 1621

* * *

[FIRST THANKSGIVING]

They began now to gather in the small harvest they had, and to fit up their houses and dwellings against winter, being all well recovered in health and strength and had all things in good plenty. For as some were thus employed in affairs abroad, others were exercised in fishing, about cod and bass and other fish, of which they took good store, of which every family had their portion. All the summer there was no want;[1] and now began to come in store of fowl, as winter approached, of which this place did abound when they came first (but afterward decreased by degrees). And besides waterfowl there was great store of wild turkeys, of which they took many, besides venison, etc. Besides they had about a peck a meal a week to a person, or now since harvest, Indian corn to that proportion. Which made many afterwards write so largely of their plenty here to their friends in England, which were not feigned but true reports.

FROM CHAPTER XIX. ANNO DOM: 1628

* * *

[THOMAS MORTON OF MERRYMOUNT][2]

About some three or four years before this time, there came over one Captain Wollaston (a man of pretty parts[3]) and with him three or four more

---

7. I.e., the *Mayflower*.
8. Medicine men.
9. *Mourt's Relation* (1622). See n. 1, p. 163.
1. Lack.
2. Almost nothing is known of either Thomas Morton or Captain Wollaston other than what Bradford tells us. By all accounts Morton left England with a bad reputation and a history of

unrest behind him. Unlike the Puritans, however, Morton relished the sensuality of the wild and took great pleasure in the American landscape. Bradford tells us that Morton did not think that "in all the world it could be paralleled" for its plenitude and beauty.
3. I.e., of a clever nature.

of some eminency, who brought with them a great many servants, with provisions and other implements for to begin a plantation. And pitched themselves in a place within the Massachusetts which they called after their Captain's name, Mount Wollaston. Amongst whom was one Mr. Morton, who it should seem had some small adventure of his own or other men's amongst them, but had little respect amongst them, and was slighted by the meanest servants. Having continued there some time, and not finding things to answer their expectations nor profit to arise as they looked for, Captain Wollaston takes a great part of the servants[4] and transports them to Virginia, where he puts them off at good rates, selling their time to other men; and writes back to one Mr. Rasdall (one of his chief partners and accounted their merchant) to bring another part of them to Virginia likewise, intending to put them off there as he had done the rest. And he, with the consent of the said Rasdall, appointed one Fitcher to be his Lieutenant and govern the remains of the Plantation till he or Rasdall returned to take further order thereabout. But this Morton abovesaid, having more craft than honesty (who had been a kind of pettifogger of Furnival's Inn) in the others' absence watches an opportunity (commons being but hard amongst them)[5] and got some strong drink and other junkets[6] and made them a feast; and after they were merry, he began to tell them he would give them good counsel. "You see," saith he, "that many of your fellows are carried to Virginia, and if you stay till this Rasdall return, you will also be carried away and sold for slaves with the rest. Therefore I would advise you to thrust out this Lieutenant Fitcher, and I, having a part in the Plantation, will receive you as my partners and consociates; so may you be free from service, and we will converse, plant, trade, and live together as equals and support and protect one another," or to like effect. This counsel was easily received, so they took opportunity and thrust Lieutenant Fitcher out o' doors, and would suffer him to come no more amongst them, but forced him to seek bread to eat and other relief from his neighbors till he could get passage for England.

After this they fell to great licentiousness and led a dissolute life, pouring out themselves into all profaneness. And Morton became Lord of Misrule,[7] and maintained (as it were) a School of Atheism. And after they had got some goods into their hands, and got much by trading with the Indians, they spent it as vainly in quaffing and drinking, both wine and strong waters in great excess (and, as some reported) £10 worth in a morning. They also set up a maypole, drinking and dancing about it many days together, inviting the Indian women for their consorts, dancing and frisking together like so many fairies, or furies, rather; and worse practices. As if they had anew revived and celebrated the feasts of the Roman goddess Flora, or the beastly practices of the mad Bacchanalians.[8] Morton likewise, to show his poetry composed sundry rhymes and verses, some tending to lasciviousness, and

4. A servant was anyone who worked for another in agriculture or domestic economy. An indentured servant was one who agreed to work for another for seven years to pay for transportation to the New World.
5. I.e., there were few responsible citizens among them. "Pettifogger": a shifty lawyer. Furnival's Inn was a lawyers' building in the city of London.
6. Delicacies; food for banqueting.
7. One who presides over games and revels, usually at Christmastime in a great person's house; here one who presides over revelry and licentiousness.
8. At the Bacchanalia, or revels in honor of Bacchus (god of wine), frenzied worshipers drank, danced, and even tore apart wild animals and devoured them. Flora was the Roman goddess of flowers and vegetation whose cult was celebrated with highly indecent farces.

others to the detraction and scandal of some persons, which he affixed to this idle or idol maypole. They changed also the name of their place, and instead of calling it Mount Wollaston they call it Merry-mount, as if this jollity would have lasted ever. But this continued not long, for after Morton was sent for England (as follows to be declared) shortly after came over that worthy gentleman Mr. John Endicott, who brought over a patent under the broad seal for the government of the Massachusetts. Who, visiting those parts, caused that maypole to be cut down and rebuked them for the profaneness and admonished them to look there should be better walking. So they or others now changed the name of their place again and called it Mount Dagon.[9]

Now to maintain this riotous prodigality and profuse excess, Morton, thinking himself lawless, and hearing what gain the French and fishermen made by trading of pieces,[1] powder and shot to the Indians, he as the head of this consortship began the practice of the same in these parts. And first he taught them how to use them, to charge and discharge, and what proportion of powder to give the piece, according to the size or bigness of the same; and what shot to use for fowl and what for deer. And having thus instructed them, he employed some of them to hunt and fowl for him, so as they became far more active in that employment than any of the English, by reason of their swiftness of foot and nimbleness of body, being also quick-sighted and by continual exercise well knowing the haunts of all sorts of game. So as when they saw the execution that a piece would do, and the benefit that might come by the same, they became mad (as it were) after them and would not stick to give any price they could attain to for them; accounting their bows and arrows but baubles in comparison of them.

*　　*　　*

This Morton having thus taught them the use of pieces, he sold them all he could spare, and he and his consorts determined to send for many out of England and had by some of the ships sent for above a score. The which being known, and his neighbors meeting the Indians in the woods armed with guns in this sort, it was a terror unto them who lived stragglingly[2] and were of no strength in any place. And other places (though more remote) saw this mischief would quickly spread over all, if not prevented. Besides, they saw they should keep no servants, for Morton would entertain any, how vile soever, and all the scum of the country or any discontents would flock to him from all places, if this nest was not broken. And they should stand in more fear of their lives and goods in short time from this wicked and debased crew than from the savages themselves.

So sundry of the chief of the straggling plantations, meeting together, agreed by mutual consent to solicit those of Plymouth (who were then of more strength than them all) to join with them to prevent the further growth of this mischief, and suppress Morton and his consorts before they grew to further head and strength. Those that joined in this action, and after contributed to the charge of sending him for England, were from Piscataqua,

9. Named after the god of the Philistines: "Then the lords of the Philistines gathered them together for to offer a great sacrifice unto Dagon their god, and to rejoice: for they said, Our god hath delivered Samson our enemy into our hand" (Judges 16.23).
1. Guns.
2. Spread out in a scattered fashion; far apart.

Naumkeag, Winnisimmet, Wessagusset, Nantasket and other places where any English were seated. Those of Plymouth being thus sought to by their messengers and letters, and weighing both their reasons and the common danger, were willing to afford them their help though themselves had least cause of fear or hurt. So, to be short, they first resolved jointly to write to him, and in a friendly and neighborly way to admonish him to forbear those courses, and sent a messenger with their letters to bring his answer.

But he was so high as he scorned all advice, and asked who had to do with him, he had and would trade pieces with the Indians, in despite of all, with many other scurrilous terms full of disdain. They sent to him a second time and bade him be better advised and more temperate in his terms, for the country could not bear the injury he did. It was against their common safety and against the King's proclamation. He answered in high terms as before; and that the King's proclamation was no law, demanding what penalty was upon it. It was answered, more than he could bear—His Majesty's displeasure. But insolently he persisted and said the King was dead and his displeasure with him, and many the like things. And threatened withal that if any came to molest him, let them look to themselves for he would prepare for them.

Upon which they saw there was no way but to take him by force; and having so far proceeded, now to give over would make him far more haughty and insolent. So they mutually resolved to proceed, and obtained of the Governor of Plymouth to send Captain Standish and some other aid with him, to take Morton by force. The which accordingly was done. But they found him to stand stiffly in his defense, having made fast his doors, armed his consorts, set divers dishes of powder and bullets ready on the table; and if they had not been over-armed with drink, more hurt might have been done. They summoned him to yield, but he kept his house and they could get nothing but scoffs and scorns from him. But at length, fearing they would do some violence to the house, he and some of his crew came out, but not to yield but to shoot; but they were so steeled[3] with drink as their pieces were too heavy for them. Himself with a carbine, overcharged and almost half filled with powder and shot, as was after found, had thought to have shot Captain Standish; but he stepped to him and put by his piece and took them. Neither was there any hurt done to any of either side, save that one was so drunk that he ran his own nose upon the point of a sword that one held before him, as he entered the house; but he lost but a little of his hot blood.[4]

Morton they brought away to Plymouth, where he was kept till a ship went from the Isle of Shoals for England, with which he was sent to the Council of New England, and letters written to give them information of his course and carriage. And also one was sent at their common charge to inform their Honors more particularly and to prosecute against him. But he fooled of the messenger, after he was gone from hence, and though he went for England yet nothing was done to him, not so much as rebuked, for aught was heard, but returned the next year. Some of the worst of the company were dispersed

3. Insensible.
4. Morton refers to Captain Standish in his *New English Canaan* (1637) as "Captain Shrimp," and tells us that it would have been easy for him to destroy these nine "worthies" like a "flock of wild geese" but that he loathed violence and asked for his freedom to leave. He suggests that he was treated brutally because the Puritans wished to shame him before the Nausets.

and some of the more modest kept the house till he should be heard from. But I have been too long about so unworthy a person, and bad a cause.

FROM CHAPTER XXIII. ANNO DOM: 1632

* * *

[PROSPERITY BRINGS DISPERSAL OF POPULATION]

Also the people of the Plantation began to grow in their outward estates, by reason of the flowing of many people into the country, especially into the Bay of the Massachusetts. By which means corn and cattle rose to a great price, by which many were much enriched and commodities grew plentiful. And yet in other regards this benefit turned to their hurt, and this accession of strength to their weakness. For now as their stocks increased and the increase vendible,[5] there was no longer any holding them together, but now they must of necessity go to their great lots. They could not otherwise keep their cattle, and having oxen grown they must have land for plowing and tillage. And no man now thought he could live except he had cattle and a great deal of ground to keep them, all striving to increase their stocks. By which means they were scattered all over the Bay quickly and the town in which they lived compactly till now was left very thin and in a short time almost desolate.

And if this had been all, it had been less, though too much; but the church must also be divided, and those that had lived so long together in Christian and comfortable fellowship must now part and suffer many divisions. First, those that lived on their lots on the other side of the Bay, called Duxbury, they could not long bring their wives and children to the public worship and church meetings here, but with such burthen as, growing to some competent number, they sued to be dismissed and become a body of themselves. And so they were dismissed about this time, though very unwillingly. But to touch this sad matter, and handle things together that fell out afterward; to prevent any further scattering from this place and weakening of the same, it was thought best to give out some good farms to special persons that would promise to live at Plymouth, and likely to be helpful to the church or commonwealth, and so tie the lands to Plymouth as farms for the same; and there they might keep their cattle and tillage by some servants and retain their dwellings here. And so some special lands were granted at a place general called Green's Harbor, where no allotments had been in the former division, a place very well meadowed and fit to keep and rear cattle good store. But alas, this remedy proved worse than the disease; for within a few years those that had thus got footing there rent themselves away, partly by force and partly wearing the rest with importunity and pleas of necessity, so as they must either suffer them to go or live in continual opposition and contention. And other still, as they conceived themselves straitened[6] or to want accommodation, broke away under one pretence or other, thinking their own conceived necessity and the example of others a warrant sufficient for them. And this I fear will be the ruin of New England, at least of the churches of God there, and will provoke the Lord's displeasure against them.

* * *

5. Saleable.   6. Financially hampered.

FROM CHAPTER XXV. ANNO DOM: 1634

* * *

[CAPTAIN STONE, THE DUTCH, AND THE CONNECTICUT INDIANS]

This year in the forepart of the same they sent forth a bark to trade at the Dutch plantation, and they met there with one Captain Stone that had lived in Christopher's, one of the West India Islands, and now had been some time in Virginia and came from thence into these parts.[7] He kept company with the Dutch Governor and I know not in what drunken fit he got leave of the Governor to seize on their[8] bark when they were ready to come away and had done their market, having to the value of £500 worth of goods aboard her. Having no occasion at all, or any color of ground for such a thing, but having made the Governor drunk so as he could scarce speak a right word, and when he urged him hereabout, he answered him, *Als't u beleeft.*[9] So he gat aboard, the chief of their men and merchant being ashore, and with some of his own men made the rest of theirs weigh anchor, set sail and carry her away towards Virginia. But divers of the Dutch seamen which had been often at Plymouth and kindly entertained there, said one to another, "Shall we suffer our friends to be thus abused and have their goods carried away before our faces, whilst our Governor is drunk?" They vowed they would never suffer it and so got a vessel or two and pursued him and brought him in again and delivered them their bark and goods again.

Afterwards Stone came into the Massachusetts and they sent and commenced suit against him for this fact; but by mediation of friends it was taken up and the suit let fall. And in the company of some other gentlemen Stone came afterwards to Plymouth and had friendly and civil entertainment amongst them with the rest. But revenge boiled within his breast (though concealed) for some conceived he had a purpose at one time to have stabbed the Governor, and put his hand to his dagger for that end; but by God's providence and the vigilance of some, was prevented.

He afterward returned to Virginia in a pinnace with one Captain Norton and some others, and, I know not for what occasion, they would needs go up Connecticut River. And how they carried themselves I know not, but the Indians knocked him[1] in the head as he lay in his cabin, and had thrown the covering over his face, whether out of fear or desperation is uncertain. This was his end; they likewise killed all the rest, but Captain Norton defended himself a long time against them all in the cook room, till by accident the gunpowder took fire which for readiness he had set in an open thing before him, which did so burn and scald him and blind his eyes as he could make no longer resistance but was slain also by them, though they much commended his valor. And having killed the men, they made a prey of what they had, and chaffered away some of their things to the Dutch that lived there. But it was not long before a quarrel fell between the Dutch and them, and they would have cut off their bark, but they slew the chief sachem with the shot of a murderer.

---

7. Morison notes that Captain John Stone was an English trader carrying cattle from Virginia to Boston. He put in at New Amsterdam for water.
8. I.e., Plymouth Plantation's ship.
9. As you please (Dutch).

1. I.e., Captain Stone. Morison notes, "This murder, and the clumsy attempt of the English to punish the Indian culprits, eventually led to the Pequot War."

I am now to relate some strange and remarkable passages. There was a company of people lived in the country up above in the River of Connecticut a great way from their trading house there, and were enemies to those Indians which lived about them, and of whom they stood in some fear, being a stout people. About a thousand of them had enclosed themselves in a fort which they had strongly palisadoed about. Three or four Dutchmen went up in the beginning of winter to live with them, to get their trade and prevent them for bringing it to the English or to fall into amity with them; but at spring to bring all down to their place. But their enterprise failed. For it pleased God to visit these Indians with a great sickness and such a mortality that of a thousand, above nine and a half hundred of them died, and many of them did rot above ground for want of burial. And the Dutchmen almost starved before they could get away, for ice and snow; but about February they got with much difficulty to their trading house; whom they kindly relieved, being almost spent with hunger and cold. Being thus refreshed by them divers days, they got to their own place and the Dutch were very thankful for this kindness.

This spring also, those Indians that lived about their trading house there,[2] fell sick of the small pox and died most miserably; for a sorer disease cannot befall them, they fear it more than the plague. For usually they that have this disease have them in abundance, and for want of bedding and linen and other helps they fall into a lamentable condition as they lie on their hard mats, the pox breaking and mattering and running one into another, their skin cleaving by reason thereof to the mats they lie on. When they turn them, a whole side will flay off at once as it were, and they will be all of a gore blood, most fearful to behold. And then being very sore, what with cold and other distempers, they die like rotten sheep. The condition of this people was so lamentable and they fell down so generally of this disease as they were in the end not able to help one another, no not to make a fire nor to fetch a little water to drink, nor any to bury the dead. But would strive as long as they could, and when they could procure no other means to make fire, they would burn the wooden trays and dishes they ate their meat in, and their very bows and arrows. And some would crawl out on all fours to get a little water, and sometimes die by the way and not be able to get in again. But of those of the English house, though at first they were afraid of the infection, yet seeing their woeful and sad condition and hearing their pitiful cries and lamentations, they had compassion of them, and daily fetched them wood and water and made them fires, got them victuals whilst they lived; and buried them when they died. For very few of them escaped, notwithstanding they did what they could for them to the hazard of themselves. The chief sachem himself now died and almost all his friends and kindred. But by the marvelous goodness and providence of God, not one of the English was so much as sick or in the least measure tainted with this disease, though they daily did these offices for them for many weeks together. And this mercy which they showed them was kindly taken and thankfully acknowledged of all the Indians that knew or heard of the same. And their masters here did much commend and reward them for the same.

2. The Plymouth trading house at Windsor.

FROM CHAPTER XXVII. ANNO DOM: 1636

* * *

[WAR THREATENED WITH THE PEQUOTS]

In the year 1634 the Pequots (a stout and warlike people) who had made wars with sundry of their neighbors and, puffed up with many victories, grew now at variance with the Narragansetts, a great people bordering upon them there. These Narragansetts held correspondence and terms of friendship with the English of the Massachusetts. Now the Pequots, being conscious of the guilt of Captain Stone's death, whom they knew to be an Englishman, as also those that were with him, and being fallen out with the Dutch, lest they should have overmany enemies at once, sought to make friendship with the English of the Massachusetts. And for that end sent both messengers and gifts unto them, as appears by some letters sent from the Governor hither.

DEAR AND WORTHY SIR, etc. To let you know somewhat of our affairs, you may understand that the Pequots have sent some of theirs to us, to desire our friendship, and offered much wampum and beaver, etc. The first messengers were dismissed without answer. With the next we had divers[3] days' conference; and taking the advice of some of our ministers and seeking the Lord in it, we concluded a peace and friendship with them, upon these conditions: That they should deliver up to us those men who were guilty of Stone's death, etc. And if we desired to plant in Connecticut, they should give up their right to us, and so we would send to trade with them as our friends—which was the chief thing we aimed at, [they] being now in war with the Dutch and the rest of their neighbors.

To this they readily agreed, and that we should mediate a peace between them and the Narragansetts, for which end they were content we should give the Narragansetts part of that present they would bestow on us. For they stood so much on their honor as they would not be seen to give anything of themselves. As for Captain Stone, they told us there were but two left of those who had any hand in his death, and that they killed him in a just quarrel. For, say they, he surprised two of our men and bound them to make them by force to show him the way up the river;[4] and he with two other coming on shore, nine Indians watched him, and when they were asleep in the night, they killed them to deliver their own men. And some of them going afterwards to the pinnace, it was suddenly blown up. We are now preparing to send a pinnace unto them, etc.

In another of his, dated the 12th of the first month, he hath this:

Our pinnace is lately returned from the Pequots; they put off but little commodity, and found them a very false people, so as they mean to have no more to do with them. I have divers other things to write unto you, etc.

Yours ever assured,

Boston, 12 of the 1st month, 1634[5]   JOHN WINTHROP

---

3. Several.
4. There is little trust to be given to their relations
in these things [Bradford's note].
5. I.e., March 12, 1635.

After these things, and as I take this year, John Oldham (of whom much is spoken before) being now an inhabitant of the Massachusetts, went with a small vessel and slenderly manned a-trading into these south parts, and upon a quarrel between him and the Indians, was cut off by them (as hath been before noted) at an island called by the Indians Munisses, but since by the English, Block Island. This, with the former about the death of Stone, and the baffling[6] of the Pequots with the English of the Massachusetts, moved them to set out some to take revenge and require satisfaction for these wrongs. But it was done so superficially, and without their acquainting those of Connecticut and other neighbors with the same, as they did little good, but their neighbors had more hurt done. For some of the murderers of Oldham fled to the Pequots, and though the English went to the Pequots and had some parley with them, yet they did but delude them, and the English returned without doing anything to purpose, being frustrate of their opportunity by the others' deceit.[7]

After the English were returned, the Pequots took their time and opportunity to cut off some of the English as they passed in boats and went on fowling, and assaulted them the next spring at their habitations, as will appear in its place. I do but touch these things, because I make no question they will be more fully and distinctly handled by themselves who had more exact knowledge of them and whom they did more properly concern.

*   *   *

FROM CHAPTER XXVIII. ANNO DOM: 1637

[THE PEQUOT WAR]

In the fore part of this year, the Pequots fell openly upon the English at Connecticut, in the lower parts of the river, and slew sundry of them as they were at work in the fields, both men and women, to the great terror of the rest, and went away in great pride and triumph, with many high threats. They also assaulted a fort at the river's mouth, though strong and well defended; and though they did not there prevail, yet it struck them with much fear and astonishment to see their bold attempts in the face of danger. Which made them in all places to stand upon their guard and to prepare for resistance, and earnestly to solicit their friends and confederates in the Bay of Massachusetts to send them speedy aid, for they looked for more forcible assaults. Mr. Vane, being then Governor, writ from their General Court to them here to join with them in this war. To which they were cordially willing, but took opportunity to write to them about some former things, as well as present, considerable hereabout. The which will best appear in the Governor's answer, which he returned to the same, which I shall here insert.

*   *   *

In the meantime, the Pequots, especially in the winter before, sought to make peace with the Narragansetts, and used very pernicious arguments to move them thereunto: as that the English were strangers and began to overspread their country, and would deprive them thereof in time, if they were

---

6. Frustration.
7. Bradford is referring to an expedition under

John Endecott. Morison notes that it did nothing other than "stir up the Pequots."

suffered to grow and increase. And if the Narragansetts did assist the English to subdue them, they did but make way for their own overthrow, for if they were rooted out, the English would soon take occasion to subjugate them. And if they would hearken to them they should not need to fear the strength of the English, for they would not come to open battle with them but fire their houses, kill their cattle, and lie in ambush for them as they went abroad upon their occasions; and all this they might easily do without any or little danger to themselves. The which course being held, they well saw the English could not long subsist but they would either be starved with hunger or be forced to forsake the country. With many the like things; insomuch that the Narragansetts were once wavering and were half minded to have made peace with them, and joined against the English. But again, when they considered how much wrong they had received from the Pequots, and what an opportunity they now had by the help of the English to right themselves; revenge was so sweet unto them as it prevailed above all the rest, so as they resolved to join with the English against them, and did.

The Court here agreed forthwith to send fifty men at their own charge; and with as much speed as possibly they could, got them armed and had made them ready under sufficient leaders, and provided a bark to carry them provisions and tend upon them for all occasions. But when they were ready to march, with a supply from the Bay, they had word to stay; for the enemy was as good as vanquished and there would be no need.

I shall not take upon me exactly to describe their proceedings in these things, because I expect it will be fully done by themselves who best know the carriage and circumstances of things. I shall therefore but touch them in general. From Connecticut, who were most sensible of the hurt sustained and the present danger, they set out a party of men, and another party met them from the Bay, at Narragansetts', who were to join with them. The Narragansetts were earnest to be gone before the English were well rested and refreshed, especially some of them which came last. It should seem their desire was to come upon the enemy suddenly and undiscovered. There was a bark of this place, newly put in there, which was come from Connecticut, who did encourage them to lay hold of the Indians' forwardness, and to show as great forwardness as they, for it would encourage them, and expedition might prove to their great advantage. So they went on, and so ordered their march as the Indians brought them to a fort[8] of the enemy's (in which most of their chief men were) before day. They approached the same with great silence and surrounded it both with English and Indians, that they might not break out; and so assaulted them with great courage, shooting amongst them, and entered the fort with all speed. And those that first entered found sharp resistance from the enemy who both shot at and grappled with them; others ran into their houses and brought out fire and set them on fire, which soon took in their mat; and standing close together, with the wind all was quickly on a flame, and thereby more were burnt to death than was otherwise slain. It burnt their bowstrings and made them unserviceable; those that scaped the fire were slain with the sword, some hewed to pieces, others run through with their rapiers, so as they were quickly dispatched and very few escaped. It was conceived they thus destroyed about 400 at this time. It was

---

8. Mystic Fort on the Mystic River.

a fearful sight to see them thus frying in the fire and the streams of blood quenching the same, and horrible was the stink and scent thereof; but the victory seemed a sweet sacrifice,[9] and they gave the praise thereof to God, who had wrought so wonderfully for them, thus to enclose their enemies in their hands and give them so speedy a victory over so proud and insulting an enemy.

The Narragansett Indians all this while stood round about, but aloof from all danger and left the whole execution to the English, except it were the stopping of any that broke away. Insulting over their enemies in this their ruin and misery, when they saw them dancing in the flames, calling them by a word in their own language, signifying "O brave Pequots!" which they used familiarly among themselves in their own praise in songs of triumph after their victories. After this service was thus happily accomplished, they marched to the waterside where they met with some of their vessels, by which they had refreshing with victuals and other necessaries. But in their march the rest of the Pequots drew into a body and accosted them, thinking to have some advantage against them by reason of a neck of land. But when they saw the English prepare for them they kept aloof, so as they neither did hurt nor could receive any.

After their refreshing, and repair together for further counsel and directions, they resolved to pursue their victory and follow the war against the rest. But the Narragansett Indians, most of them, forsook them, and such of them as they had with them for guides or otherwise, they found them very cold and backward in the business, either out of envy, or that they saw the English would make more profit of the victory than they were willing they should; or else deprive them of such advantage as themselves desired, by having them become tributaries unto them, or the like.

For the rest of this business, I shall only relate the same as it is in a letter which came from Mr. Winthrop to the Governor here, as followeth.

* * *

That I may make an end of this matter, this Sassacus[1] (the Pequots' chief sachem) being fled to the Mohawks, they cut off his head, with some other of the chief of them, whether to satisfy the English or rather the Narragansetts (who, as I have since heard, hired them to do it) or for their own advantage, I well know not; but thus this war took end. The rest of the Pequots were wholly driven from their place, and some of them submitted themselves to the Narragansetts and lived under them. Others of them betook themselves to the Mohegans under Uncas, their sachem, with the approbation of the English of Connecticut, under whose protection Uncas lived; and he and his men had been faithful to them in this war and done them very good service. But this did so vex the Narragansetts, that they had not the whole sway over them, as they have never ceased plotting and contriving how to bring them under; and because they cannot attain their ends, because of the

9. "And he shall bring it to Aaron's sons the priests: and he shall take thereout his handful of the flour thereof, and of the oil thereof, with all the frankincense thereof; and the priest shall burn the memorial of it upon the altar, to be an offering made by fire, of a sweet savour unto the Lord" (Leviticus 2.2).

1. Reportedly seventy-seven years old at the time of this war, he was the most powerful sachem in southern New England.

English who have protected them, they have sought to raise a general conspiracy against the English, as will appear in another place.

* * *

FROM CHAPTER XXXII. ANNO DOM: 1642

* * *

[A HORRIBLE CASE OF BESTIALITY]

And after the time of the writing of these things befell a very sad accident of the like foul nature in this government, this very year, which I shall now relate. There was a youth whose name was Thomas Granger. He was servant to an honest man of Duxbury, being about 16 or 17 years of age. (His father and mother lived at the same time at Scituate.) He was this year detected of buggery, and indicted for the same, with a mare, a cow, two goats, five sheep, two calves and a turkey. Horrible it is to mention, but the truth of the history requires it. He was first discovered by one that accidentally saw his lewd practice towards the mare. (I forbear particulars.) Being upon it examined and committed, in the end he not only confessed the fact with that beast at that time, but sundry times before and at several times with all the rest of the forenamed in his indictment. And this his free confession was not only in private to the magistrates (though at first he strived to deny it) but to sundry, both ministers and others; and afterwards, upon his indictment, to the whole Court and jury; and confirmed it at his execution. And whereas some of the sheep could not so well be known by his description of them, others with them were brought before him and he declared which were they and which were not. And accordingly he was cast by the jury and condemned, and after executed about the 8th of September, 1642. A very sad spectacle it was. For first the mare and then the cow and the rest of the lesser cattle were killed before his face, according to the law, Leviticus xx.15,[2] and then he himself was executed. The cattle were all cast into a great and large pit that was digged of purpose for them, and no use made of any part of them.

Upon the examination of this person and also of a former that had made some sodomitical attempts upon another, it being demanded of them how they came first to the knowledge and practice of such wickedness, the one confessed he had long used it in old England; and this youth last spoken of said he was taught it by another that had heard of such things from some in England when he was there, and they kept cattle together. By which it appears how one wicked person may infect many, and what care all ought to have what servants they bring into their families.

But it may be demanded how came it to pass that so many wicked persons and profane people should so quickly come over into this land and mix themselves amongst them? Seeing it was religious men that began the work and they came for religion's sake? I confess this may be marveled at, at least in time to come, when the reasons thereof should not be known; and the more because here was so many hardships and wants met withal. I shall therefore endeavor to give some answer hereunto.

2. "And if a man lie with a beast, he shall surely be put to death: and ye shall slay the beast."

1. And first, according to that in the gospel, it is ever to be remembered that where the Lord begins to sow good seed, there the envious man will endeavor to sow tares.[3]

2. Men being to come over into a wilderness, in which much labor and service was to be done about building and planting, etc., such as wanted help in that respect, when they could not have such as they would, were glad to take such as they could; and so, many untoward servants, sundry of them proved, that were thus brought over, both men and womenkind who, when their times were expired, became families of themselves, which gave increase hereunto.

3. Another and a main reason hereof was that men, finding so many godly disposed persons willing to come into these parts, some began to make a trade of it, to transport passengers and their goods, and hired ships for that end. And then, to make up their freight and advance their profit, cared not who the persons were, so they had money to pay them. And by this means the country became pestered with many unworthy persons who, being come over, crept into one place or other.

4. Again, the Lord's blessing usually following His people as well in outward as spiritual things (though afflictions be mixed withal) do make many to adhere to the People of God, as many followed Christ for the loaves' sake (John vi.26) and a "mixed multitude" came into the wilderness with the People of God out of Egypt of old (Exodus xii.38).[4] So also there were sent by their friends, some under hope that they would be made better; others that they might be eased of such burthens, and they kept from shame at home, that would necessarily follow their dissolute courses. And thus, by one means or other, in 20 years' time it is a question whether the greater part be not grown the worser?

FROM CHAPTER XXXIII. ANNO DOM: 1643

[THE LIFE AND DEATH OF ELDER BREWSTER]

I am to begin this year with that which was a matter of great sadness and mourning unto them all. About the 18th of April died their Reverend Elder and my dear and loving friend Mr. William Brewster, a man that had done and suffered much for the Lord Jesus and the gospel's sake, and had borne his part in weal and woe with this poor persecuted church above 36 years in England, Holland and in this wilderness, and done the Lord and them faithful service in his place and calling. And notwithstanding the many troubles and sorrows he passed through, the Lord upheld him to a great age. He was near fourscore years of age[5] (if not all out) when he died. He had this blessing added by the Lord to all the rest; to die in his bed, in peace, amongst the midst of his friends, who mourned and wept over him and ministered what help and comfort they could unto him, and he again recomforted them whilst he could. His sickness was not long, and till the last day thereof he did not

---

3. Weedy plants that grow in grainfields. "But while men slept, his enemy came and sowed tares among the wheat, and went his way" (Matthew 13.25).
4. Exodus 12.38: "And a mixed multitude went up also with them; and flocks, and herds, even very

much cattle." John 6.26:"Jesus answered them and said, 'Verily, verily, I say unto you, Ye seek me, not because ye saw the miracles, but because ye did eat of the loaves' " that Christ had miraculously multiplied to feed five thousand.
5. Brewster was born in England in 1567.

wholly keep his bed. His speech continued till somewhat more than half a day, and then failed him, and about nine or ten a clock that evening he died without any pangs at all. A few hours before, he drew his breath short, and some few minutes before his last, he drew his breath long as a man fallen into a sound sleep without any pangs or gaspings, and so sweetly departed this life unto a better.

I would now demand of any, what he was the worse for any former sufferings? What do I say, worse? Nay, sure he was the better, and they now added to his honor. "It is a manifest token," saith the Apostle, 2 Thessalonians i.5, 6, 7, "of the righteous judgment of God that ye may be counted worthy of the kingdom of God, for which ye also suffer; seeing it is a righteous thing with God to recompense tribulation to them that trouble you; and to you who are troubled, rest with us, when the Lord Jesus shall be revealed from heaven, with his mighty angels." 1 Peter iv.14: "If you be reproached for the name of Christ, happy are ye, for the spirit of glory and a God resteth upon you."

What though he wanted[6] the riches and pleasure of the world in his life, and pompous monuments at his funeral? Yet "the memorial of the just shall be blessed, when the name of the wicked shall rot" (with their marble monuments). Proverbs x.7.

I should say something of his life, if to say a little were not worse than to be silent. But I cannot wholly forbear, though happily more may be done hereafter. After he had attained some learning, viz. the knowledge of the Latin tongue and some insight in the Greek, and spent some small time at Cambridge, and then being first seasoned with the seeds of grace and virtue, he went to the Court and served that religious and godly gentleman Mr. Davison, divers[7] years when he was Secretary of State. Who found him so discreet and faithful as he trusted him above all other that were about him, and only employed him in all matters of greatest trust and secrecy; he esteemed him rather as a son than a servant, and for his wisdom and godliness, in private he would converse with him more like a friend and familiar than a master. He attended his master when he was sent in ambassage by the Queen into the Low Countries, in the Earl of Leicester's time, as for other weighty affairs of state; so to receive possession of the cautionary towns,[8] and in token and sign thereof the keys of Flushing being delivered to him in Her Majesty's name, he kept them some time and committed them to this his servant who kept them under his pillow, on which he slept the first night. And at his return the States[9] honored him with a gold chain and his master committed it to him and commanded him to wear it when they arrived in England, as they rid through the country, till they came to the Court. He afterwards remained with him till his troubles, that he was put from his place about the death of the Queen of Scots;[1] and some good time after doing him many faithful offices of service in the time of his troubles. Afterwards he went and lived in the country, in good esteem amongst his friends and the gentlemen of those parts, especially the godly and religious.

He did much good in the country where he lived in promoting and furthering religion, not only by his practice and example, and provoking and encouraging of others, but by procuring of good preachers to the places

6. Lacked.
7. Several.
8. Towns pledged as security by treaty.

9. The States General, the two-chamber legislative body of Holland.
1. In 1587.

thereabout and drawing on of others to assist and help forward in such a work. He himself most commonly deepest in the charge, and sometimes above his ability. And in this state he continued many years, doing the best good he could and walking according to the light he saw, till the Lord revealed further unto him. And in the end, by the tyranny of the bishops against godly preachers and people in silencing the one and persecuting the other, he and many more of those times began to look further into things and to see into the unlawfulness of their callings, and the burthen of many antichristian corruptions, which both he and they endeavored to cast off; as they also did as in the beginning of this treatise is to be seen.

After they were joined together in communion, he was a special stay and help unto them. They ordinarily met at his house on the Lord's Day (which was a manor of the bishop's) and with great love he entertained them when they came, making provision for them to his great charge, and continued so to do whilst they could stay in England. And when they were to remove out of the country he was one of the first in all adventures, and forwardest in any charge. He was the chief of those that were taken at Boston,[2] and suffered the greatest loss, and of the seven that were kept longest in prison and after bound over to the assizes.[3] After he came into Holland he suffered much hardship after he had spent the most of his means, having a great charge and many children; and in regard of his former breeding and course of life, not so fit for many employments as others were, especially such as were toilsome and laborious. But yet he ever bore his condition with much cheerfulness and contentation.

Towards the latter part of those twelve years spent in Holland, his outward condition was mended, and he lived well and plentifully; for he fell into a way (by reason he had the Latin tongue) to teach many students who had a desire to learn the English tongue, to teach them English; and by his method they quickly attained it with great facility, for he drew rules to learn it by after the Latin manner. And many gentlemen, both Danes and German, resorted to him as they had time from other studies, some of them being great men's sons. He also had means to set up printing by the help of some friends, and so had employment enough, and by reason of many books which would not be allowed to be printed in England, they might have had more than they could do.

But now removing into this country all these things were laid aside again, and a new course of living must be framed unto, in which he was no way unwilling to take his part, and to bear his burthen with the rest, living many times without bread or corn many months together, having many times nothing but fish and often wanting that also; and drunk nothing but water for many years together, yea till within five or six years of his death. And yet he lived by the blessing of God in health till very old age. And besides that, he would labor with his hands in the fields as long as he was able. Yet when the church had no other minister, he taught twice every Sabbath, and that both powerfully and profitably, to the great contentment of the hearers and their comfortable edification; yea, many were brought to God by his ministry. He did more in this behalf in a year than many that have their hundreds a year do in all their lives.

For his personal abilities, he was qualified above many. He was wise and

2. In England.   3. I.e., made to await trial.

discreet and well spoken, having a grave and deliberate utterance, of a very cheerful spirit, very sociable and pleasant amongst his friends, of an humble and modest mind, of a peaceable disposition, undervaluing himself and his own abilities and sometime overvaluing others. Inoffensive and innocent in his life and conversation, which gained him the love of those without as well as those within; yet he would tell them plainly of their faults and evils, both publicly and privately, but in such a manner as usually was well taken from him. He was tenderhearted and compassionate of such as were in misery, but especially of such as had been of good estate and rank and were fallen unto want and poverty either for goodness and religion's sake or by the injury and oppression of others; he would say of all men these deserved to be pitied most. And none did more offend and displease him than such as would haughtily and proudly carry and lift up themselves, being risen from nothing and having little else in them to commend them but a few fine clothes or a little riches more than others.

In teaching, he was very moving and stirring of affections,[4] also very plain and distinct in what he taught; by which means he became the more profitable to the hearers. He had a singular good gift in prayer, both public and private, in ripping up the heart and conscience before God in the humble confession of sin, and begging the mercies of God in Christ for the pardon of the same. He always thought it were better for ministers to pray oftener and divide their prayers, than be long and tedious in the same, except upon solemn and special occasions as in days of humiliation and the like. His reason was that the heart and spirits of all, especially the weak, could hardly continue and stand bent as it were so long towards God as they ought to do in that duty, without flagging and falling off.

For the government of the church, which was most proper to his office, he was careful to preserve good order in the same, and to preserve purity both in the doctrine and communion of the same, and to suppress any error or contention that might begin to rise up amongst them. And accordingly God gave good success to his endeavors herein all his days, and he saw the fruit of his labors in that behalf. But I must break off, having only thus touched a few, as it were, heads of things.

[LONGEVITY OF THE PILGRIM FATHERS]

I cannot but here take occasion not only to mention but greatly to admire the marvelous providence of God! That notwithstanding the many changes and hardships that these people went through, and the many enemies they had and difficulties they met withal, that so many of them should live to very old age! It was not only this reverend man's condition (for one swallow makes no summer as they say) but many more of them did the like, some dying about and before this time and many still living, who attained to sixty years of age, and to sixty-five, divers to seventy and above, and some near eighty as he did. It must needs be more than ordinary and above natural reason, that so it should be. For it is found in experience that change of air, famine or unwholesome food, much drinking of water, sorrows and troubles, etc., all of them are enemies to health, causes of many diseases, consumers of natural vigor and the bodies of men, and shorteners of life. And yet of all

4. Religious feelings.

these things they had a large part and suffered deeply in the same. They went from England to Holland, where they found both worse air and diet than that they came from; from thence, enduring a long imprisonment as it were in the ships at sea, into New England; and how it hath been with them here hath already been shown, and what crosses, troubles, fears, wants and sorrows they had been liable unto is easy to conjecture. So as in some sort they may say with the Apostle, 2 Corinthians xi.26, 27, they were "in journeyings often, in perils of waters, in perils of robbers, in perils of their own nation, in perils among the heathen, in perils in the wilderness, in perils in the sea, in perils among false brethren; in weariness and painfulness, in watching often, in hunger and thirst, in fasting often, in cold and nakedness."

What was it then that upheld them? It was God's visitation that preserved their spirits. Job x.12: "Thou hast given me life and grace and thy visitation hath preserved my spirit." He that upheld the Apostle upheld them. "They were persecuted, but not forsaken, cast down, but perished not." "As unknown, and yet known; as dying, and behold we live; as chastened, and yet not killed"; 2 Corinthians vi.9.

God, it seems, would have all men to behold and observe such mercies and works of His providence as these are towards His people, that they in like cases might be encouraged to depend upon God in their trials, and also to bless His name when they see His goodness towards others. Man lives not by bread only, Deuteronomy viii.3. It is not by good and dainty fare, by peace and rest and heart's ease in enjoying the contentments and good things of this world only that preserves health and prolongs life; God in such examples would have the world see and behold that He can do it without them; and if the world will shut their eyes and take no notice thereof, yet He would have His people to see and consider it. Daniel could be better liking with pulse than others were with the king's dainties. Jacob,[5] though he went from one nation to another people and passed through famine, fears and many afflictions, yet he lived till old age and died sweetly and rested in the Lord, as infinite others of God's servants have done and still shall do, through God's goodness, notwithstanding all the malice of their enemies, "when the branch of the wicked shall be cut off before his day" (Job xv.32) "and the bloody and deceitful men shall not live [out] half their days"; Psalm lv.23.

FROM CHAPTER XXXIV. ANNO DOM: 1644

[PROPOSAL TO REMOVE TO NAUSET]

Mr. Edward Winslow was chosen Governor this year.

Many having left this place[6] (as is before noted) by reason of the straitness and barrenness of the same and their finding of better accommodations elsewhere more suitable to their ends and minds; and sundry others still upon every occasion desiring their dismissions, the church began seriously to think whether it were not better jointly to remove to some other place than to be thus weakened and as it were insensibly dissolved. Many meetings and much consultation was held hereabout, and divers[7] were men's minds and opinions. Some were still for staying together in this place, alleging men might here

---

5. The father of the Chosen People (Genesis 26–50). Pulses are peas and beans. In Daniel 1 the prophet Daniel refuses to eat the "king's dainties" provided by Nebuchadnezzar, preferring "pulse to eat, and water to drink."
6. I.e., Plymouth.
7. Unlike, divided.

live if they would be content with their condition, and that it was not for want or necessity so much that they removed as for the enriching of themselves. Others were resolute upon removal and so signified that here they could not stay; but if the church did not remove, they must. Insomuch as many were swayed rather than there should be a dissolution, to condescend to a removal if a fit place could be found that might more conveniently and comfortably receive the whole, with such accession of others as might come to them for their better strength and subsistence; and some such-like cautions and limitations.

So as, with the aforesaid provisos, the greater part consented to a removal to a place called Nauset, which had been superficially viewed and the good will of the purchasers to whom it belonged obtained, with some addition thereto from the Court. But now they began to see their error, that they had given away already the best and most commodious places to others, and now wanted themselves. For this place was about 50 miles from hence, and at an outside of the country remote from all society; also that it would prove so strait as it would not be competent to receive the whole body, much less be capable of any addition or increase; so as, at least in a short time, they should be worse there than they are now here. The which with sundry other like considerations and inconveniences made them change their resolutions. But such as were before resolved upon removal took advantage of this agreement and went on, notwithstanding; neither could the rest hinder them, they having made some beginning.

And thus was this poor church left, like an ancient mother grown old and forsaken of her children, though not in their affections yet in regard of their bodily presence and personal helpfulness; her ancient members being most of them worn away by death, and these of later time being like children translated into other families, and she like a widow left only to trust in God. Thus, she that had made many rich became herself poor.[8]

1630–50   1856

8. "Now she that is a widow indeed, and desolate, trusteth in God, and continueth in supplications and prayers night and day" (1 Timothy 5.5). "As sorrowful, yet always rejoicing; as poor, yet making many rich; as having nothing, and yet possessing all things" (2 Corinthians 6.10).

THOMAS MORTON
c. 1579–1647

Little is known of Thomas Morton's life before he came to New England for the first time in 1622, but we do know that he was a capable attorney for the London-based Council for New England and a friend of many highly placed persons at the court of King Charles I; all were strong supporters of the Church of England and unsympathetic to the Puritans. He had the advantages of a traditional education provided for a young man of means and was fond of falconry and other gentlemanly sports. But the shadow of a scandal hangs over Morton's name—the murder of a business partner and the abuse of his wife were two rumors widely circulated—and persists even in the absence of particulars. His behavior in Massachusetts, however, makes it seem likely that he did something nefarious. When he was in his forties he had his eye on the fur trade in New England, and he must have decided that if he could wreak havoc on the Puritans and enrich himself at the same time, so much the better.

Morton's first visit to New England lasted only three months, but in 1625 he returned with a group led by one Captain Wollaston (nothing more is known of him) and they settled too close to Plymouth for comfort. After only one winter Wollaston decided that Virginia was a better place to spend his time. Morton never mentions him. He renamed the Wollaston settlement Merry Mount (or—as he preferred— Ma-re Mount) and began to exchange rum and guns for furs. "Mine host," as Morton liked to refer to himself, saw himself as the only civilized person in a world of spoil-sports, an assimilator of foreign culture and a man of tolerance and wit. But for Bradford and Winthrop he was Lord of Misrule, a man who entertained a flock of anarchists and "discontents" under his "licentious" roof and who posed a serious threat to the general welfare. When Morton set up a Maypole in the spring of 1627 to celebrate the death of winter and to honor—"after the old English custom"—Saints Philip and James, the community at Plymouth determined to act. It has been argued that if Morton had merely danced his time away at Merry Mount the Separatists would never have descended on him, but the combination of arming the Nauset Indians and this open display of "Bacchanalian" rites was enough for them to decide to rout him out.

Morton was arrested and returned to England in 1628; the charges brought against him were dropped. The Pilgrims could not believe their eyes when, in the company of their own London representative, he returned a year later. In 1630 they brought the same charges of arming the Nausets against him and when they deported him four months after his arrest they burned his house down for extra measure. Morton's only published work, *New English Canaan,* was written after his ignominious return to England, and in the years that followed he tried to persuade people close to Archbishop Laud and Charles I that the Puritans in New England had betrayed church and Crown and that all title to their property should be reassigned. Morton was unsuccessful, but he spent long hours devising complicated legal maneuvers from which the Puritans had a difficult time extricating themselves. It was only with Oliver Cromwell's rise to power that Morton's schemes were put to an end.

In 1643 he had the audacity to return to Massachusetts one last time, but he was powerless and without financial backing. He seemed a pitiable figure even to his enemies, but they arrested him, nevertheless, one last time in 1644. He was released in 1645; and in John Winthrop's words, "old and crazy," "poor and despised," he was last heard of in Maine, where he died "within two years" after his release.

From New English Canaan[1]

From *The Second Book.*

FROM CHAPTER I. THE GENERAL SURVEY OF THE COUNTRY

In the month of June, *Anno Salutis*[2] 1622, it was my chance to arrive in the parts of New England with 30 servants and provision of all sorts fit for a plantation; and while our houses were building, I did endeavor to take a

1. Canaan was, for the Israelites, the Promised Land. The text used here is that edited by Charles Francis Adams Jr. for the Prince Society (1883). Morton's book is in three parts; the first provides a description of "the natives, their manners and customs, with their tractable nature and love towards the English." The second book is titled "Containing a Description of the Beauty of the Country with Her Natural Endowments, Both in the Land and Sea; with the Great Lake of Iroquois" (Lake Champlain, New York).

2. In the year of our prosperity (Latin).

survey of the country. The more I looked, the more I liked it. And when I had more seriously considered of the beauty of the place, with all her fair endowments, I did not think that in all the known world it could be paralleled for so many goodly groves of trees, dainty fine round rising hillocks, delicate fair large plains, sweet crystal fountains, and clear running streams that twine in fine meanders through the meads,[3] making so sweet a murmuring noise to hear as would even lull the senses with delight asleep, so pleasantly do they glide upon the pebble stones, jetting most jocundly where they do meet, and hand in hand run down to Neptune's[4] court, to pay the yearly tribute which they owe to him as sovereign lord of all the springs. Contained within the volume of the land, [are] fowls in abundance, [and] fish in multitude. And [I] discovered, besides, millions of turtledoves on the green boughs, which sat pecking of the full ripe pleasant grapes that were supported by the lusty[5] trees, whose fruitful load did cause the arms to bend: [among] which here and there dispersed, you might see lillies and of [sic] the Daphnean-tree,[6] which made the land to me seem paradise. For in mine eye t'was Nature's masterpiece, her chiefest magazine[7] of all where lives her store. If this land be not rich, then is the whole world poor.

*   *   *

From The Third Book. [The Incident at Merry Mount]

CHAPTER XIV. OF THE REVELS OF NEW CANAAN

The inhabitants of Passonagessit[8] (having translated the name of their habitation from that ancient savage name to Ma-re Mount, and being resolved to have the new name confirmed for a memorial to after ages) did devise amongst themselves to have it performed in a solemn manner, with revels and merriment after the old English custom; [they] prepared to set up a Maypole upon the festival day of Philip and Jacob,[9] and therefore brewed a barrel of excellent beer and provided a case of bottles to be spent, with other good cheer, for all comers of that day. And because they would have it in a complete form, they had prepared a song fitting to the time and present occasion. And upon May Day they brought the Maypole to the place appointed, with drums, guns, pistols, and other fitting instruments for that purpose, and there erected it with the help of savages that came thither of purpose to see the manner of our revels. A goodly pine tree of 80 foot long was reared up, with a pair of buckhorns nailed on somewhat near unto the top of it, where it stood as a fair sea-mark for directions how to find out the way to mine host[1] of Ma-re Mount.

And because it should more fully appear to what end it was placed there, they had a poem in readiness made, which was fixed to the Maypole, to show

3. Meadows.
4. In Roman mythology the god of the sea.
5. Fertile, healthy.
6. The nymph Daphne was changed into a laurel tree.
7. Warehouse.
8. At [a place] near the little point (Algonquian, literal trans.). It was first known as Mount Wollaston and, after the departure of Captain Wollaston for Virginia, came to be called Merry Mount. Only Morton ever refers to it as "Ma-re Mount" (i.e., "a place by the sea"), because he enjoyed the pun. It is a part of present-day Quincy, Massachusetts, a

few miles south of Boston. The third book is titled "Containing a Description of the People That Are Planted There, What Remarkable Accidents Have Happened There Since They Were Settled, What Tenents [religious doctrines] They Hold, Together with the Practice of Their Church."
9. May 1 is the feast day of Saints Philip and James (Jacob being the Latin form of James), and why they are joined together on this day is not known. The raising of a Maypole was a secular holiday harking back to the Roman festivals in honor of the renewal of vegetative life.
1. I.e., Morton himself.

the new name confirmed upon that plantation, which, although it were made according to the occurrence of the time, it being enigmatically composed, puzzled the Separatists[2] most pitifully to expound it, which (for the better information of the reader) I have here inserted.

THE POEM

Rise Oedipus,[3] and, if thou canst, unfold
What means Charybdis underneath the mold,
When Scylla[4] solitary on the ground
(Sitting in form of Niobe[5]) was found,
Till Amphitrite's darling did acquaint
Grim Neptune with the tenor of her plaint,[6]
And caused him send forth Triton[7] with the sound
Of trumpet loud, at which the seas were found
So full of protean[8] forms that the bold shore
Presented Scylla a new paramour
So strong as Samson and so patient
As Job[9] himself, directed thus, by fate,
To comfort Scylla so unfortunate.
I do profess, by Cupid's beauteous mother,[1]
Here's Scogan's choice[2] for Scylla, and none other;
Though Scylla's sick with grief, because no sign
Can there be found of virtue masculine.
Asclepius[3] come; I know right well
His labor's lost when you may ring her knell.
The fatal sisters'[4] doom none can withstand,
Nor Cytherea's[5] power, who points to land
With proclamation that the first of May
At Ma-re Mount shall be kept holiday.

The setting up of this Maypole was a lamentable spectacle to the precise[6] Separatists that lived at New Plymouth. They termed it an idol; yea, they called it the Calf of Horeb[7] and stood at defiance with the place, naming it Mount Dagon, threatening to make it a woeful mount and not a merry mount.

The riddle, for want of Oedipus,[8] they could not expound, only they made some explication of part of it and said it was meant by Samson Job, the

---

2. The colonists at Plymouth, who distinguished themselves from other Puritans by separating from the Church of England, having no hope of internal reform.
3. In Greek mythology he solved the riddle of the Sphinx.
4. In Greek mythology a monster who lived in a cave opposite the whirlpool Charybdis and devoured sailors.
5. In Greek mythology the gods slew her fourteen children; she is usually depicted weeping for them.
6. Complaint, lament. "Amphitrite's darling"; a sarcastic reference to Scylla herself, whom Neptune's wife turned into a hideous monster because Neptune loved her.
7. The son of Poseidon, god of the sea, he is usually depicted with a conch shell as his horn.
8. Changing.
9. The long-suffering Old Testament patriarch. Samson was the Israelite who brought down with his own hands the temple of the Philistines as they

honored their god Dagon.
1. Venus.
2. When John Scogan (1442–1483), jester to Edward IV, was condemned to be hung, he was given an opportunity to choose the tree and escaped hanging because he could find none to suit him. "Scogan's choice" became a popular expression in Morton's time and suggested that any choice, even between two unfortunate alternatives, is better than no choice at all.
3. The Greek god of healing.
4. In Greek and Roman mythology the three women who determine human destiny.
5. Also called Aphrodite, goddess of love and beauty.
6. Strict, inflexible.
7. The idol that the Israelites falsely worshiped as their deliverer from Egypt (Exodus 32; Deuteronomy 9.16).
8. I.e., lacking Oedipus's insight.

carpenter of the ship that brought over a woman to her husband that had been there long before and thrived so well that he sent for her and her children to come to him, where shortly after he died; having no reason but because of the sound of those two words, when as (the truth is) the man they applied it to was altogether unknown to the author.

There was likewise a merry song made which (to make their revels more fashionable) was sung with a chorus, every man bearing his part, which they performed in a dance, hand in hand about the Maypole, while one of the company sang and filled out the good liquor, like Ganymede and Jupiter.[9]

THE SONG

Chorus.
    Drink and be merry, merry, merry boys;
    Let all your delight be in the Hymen's[1] joys;
    Io[2] to Hymen, now the day is come,
    About the merry Maypole take a room.
        Make green garlands, bring bottles out
        And fill sweet nectar freely about.
        Uncover thy head and fear no harm,
        For here's good liquor to keep it warm.
    Then drink and be merry, &c.
    Io to Hymen, &c.
        Nectar is a thing assigned
        By the Deity's own mind
        To cure the heart oppressed with grief,
        And of good liquors is the chief.
    Then drink, &c.
    Io to Hymen, &c.
        Give to the melancholy man
        A cup or two of't now and then;
        This physic will soon revive his blood,
        And make him be of a merrier mood.
    Then drink, &c.
    Io to Hymen, &c.
        Give to the nymph that's free from scorn
        No Irish stuff nor Scotch over worn.[3]
        Lasses in beaver coats[4] come away,
        Ye shall be welcome to us night and day.
    To drink and be merry, &c.
    Io to Hymen, &c.

This harmless mirth made by young men (that lived in hope to have wives brought over to them, that would save them a labor to make a voyage to fetch any over) was much distasted of the precise Separatists that keep much ado about the tithe of mint and cummin,[5] troubling their brains more than reason would require about things that are indifferent,[6] and from that time [they]

9. Just as the cupbearer Ganymede brought wine to the most powerful of the Roman gods.
1. In Roman mythology the god of marriage.
2. Hail.
3. No wornout Irish or Scottish cloth.
4. Native American women.

5. "Woe unto you, scribes and Pharisees, hypocrites! for ye pay tithe of mint and anise and cummin, and have omitted the weightier matters of the law, judgment, mercy, and faith" (Matthew 23.23).
6. Insignificant.

sought occasion against my honest host of Ma-re Mount, to overthrow his undertakings and to destroy his plantation quite and clean. But because they presumed [that] with their imaginary gifts (which they have out of Phaon's[7] box) they could expound hidden mysteries, to convince them of blindness as well in this as in other matters of more consequence, I will illustrate the poem according to the true intent of the authors of these revels, so much distasted by those moles.

Oedipus is generally received for[8] the absolute reader of riddles, who is invoked; Scylla and Charybdis are two dangerous places for seamen to encounter, near unto Venice, and have been by poets formerly resembled to man and wife. The like license the author challenged for a pair of his nomination, the one lamenting for the loss of the other as Niobe for her children. Amphitrite is an arm of the sea, by which the news was carried up and down of a rich widow, now to be taken up or laid down. By Triton is the fame spread that caused the suitors to muster (as it had been to Penelope[9] of Greece), and, the coast lying circular, all our passage to and fro is made more convenient by sea than land. Many aimed at this mark, but he that played Proteus[1] best and could comply with her humor must be the man that would carry her; and he had need have Samson's strength to deal with a Delilah,[2] and as much patience as Job that should come there, for a thing that I did observe in the lifetime of the former.

But marriage and hanging (they say) come by destiny, and Scogan's choice is better [than] none at all. He that played Proteus (with the help of Priapus[3]) put their noses out of joint, as the proverb is.

And this the whole company of the revelers at Ma-re Mount knew to be the true sense and exposition of the riddle that was fixed to the Maypole which the Separatists were at defiance with. Some of them affirmed that the first institution thereof was in memory of a whore, not knowing that it was a trophy erected at first in honor of Maia.[4] The Lady of Learning which [sic] they despise, vilifying the two universities[5] with uncivil terms, accounting what is there obtained by study is but unnecessary learning, not considering that learning does enable men's minds to converse with elements of a higher nature than is to be found within the habitation of the mole.

CHAPTER XV. OF A GREAT MONSTER SUPPOSED TO BE AT MA-RE MOUNT;
AND THE PREPARATION MADE TO DESTROY IT

The Separatists, envying the prosperity and hope of the plantation at Ma-re Mount (which they perceived began to come forward and to be in a good way for gain in the beaver trade), conspired together against mine host especially (who was the owner of that plantation) and made up a party against him and mustered up what aid they could, accounting of him as of a great monster.

7. An aged boatman whom Aphrodite rewarded with a chest that contained an elixir that made him young.
8. Taken as.
9. The wife of Odysseus, who refused many suitors during his twenty-year absence.
1. In Greek mythology the sea god who assumed many shapes.
2. The woman who betrayed Samson (Judges 16).
3. In Greek and Roman mythology the god of fer-

tility, whose symbol was the phallus.
4. Morton argues that the Separatists accused the revelers at Merry Mount of honoring the licentious Roman goddess Flora rather than Maia, the goddess of the spring.
5. I.e., in the Separatist confusion of Flora and Maia they reveal their contempt for the wisdom of Athena or Minerva, and in their hatred for the classical studies at Oxford and Cambridge they reveal their, for Morton, unsophisticated minds.

Many threatening speeches were given out both against his person and his habitation, which they divulged should be consumed with fire. And taking advantage of the time when his company (which seemed little to regard their threats) were gone up unto the inlands to trade with the savages for beaver, they set upon my honest host at a place called Wessaguscus,[6] where, by accident, they found him. The inhabitants there were in good hope of the subversion of the plantation at Ma-re Mount (which they principally aimed at) and the rather because mine host was a man that endeavored to advance the dignity of the Church of England, which they (on the contrary part) would labor to vilify with uncivil terms, inveighing against the sacred Book of Common Prayer[7] and mine host that used it in a laudable manner amongst his family as a practice of piety.

There he would be a means to bring sacks to their mill (such is the thirst after beaver) and [it] helped the conspirators to surprise mine host (who was there all alone), and they charged him (because they would [want to] seem to have some reasonable cause against him, to set a gloss upon[8] their malice) with criminal things, which indeed had been done by such a person, but was of their conspiracy. Mine host demanded of the conspirators who it was that was author of that information that seemed to be their ground for what they now intended. And because they answered they would not tell him, he as peremptorily replied that he would not say whether he had or he had not done as they had been informed.

The answer made no matter (as it seemed) whether it had been negatively or affirmatively made, for they had resolved what he would suffer because (as they boasted) they were now become the greater number; they had shaken off their shackles of servitude and were become masters and masterless people.

It appears they were like bears' whelps in former time when mine host's plantation was of as much strength as theirs, but now (theirs being stronger) they (like overgrown bears) seemed monstrous. In brief, mine host must endure to be their prisoner until they could contrive it so that they might send him for England (as they said), there to suffer according to the merit of the fact which they intended to father upon him, supposing (belike) it would prove a heinous crime.

Much rejoicing was made that they had gotten their capital enemy (as they concluded him) whom they purposed to hamper in such sort that he should not be able to uphold his plantation at Ma-re Mount.

The conspirators sported themselves at my honest host, that meant them no hurt, and were so jocund that they feasted their bodies and fell to tippling as if they had obtained a great prize, like the Trojans when they had the custody of Epeios' pinetree horse.[9]

Mine host feigned grief and could not be persuaded either to eat or drink, because he knew emptiness would be a means to make him as watchful as the geese kept in the Roman Capital,[1] whereon, the contrary part, the conspirators would be so drowsy that he might have an opportunity to give them a slip instead of a tester.[2]

---

6. Now Weymouth, Massachusetts.
7. Containing the prayers adopted by the Church of England and rejected by the Separatists.
8. Explain, rationalize.
9. The wooden horse used to conquer Troy was

built by Epeios.
1. When the Gauls attempted to invade Rome in 390 B.C.E. the geese on the Capitoline Hill spoiled the surprise attack by hissing.
2. A counterfeit coin rather than a true sixpence.

Six persons of the conspiracy were set to watch him at Wessaguscus. But he kept waking, and in the dead of the night (one lying on the bed for further surety), up gets mine host and got to the second door that he was to pass, which, notwithstanding the lock, he got open and shut it after him with such violence that it affrighted some of the conspirators.

The word which was given with an alarm was, "O he's gone, he's gone, what shall we do, he's gone!" The rest (half asleep) start up in amaze[3] and like rams, ran their heads one at another full butt in the dark.

Their grand leader, Captain Shrimp,[4] took on most furiously and tore his clothes for anger, to see the empty nest and their bird gone.

The rest were eager to have torn their hair from their heads, but it was so short that it would give them no hold.[5] Now Captain Shrimp thought in the loss of this prize (which he accounted his masterpiece) all his honor would be lost forever.

In the meantime mine host was got home to Ma-re Mount through the woods, eight miles round about the head of the river Monatoquit that parted the two plantations, finding his way by the help of the lightning (for it thundered as he went terribly), and there he prepared powder, three pounds dried, for his present employment, and four good guns for him and the two assistants left at his house, with bullets of several sizes, three hundred or thereabouts, to be used if the conspirators should pursue him thither; and these two persons promised their aids in the quarrel and confirmed that promise with health in good *rosa solis*.[6]

Now Captain Shrimp, the first captain in the land (as he supposed) must do some new act to repair this loss and to vindicate his reputation, who had sustained blemish by this oversight, begins now to study how to repair or survive his honor; in this manner, calling of council, they conclude.

He takes eight persons more to him, and (like the nine worthies[7] of New Canaan) they embark with preparation against Ma-re Mount where this monster of a man, as their phrase was, had his den; the whole number, had the rest not been from home, being but seven, would have given Captain Shrimp (a *quondam* drummer)[8] such a welcome as would have made him wish for a drum as big as Diogenes' tub,[9] that he might have crept into it out of sight.

Now the nine worthies are approached, and mine host prepared, having intelligence by a savage that hastened in love from Wessaguscus to give him notice of their intent.

One of mine host's men proved a craven; the other had proved his wits to purchase a little valor, before mine host had observed his posture.

The nine worthies coming before the den of this supposed monster (this seven-headed hydra, as they termed him) and began, like Don Quixote[1] against the windmill, to beat a parley and to offer quarter if mine host would yield, for they resolved to send him to England and bade him lay by[2] his arms.

But he (who was the son of a soldier), having taken up arms in his just

---

3. I.e., in astonishment.
4. Morton's favorite epithet for Captain Myles Standish, who had a ruddy complexion and was short.
5. Puritans objected to fashionable long hair.
6. A cordial red like the sun.
7. A group of heroes and kings who, to the medieval mind, represented an ideal of human conduct.

8. A one-time drummer and thus a man of low rank.
9. The Greek philosopher Diogenes (c. 412–323 B.C.E.) was indifferent to status and lived in a tub.
1. The hero of the novel by Cervantes (1547–1616). Hydra was a monster in Greek mythology.
2. Put down. "Beat a parley": suggest a conference. "Quarter": clemency.

defense, replied that he would not lay by those arms because they were so needful at sea, if he should be sent over. Yet, to save the effusion of so much worthy blood as would have issued out of the veins of these nine worthies of New Canaan if mine host should have played upon them out at his portholes (for they came within danger like a flock of wild geese, as if they had been tailed[3] one to another, as colts to be sold at a fair), mine host was content to yield upon quarter and did capitulate with them in what manner it should be for more certainty, because he knew what Captain Shrimp was.

He expressed that no violence should be offered to his person, none to his goods, nor any of his household but that he should have his arms and what else was requisite for the voyage, which their herald returns;[4] it was agreed upon and should be performed.

But mine host no sooner had set open the door and issued out, but instantly Captain Shrimp and the rest of the worthies stepped to him, laid hold of his arms, and had him down; and so eagerly was every man bent against him (not regarding any agreement made with such a carnal man), that they fell upon him as if they would have eaten him; some of them were so violent that they would have a slice with scabbard, and all for haste, until an old soldier (of the Queen's, as the proverb is) that was there by accident, clapped his gun under the weapons and sharply rebuked these worthies for their unworthy practices. So the matter was taken into more deliberate consideration.

Captain Shrimp and the rest of the nine worthies made themselves (by this outrageous riot) masters of mine host of Ma-re Mount and disposed of what he had at his plantation.

This they knew (in the eye of the savages) would add to their glory and diminish the reputation of mine honest host, whom they practiced to be rid of upon any terms, as willingly as if he had been the very hydra of the time.

CHAPTER XVI. HOW THE NINE WORTHIES PUT MINE HOST OF MA-RE
MOUNT INTO THE ENCHANTED CASTLE AT PLYMOUTH AND TERRIFIED HIM
WITH THE MONSTER BRIAREUS[5]

The nine worthies of New Canaan having now the law in their own hands (there being no general governor in the land, nor none of the separation that regarded the duty they owe their sovereign, whose natural born subjects they were, though translated out of[6] Holland from whence they had learned to work all to their own ends and make a great show of religion but no humanity), for [sic] they were now to sit in council on the cause.

And much it stood mine honest host upon to be very circumspect and to take Eacus[7] to task for that his voice was more allowed of than both the other; and had not mine host confounded all the arguments that Eacus could make in their defense and confuted him that swayed the rest, they would have made him unable to drink in such manner of merriment any more. So that following this private counsel, given him by one that knew who ruled the roost, the hurrican ceased that else would split his pinnace.[8]

A conclusion was made and sentence given that mine host should be sent

3. Tied.
4. Reports.
5. In Greek mythology a giant who fought the gods. Morton does not identify his tormentor.
6. Removed from.

7. In Greek mythology a judge in the infernal regions. Morton later identifies him as Samuel Fuller of Plymouth and names William Bradford and Myles Standish as his other two judges.
8. A small sailboat.

to England a prisoner. But when he was brought to the ships for that purpose, no man dared be so foolhardly as to undertake to carry him. So these worthies set mine host upon an island, without gun, powder, or shot, or dog, or so much as a knife to get anything to feed upon, or any other clothes to shelter him with at winter than a thin suit which he had on at that time. Home he could not get to Ma-re Mount. Upon this island he stayed a month at least and was relieved by savages that took notice that mine host was a sachem[9] of Passonagessit, and would bring bottles of strong liquor to him and unite themselves into a league of brotherhood with mine host, so full of humanity are these infidels before those Christians.

From this place for England sailed mine host in a Plymouth ship (that came into the land to fish upon the coast) that landed him safe in England at Plymouth; and he stayed in England until the ordinary time for shipping to set forth for these parts, and then returned, no man being able to tax[1] him of anything.

But the worthies (in the meantime) hoped they had been rid of him.

✻ ✻ ✻

c. 1635   1637

9. Ruling chief.
1. Charge. Morton was successful more than once

in having dismissed charges made against him by the Puritans.

JOHN WINTHROP
1588–1649

John Winthrop, the son of Adam Winthrop, a lawyer, and Anne Browne, the daughter of a tradesman, was born in Groton, England, on an estate that his father purchased from Henry VIII. It was a prosperous farm, and Winthrop had all the advantages that his father's social and economic position would allow. He went to Cambridge University for two years and married at the age of seventeen. It was probably at Cambridge University that Winthrop was exposed to Puritan ideas. Unlike Bradford and the Pilgrims, however, Winthrop was not a Separatist; that is, he wished to reform the national church from within, purging it of everything that harked back to Rome, especially the hierarchy of the clergy and all the traditional Catholic rituals. For a time Winthrop thought of becoming a clergyman himself, but instead he turned to the practice of law.

In the 1620s severe economic depression in England made Winthrop realize that he could not depend on the support of his father's estate. The ascension of Charles I to the throne—who was known to be sympathetic to Roman Catholicism and impatient with Puritan reformers—was also taken as an ominous sign for Puritans, and Winthrop was not alone in predicting that "God will bring some heavy affliction upon the land, and that speedily." Winthrop came to realize that he could not antagonize the king by expressing openly the Puritan cause without losing all that he possessed. The only recourse seemed to be to obtain the king's permission to emigrate. In March of 1629 a group of enterprising merchants, all sympathetic believers, were able to get a charter from the Council for New England for land in the New World. They called themselves "The Company of Massachusetts Bay in New England."

From four candidates, Winthrop was chosen governor in October 1629; for the next twenty years most of the responsibility for the colony rested in his hands. On April 8, 1630, an initial group of some seven hundred emigrants sailed from England. The ship carrying Winthrop was called the *Arbella*. Either just before departing from England or on the high seas, Winthrop delivered his sermon *A Model of Christian Charity*. It set out clearly and eloquently the ideals of a harmonious Christian community and reminded all those on board that they would stand as an example to the world either of the triumph or else the failure of this Christian enterprise. When Cotton Mather wrote his history of New England some fifty years after Winthrop's death, he chose Winthrop as his model of the perfect earthly ruler. Although the actual history of the colony showed that Winthrop's ideal of a perfectly selfless community was impossible to realize in fact, Winthrop emerges from the story as a man of unquestioned integrity and deep humanity.

A Model of Christian Charity[1]

1

A MODEL HEREOF

God Almighty in His most holy and wise providence, hath so disposed of the condition of mankind, as in all times some must be rich, some poor, some high and eminent in power and dignity; others mean and in subjection.

THE REASON HEREOF

First, to hold conformity with the rest of His works, being delighted to show forth the glory of His wisdom in the variety and difference of the creatures; and the glory of His power, in ordering all these differences for the preservation and good of the whole; and the glory of His greatness, that as it is the glory of princes to have many officers, so this great King will have many stewards, counting Himself more honored in dispensing His gifts to man by man, than if He did it by His own immediate hands.

Secondly, that He might have the more occasion to manifest the work of His Spirit: first upon the wicked in moderating and restraining them, so that the rich and mighty should not eat up the poor, nor the poor and despised rise up against their superiors and shake off their yoke; secondly in the regenerate, in exercising His graces, in them, as in the great ones, their love, mercy, gentleness, temperance, etc., in the poor and inferior sort, their faith, patience, obedience, etc.

Thirdly, that every man might have need of other, and from hence they might be all knit more nearly together in the bonds of brotherly affection. From hence it appears plainly that no man is made more honorable than another or more wealthy, etc., out of any particular and singular respect to himself, but for the glory of his Creator and the common good of the creature, man. Therefore God still reserves the property of these gifts to Himself as [in] Ezekiel: 16.17. He there calls wealth His gold and His silver.[2] [In]

---

1. The text is from Old South Leaflets, Old South Association, Old South Meetinghouse, Boston, Massachusetts, No. 207, edited by Samuel Eliot Morison. The original manuscript for Winthrop's sermon is lost, but a copy made during Winthrop's lifetime was published by the Massachusetts Historical Society in 1838.
2. "Thou hast also taken thy fair jewels of my gold and of my silver, which I had given thee, and madest to thyself images of men, and didst commit whoredom with them."

Proverbs: 3.9, he claims their service as His due: honor the Lord with thy riches, etc.[3] All men being thus (by divine providence) ranked into two sorts, rich and poor; under the first are comprehended all such as are able to live comfortably by their own means duly improved; and all others are poor according to the former distribution.

There are two rules whereby we are to walk one towards another: justice and mercy. These are always distinguished in their act and in their object, yet may they both concur in the same subject in each respect; as sometimes there may be an occasion of showing mercy to a rich man in some sudden danger of distress, and also doing of mere justice to a poor man in regard of some particular contract, etc.

There is likewise a double law by which we are regulated in our conversation one towards another in both the former respects: the law of nature and the law of grace, or the moral law or the law of the Gospel, to omit the rule of justice as not properly belonging to this purpose otherwise than it may fall into consideration in some particular cases. By the first of these laws man as he was enabled so withal [is] commanded to love his neighbor as himself.[4] Upon this ground stands all the precepts of the moral law, which concerns our dealings with men. To apply this to the works of mercy, this law requires two things: first, that every man afford his help to another in every want or distress; secondly, that he performed this out of the same affection which makes him careful of his own goods, according to that of our Savior. Matthew: "Whatsoever ye would that men should do to you."[5] This was practiced by Abraham and Lot in entertaining the Angels and the old man of Gibeah.[6]

The law of grace or the Gospel hath some difference from the former, as in these respects: First, the law of nature was given to man in the estate of innocency; this of the Gospel in the estate of regeneracy.[7] Secondly, the former propounds one man to another, as the same flesh and image of God; this as a brother in Christ also, and in the communion of the same spirit and so teacheth us to put a difference between Christians and others. *Do good to all, especially to the household of faith:* Upon this ground the Israelites were to put a difference between the brethren of such as were strangers though not of Canaanites.[8] Thirdly, the law of nature could give no rules for dealing with enemies, for all are to be considered as friends in the state of innocency, but the Gospel commands love to an enemy. Proof. If thine Enemy hunger, feed him; Love your Enemies, do good to them that hate you. Matthew: 5.44.

3. "Honour the Lord with thy substance, and with the firstfruits of all thine increase: So shall thy barns be filled with plenty, and thy presses shall burst out with new wine" (Proverbs 3.9–10).
4. Matthew 5.43; 19.19.
5. "Therefore all things whatsoever ye would that men should do to you, do ye even so to them: for this is the law of the prophets" (Matthew 7.12).
6. Abraham entertains the angels in Genesis 18: "And the Lord appeared unto him in the plains of Mamre; and he sat in the tent door in the heat of the day; And he lift up his eyes and looked, and, lo, three men stood by him: and when he saw them, he ran to meet them" (Genesis 18.1–2). Lot was Abraham's nephew, and he escaped the destruc-

tion of the city of Sodom because he defended two angels who were his guests from a mob (Genesis 19.1–14). In Judges 19.16–21, an old citizen of Gibeah offered shelter to a traveling priest or Levite and defended him from enemies from a neighboring city.
7. Humanity lost its natural innocence when Adam and Eve fell; that state is called unregenerate. When Christ came to ransom humankind for Adam and Eve's sin, he offered salvation for those who believed in him and who thus became regenerate, or saved.
8. People who lived in Canaan, the Land of Promise for the Israelites.

This law of the Gospel propounds likewise a difference of seasons and occasions. There is a time when a Christian must sell all and give to the poor, as they did in the Apostles' times.[9] There is a time also when a Christian (though they give not all yet) must give beyond their ability, as they of Macedonia, Corinthians: 2.8.[1] Likewise community of perils calls for extraordinary liberality, and so doth community in some special service for the Church. Lastly, when there is no other means whereby our Christian brother may be relieved in his distress, we must help him beyond our ability, rather than tempt God in putting him upon help by miraculous or extraordinary means.

This duty of mercy is exercised in the kinds, *giving, lending* and *forgiving.*—

Quest. What rule shall a man observe in giving in respect of the measure?

Ans. If the time and occasion be ordinary, he is to give out of his abundance. Let him lay aside as God hath blessed him. If the time and occasion be extraordinary, he must be ruled by them; taking this withal, that then a man cannot likely do too much, especially if he may leave himself and his family under probable means of comfortable subsistence.

Objection. A man must lay up for posterity, the fathers lay up for posterity and children and he "is worse than an infidel" that "provideth not for his own."

Ans. For the first, it is plain that it being spoken by way of comparison, it must be meant of the ordinary and usual course of fathers and cannot extend to times and occasions extraordinary. For the other place, the Apostle speaks against such as walked inordinately, and it is without question, that he is worse than an infidel who through his own sloth and voluptuousness shall neglect to provide for his family.

Objection. "The wise man's eyes are in his head" saith Solomon, "and foreseeth the plague,"[2] therefore we must forecast and lay up against evil times when he or his may stand in need of all he can gather.

Ans. This very argument Solomon useth to persuade to liberality, Ecclesiastes: "Cast thy bread upon the waters," and "for thou knowest not what evil may come upon the land."[3] Luke: 16.9. "Make you friends of the riches of iniquity."[4] You will ask how this shall be? very well. For first he that gives to the poor, lends to the Lord and He will repay him even in this life an hundred fold to him or his—The righteous is ever merciful and lendeth and his seed enjoyeth the blessing; and besides we know what advantage it will

9. In Luke, Jesus tells a ruler who asks him what he must do to gain eternal life: "sell all that thou hast, and distribute unto the poor, and thou shalt have treasure in heaven: and come, follow me" (Luke 18.22).
1. "Moreover, brethren, we do you to wit of the grace of God bestowed on the churches of Macedonia; How that in a great trial of affliction, the abundance of their joy and their deep poverty abounded unto the riches of their liberality. For to their power, I bear record, yea, and beyond their power they were willing of themselves; Praying us with much intreaty that we would receive the gift, and take upon us the fellowship of the ministering to the saints" (2 Corinthians 8.1–4).
2. Ecclesiastes 2.14. Solomon was the son of

David and successor to David as king of all Israel.
3. "Cast thy bread upon the waters: for thou shalt find it after many days. Give a portion to seven, and also to eight; for thou knowest not what evil shall be upon the earth" (Ecclesiastes 11.1–2). Winthrop either makes his own translations from the Bible or uses the King James or Geneva versions; his quotations, therefore, differ occasionally from the King James version used in these notes.
4. The passage in Luke refers to the servant who, removed from his stewardship, resolves to be received in the houses of his master's debtors and cuts their bills in half. "And I say unto you, Make to yourselves friends of the mammon of unrighteousness; that, when ye fail, they may receive you into everlasting habitations" (Luke 16.9).

be to us in the day of account when many such witnesses shall stand forth for us to witness the improvement of our talent.[5] And I would know of those who plead so much for laying up for time to come, whether they hold that to be Gospel, Matthew: 6.19: "Lay not up for yourselves treasures upon earth,"[6] etc. If they acknowledge it, what extent will they allow it? if only to those primitive times, let them consider the reason whereupon our Savior grounds it. The first is that they are subject to the moth, the rust, the thief. Secondly, they will steal away the heart; where the treasure is there will the heart be also. The reasons are of like force at all times. Therefore the exhortation must be general and perpetual, with always in respect of the love and affection to riches and in regard of the things themselves when any special service for the church or particular distress of our brother do call for the use of them; otherwise it is not only lawful but necessary to lay up as Joseph[7] did to have ready upon such occasions, as the Lord (whose stewards we are of them) shall call for them from us. Christ gives us an instance of the first, when He sent his disciples for the ass, and bids them answer the owner thus, the Lord hath need of him.[8] So when the tabernacle was to be built He sends to His people to call for their silver and gold, etc.; and yields them no other reason but that it was for His work. When Elisha comes to the widow of Sareptah and finds her preparing to make ready her pittance for herself and family, He bids her first provide for Him; he challengeth first God's part which she must first give before she must serve her own family.[9] All these teach us that the Lord looks that when He is pleased to call for His right in anything we have, our own interest we have must stand aside till His turn be served. For the other, we need look no further than to that of John: 1: "He who hath this world's goods and seeth his brother to need and shuts up his compassion from him, how dwelleth the love of God in him," which comes punctually to this conclusion: if thy brother be in want and thou canst help him, thou needst not make doubt, what thou shouldst do, if thou lovest God thou must help him.

Quest. What rule must we observe in lending?

Ans. Thou must observe whether thy brother hath present or probable, or possible means of repaying thee, if there be none of these, thou must give him according to his necessity, rather than lend him as he requires. If he hath present means of repaying thee, thou art to look at him not as an act of mercy, but by way of commerce, wherein thou art to walk by the rule of justice; but if his means of repaying thee be only probable or possible, then is he an object of thy mercy, thou must lend him, though there be danger of losing it, Deuteronomy: 15.7: "If any of thy brethren be poor," etc., "thou shalt lend him sufficient."[1] That men might not shift off this duty by the apparent hazard, He tells them that though the year of Jubilee[2] were at hand

---

5. Originally a measure of money.
6. "Lay not up for yourselves treasures upon earth, where moth and rust doth corrupt, and where thieves break through and steal: But lay up for yourselves treasures in heaven, where neither moth nor rust doth corrupt, and where thieves do not break through nor steal" (Matthew 6.19–20).
7. Joseph, the son of Jacob and Rachel, stored up the harvest in the seven good years before the famine (Genesis 41).
8. Matthew 21.5–7.
9. 1 Kings 17.8–24.

1. "If there be among you a poor man of one of thy brethren within any of thy gates in thy land which the Lord thy God giveth thee, thou shalt not harden thine heart, nor shut thine hand from thy poor brother: But thou shalt open thine hand wide unto him, and shalt surely lend him sufficient for his need, in that which he wanteth" (Deuteronomy 15.7–8).
2. According to Mosaic law, every seventh year the lands would lie fallow, all work would cease, and all debts would be canceled. The Jubilee year concluded a cycle of seven sabbatical years.

(when he must remit it, if he were not able to repay it before) yet he must lend him and that cheerfully: "It may not grieve thee to give him" saith He; and because some might object; "why so I should soon impoverish myself and my family," He adds "with all thy work,"[3] etc.; for our Savior, Matthew: 5.42: "From him that would borrow of thee turn not away."

Quest. What rule must we observe in forgiving?

Ans. Whether thou didst lend by way of commerce or in mercy, if he have nothing to pay thee, [you] must forgive, (except in cause where thou hast a surety or a lawful pledge) Deuteronomy: 15.2. Every seventh year the creditor was to quit that which he lent to his brother if he were poor as appears— verse 8: "Save when there shall be no poor with thee." In all these and like cases, Christ was a general rule, Matthew: 7.22: "Whatsoever ye would that men should do to you, do ye the same to them also."

Quest. What rule must we observe and walk by in cause of community of peril?

Ans. The same as before, but with more enlargement towards others and less respect towards ourselves and our own right. Hence it was that in the primitive church they sold all, had all things in common, neither did any man say that which he possessed was his own. Likewise in their return out of the captivity, because the work was great for the restoring of the church and the danger of enemies was common to all, Nehemiah exhorts the Jews to liberality and readiness in remitting their debts to their brethren, and disposing liberally of his own to such as wanted, and stand not upon his own due, which he might have demanded of them.[4] Thus did some of our forefathers in times of persecution in England, and so did many of the faithful of other churches, whereof we keep an honorable remembrance of them; and it is to be observed that both in Scriptures and later stories of the churches that such as have been most bountiful to the poor saints, especially in these extraordinary times and occasions, God hath left them highly commended to posterity, as Zacheus, Cornelius, Dorcas, Bishop Hooper, the Cuttler of Brussells[5] and divers others. Observe again that the Scripture gives no caution to restrain any from being over liberal this way; but all men to the liberal and cheerful practice hereof by the sweetest promises; as to instance one for many, Isaiah: 58.6: "Is not this the fast I have chosen to loose the bonds of wickedness, to take off the heavy burdens, to let the oppressed go free and to break every yoke, to deal thy bread to the hungry and to bring the poor that wander into thy house, when thou seest the naked to cover them. And then shall thy light break forth as the morning, and thy health shall grow speedily, thy righteousness shall go before God, and the glory of the Lord shall embrace thee; then thou shalt call and the Lord shall answer thee" etc. [Verse] 10: "If thou pour out thy soul to the hungry, then shall thy light spring out in darkness, and the Lord shall guide thee continually, and satisfy thy soul in drought, and make fat thy bones; thou shalt be

---

3. "The seventh year, the year of release, is at hand; and thine eye be evil against thy poor brother, and thou givest him nought; and he cry unto the Lord against thee, and it be sin unto thee. Thou shalt surely give him, and thine heart shall not be grieved when thou givest unto him: because that for this thing the Lord thy God shall bless thee in all thy works, and in all that thou puttest thine hand unto" (Deuteronomy 15.9–10).

4. Nehemiah was sent by King Artaxerxes to repair the walls of the city of Jerusalem; he saved the city as governor when he persuaded those lending money to charge no interest, and to think first of the common good (see Nehemiah 3).

5. Christian martyrs.

like a watered garden, and they shalt be of thee that shall build the old waste places" etc. On the contrary, most heavy curses are laid upon such as are straightened towards the Lord and His people, Judges: 5.[23]: "Curse ye Meroshe because ye came not to help the Lord," etc. Proverbs: [21.13]: "He who shutteth his ears from hearing the cry of the poor, he shall cry and shall not be heard." Matthew: 25: "Go ye cursed into everlasting fire" etc. "I was hungry and ye fed me not." 2 Corinthians: 9.6: "He that soweth sparingly shall reap sparingly."

Having already set forth the practice of mercy according to the rule of God's law, it will be useful to lay open the grounds of it also, being the other part of the commandment, and that is the affection from which this exercise of mercy must arise. The apostle[6] tells us that this love is the fulfilling of the law, not that it is enough to love our brother and so no further; but in regard of the excellency of his parts giving any motion to the other as the soul to the body and the power it hath to set all the faculties on work in the outward exercise of this duty. As when we bid one make the clock strike, he doth not lay hand on the hammer, which is the immediate instrument of the sound, but sets on work the first mover or main wheel, knowing that will certainly produce the sound which he intends. So the way to draw men to works of mercy, is not by force of argument from the goodness or necessity of the work; for though this course may enforce a rational mind to some present act of mercy, as is frequent in experience, yet it cannot work such a habit in a soul, as shall make it prompt upon all occasions to produce the same effect, but by framing these affections of love in the heart which will as natively bring forth the other, as any cause doth produce effect.

The definition which the Scripture gives us of love is this: "Love is the bond of perfection." First, it is a bond or ligament. Secondly it makes the work perfect. There is no body but consists of parts and that which knits these parts together gives the body its perfection, because it makes each part so contiguous to others as thereby they do mutually participate with each other, both in strength and infirmity, in pleasure and pain. To instance in the most perfect of all bodies: Christ and His church make one body. The several parts of this body, considered apart before they were united, were as disproportionate and as much disordering as so many contrary qualities or elements, but when Christ comes and by His spirit and love knits all these parts to Himself and each to other, it is become the most perfect and best proportioned body in the world. Ephesians: 4.16: "Christ, by whom all the body being knit together by every joint for the furniture thereof, according to the effectual power which is the measure of every perfection of parts," "a glorious body without spot or wrinkle," the ligaments hereof being Christ, or His love, for Christ is love (1 John: 4.8). So this definition is right: "Love is the bond of perfection."

From hence we may frame these conclusions. 1. First of all, true Christians are of one body in Christ, 1 Corinthians: 12.12, 27: "Ye are the body of Christ and members of their part." Secondly: The ligaments of this body which knit together are love. Thirdly: No body can be perfect which wants its proper ligament. Fourthly. All the parts of this body being thus united are made so contiguous in a special relation as they must needs partake of each

6. St. Paul in his Epistle to the Romans 9.31.

other's strength and infirmity; joy and sorrow, weal and woe. 1 Corinthians: 12.26: "If one member suffers, all suffer with it, if one be in honor, all rejoice with it." Fifthly. This sensibleness and sympathy of each other's conditions will necessarily infuse into each part a native desire and endeavor to strengthen, defend, preserve and comfort the other.

To insist a little on this conclusion being the product of all the former, the truth hereof will appear both by precept and pattern. 1 John: 3.10: "Ye ought to lay down your lives for the brethren." Galatians: 6.2: "bear ye one another's burthens and so fulfill the law of Christ." For patterns we have that first of our Savior who out of His good will in obedience to His father, becoming a part of this body, and being knit with it in the bond of love, found such a native sensibleness of our infirmities and sorrows as He willingly yielded Himself to death to ease the infirmities of the rest of His body, and so healed their sorrows. From the like sympathy of parts did the apostles and many thousands of the saints lay down their lives for Christ. Again, the like we may see in the members of this body among themselves. Romans: 9. Paul could have been contented to have been separated from Christ, that the Jews might not be cut off from the body. It is very observable what he professeth of his affectionate partaking with every member: "who is weak" saith he "and I am not weak? who is offended and I burn not;"[7] and again, 2 Corinthians: 7.13. "therefore we are comforted because ye were comforted." Of Epaphroditus[8] he speaketh, Philippians: 2.30. that he regarded not his own life to do him service. So Phoebe[9] and others are called the servants of the church. Now it is apparent that they served not for wages, or by constraint, but out of love. The like we shall find in the histories of the church in all ages, the sweet sympathy of affections which was in the members of this body one towards another, their cheerfulness in serving and suffering together, how liberal they were without repining, harborers without grudging and helpful without reproaching; and all from hence, because they had fervent love amongst them, which only make the practice of mercy constant and easy.

The next consideration is how this love comes to be wrought. Adam in his first estate[1] was a perfect model of mankind in all their generations, and in him this love was perfected in regard of the habit. But Adam rent himself from his creator, rent all his posterity also one from another; whence it comes that every man is born with this principle in him, to love and seek himself only, and thus a man continueth till Christ comes and takes possession of the soul and infuseth another principle, love to God and our brother. And this latter having continual supply from Christ, as the head and root by which he is united, gets the predomining in the soul, so by little and little expels the former. 1 John: 4.7. "love cometh of God and every one that loveth is borne of God," so that this love is the fruit of the new birth, and none can have it but the new creature. Now when this quality is thus formed in the souls of men, it works like the spirit upon the dry bones. Ezekiel: 37: "bone came to bone." It gathers together the scattered bones, of perfect old man

7. 2 Corinthians 11.29.
8. St. Paul tells the Philippians that he will send to them as a spiritual guide "Epaphroditus, my brother, and companion in labour, and fellow soldier, but your messenger, and he that ministered to my wants" (Philippians 2.25).
9. A Christian woman praised by St. Paul in Romans 16.1.
1. I.e., in his innocence.

Adam, and knits them into one body again in Christ, whereby a man is become again a living soul.

The third consideration is concerning the exercise of this love which is twofold, inward or outward. The outward hath been handled in the former preface of this discourse. For unfolding the other we must take in our way that maxim of philosophy *simile simili gaudet*, or like will to like; for as it is things which are turned with disaffection to each other, the ground of it is from a dissimilitude arising from the contrary or different nature of the things themselves; for the ground of love is an apprehension of some resemblance in things loved to that which affects it. This is the cause why the Lord loves the creature, so far as it hath any of His image in it; He loves His elect because they are like Himself, He beholds them in His beloved son. So a mother loves her child, because she thoroughly conceives a resemblance of herself in it. Thus it is between the members of Christ. Each discerns, by the work of the spirit, his own image and resemblance in another, and therefore cannot but love him as he loves himself. Now when the soul, which is of a sociable nature, finds anything like to itself, it is like Adam when Eve was brought to him. She must have it one with herself. This is flesh of my flesh (saith the soul) and bone of my bone. She conceives a great delight in it, therefore she desires nearness and familiarity with it. She hath a great propensity to do it good and receives such content in it, as fearing the miscarriage of her beloved she bestows it in the inmost closet of her heart. She will not endure that it shall want any good which she can give it. If by occasion she be withdrawn from the company of it, she is still looking towards the place where she left her beloved. If she heard it groan, she is with it presently. If she find it sad and disconsolate, she sighs and moans with it. She hath no such joy as to see her beloved merry and thriving. If she see it wronged, she cannot hear it without passion. She sets no bounds to her affections, nor hath any thought of reward. She finds recompense enough in the exercise of her love towards it. We may see this acted to life in Jonathan and David.[2] Jonathan a valiant man endowed with the spirit of Christ, so soon as he discovers the same spirit in David had presently his heart knit to him by this lineament of love so that it is said he loved him as his own soul. He takes so great pleasure in him, that he strips himself to adorn his beloved. His father's kingdom was not so precious to him as his beloved David. David shall have it with all his heart, himself desires no more but that he may be near to him to rejoice in his good. He chooseth to converse with him in the wilderness even to the hazard of his own life, rather than with the great courtiers in his father's palace. When he sees danger towards him, he spares neither rare pains nor peril to direct it. When injury was offered his beloved David, he would not bear it, though from his own father; and when they must part for a season only, they thought their hearts would have broke for sorrow, had not their affections found vent by abundance of tears. Other instances might be brought to show the nature of this affection, as of Ruth and Naomi,[3] and many others; but this truth is cleared enough.

If any shall object that it is not possible that love should be bred or upheld

---

2. The story of David and Jonathan is told in 1 Samuel 19ff.
3. Naomi was the mother-in-law of Ruth, whom Ruth refused to leave when her husband died, telling her, "For whither thou goest, I will go; and where thou lodgest, I will lodge" (Ruth 1.16).

without hope of requital, it is granted; but that is not our cause; for this love is always under reward. It never gives, but it always receives with advantage; first, in regard that among the members of the same body, love and affection are reciprocal in a most equal and sweet kind of commerce. Secondly, in regard of the pleasure and content that the exercise of love carries with it, as we may see in the natural body. The mouth is at all the pains to receive and mince the food which serves for the nourishment of all the other parts of the body, yet it hath no cause to complain; for first the other parts send back by several passages a due proportion of the same nourishment, in a better form for the strengthening and comforting the mouth. Secondly, the labor of the mouth is accompanied with such pleasure and content as far exceeds the pains it takes. So is it in all the labor of love among Christians. The party loving, reaps love again, as was showed before, which the soul covets more than all the wealth in the world. Thirdly: Nothing yields more pleasure and content to the soul than when it finds that which it may love fervently, for to love and live beloved is the soul's paradise, both here and in heaven. In the state of wedlock there be many comforts to bear out the troubles of that condition; but let such as have tried the most, say if there be any sweetness in that condition comparable to the exercise of mutual love.

From former considerations arise these conclusions.

First: This love among Christians is a real thing, not imaginary.

Secondly: This love is as absolutely necessary to the being of the body of Christ, as the sinews and other ligaments of a natural body are to the being of that body.

Thirdly: This love is a divine, spiritual nature free, active, strong, courageous, permanent; undervaluing all things beneath its proper object; and of all the graces, this makes us nearer to resemble the virtues of our Heavenly Father.

Fourthly: It rests in the love and welfare of its beloved. For the full and certain knowledge of these truths concerning the nature, use, and excellency of this grace, that which the Holy Ghost hath left recorded, 1 Corinthians: 13, may give full satisfaction, which is needful for every true member of this lovely body of the Lord Jesus, to work upon their hearts by prayer, meditation, continual exercise at least of the special [influence] of His grace, till Christ be formed in them and they in Him, all in each other, knit together by this bond of love.

II

It rests now to make some application of this discourse by the present design, which gave the occasion of writing of it. Herein are four things to be propounded: first the persons, secondly the work, thirdly the end, fourthly the means.

First, For the persons. We are a company professing ourselves fellow members of Christ, in which respect only though we were absent from each other many miles, and had our employments as far distant, yet we ought to account ourselves knit together by this bond of love, and live in the exercise of it, if we would have comfort of our being in Christ. This was notorious in the practice of the Christians in former times; as is testified of the Waldenses,[4] from the mouth of one of the adversaries *Æneas Sylvius*[5] "mutuo [ament] penè antequam norunt," they used to love any of their own religion even before they were acquainted with them.

Secondly, for the work we have in hand. It is by a mutual consent, through a special overvaluing providence and a more than an ordinary approbation of the Churches of Christ, to seek out a place of cohabitation and consortship under a due form of government both civil and ecclesiastical. In such cases as this, the care of the public must oversway all private respects, by which, not only conscience, but mere civil policy, doth bind us. For it is a true rule that particular estates cannot subsist in the ruin of the public.

Thirdly. The end is to improve our lives to do more service to the Lord; the comfort and increase of the body of Christ whereof we are members; that ourselves and posterity may be the better preserved from the common corruptions of this evil world, to serve the Lord and work out our salvation under the power and purity of His holy ordinances.

Fourthly, for the means whereby this must be effected. They are twofold, a conformity with the work and end we aim at. These we see are extraordinary, therefore we must not content ourselves with usual ordinary means. Whatsoever we did or ought to have done when we lived in England, the same must we do, and more also, where we go. That which the most in their churches maintain as a truth in profession only, we must bring into familiar and constant practice, as in this duty of love. We must love brotherly without dissimulation; we must love one another with a pure heart fervently. We must bear one another's burthens. We must not look only on our own things, but also on the things of our brethren, neither must we think that the Lord will bear with such failings at our hands as he doth from those among whom we have lived; and that for three reasons.

First, In regard of the more near bond of marriage between Him and us, where-in He hath taken us to be His after a most strict and peculiar manner, which will make Him the more jealous of our love and obedience. So He tells the people of Israel, you only have I known of all the families of the earth, therefore will I punish you for your transgressions. Secondly, because the Lord will be sanctified in them that come near Him. We know that there were many that corrupted the service of the Lord, some setting up altars before His own, others offering both strange fire and strange sacrifices also; yet there came no fire from heaven or other sudden judgment upon them, as did upon Nadab and Abihu,[6] who yet we may think did not sin presumptuously. Thirdly. When God gives a special commission He looks to have it strictly observed in every article. When He gave Saul a commission to destroy Amaleck, He indented with him upon certain articles,[7] and because he failed

---

4. The Waldenses took their name from Pater Valdes, an early French reformer of the church. They still survive as a religious community.
5. Aeneas Sylvius Piccolomini (1405–1464), Pope Pius II, was a historian and scholar. *Solent amare* is a closer approximation of the Latin than Morison's suggestion of *ament*.
6. "And Nadab and Abihu, the sons of Aaron, took either of them his censer, and put fire therein, and put incense thereon, and offered strange fire before the Lord, which he commanded them not.

And there went out fire from the Lord, and devoured them, and they died before the Lord" (Leviticus 10.1–2). Winthrop's point is that the chosen people are often punished more severely than unbelievers.
7. I.e., made an agreement with him on parts of a contract or agreement. Saul was instructed to destroy the Amalekites and all that they possessed, but he spared their sheep and oxen, and in doing so disobeyed the Lord's commandment and was rejected as king (1 Samuel 15.1–34).

in one of the least, and that upon a fair pretense, it lost him the kingdom which should have been his reward if he had observed his commission.

Thus stands the cause between God and us. We are entered into covenant[8] with Him for this work. We have taken out a commission, the Lord hath given us leave to draw our own articles. We have professed to enterprise these actions, upon these and those ends, we have hereupon besought Him of favor and blessing. Now if the Lord shall please to hear us, and bring us in peace to the place we desire, then hath He ratified this covenant and sealed our commission, [and] will expect a strict performance of the articles contained in it; but if we shall neglect the observation of these articles which are the ends we have propounded, and, dissembling with our God, shall fall to embrace this present world and prosecute our carnal intentions, seeking great things for ourselves and our posterity, the Lord will surely break out in wrath against us; be revenged of such a perjured people and make us know the price of the breach of such a covenant.

Now the only way to avoid this shipwreck, and to provide for our posterity, is to follow the counsel of Micah,[9] to do justly, to love mercy, to walk humbly with our God. For this end, we must be knit together in this work as one man. We must entertain each other in brotherly affection, we must be willing to abridge ourselves of our superfluities, for the supply of other's necessities. We must uphold a familiar commerce together in all meekness, gentleness, patience and liberality. We must delight in each other, make other's conditions our own, rejoice together, mourn together, labor and suffer together, always having before our eyes our commission and community in the work, our community as members of the same body. So shall we keep the unity of the spirit in the bond of peace. The Lord will be our God, and delight to dwell among us as His own people, and will command a blessing upon us in all our ways, so that we shall see much more of His wisdom, power, goodness and truth, than formerly we have been acquainted with. We shall find that the God of Israel is among us, when ten of us shall be able to resist a thousand of our enemies; when He shall make us a praise and glory that men shall say of succeeding plantations, "the Lord make it like that of of NEW ENGLAND." For we must consider that we shall be as a city upon a hill.[1] The eyes of all people are upon us, so that if we shall deal falsely with our God in this work we have undertaken, and so cause Him to withdraw His present help from us, we shall be made a story and a by-word through the world. We shall open the mouths of enemies to speak evil of the ways of God, and all professors for God's sake. We shall shame the faces of many of God's worthy servants, and cause their prayers to be turned into curses upon us till we be consumed out of the good land whither we are agoing.

And to shut up this discourse with that exhortation of Moses, that faithful servant of the Lord, in his last farewell to Israel, Deuteronomy 30.[2] Beloved,

8. A legal contract; the Israelites entered into a covenant with God in which he promised to protect them if they kept his word and were faithful to him.
9. The Book of Micah preserves the words of this 8th-century-B.C.E. prophet. Micah speaks continually of the judgment of God on his people and the necessity to hope for salvation: "I will bear the indignation of the Lord, because I have sinned against him, until he plead my cause, and execute judgment for me: he will bring me forth to the light, and I shall behold his righteousness" (Micah 7.9).
1. "Ye are the light of the world. A city that is set on a hill cannot be hid. Neither do men light a candle, and put it under a bushel, but on a candlestick; and it giveth light unto all that are in the house" (Matthew 5.14–15).
2. "And it shall come to pass, when all these things are come upon thee, the blessing and the curse,

there is now set before us life and good, death and evil, in that we are commanded this day to love the Lord our God, and to love one another, to walk in His ways and to keep His commandments and His ordinance and His laws, and the articles of our covenant with Him, that we may live and be multiplied, and that our Lord our God may bless us in the land whither we go to possess it. But if our hearts shall turn away, so that we will not obey, but shall be seduced, and worship other gods, our pleasures and profits, and serve them; it is propounded unto us this day, we shall surely perish out of the good land whither we pass over this vast sea to possess it.

> Therefore let us choose life,
> that we and our seed
> may live by obeying His
> voice and cleaving to Him,
> for He is our life and
> our prosperity.

1630   1838

From The Journal of John Winthrop[1]

[SIGHTING MOUNT DESERT ISLAND, MAINE]

[June 8, 1630] About 3 in the afternoon we had sight of land to the NW about 15 leagues, which we supposed was the Isles of Monhegen, but it proved Mount Mansell.[2] Then we tacked and stood WSW. We had now fair sunshine weather and so pleasant a sweet ether[3] as did much refresh us, and there came a smell off the shore like the smell of a garden. There came a wild pigeon into our ship and another small land bird.

[OVERCOMING SATAN]

[July 5, 1632] At Watertown there was (in the view of divers[4] witnesses) a great combat between a mouse and a snake, and after a long fight the mouse prevailed and killed the snake. The pastor of Boston, Mr. Wilson,[5] a very sincere, holy man, hearing of it gave this interpretation: that the snake was the devil, the mouse was a poor contemptible people which God had brought hither, which should overcome Satan here and dispossess him of his kingdom. Upon the same occasion he told the governor[6] that before he was resolved to come into this country he dreamed he was here, and that he saw a church arise out of the earth, which grew up and became a marvelous goodly church.

---

which I have set before thee, and thou shalt call them to mind among all the nations, whither the Lord thy God hath driven thee, and shalt return unto the Lord thy God, and shalt obey his voice according to all that I command thee this day, thou and thy children, with all thine heart, and with all thy soul; That then the Lord thy God will turn thy captivity, and have compassion upon thee, and will return and gather thee from all the nations, whither the Lord thy God hath scattered thee" (Deuteronomy 30.1–3).
1. The text used here is from *The Journal of John*

Winthrop, 1630–1649, abridged ed., edited by Richard S. Dunn and Laetitia Yeandle (1996).
2. What Winthrop saw was Mount Desert Island, Maine. The English named it after a British admiral, Sir Robert Mansell (1573–1656).
3. Air.
4. Several.
5. The Reverend John Wilson (1588–1667) was beginning a pastorate that would last thirty-seven years.
6. Winthrop himself.

[CHARGES MADE AGAINST ROGER WILLIAMS]

[December 27, 1633] The governor and assistants met at Boston and took into consideration a treatise which Mr. Williams[7] (then of Salem) had sent to them, and which he had formerly written to the governor[8] and Council of Plymouth, wherein among other things he disputes their right to the lands they possessed here, and concluded that claiming by the King's grant they could have no title, nor otherwise except they compounded[9] with the natives. For this, taking advice with some of the most judicious ministers (who much condemned Mr. Williams's error and presumption), they gave order that he should be convented[1] at the next Court to be censured, etc. There were 3 passages chiefly whereat they were much offended: 1. For that he chargeth King James to have told a solemn public lie, because in his patent he blessed God that he was the first Christian prince that had discovered this land; 2. For that he chargeth him and others with blasphemy for calling Europe Christendom or the Christian world; 3. For that he did personally apply to our present King Charles these 3 places in the Revelation, viz.[2]

Mr. Endecott[3] being absent, the governor wrote to him to let him know what was done, and withal added divers arguments to confute the said errors, wishing him to deal with Mr. Williams to retract the same, etc. Whereunto he returned a very modest and discreet answer. Mr. Williams also wrote very submissively, professing his intent to have been only to have written for the private satisfaction of the governor, etc., of Plymouth without any purpose to have stirred any further in it if the governor here had not required a copy of him; withal offering his book or any part of it to be burnt, etc. So it was left and nothing done in it.

[A SMALLPOX EPIDEMIC]

[January 20, 1634] Hall and the 2 others[4] who went to Connecticut November 3 came now home, having lost themselves and endured much misery. They informed us that the smallpox was gone as far as any Indian plantation was known to the W., and much people dead of it, by reason whereof they could have no trade. At Narragansett by the Indians' report there died 700, but beyond Pascataquack none to the E.

[A WARRANT FOR ROGER WILLIAMS]

[January 11, 1636] The governor[5] and assistants met at Boston to consult about Mr. Williams, for that they were credibly informed that notwithstanding the injunction laid upon him (upon the liberty granted him to stay till the spring) not to go about to draw others to his opinions, he did use to entertain company in his house and to preach to them, even of such points as he had been censured for; and it was agreed to send him into England by

7. Roger Williams (c. 1603–1683), who had emigrated to New England in 1630 and refused a call to the First Church of Boston because he would not preach to "an unseparated people."
8. In 1633 Edward Winslow (1595–1655) was governor in Plymouth.
9. Arranged to make a financial settlement.
1. Summoned to appear.

2. Abbreviation for videlicet: namely (Latin).
3. John Endecott (c. 1588–1665) served as governor to the Massachusetts Bay Colony's advance settlement in Salem from 1628 until Winthrop arrived.
4. Not further identified.
5. John Hays (1594–1654). Winthrop was elected governor again in 1637.

a ship then ready to depart. The reason was because he had drawn above 20 persons to his opinion and they were intended to erect a plantation about the Narragansett Bay, from whence the infection[6] would easily spread into these churches (the people being many of them much taken with the apprehension of his godliness). Whereupon a warrant was sent to him to come presently to Boston to be shipped,[7] etc. He returned answer (and divers of Salem came with it) that he could not come without hazard of his life, etc., whereupon a pinnace[8] was sent with commission to Captain Underhill, etc., to apprehend him and carry him aboard the ship (which then rode at Nantasket), but when they came at his house they found he had been gone 3 days before, but whither they could not learn.

[THE CASE OF ANNE HUTCHINSON]

[October 21, 1636] * * * One Mrs. Hutchinson,[9] a member of the church of Boston, a woman of a ready wit and bold spirit, brought over with her two dangerous errors: 1. That the person of the Holy Ghost dwells in a justified[1] person. 2. That no sanctification can help to evidence to us our justification.[2]—From these two grew many branches; as, 1, Our union with the Holy Ghost, so as a Christian remains dead to every spiritual action, and hath no gifts nor graces, other than such as are in hypocrites, nor any other sanctification but the Holy Ghost Himself.

There joined with her in these opinions a brother of hers, one Mr. Wheelwright,[3] a silenced minister sometimes in England.

[REV. JOHN COTTON EXPLAINS HIS POSITION]

[October 25, 1636] The other ministers in the bay, hearing of these things, came to Boston at the time of a general court, and entered conference in private with them, to the end they might know the certainty of these things; that if need were, they might write to the church of Boston about them, to prevent (if it were possible) the dangers which seemed hereby to hang over that and the rest of the churches. At this conference, Mr. Cotton was present, and gave satisfaction[4] to them, so as he agreed with them all in the point of sanctification, and so did Mr. Wheelwright; so as they all did hold that sanctification did help to evidence justification. The same he had delivered plainly in public, divers times; but, for the indwelling of the person of the Holy Ghost, he held that still, but not union with the person of the Holy Ghost, so as to amount to a personal union.

6. Misguided teachings. Providence Plantation in Rhode Island received its patent in 1644.
7. I.e., returned to Boston by ship.
8. John Underhill (c. 1597–1672) came to Massachusetts to organize the Massachusetts Bay Colony militia. "Pinnace": a small, light vessel, usually with two masts.
9. Anne Hutchinson (1591–1643), originally a follower of John Cotton (1584–1652), soon pursued an extreme position, believing that the elect were joined in personal union with God and superior to those lacking Inner Light. She also denied that good works were in any way a sign of God's favor, arguing that justification was by faith alone

and had nothing to do with either piety or worldly success.
1. I.e., one elected or chosen for salvation by God.
2. I.e., that proper moral conduct is no sign of justification.
3. John Wheelwright (c. 1592–1679) had been a vicar near Alford, England, where the Hutchinsons lived. He was removed from his ministry, probably because he refused to sign an oath of loyalty to the Church of England, and came to Boston in 1636.
4. Satisfied their doubts about him. Cotton's sermons were admired by the Hutchinsons and this worried his fellow ministers.

[CHARGES BROUGHT AGAINST MRS. HUTCHINSON AND OTHERS]

[November 1, 1637] * * * There was great hope that the late general assembly would have had some good effect in pacifying the troubles and dissensions about matters of religion; but it fell out otherwise. For though Mr. Wheelwright and those of his party had been clearly confuted and confounded in the assembly, yet they persisted in their opinions, and were as busy in nourishing contentions (the principal of them) as before.* * *

The court also sent for Mrs. Hutchinson, and charged her with divers matters, as her keeping two public lectures every week in her house, whereto sixty or eighty persons did usually resort, and for reproaching most of the ministers (viz., all except Mr. Cotton) for not preaching a covenant of free grace, and that they had not the seal of the spirit, nor were able ministers of the New Testament; which were clearly proved against her, though she sought to shift it off.[5] And after many speeches to and fro, at last she was so full as she could not contain, but vented her revelations; amongst which this was one, that she had it revealed to her that she should come into New England, and she should here be persecuted, and that God would ruin us and our posterity and the whole state for the same. So the court proceeded and banished her; but because it was winter, they committed her to a private house where she was well provided, and her own friends and the elders permitted to go to her, but none else.

The court called also Capt. Underhill and some five or six more of the principal, whose hands were to the said petition; and because they stood to justify it they were disfranchised, and such as had public places were put from them.

The court also ordered, that the rest, who had subscribed the petition, (and would not acknowledge their fault, and which near twenty of them did,) and some others, who had been chief stirrers in these contentions, etc., should be disarmed.[6] This troubled some of them very much, especially because they were to bring them in themselves; but at last, when they saw no remedy, they obeyed.

All the proceedings of this court against these persons were set down at large, with the reasons and other observations, and were sent into England to be published there, to the end that our godly friends might not be discouraged from coming to us, etc.* * *

[MRS. HUTCHINSON ADMONISHED FURTHER]

[March 1638] While Mrs. Hutchinson continued at Roxbury,[7] divers of the elders and others resorted to her, and finding her to persist in maintaining those gross errors beforementioned and many others to the number of thirty or thereabout, some of them wrote to the church at Boston, offering to make proof of the same before the church, etc., [March] 15; whereupon she was called, (the magistrates being desired to give her license to come,) and the lecture was appointed to begin at ten. (The general court being then at Newtown, the governor[8] and the treasurer, being members of Boston, were permitted to come down, but the rest of the court continued at Newtown.)

---

5. To qualify her statements.
6. Seventy-five people were disarmed, a severe punishment for this time and place.

7. Near Boston.
8. Winthrop himself. Newtown was shortly to be renamed Cambridge.

When she appeared, the errors were read to her. The first was that the souls of men are mortal by generation,[9] but after made immortal by Christ's purchase. This she maintained a long time; but at length she was so clearly convinced by reason and scripture, and the whole church agreeing that sufficient had been delivered for her conviction, that she yielded she had been in an error. Then they proceeded to three other errors: That there was no resurrection of these bodies, and that these bodies were not united to Christ, but every person united hath a new body, etc. These were also clearly confuted, but yet she held her own; so as the church (all but two of her sons)[1] agreed she should be admonished, and because her sons would not agree to it, they were admonished also.

Mr. Cotton pronounced the sentence of admonition with great solemnity, and with much zeal and detestation of her errors and pride of spirit. The assembly continued till eight at night, and all did acknowledge the special presence of God's spirit therein; and she was appointed to appear again the next lecture day.* * *

[MRS. HUTCHINSON BANISHED]

[March 22, 1638] Mrs. Hutchinson appeared again; (she had been licensed by the court, in regard she had given hope of her repentance, to be at Mr. Cotton's house that both he and Mr. Davenport[2] might have the more opportunity to deal with her;) and the articles being again read to her, and her answer required, she delivered it in writing, wherein she made a retractation of near all, but with such explanations and circumstances as gave no satisfaction to the church; so as she was required to speak further to them. Then she declared that it was just with God to leave her to herself, as He had done, for her slighting His ordinances, both magistracy and ministry;[3] and confessed that what she had spoken against the magistrates at the court (by way of revelation) was rash and ungrounded; and desired the church to pray for her. This gave the church good hope of her repentance; but when she was examined about some particulars, as that she had denied inherent righteousness, etc., she affirmed that it was never her judgment; and though it was proved by many testimonies that she had been of that judgment, and so had persisted and maintained it by argument against divers, yet she impudently persisted in her affirmation, to the astonishment of all the assembly. So that after much time and many arguments had been spent to bring her to see her sin, but all in vain, the church with one consent cast her out. Some moved to have her admonished once more; but, it being for manifest evil in matter of conversation, it was agreed otherwise; and for that reason also the sentence was denounced by the pastor,[4] matter of manners belonging properly to his place.

After she was excommunicated,[5] her spirits which seemed before to be somewhat dejected revived again, and she gloried in her sufferings, saying that it was the greatest happiness next to Christ that ever befell her. Indeed

9. I.e., from the beginning. Orthodox believers hold the soul immortal always.
1. Her son Edward Hutchinson and her son-in-law Thomas Savage, both of whom moved to Rhode Island.
2. John Davenport (1597–1670), a minister.

3. Because Mrs. Hutchinson's beliefs threatened both civil and ecclesiastical law.
4. John Wilson. "Admonished": warned. "Denounced": read in public.
5. Banished.

it was a happy day to the churches of Christ here, and to many poor souls who had been seduced by her, who by what they heard and saw that day were (through the grace of God) brought off quite from her errors, and settled again in the truth.

At this time the good providence of God so disposed, divers of the congregation (being the chief men of the party, her husband[6] being one) were gone to Narragansett to seek out a new place for plantation, and taking liking of one in Plymouth patent, they went thither to have it granted them; but the magistrates there, knowing their spirit, gave them a denial, but consented they might buy of the Indians an island in the Narragansett Bay.

After two or three days the governor sent a warrant to Mrs. Hutchinson to depart this jurisdiction before the last of this month, according to the order of court, and for that end set her at liberty from her former constraint, so as she was not to go forth of her own house till her departure; and upon the 28th she went by water to her farm at the Mount, where she was to take water with Mr. Wheelwright's wife and family to go to Pascataquack; but she changed her mind, and went by land to Providence, and so to the island in the Narragansett Bay which her husband and the rest of that sect had purchased of the Indians, and prepared with all speed to remove unto. For the court had ordered, that except they were gone with their families by such a time they should be summoned to the general court, etc.

[MRS. HUTCHINSON DELIVERS A CHILD]

[September 1638] * * * Mrs. Hutchinson, being removed to the Isle of Aquiday[7] in the Narragansett Bay, after her time was fulfilled that she expected deliverance of a child, was delivered of a monstrous birth. Hereupon the governor wrote to Mr. Clarke,[8] a physician and a preacher to those of the island, to know the certainty thereof, who returned him this answer: Mrs. Hutchinson, six weeks before her delivery, perceived her body to be greatly distempered and her spirits failing and in that regard doubtful of life, she sent to me etc., and not long after (in *immoderato fluore uterino*)[9] it was brought to light, and I was called to see it, where I beheld innumerable distinct bodies in the form of a globe, not much unlike the swims[1] of some fish, so confusedly knit together by so many several strings (which I conceive were the beginning of veins and nerves) so that it was impossible either to number the small round pieces in every lump, much less to discern from whence every string did fetch its original, they were so snarled one within another. The small globes I likewise opened, and perceived the matter of them (setting aside the membrane in which it was involved) to be partly wind and partly water. The governor, not satisfied with this relation, spake after with the said Mr. Clarke, who thus cleared all the doubts: The lumps were twenty-six or twenty-seven, distinct and not joined together; there came no secundine[2] after them; six of them were as great as his fist, and the smallest about the bigness of the top of his thumb. The globes were round things,

6. William Hutchinson, who along with several others laid out plans for the town of Portsmouth, Rhode Island.
7. Aquidneck Island, Rhode Island.
8. Dr. John Clarke came to Boston in 1637 and was disarmed, having been declared an antinomian.
9. In a heavy discharge from the womb (Latin).
1. Swimming bladders.
2. Afterbirth.

included in the lumps, about the bigness of a small Indian bean, and like the pearl in a man's eye. The two lumps which differed from the rest were like liver or congealed blood, and had no small globes in them, as the rest had.

[AN EARTHQUAKE AT AQUIDAY]

[March 16, 1639] * * * At Aquiday also Mrs. Hutchinson exercised[3] publicly, and she and her party (some three or four families) would have no magistracy. She sent also an admonition to the church of Boston; but the elders would not read it publicly because she was excommunicated. By these examples we may see how dangerous it is to slight the censures of the church; for it was apparent that God had given them up to strange delusions. . . . Mrs. Hutchinson and some of her adherents happened to be at prayer when the earthquake was at Aquiday, etc., and the house being shaken thereby, they were persuaded (and boasted of it) that the Holy Ghost did shake it in coming down upon them, as He did upon the apostles.

[THE DEATH OF MRS. HUTCHINSON AND OTHERS]

[September 1643] The Indians near the Dutch, having killed 15 men, began to set upon the English who dwelt under the Dutch. They came to Mrs. Hutchinson's[4] in way of friendly neighborhood, as they had been accustomed, and taking their opportunity, killed her and Mr. Collins, her son-in-law (who had been kept prisoner in Boston, as is before related), and all her family, and such [other] families as were at home; in all sixteen, and put their cattle into their houses and there burnt them. These people had cast off ordinances and churches, and now at last their own people, and for larger accommodation had subjected themselves to the Dutch and dwelt scatteringly near a mile asunder.* * *

[WINTHROP'S SPEECH TO THE GENERAL COURT]

[July 3, 1645] * * * Then was the deputy governor[5] desired by the Court to go up and take his place again upon the bench, which he did accordingly. And the Court being about to rise, he desired leave for a little speech which was to this effect.

I suppose something may be expected from me upon this charge that is befallen me, which moves me to speak now to you. Yet I intend not to intermeddle in the proceedings of the Court, or with any of the persons concerned therein. Only I bless God that I see an issue[6] of this troublesome business.

---

3. Lectured.
4. After the death of her husband, William, in 1642 Anne Hutchinson moved to Dutch territory: Pelham Bay, Long Island, now a part of the Bronx in New York.
5. Winthrop. The governor in 1645 was Thomas Dudley (1576–1653). The "little speech" that follows is one of Winthrop's most important meditations on Christian liberty. Several residents of the town of Hingham argued that "words spoken against the General Court" had been unfairly used against them by Winthrop and others, and they hoped that Winthrop would be impeached for misusing his power as deputy. Winthrop was fully acquitted.
6. Termination.

I also acknowledge the justice of the Court, and for mine own part I am well satisfied. I was publicly charged, and I am publicly and legally acquitted, which is all I did expect or desire. And though this be sufficient for my justification before men, yet not so before the Lord, who hath seen so much amiss in any dispensations (and even in this affair) as calls me to be humbled. For to be publicly and criminally charged in this Court is matter of humiliation (and I desire to make a right use of it), notwithstanding I be thus acquitted. If her father had spit in her face (saith the Lord concerning Miriam), should she not have been ashamed 7 days?[7] Shame had lain upon her whatever the occasion had been. I am unwilling to stay you from your urgent affairs, yet give me leave (upon this special occasion) to speak a little more to this assembly. It may be of some good use to inform and rectify the judgments of some of the people, and may prevent such distempers as have arisen amongst us. The great questions that have troubled the country are about the authority of the magistrates and the liberty of the people. It is yourselves who have called us to this office, and being called by you we have our authority from God in way of an ordinance, such as hath the image of God eminently stamped upon it, the contempt and violation whereof hath been vindicated with examples of divine vengeance. I entreat you to consider that when you choose magistrates you take them from among yourselves, men subject to like passions as you are. Therefore, when you see infirmities in us, you should reflect upon your own, and that would make you bear the more with us, and not be severe censurers of the failings of your magistrates when you have continual experience of the like infirmities in yourselves and others. We account him a good servant who breaks not his covenant. The covenant between you and us is the oath you have taken of us, which is to this purpose, that we shall govern you and judge your causes by the rules of God's laws and our own, according to our best skill. When you agree with a workman to build you a ship or house, etc., he undertakes as well for his skill as for his faithfulness, for it is his profession, and you pay him for both. But when you call one to be a magistrate, he doth not profess nor undertake to have sufficient skill for that office, nor can you furnish him with gifts, etc. Therefore you must run the hazard of his skill and ability. But if he fail in faithfulness, which by his oath he is bound unto, that he must answer for. If it fall out that the case be clear to common apprehension and the rule clear also, if he transgress here the error is not in the skill but in the evil of the will; it must be required of him. But if the case be doubtful, or the rule doubtful, to men of such understanding and parts as your magistrates are, if your magistrates should err here yourselves must bear it.

For the other point concerning liberty, I observe a great mistake in the country about that. There is a twofold liberty: natural (I mean as our nature is now corrupt),[8] and civil or federal. The first is common to man with beasts and other creatures. By this, man as he stands in relation to man simply, hath liberty to do what he list. It is a liberty to evil as well as to good. This liberty is incompatible and inconsistent with authority, and cannot endure

---

7. Miriam was the sister of Moses and Aaron. "And the Lord said unto Moses, If her father had but spit in her face, should she not be ashamed seven days? let her be shut out from the camp seven days, and after that let her be received in again" (Numbers 12.14).

8. Because we are fallen and subject to death.

the least restraint of the most just authority. The exercise and maintaining of this liberty makes men grow more evil, and in time to be worse than brute beasts, *omnes sumus licentia deteriores*.[9] This is that great enemy of truth and peace, that wild beast which all the ordinances of God are bent against, to restrain and subdue it.

The other kind of liberty I call civil or federal. It may also be termed moral, in reference to the covenant between God and man in the moral law, and the politic covenants and constitutions amongst men themselves. This liberty is the proper end and object of authority and cannot subsist without it, and it is a liberty to that only which is good, just, and honest. This liberty you are to stand for, with the hazard not only of your goods but of your lives, if need be. Whatsoever crosseth this is not authority, but a distemper thereof. This liberty is maintained and exercised in a way of subjection to authority. It is of the same kind of liberty wherewith Christ hath made us free.[1] The woman's own choice makes such a man her husband, yet being so chosen he is her lord and she is to be subject to him, yet in a way of liberty, not of bondage, and a true wife accounts her subjection her honor and freedom, and would not think her condition safe and free but in her subjection to her husband's authority. Such is the liberty of the church under the authority of Christ her King and husband. His yoke is so easy and sweet to her as a bride's ornaments,[2] and if through frowardness or wantonness, etc., she shake it off at any time, she is at no rest in her spirit until she take it up again. And whether her Lord smiles upon her and embraceth her in His arms, or whether He frowns, or rebukes, or smites her, she apprehends the sweetness of His love in all and is refreshed, supported, and instructed by every such dispensation of His authority over her. On the other side, you know who they are that complain of this yoke and say: let us break their bands, etc.; we will not have this man to rule over us. Even so, brethren, it will be between you and your magistrates. If you stand for your natural corrupt liberties, and will do what is good in your own eyes, you will not endure the least weight of authority, but will murmur and oppose and be always striving to shake off that yoke. But if you will be satisfied to enjoy such civil and lawful liberties, such as Christ allows you, then will you quietly and cheerfully submit unto that authority which is set over you in all the administrations of it for your good; wherein if we fail at any time, we hope we shall be willing (by God's assistance) to hearken to good advice from any of you, or in any other way of God. So shall your liberties be preserved in upholding the honor and power of authority amongst you.

The deputy governor having ended his speech, the Court arose, and the magistrates and deputies retired to attend their other affairs.* * *

---

9. We are all the worse for license (Latin). From Terence (c. 190–159 B.C.E.), *Heauton Timorumenos* (*The Self-Tormentor*) 3.1.74.

1. "Stand fast therefore in the liberty wherewith Christ hath made us free, and be not entangled again with the yoke of bondage" (Galatians 5.1).

2. "For my yoke is easy, and my burden is light" (Matthew 11.30). "And I John saw the holy city, new Jerusalem, coming down out of heaven from God, prepared as a bride adorned for her husband" (Revelation 21.2).

[A DAUGHTER RETURNED]

[July 1646] * * * A daughter of Mrs. Hutchinson was carried away by the Indians near the Dutch, when her mother and others were killed by them; and upon the peace concluded between the Dutch and the same Indians, she was returned to the Dutch governor, who restored her to her friends here. She was about 8 years old when she was taken, and continued with them about 4 years, and she had forgot her own language, and all her friends, and was loath to have come from the Indians.

1630–49   1825–26

ROGER WILLIAMS
c. 1603–1683

In his journal for January 1636, John Winthrop tells us that when the governor of Massachusetts and his assistants met to redetermine the charge of divisiveness that had been brought against Roger Williams, they agreed that they could not wait until spring to banish him from the commonwealth. They must move against him immediately, they argued, and ship him back to England. His opinions were dangerous and spreading. When they went to Salem to seize him and "carry him aboard the ship," however, they found he "had been gone three days before, but whither they could not learn." Williams had, of course, fled Massachusetts for Rhode Island. He found shelter there with the Narragansett Indians and, from that time until his death almost fifty years later, Williams and Providence Plantation were synonymous with the spirit of religious liberty. Rhode Island became a sanctuary for those who found the strictures of the Massachusetts Bay insufferable: Separatists, Baptists, Seekers, Antinomians, Jews, and Quakers were all to find a home there. In 1663 Rhode Island received a royal charter from Charles II in which freedom of conscience was guaranteed. It was something of which not even Englishmen were assured, and it became so indelibly "American" an idea that provision was made for it in our 1791 Bill of Rights.

Williams had infuriated and threatened the leaders of Massachusetts by taking four rather extreme positions, any one of which seriously undermined the theocracy that was at the heart of the Bay Colony government. He denied, first, that Massachusetts had a proper title to its land, arguing that King Charles I could not bestow a title to something that belonged to the natives. Second, he argued that no unregenerate person could be required either to pray in churches or to swear in a court of law on oath; third, that Massachusetts Bay Colony ministers, who had persuaded the king of England when they left their native country that they wished to remain a part of the national church, should not only separate from the Church of England but repent that they had ever served it; last, that civil authority was limited to civil matters and that magistrates had no jurisdiction over the soul. Williams, as the historian Perry Miller has put it, wanted to "build a wall of separation between state and church not to prevent the state from becoming an instrument of 'priestcraft,' but in order to keep the holy and pure religion of Jesus Christ from contamination by the slightest taint of earthly support." It was a disturbing position for Separatist and non-Separatist alike, and Williams has the distinction of having made himself unwelcome in both Plymouth and Boston.

In 1631 Williams and his wife, Mary, arrived in Boston aboard the ship *Lyon*. He had graduated from Cambridge University in 1627 and sometime before 1629 took holy orders and served as a chaplain to Sir William Masham at Otis in Essex County. It was there that Williams's interest in church reform developed. Years later he said that it was Archbishop Laud (who required an oath of loyalty to the Church of England from all ministers) who "pursued" him "out of this land." When he refused a call to the prestigious First Church of Boston because he "durst not officiate to an unseparated people," Massachusetts authorities must have had their first inkling of just how assured Williams was in matters of belief. It was in October 1635 that he was first accused of holding "new and dangerous opinions against the authority of magistrates."

The Massachusetts authorities did not cite Williams's attitude toward the American Indians in their charges against him, but like most of his postures, his attitude was antithetical to their own. From the beginning, he wrote, his "soul's desire was to do the natives good, and to that end to have their language." Although he was not interested in assimilating their culture, Williams nevertheless saw that the American Indians were no better or worse than the "rogues" who dealt with them, and that in fact they possessed a marked degree of civility. Williams must have known that when he prepared his *Key into the Language of America* (1634) his book would benefit those who wished to convert Native Americans to Christianity, but Williams was not primarily interested in the conversion of others. *Anyone* not regenerate was, Williams argued, outside the people of God, and to refer to the American Indians as "heathen" was "improperly sinful" and "unchristianly." Williams himself remained a Seeker and detached from the community of any church for most of his life. His great disappointment, however, was that despite his efforts to befriend the Narragansetts, they joined their brothers in King Philip's War and burned the settlements at both Warwick and Providence. By the time Williams died, sometime between January and March of 1683, the question of the future role of the Narragansetts became moot. The great tribe would never recover from the toll taken during that war.

From A Key into the Language of America[1]

To My Dear and Well-Beloved Friends and Countrymen, in Old and New England

I present you with a key; I have not heard of the like, yet framed, since it pleased God to bring that mighty continent of America to light. Others of my countrymen have often, and excellently, and lately written of the country (and none that I know beyond the goodness and worth of it).

This key, respects the native language of it, and happily may unlock some rarities concerning the natives themselves, not yet discovered.

I drew the materials in a rude lump at sea, as a private help to my own memory, that I might not, by my present absence, lightly lose what I had so dearly bought in some few years hardship, and charges among the barbarians. Yet being reminded by some, what pity it were to bury those materials in my grave at land or sea; and withal, remembering how oft I have been importuned by worthy friends of all sorts, to afford them some helps this way. I resolved (by the assistance of The Most High) to cast those materials into this key, pleasant and profitable for all, but especially for my friends residing in those parts.

1. The text is from a reprint of the first edition (1643), published by the Rhode Island and Providence Tercentenary Committee (1936).

A little key may open a box, where lies a bunch of keys.

With this I have entered into the secrets of those countries, wherever English dwell about two hundred miles, between the French and Dutch plantations; for want of this, I know what gross mistakes myself and others have run into.

There is a mixture of this language north and south, from the place of my abode, about six hundred miles; yet within the two hundred miles (afore-mentioned) their dialects do exceedingly differ; yet not so, but (within that compass) a man may, by this help, converse with thousands of natives all over the country: and by such converse it may please the Father of Mercies to spread civility, (and in His own most holy season) Christianity. For one candle will light ten thousand, and it may please God to bless a little leaven to season the mighty lump of those peoples and territories.

It is expected, that having had so much converse with these natives, I should write some little of them.

Concerning them (a little to gratify expectation) I shall touch upon four heads:

First, by what names they are distinguished.

Secondly, their original[2] and descent.

Thirdly, their religion, manners, customs, etc.

Fourthly, that great point of their conversion.

To the first, their names are of two sorts:

First, those of the English giving: as natives, savages, Indians, wildmen, (so the Dutch call them *wilden*) Abergeny[3] men, pagans, barbarians, hea-then.

Secondly, their names which they give themselves.

I cannot observe that they ever had (before the coming of the English, French or Dutch amongst them) any names to difference themselves from strangers, for they knew none; but two sorts of names they had, and have amongst themselves:

First, general, belonging to all natives, as Nínnuock, Ninnimissinnûwock, Eniskeetompaûwog, which signifies Men, Folk, or People.

Secondly, particular names, peculiar to several nations, of them amongst themselves, as Nanhiggañeŭck, Massachusêuck, Cawasumsêuck, Cowwe-sêuck, Quintikóock, Qunnipiĕuck, Pequttóog, etc.

They have often asked me, why we call them Indians, natives, etc. And understanding the reason, they will call themselves Indians, in opposition to English, etc.

For the second head proposed, their original and descent:

From Adam and Noah[4] that they spring, it is granted on all hands.

But for their later descent, and whence they came into those parts, it seems as hard to find, as to find the wellhead of some fresh stream, which running many miles out of the country to the salt ocean, hath met with many mixing streams by the way. They say themselves, that they have sprung and grown up in that very place, like the very trees of the wilderness.

They say that their great god Kautántowwìt created those parts, as I observed in the chapter of their religion. They have no clothes, books, nor

---

2. Place of origin.
3. Aboriginal.

4. After the great flood described in the Bible only Noah and his family remain.

letters, and conceive their fathers never had; and therefore they are easily persuaded that the God that made Englishmen is a greater God, because He hath so richly endowed the English above themselves. But when they hear that about sixteen hundred years ago, England and the inhabitants thereof were like unto themselves, and since have received from God, clothes, books, etc. they are greatly affected with a secret hope concerning themselves.

Wise and judicious men, with whom I have discoursed, maintain their original to be northward from Tartaria:[5] and at my now taking ship, at the Dutch plantation, it pleased the Dutch Governor, (in some discourse with me about the natives), to draw their line from Iceland, because the name Sackmakan (the name for an Indian prince, about the Dutch) is the name for a prince in Iceland.

Other opinions I could number up: under favor I shall present (not mine opinion, but) my observations to the judgment of the wise.

First, others (and myself) have conceived some of their words to hold affinity with the Hebrew.

Secondly, they constantly anoint their heads as the Jews did.

Thirdly, they give dowries for their wives, as the Jews did.

Fourthly (and which I have not so observed amongst other nations as amongst the Jews, and these:) they constantly separate their women (during the time of their monthly sickness) in a little house alone by themselves four or five days, and hold it an irreligious thing for either father or husband or any male to come near them.

They have often asked me if it be so with women of other nations, and whether they are so separated: and for their practice they plead nature and tradition. Yet again I have found a greater affinity of their language with the Greek tongue.

2. As the Greeks and other nations, and ourselves call the seven stars (or Charles' Wain, the Bear,)[6] so do they Mosk or Paukunnawaw, the Bear.

3. They have many strange relations of one Wétucks, a man that wrought great miracles amongst them, and walking upon the waters, etc., with some kind of broken resemblance to the Son of God.

Lastly, it is famous that the Sowwest (Sowaniu) is the great subject of their discourse. From thence their traditions. There they say (at the southwest) is the court of their great god Kautántowwìt: at the southwest are their forefathers' souls: to the southwest they go themselves when they die; from the southwest came their corn, and beans out of their great god Kautántowwìt's field: and indeed the further northward and westward from us their corn will not grow, but to the southward better and better. I dare not conjecture in these uncertainties. I believe they are lost, and yet hope (in the Lord's holy season) some of the wildest of them shall be found to share in the blood of the Son of God. To the third head, concerning their religion, customs, manners etc. I shall here say nothing, because in those 32 chapters of the whole book,[7] I have briefly touched those of all sorts, from their birth to their burials, and have endeavored (as the nature of the work would give way) to bring some short observations and applications home to Europe from America.

---

5. Mongolia.
6. I.e., the constellation known as Ursa Major (Great Bear), the Big Dipper, or Charlemagne's wagon ("wain").
7. I.e., the thirty-two chapters of Williams's *Key*.

Therefore fourthly, to that great point of their conversion, so much to be longed for, and by all New-English so much pretended,[8] and I hope in truth.

For myself I have uprightly labored to suit my endeavors to my pretenses: and of later times (out of desire to attain their language) I have run through varieties of intercourses[9] with them day and night, summer and winter, by land and sea, particular passages tending to this, I have related divers, in the chapter of their religion.

Many solemn discourses I have had with all sorts of nations of them, from one end of the country to another (so far as opportunity, and the little language I have could reach).

I know there is no small preparation in the hearts of multitudes of them. I know their many solemn confessions to myself, and one to another of their lost wandering conditions.

I know strong convictions upon the consciences of many of them, and their desires uttered that way.

I know not with how little knowledge and grace of Christ the Lord may save, and therefore, neither will despair, nor report much.

But since it hath pleased some of my worthy countrymen to mention (of late in print) Wequash, the Péquot captain, I shall be bold so far to second their relations, as to relate mine own hopes of him (though I dare not be so confident as others).

Two days before his death, as I passed up to Qunníhticut[1] River, it pleased my worthy friend Mr. Fenwick, (whom I visited at his house in Saybrook Fort at the mouth of that river,) to tell me that my old friend Wequash lay very sick. I desired to see him, and himself was pleased to be my guide two miles where Wequash lay.

Amongst other discourse concerning his sickness and death (in which he freely bequeathed his son to Mr. Fenwick) I closed[2] with him concerning his soul: he told me that some two or three years before he had lodged at my house, where I acquainted him with the condition of all mankind, & his own in particular; how God created man and all things; how man fell from God, and of his present enmity against God, and the wrath of God against him until repentance. Said he, "your words were never out of my heart to this present;" and said he "me much pray to Jesus Christ." I told him so did many English, French, and Dutch, who had never turned to God, nor loved Him. He replied in broken English: "Me so big naughty heart, me heart all one stone!" Savory expressions using to breathe from compunct and broken hearts, and a sense of inward hardness and unbrokenness. I had many discourses with him in his life, but this was the sum of our last parting until our General Meeting.[3]

Now, because this is the great inquiry of all men: what Indians have been converted? what have the English done in those parts? what hopes of the Indians receiving the knowledge of Christ?

And because to this question, some put an edge from the boast of the Jesuits in Canada and Maryland, and especially from the wonderful conversions made by the Spaniards and Portugals in the West-Indies, besides what I have here written, as also, beside what I have observed in the chapter of

8. Asserted, proffered (with none of the modern connotations of deceit).
9. Conversations.

1. Connecticut.
2. Came to the end of his talk.
3. I.e., Judgment Day.

their religion, I shall further present you with a brief additional discourse concerning this great point, being comfortably persuaded that that Father of Spirits, who was graciously pleased to persuade Japhet (the Gentiles) to dwell in the tents of Shem[4] (the Jews), will, in His holy season (I hope approaching), persuade these Gentiles of America to partake of the mercies of Europe, and then shall be fulfilled what is written by the prophet Malachi,[5] from the rising of the sun (in Europe) to the going down of the same (in America), My name shall be great among the Gentiles. So I desire to hope and pray,

Your unworthy countryman,
ROGER WILLIAMS

Directions for the Use of the Language

1. A dictionary or grammar way I had consideration of, but purposely avoided, as not so accommodate to the benefit of all, as I hope this form is.

2. A dialogue also I had thoughts of, but avoided for brevity's sake, and yet (with no small pains) I have so framed every chapter and the matter of it, as I may call it an implicit dialogue.

3. It is framed chiefly after the *Narragansett* dialect, because most spoken in the country, and yet (with attending to the variation of peoples and dialects) it will be of great use in all parts of the country.

4. Whatever your occasion be, either of travel, discourse, trading etc. turn to the table which will direct you to the proper chapter.

5. Because the life of all language is in the pronunciation, I have been at the pains and charges to cause the accents, tones or sounds to be affixed, (which some understand, according to the Greek language, acutes, graves, circumflexes) for example, in the second leaf[6] in the word *Ewò He*: the sound or tone must not be put on *E*, but *wò* where the grave accent is.

In the same leaf, in the word *Ascowequássin*, the sound must not be on any of the syllables, but on *quáss*, where the acute or sharp sound is.

In the same leaf in the word *Anspaumpmaûntam*, the sound must not be on any other syllable but *maûn*, where the circumflex or long sounding accent is.

6. The English for every Indian word or phrase stands in a straight line directly against the Indian: yet sometimes there are two words for the same thing (for their language is exceeding copious, and they have five or six words sometimes for one thing) and then the English stands against them both: for example in the second leaf:

Cowáunckamish & Cuckqué-namish	I pray your favor.

---

4. The eldest son of Noah. Japhet was the third son of Noah and, in some traditions, the progenitor of the Indo-European race (see Genesis 9.18).
5. "For from the rising of the sun even unto the going down of the same my name shall be great among the Gentiles" (Malachi 1.11).
6. Page.

From *An Help to the Native Language of that Part of America Called New England*

FROM CHAPTER XXI. OF RELIGION, THE SOUL, ETC.

Manìt-manittó, wock.	God, Gods.

Obs. He that questions whether God made the world, the Indians will teach him. I must acknowledge I have received in my converse[7] with them many confirmations of those two great points, Hebrews II. 6. viz:

1. That God is.
2. That He is a rewarder of all them that diligently seek Him.

They will generally confess that God made all, but them in special, although they deny not that Englishman's God made Englishmen, and the heavens and earth there! yet their Gods made them and the heaven, and earth where they dwell.

Nummusquauna-múckqun manìt.	God is angry with me?

Obs. I have heard a poor Indian lamenting the loss of a child at break of day, call up his wife and children, and all about him to lamentation, and with abundance of tears cry out! "O God thou hast taken away my child! thou art angry with me: O turn Thine anger from me, and spare the rest of my children."

If they receive any good in hunting, fishing, harvest etc. they acknowledge God in it.

Yea, if it be but an ordinary accident, a fall, etc. they will say God was angry and did it, *musquàntum manit* God is angry. But herein is their misery:

First, they branch their God-head into many gods.

Secondly, attribute it to creatures.

First, many gods: they have given me the names of thirty seven which I have, all which in their solemn worships they invocate, as:

Kautántowwìt the great Southwest God, to whose house all souls go, and from whom came their corn, beans, as they say.

Wompanand.	The Eastern god.
Chekesuwànd.	The Western God.
Wunnanaméanit.	The Northern God.
Sowwanànd.	The Southern God.
Wetuómanit.	The House God.

Even as the papists have their he and she saint protectors as St. George, St. Patrick, St. Denis, Virgin Mary, etc.

Squáuanit.	The Woman's God.
Muckquachuckquànd.	The Children's God.

Obs. I was once with a native dying of a wound, given him by some murderous English who robbed him and ran him through with a rapier, from whom in the heat of his wound, he at present escaped from them, but dying of his wound, they suffered death at New Plymouth, in New England, this native dying called much upon *Muckquachuckquànd*, which of other natives I understood (as they believed) had appeared to the dying young man, many years before, and bid him whenever he was in distress call upon him.

---

7. Conversation.

Secondly, as they have many of these fained deities; so worship they the creatures in whom they conceive doth rest some deity:

Keesuckquànd.	The Sun God.
Nanepaûshat.	The Moon God.
Paumpágussit.	The Sea.
Yotáanit.	The Fire God.

Supposing that deities be in these, etc.

* * *

They have a modest religious persuasion not to disturb any man, either themselves English, Dutch, or any in their conscience, and worship, and therefore say:

Aquiewopwaûwash.	Peace, hold your peace.
Aquiewopwaûwock.	
Peeyàuntam.	He is at prayer.
Peeyaúntamwock	They are praying.
Couwéwonck.	The soul.

Derived from *couwene* to sleep, because say they, it works and operates when the body sleeps. *Míchachunck,* the soul, in a higher notion which is of affinity, with a word signifying a looking glass, or clear resemblance, so that it hath its name from a clear sight or discerning, which indeed seems very well to suit with the nature of it.

Wuhóck.	The body
Nohòck: cohòck	My body, your body
Awaunkeesitteoúwincohòck:	
Tunna-awwa commítchichunck-	Whether goes your soul when you
kitonckquèan?	die?
An. Sowánakitaúwaw.	It goes to the southwest.

Obs. They believe that the souls of men and women go to the southwest, their great and good men and women to Kautántowwìt, his house, where they have hopes (as the Turks have of carnal joys). Murderers, thieves and liars, their souls (say they) wander restless abroad.

Now because this book (by God's good providence) may come into the hand of many fearing God, who may also have many an opportunity of occasional discourse with some of these, their wild brethren and sisters, and may speak a word for their and our glorious Maker, which may also prove some preparatory mercy to their souls: I shall propose some proper expressions concerning the creation of the world, and man's estate, and in particular theirs also, which from myself many hundreds of times, great numbers of them have heard with great delight, and great convictions; which, who knows (in God's holy season), may rise to the exalting of the Lord Jesus Christ in their conversion, and salvation?

Nétop Kunnatótemous.	Friend, I will ask you a question.
Natótema:	Speak on.
Tocketunnântum?	What think you?
Awaun Keesiteoûwin Kéesuck?	Who made the heavens?
Aûke Wechêkom?	The earth, the sea?
Míttauke.	The world.

Some will answer *Tattá,* I cannot tell, some will answer *Manittôwock,* the gods.

Tà suóg Maníttôwock	How many gods be there?
Maunaũog Mishaúnawock.	Many, great many.
Nétop machàge.	Friend, not so.
Paũsuck naũnt manìt.	There is only one God.
Cuppíssittone.	You are mistaken.
Cowauwaúnemun.	You are out of the way.

A phrase which much pleaseth them, being proper for their wandering in the woods, and similitudes greatly please them.

Kukkakótemous, wâchit-quáshouwe.	I will tell you, presently.
Kuttaunchemókous.	I will tell you news.
Paũsuck naũnt manit kéesittin kee-suck, etc.	One only God made the heavens etc.
Napannetashèmittan naugecautúm-monab nshque.	Five thousand years ago and upwards.
Naũgom naũnt wukkesittínnes wâme teâgun.	He alone made all things.
Wuche mateâg.	Out of nothing.
Quttatashuchuckqún-nacaus-keesitínnes wâme.	In six days He made all things.
Nquittaqúnne.	The first day He made the light.
Wuckéesitin wequâi.	
Néesqunne.	The second day He made the firmament.
Wuckéesitin Keésuck.	
Shúckqunnewuckéesitin Aũke kà wechêkom.	The third day He made the earth and sea.
Yóqunne wuckkéesitin Nippaũus kà Nanepaũshat.	The fourth day He made the sun and the moon.
Neenash-mamockíuwash wêquan-antíganash.	Two great lights.
Kà wáme anócksuck.	And all the stars.
Napannetashúckqunne Wuckéesit-tin pussuckseésuck wâme.	The fifth day He made all the fowl.
Keesuckquíuke	In the air, or heavens.
Ka wáme namaũsuck. Wechekom-míuke.	And all the fish in the sea.
Quttatashúkqunne wuckkeésittin penashímwock wamè.	The sixth day He made all the beasts of the field.
Wuttàke wuchè wuckeesittin pau-suck Enìn, or, Eneskéetomp.	Last of all he made one man.
Wuche mishquòck.	Of red earth,
Ka wesuonckgonnakaũnes Adam, túppautea mishquòck.	And called him Adam, or red earth.
Wuttàke wuchè, Câwit míshquock,	Then afterward, while Adam, or red earth, slept,
Wuckaudnúmmenes manìt peetaũ-gon wuche Adam.	God took a rib from Adam, or red earth.
Kà wuchè peteaũgon. Wukkeesitín-nes pausuck squâw.	And of that rib he made one woman.
Kà pawtouwúnnes Adâmuck	And brought her to Adam.
Nawônt Adam wuttúnnawaun nup-peteâgon ewò.	When Adam saw her, he said, "This is my bone."

Enadatashúckqunne, aquêi,	The seventh day He rested,
Nagaû wuchè quttatashúckqune	And, therefore, Englishmen work
anacaûsuock Englishmánuck.	six days.
Enadatashuckqunnóckat tauba-	On the seventh day they praise
taûmwock.	God.

Obs. At this relation they are much satisfied, with a reason why (as they observe) the English and Dutch, etc., labor six days, and rest and worship the seventh.

Besides, they will say, we never heard of this before: and then will relate how they have it from their fathers, that Kautántowwìt made one man and woman of a stone, which disliking, he broke them in pieces, and made another man and woman of a tree, which were the fountains of all mankind.

* * *

1643

From The Bloody Tenet of Persecution, for Cause of Conscience, in a Conference between Truth and Peace[1]

To every Courteous Reader.

While I plead the cause of *truth* and *innocency* against the bloody *doctrine* of *persecution* for cause of *conscience,* I judge it not unfit to give *alarm* to myself, and all men to prepare to be *persecuted* or hunted for cause of *conscience.*

Whether thou standest charged with ten or but two talents,[2] if thou huntest any for cause of *conscience,* how canst thou say thou followest the *Lamb of God* who so abhorred that practice?

If Paul, if Jesus Christ, were present here at London, and the question were proposed what religion would they approve of: the Papists, Prelatists,[3] Presbyterians, Independents, etc. would each say, "Of mine, of mine."

But put the second question, if one of the several sorts should by major vote attain the sword of steel: what weapons doth Christ Jesus authorize them to fight with in His cause? Do not all men hate the persecutor, and every conscience true or false complain of cruelty, tyranny? etc.

Two mountains of crying guilt lie heavy upon the backs of all that name the name of Christ in the eyes of Jews, Turks and Pagans.

First, the blasphemies of their idolatrous inventions, superstitions, and most unchristian conversations.

Secondly, the bloody, irreligious and inhumane oppressions and destructions under the mask or veil of the name of Christ, etc.

O how like is the jealous Jehovah, the consuming fire to end these present slaughters in a greater slaughter of the holy witnesses? Revelation 11.

1. The text is from *The Writings of Roger Williams,* vol. 3 (1866–74). Williams wrote this tract while in London attempting to get a patent for Providence Plantation. It is one of a series of tracts in which Williams debated John Cotton on the question of freedom of conscience. Neither the author's name nor the publisher appeared on the title page and copies were burned by order of Parliament because of its democratic implications.
2. Individuals.
3. Episcopalians.

Six years preaching of so much truth of Christ (as that time afforded in King Edward's days) kindles the flames of Queen Mary's bloody persecutions.[4]

Who can now but expect that after so many scores of years preaching and professing of more truth, and amongst so many great contentions amongst the very best of Protestants, a fiery furnace should be heat, and who sees not now the fires kindling?

I confess I have little hopes till those flames are over, that this discourse against the doctrine of persecution for cause of conscience should pass current (I say not amongst the wolves and lions, but even amongst the sheep of Christ themselves) yet *liberavi animam meam*,[5] I have not hid within my breast my soul's belief; and although sleeping on the bed either of the pleasures or profits of sin thou thinkest thy conscience bound to smite at him that dares to waken thee? Yet in the midst of all these civil and spiritual wars[6] I hope we shall agree in these particulars.

First, however, the proud (upon the advantage of an higher earth or ground) overlook the poor and cry out schismatics, heretics, etc. shall blasphemers and seducers escape unpunished, etc. Yet there is a sorer punishment in the Gospel for despising of Christ than Moses, even when the despiser of Moses was put to death without mercy, Hebrews 10.28–29. "He that believeth not shall be damned," Mark 16.16.

Secondly, whatever worship, ministry, ministration, the best and purest are practiced without faith and true persuasion that they are the true institutions of God, they are sin, sinful worships, ministries, etc. And however in civil things we may be servants unto men, yet in divine and spiritual things the poorest peasant must disdain the service of the highest prince: "Be ye not the servants of men," I Corinthians 14.

Thirdly, without search and trial no man attains this faith and right persuasion, I Thessalonians 5. "Try all things."

In vain have English Parliaments permitted English Bibles in the poorest English houses, and the simplest man or woman to search the Scriptures, if yet against their soul's persuasion from the Scripture, they should be forced (as if they lived in Spain or Rome itself without the sight of a Bible) to believe as the Church believes.

Fourthly, having tried, we must hold fast, I Thessalonians 5. upon the loss of a crown, Revelation 13. we must not let go for all the flea bitings of the present afflictions, etc. having bought truth dear, we must not sell it cheap, not the least grain of it for the whole world, no not for the saving of souls, though our own most precious; least of all for the bitter sweetening of a little vanishing pleasure.

For a little puff of credit and reputation from the changeable breath of uncertain sons of men.

For the broken bags of riches on eagles' wings: For a dream of these, any or all of these which on our deathbed vanish and leave tormenting stings behind them: Oh, how much better is it from the love of truth, from the love of the Father of Lights, from whence it comes, from the love of the Son of God, who is the way and the truth, to say as He, John 18.37: "For this end

---

4. Edward VI (r. 1547–53) and Queen Mary (r. 1553–58). Many Protestants were burned at the stake during the reign of Queen Mary.

5. I have freed my soul (Latin).
6. Civil war had broken out in England in 1642.

was I born, and for this end came I into the world that I might bear witness to the truth."

1643–44   1644

A Letter to the Town of Providence[1]

That ever I should speak or write a tittle,[2] that tends to such an infinite liberty of conscience, is a mistake, and which I have ever disclaimed and abhorred. To prevent such mistakes, I shall at present only propose this case: There goes many a ship to sea, with many hundred souls in one ship, whose weal and woe is common, and is a true picture of a commonwealth, or a human combination or society. It hath fallen out sometimes, that both Papists and Protestants, Jews and Turks, may be embarked in one ship; upon which supposal I affirm, that all the liberty of conscience, that ever I pleaded for, turns upon these two hinges—that none of the Papists, Protestants, Jews, or Turks be forced to come to the ship's prayers or worship, nor compelled from their own particular prayers or worship, if they practice any. I further add, that I never denied, that notwithstanding this liberty, the commander of this ship ought to command the ship's course, yea, and also command that justice, peace, and sobriety be kept and practiced, both among the seamen and all the passengers. If any of the seamen refuse to perform their services, or passengers to pay their freight; if any refuse to help, in person or purse, towards the common charges or defence; if any refuse to obey the common laws and orders of the ship, concerning their common peace or preservation; if any shall mutiny and rise up against their commanders and officers; if any should preach or write that there ought to be no commanders or officers, because all are equal in Christ, therefore no masters nor officers, no laws nor orders, nor corrections nor punishments; I say, I never denied, but in such cases, whatever is pretended, the commander or commanders may judge, resist, compel, and punish such transgressors, according to their deserts and merits. This if seriously and honestly minded, may, if it so please the Father of Lights, let in some light to such as willingly shut not their eyes.

I remain studious of your common peace and liberty.

Roger Williams

1655   1874

---

1. The text is from *The Writings of Roger Williams,* vol. 6 (1866–74). Williams wrote this letter after his return to Providence from England in 1654 in hopes of settling a controversy that divided the town over the question of religious autonomy and civil restraint.
2. I.e., write as much as a dot, the smallest part.

ANNE BRADSTREET
c. 1612–1672

Anne Bradstreet's father, Thomas Dudley, was the manager of the country estate of the Puritan earl of Lincoln, and his daughter was very much the apple of his eye. He took great care to see that she received an education superior to that of most young women of the time. When she was only sixteen she married the young Simon Bradstreet, a recent graduate of Cambridge University, who was associated with her father in conducting the affairs of the earl of Lincoln's estate. He also shared her father's Puritan beliefs. A year after the marriage her husband was appointed to assist in the preparations of the Massachusetts Bay Company, and the following year the Bradstreets and the Dudleys sailed with Winthrop's fleet. Bradstreet tells us that when she first "came into this country" she "found a new world and new manners," at which her "heart rose" in resistance. "But after I was convinced it was the way of God, I submitted to it and joined the church at Boston."

We know very little of Bradstreet's daily life, except that it was a hard existence. The wilderness, Samuel Eliot Morison once observed, "made men stern and silent, children unruly, servants insolent." William Bradford's wife, Dorothy, staring at the barren dunes of Cape Cod is said to have preferred the surety of drowning to the unknown life ashore. Added to the hardship of daily living was the fact that Bradstreet was never very strong. She had rheumatic fever as a child and as a result suffered recurrent periods of severe fatigue; nevertheless, she risked death by childbirth eight times. Her husband was secretary to the company and later governor of the Bay Colony; he was always involved in the colony's diplomatic missions; and in 1661 he went to England to renegotiate the Bay Company charter with Charles II. All of Simon's tasks must have added to her responsibilities at home. And like any good Puritan she added to the care of daily life the examination of her conscience. She tells us in one of the "Meditations" written for her children that she was troubled many times about the truth of the Scriptures, that she never saw any convincing miracles, and that she always wondered if those of which she read "were feigned." What proved to her finally that God exists was not her reading but the evidence of her own eyes. She is the first in a long line of American poets who took their consolation not from theology but from the "wondrous works," as she wrote, "that I see, the vast frame of the heaven and the earth, the order of all things, night and day, summer and winter, spring and autumn, the daily providing for this great household upon the earth, the preserving and directing of all to its proper end."

When Bradstreet was a young girl she had written poems to please her father, and he made much of their reading them together. After her marriage she continued writing. Quite unknown to her, her brother-in-law, John Woodbridge, pastor of the Andover church, brought with him to London a manuscript collection of her poetry and had it printed there in 1650. *The Tenth Muse* was the first published volume of poems written by a resident in the New World and was widely read. Reverend Edward Taylor, also a poet and living in the frontier community of Westfield, Massachusetts, had a copy of the second edition of Bradstreet's poems (1678) in his library. Although she herself probably took greatest pride in her long meditative poems on the ages of humankind and on the seasons, the poems that have attracted present-day readers are the more intimate ones, which reflect her concern for her family and home and the pleasures she took in everyday life rather than in the life to come. Nevertheless, Bradstreet was an ambitious poet whose imagination was firmly grounded in English religious, political, and cultural history; and, as her "Dialogue between Old England and New" attests, she was a firm believer in the Puritan experiment in America.

The text is the *Works of Anne Bradstreet,* edited by Jeannine Hensley (1967).

The Prologue

1

To sing of wars, of captains, and of kings,
Of cities founded, commonwealths begun,
For my mean[1] pen are too superior things:
Or how they all, or each their dates have run
Let poets and historians set these forth,   5
My obscure lines shall not so dim their worth.

2

But when my wond'ring eyes and envious heart
Great Bartas'[2] sugared lines do but read o'er,
Fool I do grudge the Muses[3] did not part
'Twixt him and me that overfluent store;   10
A Bartas can do what a Bartas will
But simple I according to my skill.

3

From schoolboy's tongue no rhet'ric we expect,
Nor yet a sweet consort[4] from broken strings,
Nor perfect beauty where's a main defect: 15
My foolish, broken, blemished Muse so sings,
And this to mend, alas, no art is able,
'Cause nature made it so irreparable.

4

Nor can I, like that fluent sweet tongued Greek,
Who lisped at first, in future times speak plain.[5]   20
By art he gladly found what he did seek,
A full requital of his striving pain.
Art can do much, but this maxim's most sure:
A weak or wounded brain admits no cure.

5

I am obnoxious to each carping tongue   25
Who says my hand a needle better fits,
A poet's pen all scorn I should thus wrong,
For such despite they cast on female wits:
If what I do prove well, it won't advance,
They'll say it's stol'n, or else it was by chance.   30

6

But sure the antique Greeks were far more mild
Else of our sex, why feigned they those nine

---

1. Humble.
2. Guillaume du Bartas (1544–1590), a French writer much admired by the Puritans. He was most famous as the author of *The Divine Weeks*, an epic poem translated by Joshua Sylvester and intended to recount the great moments in Christian history.

3. In Greek mythology, the nine goddesses of the arts and sciences. "Fool": i.e., like a fool.
4. Accord, harmony of sound.
5. The Greek orator Demosthenes (c. 383–322 B.C.E.) conquered a speech defect.

And poesy made Calliope's[6] own child;
So 'mongst the rest they placed the arts divine:
But this weak knot they will full soon untie.   35
The Greeks did nought, but play the fools and lie.

7

Let Greeks be Greeks, and women what they are;
Men have precedency and still excel,
It is but vain unjustly to wage war;
Men can do best, and women know it well   40
Preeminence in all and each is yours;
Yet grant some small acknowledgment of ours.

8

And oh ye high flown quills[7] that soar the skies,
And ever with your prey still catch your praise,
If e'er you deign these lowly lines your eyes   45
Give thyme or parsley wreath, I ask no bays;[8]
This mean and unrefined ore of mine
Will make your glist'ring gold but more to shine.

                                                        1650

A Dialogue between Old England and New; Concerning Their Present Troubles, Anno, 1642[1]

New England

Alas, dear Mother, fairest queen and best,
With honor, wealth, and peace, happy and blest;
What ails thee hang thy head and cross thine arms?
And sit i' th' dust, to sigh these sad alarms?
What deluge of new woes thus overwhelm   5
The glories of thy ever famous realm?
What means this wailing tone, this mournful guise?
Ah, tell thy daughter, she may sympathize.

Old England

Art ignorant indeed of these my woes?
Or must my forced tongue these griefs disclose?   10
And must myself dissect my tattered state,
Which 'mazed Christendom stands wond'ring at?
And thou a child, a limb, and dost not feel
My fainting weak'ned body now to reel?
This physic purging potion[2] I have taken   15
Will bring consumption or an ague[3] quaking,
Unless some cordial[4] thou fetch from high,

---

6. The muse of epic poetry.
7. Pens.
8. Garlands of laurel, used to crown the head of a poet.
1. Civil war broke out in England in 1642 when the Puritans determined to give greater power to Parliament than to the king. Seven years after the date of this poem Charles I was executed. "Anno": in the year (Latin).
2. A cathartic, or laxative.
3. Chill. "Consumption": a wasting away of the body.
4. A sweetened beverage, not necessarily alcoholic.

Which present help may ease my malady.
If I decease, doth think thou shalt survive?
Or by my wasting state dost think to thrive?   20
Then weigh our case, if't be not justly sad;
Let me lament alone, while thou art glad.

New England

And thus (alas) your state you much deplore
In general terms, but will not say wherefore.
What medicine shall I seek to cure this woe,   25
If th' wound's so dangerous I may not know.
But you perhaps, would have me guess it out:
What hath some Hengist like that Saxon[5] stout
By fraud or force usurped thy flow'ring crown,
Or by tempestous wars thy fields trod down?   30
Or hath Canutus,[6] that brave valiant Dane,
The regal, peaceful scepter from thee ta'en?
Or is't a Norman, whose victorious hand
With English blood bedews thy conquered land?[7]
Or is't intestine wars that thus offend?   35
Do Maud and Stephen[8] for the crown contend?
Do barons rise and side against their king,
And call in foreign aid to help the thing?
Must Edward be deposed? or is't the hour
That second Richard[9] must be clapt in th' tower?   40
Or is't the fatal jar, again begun,
That from the red white pricking roses[1] sprung?
Must Richmond's aid, the nobles now implore,
To come and break the tushes of the boar?[2]
If none of these, dear mother, what's your woe?   45
Pray do you fear Spain's bragging Armado?[3]
Doth your ally, fair France, conspire your wrack,
Or do the Scots play false behind your back?
Doth Holland[4] quit you ill for all your love?
Whence is the storm from earth or heaven above?   50
Is't drought, is't famine, or is't pestilence?

5. The Saxons were a Germanic people who settled in England when the Roman occupation of
Britain weakened. Hengest and his brother Horsa
are the best known 5th-century Jute invaders of
England.
6. Canute (c. 995), king of England, Norway, and
Denmark, was the younger son of Sweyn of Denmark; he came to England in 1013.
7. The English king Harold II was defeated by
William of Normandy in 1066.
8. Maud, or Matilda (1102–1167), queen of
England, was the daughter of Henry I. With her
brothers dead her father attempted to secure the
throne for her, but in 1135 her cousin Stephen
(1099?–1154) deposed her. In 1139 Matilda, with
her half-brother Robert, earl of Gloucester, struggled to regain the throne.
9. Richard II (1367–1400), king of England, was
forced to abdicate by his banished cousin Henry
Bolingbroke, later Henry IV, and was imprisoned
in Pontefract castle. There he was murdered or
starved himself to death. King Edward II (1284–
1327) was forced to abdicate when Queen Isabella
returned to England from France with an army of
invaders in 1326.
1. The War of the Roses involved the struggle
between the House of Lancaster (identified with
the red rose) and the House of York (identified
with the white rose) from 1455 to 1485.
2. Richard III (1452–1485), king of England—
"the wretched bloody and usurping boar," as
Shakespeare puts it in his play—was the ruthless
murderer of Edward V and his brother, and this
outrage paved the way for Henry Tudor, earl of
Richmond, a Lancastrian, to defeat him on Bos-
worth field in 1484. He became Henry VII and
married the daughter of Edward IV, uniting the
houses of Lancaster and York. "Tushes": tusks.
3. The great Spanish sailing fleet (or Armada) was
defeated in 1588 by the British navy.
4. Elizabeth I (1533–1603), queen of England,
aided the Protestant Netherlands in their wars
against Catholic Spain.

Doth feel the smart, or fear the consequence?
Your humble child entreats you, show your grief,
Though arms, nor purse she hath for your relief,
Such is her poverty, yet shall be found   55
A suppliant for your help, as she is bound.

Old England

I must confess some of those sores you name,
My beauteous body at this present maim;
But foreign foe, nor feigned friend I fear,
For they have work enough (thou know'st) elsewhere.   60
Nor is it Alcie's son, nor Henry's daughter,[5]
Whose proud contention cause this slaughter,
Nor nobles siding to make John no king,
French Lewis[6] unjustly to the crown to bring;
No Edward, Richard, to lose rule and life,   65
Nor no Lancastrians to renew old strife;
No Duke of York, nor Earl of March[7] to soil
Their hands in kindred's blood whom they did foil;
No crafty tyrant now usurps the seat,
Who nephews slew that so he might be great;[8]   70
No need of Tudor roses to unite,
None knows which is the red, or which the white;
Spain's braving fleet, a second time is sunk;
France knows how oft my fury she hath drunk
By Edward Third and Henry Fifth of fame,   75
Her lilies in mine arms avouch the same.
My sister Scotland[9] hurts me now no more
Though she hath been injurious heretofore;
What Holland is I am in some suspense,
But trust not much unto his excellence.   80
For wants, sure some I feel, but more I fear,
And for the pestilence, who knows how near;
Famine and plague, two sisters of the sword,
Destruction to a land doth soon afford;
They're for my punishment ordained on high,   85
Unless our tears prevent it speedily.
But yet I answer not what you demand,
To show the grievance of my troubled land.
Before I tell th' effect, I'll show the cause

5. Maud. "Alcie's son": Stephen, king of England (1135–1154), son of Stephen Henry, count of Blois and Chartres, and Adela, or Alice, daughter of William the Conqueror.
6. John (1167?–1216), king of England, was the son of Henry II and Eleanor of Aquitaine and ascended to the throne in 1199. He signed the Magna Carta in 1215. English barons were anxious to replace him and sought the aid of Prince Louis of France, later Louis VIII.
7. Edward (1373?–1415), duke of York, English nobleman, plotted to kill Henry IV and kidnap young Edward Mortimer, earl of March, descendant of Richard II. Sir Edmund de Mortimer (1376–1409?) was a rebel in the reign of Henry IV and allied himself with the Welshman Owen Glen-

dower.
8. A reference to Richard III, younger brother of Edward IV, whose twelve-year-old nephew was proclaimed Edward V. Richard had Edward and his younger brother killed in the Tower of London.
9. Edward III (1312–1377), king of England, assumed the title of king of France in 1340 based on a claim through his mother, Isabella. The series of wars known now as the Hundred Years' War dominated his reign. He took part in the victory at Calais in 1346. Henry V (1387–1422), king of England, invaded France in 1415 and defeated the French at Agincourt. "Lilies": the fleur-de-lis is a symbol of France. Independent Scotland's alliances with France were a source of pain during Edward's reign.

Which are my sins, the breach of sacred laws.   90
Idolatry, supplanter of a nation,
With foolish superstitious adoration,
Are liked and countenanced by men of might,
The Gospel trodden down and hath no right;
Church offices were sold and bought for gain,   95
That Pope had hope to find Rome here again.
For oaths and blasphemies, did ever ear
From Belzebub[1] himself such language hear?
What scorning of the saints of the Most High?
What injuries did daily on them lie?   100
What false reports, what nicknames[2] did they take
Not for their own, but for their Master's sake?
And thou, poor soul, wert jeered among the rest,
Thy flying for the truth was made a jest.
For Sabbath-breaking and for drunkenness,   105
Did ever land profaneness more express?
From crying blood yet cleansed am not I,
Martyrs and others, dying causelessly.
How many princely heads on blocks laid down
For nought but title to a fading crown?   110
'Mongst all the cruelties by great ones done
Oh, Edward's youths, and Clarence hapless son,
O Jane,[3] why didst thou die in flow'ring prime?
Because of royal stem, that was thy crime.
For bribery, adultery, and lies,   115
Where is the nation, I can't paralyze.
With usury, extortion, and oppression,
These be the Hydras[4] of my stout transgression.
These be the bitter fountains, heads, and roots,
Whence flowed the source, the springs, the boughs and fruits   120
Of more than thou canst hear or I relate,
That with high hand I still did perpetrate,
For these were threatened the woeful day
I mocked the preachers, put it far away;
The sermons yet upon record do stand   125
That cried destruction to my wicked land;
I then believed not, now I feel and see,
The plague of stubborn incredulity.
Some lost their livings, some in prison pent,
Some fined, from house and friends to exile went.   130
Their silent tongues to heaven did vengeance cry,
Who saw their wrongs and hath judged righteously
And will repay it sevenfold in my lap:
This is forerunner of my afterclap.[5]
Nor took I warning by my neighbor's falls.   135

1. Or Beelzebub; Satan, the prince of demons.
2. Unflattering epithets. "The saints": i.e., visible saints, those regenerate Puritans who left England for America.
3. Lady Jane Grey (1537–1554) was proclaimed queen of England but reigned only nine days. She was beheaded because her father, Henry Grey, was involved in treason. George, duke of Clarence (1449–1478), son of Richard, duke of York, was executed for treason by his brother Edward IV; Edward's sons were murdered by Richard III.
4. In Greek mythology the nine-headed monster slain by Hercules. When one head was cut off, two more replaced it.
5. A blow that comes as a surprise because the affair was thought to have ended.

I saw sad Germany's dismantled walls,
I saw her people famished, nobles slain,
Her fruitful land, a barren heath remain.
I saw, unmoved, her armies foiled and fled,
Wives forced, babes tossed, her houses calcined.[6]   140
I saw strong Rochelle[7] yielded to her foe,
Thousands of starved Christians there also.
I saw poor Ireland[8] bleeding out her last,
Such cruelties as all reports have past;
Mine heart obdurate stood not yet aghast.   145
Now sip I of that cup, and just 't may be
The bottom dregs reserved are for me.

New England

To all you've said, sad Mother, I assent,
Your fearful sins great cause there's to lament,
My guilty hands, in part, hold up with you,   150
A sharer in your punishment's my due.
But all you say amounts to this effect,
Not what you feel, but what you do expect,
Pray in plain terms, what is your present grief?
Then let's join heads and hearts for your relief.   155

Old England

Well to the matter then, there's grown of late
'Twixt king and peers a question of state,
Which is the chief, the law, or else the king.
One said, "It's he," the other no such thing.
'Tis said, my better part in Parliament   160
To ease my groaning land, showed their intent,
To crush the proud, and right to each man deal,
To help the Church and stay the commonweal.
So many obstacles came in their way,
As puts me to a stand what I should say;   165
Old customs, new prerogatives stood on,
Had they not held law fast, all had been gone,
Which by their prudence stood them in such stead
They took high Strafford[9] lower by the head.
And to their Laud be't spoke, they held i' th' tower   170
All England's metropolitan[1] that hour;

---

6. Burned. Old England is referring to the Peasant's War in Germany (1524–26), in which violent
atrocities were committed on both sides.
7. La Rochelle, one of the chief seaports of
France, on the Bay of Biscay. It was a Huguenot
(or Protestant) stronghold but fell in 1628 when
Cardinal Richelieu determined to crush the
French Protestants.
8. Under Elizabeth I's reign there were three revolutions in Ireland. It remained a Catholic country
but was under the rule of Parliament.

9. Thomas Wentworth (1593–1641), first earl of
Strafford, was the autocratic lord deputy of Ireland, and, along with Archbishop Laud, one of
Charles I's chief advisers. When the Long Parliament (1640–49) was assembled he was accused of
preparing to use Irish soldiers against English subjects and was beheaded on the order of the king.
1. Ecclesiastical head. William Laud (1573–
1645), archbishop of Canterbury, was an early
opponent of the Puritans and imposed High
Church forms of worship. He supported the earl

This done, an act they would have passed fain,
No prelate should his bishopric retain;
Here tugged they hard, indeed, for all men saw
This must be done by Gospel, not by law.   175
Next the militia they urged sore,
This was denied (I need not say wherefore).
The King, displeased, at York[2] himself absents,
They humbly beg return, show their intents;
The writing, printing, posting to and fro,   180
Shows all was done, I'll therefore let it go.
But now I come to speak of my disaster,
Contention grown,'twixt subjects and their master;
They worded it so long, they fell to blows,
That thousands lay on heaps, here bleeds my woes,   185
I that no wars so many years have known,
Am now destroyed and slaught'red by mine own;
But could the field alone this strife decide,
One battle two or three I might abide,
But these may be beginnings of more woe.   190
Who knows, but this may be my overthrow.
Oh pity me in this sad perturbation,
My plundred towns, my houses' devastation,
My weeping virgins and my young men slain;
My wealthy trading fall'n, my dearth of grain,   195
The seedtime's come, but ploughman hath no hope
Because he knows not who shall in his crop.
The poor they want their pay, their children bread,
Their woeful mothers' tears unpitied.
If any pity in thy heart remain,   200
Or any childlike love thou dost retain,
For my relief, do what there lies in thee,
And recompense that good I've done to thee.

New England

Dear Mother, cease complaints and wipe your eyes,
Shake off your dust, cheer up, and now arise;   205
You are my mother nurse, and I your flesh,
Your sunken bowels gladly would refresh;
Your griefs I pity, but soon hope to see,
Out of your troubles much good fruit to be,
To see those latter days of hoped for good,   210
Though now beclouded all with tears and blood.
After dark Popery the day did clear,
But now the sun in's brightness shall appear.
Blest be the nobles of thy noble land,
With ventured lives for truth's defence that stand.   215

---

of Strafford in the Bishop's War in Scotland (1637)
and was condemned to death by the House of
Commons in the Long Parliament.
2. Absent from London and with his army gathered at York, Charles I (1600–1649), after a defeat
by the Scottish Army of the Covenant, agreed on
October 2, 1640, to recall Parliament, the governing body, which eventually ordered his execution.
Bradstreet's poem, of course, was written before
this event took place.

Blest be thy commons, who for common good,
And thy infringed laws have boldly stood.
Blest be thy counties, who did aid thee still,
With hearts and states to testify their will.
Blest be thy preachers, who do cheer thee on,   220
O cry, "the sword of God and Gideon";[3]
And shall I not on them wish Meroz's curse,
That help thee not with prayers, arms, and purse?[4]
And for myself let miseries abound,
If mindless of thy state I e'er be found.   225
These are the days the Church's foes to crush,
To root out Popeling's head, tail, branch, and rush;
Let's bring Baal's[5] vestments forth to make a fire,
Their miters, surplices, and all their tire,[6]
Copes, rochets, crosiers,[7] and such empty trash,   230
And let their names consume, but let the flash
Light Christendom, and all the world to see
We hate Rome's whore with all her trumpery.
Go on brave Essex[8] with a loyal heart,
Not false to king, nor to the better part;   235
But those that hurt his people and his crown,
As duty binds, expell and tread them down.
And ye brave nobles chase away all fear,
And to this hopeful cause closely adhere;
O Mother, can you weep, and have such peers?   240
When they are gone, then drown yourself in tears.
If now you weep so much, that then no more
The briny ocean will o'erflow your shore.
These, these are they I trust, with Charles our King,
Out of all mists such glorious days shall bring;   245
That dazzled eyes beholding much shall wonder
At that thy settled peace, thy wealth and splendor.
Thy Church and weal[9] established in such manner,
That all shall joy, that thou displayed'st thy banner;
And discipline erected so I trust,   250
That nursing kings shall come and lick thy dust.
Then justice shall in all thy courts take place,
Without respect of person or of case;
Then bribes shall cease, and suits shall not stick long,
Patience and purse of clients oft to wrong.   255
Then high commissions shall fall to decay,
And pursuivants and catchpoles want[1] their pay.
So shall thy happy nation ever flourish,

---

3. "And the three companies blew the trumpets, and brake the pitchers, and held the lamps in their left hands, and the trumpets in their right hands to blow withal: and they cried, The sword of the Lord, and of Gideon" (Judges 7.20).
4. "Curse ye Méroz, said the angel of the Lord, curse ye bitterly the inhabitants thereof; because they came not to the help of the Lord, to the help of the Lord against the mighty" (Judges 5.23).
5. Ancient Semitic fertility god; a false god.
6. Attire.

7. Crosses. "Copes": ecclesiastical cape-like vestments. "Rochets": linen vestments resembling surplices, which are worn by bishops.
8. Robert Devereux, third earl of Essex (1591–1646), second in charge of the royal army in the first Bishop's War in Scotland in 1639, but later in command of the forces of Parliament at Edgehill in 1642.
9. Well-being, prosperity.
1. Lack. "Pursuivants": attendants. "Catchpoles": tax collectors, sheriff's officers.

When truth and righteousness they thus shall nourish,
When thus in peace, thine armies brave send out   260
To sack proud Rome and all her vassals rout;
There let thy name, thy fame, and glory shine,
As did thine ancestors' in Palestine;
And let her spoils full pay with interest be,
Of what unjustly once she polled² from thee.   265
Of all the woes thou canst let her be sped,³
And on her pour the vengeance threat'ned;
Bring forth the beast that ruled the world with's beck,⁴
And tear his flesh and set your feet on's neck;
And make his filthy den so desolate,   270
To th' 'stonishment of all that knew his state.
This done, with brandished swords to Turkey⁵ go,
For then what is't but English blades dare do,
And lay her waste for so's the sacred doom,
And do to Gog⁶ as thou hast done to Rome.   275
Oh Abraham's seed,⁷ lift up your heads on high,
For sure the day of your redemption's nigh;
The scales shall fall from your long blinded eyes,
And Him you shall adore who now despise.
Then fullness of the nations in shall flow,   280
And Jew and Gentile to one worship go;
Then follows days of happiness and rest;
Whose lot doth fall to live therein is blest:
No Canaanite shall then be found i' th' land,
And holiness on horses' bells shall stand.⁸   285
If this make way thereto, then sigh no more,
But if at all, thou didst not see't before;
Farewell, dear Mother, rightest cause prevail,
And in a while, you'll tell another tale.

1642   1650

In Honor of That High and Mighty Princess Queen Elizabeth¹
of Happy Memory

The Proem²

Although, great Queen, thou now in silence lie,
Yet thy loud herald Fame doth to the sky

2. Took away; shaved off.
3. Given.
4. By his bidding; with his command.
5. Because the Holy Land was under Turkish control.
6. "And it shall come to pass at the same time when Gog shall come against the land of Israel, saith the Lord God, that my fury shall come up in my face" (Ezekiel 38.18). Gog's country is Magog and he is identified with the Scythians.
7. The children of Abraham, who was the progenitor of the Hebrews; used here to indicate the Puritans as God's chosen people.
8. "In that day shall there be upon the bells of the horses, HOLINESS UNTO THE LORD; and the pots in the Lord's house shall be like the bowls before the altar. Yea, every pot in Jerusalem and in Judah shall be holiness unto the Lord of hosts: and all they that sacrifice shall come and take care of them, and seethe therein: and in that day there shall be no more the Canaanite in the house of the Lord of hosts" (Zechariah 14.20–21). Canaan was the promised land of the Israelites, and after their deliverance from Egypt they subjugated it.
1. Elizabeth I (1533–1603), queen of England, ascended to the throne in 1558.
2. Prelude.

Thy wondrous worth proclaim in every clime,
And so hath vowed while there is world or time.
So great's thy glory and thine excellence,   5
The sound thereof rapts[3] every human sense,
That men account it no impiety,
To say thou wert a fleshly deity.
Thousands bring offerings (though out of date)
Thy world of honors to accumulate;   10
'Mongst hundred hecatombs of roaring[4] verse,
Mine bleating stands before thy royal hearse.[5]
Thou never didst nor canst thou now disdain
T' accept the tribute of a loyal brain.
Thy clemency did erst esteem as much   15
The acclamations of the poor as rich,
Which makes me deem my rudeness is no wrong,
Though I resound thy praises 'mongst the throng.

The Poem

No Phoenix pen, nor Spenser's poetry,
No Speed's nor Camden's[6] learned history,   20
Eliza's works, wars, praise, can e'er compact;[7]
The world's the theatre where she did act.
No memories nor volumes can contain
The 'leven Olympiads[8] of her happy reign.
Who was so good, so just, so learn'd, so wise,   25
From all the kings on earth she won the prize.
Nor say I more than duly is her due,
Millions will testify that this is true.
She hath wiped off th' aspersion of her sex,
That women wisdom lack to play the rex.[9]   30
Spain's monarch, says not so, nor yet his host;
She taught them better manners, to their cost.[1]
The Salic law,[2] in force now had not been,
If France had ever hoped for such a queen.
But can you, doctors,[3] now this point dispute,   35
She's argument enough to make you mute.
Since first the Sun did run his ne'er run race,[4]
And earth had, once a year, a new old face,[5]
Since time was time, and man unmanly man,

3. Enraptures.
4. Loud. "Hecatombs": sacrificial offerings of one hundred beasts, made in ancient Greece.
5. An elaborate framework erected over a royal tomb to which verses or epitaphs were attached.
6. William Camden (1551–1623), the author of Annales, translated in 1630 as The History of the Most Renowned and Victorious Princess Elizabeth. "No Phoenix pen": perhaps a reference to the English poet Sir Philip Sidney (1554–1586), the subject of one of Bradstreet's poems, but she may also be referring to any immortal poet's work. The phoenix is a mythological bird that dies in flames and rises from its ashes. Edmund Spenser (c. 1552–1599), author of The Faerie Queen (1590, 1596), whose title honors Elizabeth. John Speed

(1552?–1629), who published his Historie of Great Britain in 1611.
7. Reduce to manageable space.
8. Four-year intervals between Olympic games; in ancient Greece dates were calculated by them. Elizabeth I reigned for forty-four years.
9. King (Latin).
1. Philip II (1527–1598) was Spain's monarch when Queen Elizabeth's navy defeated his "host" (the many ships of the Spanish Armada) in 1588.
2. A law of the Salian Franks that excluded women from succession to the French crown.
3. Learned men.
4. I.e., never-finished course.
5. I.e., earth has a new face each spring.

Come show me such a Phoenix if you can.   40
Was ever people better ruled than hers?
Was ever land more happy freed from stirs?[6]
Did ever wealth in England more abound?
Her victories in foreign coasts resound;
Ships more invincible than Spain's, her foe,   45
She wracked, she sacked, she sunk his Armado;
Her stately troops advanced to Lisbon's wall,
Don Anthony[7] in's right there to install.
She frankly helped Frank's brave distressed king;[8]
The states united[9] now her fame do sing.   50
She their protectrix was; they well do know
Unto our dread virago,[1] what they owe.
Her nobles sacrificed their noble blood,
Nor men nor coin she spared to do them good.
The rude untamed Irish, she did quell,   55
Before her picture the proud Tyrone[2] fell.
Had ever prince such counsellors as she?
Herself Minerva[3] caused them so to be.
Such captains and such soldiers never seen,
As were the subjects of our Pallas queen.   60
Her seamen through all straits the world did round;
Terra incognita[4] might know the sound.
Her Drake came laden home with Spanish gold;
Her Essex took Cadiz, their Herculean hold.[5]
But time would fail me, so my tongue would too,   65
To tell of half she did, or she could do.
Semiramis[6] to her is but obscure,
More infamy than fame she did procure.
She built her glory but on Babel's walls,[7]
World's wonder for a while, but yet it falls.   70
Fierce Tomris (Cyrus' headsman) Scythians' queen,[8]
Had put her harness off, had she but seen
Our Amazon in th' Camp of Tilbury,[9]
Judging all valor and all majesty
Within that princess to have residence,   75
And prostrate yielded to her excellence.

---

6. Disturbances.
7. Don Antonio of Crato (1531–1595), who laid claim to the Portuguese throne.
8. Henri IV (1553–1610), Protestant king of France.
9. A reference to The Netherlands, whose national assembly was called the States General. Elizabeth I came to their aid in the wars against Spain.
1. Female warrior.
2. The Irish chieftain Hugh O'Neill (c. 1540–1616), second earl of Tyrone, who was defeated by English forces in 1601.
3. The Roman goddess of war, wisdom, chastity, the arts, and justice. In Greece she is known as Pallas Athena.
4. Unknown land (Latin).
5. Robert Devereux (1566–1601), second earl of Essex, captured the Spanish port Cadiz in 1596. The hold was "Herculean" because Cadiz was

exceptionally well defended. Sir Francis Drake (1540?–1596) brought back to England Spanish gold from Chile and Peru.
6. Late-9th-century queen of Assyria; she is said to have built Babylon.
7. The tower of Babel was built to win fame for its builders (Genesis 11).
8. Tomyris was queen of the Massagetae, a Scythian tribe, whose armies in 529 B.C.E. defeated Cyrus the Great of Persia. According to some accounts, she had him beheaded and his head thrown into a pot of blood because it was a fitting end to a bloodthirsty man.
9. It is reported that Elizabeth I, dressed like the mythological female warriors known as Amazons, wore a silver breastplate when she addressed the English troops at Tilbury on the north bank of the Thames River in 1588, anticipating a Spanish invasion.

Dido, first foundress of proud Carthage walls[1]
(Who living consummates her funerals),
A great Eliza, but compared with ours,
How vanisheth her glory, wealth, and powers.   80
Profuse, proud Cleopatra, whose wrong name,[2]
Instead of glory, proved her country's shame,
Of her what worth in stories to be seen,
But that she was a rich Egyptian queen.
Zenobya,[3] potent empress of the East,   85
And of all these without compare the best,
Whom none but great Aurelius could quell;
Yet for our Queen is no fit parallel.
She was a Phoenix queen, so shall she be,
Her ashes not revived, more Phoenix she.   90
Her personal perfections, who would tell
Must dip his pen in th' Heleconian well,[4]
Which I may not, my pride doth but aspire
To read what others write and so admire.
Now say, have women worth? or have they none?   95
Or had they some, but with our Queen is't gone?
Nay masculines, you have thus taxed us long,
But she, though dead, will vindicate our wrong.
Let such as say our sex is void of reason,
Know 'tis a slander now but once was treason.   100
But happy England which had such a queen;
Yea happy, happy, had those days still been.
But happiness lies in a higher sphere,
Then wonder not Eliza moves not here.
Full fraught with honor, riches and with days   105
She set, she set, like Titan[5] in his rays.
No more shall rise or set so glorious sun
Until the heaven's great revolution;[6]
If then new things their old forms shall retain,
Eliza shall rule Albion[7] once again.   120

Her Epitaph

Here sleeps the queen, this is the royal bed
Of th' damask rose, sprung from the white and red,[8]

1. The Latin poet Virgil (70–19 B.C.E.), in his *Aeneid* (book 4), tells the tale of the fabled queen of Carthage and her self-immolation after she was abandoned by Aeneas.
2. In Greek Cleopatra—the name of the famous, but licentious, Egyptian queen (69–30 B.C.E.)—means "glory to the father." Bradstreet extends the meaning to "fatherland."
3. Queen of Palmyra in Syria, famous for her wars of expansion and defeated by the Roman emperor Aurelian in 273. She died sometime shortly after that date.
4. The Hippocrene spring on Mount Helican, home of the Muses, was the source of poetic inspiration.

5. The Latin poets' name for the sun god.
6. "And I saw a new heaven and a new earth: for the first heaven and the first earth were passed away; and there was no more sea" (Revelation 21.1).
7. England.
8. Queen Elizabeth's father, Henry VIII (1491–1547), descended from the House of Lancaster, identified with the symbol of the red rose; her mother, Anne Boleyn (1507?–1536), was from the House of York, identified with a white rose. The two houses were at war with each other for many years. Bradstreet suggests that the damask rose of Elizabeth is formed by the interweaving of these two colors.

Whose sweet perfume fills the all-filling air.
This rose is withered, once so lovely fair.
On neither tree did grow such rose before,   125
The greater was our gain, our loss the more.

Another

Here lies the pride of queens, pattern of kings,
So blaze it, Fame, here's feathers for thy wings.
Here lies the envied, yet unparalleled prince,
Whose living virtues speak (though dead long since).   130
If many worlds, as that fantastic framed,
In every one be her great glory famed.

1643   1650

To the Memory of My Dear and Ever Honored Father Thomas Dudley Esq. Who Deceased, July 31, 1653, and of His Age 77

By duty bound and not by custom led
To celebrate the praises of the dead,
My mournful mind, sore pressed, in trembling verse
Presents my lamentations at his hearse,
Who was my father, guide, instructor too,   5
To whom I ought whatever I could do.
Nor is't relation near my hand shall tie;
For who more cause to boast his worth than I?
Who heard or saw, observed or knew him better?
Or who alive than I a greater debtor?   10
Let malice bite and envy gnaw its fill,
He was my father, and I'll praise him still.
Nor was his name or life lead so obscure
That pity might some trumpeters procure
Who after death might make him falsely seem   15
Such as in life no man could justly deem.
Well known and loved, where e'er he lived, by most
Both in his native and in foreign coast,
These to the world his merits could make known,
So needs no testimonial from his own;   20
But now or never I must pay my sum;
While others tell his worth, I'll not be dumb.
One of thy Founders,[1] him New England know,
Who stayed thy feeble sides when thou wast low,
Who spent his state,[2] his strength and years with care   25
That after-comers in them might have share.
True patriot of this little commonweal,

1. Thomas Dudley came to Massachusetts in 1630.   2. I.e., estate; position in life.

Who is't can tax thee ought, but for thy zeal?
Truth's friend thou wert, to errors still a foe,
Which caused apostates to malign so.   30
Thy love to true religion e'er shall shine;
My father's God, be God of me and mine.
Upon the earth he did not build his nest,
But as a pilgrim, what he had, possessed.
High thoughts he gave no harbor in his heart,   35
Nor honors puffed him up when he had part;
Those titles loathed, which some too much do love,
For truly his ambition lay above.
His humble mind so loved humility,
He left it to his race for legacy;   40
And oft and oft with speeches mild and wise
Gave his in charge that jewel rich to prize.
No ostentation seen in all his ways,
An³ in the mean ones of our foolish days,
Which all they have and more still set to view,   45
Their greatness may be judged by what they shew.
His thoughts were more sublime, his actions wise,
Such vanities he justly did despise.
Nor wonder 'twas, low things ne'er much did move
For he a mansion had, prepared above,   50
For which he sighed and prayed and longed full sore
He might be clothed upon for evermore.
Oft spake of death, and with a smiling cheer
He did exult his end was drawing near;
Now fully ripe, as shock of wheat that's grown,   55
Death as a sickle hath him timely mown,
And in celestial barn hath housed him high,
Where storms, nor show'rs, nor ought can damnify.
His generation served, his labors cease;
And to his fathers gathered is in peace.   60
Ah happy soul,'mongst saints and angels blesst,
Who after all his toil is now at rest.
His hoary⁴ head in righteousness was found;
As joy in heaven, on earth let praise resound.
Forgotten never be his memory,   65
His blessing rest on his posterity;
His pious footsteps, followed by his race,
At last will bring us to that happy place
Where we with joy each other's face shall see,
And parted more by death shall never be.   70

His Epitaph

Within this tomb a patriot lies
That was both pious, just, and wise,
To truth a shield, to right a wall,

---

3. Though.   4. Gray-haired.

To sectaries a whip and maul,
A magazine[5] of history,   75
A prizer of good company,
In manners pleasant and severe;
The good him loved, the bad did fear,
And when his time with years was spent,
If some rejoiced, more did lament.   80

To Her Father with Some Verses

Most truly honored, and as truly dear,
If worth in me or ought[1] I do appear,
Who can of right better demand the same
Than may your worthy self from whom it came?
The principal[2] might yield a greater sum,   5
Yet handled ill, amounts but to this crumb;
My stock's so small I know not how to pay,
My bond[3] remains in force unto this day;
Yet for part payment take this simple mite,[4]
Where nothing's to be had, kings loose their right.   10
Such is my debt I may not say forgive,
But as I can, I'll pay it while I live;
Such is my bond, none can discharge but I,
Yet paying is not paid until I die.

                                                            1678

Contemplations

1

Some time now past in the autumnal tide,
When Phoebus[1] wanted but one hour to bed,
The trees all richly clad, yet void of pride,
Were gilded o'er by his rich golden head.
Their leaves and fruits seemed painted, but was true,   5
Of green, of red, of yellow, mixed hue;
Rapt were my senses at this delectable view.

2

I wist not what to wish, yet sure thought I,
If so much excellence abide below,
How excellent is He that dwells on high,   10
Whose power and beauty by His works we know?

5. Storehouse. "Sectaries": opposing believers.   3. I.e., contract.
"Maul": hammer or club.   4. The smallest possible denomination.
1. Anything at all.   1. Apollo, the sun god.
2. The capital that yields interest.

Sure He is goodness, wisdom, glory, light,
That hath this under world so richly dight;[2]
More heaven than earth was here, no winter and no night.

3

Then on a stately oak I cast mine eye,   15
Whose ruffling top the clouds seemed to aspire;
How long since thou wast in thine infancy?
Thy strength, and stature, more thy years admire,
Hath hundred winters past since thou wast born?
Or thousand since thou brakest thy shell of horn?   20
If so, all these as nought, eternity doth scorn.

4

Then higher on the glistering Sun I gazed.
Whose beams was shaded by the leafy tree;
The more I looked, the more I grew amazed,
And softly said, "What glory's like to thee?"   25
Soul of this world, this universe's eye,
No wonder some made thee a deity;
Had I not better known, alas, the same had I.

5

Thou as a bridegroom from thy chamber rushes,
And as a strong man, joys to run a race;[3]   30
The morn doth usher thee with smiles and blushes;
The Earth reflects her glances in thy face.
Birds, insects, animals with vegative,
Thy heat from death and dullness doth revive,
And in the darksome womb of fruitful nature dive.   35

6

Thy swift annual and diurnal course,
Thy daily straight and yearly oblique path,
Thy pleasing fervor and thy scorching force,
All mortals here the feeling knowledge hath.
Thy presence makes it day, thy absence night,   40
Quaternal seasons caused by thy might:
Hail creature, full of sweetness, beauty, and delight.

7

Art thou so full of glory that no eye
Hath strength thy shining rays once to behold?
And is thy splendid throne erect so high,   45
As to approach it, can no earthly mold?
How full of glory then must thy Creator be,
Who gave this bright light luster unto thee?
Admired, adored for ever, be that Majesty.

---

2. Furnished, adorned.
3. The sun "is as a bridegroom coming out of his
chamber, and rejoiceth as a strong man to run a
race" (Psalm 19.5).

8

Silent alone, where none or saw, or heard,   50
In pathless paths I lead my wand'ring feet,
My humble eyes to lofty skies I reared
To sing some song, my mazéd[4] Muse thought meet.
My great Creator I would magnify,
That nature had thus decked liberally;   55
But Ah, and Ah, again, my imbecility!

9

I heard the merry grasshopper then sing.
The black-clad cricket bear a second part;
They kept one tune and played on the same string,
Seeming to glory in their little art.   60
Shall creatures abject thus their voices raise
And in their kind resound their Maker's praise
Whilst I, as mute, can warble forth no higher lays?

10

When present times look back to ages past,
And men in being fancy those are dead,   65
It makes things gone perpetually to last,
And calls back months and years that long since fled.
It makes a man more aged in conceit
Than was Methuselah,[5] or's grandsire great,
While of their persons and their acts his mind doth treat.   70

11

Sometimes in Eden fair he seems to be,
Sees glorious Adam there made lord of all,
Fancies the apple, dangle on the tree,
That turned his sovereign to a naked thrall.[6]
Who like a miscreant's driven from that place,   75
To get his bread with pain and sweat of face,
A penalty imposed on his backsliding race.

12

Here sits our grandame in retired place,
And in her lap her bloody Cain new-born;
The weeping imp oft looks her in the face,   80
Bewails his unknown hap[7] and fate forlorn;
His mother sighs to think of Paradise,
And how she lost her bliss to be more wise,
Believing him that was, and is, father of lies.[8]

---

4. Amazed.
5. Thought to have lived 969 years (Genesis
5.27). "Conceit": apprehension, the processes of
thought.
6. Slave.

7. Fortune, circumstances.
8. By believing in the "father of lies," Eve lost Paradise in her desire to gain wisdom (Genesis 3); her
elder son, Cain, slew his brother, Abel (Genesis
4.8).

13

Here Cain and Abel come to sacrifice,   85
Fruits of the earth and fatlings⁹ each do bring.
On Abel's gift the fire descends from skies,
But no such sign on false Cain's offering;
With sullen hateful looks he goes his ways,
Hath thousand thoughts to end his brother's days,   90
Upon whose blood his future good he hopes to raise.

14

There Abel keeps his sheep, no ill he thinks;
His brother comes, then acts his fratricide:
The virgin Earth of blood her first draught drinks,
But since that time she often hath been cloyed.   95
The wretch with ghastly face and dreadful mind
Thinks each he sees will serve him in his kind,
Though none on earth but kindred near then could he find.

15

Who fancies not his looks now at the bar,
His face like death, his heart with horror fraught,   100
Nor malefactor ever felt like war,
When deep despair with wish of life hath fought,
Branded with guilt and crushed with treble woes,
A vagabond to Land of Nod¹ he goes.
A city builds, that walls might him secure from foes.   105

16

Who thinks not oft upon the father's ages,
Their long descent, how nephew's sons they saw,
The starry observations of those sages,
And how their precepts to their sons were law,
How Adam sighed to see his progeny,   110
Clothed all in his black sinful livery,
Who neither guilt nor yet the punishment could fly.

17

Our life compare we with their length of days
Who to the tenth of theirs doth now arrive?
And though thus short, we shorten many ways,   115
Living so little while we are alive;
In eating, drinking, sleeping, vain delight
So unawares comes on perpetual night,
And puts all pleasures vain unto eternal flight.

18

When I behold the heavens as in their prime,   120
And then the earth (though old) still clad in green,

---

9. Animals for slaughter.
1. An unidentified region east of Eden where Cain dwelled after slaying Abel (Genesis 4.16).

The stones and trees, insensible of time,
Nor age nor wrinkle on their front are seen;
If winter come and greenness then do fade,
A spring returns, and they more youthful made;   125
But man grows old, lies down, remains where once he's laid.

19

By birth more noble than those creatures all,
Yet seems by nature and by custom cursed,
No sooner born, but grief and care makes fall
That state obliterate he had at first;   130
Nor youth, nor strength, nor wisdom spring again,
Nor habitations long their names retain,
But in oblivion to the final day remain.

20

Shall I then praise the heavens, the trees, the earth
Because their beauty and their strength last longer?   135
Shall I wish there, or never to had birth,
Because they're bigger, and their bodies stronger?
Nay, they shall darken, perish, fade and die,
And when unmade, so ever shall they lie,
But man was made for endless immortality.   140

21

Under the cooling shadow of a stately elm
Close sat I by a goodly river's side,
Where gliding streams the rocks did overwhelm,
A lonely place, with pleasures dignified.
I once that loved the shady woods so well,   145
Now thought the rivers did the trees excel,
And if the sun would ever shine, there would I dwell.

22

While on the stealing stream I fixt mine eye,
Which to the longed-for ocean held its course,
I marked, nor crooks, nor rubs,[2] that there did lie   150
Could hinder aught,[3] but still augment its force.
"O happy flood," quoth I, "that holds thy race
Till thou arrive at thy beloved place,
Nor is it rocks or shoals that can obstruct thy pace,

23

Nor is't enough, that thou alone mayst slide   155
But hundred brooks in thy clear waves do meet,
So hand in hand along with thee they glide
To Thetis' house,[4] where all embrace and greet.
Thou emblem true of what I count the best,

2. Difficulties.
3. Anything.

4. I.e., the sea. Thetis, a sea nymph, was Achilles' mother.

O could I lead my rivulets to rest,   160
So may we press to that vast mansion, ever blest."

24
Ye fish, which in this liquid region 'bide,
That for each season have your habitation,
Now salt, now fresh where you think best to glide
To unknown coasts to give a visitation,   165
In lakes and ponds you leave your numerous fry;
So nature taught, and yet you know not why,
You wat'ry folk that know not your felicity.

25
Look how the wantons frisk to taste the air,
Then to the colder bottom straight they dive;   170
Eftsoon to Neptune's⁵ glassy hall repair
To see what trade they great ones there do drive,
Who forage o'er the spacious sea-green field,
And take the trembling prey before it yield,
Whose armor is their scales, their spreading fins their shield.   175

26
While musing thus with contemplation fed,
And thousand fancies buzzing in my brain,
The sweet-tongued Philomel⁶ perched o'er my head
And chanted forth a most melodious strain
Which rapt me so with wonder and delight,   180
I judged my hearing better than my sight,
And wished me wings with her a while to take my flight.

27
"O merry Bird," said I, "that fears no snares,
That neither toils nor hoards up in thy barn,
Feels no sad thoughts nor cruciating⁷ cares   185
To gain more good or shun what might thee harm.
Thy clothes ne'er wear, thy meat is everywhere,
Thy bed a bough, thy drink the water clear,
Reminds not what is past, nor what's to come dost fear."

28
"The dawning morn with songs thou dost prevent,⁸   190
Sets hundred notes unto thy feathered crew,
So each one tunes his pretty instrument,
And warbling out the old, begin anew,
And thus they pass their youth in summer season,
Then follow thee into a better region,   195
Where winter's never felt by that sweet airy legion."

5. Roman god of the ocean. "Eftsoon": soon afterward.
6. I.e., the nightingale. Philomela, the daughter of King Attica, was transformed into a nightingale after her brother-in-law raped her and tore out her tongue.
7. I.e., excruciating, painful.
8. Anticipate.

29

Man at the best a creature frail and vain,
In knowledge ignorant, in strength but weak,
Subject to sorrows, losses, sickness, pain,
Each storm his state, his mind, his body break,   200
From some of these he never finds cessation,
But day or night, within, without, vexation,
Troubles from foes, from friends, from dearest, near'st relation.

30

And yet this sinful creature, frail and vain,
This lump of wretchedness, of sin and sorrow,   205
This weatherbeaten vessel wracked with pain,
Joys not in hope of an eternal morrow;
Nor all his losses, crosses, and vexation,
In weight, in frequency and long duration
Can make him deeply groan for that divine translation.⁹   210

31

The mariner that on smooth waves doth glide
Sings merrily and steers his bark with ease,
As if he had command of wind and tide,
And now become great master of the seas:
But suddenly a storm spoils all the sport,   215
And makes him long for a more quiet port,
Which 'gainst all adverse winds may serve for fort.

32

So he that saileth in this world of pleasure,
Feeding on sweets, that never bit of th' sour,
That's full of friends, of honor, and of treasure,   220
Fond fool, he takes this earth ev'n for heav'n's bower.
But sad affliction comes and makes him see
Here's neither honor, wealth, nor safety;
Only above is found all with security.

33

O Time the fatal wrack¹ of mortal things,   225
That draws oblivion's curtains over kings;
Their sumptuous monuments, men know them not,
Their names without a record are forgot,
Their parts, their ports, their pomp's² all laid in th' dust
Nor wit nor gold, nor buildings scape times rust;   230
But he whose name is graved in the white stone³
Shall last and shine when all of these are gone.

1678

9. Transformation.
1. Destroyer.
2. Vanity. "Parts": features. "Ports": places of refuge.
3. "To him that overcometh will I give to eat of the

hidden manna and will give him a white stone, and
in the stone a new name written, which no man
knoweth saving he that receiveth it" (Revelation
2.17).

The Flesh and the Spirit

In secret place where once I stood
Close by the banks of Lacrim[1] flood,
I heard two sisters reason on
Things that are past and things to come;
One Flesh was called, who had her eye   5
On worldly wealth and vanity;
The other Spirit, who did rear
Her thoughts unto a higher sphere:
Sister, quoth Flesh, what liv'st thou on,
Nothing but meditation?   10
Doth contemplation feed thee so
Regardlessly to let earth go?
Can speculation satisfy
Notion[2] without reality?
Dost dream of things beyond the moon,   15
And dost thou hope to dwell there soon?
Hast treasures there laid up in store
That all in th' world thou count'st but poor?
Art fancy sick, or turned a sot[3]
To catch at shadows which are not?   20
Come, come, I'll show unto thy sense,
Industry hath its recompense.
What canst desire, but thou may'st see
True substance in variety?
Dost honor like? Acquire the same,   25
As some to their immortal fame,
And trophies[4] to thy name erect
Which wearing time shall ne'er deject.
For riches doth thou long full sore?
Behold enough of precious store.   30
Earth hath more silver, pearls, and gold,
Than eyes can see or hands can hold.
Affect's thou pleasure? Take thy fill,
Earth hath enough of what you will.
Then let not go, what thou may'st find   35
For things unknown, only in mind.

Spirit: Be still thou unregenerate[5] part,
Disturb no more my settled heart,
For I have vowed (and so will do)
Thee as a foe still to pursue.   40
And combat with thee will and must,
Until I see thee laid in th' dust.
Sisters we are, yea, twins we be,
Yet deadly feud 'twixt thee and me;
For from one father are we not,   45

1. In Latin *lacrima* means "tear."
2. Thought.
3. Fool. "Art fancy sick": i.e., do you have hallu-
cinations?
4. Monuments.
5. Unrepentant.

Thou by old Adam wast begot.
But my arise is from above,
Whence my dear Father I do love.
Thou speak'st me fair, but hat'st me sore,
Thy flatt'ring shows[6] I'll trust no more.   50
How oft thy slave, hast thou me made,
When I believed what thou hast said,
And never had more cause of woe
Than when I did what thou bad'st do.
I'll stop mine ears at these thy charms,   55
And count them for my deadly harms.
Thy sinful pleasures I do hate,
Thy riches are to me no bait,
Thine honors do, nor will I love;
For my ambition lies above.   60
My greatest honor it shall be
When I am victor over thee,
And triumph shall with laurel head,[7]
When thou my captive shalt be led,
How I do live, thou need'st not scoff,   65
For I have meat thou know'st not of;
The hidden manna[8] I do eat,
The word of life it is my meat.
My thoughts do yield me more content
Than can thy hours in pleasure spent.   70
Nor are they shadows which I catch,
Nor fancies vain at which I snatch,
But reach at things that are so high,
Beyond thy dull capacity:
Eternal substance I do see,   75
With which enrichéd I would be.
Mine eye doth pierce the heavens and see
What is invisible to thee.
My garments are not silk nor gold,
Nor such like trash which earth doth hold,   80
But royal robes I shall have on,
More glorious than the glist'ring sun;
My crown not diamonds, pearls, and gold,
But such as angels' heads enfold.
The city[9] where I hope to dwell,   85
There's none on earth can parallel;
The stately walls both high and strong,
Are made of precious jasper stone;
The gates of pearl, both rich and clear,
And angels are for porters there;   90
The streets thereof transparent gold,
Such as no eye did e'er behold;
A crystal river there doth run,

6. Exhibitions, displays.
7. In classical times a crown of laurel was a sign of victory for poets, heroes, and athletes.
8. The food sent by God to the Israelites in the wilderness (Exodus 16.15).
9. Lines 85 to 106 follow the description of the heavenly city of the New Jerusalem in Revelation 21 and 22.

Which doth proceed from the Lamb's throne.
Of life, there are the waters sure,   95
Which shall remain forever pure,
Nor sun, nor moon, they have no need,
For glory doth from God proceed.
No candle there, nor yet torchlight,
For there shall be no darksome night.   100
From sickness and infirmity
For evermore they shall be free;
Nor withering age shall e'er come there,
But beauty shall be bright and clear;
This city pure is not for thee,   105
For things unclean there shall not be.
If I of heaven may have my fill,
Take thou the world and all that will.

                                                                        1678

The Author to Her Book[1]

Thou ill-formed offspring of my feeble brain,
Who after birth didst by my side remain,
Till snatched from thence by friends, less wise than true,
Who thee abroad, exposed to public view,
Made thee in rags, halting to th' press to trudge,   5
Where errors were not lessened (all may judge).
At thy return my blushing was not small,
My rambling brat (in print) should mother call,
I cast thee by as one unfit for light,
Thy visage was so irksome in my sight;   10
Yet being mine own, at length affection would
Thy blemishes amend, if so I could:
I washed thy face, but more defects I saw,
And rubbing off a spot still made a flaw.
I stretched thy joints to make thee even feet,[2]   15
Yet still thou run'st more hobbling than is meet;
In better dress to trim thee was my mind,
But nought save homespun cloth i' th' house I find.
In this array 'mongst vulgars[3] may'st thou roam.
In critic's hands beware thou dost not come,   20
And take thy way where yet thou art not known;
If for thy father asked, say thou hadst none;
And for thy mother, she alas is poor,
Which caused her thus to send thee out of door.

                                                                        1678

1. *The Tenth Muse* was published in 1650 without
Bradstreet's knowledge. She is thought to have
written this poem in 1666 when a 2nd edition was
contemplated.
2. I.e., metrical feet; thus, to smooth out the lines.
3. The common people.

Before the Birth of One of Her Children

All things within this fading world hath end,
Adversity doth still our joys attend;
No ties so strong, no friends so dear and sweet,
But with death's parting blow is sure to meet.
The sentence past is most irrevocable,   5
A common thing, yet oh, inevitable.
How soon, my Dear, death may my steps attend,
How soon't may be thy lot to lose thy friend,
We both are ignorant, yet love bids me
These farewell lines to recommend to thee,   10
That when that knot's untied that made us one,
I may seem thine, who in effect am none.
And if I see not half my days that's due,
What nature would, God grant to yours and you;
The many faults that well you know I have   15
Let be interred in my oblivious grave;
If any worth or virtue were in me,
Let that live freshly in thy memory
And when thou feel'st no grief, as I no harms,
Yet love thy dead, who long lay in thine arms,   20
And when thy loss shall be repaid with gains
Look to my little babes, my dear remains.
And if thou love thyself, or loved'st me,
These O protect from stepdame's[1] injury.
And if chance to thine eyes shall bring this verse,   25
With some sad sighs honor my absent hearse;
And kiss this paper for thy love's dear sake,
Who with salt tears this last farewell did take.

1678

To My Dear and Loving Husband

If ever two were one, then surely we.
If ever man were loved by wife, then thee;
If ever wife was happy in a man,
Compare with me, ye women, if you can.
I prize thy love more than whole mines of gold   5
Or all the riches that the East doth hold.
Nor ought but love from thee, give recompense.
My love is such that rivers cannot quench,
Thy love is such I can no way repay,
The heavens reward thee manifold, I pray.   10
Then while we live, in love let's so persevere
That when we live no more, we may live ever.

1678

1. I.e., stepmother's.

A Letter to Her Husband,
Absent upon Public Employment

My head, my heart, mine eyes, my life, nay, more,
My joy, my magazine[1] of earthly store,
If two be one, as surely thou and I,
How stayest thou there, whilst I at Ipswich[2] lie?
So many steps, head from the heart to sever,   5
If but a neck, soon should we be together.
I, like the Earth this season, mourn in black,
My Sun is gone so far in's zodiac,
Whom whilst I 'joyed, nor storms, nor frost I felt,
His warmth such frigid colds did cause to melt.   10
My chilled limbs now numbed lie forlorn;
Return, return, sweet Sol, from Capricorn;[3]
In this dead time, alas, what can I more
Than view those fruits which through thy heat I bore?
Which sweet contentment yield me for a space,   15
True living pictures of their father's face.
O strange effect! now thou art southward gone,
I weary grow the tedious day so long;
But when thou northward to me shalt return,
I wish my Sun may never set, but burn   20
Within the Cancer[4] of my glowing breast,
The welcome house of him my dearest guest.
Where ever, ever stay, and go not thence,
Till nature's sad decree shall call thee hence;
Flesh of thy flesh, bone of thy bone,   25
I here, thou there, yet both but one.

1678

Another [Letter to Her Husband, Absent upon Public Employment]

As loving hind that (hartless) wants[1] her deer,
Scuds through the woods and fern with hark'ning ear,
Perplext, in every bush and nook doth pry,
Her dearest deer, might answer ear or eye;
So doth my anxious soul, which now doth miss   5
A dearer dear (far dearer heart) than this,
Still wait with doubts, and hopes, and failing eye,
His voice to hear or person to descry.
Or as the pensive dove doth all alone
(On withered bough) most uncouthly bemoan   10
The absence of her love and loving mate,

1. Warehouse, storehouse.
2. Ipswich, Massachusetts, is north of Boston.
3. Capricorn, the tenth sign of the zodiac, represents winter. "Sol": sun.

4. Cancer, the fourth sign of the zodiac, represents summer.
1. Lacks. "Hind": female deer. "Hartless" puns on *hart* (male deer) and *heart*.

Whose loss hath made her so unfortunate,
Ev'n thus do I, with many a deep sad groan,
Bewail my turtle[2] true, who now is gone,
His presence and his safe return still woos,   15
With thousand doleful sighs and mournful coos.
Or as the loving mullet,[3] that true fish,
Her fellow lost, nor joy nor life do wish,
But launches on that shore, there for to die,
Where she her captive husband doth espy.   20
Mine being gone, I lead a joyless life,
I have a loving peer, yet seem no wife;
But worst of all, to him can't steer my course,
I here, he there, alas, both kept by force.
Return my dear, my joy, my only love,   25
Unto thy hind, thy mullet, and thy dove,
Who neither joys in pasture, house, nor streams,
The substance gone, O me, these are but dreams.
Together at one tree, oh let us browse,
And like two turtles roost within one house,   30
And like the mullets in one river glide,
Let's still remain but one, till death divide.
    Thy loving love and dearest dear,
    At home, abroad, and everywhere.

                  1678

In Reference to Her Children, 23 June, 1659

I had eight birds hatched in one nest,
Four cocks there were, and hens the rest.
I nursed them up with pain and care,
Nor cost, nor labor did I spare,
Till at the last they felt their wing,   5
Mounted the trees, and learned to sing;
Chief of the brood then took his flight
To regions far and left me quite.
My mournful chirps I after send,
Till he return, or I do end: 10
Leave not thy nest, thy dam and sire,
Fly back and sing amidst this choir.
My second bird did take her flight,
And with her mate flew out of sight;
Southward they both their course did bend,   15
And seasons twain they there did spend,
Till after blown by southern gales,
They norward steered with filled sails.
A prettier bird was no where seen,
Along the beach among the treen.[1]   20
I have a third of color white,

2. I.e., turtledove.   1. Trees.
3. A common species of fish.

On whom I placed no small delight;
Coupled with mate loving and true,
Hath also bid her dam adieu;
And where Aurora[2] first appears,   25
She now hath perched to spend her years.
One to the academy flew
To chat among that learned crew,
Ambition moves still in his breast
That he might chant above the rest,   30
Striving for more than to do well,
That nightingales he might excel.
My fifth, whose down is yet scarce gone,
Is 'mongst the shrubs and bushes flown,
And as his wings increase in strength,   35
On higher boughs he'll perch at length.
My other three still with me nest,
Until they're grown, then as the rest,
Or[3] here or there they'll take their flight,
As is ordained, so shall they light.   40
If birds could weep, then would my tears
Let others know what are my fears
Lest this my brood some harm should catch,
And be surprised for want of watch,
Whilst pecking corn and void of care,   45
They fall un'wares in fowler's[4] snare,
Or whilst on trees they sit and sing,
Some untoward[5] boy at them do fling,
Or whilst allured with bell and glass,
The net be spread, and caught, alas.   50
Or lest by lime-twigs they be foiled,[6]
Or by some greedy hawks be spoiled.
O would my young, ye saw my breast,
And knew what thoughts there sadly rest,
Great was my pain when I you bred,   55
Great was my care when I you fed,
Long did I keep you soft and warm,
And with my wings kept off all harm,
My cares are more and fears than ever,
My throbs such now as 'fore were never.   60
Alas, my birds, you wisdom want,
Of perils you are ignorant;
Oft times in grass, on trees, in flight,
Sore accidents on you may light.
O to your safety have an eye,   65
So happy may you live and die.
Meanwhile my days in tunes I'll spend,
Till my weak lays[7] with me shall end.
In shady woods I'll sit and sing,

2. In Roman mythology the goddess of the dawn.
3. Either.
4. Bird catcher's.
5. Unruly, fractious.

6. I.e., caught by means of birdlime (a sticky substance) spread on twigs.
7. Ballads, poems.

And things that past to mind I'll bring.   70
Once young and pleasant, as are you,
But former toys (no joys) adieu.
My age I will not once lament,
But sing, my time so near is spent.
And from the top bough take my flight   75
Into a country beyond sight,
Where old ones instantly grow young,
And there with seraphims[8] set song;
No seasons cold, nor storms they see;
But spring lasts to eternity.   80
When each of you shall in your nest
Among your young ones take your rest,
In chirping language, oft them tell,
You had a dam that loved you well,
That did what could be done for young,   85
And nursed you up till you were strong,
And 'fore she once would let you fly,
She showed you joy and misery;
Taught what was good, and what was ill,
What would save life, and what would kill.   90
Thus gone, amongst you I may live,
And dead, yet speak, and counsel give:
Farewell, my birds, farewell adieu,
I happy am, if well with you.

1678

In Memory of My Dear Grandchild Elizabeth Bradstreet, Who Deceased August, 1665, Being a Year and a Half Old

1

Farewell dear babe, my heart's too much content,
Farewell sweet babe, the pleasure of mine eye,
Farewell fair flower that for a space was lent,
Then ta'en away unto eternity.
Blest babe, why should I once bewail thy fate,   5
Or sigh thy days so soon were terminate,
Sith[1] thou art settled in an everlasting state.

2

By nature trees do rot when they are grown,
And plums and apples thoroughly ripe do fall,
And corn and grass are in their season mown,   10
And time brings down what is both strong and tall.
But plants new set to be eradicate,

---

8. Winged angels.   1. Since.

And buds new blown to have so short a date,
Is by His hand alone that guides nature and fate.

1678

In Memory of My Dear Grandchild Anne Bradstreet, Who Deceased June 20, 1669, Being Three Years and Seven Months Old

With troubled heart and trembling hand I write,
The heavens have changed to sorrow my delight.
How oft with disappointment have I met,
When I on fading things my hopes have set.
Experience might 'fore this have made me wise,   5
To value things according to their price.
Was ever stable joy yet found below?
Or perfect bliss without mixture of woe?
I knew she was but as a withering flower,
That's here today, perhaps gone in an hour;   10
Like as a bubble, or the brittle glass,
Or like a shadow turning as it was.
More fool then I to look on that was lent
As if mine own, when thus impermanent.
Farewell dear child, thou ne'er shall come to me,   15
But yet a while, and I shall go to thee;
Meantime my throbbing heart's cheered up with this:
Thou with thy Savior art in endless bliss.

1678

On My Dear Grandchild Simon Bradstreet, Who Died on 16 November, 1669, Being But a Month, and One Day Old

No sooner came, but gone, and fall'n asleep.
Acquaintance short, yet parting caused us weep;
Three flowers, two scarcely blown, the last i' th' bud,
Cropped by th' Almighty's hand; yet is He good.
With dreadful awe before Him let's be mute,   5
Such was His will, but why, let's not dispute,
With humble hearts and mouths put in the dust,
Let's say He's merciful as well as just.
He will return and make up all our losses,
And smile again after our bitter crosses.   10
Go pretty babe, go rest with sisters twain;
Among the blest in endless joys remain.

1678

For Deliverance from a Fever

When sorrows had begirt me round,
And pains within and out,
When in my flesh no part was found,[1]
Then didst Thou rid[2] me out.
My burning flesh in sweat did boil,   5
My aching head did break,
From side to side for ease I toil,
So faint I could not speak.
Beclouded was my soul with fear
Of Thy displeasure sore,   10
Nor could I read my evidence
Which oft I read before.
"Hide not Thy face from me!" I cried,
"From burnings keep my soul.
Thou know'st my heart, and hast me tried;   15
I on Thy mercies roll."
"O heal my soul," Thou know'st I said,
"Though flesh consume to nought,
What though in dust it shall be laid,
To glory t' shall be brought."   20
Thou heard'st, Thy rod Thou didst remove
And spared my body frail,
Thou show'st to me Thy tender love,
My heart no more might quail.
O, praises to my mighty God,   25
Praise to my Lord, I say,
Who hath redeemed my soul from pit,[3]
Praises to Him for aye.[4]

1867

Here Follows Some Verses upon the Burning of Our House July 10th, 1666

Copied Out of a Loose Paper

In silent night when rest I took
For sorrow near I did not look
I wakened was with thund'ring noise
And piteous shrieks of dreadful voice.
That fearful sound of "Fire!" and "Fire!"   5
Let no man know is my desire.
I, starting up, the light did spy,
And to my God my heart did cry
To strengthen me in my distress

---

1. I.e., when nothing was spared.   3. Hell.
2. Cleanse. "Thou": God.   4. Ever.

And not to leave me succorless.   10
Then, coming out, beheld a space
The flame consume my dwelling place.
And when I could no longer look,
I blest His name that gave and took,[1]
That laid my goods now in the dust.   15
Yea, so it was, and so 'twas just.
It was His own, it was not mine,
Far be it that I should repine;
He might of all justly bereft
But yet sufficient for us left.   20
When by the ruins oft I past
My sorrowing eyes aside did cast,
And here and there the places spy
Where oft I sat and long did lie:
Here stood that trunk, and there that chest,   25
There lay that store I counted best.
My pleasant things in ashes lie,
And them behold no more shall I.
Under thy roof no guest shall sit,
Nor at thy table eat a bit.   30
No pleasant tale shall e'er be told,
Nor things recounted done of old.
No candle e'er shall shine in thee,
Nor bridegroom's voice e'er heard shall be.
In silence ever shall thou lie,   35
Adieu, Adieu, all's vanity.[2]
Then straight I 'gin my heart to chide,
And did thy wealth on earth abide?
Didst fix thy hope on mold'ring dust?
The arm of flesh didst make thy trust?   40
Raise up thy thoughts above the sky
That dunghill mists away may fly.
Thou hast an house on high erect,
Framed by that mighty Architect,
With glory richly furnished,   45
Stands permanent though this be fled.
It's purchaséd and paid for too
By Him who hath enough to do.
A price so vast as is unknown
Yet by His gift is made thine own;   50
There's wealth enough, I need no more,
Farewell, my pelf,[3] farewell my store.
The world no longer let me love,
My hope and treasure lies above.

                                                       1867

---

1. "The Lord gave, and the Lord hath taken away;   3. Possessions, usually in the sense of being falsely
blessed be the name of the Lord" (Job 1.21).   gained.
2. Empty, worthless.

As Weary Pilgrim

As weary pilgrim, now at rest,
  Hugs with delight his silent nest,
His wasted limbs now lie full soft
  That mirey steps have trodden oft,
Blesses himself to think upon   5
  His dangers past, and travails done.
The burning sun no more shall heat,
  Nor stormy rains on him shall beat.
The briars and thorns no more shall scratch.
  Nor hungry wolves at him shall catch.   10
He erring paths no more shall tread,
  Nor wild fruits eat instead of bread.
For waters cold he doth not long
  For thirst no more shall parch his tongue.
No rugged stones his feet shall gall,   15
  Nor stumps nor rocks cause him to fall.
All cares and fears he bids farewell
  And means in safety now to dwell.
A pilgrim I, on earth perplexed
  With sins, with cares and sorrows vext,   20
By age and pains brought to decay,
  And my clay house[1] mold'ring away.
Oh, how I long to be at rest
  And soar on high among the blest.
This body shall in silence sleep,   25
  Mine eyes no more shall ever weep,
No fainting fits shall me assail,
  Nor grinding pains my body frail,
With cares and fears ne'er cumb'red be
  Nor losses know, nor sorrows see.   30
What though my flesh shall there consume,
  It is the bed Christ did perfume,
And when a few years shall be gone,
  This mortal shall be clothed upon.
A corrupt carcass down it lies,   35
  A glorious body it shall rise.
In weakness and dishonor sown,
  In power 'tis raised by Christ alone.
Then soul and body shall unite
  And of their Maker have the sight.   40
Such lasting joys shall there behold
  As ear ne'er heard nor tongue e'er told.
Lord make me ready for that day,
  Then come, dear Bridegroom,[2] come away.

Aug. 31, 1669   1867

---

1. I.e., the body.
2. Christ is the bridegroom and the soul is married to him. "And Jesus said unto them, Can the children of the bridechamber fast, while the bridegroom is with them? as long as they have the bridegroom with them, they cannot fast" (Mark 2.19).

To My Dear Children

This book by any yet unread,
I leave for you when I am dead,
That being gone, here you may find
What was your living mother's mind.
Make use of what I leave in love,
And God shall bless you from above.

A. B.

My dear children,

I, knowing by experience that the exhortations of parents take most effect when the speakers leave to speak,[1] and those especially sink deepest which are spoke latest, and being ignorant whether on my death bed I shall have opportunity to speak to any of you, much less to all, thought it the best, whilst I was able, to compose some short matters (for what else to call them I know not) and bequeath to you, that when I am no more with you, yet I may be daily in your remembrance (although that is the least in my aim in what I now do), but that you may gain some spiritual advantage by my experience. I have not studied in this you read to show my skill, but to declare the truth, not to set forth myself, but the glory of God. If I had minded the former, it had been perhaps better pleasing to you, but seeing the last is the best, let it be best pleasing to you.

The method I will observe shall be this: I will begin with God's dealing with me from my childhood to this day.

In my young years, about 6 or 7 as I take it, I began to make conscience of my ways, and what I knew was sinful, as lying, disobedience to parents, etc., I avoided it. If at any time I was overtaken with the like evils, it was as a great trouble, and I could not be at rest till by prayer I had confessed it unto God. I was also troubled at the neglect of private duties though too often tardy that way. I also found much comfort in reading the Scriptures, especially those places I thought most concerned my condition, and as I grew to have more understanding, so the more solace I took in them.

In a long fit of sickness which I had on my bed I often communed with my heart and made my supplication to the most High who set me free from that affliction.

But as I grew up to be about 14 or 15, I found my heart more carnal,[2] and sitting loose from God, vanity and the follies of youth take hold of me.

About 16, the Lord laid His hand sore upon me and smote me with the smallpox. When I was in my affliction, I besought the Lord and confessed my pride and vanity, and He was entreated of me and again restored me. But I rendered not to Him according to the benefit received.

After a short time I changed my condition and was married, and came into this country, where I found a new world and new manners, at which my heart rose. But after I was convinced it was the way of God, I submitted to it and joined to the church at Boston.

After some time I fell into a lingering sickness like a consumption together with a lameness, which correction I saw the Lord sent to humble and try me and do me good, and it was not altogether ineffectual.

1. I.e., stop speaking.   2. I.e., worldly.

It pleased God to keep me a long time without a child, which was a great grief to me and cost me many prayers and tears before I obtained one, and after him gave me many more of whom I now take the care, that as I have brought you into the world, and with great pains, weakness, cares, and fears brought you to this, I now travail[3] in birth again of you till Christ be formed in you.

Among all my experiences of God's gracious dealings with me, I have constantly observed this, that He hath never suffered me long to sit loose from Him, but by one affliction or other hath made me look home, and search what was amiss; so usually thus it hath been with me that I have no sooner felt my heart out of order, but I have expected correction for it, which most commonly hath been upon my own person in sickness, weakness, pains, sometimes on my soul, in doubts and fears of God's displeasure and my sincerity towards Him; sometimes He hath smote a child with a sickness, sometimes chastened by losses in estate,[4] and these times (through His great mercy) have been the times of my greatest getting and advantage; yea, I have found them the times when the Lord hath manifested the most love to me. Then have I gone to searching and have said with David, "Lord, search me and try me, see what ways of wickedness are in me, and lead me in the way everlasting,"[5] and seldom or never but I have found either some sin I lay under which God would have reformed, or some duty neglected which He would have performed, and by His help I have laid vows and bonds upon my soul to perform His righteous commands.

If at any time you are chastened of God, take it as thankfully and joyfully as in greatest mercies, for if ye be His, ye shall reap the greatest benefit by it. It hath been no small support to me in times of darkness when the Almighty hath hid His face from me that yet I have had abundance of sweetness and refreshment after affliction and more circumspection[6] in my walking after I have been afflicted. I have been with God like an untoward child, that no longer than the rod has been on my back (or at least in sight) but I have been apt to forget Him and myself, too. Before I was afflicted, I went astray, but now I keep Thy statutes.[7]

I have had great experience of God's hearing my prayers and returning comfortable answers to me, either in granting the thing I prayed for, or else in satisfying my mind without it, and I have been confident it hath been from Him, because I have found my heart through His goodness enlarged in thankfulness to Him.

I have often been perplexed that I have not found that constant joy in my pilgrimage and refreshing which I supposed most of the servants of God have, although He hath not left me altogether without the witness of His holy spirit, who hath oft given me His word and set to His seal that it shall be well with me. I have sometimes tasted of that hidden manna that the world knows not, and have set up my Ebenezer,[8] and have resolved with myself that against such a promise, such tastes of sweetness, the gates of hell shall never prevail; yet have I many times sinkings and droopings, and not enjoyed that felicity that sometimes I have done. But when I have been in darkness

---

3. Toil, labor.
4. Financial losses.
5. Psalm 139.23–24.
6. Prudence.
7. Psalm 119.8.

8. In 1 Samuel 7.12, a stone monument to commemorate a victory over the Philistines. "Manna": the "bread from heaven" (Exodus 16.4) that fed the Israelites in the wilderness.

and seen no light, yet have I desired to stay myself upon the Lord, and when I have been in sickness and pain, I have thought if the Lord would but lift up the light of His countenance upon me, although He ground me to powder, it would be but light to me; yea, oft have I thought were I in hell itself and could there find the love of God toward me, it would be a heaven. And could I have been in heaven without the love of God, it would have been a hell to me, for in truth it is the absence and presence of God that makes heaven or hell.

Many times hath Satan troubled me concerning the verity of the Scriptures, many times by atheism how I could know whether there was a God; I never saw any miracles to confirm me, and those which I read of, how did I know but they were feigned? That there is a God my reason would soon tell me by the wondrous works that I see, the vast frame of the heaven and the earth, the order of all things, night and day, summer and winter, spring and autumn, the daily providing for this great household upon the earth, the preserving and directing of all to its proper end. The consideration of these things would with amazement certainly resolve me that there is an Eternal Being. But how should I know He is such a God as I worship in Trinity, and such a Savior as I rely upon? Though this hath thousands of times been suggested to me, yet God hath helped me over. I have argued thus with myself. That there is a God, I see. If ever this God hath revealed himself, it must be in His word, and this must be it or none. Have I not found that operation by it that no human invention can work upon the soul, hath not judgments befallen divers who have scorned and contemned it, hath it not been preserved through all ages maugre[9] all the heathen tyrants and all of the enemies who have opposed it? Is there any story but that which shows the beginnings of times, and how the world came to be as we see? Do we not know the prophecies in it fulfilled which could not have been so long foretold by any but God Himself?

When I have got over this block, then have I another put in my way, that admit this be the true God whom we worship, and that be his word, yet why may not the Popish religion be the right? They have the same God, the same Christ, the same word. They only interpret it one way, we another.

This hath sometimes stuck with me, and more it would, but the vain fooleries that are in their religion together with their lying miracles and cruel persecutions of the saints, which admit were they as they term them, yet not so to be dealt withal.

The consideration of these things and many the like would soon turn me to my own religion again.

But some new troubles I have had since the world has been filled with blasphemy and sectaries,[1] and some who have been accounted sincere Christians have been carried away with them, that sometimes I have said, "Is there faith upon the earth?" and I have not known what to think; but then I have remembered the works of Christ that so it must be, and if it were possible, the very elect should be deceived. "Behold," saith our Savior, "I have told you before." That hath stayed my heart, and I can now say, "Return, O my Soul, to thy rest, upon this rock Christ Jesus will I build my faith, and if I perish, I perish"; but I know all the Powers of Hell shall never prevail against it. I know whom I have trusted, and whom I have believed, and that He is able to keep that I have committed to His charge.

9. In spite of. "Contemned": despised.   1. Unbelievers, heretics.

Now to the King, immortal, eternal and invisible, the only wise God, be honor, and glory for ever and ever, Amen.

This was written in much sickness and weakness, and is very weakly and imperfectly done, but if you can pick any benefit out of it, it is the mark which I aimed at.

1867

JACOB STEENDAM
1616–c. 1671

A man of obscure origins in his native Netherlands, Jacob Steendam may have been from the North Holland port of Enkhuizen but early in his life relocated to Amsterdam, the newly independent nation's busy commercial center. There, amid the hectic activity of the merchants and stock companies exploiting the country's colonial interests overseas, Steendam found both a home and a vocation. One institution in particular, the Dutch West India Company, absorbed his personal ambitions for some fifteen years. Founded in 1621, the company was a bold but undercapitalized trading venture whose main branch was located in Amsterdam. Its merchants, nominally entitled by their charter to monopolize all commerce with Africa and the Americas, a goal they never even came near reaching, established operations in the Caribbean, on the South American mainland ("New Holland" was the optimistic name they gave to Brazil for the few years they controlled it) and along the Gold and Slave coasts of West Africa—as well as in the much-neglected region running from Manhattan up the Hudson River in North America and west into what would one day be New Jersey. Steendam, who wrote and published poetry as a diversion for much of his adult life, served the company in Africa for several years before returning in 1649 to the Dutch metropolis, where he published his love songs, emblems, odes, and spiritual verse under the title *Den Distlevink* (or The Gold-Finch).

Having severed his ties with the company, Steendam soon afterward set sail for the troubled but promising settlement of New Amsterdam, setting himself up there as a trader and farmer. A keen observer of public affairs, before long Steendam sent over for publication in The Netherlands a new series of poems concerned with the challenges facing New Netherland. The Dutch venture there was put in doubt by the virtual collapse of the company, internal colonial dissension, difficulties with the Indians, and rivalry with the English settlers to the colony's east. By 1664, when the English succeeded in conquering the Dutch colony, Steendam had left New Netherland, but even in Amsterdam his verse still dwelled on that "noblest spot of earth" where he had briefly resided. In 1661 and 1662, he published the two poems printed here, one a general description of the land and its potential and the other a straightforward pitch aimed at attracting settlers for a new Dutch venture in the Delaware valley. Steendam himself was not among the recruits for the latter. He had found brighter prospects in another area of Dutch enterprise. In 1666, two years after the Dutch lost New Netherland, he sailed for the East Indies, the domain exploited by the older and vastly more successful East India Company. He traveled to Bengal, but for most of his remaining time before his death early in the 1670s, he lived with his wife and children in Batavia, in what was later called Indonesia, where the couple ran the orphanage and where Steendam kept writing and publishing poetry.

Steendam's New Netherland poetry was first translated into English by Henry C. Murphy in *Anthology of New Netherland* (1865), from which the texts included here are adapted.

The Praise of New Netherland

Dedicated to
The Honorable Cornelis Van Ruyven:[1]
Counsellor and Secretary of the Hon. West
India Company There,
Faithful and very upright Promoter
of New Netherland.

With sharpened pen and wit, one tunes his lays,
To sing the vanity of fame and praise:
His moping thoughts, bewildered in a maze,
            In darkness wander.

What brings disgrace, what constitutes a wrong,   5
These form the burden of the tuneful song:
And honor saved, his senses then among
            The dark holes ponder.

For me, it is a nobler theme I sing.
New Netherland springs forth my heroine;   10
Where Amstel's[2] folk did erst their people bring,
            And still they flourish.

New Netherland, thou noblest spot of earth,
Where bounteous Heaven ever poureth forth
The fulness of His gifts, of greatest worth,   15
            Mankind to nourish.

Whoe'er to you a judgment fair applies,
And knowing, comprehends your qualities,
Will justify the man who, to the skies,
            Extols your glories.   20

Who studies well your natural elements,
And with the plumb of science, gains a sense
Of all the four: fails not in their defence,
            Before free juries.

Your *Air*, so clear, so sharp to penetrate,   25
The Western breezes softly moderate;
And tempering the heat, they separate
            It from all moisture.

1. The secretary for the province of New Nether-land arrived in 1653 and was personally known to Steendam, from whom he jointly purchased a Manhattan houselot in 1656. Van Ruyven later held many other offices under the Dutch and, fol-lowing the conquest in 1664, under the English before returning to The Netherlands in 1674.
2. Small river from which Amsterdam derives its name.

From damp, and mist, and fog, they set it free;
From boggy smells they give it liberty: 30
The struggling stenches made to mount on high,
             And be at peace there.

No deadly pest its purity assails,
To spread infection o'er your hills and vales,
Save when a guilty race, great sins bewails   35
             In expiating.

Your Sun, th' original of *Fire* and heat,
The common nutriment of both to eat,
Is warm and pure; in plants most delicate,
             Much sap creating.   40

Nor turf, nor dried manure,—within your door
Nor coal, extracted from earth's secret stores;
Nor sods, uplifted from the barren moors,
             For fuel given;

Which, with foul stench the brain intoxicate;   45
And thus, by fetid gas which they create,
The intellects of many, wise and great,
             Men are out-driven.

The forests do, with better means, supply
The hearth and house: the stately hickory,   50
Not planted, does the winter fell defy,—
             A valiant warden;

So closely grained, so rich with fragrant oil,
Before its blaze both wet and cold recoil;
And sweetest perfumes float around the while,   55
             Like 'n Eden's garden.

The *Water* clear and fresh, and pure and sweet,
Springs up continually beneath the feet,
And everywhere the gushing fountains meet,
             In brooks o'erflowing,   60

Which animals refresh, both tame and wild;
And plants conduce to grow on hill and field;
And these to man unnumbered comforts yield,
             And quickly growing.

The *Earth* in soils of different shades appears,   65
Black, blue and white, and red; its bosom bears
Abundant harvests; and, what pleases, spares
             Not to surrender.

No bounds exist to their variety.
They nourishment afford most plenteously   70
To creatures which, in turn, man's wants supply
                    And health engender.

O fruitful land! heaped up with blessings kind,
Whoe'er your several virtues brings to mind,—
Its proper value to each gift assigned,   75
                    Will soon discover,

If ever land perfection have attained,
That you in all things have that glory gained;
Ungrateful mortal, who, your worth disdained,
                    Would pass you over.   80

In North America, behold your *Seat*,
Where all that heart can wish you satiate,
And where oppressed with wealth inordinate,
                    You have the power,

To bless the people with whate'er they need;   85
The melancholy, from their sorrows, lead;
The light of heart, exulting pleasure cede,
                    Who never cower.

The *Ocean* laves secure the outer shore,
Which, like a dyke, is raised your fields before;   90
And streams, like arteries, all veined o'er,
                    The woods refreshing;

And rolling down from mountains and the hills,
Afford, upon their banks, fit sites for mills;
And furnish, what the heart with transport fills,   95
                    The finest fishing.

The lamprey, eel and sunfish, and the white
And yellow perch, which make your tables bright;
And "elevens" and "twelves" not scarce, but quite
                    Innumerable.   100

The bream and sturgeon, "thirteens" and gurnard;[3]
The sea-bass which a prince would not discard;
The cod and salmon,—cooked with due regard,
                    Most palatable.

The black, and rock-fish, herring, mackerel,   105
The haddock, mosbankers and roach which fill

3. Probably the porgy. As Adriaen Van der Donck reports, when the Dutch settlers first came to North America, they named many fish after similar ones they were familiar with in European waters. In some cases, as with the *knor-haan* ("gurnard"), the Old World name was inaccurate. Van der Donck adds that when the settlers caught fish they did not recognize, they humorously began numbering them. "Elevens": shad. "Twelves": striped bass. "Thirteens": drum fish.

The nets to loathing; and so many, all
                Cannot be eaten.

And thus it happens here, that in the flood
Which, rolling from the Fountain of all Good,   110
O'erwhelms weak mortal man with royal food,
                He is forgotten.

You've weak-fish, carp, and turbot; pike and plaice;
There's not a pool or tiny water trace,
Where swarm not myriads of the finny race,   115
                Easily taken.

Crabs, lobsters, mussels; oysters, too, there be
So large, that one does overbalance three
Of those of Europe; and, in quantity,
                No one can reckon.   120

The tortoise, seal and shark; and in your bay,
The mighty whale and porpoise sporting, they
The power and wondrous works of God display
                For our beholding.

And curious forms come out the shoalless deep,   125
Whose depths produced by Wisdom Infinite,
Have never slept and never more will sleep,
                His works unfolding.

The *Animals* which in the woods roam free
By thousands, and are no one's property,   130
Are reared like lambs, their flesh and skins to be
                For man's sustaining.

The beaver, and the otter, clean of limb;
The weasel, which has scarce the like of him;
The wild cat, strengthening the old, who seem,   135
                With gout complaining.

Raccoon and fox, with marten, mink and hare;
The nimble squirrels, leaping through the air
And flying; which, to craving stomachs, are
                Baits most decoying.   140

Bears, lions, wolves and other beasts of prey,
The chase has long since made to waste away,
Their maws, with naught the hunger to allay,
                Themselves destroying.

The elk, the hind and hart which, fleeing, bound   145
Far in the forest depths, and there are found;
And when at last they feel the fatal wound,
                Die hard and crying.

Of *Birds*, there is a knavish robbing crew,
Which constantly the smaller tribes pursue; 150
The hawk and eagle swoop the azure blue,
                    With sharp eyes prying.

The thieving chicken hawk, with talons fell;
The sparrow-hawk; the vigilant castrel
Watching his enemy till he may reel 155
                    And faint in flying.

The duck, the goose, the turkey, and proud swan,
The diver and the heron and the crane,
The snipe, the curlew, merlin and moorhen,
                    The foremost vieing; 160

The dove and pheasant, thievish blackbird, quail;
The widgeon, which an epicure may hail;
The teal and bob-o'-lincoln, all avail
                    For man's enjoyment.

But names are wanting wholly to explain 165
The numerous species of the feathered train;
And surely the recital were a vain,
                    Misspent employment.

The hills and valleys, fields and forests wide,
As richly are, by nature's hand, supplied 170
With *Fruits*. Of which all will be satisfied
                    By this true story.

Acorns there are, the bitter and the sweet;
And nuts of various kinds, all choice to eat;
Of these the chestnuts, with the rest compete 175
                    And win the glory.

And strawberries, which in proud scarlet shine;
The plum, the cherry, and grape clustering vine;
The ground-nut and the ground-bean,[4] both we find;
                    The artichoke, too. 180

The gooseberry, both sorts of mulberries;
The garlic, leek and wild greens and chives;
And hops and mints, with sweetest flatteries,
                    The eyes provoke do.

Within your woods, for house and ship, is found 185
Good building timber; in your untilled ground,
Do reeds and rushes and wild grass abound;
                    Upon your border

4. Plants that produce edible tubers, such as peanuts and wild beans.

Lie stones for every use; some suitable
For polishing and grinding; some as well   190
For masonry and streets. 'Tis hard to tell
          Them all in order.

Graphite, and crystal, mercury and gold;
Fuller's earth, potter's earth,[5] your hills unfold
Whatever art and science seek to mould,   195
          Or can discover.

You've *herbs*, both wholesome and medicinal,
Possessed of virtues wondrous powerful
The failing strength to raise, and wounds to heal,
          And curing fever.   200

Sweet marjoram; and sassafras, whose root,
Like cassia,[6] does the fainting soul recruit,
And o'er the fields its fragrant suckers shoot,
          Like weeds, to harrow.

So grow the plants by thousands o'er the land,   205
Along the mountain top and water strand,
It is too strange for us to understand,
          And to our sorrow.

For bee and wasp, sweet-smelling flowers bloom,
O'er all; renowned for colors and perfume;   210
More, than my Heroine[7] can yet assume
          To name, occurring.

Wherever men a helping hand accord
To nature, there, behold! the fields reward
Them, without any care; no fears unt'ward   215
          Of loss them worry'ng.

Whatever skillful science more may know,
And in your lap, from other countries, throw
For culture: these, fresh strength on you bestow,
          Without consuming.   220

You've most delicious hand and kitchen fruits,
Greens, salads, radishes and savory shoots,
And turnips; and the cabbage you produce,
          In large heads poming.[8]

The biting herb—the strong tobacco plant;   225
The carrot and the Maltese parsnip; and
The melon, pumpkin, Spanish comfrey, grant
          The sweetest pleasure.

5. Clay suitable for the production of pottery. "Fuller's earth": a hydrous silicate of alumina used for cleansing cloth.
6. Bark from the bastard cinnamon tree.
7. I.e., New Netherland; see line 10.
8. A pome is the heart of a cabbage head.

Exotics which, from foreign climes, they bear
Unto your bosom, need no special care;   230
But reach, untended, in your genial air,
               Their proper measure.

There's wheat and rye; and barley, pea, and bean;
Spelt,[9] maize and buckwheat; all these kinds of grain
Do nobly grow: for horses to sustain,   235
               Oats are awarded.

You've horses, cows, and wallowing swine and sheep;
Geese, ducks and hens; and rabbits (tame to keep)
Which will be all, both fat and choice to eat,
               And thrive unguarded.   240

Air, water, soil, of greatest purity;
And all, combined in sweetest harmony,
Unite, the ploughed up land to fructify,
               With strength unerring.

You seem the masterpiece of nature's hand;   245
Whatever does with breath of life expand,
Or comes from out the sea, or thrives on land,
               On you conferring.

And, in a country, fitted happily,
With creek and channel, river, brook and sea,   250
For every use of man. I make the plea,
               Who can deny it?

A land for trade and navigation sought;
With harbors which the earth herself has wrought,
For aid to those who are in danger brought   255
               And seek to fly it.

It is the land where milk and honey flow;
Where plants distilling perfume grow;
Where Aaron's rod with budding blossoms blow;[1]
               A very Eden.   260

Oh happy land! while envy you invite,
You soar far over all you thus excite;
And conquer whom by chance you meet in fight;
               May God protect and

Defend and save you; peace and comfort give;   265
All strife and discord from your borders drive;
So Netherland your happiness perceive
               With joy and pleasure.

9. An old type of grain related to wheat.
1. In Numbers 17, Aaron's staff miraculously buds.

So labor may in peace its fruits consume;
And Christ's true Church fresh as the lily bloom,—   270
Its mark in you irrevocably hewn,
          Henceforth forever.

Rule, doctrine, covenants, all in accord
With His pure word who is, of Lords, the Lord;
Where righteousness and truth may rest like broad   275
          And solid pillars.

So may a city, house, or kingdom stand,
Which else have laid foundations in the sand,
And envy, pride, hate, lust, and violent hand,
          Lurk in their cellars.   280

But you accept, O noblest land of all!
With thankfulness, His bounties liberal,
Who has a pleasure garden made your soil,
          That you might render

Your children an inheritance fore'er,   285
Until the Seed of Woman reappear,
For our redemption. Welcome hour! Who'll dare
          His coming hinder?
                    Noch vaster.[2]

                    1661

Spurring Verses

To the lovers of the colony and brothership, to be established on the South river of New Netherland, by Peter Cornelison Plockhoy,[1] of Zierikzee, with his associates; and the favorable privileges, for that purpose, granted by the noble Lords Burgomasters of the city of Amsterdam, the 9th of June, 1662.

You poor, who know not how your living to obtain;
You affluent, who seek in mind to be content;
Choose you New Netherland (which no one shall disdain),
Before your time and strength here fruitlessly are spent.
There have you other ends, your labor to incite;   5
Your work, will gen'rous soils, with usury, requite.

New Netherland's the flow'r, the noblest of all lands;
With richest blessings crowned, where milk and honey flow;

2. This customary signature of the poet was an elaborate pun on *Steen-dam* (stone dam, literal trans.). "*Noch vaster*": yet steadier (literal trans.); suggesting his increasing steadfastness as time passed.
1. A Dutch Mennonite (1620?–1700?) who in 1663 led a small band of settlers to a site near Cape

Henlopen on the lower Delaware ("South") River, which had been wrested from Swedish control by the Dutch in 1655. Plockhoy's own venture collapsed when the English conquered all of New Netherland in 1664–65 and put the settlers to flight. A Mennonite is a follower of the anabaptist Menno Simons.

By the most High of All, with doubly lib'ral hands
Endowed; yea, filled up full, with what may thrive and grow.　10
The air, the earth, the sea, each pregnant with its gift,
The needy, without trouble, from distress to lift.

　The birds obscure the sky, so numerous in their flight;
The animals roam wild, and flatten down the ground;
The fish swarm in the waters, and exclude the light;　15
The oysters there, than which none better can be found,
Are piled up, heap on heap, till islands they attain;
And vegetation clothes the forest, mead and plain.

　You have a portion there which costs not pains nor gold;
But if you labor give, then shall you also share　20
(With trust in Him who you from want does there uphold)
A rich reward, in time, for all your toil and care.
In cattle, grain and fruit, and every other thing;
Whereby you always have great cause His praise to sing.

　What see you in your houses, towns and Fatherland?　25
Is God not over all? the sky not ever wide?
His blessings deck the earth, like bursting veins expand
A flood of treasure wherever you abide;
They neither are to monarchies nor dukedoms bound,
They are as well in one, as other countries, found.　30

　But there, a living view does always meet your eye,
Of Eden, and the promised land of Jacob's seed;
Who would not, then, in such a tight community
Desire to be a freeman; and the rights decreed
To each and every one, by Amstel's burgher lords,　35
Enjoy? and treat with honor what their rule awards?

　Communities the groundwork are of every state;
They first the hamlet, village and the city make;
From whence proceeds the commonwealth; whose members, great
Become, an interest in the common welfare take.　40
'T is no Utopia; it rests on principles,
Which, for true liberty, prescribes you settled rules.

　You will not aliens, in those far lands, appear;
As formerly, in Egypt, e'en was Israel.
Nor have you slavery nor tyranny to fear,　45
Since Joseph's eyes do see, and on the compass fall.
The civic Fathers who on th' Y[2] perform their labors,
Are your protectors; and your countrymen are neighbors.

　New Netherland's South River,—second Amazon,
For you a pleasure garden on its banks concedes.　50
Choose you the Swanendael, where Osset[3] had his throne,

2. A river flowing through Amsterdam (also spelled Ij).
3. Gilles Oset (or Houset) commanded the first Dutch colony on the Delaware, founded in 1630–31 on what was named the Swan's dale or Swanendael.

Or any other spot your avocation needs.
You have the choice of all; and you're left free to choose;
Keep the conditions well, and you have naught to lose.

Discard the base report,[4] unworthy of your ear;   55
'Tis forged by ignorance and hate and jealous spite,
By those who are its authors, to bedim this fair
Bright morning sun before the laughing noonday light.
An accident may hinder, but not change the plan,
Whose gloss, take that away, you then may fairly scan.   60

'T was but an accident, which gives them stuff to slight
That land, which, *as I know*, no proper rival has;
In order from your purpose they may you affright,
Who there desire to live, before you thither pass.
'Tis groundless, ev'ry one may easily perceive.   65
Who now neglects the chance, great treasures does he leave.

JACOB STEENDAM,
Noch vaster.[5]

1662

4. Oset's fort at Swanendael was burned by the Indians in 1632 and the settlers were murdered. Steendam is eager to keep his readers from associating the new venture with that old "accident," as he later calls the disaster (line 59).
5. See n. 2, p. 283

ADRIAEN VAN DER DONCK
1620–1655

A native of Breda, in The Netherlands province of North Brabant, Adriaen Cornelissen Van der Donck studied law at the prestigious University of Leyden before deciding, at the age of twenty-one, to risk emigration to the Dutch colony of New Netherland. He went as an agent of the wealthy Amsterdam jewel merchant Kiliaen Van Rensselaer, absentee owner of the largest patroonship, or manor, in New Netherland. Van der Donck was the only university-trained person among the fifteen hundred or so Europeans then living in New Netherland, a weak commercial colony settled by merchants following Henry Hudson's voyage in 1609 and later put under the control of the Dutch West India Company. He thus was a plausible appointee for the job assigned to him as *schout* (judicial officer) for Rensselaerwyck, Van Rensselaer's vast but mostly undeveloped estate located in the upper Hudson valley. The temptations of the lucrative fur trade diverted the attention of Van Rensselaer's settlers from agricultural development, much to the patroon's dislike. From the beginning, Van der Donck was in competition with Van Rensselaer's other appointees and was drawn into the many disputes that festered while the patroon issued directive after directive aimed at keeping his employees and tenants hard at work. Van der Donck's first official ordinance, dictated in The Netherlands and designed to bar his master's tenants from the fur trade, thus spoke of the "great strife, uproar, quarreling, yes what is more, mutual discord" daily produced by trading rivalries among the mere hundred residents of Rensselaerwyck. By 1646, disillusioned with the social climate of Rensselaerwyck, Van der Donck relocated downriver to the northern fringes of the future New York City.

Having aided New Netherland governor Willem Kieft in the latter's war against the American Indians in the mid-1640s, Van der Donck in 1646 secured Kieft's permission to buy from its native owners a tract of some twenty-four thousand acres on the mainland just north of Manhattan. Here, in what he called *Colen Donck*, the joncker (squire) Van der Donck set about erecting an estate that he hoped might someday become a patroonship in its own right. That dream was to be forestalled by his involvement in the discord that followed soon after the arrival of the new Dutch governor, Pieter Stuyvesant, the following year. Taking on a major role in the growing opposition to Stuyvesant, Van der Donck penned the rebels' eloquent *Vertoogh van Nieu-Neder-Land* (Remonstrance of New Netherland) against him and personally took it home to The Netherlands in 1649. Lingering there until 1653, he employed part of his time writing a second and even more impressive book about his adopted country. The *Beschryvinge van Nieuw-Nederlant* (Description of New Netherland), published in 1655, bypassed most of the discord that was the focus of the *Remonstrance* and of Van der Donck's colonial experience. It centered instead on the native inhabitants of the land and on "the fruitfulness and natural advantages of the country," the wondrous abundance of plant, fish, fowl, and beast—especially the all-important beaver—that so impressed him as he went about his duties in Van Rensselaer's domain. The enthusiastic book was enriched by information derived from the trappers and American Indians and other figures its author had encountered upriver, including such legendary individuals as the Jesuit priest and Indian captive Isaac Jogues. It might have acquired even greater importance had Van der Donck's plan to use public documents not been forbidden by Stuyvesant. Van der Donck, who retired to his estate soon after returning to the colony, died of unknown causes at the age of thirty-five in the year his *Description of New Netherland* was published. His name lives on not only in his two substantial books about his new homeland but also in the city of Yonkers, founded on the lands of that estate and named for Joncker van der Donck, brief master of its fate.

From A Description of New Netherland[1]

Why This Country Is Called New Netherland

We have before related, that the Netherlanders, in the year 1609, had first discovered this country, of which they took possession as their own by right of their discovery, and finding the country fruitful and advantageously situated, possessing good and safe havens, rivers, fisheries, and many other worthy appurtenances corresponding with The Netherlands, or in truth excelling the same; for this good reason it was named New Netherland, being as much as to say, another or a new-found Netherland. Still the name depended most upon the first discovery, and upon the corresponding temperatures of the climates of the two countries, which to strangers is not so observable. We notice also that the French in the same quarter of the new world, have named their territory Canada or Nova Francia, only because they were the first Europeans who possessed the lands in those parts, for the temperature of the climate is so cold and wintry, that the snow commonly lies on the earth four or five months in succession and from four to five feet deep, which renders it costly to keep domestic animals there; and although this country lies no farther than fifty degrees north, still the air in winter is so fine, clear and sharp there, that when the snow once falls, which it commonly does

1. The text is from the first edition in English (1841), translated by Jeremiah Johnson.

about the first of December, it does not thaw away except by the power of the sun in April. If a shower of rain happens to fall in winter (which is seldom) then it forms a hard crust on the surface of the snow, that renders travelling difficult for man and beast. The air there is clear and dry, and the snow seldom melts or thaws away suddenly.

The Swedes also have a possession on the south (Delaware) river, which they name New Sweden. The climate of this place by no means corresponds with that of Sweden, as it lies in latitude 39 degrees north. But, although they have formed a settlement there, still their title is disputed,[2] for they can show no legal right or claim to their possessions.

The country having been first found or discovered by the Netherlanders, and keeping in view the discovery of the same, it is named the New Netherland. That this country was first found or discovered by the Netherlanders, is evident and clear from the fact, that the Indians or natives of the land, many of whom are still living, and with whom I have conversed, declare freely, that before the arrival of the Lowland ship, the *Half Moon*, in the year 1609, they (the natives) did not know that there were any other people in the world than those who were like themselves, much less any people who differed so much in appearance from them as we did. Their men on the breasts and about the mouth were bare, and their women like ours, hairy; going unclad and almost naked, particularly in summer, while we are always clothed and covered. When some of them first saw our ship approaching at a distance, they did not know what to think about her, but stood in deep and solemn amazement, wondering whether it were a ghost or apparition, coming down from heaven, or from hell. Others of them supposed her to be a strange fish or sea monster. When they discovered men on board, they supposed them to be more like devils than human beings. Thus they differed about the ship and men. A strange report was also spread about the country concerning our ship and visit, which created great astonishment and surprise amongst the Indians. These things we have frequently heard them declare, which we hold as certain proof that the Netherlanders were the first finders or discoverers and possessors of New Netherland. There are Indians in the country, who remember a hundred years, and if there had been any other people here before us, they would have known something of them, and if they had not seen them themselves, they would have heard an account of them from others. There are persons who believe that the Spaniards have been here many years ago, when they found the climate too cold to their liking, and again left the country; and that the maize or Turkish corn, and beans found among the Indians, were left with them by the Spaniards. This opinion or belief is improbable, as we can discover nothing of the kind from the Indians. They say that their corn and beans were received from the southern Indians, who received their seed from a people who resided still farther south, which may well be true, as the Castilians have long since resided in Florida. The maize may have been among the Indians in the warm climate long ago; however, our Indians say that they did eat roots and the bark of trees instead of bread, before the introduction of Indian corn or maize.

*   *   *

2. Even as Van der Donck's book was appearing in print in 1655, Dutch forces sent out by Governor Pieter Stuyvesant were about to dislodge the Swedes.

Of the North River[3]

We have before noticed the name of this river, with the population and advantages of the country; and, inasmuch as a particular and ample account of the same is preparing for publication, we will at once say, that this river is the most famous, and the country the most populous of any in New Netherland. There are also several colonies settled, besides the city of New Amsterdam, on the island of Manhattan, where most of the trade of this river centres. The river carries flood tides forty miles[4] up the same. Several fine creeks empty into this river, such as the Great and Small Esopus kills, Kats kill, Sleepy Haven kill, Colondonck's kill or Saw kill, Wappincke's kill, &c. We can also pass from the North river behind Manhattan island by the East river, without approaching New Amsterdam. This river still remains altogether in the possession and jurisdiction of the Netherlanders, without being invaded; but if the population did not increase and advance, there would be great danger of its long continuation. This river is rich in fishes: sturgeon, dunns, bass, sheep-heads, &c. I cannot refrain, although somewhat out of place, to relate a very singular occurrence, which happened in the month of March, 1647, at the time of a great freshet caused by the fresh water flowing down from above, by which the water of the river became nearly fresh to the bay, when at ordinary seasons the salt water flows up from twenty to twenty-four miles from the sea. At this season, two whales, of common size, swam up the river forty miles, from which place one of them returned and stranded about twelve miles from the sea, near which place four others also stranded the same year. The other run farther up the river and grounded near the great Chahoos falls,[5] about forty-three miles from the sea. This fish was tolerably fat, for although the citizens of Rensselaerwyck broiled out a great quantity of train oil,[6] still the whole river (the current being still rapid) was oily for three weeks, and covered with grease. As the fish lay rotting, the air was infected with its stench to such a degree that the smell was offensive and perceptible for two miles to leeward. For what purpose those whales ascended the river so far, it being at the time full forty miles from all salt or brackish water, it is difficult to say, unless their great desire for fish, which were plenty at this season, led them onward.

Forty-four miles from the sea this North river is divided. One part by four sprouts[7] ascends to the great falls of the Maquas kill, which is named the Chahoos, of which we will treat presently. The other part which retains the name of the North river, is navigable for boats several miles farther, and, according to the information of the Indians, rises in a great lake, from which the river of Canada also proceeds. This should be the lake of the *Iracoysen* (lake Ontario), which is as great as the Mediterranean sea, being about forty miles wide, when in the middle of the sea, no eye can see land or see over it. The lake also has extensive reed and wastelands of great breadth, wherein great multitudes of waterfowl breed in summer. When the Indians intend to cross this lake, they know certain islands which lie therein, and proceed from one to another by daylight, to the number of three or four, without which they could not find their way over the same. This, however, we relate on the

3. I.e., the Hudson River.
4. One Dutch mile equals about three English miles.
5. On the Mohawk above its junction with the

Hudson River north of Albany.
6. Whale oil obtained from boiling the blubber.
7. Divisions.

information of the Indians. They also assert that we can proceed in boats to the river of Canada, which we deem incredible.

The other arm of the North river runs by four sprouts (as we have related) to the great falls of the *Maquas kill* (Mohawk river), which the Indians name the Chahoos, and our nation the Great Falls; above which the river is again several hundred yards wide, and the falls we estimate to be one hundred and fifty or two hundred feet high.[8] The water glides over the falls as smooth as if it ran over an even wall and fell over the same. The precipice is formed of firm blue rock; near by and below the falls there stand several rocks, which appear splendid in the water, rising above it like high turf-heaps, apparently from eight, sixteen, to thirty feet high; very delightful to the eye. This place is well calculated to exalt the fancy of the poets. The ancient fabulous writers would, if they had been here, have exalted those works of nature, by the force of imagination, into the most artful and elegant descriptive illusions. The waters descend rapidly downwards from the falls, over a stony bottom, skipping, foaming and whirling boisterously about the distance of a gunshot or more; when it resumes an even course, and flows downwards. We name this the Maquas Kill, but still it is wider in most places than the Yssell[9] of The Netherlands. It however always runs one way; is navigable for boats; being tolerably deep and not rapid; but it extends above sixty miles, and runs through the Maquas' and Senecas' countries to a lake, remaining boatable all the way. The river passes through fine land, and abounds with fish. The Indians, when they travel by water, and come to trade, usually come in canoes made of the bark of trees, which they know how to construct. When they come near the falls, they land, and carry their boats and their lading some distance below the falls, and proceed on their voyage; otherwise, they would be driven over the falls and destroyed. An occurrence of this kind took place here in our time. An Indian, whom I have known, accompanied by his wife and child, with sixty beaver skins, descended the river in his canoe, in the spring, when the water runs rapid and the current is strongest, for the purpose of selling his beaver to the Netherlanders. This Indian carelessly approached too near to the falls, before he discovered his danger, and notwithstanding his utmost exertion to gain the land, his frail bark with all on board was swept over by the rapid current and down the falls; his wife and child were killed, his bark shattered to pieces, his cargo of furs damaged. But his life was preserved. I have frequently seen the Indian, and have heard him relate the perilous occurrence or adventure.

* * *

Of the Wood, the Natural Productions and Fruits of the Land

New Netherland, as in other regards, is very fruitful and fortunate in its fine woods; so much so, that the whole country is covered with wood, and in our manner of speaking, there is all too much of it, and it is always in our way. Still it comes in handy to build vessels and houses, and to fence the farms &c. The oak trees are very large; from sixty to seventy feet high without knots, and from two to three fathoms[1] thick, being of various sizes. There

8. The falls are actually seventy feet high. The Mohawk Indians lived farther inland along the river; they were members of the original Iroquois league, as were the Oneida, Onondaga, Cayuga, and Seneca peoples.

9. The north mouth (now spelled IJssel) of the Rhine, flowing from the Rhine proper into the IJsselmeer (formerly the Zuider Zee).
1. Twelve to eighteen feet.

are several kinds of oak, such as white, smooth bark, rough bark, grey bark and black bark. It is all durable wood, being as good as the oak of the Rhine or the Weser when properly worked, according to the opinion of our wood-cutters, who are judges of timber and are sawyers. The nut-wood grows as tall as the oak, but not so heavy. It is probable that this kind of wood will be useful for many purposes, for it grows straight and is tough and hard. We now use it for cogs and rounds in our mills and for threshing-flails, swivel-trees and other farming purposes. It also is excellent firewood, surpassing every other kind, and setting at naught our old adage, "The man is yet to come, who can find better wood to burn than oak." This wood is far better as well for heat as duration. It possesses a peculiar sap, which causes it to burn freely, whether green or dry. If we draw it up out of the fresh water where it has lain a long time, still, on account of its hardness, it is even then uncommonly durable on the fire. We all agree, that no turf, or other common fuel is equal to nut-wood. When it is dry, it keeps fire and sparkles like matches. Our women prefer nut-coals to turf for their stoves, because they last longer, and are not buried in ashes. This kind of wood is found all over New Netherland in such abundance, that it cannot become scarce in the first hundred years with an increased population. There also is oak and ash enough to supply its place for many purposes. The land also is so natural to produce wood, that in a few years large trees will be grown, which I can say with certainty from my own observation; and that unless there be natural changes or great improvidence, there can be no scarcity of wood in this country.

It has happened when I have been out with the natives, (*Wilden,* for so we name those who are not born of Christian parents,) that we have come to a piece of young woodland. When I have told them, in conversation, that they would do well to clear off such land, because it would bear good corn, that they said, "it is but twenty years since we planted corn there, and now it is woods again." I asked them individually if it were true, when they all answered in the affirmative. This relation was also corroborated by others. To return to the subject: this woodland was composed of oak, nut and other kinds of wood, but principally of oak and nut; and there were several trees in the same which were a fathom in circumference. The wood was so closely grown that it was difficult to pass through it on horseback. As the wood appeared young and thrifty, I give credit to the relation of the natives. I have also observed that the youngest woodlands are always covered closest with wood, and where the growth is small, the woods are so thick as to render walking through the same difficult. But where the woods are old, the timber is large and heavy, whereby the underwood is shaded, which causes it to die and perish.

The Indians have a yearly custom (which some of our Christians have also adopted) of burning the woods, plains and meadows in the fall of the year, when the leaves have fallen, and when the grass and vegetable substances are dry. Those places which are then passed over are fired in the spring in April. This practice, named by us and the Indians, "*bush burning,*" is done for several reasons: first, to render hunting easier, as the bush and vegetable growth renders walking difficult for the hunter, and the crackling of the dry substances betrays him and frightens away the game. Secondly, to thin out and clear the woods of all dead substances and grass, which grow better the ensuing spring. Thirdly, to circumscribe and enclose the game within the lines of the fire, when it is more easily taken, and also, because the game is more easily tracked over the burned parts of the woods.

The bush burning presents a grand and sublime appearance. On seeing it from without, we would imagine that not only the dry leaves, vegetables and limbs would be burnt, but that the whole woods would be consumed where the fire passes, for it frequently spreads and rages with such violence, that it is awful to behold; and when the fire approaches houses, gardens, and wooden enclosures, then great care and vigilance are necessary for their preservation, for I have seen several houses which have recently been destroyed, before the owners were apprized of their danger.

Notwithstanding the apparent danger of the entire destruction of the woodlands by the burning, still the green trees do not suffer. The outside bark is scorched three or four feet high, which does them no injury, for the trees are not killed. It however sometimes happens in the thick pine woods, wherein the fallen trees lie across each other, and have become dry, that the blaze ascends and strikes the tops of the trees, setting the same on fire, which is immediately increased by the resinous knots and leaves, which promote the blaze, and is passed by the wind from tree to tree, by which the entire tops of the trees are sometimes burnt off, while the bodies remain standing. Frequently great injuries are done by such fires, but the burning down of entire woods never happens. I have seen many instances of wood-burning in the colony of Rensselaerwyck, where there is much pine wood. Those fires appear grand at night from the passing vessels in the river, when the woods are burning on both sides of the same. Then we can see a great distance by the light of the blazing trees, the flames being driven by the wind, and fed by the tops of the trees. But the dead and dying trees remain burning in their standing positions, which appear sublime and beautiful when seen at a distance.

Hence it will appear that there actually is such an abundance of wood in New Netherland, that, with ordinary care, it will never be scarce there. There always are, however, in every country, some people so improvident, that even they may come short here, and for this reason we judge that it should not be destroyed needlessly. There, however, is such an abundance of wood, that they who cultivate the land for planting and sowing can do nothing better than destroy it, and thus clear off the land for tillage, which is done by cutting down the trees and collecting the wood into great heaps and burning the same, to get it out of their way. Yellow and white pine timber, in all their varieties, is abundant here, and we have heard the Northerners[2] say (who reside here) that the pine is as good here as the pine of Norway. But the pine does not grow as well near the salt water, except in some places. Inland, however, and high up the rivers, it grows in large forests, and it is abundant, and heavy enough for masts and spars for ships. There also are chestnuts here, like those of The Netherlands, which are spread over the woods. Chestnuts would be plentier if it were not for the Indians, who destroy the trees by stripping off the bark for covering for their houses. They, and the Netherlanders also, cut down the trees in the chestnut season, and cut off the limbs to gather the nuts, which also lessens the trees. We also find several kinds of beech trees, but those bear very little. Amongst the other trees, the water-beeches grow very large along the brooks, heavier and larger than most of the trees of the country. When those trees begin to bud, then the bark becomes a beautiful white, resembling the handsomest satin. This tree retains the leaves later than any other tree of the woods. Trees of this kind

2. Scandinavians.

are considered more ornamental and handsomer than the linden trees for the purpose of planting near houses. We can give no comparison with this species of trees, and can give the same no better name to make the wood known.[3] There also is wild ash, some trees large; and maple trees, the wood resembling cedar; white-wood trees, which grow very large,—the Indians frequently make their canoes of this wood, hence we name it *Canoe-wood*; we use it for flooring, because it is bright and free of knots. There are also two kinds of ash, with linden, birch, yew, poplar, sapine, alder, willow, thorn trees, sassafras, persimmon, mulberry, wild cherry, crab, and several other kinds of wood, the names of which are unknown to us, but the wood is suitable for a variety of purposes. Some of the trees bear fruit. The oak trees in alternate years bear many acorns of the chestnut species. The nuts grow about as large as our persimmons, but they are not as good as ours. The mulberries are better and sweeter than ours, and ripen earlier. Several kinds of plums, wild or small cherries, juniper, small kinds of apples, many hazel-nuts, black currants, gooseberries, blue India figs, and strawberries [grow] in abundance all over the country, some of which ripen at half May, and we have them until July; [so do] blueberries, raspberries, black-caps, &c., with artichokes, ground-acorns, ground beans, wild onions, and leeks like ours, with several other kinds of roots and fruits, known to the Indians, who use the same which are disregarded by the Netherlanders, because they have introduced every kind of garden vegetables, which thrive and yield well. The country also produces an abundance of fruits like the Spanish capers, which could be preserved in like manner.

1655, 1841

3. Evidently, the sycamore.

MICHAEL WIGGLESWORTH
1631–1705

It is clear from the diary that Michael Wigglesworth kept in his early twenties that the Judgment Day was never very far from his mind. When he learned, for example, that eight houses in Boston had burned, he immediately thought about how destruction "seals" God's word in his "dreadful works," and shortly after the news of his father's death was brought to him (and he had to acknowledge to himself that in his heart he was "secretly glad"), he "dreamed of the approach of the great and dreadful Day of Judgment." Wigglesworth wept, he writes, when he awoke, and determined to "follow God with tears and cries until He gave me some hopes of His gracious good will toward me." Like any sensitive believer, he was bound to have moments of doubt and joy, but ambiguity about his feelings toward his father's death never seems to have been resolved. Two months later he despaired of his "senselessness" toward this loss and bewailed his "secure, hard heart." "The death of the righteous unlamented," he notes, "is a forerunner of evil to come."

Nine years later Wigglesworth turned his dream of Judgment Day into one of the most popular poems ever written in America. Its 224 eight-line stanzas captivated the Puritan imagination, and many pious souls learned its verses by heart. Edward Taylor said that one of the reasons he loved his wife was that "the Doomsday verses much perfumed her breath." Committing it to memory would be a formidable task for anyone, but Puritans were helped by the fact that Wigglesworth used common hymn meter (alternating rhymed lines of eight and six syllables) and that the subject of his poem was familiar to them from sermons. In the first year of its publication, 1662, it sold eighteen hundred copies and it was frequently reprinted thereafter. Although Wigglesworth published other poems, nothing he wrote ever achieved the popularity of these "Doomsday verses." About one out of every twenty persons in New England bought it, and there are no complete copies of the first edition extant, for it was literally read to pieces. Its great appeal to this generation of Puritans is sometimes attributed to its "sulferousness," and it does indeed portray a vivid picture of hellfire; but its appeal can equally be laid to the fact that it assured the reader that a final order prevailed in all things, and that the regenerate would reign with Christ eternally. The poem is, finally, as comforting as it is frightening.

Wigglesworth must have been as surprised as anyone to find himself the author of a best-selling work, for nothing in his earlier career hinted at popularity. He was a neurotic young man, sometimes almost paralyzed with anxiety and self-doubt. As he was never physically strong, some of his illnesses (syphilis was one) were clearly imagined, but others were not. He came to Harvard College at sixteen, traveling from New Haven, Connecticut, where his father, recently injured, had had to give up farming. It is clear from his diary that the family expected him to do well. Wigglesworth intended to become a physician, but his introspective, bookish, and didactic nature impelled him to the ministry. In 1655 he accepted a call to the church in Malden, Massachusetts, and remained there for the next fifty years. He was not, however, a favorite of the townspeople, and he turned to writing as an alternative to his lack of success in the pulpit. Only when he jeopardized his reputation by marrying someone much younger did the attitude of his parishioners toward him soften. Nothing he ever did or did not do, however, detracted from his reputation as chief poet of the age. Samuel Sewall notes in his diary for June 10, 1705, that Mr. Michael Wigglesworth died that day in Malden: "He was the author of the poem entitled The Day of Doom, which has been so often printed; and was very useful as a physician."

From The Day of Doom[1]

I

The security
of the world
before Christ's
coming to
judgment.
Luk. 12.19

Still was the night, serene and bright,
　　when all men sleeping lay;
Calm was the season, and carnal reason[2]
　　thought so 'twould last for ay.[3]
Soul, take thine ease, let sorrow cease,　　5
　　much good thou hast in store:
This was their song, their cups among,
　　the evening before.

---

1. The text used here is from *The Day of Doom or a Poetical Description of the Great and Last Judgment with Other Poems*, edited by Kenneth B. Murdock (1929), which reprints the only complete American edition (1701).
2. The rationalizations of the flesh as opposed to spiritual "right reason."
3. Ever.

2

Wallowing in all kind of sin,
    vile wretches lay secure: 10
The best of men had scarcely then
    their lamps kept in good ure.[4]

Mat. 25.5

Virgins unwise, who through disguise
    amongst the best were numberéd,
Had closed their eyes: yea, and the wise   15
    through sloth and frailty slumberéd.

3

Like as of old, when men grow bold
    God's threat'nings to contemn,[5]

*Mat. 24.37–
38*

Who stopped their ear, and would not hear,
    when Mercy warned them: 20
But took their course, without remorse,
    till God began to pour
Destruction the world upon
    in a tempestuous shower.

4

They put away the evil day,   25
    and drowned their care and fears,
Till drowned were they, and swept away
    by vengeance unawares:

1 Thes. 5.3

So at the last, whilst men sleep fast
    in their security,   30
Surprised they are in such a snare
    as cometh suddenly.

5

*The sudden-
ness, majesty,
& terror of
Christ's
appearing.
Mat. 25.6
2 Pet. 3.10*

For at midnight brake forth a light,
    which turned the night to day,
And speedily an hideous cry   35
    did all the world dismay.
Sinners awake, their hearts do ache,
    trembling their loins surpriseth;
Amazed with fear, by what they hear,
    each one of them ariseth.   40

6

They rush from beds with giddy heads,
    and to their windows run,
Viewing this light, which shines more bright
    then doth the noon-day sun.

*Mat. 24.29–
30*

Straightway appears (they see't with tears)   45
    the Son of God most dread;
Who with His train comes on amain
    to judge both quick[6] and dead.

4. Use, condition.   6. Living. "Train": retinue. "Amain": in full force.
5. Despise.

7

Before his face the Heav'ns gave place,
    and skies are rent asunder,   50

2 Pet. 3.10

With mighty voice, and hideous noise,
    more terrible than thunder.
His brightness damps Heav'n's glorious lamps
    and makes them hide their heads,
As if afraid and quite dismayed,   55
    they quit their wonted steads.[7]

8

Ye sons of men that durst contemn
    the threat'nings of God's word,
How cheer you now? your hearts, I trow,
    are thrilled[8] as with a sword.   60
Now atheist blind, whose brutish mind
    a God could never see,
Dost thou perceive, dost now believe,
    that Christ thy Judge shall be?

9

Stout courages,[9] (whose hardiness   65
    could death and hell out-face)
Are you as bold now you behold
    your Judge draw near apace?
They cry, no, no: alas! and woe!
    our courage all is gone: 70
Our hardiness (fool hardiness)
    hath us undone, undone.

10

No heart so bold, but now grows cold
    and almost dead with fear:
No eye so dry, but now can cry,   75

Rev. 6.16

    and pour out many a tear.
Earth's potentates and powerful states,
    captains and men of might
Are quite abashed, their courage dashed
    at this most dreadful sight.   80

11

Mean[1] men lament, great men do rent
    their robes, and tear their hair:
They do not spare their flesh to tear

Mat. 24.30

    through horrible despair.
All kindreds wail: all hearts do fail: 85
    horror the world doth fill
With weeping eyes, and loud out-cries,
    yet knows not how to kill.

---

7. Accustomed places.
8. Pierced. "Trow": trust, believe.

9. Haughty and defiant souls.
1. Ordinary.

12

Rev. 6.15–16

Some hide themselves in caves and delves,
    in places under ground: 90
Some rashly leap into the deep,
    to scape by being drowned:
Some to the rocks (O senseless blocks!)
    and woody mountains run,
That there they might this fearful sight,   95
    and dreaded presence shun.

13

In vain do they to mountains say,
    "Fall on us, and us hide
From Judge's ire, more hot than fire,
    for who may it abide?"   100
No hiding place can from His face,
    sinners at all conceal,
Whose flaming eyes hid things doth 'spy,
    and darkest things reveal.

14

The Judge draws nigh, exalted high   105
    upon a lofty throne,
Mat. 25.31
Amidst the throng of angels strong,
    lo, Israel's Holy One!
The excellence of Whose presence
    and awful Majesty,   110
Amazeth Nature, and every creature,
    doth more than terrify.

15

The mountains smoke, the hills are shook,
Rev. 6.14
    the earth is rent and torn,
As if she should be clean dissolved,   115
    or from the center born.
The sea doth roar, forsakes the shore,
    and shrinks away for fear;
The wild beasts flee into the sea,
    so soon as He draws near.   120

16

Whose glory bright, whose wondrous might,
    whose power imperial,
So far surpass whatever was
    in realms terrestrial;
That tongues of men (nor Angel's pen)   125
    cannot the same express,
And therefore I must pass it by,
    lest speaking should transgress.

17

1 Thes. 4.16
Resurrection
of the dead.
Joh. 5.28–29

Before His throne a trump is blown,
   proclaiming the Day of Doom: 130
Forthwith He cries, *"Ye dead arise,*
   and unto Judgment come."
No sooner said, but 'tis obeyed;
   sepulchers opened are:
Dead bodies all rise at His call,   135
   and's mighty power declare.

18

Both sea and land, at His command,
   their dead at once surrender:
The fire and air constrained are
   also their dead to tender.   140
The mighty word of this great Lord
   links body and soul together
Both of the just, and the unjust,
   to part no more forever.

*   *   *

21

2 Cor. 5.10
The sheep
separated
from the
goats. Mat.
25

Thus everyone before the throne
   of Christ the Judge is brought,
Both righteous and impious
   that good or ill had wrought.
A separation, and differing station[2]   165
   by Christ appointed is
(To sinners sad) 'twixt good and bad,
   'twixt heirs of woe and bliss.

22

Who are
Christ's sheep.
Mat. 5.10–11

At Christ's right hand the sheep do stand,
   His holy martyrs, who   170
For His dear name suffering shame,
   calamity and woe,
Like champions stood, and with their blood
   their testimony sealed;
Whose innocence without offense,   175
   to Christ their Judge appealed.

23

Heb. 12.5–7

Next unto whom there find a room
   all Christ's afflicted ones,
Who being chastised, neither despised
   nor sank amidst their groans: 180
Who by the rod were turned to God,
   and lovéd Him the more,

2. Standing, place.

Not murmuring nor quarreling
   when they were chastened sore.

24

Luk. 7.41,47

Moreover, such as lovéd much,   185
   that had not such a trial,
As might constrain to so great pain,
   and such deep self-denial:
Yet ready were the cross to bear,
   when Christ them called thereto,   190
And did rejoice to hear His voice,
   they're counted sheep also.

25

Joh. 21.15
Mat. 19.14
Joh. 3.3

Christ's flock of lambs there also stands,
   whose faith was weak, yet true;
All sound believers (Gospel receivers)   195
   whose grace was small, but grew:
And them among an infant throng
   of babes, for whom Christ died;
Whom for His own, by ways unknown
   to men, He sanctified.   200

26

All stand before their Savior

Rev. 6.11
Phil. 3.21

   in long white robes yclad,[3]
Their countenance full of pleasance,
   appearing wondrous glad.
O glorious sight! Behold how bright   205
   dust heaps are made to shine,
Conforméd so their Lord unto,
   whose glory is divine.

27

The goats
described or
the several
sorts of repro-
bates on the
left hand.
Mat. 24.51

At Christ's left hand the goats do stand,
   all whining hypocrites,   210
Who for self-ends did seem Christ's friends,
   but fostered guileful sprites;[4]
Who sheep resembled, but they dissembled
   (their hearts were not sincere);
Who once did throng Christ's lambs among,   215
   but now must not come near.

28

Luk. 11.24,26
Heb. 6.4–6
Heb. 10.29

Apostates[5] and run-aways,
   such as have Christ forsaken,
Of whom the devil, with seven more evil,[6]
   hath fresh possession taken: 220
Sinners ingrain,[7] reserved to pain

3. Dressed.
4. Spirits.
5. Turncoats.

6. I.e., with seven accomplices more evil than he.
7. Inveterate.

and torments most severe:
Because 'gainst light they sinned with spite,
are also placéd there.

29

There also stand a num'rous band,   225
   that no profession made

Luk. 12.47
Prov. 1.24,26
Joh. 3.19

Of godliness, nor to redress
   their ways at all essayed:
Who better knew, but (sinful crew)
   Gospel and law despised;   230
Who all Christ's knocks[8] withstood like blocks
   and would not be advised.

30

Moreover, there with them appear
   a number, numberless

Gal. 3.10
1 Cor. 6.9
Rev. 21.8

Of great and small, vile wretches all,   235
   that did God's Law transgress;
Idolaters, false worshipers,
   profaners of God's name,
Who not at all thereon did call,
   or took in vain the same.   240

*   *   *

38

All silence keep, both goats and sheep,
   before the Judge's throne;

The saints
cleared & jus-
tified.

With mild aspect to His elect[9]
   then spake the Holy One: 300
"My sheep draw near, your sentence hear,
   which is to you no dread,
Who clearly now discern, and know
   your sins are pardonéd.

39

2 Cor. 5.10
Eccles. 3.17
Joh. 3.18

" 'Twas meet that ye should judgéd be,   305
   that so the world may spy
No cause of grudge, when as I judge
   and deal impartially.
Know therefore all, both great and small,
   the ground and reason why   310
These men do stand at My right hand,
   and look so cheerfully.

40

Joh. 17.6
Eph. 1.4

"These men be those My Father chose
   before the world's foundation,

---

8. Attempts to gain admittance to their souls. "Behold, I stand at the door and knock" (Revela-tion 3.20).

9. Those chosen by God for eternal life.

And to Me gave, that I should save   315
    from death and condemnation.
For whose dear sake I flesh did take,
    was of a woman born,
And did inure[1] Myself t'endure,
    unjust reproach and scorn.   320

41

"For them it was that I did pass
    through sorrows many one:
That I drank up that bitter cup,
Rev. 1.5   which made Me sigh and groan.
The cross his pain I did sustain;   325
    yea more, My Father's ire
I underwent, My blood I spent
    to save them from hell fire.

*   *   *

107

Those that   A wond'rous crowd then 'gan aloud,
pretend want   thus for themselves to say,   850
of opportunity   "We did intend, Lord to amend,
to repent.   and to reform our way:
Prov. 27.1
Jam. 4.13   Our true intent was to repent,
    and make our peace with Thee;
But sudden death stopping our breath,   855
    left us no liberty.

108

"Short was our time, for in his prime
    our youthful flower was cropped:
We died in youth, before full growth,
    so was our purpose stopped.   860
Let our good will to turn from ill,
    and sin to have forsaken,
Accepted be, O Lord, by Thee,
    and in good part be taken."

109

Are confuted   To whom the Judge: "Where you allege   865
and con-   the shortness of the space,
vinced.
Eccles. 12.1 That from your birth you lived on earth,
Rev. 2.21   to compass saving grace:
It was free grace that any space
    was given you at all   870
To turn from evil, defy the devil,
    and upon God to call.

1. Accustom.

110

Luk. 13.24
2 Cor. 6.2
Heb. 3.7–9

"One day, one week, wherein to seek
    God's face with all your hearts,
A favor was that far did pass   875
    the best of your deserts.[2]
You had a season, what was your reason
    such precious hours to waste?
What could you find, what could you mind
    that was of greater haste?   880

*   *   *

113

Luk. 13.24–
25 etc.
Phil. 2.12

"Had your intent been to repent,
    and had you it desired,   900
There would have been endeavors seen,
    before your time expired
God makes no treasure, nor hath he pleasure,
    in idle purposes:
Such fair pretenses are foul offenses,   905
    and cloaks for wickedness."

*   *   *

130

Others plead
for pardon
both from
God's mercy
and justice.
Psal. 78.38

Others argue, and not a few,
    "Is not God gracious?
His equity and clemency   1035
    are they not marvelous?
Thus we believed; are we deceived?
    cannot His mercy great,
(As hath been told to us of old)
    assuage His anger's heat?   1040

*   *   *

132

"Can God delight in such a sight
    as sinners' misery?   1050
Or what great good can this our blood
    bring unto The Most High?
Oh, Thou that dost Thy glory most

Psal. 30.9
Mic. 7.18

    in pard'ning sin display!
Lord, might it please Thee to release,   1055
    and pardon us this day?"

*   *   *

134

But all too late, grief's out of date,   1065
    when life is at an end.

2. Good deeds, merits.

The glorious King thus answering,
    all to His voice attend:

They
answered.
"God gracious is," quoth He, "like His
    no mercy can be found;   1070
His equity and clemency
    to sinners do abound.

135

Mercy that
now shines
forth in the
vessels of
mercy.
Mic. 7.18
Rom. 9.23
"As may appear by those that here
    are placed at My right hand;
Whose stripes I bore, and cleared the score,   1075
    that they might quitted stand.
For surely none, but God alone,
    whose grace transcends men's thought,
For such as those that were His foes
    like wonders would have wrought.   1080

* * *

137

Luk. 13.34
The day of
grace now
past.
"With cords of love God often strove
    your stubborn hearts to tame: 1090
Nevertheless your wickedness,
    did still resist the same.
If now at last mercy be past
    from you forevermore,
And justice come in mercy's room,   1095
    yet grudge you not therefore.

138

"If into wrath God turnéd hath
    His long long suffering,

Luk. 19.42–
43
Jud. 4
And now for love you vengeance prove,
    it is an equal thing.   1100
Your waxing worse, hath stopped the course
    of wonted[3] clemency:
Mercy refused, and grace misused,
    call for severity."

* * *

156

These words appall and daunt them all;
    dismayed, and all amort,
Like stocks[4] they stand at Christ's left hand,
    and dare no more retort.

* * *

3. Familiar, usual. "Waxing": growing.
4. Blocks of wood, speechless persons. "Amort": spiritless, inanimate.

182

Behold the
formidable
estate of all
the ungodly,
as they stand
hopeless &
helpless
before an
impartial
Judge, expect-
ing their final
sentence.
Rev. 6.16–17

Thus all men's pleas the Judge with ease
    doth answer and confute,   1450
Until that all, both great and small,
    are silencéd and mute.
Vain hopes are cropped, all mouths are stopped,
    sinners have naught to say,
But that 'tis just, and equal most   1455
    they should be damned for ay.

183

Now what remains, but that to pains
    and everlasting smart,[5]
Christ should condemn the sons of men,
    which is their just desert;   1460
Oh, rueful plights of sinful wights![6]
    oh wretches all forlorn:
'T had happy been they ne're had seen
    the sun, or not been born.

184

Yea, now it would be good they could   1465
    themselves annihilate,
And cease to be, themselves to free
    from such a fearful state.
Oh happy dogs, and swine, and frogs:
    yea serpent's generation,   1470
Who do not fear this doom to hear,
    and sentence of damnation!

185

Psal. 139.2–4
Eccles. 12.14

This is their state so desperate:
    their sins are fully known;
Their vanities and villanies   1475
    before the world are shown.
As they are gross and impious,
    so are their numbers more
Than motes i'th' air, or than their hair,
    or sands upon the shore.   1480

186

Divine justice offended is
    and satisfaction claimeth:
God's wrathful ire kindled like fire,
    against them fiercely flameth.
Their Judge severe doth quite cashier[7]   1485

Mat. 25.45

    and all their pleas off take,
That never a man, or dare, or can
    a further answer make.

5. Hurt.
6. Souls, persons.

7. Dismiss from fellowship.

187

Mat. 22.12
Rom. 2.5 6
Luk. 19.42

Their mouths are shut, each man is put
    to silence and to shame: 1490
Nor have they ought within their thought,
    Christ's justice for to blame.
The Judge is just, and plague[8] them must,
    nor will He mercy show
(For mercy's day is past away)   1495
    to any of this crew.

*   *   *

195

Unto the saints[9] with sad complaints
    should they themselves apply?

Psal. 58.10

They're not dejected, nor ought[1] affected   1555
    with all their misery.
Friends stand aloof, and make no proof
    what prayers or tears can do:

Rev. 21.4

Your godly friends are now more friends
    to Christ than unto you.   1560

196

Where tender love men's hearts did move
    unto a sympathy,
And bearing part of other's smart
    in their anxiety;

1 Cor. 6.2

Now such compassion is out of fashion   1565
    and wholly laid aside:
No friends so near, but saints to hear
    their sentence can abide.

197

One natural brother beholds another
    in this astonied[2] fit,   1570

*Compare
Prov. 1.26
with
1 Joh. 3.2 &
2 Cor. 5.16*

Yet sorrows not thereat a jot,
    nor pities him a whit.
The godly wife conceives no grief,
    nor can she shed a tear
For the sad state of her dear mate,   1575
    When she his doom doth hear.

198

He that was erst[3] a husband pierced
    with sense of wife's distress,
Whose tender heart did bear a part
    of all her grievances,   1580
Shall mourn no more as heretofore

8. Punish.
9. Those who experienced saving grace and in this
life felt assurance of salvation; not to be confused
with the canonized saints of the Catholic Church.

1. Anything, at all.
2. Dazed.
3. At one time.

because of her ill plight;
Although he see her now to be
    a damned forsaken wight.

199

The tender mother will own no other   1585
    of all her num'rus brood,
But such as stand at Christ's right hand
    acquitted through His blood.

Luk. 16.25 The pious father had now much rather
    his graceless son should lie   1590
In hell with devils, for all his evils
    burning eternally,

200

Than God most high should injury,
Psal. 58.10   by sparing him sustain;
And doth rejoice to hear Christ's voice   1595
    adjudging him to pain;
Who having all, both great and small,
    convinced and silencéd,
Did then proceed their doom to read,
    and thus it utteréd: 1600

201

The Judge   *"Ye sinful wights, and cursed sprights,*[4]
pronounceth   *that work iniquity,*
the sentence *Depart together from me forever*
of condemna-   *to endless misery;*
tion.
Mat. 25.41 *Your portion take in yonder lake,*   1605
    where fire and brimstone flameth:
Suffer the smart, which your desert
    as its due wages claimeth."

                    *   *   *

205

Luk. 13.28 They wring their hands, their caitiff[5]-hands
    and gnash their teeth for terror;
They cry, they roar for anguish sore,   1635
    and gnaw their tongues for horror.
But get away without delay,
    Christ pities not your cry:
Depart to hell, there may you yell,
Prov. 1.26   and roar eternally.   1640

206

It is put in That word, *Depart,* maugre their heart,[6]
execution.   drives every wicked one,

4. Spirits.   6. Despite their wishes.
5. Wretched.

With mighty power, the self-same hour,
    far from the Judge's throne.

Mat. 25.46   Away they're chased by the strong blast   1645
    of His death-threat'ning mouth:
They flee full fast, as if in haste,
    although they be full loath.[7]

207

As chaff that's dry, and dust doth fly
    before the northern wind: 1650
Right so are they chaséd away,
    and can no refuge find.
They hasten to the pit of woe,

Mat. 13.41–   guarded by angels stout;[8]
42   Who to fulfill Christ's holy will,   1655
    attend this wicked rout.[9]

208

HELL.   Whom having brought, as they are taught,
Mat. 25.30   unto the brink of hell
Mar. 9.43   (That dismal place far from Christ's face,
Isa. 30.33
Rev. 21.8   where death and darkness dwell: 1660
Where God's fierce ire kindleth the fire,
    and vengeance feeds the flame
With piles of wood, and brimstone flood,
    that none can quench the same),

209

Wicked men   With iron bands they bind their hands,   1665
and devils   and curséd feet together,
cast into it   And cast them all, both great and small,
forever.   into that lake forever.
Mat. 22.13 &   Where day and night, without respite,
25.46   they wail, and cry, and howl   1670
For tort'ring pain, which they sustain
    in body and in soul.

210

Rev. 14.10–   For day and night, in their despite,
11   their torment's smoke ascendeth.
Their pain and grief have no relief,   1675
    their anguish never endeth.
There must they lie, and never die,
    though dying every day:
There must they dying ever lie,
    and not consume away.   1680

*   *   *

7. Reluctant to do so.   9. Fleeing mob.
8. Resolute, brave.

218

Mar. 9.44
Rom. 2.15

Thus shall they lie, and wail, and cry,
  tormented, and tormenting
Their gallèd hearts with poisoned darts
  but now too late repenting.   1740
There let them dwell i'th' flames of hell;
  there leave we them to burn,
And back again unto the men
  whom Christ acquits, return.

219

*The saints
rejoice to see
judgment exe-
cuted upon
the wicked
world.
Psal. 58.10
Rev. 19.1–3*

The saints behold with courage bold,   1745
  and thankful wonderment,
To see all those that were their foes
  thus sent to punishment:
Then do they sing unto their King
  a song of endless praise: 1750
They praise His name, and do proclaim
  that just are all His ways.

220

*They ascend
with Christ
into heaven
triumphing.
Mat. 25.46
I Joh. 3.2
1 Cor. 13.12*

Thus with great joy and melody
  to heav'n they all ascend,
Him there to praise with sweetest lays,[1]   1755
  and hymns that never end,
Where with long rest they shall be blest,
  and nought shall them annoy:
Where they shall see as seen they be,
  and whom they love enjoy.   1760

221

*Their eternal
happiness and
incomparable
glory there.*

O glorious place! where face to face
  Jehovah may be seen,
By such as were sinners whilere[2]
  and no dark veil between.
Where the sun shine, and light divine,   1765
  of God's bright countenance,
Doth rest upon them every one,
  with sweetest influence.

222

O blessed state of the renate![3]
  O wondrous happiness,   1770
To which they're brought, beyond what thought
  can reach, or words express!
Rev. 21.4
Grief's water-course,[4] and sorrow's source,
  are turned to joyful streams.

1. Songs.
2. Once, earlier.
3. Reborn.
4. Channel bed.

Their old distress and heaviness   1775
are vanishéd like dreams.

223
For God above in arms of love
    doth dearly them embrace,
Psal. 16.11   And fills their sprights with such delights,
    and pleasures in His grace;   1780
As shall not fail, nor yet grow stale
    through frequency of use:
Nor do they fear God's favor there,
    to forfeit by abuse.

224
Heb. 12.23   For there the saints are perfect saints,   1785
    and holy ones indeed,
From all the sin that dwelt within
    their mortal bodies freed:
Made kings and priests to God through Christ's
Rev. 1.6 &   dear love's transcendency,   1790
22.5   There to remain, and there to reign
    with Him eternally.

1662

MARY ROWLANDSON
c. 1636–1711

On June 20, 1675, Metacomet, who was called Philip by the colonists, led the first of a series of attacks on colonial settlements that lasted for more than a year. Before they were over, more than twelve hundred houses had been burned, about six hundred English colonials were dead, and three thousand American Indians killed. These attacks have become known as "King Philip's War." It was the direct result of the execution in Plymouth, Massachusetts, of three of Philip's Wampanoag tribesmen, but the indirect causes were many; not the least was the fact that the native Americans were starving and desperate to retain their lands. In a sense, the war may be seen as a last-ditch effort by the Wampanoags and their allies against further expansion by the colonists. By the time the war was over, in August of 1676, with Philip slain and his wife and children sold into slavery in the West Indies, the independent power of the New England American Indians had ended.

    Probably the most famous victim of these attacks is the author of *A Narrative of the Captivity and Restoration of Mrs. Mary Rowlandson,* the wife of the minister of the town of Lancaster. With the exception of the eleven weeks she spent as a captive among the Wampanoags, however, almost everything about Mrs. Rowlandson's life remains conjectural. She was probably born in England and brought to this country at an early age. Her father, John White, was a wealthy landholder in the Massachusetts Bay Colony who settled in Lancaster. About 1656 she married Joseph Rowlandson and for the next twenty years led a busy life as mother and minister's wife. The attack on Lancaster occurred on February 20, 1676, and she was not released until the second of May, having been ransomed for twenty pounds. The following year she went with her husband to Wethersfield, Connecticut; Mr. Rowlandson died there in 1678. The town voted to pay her an annuity "so long as she remains a widow among us." For lack of any further information, most biographical entries conclude here. Recently, David Greene has verified that Mary Rowlandson married Captain Samuel Talcott in Wethersfield on August 6, 1679, and that she died in that Connecticut Valley town on January 5, 1711, thirty-five years after her famous ordeal.

Shortly after her return to Lancaster, Mrs. Rowlandson began to make a record of her life in captivity. Her *Narrative* (published in 1682) is the only evidence we have of her skill as a writer. The account of her captivity became one of the most popular prose works of the seventeenth century, both in this country and in England. It combined high adventure, heroism, and exemplary piety and is the first and, in its narrative skill and delineation of character, the best of what have become popularly known as "Indian captivities." As transformed into fictional form by writers like James Fenimore Cooper (in *The Last of the Mohicans*) and William Faulkner (in *Sanctuary*), it is a genre that has proven to be an integral part of our American literary consciousness.

A Narrative of the Captivity and Restoration of Mrs. Mary Rowlandson[1]

On the tenth of February 1675,[2] came the Indians with great numbers upon Lancaster:[3] their first coming was about sunrising; hearing the noise of some guns, we looked out; several houses were burning, and the smoke ascending to heaven. There were five persons taken in one house; the father, and the mother and a sucking child, they knocked on the head; the other two they took and carried away alive. There were two others, who being out of their garrison[4] upon some occasion were set upon; one was knocked on the head, the other escaped; another there was who running along was shot and wounded, and fell down; he begged of them his life, promising them money (as they told me) but they would not hearken to him but knocked him in head, and stripped him naked, and split open his bowels.[5] Another, seeing many of the Indians about his barn, ventured and went out, but was quickly shot down. There were three others belonging to the same garrison who were killed; the Indians getting up upon the roof of the barn, had advantage to shoot down upon them over their fortification. Thus these murderous wretches went on, burning, and destroying before them.

1. The text used is *Original Narratives of Early American History, Narratives of Indian Wars 1675–1699*, vol. 14, edited by C. H. Lincoln (1952). All copies of the first edition have been lost. Like most modern editors, Lincoln has chosen to reprint the second "addition," printed in Cambridge, Massachusetts, by Samuel Green in 1682. The full title is *The sovereignty and goodness of GOD, together with the faithfulness of his promises displayed; being a narrative of the captivity and restoration of Mrs. Mary Rowlandson, commended by her, to all that desires to know the Lord's doings to, and dealings with her. Especially to her dear children and relations. The second Addition Corrected and amended. Written by her own hand for her private use, and* now made public at the earnest desire of some friends, and for the benefit of the afflicted. *Deut. 32.39. See now that I, even I am he, and there is no god with me; I kill and I make alive, I wound and I heal, neither is there any can deliver out of my hand.*

2. A Thursday. Using the present Gregorian calendar, adopted in 1752, February 20, 1676.

3. Lancaster, Massachusetts, was a frontier town of approximately fifty families, about thirty miles west of Boston.

4. I.e., houses in the town where people gathered for defense.

5. Belly.

At length they came and beset our own house, and quickly it was the dolefulest day that ever mine eyes saw. The house stood upon the edge of a hill; some of the Indians got behind the hill, others into the barn, and others behind anything that could shelter them; from all which places they shot against the house, so that the bullets seemed to fly like hail; and quickly they wounded one man among us, then another, and then a third. About two hours (according to my observation, in that amazing time) they had been about the house before they prevailed to fire it (which they did with flax and hemp, which they brought out of the barn, and there being no defense about the house, only two flankers[6] at two opposite corners and one of them not finished); they fired it once and one ventured out and quenched it, but they quickly fired it again, and that took. Now is the dreadful hour come, that I have often heard of (in time of war, as it was the case of others), but now mine eyes see it. Some in our house were fighting for their lives, others wallowing in their blood, the house on fire over our heads, and the bloody heathen ready to knock us on the head, if we stirred out. Now might we hear mothers and children crying out for themselves, and one another, "Lord, what shall we do?" Then I took my children (and one of my sisters', hers) to go forth and leave the house: but as soon as we came to the door and appeared, the Indians shot so thick that the bullets rattled against the house, as if one had taken an handful of stones and threw them, so that we were fain to give back. We had six stout dogs belonging to our garrison, but none of them would stir, though another time, if any Indian had come to the door, they were ready to fly upon him and tear him down. The Lord hereby would make us the more acknowledge His hand, and to see that our help is always in Him. But out we must go, the fire increasing, and coming along behind us, roaring, and the Indians gaping before us with their guns, spears, and hatchets to devour us. No sooner were we out of the house, but my brother-in-law (being before wounded, in defending the house, in or near the throat) fell down dead, whereat the Indians scornfully shouted, and hallowed, and were presently upon him, stripping off his clothes, the bullets flying thick, one went through my side, and the same (as would seem) through the bowels and hand of my dear child in my arms. One of my elder sisters' children, named William, had then his leg broken, which the Indians perceiving, they knocked him on [his] head. Thus were we butchered by those merciless heathen, standing amazed, with the blood running down to our heels. My eldest sister being yet in the house, and seeing those woeful sights, the infidels hauling mothers one way, and children another, and some wallowing in their blood: and her elder son telling her that her son William was dead, and myself was wounded, she said, "And Lord, let me die with them," which was no sooner said, but she was struck with a bullet, and fell down dead over the threshold. I hope she is reaping the fruit of her good labors, being faithful to the service of God in her place. In her younger years she lay under much trouble upon spiritual accounts, till it pleased God to make that precious scripture take hold of her heart, "And he said unto me, my Grace is sufficient for thee" (2 Corinthians 12.9). More than twenty years after, I have heard her tell how sweet and comfortable that place was to her. But to return: the Indians laid hold of us, pulling me one way, and the children another, and

6. Projecting fortifications.

said, "Come go along with us"; I told them they would kill me: they answered, if I were willing to go along with them, they would not hurt me.

Oh the doleful sight that now was to behold at this house! "Come, behold the works of the Lord, what desolations he has made in the earth."[7] Of thirty-seven persons who were in this one house, none escaped either present death, or a bitter captivity, save only one, who might say as he, "And I only am escaped alone to tell the News" (Job 1.15). There were twelve killed, some shot, some stabbed with their spears, some knocked down with their hatchets. When we are in prosperity, Oh the little that we think of such dreadful sights, and to see our dear friends, and relations lie bleeding out their heart-blood upon the ground. There was one who was chopped into the head with a hatchet, and stripped naked, and yet was crawling up and down. It is a solemn sight to see so many Christians lying in their blood, some here, and some there, like a company of sheep torn by wolves, all of them stripped naked by a company of hell-hounds, roaring, singing, ranting, and insulting, as if they would have torn our very hearts out; yet the Lord by His almighty power preserved a number of us from death, for there were twenty-four of us taken alive and carried captive.

I had often before this said that if the Indians should come, I should choose rather to be killed by them than taken alive, but when it came to the trial my mind changed; their glittering weapons so daunted my spirit, that I chose rather to go along with those (as I may say) ravenous beasts, than that moment to end my days; and that I may the better declare what happened to me during that grievous captivity, I shall particularly speak of the several removes[8] we had up and down the wilderness.

The First Remove

Now away we must go with those barbarous creatures, with our bodies wounded and bleeding, and our hearts no less than our bodies. About a mile we went that night, up upon a hill within sight of the town, where they intended to lodge. There was hard by a vacant house (deserted by the English before, for fear of the Indians). I asked them whether I might not lodge in the house that night, to which they answered, "What, will you love English men still?" This was the dolefulest night that ever my eyes saw. Oh the roaring, and singing and dancing, and yelling of those black creatures in the night, which made the place a lively resemblance of hell. And as miserable was the waste that was there made of horses, cattle, sheep, swine, calves, lambs, roasting pigs, and fowl (which they had plundered in the town), some roasting, some lying and burning, and some boiling to feed our merciless enemies; who were joyful enough, though we were disconsolate. To add to the dolefulness of the former day, and the dismalness of the present night, my thoughts ran upon my losses and sad bereaved condition. All was gone, my husband gone (at least separated from me, he being in the Bay;[9] and to add to my grief, the Indians told me they would kill him as he came home-ward), my children gone, my relations and friends gone, our house and home and all our comforts—within door and without—all was gone (except my

---

7. Psalm 46.8.
8. I.e., departures; movings from place to place.

9. I.e., Boston, or Massachusetts Bay.

life), and I knew not but the next moment that might go too. There remained nothing to me but one poor wounded babe, and it seemed at present worse than death that it was in such a pitiful condition, bespeaking compassion, and I had no refreshing for it, nor suitable things to revive it. Little do many think what is the savageness and brutishness of this barbarous enemy, Ay, even those that seem to profess more than others among them, when the English have fallen into their hands.

Those seven that were killed at Lancaster the summer before upon a Sabbath day, and the one that was afterward killed upon a weekday, were slain and mangled in a barbarous manner, by one-eyed John, and Marlborough's Praying Indians, which Capt. Mosely brought to Boston, as the Indians told me.[1]

The Second Remove[2]

But now, the next morning, I must turn my back upon the town, and travel with them into the vast and desolate wilderness, I knew not whither. It is not my tongue, or pen, can express the sorrows of my heart, and bitterness of my spirit that I had at this departure: but God was with me in a wonderful manner, carrying me along, and bearing up my spirit, that it did not quite fail. One of the Indians carried my poor wounded babe upon a horse; it went moaning all along, "I shall die, I shall die." I went on foot after it, with sorrow that cannot be expressed. At length I took it off the horse, and carried it in my arms till my strength failed, and I fell down with it. Then they set me upon a horse with my wounded child in my lap, and there being no furniture upon the horse's back, as we were going down a steep hill we both fell over the horse's head, at which they, like inhumane creatures, laughed, and rejoiced to see it, though I thought we should there have ended our days, as overcome with so many difficulties. But the Lord renewed my strength still, and carried me along, that I might see more of His power; yea, so much that I could never have thought of, had I not experienced it.

After this it quickly began to snow, and when night came on, they stopped, and now down I must sit in the snow, by a little fire, and a few boughs behind me, with my sick child in my lap; and calling much for water, being now (through the wound) fallen into a violent fever. My own wound also growing so stiff that I could scarce sit down or rise up; yet so it must be, that I must sit all this cold winter night upon the cold snowy ground, with my sick child in my arms, looking that every hour would be the last of its life; and having no Christian friend near me, either to comfort or help me. Oh, I may see the wonderful power of God, that my Spirit did not utterly sink under my affliction: still the Lord upheld me with His gracious and merciful spirit, and we were both alive to see the light of the next morning.

The Third Remove[3]

The morning being come, they prepared to go on their way. One of the Indians got up upon a horse, and they set me up behind him, with my poor

1. On August 30, 1675, Captain Samuel Mosely, encouraged by a number of people who were skeptical of converted American Indians, brought to Boston by force fifteen Christianized American Indians who lived on their own lands in Marlborough, Massachusetts, and accused them of an attack on the town of Lancaster on August 22.
2. To Princeton, Massachusetts, near Mount Wachusett.
3. February 12–27; they stopped at a Native American village on the Ware River near New Braintree.

sick babe in my lap. A very wearisome and tedious day I had of it; what with my own wound, and my child's being so exceeding sick, and in a lamentable condition with her wound. It may be easily judged what a poor feeble condition we were in, there being not the least crumb of refreshing that came within either of our mouths from Wednesday night to Saturday night, except only a little cold water. This day in the afternoon, about an hour by sun, we came to the place where they intended, *viz.* an Indian town, called Wenimesset, northward of Quabaug. When we were come, Oh the number of pagans (now merciless enemies) that there came about me, that I may say as David, "I had fainted, unless I had believed, etc" (Psalm 27.13). The next day was the Sabbath. I then remembered how careless I had been of God's holy time; how many Sabbaths I had lost and misspent, and how evilly I had walked in God's sight; which lay so close unto my spirit, that it was easy for me to see how righteous it was with God to cut off the thread of my life and cast me out of His presence forever. Yet the Lord still showed mercy to me, and upheld me; and as He wounded me with one hand, so he healed me with the other. This day there came to me one Robert Pepper (a man belonging to Roxbury) who was taken in Captain Beers's fight, and had been now a considerable time with the Indians; and up with them almost as far as Albany, to see King Philip, as he told me, and was now very lately come into these parts.[4] Hearing, I say, that I was in this Indian town, he obtained leave to come and see me. He told me he himself was wounded in the leg at Captain Beer's fight; and was not able some time to go, but as they carried him, and as he took oaken leaves and laid to his wound, and through the blessing of God he was able to travel again. Then I took oaken leaves and laid to my side, and with the blessing of God it cured me also; yet before the cure was wrought, I may say, as it is in Psalm 38.5–6 "My wounds stink and are corrupt, I am troubled, I am bowed down greatly, I go mourning all the day long." I sat much alone with a poor wounded child in my lap, which moaned night and day, having nothing to revive the body, or cheer the spirits of her, but instead of that, sometimes one Indian would come and tell me one hour that "your master will knock your child in the head," and then a second, and then a third, "your master will quickly knock your child in the head."

This was the comfort I had from them, miserable comforters are ye all, as he[5] said. Thus nine days I sat upon my knees, with my babe in my lap, till my flesh was raw again; my child being even ready to depart this sorrowful world, they bade me carry it out to another wigwam (I suppose because they would not be troubled with such spectacles) whither I went with a very heavy heart, and down I sat with the picture of death in my lap. About two hours in the night, my sweet babe like a lamb departed this life on Feb. 18, 1675. It being about six years, and five months old. It was nine days from the first wounding, in this miserable condition, without any refreshing of one nature or other, except a little cold water. I cannot but take notice how at another time I could not bear to be in the room where any dead person was, but now the case is changed; I must and could lie down by my dead babe, side by side all the night after. I have thought since of the wonderful goodness of God to me in preserving me in the use of my reason and senses in that

4. Captain Beers had attempted to save the garrison of Northfield, Massachusetts, on September 4, 1675.

5. I.e., as Job said. "I have heard many such things: miserable comforters are ye all" (Job 16.2).

distressed time, that I did not use wicked and violent means to end my own miserable life. In the morning, when they understood that my child was dead they sent for me home to my master's wigwam (by my master in this writing, must be understood Quinnapin, who was a Sagamore,[6] and married King Philip's wife's sister; not that he first took me, but I was sold to him by another Narragansett Indian, who took me when first I came out of the garrison). I went to take up my dead child in my arms to carry it with me, but they bid me let it alone; there was no resisting, but go I must and leave it. When I had been at my master's wigwam, I took the first opportunity I could get to go look after my dead child. When I came I asked them what they had done with it; then they told me it was upon the hill. Then they went and showed me where it was, where I saw the ground was newly digged, and there they told me they had buried it. There I left that child in the wilderness, and must commit it, and myself also in this wilderness condition, to Him who is above all. God having taken away this dear child, I went to see my daughter Mary, who was at this same Indian town, at a wigwam not very far off, though we had little liberty or opportunity to see one another. She was about ten years old, and taken from the door at first by a Praying Ind. and afterward sold for a gun. When I came in sight, she would fall aweeping; at which they were provoked, and would not let me come near her, but bade me be gone; which was a heart-cutting word to me. I had one child dead, another in the wilderness, I knew not where, the third they would not let me come near to: "Me (as he said) have ye bereaved of my Children, Joseph is not, and Simeon is not, and ye will take Benjamin also, all these things are against me."[7] I could not sit still in this condition, but kept walking from one place to another. And as I was going along, my heart was even overwhelmed with the thoughts of my condition, and that I should have children, and a nation which I knew not, ruled over them. Whereupon I earnestly entreated the Lord, that He would consider my low estate, and show me a token for good, and if it were His blessed will, some sign and hope of some relief. And indeed quickly the Lord answered, in some measure, my poor prayers; for as I was going up and down mourning and lamenting my condition, my son came to me, and asked me how I did. I had not seen him before, since the destruction of the town, and I knew not where he was, till I was informed by himself, that he was amongst a smaller parcel of Indians, whose place was about six miles off. With tears in his eyes, he asked me whether his sister Sarah was dead; and told me he had seen his sister Mary; and prayed me, that I would not be troubled in reference to himself. The occasion of his coming to see me at this time, was this: there was, as I said, about six miles from us, a small plantation of Indians, where it seems he had been during his captivity; and at this time, there were some forces of the Ind. gathered out of our company, and some also from them (among whom was my son's master) to go to assault and burn Medfield.[8] In this time of the absence of his master, his dame brought him to see me. I took this to be some gracious answer to my earnest and unfeigned desire. The next day, viz. to this, the Indians returned from Medfield, all the company, for those that belonged to the other small company, came through the town that now we were at. But before they came to us, Oh! the outrageous roaring and hooping that there

6. A subordinate chief among the Algonquin Indians. Quinnapin was the husband of Weetamoo, and Rowlandson became her servant.

7. Jacob's lamentation in Genesis 42.36.
8. The attack on Medfield, Massachusetts, occurred on February 21.

was. They began their din about a mile before they came to us. By their noise and hooping they signified how many they had destroyed (which was at that time twenty-three). Those that were with us at home were gathered together as soon as they heard the hooping, and every time that the other went over their number, these at home gave a shout, that the very earth rung again. And thus they continued till those that had been upon the expedition were come up to the Sagamore's wigwam; and then, Oh, the hideous insulting and triumphing that there was over some Englishmen's scalps that they had taken (as their manner is) and brought with them. I cannot but take notice of the wonderful mercy of God to me in those afflictions, in sending me a Bible. One of the Indians that came from Medfield fight, had brought some plunder, came to me, and asked me, if I would have a Bible, he had got one in his basket. I was glad of it, and asked him, whether he thought the Indians would let me read? He answered, yes. So I took the Bible, and in that melancholy time, it came into my mind to read first the 28th chapter of Deuteronomy,[9] which I did, and when I had read it, my dark heart wrought on this manner: that there was no mercy for me, that the blessings were gone, and the curses come in their room, and that I had lost my opportunity. But the Lord helped me still to go on reading till I came to Chap. 30, the seven first verses, where I found, there was mercy promised again, if we would return to Him by repentance;[1] and though we were scattered from one end of the earth to the other, yet the Lord would gather us together, and turn all those curses upon our enemies. I do not desire to live to forget this Scripture, and what comfort it was to me.

Now the Ind. began to talk of removing from this place, some one way, and some another. There were now besides myself nine English captives in this place (all of them children, except one woman). I got an opportunity to go and take my leave of them. They being to go one way, and I another, I asked them whether they were earnest with God for deliverance. They told me they did as they were able, and it was some comfort to me, that the Lord stirred up children to look to Him. The woman, *viz.* goodwife[2] Joslin, told me she should never see me again, and that she could find in her heart to run away. I wished her not to run away by any means, for we were near thirty miles from any English town, and she very big with child, and had but one week to reckon, and another child in her arms, two years old, and bad rivers there were to go over, and we were feeble, with our poor and coarse entertainment. I had my Bible with me, I pulled it out, and asked her whether she would read. We opened the Bible and lighted on Psalm 27, in which Psalm we especially took notice of that, *ver. ult.*, "Wait on the Lord, Be of good courage, and he shall strengthen thine Heart, wait I say on the Lord."[3]

The Fourth Remove[4]

And now I must part with that little company I had. Here I parted from my daughter Mary (whom I never saw again till I saw her in Dorchester,

9. This chapter of Deuteronomy is concerned with blessings for obedience to God and curses for disobedience.
1. "That then the Lord thy God will turn thy captivity, and have compassion upon thee, and will return and gather thee from all the nations" (Deuteronomy 30.3).

2. I.e., the mistress of a house.
3. Verse 14. *"Ver. ult.":* last verse (Latin abbreviation).
4. February 28 to March 3. The camp was between Ware River and Miller's River in present-day Petersham, Massachusetts.

returned from captivity), and from four little cousins and neighbors, some of which I never saw afterward: the Lord only knows the end of them. Amongst them also was that poor woman before mentioned, who came to a sad end, as some of the company told me in my travel: she having much grief upon her spirit about her miserable condition, being so near her time, she would be often asking the Indians to let her go home; they not being willing to that, and yet vexed with her importunity, gathered a great company together about her and stripped her naked, and set her in the midst of them, and when they had sung and danced about her (in their hellish manner) as long as they pleased they knocked her on head, and the child in her arms with her. When they had done that they made a fire and put them both into it, and told the other children that were with them that if they attempted to go home, they would serve them in like manner. The children said she did not shed one tear, but prayed all the while. But to return to my own journey, we traveled about half a day or little more, and came to a desolate place in the wilderness, where there were no wigwams or inhabitants before; we came about the middle of the afternoon to this place, cold and wet, and snowy, and hungry, and weary, and no refreshing for man but the cold ground to sit on, and our poor Indian cheer.

Heart-aching thoughts here I had about my poor children, who were scattered up and down among the wild beasts of the forest. My head was light and dizzy (either through hunger or hard lodging, or trouble or all together), my knees feeble, my body raw by sitting double night and day, that I cannot express to man the affliction that lay upon my spirit, but the Lord helped me at that time to express it to Himself. I opened my Bible to read, and the Lord brought that precious Scripture to me. "Thus saith the Lord, refrain thy voice from weeping, and thine eyes from tears, for thy work shall be rewarded, and they shall come again from the land of the enemy" (Jeremiah 31.16). This was a sweet cordial to me when I was ready to faint; many and many a time have I sat down and wept sweetly over this Scripture. At this place we continued about four days.

The Fifth Remove[5]

The occasion (as I thought) of their moving at this time was the English army, it being near and following them. For they went as if they had gone for their lives, for some considerable way, and then they made a stop, and chose some of their stoutest men, and sent them back to hold the English army in play whilst the rest escaped. And then, like Jehu,[6] they marched on furiously, with their old and with their young: some carried their old decrepit mothers, some carried one, and some another. Four of them carried a great Indian upon a bier; but going through a thick wood with him, they were hindered, and could make no haste, whereupon they took him upon their backs, and carried him, one at a time, till they came to Banquaug river. Upon a Friday, a little after noon, we came to this river. When all the company was come up, and were gathered together, I thought to count the number

---

5. March 3 to March 5. They crossed the Banquaug or present-day Miller's River in Orange, Massachusetts. The "English army" Rowlandson refers to consisted of Massachusetts and Connect-icut forces under the command of Captain Thomas Savage.
6. King of Israel (c. 843–816 B.C.E.) who killed kings Jehoram and Ahaziah (cf. 2 Kings 9.20).

of them, but they were so many, and being somewhat in motion, it was beyond my skill. In this travel, because of my wound, I was somewhat favored in my load; I carried only my knitting work and two quarts of parched meal. Being very faint I asked my mistress to give me one spoonful of the meal, but she would not give me a taste. They quickly fell to cutting dry trees, to make rafts to carry them over the river: and soon my turn came to go over. By the advantage of some brush which they had laid upon the raft to sit upon, I did not wet my foot (which many of themselves at the other end were mid-leg deep) which cannot but be acknowledged as a favor of God to my weakened body, it being a very cold time. I was not before acquainted with such kind of doings or dangers. "When thou passeth through the waters I will be with thee, and through the rivers they shall not overflow thee" (Isaiah 43.2). A certain number of us got over the river that night, but it was the night after the Sabbath before all the company was got over. On the Saturday they boiled an old horse's leg which they had got, and so we drank of the broth, as soon as they thought it was ready, and when it was almost all gone, they filled it up again.

The first week of my being among them I hardly ate any thing; the second week I found my stomach grow very faint for want of something; and yet it was very hard to get down their filthy trash; but the third week, though I could think how formerly my stomach would turn against this or that, and I could starve and die before I could eat such things, yet they were sweet and savory to my taste. I was at this time knitting a pair of white cotton stockings for my mistress; and had not yet wrought upon a Sabbath day. When the Sabbath came they bade me go to work. I told them it was the Sabbath day, and desired them to let me rest, and told them I would do as much more tomorrow; to which they answered me they would break my face. And here I cannot but take notice of the strange providence of God in preserving the heathen. They were many hundreds, old and young, some sick, and some lame; many had papooses at their backs. The greatest number at this time with us were squaws, and they traveled with all they had, bag and baggage, and yet they got over this river aforesaid; and on Monday they set their wigwams on fire, and away they went. On that very day came the English army after them to this river, and saw the smoke of their wigwams, and yet this river put a stop to them. God did not give them courage or activity to go over after us. We were not ready for so great a mercy as victory and deliverance. If we had been God would have found out a way for the English to have passed this river, as well as for the Indians with their squaws and children, and all their luggage. "Oh that my people had hearkened to me, and Israel had walked in my ways, I should soon have subdued their enemies, and turned my hand against their adversaries" (Psalm 81.13–14).

The Sixth Remove[7]

On Monday (as I said) they set their wigwams on fire and went away. It was a cold morning, and before us there was a great brook with ice on it; some waded through it, up to the knees and higher, but others went till they came to a beaver dam, and I amongst them, where through the good provi-

7. Monday, March 6, ending near Northfield, Massachusetts.

dence of God, I did not wet my foot. I went along that day mourning and lamenting, leaving farther my own country, and traveling into a vast and howling wilderness, and I understood something of Lot's wife's temptation, when she looked back.[8] We came that day to a great swamp, by the side of which we took up our lodging that night. When I came to the brow of the hill, that looked toward the swamp, I thought we had been come to a great Indian town (though there were none but our own company). The Indians were as thick as the trees: it seemed as if there had been a thousand hatchets going at once. If one looked before one there was nothing but Indians, and behind one, nothing but Indians, and so on either hand, I myself in the midst, and no Christian soul near me, and yet how hath the Lord preserved me in safety? Oh the experience that I have had of the goodness of God, to me and mine!

The Seventh Remove[9]

After a restless and hungry night there, we had a wearisome time of it the next day. The swamp by which we lay was, as it were, a deep dungeon, and an exceeding high and steep hill before it. Before I got to the top of the hill, I thought my heart and legs, and all would have broken, and failed me. What, through faintness and soreness of body, it was a grievous day of travel to me. As we went along, I saw a place where English cattle had been. That was comfort to me, such as it was. Quickly after that we came to an English path, which so took with me, that I thought I could have freely lyen down and died. That day, a little after noon, we came to Squakeag, where the Indians quickly spread themselves over the deserted English fields, gleaning what they could find. Some picked up ears of wheat that were crickled down; some found ears of Indian corn; some found ground nuts, and others sheaves of wheat that were frozen together in the shock, and went to threshing of them out. Myself got two ears of Indian corn, and whilst I did but turn my back, one of them was stolen from me, which much troubled me. There came an Indian to them at that time with a basket of horse liver. I asked him to give me a piece. "What," says he, "can you eat horse liver?" I told him, I would try, if he would give a piece, which he did, and I laid it on the coals to roast. But before it was half ready they got half of it away from me, so that I was fain to take the rest and eat it as it was, with the blood about my mouth, and yet a savory bit it was to me: "For to the hungry soul every bitter thing is sweet."[1] A solemn sight methought it was, to see fields of wheat and Indian corn forsaken and spoiled and the remainders of them to be food for our merciless enemies. That night we had a mess of wheat for our supper.

The Eighth Remove[2]

On the morrow morning we must go over the river, *i.e.* Connecticut, to meet with King Philip. Two canoes full they had carried over; the next turn I myself was to go. But as my foot was upon the canoe to step in there was

---

8. Lot's wife looked back upon the wicked city of Sodom and was turned into a pillar of salt (cf. Genesis 19.24).
9. To Squakeag, near Beer's Plain, in Northfield,

Massachusetts.
1. Proverbs 27.7.
2. To Coasset in South Vernon, Vermont.

a sudden outcry among them, and I must step back, and instead of going over the river, I must go four or five miles up the river farther northward. Some of the Indians ran one way, and some another. The cause of this rout was, as I thought, their espying some English scouts, who were thereabout. In this travel up the river about noon the company made a stop, and sat down; some to eat, and others to rest them. As I sat amongst them, musing of things past, my son Joseph unexpectedly came to me. We asked of each other's welfare, bemoaning our doleful condition, and the change that had come upon us. We had husband and father, and children, and sisters, and friends, and relations, and house, and home, and many comforts of this life: but now we may say, as Job, "Naked came I out of my mother's womb, and naked shall I return: the Lord gave, the Lord hath taken away, blessed be the name of the Lord."[3] I asked him whether he would read. He told me he earnestly desired it, I gave him my Bible, and he lighted upon that comfortable Scripture "I shall not die but live, and declare the works of the Lord: the Lord hath chastened me sore, yet he hath not given me over to death" (Psalm 118.17–18). "Look here, mother," says he, "did you read this?" And here I may take occasion to mention one principal ground of my setting forth these lines: even as the psalmist says, to declare the works of the Lord, and His wonderful power in carrying us along, preserving us in the wilderness, while under the enemy's hand, and returning of us in safety again. And His goodness in bringing to my hand so many comfortable and suitable scriptures in my distress.[4] But to return, we traveled on till night; and in the morning, we must go over the river to Philip's crew. When I was in the canoe I could not but be amazed at the numerous crew of pagans that were on the bank on the other side. When I came ashore, they gathered all about me, I sitting alone in the midst. I observed they asked one another questions, and laughed, and rejoiced over their gains and victories. Then my heart began to fail: and I fell aweeping, which was the first time to my remembrance, that I wept before them. Although I had met with so much affliction, and my heart was many times ready to break, yet could I not shed one tear in their sight; but rather had been all this while in a maze, and like one astonished. But now I may say as Psalm 137.1, "By the Rivers of Babylon, there we sate down: yea, we wept when we remembered Zion." There one of them asked me why I wept. I could hardly tell what to say: Yet I answered, they would kill me. "No," said he, "none will hurt you." Then came one of them and gave me two spoonfuls of meal to comfort me, and another gave me half a pint of peas; which was more worth than many bushels at another time. Then I went to see King Philip. He bade me come in and sit down, and asked me whether I would smoke it (a usual compliment nowadays amongst saints and sinners)[5] but this no way suited me. For though I had formerly used tobacco, yet I had left it ever since I was first taken. It seems to be a bait the devil lays to make men lose their precious time. I remember with shame how formerly, when I had taken two or three pipes, I was presently ready for another, such a bewitching thing it is. But I thank God, He has now given me power over it; surely there are many who may be better employed than to lie sucking a stinking tobacco-pipe.

3. Job 1.21.
4. Rowlandson probably has in mind Psalm 145.4: "One generation shall praise thy works to another, and shall declare thy mighty acts."
5. I.e., among believers ("saints") as well as the unregenerate.

Now the Indians gather their forces to go against Northampton. Over night one went about yelling and hooting to give notice of the design. Whereupon they fell to boiling of ground nuts, and parching of corn (as many as had it) for their provision; and in the morning away they went. During my abode in this place, Philip spake to me to make a shirt for his boy, which I did, for which he gave me a shilling. I offered the money to my master, but he bade me keep it; and with it I bought a piece of horse flesh. Afterwards he asked me to make a cap for his boy, for which he invited me to dinner. I went, and he gave me a pancake, about as big as two fingers. It was made of parched wheat, beaten, and fried in bear's grease, but I thought I never tasted pleasanter meat in my life. There was a squaw who spake to me to make a shirt for her *sannup*,[6] for which she gave me a piece of bear. Another asked me to knit a pair of stockings, for which she gave me a quart of peas. I boiled my peas and bear together, and invited my master and mistress to dinner; but the proud gossip,[7] because I served them both in one dish, would eat nothing, except one bit that he gave her upon the point of his knife. Hearing that my son was come to this place, I went to see him, and found him lying flat upon the ground. I asked him how he could sleep so? He answered me that he was not asleep, but at prayer; and lay so, that they might not observe what he was doing. I pray God he may remember these things now he is returned in safety. At this place (the sun now getting higher) what with the beams and heat of the sun, and the smoke of the wigwams, I thought I should have been blind. I could scarce discern one wigwam from another. There was here one Mary Thurston of Medfield, who seeing how it was with me, lent me a hat to wear; but as soon as I was gone, the squaw (who owned that Mary Thurston) came running after me, and got it away again. Here was the squaw that gave me one spoonful of meal. I put it in my pocket to keep it safe. Yet notwithstanding, somebody stole it, but put five Indian corns in the room of it;[8] which corns were the greatest provisions I had in my travel for one day.

The Indians returning from Northampton, brought with them some horses, and sheep, and other things which they had taken; I desired them that they would carry me to Albany upon one of those horses, and sell me for powder: for so they had sometimes discoursed. I was utterly hopeless of getting home on foot, the way that I came. I could hardly bear to think of the many weary steps I had taken, to come to this place.

The Ninth Remove[9]

But instead of going either to Albany or homeward, we must go five miles up the river, and then go over it. Here we abode a while. Here lived a sorry Indian, who spoke to me to make him a shirt. When I had done it, he would pay me nothing. But he living by the riverside, where I often went to fetch water, I would often be putting of him in mind, and calling for my pay: At last he told me if I would make another shirt, for a papoose not yet born, he would give me a knife, which he did when I had done it. I carried the knife in, and my master asked me to give it him, and I was not a little glad that I

---

6. Husband.
7. Relation, i.e., wife.

8. I.e., five kernels of corn in place of it.
9. To the Ashuelot valley in New Hampshire.

had anything that they would accept of, and be pleased with. When we were at this place, my master's maid came home; she had been gone three weeks into the Narragansett country to fetch corn, where they had stored up some in the ground. She brought home about a peck and half of corn. This was about the time that their great captain, Naananto, was killed in the Narragansett country. My son being now about a mile from me, I asked liberty to go and see him; they bade me go, and away I went; but quickly lost myself, traveling over hills and through swamps, and could not find the way to him. And I cannot but admire at the wonderful power and goodness of God to me, in that, though I was gone from home, and met with all sorts of Indians, and those I had no knowledge of, and there being no Christian soul near me; yet not one of them offered the least imaginable miscarriage to me. I turned homeward again, and met with my master. He showed me the way to my son. When I came to him I found him not well: and withall he had a boil on his side, which much troubled him. We bemoaned one another a while, as the Lord helped us, and then I returned again. When I was returned, I found myself as unsatisfied as I was before. I went up and down mourning and lamenting; and my spirit was ready to sink with the thoughts of my poor children. My son was ill, and I could but not think of his mournful looks, and no Christian friend was near him, to do any office of love for him, either for soul or body. And my poor girl, I knew not where she was, nor whether she was sick, or well, or alive, or dead. I repaired under these thoughts to my Bible (my great comfort in that time) and that Scripture came to my hand, "Cast thy burden upon the Lord, and He shall sustain thee" (Psalm 55.22).

But I was fain to go and look after something to satisfy my hunger, and going among the wigwams, I went into one and there found a squaw who showed herself very kind to me, and gave me a piece of bear. I put it into my pocket, and came home, but could not find an opportunity to broil it, for fear they would get it from me, and there it lay all that day and night in my stinking pocket. In the morning I went to the same squaw, who had a kettle of ground nuts boiling. I asked her to let me boil my piece of bear in her kettle, which she did, and gave me some ground nuts to eat with it: and I cannot but think how pleasant it was to me. I have sometime seen bear baked very handsomely among the English, and some like it, but the thought that it was bear made me tremble. But now that was savory to me that one would think was enough to turn the stomach of a brute creature.

One bitter cold day I could find no room to sit down before the fire. I went out, and could not tell what to do, but I went in to another wigwam, where they were also sitting round the fire, but the squaw laid a skin for me, and bid me sit down, and gave me some ground nuts, and bade me come again; and told me they would buy me, if they were able, and yet these were strangers to me that I never saw before.

The Tenth Remove[1]

That day a small part of the company removed about three-quarters of a mile, intending further the next day. When they came to the place where

1. To another location in the Ashuelot valley.

they intended to lodge, and had pitched their wigwams, being hungry, I went again back to the place we were before at, to get something to eat, being encouraged by the squaw's kindness, who bade me come again. When I was there, there came an Indian to look after me, who when he had found me, kicked me all along. I went home and found venison roasting that night, but they would not give me one bit of it. Sometimes I met with favor, and sometimes with nothing but frowns.

The Eleventh Remove[2]

The next day in the morning they took their travel, intending a day's journey up the river. I took my load at my back, and quickly we came to wade over the river; and passed over tiresome and wearisome hills. One hill was so steep that I was fain to creep up upon my knees, and to hold by the twigs and bushes to keep myself from falling backward. My head also was so light that I usually reeled as I went; but I hope all these wearisome steps that I have taken, are but a forewarning to me of the heavenly rest: "I know, O Lord, that thy judgments are right, and that thou in faithfulness hast afflicted me" (Psalm 119.75).

The Twelfth Remove[3]

It was upon a Sabbath-day-morning, that they prepared for their travel. This morning I asked my master whether he would sell me to my husband. He answered me "Nux,"[4] which did much rejoice my spirit. My mistress, before we went, was gone to the burial of a papoose, and returning, she found me sitting and reading in my Bible; she snatched it hastily out of my hand, and threw it out of doors. I ran out and catched it up, and put it into my pocket, and never let her see it afterward. Then they packed up their things to be gone, and gave me my load. I complained it was too heavy, whereupon she gave me a slap in the face, and bade me go; I lifted up my heart to God, hoping the redemption was not far off; and the rather because their insolency grew worse and worse.

But the thoughts of my going homeward (for so we bent our course) much cheered my spirit, and made my burden seem light, and almost nothing at all. But (to my amazement and great perplexity) the scale was soon turned; for when we had gone a little way, on a sudden my mistress gives out; she would go no further, but turn back again, and said I must go back again with her, and she called her *sannup*, and would have had him gone back also, but he would not, but said he would go on, and come to us again in three days. My spirit was, upon this, I confess, very impatient, and almost outrageous. I thought I could as well have died as went back; I cannot declare the trouble that I was in about it; but yet back again I must go. As soon as I had the opportunity, I took my Bible to read, and that quieting Scripture came to my hand, "Be still, and know that I am God" (Psalm 46.10). Which stilled my spirit for the present. But a sore time of trial, I concluded, I had to go

2. April 1676, near Chesterfield, New Hampshire. This is as far north as Rowlandson was taken.

3. Sunday, April 9.

4. Yes.

through, my master being gone, who seemed to me the best friend that I had of an Indian, both in cold and hunger, and quickly so it proved. Down I sat, with my heart as full as it could hold, and yet so hungry that I could not sit neither; but going out to see what I could find, and walking among the trees, I found six acorns, and two chestnuts, which were some refreshment to me. Towards night I gathered some sticks for my own comfort, that I might not lie a-cold; but when we came to lie down they bade me to go out, and lie somewhere else, for they had company (they said) come in more than their own. I told them, I could not tell where to go, they bade me go look; I told them, if I went to another wigwam they would be angry, and send me home again. Then one of the company drew his sword, and told me he would run me through if I did not go presently. Then was I fain to stoop to this rude fellow, and to go out in the night, I knew not whither. Mine eyes have seen that fellow afterwards walking up and down Boston, under the appearance of a Friend Indian, and several others of the like cut. I went to one wigwam, and they told me they had no room. Then I went to another, and they said the same; at last an old Indian bade me to come to him, and his squaw gave me some ground nuts; she gave me also something to lay under my head, and a good fire we had; and through the good providence of God, I had a comfortable lodging that night. In the morning, another Indian bade me come at night, and he would give me six ground nuts, which I did. We were at this place and time about two miles from [the] Connecticut river. We went in the morning to gather ground nuts, to the river, and went back again that night. I went with a good load at my back (for they when they went, though but a little way, would carry all their trumpery with them). I told them the skin was off my back, but I had no other comforting answer from them than this: that it would be no matter if my head were off too.

The Thirteenth Remove⁵

Instead of going toward the Bay, which was that I desired, I must go with them five or six miles down the river into a mighty thicket of brush; where we abode almost a fortnight. Here one asked me to make a shirt for her papoose, for which she gave me a mess of broth, which was thickened with meal made of the bark of a tree, and to make it the better, she had put into it about a handful of peas, and a few roasted ground nuts. I had not seen my son a pretty while, and here was an Indian of whom I made inquiry after him, and asked him when he saw him. He answered me that such a time his master roasted him, and that himself did eat a piece of him, as big as his two fingers, and that he was very good meat. But the Lord upheld my Spirit, under this discouragement; and I considered their horrible addictedness to lying, and that there is not one of them that makes the least conscience of speaking of truth. In this place, on a cold night, as I lay by the fire, I removed a stick that kept the heat from me. A squaw moved it down again, at which I looked up, and she threw a handful of ashes in mine eyes. I thought I should have been quite blinded, and have never seen more, but lying down, the water run out of my eyes, and carried the dirt with it, that by the morning

5. To Hinsdale, New Hampshire, near the Connecticut River.

I recovered my sight again. Yet upon this, and the like occasions, I hope it is not too much to say with Job, "Have pity upon me, O ye my Friends, for the Hand of the Lord has touched me."[6] And here I cannot but remember how many times sitting in their wigwams, and musing on things past, I should suddenly leap up and run out, as if I had been at home, forgetting where I was, and what my condition was; but when I was without, and saw nothing but wilderness, and woods, and a company of barbarous heathens, my mind quickly returned to me, which made me think of that, spoken concerning Sampson, who said, "I will go out and shake myself as at other times, but he wist not that the Lord was departed from him."[7] About this time I began to think that all my hopes of restoration would come to nothing. I thought of the English army, and hoped for their coming, and being taken by them, but that failed. I hoped to be carried to Albany, as the Indians had discoursed before, but that failed also. I thought of being sold to my husband, as my master spake, but instead of that, my master himself was gone, and I left behind, so that my spirit was now quite ready to sink. I asked them to let me go out and pick up some sticks, that I might get alone, and pour out my heart unto the Lord. Then also I took my Bible to read, but I found no comfort here neither, which many times I was wont to find. So easy a thing it is with God to dry up the streams of Scripture comfort from us. Yet I can say, that in all my sorrows and afflictions, God did not leave me to have my impatience work towards Himself, as if His ways were unrighteous. But I knew that He laid upon me less than I deserved. Afterward, before this doleful time ended with me, I was turning the leaves of my Bible, and the Lord brought to me some Scriptures, which did a little revive me, as that [in] Isaiah 55.8: "For my thoughts are not your thoughts, neither are your ways my ways, saith the Lord." And also that [in] Psalm 37.5: "Commit thy way unto the Lord; trust also in him; and he shall bring it to pass." About this time they came yelping from Hadley, where they had killed three Englishmen, and brought one captive with them, *viz.* Thomas Read. They all gathered about the poor man, asking him many questions. I desired also to go and see him; and when I came, he was crying bitterly, supposing they would quickly kill him. Whereupon I asked one of them, whether they intended to kill him; he answered me, they would not. He being a little cheered with that, I asked him about the welfare of my husband. He told me he saw him such a time in the Bay, and he was well, but very melancholy. By which I certainly understood (though I suspected it before) that whatsoever the Indians told me respecting him was vanity and lies. Some of them told me he was dead, and they had killed him; some said he was married again, and that the Governor wished him to marry; and told him he should have his choice, and that all persuaded I was dead. So like were these barbarous creatures to him who was a liar from the beginning.[8]

As I was sitting once in the wigwam here, Philip's maid came in with the child in her arms, and asked me to give her a piece of my apron, to make a flap for it. I told her I would not. Then my mistress bade me give it, but still I said no. The maid told me if I would not give her a piece, she would tear a piece off it. I told her I would tear her coat then. With that my mistress

6. Job 19.21.
7. Judges 16.20.

8. I.e., Satan.

rises up, and take up a stick big enough to have killed me, and struck at me with it. But I stepped out, and she struck the stick into the mat of the wigwam. But while she was pulling of it out I ran to the maid and gave her all my apron, and so that storm went over.

Hearing that my son was come to this place, I went to see him, and told him his father was well, but melancholy. He told me he was as much grieved for his father as for himself. I wondered at his speech, for I thought I had enough upon my spirit in reference to myself, to make me mindless of my husband and everyone else; they being safe among their friends. He told me also, that awhile before, his master (together with other Indians) were going to the French for powder; but by the way the Mohawks met with them, and killed four of their company, which made the rest turn back again, for it might have been worse with him, had he been sold to the French, than it proved to be in his remaining with the Indians.

I went to see an English youth in this place, one John Gilbert of Springfield. I found him lying without doors, upon the ground. I asked him how he did? He told me he was very sick of a flux,[9] with eating so much blood. They had turned him out of the wigwam, and with him an Indian papoose, almost dead (whose parents had been killed), in a bitter cold day, without fire or clothes. The young man himself had nothing on but his shirt and waistcoat. This sight was enough to melt a heart of flint. There they lay quivering in the cold, the youth round like a dog, the papoose stretched out with his eyes and nose and mouth full of dirt, and yet alive, and groaning. I advised John to go and get to some fire. He told me he could not stand, but I persuaded him still, lest he should lie there and die. And with much ado I got him to a fire, and went myself home. As soon as I was got home his master's daughter came after me, to know what I had done with the Englishman. I told her I had got him to a fire in such a place. Now had I need to pray Paul's Prayer "That we may be delivered from unreasonable and wicked men" (2 Thessalonians 3.2). For her satisfaction I went along with her, and brought her to him; but before I got home again it was noised about that I was running away and getting the English youth, along with me; that as soon as I came in they began to rant and domineer, asking me where I had been, and what I had been doing? and saying they would knock him on the head. I told them I had been seeing the English youth, and that I would not run away. They told me I lied, and taking up a hatchet, they came to me, and said they would knock me down if I stirred out again, and so confined me to the wigwam. Now may I say with David, "I am in a great strait" (2 Samuel 24.14). If I keep in, I must die with hunger, and if I go out, I must be knocked in head. This distressed condition held that day, and half the next. And then the Lord remembered me, whose mercies are great. Then came an Indian to me with a pair of stockings that were too big for him, and he would have me ravel them out, and knit them fit for him. I showed myself willing, and bid him ask my mistress if I might go along with him a little way; she said yes, I might, but I was not a little refreshed with that news, that I had my liberty again. Then I went along with him, and he gave me some roasted ground nuts, which did again revive my feeble stomach.

Being got out of her sight, I had time and liberty again to look into my

9. Dysentery.

Bible; which was my guide by day, and my pillow by night. Now that comfortable Scripture presented itself to me, "For a small moment have I forsaken thee, but with great mercies will I gather thee" (Isaiah 54.7). Thus the Lord carried me along from one time to another, and made good to me this precious promise, and many others. Then my son came to see me, and I asked his master to let him stay awhile with me, that I might comb his head, and look over him, for he was almost overcome with lice. He told me, when I had done, that he was very hungry, but I had nothing to relieve him, but bid him go into the wigwams as he went along, and see if he could get any thing among them. Which he did, and it seems tarried a little too long; for his master was angry with him, and beat him, and then sold him. Then he came running to tell me he had a new master, and that he had given him some ground nuts already. Then I went along with him to his new master who told me he loved him, and he should not want. So his master carried him away, and I never saw him afterward, till I saw him at Piscataqua in Portsmouth.

That night they bade me go out of the wigwam again. My mistress's papoose was sick, and it died that night, and there was one benefit in it—that there was more room. I went to a wigwam, and they bade me come in, and gave me a skin to lie upon, and a mess of venison and ground nuts, which was a choice dish among them. On the morrow they buried the papoose, and afterward, both morning and evening, there came a company to mourn and howl with her; though I confess I could not much condole with them. Many sorrowful days I had in this place, often getting alone. "Like a crane, or a swallow, so did I chatter; I did mourn as a dove, mine eyes ail with looking upward. Oh, Lord, I am oppressed; undertake for me" (Isaiah 38.14). I could tell the Lord, as Hezekiah, "Remember now O Lord, I beseech thee, how I have walked before thee in truth."[1] Now had I time to examine all my ways: my conscience did not accuse me of unrighteousness toward one or other; yet I saw how in my walk with God, I had been a careless creature. As David said, "Against thee, thee only have I sinned":[2] and I might say with the poor publican, "God be merciful unto me a sinner."[3] On the Sabbath days, I could look upon the sun and think how people were going to the house of God, to have their souls refreshed; and then home, and their bodies also; but I was destitute of both; and might say as the poor prodigal, "He would fain have filled his belly with the husks that the swine did eat, and no man gave unto him" (Luke 15.16). For I must say with him, "Father, I have sinned against Heaven and in thy sight."[4] I remembered how on the night before and after the Sabbath, when my family was about me, and relations and neighbors with us, we could pray and sing, and then refresh our bodies with the good creatures of God; and then have a comfortable bed to lie down on; but instead of all this, I had only a little swill for the body and then, like a swine, must lie down on the ground. I cannot express to man the sorrow that lay upon my spirit; the Lord knows it. Yet that comfortable Scripture would often come to mind, "For a small moment have I forsaken thee, but with great mercies will I gather thee."[5]

1. Isaiah 38.3.
2. Psalm 51.4.
3. Luke 18.13.

4. Luke 15.21.
5. Isaiah 54.7.

The Fourteenth Remove[6]

Now must we pack up and be gone from this thicket, bending our course toward the Baytowns; I having nothing to eat by the way this day, but a few crumbs of cake, that an Indian gave my girl the same day we were taken. She gave it me, and I put it in my pocket; there it lay, till it was so moldy (for want of good baking) that one could not tell what it was made of; it fell all to crumbs, and grew so dry and hard, that it was like little flints; and this refreshed me many times, when I was ready to faint. It was in my thoughts when I put it into my mouth, that if ever I returned, I would tell the world what a blessing the Lord gave to such mean food. As we went along they killed a deer, with a young one in her, they gave me a piece of the fawn, and it was so young and tender, that one might eat the bones as well as the flesh, and yet I thought it very good. When night came on we sat down; it rained, but they quickly got up a bark wigwam, where I lay dry that night. I looked out in the morning, and many of them had lain in the rain all night, I saw by their reeking.[7] Thus the Lord dealt mercifully with me many times, and I fared better than many of them. In the morning they took the blood of the deer, and put it into the paunch, and so boiled it. I could eat nothing of that, though they ate it sweetly. And yet they were so nice[8] in other things, that when I had fetched water, and had put the dish I dipped the water with into the kettle of water which I brought, they would say they would knock me down; for they said, it was a sluttish trick.

The Fifteenth Remove

We went on our travel. I having got one handful of ground nuts, for my support that day, they gave me my load, and I went on cheerfully (with the thoughts of going homeward), having my burden more on my back than my spirit. We came to Banquang river again that day, near which we abode a few days. Sometimes one of them would give me a pipe, another a little tobacco, another a little salt: which I would change for a little victuals. I cannot but think what a wolvish appetite persons have in a starving condition; for many times when they gave me that which was hot, I was so greedy, that I should burn my mouth, that it would trouble me hours after, and yet I should quickly do the same again. And after I was thoroughly hungry, I was never again satisfied. For though sometimes it fell out, that I got enough, and did eat till I could eat no more, yet I was as unsatisfied as I was when I began. And now could I see that Scripture verified (there being many Scriptures which we do not take notice of, or understand till we are afflicted) "Thou shalt eat and not be satisfied" (Micah 6.14). Now might I see more than ever before, the miseries that sin hath brought upon us. Many times I should be ready to run against the heathen, but the Scripture would quiet me again, "Shall there be evil in a City and the Lord hath not done it?" (Amos 3.6). The Lord help me to make a right improvement of His word, and that I might learn that great lesson: "He hath showed thee (Oh Man) what is

6. The fourteenth to nineteenth removes (April 20 to April 28) retrace the path taken earlier. The "Baytowns" are the towns near Boston.

7. Steaming.
8. Fastidious.

good, and what doth the Lord require of thee, but to do justly, and love mercy, and walk humbly with thy God? Hear ye the rod, and who hath appointed it" (Micah 6.8–9).

The Sixteenth Removal

We began this remove with wading over Banquang river: the water was up to the knees, and the stream very swift, and so cold that I thought it would have cut me in sunder. I was so weak and feeble, that I reeled as I went along, and thought there I must end my days at last, after my bearing and getting through so many difficulties. The Indians stood laughing to see me staggering along; but in my distress the Lord gave me experience of the truth, and goodness of that promise, "When thou passest through the waters, I will be with thee; and through the rivers, they shall not overflow thee" (Isaiah 43.2). Then I sat down to put on my stockings and shoes, with the tears running down mine eyes, and sorrowful thoughts in my heart, but I got up to go along with them. Quickly there came up to us an Indian, who informed them that I must go to Wachusett to my master, for there was a letter come from the council to the Sagamores, about redeeming the captives, and that there would be another in fourteen days, and that I must be there ready. My heart was so heavy before that I could scarce speak or go in the path; and yet now so light, that I could run. My strength seemed to come again, and recruit my feeble knees, and aching heart. Yet it pleased them to go but one mile that night, and there we stayed two days. In that time came a company of Indians to us, near thirty, all on horseback. My heart skipped within me, thinking they had been Englishmen at the first sight of them, for they were dressed in English apparel, with hats, white neckcloths, and sashes about their waists; and ribbons upon their shoulders; but when they came near, there was a vast difference between the lovely faces of Christians, and foul looks of those heathens, which much damped my spirit again.

The Seventeenth Remove

A comfortable remove it was to me, because of my hopes. They gave me a pack, and along we went cheerfully; but quickly my will proved more than my strength; having little or no refreshing, my strength failed me, and my spirits were almost quite gone. Now may I say with David "I am poor and needy, and my heart is wounded within me. I am gone like the shadow when it declineth: I am tossed up and down like the locust; my knees are weak through fasting, and my flesh faileth of fatness" (Psalm 119.22–24). At night we came to an Indian town, and the Indians sat down by a wigwam discoursing, but I was almost spent, and could scarce speak. I laid down my load, and went into the wigwam, and there sat an Indian boiling of horses feet (they being wont to eat the flesh first, and when the feet were old and dried, and they had nothing else, they would cut off the feet and use them). I asked him to give me a little of his broth, or water they were boiling in; he took a dish, and gave me one spoonful of samp,[9] and bid me take as much of the

9. A porridge made of Indian corn.

broth as I would. Then I put some of the hot water to the samp, and drank it up, and my spirit came again. He gave me also a piece of the ruff or ridding[1] of the small guts, and I broiled it on the coals; and now may I say with Jonathan, "See, I pray you, how mine eyes have been enlightened, because I tasted a little of this honey" (1 Samuel 14.29). Now is my spirit revived again; though means be never so inconsiderable, yet if the Lord bestow His blessing upon them, they shall refresh both soul and body.

The Eighteenth Remove

We took up our packs and along we went, but a wearisome day I had of it. As we went along I saw an Englishman stripped naked, and lying dead upon the ground, but knew not who it was. Then we came to another Indian town, where we stayed all night. In this town there were four English children, captives; and one of them my own sister's. I went to see how she did, and she was well, considering her captive condition. I would have tarried that night with her, but they that owned her would not suffer it. Then I went into another wigwam, where they were boiling corn and beans, which was a lovely sight to see, but I could not get a taste thereof. Then I went to another wigwam, where there were two of the English children; the squaw was boiling horses feet; then she cut me off a little piece, and gave one of the English children a piece also. Being very hungry I had quickly eat up mine, but the child could not bite it, it was so tough and sinewy, but lay sucking, gnawing, chewing and slabbering of it in the mouth and hand. Then I took it of the child, and eat it myself, and savory it was to my taste. Then I may say as Job 6.7, "The things that my soul refused to touch are as my sorrowful meat." Thus the Lord made that pleasant refreshing, which another time would have been an abomination. Then I went home to my mistress's wigwam; and they told me I disgraced my master with begging, and if I did so any more, they would knock me in the head. I told them, they had as good knock me in head as starve me to death.

The Nineteenth Remove

They said, when we went out, that we must travel to Wachusett this day. But a bitter weary day I had of it, traveling now three days together, without resting any day between. At last, after many weary steps, I saw Wachusett hills, but many miles off. Then we came to a great swamp, through which we traveled, up to the knees in mud and water, which was heavy going to one tired before. Being almost spent, I thought I should have sunk down at last, and never got out; but I may say, as in Psalm 94.18, "When my foot slipped, thy mercy, O Lord, held me up." Going along, having indeed my life, but little spirit, Philip, who was in the company, came up and took me by the hand, and said, two weeks more and you shall be mistress again. I asked him, if he spake true? He answered, "Yes, and quickly you shall come to your master again; who had been gone from us three weeks." After many weary steps we came to Wachusett, where he was: and glad I was to see him. He

---

1. I.e., the refuse, that which he was casting away.

asked me, when I washed me? I told him not this month. Then he fetched me some water himself, and bid me wash, and gave me the glass to see how I looked; and bid his squaw give me something to eat. So she gave me a mess of beans and meat, and a little ground nut cake. I was wonderfully revived with this favor showed me: "He made them also to be pitied of all those that carried them captives" (Psalm 106.46).

My master had three squaws, living sometimes with one, and sometimes with another one, this old squaw, at whose wigwam I was, and with whom my master had been those three weeks. Another was Weetamoo[2] with whom I had lived and served all this while. A severe and proud dame she was, bestowing every day in dressing herself neat as much time as any of the gentry of the land: powdering her hair, and painting her face, going with necklaces, with jewels in her ears, and bracelets upon her hands. When she had dressed herself, her work was to make girdles of wampum and beads. The third squaw was a younger one, by whom he had two papooses. By the time I was refreshed by the old squaw, with whom my master was, Weetamoo's maid came to call me home, at which I fell aweeping. Then the old squaw told me, to encourage me, that if I wanted victuals, I should come to her, and that I should lie there in her wigwam. Then I went with the maid, and quickly came again and lodged there. The squaw laid a mat under me, and a good rug over me; the first time I had any such kindness showed me. I understood that Weetamoo thought that if she should let me go and serve with the old squaw, she would be in danger to lose not only my service, but the redemption pay also. And I was not a little glad to hear this; being by it raised in my hopes, that in God's due time there would be an end of this sorrowful hour. Then came an Indian, and asked me to knit him three pair of stockings, for which I had a hat, and a silk handkerchief. Then another asked me to make her a shift, for which she gave me an apron.

Then came Tom and Peter,[3] with the second letter from the council, about the captives. Though they were Indians, I got them by the hand, and burst out into tears. My heart was so full that I could not speak to them; but recovering myself, I asked them how my husband did, and all my friends and acquaintance? They said, "They are all very well but melancholy." They brought me two biscuits, and a pound of tobacco. The tobacco I quickly gave away. When it was all gone, one asked me to give him a pipe of tobacco. I told him it was all gone. Then began he to rant and threaten. I told him when my husband came I would give him some. Hang him rogue (says he) I will knock out his brains, if he comes here. And then again, in the same breath they would say that if there should come an hundred without guns, they would do them no hurt. So unstable and like madmen they were. So that fearing the worst, I durst not send to my husband, though there were some thoughts of his coming to redeem and fetch me, not knowing what might follow. For there was little more trust to them than to the master they served. When the letter was come, the Sagamores met to consult about the captives, and called me to them to inquire how much my husband would give to redeem me. When I came I sat down among them, as I was wont to do, as their manner is. Then they bade me stand up, and said they were the

General Court.[4] They bid me speak what I thought he would give. Now knowing that all we had was destroyed by the Indians, I was in a great strait. I thought if I should speak of but a little it would be slighted, and hinder the matter; if of a great sum, I knew not where it would be procured. Yet at a venture I said "Twenty pounds," yet desired them to take less. But they would not hear of that, but sent that message to Boston, that for twenty pounds I should be redeemed. It was a Praying Indian that wrote their letter for them. There was another Praying Indian, who told me, that he had a brother, that would not eat horse; his conscience was so tender and scrupulous (though as large as hell, for the destruction of poor Christians). Then he said, he read that Scripture to him, "There was a famine in Samaria, and behold they besieged it, until an ass's head was sold for fourscore pieces of silver, and the fourth part of a cab of dove's dung for five pieces of silver" (2 Kings 6.25). He expounded this place to his brother, and showed him that it was lawful to eat that in a famine which is not at another time. And now, says he, he will eat horse with any Indian of them all. There was another Praying Indian, who when he had done all the mischief that he could, betrayed his own father into the English hands, thereby to purchase his own life. Another Praying Indian was at Sudbury fight,[5] though, as he deserved, he was afterward hanged for it. There was another Praying Indian, so wicked and cruel, as to wear a string about his neck, strung with Christians' fingers. Another Praying Indian, when they went to Sudbury fight, went with them, and his squaw also with him, with her papoose at her back. Before they went to that fight they got a company together to pow-wow.[6] The manner was as followeth: there was one that kneeled upon a deerskin, with the company round him in a ring who kneeled, and striking upon the ground with their hands, and with sticks, and muttering or humming with their mouths. Besides him who kneeled in the ring, there also stood one with a gun in his hand. Then he on the deerskin made a speech, and all manifested assent to it; and so they did many times together. Then they bade him with the gun go out of the ring, which he did. But when he was out, they called him in again; but he seemed to make a stand; then they called the more earnestly, till he returned again. Then they all sang. Then they gave him two guns, in either hand one. And so he on the deerskin began again; and at the end of every sentence in his speaking, they all assented, humming or muttering with their mouths, and striking upon the ground with their hands. Then they bade him with the two guns go out of the ring again; which he did, a little way. Then they called him in again, but he made a stand. So they called him with greater earnestness; but he stood reeling and wavering as if he knew not whither he should stand or fall, or which way to go. Then they called him with exceeding great vehemency, all of them, one and another. After a little while he turned in, staggering as he went, with his arms stretched out, in either hand a gun. As soon as he came in they all sang and rejoiced exceedingly a while. And then he upon the deerskin, made another speech unto which they all assented in a rejoicing manner. And so they ended their business, and forthwith went to Sudbury fight. To my thinking they went without any scruple, but that they should prosper, and gain the victory. And they went out not so

4. In imitation of the colonial assembly of Massachusetts.
5. Reference to an attack on Sudbury, Massachusetts, April 18.
6. Confer.

rejoicing, but they came home with as great a victory. For they said they had killed two captains and almost an hundred men. One Englishman they brought along with them: and he said, it was too true, for they had made sad work at Sudbury, as indeed it proved. Yet they came home without that rejoicing and triumphing over their victory which they were wont to show at other times; but rather like dogs (as they say) which have lost their ears. Yet I could not perceive that it was for their own loss of men. They said they had not lost above five or six; and I missed none, except in one wigwam. When they went, they acted as if the devil had told them that they should gain the victory; and now they acted as if the devil had told them they should have a fall. Whither it were so or no, I cannot tell, but so it proved, for quickly they began to fall, and so held on that summer, till they came to utter ruin. They came home on a Sabbath day, and the *Powaw* that kneeled upon the deer-skin came home (I may say, without abuse) as black as the devil. When my master came home, he came to me and bid me make a shirt for his papoose, of a holland-laced pillowbere.[7] About that time there came an Indian to me and bid me come to his wigwam at night, and he would give me some pork and ground nuts. Which I did, and as I was eating, another Indian said to me, he seems to be your good friend, but he killed two Englishmen at Sudbury, and there lie their clothes behind you: I looked behind me, and there I saw bloody clothes, with bullet-holes in them. Yet the Lord suffered not this wretch to do me any hurt. Yea, instead of that, he many times refreshed me; five or six times did he and his squaw refresh my feeble carcass. If I went to their wigwam at any time, they would always give me something, and yet they were strangers that I never saw before. Another squaw gave me a piece of fresh pork, and a little salt with it, and lent me her pan to fry it in; and I cannot but remember what a sweet, pleasant and delightful relish that bit had to me, to this day. So little do we prize common mercies when we have them to the full.

The Twentieth Remove[8]

It was their usual manner to remove, when they had done any mischief, lest they should be found out; and so they did at this time. We went about three or four miles, and there they built a great wigwam, big enough to hold an hundred Indians, which they did in preparation to a great day of dancing. They would say now amongst themselves, that the governor would be so angry for his loss at Sudbury, that he would send no more about the captives, which made me grieve and tremble. My sister being not far from the place where we now were, and hearing that I was here, desired her master to let her come and see me, and he was willing to it, and would go with her; but she being ready before him, told him she would go before, and was come within a mile or two of the place. Then he overtook her, and began to rant as if he had been mad, and made her go back again in the rain; so that I never saw her till I saw her in Charlestown. But the Lord requited many of their ill doings, for this Indian her master, was hanged afterward at Boston. The Indians now began to come from all quarters, against their merry dancing day. Among some of them came one goodwife Kettle. I told her my heart

7. Pillowcase.
8. April 28 to May 2, to an encampment at the southern end of Wachusett Lake, Princeton, Massachusetts.

was so heavy that it was ready to break. "So is mine too," said she, but yet said, "I hope we shall hear some good news shortly." I could hear how earnestly my sister desired to see me, and I as earnestly desired to see her; and yet neither of us could get an opportunity. My daughter was also now about a mile off, and I had not seen her in nine or ten weeks, as I had not seen my sister since our first taking. I earnestly desired them to let me go and see them: yea, I entreated, begged, and persuaded them, but to let me see my daughter; and yet so hard-hearted were they, that they would not suffer it. They made use of their tyrannical power whilst they had it; but through the Lord's wonderful mercy, their time was now but short.

On a Sabbath day, the sun being about an hour high in the afternoon, came Mr. John Hoar[9] (the council permitting him, and his own foreward spirit inclining him), together with the two forementioned Indians, Tom and Peter, with their third letter from the council. When they came near, I was abroad. Though I saw them not, they presently called me in, and bade me sit down and not stir. Then they catched up their guns, and away they ran, as if an enemy had been at hand, and the guns went off apace. I manifested some great trouble, and they asked me what was the matter? I told them I thought they had killed the Englishman (for they had in the meantime informed me that an Englishman was come). They said, no. They shot over his horse and under and before his horse, and they pushed him this way and that way, at their pleasure, showing what they could do. Then they let them come to their wigwams. I begged of them to let me see the Englishman, but they would not. But there was I fain to sit their pleasure. When they had talked their fill with him, they suffered me to go to him. We asked each other of our welfare, and how my husband did, and all my friends? He told me they were all well, and would be glad to see me. Amongst other things which my husband sent me, there came a pound of tobacco, which I sold for nine shillings in money; for many of the Indians for want of tobacco, smoked hemlock, and ground ivy. It was a great mistake in any, who thought I sent for tobacco; for through the favor of God, that desire was overcome. I now asked them whether I should go home with Mr. Hoar? They answered no, one and another of them, and it being night, we lay down with that answer. In the morning Mr. Hoar invited the Sagamores to dinner; but when we went to get it ready we found that they had stolen the greatest part of the provision Mr. Hoar had brought, out of his bags, in the night. And we may see the wonderful power of God, in that one passage, in that when there was such a great number of the Indians together, and so greedy of a little good food, and no English there but Mr. Hoar and myself, that there they did not knock us in the head, and take what we had, there being not only some provision, but also trading-cloth,[1] a part of the twenty pounds agreed upon. But instead of doing us any mischief, they seemed to be ashamed of the fact, and said, it were some matchit[2] Indian that did it. Oh, that we could believe that there is nothing too hard for God! God showed His power over the heathen in this, as He did over the hungry lions when Daniel was cast into the den.[3] Mr. Hoar called them betime to dinner, but they ate very little, they being so

9. John Hoar was from Concord, Massachusetts. He had been delegated by Rowlandson's husband to represent him at the council for the Sagamore Indians, and to bargain for Rowlandson's redemption.

1. Cloth used for barter.
2. Bad.
3. The prophet Daniel was cast into a den of lions, but they did not harm him (see Daniel 6.1–29).

busy in dressing themselves, and getting ready for their dance, which was carried on by eight of them, four men and four squaws. My master and mistress being two. He was dressed in his holland[4] shirt, with great laces sewed at the tail of it; he had his silver buttons, his white stockings, his garters were hung round with shillings, and he had girdles of wampum[5] upon his head and shoulders. She had a kersey[6] coat, and covered with girdles of wampum from the loins upward. Her arms from her elbows to her hands were covered with bracelets; there were handfuls of necklaces about her neck, and several sorts of jewels in her ears. She had fine red stockings, and white shoes, her hair powdered and face painted red, that was always before black. And all the dancers were after the same manner. There were two others singing and knocking on a kettle for their music. They kept hopping up and down one after another, with a kettle of water in the midst, standing warm upon some embers, to drink of when they were dry. They held on till it was almost night, throwing out wampum to the standers by. At night I asked them again, if I should go home? They all as one said no, except[7] my husband would come for me. When we were lain down, my master went out of the wigwam, and by and by sent in an Indian called James the Printer,[8] who told Mr. Hoar, that my master would let me go home tomorrow, if he would let him have one pint of liquors. Then Mr. Hoar called his own Indians, Tom and Peter, and bid them go and see whether he would promise it before them three; and if he would, he should have it; which he did, and he had it. Then Philip[9] smelling the business called me to him, and asked me what I would give him, to tell me some good news, and speak a good word for me. I told him I could not tell what to give him. I would [give him] anything I had, and asked him what he would have? He said two coats and twenty shillings in money, and half a bushel of seed corn, and some tobacco. I thanked him for his love; but I knew the good news as well as the crafty fox. My master after he had had his drink, quickly came ranting into the wigwam again, and called for Mr. Hoar, drinking to him, and saying, he was a good man, and then again he would say, "hang him rogue." Being almost drunk, he would drink to him, and yet presently say he should be hanged. Then he called for me. I trembled to hear him, yet I was fain to go to him, and he drank to me, showing no incivility. He was the first Indian I saw drunk all the while that I was amongst them. At last his squaw ran out, and he after her, round the wigwam, with his money jingling at his knees. But she escaped him. But having an old squaw he ran to her; and so through the Lord's mercy, we were no more troubled that night. Yet I had not a comfortable night's rest; for I think I can say, I did not sleep for three nights together. The night before the letter came from the council, I could not rest, I was so full of fears and troubles, God many times leaving us most in the dark, when deliverance is nearest. Yea, at this time I could not rest night nor day. The next night I was overjoyed, Mr. Hoar being come, and that with such good tidings. The third night I was even swallowed up with the thoughts of things, *viz.* that ever I should go home again; and that I must go, leaving

4. Linen.
5. Beads of polished shells used by some American Indians as currency.
6. Coarse cloth woven from long wool and usually ribbed.

7. Unless.
8. An American Indian who assisted the Rev. John Eliot in his printing of the Bible.
9. An American Indian who aided Rowlandson earlier on the journey.

my children behind me in the wilderness; so that sleep was now almost departed from mine eyes.

On Tuesday morning they called their general court (as they call it) to consult and determine, whether I should go home or no. And they all as one man did seemingly consent to it, that I should go home; except Philip, who would not come among them.

But before I go any further, I would take leave to mention a few remarkable passages of providence, which I took special notice of in my afflicted time.

1. Of the fair opportunity lost in the long march, a little after the fort fight, when our English army was so numerous, and in pursuit of the enemy, and so near as to take several and destroy them, and the enemy in such distress for food that our men might track them by their rooting in the earth for ground nuts, whilst they were flying for their lives. I say, that then our army should want provision, and be forced to leave their pursuit and return homeward; and the very next week the enemy came upon our town, like bears bereft of their whelps, or so many ravenous wolves, rending us and our lambs to death. But what shall I say? God seemed to leave his People to themselves, and order all things for His own holy ends. Shall there be evil in the City and the Lord hath not done it?[1] They are not grieved for the affliction of Joseph, therefore shall they go captive, with the first that go captive.[2] It is the Lord's doing, and it should be marvelous in our eyes.

2. I cannot but remember how the Indians derided the slowness, and dullness of the English army, in its setting out. For after the desolations at Lancaster and Medfield, as I went along with them, they asked me when I thought the English army would come after them? I told them I could not tell. "It may be they will come in May," said they. Thus did they scoff at us, as if the English would be a quarter of a year getting ready.

3. Which also I have hinted before, when the English army with new supplies were sent forth to pursue after the enemy, and they understanding it, fled before them till they came to Banquaug river, where they forthwith went over safely; that that river should be impassable to the English. I can but admire to see the wonderful providence of God in preserving the heathen for further affliction to our poor country. They could go in great numbers over, but the English must stop. God had an over-ruling hand in all those things.

4. It was thought, if their corn were cut down, they would starve and die with hunger, and all their corn that could be found, was destroyed, and they driven from that little they had in store, into the woods in the midst of winter; and yet how to admiration did the Lord preserve them for His holy ends, and the destruction of many still amongst the English! strangely did the Lord provide for them; that I did not see (all the time I was among them) one man, woman, or child, die with hunger.

Though many times they would eat that, that a hog or a dog would hardly touch; yet by that God strengthened them to be a scourge to His people.

The chief and commonest food was ground nuts. They eat also nuts and acorns, artichokes, lilly roots, ground beans, and several other weeds and roots, that I know not.

They would pick up old bones, and cut them to pieces at the joints, and

1. Amos 3.6.   2. Amos 6.6–7.

if they were full of worms and maggots, they would scald them over the fire to make the vermine come out, and then boil them, and drink up the liquor, and then beat the great ends of them in a mortar, and so eat them. They would eat horse's guts, and ears, and all sorts of wild birds which they could catch; also bear, venison, beaver, tortoise, frogs, squirrels, dogs, skunks, rattlesnakes; yea, the very bark of trees; besides all sorts of creatures, and provision which they plundered from the English. I can but stand in admiration to see the wonderful power of God in providing for such a vast number of our enemies in the wilderness, where there was nothing to be seen, but from hand to mouth. Many times in a morning, the generality of them would eat up all they had, and yet have some further supply against they wanted. It is said, "Oh, that my People had hearkened to me, and Israel had walked in my ways, I should soon have subdued their Enemies, and turned my hand against their Adversaries" (Psalm 81.13–14). But now our perverse and evil carriages in the sight of the Lord, have so offended Him, that instead of turning His hand against them, the Lord feeds and nourishes them up to be a scourge to the whole land.

5. Another thing that I would observe is the strange providence of God, in turning things about when the Indians was at the highest, and the English at the lowest. I was with the enemy eleven weeks and five days, and not one week passed without the fury of the enemy, and some desolation by fire and sword upon one place or other. They mourned (with their black faces) for their own losses, yet triumphed and rejoiced in their inhumane, and many times devilish cruelty to the English. They would boast much of their victories; saying that in two hours time they had destroyed such a captain and his company at such a place; and boast how many towns they had destroyed, and then scoff, and say they had done them a good turn to send them to Heaven so soon. Again, they would say this summer that they would knock all the rogues in the head, or drive them into the sea, or make them fly the country; thinking surely, Agag-like, "The bitterness of Death is past."[3] Now the heathen begins to think all is their own, and the poor Christians' hopes to fail (as to man) and now their eyes are more to God, and their hearts sigh heaven-ward; and to say in good earnest, "Help Lord, or we perish." When the Lord had brought His people to this, that they saw no help in anything but Himself; then He takes the quarrel into His own hand; and though they had made a pit, in their own imaginations, as deep as hell for the Christians that summer, yet the Lord hurled themselves into it. And the Lord had not so many ways before to preserve them, but now He hath as many to destroy them.

But to return again to my going home, where we may see a remarkable change of providence. At first they were all against it, except my husband would come for me, but afterwards they assented to it, and seemed much to rejoice in it; some asked me to send them some bread, others some tobacco, others shaking me by the hand, offering me a hood and scarfe to ride in; not one moving hand or tongue against it. Thus hath the Lord answered my poor desire, and the many earnest requests of others put up unto God for me. In my travels an Indian came to me and told me, if I were willing, he and his

---

3. 1 Samuel 15.32. Agag was the king of Amalek; he was defeated by Saul and thought himself spared, but was slain by Samuel (see 1 Samuel 15).

squaw would run away, and go home along with me. I told him no: I was not willing to run away, but desired to wait God's time, that I might go home quietly, and without fear. And now God hath granted me my desire. O the wonderful power of God that I have seen, and the experience that I have had. I have been in the midst of those roaring lions, and savage bears, that feared neither God, nor man, nor the devil, by night and day, alone and in company, sleeping all sorts together, and yet not one of them ever offered me the least abuse of unchastity to me, in word or action. Though some are ready to say I speak it for my own credit; but I speak it in the presence of God, and to His Glory. God's power is as great now, and as sufficient to save, as when He preserved Daniel in the lion's den; or the three children in the fiery furnace.⁴ I may well say as his Psalm 107.12 "Oh give thanks unto the Lord for he is good, for his mercy endureth for ever." Let the redeemed of the Lord say so, whom He hath redeemed from the hand of the enemy, especially that I should come away in the midst of so many hundreds of enemies quietly and peaceably, and not a dog moving his tongue. So I took my leave of them, and in coming along my heart melted into tears, more than all the while I was with them, and I was almost swallowed up with the thoughts that ever I should go home again. About the sun going down, Mr. Hoar, and myself, and the two Indians came to Lancaster, and a solemn sight it was to me. There had I lived many comfortable years amongst my relations and neighbors, and now not one Christian to be seen, nor one house left standing. We went on to a farmhouse that was yet standing, where we lay all night, and a comfortable lodging we had, though nothing but straw to lie on. The Lord preserved us in safety that night, and raised us up again in the morning, and carried us along, that before noon, we came to Concord. Now was I full of joy, and yet not without sorrow; joy to see such a lovely sight, so many Christians together, and some of them my neighbors. There I met with my brother, and my brother-in-law, who asked me, if I knew where his wife was? Poor heart! he had helped to bury her, and knew it not. She being shot down by the house was partly burnt, so that those who were at Boston at the desolation of the town, and came back afterward, and buried the dead, did not know her. Yet I was not without sorrow, to think how many were looking and longing, and my own children amongst the rest, to enjoy that deliverance that I had now received, and I did not know whether ever I should see them again. Being recruited⁵ with food and raiment we went to Boston that day, where I met with my dear husband, but the thoughts of our dear children, one being dead, and the other we could not tell where, abated our comfort each to other. I was not before so much hemmed in with the merciless and cruel heathen, but now as much with pitiful, tender-hearted and compassionate Christians. In that poor, and distressed, and beggarly condition I was received in; I was kindly entertained in several houses. So much love I received from several (some of whom I knew, and others I knew not) that I am not capable to declare it. But the Lord knows them all by name. The Lord reward them sevenfold into their bosoms of His spirituals, for their temporals.⁶ The twenty pounds, the price of my redemption, was raised by some Boston gentlemen, and Mrs. Usher, whose bounty and reli-

4. Shadrach, Meshach, and Abednego refused to worship false gods and were cast into a fiery furnace but saved from death by an angel (see Daniel 3.13–30).

5. Refreshed.

6. Worldly goods and gifts.

gious charity, I would not forget to make mention of. Then Mr. Thomas Shepard of Charlestown received us into his house, where we continued eleven weeks; and a father and mother they were to us. And many more tender-hearted friends we met with in that place. We were now in the midst of love, yet not without much and frequent heaviness of heart for our poor children, and other relations, who were still in affliction. The week following, after my coming in, the governor and council sent forth to the Indians again; and that not without success; for they brought in my sister, and goodwife Kettle. Their not knowing where our children were was a sore trial to us still, and yet we were not without secret hopes that we should see them again. That which was dead lay heavier upon my spirit, than those which were alive and amongst the heathen: thinking how it suffered with its wounds, and I was no way able to relieve it; and how it was buried by the heathen in the wilderness from among all Christians. We were hurried up and down in our thoughts, sometime we should hear a report that they were gone this way, and sometimes that; and that they were come in, in this place or that. We kept inquiring and listening to hear concerning them, but no certain news as yet. About this time the council had ordered a day of public thanksgiving. Though I thought I had still cause of mourning, and being unsettled in our minds, we thought we would ride toward the eastward, to see if we could hear anything concerning our children. And as we were riding along (God is the wise disposer of all things) between Ipswich and Rowley we met with Mr. William Hubbard, who told us that our son Joseph was come in to Major Waldron's, and another with him, which was my sister's son. I asked him how he knew it? He said the major himself told him so. So along we went till we came to Newbury; and their minister being absent, they desired my husband to preach the thanksgiving for them; but he was not willing to stay there that night, but would go over to Salisbury, to hear further, and come again in the morning, which he did, and preached there that day. At night, when he had done, one came and told him that his daughter was come in at Providence. Here was mercy on both hands. Now hath God fulfilled that precious Scripture which was such a comfort to me in my distressed condition. When my heart was ready to sink into the earth (my children being gone, I could not tell whither) and my knees trembling under me, and I was walking through the valley of the shadow of death; then the Lord brought, and now has fulfilled that reviving word unto me: "Thus saith the Lord, Refrain thy voice from weeping, and thine eyes from tears, for thy Work shall be rewarded, saith the Lord, and they shall come again from the Land of the Enemy."[7] Now we were between them, the one on the east, and the other on the west. Our son being nearest, we went to him first, to Portsmouth, where we met with him, and with the Major also, who told us he had done what he could, but could not redeem him under seven pounds, which the good people thereabouts were pleased to pay. The Lord reward the major, and all the rest, though unknown to me, for their labor of Love. My sister's son was redeemed for four pounds, which the council gave order for the payment of. Having now received one of our children, we hastened toward the other. Going back through Newbury my husband preached there on the Sabbath day; for which they rewarded him many fold.

7. Jeremiah 31.16.

On Monday we came to Charlestown, where we heard that the governor of Rhode Island had sent over for our daughter, to take care of her, being now within his jurisdiction; which should not pass without our acknowledgments. But she being nearer Rehoboth than Rhode Island, Mr. Newman went over, and took care of her and brought her to his own house. And the goodness of God was admirable to us in our low estate, in that He raised up passionate[8] friends on every side to us, when we had nothing to recompense any for their love. The Indians were now gone that way, that it was apprehended dangerous to go to her. But the carts which carried provision to the English army, being guarded, brought her with them to Dorchester, where we received her safe. Blessed be the Lord for it, for great is His power, and He can do whatsoever seemeth Him good. Her coming in was after this manner: she was traveling one day with the Indians, with her basket at her back; the company of Indians were got before her, and gone out of sight, all except one squaw; she followed the squaw till night, and then both of them lay down, having nothing over them but the heavens and under them but the earth. Thus she traveled three days together, not knowing whither she was going; having nothing to eat or drink but water, and green hirtle-berries. At last they came into Providence, where she was kindly entertained by several of that town. The Indians often said that I should never have her under twenty pounds. But now the Lord hath brought her in upon free-cost, and given her to me the second time. The Lord make us a blessing indeed, each to others. Now have I seen that Scripture also fulfilled, "If any of thine be driven out to the outmost parts of heaven, from thence will the Lord thy God gather thee, and from thence will he fetch thee. And the Lord thy God will put all these curses upon thine enemies, and on them which hate thee, which persecuted thee" (Deuteronomy 30.4–7). Thus hath the Lord brought me and mine out of that horrible pit, and hath set us in the midst of tenderhearted and compassionate Christians. It is the desire of my soul that we may walk worthy of the mercies received, and which we are receiving.

Our family being now gathered together (those of us that were living), the South Church in Boston hired an house for us. Then we removed from Mr. Shephard's, those cordial friends, and went to Boston, where we continued about three-quarters of a year. Still the Lord went along with us, and provided graciously for us. I thought it somewhat strange to set up housekeeping with bare walls; but as Solomon says, "Money answers all things"[9] and that we had through the benevolence of Christian friends, some in this town, and some in that, and others; and some from England; that in a little time we might look, and see the house furnished with love. The Lord hath been exceeding good to us in our low estate, in that when we had neither house nor home, nor other necessaries, the Lord so moved the hearts of these and those towards us, that we wanted neither food, nor raiment for ourselves or ours: "There is a Friend which sticketh closer than a Brother" (Proverbs 18.24). And how many such friends have we found, and now living amongst? And truly such a friend have we found him to be unto us, in whose house we lived, viz. Mr. James Whitcomb, a friend unto us near hand, and afar off.

I can remember the time when I used to sleep quietly without workings in my thoughts, whole nights together, but now it is other ways with me.

---

8. Compassionate.   9. Ecclesiastes 10.19.

When all are fast about me, and no eye open, but His who ever waketh, my thoughts are upon things past, upon the awful dispensation of the Lord towards us, upon His wonderful power and might, in carrying of us through so many difficulties, in returning us in safety, and suffering none to hurt us. I remember in the night season, how the other day I was in the midst of thousands of enemies, and nothing but death before me. It is then hard work to persuade myself, that ever I should be satisfied with bread again. But now we are fed with the finest of the wheat, and, as I may say, with honey out of the rock.[1] Instead of the husk, we have the fatted calf.[2] The thoughts of these things in the particulars of them, and of the love and goodness of God towards us, make it true of me, what David said of himself, "I watered my Couch with my tears" (Psalm 6.6). Oh! the wonderful power of God that mine eyes have seen, affording matter enough for my thoughts to run in, that when others are sleeping mine eyes are weeping.

I have seen the extreme vanity of this world: One hour I have been in health, and wealthy, wanting nothing. But the next hour in sickness and wounds, and death, having nothing but sorrow and affliction.

Before I knew what affliction meant, I was ready sometimes to wish for it. When I lived in prosperity, having the comforts of the world about me, my relations by me, my heart cheerful, and taking little care for anything, and yet seeing many, whom I preferred before myself, under many trials and afflictions, in sickness, weakness, poverty, losses, crosses, and cares of the world, I should be sometimes jealous least I should have my portion in this life, and that Scripture would come to my mind, "For whom the Lord loveth he chasteneth, and scourgeth every Son whom he receiveth" (Hebrews 12.6). But now I see the Lord had His time to scourge and chasten me. The portion of some is to have their afflictions by drops, now one drop and then another; but the dregs of the cup, the wine of astonishment, like a sweeping rain that leaveth no food, did the Lord prepare to be my portion. Affliction I wanted, and affliction I had, full measure (I thought), pressed down and running over. Yet I see, when God calls a person to anything, and through never so many difficulties, yet He is fully able to carry them through and make them see, and say they have been gainers thereby. And I hope I can say in some measure, as David did, "It is good for me that I have been afflicted."[3] The Lord hath showed me the vanity of these outward things. That they are the vanity of vanities, and vexation of spirit, that they are but a shadow, a blast, a bubble, and things of no continuance. That we must rely on God Himself, and our whole dependance must be upon Him. If trouble from smaller matters begin to arise in me, I have something at hand to check myself with, and say, why am I troubled? It was but the other day that if I had had the world, I would have given it for my freedom, or to have been a servant to a Christian. I have learned to look beyond present and smaller troubles, and to be quieted under them. As Moses said, "Stand still and see the salvation of the Lord" (Exodus 14.13).

Finis.

1682

1. "He should have fed them also with the finest of the wheat: and with honey out of the rock should I have satisfied thee" (Psalm 81.16).

2. "And bring hither the fatted calf, and kill it; and let us eat, and be merry" (Luke 15.23).
3. Psalm 119.71.

EDWARD TAYLOR
c. 1642–1729

Given the importance of Edward Taylor's role in the town in which he lived for fifty-eight years, it is curious that we should know so little about his life. Taylor was probably born in Sketchly, Leicestershire County, England; his father was a "yeoman farmer"—that is, he was not a "gentleman" with large estates, but an independent landholder with title to his farm. Although his poetry contains no images that reflect his boyhood in Leicestershire, the dialect of that farming country is ever-present and gives his verse an air of provincial charm but also, it must be admitted, makes it difficult and complex for the modern reader. Taylor did not enter Harvard until he was twenty-nine years old and stayed only three years. It is assumed, therefore, that he had some university education in England, but it is not known where. We do know that he taught school and that he left his family and sailed to New England in 1668 because he would not sign an oath of loyalty to the Church of England. Rather than compromise his religious principles as a Puritan, he preferred exile in what he once called a "howling wilderness." It was at Harvard that he must have decided to leave teaching and prepare himself for the ministry.

In 1671 a delegation from the frontier town of Westfield, Massachusetts, asked Taylor to join them as their minister, and after a good deal of soul-searching he journeyed with them the hundred miles west to Westfield, where he remained the rest of his life. As by far the most educated member of that community, he served as minister, physician, and public servant. Taylor married twice and had fourteen children, many of whom died in infancy. A rigorous observer of all churchly functions, Taylor did not shy away from the religious controversies of the period. He was a strict observer of the "old" New England way, demanding a public account of conversion before admission to church membership and the right to partake of the sacrament of communion.

Taylor was a learned man as well as a pious one. Like most Harvard ministers, he knew Latin, Hebrew, and Greek. He had a passion for books and copied out in his own hand volumes that he borrowed from his college roommate, Samuel Sewall. He was known to Sewall and others as a good preacher, and on occasion he sent poems and letters to Boston friends, some parts of which were published during his lifetime. But Taylor's work as a poet was generally unknown until, in the 1930s, Thomas H. Johnson discovered that most of Taylor's poems had been deposited in the Yale University Library by Taylor's grandson, Ezra Stiles, a former president of Yale. It was one of the major literary discoveries of the twentieth century and revealed a body of work by a Puritan divine that was remarkable both in its quantity and quality.

Taylor's interest in poetry was lifelong, and he tried his hand at a variety of poetic genres: elegies on the death of public figures; lyrics in the manner of Elizabethan songs; a long poem, *God's Determinations*, in the tradition of the medieval debate; and an almost unreadable five-hundred-page *Metrical History of Christianity*, primarily a book of martyrs. But Taylor's best verse is to be found in a series called *Preparatory Meditations*. These poems, written for his own pleasure and never a part of any religious service, followed chiefly upon his preparation for a sermon to be delivered at monthly communion. They gave the poet an occasion to summarize the emotional and intellectual content of his sermon and to speak directly and fervently to God. Sometimes these poems are gnarled and difficult to follow, but they also reveal a unique voice, unmistakably Taylor's. They are written in an idiom that harks back to the verse Taylor must have known as a child in England—the Metaphysical lyrics of John Donne and George Herbert—and so delight in puns and paradoxes and a rich profusion of metaphors and images. Nothing previously discovered about Puritan literature had suggested that there was a writer in New England who had sustained such a long-term love affair with poetry.

Psalm Two[1]

(First Version)

Why do the Heathen rage? & folk
    A vain thing meditate?
Kings of the earth do set themselves
    & Rulers Counsel take
Against the Lord, & 'gainst His Christ   5
    Anointed, saying thus,
Let us asunder break Their bands,
    & cast Their Cords[2] from us.

He that doth in the heavens sit
    Shall laugh deridingly;   10
The Lord Himself shall have them in
    derision mightily.
T[h]en shall He speak in's wra[th]
    I[n] fury vex them will.
[Ye]t have I set my King un[to]   15
    Zion[3] my Holy hill.

I will declare out the dec[re]e
    The Lord hath said to me:
Thou art Mine only Son, I ha[ve]
    this day begotten Thee.   20
Ask of Me, & the heathen for
    Thine 'heritance I'll give
And th' utmost parts of th' earth f[or]
    Possession will bequeath.
Thou shalt them into pieces [wi]th   25
    A rod of iron break;
Thou shalt them dash in pieces, li[ke]
    A Potter's vessel weak.
Be wise ye Kings, instructed
    Ye Judges of the earth.   30
Serve ye the Lord with fear th[en]
    Rejoice with trembling mirth.

Kiss th' Son lest He be wroth, &
    The way ye perish must,
When His wrath but a little bu[rn].   35
    Blesst all that in Him trust.

c. 1674–75   1981

1. Taylor made two attempts at paraphrasing the Psalms, putting them into the common meter (i.e., alternating lines of eight and six syllables) used for singing hymns, but never completed paraphrasing all 150. A comparison with the King James version is useful: "Why do the heathen rage, and the people imagine a vain thing? The kings of the earth set themselves, and the rulers take counsel together, against the Lord, and against his anointed, saying, Let us break their bands asunder, and cast away their cords from us." The text used here is from *Edward Taylor's Minor Poetry*, edited by Thomas M. and Virginia L. Davis (1981).
2. Ropes.
3. The hill in Jerusalem on which Solomon's temple was built.

FROM PREPARATORY MEDITATIONS[1]

Prologue

Lord, Can a Crumb of Dust the Earth outweigh,
    Outmatch all mountains, nay, the Crystal sky?
Embosom in't designs that shall Display
    And trace into the Boundless Deity?
    Yea, hand a Pen whose moisture doth guide o'er   5
    Eternal Glory with a glorious glore.[2]

If it its Pen had of an Angel's Quill,
    And sharpened on a Precious Stone ground tight,
And dipped in liquid Gold, and moved by Skill
    In Crystal leaves should golden Letters write,   10
    It would but blot and blur, yea, jag, and jar
    Unless Thou mak'st the Pen, and Scrivener.

I am this Crumb of Dust which is designed
    To make my Pen unto Thy Praise alone,
And my dull Fancy[3] I would gladly grind   15
    Unto an Edge on Zion's[4] Precious Stone.
    And Write in Liquid Gold upon Thy Name
    My Letters till Thy glory forth doth flame.

Let not th' attempts break down my Dust, I pray,
    Nor laugh Thou them to scorn but pardon give.   20
Inspire this crumb of Dust till it display
    Thy Glory through't: and then Thy dust shall live.
    Its failings then Thou'lt overlook, I trust,
    They being Slips slipped from Thy Crumb of Dust.

Thy Crumb of Dust breathes two words from its breast,   25
    That Thou wilt guide its pen to write aright
To Prove Thou art, and that Thou art the best
    And show Thy Properties to shine most bright.
    And then Thy Works will shine as flowers on Stems
    Or as in Jewelry Shops, do gems.   30

c. 1682   1939

---

1. The full title is *Preparatory Meditations before my Approach to the Lord's Supper. Chiefly upon the Doctrine preached upon the Day of Administration [of Communion]*. Taylor administered communion once a month to those members of his congregation who had made a declaration of their faith. He wrote these meditations in private; they are primarily the result of his contemplation of the biblical texts that served as the basis for the communion sermon. A total of 217 meditations survive, dating from 1682 to 1725. The text used here is from *Poems of Edward Taylor*, edited by Donald E. Stanford (1960).
2. Glory (Scottish).
3. I.e., imagination.
4. The hill in Jerusalem on which Solomon built his temple; the City of God on earth.

Meditation 8 (First Series)

John 6.51. I am the Living Bread.[1]

I kenning through Astronomy Divine
    The World's bright Battlement,[2] wherein I spy
A Golden Path my Pencil cannot line,
    From that bright Throne unto my Threshold lie.
    And while my puzzled thoughts about it pour,   5
    I find the Bread of Life in't at my door.

When that this Bird of Paradise[3] put in
    This Wicker Cage (my Corpse) to tweedle praise
Had pecked the Fruit forbade: and so did fling
    Away its Food; and lost its golden days;   10
    It fell into Celestial Famine sore:
    And never could attain a morsel more.

Alas! alas! Poor Bird, what wilt thou do?
    The Creatures' field no food for Souls e'er gave.
And if thou knock at Angels' doors they show
    An Empty Barrel: they no soul bread have.   15
    Alas! Poor Bird, the World's White Loaf is done.
    And cannot yield thee here the smallest Crumb.

In this sad state, God's Tender Bowels[4] run
    Out streams of Grace: and He to end all strife   20
The Purest Wheat in Heaven His dear-dear son
    Grinds, and kneads up into this Bread of Life.
    Which Bread of Life from Heaven down came and stands
    Dished on Thy Table up by Angels' Hands.

Did God mold up this Bread in Heaven, and bake,   25
    Which from His Table came, and to thine goeth?
Doth He bespeak thee thus, This Soul Bread take.
    Come Eat thy fill of this thy God's White Loaf?
    It's Food too fine for Angels, yet come, take
    And Eat thy fill. It's Heaven's Sugar Cake.   30

What Grace is this knead in this Loaf? This thing
    Souls are but petty things it to admire.
Ye Angels, help: This fill would to the brim
    Heav'ns whelmed-down[5] Crystal meal Bowl, yea and higher.

1. "The Jews then murmured at him, because he said, I am the bread which came down from heaven. And they said, Is not this Jesus, the son of Joseph, whose father and mother we know? how is it then that he saith, I came down from heaven? Jesus therefore answered[,] . . . Verily, verily, I say unto you, He that believeth on me hath everlasting life. I am that bread of life" (John 6.41–48). Jesus offers a "New Covenant of Faith" in place of the "Old Covenant of Works," which Adam broke when he disobeyed God's commandment.

2. I.e., discerning, by means of "divine astronomy," the towers of heaven. Taylor goes on to suggest that there is an invisible golden path from this world to the Gates of Heaven.
3. I.e., the soul, which is like a bird kept in the body's cage.
4. Here used in the sense of the interior of the body, the "seat of the tender and sympathetic emotions," the heart.
5. Turned over. The *Oxford English Dictionary* quotes a passage from Dryden that is relevant:

This Bread of Life dropped in thy mouth, doth Cry: 35
Eat, Eat me, Soul, and thou shalt never die.

June 8, 1684   1939

Meditation 16 (First Series)

Luke 7.16. A Great Prophet is risen up.[1]

Leaf Gold, Lord of Thy Golden wedge[2] o'erlaid
    My Soul at first, Thy Grace in every part
Whose pert,[3] fierce Eye Thou such a Sight hadst made
    Whose brightsome beams could break into Thy heart
    Till Thy Cursed Foe had with my Fist mine Eye   5
    Dashed out, and did my Soul Unglorify.

I cannot see, nor Will Thy will aright.
    Nor see to wail my Woe, my loss and hue
Nor all the Shine in all the Sun can light
    My Candle, nor its heat my Heart renew.   10
    See, wail, and Will Thy Will, I must, or must
    From Heaven's sweet Shine to Hell's hot flame be thrust.

Grace then Concealed in God Himself, did roll
    Even Snowball like into a Sunball Shine
And nestles all Its beams bunched in Thy soul   15
    My Lord, that sparkle in Prophetic Lines.
    Oh! Wonder more than Wonderful! this Will
    Lighten the Eye which Sight Divine did spill.

What art Thou, Lord, this Ball of Glory bright?
    A Bundle of Celestial Beams up bound   20
In Grace's band fixed in Heaven's topmost height
    Pouring Thy golden beams thence, Circling round
    Which show Thy Glory, and Thy Glory's Way
    And Everywhere will make Celestial Day.

Lord, let Thy Golden Beams pierce through mine Eye   25
    And leave therein an Heavenly Light to glaze
My Soul with glorious Grace all o'er, whereby
    I may have Sight, and Grace in me may blaze.
    Lord ting[4] my Candle at Thy Burning rays,
    To give a gracious Glory to Thy Praise   30

Thou Lightning Eye, let some bright Beams of Thine
    Stick in my Soul, to light and liven it:

"That the earth is like a trencher and the Heavens a dish whelmed over it."
1. Taylor refers to the passage in the New Testament in which Jesus raised from the dead the only son of a widow. When the dead man spoke, fear took hold of all the witnesses to this miracle and they said: "That a great prophet is risen up among us; and, That God hath visited his people. And this rumour of him went forth throughout all Judea, and throughout all the region round about" (Luke 7.16–17).
2. In gilding it is customary to apply small squares of gold leaf to a surface; here the shape would seem to be triangular.
3. Sharp, quick to see.
4. Perhaps to "ring" with light.

Light, Life, and Glory, things that are Divine;
 I shall be graced withall for glory fit.
 My heart then stuffed with Grace, Light, Life, and Glee   35
 I'll sacrifice in Flames of Love to Thee.

March 6, 1686   1960

Meditation 22 (First Series)

Philippians 2.9. God hath highly exalted Him.[1]

When Thy Bright Beams, my Lord, do strike mine Eye,
 Methinks I then could truly Chide outright
My Hide-bound Soul that stands so niggardly
 That scarce a thought gets glorified by't.
 My Quaintest[2] metaphors are ragged Stuff,   5
 Making the Sun seem like a Mullipuff.[3]

It's my desire, Thou shouldst be glorified:
 But when Thy Glory shines before mine eye,
I pardon Crave, lest my desire be Pride,
 Or bed Thy Glory in a Cloudy Sky.   10
 The Sun grows wan; and Angels palefaced shrink,
 Before Thy Shine, which I besmear with Ink.

But shall the Bird sing forth Thy Praise, and shall
 The little Bee present her thankful Hum?
But I who see Thy shining Glory fall   15
 Before mine Eyes, stand Blockish, Dull, and Dumb?
 Whether I speak, or speechless stand, I spy,
 I fail Thy Glory: therefore pardon Cry.

But this I find; My Rhymes do better suit
 Mine own Dispraise than tune forth praise to Thee.   20
Yet being Chid, whether Consonant,[4] or Mute,
 I force my Tongue to tattle, as You see.
 That I Thy glorious Praise may Trumpet right,
 Be Thou my Song, and make, Lord, me Thy pipe.

This shining Sky will fly away apace,   25
 When Thy bright Glory splits the same to make
Thy Majesty a Pass, whose Fairest Face
 Too foul a Path is for Thy Feet to take.
 What Glory then, shall tend Thee through the Sky
 Draining the Heaven much of Angels dry?   30

1. "Let this mind be in you, which was also in Christ Jesus: Who, being in the form of God, thought it not robbery to be equal with God: But made himself no reputation, and took upon him the form of a servant, and was made in the likeness of men: And being found in fashion as a man, he humbled himself, and became obedient unto death, even the death of the cross. Wherefore God also hath highly exalted him, and given him a name which is above every name: That at the name of Jesus every knee should bow, of things in heaven, and things in earth, and things under the earth; And that every tongue should confess that Jesus Christ is Lord, to the glory of God the Father" (Philippians 2.5–11).
2. Most skilled, wise.
3. Fuzz ball.
4. Talkative, making sounds.

What Light then flame will in Thy Judgment Seat,
    'Fore which all men and Angels shall appear?
How shall Thy Glorious Righteousness them treat,
    Rend'ring to each after his Works done here?
    Then Saints with Angels Thou wilt glorify: 35
    And burn Lewd[5] Men, and Devils Gloriously.

One glimpse, my Lord, of Thy bright Judgment Day,
    And Glory piercing through, like fiery Darts,
All Devils, doth me make for Grace to pray,
    For filling Grace had I ten thousand Hearts.   40
    I'd through ten Hells to see Thy Judgment Day
    Wouldst Thou but gild my Soul with Thy bright Ray.

June 12, 1687   1960

Meditation 38 (First Series)

1 John 2.1. An Advocate with the Father.[1]

Oh! What a thing is Man? Lord, Who am I?
    That Thou shouldst give him Law (Oh! golden line)[2]
To regulate his Thoughts, Words, Life thereby.
    And judge him Wilt thereby too in Thy time.
    A Court of Justice Thou in Heaven holdst   5
    To try his Case while he's here housed on mold.[3]

How do Thy Angels lay before Thine eye
    My Deeds both White and Black I daily do?
How doth Thy Court Thou Panelist[4] there them try?
    But flesh complains. What right for this? let's know.   10
    For right, or wrong I can't appear unto't.
    And shall a sentence Pass on such a suit?

Soft; blemish not this golden Bench, or place.
    Here is no Bribe, nor Colorings[5] to hide,
Nor Pettifogger[6] to befog the Case,   15
    But Justice hath Her Glory here well tried.
    Her spotless Law all spotted Cases tends.
    Without Respect or Disrespect them ends.

God's Judge Himself: and Christ Attorney is,
    The Holy Ghost Registerer[7] is found.   20
Angels the Sergeants[8] are, all Creatures kiss
    The Book, and do as Evidences[9] abound.

5. Worthless, fallen.
1. "And if any man sin, we have an advocate with the Father, Jesus Christ the righteous: And he is the propitiation for our sins: and not for ours only, but also for the sins of the whole world" (1 John 2.1–2).
2. "Law": i.e., the Ten Commandments set forth in the Old Testament prescribing our behavior. This inheritance is our "golden line," or lineage.
3. I.e., the body will decay; only the soul is immortal.
4. I.e., impanel, as a jury.
5. Deceitful appearances.
6. Lawyer who handles trivial cases and is given to professional tricks and quibblings.
7. I.e., registrar, court recorder and keeper of records.
8. Attendants at court who maintain order.
9. Witnesses.

All Cases pass according to pure Law
And in the sentence is no Fret,[1] nor flaw.

What sayst, my Soul? Here all thy Deeds are tried.   25
    Is Christ thy Advocate to plead thy Cause?
Art thou His Client? Such shall never slide.
    He never lost His Case: He pleads such Laws
    As Carry do the same, nor doth refuse
    The Vilest sinner's Case that doth Him Choose.   30

This is His honor, not Dishonor: nay,
    No Habeas-Corpus[2] against His Clients came.
For all their Fines His Purse doth make down pay.
    He Non-Suits Satan's Suit or Casts[3] the Same.
    He'll plead thy Case, and not accept a Fee.   35
    He'll plead Sub Forma Pauperis[4] for thee.

My Case is bad. Lord, be my Advocate.
    My sin is red: I'm under God's Arrest.
Thou hast the Hint of Pleading; plead my State.
    Although it's bad Thy Plea will make it best.   40
    If Thou wilt plead my Case before the King:
    I'll Wagonloads of Love and Glory bring.

July 6, 1690   1939

Meditation 42 (First Series)

Revelation 3.21. I will give Him to sit with Me in my Throne.[1]

Apples of gold, in silver pictures shrined[2]
    Enchant the appetite, make mouths to water.
And Loveliness in Lumps, tunn'd, and enrined[3]
    In Jasper[4] Cask, when tapped, doth briskly vapor:
    Bring forth a birth of Keys t'unlock Love's Chest,   5
    That Love, like Birds, may fly to't from its nest.

Such is my Lord, and more. But what strange thing
    Am I become? Sin rusts my Lock all o'er.
Though He ten thousand Keys all on a string
    Takes out, scarce one is found unlocks the Door.   10

---

1. Malice, ill will.
2. You should have the body (Latin, literal trans.), i.e., no person may be kept in jail without the charge against him or her being quickly brought before a judge. Christ's clients are brought to trial immediately; he has himself paid for humanity's sins with his Crucifixion and covered their fines with his own blood.
3. Dismisses. He stops a suit because of insufficient evidence.
4. According to form of poverty (Latin, literal trans.), a procedure in which an impoverished person is able to sue another without threat of costs in the event that the case should be lost.

1. "To him that overcometh will I grant to sit with me in my throne, even as I also overcame, and am set down with my Father in his throne. He that hath an ear, let him hear what the Spirit saith unto the churches" (Revelation 3.21–22).
2. Enshrined, enclosed.
3. Rendered, melted down. "Tunn'd": placed in a casket.
4. A precious stone, usually green in color.

Which ope, my Love crinched[5] in a Corner lies
Like some shrunk Crickling[6] and scarce can rise.

Lord, ope the Door: rub off my Rust, Remove
My sin, and Oil my Lock. (Dust there doth shelf).
My Wards will trig[7] before Thy Key: my Love   15
Then, as enlivened, leap will on Thyself.
It needs must be, that giving hands receive
Again Receivers Hearts furled in Love Wreath.

Unkey my Heart; unlock Thy Wardrobe: bring
Out royal Robes: adorn my Soul, Lord: so,   20
My Love in rich attire shall on my King
Attend, and honor on Him well bestow.
In Glory He prepares for His a place
Whom He doth all beglory here with Grace.

He takes them to the shining threshold clear   25
Of His bright Palace, clothed in Grace's flame.
Then takes them in thereto, not only there
To have a Prospect,[8] but possess the same.
The Crown of Life, the throne of Glory's Place,
The Father's House blanched o'er with orient Grace.   30

Canaan[9] in gold print enwalled with gems:
A Kingdom rimmed with Glory round: in fine[1]
A glorious Crown paled[2] thick with all the stems
Of Grace, and of all Properties Divine.
How happy wilt Thou make me when these shall   35
As a blest Heritage unto me fall?

Adorn me, Lord, with Holy Huswifry.[3]
All blanch my Robes with Clusters of Thy Graces:
Thus lead me to Thy threshold: give mine Eye
A Peephole there to see Bright Glory's Chases.[4]   40
Then take me in: I'll pay, when I possess
Thy Throne, to Thee the Rent in Happiness.

August 2, 1691   1939

---

5. Shrunken, gnarled up.
6. Properly "crinkling," a small, withered apple.
7. Open. "Wards": the protective ridges of a lock that prevent any but the proper key to open it.
8. View, range of vision.
9. The land promised by God to Abraham; the biblical name of Jerusalem (cf. Genesis 12.5–8).
1. In essence.
2. Striped.
3. Cloth woven in the home, and the traditional task of the housewife.
4. The settings of precious stones.

Meditation 26 (Second Series)

Hebrews 9.13–14. How much more shall the Blood of Christ, etc.[1]

Unclean, Unclean: My Lord, Undone, all vile,
    Yea, all Defiled: What shall Thy Servant do?
Unfit for Thee: not fit for holy Soil,
    Nor for Communion of Saints[2] below.
    A bag of botches, Lump of Loathsomeness: 5
    Defiled by Touch, by Issue: Leproused flesh.

Thou wilt have all that enter to Thy fold
    Pure, Clean, and bright, Whiter than whitest Snow
Better refined than most refined Gold:
    I am not so: but foul: What shall I do?   10
    Shall Thy Church Doors be shut, and shut out me?
    Shall not Church Fellowship my portion be?

How can it be? Thy Churches do require
    Pure Holiness: I am all filth, alas!
Shall I defile them, tumbled thus in mire?   15
    Or they me cleanse before I current pass?[3]
    If thus they do, Where is the Nitre[4] bright
    And Soap they offer me to wash me White?

The brisk Red heifer's Ashes, when calcined,[5]
    Mixed all in running Water, is too Weak   20
To wash away my Filth: The Doves assigned
    Burnt and Sin Offerings ne'er do the feat
    But[6] as they Emblemize the Fountain Spring
    Thy Blood, my Lord, set ope to wash off Sin.

Oh! richest Grace! Are Thy Rich Veins then tapped   25
    To ope this Holy Fountain (boundless sea)
For Sinners here to laver[7] off (all sapped
    With Sin) their Sins and Sinfulness away?
    In this bright Crystal Crimson Fountain flows
    What washeth whiter than the Swan or Rose.   30

Oh! wash me, Lord, in this Choice Fountain, White
    That I may enter, and not sully here
Thy Church, whose floor is paved with Graces bright
    And hold Church Fellowship with Saints most clear.
    My Voice all sweet, with their melodious lays   35
    Shall make sweet Music blossomed with Thy praise.

June 26, 1698   1960

---

1. "For if the blood of bulls and of goats, and the ashes of an heifer sprinkling the unclean, sanctifieth to the purifying of the flesh: How much more shall the blood of Christ, who through the eternal Spirit offered himself without spot to God, purge your conscience from dead works to serve the living God?" (Hebrews 9.13–14).

2. "Visible saints," i.e., living church members.

3. I.e., pass accepted.

4. Potassium nitrate, used in whitening.

5. Burned.

6. Except, i.e., the sacrificial doves cannot cleanse his soul, but their blood serves as a symbol of ("emblemizes") the power of Christ's blood to wash us clean.

7. Wash.

FROM GOD'S DETERMINATIONS[1]

The Preface

Infinity, when all things it beheld
In Nothing, and of Nothing all did build,
Upon what Base was fixed the Lath wherein
He turned this Globe, and riggalled[2] it so trim?
Who blew the Bellows of His Furnace Vast?   5
Or held the Mold wherein the world was Cast?
Who laid its Corner Stone?[3] Or whose Command?
Where stand the Pillars upon which it stands?
Who Laced and Filleted[4] the earth so fine,
With Rivers like green Ribbons Smaragdine?[5]   10
Who made the Sea's its Selvage,[6] and its locks
Like a Quilt Ball[7] within a Silver Box?
Who Spread its Canopy? Or Curtains Spun?
Who in this Bowling Alley bowled the Sun?
Who made it always when it rises set   15
To go at once both down, and up to get?
Who th' Curtain rods made for this Tapestry?
Who hung the twinkling Lanthorns in the Sky?
Who? who did this? or who is He? Why, know
It's Only Might Almighty this did do.   20
His hand hath made this noble work which Stands
His Glorious Handiwork not made by hands.
Who spake all things from Nothing; and with ease
Can speak all things to Nothing, if He please.
Whose Little finger at His pleasure Can   25
Out mete[8] ten thousand worlds with half a Span:
Whose Might Almighty can by half a looks
Root up the rocks and rock the hills by the'roots.
Can take this mighty World up in His hand,
And shake it like a Squitchen[9] or a Wand.   30
Whose single Frown will make the Heavens shake
Like as an aspen leaf the Wind makes quake.
Oh! what a might is this Whose single frown

1. The subject of this "debate" poem is made clear in the full title: *God's determinations touching His Elect: and the Elect's combat in their conversion, and coming up to God in Christ, together with the comfortable effects thereof.* In this group of poems Taylor explores the progress of the human soul from the creation of the world and the fall from Grace to the redemption of the Christian soul through Christ's Crucifixion: Christ's mercy triumphs over justice—the punishment that humanity deserves for disobedience—and the soul is finally carried to heaven to share in the joys of the Resurrection. The text used here is from *Poems of Edward Taylor,* edited by Donald E. Stanford (1960).
2. Grooved.
3. "Where wast thou when I laid the foundations of the earth? declare, if thou hast understanding. Who hath laid the measures thereof, if thou knowest? or who hath stretched the line upon it? Whereupon are the foundations thereof fastened? or who laid the corner stone thereof; When the morning stars sang together, and all the sons of God shouted for joy? Or who shut up the sea with doors, when it brake forth, as if it had issued out of the womb?" (Job 38.4–8).
4. Encircled, bound around.
5. Emerald green.
6. The border of woven material that prevents unraveling.
7. A ball of wool that would unravel if it were not kept in a box.
8. Outmeasure.
9. Switch.

Doth shake the world as it would shake it down?
Which All from Nothing fet,[1] from Nothing, All: 35
Hath All on Nothing set, lets Nothing fall.
Gave All to Nothing Man indeed, whereby
Through Nothing man all might Him Glorify.
In Nothing then embossed the brightest Gem
More precious than all preciousness in them.   40
But Nothing man did throw down all by Sin:
And darkened that lightsome Gem in him.
      That now his Brightest Diamond is grown
      Darker by far than any Coalpit Stone.

c. 1685   1939

The Soul's Groan to Christ for Succor

Good Lord, behold this Dreadful Enemy
      Who makes me tremble with his fierce assaults;
I dare not trust, yet fear to give the lie,
      For in my soul, my soul finds many faults
      And though I justify myself to's face: 5
      I do Condemn myself before Thy Grace.

He strives to mount my sins, and them advance
      Above Thy Merits, Pardons, or Good Will
Thy Grace to lessen, and Thy Wrath t'enhance
      As if Thou couldst not pay the sinner's bill.   10
      He Chiefly injures Thy rich Grace, I find,
      Though I confess my heart to sin inclined.

Those Graces which Thy Grace enwrought in me,
      He makes as nothing but a pack of Sins.
He maketh Grace no grace, but Cruelty;   15
      Is Grace's Honeycomb a Comb of Stings?
      This makes me ready leave Thy Grace and run.
      Which if I do, I find I am undone.

I know he is Thy Cur, therefore I be
      Perplexed lest I from Thy Pasture stray.   20
He bays, and barks so veh'mently at me.
      Come rate[1] this Cur, Lord, break his teeth, I pray.
      Remember me, I humbly pray Thee first.
      Then halter up this Cur that is so Cursed.

c. 1685   1939

---

1. Made.   1. Give reproof, specifically, to a dog.

Christ's Reply

Peace, Peace, my Honey, do not Cry,
My Little Darling, wipe thine eye,
　　Oh Cheer, Cheer up, come see.
Is anything too dear,[1] my Dove,
Is anything too good, my Love,　　　　　　　　　　　5
　　To get or give for thee?

If in the several[2] thou art,
This Yelper fierce will at thee bark:
　　That thou art Mine this shows.
As Spot barks back the sheep again　　　　　　　　10
Before they to the Pound are ta'en,
　　So he and hence 'way goes.

But yet this Cur that bays so sore
Is broken-toothed, and muzzled sure,
　　Fear not, my Pretty Heart.　　　　　　　　　　　15
His barking is to make thee Cling
Close underneath thy Savior's Wing.
　　Why did my sweeten[3] start?

And if he run an inch too far,
I'll Check his Chain, and rate[4] the Cur.　　　　　　20
　　My Chick, keep close to me.
The Poles shall sooner kiss, and greet
And Parallels shall sooner meet
　　Than thou shalt harmed be.

He seeks to aggravate thy sin　　　　　　　　　　　25
And screw them to the highest pin,
　　To make thy faith to quail.
Yet mountain Sins like mites should show
And then these mites for naught should go
　　Could he but once prevail.　　　　　　　　　　　30

I smote thy sins upon the Head.
They Deadened are, though not quite dead:
　　And shall not rise again.
I'll put away the Guilt thereof,
And purge its Filthiness clear off　　　　　　　　　35
　　My Blood doth out the stain.

And though thy judgment was remiss
Thy Headstrong Will too willful is.
　　I will Renew the same.
And though thou do too frequently　　　　　　　　40

1. Difficult to get; expensive.
2. Divided, in the sense that the soul is torn between Christ and the Devil.
3. Beloved.
4. Give reproof, specifically, to a dog.

Offend as heretofore hereby,
　　I'll not severely blame.

And though thy senses do inveigle
Thy Noble Soul to tend the Beagle,
　　That t'hunt her games forth go,
I'll Lure her back to me, and Change
Those fond Affections that do range
　　As yelping beagles do.

Although thy sins increase their race,
And though when thou hast sought for Grace,
　　Thou fallst more than before,
If thou by true Repentence Rise,
And Faith makes Me Thy Sacrifice,
　　I'll pardon all, though more.

Though Satan strive to block thy way
By all his Stratagems he may:
　　Come, come though through the fire.
For Hell that Gulf of fire for sins,
Is not so hot as t'burn thy Shins.
　　Then Credit not the Liar.

Those Cursed Vermin Sins that Crawl
All o'er thy Soul, both Great and small,
　　Are only Satan's own:
Which he in his Malignity
Unto thy Soul's true Sanctity
　　In at the doors hath thrown.

And though they be Rebellion high,
Ath'ism or Apostasy;
　　Though blasphemy it be:
Unto what Quality, or Size
Excepting one, so e'er it rise.
　　Repent, I'll pardon thee.

Although thy Soul was once a Stall⁵
Rich hung with Satan's nicknacks all;
　　If thou Repent thy sin,
A Tabernacle in't I'll place
Filled with God's Spirit, and His Grace.
　　Oh, Comfortable thing!

I dare the World therefore to show
A God like Me, to anger slow:
　　Whose wrath is full of Grace.
Doth hate all Sins both Great and small:
Yet when Repented, pardons all.
　　Frowns with a Smiling Face.

5. A small booth in which things are sold.

As for thy outward Postures each,   85
Thy Gestures, Actions, and thy Speech,
   I Eye and Eying spare,
If thou repent. My Grace is more
Ten thousand times still trebled o'er
   Than thou canst want, or wear.   90

As for the Wicked Charge he makes,
That he of Every Dish first takes
   Of all thy holy things,
It's false, deny the same, and say,
That which he had he stole away   95
   Out of thy Offerings.[6]

Though to thy Grief, poor Heart, thou find
In Prayer too oft a wandering mind,
   In Sermons Spirits dull,
Though faith in fiery furnace flags,   100
And Zeal in Chilly Seasons lags,
   Temptation's powerful.

These faults are his, and none of thine
So far as thou dost them decline.
   Come, then receive My Grace.   105
And when he buffets thee therefore,
If thou My aid and Grace implore,
   I'll show a pleasant face.

But still look for Temptations Deep,
Whilst that thy Noble Spark doth keep   110
   Within a Mudwalled Cote.[7]
These White Frosts and the Showers that fall
Are but to whiten thee withall,
   Not rot the Web they smote.

If in the fire where Gold is tried   115
Thy Soul is put, and purified,
   Wilt thou lament thy loss?
If silver-like this fire refine
Thy Soul and make it brighter shine:
   Wilt thou bewail the Dross?   120

Oh! fight My Field: no Colors fear:
I'll be thy Front, I'll be thy rear.
   Fail not: My Battles fight.
Defy the Tempter, and his Mock.
Anchor thy heart on Me thy Rock.   125
   I do in thee Delight.

c. 1685   1939

6. Satan argues that humanity does nothing in a disinterested way for the love of God but only from the fear of hell. Christ argues that the soul should affirm its generous impulses and put Satan in his place.
7. Cottage.

The Joy of Church Fellowship Rightly Attended[1]

In Heaven soaring up, I dropped an Ear
    On Earth: and oh! sweet Melody!
And listening, found it was the Saints[2] who were
    Encoached for Heaven that sang for Joy.
    For in Christ's Coach they sweetly sing;   5
    As they to Glory ride therein.

Oh! joyous hearts! Enfired with holy Flame!
    Is speech thus tasseléd[3] with praise?
Will not your inward fire of Joy contain:
    That it in open flames doth blaze?   10
    For in Christ's Coach Saints sweetly sing,
    As they to Glory ride therein.

And if a string do slip, by Chance, they soon
    Do screw it up again; whereby
They set it in a more melodious Tune   15
    And a Diviner Harmony.
    For in Christ's Coach they sweetly sing
    As they to Glory ride therein.

In all their Acts, public, and private, nay
    And secret, too, they praise impart.   20
But in their Acts Divine and Worship, they
    With Hymns do offer up their Heart.
    Thus in Christ's Coach they sweetly sing
    As they to Glory ride therein.

Some few not in;[4] and some whose Time and Place   25
    Block up this Coach's way do go
As Travelers afoot, and so do trace
    The Road that gives them right thereto;
    While in this Coach these sweetly sing
    As they to Glory ride therein.   30

c. 1685   1939

Upon Wedlock, and Death of Children[1]

A Curious Knot[2] God made in Paradise,
    And drew it out enameled[3] neatly Fresh.
It was the True-Love Knot, more sweet than spice,
    And set with all the flowers of Grace's dress.

---

1. The final poem in *God's Determinations*.
2. I.e., "visible saints," those who were church members when alive.
3. Ornamented, in the sense in which tassels might be applied to a piece of fabric.
4. I.e., those who are saved but are outside the church.

1. The text used here is from *Poems of Edward Taylor*, edited by Donald E. Stanford (1960).
2. Flower bed.
3. Polished, shining.

It's Wedden's[4] Knot, that ne're can be untied: 5
No Alexander's Sword[5] can it divide.

The slips[6] here planted, gay and glorious grow:
    Unless an Hellish breath do singe their Plumes.
Here Primrose, Cowslips, Roses, Lilies blow[7]
    With Violets and Pinks that void[8] perfumes: 10
    Whose beauteous leaves o'erlaid with Honey Dew,
    And Chanting birds Chirp out sweet Music true.

When in this Knot I planted was, my Stock[9]
    Soon knotted, and a manly flower out brake.[1]
And after it, my branch again did knot,   15
    Brought out another Flower, its sweet-breathed mate.
    One knot gave one tother[2] the tother's place.
    Whence Chuckling smiles fought in each other's face.

But Oh! a glorious hand from glory came
    Guarded with Angels, soon did crop this flower[3]   20
Which almost tore the root up of the same,
    At that unlooked for, Dolesome, darksome hour.
    In Prayer to Christ perfumed it did ascend,
    And Angels bright did it to heaven 'tend.

But pausing on't, this sweet perfumed my thought: 25
    Christ would in Glory have a Flower, Choice, Prime,
And having Choice, chose this my branch forth brought.
    Lord take't. I thank Thee, Thou tak'st ought of mine:
    It is my pledge in glory, part of me
    Is now in it, Lord, glorified with Thee.   30

But praying o're my branch, my branch did sprout,
    And bore another manly flower, and gay,[4]
And after that another, sweet brake[5] out,
    The which the former hand soon got away.
    But Oh! the tortures, Vomit, screechings, groans,   35
    and six week's Fever would pierce hearts like stones.[6]

Grief o're doth flow: and nature fault would find
    Were not Thy Will, my Spell, Charm, Joy, and Gem:
That as I said, I say, take, Lord, they're Thine.
    I piecemeal pass to Glory bright in them.   40
    In joy, may I sweet flowers for glory breed,
    Whether thou get'st them green, or lets them seed.

c. 1682   1939

4. I.e., wedding's.
5. Alexander the Great cut the Gordian knot devised by the king of Phyrgia when he learned that anyone who could undo it would rule Asia.
6. Cuttings.
7. Bloom.
8. Emit.
9. Stem.
1. Samuel Taylor was born on August 27, 1675, and lived to maturity.
2. To the other.
3. Elizabeth Taylor was born on December 27, 1676, and died on December 25, 1677.
4. James Taylor was born on October 12, 1678, and lived to maturity.
5. I.e., broke out.
6. Abigail Taylor was born on August 6, 1681, and died on August 22, 1682.

[When] Let by Rain[1]

Ye Flippering[2] Soul,
    Why dost between the Nippers[3] dwell?
Not stay, Nor go. Not yea, nor yet Control.
    Doth This do well?
        Rise journey'ng when the skies fall weeping Showers.   5
        Not o'er nor under th'Clouds and Cloudy Powers.

Not yea, nor no:
    On tiptoes thus? Why sit on thorns?
Resolve the matter: Stay thyself or go.
    Be n't both ways borne.   10
        Wager thyself against thy surplice,[4] see,
        And win thy Coat: or let thy Coat Win thee.

Is this th'Effect,
    To leaven[5] thus my Spirits all?
To make my heart a Crabtree Cask direct?   15
    A Verjuiced[6] Hall?
        As Bottle Ale, whose Spirits prisoned nursed[7]
        When jogged, the bung[8] with Violence doth burst?

Shall I be made
    A sparkling Wildfire Shop   20
Where my dull Spirits at the Fireball trade[9]
    Do frisk and hop?
        And while the Hammer doth the Anvil pay,
        The fireball matter sparkles ev'ry way.

One sorry fret,[1]   25
    An anvil Spark, rose higher,
And in Thy Temple falling almost set
    The house on fire.
        Such fireballs dropping in the Temple Flame
        Burns up the building: Lord forbid the same.   30

1939

1. The text used here is from *Poems of Edward Taylor*, edited by Donald E. Stanford (1960). "Let": prevented, hindered.
2. Hesitant, indecisive.
3. Iron forcepslike instrument.
4. Outer garment.
5. Ferment.
6. Soured. Verjuice is the acid juice of green or unripe grapes.
7. Cultured, brought up.
8. Cork, stopper.
9. I.e., the blacksmith's trade. Taylor goes on to suggest that the soul is like hot metal, and when struck by the blacksmith's hammer it sends sparks flying and is thus like a "wildfire shop."
1. Irritation of mind, vexation; compared here to a spark from the blacksmith's anvil.

Upon a Wasp Chilled with Cold[1]

The Bear that breathes the Northern blast[2]
Did numb, Torpedo-like,[3] a Wasp
Whose stiffened limbs encramped, lay bathing
In Sol's[4] warm breath and shine as saving,
Which with her hands she chafes and stands   5
Rubbing her Legs, Shanks, Thighs, and hands.
Her petty toes, and fingers' ends
Nipped with this breath, she out extends
Unto the Sun, in great desire
To warm her digits at that fire.   10
Doth hold her Temples in this state
Where pulse doth beat, and head doth ache.
Doth turn, and stretch her body small,
Doth Comb her velvet Capital.[5]
As if her little brain pan were   15
A Volume of Choice precepts clear.
As if her satin jacket hot
Contained Apothecary's Shop
Of Nature's receipts,[6] that prevails
To remedy all her sad ails,   20
As if her velvet helmet high
Did turret[7] rationality.
She fans her wing up to the Wind
As if her Pettycoat were lined,
With reason's fleece, and hoists sails   25
And humming flies in thankful gales
Unto her dun Curled[8] palace Hall
Her warm thanks offering for all.

    Lord, clear my misted sight that I
May hence view Thy Divinity,   30
Some sparks whereof Thou up dost hasp[9]
Within this little downy Wasp
In whose small Corporation[1] we
A school and a schoolmaster see,
Where we may learn, and easily find   35
A nimble Spirit bravely mind
Her work in every limb: and lace
It up neat with a vital grace,
Acting each part though ne'er so small
Here of this Fustian[2] animal,   40
Till I enravished Climb into

---

1. The text used here is from *Poems of Edward Taylor*, edited by Donald E. Stanford (1960).
2. The northern constellation the Big Dipper, also called Ursa Major, or the Great Bear.
3. The torpedo is a fish, like a stingray, and discharges a shock to one who touches it, causing numbness. Sir Thomas Browne writes: "Torpedoes deliver their opium at a distance and stupify beyond themselves" (1646).
4. The sun personified.
5. Head.
6. Remedies, prescriptions. "Apothecary's Shop": what we would now call a drugstore or pharmacy.
7. Contain, encompass.
8. Dark curved.
9. Enclose, confine.
1. Body.
2. Coarse-clothed.

The Godhead on this Ladder do,
Where all my pipes inspired upraise
An Heavenly music furred[3] with praise.

1960

Huswifery[1]

Make me, O Lord, Thy Spinning Wheel complete.
    Thy Holy Word my Distaff make for me.
Make mine Affections Thy Swift Flyers neat
    And make my Soul Thy holy Spool to be.
    My conversation make to be Thy Reel   5
    And reel the yarn thereon spun of Thy Wheel.[2]

Make me Thy Loom then, knit therein this Twine:
    And make Thy Holy Spirit, Lord, wind quills:[3]
Then weave the Web Thyself. The yarn is fine.
    Thine Ordinances make my Fulling Mills.[4]   10
    Then dye the same in Heavenly Colors Choice,
    All pinked with Varnished[5] Flowers of Paradise.

Then clothe therewith mine Understanding, Will,
    Affections, Judgment, Conscience, Memory,
My Words, and Actions, that their shine may fill   15
    My ways with glory and Thee glorify.
    Then mine apparel shall display before Ye
    That I am Clothed in Holy robes for glory.

1939

A Fig for Thee, Oh! Death[1]

Thou King of Terrors with thy Ghastly eyes,
With Butter[2] teeth, bare bones, Grim looks likewise,
And Grizzly hide, and clawing Talons fell,[3]
Op'ning to Sinners Vile, Trap Door of Hell,
That on in Sin impenitently trip,   5
The Downfall[4] art of the infernal Pit,

---

3. Trimmed or embellished, as with fur.
1. Housekeeping: used here to mean weaving. In Taylor's *Treatise Concerning the Lord's Supper* (see p. 362) he considers the significance of the sacrament of communion and takes as his text a passage from the New Testament: "And he saith unto him, Friend, how camest thou in hither not having a wedding garment? And he was speechless" (Matthew 22.12). Taylor argues that the wedding garment is the proper sign of the regenerate Christian. The text used here is from *Poems of Edward Taylor,* edited by Donald E. Stanford (1960).
2. In the lines above Taylor refers to the working parts of a spinning wheel: the "distaff" holds the raw wool or flax; the "flyers" regulate the spinning; the "spool" twists the yarn; and the "reel" takes up the finished thread.
3. I.e., be like a spool or bobbin.
4. Where cloth is beaten and cleansed with fuller's earth, or soap.
5. Glossy, sparkling. "Pinked": adorned.
1. A fig is anything that is valueless, small, and contemptible. The text used here is from *Poems of Edward Taylor,* edited by Donald E. Stanford (1960).
2. Yellow.
3. Deadly.
4. Descending precipice.

Thou struck'st thy teeth deep in my Lord's bless'd side:
Who dashed it out, and all its venom 'stroyed[5]
That now thy Pounderall[6] shall only dash
My Flesh and bones to bits, and Cask shall clash.[7]   10
Thou'rt not so frightful now to me, thy knocks
Do crack my shell. Its Heavenly kernel's box
Abides most safe. Thy blows do break its shell,
Thy Teeth its Nut. Cracks are that on it fell.
Thence out its kernel fair and nut, by worms   15
Once Vitiated out, new formed forth turns
And on the wings of some bright Angel flies
Out to bright glory of God's blissful joys.
Hence thou to me with all thy Ghastly face
Art not so dreadful unto me through Grace.   20
I am resolved to fight thee, and ne'er yield,
Blood up to th'Ears; and in the battlefield
Chasing thee hence. But not for this, my flesh;
My Body, my vile harlot, it's thy Mess,[8]
Laboring to drown me into Sin's disguise   25
By Eating and by drinking, such evil joys—
Though Grace preserved me that I ne'er have
Surprised been nor tumbled in such grave.[9]
Hence for my strumpet I'll ne'er draw my Sword,
Nor thee restrain at all by Iron curb,   30
Nor for her safety will I 'gainst thee strive,
But let thy frozen grips take her Captive
And her imprison in thy dungeon Cave
And grind to powder in thy Mill the grave,
Which powder in thy Van[1] thou'st safely keep   35
Till she hath slept out quite her fatal Sleep.
When the last Cock shall Crow the Last Day[2] in,
And the Archangel's Trumpet's sound shall ring,
Then th'Eye Omniscient seek shall all there round,
Each dust death's mill had very finely ground,   40
Which in death's smoky furnace well refined
And Each to 'ts fellow hath exactly joined,
Is raised up anew and made all bright
And Crystallized; all topfull of delight,
And entertains its Soul again in bliss,   45
And Holy Angels waiting all on this,
The Soul and Body now, as two true lovers,
E'ry night how do they hug and kiss each other.
And going hand in hand thus through the skies
Up to Eternal glory glorious rise.   50
Is this the Worst thy terrors then canst, why
Then should this grimace at me terrify?
Why cam'st thou then so slowly? Mend thy pace.

5. Destroyed.
6. Pestle.
7. I.e., his body will feel the resounding blow.
8. Dinner.
9. Taylor made two versions of this poem. In the first version these difficult lines (24–28) are made clearer: "My harlot body, make thou it thy mess, / That oft ensnared me with its strumpet's guise / Of meat's and drink's dainty sensualities. / Yet grace ne'er suffer[ed] me to turn aside / As sinners oft fall in and do abide."
1. Winnowing basket, used to separate chaff from the grain.
2. I.e., when Judgment Day comes.

Thy Slowness me detains from Christ's bright face.
Although thy terrors rise to th'highst degree,   55
I still am where I was. A Fig for thee.

                                                              1960

From Treatise Concerning the Lord's Supper[1]

From Sermon VI

Doctrine: *There is no reason of approaching to the wedden feast, without the wedden garment.*

Touching these positive helps, they are such as tend to put the soul into a due state to be informed, and to receive information in its trying itself, and therefore:

You are to shrive your will and affections of all their own conclusions made beforehand of things. You stand not in a receptive frame unto the truth to be discovered, while you are prepossessed with your own persuasions. Oftentimes persons rivet their affections to raw notions picked up out of some cursory expressions let fall by such as never well concocted the same: and being thus received, they prejudice the truth and forestall the soul, that such discoveries as strike against such espoused notions will in no wise gain acceptance. For such notions frequently are with them as true as gospel; nay, and are made the standards of the market to measure all things by. And such things as will not receive countenance therefrom must be chased away, as faulty. Hence in your trying of yourselves you must shake off all such things prejudicial to truth from your wills and affections, or it is to be feared your search will be in vain. It is a snare to a man after vows to make inquiry (Proverbs 20.25). Therefore in thy search put thyself into a receptive capacity unto truth to be discovered.

You are to clear up the light of your eyes. Get clear glasses. Use good spectacles. Avoid raw notions that, like ill-concocted matter, send gross vapors into the ventricles of the brain, and so cloud the head. But get a clear head: be well insighted into the nature of the matter before you. Remove the beam,[2] mote, or gravel out of thine eye (Matthew 7.5).[3] Anoint thine eyes with Christ's eye salve (Revelation 3.18),[4] and this lies in getting a clear sight in:

The rule: and this is the holy scriptures. The thing to be tried must be brought to the rule. The trial itself lieth in two things: viz., the laying the thing to be tried unto the rule, according to which it ought to be squared; and the determination made by the conformity it hath unto the rule. Hence get good insight into the rule. Study the scriptures.

The wedden garment. For your judgment being to be made whether this

1. Edited by Norman S. Grabo (1966). Taylor prepared eight untitled sermons on the subject of the sacrament of communion and completed them in 1694. He took as his text the parable of the wedding feast in Matthew: "And he saith unto him, Friend, how camest thou in hither not having a wedding garment? And he was speechless" (Matthew 22.12). Taylor argues that the garment referred to is the sign of the garment of righteousness, the garment worn by the regenerate Christian.

2. An irritating particle in the eye.
3. "Thou hypocrite, first cast out the beam out of thine own eye; and then shalt thou see clearly to cast out the mote out of thy brother's eye."
4. "I counsel thee to buy of me gold tried in the fire, that thou mayest be rich; and white raiment, that thou mayest be clothed, and that the shame of thy nakedness do not appear; and anoint thine eyes with eyesalve, that thou mayest see."

is yours, you must have a clear insight into the nature of it, that wherever you see it you may be able to say, this is it, whether in yourselves or in others. Therefore endeavor to be well insighted in the nature of this wedden garment, and that in these things:

As to the matter it is made on. And this you have heard to be the grace of God as saving, and therefore both inherent, as the sanctifying grace of God's Spirit, as you have had it evidenced unto you, and the adherent grace of God, viz., imputed righteousness of Christ. Hence you must get a true knowledge of the nature of every grace, that so you may discern them in the web. You must know what faith is, what humility is, what hope is, what patience is, what repentance is, etc. For these are some of the fine twine of the Spirit that are woven into this web.

*   *   *

* * * Where the wedden garment is, there there is an exercise of these two properties incessantly as that of invincible hatred and love.

Invincible hatred. Now hatred is a virtue, its object hateful, viz., whatever is contrary to this wedden garment. It is so choice of it, that whatever tends to defile it hath the irreconcilable enmity of the soul rising up against it: all the enchantments of hell cannot charm this enmity. It is the property of all to be offended at what defiles his best apparel. So it is here: it's the property of the soul in the wedden garment to be utterly wroth with all array contrary to it, and all things, whatever do defile it. There is nothing can defile it but sin: there is nothing contrary to it but sin. Hence the soul that hath it hates sin. He is called to it, Psalm 97.10. Hate the very garment spotted with the flesh (Jude 23). Such as have this garment reply to this call: I hate every false way; I hate vain thoughts; I hate and abhor lying. Well then here lies the trial of the case. Dost thou hate sin? Dost thou hate sin as it is defiling thy garments? Dost thou hate sin as sin? Because it makes unclean, and unlike God? This is a casting[5] note. But if thou hatest it, thou watchest against it, keepest far from it, repentest of it, and loathest thyself as defiled by it. But if sin be not in truth hateful unto thee, thou hast not this property, and so the wedden garment is none of thine, and this is a sad word to be spoken to thee, yet it is a true word. But here is this ease to be administered to the doubting soul. You are not to conclude that you do not hate sin in that you find in you a principle of love to sin. For so long as sanctification is but in part, there will be a party holding in thee with sin. But then if thou art sanctified in part, thou wilt be grieved that thou hast no more hatred of sin, or that thou hast anything in thee that doth hinder thee that thou canst not hate sin as thou wouldst. Well then try by this; and accordingly thou mayst draw up the conclusion.

Invincible love: as it is the property of the person that hath the wedden garment to bear invincible hatred to whatever is against the wedden garment any way, so it is his property to have invincible love to it in all its respects. And therefore consider it as laid out on the wedden garment.

Invincible love runs upon the wedden garment simply and relatively.

Simply: take this wedden garment in its simple and absolute consideration and it's the object of insuperable love to everyone that hath it. The Spirit of

5. Determining or deciding.

God saith that love is strong as death. Many waters cannot quench it; neither can the floods drown it; and this love is fixed upon these wedden robes, for they are the richest robes that ever were worn. They are the best robes; they are royal robes. Joseph must be arrayed in vesture of fine linen, or rather in silk or satin[6] (Genesis 41.42). These are festival clothes, wedden clothes. The church in them is said to stand in gold of Ophir,[7] and to be all glorious within, and to be arrayed in wrought gold (Psalms 45.9, 13). Nay, the Lord Christ highly esteems this, and knows that the soul doth that hath it on, that He lays it down as a promise (Revelation 3.5). Hence it must needs be prized by such as have it. For Christ Himself saith of it, "the smell of thy garments is as Lebanon"[8] (Canticles 4.11). Now then, here is thy trial: what is thy respect to this garment? Is it low? If below what is laid out on others, if not above what goes to others, it is not thine. Everyone doth love his own above another's; if this which is in its own nature above another's is not esteemed by thee above all others, it is none of thine. And this is an hard word. But if thy love to it excels, then it is thine.

Relatively: take this wedden garment in its relative consideration, as it is related to thee, and thy love to it excels and comes upon it invincibly. And as it stands under this consideration, we are to note it in its aspect to our wear and ways.

Our wear. We love to wear it. We are never well but when we are in it. A child of God in this is like to the little children of men, ever best when he is in best clothes. Nay, he is loathsome to himself if he find himself in any respect out of this wedden garment. This is his joy and rejoicing, to be wearing this apparel. He hath the shame of his nakedness appear, if he find his wear is not this white raiment, and this is that that his glory lieth in. Here his garments are always white and shining, as a robe of solid metal, whether silver or of gold, by wearing made more shining. So it is here: the more it is worn, the more it shines. It is not worn out by wearing, but worn more bright and shining, and hence he ever lives to be wearing of it.

*　　*　　*

As to the celebration of the wedden feast, in which, what height is the love advanced unto in the soul that is invested in this wedden attire? We are not able to take an observation of love's elevation in order to the solemnizing this feast. For consider and you shall find all the beams of gospel grace communicated unto the soul through the dispensation of the Word concentrating in the preparation adorning the soul for it, as they in this wedden garment. Now this is the highest preparation under heaven that mortals arrive at, and yet this is not a preparation above this feast: nay, the highest preparation under heaven below this is a preparation below the welcome to this feast. Consider the nature of the feast, and you shall find it is the marriage feast of the King's Son. The King of Glory, King of Kings, the King Immortal and Invisible and Eternal herein celebrates the espousals made between His own and only begotten Son, and heir of all things, and the souls

6. The son of Jacob and Rachel, Joseph was made the ruler of Egypt by Pharaoh: "See, I have set thee over all the land of Egypt. And Pharaoh took off his ring from his hand, and put it upon Joseph's hand, and arrayed him in vestures of fine linen, and put a gold chain about his neck" (Genesis 41.41–42).
7. Ophir is mentioned in the Old Testament (1 Kings 10.11) as a place where fine gold was found.
8. Mountainous land noted for its fragrant cedars.

of His elect drawn up in an holy contract at the time of their particular conversions. Wherein He entertains them with the royalest dainties, and the richest provision that heaven itself affords: with that miraculous water out of the rock, and Manna,[9] the breads of heaven, angels' bread. Not that these were properly types of the festival provision in the elemental signs. For as Ames[1] saith, "there are no figures of figures, or sacraments that God hath instituted, or the scripture teacheth." But this rock notes[2] Christ, and the water the graces of the Holy Ghost communicated by Christ, and the Manna, angels' bread, some think, because the angels in their judgment were the makers of it. But now God provides the true Manna, or Bread of Life here to feast His with, not such as the angels made, but the which the God of angels Himself made. Oh! the provision here, the flesh and the blood, the precious blood of His own Son, most richly dressed, is the provision God makes now to entertain His guests with all the benefits thereof. Here is a feast, a soul feast "of fat things, a feast of wines on the lees,[3] a feast of fat things full of marrow, of wines on the lees well refined" (Isaiah 25.6). It is the richest and royalest feast that ever was made. George Neville's[4] feast at York was nothing to this for costliness. Nor was King Ahasuerus his feast (Esther 1) to be mentioned with this. This feast for the provision of it in signs, and things signified, is an epitome of all gospel grace, or all the grace of the gospel. Now then think of it. Hence how can it be that the soul dressed up in the wedden garment should not have an high esteem and an unspeakable love unto it? If thou hast not such a love, thou hast not this wedden garment. If the wedden garment is thine, thou hast lapt upon it[5] this love. Try therefore by thy love unto the wedden.

As to the celebrators of this feast. Thy love runs out to these with all its might, if thou are arrayed in this rich robe. And these that celebrate it are authors and guests.

The authors of it, the King the Father, and the Prince the Son. The Father makes the wedden for the Son and the Son acts with the Father. Now these have all loveliness in them. The Father, He is the foundation of loveliness, being the fountain of love. "Oh!" saith the soul, "whom have I in heaven but thee, and in all the earth I desire nothing in comparison of thee" (Psalm 74.25). Oh! God is all to the soul in this royal array. So the Son. Now it is the Father's design to set out the Son as most lovely, and therefore He celebrates the feast for this end. He is the lovely rose of Sharon,[6] and glorious lily of the valley. He is altogether lovely in everything, lovely in His person, lovely in His natures, lovely in His properties, lovely in His offices,[7] lovely in His titles, lovely in His practice, lovely in His purchases and lovely in His relations. And in all these, and all other things, He is altogether lovely. Now this is the Bridegroom, and His love doth mostly show itself in this feast, wherein He feasts the souls of His upon His own flesh and blood most royally served up, as the viands of their peace offering. Oh! how should the soul

9. The substance miraculously offered as food for the Children of Israel in their journey through the wilderness.
1. William Ames (1576–1633), an English theologian well known among Puritan divines.
2. Denotes.
3. Dregs; i.e., wine drunk to the last drop.
4. Neville (1433?–1476) was made archbishop of York in 1464, and the occasion was followed by a celebrated feast. Taylor was interested enough to keep a list of the dishes served.
5. Wrapped around it.
6. Sharon is the name of a fertile land along the coast of Israel. The phrase "rose of Sharon" comes from the Song of Solomon 2.1: "I am the rose of Sharon and the lily of the valleys."
7. Duties; things undertaken.

choose but love Him that hath received this wedden attire of Him. If now
thou hast no love to Him, or if thy love to other things shuffles Him into a
corner, thou hast not His wedden garment. But if thy love now runs out to
Him above all things, so that nothing can separate thee from loving Him
above all things, nay above life itself, then this robe is thine.

* * *

c. 1694   1966

FRANCIS DANIEL PASTORIUS
1651–c. 1720

Born in the south-central German duchy of Franconia, Francis Daniel Pastorius was
the only child of the prominent lawyer, judge, and author Melchior Adam Pastorius,
later adviser to the prince of Brandenburg. Following his education in law and theology at several universities—Strassburg, Basel, Jena, and Ratisbon—Francis briefly
practiced law before setting out on a grand tour in 1680 as the companion of a young
nobleman. Passing through Germany, The Netherlands, England, France, and Switzerland, he experienced firsthand much of the best in contemporary culture. He nonetheless returned deeply dissatisfied to Frankfort-on-Main in 1682. "I withdrew into
my study for a short retreat," he later wrote, "and recalled to mind all that this world-
spectacle had brought to my view, and could find no enduring pleasure in anything
therein." America was to help revive his pleasure and give him a purpose. As it happened, Frankfort at the time he returned there was a vital center for the religious
movement called Pietism, which arose in reaction against the worldly late Renaissance culture he himself had rejected. When the English Quaker William Penn,
whose own similar faith had led him to visit the Frankfort Pietists five years earlier,
reached out to such people and urged them to join his new "holy experiment" in
America in the 1680s, Pastorius quickly emerged as the agent for a group of Frankfort
residents who purchased a large tract of land in Pennsylvania.

Pastorius sailed for America in June of 1683, arrived there two months later, and
by fall had founded the first great settlement for German-speaking emigrants in America, Germantown. From that point on, he was intimately linked to the fortunes of the
town, which he served as justice, clerk, and member for the colony's Assembly.
Teacher and schoolmaster for much of his later life, he was also a scholar who built
an impressive library and wrote several published and many unpublished texts. Among
the works left in manuscript is an impressive body of verse (a considerable proportion
of it written in English) only now being discovered and printed. Baroque in mood and
image, by turns humorous and probing, it is of rising importance in its own right and
as a representative of the literary culture of the learned author's region. In his own
day, Pastorius was known as the author of a handful of modest texts reporting on
affairs among the German immigrants to their compatriots at home, especially his
*Umständige Geographische Beschreibung der zu Allerletzt Erfundenen Provintz Pen-
sylvaniae* (Circumstantial Geographical Description of the Lately Discovered Province
of Pennsylvania), edited by his father and published in Frankfort and Leipzig in 1700.
A similar, briefer account of Penn's province and of the German role in settling it
had appeared in Nürmberg eight years earlier as an appendix to a work of the author's

father. And at the start of his American career, Pastorius had sent back home an even briefer text recounting his voyage and the first impressions gathered from his new home. It is from this work, *Sichere Nachricht auss America, wegen der Landschafft Pennsylvania* (Positive Information from America Concerning the Country of Pennsylvania), issued in 1684, that the following pages are taken. Attuned to the spiritual assumptions of his fellow immigrants as he was, it is only right that Pastorius should be credited with having written the first antislavery tract penned in America. That 1688 document recorded the indignation of his countrymen, to whom the institution was unknown, with its very existence in a new homeland where they were seeking spiritual renewal and worldly peace.

From Positive Information from America, concerning the Country of Pennsylvania, from a German who has migrated thither; dated Philadelphia, March 7, 1684[1]

[PREFACE]

To fulfill my duty as well as my promise made at my departure I will somewhat more circumstantially state what I have found and noted of these lands; and since I am not unaware that by imperfect relations many of you have been misinformed, I gave my assurance beforehand that I with impartial pen and without deceptive additions will set forth faithfully both the inconveniences of the journey and the defects of this province, as well as that plentifulness of the same which has been praised by others almost to excess; for I desire nothing more in my little place than to walk in the footsteps of Him who is the way, and to follow His holy teachings, because He is the truth, in order that I may ceaselessly enjoy with Him eternal life.

[VOYAGE TO PENNSYLVANIA]

I. Accordingly I will begin with the voyage, which is certainly on the one hand dangerous on account of the terror of shipwreck, and on the other hand very burdensome on account of the bad and hard fare, so that I now from my own experience understand in a measure what David says in the 107th Psalm, that on the sea one may observe and perceive not only the wonderful works of God but also the spirit of the storm. As to my voyage hither, I sailed from Deal the tenth of June with four men servants, two maid servants, two children and one young boy. We had the whole way over, for the most part, contrary winds, and never favorable for twelve hours together, many tempests and thunderstorms, also the foremast broke twice, so that it was ten weeks before we arrived here; yet *sat citò, si sat bene*,[2] considering that it seldom happens that any persons arrive here much more quickly. The Crefelders,[3] who arrived here on October 6, were also ten weeks upon the ocean, and the ship that set out with ours from Deal was fourteen days longer on the voyage, and several people died in it. The Crefelders lost a grown girl between Rotterdam and England, which loss however was made up between

---

1. The source of the text is a translation by J. Franklin Jameson in *Narratives of Early Pennsylvania, West New Jersey, and Delaware, 1630–1707* (1912), edited by Albert Cook Myers.
2. Quickly enough if well enough (Latin).

3. A group of Quaker and Mennonite families from Crefeld, near the Dutch frontier in the lower Rhine valley in Germany, who left English waters about a month after the ship carrying Pastorius.

England and Pennsylvania by the birth of two children. On our ship, on the other hand, no one died and no one was born. Almost all the passengers were seasick for some days, I however for not more than four hours. On the other hand I underwent other accidents, namely, that the two carved lugs[4] over the ship's bell fell right upon my back, and on the 9th of July during a storm in the night I fell so severely upon my left side that for some days I had to keep to my bed. These two falls reminded me forcibly of the first fall of our original parents in Paradise, which has come down upon all their posterity, and also of many of those falls which I have undergone in this vale of misery of my exile. *Per varios casus,*[5] etc. But praised be the fatherly hand of the divine mercy which lifts us up again so many times and holds us back that we fall not entirely into the abyss of the evil one. Georg Wertmiller also fell down extremely hard, Thomas Gasper had an eruption of the body, the English maid had the erysipelas, and Isaac Dilbreck,[6] who according to outward appearance was the strongest, succumbed for the greatest length of time. So I had a small ship-hospital, although I alone of the Germans had taken my berth among the English. That one of the boatmen became insane and that our ship was shaken by the repeated assaults of a whale, I set forth at length in my last letter. The rations upon the ship were very bad. We lived *medice ac modice.*[7] Every ten persons received three pounds of butter a week, four cans of beer and two cans of water a day, two platters full of peas every noon, meat four dinners in the week and fish three, and these we were obliged to prepare with our own butter. Also we must every noon save up enough so that we might get our supper from it. The worst of all was, that both the meat and the fish were salted to such an extent and had become so rancid that we could hardly eat half of them. And had I not by the advice of good friends in England provided myself with various kinds of refreshment, it might perhaps have gone very badly. Therefore all those who hereafter intend to make the voyage hither should take good heed that they either, if there are many of them, procure their own provisions, or else agree distinctly with the captain as to both quantity and quality, how much food and of what sort they are to receive each day; and to hold him down the more completely to this agreement, one should reserve some small part of the passage money, to be paid on this side. Also when possible one should arrange with a ship which sails up to this city of Philadelphia, since in the case of the others which end their voyage at Upland,[8] one is subjected to many inconveniences.

My company consisted of many sorts of people. There was a doctor of medicine with his wife and eight children, a French captain, a Dutch cake-baker, an apothecary, a glass-blower, a mason, a smith, a wheelwright, a cabinet-maker, a cooper, a hat-maker, a cobbler, a tailor, a gardener, farmers, seamstresses, etc., in all about eighty persons besides the crew. They were not only different in respect to age (for our oldest woman was sixty years of age and the youngest child only twelve weeks) and in respect to their occupations, as I have mentioned, but were also of such different religions and

---

4. Decorative hangers.
5. Through various accidents, through so many hazards we go on toward Latium (Latin); a reference to Virgil, *Aeneid* 1.204.
6. Except for Gasper, these immigrants were servants of the Frankfort investors. All four came over on the *America* with Pastorious. "The English

maid": Frances Simson. "Erysipelas": an illness characterized by fever and inflammation of the skin.
7. Medically and moderately (Latin).
8. A settlement fifteen miles below Philadelphia near the Delaware.

behaviors that I might not unfittingly compare the ship that bore them hither with Noah's Ark, but that there were more unclean than clean (rational) animals to be found therein. In my household I have those who hold to the Roman, to the Lutheran, to the Calvinistic, to the Anabaptist, and to the Anglican church, and only one Quaker. On the 11th of August we cast the lead for the first time and perceived that we were close to the great sand bank, and so had to sail back and around and consequently to run more than a hundred leagues[9] out of our course.

On the 16th we came with joy in sight of America and on the morning of the 18th arrived in Delaware Bay, which is thirty English miles long and fifteen wide and is of such unequal depth that since our ship drew thirteen feet of water we sometimes stuck upon the sand.

[WILLIAM PENN]

On the 20th we sailed past Neu Castle, Upland and Dunicum and arrived at evening, praise God, safely at Philadelphia, where I on the following day delivered to William Penn[1] the letters that I had, and was received by him with amiable friendliness; of that very worthy man and famous ruler I might properly.

II. write many things; but my pen (though it is from an eagle, which a so-called savage lately brought to my house) is much too weak to express the high virtues of this Christian—for such he is indeed. He often invites me to his table and has me walk and ride in his always edifying company; and when I lately was absent from here a week, in order to fetch provisions from Neu Castle, and he had not seen me for that space of time, he came himself to my little house and besought me that I should at least once or twice a week be his guest. He heartily loves the [Germans], and once said openly in my presence to his councillors and those who were about him, I love the [Germans] and desire that you also should love them. Yet in any other matter I have never heard such a command from him. This however pleased me so much the better because it was entirely conformable with the command of God (see John xiii. 23). I can at present say no more than that William Penn is a man who honors God and is honored by Him, who loves what is good and is rightly beloved by all good men. I doubt not that some of them will come here and by their own experience learn, that my pen has in this case not written enough.

* * *

[THE INHABITANTS]

V. As to the inhabitants, I cannot better classify them than into the native and the engrafted. For if I were to call the former savages and the latter Christians, I should do great injustice to many of both varieties. Of the latter sort, I have already mentioned above, that the incoming ships are not altogether to be compared with Noah's Ark. The Lutheran preacher, who ought

9. About three hundred miles.
1. Son (1644–1718) of a British admiral, he promoted Quaker causes. In the early 1680s he helped arrange a Utopian experiment in the Delaware valley and then acquired vast tracts of land on his own for a "holy experiment" in what is now Pennsylvania. The experiment involved freedom of religion and equitable treatment of Native Americans. Penn went back to England in 1684, returning to America only once more, in 1699. Newcastle ("Neu Castle") is in Delaware. Tinicum ("Dunicum") is just below Philadelphia.

as a *statua Mercurialis*[2] to show the Swedes the way to heaven, is, to say it in one word, a drunkard. Also there are coiners of false money and other vicious persons here whom nevertheless, it may be hoped, the wind of God's vengeance will in his own time drive away like chaff. On the other hand there is no lack of pious, God-fearing people, and I can with truth affirm that I have nowhere in Europe seen the notice posted up, as here in our Philadelphia, that such a one has found this or that, and that the loser may call for it at his house; often however the converse, Lost this or that; he who returns it again shall receive a reward, etc.

Of these new engrafted strangers I will for the present say no more than that among them some High Germans are to be found who have lived already twenty years in this land and consequently are, so to speak, naturalized, namely, Silesians, Brandenburgers, Holsteiners, Swiss, etc., also a Nuremberg man named Jan Jaquet;[3] but will briefly give my account of those who are erroneously called savages. The first who came before my eyes were those two who at Upland came in a canoe to our ship. I presented them with a dram of brandy. They attempted to pay me for it with a sixpence, and when I refused the money they gave me their hands, and said, Thank you, brother. They are strong of limb, swarthy of body, and paint their faces, red, blue, etc., in various ways. In the summer they go quite naked, except that they cover their private parts with a piece of cloth, and now in winter hang duffels[4] upon themselves. They have coal-black hair, while the Swedish children born here have hair snow-white. I was once dining with William Penn where one of their kings sat at table with us. William Penn, who can speak their language fairly fluently, said to him that I was a German, etc. He came accordingly on the third of October, and on the twelfth of December another king and queen came to my house. Also many common persons over-run me very often, to whom however I almost always show my love with a piece of bread and a drink of beer, whereby an answering affection is awakened in them and they commonly call me "Teutschmann," also "Carissimo" (that is, brother). N. B. Their language is manly and in my opinion is little inferior to the Italian in gravity, etc. As to their manners and nature, one must so to speak sub-distinguish them into those who have associated for some time with the so-called Christians and those who are just beginning to come forth out of their burrows. For the former are crafty and deceitful, which they owe to the above-mentioned nominal Christians. *Semper enim aliquid hæret.*[5] Such a one lately pledged me his strap[6] as security that he would bring me a turkey, but in its place he brought an eagle and wished to persuade me that it was a turkey. When however I showed him that I had seen many eagles he acknowledged to a Swede who stood by that he had done it out of deception, in the belief that because we had lately come into the land I should not know such birds so accurately. Another at my fireside tested the brandy thus: he stuck his finger into it and then put the latter into the fire

2. Statue of Mercury (Latin), the god of travelers. Reference to the Reverend Jacob Fabritius (d. 1693), Lutheran preacher of Dutch or possibly Polish background, who had come to New York in 1669 and later moved to the Delaware, where in 1677 he became pastor of the Gloria Dei Swedish church.
3. Jean Paul Jacquet (c. 1615–1685), a holdover from the old state of affairs in the Delaware valley, who had been in the service of the Dutch West India Company in Brazil before emigrating to New Netherland in 1654. He was sent to the South River by the Dutch after their conquest of the Swedes in 1655 and survived the English conquest and the coming of the Quakers.
4. Coarse woolen cloth.
5. Always something adheres (Latin).
6. Used for carrying goods.

to see whether water had been mingled with the liquor. Those of the second class, on the contrary, are of a reasonable spirit, injure nobody, and we have nothing whatever to fear from them. One thing lately struck deeply into my heart when I pondered the sincere admonition of our Saviour, that we His disciples should take no thought for the morrow, because thus do the Gentiles. Ah, thought I to myself, how entirely has all been now perverted! When we Christians are not provided for a month and more how displeased are we, while these heathen in so wonderful a spirit of resignation refer their sustenance to God. Just at that time I saw four of them eating together. The earth was at once their table and their bench. A pumpkin, cooked in plain water, without butter or spice, was all their food. Their spoons were mussel-shells, with which they supped the warm water. Their plates were oak leaves, which they had no need to clean after the meal, nor, when they needed others, to give themselves much trouble about them. Now, dear friend, let us not hesitate to learn contentment from these people, that they may not hereafter shame us before the judgment-seat of Jesus Christ.

1684

SAMUEL SEWALL
1652–1730

Although Samuel Sewall was born in England, his parents had lived in Massachusetts for a number of years before their marriage, and by the time he was nine the family once more had returned to New England. On his long-remembered ocean crossing, the boy was impressed by the fact that "we had nothing to see but Water and Sky," and feared that he would "never get to Shoar again." He calmed himself, however, by reflecting that the sailors and captain hardly would have ventured to sea if they thought they "had not hopes of getting to Land again." That youthful exercise of reason suggests Sewall's later talents as a scholar, judge, and writer. Sewall was schooled at Newbury, Massachusetts, where his parents established themselves, from the time he arrived in America until his admission in 1667 to Harvard, from which he earned his bachelor's degree in 1671. He was named a fellow and tutor there before being awarded his master's degree in 1674 (his thesis concerned the nature of original sin) and served briefly as keeper of the college library. Among his classmates at college was the future poet Edward Taylor, with whom he developed a close friendship. Sewall might have followed Taylor and most of his other classmates into the ministry, but his temperament and the demands of his family's worldly business deflected him instead into secular concerns, including commerce and the law. In 1674 Sewall refused a call to a pulpit in Woodbridge, New Jersey (a Puritan community settled by emigrants from Massachusetts in 1665), and thereafter took increasing interest in the Sewall properties and in his own activities as a merchant. Still, he remained bookish and familiar with new theological subtleties all his life; and because he traveled extensively in Massachusetts, he was intimately familiar with church affairs across the province.

While at Harvard Sewall began his famous diary, continuing it until 1729, two years before his death. From the time of its partial publication in the mid-nineteenth century, Sewall's diary became a crucial source for understanding its author's life and the events that transformed Massachusetts from a Puritan colony to a stronghold of "Yankees," the term of uncertain origins that eventually would be applied to the residents of all New England. For a brief time after his Harvard experience, Sewall returned to Newbury, where the family had large landholdings, but following his marriage in 1676 to Hannah Hull, only surviving child of wealthy Boston goldsmith and merchant John Hull, he took up residence in Hull's Boston house, which was to remain Sewall's home for the remainder of his long life. John Hull entrusted his extensive business interests to his son-in-law, and on Hull's death in 1684 Sewall became a central figure in the great mercantile life of the port of Boston. He learned when to borrow and when to lend, filled his ships with American goods Londoners were eager to buy (timber, molasses, pitch), and learned to anticipate public demand in New England for English goods (metalwares, fabrics, tiles), which his agent in London purchased for him and loaded in his ships.

Sewall's learning and his status made him an obvious choice for the public positions, both military and civil, that he began to assume in 1676. Two years later, the Massachusetts General Court (or legislature) appointed him to manage the printing press established in Boston, a job he initiated by issuing John Bunyan's *Pilgrim's Progress*. He ran the press for almost three years, during which time it printed works by Puritan thinkers such as Samuel Willard (author of the posthumous *Complete Body of Divinity*), as well as Increase and Cotton Mather, along with official documents and a handful of other items. By 1683, Sewall was serving as the absentee deputy or representative for Westfield in the General Court, and the following year assumed his first judicial appointment as a member of the Court of Assistants. In 1692 Sewall became one of the justices of the Superior Court of Judicature, a position he held for more than thirty-five years, the last eleven as chief justice. But earlier that same year he already had taken on his most conspicuous public responsibility as a member of the special court, along with Nathaniel Hawthorne's ancestor John Hathorne (as the name then was spelled) and several other men, appointed to inquire into the reported instances of witchcraft in Salem and other towns. Although Sewall's service on that body, which considered a great number of cases and condemned several people to death, has long associated his name with the hysteria and intolerance that produced the trials, he also was courageous enough five years later to confess his guilt for his part in the tragedy.

In 1700, in what remains his most singular gift to the conscience of a nation that would not exist until fifty years after his death, Sewall published the first antislavery tract in America, *The Selling of Joseph*, a venture for which, as he reported, he received "frowns and harsh words" from his fellow townspeople—including merchant and slaveholder John Saffin, who published *A Brief and Candid Answer* the following year. Sewall delayed acknowledging this answer until he "saw a very severe act passing [the General Court] against Indian and Negroes" in 1705, which caused him to have reprinted in Boston an article from an English periodical arguing that the slave trade was "especially contrary to the great Law of Christianity." This was clearly an issue Judge Sewall wanted to keep before the public.

From The Diary of Samuel Sewall[1]

Satterday, Jany 2^d[, 1686.] Last night had a very unusual Dream; *viz.* That our Savior in the dayes of his Flesh when upon Earth, came to Boston and

---

1. The first entry of Sewall's diary is dated December 3, 1673, and the last entry December 25, 1728. The text used here is from *The Diary of Samuel Sewall*, edited by M. Halsey Thomas (1973). To preserve the special flavor of Sewall's style, the text has been only slightly modernized. The dates, however, have been changed to conform to the modern calendar.

abode here sometime, and moreover that He Lodged in that time at Father Hull's; upon which in my Dream had two Reflections, One was how much more Boston had to say than Rome boasting of Peter's being there. The other a sense of great Respect that I ought to have shewed Father Hull since Christ chose when in town, to take up His Quarters at his House. Admired the goodness and Wisdom of Christ in coming hither and spending some part of His short Life here. The Chronological absurdity never came into my mind, as I remember. Jan[y] 1, 1688, finished reading the Godly Learned ingenious Pareus[2] on the Revelation.

Sabbath, Augt. 10th[, 1690.] Went to see Cous. [Daniel] Quinsey; read the 102. Psal. and begin 103. pray'd, and so went home. Put up a Bill[3] at his request. Just after Contribution in the Afternoon, was call'd out, Cousin being very bad, so far as I could perceive. He desired me to pray, which I did: Afterward sent for Mr. Willard, and He pray'd, then Cousin pull'd his hand out of the Bed, and gave it to Mr. Willard. Seem'd to pray himself; but I could hear little except Jesus Christ; breath'd quick and hard, till at last abated and He quietly expired about Seven aclock. Mother Hull and I being there. I have parted with a cordial fast Friend, such an one as I shall hardly find. The Lord fit me for my Change and help me to wait till it come. Cousin was concern'd what he should doe for Patience, but God graciously furnish'd him, and has how translated Him to that State and place wherein He has no occasion for any.

Tuesday, Augt. 12[, 1690.] About 7. P.M. we lay the Body of Cous. Daniel Quinsey in my Father's Tomb. Mr. Serjeant, Dummer, H. Usher, Davis, Williams, Conney, Bearers. I led the Widow, then the Children, next, Mr. T. Brattle, Mis. Shepard, H. Newman, Mistress Margaret, Mr. Willard, Mother Hull, Mr. Parson, my wife and so on. Note. My wife[4] was so ill could hardly get home, taking some harm in going in Pattens[5] or some wrench, so had a great flux of Blood, which amaz'd us both, at last my wife bade me call Mrs. Ellis, then Mother Hull, then the Midwife, and throw the Goodness of God was brought to Bed of a Daughter between 3. and four aclock, Aug. 13th, 1690. mane Mrs. Elisabeth Weeden, Midwife. Had not Women nor other preparations as usually, being wholly surpris'd, my wife expecting to have gone a Moneth longer.

✻   ✻   ✻

Augt. 17 [, 1690.] Mr. Willard keeps his Sabbath at Roxbury, and so the Baptism of my little Daughter is deferred to the next Lord's Day.

Sabbath-day, August the four and twentieth, 1690. I publish my little Daughter's name to be Judith, held her up for Mr. Willard to baptize her. She cried not at all, though a pretty deal of water was poured on her by Mr. Willard when He baptized her: Six others were baptized at the same time; Capt. Davis's Son James, and a grown person, Margaret Clifford, two of them. I named my Daughter Judith for the sake of her Grandmother and great Grandmother, who both wore that Name, and the Signification of it very good: The Lord grant that we may have great cause to praise Him on

2. David Pareus (1548–1622), a theologian and biblical commentator and one of Sewall's favorite authors.
3. A legal petition.

4. Sewall married Hannah Hull (1658–1717) in February 1676.
5. Wearing high-heeled shoes.

her account and help her to speak the Jews Language and to forget that of Ashdod,[6] Nehemiah 13.24. And that she may follow her Grandmother Hull, as she follows Christ, being not slothfull in Business, fervent in Spirit, serving the Lord. Her Prayers and Painstaking for all my Children are incessant, voluntary, with condescension to the meanest Services night and day: that I judg'd I could in justice doe no less than endeavor her remembrance by putting her Name on one of her Grand-Daughters. I have now had my health and opportunity to offer up Nine Children to God in Baptisme. Mr. Tho. Thacher baptized the two eldest; John and Samuel; Mr. Samuel Willard baptized the Seven younger. Lord grant that I who have thus solemnly and frequently named the name of the Lord Jesus, may depart from Iniquity; and that mine may be more His than Mine, or their own.

Sept. 20[, 1690.] * * * My little Judith languishes and moans, ready to die.

Sabbath, Sept. 21[, 1690.] About 2 mane, I rise, read some Psalms and pray with my dear Daughter. Between 7. and 8. (Mr. Moodey preaches in the Forenoon,) I call Mr. Willard, and he prays. Told Mr. Walter of her condition * * * desiring him to give her a Lift towards heaven. Mr. Baily sat with me in the Afternoon. I acquainted Him. Between 7. and 8. in the evening the child died, and I hope sleeps in Jesus.

Sept. 22[, 1690.] In the even, Mr. Moodey, Allen, Mather come from Mrs. Clark's Funeral to see us. Mr. Moodey and I went before the other came, to neighbor Hord, who lay dying; where also Mr. Allen came in. Nurse Hord told her Husband who was there, and what he had to say; whether he desir'd them to pray with him: He said with some earnestness, Hold your tongue, which was repeated three times to his wive's repeated intreaties; once he said, Let me alone, or, be quiet, (whether that made a fourth or was one of the three do not remember) and, My Spirits are gon. At last Mr. Moodey took him up pretty roundly and told him he might with the same labor have given a pertinent answer. When were ready to come away Mr. Moodey bid him put forth a little Breath to ask prayer, and said twas the last time had to speak to him; At last ask'd him, doe you desire prayer, shall I pray with you, He answer'd, Ay for the Lord's sake, and thank'd Mr. Moodey when had done. His former carriage was very startling and amazing to us. About One at night he died. About 11. aclock I supposed to hear neighbor Mason at prayer with him, just as I and my wife were going to bed. Mr. Allen prayed with us when came from said Hord's.

Sept. 23[, 1690.] Tuesday, between 5. and 6. Sir[7] Moodey carries the Body of my dear Judith to the Tomb, Solomon Rainsford receives it on the Stairs and sets it in. On the Coffin is the year 1690. made with little nails. Govr Bradstreet and Lady,[8] Mrs. Moodey, Mather the Mother, Mr. Winthrop, Richards here, with many others; Ministers, Willard, Moodey, Mather.

June 2^d, 1691. Mr. Edward Taylor[9] puts his Son James to Mr. Steward, Shopkeeper of Ipswich, for Seven years, to serve him as an Apprentice, Term to begin the first of July next. Mr. Taylor desires me to represent himself in

6. I.e., be true believers and speak the language of Judah. Children of Jews who married Ashdod women were unable to speak the language of their fathers.
7. Here meaning minister.

8. Simon Bradstreet's second wife.
9. The poet from Westfield (c. 1642–1729) and Sewall's Harvard College roommate. Sewall represented the town of Westfield in the General Court of Massachusetts.

making the Indenture, if Mr. Steward desire the accomplishment of it befor He comes down again.

Monday, Dec. 7th, [1691.] I ride to New-Cambridge to see Sam.[1] He could hardly speak to me, his affections were so mov'd, having not seen me for above a fortnight; his Cough is still very bad, much increas'd by his going to Cambridge on foot in the night.* * *

April 11th, 1692. Went to Salem, where, in the Meeting-house, the persons accused of Witchcraft were examined; was a very great Assembly; 'twas awfull to see how the afflicted persons were agitated. Mr. Noyes pray'd at the beginning, and Mr. Higginson concluded. [*In the margin*], Væ,[2] Væ, Væ, Witchcraft.

July 30, 1692. Mrs. Cary makes her escape out of Cambridge-Prison, who was Committed for Witchcraft.[3]

Thorsday, Augt. 4, [1692.] At Salem, Mr. Waterhouse brings the news of the desolation at Jamaica, June 7th. 1700 persons kill'd, besides the Loss of Houses and Goods by the Earthquake.

Augt. 19th, 1692. * * * This day [*in the margin*, Dolefull Witchcraft] George Burrough, John Willard, Jnº Procter, Martha Carrier and George Jacobs were executed at Salem, a very great number of Spectators being present. Mr. Cotton Mather was there, Mr. Sims, Hale, Noyes, Chiever, &c. All of them said they were innocent, Carrier and all. Mr. Mather says they all died by a Righteous Sentence. Mr. Burrough by his Speech, Prayer, protestation of his Innocence, did much move unthinking persons, which occasions their speaking hardly[4] concerning his being executed.

Augt. 25, [1692.] Fast at the old [*First*] Church, respecting the Witchcraft, Drought, &c.

Monday, Sept. 19, 1692. About noon, at Salem, Giles Corey was press'd to death [5] for standing Mute; much pains was used with him two days, one after another, by the Court and Capt. Gardner of Nantucket who had been of his acquaintance: but all in vain.

Sept. 20, [1692.] Now I hear from Salem that about 18 years agoe, he was suspected to have stamped and press'd a man to death, but was cleared. Twas not remembred till Anne Putnam was told of it by said Corey's Spectre the Sabbath-day night before Execution.[6]

Sept. 20, 1692. The Swan[7] brings in a rich French Prize of about 300 Tuns, laden with Claret, White Wine, Brandy, Salt, Linnen Paper, &c.

Sept. 21, [1692.] A petition is sent to Town in behalf of Dorcas Hoar, who now confesses: Accordingly an order is sent to the Sheriff to forbear her Execution, notwithstanding her being in the Warrant to die to morrow. This is the first condemned person who has confess'd.[8]

1. Sewall's thirteen-year-old son, boarding at school.
2. Woe (Latin). Governor William Phips (1651–1695) appointed Sewall one of seven councillors of a court of Oyer and Terminer (i.e., to hear and determine) to judge those accused of witchcraft in Salem on May 24, 1692. The court met in Salem on June 2 and Bridget Bishop was hanged on June 10. On June 30 they met again and five more accused were executed on July 19. Unfortunately for us, Sewall kept his entries regarding the trials at Salem to a minimum.
3. Cary was given protection in New York.
4. Vigorously.
5. Corey was eighty years old at the time. Heavy stones were placed on him until he died.
6. Putnam was only twelve when she made, along with her mother, accusations against "witches."
7. A ship.
8. Confession of witchcraft automatically set the accused free.

Nov. 6[, *1692.*] Joseph threw a knop of Brass and hit his Sister Betty on the forhead so as to make it bleed and swell; upon which, and for his playing at Prayer-time, and eating when Return Thanks, I whipd him pretty smartly. When I first went in (call'd by his Grandmother) he sought to shadow and hide himself from me behind the head of the Cradle: which gave me the sorrowfull remembrance of Adam's carriage.

Apr. 16, 1695. My Appletree which I nourish from a kernel, has the growth of 1694 and is now scarce Ten inches high; removd it this Spring into the room of a young Appletree that dyed.

* * *

Monday, April 29, 1695. The morning is very warm and Sunshiny; in the Afternoon there is Thunder and Lightening, and about 2 P.M. a very extraordinary Storm of Hail, so that the ground was made white with it, as with the blossoms when fallen; 'twas as bigg as pistoll and Musquet Bullets; It broke of the Glass of the new House about 480 Quarrels [*squares*] of the Front; of Mr. Sergeant's about as much; Col. Shrimpton, Major General, Gov' Bradstreet, New Meetinghouse, Mr. Willard, &c. Mr. Cotton Mather dined with us, and was with me in the new Kitchen when this was; He had just been mentioning that more Minister Houses than others proportionably had been smitten with Lightening; enquiring what the meaning of God should be in it. Many Hail-Stones broke throw the Glass and flew to the middle of the Room, or farther: People afterward Gazed upon the House to see its Ruins. I got Mr. Mather to pray with us after this awfull Providence; He told God He had broken the brittle part of our house, and prayd that we might be ready for the time when our Clay-Tabernacles should be broken. Twas a sorrowfull thing to me to see the house so far undon again before twas finish'd. It seems at Milton[9] on the one hand, and at Lewis's [*the tavern at Lynn*] on the other, there was no Hail.

Jan' 15, [*1697.*] * * * Copy of the Bill I put up on the Fast day [January 14]; giving it to Mr. Willard as he pass'd by, and standing up at the reading of it, and bowing when finished; in the Afternoon.

Samuel Sewall, sensible of the reiterated strokes of God upon himself and family[1] and being sensible, that as to the Guilt contracted, upon the opening of the late Commission of Oyer and Terminer at Salem (to which the order for this Day relates) he is, upon many accounts, more concerned than any that he knows of, Desires to take the Blame and Shame of it, Asking pardon of Men, And especially desiring prayers that God, who has an Unlimited Authority, would pardon that Sin and all other his Sins; personal and Relative: And according to his infinite Benignity, and Soveraignty, Not Visit the Sin of him, or of any other, upon himself or any of his, nor upon the Land: But that He would powerfully defend him against all Temptations to Sin, for the future; and vouchsafe him the Efficacious, Saving Conduct of his Word and Spirit.

July 15, 1698. Mr. Edward Taylor comes to our house from Westfield.

9. Milton is south of Boston.
1. On May 22, 1696, Sewall buried a premature son born dead and on December 23 his daughter Sarah died. When his son Samuel read from Matthew 12.7 ("But if ye had known what this meaneth, I will have mercy, and not sacrifice, ye would not have condemned the guiltless") it did "awfully bring to mind," Sewall noted, "the Salem tragedy."

Monday, July 18, [1698.] I walk'd with Mr. Edward Taylor upon Cotton Hill, thence to Becon Hill, the Pasture, along the Stone-wall: As came back, we sat down on the great Rock, and Mr. Taylor told me his courting his first wife,[2] and Mr. Fitch his story of Mr. Dod's prayer to God to bring his Affection to close with a person pious, but hard-favored. Has God answered me in finding out one Godly and fit for me, and shall I part for fancy? When came home, my wife gave me Mr. Tappan's Letter concerning Eliza,[3] which caus'd me to reflect on Mr. Taylor's Discourse. And his Prayer was for pardon of error in our ways—which made me think whether it were not best to overlook all, and go on. This day John Ive, fishing in great Spiepond, is arrested with mortal sickness which renders him in a manner speechless and senseless; dies next day; buried at Charlestown on the Wednesday. Was a very debauched, atheistical man. I was not at his Funeral. Had Gloves sent me, but the knowledge of his notoriously wicked life made me sick of going; and Mr. Mather, the president, came in just as I was ready to step out, and so I staid at home, and by that means lost a Ring:[4] but hope had no loss. Follow thou Me, was I suppose more complied with, than if had left Mr. Mather's company to go to such a Funeral.

Fourth-day, June 19, 1700. * * * Having been long and much dissatisfied with the Trade of fetching Negros from Guinea; at last I had a strong Inclination to Write something about it; but it wore off. At last reading Bayne, Ephes.[5] about servants, who mentions Blackamoors; I began to be uneasy that I had so long neglected doing any thing. When I was thus thinking, in came Bro[r] Belknap to shew me a Petition he intended to present to the Gen[L] Court for the freeing a Negro and his wife, who were unjustly held in Bondage. And there is a Motion by a Boston Committee to get a Law that all Importers of Negros shall pay 40[s] *per* head, to discourage the bringing of them. And Mr. C. Mather resolves to publish a sheet to exhort Masters to labor their Conversion. Which makes me hope that I was call'd of God to Write this Apology[6] for them; Let his Blessing accompany the same.

Tuesday, June 10th[, 1701.] Having last night heard that Josiah Willard had cut off his hair (a very full head of hair) and put on a Wigg, I went to him this morning. Told his Mother what I came about, and she call'd him. I enquired of him what Extremity had forced him to put off his own hair, and put on a Wigg? He answered, none at all. But said that his Hair was streight, and that it parted behinde. Seem'd to argue that men might as well shave their hair off their head, as off their face. I answered men were men before they had hair on their faces, (half of mankind have never any). God seems to have ordain'd our Hair as a Test, to see whether we can bring our minds to be content to be at his finding: or whether we would be our own Carvers, Lords, and come no more at Him. If disliked our Skin, or Nails; 'tis no Thanks to us, that for all that, we cut them not off: Pain and danger restrain us. Your Calling is to teach men self Denial. Twill be displeasing and burdensom to good men: And they that care not what men think of them

---

2. Elizabeth Fitch died on July 7, 1689.
3. Elizabeth Tappan (or Toppan) was Sewall's niece.
4. A memorial gift. Gloves were sent as an invitation to a funeral.

5. Paul Baynes, *A Commentary upon the First Chapter of the Epistle of Saint Paul. Written to the Ephesians* (1618).
6. *The Selling of Joseph* was published on June 24, 1700.

care not what God thinks of them. Father, Bro' Simon, Mr. Pemberton, Mr. Wigglesworth, Oakes, Noyes (Oliver), Brattle of Cambridge their example. Allow me to be so far a *Censor Morum*[7] for this end of the Town. Pray'd him to read the Tenth Chapter of the Third book of Calvins Institutions. I read it this morning in course, not of choice. Told him that it was condemn'd by a Meeting of Ministers at Northampton in Mr. [Solomon] Stoddards house, when the said Josiah was there. Told him of the Solemnity of the Covenant which he and I had lately entered into, which put me upon discoursing to him. He seem'd to say would leave off his Wigg when his hair was grown. I spake to his Father of it a day or two after: He thank'd me that had discoursed his Son, and told me that when his hair was grown to cover his ears, he promis'd to leave off his Wigg. If he had known of it, would have forbidden him. His Mother heard him talk of it; but was afraid positively to forbid him; lest he should do it, and so be more faulty.

Sabbath, Nov' 30, [1701.] * * * I spent this Sabbath at Mr. Colman's, partly out of dislike to Mr. Josiah Willard's cutting off his Hair, and wearing a Wigg: He preach'd for Mr. Pemberton in the morning; He that contemns[8] the Law of Nature, is not fit to be a publisher of the Law of Grace. * * *

Lord's Day, June 10, 1705. The Learned and pious Mr. Michael Wigglesworth dies at Malden about 9. m. Had been sick about 10. days of a Fever; 73 years and 8 moneths old. He was the Author of the Poem entituled The Day of Doom, which has been so often printed: and was very useful as a Physician.

Febr. 6, [1718.] This morning wandering in my mind wh8ther to live a Single or a Married Life;[9] I had a sweet and very affectionat Meditation Concerning the Lord Jesus; Nothing was to be objected against his Person, Parentage, Relations, Estate, House, Home! Why did I not resolutely, presently close with Him! And I cry'd mightily to God that He would help me so to doe! * * *

March, 14, [1718.] Deacon Marion comes to me, sits with me a great while in the evening; after a great deal of Discourse about his Courtship— He told [me] the Olivers said they wish'd I would Court their Aunt.[1] I said little, but said twas not five Moneths since I buried my dear Wife. Had said before 'twas hard to know whether best to marry again or no; whom to marry. * * *

Sept' 5, [1720.] Mary Hirst goes to Board with Madam Oliver and her Mother Loyd. Going to Son Sewall's I there meet with Madam Winthrop, told her I was glad to meet her there, had not seen her a great while; gave her Mr. Homes's Sermon.

Sept. 30, [1720.] Mr. Colman's Lecture: Daughter Sewall acquaints Madam Winthrop that if she pleas'd to be within at 3. P.M. I would wait on her. She answer'd she would be at home.

Satterday, October 1, [1720.] I dine at Mr. Stoddard's: from thence I went to Madam Winthrop's just at 3. Spake to her, saying, my loving wife[2] died

7. Judge of morals (Latin).
8. Scorns.
9. Hannah Hull Sewall had died on October 19, 1717; they had been married almost forty-two years. Sewall married Abigail Tilley on October 29, 1719, and she died suddenly in May of 1720. Sewall's courtship of Madame Winthrop began seri-

ously in the fall of 1720. On March 29, 1722, Sewall married a widow, Mary Gibbs, and she survived him.
1. Katherine Brattle Winthrop was the widow of Chief Justice Wait Still Winthrop, Sewall's friend. Instead, he married Tilley.
2. I.e., Abigail.

so soon and suddenly, 'twas hardly convenient for me to think of Marrying again; however I came to this Resolution, that I would not make my Court to any person without first Consulting with her. Had a pleasant discourse about 7 Single persons sitting in the Fore-seat [September] 29th, viz. Mad^m Rebekah Dudley, Catharine Winthrop, Bridget Usher, Deliverance Legg, Rebekah Loyd, Lydia Colman, Elizabeth Bellingham.³ She propounded one and another for me; but none would do, said Mrs. Loyd was about her Age.

Octob^r 3, 2, [1720.] Waited on Madam Winthrop again; 'twas a little while before she came in. Her daughter Noyes⁴ being there alone with me, I said, I hoped my Waiting on her Mother would not be disagreeable to her. She answer'd she should not be against that that might be for her Comfort. I Saluted her, and told her I perceiv'd I must shortly wish her a good Time; (her mother had told me, she was with Child, and within a Moneth or two of her Time). By and by in came Mr. Airs, Chaplain of the Castle,⁵ and hang'd up his Hat, which I was a little startled at, it seeming as if he was to lodge there. At last Madam Winthrop came in. After a considerable time, I went up to her and said, if it might not be inconvenient I desired to speak with her. She assented, and spake of going into another Room; but Mr. Airs and Mrs. Noyes presently rose up, and went out, leaving us there alone. Then I usher'd in Discourse from the names in the Fore-seat; at last I pray'd that Katharine [Mrs. Winthrop] might be the person assign'd for me. She instantly took it up in way of Denyal, as if she had catch'd at an Opportunity to do it, saying she could not do it before she was asked. Said that was her mind unless she should Change it, which she believed she should not; could not leave her Children. I express'd my Sorrow that she should do it so Speedily, pray'd her Consideration, and ask'd her when I should wait upon her agen. She setting no time, I mention'd that day Sennight.⁶ Gave her Mr. Willard's Fountain open'd⁷ with the little print and verses; saying I hop'd if we did well read that book, we should meet together hereafter, if we did not now. She took the Book, and put it in her Pocket. Took Leave.

Midweek, Oct. 5, [1720.] I din'd with the Court; from thence went and visited Cousin Jonathan's wife, Lying in with her little Betty. Gave the Nurse 2^s⁸ Although I had appointed to wait upon her, M^m Winthrop, next Monday, yet I went from my Cousin Sewall's thither about 3. P.M. The Nurse told me Madam dined abroad at her daughter Noyes's, they were to go out together.
* * *

[Oct.] 6th [, 1720.] A little after 6 P.M. I went to Madam Winthrop's. She was not within. I gave Sarah Chickering the Maid 2^s, Juno, who brought in wood, 1^s Afterward the Nurse came in, I gave her 18^d,⁹ having no other small Bill. After awhile Dr. Noyes came in with his Mother; and quickly after his wife came in: They sat talking, I think, till eight aclock. I said I fear'd I might be some Interruption to their Business: Dr. Noyes reply'd pleasantly: He fear'd they might be an Interruption to me, and went away. Madam seem'd to harp upon the same string. Must take care of her Children; could not leave that House and Neighborhood where she had dwelt so long. I told her

3. Widows usually sat in a front pew reserved for them.
4. The wife of Dr. Oliver Noyes.
5. I.e., Castle Island in Boston Harbor. "Saluted": kissed.
6. A week hence.

7. Samuel Willard, The Fountain Opened, or the Great Gospel Privilege of Having Christ Exhibited to Sinful Men (1700).
8. Two shillings.
9. Pence; from the Latin denarius.

she might doe her children as much or more good by bestowing what she laid out in Hous-keeping, upon them. Said her Son would be of Age the 7th of August. I said it might be inconvenient for her to dwell with her Daughter-in-Law, who must be Mistress of the House. I gave her a piece of Mr. Belcher's Cake and Ginger-Bread wrapped up in a clean sheet of Paper; told her of her Father's kindness to me when Treasurer, and I Constable. My Daughter Judith was gon from me and I was more lonesom—might help to forward one another in our Journey to Canaan.[1] * * *

[Oct.] 10th[, 1720.] * * * In the Evening I visited Madam Winthrop, who treated me with a great deal of Curtesy; Wine, Marmalade. I gave her the News-Letter[2] about the Thanksgiving Proposals, for sake of the verses for David Jeffries. She tells me Dr. Increase Mather visited her this day, in Mr. Hutchinson's Coach. * * *

[Oct.] 12[, 1720.] At Mad^m Winthrop's Steps I took leave of Capt Hill, &c.

Mrs. Anne Cotton came to door (twas before 8.) said Madam Winthrop was within, directed me into the little Room, where she was full of work[3] behind a Stand; Mrs. Cotton came in and stood. Madam Winthrop pointed to her to set me a Chair. Madam Winthrop's Countenance was much changed from what 'twas on Monday, look'd dark and lowering. At last, the work, (black stuff or Silk) was taken away, I got my Chair in place, had some Converse, but very Cold and indifferent to what 'twas before. Ask'd her to acquit me of Rudeness if I drew off her Glove. Enquiring the reason, I told her twas great odds between handling a dead Goat, and a living Lady. Got it off. I told her I had one Petition to ask of her, that was, that she would take off the Negative she laid on me the third of October; She readily answer'd she could not, and enlarg'd upon it; She told me of it so soon as she could; could not leave her house, children, neighbors, business. I told her she might do som Good to help and support me. * * * Sarah fill'd a Glass of Wine, she drank to me, I to her, She sent Juno home with me with a good Lantern, I gave her 6^d and bid her thank her Mistress. In some of our Discourse, I told her I had rather go to the Stone-House[4] adjoining to her, than to come to her against her mind. Told her the reason why I came every other night was lest I should drink too deep draughts of Pleasure. She had talk'd of Canary,[5] her Kisses were to me better than the best Canary. * * *

Oct. 13, [1720.] I tell my Son and daughter Sewall, that the Weather was not so fair as I apprehended. * * *

Monday, [Oct.] 17, [1720.] Give Mr. Dan Willard, and Mr. Pelatiah Whittemore their Oaths to their Accounts; and Mr. John Briggs to his, as they are Attornys to Dr. Cotton Mather, Administrator to the estate of Nathan Howell deceased. In the Evening I visited Madam Winthrop, who Treated me Courteously, but not in Clean Linen as somtimes. She said, she did not know whether I would come again, or no. I ask'd her how she could so impute inconstancy to me. (I had not visited her since Wednesday night being unable to get over the Indisposition received by the Treatment received that night, and I must in it seem'd to sound like a made piece of Formality.) Gave her this day's Gazett. Heard David Jeffries say the Lord's Prayer, and some other portions of the Scriptures. He came to the door, and ask'd me to go into Chamber, where his Grandmother was tending Little Katee, to whom she

1. I.e., to paradise.
2. *The Boston News-Letter* published the governor's proclamation for Thanksgiving Day 1720.
3. I.e., her needlework.
4. A prison.
5. A sweet wine from the Canary Isles.

had given Physick; but I chose to sit below. Dr. Noyes and his wife came in, and sat a Considerable time; had been visiting Son and dâter Cooper. Juno came home with me.

[Oct.] 18, [1720.] Visited Madam Mico, who came to me in a splendid Dress. I said, It may be you have heard of my Visiting Madam Winthrop, her Sister. She answered, Her Sister had told her of it. I ask'd her good Will in the Affair. She answer'd, If her Sister were for it, she should not hinder it. I gave her Mr. Homes's Sermon. She gave me a Glass of Canary, entertain'd me with good Discourse, and a Respectfull Remembrance of my first Wife. I took Leave.

Midweek, [Oct.] 19, [1720.] Visited Madam Winthrop; Sarah told me she was at Mr. Walley's, would not come home till late. I gave her Hannah's 3 oranges with her Duty, not knowing whether I should find her or no. Was ready to go home: but said if I knew she was there, I would go thither. Sarah seemd to speak with pretty good Courage, She would be there. I went and found her there, with Mr. Walley and his wife in the little Room below. At 7 aclock I mentioned going home; at 8. I put on my Coat, and quickly waited on her home. She found occasion to speak loud to the servant, as if she had a mind to be known. Was Courteous to me; but took occasion to speak pretty earnestly about my keeping a Coach: I said 'twould cost £100. per annum: she said 'twould cost but £40. Spake much against John Winthrop, his false-heartedness. Mr. Eyre came in and sat awhile; I offer'd him Dr. Incr. Mather's Sermons, whereof Mr. Appleton's Ordination-Sermon was one; said he had them already. I said I would give him another. Exit. Came away somewhat late.

Oct. 20, [1720.] Mr. Colman preaches from Luke 15.10. Joy among the Angels: made an Excellent Discourse.

At Council, Col. Townsend spake to me of my Hood: Should get a Wigg.[6] I said twas my chief[7] Ornament: I wore it for sake of the Day. Bro[r] Odlin, and Sam, Mary, and Jane Hirst dine with us. Promis'd to wait on the Govr about 7. Madam Winthrop not being at Lecture, I went thither first; found her very Serene with her dâter Noyes, Mrs. Dering, and the widow Shipreev sitting at a little Table, she in her arm'd Chair. She drank to me, and I to Mrs. Noyes. After awhile pray'd the favor to speak with her. She took one of the Candles, and went into the best Room, clos'd the shutters, sat down upon the Couch. She told me Madam Usher had been there, and said the Coach must be set on Wheels, and not by Rusting. She spake something of my needing a Wigg. Ask'd me what her Sister said to me. I told her, She said, If her Sister were for it, She would not hinder it. But I told her, she did not say she would be glad to have me for her Brother. Said, I shall keep you in the Cold, and ask her if she would be within tomorrow night, for we had had but a running Feast. She said she could not tell whether she should, or no. I took Leave. As were drinking at the Governor's, he said: In England the Ladies minded little more than that they might have Money, and Coaches to ride in. I said, And New-England brooks its Name.[8] At which Mr. Dudley smiled. Gov[r] said they were not quite so bad here.

Friday, Oct. 21, [1720.] My Son, the Minister, came to me p. m. by

6. I.e., in addition to Sewall's judicial hood, he should acquire a wig such as English judges wear today, and to be distinguished from the periwig that Madame Winthrop wanted Sewall to wear to disguise his baldness. Sewall chose to wear a velvet cap instead.
7. Principal.
8. I.e., it is the same in New England.

appointment and we pray one for another in the Old Chamber; more espe-cially respecting my Courtship. About 6. aclock I go to Madam Winthrop's; Sarah told me her Mistress was gon out, but did not tell me whither she went. She presently order'd me a Fire; so I went in, having Dr. Sibb's Bowels[9] with me to read. I read the two first Sermons, still no body came in: at last about 9. aclock Mr. Jn⁰ Eyre came in; I took the opportunity to say to him as I had done to Mrs. Noyes before, that I hoped my Visiting his Mother would not be disagreeable to him; He answered me with much Respect. When twas after 9. aclock He of himself said he would go and call her, she was but at one of his Brothers: A while after I heard Madam Winthrop's voice, enquiring somthing about John. After a good while and Clapping the Garden door twice or thrice, she came in. I mention'd somthing of the late-ness; she banter'd me, and said I was later. She receiv'd me Courteously. I ask'd when our proceedings should be made publick: She said They were like to be no more publick than they were already. Offer'd me no Wine that I remember. I rose up at 11 aclock to come away, saying I would put on my Coat, She offer'd not to help me. I pray'd her that Juno might light me home, she open'd the Shutter, and said twas pretty light abroad; Juno was weary and gon to bed. So I came hôm by Star-light as well as I could. At my first coming in, I gave Sarah five Shillings. I writ Mr. Eyre his Name in his book with the date Octob^r 21, 1720. It cost me 8ˢ. Jehovah jireh![1] Madam told me she had visited M. Mico, Wendell, and Wᵐ Clark of the South [Church].

Octob^r 22, [*1720.*] Dâter Cooper visited me before my going out of Town, staid till about Sun set. I brought her going near as far as the Orange Tree.[2] Coming back, near Leg's Corner, Little David Jeffries saw me, and looking upon me very lovingly, ask'd me if I was going to see his Grandmother? I said, Not to-night. Gave him a penny, and bid him present my Service to his Grandmother.

Octob^r 24, [*1720.*] I went in the Hackny Coach through the Common, stop't at Madam Winthrop's (had told her I would take my departure from thence). Sarah came to the door with Katee in her Arms: but I did not think to take notice of the Child. Call'd her Mistress. I told her, being encourag'd by David Jeffries loving eyes, and sweet Words, I was come to enquire whether she could find in her heart to leave that House and Neighborhood, and go and dwell with me at the South-end; I think she said softly, Not yet. I told her It did not ly in my hands to keep a Coach. If I should, I should be in danger to be brought to keep company with her Neighbor Brooker, (he was a little before sent to prison for Debt). Told her I had an Antipathy against those who would pretend to give themselves; but nothing of their Estate. I would a proportion of my Estate with my self. And I suppos'd she would do so. As to a Perriwig, My best and greatest Friend, I could not possibly have a greater, began to find me with Hair before I was born, and had continued to do so ever since; and I could not find in my heart to go to another. She commended the book I gave her, Dr. Preston, the Church's Marriage; quoted him saying 'twas inconvenient keeping out of a Fashion commonly used. I said the Time and Tide did circumscribe my Visit. She

---

9. Dr. Richard Sibbes was the author of *Bowels Opened; or a Discovery of the Neere and Deere Love, Union, and Communion between Christ and the Church* (1641).

1. The Lord will provide (Hebrew); from Genesis 22.14.
2. An inn.

gave me a Dram of Black-Cherry Brandy, and gave me a lump of the Sugar that was in it. She wish'd me a good Journy. I pray'd God to keep her, and came away. Had a very pleasant Journy to Salem.

[October] 31, [1720.] * * * At night I visited Madam Winthrop about 6. P.M. They told me she was gone to Madam Mico's. I went thither and found she was gone; so return'd to her house, read the Epistles to the Galatians, Ephesians in Mr. Eyre's Latin Bible. After the Clock struck 8. I began to read the 103. Psalm. Mr. Wendell came in from his Warehouse. Ask'd me if I were alone? Spake very kindly to me, offer'd me to call Madam Winthrop. I told him, She would be angry, had been at M. Mico's; he help'd me on with my Coat and I came home: left the Gazett in the Bible, which told Sarah of, bid her present my Service to M. Winthrop, and tell her I had been to wait on her if she had been at home.

Nov' 1, [1720.] I was so taken up that I could not go if I would.

Midweek, Nov' 2, [1720.] Went again, and found Mrs. Alden there, who quickly went out. Gave her [Madam Winthrop] about ½ pound of Sugar Almonds, cost 3ˢ per £. Carried them on Monday. She seem'd pleas'd with them, ask'd what they cost. Spake of giving her a Hundred pounds per annum if I dy'd before her. Ask'd her what sum she would give me, if she should dy first? Said I would give her time to Consider of it. She said she heard as if I had given all to my Children by Deeds of Gift. I told her 'twas a mistake, Point-Judith was mine &c. That in England, I own'd, my Father's desire was that it should go to my eldest Son; 'twas 20£ per annum; she thought 'twas forty. I think when I seem'd to excuse pressing this, she seem'd to think 'twas best to speak of it; a long winter was coming on. Gave me a Glass or two of Canary.

Friday, Nov' 4th[, 1720.] Went again about 7. aclock; found there Mr. John Walley and his wife: sat discoursing pleasantly. I shew'd them Isaac Moses's [an Indian] Writing. Madam W. serv'd Comfeits³ to us. After awhile a Table was spread, and Supper was set. I urg'd Mr. Walley to Crave a Blessing; but he put it upon me. About 9. they went away. I ask'd Madam what fashioned Neck-lace I should present her with, She said, None at all. I ask'd her Whereabout we left off last time; mention'd what I had offer'd to give her; Ask'd her what she would give me; She said she could not Change her Condition: She had said so from the beginning; could not be so far from her Children, the Lecture. Quoted the Apostle Paul affirming that a single Life was better than Married. I answer'd That was for the present Distress. Said she had not pleasure in things of that nature as formerly: I said, you are the fitter to make me a Wife. If she held in that mind, I must go home and bewail my Rashness in making more haste than good Speed. However, considering the Supper, I desired her to be within next Monday night, if we liv'd so long. Assented. She charg'd me with saying, that she must put away Juno, if she came to me: I utterly deny'd it, it never came in my heart; yet she insisted upon it; saying it came in upon discourse about the Indian woman that obtained her Freedom this Court. About 10. I said I would not disturb the good orders of her House, and came away. She not seeming pleas'd with my Coming away. Spake to her about David Jeffries, had not seen him.

Monday, Nov' 7th[, 1720.] My son pray'd in the Old Chamber. Our time

3. Sweetmeats; fruits preserved in sugar, comfits.

had been taken up by Son and Daughter Cooper's Visit; so that I only read the 130th and 143. Psalm. Twas on the Account of my Courtship. I went to Mad. Winthrop; found her rocking her little Katee in the Cradle. I excus'd my Coming so late (near Eight). She set me an arm'd Chair and Cusheon; and so the Cradle was between her arm'd Chair and mine. Gave her the remnant of my Almonds; She did not eat of them as before; but laid them away; I said I came to enquire whether she had alter'd her mind since Friday, or remained of the same mind still. She said, Thereabouts. I told her I loved her, and was so fond[4] as to think that she loved me: She said had a great respect for me. I told her, I had made her an offer, without asking any advice; she had so many to advise with, that twas a hindrance. The Fire was come to one short Brand besides the Block, which Brand was set up in end; at last it fell to pieces, and no Recruit was made:[5] She gave me a Glass of Wine. I think I repeated again that I would go home and bewail my Rashness in making more haste than good Speed. I would endeavor to contain myself, and not go on to sollicit her to do that which she could not Consent to. Took leave of her. As came down the steps she bid me have a Care. Treated me Courteously. Told her she had enter'd the 4th year of her Widowhood. I had given her the News-Letter before: I did not bid her draw off her Glove as sometime I had done. Her Dress was not so clean as sometime it had been. Jehovah jireh!

Midweek, [Nov.] 9th[, 1720.] Dine at Bro[r] Stoddard's: were so kind as to enquire of me if they should invite M[m] Winthrop; I answer'd No. Thank'd my Sister Stoddard for her Courtesie; sat down at the Table Simeon Stoddard esqr, Mad. Stoddard, Samuel Sewall, Mr. Colman, M[m] Colman, Mr. Cooper, Mrs. Cooper, Mrs. Hannah Cooper, Mr. Samuel Sewall of Brooklin, Mrs. Sewall, Mr. Joseph Sewall, Mrs. Lydia Walley, Mr. William Stoddard. Had a noble Treat. At night our Meeting was at the Widow Belknap's. Gave each one of the Meeting one of Mr. Homes's Sermons, 12 in all; She sent her servant home with me with a Lantern. Madam Winthrop's Shutters were open as I pass'd by.

Nov[r] 11, [1720.] Went not to M[m] Winthrop's. This is the 2[d] Withdraw.[6]

Nov[r] 14, [1720.] Madam Winthrop visits my daughter Sewall with her [*granddaughter*] Katee [*Walley*].

March, 29th, [1722.] Samuel Sewall, and Mrs. Mary Gibbs were joined together in Marriage by the Rev[d] Mr. William Cooper; Mr. Sewall pray'd once. Mr. Jn[o] Cotton was at Sandwich, sent for by Madam Cotton after her Husband's death.

Lord's day, April 1, [1722.] Sat with my wife in her Pue.

April, 2, [1722.] Brought her home to my House.

April, 8, [1722.] introduc'd her into my Pue, and sat with her there.

June 15, [1725.] I accompanied my Son to Mad. Winthrop's. She was a-bed about 10. *mane.* I told her I found my Son coming to her and took the Opportunity to come with him. She thank'd me kindly, enquired how Madam Sewall did. Ask'd my Son to go to Prayer. Present Mr. John Eyre, Mrs. Noyes, Mrs. Walley and David Jeffries. At coming I said, I kiss your hand Madame

---

4. Foolish.
5. Added logs would indicate that Sewall was

expected to stay longer.
6. I.e., the second time he decided not to visit.

(her hand felt very dry). She desired me to pray that God would lift up upon her the Light of his Countenance.

Monday, Augt 2, [1725.] Mrs. Katherine Winthrop, Relict[7] of the hon^{ble} Waitstill Winthrop esqr., died, Ætatis 61. She was born in September 1664. The Escutcheons on the Hearse bore the Arms of Winthrop and Brattle, The Lion Sable.[8] *Augt 5, 1725.* Bearers, His Hon^r Lt Govr Dummer, Saml Sewall; Col. Byfield, Edw. Bromfield esqr; Simeon Stoddard esqr., Adam Winthrop esqr. Was buried in the South-burying place, in a Tomb near the North-east Corner. Will be much miss'd. After the Funeral, Many of the Council, went and wish'd Col. Fitch Joy of his daughter Martha's Marriage with Mr. James Allen. Had good Bride-Cake, good Wine, Burgundy and Canary, good Beer, Oranges, Pears.

Friday, April 28, 1727. The first half sheet of the Phenomena is wrought off.[9]

Lords day, Decr 17, [1727.] I was surprised to hear Mr. Thacher of Milton, my old Friend, pray'd for as dangerously Sick. Next day. *Decr 18, 1727.* I am inform'd by Mr. Gerrish, that my dear friend died last night; which I doubt bodes ill to Milton and the Province, his dying at this Time, though in the 77th year of his Age. *Deus avertat Omen!*[1]

Friday, Decr 22, [1727.] the day after the Fast, was inter'd. Bearers Rev^d Mr. Nehemiah Walter, Mr. Joseph Baxter; Mr. John Swift, Mr. Saml Hunt; Mr. Joseph Sewall, Mr. Thomas Prince. I was inclin'd before, and having a pair of Gloves sent me, I determined to go to the Funeral, if the Weather prov'd favorable, which it did, and I hired Blake's Coach with four Horses; my Son, Mr. Cooper and Mr. Prince went with me. Refresh'd there with Meat and Drink; got thither about half an hour past one. It was sad to see triumphed over my dear Friend! I rode in my Coach to the Burying place; not being able to get nearer by reason of the many Horses. From thence went directly up the Hill where the Smith's Shop, and so home very comfortably and easily, the ground being mollified. But when I came to my own Gate, going in, I fell down, a board slipping under my Left foot, my right Legg

---

7. Widow.
8. Black. "Escutcheons": heraldic shields.
9. Set in type. The 2nd edition of Sewall's first book, published in 1697. The full title is *Phaenomena quaedam Apocalyptica ad Aspectum Novi Orbis configurate. Or, some few lines towards a description of the New Heaven as it makes to those who stand upon the New Earth.* Although it is now hardly ever read, it contains a passage describing Plum Island, Massachusetts, which remains one of the best 17th-century American hymns to the New World:

As long as Plum Island shall faithfully keep the commanded post; notwithstanding all the hectoring words, and hard blows of the proud and boisterous ocean; as long as any salmon, or sturgeon shall swim in the streams of Merrimack; or any perch or pickrel in Crane Pond; as long as the sea-fowl shall know the time of their coming, and not neglect seasonably to visit the places of their acquaintance; as long as any cattle shall be fed with the grass growing in the meadows, which do humbly bow down themselves before Turkey Hill; as long as any sheep shall walk upon Old Town Hills, and shall from thence pleasantly look down upon the river Parker, and the fruitful marshes lying beneath; as long as any free and harmless doves shall find a white oak or other tree within the township to perch, or feed, or build a careless nest upon; and shall voluntarily present themselves to perform the office of gleaners after barley-harvest; as long as Nature shall not grow old and date, but shall constantly remember to give the rows of Indian corn their education by pairs: so long shall Christians be born there; and being first made meet, shall from thence be translated to be made partakers of the inheritance of the saints in light. Now seeing the inhabitants of Newbury, and of New England, upon the observance of their tenure, we may expect that their rich and gracious Lord will continue and confirm them in the possession of these invaluable privileges. *Let us have grace, whereby we may serve God acceptably with reverence and godly fear, for our God is a consuming fire.* Hebrews 12.28–29.

1. May God turn aside all bad things (Latin).

raised off the skin, and put me to a great deal of pain, especially when 'twas washed with Rum. It was good for me that I was thus Afflicted that my spirit might be brought into a frame more suitable to the Solemnity, which is apt to be too light; and by the loss of some of my Skin, and blood I might be awakened to prepare for my own Dissolution. Mr. Walter prayed before the Corps was carried out. I had a pair of Gloves sent me before I went, and a Ring given me there. Mr. Millar, the Church of England Minister, was there. At this Funeral I heard of the death of my good old Tenant Cap¹ Nathan Niles, that very Friday morn. I have now been at the Interment of 4 of my Class-mates. First, the Rev'd Mr. William Adams at Dedham, Midweek, Augt. 19, 1685. Second, Mr. John Bowles, at Roxbury, March 31, 1691. Was one of his Bearers. Third, Capt. Samuel Phips at Charlestown. He was laid in his Son-in-Law Lemmon's Tomb. Had a good pair of Gloves, and a gold Ring. He was Clerk of the Court and Register many years. Clerk to his death, and his Son succeeded him. Was Præcentor² many years to the congregation. Inter'd Augt. 9, 1725. Fourth, the Rev'd Mr. Thachar at Milton. Now I can go to no more Funerals of my Classmates; nor none be at mine; for the survivers, the Rev'd Mr. Samuel Mather at Windsor, and the Revᵈ Mr. Taylor at Westfield, [are] one Hundred Miles off, and are extremly enfeebled. I humbly pray that CHRIST may be graciously present with us all Three both in Life, and in Death, and then we shall safely and Comfortably walk through the shady valley that leads to Glory.

Lords-day, Decʳ 24th[, 1727.] am kept from the solemn Assembly by my bruised Shin.

October 19, 1728. Seeing this to be the same day of the week and Moneth that the Wife of my youth expired Eleven years agoe, it much affected me. I writ to my dear Son Mr. Joseph Sewall of it, desiring him to come and dine with me: or however that he would call some time to join my Condolence. He came about Noon and made an excellent Prayer in the East Chamber. Laus Deo.³ I told him of the death of the Widow Wheeler yesterday morning, which he had not heard of. When Sam came to read, I wrap'd up a Silver Cup with one ear,⁴ weighing about 3 ounces and 12 Grains, to give his Mother, which I had promis'd her. A Minister's Wife, I told her, ought not to be without such a one. I went to looke [for] silver to make such a one, and unexpectedly met with one ready made.

Ditto, die, feria Septima.⁵ I gave my dear Wife a Book of 7 Sermons, which had been my Daughter Hannah's, for whom she had labored beyond measure.

1673–1729   1878–82

2. One who leads the congregation in singing.   4. Handle.
3. Praise God (Latin).   5. Same place, the day, Sunday (Latin).

The Selling of Joseph: A Memorial[1]

Forasmuch as Liberty *is in real value next unto* Life: *None ought to part with it themselves, or deprive others of it, but upon most mature Consideration.*[2]

The Numerousness of Slaves at this day in the Province, and the Uneasiness of them under their Slavery, hath put many upon thinking whether the Foundation of it be firmly and well laid; so as to sustain the Vast Weight that is built upon it. It is most certain that all Men, as they are the Sons of *Adam*, are Coheirs; and have equal Right unto Liberty, and all other outward Comforts of Life. *God hath given the Earth* [with all its Commodities] *unto the Sons of Adam, Psal* 115.16. *And hath made of One Blood, all Nations of Men, for to dwell on all the face of the Earth, and hath determined the Times before appointed, and the bounds of their habitation: That they should seek the Lord. Forasmuch then as we are the Offspring of GOD &c. Act* 17.26, 27, 29. Now although the Title given by the last ADAM, doth infinitely better Men[']s Estates, respecting GOD and themselves; and grants them a most beneficial and inviolable Lease under the Broad Seal of Heaven, who were before only Tenants at Will:[3] Yet through the Indulgence of GOD to our First Parents after the Fall, the outward Estate of all and every of their Children, remains the same, as to one another. So that Originally, and Naturally, there is no such thing as Slavery. *Joseph* was rightfully no more a Slave to his Brethren, than they were to him: and they had no more Authority to *Sell* him, than they had to *Slay* him. And if *they* had nothing to do to Sell him; the *Ishmaelites* bargaining with them, and paying down Twenty pieces of Silver could not make a Title. Neither could *Potiphar* have any better Interest in him than the *Ishmaelites* had. *Gen.* 37.20, 27, 28. For he that shall in this case plead *Alteration of Property*, seems to have forfeited a great part of his own claim to Humanity. There is no proportion between Twenty Pieces of Silver, and LIBERTY. The Commodity it self is the Claimer. If *Arabian* Gold be imported in any quantities, most are afraid to meddle with it, though they might have it at easy rates; lest if it should have been wrongfully taken from the Owners, it should kindle a fire to the Consumption of their whole Estate. 'Tis pity there should be more Caution used in buying a Horse, or a little lifeless dust; than there is in purchasing Men and Women: Whenas they are the Offspring of GOD, and their Liberty is,

. . . . *Auro pretiosior Omni.*[4]

And seeing GOD hath said, *He that Stealeth a Man and Selleth him, or if he be found in his hand, he shall surely be put to Death.* Exod. 21.16. This Law being of Everlasting Equity, wherein Man Stealing is ranked amongst

---

1. A public remonstrance or statement. The text is derived from the first edition (1700).
2. Translated from *De Conscientia, et eius iure, vel casibus* (1623), by English theologian William Ames, the main source for Puritan ecclesiastical ideas. The last quotation in the tract includes this same passage in Ames's Latin original.

3. Renters subject to immediate expulsion from rental property, as opposed to those holding a long-term lease. Here and throughout this opening passage, Sewall uses language derived from contemporary property law and practice. "Broad Seal": seal of England, affixed to land grants and patents.
4. More precious than all the gold (Latin).

the most atrocious of Capital Crimes: What louder Cry can there be made of that Celebrated Warning,

Caveat Emptor![5]

And all things considered, it would conduce more to the Welfare of the Province, to have White Servants for a Term of Years, than to have Slaves for Life. Few can endure to hear of a Negro's being made free; and indeed they can seldom use their freedom well; yet their continual aspiring after their forbidden Liberty, renders them Unwilling Servants. And there is such a disparity in their Conditions, Colour & Hair, that they can never embody with us, and grow up into orderly Families, to the Peopling of the Land: but still remain in our Body Politick as a kind of extravasat[6] Blood. As many Negro men as there are among us, so many empty places there are in our Train Bands, and the places taken up of Men that might make Husbands for our Daughters. And the Sons and Daughters of *New England* would become more like *Jacob,* and *Rachel,*[7] if this Slavery were thrust quite out of doors. Moreover it is too well known what Temptations Masters are under, to connive at the Fornication of their Slaves; lest they should be obliged to find them Wives, or pay their Fines. It seems to be practically pleaded that they might be Lawless; 'tis thought much of, that the Law should have Satisfaction for their Thefts, and other Immoralities; by which means, *Holiness to the Lord,* is more rarely engraven upon this sort of Servitude. It is likewise most lamentable to think, how in taking Negros out of *Africa,* and Selling of them here, That which GOD has joyned together men do boldly rend asunder; Men from their Country, Husbands from their Wives, Parents from their Children. How horrible is the Uncleanness, Mortality, if not Murder, that the Ships are guilty of that bring great Crouds of these miserable Men, and Women. Methinks, when we are bemoaning the barbarous Usage of our Friends and Kinsfolk in *Africa:* it might not be unseasonable to enquire whether we are not culpable in forcing the *Africans* to become Slaves amongst our selves. And it may be a question whether all the Benefit received by *Negro* Slaves, will balance the Accompt[8] of Cash laid out upon them; and for the Redemption of our own enslaved Friends out of *Africa.* Besides all the Persons and Estates that have perished there.

Obj. 1. *These Blackamores are of the Posterity of* Cham,[9] *and therefore are under the Curse of Slavery.* Gen. 9.25, 26, 27.

Answ. Of all Offices, one would not begg this; *viz.* Uncall'd for, to be an Executioner of the Vindictive Wrath of God; the extent and duration of which is to us uncertain. If this ever was a Commission; How do we know but that it is long since out of Date? Many have found it to their Cost, that a Prophetical Denunciation of Judgment against a Person or People, would not warrant them to inflict that evil. If it would, *Hazael* might justify himself in all he did against his Master, and the *Israelites,* from 2 *Kings* 8.10, 12.

But it is possible that by cursory reading, this Text may have been mistaken. For *Canaan* is the Person Cursed three times over, without the men-

5. Let the buyer beware! (Latin).
6. Foreign, not intrinsic.
7. Famous in the Bible for their courtship and abiding love.
8. Account.
9. I.e., Ham, the second son of Noah and the father of Cush as well as of Canaan, of the latter of whom Noah in Genesis 9.25 says, "Cursed be Canaan; a servant of servants shall he be unto his brethren." Apologists for slavery often insisted that Ham was the ancestor of the African peoples.

tioning of *Cham*. Good Expositors suppose the Curse entaild on him, and that this Prophesie was accomplished in the Extirpation of the *Canaanites*, and in the Servitude of the *Gibeonites*. *Vide Pareum*.[1] Whereas the Blackmores are not descended of *Canaan*, but of *Cush*. Psal. 68.31. *Princes shall come out of Egypt* [Mizraim], *Ethiopia* [Cush] *shall soon stretch out her hands unto God*. Under which Names, all *Africa* may be comprehended; and their Promised Conversion ought to be prayed for. *Jer*. 13.23. *Can the Ethiopian change his skin?* This shows that Black Men are the Posterity of *Cush*: Who time out of mind have been distinguished by their Colour. And for want of the true, *Ovid* assigns a fabulous cause of it.

> *Sanguine tum credunt in corpora summa vocato*
> *Æthiopum populus nigrum traxisse colorem*.[2]
> Metamorph. lib. 2.

Obj. 2. *The Nigers are brought out of a Pagan Country, into places where the Gospel is Preached*.

Answ. Evil must not be done, that good may come of it. The extraordinary and comprehensive Benefit accruing to the Church of God, and to *Joseph* personally, did not rectify his brethren[']s Sale of him.

Obj. 3. *The Africans have Wars one with another: Our Ships bring lawful Captives taken in those Wars*.

Answ. For ought is known, their Wars are much such as were between *Jacob's* Sons and their Brother *Joseph*. If they be between Town and Town; Provincial, or National: Every War is upon one side Unjust. An Unlawful War can't make lawful Captives. And by Receiving, we are in danger to promote, and partake in their Barbarous Cruelties. I am sure, if some Gentlemen should go down to the *Brewsters* to take the Air, and Fish: And a stronger party from *Hull*[3] should Surprise them, and Sell them for Slaves to a Ship outward bound: they would think themselves unjustly dealt with; both by Sellers and Buyers. And yet 'tis to be feared, we have no other kind of Title to our *Nigers*. *Therefore all things whatsoever ye would that men should do to you, do ye even so to them: for this is the Law and the Prophets*. Matt. 7.12.

Obj. 4. Abraham *had Servants bought with his Money, and born in his House*.

Answ. Until the Circumstances of *Abraham's* purchase be recorded, no Argument can be drawn from it. In the mean time, Charity obliges us to conclude, that He knew it was lawful and good.

It is Observable that the *Israelites* were strictly forbidden the buying, or selling one another for Slaves. *Levit*. 25. 39. 46. *Jer*. 34 8. . . . . . . 22. And GOD gaged His Blessing in lieu of any loss they might conceipt they suffered thereby. *Deut*. 15. 18. And since the partition Wall is broken down, inordinate Self love should likewise be demolished.[4] GOD expects that

---

1. "The Godly Learned ingenious [David] Pareus," as Sewall termed him in his diary in 1686, was a German theologian whose works were favorites with Sewall.
2. Then it was, as men think, that the people of Ethiopia became dark-skinned, for the blood was called to the surface of their bodies (by the heat) (Latin).
3. A coastal town near Boston. The Brewsters are a group of islands at the outer entrance to Boston Harbor.
4. Ephesians 2.12–14: "At that time ye were without Christ, being aliens from the commonwealth of Israel, and strangers to the covenants of promise, having no hope, and without God in the world: But now in Christ Jesus ye who sometimes were far off are made nigh by the blood of Christ. For he is our peace, who hath made both one, and hath broken down the middle wall of partition between us." "Conceipt": conceive.

Christians should be of a more Ingenuous and benign frame of spirit. Christians should carry it to all the World, as the *Israelites* were to carry it one towards another. And for men obstinately to persist in holding their Neighbours and Brethren under the Rigor of perpetual Bondage, seems to be no proper way of gaining Assurance that God has given them Spiritual Freedom. Our Blessed Saviour has altered the Measures of the ancient Love-Song, and set it to a most Excellent New Tune, which all ought to be ambitious of Learning. *Matt.* 5.43, 44 *John* 13.34. These *Ethiopians,* as black as they are; seeing they are the Sons and Daughters of the First *Adam,* the Brethren and Sisters of the Last ADAM, and the Offspring of GOD; They ought to be treated with a Respect agreeable.

 Servitus perfecta voluntaria, inter Christianum & Christianum, ex parte servi patientis sæpe est licita, quia est necessaria: sed ex parte domini agentis, & procurando & exercendo, vix potest esse licita: quia non convenit regulæ illi generali: Quæcunque volueritis ut faciant vobis homines, ita & vos facite eis.[5] Matt. 7. 12.

 Perfecta servitus pœnæ, non potest jure locum habere, nisi ex delicto gravi quod ultimum supplicium aliquo modo meretur: quia Libertas ex naturali æstimatione proxime accedit ad vitam ipsam, & eidem a multis præferri solet.[6]

Ames. Cas. Consc. Lib. 5. Cap. 23. Thes. 2, 3.

1700

---

5. As long as it is voluntary, the total servitude of one Christian to another is often enough lawful on the part of the servant because it arises from his necessity. But on the part of the master who is the agent in procuring and managing [the servant], it is scarcely legal, for it does not conform to the general rule: *Whatsoever ye would that men should do to you, do ye even so to them* (Latin).

6. Total servitude, when used as a punishment, can have no place in law, unless for an offense so grave that it is deserving of the severest penalty: for liberty by common estimate is next in importance to life itself, and by many is placed even higher than life (Latin); from Ames's *De Conscientia.*

COTTON MATHER
1663–1728

Cotton Mather, as the eldest son of Increase Mather and the grandson of Richard Mather and John Cotton, was the heir apparent to the Congregational hierarchy that had dominated the churches of New England for almost fifty years. Like his father before him, Cotton Mather attended Harvard College. He was admitted at the age of twelve, and when he graduated in 1678, President Urian Oakes told the commencement audience that his hope was great that "in this youth, Cotton and Mather shall, in fact as well as name, joint together and once more appear in life." He was expected by his family to excel and did not disappoint them, but there is no doubt he had to pay a price for his ambition: he stammered badly when young, so much so that it was assumed he could never be a preacher, and he was subject all his life to nervous disorders that drove him alternatively to ecstasy and despair. His enemies often complained that he was vain and aggressive. But he was also a genius of sorts, competent in the natural sciences and gifted in the study of ancient languages. He possessed a strong mind, and by the time he had stopped writing he could boast that he had published more than four hundred separate works. A worthy successor to his father's position as pastor of the Second Church of Boston, he remained connected with that church from 1685, when he was ordained, until his death.

Like Benjamin Franklin, Mather found great satisfaction in doing good works and organized societies for building churches, supported schools for the children of slaves, and worked to establish funds for indigent clergy. But for all his worldly success, Mather's life was darkened by disappointment and tragedy. He lost two wives and saw his third wife go insane, and of his fifteen children, only two lived until his death. More than one of his contemporaries observed that he never overcame his bitterness at being rejected for the presidency of Harvard. It was the one thing his father had achieved that he could not succeed in doing.

Although he was a skillful preacher and an eminent theologian, it is his work as a historian that has earned Mather a significant place in American literature. No one has described more movingly the hopes of the first generation of Puritans, and what gives Mather's best writing its urgency is the sense that the Puritan community as he knew it was fading away. By the time that Mather was writing his history of New England, the issues that seemed most pressing to his parishioners were political and social rather than theological. In his diary of 1700 he noted that "there was hardly any but my father and myself to appear in defense of our invaded churches." Everything that Mather wrote can be seen as a call to defend the old order of church authority against the encroachment of an increasingly secular world. As an apologist for the "old New England way" there is no doubt that Mather left himself open to attack, and by the end of the seventeenth century he had become a scapegoat for the worst in Puritan culture. He is often blamed for the Salem witch trials, for example, but he never actually attended one of them; his greatest crime was in not speaking out against those who he knew had exceeded the limits of authority. Mather saw the devil's presence in Salem as a final effort to undermine and destroy religious community.

In spite of its rambling and sometimes self-indulgent nature, the *Magnalia Christi Americana* (the title may be translated as "A history of the wonderful works of Christ in America") remains Mather's most impressive work. It is described on the title page as an "ecclesiastical history of New England," and in the course of its seven books, Mather attempts to record for future readers not only a history of the New England churches and the college (Harvard) where its ministers were trained but representative biographies of "saint's" lives. Although it is true that Mather was so caught up in his vision of a glorious past that he was sometimes quite blind to the suffocating realities of the world in which he lived, no one has set forth more clearly the history of a people who transformed a wilderness into a garden and the ideal of a harmonious community that has been characterized time and again as the American dream. It is, however, in Mather's biographical sketches—his lives of Bradford, Winthrop, Eliot, and Phips—that the *Magnalia* is most arresting, for it is in his account of a particular saint's reconciliation with God on earth that New England's story is most eloquently realized.

In addition to defending Puritan beliefs and attempting to record New England's history in the epic *Magnalia,* Mather experimented in a variety of forms that served the tastes of an emergent popular literary culture. Certainly that was the case in his handling of such tales as Hannah Dustan's, since the Indian captivity narrative was to be a prolific source for later American writers eager to reach a wide public. But Mather's reach went further. His many forays into what in essence were "conduct books" (such as *Ornaments for the Daughters of Zion,* 1692, and *Bonifacius,* 1710, later reprinted as *Essays to Do Good*), even as they showed him seeking to replace the old political power of the clergy with moral chastisement and persuasion, pioneered a kind of writing that proliferated in England and America across the following century, helping ordinary people imitate the manners and values of the elite and thus rise in the world. Here, too, Mather shared an interest with Benjamin Franklin, whose *Poor Richard* provided similar guidance for commoners. Likewise, in a book such as *Pillars of Salt* (1700), a collection of solemn anecdotes about the last days of criminals condemned to execution, Mather intended to induce meditation on the awful costs of sin. Yet at the same time he unwittingly satisfied the curiosity of the ordinary reader about such transgressive characters—the ones who failed to rise, except to the gallows. The criminal biographies just beginning to pour from the English and American press at the time would soon lead to such literary inventions as Daniel Defoe's Moll Flanders, of whom Cotton Mather was in his own small way an unlikely godfather. In Mather's day, court records were usually mere summaries, often only stating the verdict, and there was virtually no press coverage of trials. Thus the fact that he gave such a man as the convicted murderer James Morgan some opportunity to speak his mind as the two of them walked together to the gallows on Boston Common and then recorded his "last speech" there, was more of an innovation than we may imagine: those Bostonians who had heard of the trial must have been eager for such details. We may suspect that Morgan was coached, or worse, that Mather put words into his mouth, but in some ways we can recognize in their dramatic exchange a voice from the underside of Puritan New England, reminding us of the social realities that existed beneath the level usually occupied by the likes of Mather. That Mather is, from our perspective, transgressive in his own way—scornful of the Indians in many texts, scornful here of the Jews (who, Mather tells Morgan, did worse to Christ than Massachusetts authorities are about to do to Morgan himself)—draws a subtle line of connection between the minister and his lowly companion.

From The Wonders of the Invisible World[1]

[A PEOPLE OF GOD IN THE DEVIL'S TERRITORIES]

The New Englanders are a people of God settled in those, which were once the devil's territories; and it may easily be supposed that the devil was exceedingly disturbed, when he perceived such a people here accomplishing the promise of old made unto our blessed Jesus, that He should have the utmost parts of the earth for His possession.[2] There was not a greater uproar among the Ephesians,[3] when the Gospel was first brought among them, than there was among the powers of the air (after whom those Ephesians walked) when first the silver trumpets of the Gospel here made the joyful sound. The devil thus irritated, immediately tried all sorts of methods to overturn this poor plantation: and so much of the church, as was fled into this wilderness, immediately found the serpent cast out of his mouth a flood for the carrying of it away. I believe that never were more satanical devices used for the unsettling of any people under the sun, than what have been employed for the extirpation of the vine which God has here planted, casting out the heathen, and preparing a room before it, and causing it to take deep root, and fill the land, so that it sent its boughs unto the Atlantic Sea eastward, and

1. In May 1692, Governor William Phips of Massachusetts appointed a court to "hear and determine" the cases against some nineteen persons in Salem, Massachusetts, accused of witchcraft. Mather had long been interested in the subject of witchcraft; and in this work, written at the request of the judges, he describes the case against the accused. Mather, like many others, saw the evidence of witchcraft as the devil's work, a last-ditch effort to undermine the Puritan ideal. Mather was himself skeptical of much of the evidence used against the accused, especially as the trials proceeded in the summer of 1692, but like a number of prominent individuals in the community, he made no public protest. First published in 1693, the text used here is taken from the reprint by John Russell Smith (1862).
2. After Jesus was baptized he went into the desert to fast for forty days; it was there that the devil tempted him and offered him the world (see Luke 4).
3. Ephesus was an ancient city of Ionia in west Asia Minor and famous for its temples to the goddess Diana. When St. Paul preached there he received hostile treatment, and riots followed the sermons of missionaries who attempted to convert the Ephesians.

its branches unto the Connecticut River westward, and the hills were covered with a shadow thereof. But all those attempts of hell have hitherto been abortive, many an Ebenezer[4] has been erected unto the praise of God, by his poor people here; and having obtained help from God, we continue to this day. Wherefore the devil is now making one attempt more upon us; an attempt more difficult, more surprising, more snarled with unintelligible circumstances than any that we have hitherto encountered; an attempt so critical, that if we get well through, we shall soon enjoy halcyon days with all the vultures of hell trodden under our feet. He has wanted his incarnate legions to persecute us, as the people of God have in the other hemisphere been persecuted: he has therefore drawn forth his more spiritual ones to make an attack upon us. We have been advised by some credible Christians yet alive, that a malefactor, accused of witchcraft as well as murder, and executed in this place more than forty years ago, did then give notice of an horrible plot against the country by witchcraft, and a foundation of witchcraft then laid, which if it were not seasonably discovered, would probably blow up, and pull down all the churches in the country. And we have now with horror seen the discovery of such a witchcraft! An army of devils is horribly broke in upon the place which is the center, and after a sort, the first-born of our English settlements: and the houses of the good people there are filled with the doleful shrieks of their children and servants, tormented by invisible hands, with tortures altogether preternatural. After the mischiefs there endeavored, and since in part conquered, the terrible plague of evil angels hath made its progress into some other places, where other persons have been in like manner diabolically handled. These our poor afflicted neighbors, quickly after they become infected and infested with these demons, arrive to a capacity of discerning those which they conceive the shapes of their troublers; and notwithstanding the great and just suspicion that the demons might impose the shapes of innocent persons in their spectral exhibitions upon the sufferers (which may perhaps prove no small part of the witch-plot in the issue), yet many of the persons thus represented, being examined, several of them have been convicted of a very damnable witchcraft: yea, more than one [and] twenty have confessed, that they have signed unto a book, which the devil showed them, and engaged in his hellish design of bewitching and ruining our land. We know not, at least I know not, how far the delusions of Satan may be interwoven into some circumstances of the confessions; but one would think all the rules of understanding human affairs are at an end, if after so many most voluntary harmonious confessions, made by intelligent persons of all ages, in sundry towns, at several times, we must not believe the main strokes wherein those confessions all agree: especially when we have a thousand preternatural things every day before our eyes, wherein the confessors do acknowledge their concernment, and give demonstration of their being so concerned. If the devils now can strike the minds of men with any poisons of so fine a composition and operation, that scores of innocent people shall unite, in confessions of a crime, which we see actually committed, it is a thing prodigious, beyond the wonders of the former ages, and it threatens no less than a sort of a dissolution upon the

---

4. Stone of help (Hebrew, literal trans.); a commemorative monument like the one Samuel erected to note victory over the Philistines (1 Samuel 7.12).

world. Now, by these confessions 'tis agreed that the devil has made a dreadful knot of witches in the country, and by the help of witches has dreadfully increased that knot: that these witches have driven a trade of commissioning their confederate spirits to do all sorts of mischiefs to the neighbors, whereupon there have ensued such mischievous consequences upon the bodies and estates of the neighborhood, as could not otherwise be accounted for: yea, that at prodigious witch-meetings, the wretches have proceeded so far as to concert and consult the methods of rooting out the Christian religion from this country, and setting up instead of it perhaps a more gross diabolism than ever the world saw before. And yet it will be a thing little short of miracle, if in so spread a business as this, the devil should not get in some of his juggles,[5] to confound the discovery of all the rest.

*　　*　　*

But I shall no longer detain my reader from his expected entertainment, in a brief account of the trials which have passed upon some of the malefactors lately executed at Salem, for the witchcrafts whereof they stood convicted. For my own part, I was not present at any of them; nor ever had I any personal prejudice at the persons thus brought upon the stage; much less at the surviving relations of those persons, with and for whom I would be as hearty a mourner as any man living in the world: The Lord comfort them! But having received a command[6] so to do, I can do no other than shortly relate the chief matters of fact, which occurred in the trials of some that were executed, in an abridgment collected out of the court papers on this occasion put into my hands. You are to take the truth, just as it was; and the truth will hurt no good man. There might have been more of these, if my book would not thereby have swollen too big; and if some other worthy hands did not perhaps intend something further in these collections; for which cause I have only singled out four or five, which may serve to illustrate the way of dealing, wherein witchcrafts use to be concerned; and I report matters not as an advocate, but as an historian.

*　　*　　*

The Trial of Martha Carrier

AT THE COURT OF OYER AND TERMINER,[7] HELD BY ADJOURNMENT AT
SALEM, AUGUST 2, 1692.

I. Martha Carrier was indicted for the bewitching certain persons, according to the form usual in such cases, pleading not guilty to her indictment; there were first brought in a considerable number of the bewitched persons who not only made the court sensible[8] of an horrid witchcraft committed upon them, but also deposed that it was Martha Carrier, or her shape, that grievously tormented them, by biting, pricking, pinching and choking of them. It was further deposed that while this Carrier was on her examination before the magistrates, the poor people were so tortured that every one expected their death upon the very spot, but that upon the binding of Carrier they were eased. Moreover the look of Carrier then laid the afflicted people

---

5. Tricks.
6. I.e., the request by the judges of the Salem trials to explain the sentencing of people accused of

witchcraft.
7. To hear and determine.
8. Aware.

for dead; and her touch, if her eye at the same time were off them, raised them again: which things were also now seen upon her trial. And it was testified that upon the mention of some having their necks twisted almost round, by the shape of this Carrier, she replied, "It's no matter though their necks had been twisted quite off."

II. Before the trial of this prisoner, several of her own children had frankly and fully confessed not only that they were witches themselves, but that this their mother had made them so. This confession they made with great shows of repentance, and with much demonstration of truth. They related place, time, occasion; they gave an account of journeys, meetings and mischiefs by them performed, and were very credible in what they said. Nevertheless, this evidence was not produced against the prisoner at the bar,[9] inasmuch as there was other evidence enough to proceed upon.

III. Benjamin Abbot gave his testimony that last March was a twelve-month, this Carrier was very angry with him, upon laying out some land near her husband's: her expressions in this anger were that she would stick as close to Abbot as the bark stuck to the tree; and that he should repent of it afore seven years came to an end, so as Doctor Prescot should never cure him. These words were heard by others besides Abbot himself; who also heard her say, she would hold his nose as close to the grindstone as ever it was held since his name was Abbot. Presently after this, he was taken with a swelling in his foot, and then with a pain in his side, and exceedingly tormented. It bred into a sore, which was lanced by Doctor Prescot, and several gallons of corruption[1] ran out of it. For six weeks it continued very bad, and then another sore bred in the groin, which was also lanced by Doctor Prescot. Another sore than bred in his groin, which was likewise cut, and put him to very great misery: he was brought unto death's door, and so remained until Carrier was taken, and carried away by the constable, from which very day he began to mend, and so grew better every day, and is well ever since.

Sarah Abbot also, his wife, testified that her husband was not only all this while afflicted in his body, but also that strange, extraordinary and unaccountable calamities befell his cattle; their death being such as they could guess at no natural reason for.

IV. Allin Toothaker testified that Richard, the son of Martha Carrier, having some difference with him, pulled him down by the hair of the head. When he rose again he was going to strike at Richard Carrier but fell down flat on his back to the ground, and had not power to stir hand or foot, until he told Carrier he yielded; and then he saw the shape of Martha Carrier go off his breast.

This Toothaker had received a wound in the wars; and he now testified that Martha Carrier told him he should never be cured. Just afore the apprehending of Carrier, he could thrust a knitting needle into his wound four inches deep; but presently after her being seized, he was thoroughly healed.

He further testified that when Carrier and he some times were at variance, she would clap her hands at him, and say he should get nothing by it; whereupon he several times lost his cattle, by strange deaths, whereof no natural causes could be given.

V. John Rogger also testified that upon the threatening words of this mali-

---

9. Court.   1. Pus; infected matter. "Lanced": cut open.

cious Carrier, his cattle would be strangely bewitched; as was more particularly then described.

VI. Samuel Preston testified that about two years ago, having some difference with Martha Carrier, he lost a cow in a strange, preternatural, unusual manner; and about a month after this, the said Carrier, having again some difference with him, she told him he had lately lost a cow, and it should not be long before he lost another; which accordingly came to pass; for he had a thriving and well-kept cow, which without any known cause quickly fell down and died.

VII. Phebe Chandler testified that about a fortnight before the apprehension of Martha Carrier, on a Lordsday, while the Psalm was singing in the Church, this Carrier then took her by the shoulder and shaking her, asked her, where she lived: she made her no answer, although as Carrier, who lived next door to her father's house, could not in reason but know who she was. Quickly after this, as she was at several times crossing the fields, she heard a voice, that she took to be Martha Carrier's, and it seemed as if it was over her head. The voice told her she should within two or three days be poisoned. Accordingly, within such a little time, one half of her right hand became greatly swollen and very painful; as also part of her face: whereof she can give no account how it came. It continued very bad for some days; and several times since she has had a great pain in her breast; and been so seized on her legs that she has hardly been able to go. She added that lately, going well to the house of God, Richard, the son of Martha Carrier, looked very earnestly upon her, and immediately her hand, which had formerly been poisoned, as is abovesaid, began to pain her greatly, and she had a strange burning at her stomach; but was then struck deaf, so that she could not hear any of the prayer, or singing, till the two or three last words of the Psalm.

VIII. One Foster, who confessed her own share in the witchcraft for which the prisoner stood indicted, affirmed that she had seen the prisoner at some of their witch-meetings, and that it was this Carrier, who persuaded her to be a witch. She confessed that the devil carried them on a pole to a witch-meeting; but the pole broke, and she hanging about Carrier's neck, they both fell down, and she then received an hurt by the fall, whereof she was not at this very time recovered.

IX. One Lacy, who likewise confessed her share in this witchcraft, now testified, that she and the prisoner were once bodily present at a witch-meeting in Salem Village; and that she knew the prisoner to be a witch, and to have been at a diabolical sacrament, and that the prisoner was the undoing of her and her children by enticing them into the snare of the devil.

X. Another Lacy, who also confessed her share in this witchcraft, now testified, that the prisoner was at the witch-meeting, in Salem Village, where they had bread and wine administered unto them.

XI. In the time of this prisoner's trial, one Susanna Sheldon in open court had her hands unaccountably tied together with a wheel-band[2] so fast that without cutting, it could not be loosed: it was done by a specter; and the sufferer affirmed it was the prisoner's.

Memorandum. This rampant hag, Martha Carrier, was the person of whom the confessions of the witches, and of her own children among the

---

2. A band or strap that goes around a wheel.

rest, agreed that the devil had promised her she should be Queen of Hebrews.

1692, 1693

FROM MAGNALIA CHRISTI AMERICANA[1]

Galeacius Secundus:[2] The Life of William Bradford, Esq., Governor of Plymouth Colony

Omnium Somnos illius vigilantia defendit; omnium otium, illius Labor; omnium Delicias, illius Industria; omnium vacationem, illius occupatio.[3]

It has been a matter of some observation, that although Yorkshire be one of the largest shires in England; yet for all the fires of martyrdom which were kindled in the days of Queen Mary,[4] it afforded no more fuel than one poor leaf; namely, John Leaf, an apprentice, who suffered for the doctrine of the Reformation at the same time and stake with the famous John Bradford.[5] But when the reign of Queen Elizabeth[6] would not admit the reformation of worship to proceed unto those degrees, which were proposed and pursued by no small number of the faithful in those days, Yorkshire was not the least of the shires in England that afforded suffering witnesses thereunto. The churches there gathered were quickly molested with such a raging persecution, that if the spirit of separation in them did carry them unto a further extreme than it should have done, one blamable cause thereof will be found in the extremity of that persecution. Their troubles made that cold country too hot for them, so that they were under a necessity to seek a retreat in the Low Countries;[7] and yet the watchful malice and fury of their adversaries rendered it almost impossible for them to find what they sought. For them to leave their native soil, their lands and their friends, and go into a strange place, where they must hear foreign language, and live meanly[8] and hardly, and in other employments than that of husbandry, wherein they had been educated, these must needs have been such discouragements as could have been conquered by none, save those who sought first the kingdom of God,

1. A History of the Wonderful Works of Christ in America (Latin). Mather's book is subtitled *The ecclesiastical History of New England from its first planting, in the year 1620, unto the year of our Lord, 1698.* The *Magnalia* contains seven books. The first book is concerned with the landing of the first Europeans in America and the founding and history of the New England settlements. The second book contains lives of governors of New England, and the lives of Bradford and Winthrop may be found there; the third book contains lives of sixty famous "Divines, by whose ministry the churches of New England have been planted and continued." Other books contain a history of Harvard College, a record of church ordinances passed in synods, and a record of "illustrious" and "wonderous" events that have been witnessed by people in New England. First published in London in 1702, the text used here is taken from that edited by Thomas Robbins, with translations from the Hebrew, Greek, and Latin by Lucius F. Robinson (1853–55).

2. The second Galeazzo (Latin). Galeazzo Caraccioli (1517–1586) was a Neapolitan nobleman who left home and country to follow the example of Calvin in Geneva.
3. His vigilance defends the sleep of all; his labor, their rest; his industry, their pleasures; and his diligence, their leisure (Latin).
4. During the reign of Mary Tudor (1553–58) an effort was made to restore Roman Catholicism to the position of a national church, and a number of Protestants were executed.
5. Bradford (1510?–1555), burned at the stake with Leaf on July 1, 1555. Their story was well known from John Foxe's *Book of Martyrs.*
6. Followed Mary Tudor to the throne (1558–1603) and by virtue of the Act of Uniformity prescribed traditional church ritual.
7. A number of English Puritans went to Holland to form their own churches without being accused of treason.
8. In poverty.

and the righteousness thereof. But that which would have made these discouragements the more unconquerable unto an ordinary faith, was the terrible zeal of their enemies to guard all ports, and search all ships, that none of them should be carried off. I will not relate the sad things of this kind then seen and felt by this people of God; but only exemplify those trials with one short story. Divers of these people having hired a Dutchman, then lying at Hull, to carry them over to Holland, he promised faithfully to take them in, between Grimsby and Hull; but they coming to the place a day or two too soon, the appearance of such a multitude alarmed the officers of the town adjoining, who came with a great body of soldiers to seize upon them. Now it happened that one boat full of men had been carried aboard, while the women were yet in a bark that lay aground in a creek at low water. The Dutchman perceiving the storm that was thus beginning ashore, swore by the sacrament that he would stay no longer for any of them; and so taking the advantage of a fair wind then blowing, he put out to sea for Zeeland[9] The women thus left near Grimsby-common, bereaved of their husbands, who had been hurried from them, and forsaken of their neighbors, of whom none durst in this fright stay with them, were a very rueful spectacle; some crying for fear, some shaking for cold, all dragged by troops of armed and angry men from one Justice to another, till not knowing what to do with them, they even dismissed them to shift as well as they could for themselves. But by their singular afflictions, and by their Christian behaviors, the cause for which they exposed themselves did gain considerably. In the meantime, the men at sea found reason to be glad that their families were not with them, for they were surprised with an horrible tempest, which held them for fourteen days together, in seven whereof they saw not sun, moon or star, but were driven upon the coast of Norway. The mariners often despaired of life, and once with doleful shrieks gave over all, as thinking the vessel was foundered: but the vessel rose again, and when the mariners with sunk hearts often cried out, "We sink! we sink!" the passengers, without such distraction of mind, even while the water was running into their mouths and ears, would cheerfully shout, "Yet, Lord, thou canst save! Yet, Lord, thou canst save!" And the Lord accordingly brought them at last safe unto their desired haven: and not long after helped their distressed relations thither after them, where indeed they found upon almost all accounts a new world, but a world in which they found that they must live like strangers and pilgrims.

Among these devout people was our William Bradford, who was born *Anno* 1588, in an obscure village called Austerfield, where the people were as unacquainted with the Bible, as the Jews do seem to have been with part of it in the days of Josiah;[1] a most ignorant and licentious people, and like unto their priest. Here, and in some other places, he had a comfortable inheritance left him of his honest parents, who died while he was yet a child, and cast him on the education,[2] first of his grandparents, and then of his uncles, who devoted him, like his ancestors, unto the affairs of husbandry. Soon a long sickness kept him, as he would afterwards thankfully say, from the vanities of youth, and made him the fitter for what he was afterwards to undergo. When he was about a dozen years old, the reading of the Scriptures began to cause great impressions upon him; and those impressions were much assisted and improved, when he came to enjoy Mr. Richard Clifton's[3]

9. I.e., The Netherlands.
1. King of Judah (c. 638–608 B.C.E.), who was ignorant of the book of the law of the God of Israel and worshiped false gods (see 2 Kings 22f.). "*Anno*": in the year (Latin).

2. I.e., made his education dependent on.
3. A Puritan minister (d. 1616) in the town of Scrooby, who also settled in Amsterdam with the Scrooby Separatists.

illuminating ministry, not far from his abode; he was then also further befriended, by being brought into the company and fellowship of such as were then called professors;[4] though the young man that brought him into it did after become a prófane and wicked apostate.[5] Nor could the wrath of his uncles, nor the scoff of his neighbors, now turned upon him, as one of the Puritans, divert him from his pious inclinations.

At last, beholding how fearfully the evangelical and apostolical church-form, whereinto the churches of the primitive times were cast by the good spirit of God, had been deformed by the apostacy of the succeeding times; and what little progress the Reformation had yet made in many parts of Christendom towards its recovery, he set himself by reading, by discourse, by prayer, to learn whether it was not his duty to withdraw from the communion of the parish-assemblies, and engage with some society of the faithful, that should keep close unto the written Word of God, as the rule of their worship. And after many distresses of mind concerning it, he took up a very deliberate and understanding resolution, of doing so; which resolution he cheerfully prosecuted, although the provoked rage of his friends tried all the ways imaginable to reclaim him from it, unto all whom his answer was:

> Were I like to endanger my life, or consume my estate by any ungodly courses, your counsels to me were very seasonable; but you know that I have been diligent and provident in my calling, and not only desirous to augment what I have, but also to enjoy it in your company; to part from which will be as great a cross as can befall me. Nevertheless, to keep a good conscience, and walk in such a way as God has prescribed in His Word; is a thing which I must prefer before you all, and above life itself. Wherefore, since 'tis for a good cause that I am like to suffer the disasters which you lay before me, you have no cause to be either angry with me, or sorry for me; yea, I am not only willing to part with every thing that is dear to me in this world for this cause, but I am also thankful that God has given me an heart so to do, and will accept me so to suffer for Him.

Some lamented him, some derided him, all dissuaded him: nevertheless, the more they did it, the more fixed he was in his purpose to seek the ordinances of the Gospel, where they should be dispensed with most of the commanded purity; and the sudden deaths of the chief relations which thus lay at him,[6] quickly after convinced him what a folly it had been to have quitted his profession, in expectation of any satisfaction from them. So to Holland he attempted a removal.

Having with a great company of Christians hired a ship to transport them for Holland, the master perfidiously betrayed them into the hands of those persecutors, who rifled and ransacked their goods, and clapped their persons into prison at Boston,[7] where they lay for a month together. But Mr. Bradford being a young man of about eighteen, was dismissed sooner than the rest, so that within a while he had opportunity with some others to get over to Zeeland, through perils, both by land and sea not inconsiderable; where he was not long ashore ere a viper seized on his hand—that is, an officer—who carried him unto the magistrates, unto whom an envious passenger had

4. I.e., those who declared their faith.
5. One who denies what he formerly professed.
6. I.e., struck out at him and tried to make him
change his beliefs.
7. In England.

accused him as having fled out of England. When the magistrates understood the true cause of his coming thither, they were well satisfied with him; and so he repaired joyfully unto his brethren at Amsterdam, where the difficulties to which he afterwards stooped in learning and serving of a Frenchman at the working of silks, were abundantly compensated by the delight wherewith he sat under the shadow of our Lord, in His purely dispensed ordinances. At the end of two years, he did, being of age to do it, convert his estate in England into money; but setting up for himself, he found some of his designs by the Providence of God frowned upon, which he judged a correction bestowed by God upon him for certain decays of internal piety, whereinto he had fallen; the consumption of his estate he thought came to prevent a consumption in his virtue. But after he had resided in Holland about half a score years, he was one of those who bore a part in that hazardous and generous enterprise of removing into New England, with part of the English church at Leyden, where, at their first landing, his dearest consort[8] accidently falling overboard, was drowned in the harbor; and the rest of his days were spent in the services, and the temptations, of that American wilderness.

Here was Mr. Bradford, in the year 1621, unanimously chosen the governor of the plantation; the difficulties whereof were such, that if he had not been a person of more than ordinary piety, wisdom and courage, he must have sunk under them. He had, with a laudable industry, been laying up a treasure of experiences, and he had now occasion to use it; indeed, nothing but an experienced man could have been suitable to the necessities of the people. The potent nations of the Indians, into whose country they were come, would have cut them off, if the blessing of God upon his conduct had not quelled them; and if his prudence, justice and moderation had not overruled them, they had been ruined by their own distempers. One specimen of his demeanor is to this day particularly spoken of. A company of young fellows that were newly arrived were very unwilling to comply with the governor's order for working abroad on the public account; and therefore on Christmas Day, when he had called upon them, they excused themselves, with a pretense that it was against their conscience to work such a day.[9] The governor gave them no answer, only that he would spare them till they were better informed; but by and by he found them all at play in the street, sporting themselves with various diversions; whereupon commanding the instruments of their games to be taken from them, he effectually gave them to understand that it was against his conscience that they should play whilst others were at work, and that if they had any devotion to the day, they should show it at home in the exercises of religion, and not in the streets with pastime and frolics; and this gentle reproof put a final stop to all such disorders for the future.

For two years together after the beginning of the colony, whereof he was now governor, the poor people had a great experiment of "man's not living by bread alone";[1] for when they were left all together without one morsel of bread for many months, one after another, still the good Providence of God relieved them, and supplied them, and this for the most part out of the sea. In this low condition of affairs, there was no little exercise for the prudence

8. Wife.
9. Puritans did not observe Christmas as a holiday.
1. Luke 4.4.

and patience of the governor, who cheerfully bore his part in all; and, that industry might not flag, he quickly set himself to settle propriety among the new planters, foreseeing that while the whole country labored upon a common stock, the husbandry and business of the plantation could not flourish, as Plato[2] and others long since dreamed that it would if a community were established. Certainly, if the spirit which dwelt in the old Puritans, had not inspired these new planters, they had sunk under the burden of these difficulties; but our Bradford had a double portion of that spirit.

The plantation was quickly thrown into a storm that almost overwhelmed it, by the unhappy actions of a minister sent over from England by the adventurers[3] concerned for the plantation; but by the blessing of Heaven on the conduct of the governor, they weathered out that storm. Only the adventurers, hereupon breaking to pieces, threw up all their concernments with the infant colony; whereof they gave this as one reason, that the planters dissembled with his Majesty and their friends in their petition, wherein they declared for a church discipline, agreeing with the French and others of the reforming churches in Europe.[4] Whereas 'twas now urged, that they had admitted into their communion a person who at his admission utterly renounced the churches of England, (which person, by the way, was that very man who had made the complaints against them) and therefore, though they denied the name of Brownists,[5] yet they were the thing. In answer hereunto, the very words written by the governor were these:

> Whereas you tax us with dissembling about the French discipline, you do us wrong, for we both hold and practice the discipline of the French and other Reformed Churches (as they have published the same in the Harmony of Confessions) according to our means, in effect and substance. But whereas you would tie us up to the French discipline in every circumstance, you derogate from the liberty we have in Christ Jesus. The Apostle Paul would have none to follow him in any thing, but wherein he follows Christ; much less ought any Christian or church in the world to do it. The French may err, we may err, and other churches may err, and doubtless do in many circumstances. That honor therefore belongs only to the infallible Word of God, and pure Testament of Christ, to be propounded and followed as the only rule and pattern for direction herein to all churches and Christians. And it is too great arrogancy for any man or church to think that he or they have so sounded the Word of God unto the bottom, as precisely to set down the church's discipline without error in substance or circumstance, that no other without blame may digress or differ in any thing from the same. And it is not difficult to show that the reformed churches differ in many circumstances among themselves.

By which words it appears how far he was free from that rigid spirit of separation, which broke to pieces the Separatists themselves in the Low

2. Greek philosopher (427?–347 B.C.E.). "propriety": i.e., property. "Common stock": property held in common.
3. English investors.
4. In Europe states were declared as either Protestant or Catholic; in France the Edict of Nantes (1598) provided liberty of conscience for all without denying the authority of the Crown.
5. Robert Browne (c. 1550–1633) was a Separatist clergyman and identified with Congregationalism, a system whereby each church is independent of any national church.

Countries, unto the great scandal of the reforming churches.[6] He was indeed a person of a well-tempered spirit, or else it had been scarce possible for him to have kept the affairs of Plymouth in so good a temper for thirty-seven years together; in every one of which he was chosen their governor, except the three years wherein Mr. Winslow, and the two years wherein Mr. Prince,[7] at the choice of the people, took a turn with him.

The leader of a people in a wilderness had need be a Moses;[8] and if a Moses had not led the people of Plymouth Colony, where this worthy person was the governor, the people had never with so much unanimity and importunity still called him to lead them. Among many instances thereof, let this one piece of self-denial be told for a memorial of him, wheresoever this history shall be considered: the patent of the colony was taken in his name, running in these terms: "To William Bradford, his heirs, associates, and assigns," but when the number of the freemen[9] was much increased, and many new townships erected, the General Court there desired of Mr. Bradford that he would make a surrender of the same into their hands, which he willingly and presently assented unto, and confirmed it according to their desire by his hand and seal, reserving no more for himself than was his proportion, with others, by agreement. But as he found the Providence of Heaven many ways recompensing his many acts of self-denial, so he gave this testimony to the faithfulness of the Divine Promises: that he had forsaken friends, houses and lands for the sake of the Gospel, and the Lord gave them him again. Here he prospered in his estate; and besides a worthy son which he had by a former wife, he had also two sons and a daughter by another, whom he married in this land.

He was a person for study as well as action; and hence, notwithstanding the difficulties through which he passed in his youth, he attained unto a notable skill in languages: the Dutch tongue was become almost as vernacular to him as the English; the French tongue he could also manage; the Latin and the Greek he had mastered; but the Hebrew he most of all studied, because he said he would see with his own eyes the ancient oracles of God in their native beauty. He was also well skilled in history, in antiquity, and in philosophy; and for theology he became so versed in it, that he was an irrefragable disputant against the errors, especially those of Anabaptism,[1] which with trouble he saw rising in his colony; wherefore he wrote some significant things for the confutation of those errors. But the crown of all was his holy, prayerful, watchful, and fruitful walk with God, wherein he was very exemplary.

At length he fell into an indispositon of body, which rendered him unhealthy for a whole winter; and as the spring advanced, his health yet more declined; yet he felt himself not what he counted sick, till one day, in the night after which, the God of Heaven so filled his mind with ineffable consolations, that he seemed little short of Paul, rapt up unto the unutterable

---

6. By the time the movement for reform had come to an end, the movement for separating ended in dissension and mutual recrimination, with particular churches arguing they were more pure than others. Two English Puritans baptized themselves on the grounds that there were no pure churches to baptize them.
7. Thomas Prince (1600–1673). Edward Winslow

(1595–1655).
8. The Hebrew lawgiver and prophet who led the Israelites out of Egypt.
9. I.e., those who are not indentured servants and are able to work for themselves.
1. Anabaptists opposed the baptism of children and advocated separation of church and state.

entertainments of Paradise.[2] The next morning he told his friends that the good spirit of God had given him a pledge of his happiness in another world, and the first fruits of his eternal glory; and on the day following he died, May 9, 1657, in the 69th year of his age—lamented by all the colonies of New England as a common blessing and father to them all.

O mihi si Similis Contingat Clausula Vitae![3]
Plato's brief description of a governor, is all that I will now leave as his character, in an

EPITAPH.

Νομεὺς Τροψὸς ἀγέλης ἀνθρωπίνης.[4]

Men are but flocks: Bradford beheld their need,
And long did them at once both rule and feed.

1702

Nehemias Americanus:[1] The Life of John Winthrop, Esq., Governor of the Massachusetts Colony

Quicunque Venti erunt, Ars nostra certe non aberit.
—Cicero[2]

Let Greece boast of her patient Lycurgus,[3] the lawgiver, by whom diligence, temperance, fortitude, and wit were made the fashions of a therefore long-lasting and renowned commonwealth: let Rome tell of her devout Numa,[4] the lawgiver, by whom the most famous commonwealth saw peace triumphing over extinguished war and cruel plunders; and murders giving place to the more mollifying exercises of his religion. Our New England shall tell and boast of her Winthrop, a lawgiver as patient as Lycurgus, but not admitting any of his criminal disorders; as devout as Numa, but not liable to any of his heathenish madnesses; a governor in whom the excellencies of Christianity made a most improving addition unto the virtues, wherein even without those he would have made a parallel for the great men of Greece, or of Rome, which the pen of a Plutarch[5] has eternized.

A stock of heroes by right should afford nothing but what is heroical; and nothing but an extreme degeneracy would make anything less to be expected from a stock of Winthrops. Mr. Adam Winthrop, the son of a worthy gentleman wearing the same name, was himself a worthy, a discreet, and a learned gentleman, particularly eminent for skill in the law, nor without remark for[6]

2. In 2 Corinthians 12.2–4 Paul describes a man (himself) who experienced a moment in which he "was caught up into paradise, and heard unspeakable words, which it is not lawful for a man to utter."
3. Oh, that such an end of life might come to me (Latin).
4. Shepherd and provider of the human flock (Greek).
1. The American Nehemiah (Latin). As governor of Judea, Nehemiah rebuilt the walls of Jerusalem (Nehemiah 1.3).
2. Whatever winds may blow, this art of ours can

never be lost (Latin). The quotation is from the Roman orator Cicero's (106–43 B.C.E.) *Epistulae ad Familiares* 12.25.5.
3. Spartan reformer (9th century B.C.E.), who reshaped the nation's constitution and made it an efficient military state.
4. Numa Pompilius (715–673 B.C.E.), second legendary king of Rome.
5. The Greek biographer (c. 46–120 C.E.), best known for his lives of Greeks and Romans.
6. I.e., notable for. Mather refers here to Winthrop's grandfather (1498–1562), father (1548–1623), and uncle William (1529–1582).

love to the gospel, under the reign of King Henry VIII, and brother to a memorable favorer of the Reformed religion in the days of Queen Mary, into whose hands the famous martyr Philpot[7] committed his papers, which afterwards made no inconsiderable part of our martyr-books. This Mr. Adam Winthrop had a son of the same name also, and of the same endowments and employments with his father; and this third Adam Winthrop was the father of that renowned John Winthrop, who was the father of New England, and the founder of a colony, which, upon many accounts, like him that founded it, may challenge the first place among the English glories of America. Our John Winthrop, thus born at the mansion-house of his ancestors, at Groton in Suffolk, on June 12, 1587,[8] enjoyed afterwards an agreeable education. But though he would rather have devoted himself unto the study of Mr. John Calvin, than of Sir Edward Cook;[9] nevertheless, the accomplishments of a lawyer were those wherewith heaven made his chief opportunities to be serviceable.

Being made, at the unusually early age of eighteen, a justice of peace, his virtues began to fall under a more general observation; and he not only so bound himself to the behavior of a Christian, as to become exemplary for a conformity to the laws of Christianity in his own conversation, but also discovered a more than ordinary measure of those qualities which adorn an officer of humane society. His justice was impartial, and used the balance to weigh not the cash, but the case of those who were before him: *prosopolatria* he reckoned as bad as *idolatria*.[1] His wisdom did exquisitely temper things according to the art of governing, which is a business of more contrivance than the seven arts of the schools; *oyer* still went before *terminer* in all his administrations.[2] His courage made him dare to do right, and fitted him to stand among the lions that have sometimes been the supporters of the throne.[3] All which virtues he rendered the more illustrious, by emblazoning them with the constant liberality and hospitality of a gentleman. This made him the terror of the wicked, and the delight of the sober, the envy of the many, but the hope of those who had any hopeful design in hand for the common good of the nation and the interests of religion.

Accordingly, when the noble design of carrying a colony of chosen people into an American wilderness was by some eminent persons undertaken, this eminent person was, by the consent of all, chosen for the Moses,[4] who must be the leader of so great an undertaking: and indeed nothing but a Mosaic spirit could have carried him through the temptations, to which either his farewell to his own land, or his travel in a strange land, must needs expose a gentleman of his education. Wherefore, having sold a fair estate of six or seven hundred[5] a year, he transported himself with the effects of it into New

7. John Philpot (1516–1555) was a Puritan martyr burned at the stake and is included in John Foxe's *Book of Martyrs* (1563). Henry VIII (1491–1547) founded the Church of England and was despised by Puritans. Mary Tudor (1516–1558) reestablished Roman Catholicism in England in 1555.
8. Should read January 12, 1588.
9. I.e., he would have preferred to study for the ministry and read John Calvin's *Institutes* (1536) rather than prepare for the law by reading Lord Chief Justice Edward Coke's *Institutes of English Law* (1628–44).
1. Worship of false gods (Latin). "*Prosopolatria*":

face worship (Latin, literal trans.); i.e., hero worship.
2. I.e., in the parlance of English law, hearing ("*oyer*") all the evidence came before judging ("*terminer*"). "Seven arts": the trivium and quadrivium of a classical education consisted of grammar, rhetoric, and logic as well as arithmetic, music, geometry, and astronomy.
3. Daniel was saved from the Babylonian lions by his faith (Daniel 6.23). King Solomon's throne had carved lions on both sides (1 Kings 10.19–20).
4. Moses led the Hebrews out of Egypt into Canaan.
5. I.e., English pounds.

England in the year 1630, where he spent it upon the service of a famous plantation, founded and formed for the seat of the most reformed Christianity: and continued there, conflicting with temptations of all sorts, as many years as the nodes of the moon take to dispatch a revolution.[6] Those persons were never concerned in a new plantation, who know not that the unavoidable difficulties of such a thing will call for all the prudence and patience of a mortal man to encounter therewithal; and they must be very insensible of the influence, which the just wrath of heaven has permitted the devils to have upon this world, if they do not think that the difficulties of a new plantation, devoted unto the evangelical worship of our Lord Jesus Christ, must be yet more than ordinary. How prudently, how patiently, and with how much resignation to our Lord Jesus Christ, our brave Winthrop waded through these difficulties, let posterity consider with admiration. And know, that as the picture of this their governor was, after his death, hung up with honor in the State House of his country, so the wisdom, courage, and holy zeal of his life, were an example well worthy to be copied by all that shall succeed him in government.

Were he now to be considered only as a Christian, we might therein propose him as greatly imitable. He was a very religious man; and as he strictly kept his heart, so he kept his house, under the laws of piety;[7] there he was every day constant in holy duties, both morning and evening, and on the Lord's days, and lectures, though he wrote not after the preacher,[8] yet such was his attention, and such his retention in hearing, that he repeated unto his family the sermons which he had heard in the congregation. But it is chiefly as a governor that he is now to be considered. Being the governor over the considerablest part of New England, he maintained the figure and honor of his place with the spirit of a true gentleman; but yet with such obliging condescension to the circumstances of the colony, that when a certain troublesome and malicious calumniator, well known in those times, printed his libelous nicknames upon the chief persons here, the worst nickname he could find for the governor was John Temperwell;[9] and when the calumnies of that ill man caused the Archbishop to summon one Mr. Cleaves[1] before the King, in hopes to get some accusation from him against the country, Mr. Cleaves gave such an account of the governor's laudable carriage in all respects, and the serious devotion wherewith prayers were both publicly and privately made for his Majesty, that the King expressed himself most highly pleased therewithal, only sorry that so worthy a person should be no better accommodated than with the hardships of America. He was, indeed, a governor, who had most exactly studied that book which, pretending to teach politics, did only contain three leaves, and but one word in each of those leaves, which word was, MODERATION. Hence, though he were a zealous enemy to all vice, yet his practice was according to his judgment thus expressed: "In the infancy of plantations, justice should be administered with more lenity than in a settled state; because people are more apt

6. Approximately the same number of years that Winthrop lived in Massachusetts: 18.6 years. In astronomy a "node" is either of two diametrically opposite points at which the orbit (or revolution) of a planet intersects the ecliptic.

7. "(For if a man know not how to rule his own house, how shall he take care of the church of God?)" (1 Timothy 3.5).

8. I.e., although he did not take the sermon down in shorthand. "Lectures": days on which less formal sermons were delivered.

9. Thomas Morton (d. 1649) in *New English Canaan* (1637), pt. 4, chap. 23.

1. George Cleaves settled in Maine in 1630 and returned to England in 1636. Archbishop William Laud (1573–1645) was an enemy of the Puritans.

then to transgress; partly out of ignorance of new laws and orders, partly out of oppression of business, and other straits. [LENTO GRADU]² was the old rule; and if the strings of a new instrument be wound up unto their height, they will quickly crack." But when some leading and learned men took offense at his conduct in this matter, and upon a conference gave it in as their opinion, "That a stricter discipline was to be used in the beginning of a plantation, than after its being with more age established and confirmed," the governor being readier to see his own errors than other men's, professed his purpose to endeavor their satisfaction with less of lenity in his adminis- trations. At that conference there were drawn up several other articles to be observed between the governor and the rest of the magistrates, which were of this import: That the magistrates, as far as might be, should aforehand ripen their consultations, to produce that unanimity in their public votes, which might make them liker to the voice of God; that if differences fell out among them in their public meetings, they should speak only to the case, without any reflection,³ with all due modesty, and but by way of question; or desire the deferring of the cause to further time; and after sentence to imitate privately no dislike; that they should be more familiar, friendly and open unto each other, and more frequent in their visitations, and not any way expose each other's infirmities, but seek the honor of each other, and all the court; that one magistrate shall not cross the proceedings of another, without first advising with him; and that they should in all their appearances abroad, be so circumstanced as to prevent all contempt of authority; and that they should support and strengthen all under-officers. All of which articles were observed by no man more than by the governor himself.

But whilst he thus did, as our New English Nehemiah, the part of a ruler in managing the public affairs of our American Jerusalem, when there were Tobijahs and Sanballats enough to vex him,⁴ and give him the experiment of Luther's observation, *Omnis qui regit est tanquam signum, in quod omnia jacula, Satan et Mundus dirigunt;*⁵ he made himself still an exacter parallel unto that governor of Israel, by doing the part of a neighbor among the distressed people of the new plantation. To teach them the frugality neces- sary for those times, he abridged himself of a thousand comfortable things, which he had allowed himself elsewhere: his habit was not that soft raiment, which would have been disagreeable to a wilderness;⁶ his table was not cov- ered with the superfluities that would have invited unto sensualities: water was commonly his own drink, though he gave wine to others. But at the same time his liberality unto the needy was even beyond measure generous; and therein he was continually causing "the blessing of him that was ready to perish to come upon him, and the heart of the widow and the orphan to sing for joy,"⁷ but none more than those of deceased ministers, whom he always treated with a very singular compassion; among the instances whereof we still enjoy with us the worthy and now aged son of that Reverend Higginson,

2. By slow degrees (Latin).
3. I.e., without imputing any ill will on the part of another.
4. Both the governor of Samaria, Sanballat, and a Persian officer, Tobijah, opposed the rebuilding of the walls of Jerusalem (Nehemiah 2.10; 4.7).
5. A man in authority is a target at which Satan

and the world launch all their darts (Latin), from Martin Luther's (1483–1546) *Loci Communes.*
6. "But what went ye out for to see? A man clothed in soft raiment? behold, they that wear soft cloth- ing are in kings' houses" (Matthew 11.8).
7. Job 29.13.

whose death left his family in a wide world soon after his arrival here, publicly acknowledging the charitable Winthrop for his foster-father.[8] It was often-times no small trial unto his faith, to think how a table for the people should be furnished when they first came into the wilderness![9] and for very many of the people his own good works were needful, and accordingly employed for the answering of his faith. Indeed, for a while the governor was the Joseph, unto whom the whole body of the people repaired when their corn failed them,[1] and he continued relieving of them with his open-handed boun-ties, as long as he had any stock to do it with; and a lively faith to see the return of the "bread after many days,"[2] and not starve in the days that were to pass till that return should be seen, carried him cheerfully through those expenses.

Once it was observable that, on February 5, 1630,[3] when he was distrib-uting the last handful of the meal in the barrel unto a poor man distressed by the "wolf at the door," at that instant they spied a ship arrived at the harbor's mouth, laden with provisions for them all. Yea, the governor sometimes made his own private purse to be the public: not by sucking into it, but by squeezing out of it; for when the public treasure had noth-ing in it, he did himself defray the charges of the public. And having learned that lesson of our Lord, "that it is better to give than to receive,"[4] he did, at the General Court, when he was a third time chosen governor, make a speech unto this purpose: That he had received gratuities from divers towns, which he accepted with much comfort and content; and he had likewise received civilities from particular persons, which he could not refuse without incivility in himself: nevertheless, he took them with a trembling heart, in regard of God's word, and the conscience of his own infirmities; and therefore he desired them that they would not hereafter take it ill if he refused such presents for the time to come. 'Twas his cus-tom also to send some of his family upon errands unto the houses of the poor, about their mealtime, on purpose to spy whether they wanted;[5] and if it were found that they wanted, he would make that the opportunity of sending supplies unto them. And there was one passage of his charity that was perhaps a little unusual: in an hard and long winter, when wood was very scarce at Boston, a man gave him a private information that a needy person in the neighborhood stole wood sometimes from his pile; where-upon the governor in a seeming anger did reply, "Does he so? I'll take a course with him; go, call that man to me; I'll warrant you I'll cure him of stealing." When the man came, the governor considering that if he had stolen, it was more out of necessity than disposition, said unto him, "Friend, it is a severe winter, and I doubt you are but meanly provided for wood; wherefore I would have you supply yourself at my woodpile till this

8. Francis Higginson (1587–1630) died after only a year's residence in Salem. His "aged son" John (1616–1708) wrote an "Attestation" prefixed to the *Magnalia*.
9. "Yea, they spake against God; they said, Can God furnish a table in the wilderness?" (Psalm 78.19).
1. "And the famine was over all the face of the earth: And Joseph opened all the storehouses, and sold unto the Egyptians; and the famine waxed sore in the land of Egypt" (Genesis 41.56).
2. "Cast thy bread upon the waters: for thou shalt

find it after many days" (Ecclesiastes 11.1).
3. Old Style. The present Gregorian calendar des-ignating January 1 as the first day of the year was adopted in England in 1752. Earlier, March 25 had served as the first day of the calendar year.
4. "I have shewed you all things, how that so labouring ye ought to support the weak, and to remember the words of the Lord Jesus, how he said, It is more blessed to give than to receive" (Acts 20.35).
5. I.e., lacked anything.

cold season be over." And he then merrily asked his friends whether he had not effectually cured this man of stealing his wood.

One would have imagined that so good a man could have had no enemies, if we had not had a daily and woeful experience to convince us that goodness itself will make enemies. It is a wonderful speech of Plato (in one of his books, *De Republica*), "For the trial of true virtue, 'tis necessary that a good man μηδέν ἀδικῶ, δοξαν εχει την μεγιστην ἀδικιας: Though he do no unjust thing, should suffer the infamy of the greatest injustice."[6] The governor had by his unspotted integrity procured himself a great reputation among the people; and then the crime of popularity was laid unto his charge by such, who were willing to deliver him from the danger of having all men speak well of him.[7] Yea, there were persons eminent both for figure and for number, unto whom it was almost essential to dislike everything that came from him; and yet he always maintained an amicable correspondence with them; as believing that they acted according to their judgment and conscience, or that their eyes were held by some temptation in the worst of all their oppositions. Indeed, his right works were so many, that they exposed him unto the envy of his neighbors,[8] and of such power was that envy, that sometimes he could not stand before it; but it was by not standing that he most effectually withstood it all.[9] Great attempts were sometimes made among the freemen to get him left out from his place in the government upon little pretenses, lest by the too frequent choice of one man, the government should cease to be by choice; and with a particular aim at him, sermons were preached at the anniversary Court of Election, to dissuade the freemen from choosing one man twice together. This was the reward of his extraordinary serviceableness! But when these attempts did succeed, as they sometimes did, his profound humility appeared in that equality of mind, wherewith he applied himself cheerfully to serve the country in whatever station their votes had allotted for him. And one year when the votes came to be numbered, there were found six less for Mr. Winthrop than for another gentleman who then stood in competition: but several other persons regularly tendering their votes before the election was published, were, upon a very frivolous objection, refused by some of the magistrates that were afraid lest the election should at last fall upon Mr. Winthrop: which, though it was well perceived, yet such was the self-denial of this patriot, that he would not permit any notice to be taken of the injury. But these trials were nothing in comparison of those harsher and harder treats which he sometimes had from the forwardness of not a few in the days of their paroxisms; and from the faction of some against him, not much unlike that of the Piazzi in Florence against the family of the Medicis:[1] all of which he at last conquered by conforming to the famous Judge's motto, *Prudens qui Patiens.*[2] The oracles of God have said, "Envy is rottenness to the bones;"[3] and Gulielmus Parisiensis[4] applies it unto rulers, who are as it were the bones of the societies which they belong unto: "Envy,"

6. From *The Republic* of Plato (427?–347 B.C.E.).
7. "Woe unto you, when all men shall speak well of you! for so did their fathers to the false prophets" (Luke 6.26).
8. "Again, I consider all travail, and every right work, that for this a man is envied of his neighbour. This is also vanity and vexation of spirit" (Ecclesiastes 4.4).
9. "Wrath is cruel, and anger is outrageous; but who is able to stand before envy?" (Proverbs 27.4).

1. In 1478 an important member of the Medici family was assassinated by one of the Piazzis, and all Italy became involved in the war that followed.
2. He is prudent who is patient (Latin), a maxim attributed to Sir Edward Coke.
3. "A sound heart is the life of the flesh: but envy the rottenness of the bones" (Proverbs 14.30).
4. William of St. Amour (d. 1272), bishop of Paris, was also known as a satirist.

says he, "is often found among them, and it is rottenness unto them." Our Winthrop encountered this envy from others, but conquered it, by being free from it himself.

Were it not for the sake of introducing the exemplary skill of this wise man, at giving soft answers, one would not choose to relate those instances of wrath which he had sometimes to encounter with; but he was for his gentleness, his forbearance, and longanimity,[5] a pattern so worthy to be written *after*, that something must here be written *of* it. He seemed indeed never to speak any other language than that of Theodosius: "If any man speak evil of the governor, if it be through lightness, 'tis to be contemned;[6] if it be through madness, 'tis to be pitied; if it be through injury, 'tis to be remitted." Behold, reader, the "meekness of wisdom" notably exemplified! There was a time when he received a very sharp letter from a gentleman who was a member of the Court,[7] but he delivered back the letter unto the messengers that brought it, with such a Christian speech as this: "I am not willing to keep such a matter of provocation by me!" Afterwards the same gentleman was compelled by scarcity of provisions to send unto him that he would sell him some of his cattle; whereupon the governor prayed him to accept what he had sent for as a token of his good will; but the gentleman returned him this answer: "Sir, your overcoming of yourself hath overcome me:" and afterwards gave demonstration of it.

The French have a saying that *"Un honesté homme, est un homme mesle!"*—a good man is a mixed man; and there hardly ever was a more sensible mixture of those two things, resolution and condescension,[8] than in this good man. There was a time when the Court of Election being, for fear of tumult, held at Cambridge, May 17, 1637, the sectarian part of the country, who had the year before gotten a governor more unto their mind,[9] had a project now to have confounded the election, by demanding that the court would consider a petition then tendered before their proceeding thereunto. Mr. Winthrop saw that this was only a trick to throw all into confusion, by putting off the choice of the governor and assistants until the day should be over; and therefore he did, with a strenuous resolution, procure a disappointment unto that mischievous and ruinous contrivance. Nevertheless, Mr. Winthrop himself being by the voice of the freemen in this exigency chosen the governor, and all of the other party left out, that ill-affected party discovered the dirt and mire, which remained with them, after the storm was over; particularly the sergeants, whose office 'twas to attend the governor, laid down their halberds;[1] but such was the condescension of this governor, as to take no present notice of this anger and contempt, but only order some of his own servants to take the halberds; and when the country manifested their deep resentments of the affront thus offered him, he prayed them to overlook it. But it was not long before a compensation was made for these things by the doubled respects which were from all parts paid unto him. Again, there was a time when the suppression of an *Antinomian* and *Familistical* faction,[2] which extremely threatened the ruin of the country, was

5. Patience.
6. Despised. Theodosius Flavius I (346–395 C.E.) was a Christian Roman emperor.
7. Thomas Dudley (1574–1653). The messengers were John Haynes and Thomas Hooker.
8. Humility.
9. Sir Henry Vane returned to England in 1637; he was sympathetic toward the views expressed by

the followers of Anne Hutchinson.
1. A weapon that is a combination spear and battle-ax.
2. Both Antinomianism and Familism (a word derived from an English religious sect called the Family of Love) hold the regenerate self above ecclesiastical and civil law.

generally thought much owing unto this renowned man; and therefore when
the friends of that faction could not wreak[3] their displeasure on him with
any politic vexations, they set themselves to do it by ecclesiastical ones.
Accordingly, when a sentence of banishment was passed on the ringleaders
of those disturbances, who

> ———Maria et Terras, Cœlumque profundum,
> Quippe ferant Rapidi, secum vertantque per Auras;[4]

many at the church of Boston, who were then that way too much inclined,
most earnestly solicited the elders of that church, whereof the governor was
a member, to call him forth as an offender, for passing of that sentence. The
elders were unwilling to do any such thing; but the governor understanding
the ferment among the people took that occasion to make a speech in the
congregation to this effect:

> BRETHREN: Understanding that some of you have desired that I should
> answer for an offense lately taken among you; had I been called upon
> so to do, I would, first, have advised with the ministers of the country,
> whether the church had power to call in question the civil court; and I
> would, secondly, have advised with the rest of the court, whether I might
> discover their counsels unto the church. But though I know that the
> reverend Elders of this church, and some others, do very well apprehend
> that the church cannot inquire into the proceedings of the court; yet,
> for the satisfaction of the weaker, who do not apprehend it, I will declare
> my mind concerning it. If the church have any such power, they have it
> from the Lord Jesus Christ; but the Lord Jesus Christ hath disclaimed
> it, not only by practice, but also by precept, which we have in his gospel,
> Matt. xx. 25, 26.[5] It is true, indeed, that magistrates, as they are church-
> members, are accountable unto the church for their failings; but that is
> when they are out of their calling. When Uzziah would go offer incense
> in the temple, the officers of the church called him to an account, and
> withstood him; but when Asa[6] put the prophet in prison, the officers of
> the church did not call him to an account for that. If the magistrate
> shall in a private way wrong any man, the church may call him to an
> account for it; but if he be in pursuance of a course of justice, though
> the thing that he does be unjust, yet he is not accountable for it before
> the church. As for myself, I did nothing in the causes of any of the
> brethren but by the advice of the Elders of the church. Moreover, in the
> oath which I have taken there is this clause: "In all cases wherein you
> are to give your vote, you shall do as in your judgment and conscience
> you shall see to be just, and for the public good." And I am satisfied, it
> is most for the glory of God, and the public good, that there has been
> such a sentence passed; yea, those brethren are so divided from the rest
> of the country in their opinions and practices, that it cannot stand with

---

3. Inflict.
4. "Rack sea and land and sky with mingled wrath.
/ In the wild tumult of their stormy path" (Virgil's
Aeneid 1.59–60).
5. "But Jesus called them unto him, and said, Ye
know that the princes of the Gentiles exercise
dominion over them, and they that are great exercise authority upon them. But it shall not be so

among you: but whosoever will be great among
you, let him be your minister."
6. Asa was the third king of Judea and put the
prophet Hanani in prison when he accused him of
not relying on the Lord (2 Chronicles 16.7–10).
Uzziah, king of Judea, was afflicted with leprosy
when he tried to burn incense on the altar in spite
of the protests of the priests (2 Chronicles 26.18).

the public peace for them to continue with us; Abraham saw that Hagar and Ishmael[7] must be sent away.

By such a speech he marvelously convinced, satisfied and mollified the uneasy brethren of the church; *Sic cunctus Pelagi cecidit Fragor*[8]———. And after a little patient waiting, the differences all so wore away, that the church, merely as a token of respect unto the governor when he had newly met with some losses in his estate, sent him a present of several hundreds of pounds.

Once more there was a time when some active spirits among the deputies of the colony, by their endeavors not only to make themselves a Court of Judicature, but also to take away the negative by which the magistrates might check their votes, had like by over-driving to have run the whole government into something too democratical. And if there was a town in Spain undermined by coneys, another town in Thrace destroyed by moles, a third in Greece ranversed[9] by frogs, a fourth in Germany subverted by rats; I must on this occasion add, that there was a country in America like to be confounded by a swine. A certain stray sow being found, was claimed by two several persons with a claim so equally maintained on both sides, that after six or seven years' hunting the business from one court unto another, it was brought at last into the General Court, where the final determination was "that it was impossible to proceed unto any judgment in the case."[1] However, in the debate of this matter, the negative of the upper-house upon the lower in that court was brought upon the stage; and agitated with so hot a zeal, that a little more, and all had been in the fire. In these agitations, the governor was informed that an offense had been taken by some eminent persons at certain passages in a discourse by him written thereabout; whereupon, with his usual condescendency, when he next came into the General Court, he made a speech of this import:

I understand that some have taken offense at something that I have lately written; which offense I desire to remove now, and begin this year in a reconciled state with you all. As for the matter of my writing, I had the concurrence of my brethren; it is a point of judgment which is not at my own disposing. I have examined it over and over again by such light as God has given me, from the rules of religion, reason and custom; and I see no cause to retract anything of it: wherefore I must enjoy my liberty in that, as you do yourselves. But for the manner, this, and all that was blameworthy in it, was wholly my own; and whatsoever I might allege for my own justification therein before men, I wave it, as now setting myself before another Judgment seat. However, what I wrote was upon great provocation, and to vindicate myself and others from great aspersion; yet that was no sufficient warrant for me to allow any distemper of spirit in myself; and I doubt I have been too prodigal of my brethren's reputation; I might have maintained my cause without casting any blemish upon others, when I made that my conclusion, "And now let religion and sound reason give judgment in the case;" it looked as if

7. Ishmael was the son of Abraham and his wife's servant Hagar. Abraham sent them into the wilderness at the insistence of his wife, Sarah (Genesis 16.1–16; 21.9–14).
8. "To silence sunk the thunder of the wave" (*Aeneid* 1.154).
9. Overturned. "Coneys": rabbits.
1. Mather refers to a case involving the merchant Robert Keayne (1595–1656) and Goody Sherman, a Boston widow, in 1643.

I arrogated too much unto myself, and too little to others. And when I made that profession, "That I would maintain what I wrote before all the world," though such words might modestly be spoken, yet I perceive an unbeseeming pride of my own heart breathing in them. For these failings, I ask pardon of God and man.

> Sic ait, et dicto citius Tumida Æquora placat,
> Collectasque fugat Nubes, Solemque reducit.[2]

This acknowledging disposition in the governor made them all acknowledge that he was truly "a man of an excellent spirit."[3] In fine, the victories of an Alexander, an Hannibal, or a Cæsar[4] over other men were not so glorious as the victories of this great man over himself, which also at last proved victories over other men.

But the stormiest of all the trials that ever befell this gentleman was in the year 1645, when he was, in title, no more than deputy governor of the colony. If the famous Cato were forty-four times called into judgment but as often acquitted; let it not be wondered, and if[5] our famous Winthrop were one time so. There happening certain seditious and mutinous practices in the town of Hingham,[6] the deputy governor, as legally as prudently, interposed his authority for the checking of them: whereupon there followed such an enchantment[7] upon the minds of the deputies in the General Court, that upon a scandalous petition of the delinquents unto them, wherein a pretended invasion made upon the liberties of the people was complained of, the deputy governor was most irregularly called forth unto an ignominious hearing before them in a vast assembly; whereto with a sagacious humilitude he consented, although he showed them how he might have refused it. The result of that hearing was, that notwithstanding the touchy jealousy of the people about their liberties lay at the bottom of all this prosecution, yet Mr. Winthrop was publicly acquitted, and the offenders were severally fined and censured. But Mr. Winthrop then resuming the place of deputy governor on the bench, saw cause to speak unto the root of the matter after this manner:[8]

I shall not now speak anything about the past proceedings of this Court, or the persons therein concerned. Only I bless God that I see an issue[9] of this troublesome affair. I am well satisfied that I was publicly accused, and that I am now publicly acquitted. But though I am justified before men, yet it may be the Lord hath seen so much amiss in my administrations, as calls me to be humbled; and indeed for me to have been thus charged by men, is itself a matter of humiliation, whereof I

2. "He speaks—but ere the word is said, / Each mounting billow droops its head, / And brightening clouds one moment stay / To pioneer returning day" (Aeneid 1.142–43).
3. "He that hath knowledge spareth his words: and a man of understanding is of an excellent spirit" (Proverbs 17.27).
4. Julius Caesar (100–44 B.C.E.), Roman general and statesman. Alexander the Great (356–323 B.C.E.), king of Macedonia. Hannibal (247–183 B.C.E.), the Carthaginian general. All were pre-Christian warriors.
5. "And if" is the archaic form of if. Cato: the

Roman orator (234–149 B.C.E.).
6. A town about twenty-five miles south of Boston. These challenges to authority were made against the captain of the town militia who was appointed by the state authorities.
7. I.e., a delusion in judgment.
8. "But ye should say, Why persecute we him, seeing the root of the matter is found in me?" (Job 19.28). Mather's version of Winthrop's speech to the General Court differs somewhat from that quoted in Winthrop's Journal.
9. End.

desire to make a right use before the Lord. If Miriam's father spit in her face, she is to be ashamed.[1] But give me leave, before you go, to say something that may rectify the opinions of many people, from whence the distempers have risen that have lately prevailed upon the body of this people. The questions that have troubled the country have been about the authority of the magistracy, and the liberty of the people. It is you who have called us unto this office; but being thus called, we have our authority from God; it is the ordinance of God, and it hath the image of God stamped upon it; and the contempt of it has been vindicated by God with terrible examples of his vengeance. I entreat you to consider, that when you choose magistrates, you take them from among yourselves, "men subject unto like passions with yourselves." If you see our infirmities, reflect on your own, and you will not be so severe censurers of ours. We count him a good servant who breaks not his covenant: the covenant between us and you is the oath you have taken of us, which is to this purpose, "that we shall govern you, and judge your causes, according to God's laws, and our own, according to our best skill." As for our skill, you must run the hazard of it; and if there be an error, not in the will, but only in skill, it becomes you to bear it. Nor would I have you to mistake in the point of your own liberty. There is a liberty of corrupt nature, which is affected both by men and beasts, to do what they list; and this liberty is inconsistent with authority, impatient of all restraint; by this liberty, *Sumus Omnes Deteriores*;[2] 'tis the grand enemy of truth and peace, and all the ordinances of God are bent against it. But there is a civil, a moral, a federal liberty, which is the proper end and object of authority; it is a liberty for that only which is just and good; for this liberty you are to stand with the hazard of your very lives; and whatsoever crosses it is not authority, but a distemper thereof. This liberty is maintained in a way of subjection to authority; and the authority set over you will in all administrations for your good be quietly submitted unto, by all but such as have a disposition to shake off the yoke, and lose their true liberty, by their murmuring at the honor and power of authority.

The spell that was upon the eyes of the people being thus dissolved, their distorted and enraged notions of things all vanished; and the people would not afterwards entrust the helm of the weather-beaten bark in any other hands but Mr. Winthrop's until he died.

Indeed, such was the mixture of distant qualities in him, as to make a most admirable temper; and his having a certain greatness of soul, which rendered him grave, generous, courageous, resolved, well-applied, and every way a gentleman in his demeanor, did not hinder him from taking sometimes the old Roman's way to avoid confusions, namely, *Cedendo*;[3] or from discouraging some things which are agreeable enough to most that wear the name of gentlemen. Hereof I will give no instances, but only oppose two passages of his life.

1. "And the Lord said unto Moses, If her father had but spit in her face, should she not be ashamed seven days? let her be shut out from the camp seven days, and after that let her be received in again" (Numbers 12.14). Miriam, Moses' sister, was punished for challenging his choice in a wife.
2. We are all the worse for it (Latin), from Terence (c. 190–159 B.C.E.), *Heauton Timorumenos* (The Self-tormentor), 3.1.74.
3. By yielding the point (Latin).

In the year 1632, the governor, with his pastor, Mr. Wilson,[4] and some other gentlemen, to settle a good understanding between the two colonies, traveled as far as Plymouth, more than forty miles, through an howling wilderness, no better accommodated in those early days than the princes that in Solomon's time saw "servants on horseback,"[5] or than genus and species in the old epigram, "going on foot."[6] The difficulty of the walk was abundantly compensated by the honorable, first reception, and then dismission, which they found from the rulers of Plymouth, and by the good correspondence thus established between the new colonies, who were like the floating bottles wearing this motto: *Si Collidimur Frangimur.*[7] But there were at this time in Plymouth two ministers,[8] leavened so far with the humors of the rigid Separation, that they insisted vehemently upon the unlawfulness of calling any unregenerate man by the name of "Goodman Such-an-One," until by their indiscreet urging of this whimsy, the place began to be disquieted.[9] The wiser people being troubled at these trifles, they took the opportunity of Governor Winthrop's being there, to have the thing publicly propounded in the congregation; who in answer thereunto, distinguished between a theological and a moral goodness; adding, that when juries were first used in England, it was usual for the crier, after the names of persons fit for that service were called over, to bid them all, "Attend, good men and true;" whence it grew to be a civil custom in the English nation, for neighbors living by one another, to call one another "Goodman Such-an-One;" and it was [a] pity now to make a stir about a civil custom, so innocently introduced. And that speech of Mr. Winthrop's put a lasting stop to the little, idle, whimsical conceits, then beginning to grow obstreperous.

Nevertheless, there was one civil custom used in (and in few but) the English nation, which this gentleman did endeavor to abolish in this country; and that was, the usage of drinking to one another. For although by drinking to one another, no more is meant than an act of courtesy, when one going to drink, does invite another to do so too, for the same ends with himself, nevertheless the governor (not altogether unlike to Cleomenes, of whom 'tis reported by Plutarch, ἄκοντι οὐδεὶς ποτήριον προσέφερε, *Nolenti poculum nunquam præbuit,*)[1] considered the impertinency and insignificancy of this usage, as to any of those ends that are usually pretended for it; and that indeed it ordinarily served for no ends at all, but only to provoke persons unto unseasonable and perhaps unreasonable drinking, and at last produce that abominable health-drinking, which the Fathers of old[2] so severely rebuked in the pagans, and which the Papists themselves do condemn, when their casuists pronounce it, *Peccatum mortale, provocare ad Æquales Calices, et Nefas Respondere.*[3] Wherefore in his own most hospitable house he left it off; not out of any silly or stingy fancy, but merely that by his example a greater temperance, with liberty of drinking, might be recommended, and

---

4. John Wilson (c. 1591–1667).
5. "I have seen servants upon horses, and princes walking as servants upon the earth" (Ecclesiastes 10.7). The Book of Ecclesiastes was mistakenly attributed to Solomon.
6. Better on foot go, than a wicked horse to ride (adage).
7. If we come into collision, we break (Latin).
8. Ralph Smith (1590–1661), Plymouth's first minister (1629–36), and Roger Williams (c. 1604–1683) were both Separatists.

9. I.e., they used the title "Goodman" to mean only regeneracy and visible sainthood.
1. Never urge the reluctant to drink (Latin). Plutarch (c. 46–120 C.E.) writes about the Spartan king Cleomenes III (r. 235–222 B.C.E.) in his *Parallel Lives.*
2. I.e., church fathers.
3. It is a deadly sin to challenge another to a drinking match, and it is impious to accept such challenges (Latin).

sundry inconveniences in drinking avoided; and his example accordingly began to be much followed by the sober people in this country, as it now also begins among persons of the highest rank in the English nation itself; until an order of court came to be made against that ceremony in drinking, and then, the old wont violently returned, with a *Nitimur in Vetitum.*[4]

Many were the afflictions of this righteous man![5] He lost much of his estate in a ship, and in an house, quickly after his coming to New England, besides the prodigious expense of it in the difficulties of his first coming hither. Afterwards his assiduous application unto the public affairs, (wherein *Ipse se non habuit, postquam Republica eum Gubernatorem habere cœpit*)[6] made him so much to neglect his own private interests, that an unjust steward[7] ran him £2,500 in debt before he was aware; for the payment whereof he was forced, many years before his decease, to sell the most of what he had left unto him in the country. Albeit, by the observable blessings of God upon the posterity of this liberal man, his children all of them came to fair estates, and lived in good fashion and credit. Moreover, he successively buried three wives; the first of which was the daughter and heiress of Mr. Forth, of Much Stambridge in Essex, by whom he had "wisdom with an inheritance;" and an excellent son. The second was the daughter of Mr. William Clopton, of London, who died with her child, within a very little while. The third was the daughter of the truly worshipful Sir John Tyndal,[8] who made it her whole care to please, first God, and then her husband; and by whom he had four sons, which survived and honored their father. And unto all these, the addition of the distempers, ever now and then raised in the country, procured unto him a very singular share of trouble; yea, so hard was the measure which he found even among pious men, in the temptations of a wilderness, that when the thunder and lightning had smitten a windmill whereof he was owner, some had such things in their heads as publicly to reproach this charitablest of men as if the voice of the Almighty had rebuked, I know not what oppression, which they judged him guilty of; which things I would not have mentioned, but that the instances may fortify the expectations of my best readers for such afflictions.

He that had been for his attainments, as they said of the blessed Macarius,[9] a παιδαριογερων, (an old man, while a young one,) and that had in his young days met with many of those ill days, whereof he could say, he had "little pleasure in them;" now found old age in its infirmities advancing earlier upon him, than it came upon his much longer-lived progenitors. While he was yet seven years off of that which we call "the grand climacterical,"[1] he felt the approaches of his dissolution; and finding he could say,

> *Non Habitus, non ipse Color, non Gressus Euntis,*
> *Non Species Eadem, quæ fuit ante, manet.*[2]

---

4. "A bias towards the forbidden usage" (Ovid's *Amores* 3.4.17).
5. "Many are the afflictions of the righteous: but the Lord delivereth him of them all" (Psalm 34.19).
6. He no longer belonged to himself, after the Republic had once made him her chief magistrate (Latin).
7. One James Luxford.
8. Winthrop married Mary Forth (1583–1615) in 1606. Much Stambridge is also known as Great Stambridge. They had six children but only one,

John (b. 1606), survived his father. Winthrop married Thomasine Clopton (1583–1616) in 1615 and Margaret Tyndal in 1618.
9. Egyptian (4th century), who had a reputation for having accomplished much while still young.
1. I.e., when he was fifty-six. "Grand climacterical"; age sixty-three.
2. "I am not what I was in form or face, / In healthful color or in vigorous pace" (Maximianus's *Elegies* 1.210–211).

He then wrote this account of himself: "Age now comes upon me, and infirmities therewithal, which makes me apprehend, that the time of my departure out of this world is not far off.[3] However, our times are all in the Lord's hand, so as we need not trouble our thoughts how long or short they may be, but how we may be found faithful when we are called for." But at last when that year came, he took a cold which turned into a fever, whereof he lay sick about a month, and in that sickness, as it hath been observed, that there was allowed unto the serpent the "bruising of the heel;"[4] and accordingly at the heel or the close of our lives the old serpent will be nibbling more than ever in our lives before; and when the devil sees that we shall shortly be, "where the wicked cease from troubling," that wicked one will trouble us more than ever; so this eminent saint now underwent sharp conflicts with the tempter, whose wrath grew great, as the time to exert it grew short; and he was buffeted with the disconsolate thoughts of black and sore desertions, wherein he could use that sad representation of his own condition:

Nuper eram Judex; Jam Judicor; Ante Tribunal
Subsistens paveo; Judicor ipse modo.[5]

But it was not long before those clouds were dispelled, and he enjoyed in his holy soul the great consolations of God! While he thus lay ripening for heaven, he did out of obedience unto the ordinance of our Lord send for the Elders of the church to pray with him; yea, they and the whole church fasted as well as prayed for him; and in that fast the venerable Cotton[6] preached on Psalm 35.13–14: "When they were sick, I humbled myself with fasting; I behaved myself as though he had been my friend or brother; I bowed down heavily, as one that mourned for his mother." From whence I find him raising that observation, "The sickness of one that is to us as a friend, a brother, a mother, is a just occasion of deep humbling our souls with fasting and prayer;" and making this application:

> Upon this occasion we are now to attend this duty for a governor, who has been to us as a friend in his counsel for all things, and help for our bodies by physic, for our estates by law, and of whom there was no fear of his becoming an enemy, like the friends of David:[7] a governor who has been unto us as a brother; not usurping authority over the church; often speaking his advice, and often contradicted, even by young men, and some of low degree; yet not replying, but offering satisfaction also when any supposed offenses have arisen; a governor who had been unto us as a mother, parent-like distributing his goods to brethren and neighbors at his first coming; and gently bearing our infirmities without taking notice of them.

Such a governor, after he had been more than ten several times by the people chosen their governor, was New England now to lose; who having,

---

3. "For I am now ready to be offered, and the time of my departure is at hand" (2 Timothy 4.6).
4. In his anger after the Fall, God tells the devil (in the form of a serpent): "And I will put enmity between thee and the woman, and between thy seed and her seed; it shall bruise thy head, and thou shalt bruise his heel" (Genesis 3.15).

5. "I once judged others, but now trembling stand / Before a dread tribunal, to be judged" (Latin).
6. John Cotton (1584–1652), Mather's grandfather and namesake.
7. King David's friends and counselors joined Absalom in his revolt against his father (2 Samuel).

like Jacob, first left his counsel and blessing with his children gathered about his bedside;[8] and, like David, "served his generation by the will of God,"[9] he "gave up the ghost," and fell asleep on March 26, 1649. Having like the dying Emperor Valentinian,[1] this above all his other victories for his triumphs, his overcoming of himself.

The words of Josephus[2] about Nehemiah, the governor of Israel, we will now use upon this governor of New England, as his

EPITAPH

'Ανηρ 'εγενετο χρηστος την φυσιν, και δικαιος.
Και περι τους ομοεθνεις φιλοτιμοτατος
Μνημεῖον αιωνιον αυτω καταλιπων, τα τῶν
'Ιεροσολυμων τειχη.

VIR FUIT INDOLE BONUS, AC JUSTUS:
ET POPULARIUM GLORIAE AMANTISSIMUS:
QUIBUS ETERNUM RELIQUIT MONUMENTUM,
Novanglorum MOENIA.[3]

1702

From Pillars of Salt[1]

[EXECUTION OF JAMES MORGAN]

On *March* II. 1686 was Executed at *Boston*, one *James Morgan*, for an horrible *Murder*. A man,[2] finding it necessary to come into his House, he Swore he would *Run a Spit into his Bowels*; and he was as bad as his word.

He was a *passionate* Fellow; and now, after his Condemnation, he much bewayl'd, his having been given to *Cursing*, in his passions.

The Reverend Person[3] who Preached, unto a great Assembly, on the Day of this poor man[']s Execution, did in the midst of his Sermon take occasion, to Read a Paper, which he had Received from the Malefactor, then present in the Assembly. It was as followeth.

I *James Morgan*, being Condemned to Dye, must needs own to the glory of God, that He is righteous, and that I have by my sins, provoked Him to destroy me before my time. I have been a great Sinner, guilty of Sabbath-

---

8. The aged patriarch Jacob was the second son of Isaac and Rebekah. In Genesis 49 he called his sons about him and told them what would befall them "in the last days" of the world.
9. "For David, after he had served his own generation by the will of God, fell on sleep, and was laid unto his fathers" (Acts 13.36).
1. Christian emperor of Rome (d. 375).
2. Jewish historian (37–100?) and author of *Antiquities of the Jews*, where the following quotation appears (book II, chap. 5).
3. He was by nature a man at once benevolent and just: most zealous for the honor of his countrymen and to them he left an imperishable monument—the walls of New England (Latin). The Latin paraphrase of the Greek substitutes *New England* for *Jerusalem*.

1. The text is derived from the first edition (1699).
2. Joseph Johnson, a butcher, died of "a wound an inch or 2 above his Navel," as Samuel Sewall reported in his diary. As Daniel A. Cohen reports in *Pillars of Salt and Monuments of Grace* (1993), he had been drinking with a pair of seamen in a Boston boarding house when the cries of a woman (as it turned out, Morgan's wife) caused them to rush to her aid. The woman told the three men that Morgan had harmed her and one of their children. When Morgan threatened the three men, they left. On hearing the woman once again cry out, they returned, at which point Morgan lunged at Johnson and ran him through with an iron spit. Johnson died four days later.
3. Increase Mather.

breaking, of Lying, and of Uncleanness; but there are especially two Sins whereby I have offended the Great God; one is that Sin of Drunkenness, which has caused me to commit many other Sins; for when in Drink, I have been often guilty of Cursing and Swearing, and quarrelling, and striking others: But the Sin which lies most heavy upon my Conscience, is, that I have despised the Word of God, and many a time refused to hear it preached. For these things, I believe God has left me to that, which has brought me to a shameful and miserable death. I do therefore beseech and warn all persons, young men especially, to take heed of these Sins, lest they provoke the Lord to do to them as He has justly done by me. And for the further peace of my own Conscience, I think my self obliged to add this unto my foregoing Confession, That *I own the Sentence* which the Honoured Court has *pass'd upon me*, to be exceeding just; inasmuch as (tho' I had no former Grudge and Malice against the man whom I have killed, yet) my Passion at the time of the Fact was so outragious, as that it hurried me on to the doing of that which makes me justly now proceeded against as a Murderer.

After the Sermon, a Minister,[4] at his Desire, went unto the place of Execution with him. And of what passed by the way, there was a Copy taken; which here Ensueth.

> *The DISCOURSE of the* MINISTER *with* JAMES MORGAN, *on the way to his Execution.*

MIN. I'm come hither to answer your desires which just now you exprest to me in the Publick, that I would give you my company at your Execution.

MOR. *Dear Sir, how much am I beholden to you! you have already done a great deal for me. Oh who am I that I have been such a vile wretch, that any Servants of God should take notice of me!*

MIN. I beseech you to make this use of it, I believe there is not one Christian this day beholding you, who would not willingly be at the greatest pains they could devise to save your precious Soul: How merciful then is that *Man* who is *God* as well as man! how unspeakably ready is the Lord Christ to save the Souls of sinners that affectionately *Look* unto him! The goodness and pitifulness of the most tender-hearted man in the world is but a shadow of what is in *Him*. The compassions of any man compared with the Bowels of a merciful *JESUS* are but as the painted Sun, or the painted Fire in comparison of the real.

MOR. *Oh that I could now look unto Him as I ought to do! Lord help me.*

MIN. Well, you are now a dying man, the last hour or two of your life is now running. You know your self now to stand just on the brink of Eternity; you shall presently be in a state of wonderful happiness or of horrible misery which must endure forever: which of those estates do you now count yourself stepping into?

MOR. *Oh Sir, I am afraid, but I am not without hope that God may have mercy on me.*

MIN. What's your ground for that hope? O see that your confidences been't[5] such as God will by and by reject.

MOR. *I don't know well what to say, but this I hope is a good sign, I have lived in many grievous sins, in* Lying, Drinking, Sabbath-breaking, *and evil*

---

4. Cotton Mather.   5. Be not.

Company-keeping; *God has made now these so bitter to my soul, that I would not commit them again, might I have my life this afternoon by doing it.*

MIN. That's a great word, God grant it may not be a word only, the good word of a good pang, without such a thro'[6] change of heart, as you must have if you would not perish everlastingly. You are not like to have any longer time in this world to try the Sincerity of your Profession.

MOR. *I know it, and I beseech you Sir to help me what you can: I hope the means used with me since my Condemnation ha'n't been lost.*

MIN. I would not have the sence of the pain and shame which your body is about to undergoe, any ways hinder your mind from being taken up about the Soul matters which I shall endeavour to set before you.

MOR. *Sir, as for the pain that my body must presently feel, I matter[7] it not: I know what pain is; but what shall I do for my poor Soul? I'm terrify'd with the Wrath of God; This, this terrifyes me, Hell terrifyes me: I should not mind my Death, if it were not for that.*

MIN. Now the Lord help me to deal faithfully with you, and the Lord help you to receive what he shall enable me to offer unto you. Mark what I say: You were born among the enemies of God, you were born with a soul as full of enmity against God, as a Toad is full of poison. You have liv'd now, how many years?

MORG. *I think about Thirty.*

MIN. And all these thirty years have you been sinning against the Holy God. Ever since you knew how to do any thing, you have every day been guilty of innumerable sins; you deserve the dreadful wrath and curse of the infinite God. But God has brought you here, to a place where you have enjoy'd the means of Grace. And here you have added unto your old Sins, most fearful Iniquities: you have been such a matchless, prodigious Transgressor, that you are now to Dy by the stroke of civil Justice; to *Dy before your time, for being wicked overmuch.* There is hardly any sort of Wickedness which you have not wallowed in. That Sin particularly which you are now to Dy for, is a most monstrous Crime. I can't possibly describe or declare the sins whereby you have made your self an astonishing Example of Impiety and punishment.

MOR. *O Sir, I have been a most hellish Sinner. I am sorry for what I have been.*

MIN. Sorry, you say: well, tell me, which of all your sins you are now most sorry for, which lies most heavy.

MOR. *I hope I am sorry for all my sins, but I must especially bewail my neglect of the means of Grace. On Sabbath dayes I us'd to lye at home, or be ill imploy'd elsewhere when I should have been at Church. This has undone me!*

MIN. And let me seriously tell you, your despising of Christ is a most dreadful sin indeed. You have for whole years together had the Call of Jesus Christ to seek an Interest in him, and you would now give all the world for that Interest, but you would take no notice of him. The Jews of Old put him to a worse death than yours will be this afternoon; and by your contempt of Christ you have said, the Jews did well to do so. How justly might he now laugh at your Calamity? And for these sins of yours, besides the direful woes and plagues that have already come upon you, you are now expos'd unto the

6. Thorough.   7. Mind.

Vengeance of eternal fire. You are in danger of being now quickly cast into these exquisite amazing Torments, in comparison of which, the anguishes which your body ever did feel, or shall feel before night, or can ever feel, are just nothing at all; and these dolorous torments are such as never had an End; as many sands as could lie between this earth and the Stars in Heaven would not be near so many as the Ages, the endless Ages of these Torments.

MOR. *But is there not Mercy for me in Christ?*

MIN. Yes, and its a wonderful thing that I have now further to tell you. Mind, I entreat you. The Son of God is become the Son of Man; the Lord Jesus Christ is both God & Man in one Person, and he is both sufficiently able & willing also, to be your Saviour. He lived a most righteous life, & this was that such as you and I might be able to say before God, *Lord, accept of me as if I had lived righteously.* He dyed at length a most cursed death, and this was that we might be able to say unto God, *Lord, let me not dye for Sin, since thy Son has dyed in my room.* This glorious Redeemer is now in the highest Heaven, pleading with God for the Salvation of His Chosen ones.— And he pours out his Spirit continually upon them that do believe on him: might you then be enabled by his Grace to carry your poor, guilty, condemned, enslaved, ignorant Soul unto Jesus Christ, and humbly put your trust in him for deliverance from the whole bad state which you are brought into. Oh then his voice is to you the same that was to the penitent Thief, *This day shalt thou be with me in Paradise.*

MOR. *Oh that I might be so! Sir, I would hear more of these things: I think, I can't better fit my self for my Death than by hearkening to these things.*

MIN. Attend then: The never-dying Spirit that lodges within you, must now within a few minutes appear before the Tribunal of the Great GOD; in what, or in whose Righteousness will you then appear? will you have this to be your Plea, *Lord, I experienced many good Motions & Desires in my Soul, and many sorrows for my sin before I dy'd*: or will you expect to have no other Plea but This, *Lord, I am vile, but thy Son is a Surety for the worst of Sinners that believe on Him; for his sake alone, have M E R C Y on me.*

MOR. *I thank God for what He has wrought in my Soul.*—

MIN. But be very careful about this matter: if you build on your own good Affections instead of Jesus Christ the only Rock, if you think they shall recommend you to God, *He that made you will not have mercy on you.*

MOR. *I would be clothed with the Righteousness of J E S U S   C H R I S T.*

MIN. But you can't sincerely desire that Christ should justify you, if you don't also desire that He should sanctify you: those two always go together. Is every lust that has hitherto had possession of your heart become so loathsome to you, that it would fill your Soul with joy to hear Jesus Christ say, *I will subdue those Iniquities of thine; I will make a holy, an heavenly, a spiritually minded person of thee.*

MOR. *I would not Sin against God any more.*

MIN. But I must deal plainly with you: You have made it sadly suspicious that your repentance is not yet as it ought to be: when men truly & throughly repent of sin, they use[8] to be in a special manner watchful against that Sin which has been their chief Sin: one of your principal sins which has indeed brought you to the Death of a *Murderer*, is *Passion*, unmortifi'd and outra-

8. Attempt.

gious *Passionateness*: Now I have been this day informed, that no longer since than the last night, upon some Dissatisfaction about the place which the Authority hath ordered you by and by to be buried in, you did express your self with a most unruly Passionateness.

MOR. *Sir, I confess it, and I was quickly sorry for it, tho' for the present I was too much disturbed: Twas my folly to be so careful about the place where my body should be laid, when my precious Soul was in such a Condition.—*

MIN. Truly you have cause to mourn for it. Secure the welfare of your soul, and this (now) pinion'd, hang'd, vile body of yours will shortly be raised unto glory, glory for evermore. And let me put you in mind of one thing more, I doubt you han't yet laid aside your unjust Grudges against the Persons concerned in your Conviction and Condemnation: You have no cause to complain of them: and you are not fit to pray, much less are you fit to dye, till you heartily wish them as well as your own soul: if you dy malicious, you die miserable.

MOR. *I heartily wish them all well, I bear Ill-will to none. What a lamentable thing is this? Ah this is that which has brought me hither!*

MIN. What do you mean?

MOR. *I over heard a man mocking and scoffing at me when I stumbled just now, he does very ill. I have done so my self. I have mock'd and scoff'd like that man, and see what it hath brought me to; he may come to the like.*

MIN. The Lord forgive that foolish hard hearted creature. But be not too much disturbed.

MOR. *Yonder! I am now come in sight of the place where I must immediately end my days. Oh what a huge Multitude of people is come together on this occasion. O Lord, O Lord, I pray thee to make my Death profitable to all this Multitude of People, that they may not sin against thee as I have done.*

MIN. Amen, Amen, ten thousand times; the Lord God Almighty say Amen to this Prayer of yours! It would indeed be an excellent thing if you would now come to receive your death with some satisfaction of soul in this thought, That much Glory is like to come to God by it: I am verily persuaded God intends to do good to many souls by means of your Execution: This a greater honour than you are worthy of.

(After the Discourse had been intermitted about a minute or two by reason of the miery way.)[9]

MOR. *I beseech you Sir speak to me. Do me all the good you can: my time grows very short: your discourse fits me for my Death more than any thing.*

MIN. I am sorry so small a thing as a plashy Street should make me loose one minute of this more than ordinary precious time; a few paces more bring you to the place which you have now in your eye, from whence you shall not come back alive. Do you find your self afraid to dy there?

MOR. *Sir, if it were not for the Condition that my Soul must by and by be in, I should not fear my death at all; but I have a little comfort from some of Gods promises about that.*

MIN. And what shall I now say? These are among the last words that I can have liberty to leave with you. Poor man, thou art now going to knock at the door of Heaven, and to beg & cry, *Lord, Lord open to me!* The only way for thee to speed, is, to open the door of thy own soul now unto the Lord Jesus

9. Muddy street.

Christ. Do this, and thou shalt undoubtedly be admitted into the Glories of His Heavenly Kingdom: You shall fare as well as *Manasseh* did before you: leave this undone, and there's nothing remains for you but the *Worm which dyeth not, and the Fire which shall not be quenched.*[1]

MOR. *Sir, shew me then again what I have to do.*

MIN. The voice, the sweet voice of the Lord Jesus Christ, (who was once hang'd on a tree, to take away the Sting and Curse of even such a Death as yours) unto all that close with him, His Heavenly voice now is, O that I and my saving work might be entertained, kindly entreated, in that poor perishing Soul of thine! Are you willing?

MOR. *I hope I am.*

MIN. His Voice further is, If I am lodged in thy Soul, I'le sprinkle my blood upon it, and on my account thou shalt find Favour with God. Do you consent to this?

MOR. *This I want.*

MIN. But this is not all that he saith, His Voice further is, If I come into thy Soul, I will change it, I will make all sin bitter to it, I will make it an holy heavenly soul. Do you value this above the proffers of all the World?

MOR. *I think I do,—and now Sir, I must go no further, Look here—what a solemn sight is this! Here lyes the Coffin which this Body of mine must presently be laid in. I thank you dear Sir, for what you have already done for me.*

MIN. When you are gone up this Ladder, my last Service for you, before you are gone off, will be to pray with you: but I would here take my leave of you. Oh that I might meet you at the Right Hand of the Lord Jesus in the Last Day. Farewell poor heart, Fare thee well. The Everlasting Arms receive thee! The Lord Jesus, the merciful Saviour of Souls take possession of thy Spirit for himself. The Great God, who is a great Forgiver, grant thee Repentance unto Life; and Glorify Himself in the Salvation of such a wounded Soul as thine for ever. With Him, and with His free, rich, marvellous, Infinite Grace, I leave you. *Farewell.*

Being Arrived unto the place of Execution, his *Last Speech* upon the Ladder, then taken in Short-Hand, was that which is here inserted.

I Pray God that I may be a warning to you all, and that I may be the last that ever shall suffer after this manner: In the fear of God I warn you to have a care of taking the Lords Name in vain. Mind and have a care of that Sin of Drunkenness, for that Sin leads to all manner of Sins and Wickedness: (mind, and have a care of breaking the sixth Commandment, where it is said, *Thou shalt not do no Murder*) for when a man is in Drink, he is ready to commit all manner of Sin, till he fills up the cup of the wrath of God, as I have done by committing that Sin of Murder. I beg of God, as I am a dying man, and to appear before the Lord within a few minutes, that you may take notice of what I say to you. Have a care of drunkenness, and ill Company, and mind all good Instruction, and don't turn your back upon the Word of God, as I have done. When I have been at meeting, I have gone out of the Meeting-house to commit sin, and to please the lust of my flesh. Don't make a mock at any poor object of pity, but bless God that he has not left you as

1. Isaiah 66.24.

he had justly done me, to commit that horrid Sin of Murder. Another thing that I have to say to you is to have a care of that house where that wickedness was committed, and where I have been partly ruined by. But here I am, and know not what will become of my poor soul, which is within a few moments of eternity. I have murder'd a poor man, who had but little time to repent, and I know not what is become of his poor soul; Oh that I may make use of this Opportunity that I have! O that I may make improvement of this little time, before I go hence and be no more. O let all mind what *I* am a saying now, I'm going out of this world. O take warning by me, and beg of God to keep you from this sin which has been my ruine. (His last words were) *O Lord, receive my Spirit, I come unto thee, O Lord, I come unto thee, O Lord, I come, I come, I come.*

*   *   *

[EXECUTION OF ELIZABETH EMERSON]

On *June* 8. 1693[.] Two Young Women, (the one *English*, t'other *Negro*) were Executed at *Boston*, for murdering their *Bastard Children*.

The *English* Young Woman,[2] gave to the Minister, who Preach'd that Afternoon, the following Paper of *Confessions*; which he took occasion, in the Sermon, to publish unto the Congregation, where she also was then present before the Lord.

I am a miserable Sinner; and I have justly provoked the Holy God to leave me unto that Folly of my own Heart, for which I am now Condemned to Dy. I cannot but see much of the *Anger* of God against me, in the Circumstances of my woful Death; He hath Fulfilled upon me, that Word of His, *Evil pursueth Sinners.* I therefore desire, Humbly to *Confess* my many Sins before God, and the World: but most particularly my *Blood Guiltiness*. Before the Birth of my *Twin-Infants*, I too much parlyed with the Temptations of the Devil, to smother my Wickedness by Murthering of them: At length, when they were Born I was not unsensible, that at least, *One* of them was alive; but such a Wretch was I, as to use a *Murderous* Carriage towards them, in the place where I lay, on purpose to dispatch them out of the World. I acknowledge that I have been more Hard hearted than the *Sea Monsters*, and yet for the Pardon of these my Sins, I would Fly to the Blood of the Lord Jesus Christ, which is the only *Fountain set open for Sin and Uncleanness*. I know not how better to Glorify God, for giving me such an Opportunity as I have had to make sure of His Mercy, than by advising and entreating the *Rising Generation* here, to take Warning by my Example; and I will therefore tell the *Sins*, that have brought me to my shameful End. I do Warn all People, and especially, *Young People*, against the Sin of *Uncleanness* in particular; 'tis that Sin that hath been my Ruine; well had it been for me, if I had

---

2. Elizabeth Emerson (1665–1693), a younger sister of famous Indian captive Hannah Dustan, had a difficult childhood—her father in 1676 was fined for "cruel and excessive beating" of her, as Laurel Thatcher Ulrich reports in *Good Wives* (1982). In her early twenties, Elizabeth had illicit relations with Timothy Swan, a young neighbor, and gave birth to a daughter out of wedlock. In 1691, still not married, she was thought to be pregnant again. Suspicious neighbors prompted an investigation which yielded two bodies in a shallow grave in the Emerson garden. She claimed that the infants had been stillborn, but a court in Boston found her guilty of murder. The other woman executed with her, whose name is not given in Mather's account, was accorded scant room in his book. Cotton Mather himself is the minister preaching on the afternoon of her execution.

answered all Temptations to that Sin as *Joseph* did, *How shall I do this Wickedness, and Sin against God?*[3]—But, I see, *Bad Company* is that, which leads to that, and all other Sins; and I therefore beg all that Love their Souls to be familiar with none but such as fear God. I believe, the chief thing that hath brought me into my present Condition, is my *Disobedience to my Parents*: I despised all their Godly Counsels and Reproofs; and I was always of an Haughty and stubborn Spirit. So that now I am become a dreadful Instance of the Curse of God belonging to *Disobedient Children*. I must Bewayl this also, that although I was *Baptised*, yet when I grew up, I forgot the *Bonds* that were laid upon me to be the Lords. Had I given my self to God, as soon as I was capable to consider that I had been in *Baptism*, set apart for him, How happy had I been! It was my *Delay* to Repent of my former Sins, that provoked God to leave me unto the Crimes, for which I am now to Dy. Had I seriously Repented of my *Uncleanness* the *First Time* I fell into it, I do suppose, I had not been left unto what followed. Let all take it from me; they little think, what they do, when they put off turning from Sin to God, and Resist the *Strivings* of the Holy Spirit. I fear, 'tis for this, that I have been given up to such *Hardness of Heart*, not only since my long *Imprisonment*, but also since my Just *Condemnation*. I now know not what will become of my Distressed, perishing Soul. But I would humbly Commit it unto the Mercy of God in Jesus Christ; *Amen*.

[EXECUTION OF AN INDIAN, CALLED ZACHARY]

In the Year, 1694. A miserable *Indian*, called *Zachary*, was Executed for *Murder*.

He understood so very little English, that it put the English Minister, who, after his Condemnation, visited him, unto an Inexpressible deal of trouble, to convey unto him, the *Principles* and the *Directions* of our Holy Religion. But the Lord so succeeded the endeavours used upon the wretched Salvage, that within a little while, he could give a sensible, tho' a Shattered, Account, of the *Fundamentals* in Christianity. And such an Impression, had the Doctrine of *Grace* upon him, that he professed himself, desirous rather to *Dy*, than to *Live* at his Old sinful rate. He seem'd, even to long for his Execution, that so he might be delivered from all disposition to Sin against God. But all his Hopes of Everlasting Salvation, he seem'd very Suitably to place, on the Obedience which the Lord Jesus Christ, had yeelded unto God in the room of Sinners.

Of this poor creature, nothing had been here mentioned, if it had not been to introduce the mention of this one passage.

He said, *That the Thing which undid him was This: He had begun to come, and hear the Preaching of the Gospel among the Indians: But he minded the Indian-Preacher, how he lived; and he saw plainly that the Preacher minded his Bottle, more than his Bible: he lov'd Rum too well, and when his Rum was in him, he would quarrel with other people, and with himself Particularly. This* (he said) *Prejuduced him against the Gospel. So he lived as a Pagan still; and would be Drunk too; and his Drunkenness had brought all this misery upon him.*

1700

3. Genesis 39.9

American Literature
1700–1820

AN EXPANDING WORLD AND UNIVERSE

By the time of Cotton Mather's death in 1728, which symbolically marks the passing of Puritanism as the colonists had experienced it, the imaginative world he and other clerical writers strove to maintain was challenged in a variety of ways. The eighteenth century saw enormous changes—economic, social, philosophical, and scientific—that inevitably affected the influence and authority of clergymen like Mather and transformed the ways in which they understood the world. Most important, many intellectuals now believed in the power of the human mind to comprehend the universe as never before, particularly through the laws of physics as they recently had been described by the great Isaac Newton (1642–1727). Inevitably, then, scripture became more a handmaiden than a guide to metaphysics. Second, and of equal importance, through the influence of the English metaphysician John Locke (1632–1704) there arose new psychological paradigms that promulgated human sympathy, rather than supernatural grace, as the basis for the moral life. As elaborated by Adam Smith and other thinkers, this reliance on human sympathy or "sentiment" as the catalyst for moral choice and action concomitantly encouraged the belief that each individual had the power to control his or her spiritual destiny. Such challenges to the theocentric world of the colonial clergy were part of the immense changes in Western thought described by historians as the Enlightenment.

The Enlightenment had political as well as scientific and religious implications. By the end of the century, colonists were in the process of establishing a polity the likes of which the world had not yet seen. There would be a religious element to this new nation, but it would be only one component of a state whose destiny, while still thought of as divinely guaranteed, was understood to be achievable on earth through the spread of democratic principles. The literature of this century reflected and extended these and other new emphases in Western thought and culture.

The eighteenth century brought a new world into being in the most basic and striking ways. The increase in population alone helps account for the greater diversity of opinion in religious as well as in political life that marked it and its literature. In 1670, for example, the population of the colonies numbered approximately 111,000. Thirty years later it was more than 250,000; by 1760, if one includes Georgia, it reached 1,600,000—and the settled area had tripled. The demand for and price of colonial goods increased in England, and vast fortunes were to be made in New England with any business connected with shipbuilding: especially timber, tar, and pitch. Virginia planters became rich through tobacco; and rice and indigo from the Carolinas were in constant demand. Further, compared with such crowded cities as London, the colonies were healthier and cheaper, and promotional literature as well as personal testimony painted British North America as a region in which one could take charge of and transform one's life. Thus those who could arrange their passage, either by paying for it outright or mortgaging it through indentured service, arrived in great numbers: Boston, for example, almost doubled in size from 1700 to 1720. The colonies were ethnically diverse; the great migration during the first half of the eighteenth century was not primarily English. Dutch and Germans came in large numbers and so did French Protestants. By this time, too, Jewish merchants and craftsmen established themselves in New York and Philadelphia.

This rapidly expanding trade—hallmark of what we now recognize as the beginning of modern consumerism—linked the colonies to other areas in what historians call the Atlantic Rim, a region encompassing Europe, Africa, and the Caribbean basin as well as North and South America. The rim had a complex, multiethnic, multiracial population united by their status as laborers. Thus even as the new and seemingly insatiable desire for goods brought great wealth to planters and merchants, it created at the other end of the social spectrum the world's first multiethnic working class, one whose members often had to endure great cruelty. The numbers of enslaved Africans increased in this period, for example, even as some of them, typified here by Olaudah Equiano, began to speak out about their experiences and condition. Other groups like the New England Indians suffered in different ways. Estimated to number 25,000 in 1600, they already had been reduced by one-third during the plague of 1616–18 and declined steadily thereafter; many Native American communities disappeared entirely during this period of expansion in the Northeast. Their fate in the southern colonies and the Caribbean islands, often linked to plantation slavery, was no better.

This economic take-off affected the very warp and woof of social organization. New England towns, for example, long viewed as pillars of stability, often were full of acrimonious debate between first settlers and newcomers as they bickered over diminishing land or the proper form and substance of worship. When the colonies' first towns were formed, for example, acreage was apportioned to settlers and allotted free; but by 1713 speculators in land were hard at work, buying as much as possible for as little as possible and selling high. Many a town history records the wrangling of splinter groups and the establishment of a "second" church and the inevitable removal of families and groups who sought richer farm lands. Under new economic and religious pressures, the idea of a "community" of mutually helpful souls was fast disappearing, and the colonists' gradual awakening to the incongruity of the slavery that they tolerated or encouraged only further stretched the capacity of their rhetoric of Christian charity.

While life in many parts of the colonies remained difficult, the hardships and dangers the first settlers faced were mostly overcome, and more and more colonists, particularly those along the coast, emulated the culture of metropolitan London. Concomitantly, once colonists began to expect the refinements made available by their extensive trading networks, they better understood what was special or unique about their experience in the New World. United by the common experience of ocean passage and the desire to make new lives for themselves, these thousands of emigrants slowly but inexorably began to realize that they had more in common as inhabitants of America than they did as citizens of a Europe that rapidly receded into memory. In 1702 no one would have dreamed of an independent union of colonies, but by the 1750s it was a distinct possibility.

ENLIGHTENMENT IDEALS

By the early eighteenth century, scientists and philosophers had posed great challenges to seventeenth-century beliefs, and the "modern" period as we understand it emerged from their efforts to conceive humans and their universe in new terms, even as they struggled to yoke this brave new world to what they learned in scripture. Indeed, scientists like Newton and philosophers like Locke sought to resolve implicit conflicts between their discoveries and traditionally held Christian truths. Because they believed that God worked in reasonable, comprehensible ways with humankind uppermost, they saw nothing heretical in arguing that the universe was an orderly system such that by the application of reason humanity would comprehend its laws, or that one's supreme obligation was to relate to one's fellows through an innate and thus natural power of sympathy. But the inevitable result of such inquiries made the universe seem more rational and benevolent than it had been represented in Puritan doctrine. Similarly, people increasingly defined their highest duties in social rather than in spiritual terms.

Because science made the world seem more comprehensible, many put less stock in revealed religion. Often these new scientists and philosophers were avowedly, or were called, Deists; they deduced the existence of a supreme being from the construction of the universe itself rather than from the Bible. "A creation," as one distinguished historian has put it, "presupposes a creator." A harmonious universe proclaimed the beneficence of God. A number of seventeenth-century modes of thought—Bradford's and Winthrop's penchant for the allegorical and emblematic, seeing every natural and human event as a message from God, for instance—seemed anachronistic and quaint. People were less interested in the metaphysical wisdom of introspective divines than in the progress of ordinary individuals, relating now to their fellow beings through emotions and experiences they shared as colonists. This no doubt accounts for the popularity of Benjamin Franklin's *Autobiography*. Many now assumed that humankind was naturally good and thus dwelt on neither the Fall nor the Incarnation, but rather on how thinking, feeling people shared the bonds of their common humanity. They were not interested in theology but in humankind's own nature, and frequently cited Alexander Pope's famous couplet:

> Know then thyself, presume not God to scan,
> The proper study of mankind is man.

Locke said that "our business" here on earth "is not to know all things, but those which concern our conduct." In suggesting that we are not born with a set of innate ideas of good or evil and that the mind is rather like a blank wax tablet (a *tabula rasa*) on which experiences are inscribed, Locke qualified traditional belief and suggested that the more that we understood and sympathized with our fellow men and women, the richer our social and spiritual lives would be.

REASON AND RELIGION: THE GREAT AWAKENING

But the old beliefs did not die easily, and as early as the 1730s a conservative reaction against the worldview of the new science and psychology followed as some intellectuals, aware of the new thought but intent on maintaining the final truth of revealed religion, resisted the religious implications of Enlightenment principles. But the genie had escaped from the bottle, and this reaction was indelibly marked by the new thought it opposed. One unexpected result, for example, was that the first half of the eighteenth century witnessed a number of religious revivals in both England and America that in part were fueled by the new emphasis on emotion as a component of human experience. Although some historians view the revivals as desperate efforts to reassert outmoded Puritan values in the face of the new, in fact the religious fires that burned so intensely between 1735 and 1750 were themselves the direct product of the new cult of feeling whose foundation Locke had laid. Now ministers as well as philosophers argued that our greatest pleasure was derived from the good we did for others, and that our sympathetic emotions (our joys as well as our tears) were not signs of human-kind's fallen state but rather a guarantee of our glorious future. The African American poet Phillis Wheatley, for example, whose poem on the death of the itinerant Methodist George Whitefield (1714–1770) made her famous, said that Whitefield prayed that "grace in every heart might dwell" and longed to see "America excell." Following his many successful religious revivals in England, Whitefield embarked on a preaching tour along the Atlantic seaboard colonies in 1739–40, a visit that was punctuated by great emotionalism. But in this he only followed the similarly "extraordinary circumstances" that had occurred in Northampton, Massachusetts, under the leadership of Jonathan Edwards in the 1730s and that have come to be synonymous with the "Great Awakening."

Edwards also had read his Locke and understood that if his parishioners were to be awakened from their spiritual slumbers they had to experience religion in a more heartfelt way, not just strive to comprehend it intellectu-ally. Thus, from his time as a young minister under the tutelage of his emi-nent grandfather, the Reverend Solomon Stoddard, Edwards began to rejuvenate the basic tenets of Calvinism, including that of unconditional election, the one doctrine most difficult for eighteenth-century minds to accept. Edwards insisted that such doctrines made sense in terms of Enlight-enment science. Hammering at his audience through what one historian has called a "rhetoric of sensation," he persuaded his congregation that God's sovereignty was not only a most reasonable doctrine but also the most "delightful," and appeared to him in an almost sensuous way as "exceeding pleasant, bright, and sweet." In carefully reasoned, calmly argued prose, as harmonious and as ordered as anything the age produced, Edwards brought many in his audience to understand that "if the great things of religion are rightly understood, they will affect the heart." Thus, while most people remember Edwards for his frightening sermon *Sinners in the Hands of an Angry God,* he was much more moved by the experience of joy that his faith brought him. More typical is his "Personal Narrative" or his apostrophe to Sara Pierpont (whom he would marry), for both testify to how experientially moving he found true religious feeling. These are foundational texts for understanding the rise of the sentimental in literature and Western culture generally.

The Awakening in turn engendered as many critics as supporters, for many believed that revivalists were too given over to "enthusiasm" at the expense of their reason. Thus Edwards and others who believed in the new light that God had shed over them had to expend much time and energy in pamphlet wars with prominent clergy such as Boston's Charles Chauncy who, from his pulpit in that city's First Church, compared the antics of the revived to the hysteria that Anne Hutchinson earlier had instigated. Heirs to a rapid expansion of print culture that fueled the controversies over revival, opponents like Edwards and Chauncy, and others on both sides of the religious question, used the presses as never before to win over public opinion. Inevitably, the fires of revival burned lower; when Edwards himself tried to consolidate his success in Northampton and in 1749 demanded from applicants personal accounts of conversion before admitting them to church membership, he was accused of being a reactionary, removed from his pulpit, and effectively silenced. He spent the next few years as a missionary to the American Indians in Stockbridge, Massachusetts, a town forty miles west of Northampton, imitating the call of the Reverend David Brainard, a young man who, had he lived, would have married Edwards's daughter Jerusha. There Edwards remained until invited to become president of the College of New Jersey. His death in Princeton was the direct result of his being inoculated against smallpox, which he had done to set an example for his frightened and superstitious students; it serves as a vivid reminder of how complicated in any one individual the response to the "new science" could become.

IMPERIAL POLITICS

If religion occupied many colonists in the first half of the eighteenth century, after 1763, when Great Britain had consolidated its empire in the New World with victory over the French in Canada, politics dominated its second half. On June 7, 1776, at the second Continental Congress, Richard Henry Lee of Virginia moved that "these united colonies are, and of a right ought to be, free and independent states." A committee was duly appointed to prepare a declaration of independence, and it was issued on July 4. Although these motions and their swiftness took some delegates by surprise—the purpose of the congress had, after all, not been to declare independence but to protest the usurpation of rights by king and Parliament and to effect a compromise with the homeland—others saw them as the inevitable consequence of the events of the preceding decade. The Stamp Act of 1764, taxing all newspapers, legal documents, and licenses, had infuriated Bostonians and resulted in the burning of the governor's palace; the Virginian Patrick Henry had taken the occasion to speak with passion against taxation without representation. In 1770 a Boston mob had been fired on by British soldiers. Three years later was the famous "Tea Party," when colonists dressed as Native Americans and dumped English tea into Boston harbor as a protest against paying taxes on it. This event tested the limits of British rule. In adopting the costume of Native Americans, these protesters declared themselves antithetical to everything British. The news of the April 1775 confrontation with the British in Concord and Lexington, Massachusetts, was still on everyone's tongue in Philadelphia when the Second Continental Congress convened that May.

Although the drama of these events and the personal suffering they caused cannot be underestimated, colonists also were transformed into revolutionaries through the power of the word. Thomas Paine's pamphlet *Common Sense*, published in January 1776, has been credited with tipping the scales toward revolution; but it was preceded by a vast literature that took to heart the arguments of the Whig opposition in England. The Whigs, the so-called country as opposed to court party, inveighed against luxury and tyranny in terms that resonated across the Atlantic. We see Whig party principles applied to the American strand in Royall Tyler's play *The Contrast* (1787). In arguing that separation from England was the only reasonable course and that "the Almighty" had planted these feelings in us "for good and wise purposes," Paine appealed to basic tenets of the Enlightenment. His clarion call to those that "love mankind," those "that dare oppose not only the tyranny but the tyrant, stand forth!" did not go unheeded. Americans needed an apologist for the Revolution, and in December 1776, when Washington's troops were at their most demoralized, it was, again, Paine's first *Crisis* paper—popularly called *The American Crisis*—that was read to all the regiments and was said to have inspired their future success.

Paine first came to America in 1774 with a note from Benjamin Franklin recommending him to publishers and editors. He was only one of a number of young writers who took advantage of the revolution in print culture that was to make authorship as we know it possible. This was, in fact, the great age of the newspaper and the moral essay; Franklin tells us that he modeled his own style on the clarity, good sense, and simplicity of the English essayists Joseph Addison and Richard Steele. The first newspaper in the colonies appeared in 1704, and by the time of the Revolution there were almost fifty papers and forty magazines. The great cry was for a "national literature" (meaning anti-British), and the political events of the 1770s were advantageous for a career in letters. Even women like Judith Sargent Murray, Sarah Wentworth Morton, and others got into the act, and all found eager audiences for their work in periodicals like Isaiah Thomas's *Massachusetts Magazine*. Although the conventions of the day required anonymity, the women used feminine pen-names, thus proclaiming the right of all women to opine in print on public events. Actually, the identity of these women writers was generally known; their literary efforts added to the campaign for a true realization of the principle of equality.

Similarly, other writers published utilitarian political and polite—aesthetically enjoyable—literature simultaneously. Philip Freneau, for example, succeeded first as a writer of satires of the British; after publishing his *Poems Written Chiefly during the Late War* (1786) he turned to newspaper work, editing the *New York Daily Advertiser* and writing anti–Federalist Party essays, making himself an enemy of Alexander Hamilton in the process. Other authors, Annis Boudinot Stockton among them, cut a different profile, publishing in local periodicals and newspapers but also contributing significantly to an extensive manuscript culture in which literary efforts were shared with a coterie of like-minded people. But, as the career of Freneau suggests, despite the amount of belletristic writing extant from the late eighteenth century, the most significant writings of the period are political, like the essays Hamilton, John Jay, and James Madison wrote for New York newspapers in 1787 and 1788 in support of the new federal constitution, collectively known as *The Federalist Papers*. They provided an eloquent defense of the framework of the republic and remind us that in good measure the uniqueness of the new United States of America resided in the language of the documents, the very words, on which the nation was based. Together with such self-consciously American works as Benjamin Franklin's *Autobiography* and Hector St. John de Crèvecoeur's *Letters from an American Farmer,* they mark the beginning of a new sense of national identity as colonists from greatly different backgrounds and of varied nationalities now found reasons to call themselves "Americans." This transformation was not easy. Washington Irving's fictional character Rip Van Winkle found the world radically different when, finally awakened from his slumbers, he tried to make sense of what he had missed, the American Revolution: "God knows, I'm not myself—I'm somebody else—that's me yonder—no—that's somebody else got into my shoes—I was myself last night, but I fell asleep on the mountain . . . and everything's changed, and I'm changed, and I can't tell what's my name, or who I am!"

Because neither the technological nor the economic infrastructure was yet in place to support a national audience, because people lived in widely separated and poorly connected villages or on remote farms, none of these early American writers, including such popular novelists as Susanna Rowson and Charles Brockden Brown, could live by their pens alone. The crisis in American life caused by the Revolution had made artists self-conscious about American subjects, but it was Washington Irving who best learned how to exploit this nascent self-consciousness, who had the distinction of being the first American writer to live on the income produced by his publications. His generation discovered ways of being American without compromising their integrity, and they successfully harnessed the world of print to their ambition to speak through the profession of authorship.

PURSUING HAPPINESS

When John Winthrop described his "model" for a Christian community, he envisioned a group of men and women working together for the common good, each of whom knew his or her place in the stable social structure decreed by God. At all times, he said, "some must be rich, some poor, some high and eminent in power and dignity," others low and "in subjection." Ideally, it was to be a community of love, all made equal by their fallen nature and their concern for the salvation of their souls, but it was to be a stable community. But President John Adams witnessed social mobility of a kind and to an extent that Winthrop would not have dreamed possible. As historians have observed, European critics of America in the eighteenth and nineteenth centuries never understood that great social change was possible without social upheaval primarily because there was no feudal hierarchy to overthrow. When Crèvecoeur wanted to distinguish America from Europe, it was the medievalism of the latter that he wished to stress. The visitor to

America, he said, "views not the hostile castle, and the haughty mansion, contrasted with the clay-built hut and miserable cabin, where cattle and men help to keep each other warm, and dwell in meanness, smoke and indigence."

Of course, in 1820, many Americans were still not free. Some of the Founding Fathers, like George Washington and Thomas Jefferson, were slave owners themselves. Men could not vote unless they owned property; women could not vote at all. Women were wards of their fathers until marriage, upon which their legal identity was merged with their husbands, so that they could not own property or keep any wages they might earn. Educated at home for domestic duties, young women were supposed to be excluded from public, intellectual life. But, by the end of the eighteenth century, a movement to educate women like men—so that they could properly imbue their young children with patriotic ideals—had gained considerable strength. Every literary woman testified in her own way to the usefulness of all women in the public sphere. Fired by Enlightenment ideals of reason and equality, women like Judith Sargent Murray and Hannah Foster began to speak and write on public subjects and to agitate for their rights as citizens.

The condition of Native Americans continued to deteriorate throughout the nineteenth century. Well understanding their vulnerability to colonial expansionist drives, many eastern tribes sided with the British during the Revolution. After the British defeat, they were exposed both to white vengeance and white greed. Entire tribes were systematically displaced from their traditional territories, pushed ever farther and farther west. Nevertheless, the same forces that earlier had undermined church authority in New England gradually affected the Americans' understanding of what constituted the good society. If, as Russel Nye once put it, the two assumptions held to be true by most eighteenth-century Americans were "the perfectibility of man, and the prospect of his future progress," American citizens had to ground those assumptions in the reality of their day-to-day relations with others whose plight had not yet been touched by the contagion of liberty. Thus much imaginative energy in the late eighteenth and early nineteenth centuries was expended in beginning to correct institutional and social injustices: the tyranny of monarchy, the tolerance of slavery, the misuse of prisons, the place of women. Even as they agitated for an extension of the principles of liberty codified by the Revolutionary generation, few doubted that with the application of intelligence the human lot could be improved. Writers like Freneau, Franklin, and Crèvecoeur argued that, if it was not too late, the transplanted European might learn something about fellowship and manners from "the noble savages" rather than from rude white settlers, slave owners, and backwoods pioneers.

For many, Franklin best represents the promise of the Enlightenment in America, even as his long and fruitful life also testified to the pitfalls that accompanied an uncritical adoption of principles that enshrined the individual's concerns above those of the community. Franklin was self-educated, social, assured, a man of the world, ambitious and public-spirited, speculative about the nature of the universe, and in matters of religion content "to observe the actual conduct of humanity rather than to debate supernatural matters that are unprovable." When Ezra Stiles asked him about his religion, he said he believed in the "creator of the universe" but he doubted the "divinity of Jesus." He would never be dogmatic about it, however, because—as he wryly put it—he expected soon "an opportunity of knowing the truth with less trouble." Franklin always presents himself as a man depending on first-hand experience, too worldly-wise to be caught off guard, and always minding "the main chance," as one character in Tyler's *The Contrast* counsels. This aspect of Franklin's persona, however, belies another side of him and of the eighteenth century: those idealistic assumptions in which the great public documents of the American Revolution, especially the Declaration of Independence, are grounded. Given the representative nature of Franklin's character, it seems right that of the documents most closely associated with the formation of the American republic—the Declaration of Independence, the treaty of alliance with France, the Treaty of Paris, and the Constitution—only he signed all four.

The fact that Americans in the last quarter of the eighteenth century held that "certain truths are self-evident, that all men are created equal, that they are endowed by their Creator with certain unalienable Rights, that among these are Life, Liberty and the pursuit of Happiness" was the result of their reading the Scottish philosophers, particularly Francis Hutcheson and Lord Kames (Henry Home), who argued that all people in all places possess a sense common to all—a moral sense—that contradicted the notion of the mind as an empty vessel awaiting experience. This idealism paved the way for writers like Bryant, Emerson, Thoreau, and Whitman, but in the 1770s its presence is found chiefly in politics and ethics. The assurance of a universal sense of right and wrong made possible both the overthrow of tyrants and the restoration of order, and it allowed humankind to make new earthly covenants, not, as was the case with Bradford and Winthrop, for the glory of God, but, as Thomas Jefferson argued, for an individual's right to happiness on earth. How Americans used and abused that right in the service of self-interest would become the theme of countless writers after 1820, as a market revolution permanently enshrined liberal principles over those of the civic republicanism that had informed the previous generation's behavior.

AMERICAN LITERATURE 1700–1820

TEXTS	CONTEXTS
1704–05 Sarah Kemble Knight keeps *The Private Journal of a Journey from Boston to New York* (pub. 1825)	
	1718 French found New Orleans
	1726–56 The "Great Awakening"
1728 William Byrd writes his *History of the Dividing Line* (pub. 1841)	
1735 "The Speech of Moses Bon Sàam" published in London periodical	
1741 Jonathan Edwards, *Sinners in the Hands of an Angry God*	1741 Vitus Bering discovers Alaska
	1755–63 French and Indian Wars
1760 Briton Hammon, *Narrative of the Uncommon Sufferings, and Surprizing Deliverance*	
1764 James Grainger, *The Sugar Cane*	
1768 Samson Occom, *A Short Narrative of My Life*	
1771–90 Benjamin Franklin continues his *Autobiography* (Part I pub. 1818)	
1773 Phillis Wheatley, *Poems on Various Subjects*	1773 Boston Tea Party
1774 John Woolman, *The Journal of John Woolman*	
1774–83 John and Abigail Adams exchange **letters** (pub. 1840, 1875)	
	1775–83 War for American Independence
1776 Thomas Paine, *Common Sense*	1776 Declaration of Independence
1780s Annis Boudinot Stockton publishes **poems** in magazines and newspapers	
1782 J. Hector St. John de Crèvecoeur, *Letters from an American Farmer*	
	1783 Britain opens "Old Northwest" to United States after Treaty of Paris ends American Revolution
1786 Philip Freneau, *Poems*	
1787 Thomas Jefferson, *Notes on the State of Virginia* • Royall Tyler, *The Contrast*	1787 U.S. Constitution adopted
1787–88 *The Federalist* papers	

Boldface title indicate works in the anthology.

TEXTS	CONTEXTS
1789 Olaudah Equiano, *The Interesting Narrative of the Life of Olaudah Equiano* • Sarah Wentworth Morton publishes her first poem; pub. *My Mind and Its Thoughts* 1823	**1789** George Washington elected first president
1790 Judith Sargent Murray, *On the Equality of the Sexes*	
1791 Susanna Rowson, *Charlotte: A Tale of Truth*	**1791** Washington D.C. established as U.S. capital
1798 Charles Brockden Brown, *Wieland*	
	1803 United States buys Louisiana Territory from France
	1812–14 Second war against England
	1819 Spain exchanges Florida for U.S. assumption of $5 million in claims

SARAH KEMBLE KNIGHT
1666–1727

Like a number of the classics of early American literature, *The Private Journal* of Mrs. Sarah Kemble Knight was not published until the nineteenth century; it at once found an enthusiastic audience eager to read documents of social history from the American past. Knight's shorthand journal, as transcribed and edited by Theodore Dwight, provides a healthy antidote to the soul-searching journals of Knight's contemporaries and reminds us of the manifold ways in which provincial Americans absorbed transatlantic models for the expression of the most common and intimate details of their lives. As such, it links her frank narrative to the similarly revealing private writings of William Byrd and others who saw around them subjects for meditation on what made a provincial culture viable and mature. Knight was a keen observer of provincial America and a woman who did not suffer fools gladly. Something of Knight's tough-mindedness was undoubtedly the result of the fact that she had to make her way in the world with considerable ingenuity and that early on in life she displayed a gift for managing other people's affairs—a gift that, unfortunately, sometimes leads to arrogance.

Knight was the daughter of the Boston merchant Thomas Kemble and Elizabeth Trerice of Charlestown, Massachusetts. She married a man much older who was a sometime sea captain and London agent for an American company. After her father died in 1689, Knight assumed full responsibility for being head of the household. While her husband was abroad, she kept a boardinghouse and taught school (hence the title "Madam Knight") and supposedly could number Benjamin Franklin and the Mather children among her pupils. Knight taught penmanship, made copies of court records, and wrote letters for people having business with the courts. Historians recently have demonstrated that such engagement in public affairs was not as exceptional as it once seemed, for in the early eighteenth century many women played significant economic roles. Thus she trained herself in the ways of the law and had a reputation for settling estates with skill. In 1704, while her husband was abroad, Knight took on herself the task of settling her cousin Caleb Trowbridge's estate on behalf of his young widow. Knight set out for New Haven, Connecticut, on Monday, October 2, 1704. From there she went to New York and returned home to Boston in March 1705. It was a hazardous journey, one not undertaken lightly in those years and almost unprecedented for a woman traveling alone.

In 1706 Knight apparently became a widow; at least her husband is not mentioned again after that date. In 1714 she followed her married daughter to Connecticut. Her last years were spent in New London, where she ran an inn and, true to her genius, made shrewd investments in property.

The text used here is from *The Journal of Madame Knight*, edited by George P. Winship (1920; reprinted 1935).

From The Private Journal of a Journey from Boston to New York

* * *

Tuesday, October the Third

About 8 in the morning, I with the post proceeded forward without observing anything remarkable; and about two, afternoon, arrived at the post's second stage,[1] where the western post met him and exchanged letters. Here, having called for something to eat, the woman brought in a twisted thing like a cable, but something[2] whiter; and laying it on the board, tugged for life to bring it into a capacity to spread; which having with great pains accomplished, she served in a dish of pork and cabbage, I suppose the remains of dinner. The sauce was of a deep purple, which I thought was boiled in her dye kettle; the bread was Indian and everything on the table service agreeable to these. I, being hungry, got a little down; but my stomach was soon cloyed, and what cabbage I swallowed served me for a cud the whole day after.

Having here discharged the ordinary[3] for self and guide (as I understood was the custom), about three, afternoon, went on with my third guide, who rode very hard; and having crossed Providence ferry, we come to a river which they generally ride through. But I dare not venture; so the post got a lad and canoe to carry me to t'other side, and he ride through and led my horse. The canoe was very small and shallow, so that when we were in, she seemed ready to take in water, which greatly terrified me, and caused me to be very circumspect, sitting with my hands fast on each side, my eyes steady, not daring so much as to lodge my tongue a hair's breadth more on one side of my mouth than t'other nor so much as think on Lot's wife,[4] for a wry thought would have overset our wherry:[5] but was soon put out of this pain, by feeling the canoe on shore, which I as soon almost saluted with my feet; and rewarding my sculler, again mounted and made the best of our way forwards. The road here was very even and the day pleasant, it being now near sunset. But the post told me we had near 14 miles to ride to the next stage (where we were to lodge). I asked him of the rest of the road, foreseeing we must travail in the night. He told me there was a bad river we were to ride through, which was so very fierce a horse could sometimes hardly stem it: but it was but narrow, and we should soon be over. I cannot express the concern of mind this relation set me in: no thoughts but those of the dangerous river could entertain my imagination, and they were as formidable as various, still tormenting me with blackest ideas of my approaching fate—sometimes seeing myself drowning, otherwhiles drowned, and at the best, like a holy sister just come out of a spiritual bath in dripping garments.

Now was the glorious luminary, with his swift coursers arrived at his stage,[6] leaving poor me with the rest of this part of the lower world in darkness, with which we were soon surrounded. The only glimmering we now had was from the spangled skies, whose imperfect reflections rendered every object formidable. Each lifeless trunk, with its shattered limbs, appeared an armed enemy; and every little stump like a ravenous devourer. Nor could I so much as discern my guide, when at any distance, which added to the terror.

Thus, absolutely lost in thought, and dying with the very thoughts of drowning, I come up with the post, who I did not see till even with his horse: he told me he stopped for me; and we rode on very deliberately a few paces,

1. A stopping place where mail was left from the previous stage of a journey and then forwarded to the next. People who traveled "post" accompanied the driver to the next stop.
2. Somewhat.
3. I.e., paid for the meal. "Ordinary": a meal served at an inn or public house.

4. I.e., not daring to look back. When Sodom was being destroyed, Lot's wife looked back and was turned into a pillar of salt (Genesis 19.26).
5. Small boat.
6. I.e., it was night. In Greek mythology the sun god Apollo rides across the sky in a chariot. "Coursers": horses.

when we entered a thicket of trees and shrubs, and I perceived by the horse's going, we were on the descent of a hill, which, as we come nearer the bottom, 'twas totally dark with the trees that surrounded it. But I knew by the going of the horse we had entered the water, which my guide told me was the hazardous river he had told me of; and he, riding up close to my side, bid me not fear—we should be over immediately. I now rallied all the courage I was mistress of, knowing that I must either venture my fate of drowning, or be left like the children in the wood.[7] So, as the post bid me, I gave reins to my nag; and sitting as steady as just before in the canoe, in a few minutes got safe to the other side, which he told me was the Narragansett country.

Here we found great difficulty in travailing, the way being very narrow, and on each side the trees and bushes gave us very unpleasant welcomes with their branches and boughs, which we could not avoid, it being so exceeding dark. My guide, as before so now, put on harder than I, with my weary bones, could follow; so left me and the way behind him. Now returned my distressed apprehensions of the place where I was: the dolesome woods, my company next to none, going I knew not whither, and encompassed with terrifying darkness; the least of which was enough to startle a more masculine courage. Added to which the reflections, as in the afternoon of the day that my call[8] was very questionable, which, till then I had not so prudently as I ought considered. Now, coming to the foot of a hill, I found great difficulty in ascending; but being got to the top, was there amply recompensed with the friendly appearance of the kind conductress of the night, just then advancing above the horizontal line. The raptures which the sight of that fair planet produced in me, caused me, for the moment, to forget my present weariness and past toils; and inspired me for most of the remaining way with very diverting thoughts, some of which, with the other occurrences of the day, I reserved to note down when I should come to my stage. My thoughts on the sight of the moon were to this purpose:

> Fair Cynthia,[9] all the homage that I may
> Unto a creature, unto thee I pay;
> In lonesome woods to meet so kind a guide,
> To me's more worth than all the world beside.
> Some joy I feel just now, when safe got o'er
> Yon surly river to this rugged shore,
> Deeming rough welcomes from these clownish trees
> Better than lodgings with Nereides.[1]
> Yet swelling fears surprise; all dark appears—
> Nothing but light can dissipate those fears.
> My fainting vitals can't lend strength to say,
> But softly whisper, O I wish 'twere day.
> The murmur hardly warmed the ambient air,
> E're thy bright aspect rescues from despair:
> Makes the old hag[2] her sable mantle loose,
> And a bright joy does through my soul diffuse.

7. Or babes in the wood; a reference to a ballad in which two children are taken out to be murdered and instead are left in the woods where they die during the night.

8. Mission.
9. The moon personified.
1. Sea nymphs, daughters of Nereus.
2. I.e., night.

> The boisterous trees now lend a passage free,
> And pleasant prospects thou giv'st light to see.

From hence we kept on, with more ease than before: the way being smooth and even, the night warm and serene, and the tall and thick trees at a distance, especially when the moon glared light through the branches, filled my imagination with the pleasant delusion of a sumptuous city, filled with famous buildings and churches, with their spiring steeples, balconies, galleries and I know not what: grandeurs which I had heard of, and which the stories of foreign countries had given me the idea of.

> Here stood a lofty church—there is a steeple,
> And there the grand parade—O see the people!
> That famous castle there, were I but nigh,
> To see the mote and bridge and walls so high—
> They're very fine! says my deluded eye.

Being thus agreeably entertained without a thought of anything but thoughts themselves, I on a sudden was roused from these pleasing imaginations, by the post's sounding his horn, which assured me he was arrived at the stage, where we were to lodge: and that music was then most musical and agreeable to me.

Being come to Mr. Havens', I was very civilly received, and courteously entertained, in a clean comfortable house; and the good woman was very active in helping off my riding clothes, and then asked what I would eat. I told her I had some chocolate, if she would prepare it; which with the help of some milk, and a little clean brass kettle, she soon effected to my satisfaction. I then betook me to my apartment, which was a little room parted from the kitchen by a single board partition; where, after I had noted the occurrences of the past day, I went to bed, which, though pretty hard, yet neat and handsome. But I could get no sleep, because of the clamor of some of the town topers in next room, who were entered into strong debate concerning the signification of the name of their country (viz.) Narragansett. One said it was named so by the Indians, because there grew a brier there, of a prodigious height and bigness, the like hardly ever known, called by the Indians narragansett; and quotes an Indian of so barbarous a name for his author, that I could not write it. His antagonist replied no—it was from a spring it had its name, which he well knew where it was, which was extreme cold in summer, and as hot as could be imagined in the winter, which was much resorted to by the natives, and by them called Narragansett (hot and cold), and that was the original of their place's name—with a thousand impertinances not worth notice, which he uttered with such a roaring voice and thundering blows with the fist of wickedness on the table, that it pierced my very head. I heartily fretted, and wished 'um tongue-tied; but with as little success as a friend of mine once, who was (as she said) kept a whole night awake, on a journey, by a country left, and a sergeant, insigne[3] and a deacon, contriving how to bring a triangle into a square. They kept calling for t'other gill,[4] which while they were swallowing, was some intermission; but presently, like oil to fire, increased the flame. I set my candle on a chest by the

---

3. I.e., ensign, lowest grade of commissioned officer. "Left": lieutenant.

4. A measure of wine.

bed side, and setting up, fell to my old way of composing my resentments, in the following manner:

> I ask thy aid, O potent rum!
> To charm these wrangling topers dumb.
> Thou hast their giddy brains possessed—
> The man confounded with the beast—
> And I, poor I, can get no rest.
> Intoxicate them with thy fumes:
> O still their tongues' till morning comes!

And I know not but my wishes took effect; for the dispute soon ended with t'other dram; and so good night! * * *

Friday, October the Sixth

I got up very early, in order to hire somebody to go with me to New Haven, being in great perplexity at the thoughts of proceeding alone; which my most hospitable entertainer observing, himself went, and soon returned with a young gentleman of the town, who he could confide in to go with me; and about eight this morning, with Mr. Joshua Wheeler my new guide, taking leave of this worthy gentleman, we advanced on towards Saybrook. The roads all along this way are very bad, encumbered with rocks and mountainous passages, which were very disagreeable to my tired carcass; but we went on with a moderate pace which made the journey more pleasant. But after about eight miles riding, in going over a bridge under which the river run very swift, my horse stumbled, and very narrowly escaped falling over into the water; which extremely frightened me. But through God's goodness I met with no harm, and mounting again, in about half a mile's riding, come to an ordinary, were well entertained by a woman of about seventy and vantage,[5] but of as sound intellectuals as one of seventeen. She entertained Mr. Wheeler with some passages of a wedding awhile ago at a place hard by, the bride's groom being about her age or something above, saying his children was dreadfully against their father's marrying, which she condemned them extremely for.

From hence we went pretty briskly forward, and arrived at Saybrook ferry about two of the clock afternoon; and crossing it, we called at an inn to bait[6] (foreseeing we should not have such another opportunity till we come to Killingsworth). Landlady come in, with her hair about her ears, and hands at full pay[7] scratching. She told us she had some mutton which she would broil, which I was glad to hear; but I suppose forgot to wash her scratches; in a little time she brought it in; but it being pickled, and my guide said it smelled strong of head[8] sauce, we left it, and paid sixpence a piece for our dinners, which was only smell.

So we put forward with all speed, and about seven at night come to Killingsworth, and were tolerably well with travelers' fare, and lodged there that night.

---

5. I.e., or more. "Ordinary": here, an inn; a place where meals are served.
6. Refresh themselves and rest the horses.
7. I.e., busily.
8. Cheese.

Saturday, October the Seventh

We set out early in the morning and being something unacquainted with the way, having asked it of some we met, they told us we must ride a mile or two and turn down a lane on the right hand, and by their direction we rode on but not yet coming to the turning, we met a young fellow and asked him how far it was to the lane which turned down towards Guilford [Connecticut]. He said we must ride a little further and turn down by the corner of Uncle Sam's lot. My guide vented his spleen at the lubber,[9] and we soon after came into the road, and keeping still on, without anything further remarkable, about two o'clock afternoon we arrived at New Haven, where I was received with all possible respects and civility. Here I discharged Mr. Wheeler with a reward to his satisfaction, and took some time to rest after so long and toilsome a journey, and informed myself of the manners and customs of the place and at the same time employed myself in the affair I went there upon.

They are governed by the same laws as we in Boston (or little differing) throughout this whole colony of Connecticut, and much the same way of church government, and many of them good, sociable people, and I hope religious too. But a little too much independent in their principles, and, as I have been told, were formerly in their zeal very rigid in their administrations towards such as their laws made offenders, even to a harmless kiss or innocent merriment among young people, whipping being a frequent and counted an easy punishment, about which as other crimes, the judges were absolute in their sentences. They told me a pleasant story about a pair of justices in those parts, which I may not omit the relation of.

A negro slave belonging to a man in the town stole a hogshead[1] from his master and gave or sold it to an Indian, native of the place. The Indian sold it in the neighborhood, and so the theft was found out. Thereupon the heathen[2] was seized and carried to the justice's house to be examined. But his Worship (it seems) was gone into the field, with a brother in office to gather in his pompions.[3] Whither the malefactor is hurried, and complaint made and satisfaction in the name of justice demanded. Their Worships can't proceed in form without a bench: whereupon they order one to be immediately erected, which, for want of fitter materials, they made with pompions—which being finished, down sets their Worships, and the malefactor called and by the senior Justice interrogated after the following manner: You, Indian, why did you steal from this man? You shouldn't do so—it's a grandy wicked thing to steal. "Hol't, hol't," cries Justice junior. "Brother, you speak negro to him. I'll ask him." "You, sirrah, why did you steal this man's hogshead?" "Hogshead?" (replies the Indian), "Me no stomany."[4] "No?" says his Worship, and pulling off his hat, patted his own head with his hand, says, "Tatapa—you, Tatapa—you; all one this. Hogshead all one this." "Hah!" says Netop, "Now me stomany that." Whereupon the company fell into a great fit of laughter, even to roaring. Silence is commanded, but to no effect: for they continued perfectly shouting. "Nay," says his Worship in an angry tone, "If it be so, *take me off the bench.*"

9. Clumsy fellow.
1. A large barrel or cask.
2. I.e., the Indian.

3. Pumpkins.
4. Understand.

Their diversions in this part of the country are on lecture days and training days[5] mostly: on the former there is riding from town to town.

And on training days the youth divert themselves by shooting at the target, as they call it (but it very much resembles a pillory[6]), where he that hits nearest the white has some yards of red ribbon presented him which being tied to his hatband, the two ends streaming down his back, he is led away in triumph with great applause as the winners of the Olympiack games. They generally marry very young: the males oftener, as I am told, under twenty than above. They generally make public weddings and have a way something singular (as they say) in some of them, *viz.* just before joining hands the bridegroom quits the place, who is soon followed by the bridesmen and, as it were, dragged back to duty—being the reverse to the former practice among us, to steel[7] man's pride.

There are great plenty of oysters all along by the seaside as far as I rode in the colony and those very good. And they generally lived very well and comfortably in their families. But too indulgent (especially the farmers) to their slaves, suffering too great familiarity from them, permitting them to sit at table and eat with them (as they say, to save time), and into the dish goes the black hoof as freely as the white hand. They told me that there was a farmer lived near the town where I lodged who had some difference with his slave concerning something the master had promised him and did not punctually perform, which caused some hard words between them. But at length they put the matter to arbitration and bound themselves to stand to the award of such as they named—which done, the arbitrators having heard the allegations of both parties, order the master to pay 40[s8] to black face and acknowledge his fault. And so the matter ended, the poor master very honestly standing to[9] the award.

There are everywhere in the towns as I passed a number of Indians the natives of the country, and are the most savage[1] of all the savages of that kind that I had ever seen: little or no care taken (as I heard upon inquiry) to make them otherwise. They have in some places lands of their own, and governed by laws of their own making;—they marry many wives and at pleasure put them away, and on the least dislike or fickle humor, on either side. Saying *"stand away"* to one another is a sufficient divorce. And, indeed, those uncomely *"stand aways"* are too much in vogue among the English in this (indulgent colony) as their records plentifully prove, and that on very trivial matters, of which some have been told me, but are not proper to be related by a female pen, though some of that foolish sex have had too large a share in the story.

If the natives commit any crime on their own precincts among themselves the English takes no cognezens[2] of. But if on the English ground they are punishable by our laws. They mourn for their dead by blacking their faces and cutting their hair after an awkerd and frightful manner, but can't bear you should mention the names of their dead relations to them. They trade

5. Days set aside for military exercises. "Lecture days": days when a less formal sermon was offered than the one prepared for Sundays.
6. A wooden frame on a post with holes for the head and arms, used as public punishment for offenders.
7. Fortify against.
8. Shillings, or two English pounds.
9. I.e., paying.
1. Unchristian.
2. Recognition; more properly, "cognizance."

most for rum, for which they would hazard their very lives, and the English fit[3] them generally as well by seasoning it plentifully with water.

They give the title of merchant to every trader who rate their goods according to the time and spetia[4] they pay in: *viz.* pay, money, pay as money, and trusting. *Pay* is grain, pork, beef, &c. at the prices set by the General Court that year; *money* is pieces of eight, rials, or Boston or Bay shillings[5] (as they call them,) or good hard money, as sometimes silver coin is termed by them; also wampum, *viz.* Indian beads which serves for change. *Pay as money* is provisions, as aforesaid, one third cheaper than as the Assembly or General Court sets it, and *trust* as they and the merchant agree for time.

Now, when the buyer comes to ask for a commodity, sometimes before the merchant answers that he has it, he says, *"Is your pay ready?"* Perhaps the chap replies "Yes." "What do you pay in?" says the merchant. The buyer having answered, then the price is set; as suppose he wants a sixpenny knife, in pay it is 12d[6]—in pay as money eight pence, and hard money its own price, *viz.* 6d. It seems a very intricate way of trade and what *Lex Mercatoria*[7] had not thought of.

Being at a merchant's house, in comes a tall country fellow, with his alfogeos[8] full of tobacco; for they seldom lose their cud, but keep chewing and spitting as long as their eyes are open. He advanced to the middle of the room, makes an awkward nod, and spitting a large deal of aromatic tincture, he gave a scrape with his shovel-like shoe, leaving a small shovel full of dirt on the floor, made a full stop, hugging his own pretty body with his hands under his arms, stood staring round him like a cat let out of a basket. At last, like the creature Balaam rode on,[9] he opened his mouth and said: "Have you any ribinen for hatbands to sell, I pray?" The questions and answers about the pay being passed, the ribin is brought and opened. Bumpkin simpers, cries "It's confounded gay I vow"; and beckning to the door, in comes Joan Tawdry, dropping about 50 curtsies, and stands by him. He shows her the ribin. *"Law, you,"* says she, *"it's right gent,* do you take it, *tis dreadful[1] pretty."* Then she inquires *"Have you any hood silk[2] I pray?"* which being brought and bought, "Have you any *thread silk to sew it with?"* says she, which being accommodated with they departed. They generally stand after they come in a great while speechless, and sometimes don't say a word till they are asked what they want, which I impute to the awe they stand in of the merchants, who they are constantly almost indebted to, and must take what they bring without liberty to choose for themselves. But they serve them as well,[3] making the merchants stay long enough for their pay.

We may observe here the great necessity and benefit both of education and conversation; for these people have as large a portion of mother wit,[4] and sometimes a larger, than those who have been brought up in cities, but for want of improvements render themselves almost ridiculous, as above. I

---

3. Fix; cheat.
4. Actual coin or money; more properly, "specie." "Rate": calculate the price of.
5. Coin minted in the Massachusetts Bay Colony. "Pieces of eight": Spanish silver coins. "Rials": former English gold coins worth ten shillings.
6. Pence; from the Latin *denarius*.
7. The law of merchants (Latin).
8. Saddlebag-like cheeks; from the Spanish *alfor-*

ges, "pouch."
9. The ass of the Old Testament prophet Balaam spoke to him (Numbers 22).
1. Extremely (slang). "Gent": genteel (slang), stylish.
2. Silk cloth suitable for a hood to cover her head.
3. I.e., treat them equally badly.
4. Native intelligence.

should be glad if they would leave such follies and am sure all that love clean houses (at least) would be glad on't too.

They are generally very plain in their dress, throughout all the colony, as I saw, and follow one another in their modes, that you may know where they belong, especially the women, meet them where you will.

Their chief red-letter day is St. Election,[5] which is annually observed according to charter, to choose their government, a blessing they can never be thankful enough for, as they will find if ever it be their hard fortune to lose it. The present governor in Connecticut is the Honorable John Winthrop, Esq. A gentleman of an ancient and honorable family whose father was governor here sometime before, and his grandfather had been governor of the Massachusetts.[6] This gentleman is a very courteous and affable person, much given to hospitality, and has by his good services gained the affection of the people as much as any who had been before him in that post.

From *December the Sixth*

* * *

The city of New York is a pleasant, well-compacted place, situated on a commodious river which is a fine harbor for shipping. The buildings brick generally, very stately and high, though not altogether like ours in Boston. The bricks in some of the houses are of divers colors and laid in checkers, being glazed look very agreeable. The inside of them are neat to admiration, the wooden work, for only the walls are plastered, and the sumers and gist[7] are planed and kept very white scowered as so is all the partitions if made of boards. The fireplaces have no jambs (as ours have) but the backs run flush with the walls, and the hearth is of tiles and is as far out into the room at the ends as before the fire, which is generally five foot in the lower rooms, and the piece over where the mantle tree should be is made as ours with joiners'[8] work, and as I suppose is fastened to iron rods inside. The house where the vendue[9] was, had chimney corners like ours, and they and the hearths were laid with the finest tile that I ever see, and the staircases laid all with white tile which is ever clean, and so are the walls of the kitchen which had a brick floor. They were making great preparations to receive their governor, Lord Cornbury from the Jerseys,[1] and for that end raised the militia to guard him on shore to the fort.

They are generally of the Church of England and have a New England gentleman for their minister, and a very fine church set out with all customary requisites. There are also a Dutch and divers conventicles as they call them, *viz.* Baptist, Quakers, etc. They are not strict in keeping the Sabbath as in Boston and other places where I had been, but seem to deal with great exactness as far as I see or deal with. They are sociable to one another and

5. With the name "St. Election" day, Knight is mockingly suggesting that the day is kept as sacred as a religious holiday.
6. In 1704 Fitz-John Winthrop (1638–1707) was the governor of Connecticut. His father, John Winthrop (1606–1676), founded New London and was governor from 1659 to 1676. Fitz-John Winthrop's grandfather, John Winthrop (1588–1649), was the first governor of the Massachusetts

Bay Colony.
7. Main beams and joists.
8. Craftsmen who constructed things by joining pieces of wood together. Their work was more finished than a carpenter's.
9. Auction.
1. Edward Hyde (1661–1723), royal governor of New York and New Jersey from 1702 to 1708.

courteous and civil to strangers and fare well in their houses. The English go very fashionable in their dress. But the Dutch, especially the middling sort, differ from our women, in their habit go loose, wear French muchets which are like a cap and a headband in one, leaving their ears bare, which are set out with jewels of a large size and many in number. And their fingers hooped with rings, some with large stones in them of many colors as were their pendants in their ears, which you should see very old women wear as well as young.

They have vendues very frequently and make their earnings very well by them, for they treat with good liquor liberally, and the customers drink as liberally and generally pay for't as well, by paying for that which they bid up briskly for, after the sack[2] has gone plentifully about, though sometimes good penny worths' are got there. Their diversions in the winter is riding sleighs about three or four miles out of town, where they have houses of entertainment at a place called the Bowery, and some go to friends' houses who handsomely treat them. Mr. Burroughs carried his spouse and daughter and myself out to one Madame Dowes, a gentlewoman that lived at a farm house, who gave us a handsome entertainment of five or six dishes and choice beer and metheglin,[3] cider, etc. all which she said was the produce of her farm. I believe we met 50 or 60 sleighs that day—they fly with great swiftness and some are so furious that they'll turn out of the path for none except a loaden cart. Nor do they spare for any diversion the place affords, and sociable to a degree, their tables being as free to their neighbors as to themselves.

Having here transacted the affair I went upon and some other that fell in the way, after about a fortnight's stay there I left New York with no little regret[.] * * *

January the Sixth

Being now well recruited and fit for business I discoursed the person I was concerned with, that we might finish in order to my return to Boston. They delayed as they had hitherto done hoping to tire my patience. But I was resolute to stay and see an end of the matter let it be never so much to my disadvantage—So January 9th they come again and promise the Wednesday following to go through with the distribution of the estate which they delayed till Thursday and then come with new amusements.[4] But at length by the mediation of that holy good gentleman, the Rev. Mr. James Pierpont, the minister of New Haven, and with the advice and assistance of other our good friends we come to an accommodation and distribution, which having finished though not till February, the man that waited on me to York taking the charge of me I set out for Boston. We went from New Haven upon the ice (the ferry being not passable thereby) and the Rev. Mr. Pierpont with Madam Prout, cousin Trowbridge and divers others were taking leave, we went onward without anything remarkable till we come to New London and lodged again at Mr. Saltonstall's—and here I dismissed my guide, and my generous entertainer provided me Mr. Samuel Rogers of that place to go home with me—I stayed a day here longer than intended by the commands

2. Wine; specifically, white wine imported from Spain or the Canaries.
3. A spiced variety of mead. The cider offered was
probably also alcoholic.
4. I.e., trifles that caused further delays.

of the honorable Governor Winthrop to stay and take a supper with him whose wonderful civility I may not omit. The next morning I crossed the ferry to Groton, having had the honor of the company, of Madam Livingston (who is the governor's daughter) and Mary Christophers and divers others to the boat—and that night lodged at Stonington and had roast beef and pumpkin sauce for supper. The next night at Haven's and had roast fowl, and the next day we come to a river which by reason of the freshets coming down was swelled so high we feared it impassable and the rapid stream was very terrifying—However we must over and that in a small canoe. Mr. Rogers assuring me of his good conduct,[5] I after a stay of near an hour on the shore for consultation, went into the canoe, and Mr. Rogers paddled about 100 yards up the creek by the shore side, turned into the swift stream and dexterously steering her in a moment we come to the other side as swiftly passing as an arrow shot out of the bow by a strong arm. I stayed on the shore till he returned to fetch our horses, which he caused to swim over, himself bringing the furniture in the canoe. But it is past my skill to express the exceeding fright all their transactions formed in me. We were now in the colony of Massachusetts and taking lodgings at the first inn we come to, had a pretty difficult passage the next day which was the second of March by reason of the sloughy[6] ways then thawed by the sun. Here I met Capt. John Richards of Boston who was going home, so being very glad of his company we rode something harder than hitherto, and missing my way in going up a very steep hill, my horse dropped down under me as dead; this new surprise no little hurt me, meeting it just at the entrance into Dedham from whence we intended to reach home that night. But was now obliged to get another horse there and leave my own, resolving for Boston that night if possible. But in going over the causeway at Dedham the Bridge being overflowed by the high waters coming down, I very narrowly escaped falling over into the river horse and all which 'twas almost a miracle I did not—now it grew late in the afternoon and the people having very much discouraged us about the sloughy way which they said we should find very difficult and hazardous, it so wrought on me being tired and dispirited and disappointed of my desires of going home, that I agreed to lodge there that night which we did at the house of one Draper, and the next day being March 3d we got safe home to Boston, where I found my aged and tender mother and my dear and only child in good health with open arms ready to receive me, and my kind relations and friends flocking in to welcome me and hear the story of my transactions and travails, I having this day been five months from home and now I cannot fully express my joy and satisfaction. But desire sincerely to adore my great Benefactor for thus graciously carrying forth and returning in safety his unworthy handmaid.

1704–05   1825

---

5. Company for safekeeping.   6. Muddy.

WILLIAM BYRD
1674–1744

William Byrd was the son of a wealthy Virginia planter, merchant, and Indian trader. His mother, Mary Horsmanden, came from a family of Royalist refugees. Like many other American provincials who viewed London as their metropolitan center, Byrd was educated in England and spent the formative years of his life in London, where he was trained to assume the responsibility of managing his father's estate. Byrd was urbane and witty and traveled in sophisticated London circles. He loved the theater and numbered Wycherley and Congreve among his many friends. The diaries that he kept during his London years tell us a great deal about his social life as a London man-about-town and his wish for acceptance not as a colonial American but as a sophisticated participant in England's imperial economy and culture. Byrd recorded his habits of eating and prayer with the same detachment that compelled him to keep track of his whoring and his reading. The London theater, however, did not spoil Byrd's appetite for provincial pleasures. Back home in Virginia he seems to have delighted in the social life of Williamsburg even if the streets were dirty, the servants drunken, and country bumpkins present. He took great pleasure in "walking" his plantation.

More than half of Byrd's life was spent in England; but in 1726, after many years of alternation during which he sought to find a wife who suited his ambitions to represent cosmopolitan culture in Virginia, he returned to Virginia to stay. In a letter written in that year to his friend Charles Boyle, earl of Orrery, Byrd described the satisfactions to be derived from the role of the Virginia planter:

> Besides the advantage of pure air, we abound in all kinds of provisions without expense (I mean we who have plantations). I have a large family of my own, and my doors are open to everybody, yet I have no bills to pay, and half-a-crown will rest undisturbed in my pockets for many moons altogether. Like one of the patriarchs, I have my flock and herds, my bondmen and bondwomen, and every sort of trade amongst my own servants, so that I live in a kind of independence on everyone but Providence. . . . Thus, my Lord, we are very happy in our Canaans if we could but forget the onions and fleshpots of Egypt.

Byrd's "New Canaan," unlike its New England counterpart, and in spite of his nod to Divine Providence, is a self-sufficient, earthly garden, combining the best of civilized and rural life. Byrd's house at Westover epitomized his ideal of the perfect plantation, and he spared no expense to fashion it. The house he rebuilt is still standing, one of the most beautiful examples of eighteenth-century architecture in America. It housed a library of some 2,600 volumes that rivaled Cotton Mather's library in Boston; its gardens were the envy of all who saw them. Byrd had a passion for land, and before he died he escalated the 26,000 acres left to him by his father into a vast holding of 179,000 acres. The cities of Richmond and Petersburg, Virginia, were created from Byrd's landholdings.

Given Byrd's position in the affairs of Virginia, it is not surprising that he was asked to accept a number of public commissions. In 1728 he accepted a commission to survey the much-disputed boundary line between Virginia and North Carolina. The diary that Byrd kept on his trip served as the sourcebook for his *History of the Dividing Line*. Although not published until 1841, Byrd's manuscript was circulated among his London friends, and its existence was known to later naturalists such as Thomas Jefferson. In its wealth of natural detail (some of it—like his description of the opossum catching and eating little birds with its claws—quite fantastic) and Indian lore, it helped to satisfy London curiosity for all things American.

From The Secret Diary of William Byrd of Westover 1709–1712[1]

[December] 31. [1710] I rose at 5 o'clock and read a chapter in Hebrew and four leaves in Lucian.[2] I said my prayers and ate boiled milk for breakfast. My daughter was very sick all night and vomited a great deal but was a little better this morning. All my sick people were better, thank God, and I had another girl come down sick from the quarters.[3] I danced my dance.[4] Then I read a sermon in Dr. Tillotson[5] and after that walked in the garden till dinner. I ate roast venison. In the afternoon I looked over my sick people and then took a walk about the plantation. The weather was very warm still. My wife walked with me and when she came back she was very much indisposed and went to bed. In the evening I read another sermon in Dr. Tillotson. About 8 o'clock the wind came to northwest and it began to be cold. I said my prayers and had good health, good thoughts, and good humor, thank God Almighty.

Some night this month I dreamed that I saw a flaming sword in the sky and called some company to see it but before they could come it was disappeared, and about a week after my wife and I were walking and we discovered in the clouds a shining cloud exactly in the shape of a dart and seemed to be over my plantation but it soon disappeared likewise. Both these appearances seemed to foretell some misfortune to me which afterwards came to pass in the death of several of my negroes after a very unusual manner. My wife about two months since dreamed she saw an angel in the shape of a big woman who told her the time was altered and the seasons were changed and that several calamities would follow that confusion. God avert His judgment from this poor country.

[January] 2. [1711] I rose at 5 o'clock and read a chapter in Hebrew and nothing in Greek because of the company that was here. I said my prayers and ate boiled milk for breakfast. I had six sick negroes come down from the quarters. About 9 o'clock my company went away. My wife was a little better and so was my child, thank God, but C-l-y was extremely ill and so was A-g-y.[6] I tended them as much as I could but God is pleased to afflict me with His judgment for my sins. His holy will be done. I ate some wild turkey. The wind was northeast and it was cold. In the afternoon I read a little English but could not be easy because poor C-l-y was so very ill. I took a melancholy walk. In the evening about 6 o'clock C-l-y died and all the people was [sic] grieved at it. I read a little English and gave the necessary orders about the sick people who were 12 in number. I said my prayers and had good health, good thoughts, and good humor, thank God Almighty.

[January] 6. [1711] I rose at 5 o'clock and read two chapters in Hebrew and six leaves in Lucian. I said my prayers and ate boiled milk for breakfast. Poor old S-r-y died this night to make up the number of the dead. God save

---

1. The text used here is taken from *The Secret Diary of William Byrd of Westover 1709–1712*, edited by Louis B. Wright and Marion Tinling (1941).
2. I.e., four pages of Lucian, a Greek satirist of the 2nd century C.E.
3. I.e., slave quarters.
4. I.e., performed my calisthenics.
5. Dr. John Tillotson (1620–1694), archbishop of Canterbury, was one of Byrd's favorite writers.
6. Both were servants.

the rest. A-g-y seemed to be a little better and so did the rest of the sick, God be praised, except Jenny and she seemed to be worse. The weather threatened rain all day. I removed several things out of the Doctor's closet[7] into mine and was very little with my cousin. I was out of humor with my wife. I ate boiled pork for dinner. In the afternoon Mrs. Dunn[8] went away in the rain. I spent most of my time in looking after my sick. In the evening it rained extremely, and all night. My cousin and I took a walk about the plantation. I said my prayers and had good health, good thoughts, and good humor, thank God Almighty.

[January] 7. [1711] I rose at 5 o'clock and read two chapters in Hebrew and some Greek in Lucian. I said my prayers and ate boiled milk for breakfast. My sick people were some worse and some well enough to go home to the quarters. Jenny and A-g-y were much as they were. The weather held up so that I and my cousin [Guy] went to church, but my wife was afflicted with the headache and stayed at home. People condoled the sickness of my family. Mr. Anderson gave us a sermon. After church I carried him home with me to dinner and to see my sick people. I ate fish for dinner. Mr. Anderson advised me to give my people cordials since other physic failed, which I did. In the afternoon I did nothing but mind them. In the evening my cousin and we talked till 8 o'clock. I said a short prayer and had good health, good thoughts, and good humor, thank God Almighty.

[January] 22. [1711] I rose at 3 o'clock and read a chapter in Hebrew and some Greek in Lucian. I said my prayers and ate boiled milk for breakfast. I danced my dance. I ordered the sloop to be unloaded. Redskin Peter pretended to be sick and I put a [branding-iron] on the place he complained of and put the [bit] upon him.[9] The boy called the Doc was sent from Falling Creek with a swollen thigh. My sick people were better, thank God Almighty. I received a courteous letter from the Governor by Tom, who brought no news. I ate boiled pork for dinner. Mr. Mumford came down after dinner and told me all was well at Appomattox. When he had got some victuals we took a walk to see the people load the sloop and afterwards about the plantation. In the evening G-r-l came and let me know things were well at Falling Creek. He brought me a letter from Tom Turpin[1] in which he agreed to stay with me for £25 a year. I ate some roast beef for supper. I neglected to say my prayers, but had good health, good thoughts, and good humor, thank God.

[January] 23. [1711] I rose at 5 o'clock and read a chapter in Hebrew and some Greek in Lucian. I said my prayers and ate boiled milk for breakfast. I danced my dance. My sick people were better, thank God, and Redskin Peter was particularly well and worked as well as anybody. * * *

[February] 6. [1711] I rose about 9 o'clock but was so bad I thought I should not have been in condition to go to Williamsburg,[2] and my wife was so kind to [say] she would stay with me, but rather than keep her from going I resolved to go if possible. I was shaved with a very dull razor, and ate some boiled milk for breakfast but neglected to say my prayers. About 10 o'clock I went to Williamsburg without the ladies. As soon as I got there it began to

7. Small private room.
8. A frequent visitor, the wife of the minister of Hungar's Parish, Northampton County, Virginia.
9. A device something like a horse's bit and fas-

tened in his mouth.
1. An overseer.
2. The colonial capital of Virginia, 1699–1779.

rain, which hindered about [sic] the company from coming. I went to the President's where I drank tea and went with him to the Governor's[3] and found him at home. Several gentlemen were there and about 12 o'clock several ladies came. My wife and her sister came about 2. We had a short council but more for form than for business. There was no other appointed in the room of [4] Colonel Digges. My cold was a little better so that I ventured among the ladies, and Colonel Carter's wife and daughter were among them. It was night before we went to supper, which was very fine and in good order. It rained so that several did not come that were expected. About 7 o'clock the company went in coaches from the Governor's house to the capitol where the Governor opened the ball with a French dance with my wife. Then I danced with Mrs. Russell and then several others and among the rest Colonel Smith's son, who made a sad freak. Then we danced country dances for an hour and the company was carried into another room where was a very fine collation of sweetmeats. The Governor was very gallant to the ladies and very courteous to the gentlemen. About 2 o'clock the company returned in the coaches and because the drive was dirty the Governor carried the ladies into their coaches. My wife and I lay at my lodgings. Colonel Carter's family and Mr. Blair were stopped by the unruliness of the horses and Daniel Wilkinson was so gallant as to lead the horses himself through all the dirt and rain to Mr. Blair's house. My cold continued bad. I neglected to say my prayers and had good thoughts, good humor, but indifferent health, thank God Almighty. It rained all day and all night. The President had the worst clothes of anybody there.

[February] 7. [1711] I rose at 8 o'clock and found my cold continued. I said my prayers and ate boiled milk for breakfast. I went to see Mr. Clayton who lay sick of the gout. About 11 o'clock my wife and I went to wait on the Governor in the President's coach. We went there to take our leave but were forced to stay all day. The Governor had made a bargain with his servants that if they would forbear to drink upon the Queen's birthday, they might be drunk this day. They observed their contract and did their business very well and got very drunk today, in such a manner that Mrs. Russell's maid was forced to lay the cloth, but the cook in that condition made a shift to send in a pretty little dinner. I ate some mutton cutlets. In the afternoon I persuaded my wife to stay all night in town and so it was resolved to spend the evening in cards. My cold was very bad and I lost my money. About 10 o'clock the Governor's coach carried us home to our lodgings where my wife was out of humor and I out of order. I said a short prayer and had good thoughts and good humor, thank God Almighty.

[December] 31. [1711] I rose about 7 o'clock and read a chapter in Hebrew and six leaves in Lucian. I said my prayers and ate boiled milk for breakfast. The weather continued warm and clear. I settled my accounts and wrote several things till dinner. I danced my dance. I ate some turkey and chine[5] for dinner. In the afternoon I weighed some money and then read some Latin in Terence[6] and then Mr. Mumford came and told me my man Tony had been very sick but he was recovered again, thank God. He told me

---

3. Col. Alexander Spotswood (1676–1740) was the English lieutenant governor of Virginia from 1710 to 1722. "President's": i.e., the house of the president of the Council of State, to which Byrd

had been appointed in 1708.
4. I.e., in place of.
5. A joint of meat; the ribs or sirloin of beef.
6. Roman playwright (c. 190–159 B.C.E).

Robin Bolling had been like to die and that he denied that he was the first to mention the imposition[7] on skins which he certainly did. Then he and I took a walk about the plantation. When I returned I was out of humor to find the negroes all at work in our chambers. At night I ate some broiled turkey with Mr. Mumford and we talked and were merry all the evening. I said my prayers and had good health, good thoughts, and good humor, thank God Almighty. My wife and I had a terrible quarrel about whipping Eugene[8] while Mr. Mumford was there but she had a mind to show her authority before company but I would not suffer it, which she took very ill; however for peace sake I made the first advance towards a reconciliation which I obtained with some difficulty and after abundance of crying. However it spoiled the mirth of the evening, but I was not conscious that I was to blame in that quarrel.

[January] 1. [1712] I lay abed till 9 o'clock this morning to bring my wife into temper again and rogered[9] her by way of reconciliation. I read nothing because Mr. Mumford was here, nor did I say my prayers, for the same reason. However I ate boiled milk for breakfast, and after my wife tempted me to eat some pancakes with her. Mr. Mumford and I went to shoot with our bows and arrows but shot nothing, and afterwards we played at billiards till dinner, and when we came we found Ben Harrison there, who dined with us. I ate some partridge for dinner. In the afternoon we played at billiards again and I won two bits. I had a letter from Colonel Duke by H-l the brick-layer who came to offer his services to work for me. Mr. Mumford went away in the evening and John Bannister with him to see his mother. I took a walk about the plantation and at night we drank some mead of my wife's making which was very good. I gave the people some cider and a dram to the negroes. I read some Latin in Terence and had good health, good thoughts, and good humor, thank God Almighty. I said my prayers.

[January] 15. [1712] I rose about 7 o'clock but read nothing because I wrote some letters and one especially to Will Randolph concerning what I learned the Governor had [been] informed concerning my saying no Governor ought to be trusted with £20,000, and he owned he had told it because I had said it and he thought it no secret, for which I marked him as a very false friend. I said my prayers and ate boiled milk for breakfast. I had a sore throat this morning. The weather was warm and the wind southwest. Mr. G-r-l made an end of putting up the curtain cornice in the library and then went and showed John to plant fruit trees. Drury Stith, Colonel Hill, Mr. Anderson, and Mr. Platt came to see me and put me in mind of the vestry. However we ate our dinner first and I ate some roast mutton. Then we went to the vestry and among other things agreed to make a well in the churchyard. In the evening I was out of humor because my wife broke open Will Randolph's letter. I read some Terence at night and wrote in my journal. Mr. G-r-l went away in the evening. I said my prayers and had good health, good thoughts, and good humor, thank God Almighty.

[January] 16. [1712] I rose about 7 o'clock and read a chapter in Hebrew and some Greek in Lucian. I said my prayers and ate boiled milk for breakfast. I danced my dance. My wife was something better and rode out because

7. Taxation.
8. A servant.

9. Had intercourse with.

it was very fine weather and not cold. We killed a beef this morning that came yesterday from Burkland where they were all well, thank God. I settled some accounts till dinner and than I ate some hash of beef. In the afternoon my wife shaved me and then I walked out to see my people plant trees and I was angry with John for mistaking Mr. G-r-l's directions. Then I showed him again and helped him plant several trees. Then I took a walk till night. When I came in my [wife] persuaded me to eat skim milk for supper. Then I read some Latin in Terence. I said my prayers and had good thoughts, good humor, and good health, thank God Almighty. I dreamed a coffin was brought into my house and thrown into the hall.

[January] 17. [1712] I rose about 7 o'clock and read a chapter in Hebrew and some Greek in Lucian. I said my prayers and ate boiled milk for breakfast. I danced my dance. When I got up I thought to ride to Falling Creek but the weather threatened snow and the wind northeast, which discouraged me from my journey. About 12 o'clock I went to see John and Tom plant the peach orchard where I stayed till dinner was ready. I ate some beefsteak. In the afternoon I looked over some books with pictures for half an hour and then went again to my people to see them plant trees. I stayed there a little time and then went to take a walk about the plantation to examine what the rest had done and was contented with the overseer's management. I also saw all the cattle, which seem to be in good condition. At night I resisted my wife's temptation to eat milk and read some Latin in Terence. I said my prayers and had good health, good thoughts, and good humor, thank God Almighty.

[January] 18. [1712] I rose about 7 o'clock and read a chapter in Hebrew and some Greek in Lucian. I said my prayers and ate boiled milk for breakfast. I danced my dance. The weather was clear and cold but the wind was northeast. I settled several accounts and then read some Latin in Terence till dinner, and then I ate some boiled beef but I was displeased with my wife for giving the child marrow against my opinion. In the afternoon I read a little more Latin and then went to see my people plant peach trees and afterwards took a great walk about the plantation and found everything in order, for which I praised God. I was entertained with seeing a hawk which had taken a small bird pursued by another hawk, so that he was forced to let go his prey. My walk lasted till the evening and at night I read some Latin in Terence. I said my prayers and had good health, good thoughts, and good humor, thank God Almighty.

[May] 22. [1712] I rose about 6 o'clock and read two chapters in Hebrew and some Greek in Lucian. I said my prayers and ate boiled milk for breakfast. I danced my dance. It rained a little this morning. My wife caused Prue to be whipped violently notwithstanding I desired not, which provoked me to have Anaka whipped likewise who had deserved it much more, on which my wife flew into such a passion that she hoped she would be revenged of me. I was moved very much at this but only thanked her for the present lest I should say things foolish in my passion. I wrote more accounts to go to England. My wife was sorry for what she had said and came to ask my pardon and I forgave her in my heart but seemed to resent, that she might be the more sorry for her folly. She ate no dinner nor appeared the whole day. I ate some bacon for dinner. In the afternoon I wrote two more accounts till the evening and then took a walk in the garden. I said my prayers and was reconciled to my wife and gave her a flourish in token of it. I had good health, good thoughts, but was a little out of humor, for which God forgive me.

1941

From History of the Dividing Line[1]

[THE OTHER BRITISH COLONIES]

Before I enter upon the journal of the line between Virginia and North Carolina, it will be necessary to clear the way to it by showing how the other British colonies on the main have, one after another, been carved out of Virginia by grants from His Majesty's royal predecessors. All that part of the northern American continent now under the dominion of the King of Great Britain and stretching quite as far as the Cape of Florida went at first under the general name of Virginia.

The only distinction in those early days was that all the coast to the southward of Chesapeake Bay was called South Virginia and all to the northward of it North Virginia.

The first settlement of this fine country was owing to that great ornament of the British nation, Sir Walter Raleigh, who obtained a grant thereof from Queen Elizabeth, of ever-glorious memory, by letters patent[2] dated March 25, 1584.

But whether that gentleman ever made a voyage thither himself is uncertain, because those who have favored the public with an account of his life mention nothing of it. However, thus much may be depended on, that Sir Walter invited sundry persons of distinction to share in his charter and join their purses with his in the laudable project of fitting out a colony to Virginia.

Accordingly, two ships were sent away that very year, under the command of his good friends Amadas and Barlow,[3] to take possession of the country in the name of his royal mistress, the Queen of England.

These worthy commanders, for the advantage of the trade winds, shaped their course first to the Caribbee Islands, thence, stretching away by the Gulf of Florida, dropped anchor not far from Roanoke Inlet. They ventured ashore near that place upon an island now called Colleton Island,[4] where they set up the arms of England and claimed the adjacent country in right of their sovereign lady, the Queen; and this ceremony being duly performed, they kindly invited the neighboring Indians to traffic with them.

These poor people at first approached the English with great caution, having heard much of the treachery of the Spaniards and not knowing but these strangers might be as treacherous as they. But at length, discovering a kind of good nature in their looks, they ventured to draw near and barter their skins and furs for the baubles and trinkets of the English.

These first adventurers made a very profitable voyage, raising at least a thousand percent upon their cargo. Amongst other Indian commodities, they

---

1. The text used here is taken from *The Prose Works of William Byrd of Westover*, edited by Louis B. Wright (1966).
2. A public letter, usually signed by a sovereign. Sir Walter Ralegh (1552?–1618), author of *The History of the World* (1614), military and naval

commander.
3. Arthur Barlow's account of his voyage with Philip Amadas was printed in Richard Hakluyt's *Principal Navigations* (1589).
4. Now Colington Island.

brought over some of that bewitching vegetable, tobacco. And this being the first that ever came to England, Sir Walter thought he could do no less than make a present of some of the brightest of it to his royal mistress for her own smoking. The Queen graciously accepted of it, but finding her stomach sicken after two or three whiffs, 'twas presently whispered by the Earl of Leicester's[5] faction that Sir Walter had certainly poisoned her. But Her Majesty, soon recovering her disorder, obliged the Countess of Nottingham and all her maids to smoke a whole pipe out amongst them.

As it happened some ages before to be the fashion to saunter to the Holy Land and go upon other Quixote adventures,[6] so it was now grown the humor to take a trip to America. The Spaniards had lately discovered rich mines in their part of the West Indies, which made their maritime neighbors eager to do so too. This modish frenzy, being still more inflamed by the charming account given of Virginia by the first adventurers, made many fond of removing to such a Paradise.

Happy was he, and still happier she, that could get themselves transported, fondly expecting their coarsest utensils in that happy place would be of massy silver.

This made it easy for the Company to procure as many volunteers as they wanted for their new colony, but, like most other undertakers who have no assistance from the public, they starved the design by too much frugality; for, unwilling to launch out at first into too much expense, they shipped off but few people at a time, and those but scantily provided. The adventurers were, besides, idle and extravagant and expected they might live without work in so plentiful a country.

These wretches were set ashore not far from Roanoke Inlet, but by some fatal disagreement or laziness were either starved or cut to pieces by the Indians.

Several repeated misadventures of this kind did for some time allay the itch of sailing to this new world, but the distemper broke out again about the year 1606. Then it happened that the Earl of Southampton[7] and several other persons eminent for their quality and estates were invited into the Company, who applied themselves once more to people the then almost abandoned colony. For this purpose they embarked about an hundred men, most of them reprobates of good families and related to some of the Company who were men of quality and fortune.

The ships that carried them made a shift to find a more direct way to Virginia and ventured through the capes into the Bay of Chesapeake. The same night they came to an anchor at the mouth of Powhatan, the same as James River, where they built a small fort at a place called Point Comfort.

This settlement stood its ground from that time forward, in spite of all the blunders and disagreement of the first adventurers and the many calamities that befell the colony afterwards. The six gentlemen who were first named of the Company by the Crown and who were empowered to choose an annual president from among themselves were always engaged in factions and quarrels, while the rest detested work more than famine. At this rate the colony

5. Robert Dudley (1532?–1588), earl of Leicester, was Elizabeth's favorite at court and a man of great political influence.
6. Foolish and impractical ventures, after the character in Cervantes's novel *Don Quixote* (1605–15).
7. Henry Wriothesley, third earl of Southampton (1573–1624), Shakespeare's patron.

must have come to nothing had it not been for the vigilance and bravery of Captain Smith,[8] who struck a terror into all the Indians round about. This gentleman took some pains to persuade the men to plant Indian corn, but they looked upon all labor as a curse. They chose rather to depend upon the musty provisions that were sent from England; and when they failed they were forced to take more pains to seek for wild fruits in the woods than they would have taken in tilling the ground. Besides, this exposed them to be knocked in the head by the Indians and gave them fluxes[9] into the bargain, which thinned the plantation very much. To supply this mortality, they were reinforced the year following with a greater number of people, amongst which were fewer gentlemen and more laborers, who, however, took care not to kill themselves with work. These found the first adventurers in a very starving condition but relieved their wants with the fresh supply they brought with them. From Kecoughtan[1] they extended themselves as far as Jamestown, where, like true Englishmen, they built a church that cost no more than fifty pounds and a tavern that cost five hundred.

They had now made peace with the Indians, but there was one thing wanting to make that peace lasting. The natives could by no means persuade themselves that the English were heartily their friends so long as they disdained to intermarry with them. And, in earnest, had the English consulted their own security and the good of the colony, had they intended either to civilize or convert these gentiles, they would have brought their stomachs to embrace this prudent alliance.

The Indians are generally tall and well proportioned, which may make full amends for the darkness of their complexions. Add to this that they are healthy and strong, with constitutions untainted by lewdness and not enfeebled by luxury. Besides, morals and all considered, I cannot think the Indians were much greater heathens than the first adventurers, who, had they been good Christians, would have had the charity to take this only method of converting the natives to Christianity. For, after all that can be said, a sprightly lover is the most prevailing missionary that can be sent amongst these or any other infidels.

Besides, the poor Indians would have had less reason to complain that the English took away their land if they had received it by way of a portion with their daughters. Had such affinities been contracted in the beginning, how much bloodshed had been prevented and how populous would the country have been, and, consequently, how considerable! Nor would the shade of the skin have been any reproach at this day, for if a Moor may be washed white in three generations, surely an Indian might have been blanched in two.

The French, for their parts, have not been so squeamish in Canada, who upon trial find abundance of attraction in the Indians. Their late grand monarch thought it not below even the dignity of a Frenchman to become one flesh with this people and therefore ordered 100 livres for any of his subjects, man or woman, that would intermarry with a native.

By this piece of policy we find the French interest very much strengthened amongst the savages and their religion, such as it is, propagated just as far

8. Captain John Smith (1580–1631), soldier and colonist, founder of Virginia.

9. Dysentery.

1. Now Hampton, Virginia.

as their love. And I heartily wish this well-concerted scheme don't hereafter give the French an advantage over His Majesty's good subjects on the northern continent of America.

About the same time New England was pared off from Virginia by letters patent bearing date April 10, 1608. Several gentlemen of the town and neighborhood of Plymouth obtained this grant, with the Lord Chief Justice Popham at their head.

Their bounds were specified to extend from 38 to 45 degrees of northern latitude, with a breadth of one hundred miles from the seashore. The first fourteen years this company encountered many difficulties and lost many men, though, far from being discouraged, they sent over numerous recruits of Presbyterians every year, who for all that had much ado to stand their ground, with all their fighting and praying.

But about the year 1620 a large swarm of dissenters[2] fled thither from the severities of their stepmother, the church. These saints,[3] conceiving the same aversion to the copper complexion of the natives with that of the first adventurers to Virginia, would on no terms contract alliances with them, afraid, perhaps, like the Jews of old, lest they might be drawn into idolatry by those strange women.

Whatever disgusted them I can't say, but this false delicacy, creating in the Indians a jealousy that the English were ill affected toward them, was the cause that many of them were cut off and the rest exposed to various distresses.

This reinforcement was landed not far from Cape Cod, where for their greater security they built a fort and near it a small town, which, in honor of the proprietors, was called New Plymouth. But they still had many discouragements to struggle with, though by being well supported from home they by degrees triumphed over them all.

Their brethren, after this, flocked over so fast that in a few years they extended the settlement one hundred miles along the coast, including Rhode Island and Martha's Vineyard.

Thus the colony throve apace and was thronged with large detachments of Independents and Presbyterians who thought themselves persecuted at home.

Though these people may be ridiculed for some pharisaical particularities in their worship and behavior, yet they were very useful subjects, as being frugal and industrious, giving no scandal or bad example, at least by any open and public vices. By which excellent qualities they had much the advantage of the southern colony, who thought their being members of the established church sufficient to sanctify very loose and profligate morals. For this reason New England improved much faster than Virginia, and in seven or eight years New Plymouth, like Switzerland, seemed too narrow a territory for its inhabitants.

*　*　*

2. English Christians who rejected the authority of the Church of England.　　3. Here, Puritan believers.

From *October*[4]

1. There was a white frost this morning on the ground, occasioned by a northwest wind, which stood our friend in dispersing all aguish[5] damps and making the air wholesome at the same time that it made it cold. Encouraged, therefore, by the weather, our surveyors got to work early and, by the benefit of clear woods and level ground, drove the line twelve miles and twelve poles.[6]

At a small distance from our camp we crossed Great Creek and about seven miles farther Nutbush Creek, so called from the many hazel trees growing upon it. By good luck, many branches of these creeks were full of reeds, to the great comfort of our horses. Near five miles from thence we encamped on a branch that runs into Nutbush Creek, where those reeds flourished more than ordinary. The land we marched over was for the most part broken and stony and in some places covered over with thickets almost impenetrable.

At night the surveyors, taking advantage of a very clear sky, made a third trial of the variation and found it still something less than three degrees; so that it did not diminish by advancing toward the west or by approaching the mountains, nor yet by increasing our distance from the sea, but remained much the same we had found it at Currituck Inlet.

One of our Indians killed a large fawn, which was very welcome, though, like Hudibras' horse,[7] it had hardly flesh enough to cover its bones.

In the low grounds the Carolina gentlemen showed us another plant, which they said was used in their country to cure the bite of the rattlesnake. It put forth several leaves in figure like a heart and was clouded so like the common Asarabacca that I conceived it to be of that family.

2. So soon as the horses could be found, we hurried away the surveyors, who advanced the line 9 miles and 254 poles. About three miles from the camp they crossed a large creek, which the Indians called Massamony, signifying in their language "Paint Creek," because of the great quantity of red ocher found in its banks. This in every fresh tinges the water, just as the same mineral did formerly, and to this day continues to tinge, the famous river Adonis[8] in Phoenicia, by which there hangs a celebrated fable.

Three miles beyond that we passed another water with difficulty called Yapatsco or Beaver Creek. Those industrious animals had dammed up the water so high that we had much ado to get over. 'Tis hardly credible how much work of this kind they will do in the space of one night. They bite young saplings into proper lengths with their foreteeth, which are exceeding strong and sharp, and afterwards drag them to the place where they intend to stop the water. Then they know how to join timber and earth together with so much skill that their work is able to resist the most violent flood than can happen. In this they are qualified to instruct their betters, it being certain their dams will stand firm when the strongest that are made by men will be carried down the stream. We observed very broad, low grounds upon this creek, with a growth of large trees and all the other signs of fertility, but

4. The boundary commission began its expedition on March 5, 1728. By October 1, they were close to present-day Bristol, Tennessee.
5. Feverish.
6. A linear measure equal to 5.5 yards.
7. In Samuel Butler's satire *Hudibras* (1663–78),

a Presbyterian minister sets out on a journey upon a starving horse.
8. It turns red each spring, or "fresh," supposedly with the blood of Adonis, who, a mortal, was beloved of Aphrodite and wounded while hunting.

seemed subject to be everywhere overflowed in a fresh. The certain way to catch these sagacious animals is this: squeeze all the juice out of the large pride[9] of the beaver and six drops out of the small pride. Powder the inward bark of sassafras and mix it with this juice; then bait therewith a steel trap and they will eagerly come to it and be taken.

About three miles and an half farther we came to the banks of another creek, called in the Saponi language Ohimpamony, signifying "Jumping Creek," from the frequent jumping of fish during the spring season.

Here we encamped, and by the time the horses were hobbled our hunters brought us no less than a brace and an half of deer, which made great plenty and consequently great content in our quarters. Some of our people had shot a great wildcat, which was that fatal moment making a comfortable meal upon a fox squirrel, and an ambitious sportsman of our company claimed the merit of killing this monster after it was dead. The wildcat is as big again as any household cat and much the fiercest inhabitant of the woods. Whenever it is disabled, it will tear its own flesh for madness. Although a panther will run away from a man, a wildcat will only make a surly retreat, now and then facing about if he be too closely pursued, and will even pursue in his turn if he observe the least sign of fear or even of caution in those that pretend to follow him. The flesh of this beast, as well as of the panther, is as white as veal and altogether as sweet and delicious.

3. We got to work early this morning and carried the line 8 miles and 160 poles. We forded several runs of excellent water and afterwards traversed a large level of high land, full of lofty walnut, poplar, and white oak trees, which are certain proofs of a fruitful soil. This level was near two miles in length and of an unknown breadth, quite out of danger of being overflowed, which is a misfortune most of the low grounds are liable to in those parts. As we marched along, we saw many buffalo tracks and abundance of their dung very fresh but could not have the pleasure of seeing them. They either smelt us out, having that sense very quick,[1] or else were alarmed at the noise that so many people must necessarily make in marching along. At the sight of a man they will snort and grunt, cock up their ridiculous short tails, and tear up the ground with a sort of timorous fury. These wild cattle hardly ever range alone but herd together like those that are tame. They are seldom seen so far north as forty degrees of latitude, delighting much in canes and reeds which grow generally more southerly.

We quartered on the banks of a creek that the inhabitants call Tewahominy or Tuskarooda[2] Creek, because one of that nation had been killed thereabouts and his body thrown into the creek.

Our people had the fortune to kill a brace of does, one of which we presented to the Carolina gentlemen, who were glad to partake of the bounty of Providence at the same time that they sneered at us for depending upon it.

4. We hurried away the surveyors about nine this morning, who extended the line 7 miles and 160 poles, notwithstanding the ground was exceedingly uneven. At the distance of five miles we forded a stream to which we gave the name of Bluewing Creek because of the great number of those fowls[3]

9. Testis.
1. Acutely.

2. Now Tuscarora.
3. I.e., blue-winged teal.

that then frequented it. About two and a half miles beyond that, we came upon Sugartree Creek, so called from the many trees of that kind[4] that grow upon it. By tapping this tree in the first warm weather in February, one may get from twenty to forty gallons of liquor, very sweet to the taste and agreeable to the stomach. This may be boiled into molasses first and afterwards into very good sugar, allowing about ten gallons of liquor to make a pound. There is no doubt, too, that a very fine spirit may be distilled from the molasses, at least as good as rum. The sugar tree delights only in rich ground, where it grows very tall, and by the softness and sponginess of the wood should be a quick grower. Near this creek we discovered likewise several spice trees, the leaves of which are fragrant and the berries they bear are black when dry and of a hot taste, not much unlike pepper. The low grounds upon the creek are very wide, sometimes on one side, sometimes on the other, though most commonly upon the opposite shore the high land advances close to the bank, only on the north side of the line it spreads itself into a great breadth of rich low ground on both sides the creek for four miles together, as far as this stream runs into Hyco River, whereof I shall presently make mention. One of our men spied three buffaloes, but his piece being loaded only with goose shot, he was able to make no effectual impression on their thick hides; however, this disappointment was made up by a brace of bucks and as many wild turkeys killed by the rest of the company. Thus Providence was very bountiful to our endeavors, never disappointing those that faithfully rely upon it and pray heartily for their daily bread.

5. This day we met with such uneven grounds and thick underwoods that with all our industry we were able to advance the line but 4 miles and 312 poles. In this small distance it intersected a large stream four times, which our Indian at first mistook for the south branch of Roanoke River; but, discovering his error soon after, he assured us 'twas a river called Hycootomony, or Turkey Buzzard River, from the great number of those unsavory birds that roost on the tall trees growing near its banks.

Early in the afternoon, to our very great surprise, the commissioners of Carolina acquainted us with their resolution to return home. This declaration of theirs seemed the more abrupt because they had not been so kind as to prepare us by the least hint of their intention to desert us. We therefore let them understand they appeared to us to abandon the business they came about with too much precipitation, this being but the fifteenth day since we came out the last time. But although we were to be so unhappy as to lose the assistance of their great abilities, yet we, who were concerned for Virginia, determined, by the grace of God, not to do our work by halves but, all deserted as we were like to be, should think it our duty to push the line quite to the mountains; and if their government should refuse to be bound by so much of the line as was run without their commissioners, yet at least it would bind Virginia and stand as a direction how far His Majesty's lands extend to the southward. In short, these gentlemen were positive, and the most we could agree upon was to subscribe plats[5] of our work as far as we had acted together; though at the same time we insisted these plats should be got ready by Monday noon at farthest, when we on the part of Virginia intended, if we were alive, to move forward without farther loss of time, the

4. I.e., sugar maples.   5. Maps.

season being then too far advanced to admit of any unnecessary or complaisant delays.

6. We lay still this day, being Sunday, on the bank of Hyco River and had only prayers, our chaplain not having spirits enough to preach. The gentlemen of Carolina assisted not at our public devotions, because they were taken up all the morning in making a formidable protest against our proceeding on the line without them. When the divine service was over, the surveyors set about making the plats of so much of the line as we had run this last campaign. Our pious friends of Carolina assisted in this work with some seeming scruple, pretending it was a violation of the Sabbath, which we were the more surprised at because it happened to be the first qualm of conscience they had ever been troubled with during the whole journey. They had made no bones of staying from prayers to hammer out an unnecessary protest, though divine service was no sooner over but an unusual fit of godliness made them fancy that finishing the plats, which was now matter of necessity, was a profanation of the day. However, the expediency of losing no time, for us who thought it our duty to finish what we had undertaken, make such a labor pardonable.

In the afternoon, Mr. Fitzwilliam, one of the commissioners for Virginia, acquainted his colleagues it was his opinion that by His Majesty's order they could not proceed farther on the line but in conjunction with the commissioners of Carolina; for which reason he intended to retire the next morning with those gentlemen. This looked a little odd in our brother commissioner; though, in justice to him as well as to our Carolina friends, they stuck by us as long as our good liquor lasted and were so kind to us as to drink our good journey to the mountains in the last bottle we had left.

7. The duplicates of the plats could not be drawn fair this day before noon, where they were countersigned by the commissioners of each government. Then those of Carolina delivered their protest, which was by this time licked into form and signed by them all. And we have been so just to them as to set it down at full length in the Appendix, that their reasons for leaving us may appear in their full strength. After having thus adjusted all our affairs with the Carolina commissioners and kindly supplied them with bread to carry them back, which they hardly deserved at our hands, we took leave both of them and our colleague, Mr. Fitzwilliam. This gentleman had still a stronger reason for hurrying him back to Williamsburg, which was that neither the General Court might lose an able judge nor himself a double salary, not despairing in the least but he should have the whole pay of commissioner into the bargain, though he did not half the work. This, to be sure, was relying more on the interest of his friends than on the justice of his cause; in which, however, he had the misfortune to miscarry when it came to be fairly considered.

It was two o'clock in the afternoon before these arduous affairs could be dispatched, and then, all forsaken as we were, we held on our course toward the west. But it was our misfortune to meet with so many thickets in this afternoon's work that we could advance no further than 2 miles and 260 poles. In this small distance we crossed the Hyco the fifth time and quartered near Buffalo Creek, so named from the frequent tokens we discovered of that American behemoth. Here the bushes were so intolerably thick that we were obliged to cover the bread bags with our deerskins, otherwise the joke of one of the Indians must have happened to us in good earnest: that in a few days we must cut up our house[6] to make bags for the bread and so be forced to expose our backs in compliment to our bellies. We computed we had then biscuit enough left to last us, with good management, seven weeks longer; and this being our chief dependence, it imported us to be very careful both in the carriage and the distribution of it.

We had now no other drink but what Adam drank in Paradise, though to our comfort we found the water excellent, by the help of which we perceived our appetites to mend, our slumbers to sweeten, the stream of life to run cool and peaceably in our veins, and if ever we dreamt of women, they were kind.

Our men killed a very fat buck and several turkeys. These two kinds of meat boiled together, with the addition of a little rice or French barley, made excellent soup, and, what happens rarely in other good things, it never cloyed, no more than an engaging wife would do, by being a constant dish. Our Indian was very superstitious in this matter and told us, with a face full of concern, that if we continued to boil venison and turkey together we should for the future kill nothing, because the spirit that presided over the woods would drive all the game out of our sight. But we had the happiness to find this an idle superstition, and though his argument could not convince us, yet our repeated experience at last, with much ado, convinced him.

We observed abundance of coltsfoot and maidenhair in many places and nowhere a larger quantity than here. They are both excellent pectoral[7] plants and seem to have greater virtues much in this part of the world than in more northern climates; and I believe it may pass for a rule in botanics that where any vegetable is planted by the hand of Nature it has more virtue than in places whereto it is transplanted by the curiosity of man.

* * *

12. We were so cruelly entangled with bushes and grapevines all day that we could advance the line no farther than five miles and twenty-eight poles. The vines grew very thick in these woods, twining lovingly round the trees almost everywhere, especially to the saplings. This makes it evident how natural both the soil and climate of this country are to vines, though I believe most to our own vines. The grapes we commonly met with were black, though there be two or three kinds of white grapes that grow wild. The black are very sweet but small, because the strength of the vine spends itself in wood, though without question a proper culture would make the same grapes both larger and sweeter. But, with all these disadvantages, I have drunk tolerable good wine pressed from them, though made without skill. There is then good reason to believe it might admit of great improvement if rightly managed.

Our Indian killed a bear, two years old, that was feasting on these grapes. He was very fat, as they generally are in that season of the year. In the fall the flesh of this animal has a high relish different from that of other creatures, though inclining nearest to that of pork, or rather of wild boar. A true woodsman prefers this sort of meat to that of the fattest venison, not only for the *haut goût*,[8] but also because the fat of it is well tasted and never rises

6. The garments covering them.
7. Good for diseases of the chest.

8. Gamy flavor (French).

in the stomach. Another proof of the goodness of this meat is that it is less apt to corrupt than any other we are acquainted with.

As agreeable as such rich diet was to the men, yet we who were not accustomed to it tasted it at first with some sort of squeamishness, that animal being of the dog kind, though a little use soon reconciled us to this American venison. And that its being of the dog kind might give us the less disgust, we had the example of that ancient and polite people, the Chinese, who reckon dog's flesh too good for any under the quality of a mandarin. This beast is in truth a very clean feeder, living, while the season lasts, upon acorns, chestnuts, and chinquapins, wild honey and wild grapes. They are naturally not carnivorous, unless hunger constrain them to it after the mast[9] is all gone and the product of the woods quite exhausted. They are not provident enough to lay up any hoard like the squirrels, nor can they, after all, live very long upon licking their paws, as Sir John Mandeville[1] and some travelers tell us, but are forced in the winter months to quit the mountains and visit the inhabitants. Their errand is then to surprise a poor hog at a pinch to keep them from starving. And to show that they are not flesh eaters by trade, they devour their prey very awkwardly. They don't kill it right out and feast upon its blood and entrails, like other ravenous beasts, but, having, after a fair pursuit, seized it with their paws, they begin first upon the rump and so devour one collop after another till they come to the vitals, the poor animal crying all the while for several minutes together. However, in so doing, Bruin acts a little imprudently, because the dismal outcry of the hog alarms the neighborhood, and 'tis odds but he pays the forfeit with his life before he can secure his retreat.

But bears soon grow weary of this unnatural diet, and about January, when there is nothing to be gotten in the woods, they retire into some cave or hollow tree, where they sleep away two or three months very comfortably. But then they quit their holes in March, when the fish begin to run up the rivers, on which they are forced to keep Lent till some fruit or berry comes in season. But bears are fondest of chestnuts, which grow plentifully toward the mountains, upon very large trees, where the soil happens to be rich. We were curious to know how it happened that many of the outward branches of those trees came to be broke off in that solitary place and were informed that the bears are so discreet as not to trust their unwieldly bodies on the smaller limbs of the tree that would not bear their weight, but after venturing as far as is safe, which they can judge to an inch, they bite off the end of the branch, which falling down, they are content to finish their repast upon the ground. In the same cautious manner they secure the acorns that grow on the weaker limbs of the oak. And it must be allowed that in these instances a bear carries instinct a great way and acts more reasonably than many of his betters, who indiscreetly venture upon frail projects that won't bear them.

13. This being Sunday, we rested from our fatigue and had leisure to reflect on the signal mercies of Providence.

The great plenty of meat wherewith Bearskin[2] furnished us in these lonely woods made us once more shorten the men's allowance of bread from five to four pounds of biscuit a week. This was the more necessary because we knew not yet how long our business might require us to be out.

---

9. A collective name for the fruit of the beech, chestnut, oak, and other forest trees.
1. Ostensible author of a mid-14th-century book of travels.
2. Their American Indian guide.

In the afternoon our hunters went forth and returned triumphantly with three brace of wild turkeys. They told us they could see the mountains distinctly from every eminence, though the atmosphere was so thick with smoke that they appeared at a greater distance than they really were.

In the evening we examined our friend Bearskin concerning the religion of his country, and he explained it to us without any of that reserve to which his nation is subject. He told us he believed there was one supreme god, who had several subaltern deities under him. And that this master god made the world a long time ago. That he told the sun, the moon, and stars their business in the beginning, which they, with good looking-after, have faithfully performed ever since. That the same power that made all things at first has taken care to keep them in the same method and motion ever since. He believed that God had formed many worlds before he formed this, but that those worlds either grew old and ruinous or were destroyed for the dishonesty of the inhabitants. That God is very just and very good, ever well pleased with those men who possess those godlike qualities. That he takes good people into his safe protection, makes them very rich, fills their bellies plentifully, preserves them from sickness and from being surprised or overcome by their enemies. But all such as tell lies and cheat those they have dealings with he never fails to punish with sickness, poverty, and hunger and, after all that, suffers them to be knocked on the head and scalped by those that fight against them.

He believed that after death both good and bad people are conducted by a strong guard into a great road, in which departed souls travel together for some time till at a certain distance this road forks into two paths, the one extremely level and the other stony and mountainous. Here the good are parted from the bad by a flash of lightning, the first being hurried away to the right, the other to the left. The right-hand road leads to a charming, warm country, where the spring is everlasting and every month is May; and as the year is always in its youth, so are the people, and particularly the women are bright as stars and never scold. That in this happy climate there are deer, turkeys, elks, and buffaloes innumerable, perpetually fat and gentle, while the trees are loaded with delicious fruit quite throughout the four seasons. That the soil brings forth corn spontaneously, without the curse of labor, and so very wholesome that none who have the happiness to eat of it are ever sick, grow old, or die. Near the entrance into this blessed land sits a venerable old man on a mat richly woven, who examines strictly all that are brought before him, and if they have behaved well, the guards are ordered to open the crystal gate and let them enter into the land of delight. The left-hand path is very rugged and uneven, leading to a dark and barren country where it is always winter. The ground is the whole year round covered with snow, and nothing is to be seen upon the trees but icicles. All the people are hungry yet have not a morsel of anything to eat except a bitter kind of potato, that gives them the dry gripes[3] and fills their whole body with loathsome ulcers that stink and are insupportably painful. Here all the women are old and ugly, having claws like a panther with which they fly upon the men that slight their passion. For it seems these haggard old furies are intolerably fond and expect a vast deal of cherishing. They talk much and exceedingly shrill, giving exquisite pain to the drum of the ear, which in that place of the

---

3. Dry heaves; vomiting.

torment is so tender that every sharp note wounds it to the quick. At the end of this path sits a dreadful old woman on a monstrous toadstool, whose head is covered with rattlesnakes instead of tresses, with glaring white eyes that strike a terror unspeakable into all that behold her. This hag pronounces sentence of woe upon all the miserable wretches that hold up their hands at her tribunal. After this they are delivered over to huge turkey buzzards, like harpies, that fly away with them to the place above-mentioned. Here, after they have been tormented a certain number of years according to their several degrees of guilt, they are again driven back into this world to try if they will mend their manners and merit a place the next time in the regions of bliss.

This was the substance of Bearskin's religion and was as much to the purpose as could be expected from a mere state of nature, without one glimpse of revelation or philosophy. It contained, however, the three great articles of natural religion: the belief of a god, the moral distinction betwixt good and evil, and the expectation of rewards and punishments in another world. Indeed, the Indian notion of a future happiness is a little gross and sensual, like Mahomet's Paradise. But how can it be otherwise in a people that are contented with Nature as they find her and have no other lights but what they receive from purblind tradition?

*   *   *

1728   1841

JONATHAN EDWARDS
1703–1758

Although it is certainly true that, as Perry Miller once put it, the real life of Jonathan Edwards is the life of a mind, the circumstances surrounding Edwards's career are not without their drama, and his rise to eminence and fall from power remain one of the most moving stories in American literature.

Edwards was born in East Windsor, Connecticut, a town not far from Hartford, the son of the Reverend Timothy Edwards and Esther Stoddard Edwards. There was little doubt from the beginning as to his career. Edwards's mother was the daughter of the Reverend Solomon Stoddard of Northampton, Massachusetts, one of the most influential and independent figures in the religious life of New England. Western Massachusetts clergymen were so anxious for his approval that he was sometimes called the "Pope of the Connecticut Valley," and his gifted grandson, the only male child in a family of eleven children, was groomed to be his heir.

Edwards was a studious and dutiful child and from an early age showed remarkable gifts of observation and exposition. When he was eleven he wrote an essay on the flying spider, which is still very readable. Most of Edwards's early education was at home. In 1716, when he was thirteen, Edwards was admitted to Yale College; he stayed on to read theology in New Haven for two years after his graduation in 1720. Like Benjamin Franklin, Edwards determined to perfect himself, and in one of his early notebooks he resolved "never to lose one moment of time, but to improve it in the most profitable way" he could. As a student he always rose at four in the morning, studied thirteen hours a day, and reserved part of each day for walking. It was a routine that Edwards varied little, even when, after spending two years in New York, he came to Northampton to assist his grandfather in his church. He married in 1727. In 1729 Solomon Stoddard died, and Edwards was named to succeed him. In the twenty-four years that Edwards lived in Northampton he managed to tend his duties as pastor of a growing congregation and deliver brilliant sermons, to write some of his most important books—concerned primarily with defining the nature of true religious experience—and watch his eleven children grow up. Until the mid-1740s his relations with the town were harmonious.

In spite of the awesome—even imposing—quality of Edwards's mind, all of his work is of a piece and, in essence, readily graspable. Edwards was trying to restore to his congregation and to his readers that original sense of religious commitment that he felt had been lost since the first days of the Puritan exodus, and he wanted to do this by transforming his congregation from mere believers who understood the logic of Christian doctrine to converted Christians who were genuinely moved by the principles of their belief. Edwards says that he read the work of the English philosopher John Locke (1632–1704) with more pleasure "than the greedy miser finds when gathering up handfuls of silver and gold, from some newly discovered treasure." For Locke confirmed Edwards's conviction that we must do more than comprehend religious ideas; we must be *moved* by them, we must know them experientially: the difference, as he says, is like that between reading the word *fire* and actually being burned. Basic to this newly felt belief is the recognition that nothing that an individual can do warrants his or her salvation—that people are motivated entirely by self-love, and that it is only supernatural grace that alters their natural depravity. In his progress as a Christian, Edwards says that he experienced several steps toward conversion but that his true conversion came only when he had achieved a "full and constant sense of the absolute sovereignty of God, and a delight in that sovereignty." The word *delight* reminds us that Edwards is trying to inculcate and describe a religious feeling that approximates a physical sensation, recognizing always that supernatural feelings and natural ones are actually very different. The word links him to the transatlantic community of those who recognized sentiment as the basic emotion that connects individuals to each other in manifold ways. In his patient and lucid prose Edwards became a master at the art of persuading his congregation that it could—and *must*—possess this intense awareness of humanity's precarious condition. The exaltation that his parishioners felt when they experienced delight in God's sovereignty was the characteristic fervid emotion of religious revivalism.

For fifteen years, beginning in 1734, this spirit of revivalism transformed complacent believers all along the eastern seaboard. This period of new religious fervor has been called the "Great Awakening," and in its early years Edwards could do no wrong. His meetinghouse was filled with newly converted believers, and the details of the spiritual life of Edwards and his congregation were the subject of inquiry by Christian believers everywhere as his works describing his own experience in the revivals were widely published and distributed in a period of expanding print culture. But in his attempt to restore the church to the position of authority it held in the years of his grandfather's reign, Edwards went too far. When he named backsliders from his pulpit—including members of the best families in town—and tried to return to the old order of communion, permitting the sacrament to be taken only by those who had publicly declared themselves to be saved, the people of the town turned against him. Residents of the Connecticut Valley everywhere were tired of religious controversy, and the hysterical behavior of a few fanatics turned many against the spirit of revivalism. On June 22, 1750, by a vote of two hundred to twenty, Edwards was dismissed from his church and effectively silenced. Although the congregation had difficulty naming a successor to Edwards, they preferred to have no sermons rather than let Edwards preach. For the next seven years he served as missionary to the Housatonnuck Indians in Stockbridge, Massachusetts, a town thirty-five miles to the west of Northampton. There he wrote his monumental treatises debating the doctrine of the freedom of the will and defining the nature of true virtue: "that consent, propensity and union of heart to Being in general, that is immediately exercised in a general good will." It was in Stockbridge that Edwards received, very reluctantly, a call to become president of the College of New Jersey (later called Princeton). Three months after his arrival in Princeton, Edwards died of smallpox, the result of the inoculation taken to prevent infection.

Personal Narrative[1]

I had a variety of concerns and exercises about my soul from my childhood; but had two more remarkable seasons of awakening[2] before I met with that change, by which I was brought to those new dispositions, and that new sense of things, that I have since had. The first time was when I was a boy, some years before I went to college, at a time of remarkable awakening in my father's congregation. I was then very much affected[3] for many months, and concerned about the things of religion, and my soul's salvation; and was abundant in duties. I used to pray five times a day in secret, and to spend much time in religious talk with other boys; and used to meet with them to pray together. I experienced I know not what kind of delight in religion. My mind was much engaged in it, and had much self-righteous pleasure; and it was my delight to abound in religious duties. I, with some of my schoolmates joined together, and built a booth in a swamp, in a very secret and retired place, for a place of prayer. And besides, I had particular secret places of my own in the woods, where I used to retire by myself; and used to be from time to time much affected. My affections seemed to be lively and easily moved, and I seemed to be in my element, when engaged in religious duties. And I am ready to think, many are deceived with such affections, and such a kind of delight, as I then had in religion, and mistake it for grace.

But in process of time, my convictions and affections wore off; and I entirely lost all those affections and delights, and left off secret prayer, at least as to any constant performance of it; and returned like a dog to his vomit, and went on in ways of sin.[4]

Indeed, I was at some times very uneasy, especially towards the latter part of the time of my being at college.[5] Till it pleased God, in my last year at college, at a time when I was in the midst of many uneasy thoughts about the state of my soul, to seize me with a pleurisy;[6] in which he brought me nigh to the grave, and shook me over the pit of hell.

1. Because of Edwards's reference to an evening in January 1739, this essay must have been written after that date. Edwards's reasons for writing it are not known, and it was not published in his lifetime. After his death his friend Samuel Hopkins had access to his manuscripts and prepared *The Life and Character of the Late Rev. Mr. Jonathan Edwards,* which was published in 1765. In that volume the *Personal Narrative* appeared in section IV as a chapter titled "An account of his conversion, experiences, and religious exercises, given by himself." The text here is from the Yale University Press *Works of Jonathan Edwards,* vol. 16, edited

by George Claghorn.
2. I.e., spiritual awakenings, renewals. "Exercises": agitations.
3. Emotionally aroused, as opposed to merely understanding rationally the arguments for Christian faith.
4. "As a dog returneth to his vomit, so a fool returneth to his folly" (Proverbs 26.11).
5. Edwards was an undergraduate at Yale from 1716 to 1720 and a divinity student from 1720 to 1722.
6. A respiratory disorder.

But yet, it was not long after my recovery, before I fell again into my old ways of sin. But God would not suffer me to go on with any quietness; but I had great and violent inward struggles: till after many conflicts with wicked inclinations, and repeated resolutions, and bonds that I laid myself under by a kind of vows to God, I was brought wholly to break off all former wicked ways, and all ways of known outward sin; and to apply myself to seek my salvation, and practice the duties of religion: but without that kind of affection and delight, that I had formerly experienced. My concern now wrought more by inward struggles and conflicts, and self-reflections. I made seeking my salvation the main business of my life. But yet it seems to me, I sought after a miserable manner: which has made me sometimes since to question, whether ever it issued in that which was saving;[7] being ready to doubt, whether such miserable seeking was ever succeeded. But yet I was brought to seek salvation, in a manner that I never was before. I felt a spirit to part with all things in the world, for an interest in Christ. My concern continued and prevailed, with many exercising things and inward struggles; but yet it never seemed to be proper to express my concern that I had, by the name of terror.

From my childhood up, my mind had been wont to be full of objections against the doctrine of God's sovereignty, in choosing whom He would to eternal life and rejecting whom he pleased; leaving them eternally to perish, and be everlastingly tormented in hell. It used to appear like a horrible doctrine to me. But I remember the time very well, when I seemed to be convinced, and fully satisfied, as to this sovereignty of God, and his justice in thus eternally disposing of men, according to his sovereign pleasure. But never could give an account, how, or by what means, I was thus convinced; not in the least imagining, in the time of it, nor a long time after, that there was any extraordinary influence of God's Spirit in it: but only that now I saw further, and my reason apprehended the justice and reasonableness of it. However, my mind rested in it; and it put an end to all those cavils and objections, that had till then abode with me, all the preceeding part of my life. And there has been a wonderful alteration in my mind, with respect to the doctrine of God's sovereignty, from that day to this; so that I scarce ever have found so much as the rising of an objection against God's sovereignty, in the most absolute sense, in showing mercy on whom he will show mercy, and hardening and eternally damning whom he will.[8] God's absolute sovereignty, and justice, with respect to salvation and damnation, is what my mind seems to rest assured of, as much as of anything that I see with my eyes; at least it is so at times. But I have oftentimes since that first conviction, had quite another kind of sense of God's sovereignty, than I had then. I have often since, not only had a conviction, but a *delightful* conviction. The doctrine of God's sovereignty has very often appeared, an exceeding pleasant, bright and sweet doctrine to me: and absolute sovereignty is what I love to ascribe to God. But my first conviction was not with this.

The first that I remember that ever I found anything of that sort of inward, sweet delight in God and divine things, that I have lived much in since, was on reading those words, 1 Tim. 1.17, "Now unto the King eternal, immortal,

---

7. I.e., truly redeeming, capable of making the penitent a "saint."
8. "Therefore hath he mercy on whom he will have mercy, and whom he will he hardeneth" (Romans 9.18).

invisible, the only wise God, be honor and glory for ever and ever, Amen."
As I read the words, there came into my soul, and was as it were diffused
through it, a sense of the glory of the divine being, a new sense, quite different from anything I ever experienced before. Never any words of Scripture
seemed to me as these words did. I thought with myself, how excellent a
Being that was; and how happy I should be, if I might enjoy that God, and
be wrapt[9] up to God in heaven, and be as it were swallowed up in him. I kept
saying, and as it were singing over these words of Scripture to myself; and
went to prayer, to pray to God that I might enjoy him; and prayed in a manner
quite different from what I used to do, with a new sort of affection. But it
never came into my thought, that there was anything spiritual, or of a saving
nature in this.

From about that time, I began to have a new kind of apprehensions and
ideas of Christ, and the work of redemption, and the glorious way of salvation
by him. I had an inward, sweet sense of these things, that at times came into
my heart; and my soul was led away in pleasant views and contemplations
of them. And my mind was greatly engaged, to spend my time in reading and
meditating on Christ; and the beauty and excellency of his person, and the
lovely way of salvation, by free grace in him. I found no books so delightful
to me, as those that treated of these subjects. Those words (Cant. 2:1) used
to be abundantly with me: "I am the rose of Sharon, the lily of the valleys."
The words seemed to me, sweetly to represent, the loveliness and beauty of
Jesus Christ. And the whole book of Canticles[1] used to be pleasant to me;
and I used to be much in reading it, about that time. And found, from time
to time, an inward sweetness, that used, as it were, to carry me away in my
contemplations; in what I know not how to express otherwise, than by a calm,
sweet abstraction of soul from all the concerns o[f] this world; and a kind of
vision, or fixed ideas and imaginations, of being alone in the mountains, or
some solitary wilderness, far from all mankind, sweetly conversing with
Christ, and wrapt and swallowed up in God. The sense I had of divine things,
would often of a sudden as it were, kindle up a sweet burning in my heart;
an ardor of my soul, that I know not how to express.

Not long after I first began to experience these things, I gave an account
to my father, of some things that had passed in my mind. I was pretty much
affected by the discourse we had together. And when the discourse was
ended, I walked abroad alone, in a solitary place in my father's pasture, for
contemplation. And as I was walking there, and looked up on the sky and
clouds; there came into my mind, a sweet sense of the glorious majesty and
grace of God, that I know not how to express. I seemed to see them both in
a sweet conjunction: majesty and meekness joined together: it was a sweet
and gentle, and holy majesty; and also a majestic meekness; an awful sweetness; a high, and great, and holy gentleness.

After this my sense of divine things gradually increased, and became more
and more lively, and had more of that inward sweetness. The appearance of
everything was altered: there seemed to be, as it were, a calm, sweet cast, or
appearance of divine glory, in almost everything. God's excellency, his wisdom, his purity and love, seemed to appear in everything; in the sun, moon
and stars; in the clouds, and blue sky; in the grass, flowers, trees; in the

9. Lifted.   1. I.e., Song of Solomon.

water, and all nature; which used greatly to fix my mind. I often used to sit and view the moon, for a long time; and so in the daytime, spent much time in viewing the clouds and sky, to behold the sweet glory of God in these things: in the meantime, singing forth with a low voice, my contemplations of the Creator and Redeemer. And scarce anything, among all the works of nature, was so sweet to me as thunder and lightning. Formerly, nothing had been so terrible to me. I used to be a person uncommonly terrified with thunder: and it used to strike me with terror, when I saw a thunderstorm rising. But now, on the contrary, it rejoiced me. I felt God at the first appearance of a thunderstorm. And used to take the opportunity at such times, to fix myself to view the clouds, and see the lightnings play, and hear the majestic and awful voice of God's thunder: which often times was exceeding entertaining, leading me to sweet contemplations of my great and glorious God. And while I viewed, used to spend my time, as it always seemed natural to me, to sing or chant forth my meditations; to speak my thoughts in soliloquies, and speak with a singing voice.

I felt then a great satisfaction as to my good estate.[2] But that did not content me. I had vehement longings of soul after God and Christ, and after more holiness; wherewith my heart seemed to be full, and ready to break: which often brought to my mind, the words of the Psalmist, Ps. 119:28, "My soul breaketh for the longing it hath." I often felt a mourning and lamenting in my heart, that I had not turned to God sooner, that I might have had more time to grow in grace. My mind was greatly fixed on divine things; I was almost perpetually in the contemplation of them. Spent most of my time in thinking of divine things, year after year. And used to spend abundance of my time, in walking alone in the woods, and solitary places, for meditation, soliloquy and prayer, and converse with God. And it was always my manner, at such times, to sing forth my contemplations. And was almost constantly in ejaculatory prayer, wherever I was. Prayer seemed to be natural to me; as the breath, by which the inward burnings of my heart had vent.

The delights which I now felt in things of religion, were of an exceeding different kind, from those forementioned, that I had when I was a boy. They were totally of another kind; and what I then had no more notion or idea of, than one born blind has of pleasant and beautiful colors. They were of a more inward, pure, soul-animating and refreshing nature. Those former delights, never reached the heart; and did not arise from any sight of the divine excellency of the things of God; or any taste of the soul-satisfying, and life-giving good, there is in them.

My sense of divine things seemed gradually to increase, till I went to preach at New York; which was about a year and a half after they began. While I was there, I felt them, very sensibly,[3] in a much higher degree, than I had done before. My longings after God and holiness, were much increased. Pure and humble, holy and heavenly Christianity, appeared exceeding amiable to me. I felt in me a burning desire to be in everything a complete Christian; and conformed to the blessed image of Christ: and that I might live in all things, according to the pure, sweet and blessed rules of the gospel. I had an eager thirsting after progress in these things. My longings after it,

---

2. Condition of being.
3. Feelingly. Edwards was in New York from August 1722 to April 1723, assisting at a Presbyterian church.

put me upon pursuing and pressing after them. It was my continual strife day and night, and constant inquiry, how I should be more holy, and live more holily, and more becoming a child of God, and disciple of Christ. I sought an increase of grace and holiness, and that I might live an holy life, with vastly more earnestness, than ever I sought grace, before I had it. I used to be continually examining myself, and studying and contriving for likely ways and means, how I should live holily, with far greater diligence and earnestness, than ever I pursued anything in my life: but with too great a dependence on my own strength, which afterwards proved a great damage to me. My experience had not then taught me, as it has done since, my extreme feebleness and impotence, every manner of way; and the innumerable and bottomless depths of secret corruption and deceit, that there was in my heart. However, I went on with my eager pursuit after more holiness; and sweet conformity to Christ.

The Heaven I desired was a heaven of holiness; to be with God, and to spend my eternity in divine love, and holy communion with Christ. My mind was very much taken up with contemplations on heaven, and the enjoyments of those there; and living there in perfect holiness, humility and love. And it used at that time to appear a great part of the happiness of heaven, that there the saints could express their love to Christ. It appeared to me a great clog and hindrance and burden to me, that what I felt within, I could not express to God, and give vent to, as I desired. The inward ardor of my soul, seemed to be hindered and pent up, and could not freely flame out as it would. I used often to think, how in heaven, this sweet principle should freely and fully vent and express itself. Heaven appeared to me exceeding delightful as a world of love. It appeared to me, that all happiness consisted in living in pure, humble, heavenly, divine love.

I remember the thoughts I used then to have of holiness. I remember I then said sometimes to myself, I do certainly know that I love holiness, such as the gospel prescribes. It appeared to me, there was nothing in it but what was ravishingly lovely. It appeared to me, to be the highest beauty and amiableness, above all other beauties: that it was a divine beauty; far purer than anything here upon earth; and that everything else, was like mire, filth and defilement, in comparison of it.

Holiness, as I then wrote down some of my contemplations on it, appeared to me to be of a sweet, pleasant, charming, serene, calm nature. It seemed to me, it brought an inexpressible purity, brightness, peacefulness and ravishment to the soul: and that it made the soul like a field or garden of God, with all manner of pleasant flowers; that is all pleasant, delightful and undisturbed; enjoying a sweet calm, and the gently vivifying beams of the sun. The soul of a true Christian, as I then wrote my meditations, appeared like such a little white flower, as we see in the spring of the year; low and humble on the ground, opening its bosom, to receive the pleasant beams of the sun's glory; rejoicing as it were, in a calm rapture; diffusing around a sweet fragrancy; standing peacefully and lovingly, in the midst of other flowers round about; all in like manner opening their bosoms, to drink in the light of the sun.

There was no part of creature-holiness, that I then, and at other times, had so great a sense of the loveliness of, as humility, brokenness of heart and poverty of spirit: and there was nothing that I had such a spirit to long for. My heart, as it were, panted after this to lie low before GOD, and in the dust; that I might be nothing, and that God might be all; that I might become as a little child.[4]

While I was there at New York, I sometimes was much affected with reflections on my past life, considering how late it was, before I began to be truly religious; and how wickedly I had lived till then: and once so as to weep abundantly, and for a considerable time together.

On January 12, 1722-3, I made a solemn dedication of myself to God, and wrote it down; giving up myself, and all that I had to God; to be for the future in no respect my own; to act as one that had no right to himself, in any respect. And solemnly vowed to take God for my whole portion and felicity; looking on nothing else as any part of my happiness, nor acting as if it were: and his law for the constant rule of my obedience; engaging to fight with all my might, against the world, the flesh and the devil, to the end of my life. But have reason to be infinitely humbled, when I consider, how much I have failed of answering my obligation.

I had then abundance of sweet religious conversation in the family where I lived, with Mr. John Smith, and his pious mother. My heart was knit in affection to those, in whom were appearances of true piety; and I could bear the thoughts of no other companions, but such as were holy, and the disciples of the blessed Jesus.

I had great longings for the advancement of Christ's kingdom in the world. My secret prayer used to be in great part taken up in praying for it. If I heard the least hint of anything that happened in any part of the world, that appeared to me, in some respect or other, to have a favorable aspect on the interest of Christ's kingdom, my soul eagerly catched at it; and it would much animate and refresh me. I used to be earnest to read public news-letters, mainly for that end; to see if I could not find some news favorable to the interest of religion in the world.

I very frequently used to retire into a solitary place, on the banks of Hudson's River, at some distance from the city, for contemplation on divine things, and secret converse with God; and had many sweet hours there. Sometimes Mr. Smith and I walked there together, to converse of the things of God; and our conversation used much to turn on the advancement of Christ's kingdom in the world, and the glorious things that God would accomplish for his church in the latter days.

I had then, and at other times, the greatest delight in the holy Scriptures, of any book whatsoever. Oftentimes in reading it, every word seemed to touch my heart. I felt an harmony between something in my heart, and those sweet and powerful words. I seemed often to see so much light, exhibited by every sentence, and such a refreshing ravishing food communicated, that I could not get along in reading. Used oftentimes to dwell long on one sentence, to see the wonders contained in it; and yet almost every sentence seemed to be full of wonders.

I came away from New York in the month of April 1723, and had a most bitter parting with Madam Smith and her son. My heart seemed to sink within me, at leaving the family and city, where I had enjoyed so many sweet and pleasant days. I went from New York to Weathersfield[5] by water. As I sailed away, I kept sight of the city as long as I could; and when I was out

4. "Verily I say unto you, Whosoever shall not receive the kingdom of God as a little child, he shall not enter therein" (Mark 10.15).

5. Wethersfield, Connecticut, is very near his father's home in Windsor.

of sight of it, it would affect me much to look that way, with a kind of melancholy mixed with sweetness. However, that night after this sorrowful parting, I was greatly comforted in God at Westchester, where we went ashore to lodge: and had a pleasant time of it all the voyage to Saybrook.[6] It was sweet to me to think of meeting dear Christians in heaven, where we should never part more. At Saybrook we went ashore to lodge on Saturday, and there kept sabbath; where I had a sweet and refreshing season, walking alone in the fields.

After I came home to Windsor, remained much in a like frame of my mind, as I had been in at New York; but only sometimes felt my heart ready to sink, with the thoughts of my friends at New York. And my refuge and support was in contemplations on the heavenly state; as I find in my diary of May 1, 1723. It was my comfort to think of that state, where there is fulness of joy; where reigns heavenly, sweet, calm and delightful love, without alloy; where there are continually the dearest expressions of this love; where is the enjoyment of the persons loved, without ever parting; where these persons that appear so lovely in this world, will really be inexpressibly more lovely, and full of love to us. And how sweetly will the mutual lovers join together to sing the praises of God and the Lamb![7] How full will it fill us with joy, to think, that this enjoyment, these sweet exercises will never cease or come to an end; but will last to all eternity!

Continued much in the same frame in the general, that I had been in at New York, till I went to New Haven, to live there as Tutor of the College; having some special season of uncommon sweetness: particularly once at Bolton, in a journey from Boston, walking out alone in the fields. After I went to New Haven, I sunk in religion; my mind being diverted from my eager and violent pursuits after holiness, by some affairs that greatly perplexed and distracted my mind.

In September 1725, was taken ill at New Haven; and endeavoring to go home to Windsor, was so ill at the North Village, that I could go no further: where I lay sick for about a quarter of a year. And in this sickness, God was pleased to visit me again with the sweet influences of his spirit. My mind was greatly engaged there on divine, pleasant contemplations, and longings of soul. I observed that those who watched with me, would often be looking out for the morning, and seemed to wish for it. Which brought to my mind those words of the Psalmist, which my soul with sweetness made its own language, "My soul waiteth for the Lord more than they that watch for the morning: I say, more than they that watch for the morning" [Ps. 130:6].[8] And when the light of the morning came, and the beams of the sun came in at the windows, it refreshed my soul from one morning to another. It seemed to me to be some image of the sweet light of God's glory.

I remember, about that time, I used greatly to long for the conversion of some that I was concerned with. It seemed to me, I could gladly honor them, and with delight be a servant to them, and lie at their feet, if they were but truly holy.

But sometime after this, I was again greatly diverted in my mind, with some temporal concerns, that exceedingly took up my thoughts, greatly to

---

6. Westchester and Saybrook are in New York and Connecticut, respectively.

7. In Revelation the symbol of Christ.
8. Psalm 130.6.

the wounding of my soul: and went on through various exercises, that it would be tedious to relate, that gave me much more experience of my own heart, than ever I had before.

Since I came to this town, I have often had sweet complacency[9] in God in views of his glorious perfections, and the excellency of Jesus Christ. God has appeared to me, a glorious and lovely being, chiefly on the account of his holiness. The holiness of God has always appeared to me the most lovely of all his attributes. The doctrines of God's absolute sovereignty, and free grace, in showing mercy to whom he would show mercy; and man's absolute dependence on the operations of God's Holy Spirit, have very often appeared to me as sweet and glorious doctrines. These doctrines have been much my delight. God's sovereignty has ever appeared to me, as great part of his glory. It has often been sweet to me to go to God, and adore him as a sovereign God, and ask sovereign mercy of him.

I have loved the doctrines of the gospel: they have been to my soul like green pastures. The gospel has seemed to me to be the richest treasure; the treasure that I have most desired, and longed that it might dwell richly in me. The way of salvation by Christ, has appeared in a general way, glorious and excellent, and most pleasant and beautiful. It has often seemed to me, that it would in a great measure spoil heaven, to receive it in any other way. That text has often been affecting and delightful to me, Is. 32:2, "A man shall be an hiding place from the wind, and a covert from the tempest," etc.

It has often appeared sweet to me, to be united to Christ; to have him for my head, and to be a member of his body: and also to have Christ for my teacher and prophet. I very often think with sweetness and longings and pantings of soul, of being a little child, taking hold of Christ, to be led by him through the wilderness of this world. That text, Matt. 18 at the beginning, has often been sweet to me, "Except ye be converted, and become as little children," etc. I love to think of coming to Christ, to receive salvation of him, poor in spirit, and quite empty of self; humbly exalting him alone; cut entirely off from my own root, and to grow into, and out of Christ: to have God in Christ to be all in all; and to live by faith in the Son of God, a life of humble, unfeigned confidence in him. That Scripture has often been sweet to me, Ps. 115:1, "Not unto us, O Lord, not unto us, but unto thy name give glory, for thy mercy, and for thy truth's sake." And those words of Christ, Luke 10:21, "In that hour Jesus rejoiced in spirit, and said, I thank thee, O Father, Lord of heaven and earth, that thou hast hid these things from the wise and prudent, and hast revealed them unto babes: even so Father, for so it seemed good in thy sight." That sovereignty of God that Christ rejoiced in, seemed to me to be worthy to be rejoiced in; and that rejoicing of Christ, seemed to me to show the excellency of Christ, and the spirit that he was of.

Sometimes only mentioning a single word, causes my heart to burn within me: or only seeing the name of Christ, or the name of some attribute of God. And God has appeared glorious to me, on account of the Trinity. It has made me have exalting thoughts of God, that he subsists in three persons; Father, Son, and Holy Ghost.

9. Contentment. "This town": Northampton, Massachusetts, where, in 1726, Edwards came to help his grandfather in conducting the affairs of his parish.

The sweetest joys and delights I have experienced, have not been those that have arisen from a hope of my own good estate; but in a direct view of the glorious things of the gospel. When I enjoy this sweetness, it seems to carry me above the thoughts of my own safe estate. It seems at such times a loss that I cannot bear, to take off my eye from the glorious, pleasant object I behold without me, to turn my eye in upon myself, and my own good estate.

My heart has been much on the advancement of Christ's kingdom in the world. The histories of the past advancement of Christ's kingdom, have been sweet to me. When I have read histories of past ages, the pleasantest thing in all my reading has been, to read of the kingdom of Christ being promoted. And when I have expected in my reading, to come to any such thing, I have lotted[1] upon it all the way as I read. And my mind has been much entertained and delighted, with the Scripture promises and prophecies, of the future glorious advancement of Christ's kingdom on earth.

I have sometimes had a sense of the excellent fullness of Christ, and his meetness and suitableness as a Savior; whereby he has appeared to me, far above all, the chief of ten thousands.[2] And his blood and atonement has appeared sweet, and his righteousness sweet; which is always accompanied with an ardency of spirit, and inward strugglings and breathings and groanings, that cannot be uttered, to be emptied of myself, and swallowed up in Christ.

Once, as I rid out into the woods for my health, *anno*[3] 1737; and having lit from my horse in a retired place, as my manner commonly has been, to walk for divine contemplation and prayer; I had a view, that for me was extraordinary, of the glory of the Son of God; as mediator between God and man; and his wonderful, great, full, pure and sweet grace and love, and meek and gentle condescension. This grace, that appeared to me so calm and sweet, appeared great above the heavens. The person of Christ appeared ineffably excellent, with an excellency great enough to swallow up all thought and conception. Which continued, as near as I can judge, about an hour; which kept me, the bigger part of the time, in a flood of tears, and weeping aloud. I felt withal, an ardency of soul to be, what I know not otherwise how to express, than to be emptied and annihilated; to lie in the dust, and to be full of Christ alone; to love him with a holy and pure love; to trust in him; to live upon him; to serve and follow him, and to be totally wrapt up in the fullness of Christ; and to be perfectly sanctified and made pure, with a divine and heavenly purity. I have several other times, had views very much of the same nature, and that have had the same effects.

I have many times had a sense of the glory of the third person in the Trinity, in his office of Sanctifier; in his holy operations communicating divine light and life to the soul. God in the communications of his Holy Spirit, has appeared as an infinite fountain of divine glory and sweetness; being full and sufficient to fill and satisfy the soul: pouring forth itself in sweet communications, like the sun in its glory, sweetly and pleasantly diffusing light and life.

I have sometimes had an affecting sense of the excellency of the word of God, as a word of life; as the light of life; a sweet, excellent, life-giving word:

1. Rejoiced.
2. "My beloved is white and ruddy, the chiefest

among ten thousand" (Song of Solomon 5.10).
3. In the year (Latin).

accompanied with a thirsting after that word, that it might dwell richly in my heart.

I have often since I lived in this town, had very affecting views of my own sinfulness and vileness; very frequently so as to hold me in a kind of loud weeping, sometimes for a considerable time together: so that I have often been forced to shut myself up.[4] I have had a vastly greater sense of my wickedness, and the badness of my heart, since my conversion, than ever I had before. It has often appeared to me, that if God should mark iniquity against me, I should appear the very worst of all mankind; of all that have been since the beginning of the world of this time: and that I should have by far the lowest place in hell. When others that have come to talk with me about their soul concerns, have expressed the sense they have had of their own wickedness, by saying that it seemed to them, that they were as bad as the devil himself; I thought their expressions seemed exceeding faint and feeble, to represent my wickedness. I thought I should wonder, that they should content themselves with such expressions as these, if I had any reason to imagine, that their sin bore any proportion to mine. It seemed to me, I should wonder at myself, if I should express my wickedness in such feeble terms as they did.

My wickedness, as I am in myself, has long appeared to me perfectly ineffable, and infinitely swallowing up all thought and imagination; like an infinite deluge, or infinite mountains over my head. I know not how to express better, what my sins appear to me to be, than by heaping infinite upon infinite, and multiplying infinite by infinite. I go about very often, for this many years, with these expressions in my mind, and in my mouth, "Infinite upon infinite. Infinite upon infinite!" When I look into my heart, and take a view of my wickedness, it looks like an abyss infinitely deeper than hell. And it appears to me, that were it not for free grace, exalted and raised up to the infinite height of all the fullness and glory of the great Jehovah,[5] and the arm of his power and grace stretched forth, in all the majesty of his power, and in all the glory of his sovereignty; I should appear sunk down in my sins infinitely below hell itself, far beyond sight of everything, but the piercing eye of God's grace, that can pierce even down to such a depth, and to the bottom of such an abyss.

And yet, I ben't in the least inclined to think, that I have a greater conviction of sin than ordinary. It seems to me, my conviction of sin is exceeding small, and faint. It appears to me enough to amaze me, that I have no more sense of my sin. I know certainly, that I have very little sense of my sinfulness. That my sins appear to me so great, don't seem to me to be, because I have so much more conviction of sin than other Christians, but because I am so much worse, and have so much more wickedness to be convinced of. When I have had these turns of weeping and crying for my sins, I thought I knew in the time of it, that my repentance was nothing to my sin.

I have greatly longed of late, for a broken heart, and to lie low before God. And when I ask for humility of God, I can't bear the thoughts of being no more humble, than other Christians. It seems to me, that though their degrees of humility may be suitable for them; yet it would be a vile self-exaltation in me, not to be the lowest in humility of all mankind. Others

4. I.e., retire to his study.   5. The name used for God in the Old Testament.

speak of their longing to be humbled to the dust. Though that may be a proper expression for them, I always think for myself, that I ought to be humbled down below hell. 'Tis an expression that it has long been natural for me to use in prayer to God. I ought to lie infinitely low before God.

It is affecting to me to think, how ignorant I was, when I was a young Christian, of the bottomless, infinite depths of wickedness, pride, hypocrisy and deceit left in my heart.

I have vastly a greater sense, of my universal, exceeding dependence on God's grace and strength, and mere good pleasure, of late, than I used formerly to have; and have experienced more of an abhorrence of my own righteousness. The thought of any comfort or joy, arising in me, on any consideration, or reflection on my own amiableness, or any of my performances or experiences, or any goodness of heart or life, is nauseous and detestable to me. And yet I am greatly afflicted with a proud and self-righteous spirit; much more sensibly, than I used to be formerly. I see that serpent rising and putting forth its head, continually, everywhere, all around me.

Though it seems to me, that in some respects I was a far better Christian, for two or three years after my first conversion, than I am now; and lived in a more constant delight and pleasure: yet of late years, I have had a more full and constant sense of the absolute sovereignty of God, and a delight in that sovereignty; and have had more of a sense of the glory of Christ, as a mediator, as revealed in the Gospel. On one Saturday night in particular, had a particular discovery of the excellency of the gospel of Christ, above all other doctrines; so that I could not but say to myself; "This is my chosen light, my chosen doctrine": and of Christ, "This is my chosen prophet." It appeared to me to be sweet beyond all expression, to follow Christ, and to be taught and enlightened and instructed by him; to learn of him, and live to him.

Another Saturday night, January 1738-9, had such a sense, how sweet and blessed a thing it was, to walk in the way of duty, to do that which was right and meet to be done, and agreeable to the holy mind of God; that it caused me to break forth into a kind of a loud weeping, which held me some time; so that I was forced to shut myself up, and fasten the doors. I could not but as it were cry out, "How happy are they which do that which is right in the sight of God! They are blessed indeed, they are the happy ones!" I had at the same time, a very affecting sense, how meet and suitable it was that God should govern the world, and order all things according to his own pleasure; and I rejoiced in it, that God reigned, and that his will was done.

c. 1740   1765

On Sarah Pierpont[1]

They say there is a young lady in [New Haven] who is beloved of that almighty Being, who made and rules the world, and that there are certain seasons in which this great Being, in some way or other invisible, comes to

1. This tribute to Sarah Pierpont was written, according to S. E. Dwight, in 1723, when she was thirteen years old and Edwards, twenty. He married her in 1727. The manuscript appeared in a blank leaf in a book, and no holograph exists. It was first published in Sereno E. Dwight's *The Life of President Edwards* (1829). The text here is from the Yale University Press *Works of Jonathan Edwards*, vol. 16, edited by George Claghorn.

her and fills her mind with exceeding sweet delight, and that she hardly cares for anything, except to meditate on him—that she expects after a while to be received up where he is, to be raised up out of the world and caught up into heaven; being assured that he loves her too well to let her remain at a distance from him always. There she is to dwell with him, and to be ravished with his love favor and delight, forever. Therefore, if you present all the world before her, with the richest of its treasures, she disregards it and cares not for it, and is unmindful of any pain or affliction. She has a strange sweetness in her mind, and sweetness of temper, uncommon purity in her affections; is most just and praiseworthy in all her actions; and you could not persuade her to do anything thought wrong or sinful, if you would give her all the world, lest she should offend this great Being. She is of a wonderful sweetness, calmness and universal benevolence of mind; especially after those times in which this great God has manifested himself to her mind. She will sometimes go about, singing sweetly, from place to [place]; and seems to be always full of joy and pleasure; and no one knows for what. She loves to be alone, and to wander in the fields and on the mountains, and seems to have someone invisible always conversing with her.

1723   1829

A Divine and Supernatural Light[1]

IMMEDIATELY IMPARTED TO THE SOUL BY THE SPIRIT OF GOD, SHOWN TO
BE BOTH A SCRIPTURAL AND RATIONAL DOCTRINE

Matthew 16.17

And Jesus answered and said unto him, Blessed art thou, Simon Barjona;[2] for flesh and blood hath not revealed it unto thee, but my Father which is in heaven.

Christ addresses these words to Peter upon occasion of his professing his faith in Him as the Son of God. Our Lord was inquiring of His disciples, whom men said that He was; not that He needed to be informed, but only to introduce and give occasion to what follows. They answer that some said He was John the Baptist, and some Elias, and others Jeremias, or one of the prophets.[3] When they had thus given an account whom others said that He was, Christ asks them, whom they said that He was? Simon Peter, whom we find always zealous and forward, was the first to answer: he readily replied to the question, Thou art Christ, the Son of the living God.

Upon this occasion, Christ says as He does to him and of him in the text: in which we may observe.

1. That Peter is pronounced blessed on this account.—Blessed art thou—"Thou art an happy man, that thou art not ignorant of this, that I am Christ, the Son of the living God. Thou art distinguishingly happy. Others are blinded, and have dark and deluded apprehensions, as you have now given an account, some thinking that I am Elias, and some that I am Jeremias, and

---

1. Edwards delivered this sermon in Northampton, Massachusetts, in 1733; it was published the following year at the request of his congregation. The text here is from *The Works of Jonathan Edwards* (1829–30), vol. 6, edited by Sereno E. Dwight.
2. The apostle Peter (Simon, son of Jona).
3. Matthew 16.14. Elias is the name used in the New Testament for the prophet Elijah.

some one thing, and some another: but none of them thinking right, all of them are misled. Happy art thou, that art so distinguished as to know the truth in this matter."

2. The evidence of this his happiness declared, viz., That God, and He only, had revealed it to him. This is an evidence of his being blessed.

First. As it shows how peculiarly favored he was of God above others; q.d.,[4] "How highly favored art thou, that others, wise and great men, the scribes, Pharisees,[5] and rulers, and the nation in general, are left in darkness, to follow their own misguided apprehensions; and that thou shouldst be singled out, as it were, by name, that My heavenly Father should thus set His love on thee, Simon Bar-jona.—This argues thee blessed, that thou shouldst thus be the object of God's distinguishing love."

Secondly. It evidences his blessedness also, as it intimates that this knowledge is above any that flesh and blood can reveal. "This is such knowledge as only my Father which is in heaven can give. It is too high and excellent to be communicated by such means as other knowledge is. Thou art blessed, that thou knowest what God alone can teach thee."

The original of this knowledge is here declared, both negatively and positively. Positively, as God is here declared the author of it. Negatively, as it is declared, that flesh and blood had not revealed it. God is the author of all knowledge and understanding whatsoever. He is the author of all moral prudence, and of the skill that men have in their secular business. Thus it is said of all in Israel that were wise-hearted and skilled in embroidering, that God had filled them with the spirit of wisdom. Exodus 28.3.[6]

God is the author of such knowledge; yet so that flesh and blood reveals it. Mortal men are capable of imparting the knowledge of human arts and sciences, and skill in temporal affairs. God is the author of such knowledge by those means: flesh and blood is employed as the mediate or second cause of it; He conveys it by the power and influence of natural means. But this spiritual knowledge, spoken of in the text, is what God is the author of, and none else: He reveals it, and flesh and blood reveals it not. He imparts this knowledge immediately, not making use of any intermediate natural causes, as He does in other knowledge.

What had passed in the preceding discourse naturally occasioned Christ to observe this; because the disciples had been telling how others did not know Him, but were generally mistaken about him, divided and confounded in their opinions of Him: but Peter had declared his assured faith, that He was the Son of God. Now it was natural to observe how it was not flesh and blood that had revealed it to him, but God; for if this knowledge were dependent on natural causes or means, how came it to pass that they, a company of poor fishermen, illiterate men, and persons of low education, attained to the knowledge of the truth, while the Scribes and Pharisees, men of vastly higher advantages, and greater knowledge and sagacity, in other matters, remained in ignorance? This could be owing only to the gracious distinguishing influence and revelation of the Spirit of God. Hence, what I would make the subject of my present discourse from these words, is this:

---

4. I.e., *quasi dicat;* as if he should say (Latin).
5. A sect hostile to Jesus and known for their arrogance and pride (Matthew 9.9–13). "Scribes": interpreters of the Jewish law.

6. This passage from Exodus refers to God's command to the people of Israel to make proper garments for Aaron's priesthood.

Doctrine

That there is such a thing as a spiritual and divine light, immediately imparted to the soul by God, of a different nature from any that is obtained by natural means. And on this subject I would,

I. Show what this divine light is.
II. How it is given immediately by God, and not obtained by natural means.
III. Show the truth of the doctrine.
And then conclude with a brief improvement.[7]

I. I would show what this spiritual and divine light is. And in order to it would show,

First, In a few things, what it is not. And here,

1. Those convictions that natural men may have of their sin and misery, is not this spiritual and divine light. Men, in a natural condition, may have convictions of the guilt that lies upon them, and of the anger of God, and their danger of divine vengeance. Such convictions are from the light of truth. That some sinners have a greater conviction of their guilt and misery than others is because some have more light, or more of an apprehension of truth than others. And this light and conviction may be from the Spirit of God; the Spirit convinces men of sin; but yet nature is much more concerned in it than in the communication of that spiritual and divine light that is spoken of in the doctrine; it is from the Spirit of God only as assisting natural principles, and not as infusing any new principles. Common grace differs from special in that it influences only by assisting of nature, and not by imparting grace, or bestowing anything above nature. The light that is obtained is wholly natural, or of no superior kind to what mere nature attains to, though more of that kind be obtained than would be obtained if men were left wholly to themselves; or, in other words, common grace only assists the faculties of the soul to do that more fully which they do by nature, as natural conscience or reason will by mere nature make a man sensible of guilt, and will accuse and condemn him when he has done amiss. Conscience is a principle natural to men; and the work that it doth naturally, or of itself, is to give an apprehension of right and wrong, and to suggest to the mind the relation that there is between right and wrong and a retribution. The Spirit of God, in those convictions which unregenerate men[8] sometimes have, assists conscience to do this work in a further degree than it would do if they were left to themselves. He helps it against those things that tend to stupify it, and obstruct its exercise. But in the renewing and sanctifying work of the Holy Ghost, those things are wrought in the soul that are above nature, and of which there is nothing of the like kind in the soul by nature; and they are caused to exist in the soul habitually, and according to such a stated constitution or law, that lays such a foundation for exercises in a continued course, as is called a principle of nature. Not only are remaining principles assisted to do their work more freely and fully, but those principles are restored that were utterly destroyed by the fall; and the mind thenceforward

7. Literally, turning something to profit; here used in the sense of the lesson to be learned.

8. Those who are not yet saved.

habitually exerts those acts that the dominion of sin had made it as wholly destitute of as a dead body is of vital acts.

The Spirit of God acts in a very different manner in the one case, from what He doth in the other. He may, indeed, act upon the mind of a natural man, but He acts in the mind of a saint[9] as an indwelling vital principle. He acts upon the mind of an unregenerate person as an extrinsic occasional agent; for, in acting upon them, He doth not unite himself to them: for, notwithstanding all His influences that they may possess, they are still sensual, having not the Spirit. Jude 19.[1] But He unites himself with the mind of a saint, takes him for His temple, actuates and influences him as a new supernatural principle of life and action. There is this difference, that the Spirit of God, in acting in the soul of a godly man, exerts and communicates Himself there in His own proper nature. Holiness is the proper nature of the Spirit of God. The Holy Spirit operates in the minds of the godly, by uniting Himself to them, and living in them, and exerting His own nature in the exercise of their faculties. The Spirit of God may act upon a creature, and yet not in acting communicate Himself. The Spirit of God may act upon inanimate creatures, as, the Spirit moved upon the face of the waters,[2] in the beginning of the creation; so the Spirit of God may act upon the minds of men many ways, and communicate Himself no more than when He acts upon an inanimate creature. For instance, He may excite thoughts in them, may assist their natural reason and understanding, or may assist other natural principles, and this without any union with the soul, but may act, as it were, upon an external object. But as He acts in His holy influences and spiritual operations, He acts in a way of peculiar communication of Himself; so that the subject is thence denominated spiritual.

2. This spiritual and divine light does not consist in any impression made upon the imagination. It is no impression upon the mind, as though one saw anything with the bodily eyes. It is no imagination or idea of an outward light or glory, or any beauty of form or countenance, or a visible luster or brightness of any object. The imagination may be strongly impressed with such things; but this is not spiritual light. Indeed when the mind has a lively discovery of spiritual things, and is greatly affected with the power of divine light, it may, and probably very commonly doth, much affect the imagination; so that impressions of an outward beauty or brightness may accompany those spiritual discoveries. But spiritual light is not that impression upon the imagination, but an exceedingly different thing. Natural men may have lively impressions on their imaginations; and we cannot determine but that the devil, who transforms himself into an angel of light, may cause imaginations of an outward beauty, or visible glory, and of sounds and speeches, and other such things; but these are things of a vastly inferior nature to spiritual light.

3. This spiritual light is not the suggesting of any new truths or propositions not contained in the word of God. This suggesting of new truths or doctrines to the mind, independent of any antecedent revelations of those propositions, either in word or writing, is inspiration; such as the prophets and apostles had, and such as some enthusiasts[3] pretend to. But this spiritual

---

9. Here, a living Christian who has passed from mere understanding of Christ's doctrine to heartfelt commitment; such people were often called "visible saints."
1. "These be they who separate themselves, sen-

sual, having not the Spirit."
2. Genesis 1.2.
3. People who erroneously claim to be inspired by the spirit of God.

light that I am speaking of, is quite a different thing from inspiration. It reveals no new doctrine, it suggests no new proposition to the mind, it teaches no new thing of God, or Christ, or another world, not taught in the Bible, but only gives a due apprehension of those things that are taught in the word of God.

4. It is not every affecting view that men have of religious things that is this spiritual and divine light. Men by mere principles of nature are capable of being affected with things that have a special relation to religion as well as other things. A person by mere nature, for instance, may be liable to be affected with the story of Jesus Christ, and the sufferings he underwent, as well as by any other tragical story. He may be the more affected with it from the interest he conceives mankind to have in it. Yea, he may be affected with it without believing it; as well as a man may be affected with what he reads in a romance, or sees acted in a stage play. He may be affected with a lively and eloquent description of many pleasant things that attend the state of the blessed in heaven, as well as his imagination be entertained by a romantic[4] description of the pleasantness of fairyland, or the like. And a common belief of the truth of such things, from education or otherwise, may help forward their affection. We read in Scripture of many that were greatly affected with things of a religious nature, who yet are there represented as wholly graceless, and many of them very ill[5] men. A person therefore may have affecting views of the things of religion, and yet be very destitute of spiritual light. Flesh and blood may be the author of this; one man may give another an affecting view of divine things with but common assistance; but God alone can give a spiritual discovery of them.—But I proceed to show.

Secondly, Positively what this spiritual and divine light is.

And it may be thus described: A true sense of the divine excellency of the things revealed in the word of God, and a conviction of the truth and reality of them thence arising. This spiritual light primarily consists in the former of these, viz., a real sense and apprehension of the divine excellency of things revealed in the word of God. A spiritual and saving conviction of the truth and reality of these things, arises from such a sight of their divine excellency and glory; so that this conviction of their truth is an effect and natural consequence of this sight of their divine glory. There is therefore in this spiritual light,

1. A true sense of the divine and superlative excellency of the things of religion; a real sense of the excellency of God and Jesus Christ, and of the work of redemption, and the ways and works of God revealed in the gospel. There is a divine and superlative glory in these things; an excellency that is of a vastly higher kind, and more sublime nature than in other things; a glory greatly distinguishing them from all that is earthly and temporal. He that is spiritually enlightened truly apprehends and sees it, or has a sense of it. He does not merely rationally believe that God is glorious, but he has a sense of the gloriousness of God in his heart. There is not only a rational belief that God is holy, and that holiness is a good thing, but there is a sense of the loveliness of God's holiness. There is not only a speculatively judging that God is gracious, but a sense how amiable God is on account of the beauty of this divine attribute.

There is a twofold knowledge of good of which God has made the mind

4. Fanciful, imaginary.　　　　　5. I.e., evil.

of man capable. The first, that which is merely notional; as when a person only speculatively judges that anything is, which by the agreement of mankind, is called good or excellent, viz., that which is most to general advantage, and between which and a reward there is a suitableness,—and the like. And the other is, that which consists in the sense of the heart; as when the heart is sensible[6] of pleasure and delight in the presence of the idea of it. In the former is exercised merely the speculative faculty, or the understanding, in distinction from the will or disposition of the soul. In the latter, the will, or inclination, or heart, are mainly concerned.

Thus there is a difference between having an opinion, that God is holy and gracious, and having a sense of the loveliness and beauty of that holiness and grace. There is a difference between having a rational judgment that honey is sweet, and having a sense of its sweetness. A man may have the former, that knows not how honey tastes; but a man cannot have the latter unless he has an idea of the taste of honey in his mind. So there is a difference between believing that a person is beautiful, and having a sense of his beauty. The former may be obtained by hearsay, but the latter only by seeing the countenance. When the heart is sensible of the beauty and amiableness of a thing, it necessarily feels pleasure in the apprehension. It is implied in a person's being heartily sensible of the loveliness of a thing, that the idea of it is pleasant to his soul; which is a far different thing from having a rational opinion that it is excellent.

2. There arises from this sense of the divine excellency of things contained in the word of God, a conviction of the truth and reality of them; and that, either indirectly or directly.

First, Indirectly, and that two ways:

1. As the prejudices of the heart, against the truth of divine things, are hereby removed; so that the mind becomes susceptive of the due force of rational arguments for their truth. The mind of man is naturally full of prejudices against divine truth. It is full of enmity against the doctrines of the gospel; which is a disadvantage to those arguments that prove their truth, and causes them to lose their force upon the mind. But when a person has discovered to him the divine excellency of Christian doctrines, this destroys the enmity, removes those prejudices, sanctifies the reason, and causes it to lie open to the force of arguments for their truth.

Hence was the different effect that Christ's miracles had to convince the disciples, from what they had to convince the Scribes and Pharisees. Not that they had a stronger reason, or had their reason more improved; but their reason was sanctified, and those blinding prejudices, that the Scribes and Pharisees were under, were removed by the sense they had of the excellency of Christ, and his doctrine.

It not only removes the hindrances of reason, but positively helps reason. It makes even the speculative notions more lively. It engages the attention of the mind, with more fixedness and intenseness to that kind of objects; which causes it to have a clearer view of them, and enables it more clearly to see their mutual relations, and occasions it to take more notice of them. The ideas themselves that otherwise are dim and obscure are by this means impressed with the greater strength, and have a light cast upon them, so that the mind can better judge of them. As he that beholds objects on the face

6. Aware.

of the earth, when the light of the sun is cast upon them, is under greater advantage to discern them in their true forms and natural relations, than he that sees them in a dim twilight.

The mind, being sensible of the excellency of divine objects, dwells upon them with delight; and the powers of the soul are more awakened and enlivened to employ themselves in the contemplation of them, and exert themselves more fully and much more to the purpose. The beauty of the objects draws on the faculties, and draws forth their exercises; so that reason itself is under far greater advantages for its proper and free exercises, and to attain its proper end, free of darkness and delusion.—But,

Secondly, A true sense of the divine excellency of the things of God's word doth more directly and immediately convince us of their truth; and that because the excellency of these things is so superlative. There is a beauty in them so divine and godlike, that it greatly and evidently distinguishes them from things merely human, or that of which men are the inventors and authors; a glory so high and great, that when clearly seen, commands assent to their divine reality. When there is an actual and lively discovery of this beauty and excellency, it will not allow of any such thought as that it is the fruit of men's invention. This is a kind of intuitive and immediate evidence. They believe the doctrines of God's word to be divine, because they see a divine, and transcendent, and most evidently distinguishing glory in them; such a glory as, if clearly seen, does not leave room to doubt of their being of God, and not of men.

Such a conviction of the truths of religion as this, arising from a sense of their divine excellency, is included in saving faith. And this original of it is that by which it is most essentially distinguished from that common assent, of which unregenerate men are capable.

II. I proceed now to the second thing proposed, viz., to show how this light is immediately given by God, and not obtained by natural means. And here,

1. It is not intended that the natural faculties are not used in it. They are the subject of this light: and in such a manner, that they are not merely passive, but active in it. God, in letting in this light into the soul, deals with man according to his nature, and makes use of his rational faculties. But yet this light is not the less immediately from God for that; the faculties are made use of as the subject, and not as the cause. As the use we make of our eyes in beholding various objects, when the sun arises, is not the cause of the light that discovers those objects to us.

2. It is not intended that outward means have no concern in this affair. It is not in this affair, as in inspiration, where new truths are suggested; for, by this light is given only a due apprehension of the same truths that are revealed in the word of God, and therefore it is not given without the word. The gospel is employed in this affair. This light is the "light of the glorious gospel of Christ" (2 Corinthians 4.3–4).[7] The gospel is as a glass, by which this light is conveyed to us (1 Corinthians 13.12): "Now we see through a glass."[8]—But,

---

7. "But if our gospel be hid, it is hid to them that are lost: In whom the god of this world hath blinded the minds of them which believe not, lest the light of the glorious gospel of Christ, who is the image of God, should shine unto them."
8. "For now we see through a glass, darkly; but then face to face."

3. When it is said that this light is given immediately by God, and not obtained by natural means, hereby is intended that it is given by God without making use of any means that operate by their own power or natural force. God makes use of means; but it is not as mediate causes to produce this effect. There are not truly any second causes of it; but it is produced by God immediately. The word of God is no proper cause of this effect, but is made use of only to convey to the mind the subject matter of this saving instruction: And this indeed it doth convey to us by natural force or influence. It conveys to our minds these doctrines; it is the cause of a notion of them in our heads, but not of the sense of their divine excellency in our hearts. Indeed a person cannot have spiritual light without the word. But that does not argue, that the word properly causes that light. The mind cannot see the excellency of any doctrine, unless that doctrine be first in the mind; but seeing the excellency of the doctrine may be immediately from the Spirit of God; though the conveying of the doctrine, or proposition, itself, may be by the word. So that the notions which are the subject matter of this light are conveyed to the mind by the word of God; but that due sense of the heart, wherein this light formally consists, is immediately by the Spirit of God. As, for instance, the notion that there is a Christ, and that Christ is holy and gracious, is conveyed to the mind by the word of God: But the sense of the excellency of Christ, by reason of that holiness and grace, is nevertheless, immediately the work of the Holy Spirit.—I come now,

III. To show the truth of the doctrine; that is, to show that there is such a thing as that spiritual light that has been described, thus immediately let into the mind by God. And here I would show, briefly, that this doctrine is both scriptural and rational.

First, It is scriptural. My text is not only full to the purpose, but it is a doctrine with which the Scripture abounds. We are there abundantly taught, that the saints differ from the ungodly in this; that they have the knowledge of God, and a sight of God, and of Jesus Christ. I shall mention but few texts out of many: 1 John 3.6: "Whosoever sinneth, hath not seen him, nor known him." 3 John 11: "He that doeth good, is of God: but he that doeth evil, hath not seen God." John 14.19: "The world seeth me no more; but ye see me." John 17.3: "And this is eternal life, that they might know thee, the only true God, and Jesus Christ whom thou hast sent." This knowledge, or sight of God and Christ, cannot be a mere speculative knowledge, because it is spoken of as that wherein they differ from the ungodly. And by these scriptures, it must not only be a different knowledge in degree and circumstances, and different in its effects, but it must be entirely different in nature and kind.

And this light and knowledge is always spoken of as immediately given of God; Matthew 11.25–27: "At that time, Jesus answered and said, I thank thee, O Father, Lord of heaven and earth, because thou hast hid these things from the wise and prudent, and hast revealed them unto babes. Even so, Father, for so it seemed good in thy sight. All things are delivered unto me of my Father: and no man knoweth the Father, save the Son, and he to whomsoever the Son will reveal him." Here this effect is ascribed exclusively to the arbitrary operation and gift of God bestowing this knowledge on whom He will, and distinguishing those with it who have the least natural advantage or means for knowledge, even babes, when it is denied to the wise and prudent. And imparting this knowledge is here appropriated to the Son of God, as His sole prerogative. And again, 2 Corinthians 4.6: "For God, who commanded the light to shine out of darkness, hath shined in our hearts, to give the light of the knowledge of the glory of God, in the face of Jesus Christ." This plainly shows, that there is a discovery of the divine superlative glory and excellency of God and Christ, peculiar to the saints: and, also, that it is as immediately from God, as light from the sun, and that it is the immediate effect of His power and will. For it is compared to God's creating the light by his powerful word in the beginning of the creation; and is said to be by the Spirit of the Lord, in the 18th verse of the preceding chapter. God is spoken of as giving the knowledge of Christ in conversion, as of what before was hidden and unseen; Galatians 1.15–16: "But when it pleased God, who separated me from my mother's womb, and called me by his grace, to reveal his son in me." The scripture also speaks plainly of such a knowledge of the word of God, as has been described as the immediate gift of God; Psalm 119.18: "Open thou mine eyes, that I may behold wondrous things out of thy law." What could the Psalmist mean, when he begged of God to open his eyes? Was he ever blind? Might he not have resort to the law, and see every word and sentence in it when he pleased? And what could he mean by those wondrous things? Were they the wonderful stories of the creation, and deluge, and Israel's passing through the Red Sea,[9] and the like? Were not his eyes open to read these strange things when he would? Doubtless, by wondrous things in God's law, he had respect to those distinguishing and wonderful excellencies, and marvelous manifestations of the divine perfections and glory contained in the commands and doctrines of the word, and those works and counsels of God that were there revealed. So the scripture speaks of a knowledge of God's dispensation, and covenant of mercy,[1] and way of grace towards His people, as peculiar to the saints, and given only by God; Psalm 25.14: "The secret of the Lord is with them that fear him; and he will show them his covenant."

And that a true and saving belief of the truth of religion is that which arises from such a discovery is, also, what the scripture teaches. As John 6.40: "And this is the will of him that sent me, that every one who seeth the Son, and believeth on him, may have everlasting life"; where it is plain that a true faith is what arises from a spiritual sight of Christ. And John 17.6–8: "I have manifested thy name unto the men which thou gavest me out of the world. Now, they have known, that all things whatsoever thou hast given me, are of thee. For I have given unto them the words which thou gavest me, and they have received them, and have known surely, that I came out from thee, and they have believed that thou didst send me"; where Christ's manifesting God's name to the disciples, or giving them the knowledge of God, was that whereby they knew that Christ's doctrine was of God, and that Christ Himself proceeded from Him, and was sent by Him. Again, John 12.44–46: "Jesus cried, and said, He that believeth on me, believeth not on me but on him that sent me. And he that seeth me, seeth him that sent me. I am come a light into the world, that whosoever believeth on me, should not abide in darkness." Their believing in Christ, and spiritually seeing Him, are parallel.

Christ condemns the Jews, that they did not know that He was the Mes-

9. The waters of the Red Sea divided for the Israelites in their exodus from Egypt (Exodus 14.21).
1. The agreement between Christ and those who believe in him that they would be saved; also known as the Covenant of Faith, as distinct from the Covenant of Works, which Adam broke.

siah, and that His doctrine was true, from an inward distinguishing taste and relish of what was divine, in Luke 12.56–57. He having there blamed the Jews, that, though they could discern the face of the sky and of the earth, and signs of the weather, that yet they could not discern those times—or, as it is expressed in Matthew, the signs of those times—adds, "yea, and why even of your ownselves, judge ye not what is right?" i.e., without extrinsic signs. Why have ye not that sense of true excellency, whereby ye may distinguish that which is holy and divine? Why have ye not that savor of the things of God, by which you may see the distinguishing glory, and evident divinity of me and my doctrine?

The apostle Peter mentions it as what gave him and his companions good and well-grounded assurance of the truth of the gospel, that they had seen the divine glory of Christ. 2 Peter 1.16: "For we have not followed cunningly devised fables, when we made known unto you the power and coming of our Lord Jesus Christ, but were eye-witnesses of his majesty." The apostle has respect to that visible glory of Christ which they saw in His transfiguration. That glory was so divine, having such an ineffable appearance and semblance of divine holiness, majesty, and grace, that it evidently denoted Him to be a divine person. But if a sight of Christ's outward glory might give a rational assurance of His divinity, why may not an apprehension of His spiritual glory do so too? Doubtless Christ's spiritual glory is in itself as distinguishing, and as plainly shows His divinity, as His outward glory—nay, a great deal more, for His spiritual glory is that wherein His divinity consists; and the outward glory of His transfiguration showed Him to be divine, only as it was a remarkable image or representation of that spiritual glory. Doubtless, therefore, he that has had a clear sight of the spiritual glory of Christ, may say, "I have not followed cunningly devised fables, but have been an eyewitness of His majesty, upon as good grounds as the apostle, when he had respect to the outward glory of Christ that he had seen." But this brings me to what was proposed next, viz., to show that,

Secondly, This doctrine is rational.[2]

1. It is rational to suppose, that there is really such an excellency in divine things—so transcendent and exceedingly different from what is in other things—that if it were seen, would most evidently distinguish them. We cannot rationally doubt but that things divine, which appertain to the supreme Being, are vastly different from things that are human; that there is a high, glorious, and godlike excellency in them that does most remarkably difference them from the things that are of men, insomuch that if the difference were but seen, it would have a convincing, satisfying influence upon anyone that they are divine. What reason can be offered against it unless we would argue that God is not remarkably distinguished in glory from men.

If Christ should now appear to any one as he did on the mount at His transfiguration,[3] or if He should appear to the world in His heavenly glory, as He will do at the Day of Judgment,[4] without doubt, His glory and majesty would be such as would satisfy everyone that He was a divine person, and that His religion was true; and it would be a most reasonable, and well grounded conviction too. And why may there not be that stamp of divinity

2. Capable of being grasped by the mind, understandable.
3. In Matthew 17.1–8, Christ appeared to Peter, James, and John shining "as the sun" and his garments "white as the light."
4. See Revelation 4.

or divine glory on the word of God, on the scheme and doctrine of the gospel, that may be in like manner distinguishing and as rationally convincing, provided it be but seen? It is rational to suppose, that when God speaks to the world, there should be something in His word vastly different from men's word. Supposing that God never had spoken to the world, but we had notice that He was about to reveal Himself from heaven and speak to us immediately Himself, or that He should give us a book of His own inditing;[5] after what manner should we expect that He would speak? Would it not be rational to suppose, that His speech would be exceeding different from men's speech, that there should be such an excellency and sublimity in His word, such a stamp of wisdom, holiness, majesty, and other divine perfections, that the word of men, yea of the wisest of men, should appear mean and base in comparison of it? Doubtless it would be thought rational to expect this, and unreasonable to think otherwise. When a wise man speaks in the exercise of His wisdom, there is something in everything He says, that is very distinguishable from the talk of a little child. So, without doubt, and much more is the speech of God, to be distinguished from that of the wisest of men; agreeable to Jeremiah 23.28–29. God, having there been reproving the false prophets that prophesied in his name, and pretended that what they spake was His word, when indeed it was their own word, says, "The prophet that hath a dream, let him tell a dream; and he that hath my word let him speak my word faithfully: what is the chaff to the wheat? saith the Lord. Is not my word like as a fire? saith the Lord: and like a hammer that breaketh the rock in pieces?"

2. If there be such a distinguishing excellency in divine things, it is rational to suppose that there may be such a thing as seeing it. What should hinder but that it may be seen? It is no argument that there is no such distinguishing excellency, or that it cannot be seen, because some do not see it, though they may be discerning men in temporal matters. It is not rational to suppose, if there be any such excellency in divine things, that wicked men should see it. Is it rational to suppose that those whose minds are full of spiritual pollution, and under the power of filthy lusts, should have any relish or sense of divine beauty or excellency; or that their minds should be susceptive of that light that is in its own nature so pure and heavenly? It need not seem at all strange that sin should so blind the mind, seeing that men's particular natural tempers and dispositions will so much blind them in secular matters; as when men's natural temper is melancholy, jealous, fearful, proud, or the like.

3. It is rational to suppose that this knowledge should be given immediately by God, and not be obtained by natural means. Upon what account should it seem unreasonable that there should be any immediate communication between God and the creature? It is strange, that men should make any matter of difficulty of it. Why should not He that made all things still have something immediately to do with the things that He has made? Where lies the great difficulty, if we own the being of a God, and that He created all things out of nothing, of allowing some immediate influence of God on the creation still? And if it be reasonable to suppose it with respect to any part of the creation, it is especially so with respect to reasonable, intelligent

5. Composition.

creatures; who are next to God in the gradation of the different orders of beings, and whose business is most immediately with God; and reason teaches that man was made to serve and glorify his Creator. And if it be rational to suppose that God immediately communicates Himself to man in any affair, it is in this. It is rational to suppose that God would reserve that knowledge and wisdom, which is of such a divine and excellent nature, to be bestowed immediately by Himself, and that it should not be left in the power of second causes. Spiritual wisdom and grace is the highest and most excellent gift that ever God bestows on any creature; in this, the highest excellency and perfection of a rational creature consists. It is also immensely the most important of all divine gifts: it is that wherein man's happiness consists, and on which his everlasting welfare depends. How rational is it to suppose that God, however He has left lower gifts to second causes, and in some sort in their power, yet should reserve this most excellent, divine, and important of all divine communications in His own hands to be bestowed immediately by Himself, as a thing too great for second causes to be concerned in. It is rational to suppose that this blessing should be immediately from God, for there is no gift or benefit that is in itself so nearly related to the divine nature. Nothing which the creature receives is so much a participation of the Deity; it is a kind of emanation of God's beauty, and is related to God as the light is to the sun. It is, therefore, congruous and fit, that when it is given of God, it should be immediately from Himself, and by Himself, according to His own sovereign will.

It is rational to suppose, that it should be beyond man's power to obtain this light by the mere strength of natural reason; for it is not a thing that belongs to reason to see the beauty and loveliness of spiritual things; it is not a speculative thing, but depends on the sense of the heart. Reason, indeed, is necessary, in order to it, as it is by reason only that we are become the subjects of the means of it; which means, I have already shown to be necessary in order to it, though they have no proper causal influence in the affair. It is by reason that we become possessed of a notion of those doctrines that are the subject matter of this divine light or knowledge; and reason may many ways be indirectly and remotely an advantage to it. Reason has also to do in the acts that are immediately consequent on this discovery: for, seeing the truth of religion from hence, is by reason, though it be but by one step, and the inference be immediate. So reason has to do in that accepting of and trusting in Christ that is consequent on it. But if we take reason strictly— not for the faculty of mental perception in general, but for ratiocination, or a power of inferring by arguments—the perceiving of spiritual beauty and excellency no more belongs to reason than it belongs to the sense of feeling to perceive colors, or to the power of seeing to perceive the sweetness of food. It is out of reason's province to perceive the beauty or loveliness of anything; such a perception does not belong to that faculty. Reason's work is to perceive truth and not excellency. It is not ratiocination that gives men the perception of the beauty and amiableness of a countenance, though it may be many ways indirectly an advantage to it; yet it is no more reason that immediately perceives it than it is reason that perceives the sweetness of honey; it depends on the sense of the heart. Reason may determine that a countenance is beautiful to others, it may determine that honey is sweet to others, but it will never give me a perception of its sweetness.

I will conclude with a very brief improvement of what has been said.

First, this doctrine may lead us to reflect on the goodness of God, that has so ordered it, that a saving evidence of the truth of the Gospel is such as is attainable by persons of mean capacities and advantages, as well as those that are of the greatest parts and learning. If the evidence of the Gospel depended only on history and such reasonings as learned men only are capable of, it would be above the reach of far the greatest part of mankind. But persons with an ordinary degree of knowledge are capable, without a long and subtle train of reasoning, to see the divine excellency of the things of religion; they are capable of being taught by the Spirit of God, as well as learned men. The evidence that is this way obtained is vastly better and more satisfying than all that can be obtained by the arguings of those that are most learned and greatest masters of reason. And babes are as capable of knowing these things as the wise and prudent; and they are often hid from these when they are revealed to those. 1 Corinthians 1.26–27: "For ye see your calling, brethren, how that not many wise men, after the flesh, not many mighty, not many noble, are called. But God hath chosen the foolish things of the world."

Secondly, This doctrine may well put us upon examining ourselves, whether we have ever had this divine light let into our souls. If there be such a thing, doubtless it is of great importance whether we have thus been taught by the Spirit of God; whether the light of the glorious gospel of Christ, who is the image of God, hath shined unto us, giving us the light of the knowledge of the glory of God in the face of Jesus Christ; whether we have seen the Son, and believed on Him, or have that faith of gospel doctrines which arises from a spiritual sight of Christ.

Thirdly, All may hence be exhorted earnestly to seek this spiritual light. To influence and move to it, the following things may be considered.

1. This is the most excellent and divine wisdom that any creature is capable of. It is more excellent than any human learning; it is far more excellent than all the knowledge of the greatest philosophers or statesmen. Yea, the least glimpse of the glory of God in the face of Christ doth more exalt and ennoble the soul than all the knowledge of those that have the greatest speculative understanding in divinity without grace. This knowledge has the most noble object that can be, viz., the divine glory and excellency of God and Christ. The knowledge of these objects is that wherein consists the most excellent knowledge of the angels, yea, of God Himself.

2. This knowledge is that which is above all others sweet and joyful. Men have a great deal of pleasure in human knowledge, in studies of natural things; but this is nothing to that joy which arises from this divine light shining into the soul. This light gives a view of those things that are immensely the most exquisitely beautiful and capable of delighting the eye of the understanding. The spiritual light is the dawning of the light of glory in the heart. There is nothing so powerful as this to support persons in affliction, and to give the mind peace and brightness in this stormy and dark world.

3. This light is such as effectually influences the inclination and changes the nature of the soul. It assimilates our nature to the divine nature, and changes the soul into an image of the same glory that is beheld. 2 Corinthians 3.18: "But we all with open face, beholding as in a glass the glory of the Lord, are changed into the same image, from glory to glory, even as by the

Spirit of the Lord." This knowledge will wean from[6] the world, and raise the inclination to heavenly things. It will turn the heart to God as the fountain of good, and to choose Him for the only portion. This light, and this only, will bring the soul to a saving close with Christ. It conforms the heart to the gospel, mortifies its enmity and opposition against the scheme of salvation therein revealed; it causes the heart to embrace the joyful tidings, and entirely to adhere to, and acquiesce in, the revelation of Christ as our Savior; it causes the whole soul to accord and symphonize with it, admitting it with entire credit and respect, cleaving to it with full inclination and affection; and it effectually disposes the soul to give up itself entirely to Christ.

4. This light, and this only, has its fruit in an universal holiness of life. No merely notional or speculative understanding of the doctrines of religion will ever bring to this. But this light, as it reaches the bottom of the heart, and changes the nature, so it will effectually dispose to an universal obedience. It shows God as worthy to be obeyed and served. It draws forth the heart in a sincere love to God, which is the only principle of a true, gracious, and universal obedience, and it convinces of the reality of those glorious rewards that God has promised to them that obey Him.

1733   1734

Letter to Rev. Dr. Benjamin Colman[1] (May 30, 1735)

[THE GREAT AWAKENING]

Dear Sir:

In answer to your desire, I here send you a particular account of the present extraordinary circumstances of this town, and the neighboring towns with respect to religion.[2] I have observed that the town for this several years have gradually been reforming; there has appeared less and less of a party spirit, and a contentious disposition, which before had prevailed for many years between two parties in the town.[3] The young people also have been reforming more and more; they by degrees left off their frolicking, and have been observably more decent in their attendance on the public worship. The winter before last there appeared a strange flexibleness in the young people of the town, and an unusual disposition to hearken to counsel, on this occasion. It had been their manner of a long time, and for aught I know, always, to make Sabbath-day nights and lecture days[4] to be especially times of diver-

6. Draw us away from.
1. Reverend Colman, pastor of the Brattle Street Church in Boston, had written to Edwards to ask him to explain some of the events concerning the religious revivals in Northampton. Edwards complied and at Colman's request expanded his original letter with a fuller account. Colman published this second letter (abridged) in an appendix to a volume of William Williams's sermons in 1736. Edwards made a copy of his first letter, and the manuscript survives in the Andover Theological Library. It was published for the first time by Clarence H. Faust and Thomas H. Johnson in their 1935 edition of *Jonathan Edwards: Representative Selections*. The text here is from the Yale University Press *Works of Jonathan Edwards*, vol. 4. The bracketed emendations are by the editor of that volume, C. C. Goen.
2. A reference to the great revival in religious feel-

ing experienced by members of his congregation in 1734. The Northampton revival was the first of a series of such revivals, now known as the "Great Awakening," which spread from Maine to Georgia. By 1750 these revivals seem to have run their course. Edwards's fullest account may be found in *A Faithful Narrative* (1737), an expanded version of his letters to Colman.
3. In a letter to the Reverend Thomas Gillespie of Scotland, July 1, 1751, Edwards refers to these two parties but does not name them. He says that "in one ecclesiastical controversy in Mr. Stoddard's days, wherein the church was divided into two parties, the heat of spirit was raised to such a height, that it came to hard blows; a member of one party met the head of the opposite party, and assaulted him and beat him unmercifully."
4. Days during the week when sermons less formal than the Sabbath sermon were given.

sion and company keeping. I then preached a sermon on the Sabbath before the lecture, to show them the unsuitableness and inconvenience of the practice, and to persuade them to reform it; and urged it on heads of families that it should be a thing agreed among them to govern their families, and keep them in at those times. And there happened to be at my house the evening after, men that belonged to the several parts of the town, to whom I moved that they should desire the heads of families, in my name, to meet together in their several neighborhoods, that they might know each others' minds, and agree every one to restrain his family; which was done, and my motion complied with throughout the town. But the parents found little or no occasion for the exercise of government in the case; for the young people declared themselves convinced by what they had heard, and willing of themselves to comply with the counsel given them; and I suppose it was almost universally complied with thenceforward.

After this there began to be a remarkable religious concern among some farm houses at a place called Pascommuck,[5] and five or six that I hoped were savingly wrought upon there. And in April [1734] there was a very sudden and awful death of a young man in town, in the very bloom of his youth, who was violently seized with a pleurisy[6] and taken immediately out of his head, and died in two days; which much affected many young people in the town. This was followed with another death of a young married woman, who was in great distress in the beginning of her illness, but was hopefully converted before her death; so that she died full of comfort, and in a most earnest and moving manner, warning and counselling others, which I believe much contributed to the solemnizing of the spirits of the young people in the town; and there began evidently to appear more of a religious concern upon people's minds. In the fall of the year I moved to the young people that they should set up religious meetings, on evenings after lectures, which they complied with; this was followed with the death of an elderly person in the town, which was attended with very unusual circumstances, which much affected many people. About that time began the great noise that there was in this part of the country about Arminianism,[7] which seemed strangely to be overruled for the promoting of religion. People seemed to be put by it upon inquiring, with concern and engagedness of mind, what was the way of salvation, and what were the terms of our acceptance with God; and what was said publicly on that occasion, however found fault with by many elsewhere, and ridiculed by some, was most evidently attended with a very remarkable blessing of heaven, to the souls of the people in this town, to the giving of them an universal satisfaction and engaging their minds with respect to the thing in question, the more earnestly to seek salvation in the way that had been made evident to them.

And then a concern about the great things of religion began, about the latter end of December and the beginning of January [1735], to prevail abundantly in the town, till in a very little time it became universal throughout the town, among old and young, and from the highest to the lowest. All seemed to be seized with a deep concern about their eternal salvation; all

5. A community three miles from Northampton, Massachusetts, a part of Edwards's congregation.
6. A respiratory disease.
7. Arminians believed that humanity was able to save itself and were, therefore, anathema to the Puritans, who believed that humanity's salvation depended entirely on God.

the talk in all companies, and upon occasions was upon the things of religion, and no other talk was anywhere relished; and scarcely a single person in the whole town was left unconcerned about the great things of the eternal world. Those that were wont to be the vainest and loosest persons in town seemed in general to be seized with strong convictions. Those that were most disposed to contemn vital and experimental[8] religion, and those that had the greatest conceit of their own reason, the highest families in the town, and the oldest persons in the town, and many little children were affected remarkably; no one family that I know of, and scarcely a person, has been exempt. And the Spirit of God went on in his saving influences, to the appearance of all human reason and charity, in a truly wonderful and astonishing manner. The news of it filled the neighboring towns with talk, and there were many in them that scoffed and made a ridicule of the religion that appeared in Northampton. But it was observable that it was very frequent and common that those of other towns that came into this town, and observed how it was here, were greatly affected, and went home with wounded spirits, and were never more able to shake off the impression that it made upon them, till at length there began to appear a general concern in several of the towns in the county.

In the month of March the people in New Hadley[9] seemed to be seized with a deep concern about their salvation, all as it were at once, which has continued in a very great degree ever since. About the same time there began to appear the like concern in the west part of Suffield, which has since spread into all parts of the town. It next began to appear at Sunderland, and soon became universal, and to a very great degree. About the same time it began to appear in part of Deerfield, called Green River, and since has filled the town. It began to appear also at a part of Hatfield, and after that the whole town in the second week in April seemed to be seized at once, and there is a great and general concern there. And there gradually got in a considerable degree of the same concern into Hadley Old Society, and Mr. Hopkins'[1] parish in [West] Springfield, but it is nothing near so great as in many other places. The next place that we heard of was Northfield, where the concern is very great and general. We have heard that there is a considerable degree of it at Longmeadow, and there is something of it in Old Springfield in some parts of the society. About three weeks ago the town of Enfield[2] were struck down as it were at once, the worst persons in the town seemed to be suddenly seized with a great degree of concern about their souls, as I have been informed. And about the same time, Mr. Bull[3] of Westfield [said] that there began to be a great alteration there, and that there had been more done in one week before that time that I spoke with him than had been done in seven years before. The people of Westfield have till now above all other places, made a scoff and derision of this concern at Northampton. There has been a great concern of a like nature at Windsor, on the west side of the [Connecticut] River, which began about the same time that it began to be general

8. I.e., religious feeling that was tested as to its depth and truth. "Contemn": despise.
9. Later called South Hadley, Massachusetts, about seven miles east of Northampton. Most of the towns mentioned in this paragraph are within a twenty-mile radius of Northampton.

1. Samuel Hopkins (1693–1755), pastor in West Springfield, Massachusetts.
2. In Connecticut, where Edwards gave his sermon "Sinners in the Hands of an Angry God."
3. Nehemiah Bull (1701–1740), pastor at Westfield, Massachusetts.

here at Northampton; and my father has told me that there is an hopeful beginning on the east side in his society.[4] Mr. Noyes[5] writes me word that there is a considerable revival of religion at New Haven; and I have been credibly informed that there is something of it at Guilford and Lyme, as there also is at Coventry, Bolton, and a society in Lebanon called The Crank. I yesterday saw Mr. White[6] of Bolton, and also last night saw a young man that belongs to [the church at] Coventry, who gave a very remarkable account of that town, of the manner in which the rude debauched young people there were suddenly seized with a concern about their souls.

As to the nature of persons' experiences, and the influences of that spirit that there is amongst us, persons when seized with concern are brought to forsake their vices, and ill practices; the looser sort are brought to forsake and to dread their former extravagances. Persons are soon brought to have done with their old quarrels; contention and intermeddling with other men's matters seems to be dead amongst us. I believe there never was so much done at confessing of faults to each other, and making up differences, as there has lately been. Where this concern comes it immediately puts an end to differences between ministers and people: there was a considerable uneasiness at New Hadley between some of the people and their minister, but when this concern came amongst them it immediately put an end to it, and the people are now universally united to their minister. There was an exceeding alienation at Sunderland, between the minister and many of the people; but when this concern came amongst them it all vanished at once, and the people are universally united in hearty affection to their minister. There were some men at Deerfield, of turbulent spirits, that kept up an uneasiness there with Mr. Ashley;[7] but one of the chief of them has lately been influenced fully and freely to confess his fault to him, and is become his hearty friend.

People are brought off from inordinate engagedness after the world, and have been ready to run into the other extreme of too much neglecting their worldly business and to mind nothing but religion. Those that are under convictions are put upon it earnestly to inquire what they shall do to be saved, and diligently to use appointed means of grace, and apply themselves to all known duty. And those that obtain hope themselves, and the charity of others concerning their good estate, generally seem to be brought to a great sense of their own exceeding misery in a natural condition, and their utter helplessness, and insufficiency for themselves, and their exceeding wickedness and guiltiness in the sight of God; it seldom fails but that each one seems to think himself worse than anybody else, and they are brought to see that they deserve no mercy of God, that all their prayers and pains are exceeding worthless and polluted, and that God, notwithstanding all that they have done, or can do, may justly execute his eternal wrath upon them, and they seem to be brought to a lively sense of the excellency of Jesus Christ and his sufficiency and willingness to save sinners, and to be much weaned in their affections from the world, and to have their hearts filled with love

4. Timothy Edwards (1669–1758), Edwards's father and pastor at East Windsor, Connecticut.
5. Joseph Noyes (1688–1761), pastor at the First Church in New Haven, Connecticut.

6. Thomas White (1701–1763), pastor at Bolton, Connecticut. Guilford, Lyme, Coventry, and Bolton are all in Connecticut.
7. The Reverend Jonathan Ashley (1712–1780).

to God and Christ, and a disposition to lie in the dust before him. They seem to have given [to] them a lively conviction of the truth of the Gospel, and the divine authority of the Holy Scriptures; though they can't have the exercise of this at all times alike, nor indeed of any other grace. They seem to be brought to abhor themselves for the sins of their past life, and to long to be holy, and to live holily, and to God's glory; but at the same time complain that they can do nothing, [for] they are poor impotent creatures, utterly insufficient to glorify their Creator and Redeemer. They commonly seem to be much more sensible of their own wickedness after their conversion than before, so that they are often humbled by it; it seems to them that they are really become more wicked, when at the same time they are evidently full of a gracious spirit. Their remaining sin seems to be their very great burden, and many of them seem to long after heaven, that there they may be rid of sin. They generally seem to be united in dear love and affection one to another, and to have a love to all mankind. I never saw the Christian spirit in love to enemies so exemplified in all my life as I have seen it within this half year. They commonly express a great concern for others' salvation; some say that they think they are far more concerned for others' conversion, after they themselves have been converted, than ever they were for their own; several have thought (though perhaps they might be deceived in it) that they could freely die for the salvation of any soul, of the meanest of mankind, of any Indian in the woods.

This town never was so full of love, nor so full of joy, nor so full of distress as it has lately been. Some persons have had those longing desires after Jesus Christ, that have been to that degree as to take away their strength, and very much to weaken them, and make them faint. Many have been even overcome with a sense of the dying love of Christ, so that the home of the body has been ready to fail under it; there was once three pious young persons in this town talking together of the dying love of Christ, till they all fainted away; though 'tis probable the fainting of the two latter was much promoted by the fainting of the first. Many express a sense of the glory of the divine perfections, and of the excellency and fullness of Jesus Christ, and of their own littleness and unworthiness, in a manner truly wonderful and almost unparalleled; and so likewise of the excellency and wonderfulness of the way of salvation by Jesus Christ. Their esteem of the Holy Scriptures is exceedingly increased. Many of them say the Bible seems to be a new book to them, as though they never read it before. There have been some instances of persons that by only an accidental sight of the Bible, have been as much moved, it seemed to me, as a lover by the sight of his sweetheart. The preaching of the Word is greatly prized by them; they say they never heard preaching before: and so are God's Sabbaths, and ordinances,[8] and opportunities of public worship. The Sabbath is longed for before it comes; some by only hearing the bell ring on some occasion in the week time, have been greatly moved, because it has put them in mind of its ringing to call the people together to worship God. But no part of public worship has commonly [had] such an effect on them as singing God's praises. They have a greater respect to ministers than they used to have; there is scarcely a minister preaches here but gets their esteem and affection.

8. Church laws and regulations.

The experiences of some persons lately amongst [us] have been beyond almost all that ever I heard or read of. There is a pious woman in this town that is a very modest bashful person, that was moved by what she heard of the experiences of others earnestly to seek to God to give her more clear manifestations of himself, and evidences of her own good estate, and God answered her request, and gradually gave her more and more of a sense of his glory and love, which she had with intermissions for several days, till one morning the week before last she had it to a more than ordinary degree, and it prevailed more and more till towards the middle of the day, till her nature began to sink under it, as she was alone in the house; but there came somebody into the house, and found her in an unusual, extraordinary frame. She expressed what she saw and felt to him; it came to that at last that they raised the neighbors, [for] they were afraid she would die; I went up to see her and found her perfectly sober and in the exercise of her reason, but having her nature seemingly overborne and sinking, and when she could speak expressing in a manner that can't be described the sense she had of the glory of God, and particularly of such and such perfections, and her own unworthiness, her longing to lie in the dust, sometimes her longing to go to be with Christ, and crying out of the excellency of Christ, and the wonderfulness of his dying love; and so she continued for hours together, though not always in the same degree. At some times she was able to discourse to those about her; but it seemed to me [that] if God had manifested a little more of himself to her she would immediately have sunk and her frame dissolved under it. She has since been at my house, and continues as full as she can hold, but looks on herself not as an eminent saint,[9] but as the worst of all, and unworthy to go to speak with a minister; but yet now beyond any great doubt of her good estate.

There are two persons that belong to other towns that have had such a sense of God's exceeding greatness and majesty, that they were as it were swallowed up; they both of them told me to that purpose that if in the time of it they had had the least fear that they were not at peace with that great God, they should immediately have died. But there is a very vast variety of degrees of spiritual discoveries, that are made to those that we hope are godly, as there is also in the steps, and method of the Spirit's operation in convincing and converting sinners, and the length of time that persons are under conviction before they have comfort.

There is an alteration made in the town in a few months that strangers can scarcely conceive of; our church I believe was the largest in New England before, but persons lately have thronged in, so that there are very few adult persons left out.[1] There have been a great multitude hopefully converted; too many, I find, for me to declare abroad with credit to my judgment. The town seems to be full of the presence of God; our young people when they get together instead of frolicking as they used to do are altogether on pious subjects; 'tis so at weddings and on all occasions. The children in this and the neighboring towns have been greatly affected and influenced by the Spirit of God, and many of them hopefully changed; the youngest in this town is between nine and ten years of age. Some of them seem to be full of love to

---

9. I.e., a "visible saint," one who feels assured of salvation.

1. In November 1736, Edwards counted 620 adult communicants.

Christ and have expressed great longings after him and willingness to die, and leave father and mother and all things in the world to go to him, together with a great sense of their unworthiness and admiration at the free grace of God towards them. And there have been many old people, many above fifty and several near seventy, that seem to be wonderfully changed and hopefully newborn. The good people that have been formerly converted in the town have many of them been wonderfully enlivened and increased.

This work seems to be upon every account an extraordinary dispensation of providence. 'Tis extraordinary upon the account of [the] universality of it in affecting all sorts, high and low, rich and poor, wise and unwise, old and young, vicious and moral; 'tis very extraordinary as to the numbers that are hopefully savingly wrought upon, and particularly the number of aged persons and children and loose livers; and also on the account of the quickness of the work of the Spirit on them, for many seem to have been suddenly taken from a loose way of living, and to be so changed as to become truly holy, spiritual, heavenly persons; 'tis extraordinary as to the degrees of gracious communications, and the abundant measures in which the Spirit of God has been poured out on many persons; 'tis extraordinary as to the extent of it, God's Spirit being so remarkably poured out on so many towns at once, and its making such swift progress from place to place. The extraordinariness of the thing has been, I believe, one principal cause that people abroad have suspected it.

There have been, as I have heard, many odd and strange stories that have been carried about the country of this affair, which it is a wonder some wise men should be so ready to believe. Some indeed under great terrors of conscience have had impressions[2] on their imaginations; and also under the power of spiritual discoveries, they have had livelily impressed ideas of Christ shedding blood for sinners, his blood running from his veins, and of Christ in his glory in heaven and such like things, but they are always taught, and have been several times taught in public not to lay the weight of their hopes on such things and many have nothing of any such imaginations. There have been several persons that have had their natures overborne under strong convictions, have trembled, and han't been able to stand, they have had such a sense of divine wrath; but there are no new doctrines embraced, but people have been abundantly established in those that we account orthodox; there is no new way of worship affected. There is no oddity of behavior prevails; people are no more superstitious about their clothes, or anything else than they used to be. Indeed, there is a great deal of talk when they are together of one another's experiences, and indeed no other is to be expected in a town where the concern of the soul is so universally the concern, and that to so great a degree. And doubtless some persons under the strength of impressions that are made on their minds and under the power of strong affections,[3] are guilty of imprudences; their zeal may need to be regulated by more prudence, and they may need a guide to their assistance; as of old when the church of Corinth had the extraordinary gifts of the Spirit, they needed to be told by the Apostle that the spirit of the prophets were subject to the prophets, and that their gifts were to be exercised with prudence, because God was not the author of confusion but of peace.[4] There is no unlovely

2. Strong effects.
3. Emotions.
4. "Let the prophets speak two or three, and let the other judge. . . . For ye may all prophesy one by one, that all may learn, and all may be comforted. And the spirits of the prophets are subjects

oddity in people's temper prevailing with this work, but on the contrary the face of things is much changed as to the appearance of a meek, humble, amiable behavior. Indeed, the Devil has not been idle, but his hand has evidently appeared in several instances endeavoring to mimic the work of the Spirit of God and to cast a slur upon it, and no wonder. And there has hereby appeared the need of the watchful eye of skillful guides, and of wisdom from above to direct them.

There lately came up hither a couple of ministers from Connecticut, viz. Mr. Lord of [North] Preston, and Mr. Owen of Groton,[5] who had heard of the extraordinary circumstances of this and the neighboring towns, who had heard the affair well represented by some, and also had heard many reports greatly to its disadvantage, who came on purpose to see and satisfy themselves; and that they might thoroughly acquaint themselves, went about and spent [the] good part of a day in hearing the accounts of many of our new converts, and examining of them, which was greatly to their satisfaction; and they took particular notice, among other things, of the modesty with which persons gave account of themselves, and said that the one-half was not told them, and could not be told them; and that if they renounced these persons' experiences they must renounce Christianity itself. And Mr. Owen said particularly as to their impressions on their imaginations, they were quite different from what had been represented, and that they were no more than might naturally be expected in such cases.

Thus, Sir, I have given you a particular account of this affair which Satan has so much misrepresented in the country.[6] This is a true account of the matter as far as I have opportunity to know, and I suppose I am under greater advantages to know than any person living. Having been thus long in the account, I forbear to make reflections, or to guess what God is about to do; I leave this to you, and shall only say, as I desire always to say from my heart, "To God be all the glory, whose work alone it is." And let him have an interest in your prayers, who so much needs divine help at this day, and is your affectionate brother and humble servant.

Jonathan Edwards

Northampton, June 3, 1735

Since I wrote the foregoing letter, there has happened a thing of a very awful nature in the town. My Uncle Hawley,[7] the last Sabbath-day morning [June 1], laid violent hands on himself, and put an end to his life, by cutting his own throat. He had been for a considerable time greatly concerned about the condition of his soul; till, by the ordering of a sovereign providence he was suffered to fall into deep melancholy, a distemper that the family are very prone to; he was much overpowered by it; the devil took the advantage and drove him into despairing thoughts. He was kept very much awake anights, so that he had but very little sleep for two months, till he seemed not to have his faculties in his own power. He was in a great measure past

to the prophets. For God is not the author of confusion, but of peace, as in all churches of the saints" (1 Corinthians 14.29–33).
5. Joseph Owen (1699–1753), pastor at Groton, Connecticut. Hezekiah Lord (1698–1761), pastor at North Preston, Connecticut.
6. There were rumors that the revival produced

not truly converted Christians, but a frenzy of uncontrolled emotions.
7. Joseph Hawley (1682–1735) married a sister of Edwards's mother. He was one of the "River Gods," as leading businessmen in this rich Connecticut River valley were called. He took his life on June 1, 1735.

a capacity of receiving advice, or being reasoned with. The coroner's inquest judged him delirious. Satan seems to be in a great rage, at this extraordinary breaking forth of the work of God. I hope it is because he knows that he has but a short time. Doubtless he had a great reach,[8] in this violent attack of his against the whole affair. We have appointed a day of fasting in the town this week, by reason of this and other appearances of Satan's rage amongst us against poor souls. I yesterday saw a woman that belongs to [the church in] Durham [Connecticut], who says there is a considerable revival of religion there.

I am yours, etc.—
J.E.

1735   1935

Sinners in the Hands of an Angry God[1]

Deuteronomy 32.35

Their foot shall slide in due time.[2]

In this verse is threatened the vengeance of God on the wicked unbelieving Israelites, who were God's visible people, and who lived under the means of grace,[3] but who, notwithstanding all God's wonderful works towards them, remained (as in verse 28)[4] void of counsel, having no understanding in them. Under all the cultivations of heaven, they brought forth bitter and poisonous fruit, as in the two verses next preceding the text.[5] The expression I have chosen for my text, "Their foot shall slide in due time," seems to imply the following things, relating to the punishment and destruction to which these wicked Israelites were exposed.

1. That they were always exposed to destruction; as one that stands or walks in slippery places is always exposed to fall. This is implied in the manner of their destruction coming upon them, being represented by their foot sliding. The same is expressed, Psalm 73.18: "Surely thou didst set them in slippery places; thou castedst them down into destruction."

2. It implies that they were always exposed to sudden unexpected destruction. As he that walks in slippery places is every moment liable to fall, he cannot foresee one moment whether he shall stand or fall the next; and when he does fall, he falls at once without warning: which is also expressed in Psalm 73.18–19: "Surely thou didst set them in slippery places; thou castedst

8. Power of influence.
1. Edwards delivered this sermon in Enfield, Connecticut, a town about thirty miles south of Northampton, on Sunday, July 8, 1741. In Benjamin Trumbull's *A Complete History of Connecticut* (1797, 1818) we are told that Edwards read his sermon in a level voice with his sermon book in his left hand, and in spite of his calm, "there was such a breathing of distress, and weeping, that the preacher was obliged to speak to the people and desire silence, that he might be heard." The text here is from *The Works of Jonathan Edwards* (1829–30), vol. 7, edited by Sereno E. Dwight.
2. "To me belongeth vengeance, and recompense; their foot shall slide in due time: for the day of their calamity is at hand, and the things that shall come

upon them make haste."
3. I.e., the Ten Commandments. For Protestants following the Westminster Confession (1646), the "means of grace" consist of "preaching of the word and the administration of the sacraments of baptism and the Lord's Supper."
4. "For they are a nation void of counsel, neither is there any understanding in them" (Deuteronomy 32.28).
5. "For their vine is of the vine of Sodom, and the fields of Gomorrah: their grapes are grapes of gall, their clusters are bitter: Their wine is the poison of dragons, and the cruel venom of asps" (Deuteronomy 32.32–33). Sodom and Gomorrah were wicked cities destroyed by a rain of fire and sulfur from heaven (Genesis 19.24).

them down into destruction: How are they brought into desolation as in a moment!"

3. Another thing implied is, that they are liable to fall of themselves, without being thrown down by the hand of another; as he that stands or walks on slippery ground needs nothing but his own weight to throw him down.

4. That the reason why they are not fallen already, and do not fall now, is only that God's appointed time is not come. For it is said that when that due time, or appointed times comes, their foot shall slide. Then they shall be left to fall, as they are inclined by their own weight. God will not hold them up in these slippery places any longer, but will let them go; and then, at that very instant, they shall fall into destruction; as he that stands on such slippery declining ground, on the edge of a pit, he cannot stand alone, when he is let go he immediately falls and is lost.

The observation from the words that I would now insist upon is this. "There is nothing that keeps wicked men at any one moment out of hell, but the mere pleasure of God." By the mere pleasure of God, I mean His sovereign pleasure, His arbitrary will, restrained by no obligation, hindered by no manner of difficulty, any more than if nothing else but God's mere will had in the least degree, or in any respect whatsoever, any hand in the preservation of wicked men one moment. The truth of this observation may appear by the following considerations.

1. There is no want of power in God to cast wicked men into hell at any moment. Men's hands cannot be strong when God rises up. The strongest have no power to resist Him, not can any deliver[6] out of His hands. He is not only able to cast wicked men into hell, but He can most easily do it. Sometimes an earthly prince meets with a great deal of difficulty to subdue a rebel, who has found means to fortify himself, and has made himself strong by the numbers of his followers. But it is not so with God. There is no fortress that is any defense from the power of God. Though hand join in hand, and vast multitudes of God's enemies combine and associate themselves, they are easily broken in pieces. They are as great heaps of light chaff before the whirlwind; or large quantities of dry stubble before devouring flames. We find it easy to tread on and crush a worm that we see crawling on the earth; so it is easy for us to cut or singe a slender thread that any thing hangs by: thus easy is it for God, when he pleases, to cast His enemies down to hell. What are we, that we should think to stand before Him, at whose rebuke the earth trembles, and before whom the rocks are thrown down?

2. They deserve to be cast into hell; so that divine justice never stands in the way, it makes no objection against God's using His power at any moment to destroy them. Yea, on the contrary, justice calls aloud for an infinite punishment of their sins. Divine justice says of the tree that brings forth such grapes of Sodom, "Cut it down, why cumbereth it the ground?" Luke 13.7. The sword of divine justice is every moment brandished over their heads, and it is nothing but the hand of arbitrary mercy, and God's will, that holds it back.

3. They are already under a sentence of condemnation to hell. They do not only justly deserve to be cast down thither, but the sentence of the law of God, that eternal and immutable rule of righteousness that God has fixed

6. I.e., rescue others.

between Him and mankind, is gone out against them, and stands against them; so that they are bound over already to hell. John 3.18: "He that believeth not is condemned already." So that every unconverted man properly belongs to hell; that is his place; from thence he is, John 8.23: "Ye are from beneath." And thither he is bound; it is the place that justice, and God's word, and the sentence of his unchangeable law assign to him.

4. They are now the objects of that very same anger and wrath of God that is expressed in the torments of hell. And the reason why they do not go down to hell at each moment is not because God, in whose power they are, is not then very angry with them as He is with many miserable creatures now tormented in hell, who there feel and bear the fierceness of His wrath. Yea, God is a great deal more angry with great numbers that are now on earth: yea, doubtless, with many that are now in this congregation, who it may be are at ease, than He is with many of those who are now in the flames of hell.

So that it is not because God is unmindful of their wickedness, and does not resent it, that He does not let loose His hand and cut them off. God is not altogether such an one as themselves, though they may imagine Him to be so. The wrath of God burns against them, their damnation does not slumber; the pit is prepared, the fire is made ready, the furnace is now hot, ready to receive them; the flames do now rage and glow. The glittering sword is whet,[7] and held over them, and the pit hath opened its mouth under them.

5. The devil stands ready to fall upon them, and seize them as his own, at what moment God shall permit him. They belong to him; he has their souls in his possession, and under his dominion. The Scripture represents them as his goods, Luke 11.12.[8] The devils watch them; they are ever by them at their right hand; they stand waiting for them, like greedy hungry lions that see their prey, and expect to have it, but are for the present kept back. If God should withdraw His hand, by which they are restrained, they would in one moment fly upon their poor souls. The old serpent is gaping for them; hell opens its mouth wide to receive them; and if God should permit it, they would be hastily swallowed up and lost.

6. There are in the souls of wicked men those hellish principles reigning that would presently kindle and flame out into hell fire, if it were not for God's restraints. There is laid in the very nature of carnal men a foundation for the torments of hell. There are those corrupt principles, in reigning power in them, and in full possession of them, that are seeds of hell fire. These principles are active and powerful, exceeding violent in their nature, and if it were not for the restraining hand of God upon them, they would soon break out, they would flame out after the same manner as the same corruptions, the same enmity does in the hearts of damned souls, and would beget the same torments as they do in them. The souls of the wicked are in Scripture compared to the troubled sea, Isaiah 57.20.[9] For the present, God restrains their wickedness by His mighty power, as He does the raging waves of the troubled sea, saying, "Hitherto shalt thou come, but no further;"[1] but if God should withdraw that restraining power, it would soon carry all before it. Sin is the ruin and misery of the soul; it is destructive in its nature; and if God should leave it without restraint, there would need nothing else to make the soul perfectly miserable. The corruption of the heart of man is

7. Sharpened.
8. "Or if he shall ask an egg, will he offer him a scorpion?"
9. "But the wicked are like the troubled sea, when it cannot rest, whose waters cast up mire and dirt."
1. Job 38.11.

immoderate and boundless in its fury; and while wicked men live here, it is like fire pent up by God's restraints, whereas if it were let loose, it would set on fire the course of nature; and as the heart is now a sink of sin, so if sin was not restrained, it would immediately turn the soul into a fiery oven, or a furnace of fire and brimstone.

7. It is no security to wicked men for one moment that there are no visible means of death at hand. It is no security to a natural[2] man that he is now in health and that he does not see which way he should now immediately go out of the world by any accident, and that there is no visible danger in any respect in his circumstances. The manifold and continual experience of the world in all ages, shows this is no evidence that a man is not on the very brink of eternity, and that the next step will not be into another world. The unseen, unthought-of ways and means of persons going suddenly out of the world are innumerable and inconceivable. Unconverted men walk over the pit of hell on a rotten covering, and there are innumerable places in this covering so weak that they will not bear their weight, and these places are not seen. The arrows of death fly unseen at noonday;[3] the sharpest sight cannot discern them. God has so many different unsearchable ways of taking wicked men out of the world and sending them to hell, that there is nothing to make it appear that God had need to be at the expense of a miracle, or go out of the ordinary course of His providence, to destroy any wicked man at any moment. All the means that there are of sinners going out of the world are so in God's hands, and so universally and absolutely subject to His power and determination, that it does not depend at all the less on the mere will of God whether sinners shall at any moment go to hell than if means were never made use of or at all concerned in the case.

8. Natural men's prudence and care to preserve their own lives, or the care of others to preserve them, do not secure them a moment. To this, divine providence and universal experience do also bear testimony. There is this clear evidence that men's own wisdom is no security to them from death; that if it were otherwise we should see some difference between the wise and politic men of the world, and others, with regard to their liableness to early and unexpected death: but how is it in fact? Ecclesiastes 2.16: "How dieth the wise man? even as the fool."

9. All wicked men's pains and contrivance which they use to escape hell, while they continue to reject Christ, and so remain wicked men, do not secure them from hell one moment. Almost every natural man that hears of hell, flatters himself that he shall escape it; he depends upon himself for his own security; he flatters himself in what he has done, in what he is now doing, or what he intends to do. Every one lays out matters in his own mind how he shall avoid damnation, and flatters himself that he contrives well for himself, and that his schemes will not fail. They hear indeed that there are but few saved, and that the greater part of men that have died heretofore are gone to hell; but each one imagines that he lays out matters better for his own escape than others have done. He does not intend to come to that place of torment; he says within himself that he intends to take effectual care, and to order matters so for himself as not to fail.

But the foolish children of men miserably delude themselves in their own

---

2. I.e., unregenerate, unsaved.
3. "Thou shalt not be afraid for the terror by night; nor for the arrow that flieth by day" (Psalm 91.5).

schemes, and in confidence in their own strength and wisdom; they trust to nothing but a shadow. The greater part of those who heretofore have lived under the same means of grace, and are now dead, are undoubtedly gone to hell; and it was not because they were not as wise as those who are now alive: it was not because they did not lay out matters as well for themselves to secure their own escape. If we could speak with them, and inquire of them, one by one, whether they expected when alive, and when they used to hear about hell, ever to be the subjects of that misery, we doubtless, should hear one and another reply, "No, I never intended to come here: I had laid out matters otherwise in my mind; I thought I should contrive well for myself: I thought my scheme good. I intended to take effectual care; but it came upon me unexpected; I did not look for it at that time, and in that manner; it came as a thief: Death outwitted me: God's wrath was too quick for me. Oh, my cursed foolishness! I was flattering myself, and pleasing myself with vain dreams of what I would do hereafter; and when I was saying, peace and safety, then suddenly destruction came upon me."

10. God has laid Himself under no obligation by any promise to keep any natural man out of hell one moment. God certainly has made no promises either of eternal life or of any deliverance or preservation from eternal death but what are contained in the covenant of grace,[4] the promises that are given in Christ, in whom all the promises are yea and amen. But surely they have no interest in the promises of the covenant of grace who are not the children of the covenant, who do not believe in any of the promises, and have no interest in the Mediator of the covenant.[5]

So that, whatever some have imagined and pretended[6] about promises made to natural men's earnest seeking and knocking, it is plain and manifest that whatever pains a natural man takes in religion, whatever prayers he makes, till he believes in Christ, God is under no manner of obligation to keep him a moment from eternal destruction.

So that, thus it is that natural men are held in the hand of God, over the pit of hell; they have deserved the fiery pit, and are already sentenced to it; and God is dreadfully provoked. His anger is as great towards them as to those that are actually suffering the executions of the fierceness of His wrath in hell, and they have done nothing in the least to appease or abate that anger, neither is God in the least bound by any promise to hold them up one moment; the devil is waiting for them, hell is gaping for them, the flames gather and flash about them, and would fain lay hold on them, and swallow them up; the fire pent up in their own hearts is struggling to break out: and they have no interest in any Mediator, there are no means within reach that can be any security to them. In short, they have no refuge, nothing to take hold of; all that preserves them every moment is the mere arbitrary will, and uncovenanted, unobliged forbearance of an incensed God.

Application

The use of this awful[7] subject may be for awakening unconverted persons in this congregation. This that you have heard is the case of every one of you

---

4. The original covenant God made with Adam is called the Covenant of Works; the second covenant Christ made with fallen humanity—declaring that if they believed in him they would be saved—is called the Covenant of Grace.

5. I.e., Christ, who took upon himself the sins of the world and suffered for them.
6. Claimed.
7. Awesome.

that are out of Christ. That world of misery, that lake of burning brimstone, is extended abroad under you. There is the dreadful pit of the glowing flames of the wrath of God; there is hell's wide gaping mouth open; and you have nothing to stand upon, nor any thing to take hold of; there is nothing between you and hell but the air; it is only the power and mere pleasure of God that holds you up.

You probably are not sensible[8] of this; you find you are kept out of hell, but do not see the hand of God in it; but look at other things, as the good state of your bodily constitution, your care of your own life, and the means you use for your own preservation. But indeed these things are nothing; if God should withdraw His hand, they would avail no more to keep you from falling, than the thin air to hold up a person that is suspended in it.

Your wickedness makes you as it were heavy as lead, and to tend downwards with great weight and pressure towards hell; and if God should let you go, you would immediately sink and swiftly descend and plunge into the bottomless gulf, and your healthy constitution, and your own care and prudence, and best contrivance, and all your righteousness, would have no more influence to uphold you and keep you out of hell, than a spider's web would have to stop a fallen rock. Were it not for the sovereign pleasure of God, the earth would not bear you one moment; for you are a burden to it; the creation groans with you; the creature is made subject to the bondage of your corruption, not willingly; the sun does not willingly shine upon you to give you light to serve sin and Satan; the earth does not willingly yield her increase to satisfy your lusts; nor is it willingly a stage for your wickedness to be acted upon; the air does not willingly serve you for breath to maintain the flame of life in your vitals, while you spend your life in the service of God's enemies. God's creatures are good, and were made for men to serve God with, and do not willingly subserve to any other purpose, and groan when they are abused to purposes so directly contrary to their nature and end. And the world would spew you out, were it not for the sovereign hand of Him who hath subjected it in hope. There are black clouds of God's wrath now hanging directly over your heads, full of the dreadful storm, and big with thunder; and were it not for the restraining hand of God, it would immediately burst forth upon you. The sovereign pleasure of God, for the present, stays His rough wind; otherwise it would come with fury, and your destruction would come like a whirlwind, and you would be like the chaff of the summer threshing floor.

The wrath of God is like great waters that are dammed for the present; they increase more and more, and rise higher and higher, till an outlet is given; and the longer the stream is stopped, the more rapid and mighty is its course when once it is let loose. It is true that judgment against your evil works has not been executed hitherto; the floods of God's vengeance have been withheld; but your guilt in the meantime is constantly increasing, and you are every day treasuring up more wrath; the waters are constantly rising, and waxing more and more mighty; and there is nothing but the mere pleasure of God that holds the waters back, that are unwilling to be stopped, and press hard to go forward. If God should only withdraw His hand from the floodgate, it would immediately fly open, and the fiery floods of the fierceness and wrath of God, would rush forth with inconceivable fury, and would come upon you with omnipotent power; and if your strength were ten thousand

8. Aware.

times greater than it is, yea, ten thousand times greater than the strength of the stoutest, sturdiest devil in hell, it would be nothing to withstand or endure it.

The bow of God's wrath is bent, and the arrow made ready on the string, and justice bends the arrow at your heart, and strains the bow, and it is nothing but the mere pleasure of God, and that of an angry God, without any promise or obligation at all, that keeps the arrow one moment from being made drunk with your blood. Thus all you that never passed under a great change of heart, by the mighty power of the Spirit of God upon your souls, all you that were never born again, and made new creatures, and raised from being dead in sin, to a state of new, and before altogether unexperienced light and life, are in the hands of an angry God. However you may have reformed your life in many things, and may have had religious affections, and may keep up a form of religion in your families and closets,[9] and in the house of God, it is nothing but His mere pleasure that keeps you from being this moment swallowed up in everlasting destruction. However unconvinced you may now be of the truth of what you hear, by and by you will be fully convinced of it. Those that are gone from being in the like circumstances with you see that it was so with them; for destruction came suddenly upon most of them; when they expected nothing of it and while they were saying, peace and safety: now they see that those things on which they depended for peace and safety, were nothing but thin air and empty shadows.

The God that holds you over the pit of hell, much as one holds a spider or some loathsome insect over the fire, abhors you, and is dreadfully provoked: His wrath towards you burns like fire; He looks upon you as worthy of nothing else but to be cast into the fire; He is of purer eyes than to bear to have you in His sight; you are ten thousand times more abominable in His eyes than the most hateful venomous serpent is in ours. You have offended Him infinitely more than ever a stubborn rebel did his prince; and yet it is nothing but His hand that holds you from falling into the fire every moment. It is to be ascribed to nothing else, that you did not go to hell the last night; that you was suffered to awake again in this world, after you closed your eyes to sleep. And there is no other reason to be given, why you have not dropped into hell since you arose in the morning, but that God's hand has held you up. There is no other reason to be given why you have not gone to hell, since you have sat here in the house of God, provoking His pure eyes by your sinful wicked manner of attending His solemn worship. Yea, there is nothing else that is to be given as a reason why you do not this very moment drop down into hell.

O sinner! Consider the fearful danger you are in: it is a great furnace of wrath, a wide and bottomless pit, full of the fire of wrath, that you are held over in the hand of that God, whose wrath is provoked and incensed as much against you, as against many of the damned in hell. You hang by a slender thread, with the flames of divine wrath flashing about it, and ready every moment to singe it, and burn it asunder; and you have no interest in any Mediator, and nothing to lay hold of to save yourself, nothing to keep off the flames of wrath, nothing of your own, nothing that you ever have done, nothing that you can do, to induce God to spare you one moment. And consider here more particularly.

---

9. Studies; rooms for meditation. "Affections": feelings.

1. Whose wrath it is: it is the wrath of the infinite God. If it were only the wrath of man, though it were of the most potent prince, it would be comparatively little to be regarded. The wrath of kings is very much dreaded, especially of absolute monarchs, who have the possessions and lives of their subjects wholly in their power, to be disposed of at their mere will. Proverbs 20.2: "The fear of a king is as the roaring of a lion: Whoso provoketh him to anger, sinneth against his own soul." The subject that very much enrages an arbitrary prince is liable to suffer the most extreme torments that human art can invent, or human power can inflict. But the greatest earthly potentates in their greatest majesty, and strength, and when clothed in their greatest terrors, are but feeble, despicable worms of the dust, in comparison of the great and almighty Creator and King of heaven and earth. It is but little that they can do, when most enraged, and when they have exerted the utmost of their fury. All the kings of the earth, before God, are as grasshoppers; they are nothing, and less than nothing: both their love and their hatred is to be despised. The wrath of the great King of kings, is as much more terrible than theirs, as His majesty is greater. Luke 12.4–5: "And I say unto you, my friends, Be not afraid of them that kill the body, and after that, have no more that they can do. But I will forewarn you whom you shall fear: fear him, which after he hath killed, hath power to cast into hell: yea, I say unto you, Fear him."

2. It is the fierceness of His wrath that you are exposed to. We often read of the fury of God; as in Isaiah 59.18: "According to their deeds, accordingly he will repay fury to his adversaries." So Isaiah 66.15: "For behold, the Lord will come with fire, and with his chariots like a whirlwind, to render his anger with fury, and his rebuke with flames of fire." And in many other places. So, Revelation 19.15: we read of "the wine press of the fierceness and wrath of Almighty God."[1] The words are exceeding terrible. If it had only been said, "the wrath of God," the words would have implied that which is infinitely dreadful: but it is "the fierceness and wrath of God." The fury of God! the fierceness of Jehovah![2] Oh, how dreadful must that be! Who can utter or conceive what such expressions carry in them! But it is also "the fierceness and wrath of Almighty God." As though there would be a very great manifestation of His almighty power in what the fierceness of His wrath should inflict, as though omnipotence should be as it were enraged, and exerted, as men are wont to exert their strength in the fierceness of their wrath. Oh! then, what will be the consequence! What will become of the poor worms that shall suffer it! Whose hands can be strong? And whose heart can endure? To what a dreadful, inexpressible, inconceivable depth of misery must the poor creature be sunk who shall be the subject of this!

Consider this, you that are here present that yet remain in an unregenerate state. That God will execute the fierceness of His anger implies that He will inflict wrath without any pity. When God beholds the ineffable extremity of your case, and sees your torment to be so vastly disproportioned to your strength, and sees how your poor soul is crushed, and sinks down, as it were, into an infinite gloom; He will have no compassion upon you, He will not forbear the executions of His wrath, or in the least lighten His hand; there shall be no moderation or mercy, nor will God then at all stay His rough

---

1. "He treadeth the winepress of the fierceness and wrath of Almighty God." 2. The name used for God in the Old Testament.

wind; He will have no regard to your welfare, nor be at all careful lest you should suffer too much in any other sense, than only that you shall not suffer beyond what strict justice requires. Nothing shall be withheld because it is so hard for you to bear. Ezekiel 8.18: "Therefore will I also deal in fury: mine eye shall not spare, neither will I have pity; and though they cry in mine ears with a loud voice, yet I will not hear them." Now God stands ready to pity you; this is a day of mercy; you may cry now with some encouragement of obtaining mercy. But when once the day of mercy is past, your most lamentable and dolorous cries and shrieks will be in vain; you will be wholly lost and thrown away of God as to any regard to your welfare. God will have no other use to put you to, but to suffer misery; you shall be continued in being to no other end; for you will be a vessel of wrath fitted to destruction; and there will be no other use of this vessel, but to be filled full of wrath. God will be so far from pitying you when you cry to Him, that it is said He will only "laugh and mock." Proverbs 1.25–26, etc.[3]

How awful are those words, Isaiah 63.3, which are the words of the great God: "I will tread them in mine anger, and will trample them in my fury, and their blood shall be sprinkled upon my garments, and I will stain all my raiment." It is perhaps impossible to conceive of words that carry in them greater manifestations of these three things, viz., contempt, and hatred, and fierceness of indignation. If you cry to God to pity you, He will be so far from pitying you in your doleful case, or showing you the least regard or favor, that instead of that, He will only tread you under foot. And though He will know that you cannot bear the weight of omnipotence treading upon you, yet He will not regard that, but He will crush you under His feet without mercy; He will crush out your blood, and make it fly and it shall be sprinkled on His garments, so as to stain all His raiment. He will not only hate you, but He will have you in the utmost contempt: no place shall be thought fit for you, but under His feet to be trodden down as the mire of the streets.

3. The misery you are exposed to is that which God will inflict to that end, that He might show what that wrath of Jehovah is. God hath had it on His heart to show to angels and men both how excellent His love is, and also how terrible His wrath is. Sometimes earthly kings have a mind to show how terrible their wrath is, by the extreme punishments they would execute on those that would provoke them. Nebuchadnezzar, that mighty and haughty monarch of the Chaldean empire, was willing to show his wrath when enraged with Shadrach, Meshech, and Abednego; and accordingly gave orders that the burning fiery furnace should be heated seven times hotter than it was before; doubtless, it was raised to the utmost degree of fierceness that human art could raise it.[4] But the great God is also willing to show His wrath, and magnify His awful majesty and mighty power in the extreme sufferings of His enemies. Romans 9.22: "What if God, willing to show his wrath, and to make his power known, endure with much long-suffering the vessels of wrath fitted to destruction?" And seeing this is His design, and what He has determined, even to show how terrible the restrained wrath, the fury and fierceness of Jehovah is, He will do it to effect. There will be something accomplished and brought to pass that will be dreadful with a

3. "But ye have set at nought all my counsel, and would none of my reproof: I also will laugh at your calamity; I will mock you when your fear cometh."
4. See Daniel 3.1–30.

witness. When the great and angry God hath risen up and executed His awful vengeance on the poor sinner, and the wretch is actually suffering the infinite weight and power of His indignation, then will God call upon the whole universe to behold that awful majesty and mighty power that is to be seen in it. Isaiah 33.12–14: "And the people shall be as the burnings of lime, as thorns cut up shall they be burnt in the fire. Hear ye that are far off, what I have done; and ye that are near, acknowledge my might. The sinners in Zion are afraid; fearfulness hath surprised the hypocrites," etc.

Thus it will be with you that are in an unconverted state, if you continue in it; the infinite might, and majesty, and terribleness of the omnipotent God shall be magnified upon you, in the ineffable strength of your torments. You shall be tormented in the presence of the holy angels, and in the presence of the Lamb; and when you shall be in this state of suffering, the glorious inhabitants of heaven shall go forth and look on the awful spectacle, that they may see what the wrath and fierceness of the Almighty is; and when they have seen it, they will fall down and adore that great power and majesty. Isaiah 66.23–24: "And it shall come to pass, that from one new moon to another, and from one sabbath to another, shall all flesh come to worship before me, saith the Lord. And they shall go forth and look upon the carcasses of the men that have transgressed against me; for their worm shall not die, neither shall their fire be quenched, and they shall be an abhorring unto all flesh."

4. It is everlasting wrath. It would be dreadful to suffer this fierceness and wrath of Almighty God one moment; but you must suffer it to all eternity. There will be no end to this exquisite horrible misery. When you look forward, you shall see a long forever, a boundless duration before you, which will swallow up your thoughts, and amaze your soul; and you will absolutely despair of ever having any deliverance, any end, any mitigation, any rest at all. You will know certainly that you must wear out long ages, millions of millions of ages, in wrestling and conflicting with this almighty merciless vengeance; and then when you have so done, when so many ages have actually been spent by you in this manner, you will know that all is but a point to what remains. So that your punishment will indeed be infinite. Oh, who can express what the state of a soul in such circumstances is! All that we can possibly say about it gives but a very feeble, faint representation of it; it is inexpressible and inconceivable: For "who knows the power of God's anger?"[5]

How dreadful is the state of those that are daily and hourly in the danger of this great wrath and infinite misery! But this is the dismal case of every soul in this congregation that has not been born again, however moral and strict, sober and religious, they may otherwise be. Oh that you would consider it, whether you be young or old! There is reason to think that there are many in this congregation now hearing this discourse that will actually be the subjects of this very misery to all eternity. We know not who they are, or in what seats they sit, or what thoughts they now have. It may be they are now at ease, and hear all these things without much disturbance, and are now flattering themselves that they are not the persons, promising themselves that they shall escape. If they knew that there was one person, and

5. "Who knoweth the power of thine anger? even according to thy fear, so is thy wrath" (Psalm 90.11).

but one, in the whole congregation, that was to be the subject of this misery, what an awful thing would it be to think of! If we knew who it was, what an awful sight would it be to see such a person! How might all the rest of the congregation lift up a lamentable and bitter cry over him! But, alas! instead of one, how many is it likely will remember this discourse in hell? And it would be a wonder, if some that are now present should not be in hell in a very short time, even before this year is out. And it would be no wonder if some persons, that now sit here, in some seats of this meetinghouse, in health, quiet and secure, should be there before tomorrow morning. Those of you that finally continue in a natural condition, that shall keep out of hell longest will be there in a little time! your damnation does not slumber; it will come swiftly, and, in all probability, very suddenly upon many of you. You have reason to wonder that you are not already in hell. It is doubtless the case of some whom you have seen and known, that never deserved hell more than you, and that heretofore appeared as likely to have been now alive as you. Their case is past all hope; they are crying in extreme misery and perfect despair; but here you are in the land of the living and in the house of God, and have an opportunity to obtain salvation. What would not those poor damned hopeless souls give for one day's opportunity such as you now enjoy!

And now you have an extraordinary opportunity, a day wherein Christ has thrown the door of mercy wide open, and stands in calling and crying with a loud voice to poor sinners; a day wherein many are flocking to Him, and pressing into the kingdom of God. Many are daily coming from the east, west, north and south; many that were very lately in the same miserable condition that you are in are now in a happy state, with their hearts filled with love to Him who has loved them, and washed them from their sins in His own blood, and rejoicing in hope of the glory of God. How awful is it to be left behind at such a day! To see so many others feasting, while you are pining and perishing! To see so many rejoicing and singing for joy of heart, while you have cause to mourn for sorrow of heart, and howl for vexation of spirit! How can you rest one moment in such a condition? Are not your souls as precious as the souls of the people at Suffield,[6] where they are flocking from day to day to Christ?

Are there not many here who have lived long in the world, and are not to this day born again? and so are aliens from the commonwealth of Israel,[7] and have done nothing ever since they have lived, but treasure up wrath against the day of wrath? Oh, sirs, your case, in an especial manner, is extremely dangerous. Your guilt and hardness of heart is extremely great. Do you not see how generally persons of your years are passed over and left, in the present remarkable and wonderful dispensation of God's mercy? You had need to consider yourselves, and awake thoroughly out of sleep. You cannot bear the fierceness and wrath of the infinite God. And you, young men, and young women, will you neglect this precious season which you now enjoy, when so many others of your age are renouncing all youthful vanities, and flocking to Christ? You especially have now an extraordinary opportunity; but if you neglect it, it will soon be with you as with those persons who spent all the precious days of youth in sin, and are now come to such a dreadful pass in blindness and hardness. And you, children, who are unconverted, do

---

6. A town in the neighborhood [Edwards's note].   7. I.e., not among the chosen people, the saved.

not you know that you are going down to hell, to bear the dreadful wrath of that God, who is now angry with you every day and every night? Will you be content to be the children of the devil, when so many other children in the land are converted, and are become the holy and happy children of the King of kings?

And let every one that is yet of Christ, and hanging over the pit of hell, whether they be old men and women, or middle-aged, or young people, or little children, now hearken to the loud calls of God's word and providence. This acceptable year of the Lord, a day of such great favors to some, will doubtless be a day of as remarkable vengeance to others. Men's hearts harden, and their guilt increases apace at such a day as this, if they neglect their souls; and never was there so great danger of such person being given up to hardness of heart and blindness of mind. God seems now to be hastily gathering in His elect in all parts of the land; and probably the greater part of adult persons that ever shall be saved, will be brought in now in a little time, and that it will be as it was on the great outpouring of the Spirit upon the Jews in the apostles' days;[8] the election will obtain, and the rest will be blinded. If this should be the case with you, you will eternally curse this day, and will curse the day that ever you was born, to see such a season of the pouring out of God's Spirit, and will wish that you had died and gone to hell before you had seen it. Now undoubtedly it is, as it was in the days of John the Baptist, the ax is in an extraordinary manner laid at the root of the trees,[9] that every tree which brings not forth good fruit, may be hewn down and cast into the fire.

Therefore, let everyone that is out of Christ, now awake and fly from the wrath to come. The wrath of Almighty God is now undoubtedly hanging over a great part of this congregation: Let everyone fly out of Sodom: "Haste and escape for your lives, look not behind you, escape to the mountain, lest you be consumed."[1]

1741

[The Beauty of the World][1]

The beauty of the world consists wholly of sweet mutual consents,[2] either within itself or with the Supreme Being. As to the corporeal world, though there are many other sorts of consents, yet the sweetest and most charming beauty of it is its resemblance of spiritual beauties. The reason is that spiritual beauties are infinitely the greatest, and bodies being but the shadows of beings, they must be so much the more charming as they shadow forth spiritual beauties. This beauty is peculiar to natural things, it surpassing the art of man.

8. In Acts 2 the apostle Peter admonishes a crowd to repent and be converted, saying, "Save yourselves from this untoward generation. Then they that gladly received his word were baptized: and the same day there were added unto them about three thousand souls" (Acts 2.40–41).

9. "And now also the ax is laid unto the root of the trees: therefore every tree which bringeth not forth good fruit is hewn down, and cast into the fire" (Matthew 3.10).

1. Genesis 19.17.

1. This fragment was found among Edwards's papers and first published, with this title, by Perry Miller in *Images or Shadows of Divine Things* (1948). The editorial emendations are by Miller.

2. Agreements.

Thus there is the resemblance of a decent trust, dependence and acknowledgment in the planets continually moving round the sun, receiving his influences by which they are made happy, bright and beautiful: a decent attendance in the secondary planets, an image of majesty, power, glory, and beneficence in the sun in the midst of all, and so in terrestrial things, as I have shown in another place.

It is very probable that that wonderful suitableness of green for the grass and plants, the blues of the sky, the white of the clouds, the colors of flowers, consists in a complicated proportion that these colors make one with another, either in their magnitude of the rays, the number of vibrations that are caused in the atmosphere, or some other way. So there is a great suitableness between the objects of different senses, as between sounds, colors, and smells; as between colors of the woods and flowers and the smells and the singing of birds, which it is probable consist in a certain proportion of the vibrations that are made in the different organs. So there are innumerable other agreeablenesses of motions, figures, etc. The gentle motions of waves, of [the] lily, etc., as it is agreeable to other things that represent calmness, gentleness, and benevolence, etc., the fields and woods seem to rejoice, and how joyful do the birds seem to be in it. How much a resemblance is there of every grace in the field covered with plants and flowers when the sun shines serenely and undisturbedly upon them, how a resemblance, I say, of every grace and beautiful disposition of mind, of an inferior towards a superior cause, preserver, benevolent benefactor, and a fountain of happiness.

How great a resemblance of a holy and virtuous soul is a calm, serene day. What an infinite number of such like beauties is there in that one thing, the light, and how complicated an harmony and proportion is it probable belongs to it.

There are beauties that are more palpable and explicable, and there are hidden and secret beauties. The former pleases, and we can tell why; we can explain the particular point for the agreement that renders the thing pleasing. Such are all artificial regularities; we can tell wherein the regularity lies that affects us. [The] latter sort are those beauties that delight us and we cannot tell why. Thus, we find ourselves pleased in beholding the color of the violets, but we know not what secret regularity or harmony it is that creates that pleasure in our minds. These hidden beauties are commonly by far the greatest, because the more complex a beauty is, the more hidden is it. In this latter fact consists principally the beauty of the world, and very much in light and colors. Thus mere light is pleasing to the mind. If it be to the degree of effulgence, it is very sensible, and mankind have agreed in it: they all represent glory and extraordinary beauty by brightness. The reason of it is either that light or our organ of seeing is so contrived that an harmonious motion is excited in the animal spirits and propogated to the brain. That mixture we call white is a proportionate mixture that is harmonious, as Sir Isaac Newton[3] has shown, to each particular simple color, and contains in it some harmony or other that is delightful. And each sort of rays play a distinct tune to the soul, besides those lovely mixtures that are found in nature. Those beauties,

3. Newton (1642–1727), in his *Opticks* (1704), explained the phenomena of color, proving that differences in color are caused by differing degrees of ability to be refracted.

how lovely is the green of the face of the earth in all manner of colors, in flowers, the color of the skies, and lovely tinctures of the morning and evening.

Corollary:[4] Hence the reason why almost all men, and those that seem to be very miserable, love life, because they cannot bear to lose sight of such a beautiful and lovely world. The ideas, that every moment whilst we live have a beauty that we take not distinct notice of, brings a pleasure that, when we come to the trial, we had rather live in much pain and misery than lose.

1948

From Images or Shadows of Divine Things[1]

3 [Roses]

Roses grow upon briers, which is to signify that all temporal sweets are mixed with bitter. But what seems more especially to be meant by it, is that true happiness, the crown of glory, is to be come at in no other way than by bearing Christ's cross by a life of mortification, self-denial and labor, and bearing all things for Christ. The rose, the chief of all flowers, is the last thing that comes out. The briery prickly bush grows before, but the end and crown of all is the beautiful and fragrant rose.

64 [Hills and Mountains]

Hills and mountains are types[2] of heaven, and often made use of as such in Scripture. These are with difficulty ascended. To ascend them, one must go against the natural tendency of the flesh that must be contradicted in all the ascent, in every step of it, and the ascent is attended with labor, sweat and weariness, and there are commonly many hideous rocks in the way. 'Tis a great deal easier descending into valleys.

This is a representation of the difficulty, labor and self-denial of the way to heaven; and how agreeable it is to descend into hell. At the bottom of valleys, especially deep valleys, there is water—either a lake or other waters. But water, as has been shown elsewhere in "Notes on Scripture," commonly signifies misery, especially that which is occasioned by the wrath of God. So in hell is a lake or gulf of misery and wrath.

77 [Rivers]

There is a wonderful analogy between what is seen in RIVERS: their gathering from innumerable small branches beginning at a great distance one

<hr/>

4. Something that naturally follows from a proved proposition.
1. Included in Edwards's manuscripts in the Yale University Library is a notebook of some 212 entries for which Edwards had suggested several titles: *The Images of Divine Things, The Shadows of Divine Things, The Book of Nature and Common Providence, The Language and Lessons of Nature.* In 1948 Perry Miller published this notebook as *Images or Shadows of Divine Things.* In these notes Edwards continues the medieval tradition of typology, a method of reading the Bible by which Old

Testament figures ("types") are fulfilled by Christ in the New Testament ("the anti-type" being that which is foreshadowed by a type). Edwards here extends the idea of typology and suggests that the physical world may be read as a sign or type, revealing ultimate spiritual truth. The text here is from the Yale University Press *Works of Jonathan Edwards,* vol. 11, edited by Wallace E. Anderson, Mason I. Lowance, and David Watters.
2. Foreshadowings, i.e., things which are fulfilled by the idea of heaven.

from another in different regions, some on the sides or tops of mountains, others in valleys, and all conspiring to one common issue, all after their very diverse and contrary courses which they held for a while, yet all gathering more and more together the nearer they come to their common end and ultimate issue, and all at length discharging themselves at one mouth into the same ocean. Here is livelily represented how all things tend to one, even to God, the boundless ocean, which they can add nothing to, as mightiest rivers that continually disembogue themselves into the ocean add nothing to it sensibly. The waters of the ocean are not raised by it; yea, all the rivers together, great and small, together with all the brooks and little streams, can't raise the waters of the ocean in the least degree.

The innumerable streams, of which great rivers are constituted, running in such infinitely various and contrary courses, livelily represent the various dispensations of divine providence. Some of them beginning at the greatest distance from the common mouth, others nearer to it, multitudes of them meeting first to constitute certain main branches of the river before they empty themselves into the main river and so into the ocean. Some of the first constituent streams never empty themselves into any of the branches at all, but empty themselves directly into the main river. Others first empty themselves into other branches, and those into others, and those still into others, and so on many times, before they yield their tribute to the main river. Several springs first constitute a brook, and then many of these brooks constitute a small river, and then several of these small rivers meet to constitute a main branch of the main river, and then all together empty into that main river. Some of the constituent branches of the main river have their head or source at the greatest distance from the mouth, others take their source much nearer the mouth: and so all along there are new heads or new sources, beginning from the head to the mouth of the main river. Some of these branches run directly contrary to others, and yet all meet at last. And the same branches don't keep the same course: their course is not continually in a right line, that which appears to us the directest course to the main river, but sometimes they run one way, sometimes another. Sometimes their course is directly contrary to what it is at others. Sometimes instead of going towards the main river they tend to, they run for a considerable space right from it. But yet nothing is lost by this, but something gained: they nevertheless fail not of emptying themselves into the main river in proper times and due place, and bring the greater tribute of waters for their crooked and contrary courses.

And so it is with the main river itself. Its course is not directly the shortest way towards the ocean to which its waters are due, but tends thither by degrees, with many windings and turnings, sometimes seeming to run from the ocean and not towards it. If a spectator were to judge by the appearances of things before his eyes, he would think the river could [not] reach the ocean. There appears such an innumerable multitude of obstacles in the way, many hills and high mountains which a person that views at a distance sees no way between. He don't discover those ways through the hideous forests, and the openings between the mountains are not to be seen till we come to them. The winding passages through mountainous countries are not to be discovered but by tracing the course of the waters themselves. But yet amidst all these obstacles these rivers find their way, and fail not at last of an arrival at the ocean at last, though they pass through so many vast regions that all seem to be full of obstacles for so long a course together. And 'tis observable that those very hills and mountains that appear like the most insurmountable obstacles, instead of obstructing the course of these rivers, do afford the greatest supplies and additions. These rivers will at last come to the ocean, and 'tis impossible to hinder; 'tis in vain for men to attempt to turn back the stream or put a stop to it. Whatever obstacles are in the way, the waters will either bear them away before them or will find a passage round them, under them, or above them.

I need not run the parallel between this and the course of God's providence through all ages, from the beginning to the end of the world, when all things shall have their final issue in God, the infinite, inexhaustible fountain whence all things come at first, as all the rivers come from the sea, and whither they all shall come at last: for of him and to him are all things, and he is the Alpha and Omega, the beginning and the end.[3] God hath provided a watercourse for the overflowing of the waters and he turns the rivers of water whithersoever it pleaseth him.

By what has been spoken of, is it particularly livelily represented and shown, after what manner all the dispensations of providence, from the beginning of the world till the coming of Christ, all pointed to Christ: all had respect to his coming, and working our redemption and setting up his kingdom in the world, and all finally issued in this great event. From time to time, in the different successive ages of the world, there began new dispensations of providence, tending to make way and forward this great event; as there are heads of new branches all along as we come nearer and nearer to the mouth of the main river. Thus in Noah[4] began a new series of dispensations of providences, in addition to what had been begun before, making further preparation for the coming of the Messiah.

☆   ☆   ☆

78 [Trees]

(See the last.) We see the reverse in TREES of what we do in [rivers]. In these, all comes from one common stock and is distributed into innumerable branches, beginning at the root where the trunk is biggest of all, and ending in the extremities of the smallest twigs. The water here, in the sap of those trees, has a contrary course from what it has in rivers, where the course begins in the extremities of the smallest branches, and ends in the mouth of the river where the river is largest, and all the waters are collected into one body.

What is observable in trees is also a lively emblem of many spiritual things, as particularly of the dispensations of providence since the coming of Christ. Christ is as it were the trunk of the tree, and all the church are his branches: "I am the vine, ye are the branches," says Christ [John 15:5]. Christ, rising from the dead, is as it were the trunk of the tree, which appears coming out of the ground. And how do we, from this one rising Head see the body of Christ multiplied. The Christian church, as distinguished from the Jewish, began in Christ's resurrection. And how many branches shot forth soon after Christ's resurrection. The apostles, after that, were endowed with power

---

3. "I am Alpha and Omega, the beginning and the ending, saith the Lord, which is, and which was, and which is to come, the Almighty" (Revelation 1.8). Alpha and omega are the first and last letters of the Greek alphabet.

4. "And God spake unto Noah, and to his sons with him, saying, And I, behold, I establish my covenant with you, and with your seed after you" (Genesis 9.8–9).

from on high; these were as it were main branches, whence all the lesser branches came. The apostle Paul, who was a branch that shot forth later than the rest,[5] exceeded all in thirstiness and fruitfulness, so that the bigger part of the future tree came from this branch. The tree went on growing, and the further it proceeded in its growth, the more abundantly did its branches multiply; till the tree filled the Roman Empire in a few hundreds of years, and will fill the whole earth at last. Thus the parable of the grain of mustard seed is verified.[6] This tree will appear more and more glorious, till it shall appear in the greatest glory of all at the end of all things, and its full ripe fruits shall be gathered in. And though there have been many winters, and may be more, wherein this tree has ceased growing, and has been in a great measure stripped of leaves and fruit and seemed to be dead or dying, yet springs and summers are appointed to follow these winters, wherein the tree shall flourish again and appear higher and larger and more abundantly multiplied in its branches and fruit than ever before.

This tree is sometimes represented as first beginning in Abraham and sometimes in David,[7] and Christ himself as the branch of those roots, but Christ is most properly the trunk or body of the tree. Indeed, the course of the sap of the tree, from its beginning in the extremities of the roots to its end in the extremity of the branches, is an emblem of the whole series and scheme of divine providence, both before and after Christ, from the beginning to the end of the world. The sap in the roots is like the water of a river, gathering from small branches into a common body; and this, as was said before, represents the course of divine providence during the times of the Old Testament, when the designs of providence as they related to Christ and the work of redemption—which is as it were the summary comprehension of all God's works of providence—was hid as it were underground. All was under a veil, and the scheme of redemption was a mystery, kept secret from the foundation of the world. But after this the mystery was revealed, and the scheme of providence was like a tree above ground, gradually displayed as the branches successively put forth themselves. Hence we may observe that God's calling of Abraham and anointing David was as it were the planting the root whence the tree should grow, and Abraham and David were main roots whence the tree grows; but Christ himself is the sprout or branch from these roots, which becomes the tree whence all other branches proceed.

156 [The Book of Scripture]

The Book of Scripture is the interpreter of the book of nature two ways: viz. by declaring to us those spiritual mysteries that are indeed signified or typified in the constitution of the natural world; and secondly, in actually making application of the signs and types in the book of nature as representations of those spiritual mysteries in many instances.

1948

5. It is generally held that Paul did not come to Jerusalem until after the death of Jesus. His conversion came when Jesus appeared to him on the road to Damascus and, therefore, later than the other apostles (Acts 9).
6. The mustard seed is very small, and the tree which eventuates from it is very large (Matthew 13.31–32).
7. David succeeded Saul as king of Israel and was the chosen heir favored by God himself (1 Samuel 16.1–13). Abraham's descendants would possess Canaan (Genesis 12.7).

BENJAMIN FRANKLIN
1706–1790

Benjamin Franklin was born on Milk Street in Boston, the tenth son in a family of fifteen children. His father, Josiah, was a tallow chandler and soap boiler who came to Boston in 1682 from Ecton in Northamptonshire, England, and was proud of his Protestant ancestors. He married Abiah Folger, whose father was a teacher to Native Americans. Josiah talked of offering his son Benjamin as his "tithe" to the church and enrolled him in Boston Grammar School as a preparation for the study of the ministry; but his plans were too ambitious, and Benjamin was forced to leave school and work for his father. He hated his father's occupation and threatened to run away to sea. A compromise was made, and when Benjamin was twelve he was apprenticed to his brother, a printer. He must have been a natural student of the printing trade; he loved books and reading, he learned quickly, and he liked to write. His brother unwittingly published Benjamin's first essay when he printed an editorial left on his desk signed "Silence Dogood." When his brother was imprisoned in 1722 for offending Massachusetts officials, Franklin carried on publication of the paper by himself.

In 1723 Franklin broke with his brother and ran away to Philadelphia. It was a serious act for an apprentice, and his brother was justly indignant and angry. But the break was inevitable; for Franklin was proud and independent by nature and too clever for his brother by far. At seventeen, with little money in his pocket but already an expert printer, he proceeded to make his way in the world, subject to the usual "errata," as he liked to call his mistakes, but confident that he could profit from lessons learned and not repeat them. His most serious error was in trusting a foolish man who wanted to be important to everyone. As a result of Governor Keith's "favors," Benjamin found himself alone and without employment in London in 1724. He returned to the colonies two years later, at the very time when the colonies' print culture experienced a remarkable take-off that marked a period of increasing dependence on the printer as a disseminator of information. Franklin, ever an astute businessman, turned this to his advantage.

Franklin had an uncanny instinct for success and knew that the new commercialism demanded that anyone in business assume a public persona that best served his and his clients' interests, even if it masked one's true self. He taught himself French, Spanish, Italian, and Latin and yet was shrewd enough to know that people did not like to do business with merchants who were smarter than they. He dressed plainly and sometimes carried his own paper in a wheelbarrow through Philadelphia streets to assure future customers that he was hardworking and not above doing things for himself. By the time he was twenty-four he was the sole owner of a successful printing shop and editor and publisher of the *Pennsylvania Gazette*. He offered his *Poor Richard's Almanac* for sale in 1733 and made it an American institution, filling it with maxims for achieving wealth and preaching hard work and thrift. In 1730 he married Deborah Read, the daughter of his first landlady, and they had two children. Franklin had two illegitimate children, and Deborah took Franklin's son William into the household. William was later to become governor of New Jersey and a Loyalist during the Revolution; Franklin addressed the first part of his *Autobiography* to him. Before he retired from business at the age of forty-two, Franklin had founded a library, invented a stove, established a fire company, subscribed to an academy that was to become the University of Pennsylvania, and served as secretary to the American Philosophical Society. It was his intention when he retired to devote himself to public affairs and his lifelong passion for the natural sciences, especially the phenomena of sound, vapors, earthquakes, and electricity.

Franklin's observations on electricity were published in London in 1751 and, despite his disclaimers in the *Autobiography*, brought him the applause of British scientists. Science was Franklin's great passion, the only thing, the American historian Charles Beard once said, about which Franklin was not ironic. His inquiring mind was challenged most by the mechanics of the ordinary phenomena of the world, and he was convinced that the mind's rational powers would enable him to solve riddles that had puzzled humankind for centuries. Franklin believed that people were naturally innocent, that all the mysteries that charmed the religious mind could be explained to our advantage and that education, properly undertaken, would transform our lives and set us free from the tyrannies of church and monarchy. Franklin had no illusions about the errata of humankind, but his metaphor suggests that we can change and alter our past in a way that the word *sins* does not.

Franklin's remaining years, however, were not spent in a laboratory, but at the diplomatic table in London, Paris, and Philadelphia, where his gift for irony served him well. For he was a born diplomat, detached, adaptable, witty, urbane, charming, and clever; and of the slightly more than forty years left to him after his retirement, more than half were spent abroad. In 1757 he went to England to represent the colonies and stayed for five years, returning in 1763. It was in England in 1768 that Franklin first noted his growing sense of alienation and the impossibility of compromise with the homeland. Parliament can make *all* laws for the colonies or *none,* he said, and "I think the arguments for the latter more numerous and weighty, than those for the former." When he returned to Philadelphia in May 1775, he was chosen as a representative to the Second Continental Congress, and he served on the committee to draft the Declaration of Independence. In October 1776, he was appointed minister to France, where he successfully negotiated a treaty of allegiance and became something of a cult hero. In 1781 he was a member of the American delegation to the Paris peace conference, and he signed the Treaty of Paris, which brought the Revolutionary War to an end. Franklin protested his too-long stay in Europe and returned to Philadelphia in 1785, serving as a delegate to the Constitutional Convention. When he died in 1790, he was one of the most beloved Americans. Twenty thousand people attended his funeral.

This hero of the eighteenth century, however, has not universally charmed our own time. To a number of readers, Franklin is a garrulous but insensitive man of the world, too adaptable for a man of integrity and too willing to please. D. H. Lawrence is only one of a number of Franklin's critics who have charged him with insensitivity and indifference to the darker recesses of the soul. There is no question but that Franklin, like Emerson, has been reduced by his admirers—the hero of those who seek only the way to wealth. But such single-mindedness does not do justice to Franklin's complexity. A reading of his finest prose will serve as a proper antidote; for the voice we find there is fully alert to the best and worst in all of humankind.

All the Franklin texts used here—with the exception of *The Autobiography*—are from *The Writings of Benjamin Franklin,* edited by Albert Henry Smyth (1907).

The Way to Wealth[1]

Preface to Poor Richard Improved

Courteous Reader,

I have heard that nothing gives an author so great pleasure, as to find his works respectfully quoted by other learned authors. This pleasure I have seldom enjoyed; for though I have been, if I may say it without vanity, an

1. Franklin composed this essay for the twenty-fifth anniversary issue of his *Almanac,* the first issue of which, under the fictitious editorship of "Richard Saunders," appeared in 1733. For this essay Franklin brought together the best of his maxims in the guise of a speech by Father Abraham. It is frequently reprinted as *The Way to Wealth,* but is also known by earlier titles: *Poor Richard Improved* and *Father Abraham's Speech.*

eminent author of almanacs annually now a full quarter of a century, my brother authors in the same way, for what reason I know not, have ever been very sparing in their applauses, and no other author has taken the least notice of me, so that did not my writings produce me some solid pudding, the great deficiency of praise would have quite discouraged me.

I concluded at length, that the people were the best judges of my merit; for they buy my works; and besides, in my rambles, where I am not personally known, I have frequently heard one or other of my adages repeated with "as Poor Richard says" at the end on 't; this gave me some satisfaction, as it showed not only that my instructions were regarded, but discovered likewise some respect for my authority; and I own, that to encourage the practice of remembering and repeating those wise sentences, I have sometimes quoted myself with great gravity.

Judge, then, how much I must have been gratified by an incident I am going to relate to you. I stopped my horse lately where a great number of people were collected at a vendue[2] of merchant goods. The hour of sale not being come, they were conversing on the badness of the times and one of the company called to a plain clean old man, with white locks, "Pray, Father Abraham, what think you of the times? Won't these heavy taxes quite ruin the country? How shall we be ever able to pay them? What would you advise us to?" Father Abraham stood up, and replied, "If you'd have my advice, I'll give it you in short, for a *word to the wise is enough, and many words won't fill a bushel*, as Poor Richard says." They joined in desiring him to speak his mind, and gathering round him, he proceeded as follows:

"Friends," says he, "and neighbors, the taxes are indeed very heavy, and if those laid on by the government were the only ones we had to pay, we might more easily discharge them; but we have many others, and much more grievous to some of us. We are taxed twice as much by our idleness, three times as much by our pride, and four times as much by our folly; and from these taxes the commissioners cannot ease or deliver us by allowing an abatement. However, let us hearken to good advice, and something may be done for us; *God helps them that help themselves*, as Poor Richard says, in his Almanac of 1733.

"It would be thought a hard government that should tax its people one-tenth part of their time, to be employed in its service. But idleness taxes many of us much more, if we reckon all that is spent in absolute sloth, or doing of nothing, with that which is spent in idle employments, or amusements, that amount to nothing. Sloth, by bringing on diseases, absolutely shortens life. *Sloth, like rust, consumes faster than labor wears; while the used key is always bright*, as Poor Richard says. *But dost thou love life, then do not squander time, for that's the stuff life is made of*, as Poor Richard says. How much more than is necessary do we spend in sleep, forgetting that *the sleeping fox catches no poultry* and that *there will be sleeping enough in the grave*, as Poor Richard says.

"*If time be of all things the most precious, wasting time must be*, as Poor Richard says, *the greatest prodigality*; since, as he elsewhere tells us, *lost time is never found again; and what we call time enough, always proves little enough*: let us then up and be doing, and doing to the purpose; so by diligence

2. Auction or sale.

shall we do more with less perplexity. *Sloth makes all things difficult, but industry all easy,* as Poor Richard says; *and he that riseth late must trot all day, and shall scarce overtake his business at night;* while *laziness travels so slowly, that poverty soon overtakes him,* as we read in Poor Richard, who adds, *drive thy business, let not that drive thee,* and *early to bed, and early to rise, makes a man healthy, wealthy, and wise.*

"So what signifies wishing and hoping for better times. We may make these times better, if we bestir ourselves. *Industry need not wish,* as Poor Richard says, *and he that lives upon hope will die fasting. There are no gains without pains; then help hands, for I have no lands,* or if I have, they are smartly taxed. And, as Poor Richard likewise observes, *he that hath a trade hath an estate; and he that hath a calling, hath an office of profit and honor;* but then the trade must be worked at, and the calling well followed, or neither the estate nor the office will enable us to pay our taxes. If we are industrious, we shall never starve; for, as Poor Richard says, *at the workingman's house hunger looks in, but dares not enter.* Nor will the bailiff or the constable enter, for *industry pays debts, while despair increaseth them,* says Poor Richard. What though you have found no treasure, nor has any rich relation left you a legacy, *diligence is the mother of good luck,* as Poor Richard says, and *God gives all things to industry. Then plow deep, while sluggards sleep, and you shall have corn to sell and to keep,* says Poor Dick. Work while it is called today, for you know not how much you may be hindered tomorrow, which makes Poor Richard says, *one today is worth two tomorrows,* and farther, *have you somewhat to do tomorrow, do it today.* If you were a servant, would you not be ashamed that a good master should catch you idle? Are you then your own master, *be ashamed to catch yourself idle,* as Poor Dick says. When there is so much to be done for yourself, your family, your country, and your gracious king, be up by peep of day; *let not the sun look down and say, inglorious here he lies.* Handle your tools without mittens; remember that *the cat in gloves catches no mice,* as Poor Richard says. 'Tis true there is much to be done, and perhaps you are weak-handed, but stick to it steadily; and you will see great effects, for *constant dropping wears away stones,* and *by diligence and patience the mouse ate in two the cable;* and *little strokes fell great oaks,* as Poor Richard says in his Almanac, the year I cannot just now remember.

"Methinks I hear some of you say, 'must a man afford himself no leisure?' I will tell thee, my friend, what Poor Richard says, *employ thy time well, if thou meanest to gain leisure; and, since thou art not sure of a minute, throw not away an hour.* Leisure is time for doing something useful; this leisure the diligent man will obtain, but the lazy man never; so that, as Poor Richard says *a life of leisure and a life of laziness are two things.* Do you imagine that sloth will afford you more comfort than labor? No, for as Poor Richard says, *trouble springs from idleness, and grievous toil from needless ease. Many without labor, would live by their wits only, but they break for want of stock.* Whereas industry gives comfort, and plenty, and respect: *fly pleasures, and they'll follow you. The diligent spinner has a large shift;*[3] *and now I have a sheep and a cow, everybody bids me good morrow;* all of which is well said by Poor Richard.

"But with our industry, we must likewise be steady, settled, and careful,

3. Wardrobe.

and oversee our own affairs with our own eyes, and not trust too much to others; for, as Poor Richard says

> *I never saw an oft-removed tree,*
> *Nor yet an oft-removed family,*
> *That throve so well as those that settled be.*

And again, *three removes*[4] *is as bad as a fire;* and again, *keep thy shop, and thy shop will keep thee;* and again, *if you would have your business done, go; if not, send.* And again,

> *He that by the plow would thrive,*
> *Himself must either hold or drive.*

And again, *the eye of a master will do more work than both his hands;* and again, *want of care does us more damage than want of knowledge;* and again, *not to oversee workmen is to leave them your purse open.* Trusting too much to others' care is the ruin of many; for, as the Almanac says, *in the affairs of this world, men are saved, not by faith, but by the want of it;* but a man's own care is profitable; for, saith Poor Dick, *learning is to the studious,* and *riches to the careful,* as well as *power to the bold,* and *heaven to the virtuous,* and farther, *if you would have a faithful servant, and one that you like, serve yourself.* And again, he adviseth to circumspection and care, even in the smallest matters, because sometimes *a little neglect may breed great mischief;* adding, *for want of a nail the shoe was lost; for want of a shoe the horse was lost; and for want of a horse the rider was lost, being overtaken and slain by the enemy; all for want of care about a horseshoe nail.*

"So much for industry, my friends, and attention to one's own business; but to these we must add frugality, if we would make our industry more certainly successful. A man may, if he knows not how to save as he gets, keep his nose all his life to the grindstone, and die not worth a groat[5] at last. *A fat kitchen makes a lean will,* as Poor Richard says; and

> *Many estates are spent in the getting,*
> *Since women for tea forsook spinning and knitting,*
> *And men for punch forsook hewing and splitting.*

If you would be wealthy, says he, in another Almanac, *think of saving as well as of getting: the Indies have not made Spain rich, because her outgoes are greater than her incomes.*

"Away then with your expensive follies, and you will not then have so much cause to complain of hard times, heavy taxes, and chargeable families; for, as Poor Dick says,

> *Women and wine, game and deceit,*
> *Make the wealth small and the wants great.*

And farther, *what maintains one vice would bring up two children.* You may think perhaps, that a little tea, or a little punch now and then, diet a little more costly, clothes a little finer, and a little entertainment now and then, can be no great matter; but remember what Poor Richard says, *many a little makes a mickle;*[6] and farther, *Beware of little expenses; a small leak will sink*

---

4. Moves.
5. A silver coin worth about four pence.

6. Lot.

a great ship; and again, *who dainties love shall beggars prove;* and moreover, *fools make feasts, and wise men eat them.*

"Here you are all got together at this vendue of fineries and knicknacks. You call them goods; but if you do not take care, they will prove evils to some of you. You expect they will be sold cheap, and perhaps they may for less than they cost; but if you have no occasion for them, they must be dear to you. Remember what Poor Richard says; *buy what thou hast no need of, and ere long thou shalt sell thy necessaries.* And again, *at a great penny-worth pause a while:* he means, that perhaps the cheapness is apparent only, and not real; or the bargain, by straightening thee in thy business, may do thee more harm than good. For in another place he says, *many have been ruined by buying good pennyworths.* Again, Poor Richard says, *'tis foolish to lay out money in a purchase of repentance;* and yet this folly is practiced every day at vendues, for want of minding the Almanac. *Wise men,* as Poor Dick says, *learn by others' harms, fools scarcely by their own; but felix quem faciunt aliena pericula cautum.*[7] Many a one, for the sake of finery on the back, have gone with a hungry belly, and half-starved their families. *Silks and satins, scarlet and velvets,* as Poor Richard says, *put out the kitchen fire.*

"These are not the necessaries of life; they can scarcely be called the conveniences; and yet only because they look pretty, how many want to have them! The artificial wants of mankind thus become more numerous than the natural; and, as Poor Dick says, *for one poor person, there are an hundred indigent.* By these, and other extravagancies, the genteel are reduced to poverty, and forced to borrow of those whom they formerly despised, but who through industry and frugality have maintained their standing; in which case it appears plainly, that *a plowman on his legs is higher than a gentleman on his knees,* as Poor Richard says. Perhaps they have had a small estate left them, which they knew not the getting of; they think, " 'Tis day, and will never be night"; that a little to be spent out of so much is not worth minding; *a child and a fool,* as Poor Richard says, *imagine twenty shillings and twenty years can never be spent* but, *always taking out of the meal-tub, and never putting in, soon comes to the bottom;* as Poor Dick says, *when the well's dry, they know the worth of water.* But this they might have known before, if they had taken his advice; *if you would know the value of money, go and try to borrow some; for, he that goes a-borrowing goes a-sorrowing;* and indeed so does he that lends to such people, when he goes to get it in again. Poor Dick farther advises, and says,

> Fond pride of dress is sure a very curse;
> E'er fancy you consult, consult your purse.

And again, *pride is as loud a beggar as want, and a great deal more saucy.* When you have bought one fine thing, you must buy ten more, that your appearance may be all of a piece; but Poor Dick says, *'tis easier to suppress the first desire, than to satisfy all that follow it.* And 'tis as truly folly for the poor to ape the rich, as for the frog to swell, in order to equal the ox.

> Great estates may venture more,
> But little boats should keep near shore.

7. A Latin version of the proverb just quoted.

'Tis, however, a folly soon punished; for *pride that dines on vanity sups on contempt*, as Poor Richard says. And in another place, *pride breakfasted with plenty, dined with poverty, and supped with infamy*. And after all, of what use is this pride of appearance, for which so much is risked so much is suffered? It cannot promote health, or ease pain; it makes no increase of merit in the person, it creates envy, it hastens misfortune.

> *What is a butterfly? At best*
> *He's but a caterpillar dressed.*
> *The gaudy fop's his picture just,*

as Poor Richard says.

"But what madness must it be to run in debt for these superfluities! We are offered, by the terms of this vendue, *six months' credit*; and that perhaps has induced some of us to attend it, because we cannot spare the ready money, and hope now to be fine without it. But, ah, think what you do when you run in debt; you give to another power over your liberty. If you cannot pay at the time, you will be ashamed to see your creditor; you will be in fear when you speak to him; you will make poor pitiful sneaking excuses, and by degrees come to lose your veracity, and sink into base downright lying; for, as Poor Richard says, *the second vice is lying, the first is running in debt*. And again, to the same purpose, *lying rides upon debt's back*. Whereas a free-born Englishman ought not to be ashamed or afraid to see or speak to any man living. But poverty often deprives a man of all spirit and virtue: *'tis hard for an empty bag to stand upright*, as Poor Richard truly says.

"What would you think of that prince, or that government, who should issue an edict forbidding you to dress like a gentleman or a gentlewoman, on pain of imprisonment or servitude? Would you not say, that you were free, have a right to dress as you please, and that such an edict would be a breach of your privileges, and such a government tyrannical? And yet you are about to put yourself under that tyranny, when you run in debt for such dress! Your creditor has authority, at his pleasure to deprive you of your liberty, by confining you in gaol[8] for life, or to sell you for a servant, if you should not be able to pay him! When you have got your bargain, you may, perhaps, think little of payment; but *creditors*, Poor Richard tells us, *have better memories than debtors*; and in another place says, *creditors are a superstitious sect, great observers of set days and times*. The day comes round before you are aware, and the demand is made before you are prepared to satisfy it, or if you bear your debt in mind, the term which at first seemed so long will, as it lessens, appear extremely short. Time will seem to have added wings to his heels as well as shoulders. *Those have a short Lent*, saith Poor Richard, *who owe money to be paid at Easter*. Then since, as he says, *The borrower is a slave to the lender, and the debtor to the creditor*, disdain the chain, preserve your freedom; and maintain your independency: be industrious and free; be frugal and free. At present, perhaps, you may think yourself in thriving circumstances, and that you can bear a little extravagance without injury; but,

> *For age and want, save while you may;*
> *No morning sun lasts a whole day,*

8. Jail.

as Poor Richard says. Gain may be temporary and uncertain, but ever while you live, expense is constant and certain; and *'tis easier to build two chimneys than to keep one in fuel*, as Poor Richard says. So, *rather go to bed supperless than rise in debt.*

> *Get what you can, and what you get hold;*
> *'Tis the stone that will turn all your lead into gold,*

as Poor Richard says. And when you have got the philosopher's stone,[9] sure you will no longer complain of bad times, or the difficulty of paying taxes.

"This doctrine, my friends, is reason and wisdom; but after all, do not depend too much upon your own industry, and frugality, and prudence, though excellent things, for they may all be blasted without the blessing of heaven; and therefore, ask that blessing humbly, and be not uncharitable to those that at present seem to want it, but comfort and help them. Remember, Job[1] suffered, and was afterwards prosperous.

"And now to conclude, *experience keeps a dear[2] school, but fools will learn in no other, and scarce in that*; for it is true, *we may give advice, but we cannot give conduct*, as Poor Richard says: however, remember this, *they that won't be counseled, can't be helped*, as Poor Richard says: and farther, that, *if you will not hear reason, she'll surely rap your knuckles.*"

Thus the old gentleman ended his harangue. The people heard it, and approved the doctrine, and immediately practiced the contrary, just as if it had been a common sermon; for the vendue opened, and they began to buy extravagantly, notwithstanding his cautions and their own fear of taxes. I found the good man had thoroughly studied my almanacs, and digested all I had dropped on these topics during the course of five and twenty years. The frequent mention he made of me must have tired any one else, but my vanity was wonderfully delighted with it, though I was conscious that not a tenth part of the wisdom was my own, which he ascribed to me, but rather the gleanings I had made of the sense of all ages and nations. However, I resolved to be the better for the echo of it; and though I had at first determined to buy stuff for a new coat, I went away resolved to wear my old one a little longer. Reader, if thou wilt do the same, thy profit will be as great as mine. I am, as ever, thine to serve thee,

Richard Saunders
July 7, 1757

1757   1758

---

9. A substance thought to transform base metals into gold, much sought after by alchemists.
1. The Old Testament patriarch whose faith was tested by suffering.
2. Expensive.

Rules by Which a Great Empire May Be Reduced to a Small One

Presented to a Late Minister,
When He Entered upon His Administration.[1]

An ancient Sage boasted, that, tho' he could not fiddle, he knew how to make a *great city* of a *little one*. The science that I, a modern simpleton, am about to communicate, is the very reverse.

I address myself to all ministers who have the management of extensive dominions, which from their very greatness are become troublesome to govern, because the multiplicity of their affairs leaves no time for *fiddling*.[2]

I. In the first place, gentlemen, you are to consider, that a great empire, like a great cake, is most easily diminished at the edges. Turn your attention, therefore, first to your *remotest* provinces; that, as you get rid of them, the next may follow in order.

II. That the possibility of this separation may always exist, take special care the provinces are never incorporated with the mother country; that they do not enjoy the same common rights, the same privileges in commerce; and that they are governed by *severer* laws, all of *your enacting*, without allowing them any share in the choice of the legislators. By carefully making and preserving such distinctions, you will (to keep to my simile of the cake) act like a wise gingerbread-baker, who, to facilitate a division, cuts his dough half through in those places where, when baked, he would have it *broken to pieces*.

III. Those remote provinces have perhaps been acquired, purchased, or conquered, at the *sole expence* of the settlers, or their ancestors, without the aid of the mother country. If this should happen to increase her *strength*, by their growing numbers, ready to join in her wars; her *commerce*, by their growing demand for her manufactures; or her *naval power*, by greater employment for her ships and seamen, they may probably suppose some merit in this, and that it entitles them to some favor; you are therefore to *forget it all, or resent it*, as if they had done you injury. If they happen to be zealous whigs,[3] friends of liberty, nurtured in revolution principles, *remember all that* to their prejudice, and resolve to punish it; for such principles, after a revolution is thoroughly established, are of *no more use*; they are even *odious* and *abominable*.

IV. However peaceably your colonies have submitted to your government, shown their affection to your interests, and patiently borne their grievances; you are to *suppose* them always inclined to revolt, and treat them accordingly. Quarter troops among them, who by their insolence may *provoke* the rising of mobs, and by their bullets and bayonets *suppress* them. By this means, like the husband who uses his wife ill *from suspicion*, you may in time convert your *suspicions* into *realities*.

V. Remote provinces must have *Governors* and *Judges*, to represent the Royal Person, and execute everywhere the delegated parts of his office and

---

1. The minister was Wills Hill, the first earl of Hillsborough and secretary of state to the colonies (1768–72).
2. Cheating.
3. Here, American supporters of independence from Britain.

authority. You ministers know, that much of the strength of government depends on the *opinion* of the people; and much of that opinion on the *choice of rulers* placed immediately over them. If you send them wise and good men for governors, who study the interest of the colonists, and advance their prosperity, they will think their King wise and good, and that he wishes the welfare of his subjects. If you send them learned and upright men for Judges, they will think him a lover of justice. This may attach your provinces more to his government. You are therefore to be careful whom you recommend for those offices. If you can find prodigals, who have ruined their fortunes, broken gamesters or stockjobbers,[4] these may do well as *governors;* for they will probably be rapacious, and provoke the people by their extortions. Wrangling proctors and pettifogging lawyers,[5] too, are not amiss; for they will be for ever disputing and quarrelling with their little parliaments. If withal they should be ignorant, wrong-headed, and insolent, so much the better. Attorneys' clerks and Newgate solicitors will do for *Chief Justices,* especially if they hold their places *during your pleasure;*[6] and all will contribute to impress those ideas of your government, that are proper for a people *you would wish to renounce it.*

VI. To confirm these impressions, and strike them deeper, whenever the injured come to the capital with complaints of maladministration, oppression, or injustice, punish such suitors with long delay, enormous expense, and a final judgment in favor of the oppressor. This will have an admirable effect every way. The trouble of future complaints will be prevented, and Governors and Judges will be encouraged to farther acts of oppression and injustice; and thence the people may become more disaffected, and at length desperate.

VII. When such Governors have crammed their coffers, and made themselves so odious to the people that they can no longer remain among them, with safety to their persons, *recall and reward* them with pensions. You may make them *baronets*[7] too, if that respectable order should not think fit to resent it. All will contribute to encourage new governors in the same practice, and make the supreme government, *detestable.*

VIII. If, when you are engaged in war, your colonies should vie in liberal aids of men and money against the common enemy, upon your simple requisition, and give far beyond their abilities, reflect that a penny taken from them by your power is more honorable to you, than a pound presented by their benevolence; despise therefore their voluntary grants, and resolve to harass them with novel taxes. They will probably complain to your parliaments, that they are taxed by a body in which they have no representative, and that this is contrary to common right. They will petition for redress. Let the Parliaments flout their claims, reject their petitions, refuse even to suffer the reading of them, and treat the petitioners with the utmost contempt. Nothing can have a better effect in producing the alienation proposed; for though many can forgive injuries, *none ever forgave contempt.*

IX. In laying these taxes, never regard the heavy burthens those remote people already undergo, in defending their own frontiers, supporting their

---

4. Gamblers or speculators.
5. I.e., shysters. "Proctors": civil lawyers.
6. I.e., at your pleasure.
7. I.e., give them noble titles. "Solicitors": lawyers.

Newgate was a London prison. The phrase "Newgate solicitors" may be akin to "ambulance chasers."

own provincial governments, making new roads, building bridges, churches, and other public edifices, which in old countries have been done to your lands by your ancestors, but which occasion constant calls and demands on the purses of a new people. Forget the *restraints* you lay on their trade for *your own* benefit, and the advantage a *monopoly* of this trade gives your exacting merchants. Think nothing of the wealth those merchants and your manufacturers acquire by the colony commerce; their increased ability thereby to pay taxes at home; their accumulating, in the price of their commodities, most of those taxes, and so levying them from their consuming customers; all this, and the employment and support of thousands of your poor by the colonists, you are *entirely to forget*. But remember to make your arbitrary tax more grievous to your provinces, by public declarations importing that your power of taxing them has *no limits*; so that when you take from them without their consent one shilling in the pound, you have a clear right to the other nineteen. This will probably weaken every idea of *security in their property,* and convince them, that under such a government they *have nothing they can call their own*; which can scarce fail of producing the *happiest consequences!*

X. Possibly, indeed, some of them might still comfort themselves, and say, "Though we have no property, we have yet *something* left that is valuable; we have constitutional *liberty,* both of person and of conscience. This King, these Lords, and these Commons, who it seems are too remote from us to know us, and feel for us, cannot take from us our *Habeas Corpus*[8] right, or our right of trial *by a jury of our neighbors;* they cannot deprive us of the exercise of our religion, alter our ecclesiastical constitution, and compel us to be Papists, if they please, or Mahometans." To annihilate this comfort, begin by laws to perplex their commerce with infinite regulations, impossible to be remembered and observed; ordain seizures of their property for every failure; take away the trial of such property by Jury, and give it to arbitrary Judges of your own appointing, and of the lowest characters in the country, whose salaries and emoluments[9] are to arise out of the duties or condemnations, and whose appointments are *during pleasure.* Then let there be a formal declaration of both Houses, that opposition to your edicts is *treason,* and that any person suspected of treason in the provinces may, according to some obsolete law, be seized and sent to the metropolis of the empire for trial; and pass an act, that those there charged with certain other offenses, shall be sent away in chains from their friends and country to be tried in the same manner for felony. Then erect a new Court of Inquisition among them, accompanied by an armed force, with instructions to transport[1] all such suspected persons; to be ruined by the expense, if they bring over evidences to prove their innocence, or be found guilty and hanged, if they cannot afford it. And, lest the people should think you cannot possibly go any farther, pass another solemn declaratory act, "that King, Lords, Commons had, hath, and of right ought to have, full power and authority to make statutes of sufficient force and validity to bind the unrepresented provinces IN ALL CASES WHATSOEVER." This will include *spiritual* with temporal, and, taken together, must operate wonderfully to your purpose; by convincing them, that they are at present under a power something like that spoken of in the scriptures, which

8. You should have the body (Latin, literal trans.); the right to know with what one is charged.
9. Payments for services rendered.

1. I.e., to deport, as criminals were to the American colonies.

can not only *kill their bodies,* but *damn their souls* to all eternity, by compelling them, if it pleases, *to worship the Devil.*

XI. To make your taxes more odious, and more likely to procure resistance, send from the capital a board of officers to superintend the collection, composed of the most *indiscreet, ill-bred,* and *insolent* you can find. Let these have large salaries out of the extorted revenue, and live in open, grating luxury upon the sweat and blood of the industrious; whom they are to worry continually with groundless and expensive prosecutions before the above-mentioned arbitrary revenue Judges; *all at the cost of the party prosecuted,* tho' acquitted, because *the King is to pay no costs.* Let these men, *by your order,* be exempted from all the common taxes and burthens of the province, though they and their property are protected by its laws. If any revenue offices are *suspected* of the least tenderness for the people, discard them. If others are justly complained of, protect and reward them. If any of the under officers behave so as to provoke the people to drub them, promote those to better offices: this will encourage others to procure for themselves such profitable drubbings, by multiplying and enlarging such provocations, and *all will work towards the end you aim at.*

XII. Another way to make your tax odious, is to misapply the produce of it. If it was originally appropriated for the *defense* of the provinces, the better support of government, and the administration of justice, where it may be *necessary,* then apply none of it to that *defense,* but bestow it where it is *not necessary,* in augmented salaries or pensions to every governor, who has distinguished himself by his enmity to the people, and by calumniating them to their sovereign. This will make them pay it more unwillingly, and be more apt to quarrel with those that collect it and those that imposed it, who will quarrel again with them, and all shall contribute to your *main purpose,* of making them *weary of your government.*

XIII. If the people of any province have been accustomed to support their own Governors and Judges to satisfaction, you are to apprehend that such Governors and Judges may be thereby influenced to treat the people kindly, and to do them justice. This is another reason for applying part of that revenue in larger salaries to such Governors and Judges, given, as their commissions are, *during your pleasure* only; forbidding them to take any salaries from their provinces; that thus the people may no longer hope any kindness from their Governors, or (in Crown cases)[2] any justice from their Judges. And, as the money thus misapplied in one province is extorted from all, probably *all will resent the misapplication.*

XIV. If the parliaments of your provinces should dare to claim rights, or complain of your administration, order them to be harrassed with *repeated dissolutions.* If the same men are continually returned by new elections, adjourn their meetings to some country village, where they cannot be accommodated, and there keep them *during pleasure;* for this, you know, is your PREROGATIVE; and an excellent one it is, as you may manage it to promote discontents among the people, diminish their respect, and *increase their disaffection.*

XV. Convert the brave, honest officers of your *navy* into pimping tidewaiters[3] and colony officers of the *customs.* Let those, who in time of war

2. Cases that were formerly appealed directly to the king.

3. Customs officers who boarded a ship before it docked.

fought gallantly in defense of the commerce of their countrymen, in peace be taught to prey upon it. Let them learn to be corrupted by great and real smugglers; but (to show their diligence) scour with armed boats every bay, harbor, river, creek, cove, or nook throughout the coast of your colonies; stop and detain every coaster, every wood-boat, every fisherman, tumble their cargoes and even their ballast inside out and upside down; and, if a penn'orth of pins is found unentered, let the whole be seized and confiscated. Thus shall the trade of your colonists suffer more from their friends in time of peace, than it did from their enemies in war. Then let these boats' crews land upon every farm in their way, rob the orchards, steal the pigs and the poultry, and insult the inhabitants. If the injured and exasperated farmers, unable to procure other justice, should attack the aggressors, drub them, and burn their boats; you are to call this *high treason and rebellion,* order fleets and armies into their country, and threaten to carry all the offenders three thousand miles to be hanged, drawn, and quartered. *O! this will work admirably!*

XVI. If you are told of discontents in your colonies, never believe that they are general, or that you have given occasion for them; therefore do not think of applying any remedy, or of changing any offensive measure. Redress no grievance, lest they should be encouraged to demand the redress of some other grievance. Grant no request that is just and reasonable, lest they should make another that is unreasonable. Take all your informations of the state of the colonies from your Governors and officers in enmity with them. Encourage and reward these *leasing-makers;*[4] secrete their lying accusations, lest they should be confuted; but act upon them as the clearest evidence; and believe nothing you hear from the friends of the people: suppose all *their* complaints to be invented and promoted by a few factious demagogues, whom if you could catch and hang, all would be quiet. Catch and hang a few of them accordingly; and the *blood of the Martyrs* shall *work miracles* in favor of your purpose.

XVII. If you see *rival nations* rejoicing at the prospect of your disunion with your provinces, and endeavoring to promote it; if they translate, publish, and applaud all the complaints of your discontented colonists, at the same time privately stimulating you to severer measures, let not that *alarm* or offend you. Why should it, since you all mean *the same thing?*

XVIII. If any colony should at their own charge erect a fortress to secure their port against the fleets of a foreign enemy, get your Governor to betray that fortress into your hands. Never think of paying what it cost the country, for that would look, at least, like some regard for justice; but turn it into a citadel to awe the inhabitants and curb their commerce. If they should have lodged in such fortress the very arms they bought and used to aid you in your conquests, seize them all; it will provoke like *ingratitude* added to *robbery.* One admirable effect of these operations will be, to discourage every other colony from erecting such defenses, and so your enemies may more easily invade them; to the great disgrace of your government, and of course *the furtherance of your project.*

XIX. Send armies into their country under pretense of protecting the inhabitants; but, instead of garrisoning the forts on their frontiers with those troops, to prevent incursions, demolish those forts, and order the troops into the heart of the country, that the savages may be encouraged to attack the

4. I.e., liars.

frontiers, and that the troops may be protected by the inhabitants. This will seem to proceed from your ill will or your ignorance, and contribute farther to produce and strengthen an opinion among them, *that you are no longer fit to govern them.*

XX. Lastly, invest the General of your army in the provinces, with great and unconstitutional powers, and free him from the control of even your own Civil Governors. Let him have troops enow[5] under his command, with all the fortresses in his possession; and who knows but (like some provincial Generals in the Roman empire, and encouraged by the universal discontent you have produced) he may take it into his head to set up for himself? If he should, and you have carefully practiced these few *excellent rules* of mine, take my word for it, all the provinces will immediately join him; and you will that day (if you have not done it sooner) get rid of the trouble of governing them, and all the *plagues* attending their *commerce* and connection from henceforth and for ever.

Q. E. D.[6]

1773

Information to Those Who Would Remove to America[1]

Many persons in Europe, having directly or by letters, expressed to the writer of this, who is well acquainted with North America, their desire of transporting and establishing themselves in that country; but who appear to have formed, through ignorance, mistaken ideas and expectations of what is to be obtained there; he thinks it may be useful, and prevent inconvenient, expensive, and fruitless removals and voyages of improper persons, if he gives some clearer and truer notions of that part of the world, than appear to have hitherto prevailed.

He finds it is imagined by numbers, that the inhabitants of North America are rich, capable of rewarding, and disposed to reward, all sorts of ingenuity; that they are at the same time ignorant of all the sciences, and consequently, that strangers, possessing talents in the belles-lettres, fine arts, etc., must be highly esteemed, and so well paid, as to become easily rich themselves; that there are also abundance of profitable offices to be disposed of, which the natives are not qualified to fill; and that, having few persons of family among them, strangers of birth must be greatly respected, and of course easily obtain the best of those offices, which will make all their fortunes; that the governments too, to encourage emigrations from Europe, not only pay the expense of personal transportation, but give lands gratis to strangers, with Negroes to work for them, utensils of husbandry, and stocks of cattle. These are all wild imaginations; and those who go to America with expectations founded upon them will surely find themselves disappointed.

5. Enough.
6. Abbreviation for *Quod erat demonstrandum:* Which was to be demonstrated (Latin); the usual conclusion to a geometry problem. I.e., "I have proved my point."
1. The title is taken from an edition of this pamph-
let published in London without Franklin's permission in 1784. Franklin's title was *Advice to Such As Would Remove to America,* and he used this title when he published his own edition in France in the same year.

The truth is, that though there are in that country few people so miserable as the poor of Europe, there are also very few that in Europe would be called rich; it is rather a general happy mediocrity that prevails. There are few great proprietors of the soil, and few tenants; most people cultivate their own lands, or follow some handicraft or merchandise; very few rich enough to live idly upon their rents or incomes, or to pay the high prices given in Europe for paintings, statues, architecture, and the other works of art, that are more curious than useful. Hence the natural geniuses, that have arisen in America with such talents, have uniformly quitted that country for Europe, where they can be more suitably rewarded. It is true, that letters and mathematical knowledge are in esteem there, but they are at the same time more common than is apprehended; there being already existing nine colleges or universities, viz., four in New England, and one in each of the provinces of New York, New Jersey, Pennsylvania, Maryland, and Virginia, all furnished with learned professors; besides a number of smaller academies; these educate many of their youth in the languages, and those sciences that qualify men for the professions of divinity, law, or physic.[2] Strangers indeed are by no means excluded from exercising those professions; and the quick increase of inhabitants everywhere gives them a chance of employ, which they have in common with the natives. Of civil offices, or employments, there are few; no superfluous ones, as in Europe; and it is a rule established in some of the states, that no office should be so profitable as to make it desirable. The 36th Article of the Constitution of Pennsylvania, runs expressly in these words: "As every freeman, to preserve his independence, (if he has not a sufficient estate) ought to have some profession, calling, trade, or farm, whereby he may honestly subsist, there can be no necessity for, nor use in, establishing offices of profit; the usual effects of which are dependence, and servility, unbecoming freemen, in the possessors and expectants; faction, contention, corruption, and disorder among the people. Wherefore, whenever an office, through increase of fees or otherwise, becomes so profitable, as to occasion many to apply for it, the profits ought to be lessened by the legislature."

These ideas prevailing more or less in all the United States, it cannot be worth any man's while, who has a means of living at home, to expatriate himself, in hopes of obtaining a profitable civil office in America; and, as to military offices, they are at an end with the war,[3] the armies being disbanded. Much less is it advisable for a person to go thither, who has no other quality to recommend him but his birth. In Europe it has indeed its value; but it is a commodity that cannot be carried to a worse market than that of America, where people do not inquire concerning a stranger, *what is he?* but, *what can he do?* If he has any useful art, he is welcome; and if he exercises it, and behaves well, he will be respected by all that know him; but a mere man of quality, who, on that account, wants to live upon the public, by some office or salary, will be despised and disregarded. The husbandman is in honor there, and even the mechanic,[4] because their employments are useful. The people have a saying, that God Almighty is Himself a mechanic, the greatest in the universe; and He is respected and admired more for the variety, ingenuity, and utility of His handyworks, than for the antiquity of His family.

2. Medicine.
3. I.e., the Revolutionary War.
4. Manual laborer. "Husbandman": farmer.

They are pleased with the observation of a Negro, and frequently mention it, that *Boccarorra* (meaning the white men) *make de black man workee, make de horse workee, make de ox workee, make eberyting workee; only de hog. He, de hog, no workee; he eat, he drink, he walk about, he go to sleep when he please; he libb like a gentleman.* According to these opinions of the Americans, one of them would think himself more obliged to a genealogist, who could prove for him that his ancestors and relations for ten generations had been plowmen, smiths, carpenters, turners, weavers, tanners,[5] or even shoe-makers, and consequently that they were useful members of society; than if he could only prove that they were gentlemen, doing nothing of value, but living idly on the labor of others, mere *fruges consumere nati,*[6] and otherwise *good for nothing,* till by their death their estates, like the carcass of the Negro's gentleman hog, come to be *cut up.*

With regard to encouragements for strangers from government, they are really only what are derived from good laws and liberty. Strangers are welcome, because there is room enough for them all, and therefore the old inhabitants are not jealous of them; the laws protect them sufficiently, so that they have no need for the patronage of great men; and every one will enjoy securely the profits of his industry. But, if he does not bring a fortune with him, he must work and be industrious to live. One or two years' residence gives him all the rights of a citizen; but the government does not at present, whatever it may have done in former times, hire people to become settlers, by paying their passages, giving land, Negroes, utensils, stock, or any other kind of emolument whatsoever. In short, America is the land of labor, and by no means what the English call *Lubberland,* and the French *Pays de Cocagne,*[7] where the streets are said to be paved with half-peck loaves, the houses tiled with pancakes, and where the fowls fly about ready roasted, crying *come eat me!*

Who then are the kind of persons to whom an emigration to America may be advantageous? And what are the advantages they may reasonably expect?

Land being cheap in that country, from the vast forests still void of inhabitants, and not likely to be occupied in an age to come, insomuch that the property of an hundred acres of fertile soil full of wood may be obtained near the frontiers, in many places, for eight or ten guineas, hearty young laboring men, who understand the husbandry of corn and cattle, which is nearly the same in that country as in Europe, may easily establish themselves there. A little money saved of the good wages they receive there, while they work for others, enables them to buy the land and begin their plantation,[8] in which they are assisted by the good will of their neighbors, and some credit. Multitudes of poor people from England, Ireland, Scotland, and Germany, have by this means in a few years become wealthy farmers, who, in their own countries, where all the lands are fully occupied, and the wages of labor low, could never have emerged from the poor condition wherein they were born.

From the salubrity of the air, the healthiness of the climate, the plenty of good provisions, and the encouragement to early marriages by the certainty of subsistence in cultivating the earth, the increase of inhabitants by natural generation is very rapid in America, and becomes still more so by the acces-

5. Those who convert hides into leather.
6. "... born / Merely to eat up the corn."—Watts" [Franklin's note].

7. I.e., never-never land. "*Lubberland*": a land of laziness.
8. Farm.

sion of strangers; hence there is a continual demand for more artisans of all the necessary and useful kinds, to supply those cultivators of the earth with houses, and with furniture and utensils of the grosser sorts, which cannot so well be brought from Europe. Tolerably good workmen in any of those mechanic arts are sure to find employ, and to be well paid for their work, there being no restraints preventing strangers from exercising any art they understand, nor any permission necessary. If they are poor, they begin first as servants or journeymen;[9] and if they are sober, industrious, and frugal, they soon become masters, establish themselves in business, marry, raise families, and become respectable citizens.

Also, persons of moderate fortunes and capitals, who, having a number of children to provide for, as desirous of bringing them up to industry,[1] and to secure estates for their posterity, have opportunities of doing it in America, which Europe does not afford. There they may be taught and practice profitable mechanic arts, without incurring disgrace on that account, but on the contrary acquiring respect by such abilities. There small capitals laid out in lands, which daily become more valuable by the increase of people, afford a solid prospect of ample fortunes thereafter for those children. The writer of this has known several instances of large tracts of land, bought, on what was then the frontier of Pennsylvania, for ten pounds per hundred acres, which after 20 years, when the settlements had been extended far beyond them, sold readily, without any improvement made upon them, for three pounds per acre. The acre in America is the same with the English acre, or the acre of Normandy.

Those, who desire to understand the state of government in America, would do well to read the constitutions of the several states, and the Articles of Confederation that binds the whole together for general purposes, under the direction of one assembly, called the Congress. These constitutions have been printed, by order of Congress, in America; two editions of them have also been printed in London; and a good translation of them into French has lately been published at Paris.

Several of the princes of Europe having of late years, from an opinion of advantage to arise by producing all commodities and manufactures within their own dominions, so as to diminish or render useless their importations, have endeavored to entice workmen from other countries by high salaries, privileges, etc. Many persons, pretending to be skilled in various great manufactures, imagining that America must be in want of them, and that the Congress would probably be disposed to imitate the prince above mentioned, have proposed to go over, on condition of having their passages paid, lands given, salaries appointed, exclusive privileges for terms of years, etc. Such persons, on reading the Articles of Confederation, will find, that the Congress have no power committed to them, or money out into their hands, for such purposes; and that if any such encouragement is given, it must be by the government of some separate state. This, however, has rarely been done in America; and, when it has been done, it has rarely succeeded, so as to establish a manufacture, which the country was not yet so ripe for as to encourage private persons to set it up; labor being generally too dear there,

9. Those who have served their apprenticeship and are paid by the day.

1. To be skillful in whatever they undertake in the way of a vocation.

and hands difficult to be kept together, every one desiring to be a master, and the cheapness of lands inclining many to leave trades for agriculture. Some indeed have met with success, and are carried on to advantage; but they are generally such as require only a few hands, or wherein great part of the work is performed by machines. Things that are bulky, and of so small value as not well to bear the expense of freight, may often be made cheaper in the country, than they can be imported; and the manufacture of such things will be profitable wherever there is a sufficient demand. The farmers in America produce indeed a good deal of wool and flax; and none is exported, it is all worked up; but it is in the way of domestic manufacture, for the use of the family. The buying up quantities of wool and flax, with the design to employ spinners, weavers, etc., and form great establishments, producing quantities of linen and woollen goods for sale, has been several times attempted in different provinces; but those projects have generally failed, goods of equal value being imported cheaper. And when the governments have been solicited to support such schemes by encouragements, in money, or by imposing duties on importation of such goods, it has been generally refused, on this principle, that, if the country is ripe for the manufacture, it may be carried on by private persons to advantage; and if not, it is a folly to think of forcing Nature. Great establishments of manufacture require great numbers of poor to do the work for small wages; these poor are to be found in Europe, but will not be found in America, till the lands are all taken up and cultivated, and the excess of people, who cannot get land, want employment. The manufacture of silk, they say, is natural in France, as that of cloth in England, because each country produces in plenty the first material; but if England will have a manufacture of silk as well as that of cloth, and France one of cloth as well as that of silk, these unnatural operations must be supported by mutual prohibitions, or high duties on the importation of each other's goods; by which means the workmen are enabled to tax the home consumer by greater prices, while the higher wages they receive makes them neither happier nor richer, since they only drink more and work less. Therefore the governments in America do nothing to encourage such projects. The people, by this means, are not imposed on, either by the merchant or mechanic. If the merchant demands too much profit on imported shoes, they buy of the shoemaker; and if he asks too high a price, they take them of the merchant; thus the two professions are checks on each other. The shoemaker, however, has, on the whole, considerable profit upon his labor in America, beyond what he had in Europe, as he can add to his price a sum nearly equal to all the expenses of freight and commission, risk or insurance, etc., necessarily charged by the merchant. And the case is the same with the workmen in every other mechanic art. Hence it is, that artisans generally live better and more easily in America than in Europe; and such as are good economists[2] make a comfortable provision for age, and for their children. Such may, therefore, remove with advantage to America.

In the long-settled countries of Europe, all arts, trades, professions, farms, etc., are so full, that it is difficult for a poor man, who has children, to place them where they may gain, or learn to gain, a decent livelihood. The artisans, who fear creating future rivals in business, refuse to take apprentices, but

2. Providers.

upon conditions of money, maintenance, or the like, which the parents are unable to comply with. Hence the youth are dragged up in ignorance of every gainful art, and obliged to become soldiers, or servants, or thieves, for a subsistence. In America, the rapid increase of inhabitants takes away that fear of rivalship, and artisans willingly receive apprentices from the hope of profit by their labor, during the remainder of the time stipulated, after they shall be instructed. Hence it is easy for poor families to get their children instructed; for the artisans are so desirous of apprentices, that many of them will even give money to the parents, to have boys from ten to fifteen years of age bound apprentices to them till the age of twenty-one; and many poor parents have, by that means, on their arrival in the country, raised money enough to buy land sufficient to establish themselves, and to subsist the rest of their family by agriculture. These contracts for apprentices are made before a magistrate, who regulates the agreement according to reason and justice, and, having in view the formation of a future useful citizen, obliges the master to engage by a written indenture, not only that, during the time of service stipulated, the apprentice shall be duly provided with meat, drink, apparel, washing, and lodging, and, at its expiration, with a complete new suit of clothes, but also that he shall be taught to read, write, and cast accounts;[3] and that he shall be well instructed in the art or profession of his master, or some other, by which he may afterwards gain a livelihood, and be able in his turn to raise a family. A copy of this indenture is given to the apprentice or his friends, and the magistrate keeps a record of it, to which recourse may be had, in case of failure by the master in any point of performance. This desire among the masters, to have more hands employed in working for them, induces them to pay the passages of young persons, of both sexes, who, on their arrival, agree to serve them one, two, three, or four years; those, who have already learned a trade, agreeing for a shorter term, in proportion to their skill, and the consequent immediate value of their service; and those, who have none, agreeing for a longer term, in consideration of being taught an art their poverty would not permit them to acquire in their own country.

The almost general mediocrity of fortune that prevails in America obliging its people to follow some business for subsistence, those vices, that arise usually from idleness, are in a great measure prevented. Industry and constant employment are great preservatives of the morals and virtue of a nation. Hence bad examples to youth are more rare in America, which must be a comfortable consideration to parents. To this may be truly added, that serious religion, under its various denominations, is not only tolerated, but respected and practiced. Atheism is unknown there; infidelity[4] rare and secret; so that persons may live to a great age in that country, without having their piety shocked by meeting with either an atheist or an infidel. And the Divine Being seems to have manifested His approbation of the mutual forbearance and kindness with which the different sects treat each other, by the remarkable prosperity with which He has been pleased to favor the whole country.

1782   1784

---

3. Calculate; add up the figures in a column.   4. Lack of religious belief.

Remarks Concerning the Savages of
North America

Savages we call them, because their manners differ from ours, which we think the perfection of civility; they think the same of theirs.

Perhaps, if we could examine the manners of different nations with impartiality, we should find no people so rude, as to be without any rules of politeness; nor any so polite, as not to have some remains of rudeness.

The Indian men, when young, are hunters and warriors; when old, counselors; for all their government is by counsel of the sages; there is no force, there are no prisons, no officers to compel obedience, or inflict punishment. Hence they generally study oratory, the best speaker having the most influence. The Indian women till the ground, dress the food, nurse and bring up the children, and preserve and hand down to posterity the memory of public transactions. These employments of men and women are accounted natural and honorable. Having few artificial wants, they have abundance of leisure for improvement by conversation. Our laborious manner of life, compared with theirs, they esteem slavish and base; and the learning, on which we value ourselves, they regard as frivolous and useless. An instance of this occurred at the Treaty of Lancaster, in Pennsylvania, *anno* 1744, between the government of Virginia and the Six Nations.[1] After the principal business was settled, the commissioners from Virginia acquainted the Indians by a speech, that there was at Williamsburg a college, with a fund for educating Indian youth; and that, if the Six Nations would send down half a dozen of their young lads to that college, the government would take care that they should be well provided for, and instructed in all the learning of the white people. It is one of the Indian rules of politeness not to answer a public proposition the same day that it is made; they think it would be treating it as a light matter, and that they show it respect by taking time to consider it, as of a matter important. They therefore deferred their answer till the day following; when their speaker began, by expressing their deep sense of the kindness of the Virginia government, in making them that offer; "for we know," says he, "that you highly esteem the kind of learning taught in those Colleges, and that the maintenance of our young men, while with you, would be very expensive to you. We are convinced, therefore, that you mean to do us good by your proposal; and we thank you heartily. But you, who are wise, must know that different nations have different conceptions of things; and you will therefore not take it amiss, if our ideas of this kind of education happen not to be the same with yours. We have had some experience of it; several of our young people were formerly brought up at the colleges of the northern provinces; they were instructed in all your sciences; but, when they came back to us, they were bad runners, ignorant of every means of living in the woods, unable to bear either cold or hunger, knew neither how to build a cabin, take a deer, or kill an enemy, spoke our language imperfectly, were therefore neither fit for hunters, warriors, nor counselors; they were totally good for nothing. We are however not the less obliged by your kind

---

1. A confederation of Iroquois tribes: Seneca, Cayuga, Oneida, Onondaga, Mohawk, and Tuscarora. "*Anno*": in the year (Latin).

offer, though we decline accepting it; and, to show our grateful sense of it, if the gentlemen of Virginia will send us a dozen of their sons, we will take great care of their education, instruct them in all we know, and make *men* of them."

Having frequent occasions to hold public councils, they have acquired great order and decency in conducting them. The old men sit in the foremost ranks, that warriors in the next, and the women and children in the hindmost. The business of the women is to take exact notice of what passes, imprint it in their memories (for they have no writing), and communicate it to their children. They are the records of the council, and they preserve traditions of the stipulations in treaties 100 years back; which, when we compare with our writings, we always find exact. He that would speak, rises. The rest observe a profound silence. When he has finished and sits down, they leave him 5 or 6 minutes to recollect, that, if he has omitted anything he intended to say, or has anything to add, he may rise again and deliver it. To interrupt another, even in common conversation, is reckoned highly indecent. How different this from the conduct of a polite British House of Commons, where scarce a day passes without some confusion, that makes the speaker hoarse in calling to *order*; and how different from the mode of conversation in many polite companies of Europe, where, if you do not deliver your sentence with great rapidity, you are cut off in the middle of it by the impatient loquacity of those you converse with, and never suffered to finish it!

The politeness of these savages in conversation is indeed carried to excess, since it does not permit them to contradict or deny the truth of what is asserted in their presence. By this means they indeed avoid disputes; but then it becomes difficult to know their minds, or what impression you make upon them. The missionaries who have attempted to convert them to Christianity all complain of this as one of the great difficulties of their mission. The Indians hear with patience the truths of the Gospel explained to them, and give their usual tokens of assent and approbation; you would think they were convinced. No such matter. It is mere civility.

A Swedish minister, having assembled the chiefs of the Susquehanah Indians, made a sermon to them, acquainting them with the principal historical facts on which our religion is founded; such as the fall of our first parents by eating an apple, the coming of Christ to repair the mischief, His miracles and suffering, etc. When he had finished, an Indian orator stood up to thank him. "What you have told us," he says, "is all very good. It is indeed bad to eat apples. It is better to make them all into cider. We are much obliged by your kindness in coming so far, to tell us these things which you have heard from your mothers. In return, I will tell you some of those we have heard from ours. In the beginning, our fathers had only the flesh of animals to subsist on; and if their hunting was unsuccessful, they were starving. Two of our young hunters, having killed a deer, made a fire in the woods to broil some part of it. When they were about to satisfy their hunger, they beheld a beautiful young woman descend from the clouds, and seat herself on that hill, which you see yonder among the blue mountains. They said to each other, it is a spirit that has smelled our broiling venison, and wishes to eat of it; let us offer some to her. They presented her with the tongue; she was pleased with the taste of it, and said, 'Your kindness shall be rewarded; come to this place after thirteen moons, and you shall find something that will be of great benefit in nourishing you and your children to the latest generations.' They did so, and, to their surprise, found plants they had never seen before; but which, from that ancient time, have been constantly cultivated among us, to our great advantage. Where her right hand had touched the ground, they found maize; where her left hand had touched it, they found kidney-beans; and where her backside had sat on it, they found tobacco." The good missionary, disgusted with this idle tale, said, "What I delivered to you were sacred truths; but what you tell me is mere fable, fiction, and falsehood." The Indian, offended, replied, "My brother, it seems your friends have not done you justice in your education; they have not well instructed you in the rules of common civility. You saw that we, who understand and practice those rules, believed all your stories; why do you refuse to believe ours?"

When any of them come into our towns, our people are apt to crowd round them, gaze upon them, and incommode them, where they desire to be private; this they esteem great rudeness, and the effect of the want of instruction in the rules of civility and good manners. "We have," say they, "as much curiosity as you, and when you come into our towns, we wish for opportunities of looking at you, but for this purpose we hide ourselves behind bushes, where you are to pass, and never intrude ourselves into your company."

Their manner of entering one another's village has likewise its rules. It is reckoned uncivil in traveling strangers to enter a village abruptly, without giving notice of their approach. Therefore, as soon as they arrive within hearing, they stop and hollow,[2] remaining there till invited to enter. Two old men usually come out to them, and lead them in. There is in every village a vacant dwelling, called *the stranger's house.* Here they are placed, while the old men go round from hut to hut, acquainting the inhabitants, that strangers are arrived, who are probably hungry and weary; and every one sends them what he can spare of victuals, and skins to repose on. When the strangers are refreshed, pipes and tobacco are brought; and then, but not before, conversation begins, with inquiries who they are, whither bound, what news, etc.; and it usually ends with offers of service, if the strangers have occasion of guides, or any necessaries for continuing their journey; and nothing is exacted for the entertainment.

The same hospitality, esteemed among them as a principal virtue, is practiced by private persons; of which Conrad Weiser, our interpreter, gave me the following instances. He had been naturalized among the Six Nations, and spoke well the Mohawk language. In going through the Indian country, to carry a message from our Governor to the Council at Onondaga, he called at the habitation of Canassatego, an old acquaintance, who embraced him, spread furs for him to sit on, placed before him some boiled beans and venison, and mixed some rum and water for his drink. When he was well refreshed, and had lit his pipe, Canassatego began to converse with him; asked how he had fared the many years since they had seen each other; whence he then came; what occasioned the journey, etc. Conrad answered all his questions; and when the discourse began to flag, the Indian, to continue it, said, "Conrad, you have lived long among the white people, and know something of their customs; I have been sometimes at Albany, and have observed, that once in seven days they shut up their shops, and assemble all in the great house; tell me what it is for? What do they do there?"

2. Cry out; announce themselves.

"They meet there," says Conrad, "to hear and learn *good things.*" "I do not doubt," says the Indian, "that they tell you so; they have told me the same; but I doubt the truth of what they say, and I will tell you my reasons. I went lately to Albany to sell my skins and buy blankets, knives, powder, rum, etc. You know I used generally to deal with Hans Hanson; but I was a little inclined this time to try some other merchant. However, I called first upon Hans, and asked him what he would give for beaver. He said he could not give any more than four shillings a pound; 'but,' says he, 'I cannot talk on business now; this is the day when we meet together to learn *good things,* and I am going to the meeting.' So I thought to myself, 'Since we cannot do any business today, I may as well go to the meeting too,' and I went with him. There stood up a man in black, and began to talk to the people very angrily. I did not understand what he said; but, perceiving that he looked much at me and at Hanson, I imagined he was angry at seeing me there; so I went out, sat down near the house, struck fire, and lit my pipe, waiting till the meeting should break up. I thought too, that the man had mentioned something of beaver, and I suspected it might be the subject of their meeting. So, when they came out, I accosted my merchant. 'Well, Hans,' says I, 'I hope you have agreed to give more than four shillings a pound.' 'No,' says he, 'I cannot give so much; I cannot give more than three shillings and sixpence.' I then spoke to several other dealers, but they all sung the same song,—three and sixpence,—three and sixpence. This made it clear to me, that my suspicion was right; and, that whatever they pretended of meeting to learn *good things,* the real purpose was to consult how to cheat Indians in the price of beaver. Consider but a little, Conrad, and you must be of my opinion. If they met so often to learn *good things,* they would certainly have learned some before this time. But they are still ignorant. You know our practice. If a white man, in traveling through our country, enters one of our cabins, we all treat him as I treat you; we dry him if he is wet, we warm him if he is cold, we give him meat and drink, that he may allay his thirst and hunger; and we spread soft furs for him to rest and sleep on; we demand nothing in return. But, if I go into a white man's house at Albany, and ask for victuals and drink, they say, 'Where is your money?' and if I have none, they say, 'Get out, you Indian dog.' You see they have not yet learned those little *good things,* that we need no meetings to be instructed in, because our mothers taught them to us when we were children; and therefore it is impossible their meetings should be, as they say, for any such purpose, or have any such effect; they are only to contrive *the cheating of Indians in the price of beaver.*"[3]

1784

3. "It is remarkable that in all ages and countries hospitality has been allowed as the virtue of those whom the civilized were pleased to call barbarians. The Greeks celebrated the Scythians for it. The Saracens possessed it eminently, and it is to this day the reigning virtue of the wild Arabs. St. Paul, too, in the relation of his voyage and shipwreck on the island of Melité says the barbarous people showed us no little kindness; for they kindled a fire, and received us every one, because of the present rain, and because of the cold" [Franklin's note]. St. Paul's account of his visit to Melita may be found in Acts 28. The Scythians were nomadic tribes of southeastern Europe known for their plundering.

The Autobiography   Franklin turned to the manuscript of *The Autobiography* on four different occasions over a period of nineteen years. The first part, addressed to his son William Franklin (1731–1813), governor of New Jersey when Franklin was writing this section, was composed while Franklin was visiting the country home of Bishop Jonathan Shipley at Twyford, a village about fifty miles from London. It was begun on July 30 and concluded on or about August 13, 1771. Franklin did not work on the manuscript again until he was living in France and was minister of the newly formed United States, about thirteen years later. The last two sections were written in August 1788 and the winter of 1789–90, when Franklin stopped because of illness. Before he died he carried his life up to the year 1758. The account ends, therefore, before Franklin's great triumphs as a diplomat and public servant.

The first part of *The Autobiography* was published in 1791 by Jacques Buisson in a French translation; William Temple Franklin, Franklin's grandson, published an edition of *The Autobiography* in 1818, but he did not possess the last section that his grandfather wrote because he unwittingly exchanged it for the French translator's Part One. It was not until 1868 that John Bigelow published *The Autobiography* as we know it, with all four sections complete.

The text for *The Autobiography* here reprinted is the first to have been taken directly from the manuscript itself (all other editors have merely corrected earlier printed texts). It was established by J. A. Leo Lemay and Paul Zall for the Norton Critical Edition of *The Autobiography* and is here reprinted with their permission. The text has been only slightly modernized. All manuscript abbreviations and symbols have been expanded. The editors note that they have omitted short dashes, which Franklin often wrote after sentences, and punctuation marks that "have been clearly superseded by revisions or additions." Careless slips have been corrected silently but may be found in the section on emendations in their complete text. Lemay and Zall have been generous in letting us consult their footnotes and biographical sketches. Every student of *The Autobiography* must also acknowledge the helpful edition of Leonard W. Labaree et al. (1964).

From The Autobiography

[PART ONE]

Twyford, at the Bishop of St. Asaph's 1771.

Dear Son,

I have ever had a Pleasure in obtaining any little Anecdotes of my Ancestors. You may remember the Enquiries I made among the Remains[1] of my Relations when you were with me in England; and the Journey I took for that purpose. Now imagining it may be equally agreeable to you to know the Circumstances of *my* Life, many of which you are yet unacquainted with; and expecting a Week's uninterrupted Leisure in my present Country Retirement, I sit down to write them for you. To which I have besides some other Inducements. Having emerg'd from the Poverty and Obscurity in which I was born and bred, to a State of Affluence and some Degree of Reputation in the World, and having gone so far thro' Life with a considerable Share of Felicity, the conducting Means I made use of, which, with the Blessing of God, so well succeeded, my Posterity may like to know, as they may find some of them suitable to their own Situations, and therefore fit to be imitated. That Felicity, when I reflected on it, has induc'd me sometimes to say,

---

1. I.e., the remaining representatives of a family. Franklin and his son toured England in 1758 and visited ancestral homes at Ecton and Banbury.

that were it offer'd to my Choice, I should have no Objection to a Repetition of the same Life from its Beginning, only asking the Advantage Authors have in a second Edition to correct some Faults of the first. So would I if I might, besides correcting the Faults, change some sinister Accidents and Events of it for others more favorable, but tho' this were denied, I should still accept the Offer. However, since such a Repetition is not to be expected, the Thing most like living one's Life over again, seems to be a *Recollection* of that Life; and to make that Recollection as durable as possible, the putting it down in Writing. Hereby, too, I shall indulge the Inclination so natural in old Men, to be talking of themselves and their own past Actions, and I shall indulge it, without being troublesome to others who thro' respect to Age might think themselves oblig'd to give me a Hearing, since this may be read or not as any one pleases. And lastly, (I may as well confess it, since my Denial of it will be believ'd by no body) perhaps I shall a good deal gratify my own *Vanity*. Indeed I scarce ever heard or saw the introductory Words, *Without Vanity I may say*, etc. but some vain thing immediately follow'd. Most People dislike Vanity in others whatever Share they have of it themselves, but I give it fair Quarter wherever I meet with it, being persuaded that it is often productive of Good to the Possessor and to others that are within his Sphere of Action: And therefore in many Cases it would not be quite absurd if a Man were to thank God for his Vanity among the other Comforts of Life.

And now I speak of thanking God, I desire with all Humility to acknowledge, that I owe the mention'd Happiness of my past Life to his kind Providence, which led me to the Means I us'd and gave them Success. My Belief of This, induces me to *hope*, tho' I must not *presume*, that the same Goodness will still be exercis'd towards me in continuing that Happiness, or in enabling me to bear a fatal Reverso,[2] which I may experience as others have done, the Complexion of my future Fortune being known to him only: and in whose Power it is to bless to us even our Afflictions.

The Notes one of my Uncles (who had the same kind of Curiosity in collecting Family Anecdotes) once put into my Hands, furnish'd me with several Particulars, relating to our Ancestors. From those Notes I learned that the Family had liv'd in the same Village, Ecton in Northamptonshire, for 300 Years, and how much longer he knew not, (perhaps from the Time when the Name *Franklin* that before was the Name of an Order of People,[3] was assum'd by them for a Surname, when others took Surnames all over the Kingdom)[4] on a Freehold of about 30 Acres, aided by the Smith's Business which had continued in the Family till his Time, the eldest Son being always bred to that Business. A Custom which he and my Father both followed as to their eldest Sons. When I search'd the Register at Ecton, I found an Account of their Births, Marriages and Burials, from the Year 1555 only, there being no Register kept in that Parish at any time preceding. By that Register I perceiv'd that I was the youngest Son of the youngest Son for 5 Generations back. My Grandfather Thomas, who was born in 1598, lived at Ecton till he grew too old to follow Business longer, when he went to live with his Son John, a Dyer at Banbury in Oxfordshire, with whom my Father serv'd an Apprenticeship. There my Grandfather died and lies buried. We

2. I.e., a backhanded stroke, a word used in dueling with rapiers.
3. A "franklin" was a freeholder—an individual who owned land but was not of noble birth.
4. Here a note [Franklin intended to insert a note here, but did not].

saw his Gravestone in 1758. His eldest Son Thomas liv'd in the House at Ecton, and left it with the Land to his only Child, a Daughter, who with her Husband, one Fisher of Wellingborough, sold it to Mr. Isted, now Lord of the Manor there.

My Grandfather had 4 Sons that grew up, viz., Thomas, John, Benjamin and Josiah. I will give you what Account I can of them at this distance from my Papers, and if those are not lost in my Absence, you will among them find many more Particulars. Thomas was bred a Smith under his Father, but being ingenious, and encourag'd in Learning (as all his Brothers likewise were,) by an Esquire[5] Palmer then the principal Gentleman in that Parish, he qualified himself for the Business of Scrivener,[6] became a considerable Man in the County Affairs, was a chief Mover of all public Spirited Undertakings for the County or Town of Northampton and his own Village, of which many Instances were told us at Ecton, and he was much taken Notice of and patroniz'd by the then Lord Halifax. He died in 1702, Jan. 6, old Stile,[7] just 4 Years to a Day before I was born. The Account we receiv'd of his Life and Character from some old People at Ecton, I remember struck you as something extraordinary from its Similarity to what you knew of mine. Had he died on the same Day, you said one might have suppos'd a Transmigration.[8]

John was bred a Dyer, I believe of Woollens. Benjamin was bred a Silk Dyer, serving an Apprenticeship at London. He was an ingenious Man. I remember him well, for when I was a Boy he came over to my Father in Boston, and lived in the House with us some Years. He lived to a great Age. His Grandson Samuel Franklin now lives in Boston. He left behind him two Quarto[9] Volumes, Manuscript of his own Poetry, consisting of little occasional Pieces address'd to his Friends and Relations, of which the following sent to me, is a Specimen.[1] He had form'd a Shorthand of his own, which he taught me, but never practicing it I have now forgot it. I was nam'd after this Uncle, there being a particular Affection between him and my Father. He was very pious, a great Attender of Sermons of the best Preachers, which he took down in his Shorthand and had with him many Volumes of them. He was also much of a Politician, too much perhaps for his Station. There fell lately into my Hands in London a Collection he had made of all the principal Pamphlets relating to Public Affairs from 1641 to 1717. Many of the Volumes are wanting, as appears by the Numbering, but there still remains 8 Volumes Folio, and 24 in Quarto and Octavo. A Dealer in old Books met with them, and knowing me by my sometimes buying of him, he brought them to me. It seems my Uncle must have left them here when he went to America, which was above 50 Years since. There are many of his Notes in the Margins.

5. An honorific originally extended to a young man of gentle birth, but extended as a courtesy to any gentleman.
6. A professional copier of documents.
7. Until 1752 England used the Julian calendar, in which the new year began on March 25. Because the Julian calendar did not have leap years, it had fallen behind the astronomical year; the English skipped eleven days when adopting the Gregorian calendar. Franklin's birthday is either January 6, 1705–06, "old Stile," or January 17, 1706, New Style.
8. The passage of the soul to another's body upon death.
9. The terms *folio, quarto,* and *octavo* designate book sizes from large to small. A single sheet folded once makes a folio, or four sides for printing; a quarto is obtained if the sheet is folded again; an octavo is the sheet folded once more.
1. Here insert it [Franklin's note, but the example was not included].

This obscure Family of ours was early in the Reformation, and continu'd Protestants thro' the Reign of Queen Mary,[2] when they were sometimes in Danger of Trouble on Account of their Zeal against Popery. They had got an English Bible,[3] and to conceal and secure it, it was fastened open with Tapes under and within the Frame of a Joint Stool.[4] When my Great Great Grandfather read in it to his Family, he turn'd up the Joint Stool upon his Knees, turning over the Leaves then under the Tapes. One of the Children stood at the Door to give Notice if he saw the Apparitor[5] coming, who was an Officer of the Spiritual Court. In that Case the Stool was turn'd down again upon its feet, when the Bible remain'd conceal'd under it as before. This Anecdote I had from my Uncle Benjamin. The Family continu'd all of the Church of England till about the End of Charles the Second's Reign,[6] when some of the Ministers that had been outed for Nonconformity, holding Conventicles[7] in Northamptonshire, Benjamin and Josiah adher'd to them, and so continu'd all their Lives. The rest of the Family remain'd with the Episcopal Church.

Josiah, my Father, married young, and carried his Wife with three Children unto New England, about 1682.[8] The Conventicles having been forbidden by Law, and frequently disturbed, induced some considerable Men of his Acquaintance to remove to that Country, and he was prevail'd with to accompany them thither, where they expected to enjoy their Mode of Religion with Freedom. By the same Wife he had 4 Children more born there, and by a second Wife ten more, in all 17, of which I remember 13 sitting at one time at his Table, who all grew up to be Men and Women, and married. I was the youngest Son and the youngest Child but two, and was born in Boston, New England.

My Mother the second Wife was Abiah Folger, a Daughter of Peter Folger, one of the first Settlers of New England, of whom honorable mention is made by Cotton Mather, in his Church History of that Country, (entitled Magnalia Christi Americana) as a *godly learned Englishman,* if I remember the Words rightly.[9] I have heard that he wrote sundry small occasional Pieces, but only one of them was printed which I saw now many Years since. It was written in 1675, in the homespun Verse of that Time and People, and address'd to those then concern'd in the Government there. It was in favor of Liberty of Conscience, and in behalf of the Baptists, Quakers, and other Sectaries,[1] that had been under Persecution; ascribing the Indian Wars and other Distresses that had befallen the Country to that Persecution, as so many Judgments of God, to punish so heinous an Offence; and exhorting a Repeal of those uncharitable Laws. The whole appear'd to me as written with a good deal of Decent Plainness and manly Freedom. The six last concluding Lines I remember, tho' I have forgotten the two first of the Stanza, but the

---

2. From 1553 to 1558, Mary, the older sister of Elizabeth I, tried to restore Roman Catholicism as the national church.
3. A Bible known as the "Geneva" version, translated by Reformed English Protestants living in Switzerland; this version, used by the Puritans, was outlawed by the Church of England.
4. A small four-legged stool.
5. An officer of an ecclesiastical court, in this case a court established to eliminate heresy.
6. Charles II (1630–1685) reigned from 1660 to 1685.

7. Secret and illegal meetings of Nonconformists, outlawed in 1664. Nonconformists refused to adopt the rituals and acknowledge the hierarchy of the Church of England.
8. More correctly, October 1683.
9. Cotton Mather's ecclesiastical history *The Wonderful Work of Christ in America,* which was published in London in 1702; the quotation is properly "an Able Godly Englishman."
1. Believers or followers of a particular religious teaching.

Purport of them was that his Censures proceeded from *Goodwill,* and therefore he would be known as the Author,

> because to be a Libeler, (says he)
> I hate it with my Heart.
> From Sherburne Town[2] where now I dwell,
> My Name I do put here,
> Without Offence, your real Friend,
> It is Peter Folgier.

My elder Brothers were all put Apprentices to different Trades. I was put to the Grammar School at Eight Years of Age, my Father intending to devote me as the Tithe[3] of his Sons to the Service of the Church. My early Readiness in learning to read (which must have been very early, as I do not remember when I could not read) and the Opinion of all his Friends that I should certainly make a good Scholar, encourag'd him in this Purpose of his. My Uncle Benjamin too approv'd of it, and propos'd to give me all his Shorthand Volumes of Sermons, I suppose as a Stock to set up with, if I would learn his Character.[4] I continu'd however at the Grammar School not quite one Year, tho' in that time I had risen gradually from the Middle of the Class of that Year to be the Head of it, and farther was remov'd into the next Class above it, in order to go with that into the third at the End of the Year. But my Father in the meantime, from a View of the Expense of a College Education which, having so large a Family, he could not well afford, and the mean Living many so educated were afterwards able to obtain, Reasons that he gave to his Friends in my Hearing, altered his first Intention, took me from the Grammar School, and sent me to a School for Writing and Arithmetic kept by a then famous Man, Mr. George Brownell, very successful in his Profession generally, and that by mild encouraging Methods. Under him I acquired fair Writing pretty soon, but I fail'd in the Arithmetic, and made no Progress in it.

At Ten Years old, I was taken home to assist my Father in his Business, which was that of a Tallow Chandler and Soap-Boiler.[5] A Business he was not bred to, but had assumed on his Arrival in New England and on finding his Dying Trade would not maintain his Family, being in little Request. Accordingly I was employed in cutting Wick for the Candles, filling the Dipping Mold, and the Molds for cast Candles, attending the Shop, going of Errands, etc. I dislik'd the Trade and had a strong Inclination for the Sea; but my Father declar'd against it; however, living near the Water, I was much in and about it, learned early to swim well, and to manage Boats, and when in a Boat or Canoe with other Boys I was commonly allow'd to govern,[6] especially in any case of Difficulty; and upon other Occasions I was generally a Leader among the Boys, and sometimes led them into Scrapes, of which I will mention one Instance, as it shows an early projecting public Spirit, tho' not then justly conducted. There was a Salt Marsh that bounded part of the Mill Pond, on the Edge of which at Highwater, we us'd to stand to fish for Minnows. By much Trampling, we had made it a mere Quagmire. My Proposal was to build a Wharf there fit for us to stand upon, and I show'd my

---

2. In the Island of Nantucket [Franklin's note].
3. I.e., as if his son were the tenth part of his income, traditionally given to the church.

4. Here, his system of shorthand.
5. Maker of candles and soap.
6. Steer.

Comrades a large Heap of Stones which were intended for a new House near the Marsh, and which would very well suit our Purpose. Accordingly in the Evening when the Workmen were gone, I assembled a Number of my Play-fellows, and working with them diligently like so many Emmets,[7] sometimes two or three to a Stone, we brought them all away and built our little Wharf. The next Morning the Workmen were surpris'd at Missing the Stones; which were found in our Wharf; Enquiry was made after the Removers; we were discovered and complain'd of; several of us were corrected by our Fathers; and tho' I pleaded the Usefulness of the Work, mine convinc'd me that nothing was useful which was not honest.

I think you may like to know something of his Person and Character. He had an excellent Constitution of Body, was of middle Stature, but well set and very strong. He was ingenious, could draw prettily, was skill'd a little in Music and had a clear pleasing Voice, so that when he play'd Psalm Tunes on his Violin and sung withal as he some times did in an Evening after the Business of the Day was over, it was extremely agreeable to hear. He had a mechanical Genius too, and on occasion was very handy in the Use of other Tradesmen's Tools. But his great Excellence lay in a sound Understanding, and solid Judgment in prudential Matters, both in private and public Affairs. In the latter indeed he was never employed, the numerous Family he had to educate and the Straitness of his Circumstances, keeping him close to his Trade, but I remember well his being frequently visited by leading People, who consulted him for his Opinion on Affairs of the Town or of the Church he belong'd to and show'd a good deal of Respect for his Judgment and Advice. He was also much consulted by private Persons about their Affairs when any Difficulty occur'd, and frequently chosen an Arbitrator between contending Parties. At his Table he lik'd to have as often as he could, some sensible Friend or Neighbor, to converse with, and always took care to start some ingenious or useful Topic for Discourse, which might tend to improve the Minds of his Children. By this means he turn'd our Attention to what was good, just, and prudent in the Conduct of Life; and little or no Notice was ever taken of what related to the Victuals on the Table, whether it was well or ill drest, in or out of season, of good or bad flavor, preferable or inferior to this or that other thing of the kind; so that I was brought up in such a perfect Inattention to those Matters as to be quite Indifferent what kind of Food was set before me; and so unobservant of it, that to this Day, if I am ask'd I can scarce tell, a few Hours after Dinner, what I din'd upon. This has been a Convenience to me in traveling, where my Companions have been sometimes very unhappy for want of a suitable Gratification of their more delicate because better instructed Tastes and Appetites.

My Mother had likewise an excellent Constitution. She suckled all her 10 Children. I never knew either my Father or Mother to have any Sickness but that of which they died, he at 89 and she at 85 Years of age. They lie buried together at Boston, where I some Years since plac'd a Marble stone over their Grave with this Inscription:

> Josiah Franklin
> And Abiah his Wife

7. Ants.

> Lie here interred.
> They lived lovingly together in Wedlock
> Fifty-five Years.
> Without an Estate or any gainful Employment,[8]
> By constant Labor and Industry,
> With God's Blessing,
> They maintained a large Family
> Comfortably;
> And brought up thirteen Children,
> And seven Grandchildren
> Reputably.
> From this Instance, Reader,
> Be encouraged to Diligence in thy Calling,
> And distrust not Providence.
> He was a pious and prudent Man,
> She a discreet and virtuous Woman.
> Their youngest Son,
> In filial Regard to their Memory,
> Places this Stone.
> J.F. born 1655—Died 1744. Ætat[9] 89
> A.F. born 1667—died 1752——85.

By my rambling Digressions I perceive myself to be grown old. I us'd to write more methodically. But one does not dress for private Company as for a public Ball. 'Tis perhaps only Negligence.

To return. I continu'd thus employ'd in my Father's Business for two Years, that is till I was 12 Years old; and my Brother John[1] who was bred to that Business having left my Father, married and set up for himself at Rhode Island, there was all Appearance that I was destin'd to supply his Place and be a Tallow Chandler. But my Dislike to the Trade continuing, my Father was under Apprehensions that if he did not find one for me more agreeable, I should break away and get to Sea, as his Son Josiah had done to his great Vexation. He therefore sometimes took me to walk with him, and see Joiners, Bricklayers, Turners, Braziers,[2] etc. at their Work, that he might observe my Inclination, and endeavor to fix it on some Trade or other on Land. It has ever since been a Pleasure to me to see good Workmen handle their Tools; and it has been useful to me, having learned so much by it, as to be able to do little Jobs myself in my House, when a Workman could not readily be got; and to construct little Machines for my Experiments while the Intention of making the Experiment was fresh and warm in my Mind. My Father at last fix'd upon the Cutler's Trade, and my Uncle Benjamin's Son Samuel who was bred to that Business in London being about that time establish'd in Boston, I was sent to be with him some time on liking. But his Expectations of a Fee with me displeasing my Father, I was taken home again.

From a Child I was fond of Reading, and all the little Money that came into my Hands was ever laid out in Books. Pleas'd with the Pilgrim's Progress, my first Collection was of John Bunyan's[3] Works, in separate little Volumes.

8. Privileged employment.
9. Aged.
1. John Franklin (1690–1756), Franklin's favorite brother; he was to become postmaster of Boston.
2. Woodworkers, bricklayers, latheworkers, brass-workers.
3. John Bunyan (1628–1688) published *Pilgrim's Progress* in 1678; his works were enormously popular and available in cheap one-shilling editions. The book is an allegory in which the hero, Chris-

I afterwards sold them to enable me to buy R. Burton's[4] Historical Collections; they were small Chapmen's Books[5] and cheap, 40 or 50 in all. My Father's little Library consisted chiefly of Books in polemic Divinity, most of which I read, and have since often regretted, that at a time when I had such a Thirst for Knowledge, more proper Books had not fallen in my Way, since it was now resolv'd I should not be a Clergyman. Plutarch's Lives[6] there was, in which I read abundently, and I still think that time spent to great Advantage. There was also a Book of Defoe's called an Essay on Projects[7] and another of Dr. Mather's call'd Essays to do Good,[8] which perhaps gave me a Turn of Thinking that had an Influence on some of the principal future Events of my Life.

This Bookish Inclination at length determin'd my Father to make me a Printer, tho' he had already one Son, (James) of that Profession. In 1717 my Brother James return'd from England with a Press and Letters[9] to set up his Business in Boston. I lik'd it much better than that of my Father, but still had a Hankering for the Sea. To prevent the apprehended Effect of such an Inclination, my Father was impatient to have me bound[1] to my Brother. I stood out some time, but at last was persuaded and signed the Indentures,[2] when I was yet but 12 Years old. I was to serve as an Apprentice till I was 21 Years of Age, only I was to be allow'd Journeyman's Wages[3] during the last Year. In a little time I made great Proficiency in the Business, and became a useful Hand to my Brother. I now had Access to better Books. An Acquaintance with the Apprentices of Booksellers enabled me sometimes to borrow a small one, which I was careful to return soon and clean. Often I sat up in my Room reading the greatest Part of the Night, when the Book was borrow'd in the Evening and to be return'd early in the Morning lest it should be miss'd or wanted. And after some time an ingenious Tradesman[4] who had a pretty[5] Collection of Books, and who frequented our Printing-House, took Notice of me, invited me to his Library, and very kindly lent me such Books as I chose to read. I now took a Fancy to Poetry, and made some little Pieces. My Brother, thinking it might turn to account encourag'd me, and put me on composing two occasional Ballads. One was called the *Light House Tragedy*, and contain'd an Account of the drowning of Capt. Worthilake with his Two Daughters; the other was a Sailor Song on the Taking of *Teach* or Blackbeard the Pirate.[6] They were wretched Stuff, in the Grubstreet Ballad Style,[7] and when they were printed he sent me about the Town to sell them. The first sold wonderfully, the Event being recent, having made a great

---

tian, flees the City of Destruction and makes his way to the Celestial City with the help of Mr. Worldly-Wiseman, Faithful, Hopeful, etc.
4. "Burton" was a pseudonym for Nathaniel Crouch (c. 1632–1725), a popularizer of British history.
5. Peddlers' books, hence inexpensive.
6. Plutarch (c. 46–120 C.E.), Greek biographer who wrote *Parallel Lives* of noted Greek and Roman figures.
7. Daniel Defoe's (1659?–1731) *Essay on Projects* (1697) offered suggestions for economic improvement (see also n. 2, p. 552).
8. Cotton Mather published *Bonifacius: An Essay upon the Good* in 1710.
9. Type.
1. Apprenticed.

2. A contract binding him to work for his brother for nine years. James Franklin (1697–1735) had learned the printer's trade in England.
3. I.e., be paid for each day's work, having served his apprenticeship.
4. Mr. Matthew Adams [Franklin's note].
5. Exceptionally fine.
6. The full texts of these ballads cannot be found; George Worthylake, lighthouse keeper on Beacon Island, Boston Harbor, and his wife and daughter were drowned on November 3, 1718; the pirate Blackbeard, Edward Teach, was killed off the Carolina coast on November 22, 1718.
7. Grub Street in London was inhabited by poor literary hacks who capitalized on poems of topical interest.

Noise. This flatter'd my Vanity. But my Father discourag'd me, by ridiculing my Performances, and telling me Verse-makers were generally Beggars; so I escap'd being a Poet, most probably a very bad one. But as Prose Writing has been of great Use to me in the Course of my Life, and was a principal Means of my Advancement, I shall tell you how in such a Situation I acquir'd what little Ability I have in that Way.

There was another Bookish Lad in the Town, John Collins by Name, with whom I was intimately acquainted. We sometimes disputed, and very fond we were of Argument, and very desirous of confuting one another. Which disputatious Turn, by the way, is apt to become a very bad Habit, making People often extremely disagreeable in Company, by the Contradiction that is necessary to bring it into Practice, and thence, besides souring and spoiling the Conversation, is productive of Disgusts and perhaps Enmities where you may have occasion for Friendship. I had caught it by reading my Father's Books of Dispute about Religion. Persons of good Sense, I have since observ'd, seldom fall into it, except Lawyers, University Men, and Men of all Sorts that have been bred at Edinburgh.[8] A Question was once some how or other started between Collins and me, of the Propriety of educating the Female Sex in Learning, and their Abilities for Study. He was of Opinion that it was improper; and that they were naturally unequal to it. I took the contrary Side, perhaps a little for Dispute sake. He was naturally more eloquent, had a ready Plenty of Words, and sometimes as I thought bore me down more by his Fluency than by the Strength of his Reasons. As we parted without settling the Point, and were not to see one another again for some time, I sat down to put my Arguments in Writing, which I copied fair and sent to him. He answer'd and I replied. Three or four Letters of a Side had pass'd, when my Father happen'd to find my Papers, and read them. Without entering into the Discussion, he took occasion to talk to me about the Manner of my Writing, observ'd that tho' I had the Advantage of my Antagonist in correct Spelling and pointing[9] (which I ow'd to the Printing-House) I fell far short in elegance of Expression, in Method and in Perspicuity, of which he convinc'd me by several Instances. I saw the Justice of his Remarks, and thence grew more attentive to the *Manner* in Writing, and determin'd to endeavor at Improvement.

About this time I met with an odd Volume of the Spectator.[1] I had never before seen any of them. I bought it, read it over and over, and was much delighted with it. I thought the Writing excellent, and wish'd if possible to imitate it. With that View, I took some of the Papers, and making short Hints of the Sentiment in each Sentence, laid them by a few Days, and then without looking at the Book, tried to complete the Papers again, by expressing each hinted Sentiment at length and as fully as it had been express'd before, in any suitable Words that should come to hand.

Then I compar'd my Spectator with the Original, discover'd some of my Faults and corrected them. But I found I wanted a Stock of Words or a Readiness in recollecting and using them, which I thought I should have acquir'd before that time, if I had gone on making Verses, since the continual

---

8. Scottish Presbyterians were noted for their argumentative nature.
9. Punctuation. Spelling and punctuation were not standardized at this time.
1. An English periodical published daily from March 1, 1711, to December 6, 1712, and revived

in 1714. It contained essays by Joseph Addison (1672–1719) and Richard Steele (1672–1729). It addressed itself primarily to matters of literature and morality. Its aim was to "enliven morality with wit" and "temper wit with morality."

Occasion for Words of the same Import but of different Length, to suit the Measure,[2] or of different Sound for the Rhyme, would have laid me under a constant Necessity of searching for Variety, and also have tended to fix that Variety in my Mind, and make me Master of it. Therefore I took some of the Tales and turn'd them into Verse: And after a time, when I had pretty well forgotten the Prose, turn'd them back again. I also sometimes jumbled my Collections of Hints into Confusion, and after some Weeks, endeavor'd to reduce them into the best Order, before I began to form the full Sentences, and complete the Paper. This was to teach me Method in the Arrangement of Thoughts. By comparing my Work afterwards with the original, I discover'd many faults and amended them; but I sometimes had the Pleasure of Fancying that in certain Particulars of small Import, I had been lucky enough to improve the Method or the Language and this encourag'd me to think I might possibly in time come to be a tolerable English Writer, of which I was extremely ambitious.

My Time for these Exercises and for Reading, was at Night after Work, or before Work began in the Morning; or on Sundays, when I contrived to be in the Printing-House alone, evading as much as I could the common Attendance on public Worship, which my Father used to exact of me when I was under his Care: And which indeed I still thought a Duty; tho' I could not, as it seemed to me, afford the Time to practice it.

When about 16 Years of Age, I happen'd to meet with a Book written by one Tryon,[3] recommending a Vegetable Diet. I determined to go into it. My Brother being yet unmarried, did not keep House, but boarded himself and his Apprentices in another Family. My refusing to eat Flesh occasioned an Inconveniency, and I was frequently chid for my singularity. I made myself acquainted with Tryon's Manner of preparing some of his Dishes, such as Boiling Potatoes or Rice, making Hasty Pudding,[4] and a few others, and then propos'd to my Brother, that if he would give me Weekly half the Money he paid for my Board, I would board myself. He instantly agreed to it, and I presently found that I could save half what he paid me. This was an additional Fund for buying Books: But I had another Advantage in it. My Brother and the rest going from the Printing-House to their Meals, I remain'd there alone, and dispatching presently my light Repast, (which often was no more than a Biscuit or a Slice of Bread, a Handful of Raisins or a Tart from the Pastry Cook's, and a Glass of Water) had the rest of the Time till their Return, for Study, in which I made the greater Progress from that greater Clearness of Head and quicker Apprehension which usually attend Temperance in Eating and Drinking. And now it was that being on some Occasion made asham'd of my Ignorance in Figures, which I had twice fail'd in learning when at School, I took Cocker's Book of Arithmetic,[5] and went thro' the whole by myself with great Ease. I also read Seller's and Sturmy's Books of Navigation,[6] and became acquainted with the little Geometry they contain, but never proceeded far in that Science. And I read about this Time Locke on Human Understanding and the Art of Thinking by Messrs. du Port Royal.[7]

2. Meter.
3. Thomas Tryon, whose *Way to Health, Wealth, and Happiness* appeared in 1682; a digest titled *Wisdom's Dictates* appeared in 1691.
4. I.e., cornmeal or oatmeal mush.
5. Edward Cocker's *Arithmetic*, published in 1677, was reprinted twenty times by 1700.

6. John Seller published *An Epitome of the Art of Navigation* in 1681. Samuel Sturmy published *The Mariner's Magazine: Or Sturmy's Mathematical and Practical Arts* in 1699.
7. John Locke (1632–1704) published *An Essay Concerning Human Understanding* in 1690. Antoine Arnauld (1612–1694) and Pierre Nicole

While I was intent on improving my Language, I met with an English Grammar (I think it was Greenwood's[8]) at the End of which there were two little Sketches of the Arts of Rhetoric and Logic, the latter finishing with a Specimen of a Dispute in the Socratic Method.[9] And soon after I procur'd Xenophon's Memorable Things of Socrates,[1] wherein there are many Instances of the same Method. I was charm'd with it, adopted it, dropped my abrupt Contradiction and positive Argumentation, and put on the humble Enquirer and Doubter. And being then, from reading Shaftesbury and Collins,[2] became a real Doubter in many Points of our Religious Doctrine, I found this Method safest for myself and very embarrassing to those against whom I used it, therefore I took a Delight in it, practic'd it continually and grew very artful and expert in drawing People even of superior Knowledge into Concessions the Consequences of which they did not foresee, entangling them in Difficulties out of which they could not extricate themselves, and so obtaining Victories that neither myself nor my Cause always deserved. I continu'd this Method some few Years, but gradually left it, retaining only the Habit of expressing myself in Terms of modest Diffidence, never using when I advance any thing that may possibly be disputed, the Words, *Certainly, undoubtedly,* or any others that give the Air of Positiveness to an Opinion; but rather say, *I conceive,* or *I apprehend* a Thing to be so or so, *It appears to me,* or *I should think it so or so for such and such Reasons,* or *I imagine* it to be so, or *it is so if I am not mistaken.* This Habit I believe has been of great Advantage to me, when I have had occasion to inculcate my Opinions and persuade Men into Measures that I have been from time to time engag'd in promoting. And as the chief Ends of Conversation are to *inform,* or to be *informed,* to *please* or to *persuade,* I wish well-meaning sensible Men would not lessen their Power of doing Good by a Positive assuming Manner that seldom fails to disgust, tends to create Opposition, and to defeat every one of those Purposes for which Speech was given us, to wit, giving or receiving Information, or Pleasure: For If you would *inform,* a positive dogmatical Manner in advancing your Sentiments, may provoke Contradiction and prevent a candid Attention. If you wish Information and Improvement from the Knowledge of others and yet at the same time express yourself as firmly fix'd in your present Opinions, modest sensible Men, who do not love Disputation, will probably leave you undisturb'd in the Possession of your Error; and by such a Manner you can seldom hope to recommend yourself in *pleasing* your Hearers, or to persuade those whose Concurrence you desire. Pope says, judiciously.

> *Men should be taught as if you taught them not,*
> *And things unknown propos'd as things forgot,*

farther recommending it to us,

(1625?–1695), of Port Royal, published the English edition of *Logic: Or the Art of Thinking* in 1687. It was originally published in Latin in 1662.
8. James Greenwood, *An Essay towards a Practical English Grammar* (1711).
9. I.e., in the form of a debate.
1. Xenophon's (434?–355 B.C.E.) *The Memorable Things of Socrates* was translated by Edward Bysshe in 1712.

2. Anthony Ashley Cooper, third earl of Shaftesbury (1671–1713), was a religious skeptic. Anthony Collins (1676–1729) argued that the world could satisfactorily be explained in terms of itself. Perhaps Franklin read Shaftesbury's *Characteristics of Men, Manners, Opinions, Times* (1711) and Collins's *A Discourse of Free Thinking* (1713).

To speak tho' sure, with seeming Diffidence.[3]

And he might have coupled with this Line that which he has coupled with another, I think less properly,

For want of Modesty is want of Sense.

If you ask why *less properly,* I must repeat the Lines;

"Immodest Words admit of *no* Defence;
For Want of Modesty is Want of Sense."[4]

Now is not *Want of Sense,* (where a Man is so unfortunate as to want it) some Apology for his *Want of Modesty?* and would not the Lines stand more justly thus?

Immodest Words admit *but this* Defence,
That Want of Modesty is Want of Sense.

This however I should submit to better Judgments.

My Brother had in 1720 or 21, begun to print a Newspaper. It was the second[5] that appear'd in America, and was called *The New England Courant.* The only one before it, was *The Boston News Letter.* I remember his being dissuaded by some of his Friends from the Undertaking, as not likely to succeed, one Newspaper being in their Judgment enough for America. At this time 1771 there are not less than five and twenty. He went on however with the Undertaking, and after having work'd in composing the Types and printing off the Sheets I was employ'd to carry the Papers thro' the Streets to the Customers. He had some ingenious Men among his Friends who amus'd themselves by writing little Pieces for this Paper, which gain'd it Credit, and made it more in Demand; and these Gentlemen often visited us. Hearing their Conversations, and their Accounts of the Approbation their Papers were receiv'd with, I was excited to try my Hand among them. But being still a Boy, and suspecting that my Brother would object to printing any Thing of mine in his Paper if he knew it to be mine, I contriv'd to disguise my Hand, and writing an anonymous Paper I put it in at Night under the Door of the Printing-House.

It was found in the Morning and communicated to his Writing Friends when they call'd in as Usual. They read it, commented on it in my Hearing, and I had the exquisite Pleasure, of finding it met with their Approbation, and that in their different Guesses at the Author none were named but Men of some Character among us for Learning and Ingenuity. I suppose now that I was rather lucky in my Judges: And that perhaps they were not really so very good ones as I then esteem'd them. Encourag'd however by this, I wrote and convey'd in the same Way to the Press several more Papers,[6] which were equally approv'd, and I kept my Secret till my small Fund of Sense for such Performances was pretty well exhausted, and then I discovered[7] it; when I

3. From Alexander Pope's *An Essay on Criticism* (1711), lines 574–75 and 567, respectively. Franklin is quoting from memory. The first line should read, "Men must be taught as if you taught them not," and the third, "And speak, tho' sure, with seeming Diffidence."
4. Franklin is mistaken here: the lines are from Wentworth Dillon, fourth earl of Roscommon (1633?–1685), from his *Essay on Translated Verse*

(1684), lines 113–14. The second line should read, "For want of decency is want of sense." "Want": lack.
5. Actually the fifth; James Franklin's paper appeared on August 7, 1721.
6. The *Silence Dogood Letters* (April 12–October 8, 1722) were the earliest essay series in America.
7. Revealed.

began to be considered a little more by my Brother's Acquaintance, and in a manner that did not quite please him, as he thought, probably with reason, that it tended to make me too vain. And perhaps this might be one Occasion of the Differences that we began to have about this Time. Tho' a Brother, he considered himself as my Master, and me as his Apprentice; and accordingly expected the same Services from me as he would from another; while I thought he demean'd me too much in some he requir'd of me, who from a Brother expected more Indulgence, Our Disputes were often brought before our Father, and I fancy I was either generally in the right, or else a better Pleader, because the Judgment was generally in my favor. But my Brother was passionate and had often beaten me, which I took extremely amiss; and thinking my Apprenticeship very tedious, I was continually wishing for some Opportunity of shortening it, which at length offered in a manner unexpected.[8]

One of the Pieces in our Newspaper, on some political Point which I have now forgotten, gave Offence to the Assembly. He was taken up, censur'd and imprison'd[9] for a Month by the Speaker's Warrant, I suppose because he would not discover his Author. I too was taken up and examin'd before the Council; but tho' I did not give them any Satisfaction, they contented themselves with admonishing me, and dismiss'd me; considering me perhaps as an Apprentice who was bound to keep his Master's Secrets. During my Brother's Confinement, which I resented a good deal, notwithstanding our private Differences, I had the Management of the Paper, and I made bold to give our Rulers some Rubs[1] in it, which my Brother took very kindly, while others began to consider me in an unfavorable Light, as a young Genius that had a Turn for Libeling and Satire.[2] My Brother's Discharge was accompanied with an Order of the House, (a very odd one) *that James Franklin should no longer print the Paper called the New England Courant.* There was a Consultation held in our Printing-House among his Friends what he should do in this Case. Some propos'd to evade the Order by changing the Name of the Paper; but my Brother seeing Inconveniences in that, it was finally concluded on as a better Way, to let it be printed for the future under the Name of *Benjamin Franklin.* And to avoid the Censure of the Assembly that might fall on him, as still printing it by his Apprentice, the Contrivance was, that my old Indenture should be return'd to me with a full Discharge on the Back of it, to be shown on Occasion; but to secure to him the Benefit of my Service I was to sign new Indentures for the Remainder of the Term, which were to be kept private. A very flimsy Scheme it was, but however it was immediately executed, and the Paper went on accordingly under my Name for several Months.[3] At length a fresh Difference arising between my Brother and me, I took upon me to assert my Freedom, presuming that he would not venture to produce the new Indentures. It was not fair in me to take this Advantage, and this I therefore reckon one of the first Errata[4] of my Life: But the Unfairness of it weigh'd little with me, when under the Impressions of Resentment, for the Blows his Passion too often urg'd him to bestow upon me. Tho' he

8. I fancy his harsh and tyrannical Treatment of me, might be a means of impressing me with that Aversion to arbitrary Power that has stuck to me thro' my whole Life [Franklin's note].
9. On June 11, 1722, the *Courant* hinted that there was collusion between local authorities and pirates raiding off Boston Harbor. James Franklin was jailed from June 12 to July 7. "Assembly": Mas-

sachusetts legislative body; the lower house, with representatives elected by towns of the Massachusetts General Court.
1. Insults, annoyances.
2. Satirizing.
3. The paper continued under Franklin's name until 1726, nearly three years after he left Boston.
4. Printer's term for errors (Latin).

was otherwise not an ill-natur'd Man: Perhaps I was too saucy and provoking.

When he found I would leave him, he took care to prevent my getting Employment in any other Printing-House of the Town, by going round and speaking to every Master, who accordingly refus'd to give me Work. I then thought of going to New York as the nearest Place where there was a Printer: and I was the rather inclin'd to leave Boston, when I reflected that I had already made myself a little obnoxious to the governing Party; and from the arbitrary Proceedings of the Assembly in my Brother's Case it was likely I might if I stay'd soon bring myself into Scrapes; and farther that my indiscreet Disputations about Religion began to make me pointed at with Horror by good People, as an Infidel or Atheist; I determin'd on the Point: but my Father now siding with my Brother, I was sensible that if I attempted to go openly, Means would be used to prevent me. My Friend Collins therefore undertook to manage a little for me. He agreed with the Captain of a New York Sloop for my Passage, under the Notion of my being a young Acquaintance of his that had got a naughty Girl with Child, whose Friends would compel me to marry her, and therefore I could not appear or come away publicly. So I sold some of my Books to raise a little Money, was taken on board privately, and as we had a fair Wind, in three Days I found myself in New York near 300 Miles from home, a Boy of but 17, without the least Recommendation to or Knowledge of any Person in the Place, and with very little Money in my Pocket.

My Inclinations for the Sea, were by this time worn out, or I might now have gratified them. But having a Trade, and supposing myself a pretty good Workman, I offer'd my Service to the Printer of the Place, old Mr. William Bradford.[5] He could give me no Employment, having little to do, and Help enough already: But, says he, my Son at Philadelphia has lately lost his principal Hand, Aquila Rose, by Death. If you go thither I believe he may employ you. Philadelphia was 100 Miles farther. I set out, however, in a Boat for Amboy;[6] leaving my Chest and Things to follow me round by Sea. In crossing the Bay we met with a Squall that tore our rotten Sails to pieces, prevented our getting into the Kill,[7] and drove us upon Long Island. In our Way a drunken Dutchman, who was a Passenger too, fell overboard; when he was sinking I reach'd thro' the Water to his shock Pate[8] and drew him up so that we got him in again. His Ducking sober'd him a little, and he went to sleep, taking first out of his Pocket a Book which he desir'd I would dry for him. It prov'd to be my old favorite Author Bunyan's Pilgrim's Progress[9] in Dutch, finely printed on good Paper with copper Cuts,[1] a Dress better than I had ever seen it wear in its own Language. I have since found that it has been translated into most of the Languages of Europe, and suppose it has been more generally read than any other Book except perhaps the Bible. Honest John was the first that I know of who mix'd Narration and Dialogue, a Method of Writing very engaging to the Reader, who in the most interesting Parts finds himself as it were brought into the Company, and present at the

5. William Bradford (1663–1752), one of the first American printers and father of Andrew Bradford (1686–1742), Franklin's future competitor in Philadelphia.
6. Perth Amboy, New Jersey.

7. The narrow channel that separates Staten Island, New York, from New Jersey.
8. Shaggy head of hair.
9. See n. 3, p. 544.
1. Engravings.

Discourse. Defoe in his Crusoe, his Moll Flanders, Religious Courtship, Family Instructor, and other Pieces, has imitated it with Success.[2] And Richardson has done the same in his Pamela,[3] etc.

When we drew near the Island we found it was at a Place where there could be no Landing, there being a great Surf on the stony Beach. So we dropped Anchor and swung round towards the Shore. Some People came down to the Water Edge and hallow'd to us, as we did to them. But the Wind was so high and the Surf so loud, that we could not hear so as to understand each other. There were Canoes on the Shore, and we made Signs and hallow'd that they should fetch us, but they either did not understand us, or thought it impracticable. So they went away, and Night coming on, we had no Remedy but to wait till the Wind should abate, and in the mean time the Boatman and I concluded to sleep if we could, and so crowded into the Scuttle[4] with the Dutchman who was still wet, and the Spray beating over the Head of our Boat, leak'd thro' to us, so that we were soon almost as wet as he. In this Manner we lay all Night with very little Rest. But the Wind abating the next Day, we made a Shift to reach Amboy before Night, having been 30 hours on the Water without Victuals, or any Drink but a Bottle of filthy Rum: The Water we sail'd on being salt.

In the Evening I found myself very feverish, and went ill to Bed. But having read somewhere that cold Water drank plentifully was good for a Fever, I follow'd the Prescription, sweat plentifully most of the Night, my Fever left me, and in the Morning crossing the Ferry, proceeded on my Journey, on foot, having 50 Miles to Burlington,[5] where I was told I should find Boats that would carry me the rest of the Way to Philadelphia.

It rain'd very hard all the Day, I was thoroughly soak'd, and by Noon a good deal tir'd, so I stopped at a poor Inn, where I stayed all Night, beginning now to wish I had never left home. I cut so miserable a Figure too, that I found by the Questions ask'd me I was suspected to be some runaway Servant, and in danger of being taken up on that Suspicion. However I proceeded the next Day, and got in the Evening to an Inn within 8 or 10 Miles of Burlington, kept by one Dr. Browne.[6]

He entered into Conversation with me while I took some Refreshment, and finding I had read a little, became very sociable and friendly. Our Acquaintance continu'd as long as he liv'd. He had been, I imagine, an itinerant Doctor, for there was no Town in England, or Country in Europe, of which he could not give a very particular Account. He had some Letters,[7] and was ingenious, but much of an Unbeliever, and wickedly undertook some Years after to travesty the Bible in doggerel Verse as Cotton had done Virgil.[8] By this means he set many of the Facts in a very ridiculous Light, and might have hurt weak minds if his Work had been publish'd: but it never was. At his House I lay that Night, and the next Morning reach'd Burlington.—But

2. Daniel Defoe (1659?–1731) published *Robinson Crusoe* in 1719, *Moll Flanders* in 1722, *Religious Courtship* in 1772, and *The Family Instructor* in 1715–18.
3. Samuel Richardson (1689–1761) published his novel *Pamela: Or Virtue Rewarded* in 1740. Franklin reprinted Richardson's first novel in 1744 and in doing so published the first novel in America.
4. A hole or opening in a ship's deck provided with a movable cover or lid.
5. Then the capital of West Jersey, about eighteen

miles north of Philadelphia.
6. Dr. John Browne (c. 1667–1737), innkeeper in Burlington, and a noted religious skeptic as well as physician.
7. I.e., education.
8. Charles Cotton (1630–1687), who parodied the first and fourth books of the *Aeneid* in his *Scarronides* (1664). The opening lines are: "I sing the Man (read it who list), / A Trojan true as ever pissed."

had the Mortification to find that the regular Boats were gone a little before my coming, and no other expected to go till Tuesday, this being Saturday. Wherefore I return'd to an old Woman in the Town of whom I had bought Gingerbread to eat on the Water, and ask'd her Advice; she invited me to lodge at her House till a Passage by Water should offer; and being tired with my foot Traveling, I accepted the Invitation. She understanding I was a Printer, would have had me stay at that Town and follow my Business, being ignorant of the Stock necessary to begin with. She was very hospitable, gave me a Dinner of Ox Cheek with great Goodwill, accepting only of a Pot of Ale in return. And I thought myself fix'd till Tuesday should come. However walking in the Evening by the Side of the River a Boat came by, which I found was going towards Philadelphia with several People in her. They took me in, and as there was no Wind, we row'd all the Way; and about Midnight not having yet seen the City, some of the Company were confident we must have pass'd it, and would row no farther, the others knew not where we were, so we put towards the Shore, got into a Creek, landed near an old Fence with the Rails of which we made a Fire, the Night being cold, in October, and there we remain'd till Daylight. Then one of the Company knew the Place to be Cooper's Creek a little above Philadelphia, which we saw as soon as we got out of the Creek, and arriv'd there about 8 or 9 aClock, on the Sunday morning, and landed at the Market Street Wharf.[9]

I have been the more particular in this Description of my Journey, and shall be so of my first Entry into that City, that you may in your Mind compare such unlikely Beginning with the Figure I have since made there. I was in my working Dress, my best Clothes being to come round by Sea. I was dirty from my Journey; my Pockets were stuff'd out with Shirts and Stockings; I knew no Soul, nor where to look for Lodging. I was fatigu'd with Traveling, Rowing and Want of Rest. I was very hungry, and my whole Stock of Cash consisted of a Dutch Dollar and about a Shilling in Copper. The latter I gave the People of the Boat for my Passage, who at first refus'd it on Account of my Rowing; but I insisted on their taking it, a Man being sometimes more generous when he has but a little Money than when he has plenty, perhaps thro' Fear of being thought to have but little. Then I walk'd up the Street, gazing about, till near the Market House I met a Boy with Bread. I had made many a Meal on Bread, and inquiring where he got it, I went immediately to the Baker's he directed me to in Second Street; and ask'd for Biscuit, intending such as we had in Boston, but they it seems were not made in Philadelphia, then I ask'd for a three-penny Loaf, and was told they had none such: so not considering or knowing the Difference of Money and the greater Cheapness nor the Names of his Bread, I bad him give me three pennyworth of any sort. He gave me accordingly three great Puffy Rolls. I was surpris'd at the Quantity, but took it, and having no Room in my Pockets, walk'd off, with a Roll under each Arm, and eating the other. Thus I went up Market Street as far as Fourth Street, passing by the Door of Mr. Read, my future Wife's Father, when she standing at the Door saw me, and thought I made as I certainly did a most awkward ridiculous Appearance. Then I turn'd and went down Chestnut Street and part of Walnut Street, eating my Roll all the Way, and coming round found myself again at Market Street Wharf, near the Boat I came in, to which I went for a Drought of the

9. October 6, 1723.

River Water, and being fill'd with one of my Rolls, gave the other two to a Woman and her Child that came down the River in the Boat with us and were waiting to go farther. Thus refresh'd I walk'd again up the Street, which by this time had many clean dress'd People in it who were all walking the same Way; I join'd them, and thereby was led into the great Meeting House of the Quakers near the Market. I sat down among them, and after looking round a while and hearing nothing said, being very drowsy thro' Labor and want of Rest the preceding Night, I fell fast asleep, and continu'd so till the Meeting broke up, when one was kind enough to rouse me. This was therefore the first House I was in or slept in, in Philadelphia.

Walking again down towards the River, and looking in the Faces of People, I met a young Quaker Man whose Countenance I lik'd, and accosting him requested he would tell me where a Stranger could get Lodging. We were then near the Sign of the Three Mariners. Here, says he, is one Place that entertains Strangers, but it is not a reputable House; if thee wilt walk with me, I'll show thee a better. He brought me to the Crooked Billet in Water Street. Here I got a Dinner. And while I was eating it, several sly Questions were ask'd me, as it seem'd to be suspected from my youth and Appearance, that I might be some Runaway. After Dinner my Sleepiness return'd: and being shown to a Bed, I lay down without undressing, and slept till Six in the Evening; was call'd to Supper; went to Bed again very early and slept soundly till the next Morning. Then I made myself as tidy as I could, and went to Andrew Bradford the Printer's. I found in the Shop the old Man his Father, whom I had seen at New York, and who traveling on horse back had got to Philadelphia before me. He introduc'd me to his Son, who receiv'd me civilly, gave me a Breakfast, but told me he did not at present want a Hand, being lately supplied with one. But there was another Printer in town lately set up, one Keimer,[1] who perhaps might employ me; if not, I should be welcome to lodge at his House, and he would give me a little Work to do now and then till fuller Business should offer.

The old Gentleman said, he would go with me to the new Printer: And when we found him, Neighbor, says Bradford, I have brought to see you a young Man of your Business, perhaps you may want such a One. He ask'd me a few Questions, put a Composing Stick[2] in my Hand to see how I work'd, and then said he would employ me soon, tho' he had just then nothing for me to do. And taking old Bradford whom he had never seen before, to be one of the Townspeople that had a Goodwill for him, enter'd into a Conversation on his present Undertaking and Prospects; while Bradford not discovering that he was the other Printer's Father; on Keimer's Saying he expected soon to get the greatest Part of the Business into his own Hands, drew him on by artful Questions and starting little Doubts, to explain all his Views, what Interest he relied on, and in what manner he intended to proceed. I who stood by and heard all, saw immediately that one of them was a crafty old Sophister,[3] and the other a mere Novice. Bradford left me with Keimer, who was greatly surpris'd when I told him who the old Man was.

Keimer's Printing-House I found, consisted of an old shatter'd Press and one small worn-out Font of English,[4] which he was then using himself, com-

---

1. Samuel Keimer (c. 1688–1742) was a printer in London before coming to Philadelphia.
2. An instrument of adjustable width in which type is set before being put on a galley.

3. Trickster, rationalizer.
4. An oversized type, not practicable for books and newspapers.

posing in it an Elegy on Aquila Rose[5] before-mentioned, an ingenious young Man of excellent Character much respected in the Town, Clerk of the Assembly,[6] and a pretty Poet. Keimer made Verses, too, but very indifferently. He could not be said to write them, for his Manner was to compose them in the Types directly out of his Head; so there being no Copy, but one Pair of Cases,[7] and the Elegy likely to require all the Letter, no one could help him. I endeavor'd to put his Press (which he had not yet us'd, and of which he understood nothing) into Order fit to be work'd with; and promising to come and print off his Elegy as soon as he should have got it ready, I return'd to Bradford's who gave me a little Job to do for the present, and there I lodged and dieted.[8] A few Days after Keimer sent for me to print off the Elegy. And now he had got another Pair of Cases, and a Pamphlet to reprint, on which he set me to work.

These two Printers I found poorly qualified for their Business. Bradford had not been bred to it, and was very illiterate; and Keimer tho' something of a Scholar, was a mere Compositor, knowing nothing of Presswork. He had been one of the French Prophets[9] and could act their enthusiastic Agitations. At this time he did not profess any particular Religion, but something of all on occasion; was very ignorant of the World, and had, as I afterwards found, a good deal of the Knave in his Composition. He did not like my Lodging at Bradford's while I work'd with him. He had a House indeed, but without Furniture, so he could not lodge me: But he got me a Lodging at Mr. Read's before-mentioned, who was the Owner of his House. And my Chest and Clothes being come by this time, I made rather a more respectable Appearance in the Eyes of Miss Read, than I had done when she first happen'd to see me eating my Roll in the Street.

I began now to have some Acquaintance among the young People of the Town, that were Lovers of Reading with whom I spent my Evenings very pleasantly and gaining Money by my Industry and Frugality, I lived very agreeably, forgetting Boston as much as I could, and not desiring that any there should know where I resided except my Friend Collins who was in my Secret, and kept it when I wrote to him. At length an Incident happened that sent me back again much sooner than I had intended.

I had a Brother-in-law, Robert Homes,[1] Master of a Sloop that traded between Boston and Delaware. He being at New Castle 40 Miles below Philadelphia, heard there of me, and wrote me a Letter, mentioning the Concern of my Friends in Boston at my abrupt Departure, assuring me of their Goodwill to me, and that everything would be accommodated to my Mind if I would return, to which he exhorted me very earnestly. I wrote an Answer to his Letter, thank'd him for his Advice, but stated my Reasons for quitting Boston fully, and in such a Light as to convince him I was not so wrong as he had apprehended. Sir William Keith[2] Governor of the Province, was then at New Castle,[3] and Captain Homes happening to be in Company

5. Journeyman printer (c. 1695–1723) for Andrew Bradford; his son Joseph apprenticed with Franklin.
6. One who has charge of the records, documents, and correspondence of any organized body; here, the Pennsylvania legislative council.
7. Two shallow trays that contain uppercase and lowercase type.
8. Boarded.

9. An English sect that preached doomsday and cultivated emotional fits.
1. Husband of Franklin's sister Mary, and a ship's captain (d. before 1743).
2. Keith (1680–1749) was governor of Pennsylvania from 1717 to 1726; he fled to England in 1728 to escape debtor's prison.
3. Delaware

with him when my Letter came to hand, spoke to him of me, and show'd him the Letter. The Governor read it, and seem'd surpris'd when he was told my Age. He said I appear'd a young Man of promising Parts, and therefore should be encouraged: The Printers at Philadelphia were wretched ones, and if I would set up there, he made no doubt I should succeed; for his Part, he would procure me the public Business, and do me every other Service in his Power. This my Brother-in-Law afterwards told me in Boston. But I knew as yet nothing of it; when one Day Keimer and I being at Work together near the Window, we saw the Governor and another Gentleman (which prov'd to be Colonel French, of New Castle) finely dress'd, come directly across the Street to our House, and heard them at the Door.

Keimer ran down immediately, thinking it a Visit to him. But the Governor enquir'd for me, came up, and with a Condescension[4] and Politeness I had been quite unus'd to, made me many Compliments, desired to be acquainted with me, blam'd me kindly for not having made myself known to him when I first came to the Place, and would have me away with him to the Tavern where he was going with Colonel French to taste as he said some excellent Madeira. I was not a little surpris'd, and Keimer star'd like a Pig poison'd. I went however with the Governor and Colonel French, to a Tavern the Corner of Third Street, and over the Madeira he propos'd my Setting up my Business, laid before me the Probabilities of Success, and both he and Colonel French assur'd me I should have their Interest and Influence in procuring the Public-Business of both Governments. On my doubting whether my Father would assist me in it, Sir William said he would give me a Letter to him, in which he would state the Advantages, and he did not doubt of prevailing with him. So it was concluded I should return to Boston in the first Vessel with the Governor's Letter recommending me to my Father.

In the meantime the Intention was to be kept secret, and I went on working with Keimer as usual, the Governor sending for me now and then to dine with him, a very great Honor I thought it, and conversing with me in the most affable, familiar, and friendly manner imaginable. About the End of April 1724, a little Vessel offer'd for Boston. I took Leave of Keimer as going to see my Friends. The Governor gave me an ample Letter, saying many flattering things of me to my Father, and strongly recommending the Project of my setting up at Philadelphia, as a Thing that must make my Fortune. We struck on a Shoal in going down the Bay and sprung a Leak, we had a blustring time at Sea, and were oblig'd to pump almost continually, at which I took my Turn. We arriv'd safe however at Boston in about a Fortnight. I had been absent Seven Months and my Friends had heard nothing of me, for my Brother Homes was not yet return'd; and had not written about me. My unexpected Appearance surpris'd the Family; all were however very glad to see me and made me Welcome, except my Brother.

I went to see him at his Printing-House: I was better dress'd than ever while in his Service, having a genteel new Suit from Head to foot, a Watch, and my Pockets lin'd with near Five Pounds Sterling in Silver. He receiv'd me not very frankly, look'd me all over, and turn'd to his Work again. The Journeymen were inquisitive where I had been, what sort of a Country it was, and how I lik'd it? I prais'd it much, and the happy Life I led in it;

4. A disregard for difference in rank or station.

expressing strongly my Intention of returning to it; and one of them asking what kind of Money we had there, I produc'd a handful of Silver and spread it before them, which was a kind of Raree-Show[5] they had not been us'd to, Paper being the Money of Boston. Then I took an Opportunity of letting them see my Watch: and lastly, (my Brother still grum and sullen) I gave them a Piece of Eight to drink[6] and took my Leave. This Visit of mine offended him extremely. For when my Mother some time after spoke to him of a Reconciliation, and of her Wishes to see us on good Terms together, and that we might live for the future as Brothers, he said, I had insulted him in such a Manner before his People that he could never forget or forgive it. In this however he was mistaken.

My Father receiv'd the Governor's Letter with some apparent Surprise; but said little of it to me for some Days; when Captain Homes returning, he show'd it to him, ask'd if he knew Keith, and what kind of a Man he was: Adding his Opinion that he must be of small Discretion, to think of setting a Boy up in Business who wanted yet 3 Years of being at Man's Estate. Homes said what he could in favor of the Project; but my Father was clear in the Impropriety of it; and at last gave a flat Denial to it. Then he wrote a civil Letter to Sir William thanking him for the Patronage he had so kindly offered me, but declining to assist me as yet in Setting up, I being in his Opinion too young to be trusted with the Management of a Business so important; and for which the Preparation must be so expensive.

My Friend and Companion Collins, who was a Clerk at the Post-Office, pleas'd with the Account I gave him of my new Country, determin'd to go thither also: And while I waited for my Father's Determination,[7] he set out before me by Land to Rhode Island, leaving his Books which were a pretty Collection of Mathematics and Natural Philosophy,[8] to come with mine and me to New York where he propos'd to wait for me. My Father, tho' he did not approve Sir William's Proposition, was yet pleas'd that I had been able to obtain so advantageous a Character from a Person of such Note where I had resided, and that I had been so industrious and careful as to equip myself so handsomely in so short a time: therefore seeing no Prospect of an Accommodation between my Brother and me, he gave his Consent to my Returning again to Philadelphia, advis'd me to behave respectfully to the People there, endeavor to obtain the general Esteem, and avoid lampooning and libeling to which he thought I had too much Inclination; telling me, that by steady Industry and a prudent Parsimony, I might save enough by the time I was One and Twenty to set me up, and that if I came near the Matter he would help me out with the Rest. This was all I could obtain, except some small Gifts as Tokens of his and my Mother's Love, when I embark'd again for New York, now with their Approbation and their Blessing.

The Sloop putting in at Newport, Rhode Island, I visited my Brother John, who had been married and settled there some Years. He received me very affectionately, for he always lov'd me. A Friend of his, one Vernon, having some Money due to him in Pennsylvania, about 35 Pounds Currency, desired I would receive it for him, and keep it till I had his Directions what to remit it in. Accordingly he gave me an Order. This afterwards occasion'd me a good

5. A sidewalk peep show; silver coins were rare in the colonies.
6. A Spanish dollar with which they could buy drinks.
7. Decision.
8. I.e., natural science.

deal of Uneasiness. At Newport we took in a Number of Passengers for New York: Among which were two young Women, Companions, and a grave, sensible Matron-like Quaker-Woman with her Attendants. I had shown an obliging Readiness to do her some little Services which impress'd her I suppose with a degree of Goodwill towards me. Therefore when she saw a daily growing Familiarity between me and the two Young Women, which they appear'd to encourage, she took me aside and said, Young Man, I am concern'd for thee, as thou has no Friend with thee, and seems not to know much of the World, or of the Snares Youth is expos'd to; depend upon it those are very bad Women, I can see it in all their Actions, and if thee art not upon thy Guard, they will draw thee into some Danger: they are Strangers to thee, and I advise thee in a friendly Concern for thy Welfare, to have no Acquaintance with them. As I seem'd at first not to think so ill of them as she did, she mention'd some Things she had observ'd and heard that had escap'd my Notice; but now convinc'd me she was right. I thank'd her for her kind Advice, and promis'd to follow it. When we arriv'd at New York, they told me where they liv'd, and invited me to come and see them: but I avoided it. And it was well I did: For the next Day, the Captain miss'd a Silver Spoon and some other Things that had been taken out of his Cabin, and knowing that these were a Couple of Strumpets, he got a Warrant to search their Lodgings, found the stolen Goods, and had the Thieves punish'd. So tho' we had escap'd a sunken Rock which we scrap'd upon in the Passage, I thought this Escape of rather more Importance to me.

At New York I found my Friend Collins, who had arriv'd there some Time before me. We had been intimate from[9] Children, and had read the same Books together. But he had the Advantage of more time for Reading, and Studying and a wonderful Genius for Mathematical Learning in which he far outstripped me. While I liv'd in Boston most of my Hours of Leisure for Conversation were spent with him, and he continu'd a sober as well as an industrious Lad; was much respected for his Learning by several of the Clergy and other Gentlemen, and seem'd to promise making a good Figure in Life: but during my Absence he had acquir'd a Habit of Sotting with[1] Brandy; and I found by his own Account and what I heard from others, that he had been drunk every day since his Arrival at New York, and behav'd very oddly. He had gam'd too and lost his Money, so that I was oblig'd to discharge[2] his Lodgings, and defray his Expences to and at Philadelphia: Which prov'd extremely inconvenient to me. The then Governor of New York, Burnet,[3] Son of Bishop Burnet, hearing form the Captain that a young Man, one of his Passengers, had a great many Books, desired he would bring me to see him. I waited upon him accordingly, and should have taken Collins with me but that he was not sober. The Governor treated me with great Civility, show'd me his Library, which was a very large one, and we had a good deal of Conversation about Books and Authors. This was the second Governor who had done me the Honor to take Notice of me, which to a poor Boy like me was very pleasing.

We proceeded to Philadelphia. I received on the Way Vernon's Money, without which we could hardly have finish'd our Journey. Collins wish'd to

9. I.e., since we were.
1. Getting stupefied on.
2. To release him from debt by paying his bills.

3. William Burnet (1688–1729), governor of New York and New Jersey from 1720 to 1728, and governor of Massachusetts from 1728 to 1729.

be employ'd in some Counting House; but whether they discover'd his Dramming by his Breath, or by his Behavior, tho' he had some Recommendations, he met with no Success in any Application, and continu'd Lodging and Boarding at the same House with me and at my Expense. Knowing I had that Money of Vernon's he was continually borrowing of me, still promising Repayment as soon as he should be in Business. At length he had got so much of it, that I was distress'd to think what I should do, in case of being call'd on to remit it. His Drinking continu'd, about which we sometimes quarrel'd, for when a little intoxicated he was very fractious. Once in a Boat on the Delaware with some other young Men, he refused to row in his Turn: I will be row'd home, says he. We will not row you, says I. You must, says he, or stay all Night on the Water, just as you please. The others said, Let us row; What signifies it? But my Mind being soured with his other Conduct, I continu'd to refuse. So he swore he would make me row, or throw me overboard; and coming along stepping on the Thwarts[4] towards me, when he came up and struck at me, I clapped my Hand under his Crotch, and rising, pitch'd him headforemost into the River. I knew he was a good Swimmer, and so was under little Concern about him; but before he could get round to lay hold of the Boat, we had with a few Strokes pull'd her out of his Reach. And ever when he drew near the Boat, we ask'd if he would row, striking a few Strokes to slide her away from him. He was ready to die with Vexation, and obstinately would not promise to row; however seeing him at last beginning to tire, we lifted him in; and brought him home dripping wet in the Evening. We hardly exchang'd a civil Word afterwards; and a West India Captain who had a Commission to procure a Tutor for the Sons of a Gentleman at Barbados,[5] happening to meet with him, agreed to carry him thither. He left me then, promising to remit me the first Money he should receive in order to discharge the Debt. But I never heard of him after.

The Breaking into this Money of Vernon's was one of the first great Errata of my Life. And this Affair show'd that my Father was not much out in his Judgment when he suppos'd me too Young to manage Business of Importance. But Sir William, on reading his Letter, said he was too prudent. There was great Difference in Persons, and Discretion did not always accompany Years, nor was Youth always without it. And since he will not set you up, says he, I will do it myself. Give me an Inventory of the Things necessary to be had from England, and I will send for them. You shall repay me when you are able; I am resolv'd to have a good Printer here, and I am sure you must succeed. This was spoken with such an Appearance of Cordiality, that I had not the least doubt of his meaning what he said. I had hitherto kept the Proposition of my Setting up a Secret in Philadelphia, and I still kept it. Had it been known that I depended on the Governor, probably some Friend that knew him better would have advis'd me not to rely on him, as I afterwards heard it as his known Character to be liberal of Promises which he never meant to keep. Yet unsolicited as he was by me, how could I think his generous Offers insincere? I believ'd him one of the best Men in the World.

I presented him an Inventory of a little Printing-House, amounting by my Computation to about 100 Pounds Sterling. He lik'd it, but ask'd me if my being on the Spot in England to choose the Types and see that everything

---

4. The seat on which an oarsman sits.   5. Island in the British West Indies.

was good of the kind, might not be of some Advantage. Then, says he, when there, you may make Acquaintances and establish Correspondences in the Bookselling, and Stationery Way. I agreed that this might be advantageous. Then says he, get yourself ready to go with Annis;[6] which was the annual Ship, and the only one at that Time usually passing between London and Philadelphia. But it would be some Months before Annis sail'd, so I continu'd working with Keimer, fretting about the Money Collins had got from me, and in daily Apprehensions of being call'd upon by Vernon, which however did not happen for some Years after.

I believe I have omitted mentioning that in my first Voyage from Boston, being becalm'd off Block Island,[7] our People set about catching Cod and haul'd up a great many. Hitherto I had stuck to my Resolution of not eating animal Food; and on this Occasion, I consider'd with my Master Tryon, the taking every Fish as a kind of unprovok'd Murder, since none of them had or ever could do us any Injury that might justify the Slaughter. All this seem'd very reasonable. But I had formerly been a great Lover of Fish, and when this came hot out of the Frying Pan, it smelt admirably well. I balanc'd some time between Principle and Inclination: till I recollected, that when the Fish were opened, I saw smaller Fish taken out of their Stomachs: Then, thought I, if you eat one another, I don't see why we mayn't eat you. So I din'd upon Cod very heartily and continu'd to eat with other People, returning only now and then occasionally to a vegetable Diet. So convenient a thing it is to be a *reasonable Creature*, since it enables one to find or make a Reason for everything one has a mind to do.

Keimer and I liv'd on a pretty good familiar Footing and agreed tolerably well: for he suspected nothing of my Setting up. He retain'd a great deal of his old Enthusiasms, and lov'd an Argumentation. We therefore had many Disputations. I us'd to work him so with my Socratic Method, and had trapann'd[8] him so often by Questions apparently so distant from any Point we had in hand, and yet by degrees led to the Point, and brought him into Difficulties and Contradictions, that at last he grew ridiculously cautious, and would hardly answer me the most common Question, without asking first, *What do you intend to infer from that?* However it gave him so high an Opinion of my Abilities in the Confuting Way, that he seriously propos'd my being his Colleague in a Project he had of setting up a new Sect. He was to preach the Doctrines, and I was to confound all Opponents. When he came to explain with me upon the Doctrines, I found several Conundrums[9] which I objected to, unless I might have my Way a little too, and introduce some of mine. Keimer wore his Beard at full Length, because somewhere in the Mosaic Law it is said, *thou shalt not mar the Corners of thy Beard.*[1] He likewise kept the seventh-day Sabbath; and these two Points were Essentials with him. I dislik'd both, but agreed to admit them upon Condition of his adopting the Doctrine of using no animal Food. I doubt, says he, my Constitution will not bear that. I assur'd him it would, and that he would be the better for it. He was usually a great Glutton, and I promis'd myself some

6. Thomas Annis, captain of the *London Hope*, the packet boat on which Franklin sailed to London in 1724.
7. Off the coast of Rhode Island.
8. Trapped.

9. Puzzles, difficult questions.
1. "Ye shall not round the corners of your heads, neither shalt thou mar the corners of thy beard" (Leviticus 19.27). Keimer probably also wore his hair long.

Diversion in half-starving him. He agreed to try the Practice if I would keep him Company. I did so and we held it for three Months. We had our Victuals dress'd and brought to us regularly by a Woman in the Neighborhood, who had from me a List of 40 Dishes to be prepar'd for us at different times, in all which there was neither Fish Flesh nor Fowl, and the Whim suited me the better at this time from the Cheapness of it, not costing us about 18 Pence Sterling each, per Week. I have since kept several Lents most strictly, leaving the common Diet for that, and that for the common, abruptly, without the least Inconvenience: So that I think there is little in the Advice of making those Changes by easy Gradations. I went on pleasantly, but Poor Keimer suffer'd grievously, tir'd of the Project, long'd for the Flesh Pots of Egypt,[2] and order'd a roast Pig. He invited me and two Women Friends to dine with him, but it being brought too soon upon table, he could not resist the Temptation, and ate it all up before we came.

I had made some Courtship during this time to Miss Read. I had a great Respect and Affection for her, and had some Reason to believe she had the same for me: but as I was about to take a long Voyage, and we were both very young, only a little above 18, it was thought most prudent by her Mother to prevent our going too far at present, as a Marriage if it was to take place would be more convenient after my Return, when I should be as I expected set up in my Business. Perhaps too she thought my Expectations not so well founded as I imagined them to be.

My chief Acquaintances at this time were, Charles Osborne, Joseph Watson, and James Ralph;[3] All Lovers of Reading. The two first were Clerks to an eminent Scrivener or Conveyancer in the Town, Charles Brockden;[4] the other was Clerk to a Merchant. Watson was a pious sensible young Man, of great integrity. The others rather more lax in their Principles of Religion, particularly Ralph, who as well as Collins had been unsettled by me, for which they both made me suffer. Osborne was sensible, candid, frank, sincere, and affectionate to his Friends; but in literary Matters too fond of Criticizing. Ralph, was ingenious, genteel in his Manners, and extremely eloquent; I think I never knew a prettier Talker. Both of them great Admirers of Poetry, and began to try their Hands in little Pieces. Many pleasant Walks we four had together, on Sundays into the Woods near Skuylkill,[5] where we read to one another and conferr'd on what we read. Ralph was inclin'd to pursue the Study of Poetry, not doubting but he might become eminent in it and make his Fortune by it, alledging that the best Poets must when they first began to write, make as many Faults as he did. Osborne dissuaded him, assur'd him he had no Genius for Poetry, and advis'd him to think of nothing beyond the Business he was bred to; that in the mercantile way tho' he had no Stock, he might by his Diligence and Punctuality recommend himself to Employment as a Factor,[6] and in time acquire wherewith to trade on his own Account. I approv'd the amusing oneself with Poetry now and then, so far

---

2. "And the whole congregation of the children of Israel murmured against Moses and Aaron in the wilderness: And the children of Israel said unto them, Would to God we had died by the hand of the Lord in the land of Egypt, when we sat by the flesh pots, and when we did eat bread to the full" (Exodus 16.2–3).
3. Charles Osborne's dates are unknown. Joseph

Watson died about 1728. James Ralph (c. 1695–1762) became well known as a political journalist.
4. Brockden (1683–1769) came to Philadelphia in 1706. "Conveyancer": one who draws up leases and deeds.
5. Schuylkill River, at Philadelphia.
6. Business agent.

as to improve one's Language, but no farther. On this it was propos'd that we should each of us at our next Meeting produce a Piece of our own Composing, in order to improve by our mutual Observations, Criticisms and Corrections. As Language and Expression was what we had in View, we excluded all Considerations of Invention,[7] by agreeing that the Task should be a Version of the 18th Psalm, which describes the Descent of a Deity.[8] When the Time of our Meeting drew nigh, Ralph call'd on me first, and let me know his Piece was ready. I told him I had been busy, and having little Inclination had done nothing. He then show'd me his Piece for my Opinion; and I much approv'd it, as it appear'd to me to have great Merit. Now, says he, Osborne never will allow the least Merit in any thing of mine, but makes 1000 Criticisms out of mere Envy. He is not so jealous of you. I wish therefore you would take this Piece, and produce it as yours. I will pretend not to have had time, and so produce nothing. We shall then see what he will say to it. It was agreed, and I immediately transcrib'd it that it might appear in my own hand. We met.

Watson's Performance was read: there were some Beauties in it: but many Defects. Osborne's was read: It was much better. Ralph did it Justice, remark'd some Faults, but applauded the Beauties. He himself had nothing to produce. I was backward, seem'd desirous of being excus'd, had not had sufficient Time to correct; etc., but no Excuse could be admitted, produce I must. It was read and repeated; Watson and Osborne gave up the Contest; and join'd in applauding it immoderately. Ralph only made some Criticisms and propos'd some Amendments, but I defended my Text. Osborne was against Ralph, and told him he was no better a Critic than Poet; so he dropped the Argument. As they two went home together, Osborne express'd himself still more strongly in favor of what he thought my Production, having restrain'd himself before as he said, lest I should think it Flattery. But who would have imagin'd, says he, that Franklin had been capable of such a Performance; such Painting, such Force! such Fire! He has even improv'd the Original! In his common Conversation, he seems to have no Choice of Words; he hesitates and blunders; and yet, good God, how he writes!

When we next met, Ralph discover'd the Trick we had played him, and Osborne was a little laughed at. This Transaction fix'd Ralph in his Resolution of becoming a Poet. I did all I could to dissuade him from it, but he continu'd scribbling Verses, till *Pope*[9] cur'd him. He became however a pretty good Prose Writer. More of him hereafter. But as I may not have occasion again to mention the other two, I shall just remark here, that Watson died in my Arms a few Years after, much lamented, being the best of our Set. Osborne went to the West Indies, where he became an eminent Lawyer and made Money, but died young. He and I had made a serious Agreement, that the one who happen'd first to die, should if possible make a friendly Visit to the other, and acquaint him how he found things in that separate State. But he never fulfill'd his Promise.

The Governor, seeming to like my Company, had me frequently to his

7. I.e., originality.
8. "He bowed the heavens also, and came down: and darkness was under his feet" (Psalm 18.9).
9. In the 2nd edition of the *Dunciad* (1728), a poem that attacks ignorance of all kinds, Alexander Pope responded to Ralph's slur against him in *Saw-*

ney: "Silence, ye Wolves: while Ralph to Cynthia howls. / And makes Night hideous—Answer him ye Owls" (book 3, lines 159–60). In the 1742 edition Pope included another dig at Ralph: "And see: The very Gazeteers give o'er, / Ev'n Ralph repents" (book 1, lines 215–16).

House; and his Setting me up was always mention'd as a fix'd thing. I was to take with me Letters recommendatory to a Number of his Friends, besides the Letter of Credit to furnish me with the necessary Money for purchasing the Press and Types, Paper, etc. For these Letters I was appointed to call at different times, when they were to be ready, but a future time was still[1] named. Thus we went on till the ship whose Departure too had been several times postponed was on the Point of sailing. Then when I call'd to take my Leave and receive the Letters, his Secretary, Dr. Bard,[2] came out to me and said the Governor was extremely busy, in writing, but would be down at New Castle before the Ship, and there the Letters would be delivered to me.

Ralph, tho' married and having one Child, had determined to accompany me in this Voyage. It was thought he intended to establish a Correspondence, and obtain Goods to sell on Commission. But I found afterwards, that thro' some Discontent with his Wife's Relations, he purposed to leave her on their Hands, and never return again. Having taken leave of my Friends, and interchang'd some Promises with Miss Read, I left Philadelphia in the Ship, which anchor'd at New Castle. The Governor was there. But when I went to his Lodging, the Secretary came to me from him with the civilest Message in the World, that he could not then see me being engag'd in Business of the utmost Importance, but should send the Letters to me on board, wish'd me heartily a good Voyage and a speedy Return, etc. I return'd on board, a little puzzled, but still not doubting.

Mr. Andrew Hamilton,[3] a famous Lawyer of Philadelphia, had taken Passage in the same Ship for himself and Son: and with Mr. Denham[4] a Quaker Merchant, and Messrs. Onion and Russel Masters of an Iron Work in Maryland, had engag'd the Great Cabin; so that Ralph and I were forc'd to take up with a Berth in the Steerage: And none on board knowing us, were considered as ordinary Persons. But Mr. Hamilton and his Son (it was James, since Governor) return'd from New Castle to Philadelphia the Father being recall'd by a great Fee to plead for a seized Ship. And just before we sail'd Colonel French coming on board, and showing me great Respect, I was more taken Notice of, and with my Friend Ralph invited by the other Gentlemen to come into the Cabin, there being now Room. Accordingly we remov'd thither.

Understanding that Colonel French had brought on board the Governor's Dispatches, I ask'd the Captain for those Letters that were to be under my Care. He said all were put into the Bag together; and he could not then come at them; but before we landed in England, I should have an Opportunity of picking them out. So I was satisfied for the present, and we proceeded on our Voyage. We had a sociable Company in the Cabin, and lived uncommonly well, having the Addition of all Mr. Hamilton's Stores, who had laid in plentifully. In this Passage Mr. Denham contracted a Friendship for me that continued during his Life. The Voyage was otherwise not a pleasant one, as we had a great deal of bad Weather.

1. Always.
2. Patrick Bard, or Baird, resided in Philadelphia as port physician after 1720.
3. Andrew Hamilton (c. 1678–1741), American-born lawyer; his successful defense of John Peter Zenger against a charge of libel established freedom of the press in the colonies and earned for Hamilton the sobriquet "the Philadelphia Lawyer." His son James Hamilton (c. 1710–1783) was governor of Pennsylvania four times between 1748 and 1773.
4. Thomas Denham (d. 1728), merchant and benefactor, left Bristol, England, in 1715.

When we came into the Channel, the Captain kept his Word with me, and gave me an Opportunity of examining the Bag for the Governor's Letters. I found none upon which my Name was put, as under my Care; I pick'd out 6 or 7 that by the Handwriting I thought might be the promis'd Letters, especially as one of them was directed to Basket[5] the King's Printer, and another to some Stationer. We arriv'd in London the 24th of December, 1724. I waited upon the Stationer who came first in my Way, delivering the Letter as from Governor Keith. I don't know such a Person, says he: but opening the Letter, O, this is from Riddlesden;[6] I have lately found him to be a complete Rascal, and I will have nothing to do with him, nor receive any Letters from him. So putting the Letter into my Hand, he turn'd on his Heel and left me to serve some Customer. I was surprised to find these were not the Governor's Letters. And after recollecting and comparing Circumstances, I began to doubt his Sincerity. I found my Friend Denham, and opened the whole Affair to him. He let me into Keith's Character, told me there was not the least Probability that he had written any Letters for me, that no one who knew him had the smallest Dependence on him, and he laughed at the Notion of the Governor's giving me a Letter of Credit, having as he said no Credit to give. On my expressing some Concern about what I should do: He advis'd me to endeavor getting some Employment in the Way of my Business. Among the Printers here, says he, you will improve yourself; and when you return to America, you will set up to greater Advantage.

We both of us happen'd to know, as well as the Stationer, that Riddlesden the Attorney, was a very Knave. He had half ruin'd Miss Read's Father by drawing him in to be bound[7] for him. By his Letter it appear'd, there was a secret Scheme on foot to the Prejudice of Hamilton, (Suppos'd to be then coming over with us,) and that Keith was concern'd in it with Riddlesden. Denham, who was a Friend of Hamilton's, thought he ought to be acquainted with it. So when he arriv'd in England, which was soon after, partly from Resentment and Ill-Will to Keith and Riddlesden, and partly from Goodwill to him: I waited on him, and gave him the Letter. He thank'd me cordially, the Information being of Importance to him. And from that time he became my Friend, greatly to my Advantage afterwards on many Occasions.

But what shall we think of a Governor's playing such pitiful Tricks, and imposing so grossly on a poor ignorant Boy! It was a Habit he had acquired. He wish'd to please everybody; and having little to give, he gave Expectations. He was otherwise an ingenious sensible Man, a pretty good Writer, and a good Governor for the People, tho' not for his Constituents the Proprietaries,[8] whose Instructions he sometimes disregarded. Several of our best Laws were of his Planning, and pass'd during his Administration.

Ralph and I were inseparable Companions. We took Lodgings together in Little Britain[9] at 3 shillings 6 pence per Week, as much as we could then afford. He found some Relations, but they were poor and unable to assist him. He now let me know his Intentions of remaining in London, and that he never meant to return to Philadelphia. He had brought no Money with

5. John Baskett (d. 1742).
6. William Riddlesden (d. before 1733), well known in Maryland as a man of "infamy."
7. I.e., as a cosigner of a document and legally bound to be responsible for his debts.
8. Members of the Penn family were the Proprietors of Pennsylvania and its legal owners. "Constituents": those who appointed him their representative; in this case, the Penn family, which retained control of Pennsylvania until the Revolution.
9. A street in London near St. Paul's Cathedral.

him, the whole he could muster having been expended in paying his Passage. I had 15 Pistoles.[1] So he borrowed occasionally of me, to subsist while he was looking out for Business. He first endeavor'd to get into the Playhouse, believing himself qualified for an Actor; but Wilkes,[2] to whom he applied, advis'd him candidly not to think of that Employment, as it was impossible he should succeed in it. Then he propos'd to Roberts, a Publisher in Paternoster Row,[3] to write for him a Weekly Paper like the Spectator, on certain Conditions, which Roberts did not approve. Then he endeavor'd to get Employment as a Hackney Writer[4] to copy for the Stationers and Lawyers about the Temple[5] but could find no Vacancy.

I immediately got into Work at Palmer's, then a famous Printing-House in Bartholomew Close;[6] and here I continu'd near a Year. I was pretty diligent; but spent with Ralph a good deal of my Earnings in going to Plays and other Places of Amusement. We had together consum'd all my Pistoles, and now just rubb'd[7] on from hand to mouth. He seem'd quite to forget his Wife and Child, and I by degrees my Engagements with Miss Read, to whom I never wrote more than one Letter, and that was to let her know I was not likely soon to return. This was another of the great Errata of my Life, which I should wish to correct if I were to live it over again. In fact, by our Expenses, I was constantly kept unable to pay my Passage.

At Palmer's I was employ'd in Composing for the second Edition of Wollaston's Religion of Nature.[8] Some of his Reasonings not appearing to me well-founded, I wrote a little metaphysical Piece, in which I made Remarks on them. It was entitled, *A Dissertation on Liberty and Necessity, Pleasure and Pain.*[9] I inscrib'd it to my Friend Ralph. I printed a small Number. I occasion'd my being more consider'd by Mr. Palmer, as a young Man of some Ingenuity, tho' he seriously expostulated with me upon the Principles of my Pamplet which to him appear'd abominable. My printing this Pamphlet was another Erratum.

While I lodg'd in Little Britain I made an Acquaintance with one Wilcox a Bookseller, whose Shop was at the next Door. He had an immense Collection of second-hand Books. Circulating Libraries were not then in Use; but we agreed that on certain reasonable Terms which I have now forgotten, I might take, read and return any of his Books. This I esteem'd a great Advantage, and I made as much Use of it as I could.

My Pamphlet by some means falling into the Hands of one Lyons,[1] a Surgeon, Author of a Book entitled *The Infallibility of Human Judgment*, it occasioned an Acquaintance between us; he took great Notice of me, call'd on me often, to converse on these Subjects, carried me to the Horns a pale Ale-House in [blank] Lane, Cheapside, and introduc'd me to Dr. Mandeville,[2] Author of the Fable of the Bees who had a Club there, of which he

1. A Spanish gold coin worth approximately eighteen shillings.
2. Robert Wilks (1665?–1732), an Irish actor, dominated London theater life from 1709 to 1730.
3. The center of the London printing business.
4. A copyist.
5. The Inner and Middle Temples were two of four buildings in London that were centers for the legal profession.
6. Just off Little Britain, and a square known for its printers and typesetters.
7. Proceeded with difficulty.
8. William Wollaston's *Religion of Nature* was first

published in 1725. Franklin set the type for the 4th edition, which appeared in April 1726.
9. Franklin's pamphlet, of which only four copies are known to survive. By denying the existence of virtue and vice Franklin laid himself open to accusations of atheism.
1. William Lyons, a surgeon and author of *The Infallibility, Dignity, and Excellence of Human Judgment* (1719).
2. Bernard Mandeville (c. 1670–1733), a Dutch physician and man of letters residing in London. His *Fable of the Bees* was published in 1723.

was the Soul, being a most facetious entertaining Companion. Lyons too introduc'd me to Dr. Pemberton, at Batson's Coffee House,[3] who promis'd to give me an Opportunity some time or other of seeing Sir Isaac Newton,[4] of which I was extremely desirous; but this never happened.

I had brought over a few Curiosities among which the principal was a Purse made of the Asbestos, which purifies by Fire. Sir Hans Sloane[5] heard of it, came to see me, and invited me to his House in Bloomsbury Square; where he show'd me all his Curiosities, and persuaded me to let him add that to the Number, for which he paid me handsomely.

In our House there lodg'd a young Woman, a Millener, who I think had a shop in the Cloisters.[6] She had been genteelly bred, was sensible and lively, and of most pleasing Conversation. Ralph read Plays to her in the Evenings, they grew intimate, she took another Lodging, and he follow'd her. They liv'd together some time, but he being still out of Business, and her Income not sufficient to maintain them with her Child, he took a Resolution of going from London, to try for a Country School, which he thought himself well qualified to undertake, as he wrote an excellent Hand, and was a Master of Arithmetic and Accounts. This however he deem'd a Business below him, and confident of future better Fortune when he should be unwilling to have it known that he once was so meanly employ'd, he chang'd his Name, and did me the Honor to assume mine. For I soon after had a Letter from him, acquainting me, that he was settled in a small Village in Berkshire, I think it was, where he taught reading and writing to 10 or a dozen Boys at 6 pence each per Week, recommending Mrs. T. to my Care, and desiring me to write to him directing for Mr. Franklin Schoolmaster at such a Place. He continu'd to write frequently, sending me large Specimens of an Epic Poem, which he was then composing, and desiring my Remarks and Corrections. These I gave him from time to time, but endeavor'd rather to discourage his Proceeding. One of Young's Satires was then just publish'd.[7] I copied and sent him a great Part of it, which set in a strong Light the Folly of pursuing the Muses with any Hope of Advancement by them. All was in vain. Sheets of the Poem continu'd to come by every Post. In the mean time Mrs. T. having on his Account lost her Friends and Business, was often in Distresses, and us'd to send for me, and borrow what I could spare to help her out of them. I grew fond of her Company, and being at this time under no Religious Restraints, and presuming on my Importance to her, I attempted Familiarities, (another Erratum) which she repuls'd with a proper Resentment, and acquainted him with my Behavior. This made a Breach between us, and when he return'd again to London, he let me know he thought I had cancel'd all the Obligations he had been under to me. So I found I was never to expect his Repaying me what I lent to him or advanc'd for him. This was however not then of much Consequence, as he was totally unable. And in the Loss of his Friendship I found myself reliev'd from a Burden. I now began to think of getting

3. Batson's in Cornhill was a favorite meeting place of physicians. Henry Pemberton (1694–1771) was a friend of Isaac Newton's and a member of the Royal Society.
4. Isaac Newton (1642–1727), best known for explaining the theories of gravity, light, and color, was president of the Royal Society from 1703 to 1727.
5. Physician and naturalist (1660–1753), was the successor to Newton as president of the Royal Society; his library and museum served as the basis for the present collection at the British Museum.
6. Probably near St. Bartholomew's Church, London.
7. Edward Young (1683–1765) published the first four parts of Love of Fame, the Universal Passion in 1725.

a little Money beforehand; and expecting better Work, I left Palmer's to work at Watts's[8] near Lincoln's Inn Fields, a still greater Printing-House. Here I continu'd all the rest of my Stay in London.

At my first Admission into this Printing-House, I took to working at Press, imagining I felt a Want of the Bodily Exercise I had been us'd to in America, where Presswork is mix'd with Composing. I drank only Water; the other Workmen, near 50 in Number, were great Guzzlers of Beer. On occasion I carried up and down Stairs a large Form of Types[9] in each hand, when others carried but one in both Hands. They wonder'd to see from this and several Instances that the Water-American as they call'd me was *stronger* than themselves who drunk *strong*[1] Beer. We had an Alehouse Boy who attended always in the House to supply the Workmen. My Companion at the Press drank every day a Pint before Breakfast, a Pint at Breakfast with his Bread and Cheese; a Pint between Breakfast and Dinner; a Pint at Dinner; a Pint in the Afternoon about Six o'clock, and another when he had done his Day's Work. I thought it a detestable Custom. But it was necessary, he suppos'd, to drink *strong* Beer that he might be *strong* to labor. I endeavor'd to convince him that the Bodily Strength afforded by Beer could only be in proportion to the Grain or Flour of the Barley dissolved in the Water of which it was made; that there was more Flour in a Penny-worth of Bread, and therefore if he would eat that with a Pint of Water, it would give him more Strength than a Quart of Beer. He drank on however, and had 4 or 5 Shillings to pay out of his Wages every Saturday Night for that muddling Liquor; an Expense I was free from. And thus these poor Devils keep themselves always under.[2]

Watts after some Weeks desiring to have me in the Composing-Room, I left the Pressmen. A new *Bienvenu*[3] or Sum for Drink, being 5 Shillings, was demanded of me by the Compositors.[4] I thought it an Imposition, as I had paid below. The Master thought so too, and forbad my Paying it. I stood out two or three Weeks, was accordingly considered as an Excommunicate, and had so many little Pieces of private Mischief done me, by mixing my Sorts,[5] transposing my Pages, breaking my Matter,[6] etc., etc. if I were ever so little out of the Room, and all ascrib'd to the Chapel[7] Ghost, which they said ever haunted those not regularly admitted, that notwithstanding the Master's Protection, I found myself oblig'd to comply and pay the Money; convinc'd of the Folly of being on ill Terms with those one is to live with continually. I was now on a fair Footing with them, and soon acquir'd considerable Influence. I propos'd some reasonable Alterations in their Chapel Laws, and carried them against all Opposition. From my Example a great Part of them, left their muddling Breakfast of Beer and Bread and Cheese, finding they could with me be supplied from a neighboring House with a large Porringer of hot Water-gruel, sprinkled with Pepper, crumb'd with Bread, and a Bit of Butter in it, for the Price of a Pint of Beer, viz., three halfpence. This was a more comfortable as well as cheaper Breakfast, and kept their Heads clearer. Those who continu'd sotting with Beer all day, were often, by not paying, out of Credit at the Alehouse, and us'd to make Interest with me to get Beer,

8. John Watts (c. 1678–1763).
9. Type set and locked in metal frames.
1. With high alcohol content.
2. I.e., in poverty.
3. Welcome (French, literal trans.).
4. Typesetters.

5. Type, letters.
6. Type set up for printing.
7. "A Printing House is always called a Chapel by the Workmen" [Franklin's note]. The workers set their own customs, practices, and fines.

their Light, as they phras'd it, *being out.* I watch'd the Pay table on Saturday Night, and collected what I stood engag'd for them, having to pay some times near Thirty Shillings a Week on their Accounts. This and my being esteem'd a pretty good Riggite,[8] that is a jocular verbal Satirist, supported my Consequence in the Society. My constant Attendance, (I never making a St. Monday),[9] recommended me to the Master; and my uncommon Quickness at Composing, occasion'd my being put upon all Work of Dispatch, which was generally better paid. So I went on now very agreeably.

My Lodging in Little Britain being too remote, I found another in Duke Street opposite to the Romish Chapel.[1] It was two pair of Stairs backwards at an Italian Warehouse. A Widow Lady kept the House; she had a Daughter and a Maid Servant, and a Journeyman who attended the Warehouse, but lodg'd abroad. After sending to enquire my Character at the House where I last lodg'd, she agreed to take me in at the same Rate, 3 Shillings 6 Pence per Week, cheaper as she said from the Protection she expected in having a Man lodge in the House. She was a Widow, an elderly Woman, had been bred a Protestant, being a Clergyman's Daughter, but was converted to the Catholic Religion by her Husband, whose Memory she much revered, had lived much among People of Distinction, and knew a 1000 Anecdotes of them as far back as the Times of Charles the second. She was lame in her Knees with the Gout, and therefore seldom stirr'd out of her Room, so sometimes wanted Company; and hers was so highly amusing to me that I was sure to spend an Evening with her whenever she desired it. Our Supper was only half an Anchovy each, on a very little Strip of Bread and Butter, and half a Pint of Ale between us. But the Entertainment was in her Conversation. My always keeping good Hours, and giving little Trouble in the Family, made her unwilling to part with me; so that when I talk'd of a Lodging I had heard of, nearer my Business, for 2 Shillings a Week, which, intent as I now was on saving Money, made some Difference; she bid me not think of it, for she would abate me two Shillings a Week for the future, so I remain'd with her at 1 Shilling 6 Pence as long as I stayed in London.

In a Garret of her House there lived a Maiden Lady of 70 in the most retired Manner, of whom my Landlady gave me this Account, that she was a Roman Catholic, had been sent abroad when young and lodg'd in a Nunnery with an Intent of becoming a Nun: but the Country not agreeing with her, she return'd to England, where there being no Nunnery, she had vow'd to lead the Life of a Nun as near as might be done in those Circumstances: Accordingly She had given all her Estate to charitable Uses, reserving only Twelve Pounds a year to live on, and out of this Sum she still gave a great deal in Charity, living herself on Watergruel only, and using no Fire but to boil it. She had lived many Years in that Garret, being permitted to remain there gratis by successive catholic Tenants of the House below, as they deem'd it a Blessing to have her there. A Priest visited her, to confess her every Day. I have ask'd her, says my Landlady, how she, as she liv'd, could possibly find so much Employment for a Confessor? O, says she, it is impossible to avoid *vain Thoughts.* I was permitted once to visit her: She was cheerful and polite, and convers'd pleasantly. The Room was clean, but had

---

8. One who makes fun of others.
9. Taking Monday off as if it were a religious holiday.

1. The Roman Catholic Chapel of St. Anselm and St. Cecilia.

no other Furniture than a Mattress, a Table with a Crucifix and Book, a Stool, which she gave me to sit on, and a Picture over the Chimney of *St. Veronica*,[2] displaying her Handkerchief with the miraculous Figure of Christ's bleeding Face on it, which she explain'd to me with great Seriousness. She look'd pale, but was never sick, and I give it as another Instance on how small an Income Life and Health may be supported.

At Watts's Printing-House I contracted an Acquaintance with an ingenious young Man, one Wygate, who having wealthy Relations, had been better educated than most Printers, was a tolerable Latinist, spoke French, and lov'd Reading. I taught him, and a Friend of his, to swim at twice going into the River, and they soon became good Swimmers. They introduc'd me to some Gentlemen from the Country who went to Chelsea by Water to see the College and Don Saltero's Curiosities.[3] In our Return, at the Request of the Company, whose Curiosity Wygate had excited, I stripped and leaped into the River, and swam from near Chelsea to Blackfriars,[4] performing on the Way many Feats of Activity both upon and under Water, that surpris'd and pleas'd those to whom they were Novelties. I had from a Child been ever delighted with this Exercise, had studied and practic'd all Thevenot's[5] Motions and Positions, added some of my own, aiming at the graceful and easy, as well as the Useful. All these I took this Occasion of exhibiting to the Company, and was much flatter'd by their Admiration. And Wygate, who was desirous of becoming a Master, grew more and more attach'd to me on that account, as well as from the Similarity of our Studies. He at length propos'd to me traveling all over Europe together, supporting ourselves every where by working at our Business. I was once inclin'd to it. But mentioning it to my good Friend Mr. Denham, with whom I often spent an Hour when I had Leisure, he dissuaded me from it; advising me to think only of returning to Pennsylvania, which he was now about to do.

I must record one Trait of this good Man's Character. He had formerly been in Business at Bristol, but fail'd in Debt to a Number of People, compounded[6] and went to America. There, by a close Application to Business as a Merchant, he acquir'd a plentiful Fortune in a few Years. Returning to England in the Ship with me, He invited his old Creditors to an Entertainment, at which he thank'd them for the easy Composition[7] they had favor'd him with, and when they expected nothing but the Treat, every Man at the first Remove[8] found under his Plate an Order on a Banker for the full Amount of the unpaid Remainder with Interest.

He now told me he was about to return to Philadelphia, and should carry over a great Quantity of Goods in order to open a Store there: He propos'd to take me over as his Clerk, to keep his Books (in which he would instruct me), copy his Letters, and attend the Store. He added, that as soon as I should be acquainted with mercantile Business he would promote me by sending me with a Cargo of Flour and Bread, etc., to the West Indies, and

2. According to tradition, as Christ bore the cross, St. Veronica wiped his face with a cloth that miraculously retained the image of his face.
3. James Salter was a former barber for Sir Hans Sloane; he kept supposed relics, like Job's tears and pieces of the True Cross, on view. He was dubbed Don Saltero by the *Tatler*. "College": i.e., Chelsea Hospital, erected on the site of the former Chelsea College.
4. I.e., more than three miles.
5. Melchisédeck de Thevenot, *The Art of Swimming* (1699).
6. Settled part payment on his debts.
7. Conditions for accepting a declaration of bankruptcy.
8. I.e., the first time the plates were cleared.

procure me Commissions from others; which would be profitable, and if I manag'd well, would establish me handsomely. The Thing pleas'd me, for I was grown tired of London, remember'd with Pleasure the happy Months I had spent in Pennsylvania, and wish'd again to see it. Therefore I immediately agreed, on the Terms of Fifty Pounds a Year, Pennsylvania Money; less indeed than my then Gettings as a Compositor, but affording a better Prospect.

I now took Leave of Printing, as I thought for ever, and was daily employ'd in my new Business; going about with Mr. Denham among the Tradesmen, to purchase various Articles, and see them pack'd up, doing Errands, calling upon Workmen to dispatch, etc., and when all was on board, I had a few Days' Leisure. On one of these Days I was to my Surprise sent for by a great Man I knew only by Name, a Sir William Wyndham and I waited upon him. He had heard by some means or other of my Swimming from Chelsey to Blackfriars, and of my teaching Wygate and another young Man to swim in a few Hours. He had two Sons about to set out on their Travels; he wish'd to have them first taught Swimming; and propos'd to gratify me handsomely if I would teach them. They were not yet come to Town and my Stay was uncertain, so I could not undertake it. But from this Incident I thought it likely, that if I were to remain in England and open a Swimming School, I might get a good deal of Money. And it struck me so strongly, that had the Overture been sooner made me, probably I should not so soon have returned to America. After Many Years, you and I had something of more Importance to do with one of these Sons of Sir William Wyndham,[9] become Earl of Egremont, which I shall mention in its Place.[1]

Thus I spent about 18 Months in London. Most Part of the Time, I work'd hard at my Business, and spent but little upon myself except in seeing Plays, and in Books. My Friend Ralph had kept me poor. He owed me about 27 Pounds; which I was now never likely to receive; a great Sum out of my small Earnings. I lov'd him notwithstanding, for he had many amiable Qualities. Tho' I had by no means improv'd my Fortune, I had pick'd up some very ingenious Acquaintance whose Conversation was of great Advantage to me, and I had read considerably.

We sail'd from Gravesend on the 23d of July 1726. For The Incidents of the Voyage, I refer you to my Journal, where you will find them all minutely related. Perhaps the most important Part of that Journal is the *Plan*[2] to be found in it which I formed at Sea for regulating my future Conduct in Life. It is the more remarkable, as being form'd when I was so young, and yet being pretty faithfully adhered to quite thro' to old Age. We landed in Philadelphia the 11th of October, where I found sundry Alterations. Keith was no longer Governor, being superseded by Major Gordon:[3] I met him walking the Streets as a common Citizen. He seem'd a little asham'd at seeing me, but pass'd without saying anything. I should have been as much asham'd at seeing Miss Read, had not her Friends despairing with Reason of my Return, after the Receipt of my Letter, persuaded her to marry another, one Rogers, a Potter, which was done in my Absence. With him however she was never

---

9. Chancellor of the exchequer and Tory leader in Parliament (1687–1740).
1. Franklin does not mention Charles Wyndham (1710–1763) again.

2. Only the "Outline" and "Preamble" of Franklin's *Plan* survive.
3. Patrick Gordon (1644–1736), governor of Pennsylvania from 1726 to 1736.

happy, and soon parted from him, refusing to cohabit with him, or bear his Name. It being now said that he had another Wife. He was a worthless Fellow tho' an excellent Workman which was the Temptation to her Friends. He got into Debt, and ran away in 1727 or 28, went to the West Indies, and died there. Keimer had got a better House, a Shop well supplied with Stationery, plenty of new Types, a number of Hands tho' none good, and seem'd to have a great deal of Business.

Mr. Denham took a Store in Water Street, where we open'd our Goods. I attended the Business diligently, studied Accounts, and grew in a little Time expert at selling. We lodg'd and boarded together, he counsel'd me as a Father, having a sincere Regard for me: I respected and lov'd him: and we might have gone on together very happily: But in the Beginning of February 1726/7 when I had just pass'd my 21st Year, we both were taken ill. My Distemper was a Pleurisy,[4] which very nearly carried me off: I suffered a good deal, gave up the Point[5] in my own mind, and was rather disappointed when I found myself recovering; regretting in some degree that I must now sometime or other have all that disagreeable Work to do over again. I forget what his Distemper was. It held him a long time, and at length carried him off. He left me a small Legacy in a nuncupative Will,[6] as a Token of his Kindness for me, and he left me once more to the wide World. For the Store was taken into the Care of his Executors, and my Employment under him ended: My Brother-in-law Homes, being now at Philadelphia, advis'd my Return to my Business. And Keimer tempted me with an Offer of large Wages by the Year to come and take the Management of his Printing-House that he might better attend his Stationer's Shop. I had heard a bad Character of him in London, from his Wife and her Friends, and was not fond of having any more to do with him. I tried for farther Employment as a Merchant's Clerk; but not readily meeting with any, I clos'd again with Keimer.

I found in *his* House these Hands; Hugh Meredith[7] a Welsh-Pennsylvanian, 30 Years of Age, bred to Country Work: honest, sensible, had a great deal of solid Observation, was something of a Reader, but given to drink: Stephen Potts,[8] a young Country Man of full Age, bred to the Same, of uncommon natural Parts[9] and great Wit and Humor, but a little idle. These he had agreed with at extreme low Wages, per Week, to be rais'd a Shilling every 3 Months, as they would deserve by improving in their Business, and the Expectation of these high Wages to come on hereafter was what he had drawn them in with. Meredith was to work at Press, Potts at Bookbinding, which he by Agreement, was to teach them, tho' he knew neither one nor t'other. John ———— a wild Irishman brought up to no Business, whose Service for 4 Years Keimer had purchas'd[1] from the Captain of a Ship. He too was to be made a Pressman. George Webb,[2] an Oxford Scholar, whose Time for 4 Years he had likewise bought, intending him for a Compositor: of whom more presently. And David Harry,[3] a Country Boy, whom he had taken Apprentice. I soon perceiv'd that the Intention of engaging me at Wages so

4. A disease of the lungs.
5. End; i.e., resigned himself to death.
6. An oral will.
7. Hugh Meredith (c. 1696–1749), later a business partner of Franklin's.
8. Later a bookseller and innkeeper (d. 1758).
9. I.e., handsome.

1. I.e., Keimer had paid for his passage in exchange for his service.
2. Later a member of Franklin's Junto Club and printer (1708–1736?).
3. A Welsh Quaker (1708–1760) and later first printer in Barbados.

much higher than he had been us'd to give, was to have these raw cheap Hands form'd thro' me, and as soon as I had instructed them, then, they being all articled to him, he should be able to do without me. I went on however, very cheerfully; put his Printing-House in Order, which had been in great Confusion, and brought his Hands by degrees to mind their Business and to do it better.

It was an odd Thing to find an Oxford Scholar in the Situation of a bought Servant. He was not more than 18 Years of Age, and gave me this Account of himself; that he was born in Gloucester, educated at a Grammar School there, had been distinguish'd among the Scholars for some apparent Superiority in performing his Part when they exhibited Plays; belong'd to the Witty Club there, and had written some Pieces in Prose and Verse which were printed in the Gloucester Newspapers. Thence he was sent to Oxford; there he continu'd about a Year, but not well-satisfied, wishing of all things to see London and become a Player. At length receiving his Quarterly Allowance of 15 Guineas, instead of discharging his Debts, he walk'd out of Town, hid his Gown in a Furz Bush,[4] and footed it to London, where having no Friend to advise him, he fell into bad Company, soon spent his Guineas, found no means of being introduc'd among the Players, grew necessitous, pawn'd his Clothes and wanted Bread. Walking the Street very hungry, and not knowing what to do with himself, a Crimp's Bill[5] was put into his Hand, offering immediate Entertainment and Encouragement to such as would bind themselves to serve in America. He went directly, sign'd the Indentures, was put into the Ship and came over; never writing a Line to acquaint his Friends what was become of him. He was lively, witty, good-natur'd and a pleasant Companion, but idle, thoughtless and imprudent to the last Degree.

John the Irishman soon ran away. With the rest I began to live very agreeably; for they all respected me, the more as they found Keimer incapable of instructing them, and that from me they learned something daily. We never work'd on a Saturday, that being Keimer's Sabbath. So I had two Days for Reading. My Acquaintance with ingenious People in the Town increased. Keimer himself treated me with great Civility and apparent Regard; and nothing now made me uneasy but my Debt to Vernon, which I was yet unable to pay, being hitherto but a poor Economist. He however kindly made no Demand of it.

Our Printing-House often wanted Sorts,[6] and there was no Letter Founder in America. I had seen Types cast at James's[7] in London, but without much Attention to the Manner: However I now contriv'd a Mold, made use of the Letters we had as Puncheons, struck the Matrices[8] in Lead, and thus supplied in a pretty tolerable way all Deficiencies. I also engrav'd several Things on occasion. I made the Ink, I was Warehouse-man and everything, in short quite a Factotum.[9]

But however serviceable I might be, I found that my Services became every Day of less Importance, as the other Hands improv'd in the Business. And when Keimer paid my second Quarter's Wages, he let me know that he felt

4. An evergreen shrub; gorse. "Gown": academic robe worn regularly by Oxford students.
5. An advertisement for free passage to the colonies for those who would work as indentured servants.
6. Letters of type.
7. Thomas James's foundry in London.
8. Molds for casting type. "Puncheons": stamping tools.
9. Jack-of-all-trades.

them too heavy, and thought I should make an Abatement. He grew by degrees less civil, put on more of the Master, frequently found Fault, was captious and seem'd ready for an Out-breaking. I went on nevertheless with a good deal of Patience, thinking that his encumber'd Circumstances were partly the Cause. At length a Trifle snapped our Connection. For a great Noise happening near the Courthouse, I put my Head out of the Window to see what was the Matter. Keimer being in the Street look'd up and saw me, call'd out to me in a loud Voice and angry Tone to mind my Business, adding some reproachful Words, that nettled me the more for their Publicity, all the Neighbors who were looking out on the same Occasion being Witnesses how I was treated. He came up immediately into the Printing-House, continu'd the Quarrel, high Words pass'd on both Sides, he gave me the Quarter's Warning we had stipulated, expressing a Wish that he had not been oblig'd to so long a Warning: I told him his Wish was unnecessary for I would leave him that Instant; and so taking my Hat walk'd out of Doors; desiring Meredith whom I saw below to take care of some Things I left, and bring them to my Lodging.

Meredith came accordingly in the Evening, when we talk'd my Affair over. He had conceiv'd a great Regard for me, and was very unwilling that I should leave the House while he remain'd in it. He dissuaded me from returning to my native Country[1] which I began to think of. He reminded me that Keimer was in debt for all he possess'd, that his Creditors began to be uneasy, that he kept his Shop miserably, sold often without Profit for ready Money, and often trusted without keeping Account. That he must therefore fail; which would make a Vacancy I might profit of. I objected my Want of Money. He then let me know, that his Father had a high Opinion of me, and from some Discourse that had pass'd between them, he was sure would advance Money to set us up, if I would enter into Partnership with him. My Time, says he, will be out with Keimer in the Spring. By that time we may have our Press and Types in from London: I am sensible I am no Workman. If you like it, Your Skill in the Business shall be set against the Stock I furnish; and we will share the Profits equally.—The Proposal was agreeable, and I consented. His Father was in Town, and approv'd of it, the more as he saw I had great Influence with his Son, had prevail'd on him to abstain long from Dram-drinking,[2] and he hop'd might break him of that wretched Habit entirely, when we came to be so closely connected. I gave an Inventory to the Father, who carried it to a Merchant; the Things were sent for; the Secret was to be kept till they should arrive, and in the mean time I was to get Work if I could at the other Printing-House. But I found no Vacancy there, and so remain'd idle a few Days, when Keimer, on a Prospect of being employ'd to print some Paper-money, in New Jersey, which would require Cuts and various Types that I only could supply, and apprehending Bradford might engage me and get the Job from him, sent me a very civil Message, that old Friends should not part for a few Words, the Effect of sudden Passion, and wishing me to return. Meredith persuaded me to comply, as it would give more Opportunity for his Improvement under my daily Instructions. So I return'd, and we went on more smoothly than for some time before. The New Jersey Job was obtain'd. I contriv'd a Copper-Plate Press for it, the first that had been seen

1. I.e., Boston.   2. Frequently drinking small measures of alcohol.

in the Country. I cut several Ornaments and Checks for the Bills. We went together to Burlington,[3] where I executed the Whole to Satisfaction, and he received so large a Sum for the Work, as to be enabled thereby to keep his Head much longer above Water.

At Burlington I made an Acquaintance with many principal People of the Province. Several of them had been appointed by the Assembly a Committee to attend the Press, and take Care that no more Bills were printed than the Law directed. They were therefore by Turns constantly with us, and generally he who attended brought with him a Friend or two for Company. My Mind having been much more improv'd by Reading than Keimer's, I suppose it was for that Reason my Conversation seem'd to be more valu'd. They had me to their Houses, introduc'd me to their Friends and show'd me much Civility, while he, tho' the Master, was a little neglected. In truth he was an odd Fish, ignorant of common Life, fond of rudely opposing receiv'd Opinions, slovenly to extreme dirtiness, enthusiastic[4] in some Points of Religion, and a little Knavish withal. We continu'd there near 3 Months, and by that time I could reckon among my acquired Friends, Judge Allen, Samuel Bustill, the Secretary of the Province, Isaac Pearson, Joseph Cooper and several of the Smiths, Members of Assembly, and Isaac Decow the Surveyor General. The latter was a shrewd sagacious old Man, who told me that he began for himself when young by wheeling Clay for the Brickmakers, learned to write after he was of Age, carried the Chain for Surveyors, who taught him Surveying, and he had now by his Industry acquir'd a good Estate; and says he, I foresee, that you will soon work this Man out of his Business and make a Fortune in it at Philadelphia. He had not then the least Intimation of my Intention to set up there or anywhere. These Friends were afterwards of great Use to me, as I occasionally was to some of them. They all continued their Regard for me as long as they lived.

Before I enter upon my public Appearance in Business, it may be well to let you know the then State of my Mind, with regard to my Principles and Morals, that you may see how far those influenc'd the future Events of my Life. My Parents had early given me religious Impressions, and brought me through my Childhood piously in the Dissenting Way.[5] But I was scarce 15 when, after doubting by turns of several Points as I found them disputed in the different Books I read, I began to doubt of Revelation itself. Some Books against Deism fell into my Hands; they were said to be the Substance of Sermons preached at Boyle's Lectures.[6] It happened that they wrought an Effect on me quite contrary to what was intended by them: For the Arguments of the Deists which were quoted to be refuted, appeared to me much Stronger than the Refutations. In short I soon became a thorough Deist. My Arguments perverted some others, particularly Collins and Ralph: but each of them having afterwards wrong'd me greatly without the least Compunction, and recollecting Keith's Conduct towards me, (who was another Freethinker) and my own towards Vernon and Miss Read which at Times gave me great Trouble, I began to suspect that this Doctrine tho' it might be true,

3. New Jersey.
4. Highly emotional.
5. I.e., in the Congregational or Presbyterian way, as opposed to the Church of England.
6. Robert Boyle (1627–1691), English physicist

and chemist, endowed annual lectures for preaching eight sermons a year against "infidels." Deism accepts a supreme being as the author of finite existence, but denies Christian doctrines of revelation and supernaturalism.

was not very useful. My London pamphlet, which had for its Motto those Lines of Dryden

> ——Whatever is, is right
> Tho' purblind Man Sees but a Part of
> The Chain, the nearest Link,
> His Eyes not carrying to the equal Beam,
> That poizes all, above.[7]

And from the Attributes of God, his infinite Wisdom, Goodness and Power concluded that nothing could possibly be wrong in the World, and that Vice and Virtue were empty Distinctions, no such Things existing: appear'd now not so clever a Performance as I once thought it; and I doubted whether some Error had not insinuated itself unperceiv'd into my Argument, so as to infect all that follow'd, as is common in metaphysical Reasonings. I grew convinc'd that *Truth, Sincerity* and *Integrity* in Dealings between Man and Man, were of the utmost Importance to the Felicity of Life, and I form'd written Resolutions, (which still remain in my Journal Book) to practice them ever while I lived. Revelation had indeed no weight with me as such; but I entertain'd an Opinion, that tho' certain Actions might not be bad *because* they were forbidden by it, or good *because* it commanded them; yet probably those Actions might be forbidden *because* they were bad for us, or commanded *because* they were beneficial to us, in their own Natures, all the Circumstances of things considered. And this Persuasion, with the kind hand of Providence, or some guardian Angel, or accidental favorable Circumstances and Situations, or all together, preserved me (thro' this dangerous Time of Youth and the hazardous Situations I was sometimes in among Strangers, remote from the Eye and Advice of my Father) without any *willful* gross Immorality or Injustice that might have been expected from my Want of Religion. I say *willful,* because the Instances I have mentioned, had something of *Necessity* in them, from my Youth, Inexperience, and the Knavery of others. I had therefore a tolerable Character to begin the World with, I valued it properly, and determin'd to preserve it.

We had not been long return'd to Philadelphia, before the New Types arriv'd from London. We settled with Keimer, and left him by his Consent before he heard of it. We found a House to hire near the Market, and took it. To lessen the Rent, (which was then but 24 Pounds a Year tho' I have since known it let for 70) we took in Thomas Godfrey a Glazier,[8] and his Family, who were to pay a considerable Part of it to us, and we to board with them. We had scarce opened our Letters and put our Press in Order, before George House, an Acquaintance of mine, brought a Countryman to us; whom he had met in the Street enquiring for a Printer. All our Cash was now expended in the Variety of Particulars we had been obliged to procure, and this Countryman's Five Shillings, being our First Fruits and coming so seasonably, gave me more Pleasure than any Crown[9] I have since earn'd; and from the Gratitude I felt towards House, has made me often more ready than perhaps I should otherwise have been to assist young Beginners.

7. The first line is not from John Dryden (1631–1700) but from Alexander Pope's *Essay on Man* (1733), Epistle I, line 294; however, Dryden's line is close: "Whatever is, is in its Causes just." The rest of the poem is recalled accurately from Dryden's *Oedipus* (3.1.244–48).
8. A man who sets glass for windowpanes.
9. A coin worth five shillings.

There are Croakers in every Country always boding its Ruin. Such a one then lived in Philadelphia, a Person of Note, an elderly Man, with a wise Look and very grave Manner of Speaking. His Name was Samuel Mickle. This Gentleman, a Stranger to me, stopped one Day at my Door, and ask'd me if I was the young Man who had lately opened a new Printing-House: Being answer'd in the Affirmative; He said he was sorry for me; because it was an expensive Undertaking, and the Expense would be lost, for Philadelphia was a sinking¹ Place, the People already half Bankrupts or near being so; all Appearances of the contrary such as new Buildings and the Rise of Rents, being to his certain Knowledge fallacious, for they were in fact among the Things that would soon ruin us. And he gave me such a Detail of Misfortunes now existing or that were soon to exist, that he left me half-melancholy. Had I known him before I engag'd in this Business, probably I never should have done it. This Man continu'd to live in this decaying Place, and to declaim in the same Strain, refusing for many Years to buy a House there, because all was going to Destruction, and at last I had the Pleasure of seeing him give five times as much for one as he might have bought it for when he first began his Croaking.

I should have mention'd before, that in the Autumn of the preceding Year, I had form'd most of my ingenious Acquaintance into a Club, for mutual Improvement, which we call'd the Junto.² We met on Friday Evenings. The Rules I drew up, requir'd that every Member in his Turn should produce one or more Queries on any Point of Morals, Politics or Natural Philosophy, to be discuss'd by the Company, and once in three Months produce and read an Essay of his own Writing on any Subject he pleased. Our Debates were to be under the Direction of a President, and to be conducted in the sincere Spirit of Enquiry after Truth, without fondness for Dispute, or Desire of Victory; and to prevent Warmth, all expressions of Positiveness in Opinion, or of direct Contradiction, were after some time made contraband and prohibited under small pecuniary Penalties. The first Members were, Joseph Breintnall,³ a Copier of Deeds for the Scriveners; a good-natur'd friendly middle-ag'd Man, a great Lover of Poetry, reading all he could meet with, and writing some that was tolerable; very ingenious in many little Nicknackeries, and of sensible Conversation. Thomas Godfrey,⁴ a self-taught Mathematician, great in his Way, and afterwards Inventor of what is now call'd Hadley's Quadrant.⁵ But he knew little out of his way, and was not a pleasing Companion, as like most Great Mathematicians I have met with, he expected unusual Precision in everything said, or was forever denying or distinguishing upon Trifles, to the Disturbance of all Conversation. He soon left us. Nicholas Scull,⁶ a Surveyor, afterwards Surveyor-General, Who lov'd Books, and sometimes made a few Verses. William Parsons,⁷ bred a Shoemaker, but loving Reading, had acquir'd a considerable Share of Mathematics, which he first studied with a View to Astrology that he afterwards laughed at. He also became Surveyor General. William Maugridge, a Joiner,⁸ and a most

1. Economically declining.
2. I.e., a small, select group (the name is taken from the Spanish word *junta*, "fraternity").
3. Briental (d. 1746) shared Franklin's interest in science.
4. Godfrey (1704–1749).

5. An instrument for measuring altitudes in navigation and astronomy.
6. Nicholas Scull II (1687–1761).
7. Parsons (1701–1757) became surveyor general in 1741 and librarian of the Library Company.
8. A ship's carpenter (d. 1766).

exquisite Mechanic, and a solid sensible Man. Hugh Meredith, Stephen Potts, and George Webb, I have Characteris'd before. Robert Grace,[9] a young Gentleman of some Fortune, generous, lively and witty, a Lover of Punning and of his Friends. And William Coleman,[1] then a Merchant's Clerk, about my Age, who had the coolest clearest Head, the best Heart, and the exactest Morals, of almost any Man I ever met with. He became afterwards a Merchant of great Note, and one of our Provincial Judges: Our Friendship continued without Interruption to his Death, upwards of 40 Years. And the Club continu'd almost as long and was the best School of Philosophy, Morals and Politics that then existed in the Province; for our Queries which were read the Week preceding their Discussion, put us on reading with Attention upon the several Subjects, that we might speak more to the purpose: and here too we acquired better Habits of Conversation, everything being studied in our Rules which might prevent our disgusting each other. From hence the long Continuance of the Club, which I shall have frequent Occasion to speak farther of hereafter; But my giving this Account of it here, is to show something of the Interest I had, everyone of these exerting themselves in recommending Business to us.

Breintnall particularly procur'd us from the Quakers, the Printing 40 Sheets of their History, the rest being to be done by Keimer: and upon this we work'd exceeding hard, for the Price was low. It was a Folio, Pro Patria Size, in Pica with Long Primer Notes.[2] I compos'd of it a Sheet a Day, and Meredith work'd it off at Press. It was often 11 at Night and sometimes later, before I had finish'd my Distribution[3] for the next day's Work: For the little Jobs sent in by our other Friends now and then put us back. But so determin'd I was to continue doing a Sheet a Day of the Folio, that one Night when having impos'd my Forms,[4] I thought my Day's Work over, one of them by accident was broken and two Pages reduc'd to Pie,[5] I immediately distributed and compos'd it over again before I went to bed. And this Industry visible to our Neighbors began to give us Character and Credit; particularly I was told, that mention being made of the new Printing Office at the Merchants' Every-night-Club, the general Opinion was that it must fail, there being already two Printers in the Place, Keimer and Bradford; but Doctor Baird (whom you and I saw many Years after at his native Place, St. Andrews in Scotland) gave a contrary Opinion; for the Industry of that Franklin, says he, is superior to anything I ever saw of the kind: I see him still at work when I go home from Club; and he is at Work again before his Neighbors are out of bed. This struck the rest, and we soon after had Offers from one of them to supply us with Stationery. But as yet we did not choose to engage in Shop Business.

I mention this Industry the more particularly and the more freely, tho' it seems to be talking in my own Praise, that those of my Posterity who shall read it, may know the Use of that Virtue, when they see its Effects in my Favor throughout this Relation.

9. Franklin's landlord for thirty-seven years.
1. Coleman (1704–1769).
2. A book of large size, with the main text in twelve-point type and the notes in ten-point type.
3. I.e., of type, returning letters to their cases so that they may be used again.
4. Locked the type into its form and readied it for printing.
5. A confused pile.

George Webb, who had found a Friend that lent him wherewith to purchase his Time of Keimer, now came to offer himself as a Journeyman to us. We could not then employ him, but I foolishly let him know, as a Secret, that I soon intended to begin a Newspaper, and might then have Work for him. My Hopes of Success as I told him were founded on this, that the then only Newspaper,[6] printed by Bradford was a paltry thing, wretchedly manag'd, no way entertaining; and yet was profitable to him. I therefore thought a good Paper could scarcely fail of good Encouragement. I requested Webb not to mention it, but he told it to Keimer, who immediately, to be beforehand with me, published Proposals for Printing one himself, on which Webb was to be employ'd. I resented this, and to counteract them, as I could not yet begin our Paper, I wrote several Pieces of Entertainment for Bradford's Paper, under the Title of the Busy Body which Breintnall continu'd some Months.[7] By this means the Attention of the Public was fix'd on that Paper, and Keimer's Proposals which we burlesqu'd and ridicul'd, were disregarded. He began his Paper however, and after carrying it on three Quarters of a Year, with at most only 90 Subscribers, he offer'd it to me for a Trifle, and I having been ready some time to go on with it, took it in hand directly, and it prov'd in a few Years extremely profitable to me.[8]

I perceive that I am apt to speak in the singular Number, though our Partnership still continu'd. The Reason may be, that in fact the whole Management of the Business lay upon me. Meredith was no Compositor, a poor Pressman, and seldom sober. My Friends lamented my Connection with him, but I was to make the best of it.

Our first Papers made a quite different Appearance from any before in the Province, a better Type and better printed: but some spirited Remarks of my Writing on the Dispute then going on between Governor Burnet[9] and the Massachusetts Assembly, struck the principal People, occasion'd the Paper and the Manager of it to be much talk'd of, and in a few Weeks brought them all to be our Subscribers. Their Example was follow'd by many, and our Number went on growing continually. This was one of the first good Effects of my having learned a little to scribble. Another was, that the leading Men, seeing a Newspaper now in the hands of one who could also handle a Pen, thought it convenient to oblige and encourage me. Bradford still printed the Votes and Laws and other Public Business. He had printed an Address of the House[1] to the Governor in a coarse blundering manner; We reprinted it elegantly and correctly, and sent one to every Member. They were sensible of the Difference, it strengthen'd the Hands of our Friends in the House, and they voted us their Printers for the Year ensuing.

Among my Friends in the House I must not forget Mr. Hamilton[2] beforementioned, who was then returned from England and had a Seat in it. He interested himself[3] for me strongly in that Instance, as he did in many others afterwards, continuing his Patronage till his Death. Mr. Vernon about this time put me in mind of the Debt I ow'd him: but did not press me. I wrote

6. The *American Weekly Mercury*.
7. From February 4, 1728, to September 25, 1729.
8. Franklin took over Keimer's *The Universal Instructor in All Arts and Sciences: and Pennsylvania Gazette* in October 1729 and shortened the name to the *Pennsylvania Gazette*.

9. See n. 3, p. 558.
1. I.e., the Pennsylvania Assembly.
2. Andrew Hamilton (see n. 3, p. 563).
3. "I got his Son once £500" [Franklin's note]. Franklin was able to get the legislature to pay Governor James Hamilton his salary when they were at odds with him.

him an ingenuous Letter of Acknowledgments, crav'd his Forbearance a little longer which he allow'd me, and as soon as I was able I paid the Principal with Interest and many Thanks. So that Erratum was in some degree corrected.

But now another Difficulty came upon me, which I had never the least Reason to expect. Mr. Meredith's Father, who was to have paid for our Printing-House according to the Expectations given me, was able to advance only one Hundred Pounds, Currency, which had been paid, and a Hundred more was due to the Merchant; who grew impatient and su'd us all. We gave Bail, but saw that if the Money could not be rais'd in time, the Suit must come to a Judgment and Execution, and our hopeful Prospects must with us be ruined, as the Press and Letters must be sold for Payment, perhaps at half-Price. In this Distress two true Friends whose Kindness I have never forgotten nor ever shall forget while I can remember anything, came to me separately unknown to each other, and without any Application from me, offering each of them to advance me all the Money that should be necessary to enable me to take the whole Business upon myself if that should be practicable, but they did not like my continuing the Partnership with Meredith, who as they said was often seen drunk in the Streets, and playing at low Games in Alehouses, much to our Discredit. These two Friends were *William Coleman* and *Robert Grace*.

I told them I could not propose a Separation while any Prospect remain'd of the Merediths fulfilling their Part of our Agreement. Because I thought myself under great Obligations to them for what they had done and would do if they could. But if they finally fail'd in their Performance, and our Partnership must be dissolv'd, I should then think myself at Liberty to accept the Assistance of my Friends. Thus the matter rested for some time. When I said to my Partner, perhaps your Father is dissatisfied at the Part you have undertaken in this Affair of ours, and is unwilling to advance for you and me what he would for you alone: If that is the Case, tell me, and I will resign the whole to you and go about my Business. No—says he, my Father has really been disappointed and is really unable; and I am unwilling to distress him farther. I see this is a Business I am not fit for. I was bred a Farmer, and it was a Folly in me to come to Town and put myself at 30 Years of Age an Apprentice to learn a new Trade. Many of our Welsh People are going to settle in North Carolina where Land is cheap: I am inclin'd to go with them, and follow my old Employment. You may find Friends to assist you. If you will take the Debts of the Company upon you, return to my Father the hundred Pound he has advanc'd, pay my little personal Debts, and give me Thirty Pounds and a new Saddle, I will relinquish the Partnership and leave the whole in your Hands. I agreed to this Proposal. It was drawn up in Writing, sign'd and seal'd immediately. I gave him what he demanded and he went soon after to Carolina; from whence he sent me next Year two long Letters, containing the best Account that had been given of that Country, the Climate, Soil, Husbandry, etc., for in those Matters he was very judicious. I printed them in the Papers,[4] and they gave great Satisfaction to the Public.

As soon as he was gone, I recurr'd to my two Friends; and because I would not give an unkind Preference to either, I took half what each had offered

4. In the *Pennsylvania Gazette*, May 6 and 13, 1732.

and I wanted, of one, and half of the other; paid off the Company Debts, and went on with the Business in my own Name, advertising that the Partnership was dissolved. I think this was in or about the Year 1729.[5]

About this Time there was a Cry among the People for more Paper-Money, only 15,000 Pounds being extant in the Province and that soon to be sunk.[6] The wealthy Inhabitants oppos'd any Addition, being against all Paper Currency, from an Apprehension that it would depreciate as it had done in New England to the Prejudice of all Creditors. We had discuss'd this Point in our Junto, where I was on the Side of an Addition, being persuaded that the first small Sum struck in 1723 had done much good, by increasing the Trade, Employment, and Number of Inhabitants in the Province, since I now saw all the old Houses inhabited, and many new ones building, where as I remember'd well, that when I first walk'd about the Streets of Philadelphia, eating my Roll, I saw most of the Houses in Walnut Street between Second and Front Streets with Bills[7] on their Doors, to be let; and many likewise in Chestnut Street, and other Streets; which made me then think the Inhabitants of the City were one after another deserting it. Our Debates possess'd me so fully of the Subject, that I wrote and printed an anonymous Pamphlet on it, entitled, *The Nature and Necessity of a Paper Currency*.[8] It was well receiv'd by the common People in general; but the Rich Men dislik'd it; for it increas'd and strengthen'd the Clamor for more Money; and they happening to have no Writers among them that were able to answer it, their Opposition slacken'd, and the Point was carried by a Majority in the House. My Friends there, who conceiv'd I had been of some Service, thought fit to reward me, by employing me in printing the Money,[9] a very profitable Job, and a great Help to me. This was another Advantage gain'd by my being able to write. The Utility of this Currency became by Time and Experience so evident, as never afterwards to be much disputed, so that it grew soon to 55,000 Pounds, and in 1739 to 80,000 Pounds, since which it arose during War to upwards of 350,000 Pounds—Trade, Building and Inhabitants all the while increasing. Tho' I now think there are Limits beyond which the Quantity may be hurtful.

I soon after obtain'd, thro' my Friend Hamilton, the Printing of the New Castle[1] Paper Money, another profitable Job, as I then thought it; small Things appearing great to those in small Circumstances. And these to me were really great Advantages, as they were great Encouragements. He procured me also the Printing of the Laws and Votes of that Government which continu'd in my Hands as long as I follow'd the Business.

I now open'd a little Stationer's Shop.[2] I had in it Blanks of all Sorts the correctest that ever appear'd among us, being assisted in that by my Friend Breintnall; I had also Paper, Parchment, Chapmen's Books,[3] etc. One Whitmarsh[4] a Compositor I had known in London, an excellent Workman now

---

5. More accurately, July 14, 1730.
6. Destroyed. In 1723 paper money had become so scarce that the Assembly issued new money secured by real estate mortgages; when the mortgages were paid off, the bills were "sunk." But by 1729 the value of the currency was so low that the money was recalled before the mortgages were paid.
7. Signs.
8. *A Modest Inquiry into the Nature and Necessity*

of a Paper Currency (April 3, 1729).
9. Franklin received the contract to print money in 1731.
1. New Castle, Delaware. Delaware had a separate legislature but the same proprietary governor as Pennsylvania.
2. In July 1730.
3. Inexpensive paper pamphlets.
4. Thomas Whitmarsh (d. 1733); the following year Whitmarsh went to South Carolina.

came to me and work'd with me constantly and diligently, and I took an Apprentice the Son of Aquila Rose. I began now gradually to pay off the Debt I was under for the Printing-House. In order to secure my Credit and Character as a Tradesman, I took care not only to be in *Reality* Industrious and frugal, but to avoid all *Appearances* of the contrary. I dressed plainly; I was seen at no Places of idle Diversion; I never went out a-fishing or shooting; a Book, indeed, sometimes debauch'd me from my Work; but that was seldom, snug, and gave no Scandal: and to show that I was not above my Business, I sometimes brought home the Paper I purchas'd at the Stores, thro' the Streets on a Wheelbarrow. Thus being esteem'd an industrious thriving young Man, and paying duly for what I bought, the Merchants who imported Stationery solicited my Custom, others propos'd supplying me with Books, and I went on swimmingly. In the mean time Keimer's Credit and Business declining daily, he was at last forc'd to sell his Printing-House to satisfy his Creditors. He went to Barbados, and there lived some Years, in very poor Circumstances.

His Apprentice David Harry, whom I had instructed while I work'd with him, set up in his Place at Philadelphia, having bought his Materials. I was at first apprehensive of a powerful Rival in Harry, as his Friends were very able, and had a good deal of Interest. I therefore propos'd a Partnership to him; which he, fortunately for me, rejected with Scorn. He was very proud, dress'd like a Gentleman, liv'd expensively, took much Diversion and Pleasure abroad, ran in debt, and neglected his Business, upon which all Business left him; and finding nothing to do, he follow'd Keimer to Barbados; taking the Printing-House with him. There this Apprentice employ'd his former Master as a Journeyman. They quarrel'd often. Harry went continually behind-hand, and at length was forc'd to sell his Types, and return to his Country Work in Pennsylvania. The Person that bought them employ'd Keimer to use them, but in a few years he died. There remain'd now no Competitor with me at Philadelphia, but the old one, Bradford, who was rich and easy, did a little Printing now and then by straggling Hands, but was not very anxious about the Business. However, as he kept the Post Office, it was imagined he had better Opportunities of obtaining News, his Paper was thought a better Distributer of Advertisements than mine, and therefore had many more, which was a profitable thing to him and a Disadvantage to me. For tho' I did indeed receive and send Papers by the Post, yet the public Opinion was otherwise; for what I did send was by Bribing the Riders[5] who took them privately: Bradford being unkind enough to forbid it: which occasion'd some Resentment on my Part; and I thought so meanly of him for it, that when I afterwards came into his Situation,[6] I took care never to imitate it.

I had hitherto continu'd to board with Godfrey who lived in Part of my House with his Wife and Children, and had one Side of the Shop for his Glazier's Business, tho' he work'd little, being always absorb'd in his Mathematics. Mrs. Godfrey projected a Match for me with a Relation's Daughter, took Opportunities of bringing us often together, till a serious Courtship on my Part ensu'd, the Girl being in herself very deserving. The old Folks

5. I.e., the postal riders or carriers. Franklin did this to have his papers delivered on the same day as Bradford's.

6. Franklin assumed Bradford's office as postmaster of Philadelphia in October 1737.

encourag'd me by continual Invitations to Supper, and by leaving us together, till at length it was time to explain. Mrs. Godfrey manag'd our little Treaty. I let her know that I expected as much Money with their Daughter as would pay off my Remaining Debt for the Printing-House, which I believe was not then above a Hundred Pounds.[7] She brought me Word they had no such Sum to spare. I said they might mortgage their House in the Loan Office. The Answer to this after some Days was, that they did not approve the Match; that on Enquiry of Bradford they had been inform'd the Printing Business was not a profitable one, the Types would soon be worn out and more wanted, that S. Keimer and D. Harry had fail'd one after the other, and I should probably soon follow them; and therefore I was forbidden the House, and the Daughter shut up.

Whether this was a real Change of Sentiment, or only Artifice, on a Supposition of our being too far engag'd in Affection to retract, and therefore that we should steal a Marriage, which would leave them at Liberty to give or withhold what they pleas'd, I know not: But I suspected the latter, resented it, and went no more. Mrs. Godfrey brought me afterwards some more favorable Accounts of their Disposition, and would have drawn me on again: But I declared absolutely my Resolution to have nothing more to do with that Family. This was resented by the Godfreys, we differ'd, and they removed, leaving me the whole House, and I resolved to take no more Inmates. But this Affair having turn'd my Thoughts to Marriage, I look'd round me, and made Overtures of Acquaintance in other Places; but soon found that the Business of a Printer being generally thought a poor one, I was not to expect Money with a Wife unless with such a one, as I should not otherwise think agreeable. In the mean time, that hard-to-be-govern'd Passion of Youth, had hurried me frequently into Intrigues with low Women that fell in my Way, which were attended with some Expense and great Inconvenience, besides a continual Risk to my Health by a Distemper[8] which of all Things I dreaded, tho' by great good Luck I escaped it.

A friendly Correspondence as Neighbors and old Acquaintances, had continued between me and Mrs. Read's Family who all had a Regard for me from the time of my first Lodging in their House. I was often invited there and consulted in their Affairs, wherein I sometimes was of Service. I pitied poor Miss Read's unfortunate Situation, who was generally dejected, seldom cheerful, and avoided Company. I consider'd my Giddiness and Inconstancy when in London as in a great degree the Cause of her Unhappiness; tho' the Mother was good enough to think the Fault more her own than mine, as she had prevented our Marrying before I went thither, and persuaded the other Match in my Absence. Our mutual Affection was revived, but there were now great Objections to our Union. That Match was indeed look'd upon as invalid, a preceding Wife being said to be living in England; but this could not easily be prov'd, because of the Distance, etc. And tho' there was a Report of his Death, it was not certain. Then, tho' it should be true, he had left many Debts which his Successor might be call'd upon to pay. We ventured however, over all these Difficulties, and I took her to Wife Sept. 1, 1730.[9] None of the Inconveniencies happened that we had apprehended, she prov'd

7. Franklin's expectations were not unusual: marriages were often arranged on agreeable financial considerations.
8. I.e., syphilis.

9. Because there was no proof that John Rogers, Deborah Read's first husband, was dead, she and Franklin entered into a common-law marriage without civil ceremony.

a good and faithful Helpmate, assisted me much by attending the Shop, we throve together, and have ever mutually endeavor'd to make each other happy. Thus I corrected that great Erratum as well as I could.

About this Time our Club meeting, not at a Tavern, but in a little Room of Mr. Grace's set apart for that Purpose; a Proposition was made by me, that since our Books were often referr'd to in our Disquisitions upon the Queries, it might be convenient to us to have them all together where we met, that upon Occasion they might be consulted; and by thus clubbing our Books to a common Library, we should, while we lik'd to keep them together, have each of us the Advantage of using the Books of all the other Members, which would be nearly as beneficial as if each owned the whole. It was lik'd and agreed to, and we fill'd one End of the Room with such Books as we could best spare. The Number was not so great as we expected; and tho' they had been of great Use, yet some Inconveniencies occurring for want of due Care of them, the Collection after about a Year was separated, and each took his Books home again.

And now I set on foot my first Project of a public Nature, that for a Subscription Library. I drew up the Proposals, got them put into Form by our great Scrivener Brockden, and by the help of my Friends in the Junto, procur'd Fifty Subscribers of 40 Shillings each to begin with and 10 Shillings a Year for 50 Years, the Term our Company was to continue. We afterwards obtain'd a Charter, the Company being increas'd to 100. This was the Mother of all the North American Subscription Libraries now so numerous. It is become a great thing itself, and continually increasing. These Libraries have improv'd the general Conversation of the Americans, made the common Tradesmen and Farmers as intelligent as most Gentlemen from other Countries, and perhaps have contributed in some degree to the Stand so generally made throughout the Colonies in Defense of their Privileges.

Memo.

Thus far was written with the Intention express'd in the Beginning and therefore contains several little family Anecdotes of no Importance to others. What follows was written many Years after in compliance with the Advice contain'd in these Letters, and accordingly intended for the Public. The Affairs of the Revolution occasion'd the Interruption.

[Part Two][1]

LETTER FROM MR. ABEL JAMES,[2] WITH NOTES ON MY LIFE, (RECEIVED IN PARIS)

My dear and honored Friend.

I have often been desirous of writing to thee, but could not be reconciled to the Thought that the Letter might fall into the Hands of the British,[3] lest some Printer or busy Body should publish some Part of the Contents and give our Friends Pain and myself Censure.

1. Franklin wrote the second part of his autobiography at the Hôtel de Valentenois in Passy, a Paris suburb. He had been sent to Paris as American representative to the peace treaty, ending the war with Britain, September 3, 1783. Franklin remained in Paris until July 1785, when Thomas Jefferson replaced him as minister.
2. A Quaker merchant in Philadelphia (c. 1726–1790).
3. James's letter was written in 1782, when Britain was still at war with the colonies.

Some Time since there fell into my Hands to my great Joy about 23 Sheets in thy own handwriting containing an Account of the Parentage and Life of thyself, directed to thy Son ending in the Year 1730 with which there were Notes[4] likewise in thy writing, a Copy of which I enclose in Hopes it may be a means if thou continuedst it up to a later period, that the first and latter part may be put together; and if it is not yet continued, I hope thou wilt not delay it. Life is uncertain as the Preacher tells us, and what will the World say if kind, humane and benevolent Ben Franklin should leave his Friends and the World deprived of so pleasing and profitable a Work, a Work which would be useful and entertaining not only to a few, but to millions.

The Influence Writings under that Class have on the Minds of Youth is very great, and has no where appeared so plain as in our public Friends' Journals. It almost insensibly leads the Youth into the Resolution of endeavoring to become as good and as eminent as the Journalist. Should thine for Instance when published, and I think it could not fail of it, lead the Youth to equal the Industry and Temperance of thy early Youth, what a Blessing with that Class would such a Work be. I know of no Character living nor many of them put together, who has so much in his Power as Thyself to promote a greater Spirit of Industry and early Attention to Business, Frugality and Temperance with the American Youth. Not that I think the Work would have no other Merit and Use in the World, far from it, but the first is of such vast Importance, that I know nothing that can equal it.

The foregoing letter and the minutes accompanying it being shown to a friend, I received from him the following:

LETTER FROM MR. BENJAMIN VAUGHAN[5]

MY DEAREST SIR,   *Paris, January* 31, 1783.

When I had read over your sheets of minutes of the principal incidents of your life, recovered for you by your Quaker acquaintance; I told you I would send you a letter expressing my reasons why I thought it would be useful to complete and publish it as he desired. Various concerns have for some time past prevented this letter being written, and I do not know whether it was worth any expectation: happening to be at leisure however at present, I shall by writing at least interest and instruct myself; but as the terms I am inclined to use may tend to offend a person of your manners, I shall only tell you how I would address any other person, who was as good and as great as yourself, but less diffident. I would say to him, Sir, I *solicit* the history of your life from the following motives.

Your history is so remarkable, that if you do not give it, somebody else will certainly give it; and perhaps so as nearly to do as much harm, as your own management of the thing might do good.

It will moreover present a table of the internal circumstances of your country, which will very much tend to invite to it settlers of virtuous and

4. Franklin's outline for his *Autobiography*, written in 1771. Reprinted in the Yale University edition (1964).
5. The wealthy son (1751–1835) of a Jamaican

merchant and Maine mother; private secretary to Lord Shelburne, and personal emissary to Franklin during the Paris peace talks (1782–85).

manly minds. And considering the eagerness with which such information is sought by them, and the extent of your reputation, I do not know of a more efficacious advertisement than your Biography would give.

All that has happened to you is also connected with the detail of the manners and situation of *a rising* people; and in this respect I do not think that the writings of Caesar and Tacitus[6] can be more interesting to a true judge of human nature and society.

But these, Sir, are small reasons in my opinion, compared with the chance which your life will give for the forming of future great men; and in conjunction with your *Art of Virtue,*[7] (which you design to publish) of improving the features of private character, and consequently of aiding all happiness both public and domestic.

The two works I allude to, Sir, will in particular give a noble rule and example of *self-education.* School and other education constantly proceed upon false principles, and show a clumsy apparatus pointed at a false mark; but your apparatus is simple, and the mark a true one; and while parents and young persons are left destitute of other just means of estimating and becoming prepared for a reasonable course in life, your discovery that the thing is in many a man's private power, will be invaluable!

Influence upon the private character late in life, is not only an influence late in life, but a weak influence. It is in *youth* that we plant our chief habits and prejudices; it is in youth that we take our party[8] as to profession, pursuits, and matrimony. In youth therefore the turn is given; in youth the education even of the next generation is given; in youth the private and public character is determined: and the term of life extending from youth to age, life ought to begin well from youth; and more especially *before* we take our party as to our principal objects.

But your Biography will not merely teach self-education, but the education of *a wise man*; and the wisest man will receive lights and improve his progress, by seeing detailed the conduct of another wise man. And why are weaker men to be deprived of such helps, when we see our race has been blundering on in the dark, almost without a guide in this particular, from the farthest trace of time. Show then, Sir, how much is to be done, *both to sons and fathers*; and invite all wise men to become like yourself; and other men to become wise.

When we see how cruel statesmen and warriors can be to the humble race, and how absurd distinguished men can be to their acquaintance, it will be instructive to observe the instances multiply of pacific acquiescing manners; and to find how compatible it is to be great and *domestic*; enviable and yet *good-humored*.

The little private incidents which you will also have to relate, will have considerable use, as we want above all things, *rules of prudence in ordinary affairs*; and it will be curious to see how you have acted in these. It will be so far a sort of key to life, and explain many things that all men

6. Gaius Julius Caesar (100–44 B.C.E.) and Publius Cornelius Tacitus (late 1st and early 2nd centuries C.E.).
7. Vaughan is referring to Franklin's intention to write "a little work for the benefit of youth" to be called *The Art of Virtue*. Part Two of the *Autobiography* is, in part, an answer to Vaughan's reminder.
8. Make our decision.

ought to have once explained to them, to give them a chance of becoming wise by foresight.

The nearest thing to having experience of one's own, is to have other people's affairs brought before us in a shape that is interesting; this is sure to happen from your pen. Your affairs and management will have an air of simplicity or importance that will not fail to strike; and I am convinced you have conducted them with as much originality as if you had been conducting discussions in politics or philosophy; and what more worthy of experiments and system, (its importance and its errors considered) than human life!

Some men have been virtuous blindly, others have speculated fantastically, and others have been shrewd to bad purposes; but you, Sir, I am sure, will give under your hand, nothing but what is at the same moment, wise, practical, and good.

Your account of yourself (for I suppose the parallel I am drawing for Dr. Franklin, will hold not only in point of character but of private history), will show that you are ashamed of no origin; a thing the more important, as you prove how little necessary all origin is to happiness, virtue, or greatness.

As no end likewise happens without a means, so we shall find, Sir, that even you yourself framed a plan by which you became considerable; but at the same time we may see that though the event is flattering, the means are as simple as wisdom could make them; that is, depending upon nature, virtue, thought, and habit.

Another thing demonstrated will be the propriety of every man's waiting for his time for appearing upon the stage of the world. Our sensations being very much fixed to the moment, we are apt to forget that more moments are to follow the first, and consequently that man should arrange his conduct so as to suit the *whole* of a life. Your attribution appears to have been applied to your *life,* and the passing moments of it have been enlivened with content and enjoyment, instead of being tormented with foolish impatience or regrets. Such a conduct is easy for those who make virtue and themselves their standard, and who try to keep themselves in countenance by examples of other truly great men, of whom patience is so often the characteristic.

Your Quaker correspondent, Sir (for here again I will suppose the subject of my letter resembling Dr. Franklin,) praised your frugality, diligence, and temperance, which he considered as a pattern for all youth: but it is singular that he should have forgotten your modesty, and your disinterestedness, without which you never could have waited for your advancement, or found your situation in the mean time comfortable; which is a strong lesson to show the poverty of glory, and the importance of regulating our minds.

If this correspondent had known the nature of your reputation as well as I do, he would have said; your former writings and measures would secure attention to your Biography, and Art of Virtue; and your Biography and Art of Virtue, in return, would secure attention to them. This is an advantage attendant upon a various character, and which brings all that belongs to it into greater play; and it is the more useful, as perhaps more persons are at a loss for the *means* of improving their

minds and characters, than they are for the time or the inclination to
do it.

But there is one concluding reflection, Sir, that will show the use of
your life as a mere piece of biography. This style of writing seems a little
gone out of vogue, and yet it is a very useful one; and your specimen of
it may be particularly serviceable, as it will make a subject of comparison
with the lives of various public cut-throats and intriguers, and with
absurd monastic self-tormentors, or vain literary triflers. If it encourages
more writings of the same kind with your own, and induces more men
to spend lives fit to be written; it will be worth all Plutarch's Lives put
together.

But being tired of figuring to myself a character of which every feature
suits only one man in the world, without giving him the praise of it; I
shall end my letter, my dear Dr. Franklin, with a personal application to
your proper self.

I am earnestly desirous then, my dear Sir, that you should let the world
into the traits of your genuine character, as civil broils may otherwise
tend to disguise or traduce it. Considering your great age, the caution
of your character, and your peculiar style of thinking, it is not likely that
any one besides yourself can be sufficiently master of the facts of your
life, or the intentions of your mind.

Besides all this, the immense revolution of the present period, will
necessarily turn our attention towards the author of it; and when virtuous principles have been pretended in it, it will be highly important to
show that such have really influenced; and, as your own character will
be the principal one to receive a scrutiny, it is proper (even for its effects
upon your vast and rising country, as well as upon England and upon
Europe), that it should stand respectable and eternal. For the furtherance of human happiness, I have always maintained that it is necessary
to prove that man is not even at present a vicious and detestable animal;
and still more to prove that good management may greatly amend him;
and it is for much the same reason, that I am anxious to see the opinion
established, that there are fair characters existing among the individuals
of the race; for the moment that all men, without exception, shall be
conceived abandoned, good people will cease efforts deemed to be hopeless, and perhaps think of taking their share in the scramble of life, or
at least of making it comfortable principally for themselves.

Take then, my dear Sir, this work most speedily into hand: show yourself good as you are good, temperate as you are temperate; and above all
things, prove yourself as one who from your infancy have loved justice,
liberty, and concord, in a way that has made it natural and consistent
for you to have acted, as we have seen you act in the last seventeen years
of your life. Let Englishmen be made not only to respect, but even to
love you. When they think well of individuals in your native country,
they will go nearer to thinking well of your country; and when your
countrymen see themselves well thought of by Englishmen, they will go
nearer to thinking well of England. Extend your views even further; do
not stop at those who speak the English tongue, but after having settled
so many points in nature and politics, think of bettering the whole race
of men.

As I have not read any part of the life in question, but know only the character that lived it, I write somewhat at hazard. I am sure however, that the life, and the treatise I allude to (on the *Art of Virtue*), will necessarily fullfil the chief of my expectations; and still more so if you take up the measure of suiting these performances to the several views above stated. Should they even prove unsuccessful in all that a sanguine admirer of yours hopes from them, you will at least have framed pieces to interest the human mind; and whoever gives a feeling of pleasure that is innocent to man, has added so much to the fair side of a life otherwise too much darkened by anxiety, and too much injured by pain.

In the hope therefore that you will listen to the prayer addressed to you in this letter, I beg to subscribe myself, my dearest Sir, etc., etc.

Signed   BENJ. VAUGHAN.

CONTINUATION OF THE ACCOUNT OF MY LIFE.
BEGUN AT PASSY, 1784.

It is some time since I receiv'd the above Letters, but I have been too busy till now to think of complying with the Request they contain. It might too be much better done if I were at home among my Papers, which would aid my Memory, and help to ascertain Dates. But my Return being uncertain, and having just now a little Leisure, I will endeavor to recollect and write what I can; if I live to get home, it may there be corrected and improv'd.

Not having any Copy here of what is already written, I know not whether an Account is given of the means I used to establish the Philadelphia public Library, which from a small Beginning is now become so considerable, though I remember to have come down to near the Time of that Transaction, 1730. I will therefore begin here, with an Account of it, which may be struck out if found to have been already given.

At the time I establish'd myself in Pennsylvania, there was not a good Bookseller's Shop in any of the Colonies to the Southward of Boston. In New York and Philadelphia the Printers were indeed Stationers, they sold only Paper, etc., Almanacs, Ballads, and a few common School Books. Those who lov'd Reading were oblig'd to send for their Books from England. The Members of the Junto had each a few. We had left the Alehouse where we first met, and hired a Room to hold our Club in. I propos'd that we should all of us bring our Books to that Room, where they would not only be ready to consult in our Conferences, but become a common Benefit, each of us being at Liberty to borrow such as he wish'd to read at home. This was accordingly done, and for some time contented us. Finding the Advantage of this little Collection, I propos'd to render the Benefit from Books more common by commencing a Public Subscription Library. I drew a Sketch of the Plan and Rules that would be necessary, and got a skillful Conveyancer Mr. Charles Brockden[9] to put the whole in Form of Articles of Agreement to be subscribed, by which each Subscriber engag'd to pay a certain Sum down for the first Purchase of Books and an annual Contribution for increasing them. So few were the Readers at that time in Philadelphia, and the Majority of us so poor, that I was not able with great Industry to find more than Fifty

---

9. Philadelphia's leading drafter of legal documents (1683–1769). "Conveyancer": an attorney who specializes in the transfer of real estate and property.

Persons, mostly young Tradesmen, willing to pay down for this purpose Forty shillings each, and Ten Shillings per Annum. On this little Fund we began. The Books were imported. The Library was open one Day in the Week for lending them to the Subscribers, on their Promissory Notes to pay Double the Value if not duly returned. The Institution soon manifested its Utility, was imitated by other Towns and in other Provinces, the Libraries were augmented by Donations, Reading became fashionable, and our People having no public Amusements to divert their Attention from Study became better acquainted with Books, and in a few Years were observ'd by Strangers to be better instructed and more intelligent than People of the same Rank generally are in other Countries.

When we were about to sign the above-mentioned Articles, which were to be binding on us, our Heirs, etc., for fifty Years, Mr. Brockden, the Scrivener, said to us, "You are young Men, but it is scarce probable that any of you will live to see the Expiration of the Term fix'd in this Instrument." A Number of us, however, are yet living. But the Instrument was after a few Years rendered null by a Charter that incorporated and gave Perpetuity to the Company.

The Objections, and Reluctances I met with in Soliciting the Subscriptions, made me soon feel the Impropriety of presenting oneself as the Proposer of any useful Project that might be suppos'd to raise one's Reputation in the smallest degree above that of one's Neighbors, when one has need of their Assistance to accomplish that Project. I therefore put myself as much as I could out of sight, and stated it as a Scheme of *a Number of Friends*, who had requested me to go about and propose it to such as they thought Lovers of Reading. In this way my Affair went on more smoothly, and I ever after practic'd it on such Occasions; and from my frequent Successes, can heartily recommend it. The present little Sacrifice of your Vanity will afterwards be amply repaid. If it remains a while uncertain to whom the Merit belongs, someone more vain than yourself will be encourag'd to claim it, and then even Envy will be dispos'd to do you Justice, by plucking those assum'd Feathers, and restoring them to their right Owner.

This Library afforded me the Means of Improvement by constant Study, for which I set apart an Hour or two each Day; and thus repair'd in some Degree the Loss of the Learned Education my Father once intended for me. Reading was the only Amusement I allow'd myself. I spent no time in Taverns, Games, or Frolics of any kind. And my Industry in my Business continu'd as indefatigable as it was necessary. I was in debt for my Printing-House, I had a young Family[1] coming on to be educated, and I had to contend with for Business two Printers who were establish'd in the Place before me. My Circumstances however grew daily easier: my original Habits of Frugality continuing. And My Father having among his Instructions to me when a Boy, frequently repeated a Proverb of Solomon, *"Seest thou a Man diligent in his Calling, he shall stand before Kings, he shall not stand before mean Men."*[2] I from thence consider'd Industry as a Means of obtaining Wealth and Distinction, which encourag'd me: tho' I did not think that I should ever literally stand before Kings, which however has since happened; for I have stood before five,[3] and even had the honor of sitting down with one, the King of Denmark, to Dinner.

---

1. Franklin had three children: William, born c. 1731; Francis, born in 1732; Sarah, born in 1743.
2. Proverbs 22.29.

3. Louis XV and Louis XVI of France, George II and George III of England, and Christian VI of Denmark.

We have an English Proverb that says,

> He that would thrive
> Must ask his Wife,[4]

it was lucky for me that I had one as much dispos'd to Industry and Frugality as myself. She assisted me cheerfully in my Business, folding and stitching Pamphlets, tending Shop, purchasing old Linen Rags for the Paper-makers, etc., etc. We kept no idle Servants, our Table was plain and simple, our Furniture of the cheapest. For instance my Breakfast was a long time Bread and Milk, (no Tea,) and I ate it out of a two penny earthen Porringer[5] with a Pewter Spoon. But mark how Luxury will enter Families, and make a Progress, in Spite of Principle. Being Call'd one Morning to Breakfast, I found it in a China[6] Bowl with a Spoon of Silver. They had been bought for me without my Knowledge by my Wife, and had cost her the enormous Sum of three and twenty Shillings, for which she had no other Excuse or Apology to make, but that she thought *her* Husband deserv'd a Silver Spoon and China Bowl as well as any of his Neighbors. This was the first Appearance of Plate[7] and China in our House, which afterwards in a Course of Years as our Wealth increas'd, augmented gradually to several Hundred Pounds in Value.

I had been religiously educated as a Presbyterian, and tho' some of the Dogmas of that Persuasion, such as the Eternal Decrees of God, Election, Reprobation,[8] etc., appear'd to me unintelligible, others doubtful, and I early absented myself from the Public Assemblies of the Sect, Sunday being my Studying-Day, I never was without some religious Principles; I never doubted, for instance, the Existence of the Deity, that he made the World, and govern'd it by his Providence; that the most acceptable Service of God was the doing Good to Man; that our Souls are immortal; and that all Crime will be punished and Virtue rewarded either here or hereafter; these I esteem'd the Essentials of every Religion, and being to be found in all the Religions we had in our Country I respected them all, tho' with different degrees of Respect as I found them more or less mix'd with other Articles which without any Tendency to inspire, promote or confirm Morality, serv'd principally to divide us and make us unfriendly to one another. This Respect to all, with an Opinion that the worst had some good Effects, induc'd me to avoid all Discourse that might tend to lessen the good Opinion another might have of his own Religion; and as our Province increas'd in People and new Places of worship were continually wanted, and generally erected by voluntary Contribution, my Mite[9] for such purpose, whatever might be the Sect, was never refused.

Tho' I seldom attended any Public Worship, I had still an Opinion of its Propriety, and of its Utility when rightly conducted, and I regularly paid my annual Subscription for the Support of the only Presbyterian Minister or Meeting we had in Philadelphia. He us'd to visit me sometimes as a Friend, and admonish me to attend his Administrations, and I was now and then prevail'd on to do so, once for five Sundays successively. Had he been, *in my Opinion,* a good Preacher perhaps I might have continued, notwithstanding

4. More commonly: "He that will thrive must ask leave of his wife."
5. Bowl.
6. I.e., porcelain.
7. Silver.
8. Punishment. "Election": God's choosing who is to be saved and who is to be damned.
9. Small contribution.

the occasion I had for the Sunday's Leisure in my Course of Study: But his Discourses were chiefly either polemic Arguments, or Explications of the peculiar Doctrines of our Sect, and were all to me very dry, uninteresting and unedifying, since not a single moral Principle was inculcated or enforc'd, their Aim seeming to be rather to make us Presbyterians than good Citizens. At length he took for his Text that Verse of the 4th Chapter of Philippians, *Finally, Brethren, Whatsoever Things are true, honest, just, pure, lovely, or of good report, if there be any virtue, or any praise, think on these Things;*[1] and I imagin'd in a Sermon on such a Text, we could not miss of having some Morality: But he confin'd himself to five Points only as meant by the Apostle, viz., 1. Keeping holy the Sabbath Day. 2. Being diligent in Reading the Holy Scriptures. 3. Attending duly the Public Worship. 4. Partaking of the Sacrament. 5. Paying a due Respect to God's Ministers. These might be all good Things, but as they were not the kind of good Things that I expected from that Text, I despaired of ever meeting with them from any other, was disgusted, and attended his Preaching no more. I had some Years before compos'd a little Liturgy or Form of Prayer for my own private Use, viz., in 1728, entitled, *Articles of Belief and Acts of Religion.*[2] I return'd to the Use of this, and went no more to the public Assemblies. My Conduct might be blameable, but I leave it without attempting farther to excuse it, my present purpose being to relate Facts, and not to make Apologies for them.

It was about this time that I conceiv'd the bold and arduous Project of arriving at moral Perfection. I wish'd to live without committing any Fault at anytime; I would conquer all that either Natural Inclination, Custom, or Company might lead me into. As I knew, or thought I knew, what was right and wrong, I did not see why I might not *always* do the one and avoid the other. But I soon found I had undertaken a Task of more Difficulty than I had imagined: While my Care was employ'd in guarding against one Fault, I was often surpris'd by another. Habit took the Advantage of Inattention. Inclination was sometimes too strong for Reason. I concluded at length, that the mere speculative Conviction that it was our Interest to be completely virtuous, was not sufficient to prevent our Slipping, and that the contrary Habits must be broken and good Ones acquired and established, before we can have any Dependence on a steady uniform Rectitude of Conduct. For this purpose I therefore contriv'd the following Method.

In the various Enumerations of the moral Virtues I had met with in my Reading, I found the Catalog more or less numerous, as different Writers included more or fewer Ideas under the same Name. Temperance, for Example, was by some confin'd to Eating and Drinking, while by others it was extended to mean the moderating every other Pleasure, Appetite, Inclination or Passion, bodily or mental, even to our Avarice and Ambition. I propos'd to myself, for the sake of Clearness, to use rather more Names with fewer Ideas annex'd to each, than a few Names with more Ideas; and I included after Thirteen Names of Virtues all that at that time occurr'd to me as necessary or desirable, and annex'd to each a short Precept, which fully express'd the Extent I gave to its Meaning.

1. A paraphrase of Philippians 4.8.
2. Only the first part of Franklin's *Articles of Belief and Acts of Religion* survives. It can be found in

The Papers of Benjamin Franklin, vol. 1, edited by Leonard W. Labaree et al. (1964).

These Names of Virtues with their Precepts were

1. TEMPERANCE.
Eat not to Dullness. Drink not to Elevation.

2. SILENCE.
Speak not but what may benefit others or yourself. Avoiding trifling Conversation.

3. ORDER.
Let all your Things have their Places. Let each Part of your Business have its Time.

4. RESOLUTION.
Resolve to perform what you ought. Perform without fail what you resolve.

5. FRUGALITY.
Make no Expense but to do good to others or yourself: i.e., Waste nothing.

6. INDUSTRY.
Lose no Time. Be always employ'd in something useful. Cut off all unnecessary Actions.

7. SINCERITY.
Use no hurtful Deceit. Think innocently and justly; and, if you speak; speak accordingly.

8. JUSTICE.
Wrong none, by doing Injuries or omitting the Benefits that are your Duty.

9. MODERATION.
Avoid Extremes. Forbear resenting Injuries so much as you think they deserve.

10. CLEANLINESS.
Tolerate no Uncleanness in Body, Clothes or Habitation.

11. TRANQUILITY.
Be not disturbed at Trifles, or Accidents common or unavoidable.

12. CHASTITY.
Rarely use Venery but for Health or Offspring; Never to Dullness, Weakness, or the Injury of your own or another's Peace or Reputation.

13. HUMILITY.
Imitate Jesus and Socrates.

My intention being to acquire the *Habitude*[3] of all these Virtues, I judg'd it would be well not to distract my Attention by attempting the whole at once, but to fix it on one of them at a time, and when I should be Master of that, then to proceed to another, and so on till I should have gone thro' the thirteen. And as the previous Acquisition of some might facilitate the Acquisition of certain others, I arrang'd them with that View as they stand above. *Temperance* first, as it tends to procure that Coolness and Clearness of Head, which is so necessary where constant Vigilance was to be kept up, and Guard maintained, against the unremitting Attraction of ancient Habits, and the

---

3. I.e., making these virtues an integral part of his nature.

Form of the Pages

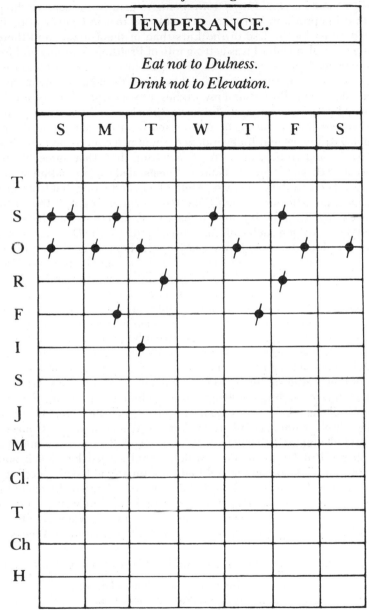

Force of perpetual Temptations. This being acquir'd and establish'd, *Silence* would be more easy, and my Desire being to gain Knowledge at the same time that I improv'd in Virtue, and considering that in Conversation it was obtain'd rather by the Use of the Ears than of the Tongue, and therefore wishing to break a Habit I was getting into of Prattling, Punning and Joking, which only made me acceptable to trifling Company, I gave *Silence* the second Place. This, and the next, *Order,* I expected would allow me more Time for attending to my Project and my studies; RESOLUTION once become habitual, would keep me firm in my Endeavors to obtain all the subsequent Virtues; *Frugality* and *Industry,* by freeing me from my remaining Debt, and producing Affluence and Independence would make more easy the Practice of *Sincerity* and *Justice,* etc., etc. Conceiving then that agreeable to the Advice of Pythagoras[4] in his Golden Verses, daily Examination would be necessary, I contriv'd the following Method for conducting that Examination.

I made a little Book in which I allotted a Page for each of the Virtues. I rul'd each Page with red Ink so as to have seven Columns, one for each Day of the Week, marking each Column with a Letter for the Day. I cross'd these Columns with thirteen red Lines, marking the Beginning of each Line with the first Letter of one of the Virtues, on which Line and in its proper Column I might mark by a little black Spot every Fault I found upon Examination, to have been committed respecting that Virtue upon that Day.

I determined to give a Week's strict Attention to each of the Virtues successively. Thus in the first Week my great Guard was to avoid every the least Offence against Temperance, leaving the other Virtues to their ordinary Chance, only marking every Evening the Faults of the Day. Thus if in the first Week I could keep my first Line marked T clear of Spots, I suppos'd the Habit of that Virtue so much strengthen'd and its opposite weaken'd, that I might venture extending my Attention to include the next, and for the following Week keep both Lines clear of Spots. Proceeding thus to the last, I could go thro' a Course complete in Thirteen Weeks, and four Courses in a Year. And like him who having a Garden to weed, does not attempt to eradicate all the bad Herbs at once, which would exceed his Reach and his Strength, but works on one of the Beds at a time, and having accomplish'd the first proceeds to a second; so I should have, (I hoped) the encouraging Pleasure of seeing on my Pages the Progress I made in Virtue, by clearing successively my Lines of their Spots, till in the End by a Number of Courses, I should be happy in viewing a clean Book after a thirteen Weeks' daily Examination.

This my little Book had for its Motto these Lines from *Addison's Cato,*[5]

> *Here will I hold: If there is a Pow'r above us,*
> *(And that there is, all Nature cries aloud*
> *Thro' all her Works) he must delight in Virtue,*
> *And that which he delights in must be happy.*

4. Pythagoras (6th century B.C.E.) was a Greek philosopher and mathematician. Franklin added a note here: "Insert those Lines that direct it in a Note," and wished to include verses translated: "Let sleep not close your eyes till you have thrice examined the transactions of the day: where have I strayed, what have I done, what good have I omitted?"

5. Joseph Addison, *Cato, a Tragedy* (1713; 5.1.15–18). Franklin also used these lines as an epigraph for his *Articles of Belief and Acts of Religion.*

Another from *Cicero*.[6]

> *O Vitæ Philosophia Dux! O Virtutum indagatrix, expultrixque vitiorum! Unus dies bene, et ex preceptis tuis actus, peccanti immortalitati est anteponendus.*

Another from the Proverbs of Solomon speaking of Wisdom or Virtue;

> Length of Days is in her right hand, and in her Left Hand Riches and Honors; Her Ways are Ways of Pleasantness, and all her Paths are Peace.
>
> III, 16, 17

And conceiving God to be the Fountain of Wisdom, I thought it right and necessary to solicit his Assistance for obtaining it; to this End I form'd the following little Prayer, which was prefix'd to my Tables of Examination, for daily Use.

> *O Powerful Goodness! bountiful Father! merciful Guide! Increase in me that Wisdom which discovers my truest Interests; Strengthen my Resolutions to perform what that Wisdom dictates. Accept my kind Offices to thy other Children, as the only Return in my Power for thy continual Favors to me.*

I us'd also sometimes a little Prayer which I took from *Thomson's*[7] Poems, viz.,

> *Father of Light and Life, thou Good supreme,*
> *O teach me what is good, teach me thy self!*
> *Save me from Folly, Vanity and Vice,*
> *From every low Pursuit, and fill my Soul*
> *With Knowledge, conscious Peace, and Virtue pure,*
> *Sacred, substantial, neverfading Bliss!*

The Precept of *Order* requiring that *every Part of my Business should have its allotted Time*, one Page in my little Book contain'd the following Scheme of Employment for the Twenty-four Hours of a natural Day.

I enter'd upon the Execution of this Plan for Self-examination, and continu'd it with occasional Intermissions for some time. I was surpris'd to find myself so much fuller of Faults than I had imagined, but I had the Satisfaction of seeing them diminish. To avoid the Trouble of renewing now and then my little Book, which by scraping out the Marks on the Paper of old Faults to make room for new Ones in a new Course, became full of Holes: I transferr'd my Tables and Precepts to the Ivory Leaves of a Memorandum Book, on which the Lines were drawn with red Ink that made a durable Stain, and on those Lines I mark'd my Faults with a black Lead Pencil, which Marks I could easily wipe out with a wet Sponge. After a while I went thro' one Course only in a Year, and afterwards only one in several Years; till at length I omitted them entirely, being employ'd in Voyages and Business

---

6. Marcus Tullius Cicero (106–43 B.C.E.), Roman philosopher and orator. The quotation is from *Tusculan Disputations* (5.2.5), but several lines are omitted after *vitiorum*: Oh, philosophy, guide of life: Oh, searcher out of virtues and expeller of vices! . . . One day lived well and according to thy precepts is to be preferred to an eternity of sin (Latin).

7. James Thomson (1700–1748), *The Seasons*, "Winter" (1726), lines 218–23.

abroad with a Multiplicity of Affairs, that interfered. But I always carried my little Book with me.

My Scheme of ORDER, gave me the most Trouble, and I found, that tho' it might be practicable where a Man's Business was such as to leave him the Disposition of his Time, that of a Journeyman Printer for instance, it was not possible to be exactly observ'd by a Master, who must mix with the World, and often receive People of Business at their own Hours. *Order* too, with regard to Places for Things, Papers, etc., I found extremely difficult to acquire. I had not been early accustomed to it, and having an exceeding good Memory, I was not so sensible of the Inconvenience attending Want of Method. This Article therefore cost me so much painful Attention and my Faults in it vex'd me so much, and I made so little Progress in Amendment, and had such frequent Relapses, that I was almost ready to give up the Attempt, and content myself with a faulty Character in that respect. Like the Man who in buying an Ax of a Smith my Neighbor, desired to have the whole of its Surface as bright as the Edge; the Smith consented to grind it bright for him if he would turn the Wheel. He turn'd while the Smith press'd the broad Face of the Ax hard and heavily on the Stone, which made the Turning of it very fatiguing. The Man came every now and then from the Wheel to see how the Work went on; and at length would take his Ax as it was without farther Grinding. No, says the Smith, Turn on, turn on; we shall have it bright by and by; as yet 'tis only speckled. Yes, says the Man; but—I *think I like a speckled Ax best.*—And I believe this may have been the Case with many who having for want of some such Means as I employ'd found the Difficulty of obtaining good, and breaking bad Habits, in other Points of Vice and Virtue, have given up the Struggle, and concluded that *a speckled Ax was best.* For something that pretended to be Reason was every now and then suggesting to me, that such extreme Nicety as I exacted of myself might be a kind of Foppery in Morals, which if it were known would make me ridiculous; that a perfect Character might be attended with the Inconvenience of being envied and hated; and that a benevolent Man should allow a few Faults in himself, to keep his Friends in Countenance.

In Truth I found myself incorrigible with respect to *Order;* and now I am grown old, and my Memory bad, I feel very sensibly the want of it. But on the whole, tho' I never arrived at the Perfection I had been so ambitious of obtaining, but fell far short of it, yet I was by the Endeavor made a better and a happier Man than I otherwise should have been, if I had not attempted it; As those who aim at perfect Writing by imitating the engraved Copies,[8] tho' they never reach the wish'd for Excellence of those Copies, their Hand is mended by the Endeavor, and is tolerable while it continues fair and legible.

And it may be well my Posterity should be informed, that to this little Artifice, with the Blessing of God, their Ancestor ow'd the constant Felicity of his Life down to his 79th Year in which this is written. What Reverses may attend the Remainder is in the Hand of Providence: But if they arrive, the Reflection on past Happiness enjoy'd ought to help his Bearing them with more Resignation. To *Temperance* he ascribes his long-continu'd Health, and what is still left to him of a good Constitution. To *Industry* and

8. I.e., the models in the printed book.

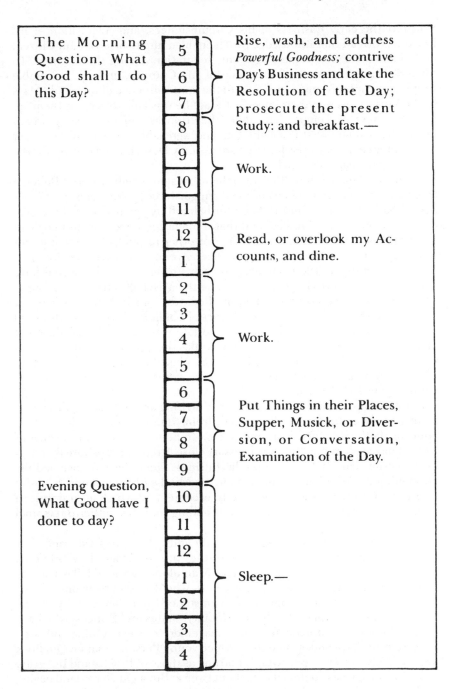

The Morning Question, What Good shall I do this Day?

5	Rise, wash, and address *Powerful Goodness;* contrive Day's Business and take the Resolution of the Day; prosecute the present Study: and breakfast.—
6	
7	
8	
9	Work.
10	
11	
12	Read, or overlook my Accounts, and dine.
1	
2	
3	
4	Work.
5	
6	Put Things in their Places, Supper, Musick, or Diversion, or Conversation, Examination of the Day.
7	
8	
9	

Evening Question, What Good have I done to day?

10	
11	
12	
1	Sleep.—
2	
3	
4	

Frugality the early Easiness of his Circumstances, and Acquisition of his Fortune, with all that Knowledge which enabled him to be an useful Citizen, and obtain'd for him some Degree of Reputation among the Learned. To *Sincerity* and *Justice* the Confidence of his Country, and the honorable Employs it conferr'd upon him. And to the joint Influence of the whole Mass of the Virtues, even in their imperfect State he was able to acquire them, all that Evenness of Temper, and that Cheerfulness in Conversation which makes his Company still sought for, and agreeable even to his younger Acquaintance. I hope therefore that some of my Descendants may follow the Example and reap the Benefit.

It will be remark'd[9] that, tho' my Scheme was not wholly without Religion there was in it no Mark of any of the distinguishing Tenets of any particular Sect. I had purposely avoided them; for being fully persuaded of the Utility and Excellency of my Method, and that it might be serviceable to People in all Religions, and intending some time or other to publish it, I would not have anything in it that should prejudice anyone of any Sect against it. I purposed writing a little Comment on each Virtue, in which I would have shown the Advantages of possessing it, and the Mischiefs attending its opposite Vice; and I should have called my Book the ART *of Virtue*, because it would have shown the *Means and Manner* of obtaining Virtue; which would have distinguish'd it from the mere Exhortation to be good, that does not instruct and indicate the Means; but is like the Apostle's Man of verbal Charity, who only, without showing to the Naked and the Hungry *how* or where they might get Clothes or Victuals, exhorted them to be fed and clothed. *James II, 15, 16.*[1]

But it so happened that my Intention of writing and publishing this Comment was never fulfilled. I did indeed, from time to time put down short Hints of the Sentiments, Reasonings, etc., to be made use of in it; some of which I have still by me: But the necessary close Attention to private Business in the earlier part of Life, and public Business since, have occasioned my postponing it. For it being connected in my Mind with a *great and extensive Project* that required the whole Man to execute, and which an unforeseen Succession of Employs prevented my attending to, it has hitherto remain'd unfinish'd.

In this Piece it was my Design to explain and enforce this Doctrine, that vicious Actions are not hurtful because they are forbidden, but forbidden because they are hurtful, the Nature of Man alone consider'd: That it was therefore every one's Interest to be virtuous, who wish'd to be happy even in this World. And I should from this Circumstance (there being always in the World a Number of rich Merchants, Nobility, States and Princes, who have need of honest Instruments for the Management of their Affairs, and such being so rare) have endeavored to convince young Persons, that no Qualities were so likely to make a poor Man's Fortune as those of Probity and Integrity.

My List of Virtues contain'd at first but twelve: But a Quaker Friend having kindly inform'd me that I was generally thought proud; that my Pride show'd itself frequently in Conversation; that I was not content with being in the right when discussing any Point, but was overbearing and rather insolent; of

9. Observed.
1. "If a brother or sister be naked, and destitute of daily food, And one of you say unto them, Depart in peace, be ye warmed and filled: notwithstanding ye give them not those things which are needful to the body; what doth it profit?"

which he convinc'd me by mentioning several Instances; I determined endeavoring to cure myself if I could of this Vice or Folly among the rest, and I added *Humility* to my List, giving an extensive Meaning to the Word. I cannot boast of much Success in acquiring the *Reality* of this Virtue; but I had a good deal with regard to the *Appearance* of it. I made it a Rule to forbear all direct Contradiction to the Sentiments of others, and all positive Assertion of my own. I even forbid myself, agreeable to the old Laws of our Junto, the Use of every Word or Expression in the Language that imported[2] a fix'd Opinion; such as *certainly, undoubtedly,* etc., and I adopted instead of them, I *conceive,* I *apprehend,* or I *imagine* a thing to be so or so, or it so appears to me at present. When another asserted something that I thought an Error, I denied myself the Pleasure of contradicting him abruptly, and of showing immediately some Absurdity in his Proposition; and in answering I began by observing that in certain Cases or Circumstances his Opinion would be right, but that in the present case there *appear'd* or *seem'd* to me some Difference, etc., I soon found the Advantage of this Change in my Manners. The Conversations I engag'd in went on more pleasantly. The modest way in which I propos'd my Opinions, procur'd them a readier Reception and less Contradiction; I had less Mortification when I was found to be in the wrong, and I more easily prevail'd with others to give up their Mistakes and join with me when I happen'd to be in the right. And this Mode, which I at first put on, with some violence to natural Inclination, became at length so easy and so habitual to me, that perhaps for these Fifty Years past no one has ever heard a dogmatical Expression escape me. And to this Habit (after my Character of Integrity) I think it principally owing, that I had early so much Weight with my Fellow Citizens, when I proposed new Institutions, or Alterations in the old; and so much Influence in public Councils when I became a Member. For I was but a bad Speaker, never eloquent, subject to much Hesitation in my choice of Words, hardly correct in Language, and yet I generally carried my Points.

In reality there is perhaps no one of our natural Passions so hard to subdue as *Pride.* Disguise it, struggle with it, beat it down, stifle it, mortify it as much as one pleases, it is still alive, and will every now and then peep out and show itself. You will see it perhaps often in this History. For even if I could conceive that I had completely overcome it, I should probably be proud of my Humility.

Thus far written at Passy, 1784.

From [*Part Three*][3]

I am now about to write at home, August 1788, but cannot have the help expected from my Papers, many of them being lost in the War. I have however found the following.

Having mentioned a *great and extensive Project* which I had conceiv'd, it seems proper that some Account should be here given of that Project and its Object. Its first Rise in my Mind appears in the following little Paper, accidentally preserv'd, viz.,

2. Suggested.
3. Franklin wrote the third part of his autobiog- raphy in Philadelphia, between August 1788 and the end of May 1789.

OBSERVATIONS on my Reading
History in Library, May 9, 1731.

"That the great Affairs of the World, the Wars, Revolutions, etc., are carried on and effected by Parties.

"That the View of these Parties is their present general Interest, or what they take to be such.

"That the different Views of these different Parties, occasion all Confusion.

"That while a Party is carrying on a general Design, each Man has his particular private Interest in View.

"That as soon as a Party has gain'd its general Point, each Member becomes intent upon his particular Interest, which thwarting others, breaks that Party into Divisions, and occasions more Confusion.

"That few in Public Affairs act from a mere View of the Good of their Country, whatever they may pretend; and tho' their Actings bring real Good to their Country, yet Men primarily consider'd that their own and their Country's Interest was united, and did not act from a Principle of Benevolence.

"That fewer still in public Affairs act with a View to the Good of Mankind.

"There seems to me at present to be great Occasion for raising an united Party for Virtue, by forming the Virtuous and good Men of all Nations into a regular Body, to be govern'd by suitable good and wise Rules, which good and wise Men may probably be more unanimous in their Obedience to, than common People are to common Laws.

"I at present think, that whoever attempts this aright, and is well qualified, cannot fail of pleasing God, and of meeting with Success.   B. F."

Revolving this Project in my Mind, as to be undertaken hereafter when my Circumstances should afford me the necessary Leisure, I put down from time to time on Pieces of Paper such Thoughts as occur'd to me respecting it. Most of these are lost; but I find one purporting to be the Substance of an intended Creed, containing as I thought the Essentials of every known Religion, and being free of everything that might shock the Professors of any Religion. It is express'd in these Words, viz.,

"That there is one God who made all things.

"That he governs the World by his Providence.

"That he ought to be worshiped by Adoration, Prayer and Thanksgiving.

"But that the most acceptable Service of God is doing Good to Man.

"That the Soul is immortal.

"And that God will certainly reward Virtue and punish Vice either here or hereafter."

My Ideas at that time were, that the Sect should be begun and spread at first among young and single Men only; that each Person to be initiated should not only declare his Assent to such Creed, but should have exercis'd himself with the Thirteen Weeks' Examination and Practice of the Virtues as in the before-mention'd Model; that the Existance of such a Society should be kept a Secret till it was become considerable, to prevent Solicitations for the Admission of improper Persons; but that the Members should each of them search among his Acquaintance for ingenuous well-disposed Youths, to whom with prudent Caution the Scheme should be gradually communicated: That the Members should engage to afford their Advice, Assistance and Support to each other in promoting one another's Interest, Business and Advancement in Life: That for Distinction we should be call'd the Society of the *Free and Easy*; Free, as being by the general Practice and Habit of the Virtues, free from the Dominion of Vice, and particularly by the Practice of Industry and Frugality, free from Debt, which exposes a Man to Confinement and a Species of Slavery to his Creditors. This is as much as I can now recollect of the Project, except that I communicated it in part to two young Men, who adopted it with some Enthusiasm. But my then narrow Circumstances, and the Necessity I was under of sticking close to my Business, occasion'd my Postponing the farther Prosecution of it at that time, and my multifarious Occupations public and private induc'd me to continue postponing, so that it has been omitted till I have no longer Strength or Activity left sufficient for such an Enterprise: Tho' I am still of Opinion that it was a practicable Scheme, and might have been very useful, by forming a great Number of good Citizens: And I was not discourag'd by the seeming Magnitude of the Undertaking, as I have always thought that one Man of tolerable Abilities may work great Changes, and accomplish great Affairs among Mankind, if he first forms a good Plan, and, cutting off all Amusements or other Employments that would divert his Attention, makes the Execution of that same Plan his sole Study and Business.

In 1732 I first published my Almanac, under the Name of *Richard Saunders*; it was continu'd by me about 25 Years, commonly call'd *Poor Richard's* Almanac. I endeavor'd to make it both entertaining and useful, and it accordingly came to be in such Demand that I reap'd considerable Profit from it, vending[4] annually near ten Thousand. And observing that it was generally read, scarce any Neighborhood in the Province being without it, I consider'd it as a proper Vehicle for conveying Instruction among the common People, who bought scarce any other Books. I therefore filled all the little Spaces that occur'd between the Remarkable Days in the Calendar, with Proverbial Sentences, chiefly such as inculcated Industry and Frugality, as the Means of procuring Wealth and thereby securing Virtue, it being more difficult for a Man in Want to act always honestly, as (to use here one of those Proverbs) *it is hard for an empty Sack to stand upright*. These Proverbs, which contained the Wisdom of many Ages and Nations, I assembled and form'd into a connected Discourse prefix'd to the Almanac of 1757, as the Harangue of a wise old Man to the People attending an Auction.[5] The bringing all these scatter'd Counsels thus into a Focus, enabled them to make greater Impression. The Piece being universally approved was copied in all the Newspapers of the Continent, reprinted in Britain on a Broadside[6] to be stuck up in Houses, two Translations were made of it in French, and great Numbers bought by the Clergy and Gentry to distribute gratis among their poor Parishioners and Tenants. In Pennsylvania, as it discouraged useless Expense in foreign Superfluities, some thought it had its share of Influence in producing that growing Plenty of Money which was observable for several Years after its Publication.

---

4. Selling. *Poor Richard's Almanac* was first published on December 19, 1732. Richard Saunders was a London almanac maker of the 17th century. Franklin may also have had in mind a London almanac published from 1661 to 1776 called *Poor Robin*.
5. This is the famous preface to the twenty-fifth anniversary edition called *Father Abraham's Speech* or *The Way to Wealth*.
6. A sheet of paper with printing on only one side.

I consider'd my Newspaper also as another Means of communicating Instruction, and in that View frequently reprinted in it Extracts from the Spectator[7] and other moral Writers, and sometimes publish'd little Pieces of my own which had been first compos'd for Reading in our Junto. Of these are a Socratic Dialogue tending to prove, that, whatever might be his Parts and Abilities, a vicious Man could not properly be called a Man of Sense. And a Discourse on Self-denial, showing that Virtue was not Secure, till its Practice became a Habitude, and was free from the Opposition of contrary Inclinations. These may be found in the Papers about the beginning of 1735.[8] In the Conduct of my Newspaper I carefully excluded all Libeling and Personal Abuse, which is of late Years become so disgraceful to our Country. Whenever I was solicited to insert anything of that kind, and the Writers pleaded as they generally did, the Liberty of the Press, and that a Newspaper was like a Stage Coach in which any one who would pay had a Right to a Place, my Answer was, that I would print the Piece separately if desired, and the Author might have as many Copies as he pleased to distribute himself, but that I would not take upon me to spread his Detraction, and that having contracted with my Subscribers to furnish them with what might be either useful or entertaining, I could not fill their Papers with private Altercation in which they had no Concern without doing them manifest Injustice. Now many of our Printers make no scruple of gratifying the Malice of Individuals by false Accusations of the fairest Characters among ourselves, augmenting Animosity even to the producing of Duels, and are moreover so indiscrete as to print scurrilous Reflections on the Government of neighboring States, and even on the Conduct of our best national Allies, which may be attended with the most pernicious Consequences. These Things I mention as a Caution to young Printers, and that they may be encouraged not to pollute their Presses and disgrace their Profession by such infamous Practices, but refuse steadily; as they may see by my Example, that such a Course of Conduct will not on the whole be injurious to their Interests.

In 1733, I sent one of my Journeymen to Charleston South Carolina where a Printer was wanting. I furnish'd him with a Press and Letters, on an Agreement of Partnership, by which I was to receive One Third of the Profits of the Business, paying One Third of the Expense. He was a Man of Learning and honest, but ignorant in Matters of Account;[9] and tho' he sometimes made me Remittances, I could get no Account from him, nor any satisfactory State of our Partnership while he lived. On his Decease, the Business was continued by his Widow, who being born and bred in Holland, where as I have been inform'd the Knowledge of Accounts makes a Part of Female Education, she not only sent me as clear a State as she could find of the Transactions past, but continu'd to account with the greatest Regularity and Exactitude every Quarter afterwards; and manag'd the Business with such Success that she not only brought up reputably a Family of Children, but at the Expiration of the Term was able to purchase of me the Printing-House and establish her Son in it. I mention this affair chiefly for the Sake of recommending that Branch of Education for our young Females, as likely to be of more Use to them and their Children in Case of Widowhood than either Music or Dancing, by preserving them from Losses by Imposition of

7. See n. 1, p. 546.
8. I.e., in the *Pennsylvania Gazette*, February 11 and 18, 1735.
9. Bookkeeping.

crafty Men, and enabling them to continue perhaps a profitable mercantile House with establish'd Correspondence till a Son is grown up fit to undertake and go on with it, to the lasting Advantage and enriching of the Family.

About the Year 1734, there arrived among us from Ireland, a young Presbyterian Preacher named Hemphill,[1] who delivered with a good Voice, and apparently extempore, most excellent Discourses, which drew together considerable Numbers of different Persuasions, who join'd in admiring them. Among the rest I became one of his constant Hearers, his Sermons pleasing me as they had little of the dogmatical kind, but inculcated strongly the Practice of Virtue, or what in the religious Style are called Good Works. Those however, of our Congregation, who considered themselves as orthodox Presbyterians, disapprov'd his Doctrine, and were join'd by most of the old Clergy, who arraign'd him of Heterodoxy before the Synod,[2] in order to have him silenc'd. I became his zealous Partisan, and contributed all I could to raise a Party[3] in his Favor; and we combated for him a while with some Hopes of Success. There was much Scribbling pro and con upon the Occasion; and finding that tho' an elegant Preacher he was but a poor Writer, I lent him my Pen and wrote for him two or three Pamphlets, and one Piece in the Gazette of April 1735. Those Pamphlets, as is generally the Case with controversial Writings, tho' eagerly read at the time, were soon out of Vogue, and I question whether a single Copy of them now exists.

During the Contest an unlucky Occurrence hurt his Cause exceedingly. One of our Adversaries having heard him preach a Sermon that was much admired, thought he had somewhere read that Sermon before, or at least a part of it. On Search he found that Part quoted at length in one of the British Reviews, from a Discourse of Dr. Foster's.[4] This Detection gave many of our Party Disgust, who accordingly abandoned his Cause, and occasion'd our more speedy Discomfiture in the Synod. I stuck by him, however, as I rather approv'd his giving us good Sermons compos'd by others, than bad ones of his own Manufacture; tho' the latter was the Practice of our common Teachers. He afterwards acknowledg'd to me that none of those he preach'd were his own; adding that his Memory was such as enabled him to retain and repeat any Sermon after one Reading only. On our Defeat he left us, in search elsewhere of better Fortune, and I quitted the Congregation, never joining it after, tho' I continu'd many Years my Subscription for the Support of its Ministers.

I had begun in 1733 to study Languages. I soon made myself so much a Master of the French as to be able to read the Books with Ease. I then undertook the Italian. An Acquaintance who was also learning it, us'd often to tempt me to play Chess with him. Finding this took up too much of the Time I had to spare for Study, I at length refus'd to play anymore, unless on this Condition, that the Victor in every Game, should have a Right to impose a Task, either in Parts of the Grammar to be got by heart, or in Translation, etc., which Tasks the Vanquish'd was to perform upon Honor before our next Meeting. As we play'd pretty equally we thus beat one another into that Language. I afterwards with a little Pains-taking acquir'd as much of the Spanish as to read their Books also.

I have already mention'd that I had only one Year's Instruction in a Latin

1. Samuel Hemphill, Irish Presbyterian minister who preached in Philadelphia in 1734.
2. The governing body of the Presbyterian church.
3. A group of supporters.
4. James Foster (1697–1735), well-known London Baptist preacher.

School, and that when very young, after which I neglected that Language entirely.—But when I had attained an Acquaintance with the French, Italian and Spanish, I was surpris'd to find, on looking over a Latin Testament,[5] that I understood so much more of that Language than I had imagined; which encouraged me to apply myself again to the Study of it, and I met with the more Success, as those preceding Languages had greatly smooth'd my Way. From these Circumstances I have thought, that there is some Inconsistency in our common Mode of Teaching Languages. We are told that it is proper to begin first with the Latin, and having acquir'd that, it will be more easy to attain those modern languages which are deriv'd from it; and yet we do not begin with the Greek in order more easily to acquire the Latin. It is true, that if you can clamber[6] and get to the Top of a Staircase without using the Steps, you will more easily gain them in descending: but certainly if you begin with the lowest you will with more Ease ascend to the Top. And I would therefore offer it to the Consideration of those who superintend the Educating of our Youth, whether, since many of those who begin with the Latin, quit the same after spending some Years, without having made any great Proficiency, and what they have learned becomes almost useless, so that their time has been lost, it would not have been better to have begun them with the French, proceeding to the Italian, etc., for tho' after spending the same time they should quit the Study of Languages, and never arrive at the Latin, they would however have acquir'd another Tongue or two that being in modern Use might be serviceable to them in common Life.

After ten Years' Absence from Boston, and having become more easy in my Circumstances, I made a Journey thither to visit my Relations, which I could not sooner well afford. In returning I call'd at Newport, to see my Brother then settled there with his Printing-House. Our former Differences were forgotten, and our Meeting was very cordial and affectionate. He was fast declining in his Health, and requested of me that in case of his Death which he apprehended not far distant, I would take home his Son, then but 10 Years of Age, and bring him up to the Printing Business. This I accordingly perform'd, sending him a few Years to School before I took him into the Office. His Mother carried on the Business till he was grown up, when I assisted him with an Assortment of new Types, those of his Father being in a Manner worn out.—Thus it was that I made my Brother ample Amends for the Service I had depriv'd him of by leaving him so early.

In 1736 I lost one of my Sons,[7] a fine Boy of 4 Years old, by the Smallpox taken in the common way. I long regretted bitterly and still regret that I had not given it to him by Inoculation. This I mention for the Sake of Parents, who omit that Operation on the Supposition that they should never forgive themselves if a Child died under it; my Example showing that the Regret may be the same either way, and that therefore the safer should be chosen.

Our Club, the Junto, was found so useful, and afforded such Satisfaction to the Members, that several were desirous of introducing their Friends, which could not well be done without exceeding what we had settled as a convenient Number, viz., Twelve. We had from the Beginning made it a Rule to keep our Institution a Secret, which was pretty well observ'd. The Intention was, to avoid Applications of improper Persons for Admittance, some of

---

5. I.e., a copy of the New Testament in Latin.
6. Climb with difficulty; scramble.
7. Francis Folger Franklin, who died from small-
pox before he had been inoculated. Franklin did not have him inoculated because Francis was recovering from an intestinal disorder.

whom perhaps we might find it difficult to refuse. I was one of those who were against any Addition to our Number, but instead of it made in Writing a Proposal, that every Member separately should endeavor to form a subordinate Club, with the same Rules respecting Queries,[8] etc., and without informing them of the Connection with the Junto. The Advantages propos'd were the Improvement of so many more young Citizens by the Use of our Institutions; Our better Acquaintance with the general Sentiments of the Inhabitants on any Occasion, as the Junto-Member might propose what Queries we should desire, and was to report to Junto what pass'd in his separate Club; the Promotion of our particular Interests in Business by more extensive Recommendations; and the Increase of our Influence in public Affairs and our Power of doing Good by spreading thro' the several Clubs the Sentiments of the Junto. The Project was approv'd, and every Member undertook to form his Club: but they did not all succeed. Five or six only were completed, which were call'd by different Names, as the Vine, the Union, the Band, etc. They were useful to themselves, and afforded us a good deal of Amusement, Information, and Instruction, besides answering in some considerable Degree our Views of influencing the public Opinion on particular Occasions, of which I shall give some Instances in course of time as they happened.

My first Promotion was my being chosen in 1736 Clerk of the General Assembly. The Choice was made that Year without Opposition, but the Year following when I was again propos'd (the Choice, like that of the Members being annual) a new Member made a long Speech against me in order to favor some other Candidate. I was however chosen; which was the more agreeable to me, as besides the Pay for immediate Service as Clerk, the Place gave me a better Opportunity of keeping up an Interest among the Members, which secur'd to me the Business of Printing the Votes, Laws, Paper Money, and other occasional Jobs for the Public, that on the whole were very profitable. I therefore did not like the Opposition of this new Member, who was a Gentleman of Fortune, and Education, with Talents that were likely to give him in time great Influence in the House, which indeed afterwards happened. I did not however aim at gaining his Favor by paying any servile Respect to him, but after some time took this other Method. Having heard that he had in his Library a certain very scarce and curious Book, I wrote a Note to him expressing my Desire of perusing that Book, and requesting he would do me the Favor of lending it to me for a few Days. He sent it immediately; and I return'd it in about a Week, with another Note expressing strongly my Sense of the Favor. When we next met in the House he spoke to me, (which he had never done before) and with great Civility. And he ever afterwards manifested a Readiness to serve me on all Occasions, so that we became great Friends, and our Friendship continu'd to his Death. This is another Instance of the Truth of an old Maxim I had learned, which says, *He that has once done you a Kindness will be more ready to do you another, than he whom you yourself have obliged.* And it shows how much more profitable it is prudently to remove, than to resent, return and continue inimical Proceedings.

In 1737, Colonel Spotswood,[9] late Governor of Virginia, and then Post-

---

8. I.e., questions to be discussed.
9. Alexander Spotswood (1676–1740), military

leader and lieutenant governor of Virginia from 1710 to 1722.

master General, being dissatisfied with the Conduct of his Deputy at Philadelphia, respecting some Negligence in rendering, and Inexactitude of his Accounts, took from him the Commission and offered it to me.[1] I accepted it readily, and found it of great Advantage; for tho' the Salary was small, it facilitated the Correspondence that improv'd my Newspaper, increas'd the Number demanded, as well as the Advertisements to be inserted, so that it came to afford me a very considerable Income. My old Competitor's Newspaper declin'd proportionably, and I was satisfied without retaliating his Refusal, while Postmaster, to permit my Papers being carried by the Riders. Thus He suffer'd greatly from his Neglect in due Accounting; and I mention it as a Lesson to those young Men who may be employ'd in managing Affairs for others that they should always render Accounts and make Remittances with great Clearness and Punctuality. The Character of observing Such a Conduct is the most powerful of all Recommendations to new Employments and Increase of Business.

I began now to turn my Thoughts a little to public Affairs, beginning however with small Matters. The City Watch[2] was one of the first Things that I conceiv'd to want Regulation. It was managed by the Constables of the respective Wards in Turn. The Constable warn'd a Number of Housekeepers to attend[3] him for the Night. Those who chose never to attend paid him Six Shillings a Year to be excus'd, which was suppos'd to be for hiring Substitutes; but was in Reality much more than was necessary for that purpose, and made the Constableship a Place of Profit. And the Constable for a little Drink often got such Ragamuffins about him as a Watch, that reputable Housekeepers did not choose to mix with. Walking the Rounds too was often neglected, and most of the Night spent in Tippling. I thereupon wrote a Paper to be read in Junto, representing these Irregularities, but insisting more particularly on the Inequality of this Six Shilling Tax of the Constables, respecting the Circumstances of those who paid it, since a poor Widow Housekeeper, all whose Property to be guarded by the Watch did not perhaps exceed the Value of Fifty Pounds, paid as much as the wealthiest Merchant who had Thousands of Pounds worth of Goods in his Stores. On the whole I proposed as a more effectual Watch, the Hiring of proper Men to serve constantly in that Business; and as a more equitable Way of supporting the Charge, the levying a Tax that should be proportion'd to Property. This Idea being approv'd by the Junto, was communicated to the other Clubs, but as arising in each of them. And tho' the Plan was not immediately carried into Execution, yet by preparing the Minds of People for the Change, it paved the Way for the Law obtain'd a few Years after,[4] when the Members of our Clubs were grown into more Influence.

About this time I wrote a Paper, (first to be read in Junto but it was afterwards publish'd)[5] on the different Accidents and Carelessnesses by which Houses were set on fire, with Cautions against them, and Means proposed of avoiding them. This was much spoken of as a useful Piece, and gave rise to a Project, which soon followed it, of forming a Company for the more ready Extinguishing of Fires, and mutual Assistance in Removing and Secur-

---

1. For the last nine years of his office, Bradford did not submit accounts; he was succeeded by Franklin in October 1737.
2. I.e., the night watch or patrol.

3. Accompany.
4. Actually, seventeen years later.
5. In the *Pennsylvania Gazette*, February 4, 1735.

ing of Goods when in Danger.[6] Associates in this Scheme were presently found amounting to Thirty. Our Articles of Agreement oblig'd every Member to keep always in good Order and fit for Use, a certain Number of Leather Buckets, with strong Bags and Baskets (for packing and transporting of Goods), which were to be brought to every Fire; and we agreed to meet once a Month and spend a social Evening together, in discoursing, and communicating such Ideas as occurr'd to us upon the Subject of Fires as might be useful in our Conduct on such Occasions. The Utility of this Institution soon appear'd, and many more desiring to be admitted than we thought convenient for one Company, they were advised to form another; which was accordingly done. And this went on, one new Company being formed after another, till they became so numerous as to include most of the Inhabitants who were Men of Property; and now at the time of my Writing this, tho' upwards of Fifty Years since its Establishment, that which I first formed, called the Union Fire Company, still subsists and flourishes, tho' the first Members are all deceas'd but myself and one who is older by a Year than I am. The small Fines that have been paid by Members for Absence at the Monthly Meetings, have been applied to the Purchase of Fire Engines, Ladders, Firehooks, and other useful Implements for each Company, so that I question whether there is a City in the World better provided with the Means of putting a Stop to beginning Conflagrations; and in fact since these Institutions, the City has never lost by Fire more than one or two Houses at a time, and the Flames have often been extinguish'd before the House in which they began has been half-consumed.

In 1739 arriv'd among us from England the Rev. Mr. Whitefield,[7] who had made himself remarkable there as an itinerant Preacher. He was at first permitted to preach in some of our Churches; but the Clergy taking a Dislike to him, soon refus'd him their Pulpits and he was oblig'd to preach in the Fields. The Multitudes of all Sects and Denominations that attended his Sermons were enormous and it was matter of Speculation to me who was one of the Number, to observe the extraordinary Influence of his Oratory on his Hearers, and how much they admir'd and respected him, notwithstanding his common Abuse of them, by assuring them they were naturally *half Beasts and half Devils*. It was wonderful to see the Change soon made in the Manners of our Inhabitants; from being thoughtless or indifferent about Religion, it seem'd as if all the World were growing Religious; so that one could not walk thro' the Town in an Evening without Hearing Psalms sung in different Families of every Street. And it being found inconvenient to assemble in the open Air, subject to its Inclemencies, the Building of a House to meet in was no sooner propos'd and Persons appointed to receive Contributions, but sufficient Sums were soon receiv'd to procure the Ground and erect the Building which was 100 feet long and 70 broad, about the Size of Westminster Hall;[8] and the Work was carried on with such Spirit as to be finished in a much shorter time than could have been expected. Both House and Ground were vested in Trustees, expressly for the Use of any Preacher of any religious Persuasion who might desire to say something to the People of

6. The Union Fire Company articles of incorporation were signed in December 1736.
7. George Whitefield (1714–1770), a popular Methodist preacher whose visit to the colonies coincided with the spiritual revival known as the "Great Awakening."
8. In London.

Philadelphia, the Design in building not being to accommodate any particular Sect, but the Inhabitants in general, so that even if the Mufti of Constantinople were to send a Missionary to preach Mahometanism to us, he would find a Pulpit at his Service.[9]

Mr. Whitefield, in leaving us, went preaching all the Way thro' the Colonies to Georgia. The Settlement of that Province had lately been begun; but instead of being made with hardy industrious Husbandmen accustomed to Labor, the only People fit for such an Enterprise, it was with Families of broken[1] Shopkeepers and other insolvent Debtors, many of indolent and idle habits, taken out of the Jails, who being set down in the Woods, unqualified for clearing Land, and unable to endure the Hardships of a new Settlement, perished in Numbers, leaving many helpless Children unprovided for. The Sight of their miserable Situation inspired the benevolent Heart of Mr. Whitefield with the Idea of building an Orphan House there, in which they might be supported and educated. Returning northward he preach'd up this charity, and made large Collections;—for his Eloquence had a wonderful Power over the Hearts and Purses of his Hearers, of which I myself was an Instance. I did not disapprove of the Design, but as Georgia was then destitute of Materials and Workmen, and it was propos'd to send them from Philadelphia at a great Expense, I thought it would have been better to have built the House here and brought the Children to it. This I advis'd, but he was resolute in his first Project, and rejected my Counsel, and I thereupon refus'd to contribute.

I happened soon after to attend one of his Sermons, in the Course of which I perceived he intended to finish with a Collection, and I silently resolved he should get nothing from me. I had in my Pocket a Handful of Copper Money, three or four silver Dollars, and five Pistoles in Gold. As he proceeded I began to soften, and concluded to give the Coppers. Another Stroke of his Oratory made me asham'd of that, and determin'd me to give the Silver; and he finish'd so admirably, that I emptied my Pocket wholly into the Collector's Dish, Gold and all. At this Sermon there was also one of our Club, who being of my Sentiments respecting the Building in Georgia, and suspecting a Collection might be intended, had by Precaution emptied his Pockets before he came from home; towards the Conclusion of the Discourse however, he felt a strong Desire to give, and apply'd to a Neighbor who stood near him to borrow some Money for the Purpose. The Application was unfortunately to perhaps the only Man in the Company who had the firmness not to be affected by the Preacher. His Answer was, *At any other time, Friend Hopkinson,*[2] *I would lend to thee freely; but not now; for thee seems to be out of thy right Senses.*

Some of Mr. Whitefield's Enemies affected to suppose that he would apply these Collections to his own private Emolument; but I, who was intimately acquainted with him, (being employ'd in printing his Sermons and Journals,[3] etc.) never had the least Suspicion of his Integrity, but am to this day decidedly of Opinion that he was in all his Conduct, a perfectly *honest Man*. And

9. The building was called "New Building" and was later used by the University of Pennsylvania, then called the Academy and College of Philadelphia. "Mufti": a judge who interprets Muslim religious law.

1. Bankrupt.
2. Thomas Hopkinson (1709–1761), first president of the American Philosophical Society.
3. Franklin printed a number of Whitefield's books and journals from 1739 to 1741.

methinks my Testimony in his Favor ought to have the more Weight, as we had no religious Connection. He us'd indeed sometimes to pray for my Conversion, but never had the Satisfaction of believing that his Prayers were heard. Ours was a mere civil Friendship, sincere on both Sides, and lasted to his Death.

The following Instance will show something of the Terms on which we stood. Upon one of his Arrivals from England at Boston, he wrote to me that he should come soon to Philadelphia, but knew not where he could lodge when there, as he understood his old kind Host Mr. Benezet[4] was remov'd to Germantown. My Answer was; You know my House, if you can make shift with its scanty Accommodations you will be most heartily welcome. He replied, that if I made that kind Offer for Christ's sake, I should not miss of a Reward.—And I return'd, *Don't let me be mistaken; it was not for Christ's sake, but for your sake.* One of our common Acquaintance jocosely remark'd, that knowing it to be the Custom of the Saints,[5] when they receiv'd any favor, to shift the Burthen of the Obligation from off their own Shoulders, and place it in Heaven, I had contriv'd to fix it on Earth.

The last time I saw Mr. Whitefield was in London, when he consulted me about his Orphan House Concern, and his Purpose of appropriating it to the Establishment of a College.

He had a loud and clear Voice, and articulated his Words and Sentences so perfectly that he might be heard and understood at a great Distance, especially as his Auditors, however numerous, observ'd the most exact Silence. He preach'd one Evening from the Top of the Court House Steps, which are in the Middle of Market Street, and on the West Side of Second Street which crosses it at right angles. Both Streets were fill'd with his Hearers to a considerable Distance. Being among the hindmost in Market Street, I had the Curiosity to learn how far he could be heard, by retiring backwards down the Street towards the River, and I found his Voice distinct till I came near Front Street,[6] when some Noise in that Street, obscur'd it. Imagining then a Semicircle, of which my Distance should be the Radius, and that it were fill'd with Auditors, to each of whom I allow'd two square feet, I computed that he might well be heard by more than Thirty Thousand. This reconcil'd me to the Newspaper Accounts of his having preach'd to 25,000 People in the Fields, and to the ancient Histories of Generals haranguing whole Armies, of which I had sometimes doubted.

By hearing him often I came to distinguish easily between Sermons newly compos'd, and those which he had often preach'd in the Course of his Travels. His Delivery of the latter was so improv'd by frequent Repetitions, that every Accent, every Emphasis, every Modulation of Voice, was so perfectly well turn'd and well plac'd, that without being interested in the Subject, one could not help being pleas'd with the Discourse, a Pleasure of much the same kind with that receiv'd from an excellent Piece of Music. This is an Advantage itinerant Preachers have over those who are stationary: as the latter cannot well improve their Delivery of a Sermon by so many Rehearsals.

His Writing and Printing from time to time gave great Advantage to his

---

4. John Stephen Benezet (1683–1751) came to Philadelphia as a Quaker but became a Moravian, or a member of the Church of United Brethren, when he moved to Germantown.

5. Living church members who feel they are saved.

6. About five hundred feet from the courthouse.

Enemies. Unguarded Expressions and even erroneous Opinions delivered in Preaching might have been afterwards explain'd, or qualified by supposing others that might have accompanied them; or they might have been denied; but *litera scripta manet.*[7] Critics attack'd his Writings violently, and with so much Appearance of Reason as to diminish the Number of his Votaries,[8] and prevent their Increase: So that I am of Opinion, if he had never written anything he would have left behind him a much more numerous and important Sect. And his Reputation might in that case have been still growing, even after his Death; as there being nothing of his Writings on which to found a Censure; and give him a lower Character, his Proselytes would be left at Liberty to feign for him as great a Variety of Excellencies, as their enthusiastic Admiration might wish him to have possessed.

* * *

1771–90   1868

7. *Vox audita perit, litera scripta manet:* The spo-   (Latin).
ken word passes away, the written word remains   8. Those devoted to him; disciples.

JOHN WOOLMAN
1720–1772

In a catalog of American writers John Woolman stands almost alone as a model of unqualified integrity, decency, and forthrightness. Woolman was a kind of latter-day "visible saint," a man both in the world and apart from it, who combined something of Franklin's practicality with Thoreau's passion for sincerity.

Woolman was born on his family's farm in Burlington County, New Jersey, a few miles east of Philadelphia. The nearest town was Mount Holly, New Jersey, a community settled mostly by English Quakers. It was an area close enough to Pennsylvania to benefit from William Penn's generous invitation to all persecuted believers to settle on his lands. After 1681 large numbers of Quakers, Baptists, and Mennonites settled in these regions. Although it may be argued that Quaker beliefs were a logical outgrowth of the Puritan movement for reforming the Church of England, Puritans despised Quakers because Quakers saw Christ's sacrifice as an act of redemption for all humankind. Quakers rejected Calvinist doctrines of election and predestination, and trusted in an "inner light," which Puritans saw as merely willful and antiauthoritarian. Quakers were not shy about their beliefs and, starting with George Fox (1624–1691), their founder, often found themselves in conflict with established order. This sense of alienation made Quaker communities like Mount Holly especially close knit. Woolman went to the Mount Holly village school and, until he was twenty-one, worked for his father on the family farm. He then moved to Mount Holly to tend a retail store and later set up in business for himself. Woolman's success in business was disturbing to him (mostly for what it said about human unresourcefulness), and it offended his Quaker belief in simplicity. He deliberately cut back his business and devoted himself more to tailoring. Woolman taught himself a number of other useful things: he was a surveyor, a teacher, and a farmer, and he studied enough law to become adept at making wills and deeds.

It was while writing a bill of sale for a slave that Woolman first became aware of the conflict between public law and private conscience that was to absorb him for the rest of his life. Although he tells us that on that first occasion he remained silent, "gave way," and wrote the bill of sale, he was never to make that mistake again. The next time he informed the owner that slavery and a religious conscience were incompatible. Woolman thereafter found his true vocation in "speaking up," both to Friends in their homes and at Quaker meetings, where his gift for articulating his religious concerns qualified him to lead. Woolman was scrupulous in calling attention to all those things in daily life that are compromises with the "true ministry" of Christ. At twenty-three he set out on a number of missions to share his convictions with fellow believers. He traveled extensively from North Carolina to New Hampshire; his last call was a trip to England, where he died in York of smallpox. In all his "conversations" with Friends, Woolman warned of the dangers of a materialist society, of the exploitation of workers, of military conscription, of paying taxes to support wars, and above all, of the corruptions of slavery. He was, as the philosopher A. N. Whitehead once put it, the "first Apostle of human freedom."

Woolman's *Journal* has never been out of print since it was first published in 1774. Almost everyone who has read it has become an admirer of the man and his writing. Charles Lamb, the English essayist, once observed that it was the only American book he had ever read twice. It has been admired not only for the life and temperament it reveals but for the directness and simplicity of its style. John Greenleaf Whittier, himself a Quaker, said that Woolman "wrote as he believed, from an inward spiritual prompting; and with all his unaffected humility he evidently felt that his work was done in the clear radiance of 'the light which never was on land or sea.' "

The text used is from *The Journal and Major Essays of John Woolman*, edited by Phillips P. Moulton (1971).

From The Journal of John Woolman

[EARLY LIFE AND VOCATION]

I have often felt a motion of love to leave some hints in writing of my experience of the goodness of God, and now, in the thirty-sixth year of my age, I begin this work. I was born in Northampton, in Burlington County in West Jersey, A.D. 1720, and before I was seven years old I began to be acquainted with the operations of divine love. Through the care of my parents, I was taught to read near as soon as I was capable of it, and as I went from school one Seventh Day,[1] I remember, while my companions went to play by the way, I went forward out of sight; and sitting down, I read the twenty-second chapter of the Revelations: "He showed me a river of water, clear as crystal, proceeding out of the throne of God and the Lamb, etc." And in reading it my mind was drawn to seek after that pure habitation which I then believed God had prepared for His servants. The place where I sat and the sweetness that attended my mind remains fresh in my memory.

This and the like gracious visitations[2] had that effect upon me, that when boys used ill language it troubled me, and through the continued mercies of God I was preserved from it. The pious instructions of my parents were often fresh in my mind when I happened amongst wicked children, and was of use

---

1. I.e., Saturday. Quakers, or members of the Religious Society of Friends, substituted numbers for the days of the week both for the sake of simplicity and to discard the names of the pagan gods (e.g.,

Saturday was named in honor of Saturn).
2. I.e., similar moments when he felt God's presence again.

to me. My parents, having a large family of children, used frequently on First Days after meeting[3] to put us to read in the Holy Scriptures or some religious books, one after another, the rest sitting by without much conversation, which I have since often thought was a good practice. From what I had read and heard, I believed there had been in past ages people who walked in uprightness before God in a degree exceeding any that I knew, or heard of, now living; and the apprehension of there being less steadiness and firmness amongst people in this age than in past ages often troubled me while I was a child.

I had a dream about the ninth year of my age as follows: I saw the moon rise near the west and run a regular course eastward, so swift that in about a quarter of an hour she reached our meridian, when there descended from her a small cloud on a direct line to the earth, which lighted on a pleasant green about twenty yards from the door of my father's house (in which I thought I stood) and was immediately turned into a beautiful green tree. The moon appeared to run on with equal swiftness and soon set in the east, at which time the sun arose at the place where it commonly does in the summer, and shining with full radiance in a serene air, it appeared as pleasant a morning as ever I saw.

All this time I stood still in the door in an awful[4] frame of mind, and I observed that as heat increased by the rising sun, it wrought so powerfully on the little green tree that the leaves gradually withered; and before noon it appeared dry and dead. There then appeared a being, small of size, full of strength and resolution, moving swift from the north, southward, called a sun worm.[5]

Another thing remarkable in my childhood was that once, going to a neighbor's house, I saw on the way a robin sitting on her nest; and as I came near she went off, but having young ones, flew about and with many cries expressed her concern for them. I stood and threw stones at her, till one striking her, she fell down dead. At first I was pleased with the exploit, but after a few minutes was seized with horror, as having in a sportive way killed an innocent creature while she was careful for her young. I beheld her lying dead and thought those young ones for which she was so careful must now perish for want of their dam to nourish them; and after some painful considerations on the subject, I climbed up the tree, took all the young birds and killed them, supposing that better than to leave them to pine away and die miserably, and believed in this case that Scripture proverb was fulfilled, "The tender mercies of the wicked are cruel."[6] I then went on my errand, but for some hours could think of little else but the cruelties I had committed, and was much troubled.

Thus He whose tender mercies are over all His works hath placed a principle in the human mind which incites to exercise goodness toward every living creature; and this being singly attended to, people become tenderhearted and sympathizing, but being frequently and totally rejected, the mind shuts itself up in a contrary disposition.

About the twelfth year of my age, my father being abroad, my mother

3. Quakers refer to their assemblies as "meetings" and their church as a "meetinghouse." It is the custom for worshipers to remain silent until someone is moved to speak.

4. Full of awe.
5. I.e., sun snake, an imaginary creature.
6. Proverbs 12.10.

reproved me for some misconduct, to which I made an undutiful reply; and the next First Day as I was with my father returning from meeting, he told me he understood I had behaved amiss to my mother and advised me to be more careful in future. I knew myself blameable, and in shame and confusion remained silent. Being thus awakened to a sense of my wickedness, I felt remorse in my mind, and getting home I retired and prayed to the Lord to forgive me, and do not remember that I ever after that spoke unhandsomely to either of my parents, however foolish in other things.

Having attained the age of sixteen years, I began to love wanton company, and though I was preserved from profane language or scandalous conduct, still I perceived a plant in me which produced much wild grapes. Yet my merciful Father forsook me not utterly, but at times through His grace I was brought seriously to consider my ways, and the sight of my backsliding affected me with sorrow. But for want of rightly attending to the reproofs of instruction, vanity was added to vanity, and repentance to repentance; upon the whole my mind was more and more alienated from the Truth,[7] and I hastened toward destruction. While I meditate on the gulf toward which I traveled and reflect on my youthful disobedience, for these things I weep; mine eye runneth down with water.

Advancing in age the number of my acquaintance increased, and thereby my way grew more difficult. Though I had heretofore found comfort in reading the Holy Scriptures and thinking on heavenly things, I was now estranged therefrom. I knew I was going from the flock of Christ and had no resolution to return; hence serious reflections were uneasy to me and youthful vanities and diversions my greatest pleasure. Running in this road I found many like myself, and we associated in that which is reverse to true friendship.[8]

But in this swift race it pleased God to visit me with sickness, so that I doubted of recovering. And then did darkness, horror, and amazement with full force seize me, even when my pain and distress of body was very great. I thought it would have been better for me never to have had a being than to see the day which I now saw. I was filled with confusion, and in great affliction both of mind and body I lay and bewailed myself. I had not confidence to lift up my cries to God, whom I had thus offended, but in a deep sense of my great folly I was humbled before Him, and at length that Word which is as a fire and a hammer broke and dissolved my rebellious heart. And then my cries were put up in contrition, and in the multitude of His mercies I found inward relief, and felt a close engagement that if He was pleased to restore my health, I might walk humbly before Him.

After my recovery this exercise remained with me a considerable time; but by degrees giving way to youthful vanities, they gained strength, and getting with wanton[9] young people I lost ground. The Lord had been very gracious and spoke peace to me in the time of my distress, and I now most ungratefully turned again to folly, on which account at times I felt sharp reproof but did not get low enough to cry for help. I was not so hardy as to commit things scandalous, but to exceed in vanity and promote mirth was my chief study. Still I retained a love and esteem for pious people, and their company brought an awe upon me.

7. I.e., ultimate spiritual reality.
8. I.e., those ideals basic to the Religious Society of Friends.

9. Frivolous, unthinking. "Exercise": religious experience.

My dear parents several times admonished me in the fear of the Lord, and their admonition entered into my heart and had a good effect for a season, but not getting deep enough to pray rightly, the tempter when he came found entrance. I remember once, having spent a part of the day in wantonness, as I went to bed at night there lay in a window near my bed a Bible, which I opened, and first cast my eye on the text, "We lie down in our shame, and our confusion covers us."[1] This I knew to be my case, and meeting with so unexpected a reproof, I was somewhat affected with it and went to bed under remorse of conscience, which I soon cast off again.

Thus time passed on; my heart was replenished with mirth and wantonness, while pleasing scenes of vanity were presented to my imagination till I attained the age of eighteen years, near which time I felt the judgments of God in my soul like a consuming fire, and looking over my past life the prospect was moving. I was often sad and longed to be delivered from those vanities; then again my heart was strongly inclined to them, and there was in me a sore conflict. At times I turned to folly, and then again sorrow and confusion took hold of me. In a while I resolved totally to leave off some of my vanities, but there was a secret reserve in my heart of the more refined part of them, and I was not low enough to find true peace. Thus for some months I had great trouble, there remaining in me an unsubjected will which rendered my labors fruitless, till at length through the merciful continuance of heavenly visitations I was made to bow down in spirit before the Lord.

I remember one evening I had spent some time in reading a pious author, and walking out alone I humbly prayed to the Lord for His help, that I might be delivered from all those vanities which so ensnared me. Thus being brought low, He helped me; and as I learned to bear the cross I felt refreshment to come from His presence; but not keeping in that strength which gave victory, I lost ground again, the sense of which greatly affected me; and I sought deserts and lonely places and there with tears did confess my sins to God and humbly craved help of Him. And I may say with reverence He was near to me in my troubles, and in those times of humiliation opened my ear to discipline.

I was now led to look seriously at the means by which I was drawn from the pure Truth, and learned this: that if I would live in the life which the faithful servants of God lived in, I must not go into company as heretofore in my own will, but all the cravings of sense must be governed by a divine principle. In times of sorrow and abasement these instructions were sealed upon me, and I felt the power of Christ prevail over selfish desires, so that I was preserved in a good degree of steadiness. And being young and believing at that time that a single life was best for me, I was strengthened to keep from such company as had often been a snare to me.

I kept steady to meetings, spent First Days after noon chiefly in reading the Scriptures and other good books, and was early convinced in my mind that true religion consisted in an inward life, wherein the heart doth love and reverence God the Creator and learn to exercise true justice and goodness, not only toward all men but also toward the brute creatures; that as the mind was moved on an inward principle to love God as an invisible, incomprehensible being, on the same principle it was moved to love Him in

1. Jeremiah 3.25.

all His manifestations in the visible world; that as by His breath the flame of life was kindled in all animal and sensitive creatures, to say we love God as unseen and at the same time exercise cruelty toward the least creature moving by His life, or by life derived from Him, was a contradiction in itself.

I found no narrowness respecting sects and opinions, but believed that sincere, upright-hearted people in every Society who truly loved God were accepted of Him.

As I lived under the cross and simply followed the openings[2] of Truth, my mind from day to day was more enlightened; my former acquaintance was left to judge of me as they would, for I found it safest for me to live in private and keep these things sealed up in my own breast.

While I silently ponder on that change wrought in me, I find no language equal to it nor any means to convey to another a clear idea of it. I looked upon the works of God in this visible creation and an awfulness covered me; my heart was tender and often contrite, and a universal love to my fellow creatures increased in me. This will be understood by such who have trodden in the same path. Some glances of real beauty may be seen in their faces who dwell in true meekness. There is a harmony in the sound of that voice to which divine love gives utterance, and some appearance of right order in their temper and conduct whose passions are fully regulated. Yet all these do not fully show forth that inward life to such who have not felt it, but this white stone and new name is known rightly to such only who have it.[3]

Now though I had been thus strengthened to bear the cross, I still found myself in great danger, having many weaknesses attending me and strong temptations to wrestle with, in the feelings whereof I frequently withdrew into private places and often with tears besought the Lord to help me, whose gracious ear was open to my cry.

All this time I lived with my parents and wrought[4] on the plantation, and having had schooling pretty well for a planter, I used to improve in winter evenings and other leisure times. And being now in the twenty-first year of my age, a man in much business shopkeeping and baking asked me if I would hire with him to tend shop and keep books. I acquainted my father with the proposal, and after some deliberation it was agreed for me to go.

At home I had lived retired, and now having a prospect of being much in the way of company, I felt frequent and fervent cries in my heart to God, the Father of Mercies, that He would preserve me from all taint and corruption, that in this more public employ I might serve Him, my gracious Redeemer, in that humility and self-denial with which I had been in a small degree exercised in a very private life.

The man who employed me furnished a shop in Mount Holly, about five miles from my father's house and six from his own, and there I lived alone and tended his shop. Shortly after my settlement here I was visited by several young people, my former acquaintance, who knew not but vanities would be as agreeable to me now as ever; and at these times I cried to the Lord in secret for wisdom and strength, for I felt myself encompassed with difficul-

2. Quakers referred to "openings" as direct messages from God; they came to those who lived in habitual expectation of them. "Under the Cross": i.e., mindful of Christ and in humility.
3. "To him that overcometh will I give to eat of the hidden manna, and will I give him a white stone, and in the stone a new name written, which no man knoweth saving he that receiveth it" (Revelation 2.17).
4. Worked.

616 / John Woolman

ties and had fresh occasion to bewail the follies of time past in contracting a familiarity with a libertine people. And as I had now left my father's house outwardly, I found my Heavenly Father to be merciful to me beyond what I can express.

By day I was much amongst people and had many trials to go through, but in evenings I was mostly alone and may with thankfulness acknowledge that in those times the spirit of supplication was often poured upon me, under which I was frequently exercised and felt my strength renewed.

In a few months after I came here, my master bought[5] several Scotch menservants from on board a vessel and brought them to Mount Holly to sell, one of which was taken sick and died. The latter part of his sickness he, being delirious, used to curse and swear most sorrowfully, and after he was buried I was left to sleep alone the next night in the same chamber where he died. I perceived in me a timorousness. I knew, however, I had not injured the man but assisted in taking care of him according to my capacity, and was not free to ask anyone on that occasion to sleep with me. Nature was feeble, but every trial was a fresh incitement to give myself up wholly to the service of God, for I found no helper like Him in times of trouble.

After a while my former acquaintance gave over expecting me as one of their company, and I began to be known to some whose conversation was helpful to me. And now, as I had experienced the love of God through Jesus Christ to redeem me from many pollutions and to be a succor to me through a sea of conflicts, with which no person was fully acquainted, and as my heart was often enlarged in this heavenly principle, I felt a tender compassion for the youth who remained entangled in snares like those which had entangled me. From one month to another this love and tenderness increased, and my mind was more strongly engaged for the good of my fellow creatures.

I went to meetings in an awful frame of mind and endeavored to be inwardly acquainted with the language of the True Shepherd. And one day being under a strong exercise of spirit, I stood up and said some words in a meeting, but not keeping close to the divine opening,[6] I said more than was required of me; and being soon sensible of my error, I was afflicted in mind some weeks without any light or comfort, even to that degree that I could take satisfaction in nothing. I remembered God and was troubled, and in the depth of my distress He had pity upon me and sent the Comforter. I then felt forgiveness for my offense, and my mind became calm and quiet, being truly thankful to my gracious Redeemer for His mercies. And after this, feeling the spring of divine love opened and a concern[7] to speak, I said a few words in a meeting, in which I found peace. This I believe was about six weeks from the first time, and as I was thus humbled and disciplined under the cross, my understanding became more strengthened to distinguish the language of the pure Spirit which inwardly moves upon the heart[8] and taught [me] to wait in silence sometimes many weeks together, until I felt that rise which prepares the creature to stand like a trumpet through which the Lord speaks to His flock.

5. I.e., bought the indentures of menservants. It was common to pay for passage to America by contracting to work for several years as an indentured servant. These contracts were negotiable.
6. I.e., he did not focus on the divine truth that inspired him to stand and speak, and spoke with "worldly wisdom."

7. For Quakers, something that is felt so deeply that one is compelled to do something about it almost against one's will.
8. Quakers distinguish between true inner light, which is characterized by "disciplined understanding," and mere selfish desires.

From an inward purifying, and steadfast abiding under it, springs a lively operative desire for the good of others. All faithful people are not called to the public ministry, but whoever are, are called to minister of that which they have tasted and handled spiritually. The outward modes of worship are various, but wherever men are true ministers of Jesus Christ it is from the operation of His spirit upon their hearts, first purifying them and thus giving them a feeling sense of the conditions of others. This truth was early fixed in my mind, and I was taught to watch the pure opening and to take heed lest while I was standing to speak, my own will should get uppermost and cause me to utter words from worldly wisdom and depart from the channel of the true gospel ministry.

In the management of my outward affairs I may say with thankfulness I found Truth to be my support, and I was respected in my master's family, who came to live in Mount Holly within two year after my going there.

About the twenty-third year of my age, I had many fresh and heavenly openings in respect to the care and providence of the Almighty over his creatures in general, and over man as the most noble amongst those which are visible. And being clearly convinced in my judgment that to place my whole trust in God was best for me, I felt renewed engagements that in all things I might act on an inward principle of virtue and pursue worldly business no further than as Truth opened my way therein.

About the time called Christmas I observed many people from the country and dwellers in town who, resorting to the public houses, spent their time in drinking and vain sports, tending to corrupt one another, on which account I was much troubled. At one house in particular there was much disorder, and I believed it was a duty laid on me to go and speak to the master of that house. I considered I was young and that several elderly Friends in town had opportunity to see these things, and though I would gladly have been excused, yet I could not feel my mind clear.

The exercise was heavy, and as I was reading what the Almighty said to Ezekiel[9] respecting his duty as a watchman, the matter was set home more clearly; and then with prayer and tears I besought the Lord for His assistance, who in loving-kindness gave me a resigned heart. Then at a suitable opportunity I went to the public house, and seeing the man amongst a company, I went to him and told him I wanted to speak with him; so we went aside, and there in the fear and dread of the Almighty I expressed to him what rested on my mind, which he took kindly, and afterward showed more regard to me than before. In a few years after, he died middle-aged, and I often thought that had I neglected my duty in that case it would have given me great trouble, and I was humbly thankful to my gracious Father, who had supported me herein.

My employer, having a Negro woman, sold her and directed me to write a bill of sale, the man being waiting who bought her. The thing was sudden, and though the thoughts of writing an instrument of slavery for one of my fellow creatures felt uneasy,[1] yet I remembered I was hired by the year, that it was my master who directed me to do it, and that it was an elderly man, a member of our Society, who bought her; so through weakness I gave way and wrote it, but at the executing it, I was so afflicted in my mind that I said

9. A priest and prophet. "Son of man, I have made thee a watchman unto the house of Israel: therefore hear the word at my mouth, and give them warning from me" (Ezekiel 3.17).
1. I.e., he contradicted his sense of right and felt ill at ease with his conscience.

before my master and the Friend that I believed slavekeeping to be a practice inconsistent with the Christian religion. This in some degree abated my uneasiness, yet as often as I reflected seriously upon it I thought I should have been clearer if I had desired to be excused from it as a thing against my conscience, for such it was. And some time after this a young man of our Society spake to me to write an instrument of slavery, he having lately taken a Negro into his house. I told him I was not easy to write it, for though many kept slaves in our Society, as in others, I still believed the practice was not right, and desired to be excused from writing [it]. I spoke to him in good will, and he told me that keeping slaves was not altogether agreeable to his mind, but that the slave being a gift made to his wife, he had accepted of her.

1774

From Some Considerations on the Keeping of Negroes

[PART ONE][1]

Recommended to the Professors[2] of Christianity of Every Denomination

INTRODUCTION

Customs generally approved and opinions received by youth from their superiors become like the natural produce of a soil, especially when they are suited to favorite inclinations. But as the judgments of God are without partiality, by which the state of the soul must be tried, it would be the highest wisdom to forego customs and popular opinions, and try the treasures of the soul by the infallible standard: Truth.

Natural affection needs a careful examination. Operating upon us in a soft manner, it kindles desires of love and tenderness, and there is danger of taking it for something higher. To me it appears an instinct like that which inferior creatures have; each of them, we see, by the ties of nature love self best. That which is a part of self they love by the same tie or instinct. In them it in some measure does the offices of reason, by which, among other things, they watchfully keep and orderly feed their helpless offspring. Thus natural affection appears to be a branch of self-love, good in the animal race, in us likewise with proper limitations, but otherwise is productive of evil by exciting desires to promote some by means prejudicial to others.

Our blessed Savior seems to give a check to this irregular fondness in nature and, at the same time, a precedent for us: "Who is my mother, and who are my brethren?"—thereby intimating that the earthly ties of relationship are, comparatively, inconsiderable to such who, through a steady course of obedience, have come to the happy experience of the Spirit of God bearing witness with their spirits that they are His children: "And he stretched forth his hands toward his disciples and said, 'Behold my mother and my brethren; for whosoever shall do the will of my Father which is in heaven (arrives at the more noble part of true relationship)[3] the same is my brother, and sister, and mother.'" Matthew 12.48[–50].

1. Woolman's essay was written after a visit to southern Maryland, Virginia, and North Carolina.
2. Believers.

3. A phrase inserted by Woolman in the quotation from Matthew.

This doctrine agrees well with a state truly complete, where love necessarily operates according to the agreeableness of things on principles unalterable and in themselves perfect. If endeavoring to have my children eminent amongst men after my death be that which no reasons grounded on those principles can be brought to support, then to be temperate in my pursuit after gain and to keep always within the bounds of those principles is an indispensable duty, and to depart from it a dark unfruitful toil.

In our present condition, to love our children is needful; but except this love proceeds from the true heavenly principle which sees beyond earthly treasures, it will rather be injurious than of any real advantage to them. Where the fountain is corrupt, the streams must necessarily be impure.

That important injunction of our Savior (Matthew 6.33),[4] with the promise annexed, contains a short but comprehensive view of our duty and happiness. If then the business of mankind in this life is to first seek another, if this cannot be done but by attending to the means, if a summary of the means is not to do that to another which (in like circumstances) we would not have done unto us, then these are points of moment and worthy of our most serious consideration.

What I write on this subject is with reluctance, and the hints given are in as general terms as my concern would allow. I know it is a point about which in all its branches men that appear to aim well are not generally agreed, and for that reason I chose to avoid being very particular. If I may happily have let drop anything that may excite such as are concerned in the practice to a close thinking on the subject treated of, the candid amongst them may easily do the subject such further justice as, on an impartial inquiry, it may appear to deserve; and such an inquiry I would earnestly recommend.

SOME CONSIDERATIONS ON THE KEEPING OF NEGROES

"Forasmuch as ye did it to the least of these my brethren, ye did it unto me." Matthew 25.40.

As many times there are different motives to the same actions, and one does that from a generous heart which another does for selfish ends, the like may be said in this case.

There are various circumstances amongst them that keep Negroes, and different ways by which they fall under their care; and, I doubt not, there are many well-disposed persons amongst them who desire rather to manage wisely and justly in this difficult matter than to make gain of it. But the general disadvantage which these poor Africans lie under in an enlightened Christian country having often filled me with real sadness, and been like undigested matter on my mind, I now think it my duty, through divine aid, to offer some thoughts thereon to the consideration of others.

When we remember that all nations are of one blood (Genesis 3.20);[5] that in this world we are but sojourners; that we are subject to the like afflictions and infirmities of body, the like disorders and frailties in mind, the like temptations, the same death and the same judgment; and that the All-wise Being is judge and Lord over us all, it seems to raise an idea of a general brotherhood and a disposition easy to be touched with a feeling of each other's

4. "But seek ye first the kingdom of God, and his righteousness; and all these things shall be added unto you."

5. "And Adam called his wife's name Eve; because she was the mother of all living."

afflictions. But when we forget those things and look chiefly at our outward circumstances, in this and some ages past, constantly retaining on our minds the distinction betwixt us and them with respect to our knowledge and improvement in things divine, natural, and artificial, our breasts being apt to be filled with fond notions of superiority, there is danger of erring in our conduct toward them.

We allow them to be of the same species with ourselves; the odds is we are in a higher station and enjoy greater favors than they. And when it is thus that our Heavenly Father endoweth some of His children with distinguished gifts, they are intended for good ends. But if those thus gifted are thereby lifted up above their brethren, not considering themselves as debtors to the weak nor behaving themselves as faithful stewards, none who judge impartially can suppose them free from ingratitude. When a people dwell under the liberal distribution of favors from heaven, it behooves them carefully to inspect their ways and consider the purposes for which those favors were bestowed, lest through forgetfulness of God and misusing His gifts they incur His heavy displeasure, whose judgments are just and equal, who exalteth and humbleth to the dust as He seeth meet.

It appears by Holy Record that men under high favors have been apt to err in their opinions concerning others. Thus Israel, according to the description of the prophet (Isaiah 65.5), when exceedingly corrupted and degenerated, yet remembered they were the chosen people of God and could say, "Stand by thyself, come not near me, for I am holier than thou." That this was no chance language, but their common opinion of other people, more fully appears by considering the circumstances which attended when God was beginning to fulfill His precious promises concerning the gathering of the Gentiles.

The Most High, in a vision, undeceived Peter, first prepared his heart to believe, and at the house of Cornelius showed him of a certainty that God was no respecter of persons. The effusion of the Holy Ghost upon a people with whom they, the Jewish Christians, would not so much as eat was strange to them. All they of the circumcision were astonished to see it, and the apostles and brethren of Judea contended with Peter about it, till he having rehearsed the whole matter and fully shown that the Father's love was unlimited, they are thereat struck with admiration and cry out, "Then hath God also to the Gentiles granted repentance unto life!" [Acts 11.18]

The opinion of peculiar favors being confined to them was deeply rooted, or else the above instance had been less strange to them, for these reasons: First, they were generally acquainted with the writings of the prophets, by whom this time was repeatedly spoken of and pointed at. Secondly, our blessed Lord shortly before expressly said, "I have other sheep, not of this fold; them also must I bring," etc. [John 10.16]. Lastly, His words to them after His resurrection, at the very time of His ascension, "Ye shall be witnesses to me not only in Jerusalem, Judea, and Samaria, but to the uttermost parts of the earth" [Acts 1.8].

Those concurring circumstances, one would think, might have raised a strong expectation of seeing such a time. Yet when it came, it proved matter of offense and astonishment.

To consider mankind otherwise than brethren, to think favors are peculiar to one nation and exclude others, plainly supposes a darkness in the understanding. For as God's love is universal, so where the mind is sufficiently influenced by it, it begets a likeness of itself and the heart is enlarged towards all men. Again, to conclude a people froward,[6] perverse, and worse by nature than others (who ungratefully receive favors and apply them to bad ends), this will excite a behavior toward them unbecoming the excellence of true religion.

To prevent such error let us calmly consider their circumstance, and, the better to do it, make their case ours. Suppose, then, that our ancestors and we have been exposed to constant servitude in the most servile and inferior employments of life; that we had been destitute of the help of reading and good company; that amongst ourselves we had had few wise and pious instructors; that the religious amongst our superiors seldom took notice of us; that while others in ease have plentifully heaped up the fruit of our labor, we had received barely enough to relieve nature, and being wholly at the command of others had generally been treated as a contemptible, ignorant part of mankind. Should we, in that case, be less abject than they now are? Again, if oppression be so hard to bear that a wise man is made mad by it (Ecclesiastes 7.7), then a series of those things altering the behavior and manners of a people is what may reasonably be expected.

When our property is taken contrary to our mind by means appearing to us unjust, it is only through divine influence and the enlargement of heart from thence proceeding that we can love our reputed oppressors. If the Negroes fall short in this, an uneasy, if not a disconsolate, disposition will be awakened and remain like seeds in their minds, producing sloth and many other habits appearing odious to us, with which being free men they perhaps had not been chargeable. These and other circumstances, rightly considered, will lessen that too great disparity which some make between us and them.

Integrity of heart hath appeared in some of them, so that if we continue in the word of Christ (previous to discipleship, John 8.31)[7] and our conduct towards them be seasoned with His love, we may hope to see the good effect of it, the which, in a good degree, is the case with some into whose hands they have fallen. But that too many treat them otherwise, not seeming conscious of any neglect, is, alas! too evident.

When self-love presides in our minds our opinions are biased in our own favor. In this condition, being concerned with a people so situated that they have no voice to plead their own cause, there's danger of using ourselves to an undisturbed partiality till, by long custom, the mind becomes reconciled with it and the judgment itself infected.

To humbly apply to God for wisdom, that we may thereby be enabled to see things as they are and ought to be, is very needful; hereby the hidden things of darkness may be brought to light and the judgment made clear. We shall then consider mankind as brethren. Though different degrees and a variety of qualifications and abilities, one dependent on another, be admitted, yet high thoughts will be laid aside, and all men treated as becometh the sons of one Father, agreeable to the doctrine of Christ Jesus.

He hath laid down the best criterion by which mankind ought to judge of their own conduct, and others judge for them of theirs, one towards

---

6. Contrary.
7. "Then said Jesus to those Jews which believed on him. If ye continue in my word, then are ye my disciples indeed."

another—viz., "Whatsoever ye would that men should do unto you, do ye even so to them." I take it that all men by nature are equally entitled to the equity of this rule and under the indispensable obligations of it. One man ought not to look upon another man or society of men as so far beneath him but that he should put himself in their place in all his actions towards them, and bring all to this test—viz., How should I approve of this conduct were I in their circumstance and they in mine? —Arscott's *Considerations*, Part III, Fol. 107.[8]

This doctrine, being of a moral unchangeable nature, hath been likewise inculcated in the former dispensation:[9] "If a stranger sojourn with thee in your land, ye shall not vex him; but the stranger that dwelleth with you shall be as one born amongst you, and thou shalt love him as thyself." Leviticus 19.33, 34. Had these people come voluntarily and dwelt among us, to have called them strangers would be proper. And their being brought by force, with regret and a languishing mind, may well raise compassion in a heart rightly disposed. But there is nothing in such treatment which upon a wise and judicious consideration will any ways lessen their right of being treated as strangers. If the treatment which many of them meet with be rightly examined and compared with those precepts, "Thou shalt not vex him nor oppress him; he shall be as one born amongst you, and thou shalt love him as thyself" (Leviticus 19.33; Deuteronomy 27.19), there will appear an important difference betwixt them.

It may be objected there is cost of purchase and risk of their lives to them who possess 'em, and therefore needful that they make the best use of their time. In a practice just and reasonable such objections may have weight; but if the work be wrong from the beginning, there's little or no force in them. If I purchase a man who hath never forfeited his liberty, the natural right of freedom is in him. And shall I keep him and his posterity in servitude and ignorance? How should I approve of that conduct were I in his circumstances and he in mine? It may be thought that to treat them as we would willingly be treated, our gain by them would be inconsiderable; and it were, in diverse respects, better that there were none in our country.

We may further consider that they are now amongst us, and those of our nation the cause of their being here, that whatsoever difficulty accrues thereon we are justly chargeable with, and to bear all inconveniences attending it with a serious and weighty concern of mind to do our duty by them is the best we can do. To seek a remedy by continuing the oppression because we have power to do it and see others do it, will, I apprehend, not be doing as we would be done by.

How deeply soever men are involved in the most exquisite difficulties, sincerity of heart and upright walking before God, freely submitting to His

8. "This quotation, slightly altered, is found in Alexander Arscott, *Some Considerations Relating to the Present State of the Christian Religion, wherein the Nature, End, and Design of Christianity, as well as the Principle Evidence of the Truth of it, are Explained and Recommended out of the Holy Scriptures; with a General Appeal to the Experience of all Men for Confirmation thereof,* Part III (London, 1734), p. 78. Arscott (1676–1737), an Oxford graduate, was a schoolmaster. About 1700, to the great dismay of his parents, he became a Quaker. He served many years as clerk of the London Yearly Meeting. He intended this volume as an apologetic for Christianity based on both Scripture and reason, apart from the special point of view of the Friends. All three parts were reprinted in Philadelphia, the first two by Benjamin Franklin in 1732, the third by A. Bradford in 1738" [Moulton's note].

9. I.e., the Old Testament.

providence, is the most sure remedy. He only is able to relieve not only persons but nations in their greatest calamities. David, in a great strait when the sense of his past error and the full expectation of an impending calamity as the reward of it were united to the aggravating his distress, after some deliberation saith, "Let me fall now into the hands of the Lord, for very great are his mercies; let me not fall into the hand of man." 1 Chronicles 21.13.

To act continually with integrity of heart above all narrow or selfish motives is a sure token of our being partakers of that salvation which God hath appointed for walls and bulwarks (Isaiah 5.26; Romans 15.8), and is, beyond all contradiction, a more happy situation than can ever be promised by the utmost reach of art and power united, not proceeding from heavenly wisdom.

A supply to nature's lawful wants, joined with a peaceful, humble mind, is the truest happiness in this life. And if here we arrive to this and remain to walk in the path of the just, our case will be truly happy. And though herein we may part with or miss of some glaring shows of riches and leave our children little else but wise instructions, a good example, and the knowledge of some honest employment, these, with the blessing of providence, are sufficient for their happiness, and are more likely to prove so than laying up treasures for them which are often rather a snare than any real benefit, especially to them who, instead of being exampled to temperance, are in all things taught to prefer the getting of riches and to eye the temporal distinctions they give as the principal business of this life. These readily overlook the true happiness of man as it results from the enjoyment of all things in the fear of God, and miserably substituting an inferior good, dangerous in the acquiring and uncertain in the fruition, they are subject to many disappointments; and every sweet carries its sting.

It is the conclusion of our blessed Lord and His apostles, as appears by their lives and doctrines, that the highest delights of sense or most pleasing objects visible ought ever to be accounted infinitely inferior to that real intellectual happiness suited to man in his primitive innocence and now to be found in true renovation of mind, and that the comforts of our present life, the things most grateful to us, ought always to be received with temperance and never made the chief objects of our desire, hope, or love, but that our whole heart and affections be principally looking to that city "which hath foundations, whose maker and builder is God" [Hebrews 11.10].

Did we so improve the gifts bestowed on us that our children might have an education suited to these doctrines, and our example to confirm it, we might rejoice in hopes of their being heirs of an inheritance incorruptible. This inheritance, as Christians, we esteem the most valuable; and how then can we fail to desire it for our children? Oh, that we were consistent with ourselves in pursuing means necessary to obtain it!

It appears by experience that where children are educated in fullness,[1] ease, and idleness, evil habits are more prevalent than is common amongst such who are prudently employed in the necessary affairs of life. And if children are not only educated in the way of so great temptation, but have also the opportunity of lording it over their fellow creatures and being masters of men in their childhood, how can we hope otherwise than that their

1. Affluence.

tender minds will be possessed with thoughts too high for them?—which by continuance, gaining strength, will prove like a slow current, gradually separating them from (or keeping from acquaintance with) that humility and meekness in which alone lasting happiness can be enjoyed.

Man is born to labor, and experience abundantly showeth that it is for our good. But where the powerful lay the burden on the inferior, without affording a Christian education and suitable opportunity of improving the mind, and a treatment which we in their case should approve—that themselves may live at ease and fare sumptuously and lay up riches for their posterity—this seems to contradict the design of Providence and, I doubt, is sometimes the effect of a perverted mind. For while the life of one is made grievous by the rigor of another, it entails misery on both.

Amongst the manifold works of Providence displayed in the different ages of the world, these which follow (with many others) may afford instruction:

Abraham[2] was called of God to leave his country and kindred, to sojourn amongst strangers. Through famine and danger of death he was forced to flee from one kingdom to another. He at length not only had assurance of being the father of many nations, but became a mighty prince. Genesis 23.6.

Remarkable was the dealings of God with Jacob[3] in a low estate. The just sense he retained of them after his advancement appears by his words: "I am not worthy of the least of all thy mercies." Genesis 32.10; 48.15.

The numerous afflictions of Joseph[4] are very singular, the particular providence of God therein no less manifest. He at length became governor of Egypt and famous for wisdom and virtue.

The series of troubles David[5] passed through, few amongst us are ignorant of; and yet he afterwards became as one of the great men of the earth.

Some evidences of the divine wisdom appears in those things, in that such who are intended for high stations have first been very low and dejected, that Truth might be sealed on their hearts, and that the characters there imprinted by bitterness and adversity might in after years remain, suggesting compassionate ideas and, in their prosperity, quicken their regard to those in the like condition, which yet further appears in the case of Israel. They were well acquainted with grievous sufferings, a long and rigorous servitude, then through many notable events were made chief amongst the nations. To them we find a repetition of precepts to the purpose above-said. Though for ends agreeable to infinite wisdom they were chosen as a peculiar people for a time, yet the Most High acquaints them that his love is not confined, but extends to the stranger, and to excite their compassion, reminds them of times past: "Ye were strangers in the land of Egypt." Deuteronomy 10.19. Again, "Thou shalt not oppress a stranger, for ye know the heart of a stranger, seeing ye were strangers in the land of Egypt." Exodus 23.9.

If we call to mind our beginning, some of us may find a time wherein our fathers were under afflictions, reproaches, and manifold sufferings. Respecting our progress in this land, the time is short since our beginning was small and number few, compared with the native inhabitants. He that sleeps not

2. The first of the Old Testament patriarchs.
3. Old Testament patriarch and grandson of Abraham; his twelve sons became the founders of the twelve tribes of Israel.
4. One of the sons of Jacob; his brothers sold him into slavery in Egypt.
5. As a youth David slew the giant Goliath, and Saul, the jealous king, tried to kill him; after he became the second king of the Hebrews, his son Absalom revolted against him.

by day nor night hath watched over us and kept us as the apple of His eye. His almighty arm hath been round about us and saved us from dangers.

The wilderness and solitary deserts in which our fathers passed the days of their pilgrimage are now turned into pleasant fields. The natives are gone from before us, and we establish peaceably in the possession of the land, enjoying our civil and religious liberties. And while many parts of the world have groaned under the heavy calamities of war, our habitation remains quiet and our land fruitful.

When we trace back the steps we have trodden and see how the Lord hath opened a way in the wilderness for us, to the wise it will easily appear that all this was not done to be buried in oblivion, but to prepare a people for more fruitful returns, and the remembrance thereof ought to humble us in prosperity and excite in us a Christian benevolence towards our inferiors.

If we do not consider these things aright, but through a stupid indolence conceive views of interest separate from the general good of the great brotherhood, and in pursuance thereof treat our inferiors with rigor, to increase our wealth and gain riches for our children, what then shall we do when God riseth up; and when He visiteth, what shall we answer Him? Did not He that made us make them, and "did not one fashion us in the womb?" Job 31.14[–15].

To our great Master we stand or fall; to judge or condemn is most suitable to His wisdom and authority. My inclination is to persuade and entreat, and simply give hints of my way of thinking.

If the Christian religion be considered, both respecting its doctrines and the happy influence which it hath on the minds and manners of all real Christians, it looks reasonable to think that the miraculous manifestation thereof to the world is a kindness beyond expression. Are we the people thus favored? Are we they whose minds are opened, influenced, and governed by the spirit of Christ and thereby made sons of God? Is it not a fair conclusion that we, like our Heavenly Father, ought in our degree to be active in the same great cause—of the eternal happiness of at least our whole families, and more, if thereto capacitated?[6]

If we, by the operation of the Spirit of Christ, become heirs with Him in the kingdom of His Father, and are redeemed from the alluring counterfeit joys of this world, and the joy of Christ remain in us; to suppose that one remaining in this happy condition can, for the sake of earthly riches, not only deprive his fellow creatures of the sweetness of freedom (which, rightly used, is one of the greatest temporal blessings), but therewith neglect using proper means for their acquaintance with the Holy Scriptures and the advantage of true religion, seems, at least, a contradiction to reason.

Whoever rightly advocates the cause of some thereby promotes the good of all. The state of mankind was harmonious in the beginning; and though sin hath introduced discord, yet through the wonderful love of God in Christ Jesus our Lord, the way is open for our redemption, and means appointed to restore us to primitive harmony.

That if one suffer by the unfaithfulness of another, the mind, the most noble part of him that occasions the discord, is thereby alienated from its true and real happiness. Our duty and interest is inseparably united, and

6. Enabled.

when we neglect or misuse our talents we necessarily depart from the heavenly fellowship and are in the way to the greatest of evils. Therefore, to examine and prove ourselves, to find what harmony the power presiding in us bears with the divine nature, is a duty not more incumbent and necessary than it would be beneficial.

In Holy Writ the Divine Being saith of Himself, " 'I am the Lord, which exercise loving-kindness, judgment, and righteousness in the earth; for in these things I delight,' saith the Lord." Jeremiah 9.24. Again, speaking in the way of man to show His compassion to Israel, whose wickedness had occasioned a calamity, and then being humbled under it, it is said, "His soul was grieved for their miseries." Judges 10.16.

If we consider the life of our blessed Savior when on earth, as it is recorded by His followers, we shall find that one uniform desire for the eternal and temporal good of mankind discovered itself in all His actions. If we observe men, both apostles and others in many different ages, who have really come to the unity of the spirit and the fellowship of the saints, there still appears the like disposition; and in them the desire of the real happiness of mankind has out-balanced the desire of ease, liberty, and many times life itself.

If upon a true search we find that our natures are so far renewed that to exercise righteousness and loving-kindness (according to our ability) towards all men, without respect of persons, is easy to us or is our delight; if our love be so orderly and regular that he who doth the will of our Father who is in heaven appears in our view to be our nearest relation, our brother and sister and mother; if this be our case, there is a good foundation to hope that the blessing of God will sweeten our treasures during our stay in this life, and our memory be savory when we are entered into rest.

To conclude, 'tis a truth most certain that a life guided by wisdom from above, agreeable with justice, equity, and mercy, is throughout consistent and amiable, and truly beneficial to society. The serenity and calmness of mind in it affords an unparalleled comfort in this life, and the end of it is blessed. And, no less true, that they who in the midst of high favors remain ungrateful, and under all the advantages that a Christian can desire are selfish, earthly, and sensual, do miss the true fountain of happiness and wander in a maze of dark anxiety, where all their treasures are insufficient to quiet their minds. Hence, from an insatiable craving they neglect doing good with what they have acquired, and too often add oppression to vanity, that they may compass more.

"Oh, that they were wise, that they understood this, that they would consider their latter end!" Deuteronomy 32.29.

1746   1754

JAMES GRAINGER
c. 1721–1766

Eighteenth-century poetry from the British colonies was inextricably tied to contemporary British poetry generally, finding its audiences as often in English coffeehouses and estates as in the colonies themselves. Nowhere is this more apparent than in James Grainger's *The Sugar Cane* (1764), which is indebted to a long tradition of "georgics"—a type of poem, derived from Virgil's *Georgics*, that celebrated agricultural production as the foundation of a healthy, prosperous civilization. By the eighteenth century, such verse regularly connected agriculture to mercantilism, praising the colonies for their contributions of tobacco, rice, and sugar planting to the course of empire. Based on Grainger's firsthand experience at Bassterre on the island of St. Christopher (now St. Kitts), *The Sugar Cane* offers an unparalleled look at the planter's life in a region that supplied this commodity to an eager world while adding substantial income to England's treasury.

Even before he came to the Caribbean, Grainger had many accomplishments. Born around 1721 in Scotland, he was educated at the University of Edinburgh, eventually receiving his M.D. in 1753. He established a medical practice in London and soon became an eager, though minor, participant in the city's vibrant club scene. He contributed essays and poems to various periodicals, and his circle of friends and admirers included many of England's chief literary lights, Oliver Goldsmith, Samuel Johnson, Joshua Reynolds, and William Shenstone among them. But like many of his contemporaries, he contracted the fever of speculation, and in 1759 he embarked for St. Christopher with thoughts of improving his estate. He also hoped to learn about the civil and natural history of England's transatlantic empire.

After his arrival on St. Christopher he evidently invested in slaves but soon decided that his fortune could be better served through marriage to a wealthy inhabitant. His new in-laws made him overseer of their considerable properties, and thus he acquired the in-depth knowledge of the cultivation of sugar cane that informs his most famous work. Returning to England briefly in 1763 Grainger launched his new work and shared parts of it with his literary coterie. James Boswell, the first biographer of Johnson, reports, for example, that Grainger presented his lengthy narrative poem on the sugar cane to eager literati—the irascible Dr. Johnson included—at Reynolds's estate. Soon thereafter Grainger published his georgic to a public eager to hear not only about how this staple was cultivated but also of the island's topography and natural history. He then returned to the Caribbean, where he spent the remainder of his life.

Following georgic conventions, Grainger divides *The Sugar Cane* into several books. The first treats the details of planting, the second describes the damage weather and vermin can do to the crop, the third considers harvesting and refining the product, and the fourth (printed here) discusses slavery as the engine that runs the plantation economy. Throughout, he supplies long, informative footnotes about the flora and fauna, and topography, thus grounding his literary endeavor solidly in the Enlightenment science and medicine in which he was trained.

Readers today will find the fourth book, "On the Genius of Africa," the most compelling, for in it Grainger displays his conflicted feelings about the relationship of slavery to England's success as an imperial power and to the Enlightenment principle of human progress generally. The book describes not only the practical considerations attendant on those who buy and use Africans for labor in the Caribbean but also offers many suggestions for ameliorating the slaves' plight. In the end, however, even as Grainger wishes for the eventual abolition of slavery, he rationalizes England's complicity in the institution on economic grounds.

As Grainger struggles in book IV with the demon of slavery, he also provides a remarkable glimpse into the multiethnicity of Africans brought to the Caribbean for forced labor. Like Olaudah Equiano later in the century, Grainger makes the reader aware that one cannot speak glibly of "African" slaves. Those Africans who worked the sugar plantations, like those who tended tobacco in the Chesapeake, came from many parts of Africa and brought diverse languages and customs with them. Recorded and elaborated in Grainger's poetry and footnotes, this cultural heritage, violently thrown into the mash of early American identity, reminds us again of the complex polyphone culture of the Atlantic Rim.

From The Sugar Cane: A Poem, in Four Books[1]

Book IV. *On the Genius of Africa*

ARGUMENT

Invocation to the Genius of Africa. Address. Negroes when bought should be young, and strong. The Congo-negroes are fitter for the house and trades, than for the field. The Gold-Coast, but especially the Papaw-negroes, make the best field-negroes: but even these, if advanced in years, should not be purchased. The marks of a sound negroe at a negroe sale. Where the men do nothing but hunt, fish or fight, and all field drudgery is left to the women; these are to be preferred to their husbands. The Minnahs make good tradesmen, but addicted to suicide. The Mundingos,[2] in particular, subject to worms; and the Congas, to dropsical disorders. How salt-water, or new negroes should be seasoned. Some negroes eat dirt. Negroes should be habituated by gentle degrees to field labour. This labour, when compared to that in lead-mines, or of those who work in the gold and silver mines of South America, is not only less toilsome, but far more healthy. Negroes should always be treated with humanity. Praise of freedom. Of the dracunculus, or dragon-worm. Of chigres. Of the yaws. Might not this disease be imparted by inoculation? Of worms, and their multiform appearance. Praise of commerce. Of the imaginary disorders of negroes, especially those caused by their conjurers or Obiamen.[3] The composition and supposed virtues of a magic-phiol. Field-negroes should not begin to work before six in the morning, and should leave off between eleven and twelve; and beginning again at two, should finish before sun-set. Of the weekly allowance of negroes. The young, the old, the sickly, and even the lazy, must have their victuals prepared for them. Of negroe-ground, and its various productions. To be fenced in, and watched. Of an American garden. Of the situation of the negroe-huts. How best defended from fire. The great negroe-dance described. Drumming, and intoxicating spirits not to be allowed. Negroes should be made to marry in their masters plantation. Inconveniences arising from the contrary practice. Negroes to be cloathed once a year, and before Christmas. Praise of Lewis XIV. for the Code Noir.[4] A body of laws of this kind recommended to the English sugar colonies. Praise of the river Thames. A moon-light landscape and vision.

       Genius of Africk! whether thou bestrid'st
    The castled elephants or at the source,

1. The text is based on *The Sugar Cane: A Poem, in Four Books*, published in London in 1764.
2. The Mande, an important West African tribe. The Minnahs are inhabitants of Minna and its surroundings, in Nigeria.

3. Folk magicians associated with many West African religions.
4. A set of laws governing slaveholders, during the reign of Louis XIV of France (1643–1715).

(While howls the desert fearfully around,)
Of thine own Niger,[5] sadly thou reclin'st
Thy temples shaded by the tremulous palm,   5
Or quick papàw,[6] whose top is necklac'd round
With numerous rows of party-colour'd fruit:
Or hear'st thou rather from the rocky banks
Of Rio Grandê, or black Sanaga?[7]
Where dauntless thou the headlong torrent brav'st   10
In search of gold, to brede thy wooly locks,
Or with bright ringlets ornament thine ears,
Thine arms, and ankles: O attend my song.
A muse that pities thy distressful state;
Who sees, with grief, thy sons in fetters bound;   15
Who wished freedom to the race of man;
Thy nod assenting craves: dread Genius, come!

    Yet vain they presence, vain thy favouring nod;
Unless once more the muses; that erewhile
Upheld me fainting in my past career,   20
Through Caribbe's cane-isles; kind condescend
To guide my footsteps, through parch'd Libya's wilds;
And bind my sun-burnt brow with other bays,
Than ever deck'd the Sylvan bard before.

    Say, will my Melvil,[8] from the public care,   25
Withdraw one moment, to the muses shrine?
Who smit with thy fair fame, industrious cull
An Indian wreath to mingle with thy bays,
And deck the hero, and the scholar's brow!
Wilt thou, whose mildness smooths the face of war,   30
Who round the victor-blade the myrtle twin'st,
And mak'st subjection loyal and sincere;
O wilt thou gracious hear the unartful strain,
Whose mild instructions teach, no trivial theme,
What care the jetty African requires?   35
Yes, thou wilt deign to hear; a man thou art
Who deem'st nought foreign that belongs to man.

    In mind, and aptitude for useful toil,
The negroes differ: muse that difference sing.

    Whether to wield the hoe, or guide the plane;   40
Or for domestic uses thou intend'st
The sunny Libyan: from what clime they spring,
It not imports; if strength and youth be theirs.

    Yet those from Congo's wide-extended plains,
Through which the long Zaire winds with chrystal stream,   45
Where lavish Nature sends indulgent forth

5. West African river.
6. Papaya tree.
7. Rivers in West Africa, primarily in Guinea and
Cameroon, respectively.
8. A physician in Tobias Smollett's novel, *The Adventures of Ferdinand Count Fathom* (1753).

Fruits of high favour, and spontaneous seeds
Of bland nutritious quality, ill bear
The toilsome field; but boast a docile mind,
And happiness of features. These, with care, 50
Be taught each nice mechanic art: or train'd
To houshold offices: their ductile souls
Will all thy care, and all they gold repay.

 But, if the labours of the field demand
Thy chief attention; and the ambrosial cane 55
Thou long'st to see, with spiry frequence, shade
Many an acre: planter, chuse the slave,
Who sails from barren climes; where want alone,
Offspring of rude necessity, compells
The sturdy native, or to plant the soil, 60
Or stem vast rivers, for his daily food.

 Such are the children of the Golden Coast;
Such the Papaws, of negroes far the best:
And such the numerous tribes, that skirt the shore,
From rapid Volta to the distant Rey.⁹ 65

 But, planter, from what coast soe'er they sail,
Buy not the old: they ever sullen prove;
With heart-felt anguish, they lament their home;
They will not, cannot work; they never learn
Thy native language; they are prone to ails; 70
And oft by suicide their being end.—

 Must thou from Africk reinforce thy gang?—
Let health and youth their every sinew firm;
Clear roll their ample eye; their tongue be red;
Broad swell their chest; their shoulders wide expand; 75
Not prominent their belly; clean and strong
Their thighs and legs, in just proportion rise.
Such soon will brave the fervours of the clime;
And free from ails, that kill thy negroe-train,
A useful servitude will long support. 80

 Yet, if thine own, thy childrens life, be dear;
Buy not a Cormantee,¹ tho' healthy, young.
Of breed too generous for the servile field;
They, born to freedom in their native land,
Chuse death before dishonourable bonds: 85
Or, fir'd with vengeance, at the midnight hour,
Sudden they seize thine unsuspecting watch,
And thine own poinard bury in they breast.

 At home, the men, in many a sylvan realm,
Their rank tobacco, charm of sauntering minds, 90

9. Rivers in West Africa.
1. Inhabitant of the area in present-day Ghana, the site of a notorious port for slavers.

From clayey tubes inhale; or, vacant, beat
For prey the forest; or, in war's dread ranks,
Their country's foes affront: while, in the field,
Their wives plant rice, or yams, or lofty maize,
Fell hunger to repel. Be these thy choice: 95
They, hardy, with the labours of the Cane
Soon grow familiar; while unusual toil,
And new severities their husbands kill.

    The slaves from Minnah are of stubborn breed:
But, when the bill, or hammer, they affect;   100
They soon perfection reach. But fly, with care,
The Moco-nation;[2] they themselves destroy.

    Worms lurk in all: yet, pronest they to worms,
Who from Mundingo sail. When therefore such
Thou buy'st, for sturdy and laborious they,   105
Straight let some learned leach[3] strong medicines give,
Till food and climate both familiar grow.
Thus, tho' from rise to set, in Phoebus'[4] eye,
They toil, unceasing; yet, at night, they'll sleep,
Lap'd in Elysium;[5] and, each day, at dawn,   110
Spring from their couch, as blythsome as the sun.

    One precept more, it much imports to know.—
The Blacks, who drink the Quanza's[6] lucid stream,
Fed by ten thousand springs, are prone to bloat,
Whether at home or in these ocean-isles;   115
And tho' nice art the water may subdue,
Yet many die; and few, for many a year,
Just strength attain to labour for their lord.

    Would'st thou secure thine Ethiop[7] from those ails,
Which change of climate, change of waters breed,   120
And food unusual? let Machaon draw
From each some blood, as age and sex require;
And well with vervain, well with sempre-vive,[8]
Unload their bowels.—These, in every hedge,
Spontaneous grow.—Nor will it not conduce   125
To give what chemists, in mysterious phrase,
Term the white eagle; deadly foe to worms.
But chief do thou, my friend, with hearty food,
Yet easy of digestion, likest that
Which they at home regal'd on; renovate   130
Their sea-worn appetites. Let gentle work,
Or rather playful exercise, amuse
The novel gang: and far be angry words;
Far ponderous chains; and far disheartening blows.—

---

2. People who came from the area near Mocha, on the Red Sea.
3. A physician, because he used leeches to bleed his patients.
4. Or Phoebus Apollo, the Greek god of the sun.
5. In Greek mythology, the place in the afterlife where the good souls go.
6. Or Kwanza, a river in southwestern Africa.
7. An African, derived from Ethiopia.
8. Herbs used for medicinal purposes.

From fruits restrain their eagerness; yet if   135
The acajou, haply, in thy garden bloom,
With cherries,⁹ or of white or purple hue,
Thrice wholesome fruit in this relaxing clime!
Safely thou may'st their appetite indulge.
Their arid skins will plump, their features shine: 140
No rheums, no dysenteric ails torment:
The thirsty hydrops¹ flies.—'Tis even averr'd,
(Ah, did experience sanctify the fact;
How many Lybians now would dig the soil,
Who pine in hourly agonies away!)   145
This pleasing fruit, if turtle join its aid,
Removes that worst of ails, disgrace of art,
The loathsome leprosy's infectious bane.

    There are, the muse hath oft abhorrent seen,
Who swallow dirt; (so the chlorotic fair   150
Oft chalk prefer to the most poignant cates:)²
Such, dropsy bloats, and to sure death consigns;
Unless restrain'd from this unwholesome food,
By soothing words, by menaces, by blows:
Nor yet will threats, or blows, or soothing words,   155
Perfect their cure; unless thou, Paean,³ design'st
By medicine's power their cravings to subdue.

    To easy labour first inure thy slaves;
Extremes are dangerous. With industrious search,
Let them fit grassy provender collect   160
For thy keen stomach'd herds.—But when the earth
Hath made her annual progress round the sun,
What time the conch⁴ or bell resounds, they may
All to the Cane-ground, with thy gang, repair.

    Nor, Negroe, at thy destiny repine,   165
Tho' doom'd to toil from dawn to setting sun.
How far more pleasant is thy rural task,
Than theirs who sweat, sequester'd from the day,
In dark tartarean caves, sunk far beneath
The earth's dark surface, where sulphureous flames,   170
Oft from their vapoury prisons bursting wild,

9. The tree which produces this wholesome fruit is tall, shady, and of quick growth. Its Indian name is *Acajou*; hence corruptly called *Cashew* by the English. The fruit has no resemblance to a cherry, either in shape or size; and bears, at its lower extremity, a nut (which the Spaniards name *Anacardo*, and physicians *Anacardium*) that resembles a large kidney-bean. Its kernal is as grateful as an almond, and more easy of digestion. Between its rinds is contained a highly caustic oil; which, being held to a candle, emits bright salient sparkles, in which the American fortune-tellers pretended they saw spirits who gave answers to whatever questions were put to them by their ignorant followers. This oil is used as a cosmetic by the ladies, to remove freckles and sun-burning; but the pain they nec-essarily suffer makes its use not very frequent. This tree also produces a gum not inferior to Gum-Arabic; and its bark is an approved astringent. The juice of the cherry stains exceedingly. The long citron, or amber-coloured, is the best. The cashew-nuts, when unripe, are of a green colour; but, ripe, they assume that of a pale olive. This tree bears fruit but once a year [Grainger's note].
1. The presence of a large amount of fluids in the body, now called edema.
2. Delicious foods.
3. Title of Apollo.
4. Plantations that have no bells assemble their Negroes by sounding a conch-shell [Grainger's note].

To dire explosion give the cavern'd deep,
And in dread ruin all its inmates whelm?—
Nor fateful only is the bursting flame;
The exhalations of the deep-dug mine,   175
Tho' slow, shake from their wings as sure a death.
With what intense severity of pain
Hath the afflicted muse, in Scotia, seen
The miners rack'd, who toil for fatal lead?
What cramps, what palsies shake their feeble limbs,   180
Who, on the margin of the rocky Drave,
Trace silver's fluent ore? Yet white men these!

    How far more happy ye, than those poor slaves,
Who, whilom, under native, gracious chiefs,
Incas and emperors, long time enjoy'd   185
Mild government, with every sweet of life,
In blissful climates? See them dragg'd in chains,
By proud insulting tyrants, to the mines
Which once they call'd their own, and then despis'd!
See, in the mineral bosom of their land,   190
How hard they toil! how soon their youthful limbs
Feel the decrepitude of age! how soon
Their teeth desert their sockets! and how soon
Shaking paralysis unstrings their frame!
Yet scarce, even then, are they allow'd to view   195
The glorious God of day, of whom they beg,
With earnest hourly supplications, death;
Yet death slow comes, to torture them the more!

    With these compar'd, ye sons of Afric, say,
How far more happy is your lot? Bland health,   200
Of ardent eye, and limb robust, attends
Your custom'd labour; and, should sickness seize,
With what solicitude are ye not nurs'd!—
Ye Negroes, then, your pleasing task pursue;
And, by your toil, deserve your master's care.   205

    When first your Blacks are novel to the hoe;
Study their humours: Some, soft-soothing words;
Some, presents; and some, menaces subdue;
And some I've known, so stubborn is their kind,
Whom blows, alas! could win alone to toil.   210

    Yet, planter, let humanity prevail.—
Perhaps thy Negroe, in his native land,
Possest large fertile plains, and slaves, and herds:
Perhaps, whene'er he deign'd to walk abroad,
The richest silks, from where the Indus rolls,   215
His limbs invested in their gorgeous pleats:
Perhaps he wails his wife, his children, left
To struggle with adversity: Perhaps
Fortune, in battle for his country fought,

Gave him a captive to his deadliest foe: 220
Perhaps, incautious, in his native fields,
(On pleasurable scenes his mind intent)
All as he wandered; from the neighbouring grove,
Fell ambush dragg'd him to the hated main.—
Were they even sold for crimes; ye polish'd, say!   225
Ye, to whom Learning opes her amplest page!
Ye, whom the knowledge of a living God
Should lead to virtue! Are ye free from crimes?
Ah pity, then, these uninstructed swains;
And still let mercy soften the decrees   230
Of rigid justice, with her lenient hand.
Oh, did the tender muse possess the power;
Which monarchs have, and monarchs oft abuse:
'Twould be the fond ambition of her soul,
To quell tyrannic sway; knock off the chains   235
Of heart-debasing slavery; give to man,
Of every colour and of every clime,
Freedom, which stamps him image of his God.
Then laws, Oppression's scourge, fair Virtue's prop,
Offspring of Wisdom! should impartial reign,   240
To knit the whole in well-accorded strife:
Servants, not slaves; of choice, and not compell'd;
The Blacks should cultivate the Cane-land isles.

        Say, shall the muse the various ills recount,
Which Negroe-nations feel? Shall she describe   245
The worm that subtly winds into their flesh,
All as they bathe them in their native streams?
There, with fell increment, it soon attains
A direful length of harm. Yet, if due skill,
And proper circumspection are employed,   250
It may be won its volumes to wind round
A leaden cylinder: But, O, beware,
No rashness practise; else 'twill surely snap,
And suddenly, retreating, dire produce
An annual lameness to the tortured Moor.   255

        Nor only is the dragon worm to dread:
Fell, winged insects,[5] which the visual ray
Scarcely discerns, their sable feet and hands
Oft penetrate; and, in the fleshy nest,
Myriads of young produce; which soon destroy   260
The parts they breed in; if assiduous care,
With art, extract not the prolific foe.

5. These, by the English, are called *Chigoes* or *Chigres*. They chiefly perforate the toes, and sometimes the fingers; occasioning an itching, which some people think not unpleasing, and are at pains to get, by going to the copper-holes, or mill-round, where chigres most abound. They lay their nits in a bag, about the size of a small pea, and are partly contained therein themselves. This the Negroes extract without bursting, by means of a needle, and filling up the place with a little snuff; it soon heals, if the person has a good constitution. One species of them is supposed to be poisonous; but, I believe, unjustly. When they bury themselves near a tendon, especially if the person is in a bad habit of body, they occasion troublesome sores. The South-Americans call them *Miguas* [Grainger's note].

Or, shall she sing, and not debase her lay,
The pest peculiar to the Aethiop-kind,
The yaw's[6] infectious bane?—The infected far   265
In huts, to leeward, lodge; or near the main.
With heartening food, with turtle, and with conchs;
The flowers of sulphur, and hard niccars[7] burnt,
The lurking evil from the blood expel,
And throw it on the surface: There in spots   270
Which cause no pain, and scanty ichor[8] yield,
It chiefly breaks about the arms and hips,
A virulent contagion!—When no more
Round knobby spots deform, but the disease
Seems at a pause; then let the learned leach   275
Give, in due dose, live-silver[9] from the mine;
Till copious spitting the whole taint exhaust.—
Nor thou repine, tho' half-way round the sun,
This globe, her annual progress shall absolve;
Ere, clear'd, they slave from all infection shine.   280
Nor then be confident; successive crops
Of defoedations[1] oft will spot the skin:
These thou, with turpentine and guaiac pods,
Reduc'd by coction to a wholesome draught,
Total remove, and give the blood its balm.   285

      Say, as this malady but once infests
The sons of Guinea, might not skill ingraft
(Thus, the small-pox are happily convey'd;)
This ailment early to thy Negroe-train?

      Yet, of the ills which torture Libya's sons,   290
Worms tyrannize the worst. They, Proteus[2]-like,
Each symptom of each malady assume;
And, under every mask, the assassins kill.
Now, in the guise of horrid spasms; they writhe
The tortured body, and all sense o'er-power.   295
Sometimes, like Mania, with her head downcast,
They cause the wretch in solitude to pine;
Or frantic, bursting from the strongest chains,
To frown with look terrific, not his own.
Sometimes like Ague, with a shivering mien,   300
The teeth gnash fearful, and the blood runs chill:
Anon the ferment maddens in the veins,
And a false vigour animates the frame.
Again, the dropsy's bloated mask they steal;
Or, "melt with minings of the hectic fire."[3]   305

6. A tropical skin disease.
7. The botanical name of this medicinal shrub is
Guilandina. The fruit resembles marbles, though
not so round. Their shell is hard and smooth, and
contains a farinaceous nut, of admirable use in
seminal weaknesses. They are also given to throw
out the yaws [Grainger's note].

8. Fluid discharged from an infected wound.
9. Quicksilver, mercury.
1. A pollution.
2. Greek god of the sea, who could change his
shape at will.
3. The quotation is from John Armstrong's *The Art
of Preserving Health: A Poem* (1744), 3.202.

Say, to such various mimic forms of death;
What remedies shall puzzle art oppose?—
Thanks to the Almighty, in each path-way hedge,
Rank cow-itch⁴ grows, whose sharp unnumber'd stings,
Sheath'd in Melasses, from their dens expell,   310
Fell dens of death, the reptile lurking foe.—
A powerful vermifuge, in skilful hands,
The worm-grass proves; yet, even in hands of skill,
Sudden, I've known it dim the visual ray
For a whole day and night. There are who use   315
(And sage Experience justifies the use)
The mineral product of the Cornish mine,⁵
Which in old times, ere Britain laws enjoyed,
The polish'd Tyrians,⁶ monarchs of the main,
In their swift ships convey'd to foreign realms: 320
The sun by day, by night the northern star,
Their course conducted.—Mighty commerce, hail!
By thee the sons of Attic's sterile land,
A scanty number, laws impos'd on Greece:
Nor aw'd they Greece alone; vast Asia's King,   325
Tho' girt by rich arm'd myriads, at their frown
Felt his heart whither on his farthest throne.
Perennial source of population thou!
While scanty peasants plough the flowery plains
Of purple Enna; from the Belgian fens,   330
What swarms of useful citizens spring up,
Hatch'd by thy fostering wing. Ah where is flown
That dauntless free-born spirit, which of old,
Taught them to shake off the tyrannic yoke
Of Spains insulting King; on whose wide realms,   335
The sun still shone with undiminished beam?
Parent of wealth! in vain, coy nature hoards
Her gold and diamonds; toil, thy firm compeer,
And industry of unremitting nerve,
Scale the cleft mountain, the loud torrent brave,   340
Plunge to the center, and thro' Nature's wiles,
(Led on by skill of penetrative soul)
Her following close, her secret treasures find,
To pour them plenteous on the laughing world.
On thee Sylvanus,⁷ thee each rural god,   345
On thee chief Ceres,⁸ with unfailing love

4. This extraordinary vine should not be permitted to grow in a Cane-piece; for Negroes have been known to fire the Canes, to save themselves from the torture which attends working in grounds where it has abounded. Mixed with melasses [i.e., molasses], it is a safe and excellent vermifuge [anti-worm medicine]. Its seeds, which resemble black-ish small beans, are purgative. Its flower is purple; and its pods, on which the stinging brown *Setae* are found, are as large as a full-grown English field-pea [Grainger's note].
5. Tin-filings are a better vermifuge than tin in powder. The western parts of Britain, and the neighbouring isles, have been famous for this useful metal from the remotest antiquity; for we find from Strabo, that the Phaenicians [i.e., Phoeni-cians] made frequent voyages to those parts (which they called *Cassiterides* [ancient name for the Scilly Isles off Cornwall, England] from stannum) in quest of that commodity, which turned out so beneficial to them, that a pilot of that nation stranded his vessel, rather than show a Roman ship, that watched him, the way to those mines. For this public spirited action he was amply rewarded, says that accurate writer, upon his return to his country. The Romans, however, soon made themselves masters of the secret, and shared with them in the profit of that merchandize [Grainger's note].
6. The Phoenicians, who came from Tyre.
7. Roman god of the forests.
8. Roman goddess of the harvest.

And fond distinction, emulously gaze.
In vain hath nature pour'd vast seas between
Far-distant kingdoms; endless storms in vain
With double night brood o'er them; thou dost throw,   350
O'er far-divided nature's realms, a chain
To bind in sweet society mankind.
By thee white Albion,[9] once a barbarous clime,
Grew fam'd for arms, for wisdom, and for laws;
By thee she holds the balance of the world,   355
Acknowledg'd now sole empress of the main.
Coy though thou art, and mutable of love,
There may'st thou ever fix thy wandering steps;
While Eurus[1] rules the wide atlantic foam!
By thee, thy favorite, great Columbus found   360
That world, where now thy praises I rehearse
To the resounding main and palmy shore;
And Lusitania's chiefs those realms explor'd,
Whence negroes spring, the subject of my song.

     Nor pine the Blacks, alone, with real ills,   365
That baffle oft the wisest rules of art:
They likewise feel imaginary woes;
Woes no less deadly. Luckless he who owns
The slave, who thinks himself bewitch'd; and whom,
In wrath, a conjuror's snake-mark'd[2] staff hath struck! 370
They mope, love silence, every friend avoid;
They inly pine; all aliment reject;
Or insufficient for nutrition take:
Their features droop; a sickly yellowish hue
Their skin deforms; their strength and beauty fly.   375
Then comes the feverish fiend, with firy eyes,
Whom drowth, convulsions, and whom death surround,
Fatal attendants! if some subtle slave
(Such, Obia-men are stil'd) do not engage,
To save the wretch by antidote or spell.   380

     In magic spells, in Obia, all the sons
Of sable Africk trust:—Ye, sacred nine!
(For ye each hidden preparation know)
Transpierce the gloom, which ignorance and fraud
Have render'd awful; tell the laughing world   385
Of what these wonder-working charms are made.

     Fern root cut small, and tied with many a knot;
Old teeth extracted from a white man's skull;
A lizard's skeleton; a serpent's head:

9. England.
1. The east wind.
2. The negroe-conjurors, or Obia-men, as they are called, carry about them a staff, which is marked with frogs, snakes, &c. The blacks imagine that its blow, if not mortal, will at least occasion long and troublesome disorders. A belief in magic is inseparable from human nature, but those nations are most addicted thereto, among whom learning, and of course, philosophy have least obtained. As in all other countries, so in Guinea, the conjurors, as they have more understanding, so are they almost always more wicked than the common herd of their deluded countrymen; and as the negroe-magicians can do mischief, so they can also do good on a plantation, provided they are kept by the white people in proper subordination [Grainger's note].

These mix'd with salt, and water from the spring,   390
Are in a phial pour'd; o'er these the leach
Mutters strange jargon, and wild circles forms.

    Of this possest, each negroe deems himself
Secure from poison; for to poison they
Are infamously prone: and arm'd with this,   395
Their sable country daemons they defy,
Who fearful haunt them at the midnight hour,
To work them mischief. This, diseases fly;
Diseases follow: such its wonderous power!
This o'er the threshold of their cottage hung,   400
No thieves break in; or, if they dare to steal,
Their feet in blotches, which admit no cure,
Burst loathsome out: but should its owner filch,
As slaves were ever of the pilfering kind,
This from detection screens;—so conjurors swear.   405

    'Till morning dawn, and Lucifer withdraw
His beamy chariot; let not the loud bell
Call forth thy negroes from their rushy couch:
And ere the sun with mid-day fervour glow,
When every broom-bush[3] opes her yellow flower;   410
Let thy black labourers from their toil desist:
Nor till the broom her every petal lock,
Let the loud bell recall them to the hoe.
But when the jalap her bright tint displays,
When the solanum[4] fills her cup with dew,   415
And crickets, snakes, and lizards 'gin their coil;
Let them find shelter in their cane-thatch'd huts:
Or, if constrain'd unusual hours to toil,
(For even the best must sometimes urge their gang)
With double nutriment reward their pains.   420

    Howe'er insensate some may deem their slaves,
Nor 'bove the bestial rank; far other thoughts
The muse, soft daughter of humanity!
Will ever entertain.—The Ethiop knows,
The Ethiop feels, when treated like a man;   425
Nor grudges, should necessity compel,
By day, by night, to labour for his lord.

    Not less inhuman, than unthrifty those;
Who, half the year's rotation round the sun,
Deny subsistence to their labouring slaves.   430

---

3. This small plant, which grows in every pasture, may, with propriety, be termed an American clock; for it begins every forenoon at eleven to open its yellow flowers, which about one are fully expanded, and at two closed. The jalap, or marvel of Peru, unfolds its petals between five and six in the evening, which shut again as soon as night comes on, to open again in the cool of the morning. This plant is called four o'clock by the natives, and bears either a yellow or purple-coloured flower [Grainger's note].
4. So some authors name the fire-weed, which grows every where, and is the *datura* of Linnaeus; whose virtues Dr. Stork, at Vienna, has greatly extolled in a late publication. It bears a white monopetalous flower, which opens always about sun-set [Grainger's note].

But would'st thou see thy negroe-train encrease,
Free from disorders; and thine acres clad
With groves of sugar: every week dispense
Or English beans, or Carolinian rice;
Ïerne's[5] beef, or Pensilvanian flour;   435
Newfoundland cod, or herrings from the main
That howls tempestuous round the Scotian isles!

    Yet some there are so lazily inclin'd,
And so neglectful of their food, that thou,
Would'st thou preserve them from the jaws of death;   440
Daily, their wholesome viands must prepare:
With these let all the young, and childless old,
And all the morbid share;—so heaven will bless,
With manifold encrease, thy costly care.

    Suffice not this; to every slave assign   445
Some mountain-ground: or, if waste broken land
To thee belong, that broken land divide.
This let them cultivate, one day, each week;
And there raise yams, and there cassada's root:[6]
From a good daemon's staff cassada sprang,   450
Tradition says, and Caribbees[7] believe;
Which into three the white-rob'd genius broke,
And bade them plant, their hunger to repel.
There let angola's bloomy bush supply,[8]
For many a year, with wholesome pulse their board.   455
There let the bonavist,[9] his fringed pods
Throw liberal o'er the prop; while ochra bears
Aloft his slimy pulp, and help disdains.
There let potatos[1] mantle o'er the ground;
Sweet as the cane-juice is the root they bear.   460
There too let eddas[2] spring in order meet.

5. Ireland's.
6. To an antient Caribbean, bemoaning the savage uncomfortable life of his countrymen, a diety clad in white apparel appeared, and told him, he would have come sooner to have taught him the ways of civil life, had he been addressed before. He then showed him sharp-cutting stones to fell trees and build houses; and bade him cover them with the palm leaves. Then he broke his staff in three; which, being planted, soon after produced cassada. See Ogilvy's America. [John Ogilby, *America: being the Latest and Most Accurate Description of the New World* (London: Tho. Johnson, 1670)] [Grainger's note].
7. The Caribs, natives of the Caribbean.
8. This is called *Pidgeon-pea*, and grows on a sturdy shrub, that will last for years. It is justly reckoned among the most wholesome legumens. The juice of the leaves, dropt into the eye, will remove incipient films. The botanic name is *Cytisus* [Grainger's note].
9. This is the Spanish name of a plant, which produces an excellent bean. It is a parasitical plant. There are five sorts of bonavist, the green, the white, the moon-shine, the small or common; and, lastly, the black and red. The flowers of all are white and papilionaceous; except the last, whose blossoms are purple. They commonly bear in six weeks. Their pulse is wholesome, though somewhat flatulent; especially those from the black and red. The pods are flattish, two or three inches long; and contain from three to five seeds in partitional cells [Grainger's note].
1. I cannot positively say, whether these vines are of Indian original or not; but as in their fructification, they differ from potatos at home, they probably are not European. They are sweet. There are four kinds, the red, the white, the long, and round. The juice of each may be made into a pleasant cool drink; and, being distilled, yield an excellent spirit [Grainger's note].
2. This wholesome root, in some of the islands, is called *Edda*: Its botanical name is *Arum maximum Aegytiacum*. There are three species of tanies, the blue, the scratching, and that which is commonly roasted. The blossoms of all three are very fragrant, in a morning or evening. The young leaves, as well as the spiral stalks which support the flower, are eaten by the Negroes as a salad. The root makes a good broth in dysenteric complaints. They are seldom so large as the yam, but most people think them preferable in point of taste. The French call

With Indian cale,[3] and foodful calaloo.[4]
While mint, thyme, balm, and Europe's coyer herbs,
Shoot gladsome forth, not reprobate the clime.

This tract secure, with hedges or of limes,   465
Or bushy citrons, or the shapely tree[5]
That glows at once with aromatic blooms,
And golden fruit mature. To these be join'd,
In comely neighbourhood, the cotton shrub;
In this delicious clime the cotton bursts   470
On rocky soils.—The coffee also plant;
White as the skin of Albion's lovely fair,
Are the thick snowy fragrant blooms it boasts:
Nor wilt thou, cocô, thy rich pods refuse;
Tho' years, and heat, and moisture they require,   475
Ere the stone grind them to the food of health.
Of thee, perhaps, and of thy various sorts,
And that kind sheltering tree, thy mother nam'd,
With crimson flowerets prodigally grac'd;
In future times, the enraptur'd muse may sing: 480
If public favour crown her present lay.

But let some antient, faithful slave erect
His sheltered mansion near; and with his dog,
His loaded gun, and cutlass, guard the whole:
Else negroe-fugitives, who skulk 'mid rocks   485
And shrubby wilds, in bands will soon destroy
Thy labourer's honest wealth; their loss and yours.

Perhaps, of Indian gardens I could sing,
Beyond what bloom'd on blest Phaeacia's isle,[6]
Or eastern climes admir'd in days of yore: 490
How Europe's foodful, culinary plants;
How gay Pomona's ruby-tinctured births;
And gawdy Flora's various-vested train;
Might be instructed to unlearn their clime,
And by due discipline adopt the sun.   495
The muse might tell what culture will entice
The ripened melon, to perfume each month;
And with the anana[7] load the fragrant board.
The muse might tell, what trees will best exclude
("Insuperable height of airiest shade")[8]   500
With their vast umbrage the noon's fervent ray.
Thee, verdant mammey,[9] first, her song should praise:

this plant *Tayove*. It produces eatable roots every four months, for one year only [Grainger's note].
3. This green, which is a native of the New World, equals any of the greens in the Old [Grainger's note].
4. Another species of Indian pot herb, no less wholesome than the preceding. These, with mezamby, and the Jamaica pickle-weed, yield to no esculent plants in Europe. This is an Indian name [Grainger's note].

5. The orange tree [Grainger's note].
6. Island of Scheria in the Ionian Sea, where the Phaeacians, mentioned in Homer's *Odyssey*, lived.
7. Pineapple.
8. From John Milton's *Paradise Lost* 4.138.
9. This is a lofty, shady, and beautiful tree. Its fruit is as large as the largest melon, and of an exquisite smell, greatly superior to it in point of taste. Within the fruit are contained one or two large stones, which when distilled, give to spirits a ratafia-

Thee, the first natives of these Ocean-isles,
Fell anthropophagi,¹ still sacred held;
And from thy large high-flavour'd fruit abstain'd,   505
With pious awe; for thine high-flavour'd fruit
The airy phantoms of their friends deceas'd
Joy'd to regale on.—Such their simple creed.
The tamarind² likewise should adorn her theme,
With whose tart fruit the sweltering fever loves   510
To quench his thirst, whose breezy umbrage soon
Shades the pleas'd planter, shades his children long.
Nor, lofty cassia,³ should she not recount
Thy woodland honours! See, what yellow flowers
Dance in the gale, and scent the ambient air;   515
While thy long pods, full-fraught with nectared sweets,
Relieve the bowels from their lagging load.
Nor chirimoia,⁴ though these torrid isles
Boast not thy fruit, to which the anana yields
In taste and flavour, wilt thou coy refuse   520
Thy fragrant shade to beautify the scene.
But, chief of palms, and pride of Indian-groves,
Thee, fair palmeto,⁵ should her song resound:
What swelling columns, form'd by Jones or Wren,
Or great Palladio,⁶ may with thee compare?   525
Not nice-proportion'd, but of size immense,
Swells the wild fig-tree, and should claim her lay:
For, from its numerous bearded twigs proceed
A filial train, stupendous as their fire,
In quick succession; and, o'er many a rood,   530
Extend their uncouth limbs; which not the bolt

flavour [ratafia is a sweet liqueur], and therefore the French call them *Les apricots de St. Domingue*: accordingly, the *l'eau des noiaux*, one of the best West-Indian cordials, is made from them. The fruit, eaten raw, is of an aperient quality; and made into sweet-meats, &c. is truly exquisite. This tree, contrary to most others in the New World, shoots up to a pyramidal figure: the leaves are uncommonly green; and it produces fruit, but once a year. The name is Indian. The English commonly call it *Mammey-sapota*. There are two species of it, the sweet, and the tart. The botanical name is *Achras* [Grainger's note].
1. Cannibals.
2. This large, shady, and beautiful tree grows fast even in the driest soils, and lasts long, and yet its wood is hard, and very fit for mechanical uses. The leaves are smaller than those of senna, and pennated: they taste sourish, as does the pulp, which is contained in pods four or five inches long. They bear once a year. An excellent vinegar may be made from the fruit; but the Creoles chiefly preserve it with sugar, as the Spaniards with salt. A pleasant syrup may be made from it. The name is, in Arabic, *Tamara*. The Antients were not acquainted therewith; for the Arabians first introduced tamarinds into physic; it is a native of the East as well as of the West-Indies and South-America, where different provinces call it by different names. Its cathartic qualities are well known. It is good in sea-sickness. The botanical name is *Tamarindus* [Grainger's note].

3. Both this tree and its mild purgative pulp are sufficiently known [Grainger's note].
4. An African fruit tree.
5. This being the most beautiful of palms, nay, perhaps, superior to any other known tree in the world, has with propriety obtained the name of *Royal*. The botanical name is *Palma Maxima*. It will shoot up perpendicularly to an hundred feet or more. The stem is perfectly circular only towards the root, and immediately under the branches at top, it bulges out. The bark is smooth, and of an ash-brown colour, except at the top where it is green. It grows very fast, and the seed from whence it springs is not bigger than an acorn. In this, as in all the palm-genus, what the natives call Cabbage is found; but it resembles in taste an almond, and is in fact the pith of the upper, or greenish part of the stem. But it would be the most unpardonable luxury to cut down so lovely a tree, for so mean a gratification; especially as the wild, or mountain cabbage tree, sufficiently supplies the table with that esculent. I never ride past the charming vista of royal palms on the Cayon-estate of Daniel Mathew, Esq; in St. Christopher, without being put in mind of the pillars of the Temple of the Sun at Palmyra. This tree grows on the tops of hills, as well as in valleys; its hard cortical part makes very durable laths for houses. There is a smaller species not quite so beautiful [Grainger's note].
6. Important architects. Inigo Jones (1573–1652); Christopher Wren (1632–1723); Andrea Palladio (1508–1580).

Of heaven can scathe; nor yet the all-wasting rage
Of Typhon, or of hurricane, destroy
Nor should, tho' small, the anata[7] not be sung:
Thy purple dye, the silk and cotton fleece   535
Delighted drink; thy purple dye the tribes
Of Northern-Ind,[8] a fierce and wily race,
Carouse, assembled; and with it they paint
Their manly make in many a horrid form,
To add new terrors to the face of war.   540
The muse might teach to twine the verdant arch,
And the cool alcove's lofty room adorn,
With ponderous granadillas,[9] and the fruit
Call'd water-lemon; grateful to the taste:
Nor should she not pursue the mountain-streams,   545
But pleas'd decoy them from their shady haunts,
In rills, to visit every tree and herb;
Or fall o'er fern-clad cliffs, with foaming rage;
Or in huge basons float, a fair expanse;
Or, bound in chains of artificial force,   550
Arise thro' sculptured stone, or breathing brass.—
But I'm in haste to furl my wind-worn sails,
And anchor my tir'd vessel on the shore.

It much imports to build thy Negroe-huts,
Or on the sounding margin of the main,   555
Or on some dry hill's gently-sloping sides,
In streets, at distance due.—When near the beach,
Let frequent coco cast its wavy shade;
'Tis Neptune's tree; and, nourish'd by the spray,
Soon round the bending stem's aerial height,   560
Clusters of mighty nuts, with milk and fruit
Delicious fraught, hang clattering in the sky.
There let the bay-grape,[1] too, its crooked limbs
Project enormous; of impurpled hue
Its frequent clusters grow. And there, if thou   565
Woud'st make the sand yield salutary food,
Let Indian millet[2] rear its corny reed,

7. Or *Anotto*, or *Arnotta*; thence corruptly called Indian Otter, by the English. The tree is about the size of an ordinary apple-tree. The French call it *Rocou*; and send the farina home as a paint, &c. for which purpose the tree is cultivated by them in their islands. The flower is pentapetalous, of a bluish and spoon-like appearance. The yellow filaments are tipped with purplish apices. The style proves the rudiment of the succeeding pod, which is of a conic shape, an inch and a half long. This is divided into many cells, which contain a great number of small seeds, covered with a red farina [Grainger's note]. [Now known as *annatto*.]
8. Native Americans.
9. This is the Spanish name, and is a species of the *passiflora*, or passion-flower, called by Linnaeus *Musa*. The seeds and pulp, through which the seeds are dispersed, are cooling, and grateful to the palate. This, as well as the water-lemon, bell-apple, or honeysuckle, as it is named, being parasitical plants, are easily formed into cooling arbors, than which nothing can be more grateful in warm climates. Both fruits are wholesome. The granadilla is commonly eat with sugar, on account of its tartness, and yet the pulp is viscid. Plumier calls it *Granadilla, late-folia, fructu maliformi.* It grows best in shady places. The unripe fruit makes an excellent pickle [Grainger's note.]
1. Or sea side grape, as it is more commonly called. This is a large, crooked, and shady tree, (the leaves being broad, thick, and almost circular;) and succeeds best in sandy places. It bears large clusters of grapes once a year; which, when ripe, are not disagreeable. The stones, seeds, or *acini*, contained in them, are large in proportion; and, being reduced to a powder, are an excellent astringent. The bark of the tree has the same property. The grapes, steept in water and fermented with sugar, make an agreeable wine [Grainger's note].
2. Or maise. This is commonly called Guinea-corn, to distinguish it from the great or Indian-corn, that grows in the southern parts of North-America. It soon shoots up to a great height, often twenty feet high, and will ratoon like the

Like arm'd battalions in array of war.
But, round the upland huts, bananas plant;
A wholesome nutriment bananas yield,   570
And sun-burnt labour loves its breezy shade.
Their graceful screen let kindred plantanes join,
And with their broad vans shiver in the breeze;
So flames design'd, or by imprudence caught,
Shall spread no ruin to the neighbouring roof.   575

    Yet nor the sounding margin of the main,
Nor gently sloping side of breezy hill,
Nor streets, at distance due, imbower'd in trees;
Will half the health, or half the pleasure yield,
Unless some pitying naiad deign to lave,   580
With an unceasing stream, thy thirsty bounds.

    On festal days; or when their work is done;
Permit thy slaves to lead the choral dance,
To the wild banshaw's[3] melancholy sound.
Responsive to the sound, head feet and frame   585
Move aukwardly harmonious; hand in hand
Now lock'd, the gay troop circularly wheels,
And frisks and capers with intemperate joy.
Halts the vast circle, all clap hands and sing;
While those distinguish'd for their heels and air,   590
Bound in the center, and fantastic twine.
Meanwhile some stripling, from the choral ring,
Trips forth; and, not ungallantly, bestows
On her who nimblest hath the greensward beat,
And whose flush'd beauties have inthrall'd his soul,   595
A silver token of his fond applause.
Anon they form in ranks; nor inexpert
A thousand tuneful intricacies weave,
Shaking their sable limbs; and oft a kiss
Steal from their partners; who, with neck reclin'd,   600
And semblant scorn, resent the ravish'd bliss.
But let not thou the drum their mirth inspire;
Nor vinous spirits: else, to madness fir'd,
(What will not bacchanalian frenzy dare?)
Fell acts of blood, and vengeance they pursue.   605

    Compel by threats, or win by soothing arts,
Thy slaves to wed their fellow slaves at home;
So shall they not their vigorous prime destroy,
By distant journeys, at untimely hours,
When muffled midnight decks her raven-hair   610
With the white plumage of the prickly vine[4]

---

other; but its blades are not so nourishing to horses
as those of the great corn, although its seeds are
more so, and rather more agreeable to the taste.
The Indians, Negroes, and poor white people,
make many (not unsavoury) dishes with them. It is
also called *Turkey wheat*. The turpentine tree will
also grow in the sand, and is most useful upon a

plantation [Grainger's note].
3. This is a sort of rude guitar, invented by the
Negroes. It produces a wild pleasing melancholy
sound [Grainger's note].
4. This beautiful white rosaceous flower is as large
as the crown of one's hat, and only blows at midnight. The plant, which is prickly and attaches

Would'st thou from countless ails preserve thy gang;
To every Negroe, as the candle-weed[5]
Expands his blossoms to the cloudy sky,
And moist Aquarius melts in daily showers;   615
A woolly vestment give, (this Wiltshire weaves)
Warm to repel chill Night's unwholesome dews:
While strong coarse linen, from the Scotian loom,
Wards off the fervours of the burning day.

The truly great, tho' from a hostile clime,   620
The sacred Nine embalm; then, Muses, chant,
In grateful numbers, Gallic Lewis' praise:
For private murder quell'd; for laurel'd arts,
Invented, cherish'd in his native realm;
For rapine punish'd; for grim famine fed;   625
For sly chicane expell'd the wrangling bar;
And rightful Themis[6] seated on her throne:
But, chief, for those mild laws his wisdom fram'd,
To guard the Aethiop from tyrannic sway!

Did such, in these green isles which Albion claims,   630
Did such obtain; the muse, at midnight-hour,
This last brain-racking study had not ply'd:
But, sunk in slumbers of immortal bliss,
To bards had listened on a fancied Thames!

All hail, old father Thames! tho' not from far   635
Thy springing waters roll; nor countless streams,
Of name conspicuous swell thy watery store;
Tho' thou, no Plata,[7] to the sea devolve
Vast humid offerings; thou art king of streams:
Delighted Commerce broods upon thy wave;   640
And every quarter of this sea-girt globe
To thee due tribute pays; but chief the world
By great Columbus found, where now the muse
Beholds, transported, slow vast fleecy clouds,
Alps pil'd on Alps romantically high,   645
Which charm the sight with many a pleasing form.
The moon, in virgin-glory, gilds the pole,
And tips yon tamarinds, tips yon Cane-crown'd vale,
With fluent silver; while unnumbered stars
Gild the vast concave with their lively beams.   650
The main, a moving burnish'd mirror, shines;
No noise is heard, save when the distant surge
With drouzy murmurings breaks upon the shore!—

---

itself firmly to the sides of houses, trees, &c. produces a fruit, which some call *Wythe Apple*, and others with more propriety, *Mountain strawberry*. But though it resembles the large Chili-strawberry in looks and size; yet being inelegant of taste, it is seldom eaten. The botanical name is *Cereus scandens minor*. The rind of the fruit is here and there studded with tufts of small sharp prickles [Grainger's note].
5. This shrub, which produces a yellow flower somewhat resembling a narcissus, makes a beautiful hedge, and blows about November. It grows wild every where. It is said to be diuretic, but this I do not know from experience [Grainger's note].
6. Greek goddess, associated with the seasons and the Fates.
7. One of the largest rivers of South America [Grainger's note].

Ah me, what thunders roll! the sky's on fire!
Now sudden darkness muffles up the pole! 655
Heavens! what wild scenes, before the affrighted sense,
Imperfect swim!—See! in that flaming scroll,
Which Time unfolds, the future germs bud forth,
Of mighty empires! independent realms!—
And must Britannia, Neptune's favorite queen, 660
Protect'ress of true science, freedom, arts;
Must she, ah! must she, to her offspring crouch?
Ah, must my Thames, old Ocean's favourite son,
Resign his trident to barbaric streams;
His banks neglected, and his waves unsought, 665
No bards to sing them, and no fleets to grace?—
Again the fleecy clouds amuse the eye,
And sparkling stars the vast horizon gild—
She shall not crouch; if Wisdom guide the helm,
Wisdom that bade loud Fame, with justest praise, 670
Record her triumphs! bade the lacquaying winds
Transport, to every quarter of the globe,
Her winged navies! bade the scepter'd sons
Of earth acknowledge her pre-eminence!—
She shall not crouch; if these Cane ocean-isles, 675
Isles which on Britain for their all depend,
And must for ever; still indulgent share
Her fostering smile: and other isles be given,
From vanquish'd foes.—And, see, another race!
A golden aera dazzles my fond sight! 680
That other race, that long'd-for aera, hail!
The British George now reigns, the Patriot King!
Britain shall ever triumph o'er the main.

1764

SAMSON OCCOM
1723–1792

Born in New London, Connecticut, Samson Occom was a Mohegan, a member of the northernmost branch of the Pequot tribe. In 1725, two years after Occom's birth, the Mohegans numbered no more than 351 persons; disease and the stress of the colonists' encroachment had caused the tribe to dwindle. When he was sixteen, Occom writes, Christian evangelical preachers came among the Indians and so impressed him that he eventually was moved to conversion. In 1743 Occom was accepted as a pupil by the Reverend Eleazar Wheelock, known to be particularly interested in training young Indian men to become missionaries to their brethren.

Wheelock was following in the footsteps of other missionaries to the Indians such as John Eliot of the Massachusetts Bay Colony in the mid-seventeenth century, the Mayhews of Martha's Vineyard toward the end of the seventeenth century, James Fitch of Norwich, Connecticut, and John Sergeant (whose successor, and Wheelock's contemporary, was Jonathan Edwards) at Stockbridge, Massachusetts, early in the eighteenth century. Like them, Wheelock was surely sincere in his desire to bring the Indians into the fold of Christianity, and, also like them, he was as surely aware of the advantage to the colonists of having Indian converts. Christian Indians, he wrote, would serve as "a far better defense than all our expensive Fortresses" against those native people still hostile to the settlers. With these ends in mind, Wheelock founded his Moors Indian-Charity School in 1754.

Occom, whose studies with Wheelock predated the formal establishment of the school by more than a decade, left him to become a teacher and missionary: first to the Indians in New London, and then to the Indians of Montauk, Long Island, with whom he remained for eleven years. It was there that he met and married Mary Fowler, a Montauk, with whom he had ten children. It was on Long Island as well that he was ordained a minister by the Presbytery of Suffolk in 1759.

Occom had kept in regular touch with his mentor, and in 1765 he traveled to England along with the Reverend Nathaniel Whitaker to raise funds for Wheelock's Indian school. In England and Scotland, Occom delivered some three hundred sermons and collected nearly twelve thousand pounds. Upon his return from England, Occom found his family sickly and in extreme poverty, despite Wheelock's promise to care for them in his absence. When Wheelock asked him to set out on a mission to the Iroquois, Occom refused. Then, when he learned that Wheelock intended to use the money he had helped raise to move the charity school from Lebanon, Connecticut, to Hanover, New Hampshire, where it was to become Dartmouth College, Occom angrily wrote Wheelock that the new school would soon "be Naturally ashamed to suckle the Tawnees [the Indians] for she is already equal in Power, Honor and Authority to any College in Europe, [sic] I think your College has too much Worked by Grandeur for the Poor Indians, they'll never have much benefit of it." He was right; Dartmouth soon ceased to minister to Indian students, and Occom and Wheelock broke off their long relation.

In dire straits financially, having broken with Wheelock, and feeling the vulnerability of his position as an "Indian preacher" in the church, Occom wrote a ten-page autobiography by way of self-justification. Dated September 17, 1768, the text remained unpublished in the Dartmouth archives until 1982. The autobiography, one of the earliest texts written by a Native American, gives fascinating details of the day-to-day life of a rural minister in the eighteenth century. Occom attends to his garden, his animals, and his parish; he preaches to the Indians and he teaches their children, shrewdly innovating to help those "who were Some what Dull" to learn their letters. Occom, however, is an *Indian* preacher and teacher who does not shrink from wondering whether criticisms leveled against him are simply because, as he writes, "I am a poor Indian."

Occom's unpublished autobiography was read by very few, but he soon was to have a local audience as large as any he had had abroad. In September 1772, he preached a sermon promoting morality and condemning the effects of strong drink before the execution, for the crime of murder, of Moses Paul, a Mohegan and formerly a convert to Christianity. Published the same year as its delivery, Occom's *Sermon at the Execution of Moses Paul* was sufficiently popular to run through some nineteen editions, which extended into the nineteenth century. Occom's only other publication was *A Choice Collection of Hymns and Spiritual Songs, Intended for the Edification of Sincere Christians of All Denominations* (1774).

As the American colonists approached the Revolutionary War with England, it was Occom's sense that neutrality was best for the Indians, and he urged his brethren "not to intermeddle in these Quarrils among the White People." In the years after American independence was achieved, Occom served as minister to the Indians at New Stockbridge; he was a teacher of the Tuscarora in New York State at the time of his death in 1792.

A Short Narrative of My Life[1]

From my Birth till I received the Christian Religion

I was Born a Heathen and Brought up In Heathenism, till I was between 16 & 17 years of age, at a Place Calld Mohegan, in New London, Connecticut, in New England. My Parents Livd a wandering life, for did all the Indians at Mohegan, they Chiefly Depended upon Hunting, Fishing, & Fowling for their Living and had no Connection with the English, excepting to Traffic[2] with them in their small Trifles; and they Strictly maintained and followed their Heathenish Ways, Customs & Religion, though there was Some Preaching among them. Once a Fortnight, in ye[3] Summer Season, a Minister from New London used to come up, and the Indians to attend; not that they regarded the Christian Religion, but they had Blankets given to them every Fall of the Year and for these things they would attend and there was a Sort of School kept, when I was quite young, but I believe there never was one that ever Learnt to read any thing,—and when I was about 10 Years of age there was a man who went about among the Indian Wigwams, and wherever he Could find the Indian Children, would make them read; but the Children Used to take Care to keep out of his way;—and he used to Catch me Some times and make me Say over my Letters; and I believe I learnt Some of them. But this was Soon over too; and all this Time there was not one amongst us, that made a Profession of Christianity—Neither did we Cultivate our Land, nor kept any Sort of Creatures except Dogs, which we used in Hunting; and we Dwelt in wigwams. These are a Sort of Tents, Covered with Matts, made of Flags.[4] And to this Time we were unacquainted with the English Tongue in general though there were a few, who understood a little of it.

From the Time of our Reformation till I left Mr. Wheelocks

When I was 16 years of age, we heard a Strange Rumor among the English, that there were Extraordinary Ministers Preaching from Place to Place and a Strange Concern among the White People. This was in the Spring of the Year. But we Saw nothing of these things, till Some Time in the Summer, when Some Ministers began to visit us and Preach the Word of God; and the Common People all Came frequently and exhorted us to the things of God, which it pleased the Lord, as I humbly hope, to Bless and accompany with Divine Influence to the Conviction and Saving Conversion of a Number of us; amongst whom I was one that was Imprest with the things we had heard. These Preachers did not only come to us, but we frequently went to their meetings and Churches. After I was awakened[5] & converted, I went to all the meetings, I could come at; & Continued under Trouble of Mind about 6 months; at which time I began to Learn the English Letters; got me a Primer, and used to go to my English Neighbours frequently for Assistance

1. The text, an unedited transcription of Occom's autobiography that preserves the original spelling and punctuation, is from *The Elders Wrote: An Anthology of Early Prose by North American Indians, 1768–1931* (1982), edited by Bernd Peyer.

2. To trade.
3. The.
4. The long, sword-shaped leaves of a variety of plants of the flag family.
5. I.e., spiritually awakened to a sense of sin.

in Reading, but went to no School. And when I was 17 years of age, I had, as I trust, a Discovery of the way of Salvation through Jesus Christ, and was enabl'd to put my trust in him alone for Life & Salvation. From this Time the Distress and Burden of my mind was removed, and I found Serenity and Pleasure of Soul, in Serving God. By this time I just began to Read in the New Testament without Spelling,—and I had a Stronger Desire Still to Learn to read the Word of God, and at the Same Time had an uncommon Pity and Compassion to my Poor Brethren According to the Flesh. I used to wish I was capable of Instructing my poor Kindred. I used to think, if I Could once Learn to Read I would Instruct the poor Children in Reading,—and used frequently to talk with our Indians Concerning Religion. This continued till I was in my 19th year: by this Time I Could Read a little in the Bible. At this Time my Poor Mother was going to Lebanon, [Connecticut,] and having had Some Knowledge of Mr. Wheelock and hearing he had a Number of English youth under his Tuition,[6] I had a great Inclination to go to him and be with him a week or a Fortnight, and Desired my Mother to Ask Mr. Wheelock whether he would take me a little while to Instruct me in Reading. Mother did so; and when She Came Back, She Said Mr. Wheelock wanted to See me as Soon as possible. So I went up, thinking I Should be back again in a few Days; when I got up there, he received me With kindness and Compassion and in Stead of Staying a Forthnight or 3 Weeks, I Spent 4 Years with him.—After I had been with him Some Time, he began to acquaint his Friends of my being with him, and of his Intentions of Educating me, and my Circumstances. And the good People began to give Some Assistance to Mr. Wheelock, and gave me Some old and Some New Clothes. Then he represented the Case to the Honorable Commissioners at Boston, who were Commission'd by the Honorable Society in London for Propagating the gospel among the Indians in New England and parts adjacent, and they allowed him 60 £ in old Tender, which was about 6 £ Sterling,[7] and they Continu'd it 2 or 3 years, I can't tell exactly.—While I was at Mr. Wheelock's, I was very weakly and my Health much impaired, and at the End of 4 Years, I over Strained my Eyes to such a Degree, I Could not persue my Studies any Longer; and out of these 4 years I Lost Just about one year;—And was obliged to quit my Studies.

From the Time I left Mr. Wheelock till I went to Europe

As soon as I left Mr. Wheelock, I endeavored to find Some Employ among the Indians; went to Nahantuck, thinking they may want a School Master, but they had one; then went to Narraganset, and they were Indifferent about a School, and went back to Mohegan, and heard a number of our Indians were going to Montauk, on Long Island, and I went with them, and the Indians there were very desirous to have me keep a School amongst them, and I Consented, and went back a while to Mohegan and Some time in November I went on the Island, I think it is 17 years ago last November. I agreed to keep School with them Half a Year, and left it with them to give me what they Pleased; and they took turns to Provide Food for me. I had

6. Tutelage, instruction.
7. About $1,200 in today's currency. Occom throughout the *Narrative* refers regularly to his income and his expenses, giving figures in several different currencies (pounds, shillings, "old Tender," and "York currency") in use in his time.

near 30 Scholars this winter; I had an evening School too for those that could not attend the Day School—and began to Carry on their meetings, they had a Minister, one Mr. Horton, the Scotch Society's Missionary; but he Spent, I think two thirds of his Time at Sheenecock, 30 Miles from Montauk. We met together 3 times for Divine Worship every Sabbath and once on every Wednesday evening. I (used) to read the Scriptures to them and used to expound upon Some particular Passages in my own Tongue. Visited the Sick and attended their Burials.—When the half year expired, they Desired me to Continue with them, which I complied with, for another half year, when I had fulfilled that, they were urgent to have me Stay Longer. So I continued amongst them till I was Married, which was about 2 years after I went there. And Continued to Instruct them in the Same manner as I did before. After I was married a while, I found there was need of a Support more than I needed while I was Single,—and made my Case Known to Mr. Buell[8] and to Mr. Wheelock, and also the Needy Circumstances and the Desires of these Indians of my Continuing amongst them, and the Commissioners were so good as to grant £ 15 a year Sterling—And I kept on in my Service as usual, yea I had additional Service; I kept School as I did before and Carried on the Religious Meetings as often as ever, and attended the Sick and their Funerals, and did what Writings they wanted, and often Sat as a Judge to reconcile and Decide their Matters Between them, and had visitors of Indians from all Quarters; and, as our Custom is, we freely Entertain all Visitors. And was fetched often from my Tribe and from others to see into their Affairs Both Religious, Temporal,—Besides my Domestic Concerns. And it Pleased the Lord to Increase my Family fast—and Soon after I was Married, Mr. Horton left these Indians and the Shenecock & after this I was (alone) and then I had the whole care of these Indians at Montauk, and visited the Shenecock Indians often. Used to set out Saturdays towards Night and come back again Mondays. I have been obliged to Set out from Home after Sun Set, and Ride 30 Miles in the Night, to Preach to these Indians. And Some Indians at Shenecock Sent their Children to my School at Montauk, I kept one of them Some Time, and had a Young Man a half year from Mohegan, a Lad from Nahantuck, who was with me almost a year; and had little or nothing for keeping them.

My Method in the School was, as Soon as the Children got together, and took their proper Seats, I Prayed with them, then began to hear them. I generally began (after some of them Could Spell and Read,) With those that were yet in their Alphabets, So around, as they were properly Seated till I got through and I obliged them to Study their Books, and to help one another. When they could not make out a hard word they Brought it to me— and I usually heard them, in the Summer Season 8 Times a Day 4 in the morning, and in ye after Noon.—In the Winter Season 6 Times a Day, As Soon as they could Spell, they were obliged to Spell when ever they wanted to go out. I concluded with Prayer; I generally heard my Evening Scholars 3 Times Round, And as they go out the School, every one, that Can Spell, is obliged to Spell a Word, and to go out Leisurely one after another. I Cate-

8. The Reverend Samuel Buell (1716–1798) was a Presbyterian minister, ordained, as was Occom, on Long Island. The renowned Jonathan Edwards had preached Buell's ordination sermon, and Buell preached Occom's. Buell later wrote of Occom, "He is the glory of the Indian nation."

chised 3 or 4 Times a Week according to the Assembly's Shout or Catechism, and many Times Proposed Questions of my own, and in my own Tongue. I found Difficulty with Some Children, who were Some what Dull, most of these can soon learn to Say over their Letters, they Distinguish the Sounds by the Ear, but their Eyes can't Distinguish the Letters, and the way I took to cure them was by making an Alphabet on Small bits of paper, and glued them on Small Chips of Cedar after this manner A B & C. I put these on Letters in order on a Bench then point to one Letter and bid a Child to take notice of it, and then I order the Child to fetch me the Letter from the Bench; if he Brings the Letter, it is well, if not he must go again and again till he brings ye right Letter. When they can bring any Letters this way, then I just Jumble them together, and bid them to set them in Alphabetical order, and it is a Pleasure to them; and they soon Learn their Letters this way.—I frequently Discussed or Exhorted my Scholars, in Religious matters.—My Method in our Religious Meetings was this; Sabbath Morning we Assemble together about 10 o'C and begin with Singing; we generally Sung Dr. Watt's Psalms or Hymns. I distinctly read the Psalm or Hymn first, and then gave the meaning of it to them, after that Sing, then Pray, and Sing again after Prayer. Then proceed to Read from Suitable portion of Scripture, and so Just give the plain Sense of it in Familiar Discourse and apply it to them. So continued with Prayer and Singing. In the after Noon and Evening we Proceed in the Same Manner, and so in Wednesday Evening. Some Time after Mr. Horton left these Indians, there was a remarkable revival of religion among these Indians and many were hopefully converted to the Saving knowledge of God in Jesus. It is to be observed before Mr. Horton left these Indians they had Some Prejudices infused in their minds, by Some Enthusiastical Exhorters from New England, against Mr. Horton, and many of them had left him; by this means he was Discouraged, and was disposed from these Indians. And being acquainted with the Enthusiasts in New England & the make and the Disposition of the Indians I took a mild way to reclaim them. I opposed them not openly but let them go on in their way, and whenever I had an opportunity, I would read Such pages of the Scriptures, and I thought would confound their Notions, and I would come to them with all Authority, Saying "these Saith the Lord"; and by this means, the Lord was pleased to Bless my poor Endeavours, and they were reclaimed, and Brought to hear almost any of the ministers.——I am now to give an Account of my Circumstances and manner of Living. I Dwelt in a Wigwam, a Small Hut with Small Poles and Covered with Matts made of Flags, and I was obligd to remove twice a Year, about 2 miles Distance, by reason of the Scarcity of wood, for in one Neck of Land they Planted their Corn, and in another, they had their wood, and I was obligd to have my Corn carted and my Hay also,—and I got my Ground Plow'd every year, which Cost me about 12 shillings an acre; and I kept a Cow and a Horse, for which I paid 21 shillings every year York currency,[9] and went 18 miles to Mill for every Dust of meal we used in my family. I Hired or Joined with my Neighbours to go to Mill, with a Horse or ox Cart, or on Horse Back, and Some time went myself. My Family Increasing fast, and my Visitors also. I was obligd to contrive every way to Support my Family; I took all opportunities, to get

9. Just less than $50 in today's currency.

Some thing to feed my Family Daily. I Planted my own Corn, Potatoes, and Beans; I used to be out hoeing my Corn Some times before Sun Rise and after my School is Dismist, and by this means I was able to raise my own Pork, for I was allowed to keep 5 Swine. Some mornings & Evenings I would be out with my Hook and Line to Catch fish and in the Fall of Year and in the Spring, I used my gun, and fed my Family with Fowls. I Could more than pay for my Powder & Shot with Feathers.[1] At other Times I Bound old Books for Easthampton People, made wooden Spoons and Ladles, Stocked Guns, & worked on Cedar to make Pails, (Piggins),[2] and Churns & C. Besides all these Difficulties I met with advers Providence, I bought a Mare, had it but a little while, and she fell into the Quick Sand and Died. After a while Bought another, I kept her about half year, and she was gone, and I never have heard of nor seen her from that Day to this; it was Supposed Some Rogue Stole her. I got another and Died with a Distemper, and last of all I Bought a Young Mare, and kept her till She had one Colt, and She broke her Leg and Died, and Presently after the Cold[3] Died also. In the whole I Lost 5 Horse Kind; all these Losses helped to pull me down; and by this Time I got greatly in Debt and acquainted my Circumstances to Some of my Friends, and they Represented my Case to the Commissioners of Boston, and Interceded with them for me, and they were pleased to vote 15 £ for my Help, and Soon after Sent a Letter to my good Friend at New London, acquainting him that they had Superseded[4] their Vote; and my Friends were so good as to represent my Needy Circumstances Still to them, and they were so good at Last, as to Vote £ 15 and Sent it, for which I am very thankful; and the Revd Mr. Buell was so kind as to write in my behalf to the gentlemen of Boston; and he told me they were much Displeased with him, and heard also once again that they blamed me for being Extravagant; I Can't Conceive how these gentlemen would have me Live. I am ready to (forgive) their Ignorance, and I would wish they had Changed Circumstances with me but one month, that they may know, by experience what my Case really was; but I am now fully convinced, that it was not Ignorance, For I believe it can be proved to the world that these Same Gentlemen gave a young Missionary a Single man, *one Hundred Pounds* for one year, and fifty Pounds for an Interpreter, and thirty Pounds for an Introducer; so it Cost them one Hundred & Eighty Pounds in one Single Year, and they Sent too where there was no Need of a Missionary.

Now you See what difference they made between me and other missionaries; they gave me 180 Pounds for 12 years Service, which they gave for one years Services in another Mission.—In my Service (I speak like a fool, but I am Constrained) I was my own Interpreter. I was both a School master and Minister to the Indians, yea I was their Ear, Eye & Hand, as Well as Mouth. I leave it with the World, as wicked as it is, to Judge whether I ought not to have had half as much, they gave a young man Just mentioned which would have been but £ 50 a year; and if they ought to have given me that, I am not under obligations to them, I owe them nothing at all; what can be

---

1. Either he could trade feathers (used to stuff pillows, mattresses, etc.) for his powder and shot or he could earn enough by selling feathers to pay for them.

2. Small pails.
3. I.e., the colt.
4. Annulled.

the Reason that they used me after this manner? I can't think of any thing, but this as a Poor Indian Boy Said, Who was Bound out to an English Family, and he used to Drive Plow for a young man, and he whipt and Beat him allmost every Day, and the young man found fault with him, and Complained of him to his master and the poor Boy was Called to answer for himself before his master, and he was asked, what it was he did, that he was So Complained of and beat almost every Day. He Said, he did not know, but he Supposed it was because he could not drive any better; but says he, I Drive as well as I know how; and at other Times he Beats me, because he is of a mind to beat me; but says he believes he Beats me for the most of the Time "because I am an Indian."

So I am *ready* to Say, they have used me thus, because I Can't Influence the Indians so well as other missionaries; but I can assure them I have endeavoured to teach them as well as I know how;—but I *must Say*, "I believe it is because I am a poor Indian." I Can't help that God has made me So; I did not make my self so.—

1768   1982

MOSES BON SÀAM
fl. 1735

Always the region from which colonists took the greatest wealth for the home country, the Caribbean oddly has remained understudied as an incubator of early American literature. Although the identity of the writer of "The Speech of Moses Bon Sàam" is uncertain, the text stands as one of the earliest representations of the African presence in British America, declaring the centrality of the British West Indies to England's overarching plans for colonization and exploitation of the New World. Preceded only by the anonymous "Speech Made by a Black of Guardaloupe" (1709), "The Speech of Moses Bon Sàam" signals both the range of England's interests in the New World and the manner in which it charted its course of empire, on the backs of African slaves, in this case, in Jamaica.

"The Speech of Moses Bon Sàam" first appeared in the London periodical the *Prompter* on January 10, 1735, and soon thereafter was picked up by other journals, suggesting the English reading public's deep interest in Caribbean affairs. Its sharp indictment of the use of enslaved Africans on English sugar plantations quickly engendered several responses defending slavery as central to England's transatlantic empire. Most notable of these was "The Speech of Campo-bello" (1736), purportedly written by a freed slave but actually penned by Robert Roberts, an unabashed apologist for the peculiar institution. Clearly, investors in and supporters of England's colonial ventures already knew that they sat on a tinderbox and saw in the speech a dangerous spark requiring rapid dousing.

Purportedly "The Speech of Moses Bon Sàam" was sent to the *Prompter* by an English merchant who had it from a letter of a white inhabitant of Jamaica, who himself had heard the old slave utter the words. But some of the responses suggest that Londoners regarded the speech as the mere fabrication of an antislavery zealot. If indeed written by a slave, it represents a remarkable example of the attitudes of the

Maroons, Africans who had escaped to the hinterlands of islands like Jamaica and Barbados and established the culture that subsequently formed so large a part of Caribbean identity.

One argument for the authenticity of "The Speech of Moses Bon Sàam" resides in the author's deep knowledge of Maroon life. But equally of interest are his claim that what sets apart the two races on Jamaica is not so much skin color as education and his use of biblical parallels to explain the plight of the enslaved Africans. Further, his calls for moderation and patience among his followers, rather than for the immediate action against the lowland plantation owners clearly urged by some, marks him as an astute strategist of the Maroon's situation. Thus he believed that only when his group was unified in purpose and numerically superior to their oppressors should they make their move against them. The first in a line of black leaders perhaps best typified by Nat Turner, who read in the Bible a prophecy of their eventual deliverance, Moses Bon Saàm, or those whose leadership he was meant to represent, found in the white slaveholders' Christianity a tool against their oppressors.

The Speech of Moses Bon Sàam[1]

A Free Negro, to the revolted Slaves in one of the most considerable Colonies of the West Indies *At the Head of those Revolted Slaves, who have betaken themselves to the Mountains, in one of the most considerable Colonies in the* West-Indies. *Taken from the* London Magazine *for the Month of* January, 1735, *p. 13.*

Dear Fellows in Arms, and Brothers in Adversity!

HAD your *Sufferings* been less painful, I might have enjoyed my own *Ease*, in an Exemption from Danger. But in vain did my Courage once exerted, as you have heard, in Defence of a *Master*, redeem me from the *Name* of a *Slave!* I found no Blessing in Freedom; tormented with a livelier Sense of your Groans, because no longer a *Partaker* of your Misery.

While I was, formerly, one of your Number, and but a Wretch, among Wretches, I wanted *Sentiments* to reflect, with *Justness*, on the Wrongs we are accustom'd to suffer. Whether ignorant of the *Bliss* of others, I *discern* not my own *Misery*: Or, that the Part I was condemn'd to bear, in so general a Calamity, had deaden'd in my Heart that *Pity*, which has been *awaken'd* by my Change of Fortune. But, I have *since* been *taught* your Wretchedness, by sixteen Years of Liberty; not spent in *Ease* and *Luxury*, like the Lives of your Oppressors; but in long, laborious Diligence in Pursuit of their *Arts*, and *Capacity*; whereby to know, and make known, that only Education, and Accident, *not* Difference of *Genius*, have been the Cause of this provoking *Superiority*, that bids the Pride of a *white* Man despise and trample on a *black* one.

What Preference, in the Name of that *mysterious God*, whom these Insulters of our *Colour* pretend to worship; what wild imaginary Superiority of Dignity has their pale sickly *Whiteness* to boast of, when compar'd with our *Majestick Glossiness!* If there is Merit in *Delicacy*, we have *Skins* as soft as their *Velvets*: If in *Manliness*, Consider your *Shape*, your *Strength*, and your *Movement!* Are they not all easier, firmer, and more graceful? Let a *white*

1. The text used here is from *Caribbeana: An Anthology of English Literature from the West Indies, 1657–1777*, edited by Thomas Krise, and is based on a version of this text reprinted from the *London Magazine* as an appendix to Robert Roberts's "The Speech of Campo-bello."

Man expose his feeble Face to the *Winds*; let him climb Hills *against Rains*: Let him go burn his uncover'd Temples in the Heat of High-Noon, as *we* do. Will he *bear* it too, as *we* do? No: The Variations of his changeable *Countenance* will make manifest the *Faintness* he was born to. He will be *sick*, and grow *pale*, and *red*, by Turns: He will be *haggard, rough,* and *Sun-burnt*. Tho' terrible and haughty to his Slaves, he will *lose* all Fierceness in his Eye, by the smallest Struggle with those *Elements*, which *we* are *Proof* against the *Rage* of.

The whole *Advantage*, then, of these proud *Spoilers* of the *Works of God*, who dare make *Beasts* of human Forms, as noble and more manly than their own, in *what* consists it, but superior *Happiness?* They are not wiser by *Nature*, but more exercis'd in *Art*, than *we* are. They are not *braver*, but more *crafty*, and assist their Anger by *Discipline*. They have *Rules* and *Modes* in War; which actuate, as by one *Soul*, the most numerous *Bodies* of arm'd People. While *we*, depriv'd of such *Improvement*, and acting resolutely, but not dependently, *divide* and *lose* our Firmness. You saw the Representation of it, but last Week, in an Example, from this neighbouring *River*. As if the *God*, that animates your Purpose, had *commanded* it to *overflow*, for your Instruction and Warning! Observe, how narrow it looks at present: Yet, because it runs confin'd, *within* its *Banks*, hark! How *roaringly* it rushes down upon the Low-Lands of our Enemy! And with how steady and resistless a Torrent! The other Day, you saw it *broader*: For it rose among the Woods, and almost floated our *Savannah*. But, was it the *louder*, for such *Breadth*? Was it, then, *thus foaming* and *terrible*? Far from it; you can all remember, as I do, that it was then *flat, tame,* and *muddy*; and had neither *Violence* nor *Tendency*.

As soon as I became able to *read*, I discover'd, in the *holiest* of all Books, in the *Fountain* of white Men's Religion; I discover'd there, with a Mixture of Amazement and *prophetic* Joy, that the very Man, from whom they had deriv'd the *Name* they had given me, of *Moses*, had been the happy *Deliverer* of a *Nation!* Of a Nation *chosen* and *belov'd* by *God!* the Deliverer of this chosen Nation, from just such a *Slavery as ours!* Just so unfair, oppressive, and unnatural; and, in every Act and Circumstance, resembling that, which you and your Forefathers have *groan'd* under! Innumerable Thousands of his captive Countrymen were as darkly ignorant as *you* are: All unknowing their own Rights; and forc'd, like you, to *labour* for ungrateful, and merciless *Masters*: Till this first *Moses*, this great Giver of *my* Name, was called out by *Heaven*; and thro' a Course of miraculous Events, instructed in the *Arts* and *Learning* of those insolent *Enslavers*: That so he might be worthy, in the Fullness of *God's Time*, to stand out, *his Instrument*, for the Redemption of a *People*.

What now will our Task-masters pretend to object against the *Lawfulness* of our Revolt? If they say our *Forefathers were Slaves*: So were the Ancestors of those Heroes, whom *their Moses*, their almost worship'd *Moses*, deliver'd from Slavery. Will they urge, *that they have paid a Price; and, therefore, claim us as their Property?* Grant them the *Life* of a *first* unhappy Captive, to repay this Claim of his proud Purchaser. But did they also *buy* his *Race*? Must the *Children's Children* of this *Wretch's Children* be *begotten*, and *transmitted* to *Slavery*, because that single Wretch himself was unsuccessful in a Battle, and had been put to *Sale* instead of *Slaughter*?

Perish the provoking Image of so *shameless* a Pretension! Let them recollect, how soon the *Profits*, which they too well knew to *make*, from any one of our poor Father's *Toils*, repaid them for his barbarous Purchase. Let them *tell us*, (if they dare see *Truth*, in any Light that shews them not their *Interest*) whether all the *Pomp*, the *Pride*, the *Wantonness*, of that Prosperity we see them live in, is not the *Purchase of our* Sweat, *our* Tears, and *our* Distresses? And shall they derive their very *Luxury* from Wretches, to whom they grudge the *Bread* of Nourishment? Shall they *rejoice*, but by *our Affliction*, yet deny their *Pity* to our Agonies?

Indulge me, dear Friends! Your Permission, to *stop here* and *weep*. I know it is a *Weakness*: And it shall posses me but a Moment. I will recover my Voice as soon as I am *able*; and go on to *enumerate* your *Miseries*!

Alas! It is not *possible*! It is *too terrible* a Task! I have neither Patience nor Breath enough to *find Names* for your *Sorrows*! Wou'd to Heaven I cou'd as easily banish them from my Memory, as I can forbear to disgrace you by their Description! But *Fancy* will not suffer me to *forget* them. Imagination, officious to *torment* me, invades my *Sleep* with your *Shriekings*. My very Dreams are made *bloody* by your *Whips*. I am insulted by the *Scoffs*, the *Cruelties*, the grinding, biting, *Insolence*, which we train up our poor Children to the Taste of! Why rejoic'd we at their Birth, unhappy, innocent, *Bleeders*? Or, why do they *smile* in our *Faces*, since we intend them but for *Anguish* and *Agony*? Yet, they *know* we have *no Comfort* to *give* them. *Such as is ours*, they *inherit*! *Happier* Parents bequeath *Money*, and *Vanity*, and *Indolence*, to their Offspring. Alas! *these* are *Legacies*, for *Freemen*! *We* have nothing but our *Shame* to bestow on our Posterity: Nothing, but the *Shame* of our *Baseness*, who have lengthen'd out our *Slavery* to *out-last* even *Life*, by assigning them our Children, on whom to practice our *Tortures*. But I have *done* with the *Horrors* of *this Subject*: You have awaken'd me, by that lamentable *Howl*, into a *Repentance* that I touch'd you *too sensibly*. Let us think then no more upon what we *have suffer'd*. Let us resolve to *suffer no longer*.

In the *Fastnesses* of these *inaccessible Mountains*, and among Forests, so dark and impenetrable, we shall have *little* to *fear*, if we but continue on the *Defensive*. Here are *Savannahs* for Cattle; and *burnt Woods* for Corn: and as other things, which we *have not*, will be wanted, there are so many Outlets and Descents, on every Side, for *Excursion*, that we can break down, unexpected, upon the scatter'd Plantations below us; and return with whatever we *wish*, from the *Store-houses* of our *Enemy*. Let us therefore repress *Malice* and *Cruelty*: Let us rather study to support our *new Liberty*, than *revenge* our *past Slavery*. While we *train* and *confirm* our Forces, by the Discipline and Exercise they are beginning to practice, we shall grow stronger, both by our *Skill*, and our *Numbers*: For all of our Colour, whose Hearts have not *whiten'd* themselves, in Terror of their imperious Torturers, will borrow Safety from the *Night*, and escape to us from every Quarter. Or, should such Opportunities be taken from them, by the Vigilance of their Masters, we can encourage, and draw them with us, as often as we make *Incursions*, thereby weakening at once our Enemy, and encreasing our own *Strength*, till our very *Numbers* shall have made us *invincible*.

I know there are some rash Spirits among us, who affirm that much *more* is *possible*: Perhaps it may be so, to our *Courage*; but it ought to be unattempted by our *Prudence*. For, even cou'd we extirpate our Enemies, and drive them out of the Island, it wou'd be found an unsurmountable Difficulty, *without Ships*, and unskill'd in *Navigation*, to maintain our Possession of the cultivated and *open* Coasts, against perpetual fresh Supplies, which wou'd be pour'd in, by their Fleets, for Recovery of *rich* Townships, and Settlements. Whereas, *here*, we shall have only their *Pride* to contend with: Their *Avarice* will not envy us our *Mountains*, where, yet, we have every *Art*, within ourselves, that can be necessary for our Support and Security. They *taught* us these *Arts*, for our *Misery*: But *God*, more just, and more merciful, has *turn'd* them to our *Benefit*.

I have shewn *Sulphur* and *Saltpetre* to your Captains, in several Places, upon our Hills. You have Hand-mills in every Company, for preparing your *Gun-powder*, that most precious of all your Possessions. You might every where find *Iron*; but that it abounds in your *Enemies Warehouses*. Having *Artists* too, who are *capable*, we might *forge* our own *Arms*, if so much trouble were necessary: But there is a *nearer* Way to obtain 'em. It is but to prevent the *Return* of those who shall *dare* to *invade* us, and the *Arms*, which *they* bring for our *Ruin*, will enlarge and perpetuate our *Protection*.

Let us understand then, and accept *God's Bounty*. Let us *divide*, and *appropriate*, the Highlands. Let us *plant*, and *possess*, for Posterity. Cultivating *Law*, too, as well as *Land*, let us, by submitting to *Government*, become too *generous* for *Slavery*. As often as the Enemy, from the *Coasts* of the Island, shall attempt to dislodge us from its *Centre*, let 'em find us too *strong* for their *Anger*. But if they content themselves with *their own*, and leave us in *Possession* of our *Lot*, let them acknowledge us *too kind* for their *Cruelty*. They must always *want* the *Cattle*, which we can never be depriv'd of, but in *Traffick*: And we may receive, in *Exchange*, a thousand Things, for our *Ease*; which it will be more for their Benefit to *sell* us, than provoke us to *conquer*.

Be of *Comfort* therefore, my Friends! and *hope all things from Patience*. Even *Time* that runs on encreasing, till it shall be *lost* in *Eternity*, forms its *Progress* but *slowly*. Tho' *Ages* appear *vast Spaces*, they have all been measur'd by *Moments*. Be not, therefore, *too hasty*. Content yourselves to be thought *weak*, for a *while*, till you have secur'd and deepen'd your *Foundation*. The Building will rise, *stronger*, more *broad*, and more *beautiful*. You have all heard talk of the *Dutch*; those Rivals in Riches and Power, to the most considerable Princes of the Earth! What were *these*, about a hundred Years past, but a Kind of *white Slaves*, to a Monarch, who *now* calls them his *Brothers*? Keep this inspiring *Example* in your *Eye*; and assure yourselves, that the proudest of your Enemies will *embrace* you, in spite of your *Colour*, when they foresee *Destruction* in your *Anger*; but *Ease* and *Security*, in your *Friendship*.

1735

J. HECTOR ST. JOHN DE CRÈVECOEUR
1735–1813

Crèvecoeur was a man with a mysterious past, and a number of details of his life have puzzled his biographers. He was born Michel-Guillaume Jean de Crèvecoeur in Caen, Normandy, in 1735. When he was nineteen, he sailed to England, where he lived with distant relatives. He planned to marry, but his fiancée died before the ceremony could take place, and in 1755 he went to Canada; he enlisted in the Canadian militia, served the government as a surveyor and cartographer, and was wounded in the defense of Quebec. His military career came to an end in 1759, at which time he traveled to New York and changed his name to Hector St. John, later expanding his surname to St. John de Crèvecoeur and adding an initial. For the next ten years Crèvecoeur traveled extensively in the colonies as a surveyor and trader with American Indians. In 1769 he bought land in Orange County, New York, and, newly married, settled into the life of an American farmer.

Given Crèvecoeur's restlessness, it is hard to know whether he would have been happy forever at Pine Hill, but the advent of the American Revolution and his Tory sympathies were enough to determine his return to France. He claimed that he wished to reestablish ownership of family lands, and it is ironic, given his political sympathies, that he was arrested and imprisoned as a rebel spy when he tried to sail from the port of New York. Not until 1780 did Crèvecoeur succeed in reaching London. He remained in France until 1783, when he returned as French consul to New York, Connecticut, and New Jersey, only to learn that his farm had been burned in an Indian attack, his wife was dead, and his children were housed with strangers.

Crèvecoeur was a great success as a diplomat—he was made an honorary citizen of a number of American cities, and the town of St. Johnsbury, Vermont, was named in his honor—but he did not remain long in America. He returned to France in 1785 and after 1790 remained there permanently, first living in Paris and retiring, after 1793, to Normandy. He died at his daughter's home outside Paris.

The first year that Crèvecoeur spent at Pine Hill he began to write a series of essays about America based on his travels and experience as a farmer. In some he assumed the persona of "Farmer James," which lends an air of fiction to what otherwise appear straightforward letters. He brought them to London in 1780 and, suppressing those essays most unsympathetic to the American cause, sold them to the bookseller Thomas Davies. *Letters from an American Farmer* appeared in 1782 and was an immediate success. Crèvecoeur found himself a popular hero when the expanded French edition (1784) appeared. Its publication followed close enough on the American Revolution to satisfy an almost insatiable demand for things American and confirmed, for most readers, a vision of a new land, rich and promising, where industry prevailed over class and fashion. George Washington said the book was "too flattering" to be true, but careful readers of the twelve letters will note an ambiguous attitude throughout: Crèvecoeur's hymn to the land does not make him blind to the ignorant frontier settlers or the calculating slaveholder. His final letter, "Distresses of a Frontiersman," affirms the possibility of a harmonious relationship with nature, but he writes from an American Indian village and with no successful historical models in mind.

From Letters from an American Farmer[1]

From *Letter III. What Is an American*

I wish I could be acquainted with the feelings and thoughts which must agitate the heart and present themselves to the mind of an enlightened Eng-

1. From *Letters from an American Farmer,* edited by Albert Boni and Charles Boni (1925).

lishman, when he first lands on this continent. He must greatly rejoice that he lived at a time to see this fair country discovered and settled; he must necessarily feel a share of national pride, when he views the chain of settlements which embellishes these extended shores. When he says to himself, this is the work of my countrymen, who, when convulsed by factions,[2] afflicted by a variety of miseries and wants, restless and impatient, took refuge here. They brought along with them their national genius,[3] to which they principally owe what liberty they enjoy, and what substance they possess. Here he sees the industry of his native country displayed in a new manner, and traces in their works the embryos of all the arts, sciences, and ingenuity which flourish in Europe. Here he beholds fair cities, substantial villages, extensive fields, an immense country filled with decent houses, good roads, orchards, meadows, and bridges, where an hundred years ago all was wild, woody, and uncultivated! What a train of pleasing ideas this fair spectacle must suggest; it is a prospect which must inspire a good citizen with the most heartfelt pleasure. The difficulty consists in the manner of viewing so extensive a scene. He is arrived on a new continent; a modern society offers itself to his contemplation, different from what he had hitherto seen. It is not composed, as in Europe, of great lords who possess everything, and of a herd of people who have nothing. Here are no aristocratical families, no courts, no kings, no bishops, no ecclesiastical dominion, no invisible power giving to a few a very visible one; no great manufacturers employing thousands, no great refinements of luxury. The rich and the poor are not so far removed from each other as they are in Europe. Some few towns excepted, we are all tillers of the earth, from Nova Scotia to West Florida. We are a people of cultivators, scattered over an immense territory, communicating with each other by means of good roads and navigable rivers, united by the silken bands of mild government, all respecting the laws, without dreading their power, because they are equitable. We are all animated with the spirit of an industry which is unfettered and unrestrained, because each person works for himself. If he travels through our rural districts he views not the hostile castle, and the haughty mansion, contrasted with the clay-built hut and miserable cabin, where cattle and men help to keep each other warm, and dwell in meanness, smoke, and indigence. A pleasing uniformity of decent competence appears throughout our habitations. The meanest of our log-houses is a dry and comfortable habitation. Lawyer or merchant are the fairest titles our towns afford; that of a farmer is the only appellation of the rural inhabitants of our country. It must take some time ere he can reconcile himself to our dictionary, which is but short in words of dignity, and names of honor. There, on a Sunday, he sees a congregation of respectable farmers and their wives, all clad in neat homespun, well mounted, or riding in their own humble wagons. There is not among them an esquire, saving the unlettered magistrate. There he sees a parson as simple as his flock, a farmer who does not riot[4] on the labor of others. We have no princes, for whom we toil, starve, and bleed; we are the most perfect society now existing in the world. Here man is free as he ought to be; nor is this pleasing equality so transitory as many others are. Many ages will not see the shores of our great lakes replen-

2. Disputes.
3. Spirit; distinctive national character.

4. I.e., indulge himself.

ished with inland nations, nor the unknown bounds of North America entirely peopled. Who can tell how far it extends? Who can tell the millions of men whom it will feed and contain? for no European foot has as yet traveled half the extent of this mighty continent!

The next wish of this traveler will be to know whence came all these people? They are a mixture of English, Scotch, Irish, French, Dutch, Germans and Swedes. From this promiscuous breed, that race now called Americans have arisen. The eastern provinces[5] must indeed be excepted, as being the unmixed descendants of Englishmen. I have heard many wish that they had been more intermixed also: for my part, I am no wisher, and think it much better as it has happened. They exhibit a most conspicuous figure in this great and variegated picture; they too enter for a great share in the pleasing perspective displayed in these thirteen provinces. I know it is fashionable to reflect[6] on them, but respect them for what they have done; for the accuracy and wisdom with which they have settled their territory; for the decency of their manners; for their early love of letters; their ancient college,[7] the first in this hemisphere; for their industry, which to me who am but a farmer is the criterion of everything. There never was a people, situated as they are, who with so ungrateful a soil have done more in so short a time. Do you think that the monarchical ingredients which are more prevalent in other governments have purged them from all foul stains? Their histories assert the contrary.

In this great American asylum, the poor of Europe have by some means met together, and in consequence of various causes; to what purpose should they ask one another what countrymen they are? Alas, two thirds of them had no country. Can a wretch who wanders about, who works and starves, whose life is a continual scene of sore affliction or pinching penury, can that man call England or any other kingdom his country? A country that had no bread for him, whose fields procured him no harvest, who met with nothing but the frowns of the rich, the severity of the laws, with jails and punishments; who owned not a single foot of the extensive surface of this planet? No! Urged by a variety of motives, here they came. Everything has tended to regenerate them; new laws, a new mode of living, a new social system; here they are become men: in Europe they were as so many useless plants, wanting vegetative mold and refreshing showers; they withered, and were mowed down by want, hunger, and war; but now by the power of transplantation, like all other plants they have taken root and flourished! Formerly they were not numbered in any civil lists[8] of their country, except in those of the poor; here they rank as citizens. By what invisible power has this surprising metamorphosis been performed? By that of the laws and that of their industry. The laws, the indulgent laws, protect them as they arrive, stamping on them the symbol of adoption; they receive ample rewards for their labors; these accumulated rewards procure them lands; those lands confer on them the title of freemen, and to that title every benefit is affixed which men can possibly require. This is the great operation daily performed by our laws. From whence proceed these laws? From our government. Whence the government? It is derived from the original genius and strong desire of the people

5. New England.
6. Censure or blame.
7. Harvard College was founded in 1636.

8. Recognized employees of the civil government: ambassadors, judges, secretaries, etc.

ratified and confirmed by the crown. This is the great chain which links us all, this is the picture which every province exhibits, Nova Scotia excepted. There the crown has done all;[9] either there were no people who had genius, or it was not much attended to: the consequence is that the province is very thinly inhabited indeed; the power of the crown in conjunction with the mosquitoes has prevented men from settling there. Yet some parts of it flourished once, and it contained a mild, harmless set of people. But for the fault of a few leaders, the whole were banished. The greatest political error the crown ever committed in America was to cut off men from a country which wanted nothing but men!

What attachment can a poor European emigrant have for a country where he had nothing? The knowledge of the language, the love of a few kindred as poor as himself, were the only cords that tied him: his country is now that which gives him land, bread, protection, and consequence: *Ubi panis ibi patria*[1] is the motto of all emigrants. What then is the American, this new man? He is either a European, or the descendant of a European, hence that strange mixture of blood, which you will find in no other country. I could point out to you a family whose grandfather was an Englishman, whose wife was Dutch, whose son married a French woman, and whose present four sons have now four wives of different nations. *He* is an American, who, leaving behind him all his ancient prejudices and manners, receives new ones from the new mode of life he has embraced, the new government he obeys, and the new rank he holds. He becomes an American by being received in the broad lap of our great *Alma Mater*.[2] Here individuals of all nations are melted into a new race of men, whose labors and posterity will one day cause great changes in the world. Americans are the western pilgrims, who are carrying along with them that great mass of arts, sciences, vigor, and industry which began long since in the east; they will finish the great circle. The Americans were once scattered all over Europe; here they are incorporated into one of the finest systems of population which has ever appeared, and which will hereafter become distinct by the power of the different climates they inhabit. The American ought therefore to love this country much better than that wherein either he or his forefathers were born. Here the rewards of his industry follow with equal steps the progress of his labor; his labor is founded on the basis of nature, *self-interest;* can it want a stronger allurement? Wives and children, who before in vain demanded of him a morsel of bread, now, fat and frolicsome, gladly help their father to clear those fields whence exuberant crops are to arise to feed and to clothe them all; without any part being claimed, either by a despotic prince, a rich abbot, or a mighty lord. Here religion demands but little of him; a small voluntary salary to the minister, and gratitude to God; can he refuse these? The American is a new man, who acts upon new principles; he must therefore entertain new ideas, and form new opinions. From involuntary idleness, servile dependence, penury, and useless labor, he has passed to toils of a very different nature, rewarded by ample subsistence.—This is an American.

British America is divided into many provinces, forming a large association, scattered along a coast 1,500 miles extent and about 200 wide. This

9. In 1755 the French Acadians were banished from Nova Scotia by the British, who had taken it in 1710.

1. Where there is bread, there is one's fatherland (Latin).
2. Dear mother (Latin, literal trans.).

society I would fain examine, at least such as it appears in the middle provinces; if it does not afford that variety of tinges and gradations which may be observed in Europe, we have colors peculiar to ourselves. For instance, it is natural to conceive that those who live near the sea must be very different from those who live in the woods; the intermediate space will afford a separate and distinct class.

Men are like plants; the goodness and flavor of the fruit proceeds from the peculiar soil and exposition in which they grow. We are nothing but what we derive from the air we breathe, the climate we inhabit, the government we obey, the system of religion we profess, and the nature of our employment. Here you will find but few crimes; these have acquired as yet no root among us. I wish I was able to trace all my ideas; if my ignorance prevents me from describing them properly, I hope I shall be able to delineate a few of the outlines, which are all I propose.

Those who live near the sea feed more on fish than on flesh, and often encounter that boisterous element. This renders them more bold and enterprising; this leads them to neglect the confined occupations of the land. They see and converse with a variety of people, their intercourse with mankind becomes extensive. The sea inspires them with a love of traffic, a desire of transporting produce from one place to another; and leads them to a variety of resources which supply the place of labor. Those who inhabit the middle settlements, by far the most numerous, must be very different; the simple cultivation of the earth purifies them, but the indulgences of the government, the soft remonstrances of religion, the rank of independent freeholders, must necessarily inspire them with sentiments, very little known in Europe among people of the same class. What do I say? Europe has no such class of men; the early knowledge they acquire, the early bargains they make, give them a great degree of sagacity. As freemen they will be litigious; pride and obstinancy are often the cause of lawsuits; the nature of our laws and governments may be another. As citizens it is easy to imagine that they will carefully read the newspapers, enter into every political disquisition, freely blame or censure governors and others. As farmers they will be careful and anxious to get as much as they can, because what they get is their own. As northern men they will love the cheerful cup. As Christians, religion curbs them not in their opinions; the general indulgence leaves everyone to think for themselves in spiritual matters; the laws inspect our actions, our thoughts are left to God. Industry, good living, selfishness, litigiousness, country politics, the pride of freemen, religious indifference are their characteristics. If you recede still farther from the sea, you will come into more modern settlements; they exhibit the same strong lineaments, in a ruder appearance. Religion seems to have still less influence, and their manners are less improved.

Now we arrive near the great woods, near the last inhabited districts;[3] there men seem to be placed still farther beyond the reach of government, which in some measure leaves them to themselves. How can it pervade every corner; as they were driven there by misfortunes, necessity of beginnings, desire of acquiring large tracts of land, idleness, frequent want of economy,[4] ancient debts; the reunion of such people does not afford a very pleasing spectacle.

---

3. I.e., the frontier; the land west of the original colonies and east of the Mississippi.

4. I.e., they were improvident and spent beyond their means.

When discord, want of unity and friendship; when either drunkenness or idleness prevail in such remote districts; contention, inactivity, and wretchedness must ensue. There are not the same remedies to these evils as in a long-established community. The few magistrates they have are in general little better than the rest; they are often in a perfect state of war; that of man against man, sometimes decided by blows, sometimes by means of the law; that of man against every wild inhabitant of these venerable woods, of which they are come to dispossess them. There men appear to be no better than carnivorous animals of a superior rank, living on the flesh of wild animals when they can catch them, and when they are not able, they subsist on grain. He who would wish to see America in its proper light, and have a true idea of its feeble beginnings and barbarous rudiments, must visit our extended line of frontiers where the last settlers dwell, and where he may see the first labors of settlement, the mode of clearing the earth, in all their different appearances; where men are wholly left dependent on their native tempers and on the spur of uncertain industry, which often fails when not sanctified by the efficacy of a few moral rules. There, remote from the power of example and check of shame, many families exhibit the most hideous parts of our society. They are a kind of forlorn hope, preceding by ten or twelve years the most respectable army of veterans which come after them. In that space, prosperity will polish some, vice and the law will drive off the rest, who uniting again with others like themselves will recede still farther; making room for more industrious people, who will finish their improvements, convert the loghouse into a convenient habitation, and rejoicing that the first heavy labors are finished, will change in a few years that hitherto barbarous country into a fine fertile, well-regulated district. Such is our progress, such is the march of the Europeans toward the interior parts of this continent. In all societies these are offcasts; this impure part serves as our precursors or pioneers; my father himself was one of that class,[5] but he came upon honest principles, and was therefore one of the few who held fast; by good conduct and temperance, he transmitted to me his fair inheritance, when not above one in fourteen of his contemporaries had the same good fortune.

Forty years ago his smiling country was thus inhabited; it is now purged, a general decency of manners prevails throughout, and such has been the fate of our best countries.

Exclusive of those general characteristics, each province has its own, founded on the government, climate, mode of husbandry, customs, and peculiarity of circumstances. Europeans submit insensibly to these great powers, and become, in the course of a few generations, not only Americans in general, but either Pennsylvanians, Virginians, or provincials under some other name. Whoever traverses the continent must easily observe those strong differences, which will grow more evident in time. The inhabitants of Canada, Massachusetts, the middle provinces, the southern ones will be as different as their climates; their only points of unit will be those of religion and language.

As I have endeavored to show you how Europeans become Americans, it may not be disagreeable to show you likewise how the various Christian sects introduced wear out, and how religious indifference becomes prevalent.

5. His father never came to America.

When any considerable number of a particular sect happen to dwell contiguous to each other, they immediately erect a temple, and there worship the Divinity agreeably to their own peculiar ideas. Nobody disturbs them. If any new sect springs up in Europe it may happen that many of its professors[6] will come and settle in America. As they bring their zeal with them, they are at liberty to make proselytes if they can, and to build a meeting and to follow the dictates of their consciences; for neither the government nor any other power interferes. If they are peaceable subjects, and are industrious, what is it to their neighbors how and in what manner they think fit to address their prayers to the Supreme Being? But if the sectaries are not settled close together, if they are mixed with other denominations, their zeal will cool for want of fuel, and will be extinguished in a little time. Then the Americans become as to religion what they are as to country, allied to all. In them the name of Englishman, Frenchman, and European is lost, and in like manner, the strict modes of Christianity as practiced in Europe are lost also. This effect will extend itself still farther hereafter, and though this may appear to you as a strange idea, yet it is a very true one. I shall be able perhaps hereafter to explain myself better; in the meanwhile, let the following example serve as my first justification.

Let us suppose you and I to be traveling; we observe that in this house, to the right, lives a Catholic, who prays to God as he has been taught, and believes in transubstantiation;[7] he works and raises wheat, he has a large family of children, all hale and robust; his belief, his prayers offend nobody. About one mile farther on the same road, his next neighbor may be a good honest plodding German Lutheran, who addresses himself to the same God, the God of all, agreeably to the modes he has been educated in, and believes in consubstantiation;[8] by so doing he scandalizes nobody; he also works in his fields, embellishes the earth, clears swamps, etc. What has the world to do with his Lutheran principles? He persecutes nobody, and nobody persecutes him, he visits his neighbors, and his neighbors visit him. Next to him lives a seceder, the most enthusiastic of all sectaries;[9] his zeal is hot and fiery, but separated as he is from others of the same complexion, he has no congregation of his own to resort to, where he might cabal and mingle religious pride with worldly obstinacy. He likewise raises good crops, his house is handsomely painted, his orchard is one of the fairest in the neighborhood. How does it concern the welfare of the country, or of the province at large, what this man's religious sentiments are, or really whether he has any at all? He is a good farmer, he is a sober, peaceable, good citizen: William Penn[1] himself would not wish for more. This is the visible character, the invisible one is only guessed at, and is nobody's business. Next again lives a Low Dutchman, who implicitly believes the rules laid down by the synod of Dort.[2]

---

6. Believers.
7. The doctrine followed by Roman Catholics that the substance of the bread and wine used in the sacrament of communion is changed at the consecration to the substance of the body and blood of Christ.
8. As distinguished from transubstantiation; the doctrine that affirms that Christ's body is not present in or under the elements of bread and wine, but that the bread and wine are signs of Christ's presence through faith.

9. One who dissents or withdraws from an established church. "Seceder": a Presbyterian who has separated from the established Church of Scotland.
1. English Quaker and founder of Pennsylvania (1644–1718).
2. The Synod of Dort met in Holland in 1618 and attempted to settle disputes between Protestant reformed churches. "Low Dutchman": someone from Holland, not Belgium.

He conceives no other idea of a clergyman than that of a hired man; if he does his work well he will pay him the stipulated sum; if not he will dismiss him, and do without his sermons, and let his church be shut up for years. But notwithstanding this coarse idea, you will find his house and farm to be the neatest in all the country; and you will judge by his wagon and fat horses that he thinks more of the affairs of this world than of those of the next. He is sober and laborious, therefore he is all he ought to be as to the affairs of this life; as for those of the next, he must trust to the great Creator. Each of these people instruct their children as well as they can, but these instructions are feeble compared to those which are given to the youth of the poorest class in Europe. Their children will therefore grow up less zealous and more indifferent in matters of religion than their parents. The foolish vanity, or rather the fury of making proselytes, is unknown here; they have no time, the seasons call for all their attention, and thus in a few years, this mixed neighborhood will exhibit a strange religious medley, that will be neither pure Catholicism nor pure Calvinism. A very perceptible indifference, even in the first generation, will become apparent; and it may happen that the daughter of the Catholic will marry the son of the seceder, and settle by themselves at a distance from their parents. What religious education will they give their children? A very imperfect one. If there happens to be in the neighborhood any place of worship, we will suppose a Quaker's meeting; rather than not show their fine clothes, they will go to it, and some of them may perhaps attach themselves to that society. Others will remain in a perfect state of indifference; the children of these zealous parents will not be able to tell what their religious principles are, and their grandchildren still less. The neighborhood of a place of worship generally leads them to it, and the action of going thither is the strongest evidence they can give of their attachment to any sect. The Quakers are the only people who retain a fondness for their own mode of worship; for be they ever so far separated from each other, they hold a sort of communion with the society, and seldom depart from its rules, at least in this country. Thus all sects are mixed as well as all nations; thus religious indifference is imperceptibly disseminated from one end of the continent to the other; which is at present one of the strongest characteristics of the Americans. Where this will reach no one can tell, perhaps it may leave a vacuum fit to receive other systems. Persecution, religious pride, the love of contradiction are the food of what the world commonly calls religion. These motives have ceased here; zeal in Europe is confined; here it evaporates in the great distance it has to travel; there it is a grain of powder inclosed, here it burns away in the open air, and consumes without effect.

But to return to our back settlers. I must tell you that there is something in the proximity of the woods which is very singular. It is with men as it is with the plants and animals that grow and live in the forests; they are entirely different from those that live in the plains. I will candidly tell you all my thoughts but you are not to expect that I shall advance any reasons. By living in or near the woods, their actions are regulated by the wildness of the neighborhood. The deer often come to eat their grain, the wolves to destroy their sheep, the bears to kill their hogs, the foxes to catch their poultry. This surrounding hostility immediately puts the gun into their hands; they watch these animals, they kill some; and thus by defending their property, they soon become professed hunters; this is the progress; once hunters, farewell to the plow. The chase renders them ferocious, gloomy, and unsociable; a hunter wants no neighbor, he rather hates them, because he dreads the competition. In a little time their success in the woods makes them neglect their tillage. They trust to the natural fecundity of the earth, and therefore do little; carelessness in fencing often exposes what little they sow to destruction; they are not at home to watch; in order therefore to make up the deficiency, they go oftener to the woods. That new mode of life brings along with it a new set of manners, which I cannot easily describe. These new manners, being grafted on the old stock, produce a strange sort of lawless profligacy, the impressions of which are indelible. The manners of the Indian natives are respectable, compared with this European medley. Their wives and children live in sloth and inactivity; and having no proper pursuits, you may judge what education the latter receive. Their tender minds have nothing else to contemplate but the example of their parents; like them they grow up a mongrel breed, half civilized, half savage, except nature stamps on them some constitutional propensities. That rich, that voluptuous sentiment is gone that struck them so forcibly; the possession of their freeholds[3] no longer conveys to their minds the same pleasure and pride. To all these reasons you must add their lonely situation, and you cannot imagine what an effect on manners the great distances they live from each other has! Consider one of the last settlements in its first view: of what is it composed? Europeans who have not that sufficient share of knowledge they ought to have, in order to prosper; people who have suddenly passed from oppression, dread of government, and fear of laws into the unlimited freedom of the woods. This sudden change must have a very great effect on most men, and on that class particularly. Eating of wild meat, whatever you may think, tends to alter their temper: though all the proof I can adduce is that I have seen it: and having no place of worship to resort to, what little society this might afford is denied them. The Sunday meetings, exclusive of religious benefits, were the only social bonds that might have inspired them with some degree of emulation in neatness. Is it then surprising to see men thus situated, immersed in great and heavy labors, degenerate a little? It is rather a wonder the effect is not more diffusive. The Moravians[4] and the Quakers are the only instances in exception to what I have advanced. The first never settle singly, it is a colony of the society which emigrates; they carry with them their forms, worship, rules, and decency: the others never begin so hard, they are always able to buy improvements, in which there is a great advantage, for by that time the country is recovered from its first barbarity. Thus our bad people are those who are half cultivators and half hunters; and the worst of them are those who have degenerated altogether into the hunting state. As old plowmen and new men of the woods, as Europeans and new-made Indians, they contract the vices of both; they adopt the moroseness and ferocity of a native, without his mildness, or even his industry at home. If manners are not refined, at least they are rendered simple and inoffensive by tilling the earth; all our wants are supplied by it, our time is divided between labor and rest, and leaves none of the commission of great misdeeds. As hunters it is divided

3. Land held outright for a specified period of time.
4. Followers of Jacob Hutter, who was executed in 1536. They were Christian family communities who gave up private property and were noted for their industry and thrift. They suffered a number of persecutions in the 17th century and emigrated to other lands.

between the toil of the chase, the idleness of repose, or the indulgence of inebriation. Hunting is but a licentious idle life, and if it does not always pervert good dispositions; yet, when it is united with bad luck, it leads to want: want stimulates that propensity to rapacity and injustice, too natural to needy men, which is the fatal gradation. After this explanation of the effects which follow by living in the woods, shall we yet vainly flatter ourselves with the hope of converting the Indians? We should rather begin with converting our back-settlers; and now if I dare mention the name of religion, its sweet accents would be lost in the immensity of these woods. Men thus placed are not fit either to receive or remember its mild instructions; they want[5] temples and ministers, but as soon as men cease to remain at home, and begin to lead an erratic life, let them be either tawny or white, they cease to be its disciples.

* * *

Europe contains hardly any other distinctions but lords and tenants; this fair country alone is settled by freeholders, the possessors of the soil they cultivate, members of the government they obey, and the framers of their own laws, by means of their representatives. This is a thought which you have taught me to cherish; our difference from Europe, far from diminishing, rather adds to our usefulness and consequence as men and subjects. Had our forefathers remained there, they would only have crowded it, and perhaps prolonged those convulsions which had shook it so long. Every industrious European who transports himself here may be compared to a sprout growing at the foot of a great tree; it enjoys and draws but a little portion of sap; wrench it from the parent roots, transplant it, and it will become a tree bearing fruit also. Colonists are therefore entitled to the consideration due to the most useful subjects; a hundred families barely existing in some parts or Scotland will here in six years cause an annual exportation of 10,000 bushels of wheat; 100 bushels being but a common quantity for an industrious family to sell, if they cultivated good land. It is here then that the idle may be employed, the useless become useful, and the poor become rich; but by riches I do not mean gold and silver, we have but little of those metals; I mean a better sort of wealth, cleared lands, cattle, good houses, good clothes, and an increase of people to enjoy them.

There is no wonder that this country has so many charms, and presents to Europeans so many temptations to remain in it. A traveler in Europe becomes a stranger as soon as he quits his own kingdom; but it is otherwise here. We know, properly speaking, no strangers; this is every person's country; the variety of our soils, situations, climates, governments, and produce hath something which must please everybody. No sooner does a European arrive, no matter of what condition, than his eyes are opened upon the fair prospect; he hears his language spoken, he retraces many of his own country manners, he perpetually hears the names of families and towns with which he is acquainted; he sees happiness and prosperity in all places disseminated; he meets with hospitality, kindness, and plenty everywhere; he beholds hardly any poor; he seldom hears of punishments and executions; and he wonders at the elegance of our towns, those miracles of industry and freedom. He

5. Lack.

cannot admire enough our rural districts, our convenient roads, good taverns, and our many accommodations; he involuntarily loves a country where everything is so lovely.

* * *

After a foreigner from any part of Europe is arrived, and become a citizen, let him devoutly listen to the voice of our great parent, which says to him, "Welcome to my shores, distressed European; bless the hour in which thou didst see my verdant fields, my fair navigable rivers, and my green mountains!—If thou wilt work, I have bread for thee; if thou wilt be honest, sober, and industrious, I have greater rewards to confer on thee—ease and independence. I will give thee fields to feed and clothe thee; a comfortable fireside to sit by, and tell thy children by what means thou hast prospered; and a decent bed to repose on. I shall endow thee beside with the immunities of a freeman. If thou wilt carefully educate thy children, teach them gratitude to God, and reverence to that government, the philanthropic government, which has collected here so many men and made them happy. I will also provide for thy progeny; and to every good man this ought to be the most holy, the most powerful, the most earnest wish he can possibly form, as well as the most consolatory prospect when he dies. Go thou and work and till; thou shalt prosper, provided thou be just, grateful, and industrious."

From Letter IV. Description of the Island of Nantucket, with the Manners, Customs, Policy, and Trade of the Inhabitants

The greatest compliment that can be paid to the best of kings, to the wisest ministers, or the most patriotic rulers, is to think, that the reformation of political abuses, and the happiness of their people are the primary objects of their attention. But alas! how disagreeable must the work of reformation be; how dreaded the operation; for we hear of no amendment: on the contrary, the great number of European emigrants, yearly coming over here, informs us, that the severity of taxes, the injustice of laws, the tyranny of the rich, and the oppressive avarice of the church; are as intolerable as ever. Will these calamities have no end? Are not the great rulers of the earth afraid of losing, by degrees, their most useful subjects? This country, providentially intended for the general asylum of the world, will flourish by the oppression of their people; they will every day become better acquainted with the happiness we enjoy, and seek for the means of transporting themselves here, in spite of all obstacles and laws. To what purpose then have so many useful books and divine maxims been transmitted to us from preceding ages?—Are they all vain, all useless? Must human nature ever be the sport of the few, and its many wounds remain unhealed? How happy are we here, in having fortunately escaped the miseries which attended our fathers; how thankful ought we to be, that they reared us in a land where sobriety and industry never fail to meet with the most ample rewards! You have, no doubt, read several histories of this continent, yet there are a thousand facts, a thousand explanations overlooked. Authors will certainly convey to you a geographical knowledge of this country; they will acquaint you with the eras of the several settlements, the foundations of our towns, the spirit of our different charters, etc., yet they do not sufficiently disclose the genius of the people, their various customs, their modes of agriculture, the innumerable resources which the industrious have of raising themselves to a comfortable and easy situation. Few of these writers have resided here, and those who have, had not pervaded every part of the country, nor carefully examined the nature and principles of our association. It would be a task worthy a speculative genius, to enter intimately into the situation and characters of the people, from Nova Scotia to West Florida; and surely history cannot possibly present any subject more pleasing to behold. Sensible how unable I am to lead you through so vast a maze, let us look attentively for some small unnoticed corner; but where shall we go in quest of such an one? Numberless settlements, each distinguished by some peculiarities, present themselves on every side; all seem to realize the most sanguine wishes that a good man could form for the happiness of his race. Here they live by fishing on the most plentiful coasts in the world; there they fell trees, by the sides of large rivers, for masts and lumber; here others convert innumerable logs into the best boards; there again others cultivate the land, rear cattle, and clear large fields. Yet I have a spot in my view, where none of these occupations are performed, which will, I hope, reward us for the trouble of inspection; but though it is barren in its soil, insignificant in its extent, inconvenient in its situation, deprived of materials for building; it seems to have been inhabited merely to prove what mankind can do when happily governed! Here I can point out to you exertions of the most successful industry; instances of native sagacity unassisted by science; the happy fruits of a well directed perseverance. It is always a refreshing spectacle to me, when in my review of the various component parts of this immense *whole,* I observe the labors of its inhabitants singularly rewarded by nature; when I see them emerged out of their first difficulties, living with decency and ease, and conveying to their posterity that plentiful subsistence, which their fathers have so deservedly earned. But when their prosperity arises from the goodness of the climate, and fertility of the soil; I partake of their happiness, it is true; yet stay but a little while with them, as they exhibit nothing but what is natural and common. On the contrary, when I meet with barren spots fertilized, grass growing where none grew before; grain gathered from fields which had hitherto produced nothing better than brambles; dwellings raised where no building materials were to be found; wealth acquired by the most uncommon means: there I pause, to dwell on the favorite object of my speculative inquiries. Willingly do I leave the former to enjoy the odoriferous furrow, or their rich valleys, with anxiety repairing to the spot, where so many difficulties have been overcome; where extraordinary exertions have produced extraordinary effects, and where every natural obstacle has been removed by a vigorous industry.

I want not to record the annals of the island of Nantucket—its inhabitants have no annals, for they are not a race of warriors. My simple wish is to trace them throughout their progressive steps, from their arrival here to this present hour; to inquire by what means they have raised themselves from the most humble, the most insignificant beginnings, to the ease and the wealth they now possess; and to give you some idea of their customs, religion, manners, policy, and mode of living.

This happy settlement was not founded on intrusion, forcible entries, or blood, as so many others have been; it drew its origin from necessity on the one side, and from good will on the other; and ever since, all has been a scene of uninterrupted harmony.—Neither political, nor religious broils; neither disputes with the natives, nor any other contentions, have in the least agitated or disturbed its detached society. Yet the first founders knew nothing either of Lycurgus or Solon;[6] for this settlement has not been the work of eminent men or powerful legislators, forcing nature by the accumulated labors of art. This singular establishment has been effected by means of that native industry and perseverance common to all men, when they are protected by a government which demands but little for its protection; when they are permitted to enjoy a system of rational laws founded on perfect freedom. The mildness and humanity of such a government necessarily implies that confidence which is the source of the most arduous undertakings and permanent success. Would you believe that a sandy spot, of about twenty-three thousand acres, affording neither stones nor timber, meadows nor arable [soil], yet can boast of an handsome town, consisting of more than 500 houses, should possess above 200 sail of vessels, constantly employ upwards of 2000 seamen, feed more than 15,000 sheep, 500 cows, 200 horses; and has several citizens worth 20,000£ sterling! Yet all these facts are uncontroverted. Who would have imagined that any people should have abandoned a fruitful and extensive continent, filled with the riches which the most ample vegetation affords; replete with good soil, enameled meadows, rich pastures, every kind of timber, and with all other materials necessary to render life happy and comfortable: to come and inhabit a little sand-bank, to which nature had refused those advantages; to dwell on a spot where there scarcely grew a shrub to announce, by the budding of its leaves, the arrival of the spring, and to warn by their fall the proximity of winter. Had this island been contiguous to the shores of some ancient monarchy, it would only have been occupied by a few wretched fishermen, who, oppressed by poverty, would hardly have been able to purchase or build little fishing barks; always dreading the weight of taxes, or the servitude of men of war. Instead of that boldness of speculation for which the inhabitants of this island are so remarkable, they would fearfully have confined themselves, within the narrow limits of the most trifling attempts; timid in their excursions, they never could have extricated themselves from their first difficulties. This island, on the contrary, contains 5000 hardy people, who boldly derive their riches from the element that surrounds them, and have been compelled by the sterility of the soil to seek abroad for the means of subsistence. You must not imagine, from the recital of these facts, that they enjoyed any exclusive privileges or royal charters, or that they were nursed by particular immunities in the infancy of their settlement. No, their freedom, their skill, their probity, and perseverance, have accomplished every thing, and brought them by degrees to the rank they now hold.

From this first sketch, I hope that my partiality to this island will be justified. Perhaps you hardly know that such an one exists in the neighborhood of Cape Cod. What has happened here, has and will happen everywhere else. Give mankind the full rewards of their industry, allow them to enjoy the fruit of their labor under the peaceable shade of their vines and fig trees, leave their native activity unshackled and free, like a fair stream without dams or

6. One of the seven wise men of Greece (638?–559 B.C.E.). Lycurgus, 9th-century B.C.E. lawgiver who laid the groundwork for Sparta's military preparedness.

other obstacles; the first will fertilize the very sand on which they tread, the other exhibit a navigable river, spreading plenty and cheerfulness wherever the declivity of the ground leads it. If these people are not famous for tracing the fragrant furrow on the plain, they plough the rougher ocean, they gather from its surface, at an immense distance, and with Herculean labors,[7] the riches it affords; they go to hunt and catch that huge fish which by its strength and velocity one would imagine ought to be beyond the reach of man. This island has nothing deserving of notice but its inhabitants; here you meet with neither ancient monuments, spacious halls, solemn temples, nor elegant dwellings; not a citadel, nor any kind of fortification, not even a battery[8] to rend the air with its loud peals on any solemn occasion. As for their rural improvements, they are many, but all of the most simple and useful kind.

* * *

Nantucket is a great nursery of seamen, pilots, coasters, and bank-fishermen; as a country belonging to the province of Massachusetts, it has yearly the benefit of a court of Common Pleas, and their appeal lies to the supreme court at Boston. I observed before, that the Friends[9] compose two thirds of the magistracy of this island; thus they are the proprietors of its territory, and the principal rulers of its inhabitants; but with all this apparatus of law, its coercive powers are seldom wanted or required. Seldom is it that any individual is amerced[1] or punished; their jail conveys no terror; no man has lost his life here judicially since the foundation of this town, which is upwards of an hundred years. Solemn tribunals, public executions, humiliating punishments, are altogether unknown. I saw neither governors, nor any pageantry of state; neither ostentatious magistrates, nor any individuals clothed with useless dignity: no artificial phantoms subsist here either civil or religious; no gibbets loaded with guilty citizens offer themselves to your view; no soldiers are appointed to bayonet their compatriots into servile compliance. But how is a society composed of 5000 individuals preserved in the bonds of peace and tranquility? How are the weak protected from the strong?—I will tell you. Idleness and poverty, the causes of so many crimes, are unknown here; each seeks in the prosecution of his lawful business that honest gain which supports them; every period of their time is full, either on shore or at sea. A probable expectation of reasonable profits, or of kindly assistance, if they fail of success, renders them strangers to licentious expedients. The simplicity of their manners shortens the catalogues of their wants; the law at a distance is ever ready to exert itself in the protection of those who stand in need of its assistance. The greatest part of them are always at sea, pursuing the whale or raising the cod from the surface of the banks: some cultivate their little farms with the utmost diligence; some are employed in exercising various trades; others again in providing every necessary resource in order to refit their vessels, or repair what misfortunes may happen, looking out for future markets, etc. Such is the rotation of those different scenes of business which fill the measure of their days; of that part of their lives at least which is enlivened by health, spirits, and vigor. It is but

7. Hercules, the greatest legendary hero of the ancient world, won immortality by performing twelve labors set by Eurystheus, ruler of Mycenae and Tiryns.

8. A platform on which guns are mounted.
9. Quakers.
1. Fined.

seldom that vice grows on a barren sand like this, which produces nothing without extreme labor. How could the common follies of society take root in so despicable a soil; they generally thrive on its exuberant juices: here there are none but those which administer to the useful, to the necessary, and to the indispensable comforts of life. This land must necessarily either produce health, temperance, and a great equality of conditions, or the most abject misery. Could the manners of luxurious countries be imported here, like an epidemical disorder they would destroy every thing; the majority of them could not exist a month, they would be obliged to emigrate. As in all societies except that of the natives, some difference must necessarily exist between individual and individual, for there must be some more exalted than the rest either by their riches or their talents; so in *this*, there are what you might call the high, the middling, and the low; and this difference will always be more remarkable among people who live by sea excursions than among those who live by the cultivation of their land. The first run greater hazard, and adventure more: the profits and the misfortuncs attending this mode of life must necessarily introduce a greater disparity than among the latter, where the equal division of the land offers no short road to superior riches. The only difference that may arise among them is that of industry, and perhaps of superior goodness of soil; the gradations I observed here, are founded on nothing more than the good or ill success of their maritime enterprises, and do not proceed from education; that is the same throughout every class, simple, useful, and unadorned like their dress and their houses. This necessary difference in their fortunes does not however cause those heart burnings, which in other societies generate crimes. The sea which surrounds them is equally open to all, and presents to all an equal title to the chance of good fortune. A collector from Boston is the only king's officer who appears on these shores to receive the trifling duties which this community owes to those who protect them, and under the shadow of whose wings they navigate to all parts of the world.

From *Letter IX. Description of Charles-Town; Thoughts on Slavery; on Physical Evil; A Melancholy Scene*

Charles-Town is, in the north, what Lima is in the south; both are capitals of the richest provinces of their respective hemispheres: you may therefore conjecture, that both cities must exhibit the appearances necessarily resulting from riches. Peru abounding in gold, Lima is filled with inhabitants who enjoy all those gradations of pleasure, refinement, and luxury, which proceed from wealth. Carolina produces commodities, more valuable perhaps than gold, because they are gained by greater industry; it exhibits also on our northern stage, a display of riches and luxury, inferior indeed to the former, but far superior to what are to be seen in our northern towns. Its situation is admirable, being built at the confluence of two large rivers, which receive in their course a great number of inferior streams; all navigable in the spring, for flat-boats. Here the produce of this extensive territory concenters; here therefore is the seat of the most valuable exportation; their wharfs, their docks, their magazines,[2] are extremely convenient to facilitate this great commercial business. The inhabitants are the gayest in America; it is called the

2. Warehouses.

center of our beau monde, and it [is] always filled with the richest planters of the province, who resort hither in a quest of health and pleasure. Here are always to be seen a great number of valetudinarians from the West Indies, seeking for the renovation of health, exhausted by the debilitating nature of their sun, air, and modes of living. Many of these West Indians have I seen, at thirty, loaded with the infirmities of old age; for nothing is more common in those countries of wealth, than for persons to lose the abilities of enjoying the comforts of life, at a time when we northern men just begin to taste the fruits of our labor and prudence. The round of pleasure, and the expenses of those citizens' tables, are much superior to what you would imagine: indeed the growth of this town and province has been astonishingly rapid. It is [a] pity that the narrowness of the neck on which it stands prevents it from increasing; and which is the reason why houses are so dear. The heat of the climate, which is sometimes very great in the interior parts of the country, is always temperate in Charles-Town; though sometimes when they have no sea breezes the sun is too powerful. The climate renders excesses of all kinds very dangerous, particularly those of the table; and yet, insensible or fearless of danger, they live on, and enjoy a short and a merry life: the rays of their sun seem to urge them irresistably to dissipation and pleasure: on the contrary, the women, from being abstemious, reach to a longer period of life, and seldom die without having had several husbands. An European at his first arrival must be greatly surprised when he sees the elegance of their houses, their sumptuous furniture, as well as the magnificence of their tables. Can he imagine himself in a country, the establishment of which is so recent?

The three principal classes of inhabitants are, lawyers, planters, and merchants; this is the province which has afforded to the first the richest spoils, for nothing can exceed their wealth, their power, and their influence. They have reached the *ne plus ultra*[3] of worldly felicity; no plantation is secured, no title is good, no will is valid, but what they dictate, regulate, and approve. The whole mass of provincial property is become tributary to this society; which, far above priests and bishops, disdain to be satisfied with the poor Mosaical portion of the tenth.[4] I appeal to the many inhabitants, who, while contending perhaps for their right to a few hundred acres, have lost by the mazes of the law their whole patrimony. These men are more properly law givers than interpreters of the law; and have united here, as well as in most other provinces, the skill and dexterity of the scribe with the power and ambition of the prince: who can tell where this may lead in a future day? The nature of our laws, and the spirit of freedom, which often tends to make us litigious, must necessarily throw the greatest part of the property of the colonies into the hands of these gentlemen. In another century, the law will possess in the north, what now the church possesses in Peru and Mexico.

While all is joy, festivity, and happiness in Charles-Town, would you imagine that scenes of misery overspread in the country? Their ears by habit are become deaf, their hearts are hardened; they neither see, hear, nor feel for the woes of their poor slaves, from whose painful labors all their wealth proceeds. Here the horrors of slavery, the hardship of incessant toils, are

3. No more beyond (Latin, literal trans.); the point of highest achievement.
4. The practice of tithing (offering one-tenth of one's worldly goods to God) was begun by Abraham (Genesis 14.20). It is "Mosaical" because the first five books of the Old Testament are traditionally ascribed to Moses.

unseen; and no one thinks with compassion of those showers of sweat and of tears which from the bodies of Africans, daily drop, and moisten the ground they till. The cracks of the whip urging these miserable beings to excessive labor, are far too distant from the gay capital to be heard. The chosen race eat, drink, and live happy, while the unfortunate one grubs up the ground, raises indigo, or husks the rice; exposed to a sun full as scorching as their native one; without the support of good food, without the cordials of any cheering liquor. This great contrast has often afforded me subjects of the most afflicting meditation. On the one side, behold a people enjoying all that life affords most bewitching and pleasurable, without labor, without fatigue, hardly subjected to the trouble of wishing. With gold, dug from Peruvian mountains, they order vessels to the coasts of Guinea; by virtue of that gold, wars, murders, and devastations are committed in some harmless, peaceable African neighborhood, where dwelt innocent people, who even knew not but that all men were black. The daughter torn from her weeping mother, the child from the wretched parents, the wife from the loving husband; whose families swept away and brought through storms and tempests to this rich metropolis! There, arranged like horses at a fair, they are branded like cattle, and then driven to toil, to starve, and to languish for a few years on the different plantations of these citizens. And for whom must they work? For persons they know not, and who have no other power over them than that of violence; no other right than what this accursed metal has given them! Strange order of things! Oh, Nature, where are thou?—Are not these blacks thy children as well as we? On the other side, nothing is to be seen but the most diffusive misery and wretchedness, unrelieved even in thought or wish! Day after day they drudge on without any prospect of ever reaping for themselves; they are obliged to devote their lives, their limbs, their will, and every vital exertion to swell the wealth of masters; who look not upon them with half the kindness and affection with which they consider their dogs and horses. Kindness and affection are not the portion of those who till the earth, who carry the burdens, who convert the logs into useful boards. This reward, simple and natural as one would conceive it, would border on humanity; and planters must have none of it!

*　　*　　*

A clergyman settled a few years ago at George-Town, and feeling as I do now, warmly recommended to the planters, from the pulpit, a relaxation of severity; he introduced the benignity of Christianity, and pathetically made use of the admirable precepts of that system to melt the hearts of his congregation into a greater degree of compassion toward their slaves than had been hitherto customary; "Sir (said one of his hearers) we pay you a genteel salary to read to us the prayers of the liturgy, and to explain to us such parts of the Gospel as the rule of the church directs; but we do not want you to teach us what we are to do with our blacks." The clergyman found it prudent to withhold any farther admonition. Whence this astonishing right, or rather this barbarous custom, for most certainly we have no kind of right beyond that of force? We are told, it is true, that slavery cannot be so repugnant to human nature as we at first imagine, because it has been practiced in all ages, and in all nations: the Lacedemonians[5] themselves, those great asser-

5. Another name for the Spartans, who enslaved the people of Helos, a town in Laconia.

tors of liberty, conquered the Helotes with the design of making them their slaves; the Romans, whom we consider as our masters in civil and military policy, lived in the exercise of the most horrid oppression; they conquered to plunder and to enslave. What a hideous aspect the face of the earth must then have exhibited! Provinces, towns, districts, often depopulated; their inhabitants driven to Rome, the greatest market in the world, and there sold by thousands! The Roman dominions were tilled by the hands of unfortunate people, who had once been, like their victors free, rich, and possessed of every benefit society can confer; until they became subject to the cruel right of war, and to lawless force. Is there then no superintending power who conducts the moral operations of the world, as well as the physical? The same sublime hand which guides the planets round the sun with so much exactness, which preserves the arrangement of the whole with such exalted wisdom and paternal care, and prevents the vast system from falling into confusion; doth it abandon mankind to all the errors, the follies, and the miseries, which their most frantic rage, and their most dangerous vices and passions can produce?

* * *

Everywhere one part of the human species are taught the art of shedding the blood of the other; of setting fire to their dwellings; of leveling the works of their industry: half of the existence of nations regularly employed in destroying other nations. What little political felicity is to be met with here and there, has cost oceans of blood to purchase; as if good was never to be the portion of unhappy man. Republics, kingdoms, monarchies, founded either on fraud or successful violence, increase by pursuing the steps of the same policy, until they are destroyed in their turn, either by the influence of their own crimes, or by more successful but equally criminal enemies.

If from this general review of human nature, we descend to the examination of what is called civilized society; there the combination of every natural and artificial want, makes us pay very dear for what little share of political felicity we enjoy. It is a strange heterogeneous assemblage of vices and virtues, and of a variety of other principles, forever at war, forever jarring, forever producing some dangerous, some distressing extreme. Where do you conceive then that nature intended we should be happy? Would you prefer the state of men in the woods, to that of men in a more improved situation? Evil preponderates in both; in the first they often eat each other for want of food, and in the other they often starve each other for want of room. For my part, I think the vices and miseries to be found in the latter, exceed those of the former; in which real evil is more scarce, more supportable, and less enormous. Yet we wish to see the earth peopled; to accomplish the happiness of kingdoms, which is said to consist in numbers. Gracious God! to what end is the introduction of so many beings into a mode of existence in which they must grope amidst as many errors, commit as many crimes, and meet with as many diseases, wants, and sufferings!

The following scene will I hope account for these melancholy reflections, and apologize for the gloomy thoughts with which I have filled this letter: my mind is, and always has been, oppressed since I became a witness to it. I was not long since invited to dine with a planter who lived three miles from ———, where he then resided. In order to avoid the heat of the sun, I resolved to go on foot, sheltered in a small path, leading through a pleasant wood. I was leisurely traveling along, attentively examining some peculiar plants which I had collected, when all at once I felt the air strongly agitated; though the day was perfectly calm and sultry. I immediately cast my eyes toward the cleared ground, from which I was but at a small distance, in order to see whether it was not occasioned by a sudden shower; when at that instant a sound resembling a deep rough voice, uttered, as I thought, a few inarticulate monosyllables. Alarmed and surprised, I precipitately looked all round, when I perceived at about six rods distance something resembling a cage, suspended to the limbs of a tree; all the branches of which appeared covered with large birds of prey, fluttering about, and anxiously endeavoring to perch on the cage. Actuated by an involuntary motion of my hands, more than by any design of my mind, I fired at them; they all flew to a short distance, with a most hideous noise: when, horrid to think and painful to repeat, I perceived a Negro, suspended in the cage, and left there to expire! I shudder when I recollect that the birds had already picked out his eyes, his cheek bones were bare; his arms had been attacked in several places, and his body seemed covered with a multitude of wounds. From the edges of the hollow sockets and from the lacerations with which he was disfigured, the blood slowly dropped, and tinged the ground beneath. No sooner were the birds flown, than swarms of insects covered the whole body of this unfortunate wretch, eager to feed on his mangled flesh and to drink his blood. I found myself suddenly arrested by the power of affright and terror; my nerves were convulsed; I trembled, I stood motionless, involuntarily contemplating the fate of this Negro, in all its dismal latitude. The living specter, though deprived of his eyes, could still distinctly hear, and in his uncouth dialect begged me to give him some water to allay his thirst. Humanity herself would have recoiled back with horror; she would have balanced whether to lessen such reliefless distress, or mercifully with one blow to end this dreadful scene of agonizing torture! Had I had a ball in my gun, I certainly should have dispatched him; but finding myself unable to perform so kind an office, I sought, though trembling, to relieve him as well as I could. A shell ready fixed to a pole, which had been used by some Negroes, presented itself to me; filled it with water, and with trembling hands I guided it to the quivering lips of the wretched sufferer. Urged by the irresistible power of thirst, he endeavored to meet it, as he instinctively guessed its approach by the noise it made in passing through the bars of the cage. "Tankè, you whitè man, tankè you, putè somè poison and givè me." "How long have you been hanging there?" I asked him. "Two days, and me no die; the birds, the birds; aaah me!" Oppressed with the reflections which this shocking spectacle afforded me, I mustered strength enough to walk away, and soon reached the house at which I intended to dine. There I heard that the reason for this slave being thus punished was on account of his having killed the overseer of the plantation. They told me that the laws of self-preservation rendered such executions necessary; and supported the doctrine of slavery with the arguments generally made use of to justify the practice; with the repetition of which I shall not trouble you at present.

Adieu.

From Letter X. On Snakes; and on the Humming Bird

* * *

As I was one day sitting solitary and pensive in my primitive arbor, my attention was engaged by a strange sort of rustling noise at some paces distant. I looked all around without distinguishing anything, until I climbed one of my great hemp stalks; when to my astonishment, I beheld two snakes of considerable length, the one pursuing the other with great celerity through a hemp stubble field. The aggressor was of the black kind, six feet long; the fugitive was a water snake, nearly of equal dimensions. They soon met, and in the fury of their first encounter, they appeared in an instant firmly twisted together; and whilst their united tails beat the ground, they mutually tried with open jaws to lacerate each other. What a fell[6] aspect did they present! their heads were compressed to a very small size, their eyes flashed fire; and after this conflict had lasted about five minutes, the second found means to disengage itself from the first, and hurried toward the ditch. Its antagonist instantly assumed a new posture, and half creeping and half erect, with a majestic mien, overtook and attacked the other again, which placed itself in the same attitude, and prepared to resist. The scene was uncommon and beautiful; for thus opposed they fought with their jaws, biting each other with the utmost rage; but notwithstanding this appearance of mutual courage and fury, the water snake still seemed desirous of retreating toward the ditch, its natural element. This was no sooner perceived by the keen-eyed black one, than twisting its tail twice round a stalk of hemp, and seizing its adversary by the throat, not by means of its jaws, but by twisting its own neck twice round that of the water snake, pulled it back from the ditch. To prevent a defeat the latter took hold likewise of a stalk on the bank, and by the acquisition of that point of resistance became a match for its fierce antagonist. Strange was this to behold; two great snakes strongly adhering to the ground mutually fastened together by means of the writhings which lashed them to each other, and stretched at their full length, they pulled but pulled in vain, and in the moments of greatest exertions that part of their bodies which was entwined, seemed extremely small, while the rest appeared inflated, and now and then convulsed with strong undulations, rapidly following each other. Their eyes seemed on fire, and ready to start out of their heads; at one time the conflict seemed decided; the water-snake bent itself into two great folds, and by that operation rendered the other more than commonly outstretched; the next minute the new struggles of the black one gained an unexpected superiority, it acquired two great folds likewise, which necessarily extended the body of its adversary in proportion as it had contracted its own. These efforts were alternate; victory seemed doubtful, inclining sometimes to the one side and sometimes to the other; until at last the stalk to which the black snake fastened, suddenly gave way, and in consequence of this accident they both plunged into the ditch. The water did not extinguish their vindictive rage; for by their agitations I could trace, though not distinguish their mutual attacks. They soon reappeared on the surface twisted together, as in their first onset; but the black snake seemed to retain

6. Evil.

its wonted superiority, for its head was exactly fixed above that of the other, which it incessantly pressed down under the water, until it was stifled, and sunk. The victor no sooner perceived its enemy incapable of farther resistance, than abandoning it to the current, it returned on shore and disappeared.

From *Letter XII. Distresses of a Frontier Man*

I wish for a change of place; the hour is come at last, that I must fly from my house and abandon my farm! But what course shall I steer, enclosed as I am? The climate best adapted to my present situation and humor[7] would be the polar regions, where six months day and six months night divide the dull year: nay, a simple Aurora Borealis would suffice me, and greatly refresh my eyes, fatigued now by so many disagreeable objects. The severity of those climates, that great gloom, where melancholy dwells, would be perfectly analogous to the turn of my mind. Oh, could I remove my plantation to the shores of the Oby, willingly would I dwell in the hut of a Samoyede,[8] with cheerfulness would I go and bury myself in the cavern of a Laplander. Could I but carry my family along with me, I would winter at Pello, or Tobolsky,[9] in order to enjoy the peace and innocence of that country. But let me arrive under the pole, or reach the antipodes,[1] I never can leave behind me the remembrance of the dreadful scenes to which I have been a witness; therefore never can I be happy! Happy, why would I mention that sweet, that enchanting word? Once happiness was our portion; now it is gone from us, and I am afraid not to be enjoyed again by the present generation! Whichever way I look, nothing but the most frightful precipices present themselves to my view, in which hundreds of my friends and acquaintances have already perished: of all animals that live on the surface of this planet, what is man when no longer connected with society; or when he finds himself surrounded by a convulsed and a half-dissolved one? He cannot live in solitude, he must belong to some community bound by some ties, however imperfect. Men mutually support and add to the boldness and confidence of each other; the weakness of each is strengthened by the force of the whole. I had never before these calamitous times formed any such ideas; I lived on, labored and prospered, without having ever studied on what the security of my life and the foundation of my prosperity were established: I perceived them just as they left me. Never was a situation so singularly terrible as mine, in every possible respect, as a member of an extensive society, as a citizen of an inferior division of the same society, as a husband, as a father, as a man who exquisitely feels for the miseries of others as well as for his own! But alas! so much is everything now subverted among us, that the very word misery, with which we were hardly acquainted before, no longer conveys the same ideas; or rather tired with feeling for the miseries of others, everyone feels now for himself alone. When I consider myself as connected in all these characters, as bound by so many cords, all uniting in my heart, I am seized with a fever of the mind, I am transported beyond that degree of calmness which is necessary to delineate our thoughts. I feel as if my reason wanted

7. Temperament.
8. Siberian nomadic inhabitants of the shores of the Arctic Ocean near Tobolsk. The Oby is a river in Siberia.
9. In Siberia.
1. Places opposite to each other on the globe.

to leave me, as if it would burst its poor weak tenement: again I try to compose myself, I grow cool, and preconceiving the dreadful loss, I endeavor to retain the useful guest.

* * *

Must I then bid farewell to Britain, to that renowned country? Must I renounce a name so ancient and so venerable? Alas, she herself, that once indulgent parent, forces me to take up arms against her. She herself first inspired the most unhappy citizens of our remote districts with the thoughts of shedding the blood of those whom they used to call by the name of friends and brethren. That great nation which now convulses the world; which hardly knows the extent of her Indian kingdoms; which looks toward the universal monarchy of trade, of industry, of riches, of power: why must she strew our poor frontiers with the carcasses of her friends, with the wrecks of our insignificant villages, in which there is no gold? When, oppressed by painful recollection, I revolve all these scattered ideas in my mind; when I contemplate my situation, and the thousand streams of evil with which I am surrounded; when I descend into the particular tendency even of the remedy I have proposed, I am convulsed—convulsed sometimes to that degree, as to be tempted to exclaim—Why has the master of the world permitted so much indiscriminate evil throughout every part of this poor planet, at all times, and among all kinds of people? It ought surely to be the punishment of the wicked only. I bring that cup to my lips, of which I must soon taste, and shudder at its bitterness. What then is life, I ask myself, is it a gracious gift? No, it is too bitter; a gift means something valuable conferred, but life appears to be a mere accident, and of the worst kind: we are born to be victims of diseases and passions, of mischances and death: better not to be than to be miserable.—Thus impiously I roam, I fly from one erratic thought to another, and my mind, irritated by these acrimonious reflections, is ready sometimes to lead me to dangerous extremes of violence. When I recollect that I am a father, and a husband, the return of these endearing ideas strikes deep into my heart. Alas! they once made it to glow with pleasure and with every ravishing exultation; but now they fill it with sorrow. At other times, my wife industriously rouses me out of these dreadful meditations, and soothes me by all the reasoning she is mistress of; but her endeavors only serve to make me more miserable, by reflecting that she must share with me all these calamities, the bare apprehensions of which I am afraid will subvert her reason. Nor can I with patience think that a beloved wife, my faithful helpmate, throughout all my rural schemes, the principal hand which has assisted me in rearing the prosperous fabric of ease and independence I lately possessed, as well as my children, those tenants of my heart, should daily and nightly be exposed to such a cruel fate. Self-preservation is above all political precepts and rules, and even superior to the dearest opinions of our minds; a reasonable accommodation of ourselves to the various exigencies of the times in which we live is the most irresistible precept. To this great evil I must seek some sort of remedy adapted to remove or to palliate it; situated as I am, what steps should I take that will neither injure nor insult any of the parties, and at the same time save my family from that certain destruction which awaits it if I remain here much longer. Could I insure them bread, safety, and subsistence, not the bread of idleness, but that earned by proper labor as heretofore; could this be accomplished by the sacrifice of my life, I would willingly give it up. I attest before heaven that it is only for these I would wish to live and to toil: for these whom I have brought into this miserable existence. I resemble, methinks, one of the stones of a ruined arch, still retaining that pristine form that anciently fitted the place I occupied, but the center is tumbled down; I can be nothing until I am replaced, either in the former circle or in some stronger one. I see one on a smaller scale, and at a considerable distance, but it is within my power to reach it: and since I have ceased to consider myself as a member of the ancient state now convulsed, I willingly descend into an inferior one. I will revert into a state approaching nearer to that of nature, unencumbered either with voluminous laws or contradictory codes, often galling the very necks of those whom they protect; and at the same time sufficiently remote from the brutality of unconnected savage nature. Do you, my friend, perceive the path I have found out? it is that which leads to the tenants of the great —— village of ——, where, far removed from the accursed neighborhood of Europeans, its inhabitants live with more ease, decency, and peace than you imagine: where, though governed by no laws, yet find, in uncontaminated simple manners all that laws can afford. Their system is sufficiently complete to answer all the primary wants of man and to constitute him a social being, such as he ought to be in the great forest of nature. There it is that I have resolved at any rate to transport myself and family: an eccentric thought, you may say, thus to cut asunder all former connections, and to form new ones with a people whom nature has stamped with such different characteristics! But as the happiness of my family is the only object of my wishes, I care very little where we be, or where we go, provided that we are safe and all united together.

* * *

You may therefore, by means of anticipation, behold me under the Wigwam;[2] I am so well acquainted with the principal manners of these people, that I entertain not the least apprehension from them. I rely more securely on their strong hospitality than on the witnessed compacts of many Europeans. As soon as possible after my arrival, I design to build myself a wigwam, after the same manner and size with the rest, in order to avoid being thought singular, or giving occasion for any railleries; though these people are seldom guilty of such European follies. I shall erect it hard by the lands which they propose to allot me, and will endeavor that my wife, my children, and myself may be adopted soon after our arrival. Thus becoming truly inhabitants of their village, we shall immediately occupy that rank within the pale[3] of their society which will afford us all the amends we can possibly expect for the loss we have met with by the convulsions of our own. According to their customs we shall likewise receive names from them, by which we shall always be known. My youngest children shall learn to swim and to shoot with the bow, that they may acquire such talents as will necessarily raise them into some degree of esteem among the Indian lads of their own age; the rest of us must hunt with the hunters. I have been for several years an expert marks-

2. I.e., living as an American Indian. A wigwam is a hut or lodge, usually built of poles and covered with skins, mats, or bark.
3. Bounds.

man; but I dread lest the imperceptible charm of Indian education may seize my younger children and give them such a propensity to that mode of life as may preclude their returning to the manners and customs of their parents. I have but one remedy to prevent this great evil; and that is, to employ them in the labor of the fields as much as I can; I am even resolved to make their daily subsistence depend altogether on it. As long as we keep ourselves busy in tilling the earth, there is no fear of any of us becoming wild; it is the chase and the food it procures that have this strange effect. Excuse a simile—those hogs which range in the woods, and to whom grain is given once a week, preserve their former degree of tameness; but if, on the contrary, they are reduced to live on ground nuts, and on what they can get, they soon become wild and fierce. For my part, I can plow, sow, and hunt, as occasion may require; but my wife, deprived of wool and flax, will have no room for industry,[4] what is she then to do? like the other squaws, she must cook for us the nasaump, the ninchické,[5] and such other preparations of corn as are customary among these people. She must learn to bake squashes and pumpkins under the ashes; to slice and smoke the meat of our own killing, in order to preserve it; she must cheerfully adopt the manners and customs of her neighbors, in their dress, deportment, conduct, and internal economy, in all respects. Surely if we can have fortitude enough to quit all we have, to remove so far, and to associate with people so different from us, these necessary compliances are but part of the scheme. The change of garments, when those they carry with them are worn out, will not be the least of my wife's and daughter's concerns: though I am in hopes that self-love will invent some sort of reparation. Perhaps you would not believe that there are in the woods looking-glasses, and paint of every color; and that the inhabitants take as much pains to adorn their faces and their bodies, to fix their bracelets of silver, and plait their hair, as our forefathers the Picts[6] used to do in the time of the Romans. Not that I would wish to see either my wife or daughter adopt those savage customs; we can live in great peace and harmony with them without descending to every article; the interruption of trade hath, I hope, suspended this mode of dress. My wife understands inoculation[7] perfectly well, she inoculated all our children one after another, and has successfully performed the operation on several scores of people, who, scattered here and there through our woods, were too far removed from all medical assistance. If we can persuade but one family to submit to it, and it succeeds, we shall then be as happy as our situation will admit of; it will raise her into some degree of consideration, for whoever is useful in any society will always be respected. If we are so fortunate as to carry one family through a disorder, which is the plague among these people, I trust to the force of example, we shall then become truly necessary, valued, and beloved; we indeed owe every kind office to a society of men who so readily offer to admit us into their social partnership, and to extend to my family the shelter of their village, the strength of their adoption, and even the dignity of their names. God grant us a prosperous beginning, we may then hope to be of more service to them than even missionaries who have been sent to preach to them a Gospel they cannot understand.

4. Household work.
5. Varieties of cornmeal mush. "Nasaump": more commonly known as *samp*.

6. Ancient people of northern Britain.
7. I.e., the injection of a virus or bacterium into the body to establish immunity.

As to religion, our mode of worship will not suffer much by this removal from a cultivated country, into the bosom of the woods; for it cannot be much simpler than that which we have followed here these many years: and I will with as much care as I can, redouble my attention, and twice a week, retrace to them the great outlines of their duty to God and to man. I will read and expound to them some part of the decalogue,[8] which is the method I have pursued ever since I married.

*   *   *

Thus then in the village of ——, in the bosom of that peace it has enjoyed ever since I have known it, connected with mild hospitable people, strangers to *our* political disputes, and having none among themselves; on the shores of a fine river, surrounded with woods, abounding with game; our little society united in perfect harmony with the new adoptive one, in which we shall be incorporated, shall rest I hope from all fatigues, from all apprehensions, from our present terrors, and from our long watchings. Not a word of politics shall cloud our simple conversation; tired either with the chase or the labor of the field, we shall sleep on our mats without any distressing want, having learnt to retrench every superfluous one: we shall have but two prayers to make to the Supreme Being, that He may shed His fertilizing dew on our little crops, and that He will be pleased to restore peace to our unhappy country. These shall be the only subject of our nightly prayers, and of our daily ejaculations:[9] and if the labor, the industry, the frugality, the union of men can be an agreeable offering to Him, we shall not fail to receive His paternal blessings. There I shall contemplate Nature in her most wild and ample extent; I shall carefully study a species of society, of which I have at present but very imperfect ideas; I will endeavor to occupy with propriety that place which will enable me to enjoy the few and sufficient benefits it confers. The solitary and unconnected mode of life I have lived in my youth must fit me for this trial, I am not the first who has attempted it; Europeans did not, it is true, carry to the wilderness numerous families; they went there as merely speculators; I, as a man seeking a refuge from the desolation of war. They went there to study the manner of the aborigines; I to conform to them, whatever they are; some went as visitors, as travelers; I as a sojourner, as a fellow hunter and laborer, go determined industriously to work up among them such a system of happiness as may be adequate to my future situation, and may be a sufficient compensation for all my fatigues and for the misfortunes I have borne: I have always found it at home, I may hope likewise to find it under the humble roof of my wigwam.

O Supreme Being! if among the immense variety of planets, inhabited by Thy creative power, Thy paternal and omnipotent care deigns to extend to all the individuals they contain; if it be not beneath Thy infinite dignity to cast Thy eye on us wretched mortals; if my future felicity is not contrary to the necessary effects of those secret causes which Thou hast appointed, receive the supplications of a man, to whom in Thy kindness Thou hast given a wife and an offspring: View us all with benignity, sanctify this strong conflict of regrets, wishes, and other natural passions; guide our steps through these unknown paths, and bless our future mode of life. If it is good and

8. The Ten Commandments.   9. Prayers.

well meant, it must proceed from Thee; Thou knowest, O Lord, our enterprise contains neither fraud, nor malice, nor revenge. Bestow on me that
energy of conduct now become so necessary, that it may be in my power to
carry the young family Thou hast given me through this great trial with safety
and in Thy peace. Inspire me with such intentions and such rules of conduct
as may be most acceptable to Thee. Preserve, O God, preserve the companion of my bosom, the best gift Thou hast given me: endue her with courage
and strength sufficient to accomplish this perilous journey. Bless the children of our love, those portions of our hearts; I implore Thy divine assistance,
speak to their tender minds, and inspire them with the love of that virtue
which alone can serve as the basis of their conduct in this world, and of their
happiness with Thee. Restore peace and concord to our poor afflicted country, assuage the fierce storm which has so long ravaged it. Permit, I beseech
Thee, O Father of Nature, that our ancient virtues, and our industry, may
not be totally lost: and that as a reward for the great toils we have made on
this new land, we may be restored to our ancient tranquillity, and enabled
to fill it with successive generations, that will constantly thank Thee for the
ample subsistence Thou hast given them.

The unreserved manner in which I have written must give you a convincing
proof of that friendship and esteem, of which I am sure you never yet
doubted. As members of the same society, as mutually bound by the ties of
affection and old acquaintance, you certainly cannot avoid feeling for my
distresses; you cannot avoid mourning with me over that load of physical
and moral evil with which we are all oppressed. My own share of it I often
overlook when I minutely contemplate all that hath befallen our native country.

c. 1769–80   1782

JOHN ADAMS
1735–1826

ABIGAIL ADAMS
1744–1818

Abigail Smith and John Adams were married on October 25, 1764, and they remained
partners in marriage until Abigail's death fifty-four years later. She was the daughter
of a wealthy Congregational minister from Weymouth, Massachusetts, on the South
Shore, and he—a man who was to become second president of the United States—
the son of a farmer from nearby Braintree (now a part of Quincy, Massachusetts).
Abigail had no formal schooling of any kind because, as she often explained, she was
frequently ill as a child. Although this was undoubtedly true, she observed in later
years that girls and boys in her youth were not treated equally and that "daughters"
were "wholly neglected in point of Literature." She grew up in her grandmother's
house where "instruction and amusement" were blended together. With a remarkable
native intelligence, easy access to her father's library, and a good ear for assimilating
conversation heard in the parsonage, she could boast of a superior mind in spite of
her remarkable spelling. She did not ever suffer fools gladly and seems early in life
to have understood how politicians get ahead in the world.

John Adams graduated from Harvard College in the class of 1755. He taught school for a short time in Worcester, but the roles of teacher and preacher were too closely joined for his taste and he was made uncomfortable by association with any "frigid" Calvinism. He took up the study of law, instead, and was admitted to the Boston bar in 1758. He met Abigail the following year. Although he preferred a country to a city law practice and treasured his Braintree farm, he found it impossible to support a growing family (the Adamses eventually had four children) on a country clientele. In 1768 they moved to Boston. John Adams's earlier opposition to the Stamp Act of 1765 and his defense of Massachusetts radicals like John Hancock identified him as one who would support the cause of independence, and in June 1774 he was elected as a Massachusetts delegate to the First Congress of the Colonies, scheduled to meet in Philadelphia, later known as the First Continental Congress. He left Braintree on August 10, and for the next twenty-six years, ten of them spent abroad, he was a famous and sometimes controversial figure in American public life. He was elected vice president for two terms (1788 and 1792) and president in 1796. After losing the election of 1800 to Thomas Jefferson, he retired to Braintree at last, anxious to lead the Arcadian life he spoke so wistfully about while holding public office. It was Abigail, as usual, who oversaw the daily life of the farm: she was always an astute manager of money, property, animals, and people.

From the time that John Adams left Massachusetts in 1774 until he returned from Paris in 1783, more than three hundred letters passed between this couple. They were lovingly saved, and many of them were published by their grandson in the middle of the nineteenth century. They provide not only an extraordinary document of a long and happy marriage but a vivid portrait of a nation seeking its identity.

From The Letters of John and Abigail Adams[1]

Abigail Adams to John Adams

[CLASSICAL PARALLELS]

Braintree August 19 1774

The great distance between us, makes the time appear very long to me. It seems already a month since you left me.[2] The great anxiety I feel for my Country, for you and for our family renders the day tedious, and the night unpleasant. The Rocks and quick Sands appear upon every Side. What course you can or will take is all wrapt in the Bosom of futurity. Uncertainty and expectation leave the mind great Scope. Did ever any Kingdom or State regain their Liberty, when once it was invaded without Blood shed? I cannot think of it without horror.

Yet we are told that all the Misfortunes of Sparta[3] were occasiond by their too great Sollicitude for present tranquility, and by an excessive love of peace they neglected the means of making it sure and lasting. They ought to have reflected says Polibius[4] that as there is nothing more desirable, or advantages than peace, when founded in justice and honour, so there is nothing more

1. The text used here is taken from *Adams Family Correspondence* (1963), 2 vols., edited by L. H. Butterfield. The original spelling remains unchanged. Words in angle brackets identify the writer's earlier choice of a word.
2. In June 1774, John was chosen as one of five delegates from Massachusetts to the Continental Congress to be held in Philadelphia. He left Braintree, Massachusetts (now Quincy), on August 10. Massachusetts was in a state of near-rebellion.
3. When Philip of Macedon (see n. 6) invaded Greece, the Greek citizens of the city of Sparta were concerned only with protecting their own territory, and as a consequence Greece fell.
4. Polybius (c. 205–125 B.C.E.), Greek historian and author of a history of Rome.

shameful and at the same time more pernicious when attained by bad measures, and purchased at the price of liberty.

I have received a most charming Letter from our Friend Mrs. W[arre]n.[5] She desires me to tell you that her best wishes attend you thro your journey both as a Friend and patriot—hopes you will have no uncommon difficulties to surmount or Hostile Movements to impeade you—but if the Locrians should interrupt you, she hop[e]s you will beware that no future Annals may say you chose an ambitious Philip for your Leader, who subverted the noble order of the American Amphyctions, and built up a Monarchy on the Ruins of the happy institution.[6]

I have taken a very great fondness for reading Rollin's[7] ancient History since you left me. I am determined to go thro with it if possible in these my days of solitude. I find great pleasure and entertainment from it, and I have perswaided Johnny[8] to read me a page or two every day, and hope he will from his desire to oblige me entertain a fondness for it.—We have had a charming rain which lasted 12 hours and has greatly revived the dying fruits of the earth.

I want much to hear from you. I long impatiently to have you upon the Stage of action. The first of September or the month of September, perhaps may be of as much importance to Great Britan as the Ides of March were to Ceaser.[9] I wish you every Publick as well, as private blessing, and that wisdom which is profitable both for instruction and edification to conduct you in this difficult day.—The little flock remember Pappa, and kindly wish to see him. So does your most affectionate

Abigail Adams

1774   1848

John Adams to Abigail Adams

[PRAYERS AT THE CONGRESS]

Phyladelphia Septr. 16. 1774

Having a Leisure Moment, while the Congress is assembling, I gladly embrace it to write you a Line.

When the Congress first met, Mr. Cushing[1] made a Motion, that it should be opened with Prayer. It was opposed by Mr. Jay of N. York and Mr. Rutledge[2] of South Carolina, because we were so divided in religious Sentiments, some Episcopalians, some Quakers, some Anabaptists, some Presbyterians, and some Congregationalists, so that We could not join in the same Act of Worship.—Mr. S. Adams[3] arose and said he was no Bigot, and could hear a

---

5. Mercy Otis Warren (1728–1814), well known as a correspondent and friend of the leading political figures of her day; wife of James Warren (1726–1808).
6. Philip II, king of Macedon (382–336 B.C.E.), transformed democratic Greece into a monarchy. In 338 B.C.E. he invaded Greece under the pretext that the Locrian town of Amphissa had resisted the authority of a neighboring council of states known as the Amphictionic League.
7. Charles Rollin (1661–1741) was rector of the University of Paris. John owned the 5th edition (1768) of his *Ancient History*.

8. Their seven-year-old son.
9. Julius Caesar's death, in 44 B.C.E., fell, as predicted, on the Ides of March. In the ancient Roman calendar the Ides fell usually on the thirteenth of the month, but on the fifteenth of March, May, July, and October.
1. Thomas Cushing (1725–1788), a Massachusetts delegate to the Continental Congress.
2. John Jay (1745–1829), jurist. John Rutledge (1739–1800), later governor of South Carolina.
3. Samuel Adams (1722–1803), a Massachusetts patriot.

Prayer from a Gentleman of Piety and Virtue, who was at the same Time a Friend to his Country. He was a Stranger in Phyladelphia, but had heard that Mr. Duchè[4] (Dushay they pronounce it) deserved that Character, and therefore he moved that Mr. Duchè, an episcopal Clergyman, might be desired, to read Prayers to the Congress, tomorrow Morning. The Motion was seconded and passed in the Affirmative. Mr. Randolph our President, waited on[5] Mr. Duchè, and received for Answer that if his Health would permit, he certainly would. Accordingly next Morning he appeared with his Clerk and in his Pontificallibus, and read several Prayers, in the established Form;[6] and then read the Collect for the seventh day of September, which was the Thirty fifth Psalm.[7]—You must remember this was the next Morning after we heard the horrible Rumour, of the Cannonade[8] of Boston.—I never saw a greater Effect upon an Audience. It seemed as if Heaven had ordained that Psalm to be read on that Morning.

After this Mr. Duchè, unexpected to every Body struck out into an extemporary Prayer, which filled the Bosom of every Man present. I must confess I never heard a better Prayer or one, so well pronounced. Episcopalian as he is, Dr. Cooper[9] himself never prayed with such fervour, such Ardor, such Earnestness and Pathos, and in Language so elegant and sublime—for America, for the Congress, for The Province of Massachusetts Bay, and especially the Town of Boston. It has had an excellent Effect upon every Body here.

I must beg you to read that Psalm. If there was any Faith in the sortes Virgilianæ, or sortes Homericæ, or especially the Sortes biblicæ, it would be thought providential.[1]

It will amuse your Friends to read this Letter and the 35th. Psalm to them. Read it to your Father and Mr. Wibirt.—I wonder what our Braintree Churchmen would think of this?—Mr. Duchè is one of the most ingenious[2] Men, and best Characters, and greatest orators in the Episcopal order, upon this Continent—Yet a Zealous Friend of Liberty and his Country.

I long to see my dear Family. God bless, preserve and prosper it. Adieu.

John Adams

1774   1875

Abigail Adams to John Adams

[THE FIRST SCENE OF THE INFERNAL PLOT DISCLOSED]

Braintree october 16 1774

My Much Loved Friend

I dare not express to you at 300 hundred miles distance how ardently I long for your return. I have some very miserly Wishes; and cannot consent to your

---

4. The Reverend Jacob Duché (1737–1798), assistant rector of Christ Church and St. Peter's in Philadelphia. He later supported the Crown and fled to England.
5. Made a formal call on. Peyton Randolph (1721?–1775), from Virginia, was president of the Continental Congress.
6. I.e., in the form set down by the Church of England. "Pontificallibus": priestly attire.
7. "Plead my cause, O Lord, with them that strive with me: fight against them that fight against me" (Psalm 35.1). "Collect": the prayer assigned to be

read before the Epistle.
8. Bombardment.
9. Samuel Cooper (1725–1783), minister of the Brattle Street Church, Boston.
1. The Bible and the works of the Roman poet Virgil (70–19 B.C.E.) and the Greek epic poet Homer were thought to have magical properties: a passage opened to at random (in Latin the sortes, or "chance oracles") had relevance to one's life and future.
2. Showing discernment.

spending one hour in Town till at least I have had you 12. The Idea plays about my Heart, unnerves my hand whilst I write, awakens all the tender sentiments that years have encreased and matured, and which when with me were every day dispensing to you.[3] The whole collected stock of ⟨nine⟩ ten weeks absence knows not how to brook[4] any longer restraint, but will break forth and flow thro my pen. May the like sensations enter thy breast, and (in spite of all the weighty cares of State) Mingle themselves with those I wish to communicate, for in giving them utterance I have felt more sincere pleasure than I have known since the 10 of August.[5]—Many have been the anxious hours I have spent since that day—the threatning aspect of our publick affairs, the complicated distress of this province, the Arduous and perplexed Business in which you are engaged, have all conspired to agitate my bosom, with fears and apprehensions to which I have heretofore been [a] stranger, and far from thinking the Scene closed, it looks [as] tho the curtain was but just drawn and only the first Scene of the infernal plot disclosed and whether the end will be tragical Heaven alone knows. You cannot be, I know, nor do I wish to see you an inactive Spectator, but if the Sword be drawn I bid adieu to all domestick felicity, and look forward to that Country where there is neither wars nor rumors of War in a firm belief that thro the mercy of its Kings we shall both rejoice there together.

I greatly fear that the arm of treachery and violence is lifted over us as a Scourge and heavy punishment from heaven for our numerous offences, and for the misimprovement of our great advantages. If we expect to inherit the blessings of our Fathers, we should return a little more to their primitive Simplicity of Manners, and not sink into inglorious ease. We have too many high sounding words, and too few actions that correspond with them. I have spent one Sabbeth in Town since you left me. I saw no difference in respect to ornaments, &c. &c. but in the Country you must look for that virtue, of which you find but small Glimerings in the Metropolis. Indeed they have not the advantages, nor the resolution to encourage our own Manufactories which people in the country have. To the Mercantile part, tis considerd as throwing away their own Bread; but they must retrench their expenses and be content with a small share of gain for they will find but few who will wear their Livery. As for me I will seek wool and flax and work willingly with my Hands, and indeed their is occasion for all our industry and economy.

You mention the removal of our Books &c. from Boston.[6] I believe they are safe there, and it would incommode the Gentlemen to remove them, as they would not then have a place to repair to for study. I suppose they would not chuse to be at the expence of bording out. Mr. Williams I believe keeps pretty much with his mother. Mr. Hills father had some thoughts of removing up to Braintree provided he could be accommodated with a house, which he finds very difficult.

Mr. Cranch's[7] last determination was to tarry in Town unless any thing new takes place. His Friends in Town oppose his Removal so much that he is determined to stay. The opinion you have entertaind of General Gage[8] is

3. I.e., being dispensed to you.
4. Tolerate.
5. When John left Braintree for Philadelphia.
6. The Adamses maintained a house in Boston, where John's law clerks Williams and Hills were resident.
7. Richard Cranch (1726–1811), Abigail's brother-in-law.
8. General Thomas Gage (1721–1787) was the British governor of Massachusetts in 1774. He left Boston in 1775.

I believe just, indeed he professes to act only upon the Defensive. The People in the Co[untr]y begin to be very anxious for the congress to rise.[9] They have no idea of the Weighty Buisness you have to transact, and their Blood boils with indignation at the Hostile prepairations they are constant Witnesses of. Mr. Quincys[1] so secret departure is Matter of various Specculation—some say he is deputed by the congress, others that he is gone to Holland, and the Tories says he is gone to be hanged.

I rejoice at the favourable account you give me of your Health; May it be continued to you. My Health is much better than it was last fall. Some folks say I grow very fat.—I venture to write most any thing in this Letter, because I know the care of the Bearer. He will be most sadly disappointed if you should be broke up before he arrives, as he is very desirous of being introduced by you to a Number of Gentlemen of respectable characters. I almost envy him, that he should see you, before I can.

Mr. Thaxter and Rice[2] present their Regards to you. Unkle Quincy too sends his Love to you, he is very good to call and see me, and so have many other of my Friends been. Coll. Warren and Lady were here a monday, and send their Love to you. The Coll. promiss'd to write. Mrs. Warren will spend a Day or two on her return with me. I told Betsy to write to you. She says she would if you were her *Husband*.

Your Mother sends her Love to you, and all your family too numerous to name desire to be rememberd. You will receive Letters from two, who are as earnest to write to Pappa as if the welfare of a kingdom depended upon it. If you can give any guess within a month let me know when you think of returning to Your most Affectionate

Abigail Adams

1774   1848

John Adams to Abigail Adams

[DR. FRANKLIN]

July 23 1775

My Dear

You have more than once in your Letters mentioned Dr. Franklin,[3] and in one intimated a Desire that I should write you something concerning him.

Dr. Franklin has been very constant in his Attendance on Congress from the Beginning. His Conduct has been composed and grave and in the Opinion of many Gentlemen very reserved. He has not assumed any Thing, nor affected to take the lead; but has seemed to choose that the Congress should pursue their own Principles and sentiments and adopt their own Plans: Yet he has not been backward: has been very usefull, on many occasions, and discovered[4] a Disposition entirely American. He does not hesitate at our boldest Measures, but rather seems to think us, too irresolute, and backward. He thinks us at present in an odd State, neither in Peace nor War, neither

9. Adjourn.
1. Josiah Quincy Jr. (1744–1775), a lawyer, sailed secretly to England to argue the American cause to British friendly to the colonies.

2. John Thaxter Jr. and Nathan Rice, law clerks.
3. Benjamin Franklin (1706–1790) returned to Philadelphia from England in 1775.
4. Revealed.

dependent nor independent. But he thinks that We shall soon assume a Character more decisive.

He thinks, that We have the Power of preserving ourselves, and that even if We should be driven to the disagreable Necessity of assuming a total Independency, and set up a separate state, We could maintain it. The People of England, have thought that the Opposition in America, was wholly owing to Dr. Franklin: and I suppose their scribblers will attribute the Temper, and Proceedings of this Congress to him: but there cannot be a greater Mistake. He has had but little share farther than to co operate and assist. He is however a great and good Man. I wish his Colleagues from this City were All like him, particularly one,[5] whose Abilities and Virtues, formerly trumpeted so much in America, have been found wanting.

There is a young Gentleman from Pensylvania whose Name is Wilson, whose Fortitude, Rectitude, and Abilities too, greatly outshine his Masters. Mr. Biddle, the Speaker, has been taken off, by Sickness. Mr. Mifflin is gone to the Camp, Mr. Morton is ill too, so that this Province has suffered by the Timidity of two overgrown Fortunes.[6] The Dread of Confiscation, or Caprice, I know not what has influenced them too much: Yet they were for taking Arms and pretended to be very valiant.—This Letter must be secret my dear—at least communicated with great Discretion. Yours,

John Adams

1775   1875

John Adams to Abigail Adams

[PREJUDICE IN FAVOR OF NEW ENGLAND]

Octr. 29. 1775

There is, in the human Breast, a social Affection, which extends to our whole Species. Faintly indeed; but in some degree. The Nation, Kingdom, or Community to which We belong is embraced by it more vigorously. It is stronger still towards the Province to which we belong, and in which We had our Birth. It is stronger and stronger, as We descend to the County, Town, Parish, Neighbourhood, and Family, which We call our own.—And here We find it often so powerfull as to become partial, to blind our Eyes, to darken our Understandings and pervert our Wills.

It is to this Infirmity, in my own Heart, that I must perhaps attribute that local Attachment, that partial Fondness, that overweening Prejudice in favour of New England, which I feel very often and which I fear sometimes, leads me to expose myself to just Ridicule.

New England has in many Respects the Advantage of every other Colony in America, and indeed of every other Part of the World, that I know any Thing of.

1. The People are purer English Blood, less mixed with Scotch, Irish, Dutch, French, Danish, Sweedish &c. than any other; and descended from

---

5. John is referring to John Dickinson (1732–1808), elected to the Continental Congress by the Pennsylvania Assembly.
6. James Wilson (1742–1798), a lawyer, was elected to the Second Continental Congress by the Pennsylvania Assembly along with Thomas Willing

(1732–1821), a banker, and Franklin. Edward Biddle (n.d.) and John Morton (1724?–1777) were often ill. Thomas Mifflin (1744–1800) left for the army. The "two overgrown fortunes" referred to are those of Dickinson and Willing.

Englishmen too who left Europe, in purer Times than the present and less tainted with Corruption than those they left behind them.

2. The Institutions in New England for the Support of Religion, Morals and Decency, exceed any other, obliging every Parish to have a Minister, and every Person to go to Meeting &c.[7]

3. The public Institutions in New England for the Education of Youth, supporting Colledges at the public Expence and obliging Towns to maintain Grammar schools, is not equalled and never was in any Part of the World.

4. The Division of our Territory, that is our Counties into Townships, empowering Towns to assemble, choose officers, make Laws, mend roads, and twenty other Things, gives every Man an opportunity of shewing and improving that Education which he received at Colledge or at school, and makes Knowledge and Dexterity at public Business common.

5. Our Laws for the Distribution of Intestate Estates[8] occasions a frequent Division of landed Property and prevents Monopolies, of Land.

But in opposition to these We have laboured under many Disadvantages. The exorbitant Prerogatives of our Governors &c. which would have overborn our Liberties, if it had not been opposed by the five preceding Particulars.

1775   1875

Abigail Adams to John Adams

[THE BUILDING UP A GREAT EMPIRE]

November 27 1775

Tis a fortnight to Night since I wrote you a line during which, I have been confined with the Jaundice, Rhumatism and a most voilent cold; I yesterday took a puke which has releived me, and I feel much better to day. Many, very many people who have had the dysentery, are now afflicted both with the Jaundice and Rhumatisim, some it has left in Hecticks, some in dropsies.[9]

The great and incessant rains we have had this fall, (the like cannot be recollected) may have occasiond some of the present disorders. The Jaundice is very prevelant in the Camp.[1] We have lately had a week of very cold weather, as cold as January, and a flight of snow, which I hope will purify the air of some of the noxious vapours. It has spoild many hundreds of Bushels of Apples, which were designd for cider, and which the great rains had prevented people from making up. Suppose we have lost 5 Barrels by it.

Col. Warren[2] returnd last week to Plymouth, so that I shall not hear any thing from you till he goes back again which will not be till the last of ⟨next⟩ this month.

He Damp'd my Spirits greatly by telling me that the Court had prolonged your Stay an other month.[3] I was pleasing myself with the thoughts that you would soon be upon your return. Tis in vain to repine. I hope the publick will reap what I sacrifice.

I wish I knew what mighty things were fabricating.[4] If a form of Goverment

---

7. I.e., to attend a Congregational church unless specifically exempted.
8. The distribution of property when no will exists.
9. With fevers and an unnatural retention of water in any part of the body.
1. Army.

2. Col. James Warren; see n. 5, p. 684.
3. On November 11, the Massachusetts House of Representatives extended the commissions of the delegates to the Continental Congress.
4. Being made.

is to be established here what one will be assumed? Will it be left to our assemblies to chuse one? and will not many men have many minds? and shall we not run into Dissentions among ourselves?

I am more and more convinced that Man is a dangerous creature, and that power whether vested in many or a few is ever grasping, and like the grave cries give, give. The great fish swallow up the small, and he who is most strenuous for the Rights of the people, when vested with power, is as eager after the perogatives of Government. You tell me of degrees of perfection to which Humane Nature is capable of arriving, and I believe it, but at the same time lament that our admiration should arise from the scarcity of the instances.

The Building up a Great Empire, which was only hinted at by my correspondent may now I suppose be realized even by the unbelievers. Yet will not ten thousand Difficulties arise in the formation of it? The Reigns of Government have been so long slakned, that I fear the people will not quietly submit to those restraints which are necessary for the peace, and security, of the community; if we seperate from Brittain, what Code of Laws will be established. How shall we be governd so as to retain our Liberties? Can any government be free which is not adminstred by general stated Laws? Who shall frame these Laws? Who will give them force and energy? Tis true your Resolution[s] as a Body have heithertoo had the force of Laws. But will they continue to have?

When I consider these things and the prejudices of people in favour of Ancient customs and Regulations, I feel anxious for the fate of our Monarchy or Democracy or what ever is to take place. I soon get lost in a Labyrinth of perplexities, but whatever occurs, may justice and righteousness be the Stability of our times, and order arise out of confusion. Great difficulties may be surmounted, by patience and perserverance.

I believe I have tired you with politicks. As to news we have not any at all. I shudder at the approach of winter when I think I am to remain desolate. Suppose your weather is warm yet. Mr. Mason[5] and Thaxter live with me, and render some part of my time less disconsolate. Mr. Mason is a youth who will please you, he has Spirit, taste and Sense. His application to his Studies is constant and I am much mistaken if he does not make a very good figure in his profession.

I have with me now, the only Daughter of your Brother;[6] I feel a tenderer affection for her as she has lost a kind parent. Though too young to be sensible of her own loss, I can pitty her. She appears to be a child of a very good Disposition—only wants to be a little used to company.

Our Little ones send Duty to pappa and want much to see him. Tom says he wont come home till the Battle is over—some strange notion he has got into his head. He has got a political cread to say to him when he returns.

I must bid you good night. Tis late for one who am much of an invalid. I was dissapointed last week in receiving a packet by the post, and upon unsealing it found only four news papers. I think you are more cautious than

5. Jonathan Mason Jr., law clerk.
6. Susanna Adams (1766–1826), daughter of Elihu and Thankful Adams.

you need be. All Letters I believe have come safe to hand. I have Sixteen from you, and wish I had as many more. Adieu. Yours.

1775   1848

John Adams to Abigail Adams

[THESE COLONIES ARE FREE AND INDEPENDENT STATES]

Philadelphia July 3. 1776

Your Favour of June 17. dated at Plymouth, was handed me, by Yesterdays Post. I was much pleased to find that you had taken a Journey to Plymouth, to see your Friends in the long Absence of one whom you may wish to see. The Excursion will be an Amusement, and will serve your Health. How happy would it have made me to have taken this Journey with you?

I was informed, a day or two before the Receipt of your Letter, that you was gone to Plymouth, by Mrs. Polly Palmer,[7] who was obliging enough in your Absence, to inform me, of the Particulars of the Expedition to the lower Harbour against the Men of War. Her Narration is executed, with a Precision and Perspicuity, which would have become the Pen of an accomplished Historian.

I am very glad you had so good an opportunity of seeing one of our little American Men of War. Many Ideas, new to you, must have presented themselves in such a Scene; and you will in future, better understand the Relations of Sea Engagements.

I rejoice extreamly at Dr. Bulfinches[8] Petition to open an Hospital. But I hope, the Business will be done upon a larger Scale. I hope, that one Hospital will be licensed in every County, if not in every Town. I am happy to find you resolved, to be with the Children, in the first Class. Mr. Whitney and Mrs. Katy Quincy,[9] are cleverly through Innoculation, in this City.

I have one favour to ask, and that is, that in your future Letters, you would acknowledge the Receipt of all those you may receive from me, and mention their Dates. By this Means I shall know if any of mine miscarry.

The Information you give me of our Friends refusing his Appointment, has given me much Pain, Grief and Anxiety.[1] I believe I shall be obliged to follow his Example. I have not Fortune enough to support my Family, and what is of more Importance, to support the Dignity of that exalted Station. It is too high and lifted up, for me; who delight in nothing so much as Retreat, Solitude, Silence, and Obscurity. In private Life, no one has a Right to censure me for following my own Inclinations, in Retirement, Simplicity, and Frugality: in public Life, every Man has a Right to remark as he pleases, at least he thinks so.

Yesterday the greatest Question was decided, which ever was debated in America, and a greater perhaps, never was or will be decided among Men. A Resolution was passed without one dissenting Colony "that these united Colonies, are, and of right ought to be free and independent States, and as

7. Miss Mary Palmer (Mrs. here stands for "Mistress") (1746–1791), a niece of the Cranches'.
8. Dr. Thomas Bulfinch (n.d.) inoculated Abigail Adams against smallpox.
9. Katherine Quincy (1733–1804), a relative of Abigail's. Reverend Whitney was from Massachusetts.
1. In an earlier letter, Abigail had informed John that James Warren had declined an appointment as associate justice of the Massachusetts Superior Court.

such, they have, and of Right ought to have full Power to make War, conclude Peace, establish Commerce, and to do all the other Acts and Things, which other States may rightfully do." You will see in a few days a Declaration setting forth the Causes, which have impell'd Us to this mighty Revolution, and the Reasons which will justify it, in the Sight of God and Man.[2] A Plan of Confederation will be taken up in a few days.

When I look back to the Year 1761, and recollect the Argument concerning Writs of Assistance, in the Superiour Court, which I have hitherto considered as the Commencement of the Controversy,[3] between Great Britain and America, and run through the whole Period from that Time to this, and recollect the series of political Events, the Chain of Causes and Effects, I am surprized at the Suddenness, as well as Greatness of this Revolution. Britain has been fill'd with Folly, and America with Wisdom, at least this is my Judgment.—Time must determine. It is the Will of Heaven, that the two Countries should be sundered forever. It may be the Will of Heaven that America shall suffer Calamities still more wasting and Distresses yet more dreadfull. If this is to be the Case, it will have this good Effect, at least: it will inspire Us with many Virtues, which We have not, and correct many Errors, Follies, and Vices, which threaten to disturb, dishonour, and destroy Us.—The Furnace of Affliction produces Refinement, in States as well as Individuals. And the new Governments we are assuming, in every Part, will require a Purification from our Vices, and an Augmentation of our Virtues or they will be no Blessings. The People will have unbounded Power. And the People are extreamly addicted to Corruption and Venality, as well as the Great.—I am not without Apprehensions from this Quarter. But I must submit all my Hopes and Fears, to an overruling Providence, in which, unfashionable as the Faith may be, I firmly believe.

1776   1792

John Adams to Abigail Adams

[REFLECTIONS ON THE DECLARATION OF INDEPENDENCE]

Philadelphia July 3d. 1776

Had a Declaration of Independency been made seven Months ago, it would have been attended with many great and glorious Effects.[4] . . . We might before this Hour, have formed Alliances with foreign States.—We should have mastered Quebec and been in Possession of Canada. . . . You will perhaps wonder, how such a Declaration would have influenced our Affairs, in Canada, but if I could write with Freedom I could easily convince you, that it would, and explain to you the manner how.—Many Gentlemen in high Stations and of great Influence have been duped, by the ministerial

2. The editors of the *Adams Family Correspondence* note that this letter "and the next one of the same date were written *between* the act of independence itself and the adoption of the statement designed to 'justify it in the sight of God and man.' "
3. Writs of assistance were general search warrants and, as such, a threat to civil liberty.
4. Here and below the ellipses are in the manu-script. On June 7, Richard Henry Lee (1732–1794), from Virginia, moved "that these United Colonies are, and of right ought to be, Free and Independent States." Lee's motion was carried on July 2 after vigorous debate. A committee was appointed to prepare a formal declaration and this document, written largely by Thomas Jefferson, was adopted July 4, 1776.

Bubble of Commissioners to treat. . . . And in real, sincere Expectation of this Event, which they so fondly wished, they have been slow and languid, in promoting Measures for the Reduction[5] of that Province. Others there are in the Colonies who really wished that our Enterprise in Canada would be defeated, that the Colonies might be brought into Danger and Distress between two Fires, and be thus induced to submit. Others really wished to defeat the Expedition to Canada, lest the Conquest of it, should elevate the Minds of the People too much to hearken to those Terms of Reconciliation which they believed would be offered Us. These jarring Views, Wishes and Designs, occasioned an opposition to many salutary Measures, which were proposed for the Support of that Expedition, and caused Obstructions, Embarrassments and studied Delays, which have finally, lost Us the Province.

All these Causes however in Conjunction would not have disappointed Us, if it had not been for a Misfortune, which could not be foreseen, and perhaps could not have been prevented, I mean the Prevalence of the small Pox among our Troops. . . . This fatal Pestilence compleated our Destruction.— It is a Frown of Providence upon Us, which We ought to lay to heart.

But on the other Hand, the Delay of this Declaration to this Time, has many great Advantages attending it.—The Hopes of Reconciliation, which were fondly entertained by Multitudes of honest and well meaning tho weak and mistaken People, have been gradually and at last totally extinguished.— Time has been given for the whole People, maturely to consider the great Question of Independence and to ripen their Judgments, dissipate their Fears, and allure their Hopes, by discussing it in News Papers and Pamphletts, by debating it, in Assemblies, Conventions, Committees of Safety and Inspection, in Town and County Meetings, as well as in private Conversations, so that the whole People in every Colony of the 13, have now adopted it, as their own Act.—This will cement the Union, and avoid those Heats and perhaps Convulsions which might have been occasioned, by such a Declaration Six Months ago.

But the Day is past. The Second Day of July 1776, will be the most memorable Epocha, in the History of America.—I am apt to believe that it will be celebrated, by succeeding Generations, as the great anniversary Festival. It ought to be commemorated, as the Day of Deliverance by solemn Acts of Devotion to God Almighty. It ought to be solemnized with Pomp and Parade, with Shews, Games, Sports, Guns, Bells, Bonfires and Illuminations from one End of this Continent to the other from this Time forward forever more.

You will think me transported with Enthusiasm but I am not.—I am well aware of the Toil and Blood and Treasure, that it will cost Us to maintain this Declaration, and support and defend these States.—Yet through all the Gloom I can see the Rays of ravishing Light and Glory. I can see that the End is more than worth all the Means. And that Posterity will tryumph in that Days Transaction, even altho We should rue it, which I trust in God We shall not.

1776   1792

5. Conquest. "To treat": to negotiate.

Abigail Adams to John Adams

[THE DECLARATION. SMALLPOX. THE GREY HORSE]

* * *

Sunday july 14 [1776]

By yesterdays post I received two Letters dated 3 and 4 of July and tho your Letters never fail to give me pleasure, be the subject what it will, yet it was greatly heightned by the prospect of the future happiness and glory of our Country; nor am I a little Gratified when I reflect that a person so nearly connected with me has had the Honour of being a principal actor, in laying a foundation for its future Greatness. May the foundation of our new constitution, be justice, Truth and Righteousness. Like the wise Mans house may it be founded upon those Rocks and then neither storms or temptests will overthrow it.[6]

I cannot but feel sorry that some of the most Manly Sentiments in the Declaration are Expunged from the printed coppy. Perhaps wise reasons induced it.

Poor Canady I lament Canady but we ought to be in some measure sufferers for the past folly of our conduct. The fatal effects of the small pox there, has led almost every person to consent to Hospitals in every Town. In many Towns, already arround Boston the Selectmen have granted Liberty for innoculation. I hope the necessity is now fully seen.

I had many dissagreable Sensations at the Thoughts of comeing myself, but to see my children thro it I thought my duty, and all those feelings vanished as soon as I was innoculated and I trust a kind providence will carry me safely thro. Our Friends from Plymouth came into Town yesterday. We have enough upon our hands in the morning. The Little folks are very sick then and puke every morning but after that they are comfortable. I shall write you now very often. Pray inform me constantly of every important transaction. Every expression of tenderness is a cordial to my Heart. Unimportant as they are to the rest of the world, to me they are *every Thing*.

We have had during all the month of June a most severe Drougth which cut of all our promising hopes of english Grain and the first crop of Grass, but since july came in we have had a plenty of rain and now every thing looks well. There is one Misfortune in our family which I have never mentioned in hopes it would have been in my power to have remedied it, but all hopes of that kind are at an end. It is the loss of your Grey Horse. About 2 months ago, I had occasion to send Jonathan[7] of an errant to my unkle Quincys (the other Horse being a plowing). Upon his return a little below the church she trod upon a rolling stone and lamed herself to that degree that it was with great difficulty that she could be got home. I immediately sent for Tirrel[8] and every thing was done for her by Baths, ointments, politceing, Bleeding &c. that could be done. Still she continued extreem lame tho not so bad as at first. I then got her carried to Domet[9] but he pronounces her incurable, as a callous is grown upon her footlock joint. You can hardly tell, not even by

---

6. Matthew 7.24–25 describes "a wise man, which built his house upon a rock: And the rain descended, and the winds blew, and beat upon that house; and it fell not: for it was founded upon a rock."

7. Abigail's servant or farm boy.

8. A veterinarian from Braintree.

9. Another veterinarian.

your own feelings how much I lament her. She was not with foal, as you immagined, but I hope she is now as care has been taken in that Respect.

I suppose you have heard of a fleet which came up pretty near the Light and kept us all with our mouths open ready to catch them, but after staying near a week and makeing what observations they could set sail and went of to our great mortification who were [prepared?][1] for them in every respect. If our Ship of 32 Guns which [was] Built at Portsmouth and waiting only for Guns and an other of [. . .] at Plimouth in the same state, had been in readiness we should in all probability been Masters of them. Where the blame lies in that respect I know not, tis laid upon Congress, and Congress is also blamed for not appointing us a General.—But Rome was not Built in a day.

I hope the Multiplicity of cares and avocations which invellope you will not be too powerfull for you. I have many anxietyes upon that account. Nabby and Johnny send duty and desire Mamma to say that an inflamation in their Eyes which has been as much of a distemper as the small pox, has prevented their writing, but they hope soon to be able to acquaint Pappa of their happy recovery from the Distemper.—Mr. C[ranch] and wife, Sister B[etsy] and all our Friend[s] desire to be rememberd to you and foremost in that Number stands your

Portia

PS   A little India herb[2] would have been mighty agreable now.

1776   1875

John Adams to Abigail Adams

[DO MY FRIENDS THINK I HAVE FORGOTTEN MY WIFE AND CHILDREN?]

Philadelphia July 20, 1776

This has been a dull day to me: I waited the Arrival of the Post with much Solicitude and Impatience, but his Arrival made me more solicitous still.— "To be left at the Post Office" in your Hand Writing, on the back of a few Lines from the Dr.[3] were all that I could learn of you, and my little Folks. If you was too busy to write, I hoped that some kind Hand would have been found to let me know something about you.

Do my Friends think that I have been a Politician so long as to have lost all feeling? Do they suppose I have forgotten my Wife and Children? Or are they so panic struck with the Loss of Canada, as to be afraid to correspond with me? Or have they forgotten that you have an Husband and your Children a Father? What have I done, or omitted to do, that I should be thus forgotten and neglected in the most tender and affecting scæne of my Life! Dont mistake me, I dont blame you. Your Time and Thoughts must have been wholly taken up, with your own and your Families situation and Necessities.—But twenty other Persons might have informed me.

I suspect, that you intended to have run slyly, through the small Pox with the family, without letting me know it, and then have sent me an Account that you were all well. This might be a kind Intention, and if the design had

1. The manuscript is torn here and below.
2. Tea, an import of the British East India company.

3. Dr. Cotton Tufts (1732–1815), Abigail's uncle by marriage.

succeeded, would have made me very joyous. But the secret is out, and I am left to conjecture. But as the Faculty[4] have this distemper so much under Command I will flatter myself with the Hope and Expectation of soon hearing of your Recovery.

1776   1875

Abigail Adams to John Adams

[SMALLPOX. THE PROCLAMATION FOR INDEPENDENCE READ ALOUD]

July 21 1776 Boston

I have no doubt but that my dearest Friend is anxious to know how his Portia does, and his little flock of children under the opperation of a disease once so formidable.

I have the pleasure to tell him that they are all comfortable tho some of them complaining. Nabby has been very ill, but the Eruption begins to make its appearance upon her, and upon Johnny. Tommy is so well that the Dr. innoculated him again to day fearing it had not taken. Charlly has no complaints yet, tho his arm has been very soar.

I have been out to meeting this forenoon, but have so many dissagreable Sensations this afternoon that I thought it prudent to tarry at home. The Dr. says they are very good feelings. Mr. Cranch has passed thro the preparation and the Eruption is comeing out cleverly[5] upon him without any Sickness at all. Mrs. Cranch is cleverly and so are all her children. Those who are broke out are pretty full for the new method as tis call'd, the Suttonian[6] they profess to practice upon. I hope to give you a good account when I write next, but our Eyes are very weak and the Dr. is not fond of either writing or reading for his patients. But I must transgress a little.

I received a Letter from you by wedensday Post 7 of July and tho I think it a choise one in the Litterary Way, containing many usefull hints and judicious observations which will greatly assist me in the future instruction of our Little ones, yet it Lacked some essential engrediants to make it compleat. Not one word respecting yourself, your Health or your present Situation. My anxiety for your welfare will never leave me but with my parting Breath, tis of more importance to me than all this World contains besides. The cruel Seperation to which I am necessatated cuts of half the enjoyments of life, the other half are comprised in the hope I have that what I do and what I suffer may be serviceable to you, to our Little ones and our Country; I must beseach you therefore for the future never to omit what is so essential to my happiness.

Last Thursday[7] after hearing a very Good Sermon I went with the Multitude into Kings Street to hear the proclamation for independance read and proclamed. Some Field peices with the Train[8] were brought there, the troops appeard under Arms and all the inhabitants assembled there (the small pox prevented many thousand from the Country). When Col. Crafts read from the Belcona[9] of the State House the Proclamation, great attention was given

4. The medical profession.
5. Completely. "Cleverly" can also mean "healthy," as below.
6. Named after Daniel Sutton (1735–1819) of Essex, Massachusetts. His method required only a

small puncture instead of the customary gash to infect the subject.
7. July 18, 1776.
8. I.e., field guns with their vehicles.
9. Balcony. Col. Thomas Crafts (n.d.).

to every word. As soon as he ended, the cry from the Belcona, was God Save our American States and then 3 cheers which rended the air, the Bells rang, the privateers[1] fired, the forts and Batteries, the cannon were discharged, the platoons followed and every face appeard joyfull. Mr. Bowdoin then gave a Sentiment,[2] Stability and perpetuity to American independance. After dinner the kings arms were taken down from the State House and every vestage of him from every place in which it appeard and burnt in King Street. Thus ends royall Authority in this State, and all the people shall say Amen.

I have been a little surprized that we collect no better accounts with regard to the horrid conspiricy at New York, and that so little mention has been made of it here. It made a talk for a few days but now seems all hushed in Silence. The Tories say that it was not a conspiricy but an association, and pretend that there was no plot to assasinate the General.[3] Even their hardned Hearts ⟨Blush⟩ feel——the discovery. We have in Gorge a match for a Borgia and a Catiline,[4] a Wretch Callous to every Humane feeling. Our worthy preacher told us that he believed one of our Great Sins for which a righteous God has come out in judgment against us, was our Biggoted attachment to so wicked a Man. May our repentance be sincere.

Monday morg. july 22

I omitted many things yesterday in order to be better informed. I have got Mr. Cranch to inquire and write you, concerning a French Schooner from Martineco which came in yesterday and a prize from Ireland. My own infirmities prevents my writing. A most Excruciating pain in my head and every Limb and joint I hope portends a speedy Eruption and prevents my saying more than that I am forever Yours.

The children are not yet broke out. Tis the Eleventh Day with us.

1776   1875

John Adams to Abigail Adams

[MY COUNTRYMEN WANT ART AND ADDRESS]

Aug. 3. 1776

The Post was later than usual to day, so that I had not yours of July 24 till this Evening. You have made me very happy, by the particular and favourable Account you give me of all the Family. But I dont understand how there are so many who have no Eruptions, and no Symptoms. The Inflammation in the Arm might do, but without that, there is no small Pox.

I will lay a Wager, that your whole Hospital have not had so much small Pox, as Mrs. Katy Quincy. Upon my Word she has had an Abundance of it, but is finely recovered, looks as fresh as a Rose, but pitted all over, as thick as ever you saw any one. I this Evening presented your Compliments and Thanks to Mr. Hancock[5] for his polite offer of his House, and likewise your Compliments to his Lady and Mrs. Katy.

1. Privately owned armed vessels with a government commission.
2. A personal reflection. James Bowdoin Sr. (1726–1790), proposed by John for governor of Massachusetts (1785–87).
3. George Washington.
4. King George III of England (1738–1820) is compared to the Italian statesman and cardinal Cesare Borgia (1475–1507), famous for his cruelty, and to Catiline (108?–62 B.C.E.), Roman politician and conspirator against the state.
5. John Hancock (1737–1793), another delegate from Massachusetts.

Aug. 4

Went this Morning to the Baptist Meeting, in Hopes of hearing Mr. Still-man,[6] but was dissappointed. He was there, but another Gentleman preached. His Action was violent to a degree bordering on fury. His Gestures, unnatural, and distorted. Not the least Idea of Grace in his Motions, or Elegance in his Style. His Voice was vociferous and boisterous, and his Composition almost wholly destitute of Ingenuity. I wonder extreamly at the Fondness of our People for schollars educated at the Southward and for southern Preachers. There is no one Thing, in which We excell them more, than in our University, our schollars, and Preachers. Particular Gentlemen here, who have improved upon their Education by Travel, shine. But in general, old Massachusetts outshines her younger sisters, still. In several Particulars, they have more Wit, than We. They have Societies; the philosophical Society particularly, which excites a scientific Emulation, and propagates their Fame. If ever I get through this Scene of Politicks and War, I will spend the Remainder of my days, in endeavouring to instruct my Countrymen in the Art of making the most of their Abilities and Virtues, an Art, which they have hitherto, too much neglected. A philosophical society shall be established at Boston, if I have Wit and Address enough to accomplish it, sometime or other.—Pray set Brother[7] Cranch's Philosophical Head to plodding upon this Project. Many of his Lucubrations would have been published and preserved, for the Benefit of Mankind, and for his Honour, if such a Clubb had existed.

My Countrymen want Art and Address.[8] They want Knowledge of the World. They want the exteriour and superficial Accomplishments of Gentlemen, upon which the World has foolishly set so high a Value. In solid Abilities and real Virtues, they vastly excell in general, any People upon this Continent. Our N. England People are Aukward and bashfull; yet they are pert, ostentatious and vain, a Mixture which excites Ridicule and gives Disgust. They have not the faculty of shewing themselves to the best Advantage, nor the Art of concealing this faculty. An Art and Faculty which some People possess in the highest degree. Our Deficiencies in these Respects, are owing wholly to the little Intercourse We have had with strangers, and to our Inexperience in the World. These Imperfections must be remedied, for New England must produce the Heroes, the statesmen, the Philosophers, or America will make no great Figure for some Time.

Our Army is rather sickly at N. York, and We live in daily Expectation of hearing of some great Event. May God almighty grant it may be prosperous for America.—Hope is an Anchor and a Cordial. Disappointment however will not disconcert me.

If you will come to Philadelphia in September, I will stay, as long as you please. I should be as proud and happy as a Bridegroom. Yours.

1776   1875

---

6. The Reverend Samuel Stillman (1738–1807), pastor of the First Baptist Church of Boston from 1765 to 1807.

7. I.e., brother-in-law.
8. I.e., lack skill and dexterity.

ANNIS BOUDINOT STOCKTON
1736–1801

British Americans, hoping to demonstrate their familiarity with the norms that defined a person of learning and sociability, expressed themselves in many of the same poetic forms—elegies, odes, epithalamiums, sonnets, satire, pastoral, for example—that defined English literature in the Augustan Age. But to think of authorship primarily in terms of print publication greatly limits our understanding of such eighteenth-century writing. In fact, colonial Americans prepared a considerable amount of belletristic literature for oral presentation or manuscript circulation among friends and like-minded acquaintances. Some of these provincials took as their model the famous English social clubs in which politics and literature were mixed in the headiest concoctions. At such American incarnations of club culture as the Tuesday Club of Annapolis, Maryland (1745–56), whose elaborate history was left in manuscript by Dr. Alexander Hamilton, both women and men shared hospitality, conversation, and writing. Equally important, writers who traveled in such circles often prepared fair copies of poetry for literati at a distance from their meetings. For these literary types, manuscripts were the equivalent of print.

This kind of literary culture existed all along the Atlantic seaboard but flourished particularly in large port cities or near the few institutions of higher learning that dotted the provincial landscape. The center of one such circle was Princeton, New Jersey, where the poet Annis Boudinot Stockton opened her husband's family manor, Morven, to intellectuals and politicians in the region. Daughter of a well-to-do Philadelphia family that had recently moved to Princeton, Annis married the attorney Richard Stockton, scion of a prominent local family, in 1757 or early 1758. Richard quickly became a favorite of New Jersey governor William Franklin and through such patronage held various offices in the colonial government. Eventually espousing the patriots' cause, he signed the Declaration of Independence. The Stocktons' intellectual and political network ensured their high visibility, and Annis used her social position to establish a literary salon on the model of that of her childhood friend Elizabeth Graeme Fergusson in Philadelphia.

Like so many other colonists with close ties to British government, the Stocktons found their lives overturned by the turmoil of politics and war. Forced to leave Morven as battles raged nearby, they soon found themselves under suspicion by the Crown, and, subsequently, Richard was jailed and made to sign an oath not to participate further in resistance to the king. After General Washington recaptured the area, the Stocktons were able to return to their home, which Annis reopened to the kind of company, including Washington himself, that she had known since her youth in Philadelphia. After the death of her husband in 1781 deprived her of her staunchest supporter, poetry continued to bring her solace; several of her most moving poems were written on anniversaries of his death.

Stockton's skill as a poet was not totally unknown in the wider world, for eventually she published twenty-one poems in monthly magazines or weekly newspapers (she signed them "Mrs. A.S." or "Mrs. S."), most in the 1780s. The bulk of her oeuvre, however, remained in manuscript, primarily in a volume titled *Only for the Eye of a Friend*, recently acquired by the New Jersey Historical Society. Her poems' subjects vary from the overtly political to the deeply personal, and all display the wit and intelligence that characterizes the best eighteenth-century writing. In one selection printed here she indicts males for not welcoming women's poetic efforts, stinging verse reminiscent of Anne Bradstreet's "Prologue" to her first book. Other poems, including one on the topic of sensibility—perhaps *the* topic of the age—speak eloquently of the subject of female friendship and the obligations incumbent on it. Another poem celebrates Washington's presidency and demonstrates how cleverly Stockton was able to negotiate the boundaries between public and private life, as she wrote movingly of her acquaintance and hero. Clearly, as these selections indicate, Stockton thought that writing was indeed publication, albeit in a form that prevented her widespread recognition. Testament to a culture that prided itself on its sense and sensibility, her verse and its appreciation by those in her circle remind us that, despite the undeniable restrictions on eighteenth-century women, some found an audience that valued their skill and intelligence.

The texts are from *Only for the Eye of a Friend: The Poems of Annis Boudinot Stockton* (1995), edited by Carla Mulford.

A Sarcasm[1] against the ladies in a newspaper; An impromptu answer

A Sarcasm against the ladies in a newspaper

Woman are books in which we often spy
Some bloted lines and sometimes lines awry
And tho perhaps some strait ones intervene
In all of them erata may be seen   5
If it be so I wish my wife were
An almanack—to change her every year

An impromptu answer

"Woman are books"—in this I do agree
But men there are that cant read A B C   10
And more who have not genius to discern
The beauties of those books they attempt to learn
For these an almanack may always hold
As much of Science as *they* can unfold—
But thank our stars, our Critics are not *these*   15
The men of sense and taste we always please
Who know to choose and then to prize their books
Nor leave the strait lines for to search for crooks
And from these books their noblest pleasures flow
Altho perfections never found below   20
With them into a world of error thrown
And our eratas place against their own

Emelia

c. 1756   1995

To my Burrissa—[1]

Lovliest of Women! Could I gain
Thy Friendship, which I prize
Above the treasures of the Main

---

1. Here, a jest, a jocular presentation.
1. To Stockton's friend and fellow writer, Esther Edwards Burr, wife of the president of the College of New Jersey (Princeton) and part of her literary circle.

Compleat would be my Joys
Burrissa Oh my soul aspires   5
And clames a kin with yours
A daring Emulation Fires
My Mind and all its powers
Pardon the Bold attempt it means
Only to Copy you   10
And thro' Lifes Various Shiftings Scenes
Will hold thee Still in View
O let thy Virtue be my guide
Thy presepts I'll improve
Do thou ore all my ways preside   15
Reprove me & I'll Love—
When first I knew thy Heavenly Mind
I felt the Sacred Flame
Of Friendship rising in my Brest
But Darest not it proclaime   20
But now Impatient of restraint
My Eyes Declare Its force
And Every friendly Look attests
From whence they take their siource—

April 11, 1757   1995

To Laura—a card.—[1]

Permit a sister muse to soar
To heights she never knew before,
     And then look up to thee;
For sure each female virtue join'd,
Conspire to make thy lovely mind   5
     The seat of harmony.

Thy fame has reach'd the calm retreat,
Where I, secluded from the great,
     Have leisure for my lays;
It rais'd ambition in my breast,   10
Not such as envious souls possess,
     Who hate another's praise.

But that which makes me strive to gain,
And ever-grateful I'd retain,
     Thy friendship as a prize;   15
For friendship soars above low rules,
The formal fetters of the schools,
     She wisely can despise—

So may fair Laura kindly condescend
And to her bosom take another friend.   20

c. May 1757   1995

1. To Stockton's friend Elizabeth Graeme Ferguson, an accomplished Philadelphia writer.

An ode on the birth day of the illustrious George Washington, President of the United States

Fair rise the Morn that gave our heroe birth,
And with it peace descend to bless the earth,
And hail his natal day—
Fly discord far from these enlighten'd shores
Let not fell Atte[1] with destructive powers,   5
Shed one malignant ray.—
But let the loves and all the graces Come,
Let nature smiling Shed a rich perfume,
And antedate the Spring—
With Myrtle[2] crown'd fair Freedom hail the morn,   10
On which *your* friend our much lov'd chief was born,
And all ye Muses Sing.—
Let venal bards a despots brow adorn,
In every wreath they find a rugged thorn,
And praise a Satire proves—   15
But our bright theme will make the garland shine,
To sweetest flowers his virtues we Combine,
And add to those our loves—
What noble qualities enrich his mind;
His ardent zeal his policy refine'd,   20
His watchfulness and care—
When e'er his Country needs a faithful guard,
No dire event can find him unprepar'd,
For arts of peace or war.—
When Savage herds invade our fertile plains,   25
And undistinguishd Scalp the peaceful swains,
His energy is seen—
Collects the heroes from their rural home,
Their long neglected helmets they assume,
And peace is heard again.—   30
When ancient nations past their zenith drive
To that fixed point at which they must arrive,
And all their glory cloud—
Contending armies croud the ensanguind field,
The glittering arms are seen the sword the shield,   35
And garments rolld in blood—
On Natures theatre almost alone—
Columbia Sitting on a peaceful throne—
Reclines her beauteous form,
Upon the bosom of her favourite Son—   40
Sees him Compleat the work which he began—
And turn the impending storm.
Long may this bright auspicious day appear,
And gild with lucid rays our hemisphere,
Reflecting on his breast—   45

1. Daughter of Zeus, who exemplified moral obtuseness, the inability to distinguish between right and wrong.
2. One of the leaves used to crown a poet.

That Conscious peace that ever must arise,
From goodness usefulness and great emprize,
By which his Countries blest.—
And when the arbiter of life and death,
Shall send his angel to demand his breath,   50
And Speed his heavenly flight—
May humble hope and Sacred Joy impart,
Streams of celestial pleasure to his heart,
   Incommunicably bright.—

c. February 1790   1995

Sensibility[,] an ode

Sweet Sensibility Celestial power
Raise in my heart thy altar and thy throne
Nor punish me with one unfeeling hour
But temper all my soul, and mark me for thy own
Give me to feel the tender trembling tear   5
Glide down my cheek at sight of human woe
And when I cant relieve the pang severe
The melting sigh of sympathy to know
To stretch the hand to sorrows tutor'd child
To wipe the tear from off the orphans eye   10
To turn from error by instruction mild
And snatch from vice the offspring of the sky
By thee inspir'd oh may I never dare
To join the herd in scandals groveling vale
Repeat the whisper in my neighbours ear   15
And give a sanction to the slanderous tale
But let me feel the sisters mothers heart
When e'er I view my species' go astray
Nor with the pride of virtue plant a dart
To fright returning prodigals away.—   20
And may I too participate each Joy
That mixes with the cup of human life
Nor by the stoics[1] frown the balm alloy
The balm that sweetens all this mortal strife
May sprightly wit and true benevolence   25
Give relish to each good which heaven bestows
May cheerfulness with smiling innocence
Increase the charms that o'er creation glows
Nor to these only do thy laws extend
For love and friendship claim an ample part   30
Ah now I feel them with my being blend
And with my Anna's image fill my heart

                             1995

---

1. School of Greek philosophy founded by Zeno that emphasized a detachment from passion and luxury as the way to align oneself with the natural order.

Tears of friendship[.] Elegy the third.—to a friend just
married, and who had promised to write, on parting, but had
neglected it.—

Why has my Anna thus forgot her friend?
Did we not meet at friendship's sacred shrine?
Did not our mutual vows of truth ascend,
A grateful offering to the power divine?—
But ah! ev'n there, I saw the palsian queen[1]   5
With strong resentment in her beauteous eyes;
She walk'd disorder'd near her sister's fane,
"Cupid, my son, this must not be! she cries;
Was not this Anna to our altars led,
By Hymen[2] lately with a favour'd swain?   10
Did not his purple wings the pair o'erspread?
And must his golden torch be lit in vain?
Must she neglect my rites and sacrifice
Before my rival, with a female friend?
Cupid, it must not be; part them she cries,   15
And soon their airy schemes of bliss will end.
'Tis done, and memory with a pang severe,
Now swells my heart with many a rising sigh;
Tho' you, my Anna, check'd the parting tear,
'Twas paid with interest when you pass'd me by.   20

1. The Greek goddess Pallas Athena, patron of   2. Roman god of marriage.
Athens, who had great beauty.

THOMAS PAINE
1737–1809

The author of two of the most popular books in eighteenth-century America, and the
most persuasive rhetorician of the cause for independence, Thomas Paine was born
in England in 1737, the son of a Quaker father and an Anglican mother, and did not
come to America until he was thirty-seven years old. Paine's early years prepared him
to be a supporter of the Revolution. The discrepancy between his high intelligence
and the limitations imposed on him by poverty and caste made him long for a new
social order. He once said that a sermon he heard at the age of eight impressed him
with the cruelty inherent in Christianity and made him a rebel forever. When he
arrived in Philadelphia with letters of introduction from Benjamin Franklin, recommending him as an "ingenious, worthy young man," he had already had a remarkably
full life. Until he was thirteen he went to grammar school and then was apprenticed
in his father's corset shop; at nineteen he ran away from home to go to sea. From
1757 to 1774 he was a corset maker, a tobacconist and grocer, a schoolteacher, and
an exciseman (a government employee who taxed goods). His efforts to organize the
excisemen and make Parliament raise their salary was unprecedented. He lost his job
when he admitted he had stamped as examined goods that had not been opened. His

first wife died less than a year after his marriage, and he was separated from his second wife after three years. Scandals about his private life and questions about his integrity when he was employed as an exciseman provided his critics with ammunition for the rest of his life. Franklin was right, however, in recognizing Paine's genius; for, like Franklin himself, he was a remarkable man, self-taught and curious about everything, from the philosophy of law to natural science.

In Philadelphia he found himself as a journalist, and he made his way quickly in that city, first as a spokesman against slavery and then as the anonymous author of *Common Sense*, the first pamphlet published in the colonies to urge immediate independence from Britain. Paine was obviously the right man in the right place at the right time. Relations with England were at their lowest ebb: Boston was under siege, and the Second Continental Congress had convened in Philadelphia. *Common Sense* sold almost half a million copies, and its authorship (followed by the charge of traitor) could not be kept a secret for long. Paine enlisted in the Revolutionary Army and served as an aide-de-camp in battles in New York, New Jersey, and Pennsylvania. He followed the triumph of *Common Sense* with the first of sixteen pamphlets titled *Crisis*. The first *Crisis* paper ("These are the times that try men's souls") was read to Washington's troops at Trenton and did much to shore up the spirits of the Revolutionary soldiers.

Paine received a number of political appointments as rewards for his services as a writer for the American cause, but he misused his privileges and lost the most lucrative offices. He was too indiscreet and hot tempered for public employment. In 1787 he returned to England, determined to get financial assistance to construct an iron bridge for which he had devised plans. It came to nothing. But in England he wrote his second most successful work, his *Rights of Man* (1791–92), an impassioned plea against hereditary monarchy, the traditional institution Paine never tired of arguing against. Paine was charged with treason and fled to France, where he was made a citizen and lionized as a spokesman for revolution. The horrors of the French Revolution, however, brought home to Paine the fact that the mere overthrow of monarchy did not usher in light and order. When he protested the execution of Louis XVI, he was accused of sympathy with the Crown and imprisoned. He was saved from trial by the American ambassador, James Monroe, who offered him American citizenship and safe passage back to New York.

Paine spent the last years of his life in New York City and in New Rochelle, New York. They were unhappy, impoverished years, and his reputation suffered enormously as a result of *The Age of Reason* (1794). Paine's attempt to define his beliefs was viewed as an attack on Christianity and, by extension, on conventional society. He was ridiculed and despised. Even George Washington, who had supported Paine's early writing, thought English criticism of him was "not a bad thing." Paine had clearly outlived his time or was living ahead of it, for soon enough his deistic ideas assumed new life and form in American Romanticism. He was buried on his farm at New Rochelle after his request for a Quaker grave site was refused. Ten years later an enthusiastic admirer exhumed his bones with the intention of having him reburied in England. The admirer's plans came to nothing, and the whereabouts of Paine's remains is, at present, unknown.

Paine's great gift as a stylist was "plainness." He said he needed no "ceremonious expressions." "It is my design," he wrote, "to make those who can scarcely read understand," to put arguments in a language "as plain as the alphabet," and to shape everything "to fit the powers of thinking and the turn of language to the subject, so as to bring out a clear conclusion that shall hit the point in question and nothing else."

From Common Sense[1]

Introduction

Perhaps the sentiments contained in the following pages are not yet sufficiently fashionable to procure them general favor; a long habit of not thinking a thing wrong gives it a superficial appearance of being right, and raises at first a formidable outcry in defence of custom. But the tumult soon subsides. Time makes more converts than reason.

As a long and violent abuse of power is generally the means of calling the right of it in question (and in matters too which might never have been thought of, had not the sufferers been aggravated into the inquiry), and as the King of England hath undertaken in his own right, to support the Parliament in what he calls theirs, and as the good people of this country are grievously oppressed by the combination, they have an undoubted privilege to inquire into the pretensions of both, and equally to reject the usurpation of either.

In the following sheets, the author hath studiously avoided everything which is personal among ourselves. Compliments as well as censure to individuals make no part thereof. The wise and the worthy need not the triumph of a pamphlet; and those whose sentiments are injudicious or unfriendly will cease of themselves, unless too much pains is bestowed upon their conversions.

The cause of America is in a great measure the cause of all mankind. Many circumstances have, and will, arise which are not local, but universal, and through which the principles of all lovers of mankind are affected, and in the event of which their affections are interested. The laying a country desolate with fire and sword, declaring war against the natural rights of all mankind, and extirpating the defenders thereof from the face of the earth, is the concern of every man to whom nature hath given the power of feeling; of which class, regardless of party censure, is

The Author

From III. Thoughts on the Present State of American Affairs

In the following pages I offer nothing more than simple facts, plain arguments, and common sense: and have no other preliminaries to settle with the reader, than that he will divest himself of prejudice and prepossession, and suffer his reason and his feelings to determine for themselves: that he will put on, or rather that he will not put off, the true character of a man, and generously enlarge his views beyond the present day.

Volumes have been written on the subject of the struggle between England and America. Men of all ranks have embarked in the controversy, from different motives, and with various designs; but all have been ineffectual, and the period of debate is closed. Arms as the last resource decide the contest;

---

1. The full title is *Common Sense: Addressed to the Inhabitants of America, on the following Interesting Subjects: viz.: I. Of the Origin and Design of Government in General; with Concise Remarks on the English Constitution. II. Of Monarchy and Hered-* *itary Succession. III. Thoughts on the Present State of American Affairs. IV. Of the Present Ability of America; with some Miscellaneous Reflections.* The text used here is from *The Writings of Thomas Paine* (1894–96), vol. 1, edited by M. D. Conway.

the appeal was the choice of the King, and the continent has accepted the challenge.

It hath been reported of the late Mr. Pelham[2] (who though an able minister was not without his faults) that on his being attacked in the House of Commons on the score that his measures were only of a temporary kind, replied, "they will last my time." Should a thought so fatal and unmanly possess the colonies in the present contest, the name of ancestors will be remembered by future generations with detestation.

The sun never shined on a cause of greater worth. 'Tis not the affair of a city, a county, a province, or a kingdom; but of a continent—of at least one eighth part of the habitable globe. 'Tis not the concern of a day, a year, or an age; posterity are virtually involved in the contest, and will be more or less affected even to the end of time, by the proceedings now. Now is the seed time of continental union, faith and honor. The least fracture now will be like a name engraved with the point of a pin on the tender rind of a young oak; the wound would enlarge with the tree, and posterity read it in full grown characters.

By referring the matter from argument to arms, a new era for politics is struck—a new method of thinking hath arisen. All plans, proposals, etc., prior to the nineteenth of April, i.e., to the commencement of hostilities,[3] are like the almanacs of the last year; which though proper then, are superseded and useless now. Whatever was advanced by the advocates on either side of the question then, terminated in one and the same point, viz., a union with Great Britain; the only difference between the parties was the method of effecting it; the one proposing force, the other friendship; but it hath so far happened that the first hath failed, and the second hath withdrawn her influence.

As much hath been said of the advantages of reconciliation, which, like an agreeable dream, hath passed away and left us as we were, it is but right that we should examine the contrary side of the argument, and inquire into some of the many material injuries which these colonies sustain, and always will sustain, by being connected with and dependent on Great Britain. To examine that connection and dependence, on the principles of nature and common sense, to see what we have to trust to, if separated, and what we are to expect, if dependent.

I have heard it asserted by some, that as America has flourished under her former connection with Great Britain, the same connection is necessary towards her future happiness, and will always have the same effect. Nothing can be more fallacious than this kind of argument. We may as well assert that because a child has thrived upon milk, that it is never to have meat, or that the first twenty years of our lives is to become a precedent for the next twenty. But even this is admitting more than is true; for I answer roundly, that America would have flourished as much, and probably much more, had no European power taken any notice of her. The commerce by which she hath enriched herself are the necessaries of life, and will always have a market while eating is the custom of Europe.

2. Henry Pelham (1696–1754), prime minister of Britain (1743–54).
3. The "Minutemen" of Lexington, Massachusetts, defended their ammunition stores against the British on April 19, 1775, and engaged in the first armed conflict of the American Revolution.

But she has protected us, say some. That she hath engrossed[4] us is true, and defended the continent at our expense as well as her own, is admitted; and she would have defended Turkey from the same motive, viz., for the sake of trade and dominion.

Alas! we have been long led away by ancient prejudices and made large sacrifices to superstition. We have boasted the protection of Great Britain without considering that her motive was interest not attachment; and that she did not protect us from our enemies on our account; but from her enemies on her own account, from those who had no quarrel with us on any other account, and who will always be our enemies on the same account. Let Britain waive her pretensions to the continent, or the continent throw off the dependence, and we should be at peace with France and Spain, were they at war with Britain. The miseries of Hanover's last war[5] ought to warn us against connections.

It hath lately been asserted in Parliament, that the colonies have no relation to each other but through the parent country, i.e., that Pennsylvania and the Jerseys,[6] and so on for the rest, are sister colonies by the way of England; this is certainly a very roundabout way of proving relationship, but it is the nearest and only true way of proving enmity (or enemyship, if I may so call it). France and Spain never were, nor perhaps ever will be, our enemies as Americans, but as our being the subjects of Great Britain.

But Britain is the parent country, say some. Then the more shame upon her conduct. Even brutes do not devour their young, nor savages make war upon their families; wherefore, the assertion, if true, turns to her reproach; but it happens not to be true, or only partly so, and the phrase parent or mother country hath been jesuitically[7] adopted by the King and his parasites, with a low papistical design of gaining an unfair bias on the credulous weakness of our minds. Europe, and not England, is the parent country of America. This new world hath been the asylum for the persecuted lovers of civil and religious liberty from every part of Europe. Hither have they fled, not from the tender embraces of the mother, but from the cruelty of the monster; and it is so far true of England, that the same tyranny which drove the first emigrants from home, pursues their descendants still.

In this extensive quarter of the globe, we forget the narrow limits of three hundred and sixty miles (the extent of England) and carry our friendship on a larger scale; we claim brotherhood with every European Christian, and triumph in the generosity of the sentiment.

It is pleasant to observe by what regular gradations we surmount the force of local prejudices, as we enlarge our acquaintance with the world. A man born in any town in England divided into parishes, will naturally associate most with his fellow parishioners (because their interests in many cases will be common) and distinguish him by the name of neighbor; if he meet him but a few miles from home, he drops the narrow idea of a street, and salutes him by the name of townsman; if he travel out of the county and meet him in any other, he forgets the minor divisions of street and town, and calls him

4. Dominated.
5. King George III of Great Britain was a descendant of the Prussian House of Hanover. Paine is referring to the Seven Years' War (1756–63), which originally involved Prussia and Austria and grew to involve all the major European powers.

American losses in what is also called the French and Indian Wars were heavy, even though the war was settled in Britain's favor.
6. The colony was divided into East and West Jersey.
7. I.e., cunningly.

countryman, i.e., countyman: but if in their foreign excursions they should associate in France, or any other part of Europe, their local remembrance would be enlarged into that of Englishmen. And by a just parity of reasoning, all Europeans meeting in America, or any other quarter of the globe, are countrymen; for England, Holland, Germany, or Sweden, when compared with the whole, stand in the same places on the larger scale, which the divisions of street, town, and county do on the smaller ones; distinctions too limited for continental minds. Not one third of the inhabitants, even of this province,[8] are of English descent. Wherefore, I reprobate the phrase of parent or mother country applied to England only, as being false, selfish, narrow and ungenerous.

But, admitting that we were all of English descent, what does it amount to? Nothing. Britain, being now an open enemy, extinguishes every other name and title: and to say that reconciliation is our duty is truly farcical. The first King of England of the present line (William the Conqueror) was a Frenchman, and half the peers of England are descendants from the same country; wherefore, by the same method of reasoning, England ought to be governed by France.

Much hath been said of the united strength of Britain and the colonies, that in conjunction they might bid defiance to the world: but this is mere presumption; the fate of war is uncertain, neither do the expressions mean anything; for this continent would never suffer itself to be drained of inhabitants to support the British arms in either Asia, Africa, or Europe.

Besides, what have we to do with setting the world at defiance? Our plan is commerce, and that, well attended to, will secure us the peace and friendship of all Europe; because it is the interest of all Europe to have America a free port. Her trade will always be a protection, and her barrenness of gold and silver secure her from invaders.

I challenge the warmest advocate for reconciliation to show a single advantage that this continent can reap by being connected with Great Britain. I repeat the challenge; not a single advantage is derived. Our corn[9] will fetch its price in any market in Europe, and our imported goods must be paid for buy them where we will.

But the injuries and disadvantages which we sustain by that connection, are without number; and our duty to mankind at large, as well as to ourselves, instruct us to renounce the alliance: because, any submission to, or dependence on, Great Britain tends directly to involve this continent in European wars and quarrels, and set us at variance with nations who would otherwise seek our friendship, and against whom we have neither anger nor complaint. As Europe is our market for trade, we ought to form no partial connection with any part of it. It is the true interest of America to steer clear of European contentions, which she never can do, while, by her dependence on Britain, she is made the makeweight in the scale of British politics.

Europe is too thickly planted with kingdoms to be long at peace, and whenever a war breaks out between England and any foreign power, the trade of America goes to ruin, because of her connection with Britain. The next war may not turn out like the last,[1] and should it not, the advocates for

8. I.e., Pennsylvania.
9. I.e., wheat, not what Americans now call corn.

1. The Seven Years' War concluded with the Treaty of Paris (1763), by which Britain gained Canada from France.

reconciliation now will be wishing for separation then, because neutrality in that case would be a safer convoy than a man of war. Everything that is right or reasonable pleads for separation. The blood of the slain, the weeping voice of nature cries, " 'Tis time to part." Even the distance at which the Almighty hath placed England and America is a strong and natural proof that the authority of the one over the other was never the design of Heaven. The time likewise at which the continent was discovered adds weight to the argument, and the manner in which it was peopled increases the force of it. The Reformation was preceded by the discovery of America: as if the Almighty graciously meant to open a sanctuary to the persecuted in future years, when home should afford neither friendship nor safety.

The authority of Great Britain over this continent is a form of government which sooner or later must have an end: and a serious mind can draw no true pleasure by looking forward, under the painful and positive conviction that what he calls "the present constitution" is merely temporary. As parents, we can have no joy, knowing that this government is not sufficiently lasting to insure anything which we may bequeath to posterity: and by a plain method of argument, as we are running the next generation into debt, we ought to do the work of it, otherwise we use them meanly and pitifully. In order to discover the line of our duty rightly, we should take our children in our hand, and fix our station a few years farther into life; that eminence will present a prospect which a few present fears and prejudices conceal from our sight.

Though I would carefully avoid giving unnecessary offense, yet I am inclined to believe that all those who espouse the doctrine of reconciliation may be included within the following descriptions.

Interested men who are not to be trusted, weak men who cannot see, prejudiced men who will not see, and a certain set of moderate men who think better of the European world than it deserves; and this last class, by an ill-judged deliberation, will be the cause of more calamities to this continent than all the other three.

It is the good fortune of many to live distant from the scene of present sorrow; the evil is not sufficiently brought to their doors to make them feel the precariousness with which all American property is possessed. But let our imaginations transport us a few moments to Boston;[2] that seat of wretchedness will teach us wisdom, and instruct us forever to renounce a power in whom we can have no trust. The inhabitants of that unfortunate city, who but a few months ago were in ease and affluence, have now no other alternative than to stay and starve, or turn out to beg. Endangered by the fire of their friends if they continue within the city, and plundered by the soldiery if they leave it, in their present situation they are prisoners without the hope of redemption, and in a general attack for their relief they would be exposed to the fury of both armies.

Men of passive tempers look somewhat lightly over the offenses of Great Britain, and, still hoping for the best, are apt to call out, "Come, come, we shall be friends again for all this." But examine the passions and feelings of mankind: bring the doctrine of reconciliation to the touchstone of nature, and then tell me whether you can hereafter love, honor, and faithfully serve

---

2. Boston was under British military occupation and was blockaded for six months.

the power that hath carried fire and sword into your land? If you cannot do all these, then are you only deceiving yourselves, and by your delay bringing ruin upon posterity. Your future connection with Britain, whom you can neither love nor honor, will be forced and unnatural, and, being formed only on the plan of present convenience, will in a little time fall into a relapse more wretched than the first. But if you say, you can still pass the violations over, then I ask, hath your house been burnt? Hath your property been destroyed before your face? Are your wife and children destitute of a bed to lie on, or bread to live on? Have you lost a parent or a child by their hands, and yourself the ruined and wretched survivor? If you have not, then are you not a judge of those who have. But if you have, and can still shake hands with the murderers, then are you unworthy the name of husband, father, friend, or lover, and whatever may be your rank or title in life, you have the heart of a coward, and the spirit of a sycophant.

This is not inflaming or exaggerating matters, but trying them by those feelings and affections which nature justifies, and without which we should be incapable of discharging the social duties of life, or enjoying the felicities of it. I mean not to exhibit horror for the purpose of provoking revenge, but to awaken us from fatal and unmanly slumbers, that we may pursue determinately some fixed object. 'Tis not in the power of Britain or of Europe to conquer America, if she doth not conquer herself by delay and timidity. The present winter is worth an age if rightly employed, but if lost or neglected the whole continent will partake of the misfortune; and there is no punishment which that man doth not deserve, be he who, or what, or where he will, that may be the means of sacrificing a season so precious and useful.

'Tis repugnant to reason, to the universal order of things, to all examples from former ages, to suppose that this continent can long remain subject to any external power. The most sanguine in Britain doth not think so. The utmost stretch of human wisdom cannot, at this time, compass a plan, short of separation, which can promise the continent even a year's security. Reconciliation is now a fallacious dream. Nature hath deserted the connection, and art cannot supply her place. For, as Milton wisely expresses, "never can true reconcilement grow where wounds of deadly hate have pierced so deep."[3]

* * *

A government of our own is our natural right: and when a man seriously reflects on the precariousness of human affairs, he will become convinced that it is infinitely wiser and safer to form a constitution of our own in a cool deliberate manner, while we have it in our power, than to trust such an interesting event to time and chance. If we omit it now, some Massanello[4] may hereafter arise, who, laying hold of popular disquietudes, may collect together the desperate and the discontented, and by assuming to themselves the powers of government, finally sweep away the liberties of the continent like a deluge. Should the government of America return again into the hands of Britain, the tottering situation of things will be a temptation for some

3. *Paradise Lost* (1667), 4.98–99.
4. Thomas Anello, otherwise Massanello, a fisherman of Naples, who after spiriting up his countrymen in the public market place, against the oppression of the Spaniards, to whom the place was then subject, prompted them to revolt, and in the space of a day became King [Paine's note].

desperate adventurer to try his fortune; and in such a case, what relief can Britain give? Ere she could hear the news, the fatal business might be done; and ourselves suffering like the wretched Britons under the oppression of the conqueror. Ye that oppose independence now, ye know not what ye do: ye are opening a door to eternal tyranny by keeping vacant the seat of government. There are thousands and tens of thousands, who would think it glorious to expel from the continent that barbarous and hellish power, which hath stirred up the Indians and the Negroes to destroy us; the cruelty hath a double guilt: it is dealing brutally by us, and treacherously by them.

To talk of friendship with those in whom our reason forbids us to have faith, and our affections wounded through a thousand pores instruct us to detest, is madness and folly. Every day wears out the little remains of kindred between us and them; and can there be any reason to hope, that as the relationship expires, the affection will increase, or that we shall agree better when we have ten times more and greater concerns to quarrel over than ever?

Ye that tell us of harmony and reconciliation, can ye restore to us the time that is past? Can ye give to prostitution its former innocence? Neither can ye reconcile Britain and America. The last cord now is broken, the people of England are presenting addresses against us. There are injuries which nature cannot forgive; she would cease to be nature if she did. As well can the lover forgive the ravisher of his mistress, as the continent forgive the murders of Britain. The Almighty hath implanted in us these unextinguishable feelings for good and wise purposes. They are the guardians of His image in our hearts. They distinguish us from the herd of common animals. The social compact would dissolve, and justice be extirpated from the earth, or have only a casual existence were we callous to the touches of affection. The robber and the murderer would often escape unpunished, did not the injuries which our tempers sustain provoke us into justice.

O! ye that love mankind! Ye that dare oppose not only the tyranny but the tyrant, stand forth! Every spot of the old world is overrun with oppression. Freedom hath been hunted round the globe. Asia and Africa have long expelled her. Europe regards her like a stranger, and England hath given her warning to depart. O! receive the fugitive, and prepare in time an asylum for mankind.

1776

The Crisis,[1] No. 1

These are the times that try men's souls. The summer soldier and the sunshine patriot will, in this crisis, shrink from the service of their country; but he that stands it now, deserves the love and thanks of man and woman. Tyranny, like hell, is not easily conquered; yet we have this consolation with

1. The first of sixteen pamphlets that appeared under this title. Paine sometimes referred to this particular essay as *The American Crisis*. There were three pamphlet editions in one week: one undated, one dated December 19, and the one reprinted here, dated December 23. The text used here is from *The Writings of Thomas Paine 1894–96*, vol. 1, edited by M. D. Conway.

us, that the harder the conflict, the more glorious the triumph. What we obtain too cheap, we esteem too lightly: it is dearness only that gives every-thing its value. Heaven knows how to put a proper price upon its goods; and it would be strange indeed if so celestial an article as freedom should not be highly rated. Britain, with an army to enforce her tyranny, has declared that she has a right (not only to tax) but "to bind us in all cases whatsoever," and if being bound in that manner is not slavery, then is there not such a thing as slavery upon earth. Even the expression is impious; for so unlimited a power can belong only to God.

Whether the independence of the continent was declared too soon, or delayed too long, I will not now enter into as an argument; my own simple opinion is, that had it been eight months earlier, it would have been much better. We did not make a proper use of last winter, neither could we, while we were in a dependent state. However, the fault, if it were one, was all our own;[2] we have none to blame but ourselves. But no great deal is lost yet. All that Howe[3] has been doing for this month past is rather a ravage than a conquest, which the spirit of the Jerseys,[4] a year ago, would have quickly repulsed, and which time and a little resolution will soon recover.

I have as little superstition in me as any man living, but my secret opinion has ever been, and still is, that God Almighty will not give up a people to military destruction, or leave them unsupportedly to perish, who have so earnestly and so repeatedly sought to avoid the calamities of war, by every decent method which wisdom could invent. Neither have I so much of the infidel in me as to suppose that He has relinquished the government of the world, and given us up to the care of devils; and as I do not, I cannot see on what grounds the King of Britain can look up to heaven for help against us: a common murderer, a highwayman, or a housebreaker has as good a pre-tense as he.

'Tis surprising to see how rapidly a panic will sometimes run through a country. All nations and ages have been subject to them: Britain has trembled like an ague[5] at the report of a French fleet of flat-bottomed boats; and in the fourteenth century the whole English army, after ravaging the kingdom of France, was driven back like men petrified with fear; and this brave exploit was performed by a few broken forces collected and headed by a woman, Joan of Arc.[6] Would that heaven might inspire some Jersey maid to spirit up her countrymen, and save her fair fellow sufferers from ravage and ravish-ment! Yet panics, in some cases, have their uses; they produce as much good as hurt. Their duration is always short; the mind soon grows through them, and acquires a firmer habit than before. But their peculiar advantage is that they are the touchstones of sincerity and hypocrisy, and bring things and men to light, which might otherwise have lain forever undiscovered. In fact, they have the same effect on secret traitors, which an imaginary apparition

2. "The present winter is worth an age, if rightly employed; but, if lost or neglected, the whole con-tinent will partake of the evil; and there is no punishment that man does not deserve, be he who, or what, or where he will, that may be the means of sacrificing a season so precious and useful" [Paine's note, taken from *Common Sense*]. Paine wanted an immediate declaration of indepen-dence, uniting the colonies and enlisting the aid of France and Spain.
3. Lord William Howe (1729–1814) was com-mander of the British Army in America from 1775 to 1778.
4. The colony was divided into East and West Jer-sey.
5. I.e., like one who is chilled.
6. She led the French to victory over the English in 1429 (not the "fourteenth century").

would have upon a private murderer. They sift out the hidden thoughts of man, and hold them up in public to the world. Many a disguised tory[7] has lately shown his head, that shall penitentially solemnize with curses the day on which Howe arrived upon the Delaware.

As I was with the troops at Fort Lee, and marched with them to the edge of Pennsylvania, I am well acquainted with many circumstances, which those who live at a distance know but little or nothing of. Our situation there was exceedingly cramped, the place being a narrow neck of land between the North River[8] and the Hackensack. Our force was inconsiderable, being not one fourth so great as Howe could bring against us. We had no army at hand to have relieved the garrison, had we shut ourselves up and stood on our defense. Our ammunition, light artillery, and the best part of our stores had been removed on the apprehension that Howe would endeavor to penetrate the Jerseys, in which case Fort Lee could be of no use to us; for it must occur to every thinking man, whether in the army or not, that these kind of field forts are only for temporary purposes, and last in use no longer than the enemy directs his force against the particular object, which such forts are raised to defend. Such was our situation and condition at Fort Lee on the morning of the 20th of November, when an officer arrived with information that the enemy with 200 boats had landed about seven miles above: Major General Green,[9] who commanded the garrison, immediately ordered them under arms, and sent express to General Washington at the town of Hackensack, distant, by the way of the ferry, six miles. Our first object was to secure the bridge over the Hackensack, which laid up the river between the enemy and us, about six miles from us, and three from them. General Washington arrived in about three quarters of an hour, and marched at the head of the troops towards the bridge, which place I expected we should have a brush for; however, they did not choose to dispute it with us, and the greatest part of our troops went over the bridge, the rest over the ferry, except some which passed at a mill on a small creek, between the bridge and the ferry, and made their way through some marshy grounds up to the town of Hackensack, and there passed the river. We brought off as much baggage as the wagons could contain, the rest was lost. The simple object was to bring off the garrison, and march them on till they could be strengthened by the Jersey or Pennsylvania militia, so as to be enabled to make a stand. We staid four days at Newark, collected our outposts with some of the Jersey militia, and marched out twice to meet the enemy, on being informed that they were advancing, though our numbers were greatly inferior to theirs. Howe, in my little opinion, committed a great error in generalship in not throwing a body of forces off from Staten Island through Amboy, by which means he might have seized all our stores at Brunswick, and intercepted our march into Pennsylvania; but if we believe the power of hell to be limited, we must likewise believe that their agents are under some providential control.[1]

I shall not now attempt to give all the particulars of our retreat to the Delaware; suffice it for the present to say, that both officers and men, though

7. I.e., supporter of the king.
8. I.e., the Hudson River.
9. Paine was aide-de-camp to Major General Nathanael Greene (1742–1786).
1. The American losses were larger than Paine

implies. General Howe took three thousand prisoners and a large store of military supplies when he captured Fort Lee. Paine wrote *The Crisis, No. 1* while serving with Washington's army as it retreated through New Jersey.

greatly harassed and fatigued, frequently without rest, covering, or provision, the inevitable consequences of a long retreat, bore it with a manly and martial spirit. All their wishes centered in one, which was that the country would turn out and help them to drive the enemy back. Voltaire has remarked that King William never appeared to full advantage but in difficulties and in action;[2] the same remark may be made on General Washington, for the character fits him. There is a natural firmness in some minds which cannot be unlocked by trifles, but which, when unlocked, discovers a cabinet[3] of fortitude; and I reckon it among those kind of public blessings, which we do not immediately see, that God hath blessed him with uninterrupted health, and given him a mind that can even flourish upon care.

I shall conclude this paper with some miscellaneous remarks on the state of our affairs; and shall begin with asking the following question: Why is it that the enemy have left the New England provinces, and made these middle ones the seat of war? The answer is easy: New England is not infested with tories, and we are. I have been tender in raising the cry against these men, and used numberless arguments to show them their danger, but it will not do to sacrifice a world either to their folly or their baseness. The period is now arrived, in which either they or we must change our sentiments, or one or both must fall. And what is a tory? Good God! what is he? I should not be afraid to go with a hundred whigs[4] against a thousand tories, were they to attempt to get into arms. Every tory is a coward; for servile, slavish, self-interested fear is the foundation of toryism; and a man under such influence, though he may be cruel, never can be brave.

But, before the line of irrecoverable separation be drawn between us, let us reason the matter together: Your conduct is an invitation to the enemy, yet not one in a thousand of you has heart enough to join him. Howe is as much deceived by you as the American cause is injured by you. He expects you will all take up arms, and flock to his standard, with muskets on your shoulders. Your opinions are of no use to him, unless you support him personally, for 'tis soldiers, and not tories, that he wants.

I once felt all that kind of anger, which a man ought to feel, against the mean principles that are held by the tories: a noted one, who kept a tavern at Amboy,[5] was standing at his door, with as pretty a child in his hand, about eight or nine years old, as I ever saw, and after speaking his mind as freely as he thought was prudent, finished with this unfatherly expression, "Well! give me peace in my day." Not a man lives on the continent but fully believes that a separation must some time or other finally take place, and a generous parent should have said, "If there must be trouble, let it be in my day, that my child may have peace"; and this single reflection, well applied, is sufficient to awaken every man to duty. Not a place upon earth might be so happy as America. Her situation is remote from all the wrangling world, and she has nothing to do but to trade with them. A man can distinguish himself between temper and principle, and I am as confident, as I am that God governs the world, that America will never be happy till she gets clear of foreign dominion. Wars, without ceasing, will break out till that period

2. Voltaire (1694–1778) made this remark about King William III of England (1650–1702) in his *History of Louis the Fourteenth* (1751).
3. Storehouse.
4. Supporters of the Revolution.
5. Paine was stationed at Perth Amboy, New Jersey, while in the Continental Army.

arrives, and the continent must in the end be conqueror; for though the flame of liberty may sometimes cease to shine, the coal can never expire.

America did not, nor does not, want force; but she wanted a proper application of that force. Wisdom is not the purchase of a day, and it is no wonder that we should err at the first setting off. From an excess of tenderness, we were unwilling to raise an army, and trusted our cause to the temporary defense of a well-meaning militia. A summer's experience has now taught us better; yet with those troops, while they were collected, we were able to set bounds to the progress of the enemy, and thank God! they are again assembling. I always considered militia as the best troops in the world for a sudden exertion, but they will not do for a long campaign. Howe, it is probable, will make an attempt on this city;[6] should he fail on this side of the Delaware, he is ruined: if he succeeds, our cause is not ruined. He stakes all on his side against a part on ours; admitting he succeeds, the consequence will be that armies from both ends of the continent will march to assist their suffering friends in the middle states; for he cannot go everywhere, it is impossible. I consider Howe as the greatest enemy the tories have; he is bringing a war into their country, which, had it not been for him and partly for themselves, they had been clear of. Should he now be expelled, I wish with all the devotion of a Christian, that the names of whig and tory may never more be mentioned; but should the tories give him encouragement to come, or assistance if he come, I as sincerely wish that our next year's arms may expel them from the continent, and the congress appropriate their possessions to the relief of those who have suffered in well-doing. A single successful battle next year will settle the whole. America could carry on a two years' war by the confiscation of the property of disaffected persons, and be made happy by their expulsion. Say not that this is revenge; call it rather the soft resentment of a suffering people, who, having no object in view but the good of all, have staked their own all upon a seemingly doubtful event. Yet it is folly to argue against determined hardness; eloquence may strike the ear, and the language of sorrow draw forth the tear of compassion, but nothing can reach the heart that is steeled with prejudice.

Quitting this class of men, I turn with the warm ardor of a friend to those who have nobly stood, and are yet determined to stand the matter out: I call not upon a few, but upon all: not on this state or that state, but on every state: up and help us; lay your shoulders to the wheel; better have too much force than too little, when so great an object is at stake. Let it be told to the future world that in the depth of winter, when nothing but hope and virtue could survive, that the city and the country, alarmed at one common danger, came forth to meet and to repulse it. Say not that thousands are gone, turn out your tens of thousands;[7] throw not the burden of the day upon Providence, but "show your faith by your works"[8] that God may bless you. It matters not where you live, or what rank of life you hold, the evil or the blessing will reach you all. The far and the near, the home counties and the back,[9] the rich and poor will suffer or rejoice alike. The heart that feels not now is dead: the blood of his children will curse his cowardice who shrinks back at a time when a little might have saved the whole, and made them

6. I.e., Philadelphia.
7. "Saul hath slain his thousands, and David his ten thousands" (1 Samuel 18.7).

8. "Shew me thy faith without thy works, and I will shew thee my faith by my works" (James 2.18).
9. I.e., the backwoods.

happy. I love the man that can smile in trouble, that can gather strength from distress, and grow brave by reflection. 'Tis the business of little minds to shrink; but he whose heart is firm, and whose conscience approves his conduct, will pursue his principles unto death. My own line of reasoning is to myself as straight and clear as a ray of light. Not all the treasures of the world, so far as I believe, could have induced me to support an offensive war, for I think it murder; but if a thief breaks into my house, burns and destroys my property, and kills or threatens to kill me, or those that are in it, and to "bind me in all cases whatsoever"[1] to his absolute will, am I to suffer it? What signifies it to me, whether he who does it is a king or a common man; my countryman or not my countryman; whether it be done by an individual villain, or an army of them? If we reason to the root of things we shall find no difference; neither can any just cause be assigned why we should punish in the one case and pardon in the other. Let them call me rebel, and welcome, I feel no concern from it; but I should suffer the misery of devils were I to make a whore of my soul by swearing allegiance to one whose character is that of a sottish, stupid, stubborn, worthless, brutish man. I conceive likewise a horrid idea in receiving mercy from a being, who at the last day shall be shrieking to the rocks and mountains to cover him, and fleeing with terror from the orphan, the widow, and the slain of America.

There are cases which cannot be overdone by language, and this is one. There are persons, too, who see not the full extent of the evil which threatens them; they solace themselves with hopes that the enemy, if he succeed, will be merciful. It is the madness of folly to expect mercy from those who have refused to do justice; and even mercy, where conquest is the object, is only a trick of war; the cunning of the fox is as murderous as the violence of the wolf, and we ought to guard equally against both. Howe's first object is, partly by threats and partly by promises, to terrify or seduce the people to deliver up their arms and receive mercy. The ministry recommended the same plan to Gage,[2] and this is what the tories call making their peace, "a peace which passeth all understanding"[3] indeed! A peace which would be the immediate forerunner of a worse ruin than any we have yet thought of. Ye men of Pennsylvania, do reason upon these things! Were the back counties to give up their arms, they would fall an easy prey to the Indians, who are all armed: this perhaps is what some tories would not be sorry for. Were the home counties to deliver up their arms, they would be exposed to the resentment of the back counties, who would then have it in their power to chastise their defection at pleasure. And were any one state to give up its arms, that state must be garrisoned by all Howe's army of Britons and Hessians[4] to preserve it from the anger of the rest. Mutual fear is the principal link in the chain of mutual love, and woe be to that state that breaks the compact. Howe is mercifully inviting you to barbarous destruction, and men must be either rogues or fools that will not see it. I dwell not upon the vapors of imagination: I bring reason to your ears, and, in language as plain as A, B, C, hold up truth to your eyes.

1. From the Declaratory Act of Parliament, February 24, 1766, establishing British authority over the American colonies.
2. General Thomas Gage (1721–1787), who commanded the British armies in America from 1763 to 1775, before Howe.
3. "And the peace of God, which passeth all understanding, shall keep your hearts and minds through Christ Jesus" (Philippians 4.7).
4. German mercenaries.

I thank God that I fear not. I see no real cause for fear. I know our situation well, and can see the way out of it. While our army was collected, Howe dared not risk a battle; and it is no credit to him that he decamped from the White Plains,[5] and waited a mean opportunity to ravage the defenseless Jerseys; but it is great credit to us, that, with a handful of men, we sustained an orderly retreat for near an hundred miles, brought off our ammunition, all our field pieces, the greatest part of our stores, and had four rivers to pass. None can say that our retreat was precipitate, for we were near three weeks in performing it, that the country[6] might have time to come in. Twice we marched back to meet the enemy, and remained out till dark. The sign of fear was not seen in our camp, and had not some of the cowardly and disaffected inhabitants spread false alarms through the country, the Jerseys had never been ravaged. Once more we are again collected and collecting; our new army at both ends of the continent is recruiting fast, and we shall be able to open the next campaign with sixty thousand men, well armed and clothed. This is our situation, and who will may know it. By perseverance and fortitude we have the prospect of a glorious issue; by cowardice and submission, the sad choice of a variety of evils—a ravaged country—a depopulated city—habitations without safety, and slavery without hope—our homes turned into barracks and bawdyhouses for Hessians, and a future race to provide for, whose fathers we shall doubt of. Look on this picture and weep over it! and if there yet remains one thoughtless wretch who believes it not, let him suffer it unlamented.

Common Sense

1776

From The Age of Reason[1]

Chapter I. The Author's Profession of Faith

It has been my intention, for several years past, to publish my thoughts upon religion; I am well aware of the difficulties that attend the subject, and from that consideration had reserved it to a more advanced period of life. I intended it to be the last offering I should make to my fellow citizens of all nations, and that at a time when the purity of the motive that induced me to it could not admit of a question, even by those who might disapprove the work.

The circumstance that has now taken place in France,[2] of the total abolition of the whole national order of priesthood, and of everything appertaining to compulsive systems of religion, and compulsive articles of faith, has not only precipitated my intention, but rendered a work of this kind exceedingly necessary lest, in the general wreck of superstition, of false systems of government, and false theology, we lose sight of morality, of humanity, and of the theology that is true.

5. At White Plains, New York, on October 28, 1776, General Howe successfully overcame Washington's troops but failed to take full advantage of his victory.
6. I.e., the local volunteers.
1. The text used here is from The Writings of Tho-

mas Paine (1894–96), vol. 4, edited by M. D. Conway.
2. By 1792 leaders of the French Revolution had discredited the Roman Catholic Church in France and closed the churches.

As several of my colleagues and others of my fellow citizens of France have given me the example of making their voluntary and individual profession of faith, I also will make mine; and I do this with all that sincerity and frankness with which the mind of man communicates with itself.

I believe in one God, and no more; and I hope for happiness beyond this life.

I believe the equality of man, and I believe that religious duties consist in doing justice, loving mercy, and endeavoring to make our fellow creatures happy.

But, lest it should be supposed that I believe many other things in addition to these, I shall, in the progress of this work, declare the things I do not believe, and my reasons for not believing them.

I do not believe in the creed professed by the Jewish church, by the Roman church, by the Greek church, by the Turkish church, by the Protestant church, nor by any church that I know of. My own mind is my own church.

All national institutions of churches, whether Jewish, Christian, or Turkish, appear to me no other than human inventions set up to terrify and enslave mankind, and monopolize power and profit.

I do not mean by this declaration to condemn those who believe otherwise; they have the same right to their belief as I have to mine. But it is necessary to the happiness of man that he be mentally faithful to himself. Infidelity does not consist in believing, or in disbelieving; it consists in professing to believe what he does not believe.

It is impossible to calculate the moral mischief, if I may so express it, that mental lying has produced in society. When a man has so far corrupted and prostituted the chastity of his mind as to subscribe his professional belief to things he does not believe, he has prepared himself for the commission of every other crime. He takes up the trade of a priest for the sake of gain, and, in order to qualify himself for that trade, he begins with a perjury. Can we conceive anything more destructive to morality than this?

Soon after I had published the pamphlet *Common Sense,* in America, I saw the exceeding probability that a revolution in the system of government would be followed by a revolution in the system of religion. The adulterous connection of church and state, wherever it had taken place, whether Jewish, Christian, or Turkish, had so effectually prohibited, by pains and penalties, every discussion upon established creeds and upon first principles of religion, that until the system of government should be changed, those subjects could not be brought fairly and openly before the world; but that whenever this should be done, a revolution in the system of religion would follow. Human inventions and priestcraft would be detected; and man would return to the pure, unmixed, and unadulterated belief of one God, and no more.

Chapter II. Of Missions and Revelations

Every national church or religion has established itself by pretending some special mission from God, communicated to certain individuals. The Jews have their Moses; the Christians their Jesus Christ, their apostles and saints; and the Turks their Mahomet; as if the way to God was not open to every man alike.

Each of those churches shows certain books, which they call revelation, or the Word of God. The Jews say that their Word of God was given by God to Moses face to face; the Christians say that their Word of God came by divine inspiration; and the Turks say that their Word of God (the Koran) was brought by an angel from heaven. Each of those churches accuses the other of unbelief; and, for my own part, I disbelieve them all.

As it is necessary to affix right ideas to words, I will, before I proceed further into the subject, offer some observations on the word revelation. Revelation when applied to religion, means something communicated immediately from God to man.

No one will deny or dispute the power of the Almighty to make such a communication if He pleases. But admitting, for the sake of a case, that something has been revealed to a certain person, and not revealed to any other person, it is revelation to that person only. When he tells it to a second person, a second to a third, a third to a fourth, and so on, it ceases to be a revelation to all those persons. It is revelation to the first person only, and hearsay to every other, and, consequently, they are not obliged to believe it.

It is a contradiction in terms and ideas to call anything a revelation that comes to us at secondhand, either verbally or in writing. Revelation is necessarily limited to the first communication. After this, it is only an account of something which that person says was a revelation made to him; and though he may find himself obliged to believe it, it cannot be incumbent on me to believe it in the same manner, for it was not a revelation made to me, and I have only his word for it that it was made to him.

When Moses told the children of Israel that he received the two tables of the commandments from the hand of God, they were not obliged to believe him, because they had no other authority for it than his telling them so; and I have no other authority for it than some historian telling me so, the commandments carrying no internal evidence of divinity with them. They contain some good moral precepts such as any man qualified to be a lawgiver or a legislator could produce himself, without having recourse to supernatural intervention.[3]

When I am told that the Koran was written in Heaven, and brought to Mahomet by an angel, the account comes to near the same kind of hearsay evidence and secondhand authority as the former. I did not see the angel myself, and therefore I have a right not to believe it.

When also I am told that a woman, called the Virgin Mary, said, or gave out, that she was with child without any cohabitation with a man, and that her betrothed husband, Joseph, said that an angel told him so, I have a right to believe them or not: such a circumstance required a much stronger evidence than their bare word for it: but we have not even this; for neither Joseph nor Mary wrote any such matter themselves. It is only reported by others that they said so. It is hearsay upon hearsay, and I do not choose to rest my belief upon such evidence.

It is, however, not difficult to account for the credit that was given to the story of Jesus Christ being the Son of God. He was born when the heathen mythology had still some fashion and repute in the world, and that mythology had prepared the people for the belief of such a story. Almost all the extra-

3. It is, however, necessary to except the declaration which says that God *visits the sins of the fathers upon the children*. This is contrary to every principle of moral justice [Paine's note].

ordinary men that lived under the heathen mythology were reputed to be the sons of some of their gods. It was not a new thing at that time to believe a man to have been celestially begotten; the intercourse of gods with women was then a matter of familiar opinion. Their Jupiter,[4] according to their accounts, had cohabited with hundreds; the story therefore had nothing in it either new, wonderful, or obscene; it was conformable to the opinions that then prevailed among the people called Gentiles, or mythologists, and it was those people only that believed it. The Jews, who had kept strictly to the belief of one god, and no more, and who had always rejected the heathen mythology, never credited the story.

It is curious to observe how the theory of what is called the Christian Church, sprung out of the tail of the heathen mythology. A direct incorporation took place in the first instance, by making the reputed founder to be celestially begotten. The trinity of gods that then followed was no other than a reduction of the former plurality, which was about twenty or thirty thousand. The statue of Mary succeeded the statue of Diana of Ephesus.[5] The deification of heroes changed into the canonization of saints. The mythologists had gods for everything; the Christian mythologists had saints for everything. The church became as crowded with the one, as the Pantheon[6] had been with the other; and Rome was the place of both. The Christian theory is little else than the idolatry of the ancient mythologists, accommodated to the purposes of power and revenue; and it yet remains to reason and philosophy to abolish the amphibious fraud.

Chapter XI. Of the Theology of the Christians, and the True Theology

As to the Christian system of faith, it appears to me as a species of atheism; a sort of religious denial of God. It professes to believe in a man rather than in God. It is a compound made up chiefly of man-ism with but little deism, and is as near to atheism as twilight is to darkness. It introduces between man and his Maker an opaque body, which it calls a redeemer, as the moon introduces her opaque self between the earth and the sun, and it produces by this means a religious or an irreligious eclipse of light. It has put the whole orbit of reason into shade.

The effect of this obscurity has been that of turning everything upside down, and representing it in reverse; and among the revolutions it has thus magically produced, it has made a revolution in theology.

That which is now called natural philosophy, embracing the whole circle of science, of which astronomy occupies the chief place, is the study of the works of God, and of the power and wisdom of God in His works, and is the true theology.

As to the theology that is now studied in its place, it is the study of human opinions and of human fancies concerning God. It is not the study of God Himself in the works that He has made, but in the works or writings that man has made; and it is not among the least of the mischiefs that the Christian system has done to the world, that it has abandoned the original and

---

4. Roman god of the heavens and king of the gods.
5. There was a temple built to honor the goddess Artemis (identified by the Romans with Diana) at Ephesus, an Ionian city in Asia Minor, which was

one of the seven wonders of the ancient world. Artemis of Ephesus was worshiped as a fertility goddess.
6. A temple in Rome dedicated to all the gods.

beautiful system of theology, like a beautiful innocent, to distress and reproach, to make room for the hag of superstition.

The Book of Job and the 19th Psalm, which even the church admits to be more ancient than the chronological order in which they stand in the book called the Bible,[7] are theological orations conformable to the original system of theology. The internal evidence of those orations proves to a demonstration that the study and contemplation of the works of creation, and of the power and wisdom of God revealed and manifested in those works, made a great part of the religious devotion of the times in which they were written; and it was this devotional study and contemplation that led to the discovery of the principles upon which what are now called sciences are established; and it is to the discovery of these principles that almost all the arts that contribute to the convenience of human life owe their existence. Every principal art has some science for its parent, though the person who mechanically performs the work does not always, and but very seldom, perceive the connection.

It is a fraud of the Christian system to call the sciences human inventions; it is only the application of them that is human. Every science has for its basis a system of principles as fixed and unalterable as those by which the universe is regulated and governed. Man cannot make principles; he can only discover them.

For example: every person who looks at an almanac sees an account when an eclipse will take place, and he sees also that it never fails to take place according to the account there given. This shows that man is acquainted with the laws by which the heavenly bodies move. But it would be something worse than ignorance, were any church on earth to say that those laws are an human invention.

It would also be ignorance, or something worse, to say that the scientific principles, by the aid of which man is enabled to calculate and foreknow when an eclipse will take place, are an human invention. Man cannot invent anything that is eternal and immutable; and the scientific principles he employs for this purpose must, and are, of necessity, as eternal and immutable as the laws by which the heavenly bodies move, or they could not be used as they are to ascertain the time when, and the manner how, an eclipse will take place.

The scientific principles that man employs to obtain the foreknowledge of an eclipse, or of anything else relating to the motion of the heavenly bodies, are contained chiefly in that part of science that is called trigonometry, or the properties of a triangle, which, when applied to the study of the heavenly bodies, is called astronomy; when applied to direct the course of a ship on the ocean, it is called navigation; when applied to the construction of figures drawn by a rule and compass, it is called geometry; when applied to the construction of plans of edifices, it is called architecture; when applied to the measurement of any portion of the surface of the earth, it is called land surveying. In fine, it is the soul of science. It is an eternal truth: it contains

7. In the order of the Old Testament, Job comes before the Book of Psalms, but the author of Job alludes to some lines of the Psalms, which must have come earlier. Paine thinks that both Job and Psalm 19 ("The heavens declare the glory of God; and the firmament sheweth his handiwork") conform "to the original system of theology," because they convey immediate responses to the world that God made.

the mathematical demonstration of which man speaks, and the extent of its uses are unknown.

It may be said, that man can make or draw a triangle, and therefore a triangle is an human invention.

But the triangle, when drawn, is no other than the image of the principle: it is a delineation to the eye, and from thence to the mind, of a principle that would otherwise be imperceptible. The triangle does not make the principle any more than a candle taken into a room that was dark makes the chairs and tables that before were invisible. All the properties of a triangle exist independently of the figure, and existed before any triangle was drawn or thought of by man. Man had no more to do in the formation of those properties or principles than he had to do in making the laws by which the heavenly bodies move; and therefore the one must have the same divine origin as the other.

In the same manner as, it may be said, that man can make a triangle, so also, may it be said, he can make the mechanical instrument called a lever. But the principle by which the lever acts is a thing distinct from the instrument, and would exist if the instrument did not; it attaches itself to the instrument after it is made; the instrument, therefore, can act no otherwise than it does act; neither can all the efforts of human invention make it act otherwise. That which, in all such cases, man calls the effect, is no other than the principle itself rendered perceptible to the senses.

Since, then, man cannot make principles, from whence did he gain a knowledge of them, so as to be able to apply them, not only to things on earth, but to ascertain the motion of bodies so immensely distant from him as all the heavenly bodies are? From whence, I ask, could he gain that knowledge, but from the study of the true theology?

It is the structure of the universe that has taught this knowledge to man. That structure is an ever-existing exhibition of every principle upon which every part of mathematical science is founded. The offspring of this science is mechanics; for mechanics is no other than the principles of science applied practically. The man who proportions the several parts of a mill uses the same scientific principles as if he had the power of constructing an universe, but as he cannot give to matter that invisible agency by which all the component parts of the immense machine of the universe have influence upon each other, and act in motional unison together, without any apparent contact, and to which man has given the name of attraction, gravitation, and repulsion, he supplies the place of that agency by the humble imitation of teeth and cogs. All the parts of man's microcosm must visibly touch. But could he gain a knowledge of that agency, so as to be able to apply it in practice, we might then say that another canonical book[8] of the word of God had been discovered.

If man could alter the properties of the lever, so also could he alter the properties of the triangle: for a lever (taking that sort of lever which is called a steelyard, for the sake of explanation) forms, when in motion, a triangle. The line it descends from (one point of that line being in the fulcrum), the line it descends to, and the chord of the arc, which the end of the lever describes in the air, are the three sides of a triangle. The other arm of the

8. I.e., a book that would form a part of Scripture.

lever describes also a triangle; and the corresponding sides of those two triangles, calculated scientifically, or measured geometrically—and also the sines, tangents, and secants generated from the angles, and geometrically measured—have the same proportions to each other as the different weights have that will balance each other on the lever, leaving the weight of the lever out of the case.

It may also be said that man can make a wheel and axis; that he can put wheels of different magnitudes together, and produce a mill. Still the case comes back to the same point, which is, that he did not make the principle that gives the wheels those powers. This principle is as unalterable as in the former cases, or rather it is the same principle under a different appearance to the eye.

The power that two wheels of different magnitudes have upon each other is in the same proportion as if the semidiameter of the two wheels were joined together and made into that kind of lever I have described, suspended at the part where the semidiameters join; for the two wheels, scientifically considered, are no other than the two circles generated by the motion of the compound lever.

It is from the study of the true theology that all our knowledge of science is derived; and it is from that knowledge that all the arts have originated.

The Almighty lecturer, by displaying the principles of science in the structure of the universe, has invited man to study and to imitation. It is as if He had said to the inhabitants of this globe that we call ours, "I have made an earth for man to dwell upon, and I have rendered the starry heavens visible, to teach him science and the arts. He can now provide for his own comfort, and learn from my munificence to all, to be kind to each other."

Of what use is it, unless it be to teach man something, that his eye is endowed with the power of beholding, to an incomprehensible distance, an immensity of worlds revolving in the ocean of space? Or of what use is it that this immensity of worlds is visible to man? What has man to do with the Pleiades, with Orion, with Sirius, with the star he calls the North Star, with the moving orbs he has named Saturn, Jupiter, Mars, Venus, and Mercury, if no uses are to follow from their being visible? A less power of vision would have been sufficient for man, if the immensity he now possesses were given only to waste itself, as it were, on an immense desert of space glittering with shows.

It is only by contemplating what he calls the starry heavens, as the book and school of science, that he discovers any use in their being visible to him, or any advantage resulting from his immensity of vision. But when he contemplates the subject in this light, he sees an additional motive for saying, that nothing was made in vain; for in vain would be this power of vision if it taught man nothing.

1793   1794

THOMAS JEFFERSON
1743–1826

President of the United States, first secretary of state, and minister to France, governor of Virginia, and congressman, Thomas Jefferson once said that he wished to be remembered for only three things: drafting the Declaration of Independence, writing and supporting the Virginia Statute for Religious Freedom (1786), and founding the University of Virginia. Jefferson might well have included a number of other accomplishments in this list: he was a remarkable architect and designed the Virginia state capitol, his residence Monticello, and the original buildings for the University of Virginia; he farmed thousands of acres and built one of the most beautiful plantations in America; he had a library of some ten thousand volumes, which served as the basis for the Library of Congress, and a collection of paintings and sculpture that made him America's greatest patron of the arts; and he was known the world over for his spirit of scientific inquiry and as the creator of a number of remarkable inventions. The three acts for which he wished to be remembered, however, have this in common: they all testify to Jefferson's lifelong passion to liberate the human mind from tyranny, whether imposed by the state, the church, or our own ignorance.

Jefferson was born at Shadwell, in what is now Albermarle County, Virginia. His mother, Jane Randolph, came from one of the most distinguished families in Virginia. Peter Jefferson, his father, was a county official and surveyor. He made the first accurate map of Virginia, something of which Jefferson was always proud. When his father died Thomas was only fourteen. Peter Jefferson left his son 2,750 acres of land, and Jefferson added to this acreage until he died; at one time he owned almost ten thousand acres. Jefferson tells us in his *Autobiography* that his father's education had been "quite neglected" but that he was always "eager after information" and determined to improve himself. In 1760, when Jefferson entered the College of William and Mary in Williamsburg, Virginia, he had mastered Latin and Greek, played the violin respectably, and was a skilled horseman. Williamsburg was the capital of Virginia as well as a college town, and Jefferson was fortunate enough to make the acquaintance of three men who strongly influenced his life: Governor Francis Fauquier, a fellow of the Royal Society; George Wythe, one of the best teachers of law in the country; and Dr. William Small, an emigrant from Scotland who taught mathematics and philosophy and who introduced Jefferson, as Garry Wills has put it, "to the invigorating realms of the Scottish Enlightenment," especially the work of Francis Hutcheson, author of *An Inquiry into the Original of Our Ideas of Beauty and Virtue* (1725), and Lord Kames (Henry Home), author of *Essays on the Principles of Morality and Natural Religion* (1751).

Jefferson stayed on in Williamsburg to read law after graduation and was admitted to the bar. In 1769 he was elected to the Virginia House of Burgesses and began a distinguished career in the legislature. In 1774 he wrote an influential and daring pamphlet called *A Summary View of the Rights of British America*, denying all parliamentary authority over America and arguing that ties to the British monarchy were voluntary and not irrevocable. Jefferson's reputation as a writer preceded him to Philadelphia, where he was a delegate to the Second Continental Congress, and on June 11, 1776, he was appointed to join Benjamin Franklin, John Adams, Roger Sherman, and Robert Livingston in drafting a declaration of independence. Although committee members made suggestions, the draft was very much Jefferson's own. As Wills has recently shown, Jefferson was unhappy with the changes made by Congress to his draft, and rightly so; for congressional changes went contrary to some of his basic arguments. Jefferson wished to place the British *people* on record as the ultimate cause of the Revolution, because they tolerated a corrupt Parliament and king; and he wished to include a strong statement against slavery. Congress tolerated neither passage. Jefferson was justified, however, in asking that he be remembered as the author of the Declaration. It was, as Dumas Malone, Jefferson's biographer, once put it, a "dangerous but glorious opportunity." Whether as the result of these frustrations or merely Jefferson's wish to be nearer his family, he left the Congress in September 1776 and entered the Virginia House of Delegates. In 1779 he was elected governor, and although reelected the following year, Jefferson's term of office came to an ignominious end when he resigned. After the British captured Richmond in 1781, Jefferson and the legislature moved to Charlottesville, and he and the legislators barely escaped imprisonment when the pursuing British Army descended on them at Monticello. Jefferson's resignation and the lack of preparations for the defense of the city were held against him, and it was some time before he regained the confidence of Virginians.

From 1781 to 1784 Jefferson withdrew from public life and remained at Monticello, completing his only book, *Notes on the State of Virginia*. In 1784 he was appointed minister to France and served with Benjamin Franklin on the commission that signed the Treaty of Paris, ending the Revolutionary War. He returned to Monticello in 1789, and in 1790 Washington appointed him the first secretary of state under the newly adopted Constitution. After three years he announced his retirement once again and withdrew to Monticello, where he rotated his crops and built a grist mill. But Jefferson's political blood was too thick for retirement, and in 1796 he ran for the office of president, losing to John Adams and taking the office of vice president instead. In 1800 he was elected president, the first to be inaugurated in Washington. He named Benjamin Latrobe surveyor of public buildings and worked with Latrobe in planning a great city.

When Jefferson returned to Monticello in 1809, he knew that his public life was over. For the final seventeen years of his life he kept a watchful eye on everything that grew in Monticello. But Jefferson was never far from the world. He rose every morning to attack his voluminous correspondence. The Library of Congress holds more than fifty-five thousand Jefferson manuscripts and letters, and the most recent edition of his writings will run to sixty volumes. Jefferson left no treatise on political philosophy and, in a sense, was no political thinker. He was always more interested in the practical consequences of ideas. Although in drafting the Declaration and elsewhere he had argued for the freedom of slaves, he partook of the same prejudices as most of his contemporaries in the colonies and then the United States. Unable to imagine blacks integrated into American society, he counseled their colonization in a separate place. He remained an agrarian aristocrat all his life, and it is to the liberty of mind and the values of the land that he always returned. As Dumas Malone puts it, he was a "homely aristocrat in manner of life and personal tastes; he distrusted all rulers and feared the rise of an industrial proletariat, but more than any of his eminent contemporaries, he trusted the common man, if measurably enlightened and kept in rural virtue." Jefferson died a few hours before John Adams on the Fourth of July, 1826.

From The Autobiography of Thomas Jefferson[1]

From *The Declaration of Independence*

* * *

It appearing in the course of these debates, that the colonies of New York, New Jersey, Pennsylvania, Delaware, Maryland, and South Carolina were

1. On June 7, 1776, Richard Henry Lee of Virginia proposed to the Second Continental Congress, meeting in Philadelphia, that "these united Colonies are, and of a right ought to be, free and independent states." On June 11, a committee of five—John Adams of Massachusetts, Benjamin Franklin of Pennsylvania, Roger Sherman of Connecticut, Robert Livingston of New York, and Thomas Jefferson of Virginia—was instructed to draft a declaration of independence. The draft presented to Congress on June 28 was primarily the work of Jefferson. Lee's resolution was passed on July 2, and the Declaration was adopted on July 4 with the changes noted by Jefferson in this text,

not yet matured for falling from the parent stem, but that they were fast advancing to that state, it was thought most prudent to wait a while for them, and to postpone the final decision to July 1st; but, that this might occasion as little delay as possible, a committee was appointed to prepare a Declaration of Independence. The committee were John Adams, Dr. Franklin, Roger Sherman, Robert R. Livingston, and myself. Committees were also appointed, at the same time, to prepare a plan of confederation for the colonies, and to state the terms proper to be proposed for foreign alliance. The committee for drawing the Declaration of Independence, desired me to do it. It was accordingly done, and being approved by them, I reported it to the House on Friday, the 28th of June, when it was read, and ordered to lie on the table. On Monday, the 1st of July, the House resolved itself into a committee of the whole, and resumed the consideration of the original motion made by the delegates of Virginia, which, being again debated through the day, was carried in the affirmative by the votes of New Hampshire, Connecticut, Massachusetts, Rhode Island, New Jersey, Maryland, Virginia, North Carolina and Georgia. South Carolina and Pennsylvania voted against it. Delaware had but two members present, and they were divided. The delegates from New York declared they were for it themselves, and were assured their constituents were for it; but that their instructions having been drawn near a twelve-month before, when reconciliation was still the general object, they were enjoined by them to do nothing which should impede that object. They, therefore, thought themselves not justifiable in voting on either side, and asked leave to withdraw from the question: which was given them. The committee rose and reported their resolution to the House. Mr. Edward Rutledge, of South Carolina, then requested the determination might be put off to the next day, as he believed his colleagues, though they disapproved of the resolution, would then join in it for the sake of unanimity. The ultimate question, whether the House would agree to the resolution of the committee, was accordingly postponed to the next day, when it was again moved, and South Carolina concurred in voting for it. In the meantime, a third member had come post[2] from the Delaware counties, and turned the vote of that colony in favor of the resolution. Members of a different sentiment attending that morning from Pennsylvania also, her vote was changed, so that the whole twelve colonies who were authorized to vote at all, gave their voices for it; and, within a few days, the convention of New York approved of it, and thus supplied the void occasioned by the withdrawing of her delegates from the vote.

Congress proceeded the same day to consider the Declaration of Independence, which had been reported and lain on the table the Friday preceding, and on Monday referred to a committee of the whole. The pusillanimous idea that we had friends in England worth keeping terms with, still haunted the minds of many. For this reason, those passages which conveyed censures on the people of England were struck out, lest they should give them offense. The clause too, reprobating the enslaving the inhabitants of Africa, was struck out in complaisance to South Carolina and Georgia, who had never attempted to restrain the importation of slaves, and who, on the contrary,

taken from his *Autobiography*. On August 2 a copy in parchment was signed by all the delegates but three; they signed later. The text used here is from *The Writings of Thomas Jefferson*, edited by A. A. Lipscomb and A. E. Bergh (1903).
2. Speedily, posthaste.

still wished to continue it. Our northern brethren also, I believe, felt a little tender under those censures; for though their people had very few slaves themselves, yet they had been pretty considerable carriers of them to others. The debates, having taken up the greater parts of the 2d, 3d, and 4th days of July, were, on the evening of the last, closed; the Declaration was reported by the committee, agreed to by the House, and signed by every member present, except Mr. Dickinson.[3] As the sentiments of men are known not only by what they receive, but what they reject also, I will state the form of the Declaration as originally reported. The parts struck out by Congress shall be distinguished by a black line drawn under them, and those inserted by them shall be placed in the margin, or in a concurrent column.

A DECLARATION BY THE REPRESENTATIVES OF THE UNITED STATES OF AMERICA, IN GENERAL CONGRESS ASSEMBLED.

When, in the course of human events, it becomes necessary for one people to dissolve the political bands which have connected them with another, and to assume among the powers of the earth the separate and equal station to which the laws of nature and of nature's God entitle them, a decent respect to the opinions of mankind requires that they should declare the causes which impel them to the separation.

We hold these truths to be self evident: that all men are created equal;[4] that they are endowed by their Creator with inherent and inalienable rights; that among these are life, liberty, and the pursuit of happiness;[5] that to secure these rights, governments are instituted among men, deriving their just powers from the consent of the governed; that whenever any form of government becomes destructive of these ends, it is the right of the people to alter or to abolish it, and to institute new government, laying its foundation on such principles, and organizing its powers in such form, as to them shall seem most likely to effect their safety and happiness. Prudence, indeed, will dictate that governments long established should not be changed for light and transient causes; and accordingly all experience hath shown that mankind are more disposed to suffer while evils are sufferable, than to right themselves by abolishing the forms to which they are accustomed. But when a long train of abuses and usurpations, begun at a distinguished[6] period and pursuing invariably the same object,

(margin: certain)

3. John Dickinson of Pennsylvania, who opposed it.
4. Garry Wills, in his study of the Declaration (*Inventing America,* 1978), tells us that Jefferson means *equal* in possessing a moral sense: "The moral sense is not only man's *highest* faculty, but the one that is *equal* to all men."
5. In his *Second Treatise on Government* (1689) John Locke defined man's natural rights to "life, liberty, and property." Jefferson's substitution of "pursuit of happiness" has puzzled a number of critics. Wills suggests that Jefferson was less influenced by Locke than by the Scottish philosophers,

particularly Francis Hutcheson and his *Inquiry into the Original of Our Ideas of Beauty and Virtue* (1725). Wills tells us that "the pursuit of happiness is a phenomenon both obvious and paradoxical. It supplies us with the ground of human right and the goal of human virtue. It is the basic drive of the self, and the only means given for transcending the self.... Men in the eighteenth century felt they could become conscious of their freedom only by discovering how they were bound: When they found what they *must* pursue, they knew they had a *right* to pursue it."
6. I.e., discernible.

evinces a design to reduce them under absolute despotism, it is their right, it is their duty to throw off such government, and to provide new guards for their future security. Such has been the patient sufferance of these colonies; and such is now the necessity which constrains them to expunge their former systems of government. The history of the present king of Great Britain[7] is a history of unremitting injuries and usurpations, among which appears no solitary fact to contradict the uniform tenor of the rest, but all have in direct object the establishment of an absolute tyranny over these states. To prove this, let facts be submitted to a candid world for the truth of which we pledge a faith yet unsullied by falsehood.

                                                          alter, repeated, all having

He has refused his assent to laws the most wholesome and necessary for the public good.

He has forbidden his governors to pass laws of immediate and pressing importance, unless suspended in their operation till his assent should be obtained; and, when so suspended, he has utterly neglected to attend to them.

He has refused to pass other laws for the accommodation of large districts of people, unless those people would relinquish the right of representation in the legislature, a right inestimable to them, and formidable to tyrants only.

He has called together legislative bodies at places unusual, uncomfortable, and distant from the depository of their public records, for the sole purpose of fatiguing them into compliance with his measures.

He has dissolved representative houses repeatedly and continually for opposing with manly firmness his invasions on the rights of the people.

He has refused for a long time after such dissolutions to cause others to be elected, whereby the legislative powers, incapable of annihilation, have returned to the people at large for their exercise, the state remaining, in the meantime, exposed to all the dangers of invasion from without and convulsions within.

He has endeavored to prevent the population of these states; for that purpose obstructing the laws for naturalization of foreigners, refusing to pass others to encourage their migrations hither, and raising the conditions of new appropriations of lands.

He has suffered the administration of justice totally to cease in some of these states refusing his assent to laws for establishing judiciary powers.   *obstructed by*

He has made our judges dependent on his will alone for the tenure of their offices, and the amount and payment of their salaries.

He has erected a multitude of new offices, by a self-assumed

7. King George III (1738–1820).

power and sent hither swarms of new officers to harass our people and eat out their substance.

He has kept among us in times of peace standing armies and ships of war without the consent of our legislatures.

He has affected to render the military independent of, and superior to, the civil power.

He has combined with others[8] to subject us to a jurisdiction foreign to our constitutions and unacknowledged by our laws, giving his assent to their acts of pretended legislation for quartering large bodies of armed troops among us; for protecting them by a mock trial from punishment for any murders which they should commit on the inhabitants of these states; for cutting off our trade with all parts of the world; for imposing taxes on us without our consent; for depriving us [ ] of the benefits of trial by jury; for transporting us beyond seas to be tried for pretended offenses; for abolishing the free system of English laws in a neighboring province,[9] establishing therein an arbitrary government, and enlarging its boundaries, so as to render it at once an example and fit instrument for introducing the same absolute rule into these states; for taking away our charters, abolishing our most valuable laws, and altering fundamentally the forms of our governments; for suspending our own legislatures, and declaring themselves invested with power to legislate for us in all cases whatsoever.

[margin: in many cases]

[margin: colonies;]

He has abdicated government here withdrawing his governors, and declaring us out of his allegiance and protection.

[margin: by declaring us out of his protection, and waging war against us.]

He has plundered our seas, ravaged our coasts, burnt our towns, and destroyed the lives of our people.

He is at this time transporting large armies of foreign mercenaries[1] to complete the works of death, desolation and tyranny already begun with circumstances of cruelty and perfidy [ ] unworthy the head of a civilized nation.

[margin: scarcely paralleled in the most barbarous ages, and totally]

He has constrained our fellow citizens taken captive on the high seas, to bear arms against their country, to become the executioners of their friends and brethren, or to fall themselves by their hands.

He has [ ] endeavored to bring on the inhabitants of our frontiers, the merciless Indian savages, whose known rule of warfare is an undistinguished destruction of all ages, sexes and conditions of existence.

[margin: excited domestic insurrection among us, and has]

He has incited treasonable insurrections of our fellow citizens, with the allurements of forfeiture and confiscation of our property.

He has waged cruel war against human nature itself, violating its most sacred rights of life and liberty in the persons

8. I.e., the British Parliament.
9. The Quebec Act of 1774 recognized the Roman Catholic religion in Quebec and extended the borders of the province to the Ohio River; it restored French civil law and thus angered the New England colonies. It was often referred to as one of the "intolerable acts."
1. German soldiers hired by the king for colonial service.

of a distant people who never offended him, captivating and carrying them into slavery in another hemisphere, or to incur miserable death in their transportation thither. This piratical warfare, the opprobrium of INFIDEL powers, is the warfare of the CHRISTIAN king of Great Britain. Determined to keep open a market where MEN should be bought and sold, he has prostituted his negative for suppressing every legislative attempt to prohibit or to restrain this execrable commerce. And that this assemblage of horrors might want no fact of distinguished die, he is now exciting those very people to rise in arms among us, and to purchase that liberty of which he has deprived them, by murdering the people on whom he also obtruded them: thus paying off former crimes committed against the LIBERTIES of one people, with crimes which he urges them to commit against the LIVES of another.

In every stage of these oppressions we have petitioned for redress in the most humble terms: our repeated petitions have been answered only by repeated injuries.

A prince whose character is thus marked by every act which may define a tyrant is unfit to be the ruler of a [ ] people who mean to be free. Future ages will scarcely believe that the hardiness of one man adventured, within the short compass of twelve years only, to lay a foundation so broad and so undisguised for tyranny over a people fostered and fixed in principles of freedom. [margin: free]

Nor have we been wanting in attentions to our British brethren. We have warned them from time to time of attempts by their legislature to extend a jurisdiction over these our states. We have reminded them of the circumstances of our emigration and settlement here, no one of which could warrant so strange a pretension: that these were effected at the expense of our own blood and treasure, unassisted by the wealth or the strength of Great Britain: that in constituting indeed our several forms of government, we had adopted one common king, thereby laying a foundation for perpetual league and amity with them: but that submission to their parliament was no part of our constitution, nor ever in idea, if history may be credited: and, we [ ] appealed to their native justice and magnanimity as well as to the ties of our common kindred to disavow these usurpations which were likely to interrupt our connection and correspondence. They too have been deaf to the voice of justice and of consanguinity, and when occasions have been given them, by the regular course of their laws, of removing from their councils the disturbers of our harmony, they have, by their free election, reestablished them in power. At this very time too, they are permitting their chief magistrate to send over not only soldiers of our common blood, but Scotch and foreign mercenaries to invade and destroy us. These facts have given the last stab to agonizing affection, and manly spirit bids us to renounce forever these unfeeling brethren. We must [margin: an unwarrant-able/us] [margin: have and we have conjured them by would inevitably]

endeavor to forget our former love for them, and hold them
as we hold the rest of mankind, enemies in war, in peace
friends. We might have been a free and a great people
together; but a communication of grandeur and of freedom, it
seems, is below their dignity. Be it so, since they will have it.
The road to happiness and to glory is open to us, too. We will
tread it apart from them, and acquiesce in the necessity which
denounces[2] our eternal separation [   ]!

We must therefore and hold them as we hold the rest of mankind, enemies in war, in peace friends.

We therefore the representatives of the United States of America in General Congress assembled, do in the name, and by the authority of the good people of these states reject and renounce all allegiance and subjection to the kings of Great Britain and all others who may hereafter claim by, through or under them; we utterly dissolve all political connection which may heretofore have subsisted between us and the people or parliament of Great Britain: and finally we do assert and declare these colonies to be free and independent states, and that as free and independent states, they have full power to levy war, conclude peace, contract alliances, establish commerce, and to do all other acts and things which independent states may of right do.

And for the support of this declaration, we mutually pledge to each other our lives, our fortunes, and our sacred honor.

We, therefore, the representatives of the United States of America in General Congress assembled, appealing to the supreme judge of the world for the rectitude of our intentions, do in the name, and by the authority of the good people of these colonies, solemnly publish and declare, that these united colonies are, and of right ought to be free and independent states; that they are absolved from all allegiance to the British crown, and that all political connection between them and the state of Great Britain is, and ought to be, totally dissolved; and that as free and independent states, they have full power to levy war, conclude peace, contract alliances, establish commerce, and to do all other acts and things which independent states may of right do.

And for the support of this declaration, with a firm reliance on the protection of divine providence, we mutually pledge to each other our lives, our fortunes, and our sacred honor.

The Declaration thus signed on the 4th, on paper, was engrossed[3] on parchment, and signed again on the 2d of August.

1821   1829

---

2. Proclaims.

3. Written in a legal hand.

From Notes on the State of Virginia[1]

From *Query V. Cascades*

* * *

[NATURAL BRIDGE][2]

The *Natural bridge,* the most sublime of Nature's works, though not comprehended under the present head,[3] must not be pretermitted.[4] It is on the ascent of a hill, which seems to have been cloven through its length by some great convulsion. The fissure, just at the bridge, is by some admeasurements, 270 feet deep, by others only 205. It is about 45 feet wide at the bottom, and 90 feet at the top; this of course determines the length of the bridge, and its height from the water. Its breadth in the middle, is about 60 feet, but more at the ends, and the thickness of the mass at the summit of the arch, about 40 feet. A part of this thickness is constituted by a coat of earth, which gives growth to many large trees. The residue, with the hill on both sides, is one solid rock of limestone. The arch approaches the Semi-elliptical form; but the larger axis of the ellipsis, which would be the cord of the arch, is many times longer than the semi-axis which gives its height. Though the sides of this bridge are provided in some parts with a parapet of fixed rocks, yet few men have resolution to walk to them and look over into the abyss. You involuntarily fall on your hands and feet, creep to the parapet and peep over it. Looking down from this height about a minute gave me a violent headache. This painful sensation is relieved by a short, but pleasing view of the Blue ridge along the fissure downwards, and upwards by that of the Short hills, which, with the Purgatory mountain is a divergence from the North ridge; and, descending then to to the valley below, the sensation becomes delightful in the extreme. It is impossible for the emotions, arising from the sublime, to be felt beyond what they are here: so beautiful an arch, so elevated, so light, and springing, as it were, up to heaven, the rapture of the Spectator is really indescribable! The fissure continues deep and narrow and, following the margin of the stream upwards about three eighths of a mile you arrive at a limestone cavern, less remarkable, however, for height and extent than those before described. Its entrance into the hill is but a few feet above the bed of the stream. This bridge is in the county of Rockbridge, to which it has given name, and affords a public and commodious passage over a valley, which cannot be crossed elsewhere for a considerable distance. The stream passing under it is called Cedar Creek. It is a water of James River, and sufficient in the driest seasons to turn a grist-mill, though its fountain is not more than two miles above.

---

1. In 1781, the year Jefferson resigned as governor of Virginia, he received a request from the Marquis de Barbé-Marbois, secretary of the French legation at Philadelphia, to answer twenty-three questions concerning the geographical boundaries, the ecology, and the social history of Virginia. Jefferson took the occasion to make some observations on slavery, manufacturing, and government. He wanted especially to counter the notion, prevalent among European naturalists, that species in North America had degenerated and were inferior to Old World types. Jefferson's replies were published privately in 1784–85. The threat of an unauthorized French translation prompted Jefferson to publish an authorized edition in London in 1787. The text used here is from the Norton edition, edited by William Peden (1954).
2. Jefferson owned the land near Lexington, Virginia, on which the Natural Bridge stands.
3. I.e., it is not a cascade.
4. Omitted.

Query XVII. Religion

The first settlers in this country were emigrants from England, of the English church, just at a point of time when it was flushed with complete victory over the religious of all other persuasions. Possessed, as they became, of the powers of making, administering, and executing the laws, they showed equal intolerance in this country with their Presbyterian brethren, who had emigrated to the northern government. The poor Quakers were flying from persecution in England. They cast their eyes on these new countries as asylums of civil and religious freedom; but they found them free only for the reigning sect. Several acts of the Virginia assembly of 1659, 1662, and 1693, had made it penal in parents to refuse to have their children baptized; had prohibited the unlawful assembling of Quakers; had made it penal for any master of a vessel to bring a Quaker into the state; had ordered those already here, and such as should come thereafter, to be imprisoned till they should abjure the country; provided a milder punishment for their first and second return, but death for their third; had inhibited all persons from suffering their meetings in or near their houses, entertaining them individually, or disposing of books which supported their tenets. If no capital execution took place here, as did in New England, it was not owing to the moderation of the church, or spirit of the legislature, as may be inferred from the law itself; but to historical circumstances which have not been handed down to us. The Anglicans retained full possession of the country about a century. Other opinions began then to creep in, and the great care of the government to support their own church, having begotten an equal degree of indolence in its clergy, two-thirds of the people had become dissenters at the commencement of the present revolution. The laws indeed were still oppressive on them, but the spirit of the one party had subsided into moderation, and of the other had risen to a degree of determination which commanded respect.

The present state of our laws on the subject of religion is this. The convention of May 1776, in their declaration of rights, declared it to be a truth, and a natural right, that the exercise of religion should be free; but when they proceeded to form on that declaration the ordinance of government, instead of taking up every principle declared in the bill of rights, and guarding it by legislative sanction, they passed over that which asserted our religious rights, leaving them as they found them.[5] The same convention, however, when they met as a member of the general assembly in October 1776, repealed all *acts of parliament* which had rendered criminal the maintaining any opinions in matters of religion, the forbearing to repair to church, and the exercising any mode of worship; and suspended the laws giving salaries to the clergy, which suspension was made perpetual in October 1779. Statutory oppressions in religion being thus wiped away, we remain at present under those only imposed by the common law, or by our own acts of assembly. At the common law, *heresy* was a capital offense, punishable by burning. Its definition was left to the ecclesiastical judges, before whom the conviction was, till the statute of the 1 El. c. 1.[6] circumscribed it, by declaring, that nothing should be deemed heresy, but what had been so determined by authority of the canonical scriptures, or by one of the four first general coun-

---

5. Jefferson is referring to Article XVI of Virginia's Declaration of Rights.

6. That is, chapter 1 of the first year (1558–1559) of the reign of Elizabeth [Peden's note].

cils, or by some other council having for the grounds of their declaration the express and plain words of the scriptures. Heresy, thus circumscribed, being an offense at the common law, our act of assembly of October 1777, c. 17. gives cognizance of it to the general court, by declaring, that the jurisdiction of that court shall be general in all matters at the common law. The execution is by the writ *De hæretico comburendo.*[7] By our own act of assembly of 1705, c. 30, if a person brought up in the Christian religion denies the being of a God, or the Trinity, or asserts there are more Gods than one, or denies the Christian religion to be true, or the scriptures to be of divine authority, he is punishable on the first offense by incapacity to hold any office or employment ecclesiastical, civil, or military; on the second by disability to sue, to take any gift or legacy, to be guardian, executor, or administrator, and by three years' imprisonment, without bail. A father's right to the custody of his own children being founded in law on his right of guardianship, this being taken away, they may of course be severed from him, and put, by the authority of a court, into more orthodox hands. This is a summary view of that religious slavery, under which a people have been willing to remain, who have lavished their lives and fortunes for the establishment of their civil freedom.

The error seems not sufficiently eradicated, that the operations of the mind, as well as the acts of the body, are subject to the coercion of the laws.[8] But our rulers can have authority over such natural rights only as we have submitted to them. The rights of conscience we never submitted, we could not submit. We are answerable for them to our God. The legitimate powers of government extend to such acts only as are injurious to others. But it does me no injury for my neighbor to say there are twenty gods, or no god. It neither picks my pocket nor breaks my leg. If it be said, his testimony in a court of justice cannot be relied on, reject it then, and be the stigma on him. Constraint may make him worse by making him a hypocrite, but it will never make him a truer man. It may fix him obstinately in his errors, but will not cure them. Reason and free enquiry are the only effectual agents against error. Give a loose to them, they will support the true religion, by bringing every false one to their tribunal, to the test of their investigation. They are the natural enemies of error, and of error only. Had not the Roman government permitted free inquiry, Christianity could never have been introduced. Had not free inquiry been indulged, at the era of the Reformation, the corruptions of Christianity could not have been purged away. If it be restrained now, the present corruptions will be protected, and new ones encouraged. Was the government to prescribe to us our medicine and diet, our bodies would be in such keeping as our souls are now. Thus in France the emetic was once forbidden as a medicine, and the potato as an article of food. Government is just as infallible too when it fixes systems in physics. Galileo[9] was sent to the Inquisition for affirming that the earth was a sphere: the government had declared it to be as flat as a trencher, and Galileo was obliged to abjure his error. This error however at length prevailed, the earth became a globe, and Descartes[1] declared it was whirled round its axis by a

---

7. On the burning of a heretic (Latin).
8. "Furneaux passim" [Jefferson's note]. Philip Furneaux (1726–1783), English minister and author of *Letters to the Honorable Mr. Justice Blackstone* (1770).

9. Italian scientist (1564–1642), taught mathematics at Padua and appeared before the Inquisition in 1632.
1. René Descartes (1596–1650), French scientist and philosopher.

vortex. The government in which he lived was wise enough to see that this was no question of civil jurisdiction, or we should all have been involved by authority in vortices. In fact, the vortices have been exploded, and the Newtonian principle of gravitation is now more firmly established, on the basis of reason, than it would be were the government to step in, and to make it an article of necessary faith. Reason and experiment have been indulged, and error has fled before them. It is error alone which needs the support of government. Truth can stand by itself. Subject opinion to coercion: whom will you make your inquisitors? Fallible men; men governed by bad passions, by private as well as public reasons. And why subject it to coercion? To produce uniformity. But is uniformity of opinion desirable? No more than of face and stature. Introduce the bed of Procrustes[2] then, and as there is danger that the large men may beat the small, make us all of a size, by lopping the former and stretching the latter. Difference of opinion is advantageous in religion. The several sects perform the office of a Censor morum[3] over each other. Is uniformity attainable? Millions of innocent men, women, and children, since the introduction of Christianity, have been burnt, tortured, fined, imprisoned; yet we have not advanced one inch towards uniformity. What has been the effect of coercion? To make one half the world fools, and the other half hypocrites. To support roguery and error all over the earth. Let us reflect that it is inhabited by a thousand millions of people. That these profess probably a thousand different systems of religion. That ours is but one of that thousand. That if there be but one right, and ours that one, we should wish to see the 999 wandering sects gathered into the fold of truth. But against such a majority we cannot effect this by force. Reason and persuasion are the only practicable instruments. To make way for these, free inquiry must be indulged; and how can we wish others to indulge it while we refuse it ourselves. But every state, says an inquisitor, has established some religion. No two, say I, have established the same. Is this a proof of the infallibility of establishments? Our sister states of Pennsylvania and New York, however, have long subsisted without any establishment at all. The experiment was new and doubtful when they made it. It has answered beyond conception. They flourish infinitely. Religion is well supported; of various kinds, indeed, but all good enough; all sufficient to preserve peace and order: or if a sect arises, whose tenets would subvert morals, good sense has fair play, and reasons and laughs it out of doors, without suffering the state to be troubled with it. They do not hang more malefactors than we do. They are not more disturbed with religious dissensions. On the contrary, their harmony is unparalleled, and can be ascribed to nothing but their unbounded tolerance, because there is no other circumstance in which they differ from every nation on earth. They have made the happy discovery, that the way to silence religious disputes, is to take no notice of them. Let us too give this experiment fair play, and get rid, while we may, of those tyrannical laws. It is true, we are as yet secured against them by the spirit of the times. I doubt whether the people of this country would suffer an execution for heresy, or a three years' imprisonment for not comprehending the mysteries of the Trinity. But is the spirit of the people an infallible, a permanent reli-

2. A highwayman in classical mythology who either stretched or cut off the legs of his captors to fit his iron bed.
3. Critic of morals or customs (Latin).

ance? Is it government? Is this the kind of protection we receive in return for the rights we give up? Besides, the spirit of the times may alter, will alter. Our rulers will become corrupt, our people careless. A single zealot may commence persecutor, and better men be his victims. It can never be too often repeated, that the time for fixing every essential right on a legal basis is while our rulers are honest, and ourselves united. From the conclusion of this war we shall be going downhill. It will not then be necessary to resort every moment to the people for support. They will be forgotten, therefore, and their rights disregarded. They will forget themselves, but in the sole faculty of making money, and will never think of uniting to effect a due respect for their rights. The shackles, therefore, which shall not be knocked off at the conclusion of this war, will remain on us long, will be made heavier and heavier, till our rights shall revive or expire in a convulsion.

Query XIX. Manufactures

We never had an interior trade of any importance. Our exterior commerce has suffered very much from the beginning of the present contest. During this time we have manufactured within our families the most necessary articles of clothing. Those of cotton will bear some comparison with the same kinds of manufacture in Europe; but those of wool, flax and hemp are very coarse, unsightly, and unpleasant: and such is our attachment to agriculture, and such our preference for foreign manufactures, that be it wise or unwise, our people will certainly return as soon as they can, to the raising raw materials, and exchanging them for finer manufactures than they are able to execute themselves.

The political economists of Europe have established it as a principle that every state should endeavor to manufacture for itself: and this principle, like many others, we transfer to America, without calculating the difference of circumstance which should often produce a difference of result. In Europe the lands are either cultivated, or locked up against the cultivator. Manufacture must therefore be resorted to of necessity not of choice, to support the surplus of their people. But we have an immensity of land courting the industry of the husbandman.[4] Is it best then that all our citizens should be employed in its improvement, or that one half should be called off from that to exercise manufactures and handicraft arts for the other? Those who labor in the earth are the chosen people of God, if ever He had a chosen people, whose breasts He has made his peculiar deposit for substantial and genuine virtue. It is the focus in which He keeps alive that sacred fire, which otherwise might escape from the face of the earth. Corruption of morals in the mass of cultivators is a phenomenon of which no age nor nation has furnished an example. It is the mark set on those, who not looking up to heaven, to their own soil and industry, as does the husbandman, for their subsistence, depend for it on the casualties and caprice of customers. Dependence begets subservience and venality, suffocates the germ of virtue, and prepares fit tools for the designs of ambition. This, the natural progress and consequence of the arts, has sometimes perhaps been retarded by accidental circumstances: but, generally speaking, the proportion which the aggregate of the

4. Farmer.

other classes of citizens bears in any state to that of its husbandmen is the proportion of its unsound to its healthy parts, and is a good enough barometer whereby to measure its degree of corruption. While we have land to labor then, let us never wish to see our citizens occupied at a workbench, or twirling a distaff.[5] Carpenters, masons, smiths are wanting in husbandry: but, for the general operations of manufacture, let our workshops remain in Europe. It is better to carry provisions and materials to workmen there, than bring them to the provisions and materials, and with them their manners and principles. The loss by the transportation of commodities across the Atlantic will be made up in happiness and permanence of government. The mobs of great cities add just so much to the support of pure government as sores do to the strength of the human body. It is the manners and spirit of a people which preserve a republic in vigor. A degeneracy in these is a canker which soon eats to the heart of its laws and constitution.

1780–81   1787

5. A short stick on which wool or flax is wound.

THE FEDERALIST

When Richard Henry Lee, a Virginia delegate to the Continental Congress, proposed on June 7, 1776, his resolution for independence from Britain, he also suggested that a "plan of confederation be prepared and transmitted to the respective colonies for their consideration and approbation." On July 12, 1776, the Articles of Confederation were presented to Congress; they were debated for a year; they were ratified and adopted as the bylaws of the nation on March 1, 1781. The central question before the Constitutional Convention meeting in Philadelphia six years later was whether to try to salvage these articles by a number of complicated amendments or to draw up the framework of a new national government. Delegates to the convention decided upon the latter and, in September 1787, received copies of the proposed Constitution which they, in turn, were to submit to their state legislatures for ratification. Advocates of the new Constitution, dubbed Federalists, and their Antifederalist opponents quickly rose to the occasion, and a great debate followed. Many were fearful at what they saw as the loss of states' rights and the power of a large, impersonal government to dominate the lives of individual citizens, and they cited the absence of a bill of rights; others thought that the Constitution favored urban over rural populations; others bemoaned the end of the slave trade.

The debate took ten months, and in the state of New York, where adoption was not inevitable and a number of states' rights supporters objected to strengthening the power of the federal government, serious discussion ensued. The debate produced a number of significant documents, none more lasting than the eighty-five essays that appeared in New York newspapers from October 1787 to April 1788, signed with the pen name Publius and later collected in two volumes called *The Federalist*. These essays were written by Alexander Hamilton (1757–1804), a brilliant and quick-tempered man who was a secretary and aide to General Washington and, later, secretary of the treasury; John Jay (1745–1829), first chief justice of the United States Supreme Court and governor of the state of New York; and James Madison (1751–1836), fourth president of the United States, a Virginian, and a lawyer of distinction.

The pseudonym Publius was used for the sake of anonymity, but the authorship was generally known.

As originally conceived, *The Federalist* had only one purpose: to persuade reluctant New Yorkers to adopt the proposed new Constitution. It did not set out to define the nature of government; yet it has turned out to be more lasting than most political treatises. Its essential argument is that individuals have a natural right to "liberty, dignity, and happiness" and that to ensure these rights government must "secure the public good, and private rights, against the dangers of a majority," at the same time preserving the "spirit and form of a popular government." This difficult balancing that *The Federalist* argues goes to the very heart of American democracy.

From The Federalist[1]

No. 1 [*Alexander Hamilton*]

To the People of the State of New York.   October 27, 1787
After an unequivocal experience of the inefficacy of the subsisting[2] federal government, you are called upon to deliberate on a new Constitution for the United States of America. The subject speaks its own importance; comprehending in its consequences nothing less than the existence of the Union, the safety and welfare of the parts of which it is composed, the fate of an empire, in many respects, the most interesting in the world. It has been frequently remarked that it seems to have been reserved to the people of this country, by their conduct and example, to decide the important question whether societies of men are really capable or not of establishing good government from reflection and choice, or whether they are forever destined to depend, for their political constitutions, on accident and force. If there be any truth in the remark, the crisis at which we are arrived may with propriety be regarded as the era in which that decision is to be made; and a wrong election of the part we shall act, may, in this view, deserve to be considered as the general misfortune of mankind.

This idea will add the inducements of philanthropy to those of patriotism to heighten the solicitude, which all considerate and good men must feel for the event. Happy will it be if our choice should be directed by a judicious estimate of our true interests, unperplexed and unbiased by considerations not connected with the public good. But this is a thing more ardently to be wished than seriously to be expected. The plan offered to our deliberations affects too many particular interests, innovates[3] upon too many local institutions, not to involve in its discussion a variety of objects foreign to its merits, and of views, passions and prejudices little favorable to the discovery of truth.

Among the most formidable of the obstacles which the new Constitution will have to encounter may readily be distinguished the obvious interest of a certain class of men in every state to resist all changes which may hazard a diminution of the power, emolument and consequence of the offices they hold under the state establishments—and the perverted ambition of another class of men, who will either hope to aggrandize themselves by the confusions of their country, or will flatter themselves with fairer prospects of elevation

1. The text used here is from *The Federalist* (1961), edited by Jacob E. Cooke.   2. Existing; present.
3. Makes changes.

from the subdivision of the empire into several partial confederacies, than from its union under one government.

It is not, however, my design to dwell upon observations of this nature. I am well aware that it would be disingenuous to resolve indiscriminately the opposition of any set of men (merely because their situations might subject them to suspicion) into interested or ambitious views: candor will oblige us to admit, that even such men may be actuated by upright intentions; and it cannot be doubted that much of the opposition which has made its appearance, or may hereafter make its appearance, will spring from sources, blameless at least, if not respectable, the honest errors of minds led astray by preconceived jealousies and fears. So numerous indeed and so powerful are the causes, which serve to give a false bias to the judgment, that we upon many occasions see wise and good men on the wrong as well as on the right side of questions of the first magnitude to society. This circumstance, if duly attended to, would furnish a lesson of moderation to those, who are ever so much persuaded of their being in the right in any controversy. And a further reason for caution, in this respect, might be drawn from the reflection that we are not always sure that those who advocate the truth are influenced by purer principles than their antagonists. Ambition, avarice, personal animosity, party opposition, and many other motives, not more laudable than these, are apt to operate as well upon those who support as upon those who oppose the right side of a question. Were there not even these inducements to moderation, nothing could be more ill judged than that intolerant spirit, which has, at all times, characterized political parties. For, in politics as in religion, it is equally absurd to aim at making proselytes by fire and sword. Heresies in either can rarely be cured by persecution.

And yet however just these sentiments will be allowed to be, we have already sufficient indications that it will happen in this as in all former cases of great national discussion. A torrent of angry and malignant passions will be let loose. To judge from the conduct of the opposite parties, we shall be led to conclude that they will mutually hope to evince the justness of their opinions, and to increase the number of their converts by the loudness of their declamations, and by the bitterness of their invectives. An enlightened zeal for the energy and efficiency of government will be stigmatized, as the offspring of a temper fond of despotic power and hostile to the principles of liberty. An overscrupulous jealousy of danger to the rights of the people, which is more commonly the fault of the head than of the heart, will be represented as mere pretense and artifice; the bait for popularity at the expense of public good. It will be forgotten, on the one hand, that jealousy is the usual concomitant of violent love, and that the noble enthusiasm of liberty is too apt to be infected with a spirit of narrow and illiberal distrust. On the other hand, it will be equally forgotten that the vigor of government is essential to the security of liberty; that in the contemplation of a sound and well-informed judgment, their interest can never be separated; and that a dangerous ambition more often lurks behind the specious mask of zeal for the rights of the people than under the forbidding appearance of zeal for the firmness and efficiency of government. History will teach us that the former has been found a much more certain road to the introduction of despotism than the latter, and that of those men who have overturned the liberties of republics the greatest number have begun their career by paying an obsequious court to the people, commencing demagogues and ending tyrants.

In the course of the preceding observations I have had an eye, my fellow citizens, to putting you upon your guard against all attempts, from whatever quarter, to influence your decision in a matter of the utmost moment to your welfare by any impressions other than those which may result from the evidence of truth. You will, no doubt, at the same time, have collected from the general scope of them that they proceed from a source not unfriendly to the new Constitution. Yes, my countrymen, I own to you, that, after having given it an attentive consideration, I am clearly of opinion it is your interest to adopt it. I am convinced that this is the safest course for your liberty, your dignity, and your happiness. I effect not reserves, which I do not feel. I will not amuse you with an appearance of deliberation, when I have decided. I frankly acknowledge to you my convictions, and I will freely lay before you the reasons on which they are founded. The consciousness of good intentions disdains ambiguity. I shall not however multiply professions on this head. My motives must remain in the depository of my own breast: my arguments will be open to all, and may be judged of by all. They shall at least be offered in a spirit which will not disgrace the cause of truth.

I propose in a series of papers to discuss the following interesting particulars—the utility of the Union to your political prosperity—the insufficiency of the present confederation to preserve that Union—the necessity of a government at least equally energetic with the one proposed to the attainment of this object—the conformity of the proposed constitution to the true principles of republican government—its analogy to your own state constitution—and lastly, the additional security which its adoption will afford to the preservation of that species of government, to liberty and to property.

In the progress of this discussion I shall endeavor to give a satisfactory answer to all the objections which shall have made their appearance that may seem to have any claim to your attention.

It may perhaps be thought superfluous to offer arguments to prove the utility of the Union, a point, no doubt, deeply engraved on the hearts of the great body of the people in every state, and one, which it may be imagined, has no adversaries. But the fact is that we already hear it whispered in the private circles of those who oppose the new constitution that the thirteen states are of too great extent for any general system, and that we must of necessity resort to separate confederacies of distinct portions of the whole.[4] This doctrine will, in all probability, be gradually propagated, till it has votaries enough to countenance an open avowal of it. For nothing can be more evident, to those who are able to take an enlarged view of the subject, than the alternative of an adoption of the new Constitution, or a dismemberment of the Union. It will therefore be of use to begin by examining the advantages of that Union, the certain evils and the probable dangers to which every state will be exposed from its dissolution. This shall accordingly constitute the subject of my next address.

Publius[5]

4. The same idea, tracing the arguments to their consequences, is held out in several of the late publications against the new Constitution [Publius's note].

5. A Latin proper name and the collective pseudonym adopted by Hamilton, Madison, and Jay as the authors of The Federalist; their authorship was well known.

No. 10 [James Madison]

To the People of the State of New York.   November 22, 1787
Among the numerous advantages promised by a well-constructed Union, none deserves to be more accurately developed than its tendency to break and control the violence of faction. The friend of popular governments never finds himself so much alarmed for their character and fate as when he contemplates their propensity to this dangerous vice. He will not fail therefore to set a due value on any plan which, without violating the principles to which he is attached, provides a proper cure for it. The instability, injustice and confusion introduced into the public councils have in truth been the mortal diseases under which popular governments have everywhere perished; as they continue to be the favorite and fruitful topics from which the adversaries to liberty derive their most specious declamations. The valuable improvements made by the American constitutions on the popular models, both ancient and modern, cannot certainly be too much admired; but it would be an unwarrantable partiality to contend that they have as effectually obviated the danger on this side as was wished and expected. Complaints are everywhere heard from our most considerate and virtuous citizens, equally the friends of public and private faith and of public and personal liberty; that our governments are too unstable; that the public good is disregarded in the conflicts of rival parties; and that measures are too often decided not according to the rules of justice and the rights of the minor party, but by the superior force of an interested and overbearing majority. However anxiously we may wish that these complaints had no foundation, the evidence of known facts will not permit us to deny that they are in some degree true. It will be found indeed, on a candid review of our situation, that some of the distresses under which we labor have been erroneously charged on the operation of our governments; but it will be found, at the same time, that other causes will not alone account for many of our heaviest misfortunes; and particularly, for that prevailing and increasing distrust of public engagements, and alarm for private rights, which are echoed from one end of the continent to the other. These must be chiefly, if not wholly, effects of the unsteadiness and injustice with which a factious spirit has tainted our public administrations.

By a faction I understand a number of citizens, whether amounting to a majority or minority of the whole, who are united and actuated by some common impulse of passion or of interest, adverse to the rights of other citizens, or to the permanent and aggregate interests of the community.

There are two methods of curing the mischiefs of faction: the one, by removing its causes; the other, by controlling its effects.

There are again two methods of removing the causes of faction: the one by destroying the liberty which is essential to its existence; the other, by giving to every citizen the same opinions, the same passions, and the same interests.

It could never be more truly said than of the first remedy, that it is worse than the disease. Liberty is to faction, what air is to fire, an aliment[6] without which it instantly expires. But it could not be a less folly to abolish liberty,

6. Nutriment; sustenance.

which is essential to political life, because it nourishes faction, than it would be to wish the annihilation of air, which is essential to animal life, because it imparts to fire its destructive agency.

The second expedient is as impracticable as the first would be unwise. As long as the reason of man continues fallible, and he is at liberty to exercise it, different opinions will be formed. As long as the connection subsists between his reason and his self-love, his opinions and his passions will have a reciprocal influence on each other; and the former will be objects to which the latter will attach themselves. The diversity in the faculties of men from which the rights of property originate is not less an insuperable obstacle to a uniformity of interests. The protection of these faculties is the first object of government. From the protection of different and unequal faculties of acquiring property, the possession of different degrees and kinds of property immediately results: and from the influence of these on the sentiments and views of the respective proprietors ensues a division of the society into different interests and parties.

The latent causes of faction are thus sown in the nature of man; and we see them everywhere brought into different degrees of activity, according to the different circumstances of civil society. A zeal for different opinions concerning religion, concerning government and many other points, as well of speculation as of practice; an attachment to different leaders ambitiously contending for pre-eminence and power; or to persons of other descriptions whose fortunes have been interesting to the human passions have in turn divided mankind into parties, inflamed them with mutual animosity, and rendered them much more disposed to vex and oppress each other than to cooperate for their common good. So strong is this propensity of mankind to fall into mutual animosities that where no substantial occasion presents itself, the most frivolous and fanciful distinctions have been sufficient to kindle their unfriendly passions and excite their most violent conflicts. But the most common and durable source of factions has been the various and unequal distribution of property. Those who hold and those who are without property have ever formed distinct interests in society. Those who are creditors and those who are debtors fall under a like discrimination. A landed interest, a manufacturing interest, a mercantile interest, a monied interest, with many lesser interests, grow up of necessity in civilized nations, and divide them into different classes, actuated by different sentiments and views. The regulation of these various and interfering interests forms the principal task of modern legislation, and involves the spirit of party and faction in the necessary and ordinary operations of government.

No man is allowed to be a judge in his own cause, because his interest would certainly bias his judgment and, not improbably, corrupt his integrity. With equal, nay with greater, reason a body of men are unfit to be both judges and parties at the same time; yet what are many of the most important acts of legislation but so many judicial determinations, not indeed concerning the rights of single persons, but concerning the rights of large bodies of citizens; and what are the different classes of legislators but advocates and parties to the causes which they determine? Is a law proposed concerning private debts? It is a question to which the creditors are parties on one side and the debtors on the other. Justice ought to hold the balance between them. Yet the parties are and must be themselves the judges; and the most numerous party, or, in other words, the most powerful faction, must be expected to prevail. Shall domestic manufactures be encouraged, and in what degree, by restrictions on foreign manufactures? are questions which would be differently decided by the landed and the manufacturing classes; and probably by neither, with a sole regard to justice and the public good. The apportionment of taxes on the various descriptions of property is an act which seems to require the most exact impartiality; yet, there is perhaps no legislative act in which greater opportunity and temptation are given to a predominant party to trample on the rules of justice. Every shilling with which they overburden the inferior number is a shilling saved to their own pockets.

It is in vain to say that enlightened statesmen will be able to adjust these clashing interests and render them all subservient to the public good. Enlightened statesmen will not always be at the helm; nor, in many cases, can such an adjustment be made at all, without taking into view indirect and remote considerations, which will rarely prevail over the immediate interest which one party may find in disregarding the rights of another, or the good of the whole.

The inference to which we are brought is that the *causes* of faction cannot be removed, and that relief is only to be sought in the means of controlling its *effects*.

If a faction consists of less than a majority, relief is supplied by the republican principle, which enables the majority to defeat its sinister views by regular vote. It may clog the administration, it may convulse the society, but it will be unable to execute and mask its violence under the forms of the Constitution. When a majority is included in a faction, the form of popular government on the other hand enables it to sacrifice to its ruling passion or interest both the public good and the rights of other citizens. To secure the public good and private rights against the danger of such a faction, and at the same time to preserve the spirit and the form of popular government, is then the great object to which our inquiries are directed. Let me add that it is the great desideratum[7] by which alone this form of government can be rescued from the opprobrium under which it has so long labored and be recommended to the esteem and adoption of mankind.

By what means is this object attainable? Evidently by one of two only. Either the existence of the same passion or interest in a majority at the same time must be prevented; or the majority, having such co-existent passion or interest, must be rendered, by their number and local situation, unable to concert and carry into effect schemes of oppression. If the impulse and the opportunity be suffered to coincide, we well know that neither moral nor religious motives can be relied on as an adequate control. They are not found to be such on the injustice and violence of individuals, and lose their efficacy in proportion to the number combined together; that is, in proportion as their efficacy becomes needful.

From this view of the subject, it may be concluded, that a pure democracy, by which I mean a society consisting of a small number of citizens who assemble and administer the government in person, can admit of no cure for the mischiefs of faction. A common passion or interest will, in almost every case, be felt by a majority of the whole; a communication and concert results

---

7. Thing which is desired; that which is felt to be missing and needed (Latin).

from the form of government itself; and there is nothing to check the inducements to sacrifice the weaker party, or an obnoxious individual. Hence it is that such democracies have ever been spectacles of turbulence and contention; have ever been found incompatible with personal security, or the rights of property; and have in general been as short in their lives, as they have been violent in their deaths. Theoretic politicians, who have patronized this species of government, have erroneously supposed that by reducing mankind to a perfect equality in their political rights, they would, at the same time, be perfectly equalized and assimilated in their possessions, their opinions, and their passions.

A republic, by which I mean a government in which the scheme of representation takes place, opens a different prospect, and promises the cure for which we are seeking. Let us examine the points in which it varies from pure democracy, and we shall comprehend both the nature of the cure, and the efficacy which it must derive from the Union.

The two great points of difference between a democracy and a republic are, first, the delegation of the government, in the latter, to a small number of citizens elected by the rest: secondly, the greater number of citizens, and greater sphere of country, over which the latter may be extended.

The effect of the first difference is, on the one hand, to refine and enlarge the public views by passing them through the medium of a chosen body of citizens, whose wisdom may best discern the true interest of their country, and whose patriotism and love of justice will be least likely to sacrifice it to temporary or partial considerations. Under such a regulation, it may well happen that the public voice pronounced by the representatives of the people will be more consonant to the public good than if pronounced by the people themselves convened for the purpose. On the other hand, the effect may be inverted. Men of factious tempers, of local prejudices, or of sinister designs may, by intrigue, by corruption or by other means, first obtain the suffrages,[8] and then betray the interests of the people. The question resulting is whether small or extensive republics are most favorable to the election of proper guardians of the public weal: and it is clearly decided in favor of the latter by two obvious considerations.

In the first place it is to be remarked that however small the republic may be, the representatives must be raised to a certain number in order to guard against the cabals[9] of a few; and that however large it may be, they must be limited to a certain number in order to guard against the confusion of a multitude. Hence the number of representatives in the two cases, not being in proportion to that of the constituents, and being proportionally greatest in the small republic, it follows, that if the proportion of fit characters be not less in the large than in the small republic, the former will present a greater option, and consequently a greater probability of a fit choice.

In the next place, as each representative will be chosen by a greater number of citizens in the large than in the small republic, it will be more difficult for unworthy candidates to practice with success the vicious arts, by which elections are too often carried; and the suffrages of the people being more free will be more likely to center on men who possess the most attractive merit, and the most diffusive and established characters.

8. Votes.   9. Plots.

It must be confessed that in this, as in most other cases, there is a mean, on both sides of which inconveniencies will be found to lie. By enlarging too much the number of electors, you render the representative too little acquainted with all their local circumstances and lesser interests; as by reducing it too much, you render him unduly attached to these, and too little fit to comprehend and pursue great and national objects. The federal Constitution forms a happy combination in this respect; the great and aggregate interests being referred to the national, the local, and, particular, to the state legislatures.

The other point of difference is the greater number of citizens and extent of territory which may be brought within the compass of republican, than of democratic[1] government; and it is this circumstance principally which renders factious combinations less to be dreaded in the former than in the latter. The smaller the society, the fewer probably will be the distinct parties and interests composing it; the fewer the distinct parties and interests, the more frequently will a majority be found of the same party; and the smaller the number of individuals composing a majority, and smaller the compass within which they are placed, the more easily will they concert and execute their plans of oppression. Extend the sphere, and you take in a greater variety of parties and interests; you make it less probable that a majority of the whole will have a common motive to invade the rights of other citizens; or if such a common motive exists, it will be more difficult for all who feel it to discover their own strength, and to act in unison with each other. Besides other impediments, it may be remarked, that where there is a consciousness of unjust or dishonorable purposes, communication is always checked by distrust, in proportion to the number whose concurrence is necessary.

Hence it clearly appears that the same advantage which a republic has over a democracy, in controlling the effects of faction, is enjoyed by a large over a small republic—is enjoyed by the Union over the states composing it. Does this advantage consist in the substitution of representatives, whose enlightened views and virtuous sentiments render them superior to local prejudices, and to schemes of injustice? It will not be denied, that the representation of the Union will be most likely to possess these requisite endowments. Does it consist in the greater security afforded by a greater variety of parties, against the event of any one party being able to outnumber and oppress the rest? In an equal degree does the increased variety of parties, comprised within the Union, increase this security? Does it, in fine,[2] consist in the greater obstacles opposed to the concert and accomplishment of the secret wishes of an unjust and interested majority? Here, again, the extent of the Union gives it the most palpable advantage.

The influence of factious leaders may kindle a flame within their particular states, but will be unable to spread a general conflagration through the other states: a religious sect may degenerate into a political faction in a part of the confederacy, but the variety of sects dispersed over the entire face of it must secure the national councils against any danger from that source: a rage for paper money, for an abolition of debts, for an equal division of property, or for any other improper or wicked project, will be less apt to pervade the whole

1. Republicans are Federalists and are willing to have an elected few represent the whole; Democrats are anti-Federalists and are carefully guarding the individual's right to vote.
2. In conclusion.

body of the Union than a particular member of it; in the same proportion as such a malady is more likely to taint a particular county or district than an entire state.

In the extent and proper structure of the Union, therefore, we behold a republican remedy for the diseases most incident to republican government. And according to the degree of pleasure and pride we feel in being republicans, ought to be our zeal in cherishing the spirit, and supporting the character of Federalists.

Publius

1787   1788

OLAUDAH EQUIANO
1745?–1797

The Interesting Narrative of the Life of Olaudah Equiano, or Gustavus Vassa, the African was published in London in 1789 and found an enthusiastic American audience when it was reprinted in New York in 1791. In the next five years it went through eight more editions, and it was reprinted again in the nineteenth century. This publication history suggests its centrality to the antislavery cause. To offset its importance, proslavery apologists questioned the *Narrative*'s veracity, attacking in particular Equiano's claim to have been born in Africa. Scholars agree that Equiano himself left conflicting evidence about his origins; but no black voice before Frederick Douglass spoke so movingly to American readers about inhumanity, and no work before Douglass's own *Narrative* had such an impact. Incorporating the vocabulary and ideals of the Enlightenment—particularly the belief that sentiment linked all human beings and thus argued for the university of human rights—Equiano spoke for the countless disenfranchised and exploited workers whose labor fueled the new mercantilism. In a literature replete with self-made figures who voyage from innocence to experience— some fictive, some not—Equiano's story stands, in view of the actual horrors he suffered, in a class quite by itself. He defined himself as neither African American (his first owner in the New World was a Virginian) nor Anglo African (with London as his adopted home), and he stands as an exemplary inhabitant of the Atlantic Rim, someone who at various times called Africa, North America, South America, and Europe his home.

Equiano writes that he was born in about 1745 in what is now Nigeria, in an unlocated Ibo village called Essaka; he was sold to British slavers in 1756 and transported first to the Barbadoes in the West Indies and then to a plantation in Virginia. He was with his second owner, Lt. Michael Henry Pascal, throughout the Seven Years' War between England and France and was present at the siege of Fort Louisburg on Cape Breton Island in Nova Scotia. Eventually, he was sold to a Quaker merchant from Philadelphia, Robert King, who carried on much of his business in the West Indies. King often traded in "live cargo," or slaves, and Equiano saw much that made him grateful for his Quaker master's treatment of him, without having any illusions about what the loss of freedom entailed. He saw the ugliest side of American life in both the North and the South. Even in Philadelphia, a city built on the premise of "brotherly love," Equiano observed that the freed black was treated with profound contempt, "plundered" and "universally insulted," with no possibility of redress. King, however, did make it possible for Equiano to purchase his freedom in 1766. Once having gained his freedom by paying forty pounds—earned by his own instincts for enterprise, carrying on his own business while managing King's—he never set foot on American soil again.

It was Equiano's intention to settle in London for the rest of his life. He made his living there as a free servant, a musician (he played the French horn), and a barber. But Equiano's skill as a seaman, and his always remarkable curiosity, made him restless for new adventures, and before he died he had traveled as far as Turkey; had heard opera in Rome; and had seen Jamaica, Honduras, and Nicaragua. In 1783 Equiano brought the case of the infamous ship *Zong* to the British public: the owners had thrown overboard 132 shackled slaves and later made insurance claims against their loss. He lectured widely on the abolition of slavery and approved a project to resettle poor blacks in Sierra Leone, Africa. He was, in fact, given an official post in this undertaking, but lost it after he made accusations of misdeeds against some officials. Although he always spoke about his desire to return to the place of his birth, Africa always lay beyond his reach. In a letter written to his hosts in Birmingham, England, after lecturing there, he wrote:

> These acts of kindness and hospitality have filled me with a longing desire to see these worthy friends on my own estate in Africa, where the richest produce of it should be devoted to their entertainment. There they should partake of the luxuriant pineapples, and the well-flavored virgin palm-wine, and to heighten the bliss I would burn a certain tree, that would afford us light as clear and brilliant as the virtue of my guests.

In 1792 Equiano married Susanna Cullen, and their marriage was duly noticed in the London *Gentleman's Magazine*. He died on March 31, 1797, and one of his daughters died shortly after him.

From The Interesting Narrative of the Life of Olaudah Equiano, or Gustavas Vassa, the African, Written by Himself[1]

From *Chapter I*

I believe it is difficult for those who publish their own memoirs to escape the imputation of vanity; nor is this the only disadvantage under which they labor: it is also their misfortune, that what is uncommon is rarely, if ever, believed, and what is obvious we are apt to turn from with disgust, and to charge the writer with impertinence. People generally think those memoirs only worthy to be read or remembered which abound in great or striking events; those, in short, which in a high degree excite either admiration or pity: all others they consign to contempt and oblivion. It is therefore, I confess, not a little hazardous in a private and obscure individual, and a stranger too, thus to solicit the indulgent attention of the public; especially when I own[2] I offer here the history of neither a saint, a hero, nor a tyrant. I believe there are few events in my life, which have not happened to many: it is true the incidents of it are numerous; and, did I consider myself an European, I might say my sufferings were great: but when I compare my lot with that of most of my countrymen, I regard myself as a *particular favorite of Heaven,* and acknowledge the mercies of Providence in every occurrence

1. The text used here is taken from the 1st edition, published in two volumes for the author in London in 1789. The original paragraphing has been altered to facilitate reading.
2. Acknowledge.

of my life. If, then, the following narrative does not appear sufficiently interesting to engage general attention, let my motive be some excuse for its
publication. I am not so foolishly vain as to expect from it either immortality
or literary reputation. If it affords any satisfaction to my numerous friends,
at whose request it has been written, or in the smallest degree promotes the
interests of humanity, the ends for which it was undertaken will be fully
attained, and every wish of my heart gratified. Let it therefore be remembered, that, in wishing to avoid censure, I do not aspire to praise.

That part of Africa, known by the name of Guinea, to which the trade for
slaves is carried on, extends along the coast above 3400 miles, from Senegal
to Angola, and includes a variety of kingdoms. Of these the most considerable
is the kingdom of Benin, both as to extent and wealth, the richness and
cultivation of the soil, the power of its king, and the number and warlike
disposition of the inhabitants. It is situated nearly under the line,[3] and
extends along the coast about 170 miles, but runs back into the interior part
of Africa to a distance hitherto, I believe, unexplored by any traveler; and
seems only terminated at length by the empire of Abyssinnia, near 1500 miles
from its beginning. This kingdom is divided into many provinces or districts:
in one of the most remote and fertile of which, I was born, in the year 1745,
situated in a charming fruitful vale, named Essaka. The distance of this
province from the capital of Benin and the sea coast must be very considerable: for I had never heard of white men or Europeans, nor of the sea; and
our subjection to the king of Benin was little more than nominal; for every
transaction of the government, as far as my slender observation extended,
was conducted by the chief or elders of the place. The manners and government of a people who have little commerce with other countries, are generally very simple; and the history of what passes in one family or village,
may serve as a specimen of the whole nation. My father was one of those
elders or chiefs I have spoken of, and was styled Embrenche; a term, as I
remember, importing the highest distinction, and signifying in our language
a *mark* of grandeur. This mark is conferred on the person entitled to it, by
cutting the skin across at the top of the forehead, and drawing it down to
the eyebrows: and while it is in this situation applying a warm hand, and
rubbing it until it shrinks up into a thick *weal* across the lower part of the
forehead. Most of the judges and senators were thus marked; my father had
long borne it: I had seen it conferred on one of my brothers, and I also was
destined to receive it by my parents. Those Embrenche or chief men, decided
disputes and punished crimes; for which purpose they always assembled
together. The proceedings were generally short: and in most cases the law
of retaliation prevailed. * * *

We are almost a nation of dancers, musicians and poets. Thus every great
event, such as a triumphant return from battle, or other cause of public
rejoicing, is celebrated in public dances, which are accompanied with songs
and music suited to the occasion. The assembly is separated into four divisions, which dance either apart or in succession, and each with a character
peculiar to itself. The first division contains the married men, who in their
dances frequently exhibit feats of arms, and the representation of a battle.
To these succeed the married women, who dance in the second division. The

3. I.e., the equator.

young men occupy the third: and the maidens the fourth. Each represents some interesting scene of real life, such as a great achievement, domestic employment, a pathetic story, or some rural sport; and as the subject is generally founded on some recent event, it is therefore ever new. This gives our dances a spirit and variety which I have scarcely seen elsewhere.[4]

* * *

Chapter II

I hope the reader will not think I have trespassed on his patience in introducing myself to him, with some account of the manners and customs of my country. They had been implanted in me with great care, and made an impression on my mind, which time could not erase, and which all the adversity and variety of fortune I have since experienced, served only to rivet and record; for, whether the love of one's country be real or imaginary, or a lesson of reason, or an instinct of nature, I still look back with pleasure on the first scenes of my life, though that pleasure has been for the most part mingled with sorrow.

I have already acquainted the reader with the time and place of my birth. My father, besides many slaves, had a numerous family, of which seven lived to grow up, including myself and a sister, who was the only daughter. As I was the youngest of the sons, I became, of course, the greatest favorite with my mother, and was always with her; and she used to take particular pains to form my mind. I was trained up from my earliest years in the art of war: my daily exercise was shooting and throwing javelins; and my mother adorned me with emblems, after the manner of our greatest warriors. In this way I grew up till I was turned the age of eleven, when an end was put to my happiness in the following manner:—generally when the grown people in the neighborhood were gone far in the fields to labor, the children assembled together in some of the neighboring premises to play; and commonly some of us used to get up a tree to look out for any assailant, or kidnapper, that might come upon us—for they sometimes took those opportunities of our parents' absence, to attack and carry off as many as they could seize. One day as I was watching at the top of a tree in our yard, I saw one of those people come into the yard of our next neighbor but one to kidnap, there being many stout[5] young people in it. Immediately on this I gave the alarm of the rogue, and he was surrounded by the stoutest of them, who entangled him with cords, so that he could not escape till some of the grown people came and secured him. But, alas! ere long it was my fate to be thus attacked, and to be carried off, when none of the grown people were nigh. One day, when all our people were gone out to their works as usual, and only I and my dear sister were left to mind the house, two men and a woman got over our walls, and in a moment seized us both, and, without giving us time to cry out, or make resistance, they stopped our mouths, and ran off with us into the nearest wood. Here they tied our hands, and continued to carry us as far as they could, till night came on, when we reached a small house, where the robbers halted for refreshment, and spent the night. We were then unbound, but were unable to take any food; and, being quite overpowered

4. When I was in Smyrna I have frequently seen the Greeks dance after this manner [Equiano's note].
5. Strong.

by fatigue and grief, our only relief was some sleep, which allayed our misfortune for a short time. The next morning we left the house, and continued traveling all the day. For a long time we had kept the woods, but at last we came into a road which I believed I knew. I had now some hopes of being delivered; for we had advanced but a little way before I discovered some people at a distance, on which I began to cry out for their assistance; but my cries had no other effect than to make them tie me faster and stop my mouth, and then they put me into a large sack. They also stopped my sister's mouth, and tied her hands; and in this manner we proceeded till we were out of sight of these people. When we went to rest the following night, they offered us some victuals, but we refused it; and the only comfort we had was in being in one another's arms all that night, and bathing each other with our tears. But alas! we were soon deprived of even the small comfort of weeping together. The next day proved a day of greater sorrow than I had yet experienced; for my sister and I were then separated, while we lay clasped in each other's arms. It was in vain that we besought them not to part us; she was torn from me, and immediately carried away, while I was left in a state of distraction not to be described. I cried and grieved continually; and for several days did not eat any thing but what they forced into my mouth. At length, after many days traveling, during which I had often changed masters, I got into the hands of a chieftain, in a very pleasant country. This man had two wives and some children, and they all used me extremely well, and did all they could to comfort me; particularly the first wife, who was something like my mother. Although I was a great many days' journey from my father's house, yet these people spoke exactly the same language with us. This first master of mine, as I may call him, was a smith,[6] and my principal employment was working his bellows, which were the same kind as I had seen in my vicinity. They were in some respects not unlike the stoves here in gentlemen's kitchens, and were covered over with leather; and in the middle of that leather a stick was fixed, and a person stood up, and worked it in the same manner as is done to pump water out of a cask with a hand pump. I believe it was gold he worked, for it was of a lovely bright yellow color, and was worn by the women on their wrists and ankles. I was there I suppose about a month, and they at last used to trust me some little distance from the house. This liberty I used in embracing every opportunity to inquire the way to my own home; and I also sometimes, for the same purpose, went with the maidens, in the cool of the evenings, to bring pitchers of water from the springs for the use of the house. I had also remarked where the sun rose in the morning, and set in the evening, as I had traveled along; and I had observed that my father's house was towards the rising of the sun. I therefore determined to seize the first opportunity of making my escape, and to shape my course for that quarter; for I was quite oppressed and weighed down by grief after my mother and friends; and my love of liberty, ever great, was strengthened by the mortifying circumstance of not daring to eat with the free-born children, although I was mostly their companion. While I was projecting my escape one day, an unlucky event happened, which quite disconcerted my plan, and put an end to my hopes. I used to be sometimes employed in assisting an elderly slave to cook and take care of the poultry;

6. A metalworker; here, a goldsmith.

and one morning, while I was feeding some chickens, I happened to toss a small pebble at one of them, which hit it on the middle, and directly killed it. The old slave, having soon after missed the chicken, inquired after it; and on my relating the accident (for I told her the truth, for my mother would never suffer me to tell a lie), she flew into a violent passion, and threatened that I should suffer for it; and, my master being out, she immediately went and told her mistress what I had done. This alarmed me very much, and I expected an instant flogging, which to me was uncommonly dreadful, for I had seldom been beaten at home. I therefore resolved to fly; and accordingly I ran into a thicket that was hard by, and hid myself in the bushes. Soon afterwards my mistress and the slave returned, and, not seeing me, they searched all the house, but not finding me, and I not making answer when they called to me, they thought I had run away, and the whole neighborhood was raised in the pursuit of me. In that part of the country, as in ours, the houses and villages were skirted with woods, or shrubberies, and the bushes were so thick that a man could readily conceal himself in them, so as to elude the strictest search. The neighbors continued the whole day looking for me, and several times many of them came within a few yards of the place where I lay hid. I expected every moment, when I heard a rustling among the trees, to be found out, and punished by my master; but they never discovered me, though they were often so near that I even heard their conjectures as they were looking about for me; and I now learned from them that any attempts to return home would be hopeless. Most of them supposed I had fled towards home; but the distance was so great, and the way so intricate, that they thought I could never reach it, and that I should be lost in the woods. When I heard this I was seized with a violent panic, and abandoned myself to despair. Night, too, began to approach, and aggravated all my fears. I had before entertained hopes of getting home, and had determined when it should be dark to make the attempt; but I was now convinced it was fruitless, and began to consider that, if possibly I could escape all other animals, I could not those of the human kind; and that, not knowing the way, I must perish in the woods. Thus was I like the hunted deer—

—"Every leaf and every whisp'ring breath,
Convey'd a foe, and every foe a death."

I heard frequent rustlings among the leaves, and being pretty sure they were snakes, I expected every instant to be stung by them. This increased my anguish, and the horror of my situation became now quite insupportable. I at length quitted the thicket, very faint and hungry, for I had not eaten or drank any thing all the day, and crept to my master's kitchen, from whence I set out at first, which was an open shed, and laid myself down in the ashes with an anxious wish for death, to relieve me from all my pains. I was scarcely awake in the morning, when the old woman slave, who was the first up, came to light the fire, and saw me in the fire place. She was very much surprised to see me, and could scarcely believe her own eyes. She now promised to intercede for me, and went for her master, who soon after came, and, having slightly reprimanded me, ordered me to be taken care of, and not ill treated.

Soon after this, my master's only daughter, and child by his first wife, sickened and died, which affected him so much that for some time he was almost frantic, and really would have killed himself, had he not been watched and prevented. However, in short time afterwards he recovered, and I was again sold. I was now carried to the left of the sun's rising, through many dreary wastes and dismal woods, amidst the hideous roarings of wild beasts. The people I was sold to used to carry me very often, when I was tired, either on their shoulders or on their backs. I saw many convenient well built sheds along the road, at proper distances, to accommodate the merchants and travelers, who lay in those buildings along with their wives, who often accompany them; and they always go well armed.

From the time I left my own nation, I always found somebody that understood me till I came to the sea coast. The languages of different nations did not totally differ, nor were they so copious as those of the Europeans, particularly the English. They were therefore, easily learned; and, while I was journeying thus through Africa, I acquired two or three different tongues. In this manner I had been traveling for a considerable time, when, one evening, to my great surprise, whom should I see brought to the house where I was but my dear sister! As soon as she saw me, she gave a loud shriek, and ran into my arms—I was quite overpowered: neither of us could speak; but, for a considerable time, clung to each other in mutual embraces, unable to do any thing but weep. Our meeting affected all who saw us; and, indeed, I must acknowledge, in honor of those sable destroyers of human rights, that I never met with any ill treatment, or saw any offered to their slaves, except tying them, when necessary, to keep them from running away. When these people knew we were brother and sister, they indulged us to be together; and the man, to whom I supposed we belonged, lay with us, he in the middle, while she and I held one another by the hands across his breast all night; and thus for a while we forgot our misfortunes, in the joy of being together; but even this small comfort was soon to have an end; for scarcely had the fatal morning appeared when she was again torn from me forever! I was now more miserable, if possible, than before. The small relief which her presence gave me from pain was gone, and the wretchedness of my situation was redoubled by my anxiety after her fate, and my apprehensions lest her sufferings should be greater than mine, when I could not be with her to alleviate them. Yes, thou dear partner of all my childish sports! thou sharer of my joys and sorrows! happy should I have ever esteemed myself to encounter every misery for you and to procure your freedom by the sacrifice of my own.— Though you were early forced from my arms, your image has been always riveted in my heart, from which neither time nor fortune have been able to remove it; so that, while the thoughts of your sufferings have damped my prosperity, they have mingled with adversity and increased its bitterness. To that Heaven which protects the weak from the strong, I commit the care of your innocence and virtues, if they have not already received their full reward, and if your youth and delicacy have not long since fallen victims to the violence of the African trader, the pestilential stench of a Guinea ship, the seasoning in the European colonies, or the lash and lust of a brutal and unrelenting overseer.

I did not long remain after my sister. I was again sold, and carried through a number of places, till after traveling a considerable time, I came to a town called Tinmah, in the most beautiful country I had yet seen in Africa. It was extremely rich, and there were many rivulets which flowed through it, and supplied a large pond in the center of the town, where the people washed.

Here I first saw and tasted cocoa nuts, which I thought superior to any nuts I had ever tasted before; and the trees which were loaded, were also interspersed among the houses, which had commodious shades adjoining, and were in the same manner as ours, the insides being neatly plastered and whitewashed. Here I also saw and tasted for the first time, sugar cane. Their money consisted of little white shells, the size of the finger nail. I was sold here for one hundred and seventy-two of them, by a merchant who lived and brought me there. I had been about two or three days at his house, when a wealthy widow, a neighbor of his, came there one evening, and brought with her an only son, a young gentleman about my own age and size. Here they saw me; and, having taken a fancy to me, I was bought of the merchant, and went home with them. Her house and premises were situated close to one of those rivulets I have mentioned, and were the finest I ever saw in Africa: they were very extensive, and she had a number of slaves to attend her. The next day I was washed and perfumed, and when mealtime came, I was led into the presence of my mistress, and ate and drank before her with her son. This filled me with astonishment; and I could scarce help expressing my surprise that the young gentleman should suffer[7] me, who was bound, to eat with him who was free; and not only so, but that he would not at any time either eat or drink till I had taken first, because I was the eldest, which was agreeable to our custom. Indeed, every thing here, and all their treatment of me, made me forget that I was a slave. The language of these people resembled ours so nearly, that we understood each other perfectly. They had also the very same customs as we. There were likewise slaves daily to attend us, while my young master and I, with other boys, sported with our darts and bows and arrows, as I had been used to do at home. In this resemblance to my former happy state, I passed about two months; and I now began to think I was to be adopted into the family, and was beginning to be reconciled to my situation, and to forget by degrees my misfortunes, when all at once the delusion vanished; for, without the least previous knowledge, one morning early, while my dear master and companion was still asleep, I was awakened out of my reverie to fresh sorrow, and hurried away even amongst the uncircumcised.

Thus, at the very moment I dreamed of the greatest happiness, I found myself most miserable; and it seemed as if fortune wished to give me this taste of joy only to render the reverse more poignant.—The change I now experienced, was as painful as it was sudden and unexpected. It was a change indeed, from a state of bliss to a scene which is inexpressible by me, as it discovered to me an element I had never before beheld, and till then had no idea of, and wherein such instances of hardship and cruelty continually occurred, as I can never reflect on but with horror.

All the nations and people I had hitherto passed through, resembled our own in their manners, customs, and language: but I came at length to a country, the inhabitants of which differed from us in all those particulars. I was very much struck with this difference, especially when I came among a people who did not circumcise, and ate without washing their hands. They cooked also in iron pots, and had European cutlasses and cross bows, which were unknown to us, and fought with their fists among themselves. Their

7. Allow.

women were not so modest as ours, for they ate, and drank, and slept with their men. But above all, I was amazed to see no sacrifices or offerings among them. In some of those places the people ornamented themselves with scars, and likewise filed their teeth very sharp. They wanted sometimes to ornament me in the same manner, but I would not suffer them; hoping that I might some time be among a people who did not thus disfigure themselves, as I thought they did. At last I came to the banks of a large river which was covered with canoes, in which the people appeared to live with their household utensils, and provisions of all kinds. I was beyond measure astonished at this, as I had never before seen any water larger than a pond or a rivulet: and my surprise was mingled with no small fear when I was put into one of these canoes, and we began to paddle and move along the river. We continued going on thus till night, and when we came to land, and made fires on the banks, each family by themselves; some dragged their canoes on shore, others stayed and cooked in theirs, and laid in them all night. Those on the land had mats, of which they made tents, some in the shape of little houses; in these we slept; and after the morning meal, we embarked again and proceeded as before. I was often very much astonished to see some of the women, as well as the men, jump into the water, dive to the bottom, come up again, and swim about.—Thus I continued to travel, sometimes by land, sometimes by water, through different countries and various nations, till, at the end of six or seven months after I had been kidnapped, I arrived at the sea coast. It would be tedious and uninteresting to relate all the incidents which befell me during this journey, and which I have not yet forgotten; of the various hands I passed through, and the manners and customs of all the different people among whom I lived—I shall therefore only observe, that in all the places where I was, the soil was exceedingly rich; the pumpkins, eadas,[8] plantains, yams, etc., etc., were in great abundance, and of incredible size. There were also vast quantities of different gums, though not used for any purpose, and every where a great deal of tobacco. The cotton even grew quite wild, and there was plenty of red-wood. I saw no mechanics[9] whatever in all the way, except such as I have mentioned. The chief employment in all these countries was agriculture, and both the males and females, as with us, were brought up to it, and trained in the arts of war.

The first object which saluted my eyes when I arrived on the coast, was the sea, and a slave ship, which was then riding at anchor, and waiting for its cargo. These filled me with astonishment, which was soon converted into terror, when I was carried on board. I was immediately handled, and tossed up to see if I were sound, by some of the crew; and I was now persuaded that I had gotten into a world of bad spirits, and that they were going to kill me. Their complexions, too, differing so much from ours, their long hair, and the language they spoke (which was very different from any I had ever heard), united to confirm me in this belief. Indeed, such were the horrors of my views and fears at the moment, that, if ten thousand worlds had been my own, I would have freely parted with them all to have exchanged my condition with that of the meanest slave in my own country. When I looked round the ship too, and saw a large furnace of copper boiling, and a multitude of

8. More commonly spelled "eddoes": edible roots found in the tropics.   9. Artisans, manual workers.

black people of every description chained together, every one of their countenances expressing dejection and sorrow, I no longer doubted of my fate;
and, quite overpowered with horror and anguish, I fell motionless on the
deck and fainted. When I recovered a little, I found some black people about
me, who I believed were some of those who had brought me on board, and
had been receiving their pay; they talked to me in order to cheer me, but all
in vain. I asked them if we were not to be eaten by those white men with
horrible looks, red faces, and long hair. They told me I was not: and one of
the crew brought me a small portion of spirituous liquor in a wine glass, but,
being afraid of him, I would not take it out of his hand. One of the blacks,
therefore, took it from him and gave it to me, and I took a little down my
palate, which, instead of reviving me, as they thought it would, threw me
into the greatest consternation at the strange feeling it produced, having
never tasted any such liquor before. Soon after this, the blacks who brought
me on board went off, and left me abandoned to despair.

I now saw myself deprived of all chance of returning to my native country,
or even the least glimpse of hope of gaining the shore, which I now considered as friendly; and I even wished for my former slavery in preference to
my present situation, which was filled with horrors of every kind, still heightened by my ignorance of what I was to undergo. I was not long suffered to
indulge my grief; I was soon put down under the decks, and there I received
such a salutation in my nostrils as I had never experienced in my life: so that,
with the loathsomeness of the stench, and crying together, I became so sick
and low that I was not able to eat, nor had I the least desire to taste any
thing. I now wished for the last friend, death, to relieve me; but soon, to my
grief, two of the white men offered me eatables; and, on my refusing to eat,
one of them held me fast by the hands, and laid me across, I think the
windlass, and tied my feet, while the other flogged me severely. I had never
experienced any thing of this kind before, and although not being used to
the water, I naturally feared that element the first time I saw it, yet, nevertheless, could I have got over the nettings, I would have jumped over the
side, but I could not; and besides, the crew used to watch us very closely
who were not chained down to the decks, lest we should leap into the water;
and I have seen some of these poor African prisoners most severely cut, for
attempting to do so, and hourly whipped for not eating. This indeed was
often the case with myself. In a little time after, amongst the poor chained
men, I found some of my own nation, which in a small degree gave ease to
my mind. I inquired of these what was to be done with us? They gave me to
understand we were to be carried to these white people's country to work for
them. I then was a little revived, and thought, if it were no worse than working, my situation was not so desperate; but still I feared I should be put to
death, the white people looked and acted, as I thought, in so savage a manner; for I had never seen among any people such instances of brutal cruelty;
and this not only shown towards us blacks, but also to some of the whites
themselves. One white man in particular I saw, when we were permitted to
be on deck, flogged so unmercifully with a large rope near the foremast, that
he died in consequence of it; and they tossed him over the side as they would
have done a brute. This made me fear these people the more; and I expected
nothing less than to be treated in the same manner. I could not help expressing my fears and apprehensions to some of my countrymen; I asked them if

these people had no country, but lived in this hollow place (the ship)? They told me they did not, but came from a distant one. "Then," said I, "how comes it in all our country we never heard of them?" They told me because they lived so very far off. I then asked where were their women? had they any like themselves? I was told they had. "And why," said I, "do we not see them?" They answered, because they were left behind. I asked how the vessel could go? they told me they could not tell; but that there was cloth put upon the masts by the help of the ropes I saw, and then the vessel went on; and the white men had some spell or magic they put in the water when they liked, in order to stop the vessel. I was exceedingly amazed at this account, and really thought they were spirits. I therefore wished much to be from amongst them, for I expected they would sacrifice me; but my wishes were vain—for we were so quartered that it was impossible for any of us to make our escape.

While we stayed on the coast I was mostly on deck; and one day, to my great astonishment, I saw one of these vessels coming in with the sails up. As soon as the whites saw it, they gave a great shout, at which we were amazed; and the more so, as the vessel appeared larger by approaching nearer. At last, she came to an anchor in my sight, and when the anchor was let go, I and my countrymen who saw it, were lost in astonishment to observe the vessel stop—and were now convinced it was done by magic. Soon after this the other ship got her boats out, and they came on board of us, and the people of both ships seemed very glad to see each other.—Several of the strangers also shook hands with us black people, and made motions with their hands, signifying I suppose, we were to go to their country, but we did not understand them.

At last, when the ship we were in had got in all her cargo, they made ready with many fearful noises, and we were all put under deck, so that we could not see how they managed the vessel. But this disappointment was the least of my sorrow. The stench of the hold while we were on the coast was so intolerably loathsome, that it was dangerous to remain there for any time, and some of us had been permitted to stay on the deck for the fresh air; but now that the whole ship's cargo were confined together, it became absolutely pestilential. The closeness of the place, and the heat of the climate, added to the number in the ship, which was so crowded that each had scarcely room to turn himself, almost suffocated us. This produced copious perspirations, so that the air soon became unfit for respiration, from a variety of loathsome smells, and brought on a sickness among the slaves, of which many died—thus falling victims to the improvident avarice, as I may call it, of their purchasers. This wretched situation was again aggravated by the galling of the chains, now become insupportable, and the filth of the necessary tubs, into which the children often fell, and were almost suffocated. The shrieks of the women, and the groans of the dying, rendered the whole a scene of horror almost inconceivable. Happily perhaps, for myself, I was soon reduced so low here that it was thought necessary to keep me almost always on deck; and from my extreme youth I was not put in fetters. In this situation I expected every hour to share the fate of my companions, some of whom were almost daily brought upon deck at the point of death, which I began to hope would soon put an end to my miseries. Often did I think many of the inhabitants of the deep much more happy than myself. I envied them the freedom they enjoyed, and as often wished I could change my condition for theirs. Every circumstance I met with, served only to render my state more painful, and heightened my apprehensions, and my opinion of the cruelty of the whites.

One day they had taken a number of fishes; and when they had killed and satisfied themselves with as many as they thought fit, to our astonishment who were on deck, rather than give any of them to us to eat, as we expected, they tossed the remaining fish into the sea again, although we begged and prayed for some as well as we could, but in vain; and some of my countrymen, being pressed by hunger, took an opportunity, when they thought no one saw them, of trying to get a little privately; but they were discovered, and the attempt procured them some very severe floggings. One day, when we had a smooth sea and moderate wind, two of my wearied countrymen who were chained together (I was near them at the time), preferring death to such a life of misery, somehow made through the nettings and jumped into the sea: immediately, another quite dejected fellow, who, on account of his illness, was suffered to be out of irons, also followed their example; and I believe many more would very soon have done the same, if they had not been prevented by the ship's crew, who were instantly alarmed. Those of us that were the most active, were in a moment put down under the deck, and there was such a noise and confusion amongst the people of the ship as I never heard before, to stop her, and get the boat out to go after the slaves. However, two of the wretches were drowned, but they got the other, and afterwards flogged him unmercifully, for thus attempting to prefer death to slavery. In this manner we continued to undergo more hardships than I can now relate, hardships which are inseparable from this accursed trade. Many a time we were near suffocation from the want of fresh air, which we were often without for whole days together. This, and the stench of the necessary tubs, carried off many.

During our passage, I first saw flying fishes, which surprised me very much; they used frequently to fly across the ship, and many of them fell on the deck. I also now first saw the use of the quadrant; I had often with astonishment seen the mariners make observations with it, and I could not think what it meant. They at last took notice of my surprise; and one of them, willing to increase it, as well as to gratify my curiosity, made me one day look through it. The clouds appeared to me to be land, which disappeared as they passed along. This heightened my wonder; and I was now more persuaded than ever, that I was in another world, and that every thing about me was magic. At last, we came in sight of the island of Barbadoes,[1] at which the whites on board gave a great shout, and made many signs of joy to us. We did not know what to think of this; but as the vessel drew nearer, we plainly saw the harbor, and other ships of different kinds and sizes, and we soon anchored amongst them, off Bridgetown. Many merchants and planters now came on board, though it was in the evening. They put us in separate parcels,[2] and examined us attentively. They also made us jump, and pointed to the land, signifying we were to go there. We thought by this, we should be eaten by these ugly men, as they appeared to us; and, when soon after we were all put down under the deck again, there was much dread and trembling among us, and nothing but bitter cries to be heard all the night from these appre-

1. In the West Indies.   2. Groups.

hensions, insomuch, that at last the white people got some old slaves from the land to pacify us. They told us we were not to be eaten, but to work, and were soon to go on land, where we should see many of our country people. This report eased us much. And sure enough, soon after we were landed, there came to us Africans of all languages.

We were conducted immediately to the merchant's yard, where we were all pent up together, like so many sheep in a fold, without regard to sex or age. As every object was new to me, every thing I saw filled me with surprise. What struck me first, was, that the houses were built with bricks and stories,[3] and in every other respect different from those I had seen in Africa; but I was still more astonished on seeing people on horseback. I did not know what this could mean; and, indeed, I thought these people were full of nothing but magical arts. While I was in this astonishment, one of my fellow prisoners spoke to a countryman of his, about the horses, who said they were the same kind they had in their country. I understood them, though they were from a distant part of Africa; and I thought it odd I had not seen any horses there; but afterwards, when I came to converse with different Africans, I found they had many horses amongst them, and much larger than those I then saw.

We were not many days in the merchant's custody, before we were sold after their usual manner, which is this:—On a signal given (as the beat of a drum), the buyers rush at once into the yard where the slaves are confined, and make choice of that parcel they like best. The noise and clamor with which this is attended, and the eagerness visible in the countenances of the buyers, serve not a little to increase the apprehension of terrified Africans, who may well be supposed to consider them as the ministers of that destruction to which they think themselves devoted. In this manner, without scruple, are relations and friends separated, most of them never to see each other again. I remember, in the vessel in which I was brought over, in the men's apartment, there were several brothers, who, in the sale, were sold in different lots; and it was very moving on this occasion, to see and hear their cries at parting. O, ye nominal Christians![4] might not an African ask you—Learned you this from your God, who says unto you, Do unto all men as you would men should do unto you? Is it not enough that we are torn from our country and friends, to toil for your luxury and lust of gain? Must every tender feeling be likewise sacrificed to your avarice? Are the dearest friends and relations, now rendered more dear by their separation from their kindred, still to be parted from each other, and thus prevented from cheering the gloom of slavery, with the small comfort of being together, and mingling their sufferings and sorrows? Why are parents to lose their children, brothers their sisters, or husbands their wives? Surely, this is a new refinement in cruelty, which, while it has no advantage to atone for it, thus aggravates distress, and adds fresh horrors even to the wretchedness of slavery.

From *Chapter III*

I now totally lost the small remains of comfort I had enjoyed in conversing with my countrymen; the women too, who used to wash and take care of me were all gone different ways, and I never saw one of them afterwards.

---

3. I.e., the buildings were two-storied.   4. Christians in name only.

I stayed in this island for a few days; I believe it could not be above a fortnight; when I, and some few more slaves, that were not salable amongst the rest, from very much fretting, were shipped off in a sloop for North America. On the passage we were better treated than when we were coming from Africa, and we had plenty of rice and fat pork. We were landed up a river a good way from the sea, about Virginia county, where we saw few or none of our native Africans, and not one soul who could talk to me. I was a few weeks weeding grass, and gathering stones in a plantation; and at last all my companions were distributed different ways, and only myself was left. I was now exceedingly miserable, and thought myself worse off than any of the rest of my companions; for they could talk to each other, but I had no person to speak to that I could understand. In this state, I was constantly grieving and pining,[5] and wishing for death rather than any thing else. While I was in this plantation, the gentleman, to whom I suppose the estate belonged, being unwell, I was one day sent for to his dwelling house to fan him; when I came into the room where he was I was very much affrighted at some things I saw, and the more so as I had seen a black woman slave as I came through the house, who was cooking the dinner, and the poor creature was cruelly loaded with various kinds of iron machines; she had one particularly on her head, which locked her mouth so fast that she could scarcely speak; and could not eat nor drink. I was much astonished and shocked at this contrivance, which I afterwards learned was called the iron muzzle. Soon after I had a fan put in my hand, to fan the gentleman while he slept; and so I did indeed with great fear. While he was fast asleep I indulged myself a great deal in looking about the room, which to me appeared very fine and curious. The first object that engaged my attention was a watch which hung on the chimney, and was going. I was quite surprised at the noise it made, and was afraid it would tell the gentleman any thing I might do amiss; and when I immediately after observed a picture hanging in the room, which appeared constantly to look at me, I was still more affrighted, having never seen such things as these before. At one time I thought it was something relative to magic; and not seeing it move, I thought it might be some way the whites had to keep their great men when they died, and offer them libations as we used to do our friendly spirits. In this state of anxiety I remained till my master awoke, when I was dismissed out of the room, to my no small satisfaction and relief; for I thought that these people were all made up of wonders. In this place I was called Jacob; but on board the African Snow, I was called Michael. I had been some time in this miserable forlorn, and much dejected state, without having any one to talk to, which made my life a burden, when the kind and unknown hand of the Creator (who in very deed leads the blind in a way they know not) now began to appear, to my comfort; for one day the captain of a merchant ship, called the Industrious Bee, came on some business to my master's house. This gentleman, whose name was Michael Henry Pascal, was a lieutenant in the royal navy, but now commanded this trading ship, which was somewhere in the confines of the county many miles off. While he was at my master's house, it happened that he saw me, and liked me so well that he made a purchase of me. I think I have often heard him say he gave thirty or forty pounds sterling for me; but

5. Suffering.

I do not remember which. However, he meant me for a present to some of his friends in England: and as I was sent accordingly from the house of my then master (one Mr. Campbell), to the place where the ship lay; I was conducted on horseback by an elderly black man (a mode of traveling which appeared very odd to me). When I arrived I was carried on board a fine large ship, loaded with tobacco, etc., and just ready to sail for England. I now thought my condition much mended; I had sails to lie on, and plenty of good victuals to eat; and everybody on board used me very kindly, quite contrary to what I had seen of any white people before; I therefore began to think that they were not all of the same disposition. A few days after I was on board we sailed for England. I was still at a loss to conjecture my destiny. By this time, however, I could smatter a little imperfect English; and I wanted to know as well as I could where we were going. Some of the people of the ship used to tell me they were going to carry me back to my own country, and this made me very happy. I was quite rejoiced at the idea of going back; and thought if I could get home what wonders I should have to tell. But I was reserved for another fate, and was soon undeceived when we came within sight of the English coast. While I was on board this ship, my captain and master named me *Gustavus Vassa*. I at that time began to understand him a little, and refused to be called so, and told him as well as I could that I would be called Jacob; but he said I should not, and still called me Gustavus: and when I refused to answer to my new name, which I at first did, it gained me many a cuff; so at length I submitted, and by which I have been known ever since. The ship had a very long passage; and on that account we had very short allowance of provisions. Towards the last, we had only one pound and a half of bread per week, and about the same quantity of meat, and one quart of water a day. We spoke with only one vessel the whole time we were at sea, and but once we caught a few fishes. In our extremities the captain and people told me in jest they would kill and eat me; but I thought them in earnest, and was depressed beyond measure, expecting every moment to be my last. While I was in this situation, one evening they caught, with a good deal of trouble, a large shark, and got it on board. This gladdened my poor heart exceedingly, as I thought it would serve the people to eat instead of their eating me; but very soon, to my astonishment, they cut off a small part of the tail, and tossed the rest over the side. This renewed my consternation; and I did not know what to think of these white people, though I very much feared they would kill and eat me. There was on board the ship a young lad who had never been at sea before, about four or five years older than myself: his name was Richard Baker. He was a native of America, had received an excellent education, and was of a most amiable temper. Soon after I went on board, he showed me a great deal of partiality and attention, and in return I grew extremely fond of him. We at length became inseparable; and, for the space of two years, he was of very great use to me, and was my constant companion and instructor. Although this dear youth had many slaves of his own, yet he and I have gone through many sufferings together on shipboard; and we have many nights lain in each other's bosoms when we were in great distress. Thus such a friendship was cemented between us as we cherished till his death, which, to my very great sorrow, happened in the year 1759, when he was up the Archipelago, and on board his Majesty's ship the Preston: an event which I have never ceased to regret, as I lost at once a kind interpreter, an agreeable companion, and a faithful friend; who, at the age of fifteen, discovered a mind superior to prejudice; and who was not ashamed to notice, to associate with, and to be the friend and instructor of one who was ignorant, a stranger, of a different complexion, and a slave!

* * *

From *Chapter IV*

It was now between two and three years since I first came to England, a great part of which I had spent at sea; so that I became inured[6] to that service, and began to consider myself as happily situated, for my master treated me always extremely well; and my attachment and gratitude to him were very great. From the various scenes I had beheld on shipboard, I soon grew a stranger to terror of every kind, and was, in that respect at least, almost an Englishman. I have often reflected with surprise that I never felt half the alarm at any of the numerous dangers I have been in, that I was filled with at the first sight of the Europeans, and at every act of theirs, even the most trifling, when I first came among them, and for some time afterwards. That fear, however, which was the effect of my ignorance, wore away as I began to know them. I could now speak English tolerably well, and I perfectly understood every thing that was said. I not only felt myself quite easy with these new countrymen, but relished their society and manners. I no longer looked upon them as spirits, but as men superior to us; and therefore I had the stronger desire to resemble them, to imbibe their spirit, and imitate their manners. I therefore embraced every occasion of improvement, and every new thing that I observed I treasured up in my memory. I had long wished to be able to read and write; and for this purpose I took every opportunity to gain instruction, but had made as yet very little progress. However, when I went to London with my master, I had soon an opportunity of improving myself, which I gladly embraced. Shortly after my arrival, he sent me to wait upon the Miss Guerins, who had treated me with much kindness when I was there before; and they sent me to school.

While I was attending these ladies, their servants told me I could not go to Heaven unless I was baptized. This made me very uneasy, for I had now some faint idea of a future state. Accordingly I communicated my anxiety to the eldest Miss Guerin, with whom I was become a favorite, and pressed her to have me baptized; when to my great joy, she told me I should. She had formerly asked my master to let me be baptized, but he had refused. However she now insisted on it; and he being under some obligation to her brother, complied with her request. So I was baptized in St. Margaret's church, Westminster, in February, 1759, by my present name. The clergyman at the same time, gave me a book, called a Guide to the Indians, written by the Bishop of Sodor and Man.[7] On this occasion, Miss Guerin did me the honor to stand as god-mother, and afterwards gave me a treat. I used to attend these ladies about the town, in which service I was extremely happy; as I had thus many opportunities of seeing London, which I desired of all things. I was sometimes, however, with my master at his rendezvous house,[8] which was at the foot of Westminster bridge. Here I used to enjoy myself in playing about the

6. Accustomed.
7. Present-day Hebrides and the Isle of Man.
8. Private residence.

bridge stairs, and often in the waterman's wherries,[9] with other boys. On one of these occasions there was another boy with me in a wherry, and we went out into the current of the river; while we were there, two more stout boys came to us in another wherry, and abusing us for taking the boat, desired me to get into the other wherry boat. Accordingly, I went to get out of the wherry I was in, but just as I had got one of my feet into the other boat, the boys shoved it off, so that I fell into the Thames; and, not being able to swim, I should unavoidably have been drowned, but for the assistance of some watermen who providentially came to my relief.

The Namur being again got ready for sea, my master, with his gang,[1] was ordered on board; and, to my no small grief, I was obliged to leave my school-master, whom I liked very much, and always attended while I stayed in London, to repair on board with my master. Nor did I leave my kind patronesses, the Miss Guerins, without uneasiness and regret. They often used to teach me to read, and took great pains to instruct me in the principles of religion and the knowledge of God. I therefore parted from those amiable ladies with reluctance, after receiving from them many friendly cautions how to conduct myself, and some valuable presents.

When I came to Spithead,[2] I found we were destined for the Mediterranean, with a large fleet, which was now ready to put to sea. We only waited for the arrival of the Admiral, who soon came on board. And about the beginning of the spring of 1759, having weighed anchor, and got under way, sailed for the Mediterranean; and in eleven days, from the Land's End, we got to Gibralter. While we were here I used to be often on shore, and got various fruits in great plenty, and very cheap.

I had frequently told several people, in my excursions on shore, the story of my being kidnapped with my sister, and of our being separated, as I have related before; and I had as often expressed my anxiety for her fate, and my sorrow at having never met her again. One day, when I was on shore, and mentioning these circumstances to some persons, one of them told me he knew where my sister was, and if I would accompany him, he would bring me to her. Improbable as this story was, I believed it immediately, and agreed to go with him, while my heart leaped for joy; and, indeed, he conducted me to a black young woman, who was so like my sister, that at first sight, I really thought it was her; but I was quickly undeceived. And, on talking to her, I found her to be of another nation.

While we lay here, the Preston came in from the Levant.[3] As soon as she arrived, my master told me I should now see my old companion, Dick, who was gone in her when she sailed for Turkey. I was much rejoiced at this news, and expected every minute to embrace him; and when the captain came on board of our ship, which he did immediately after, I ran to inquire after my friend; but, with inexpressible sorrow, I learned from the boat's crew that the dear youth was dead! and that they had brought his chest, and all his other things, to my master. These he afterwards gave to me, and I regarded them as a memorial of my friend, whom I loved, and grieved for, as a brother.

9. Small rowboats.
1. I.e., crew.
2. On the southern coast of England; a common

rendezvous for the British fleet.
3. The eastern shore of the Mediterranean.

* * *

After our ship was fitted out again for service, in September she went to Guernsey,[4] where I was very glad to see my old hostess, who was now a widow, and my former little charming companion, her daughter. I spent some time here very happily with them, till October, when we had orders to repair to Portsmouth. We parted from each other with a great deal of affection; and I promised to return soon, and see them again, not knowing what all powerful fate had determined for me. Our ship having arrived at Portsmouth, we went into the harbor, and remained there till the latter end of November, when we heard great talk about a peace;[5] and, to our very great joy, in the beginning of December we had orders to go up to London with our ship, to be paid off. We received this news with loud huzzas, and every other demonstration of gladness; and nothing but mirth was to be seen throughout every part of the ship. I, too, was not without my share of the general joy on this occasion. I thought now of nothing but being freed, and working for myself, and thereby getting money to enable me to get a good education; for I always had a great desire to be able at least to read and write; and while I was on ship-board, I had endeavored to improve myself in both. While I was in the Etna,[6] particularly, the captain's clerk taught me to write, and gave me a smattering of arithmetic, as far as the Rule of Three.[7] There was also one Daniel Queen, about forty years of age, a man very well educated, who messed[8] with me on board this ship, and he likewise dressed and attended the captain. Fortunately this man soon became very much attached to me, and took very great pains to instruct me in many things. He taught me to shave and dress hair a little, and also to read in the Bible, explaining many passages to me, which I did not comprehend. I was wonderfully surprised to see the laws and rules of my own country written almost exactly here; a circumstance which I believe tended to impress our manners and customs more deeply on my memory. I used to tell him of this resemblance, and many a time we have sat up the whole night together at this employment. In short, he was like a father to me, and some even used to call me after his name; they also styled me the black Christian. Indeed, I almost loved him with the affection of a son. Many things I have denied myself that he might have them; and when I used to play at marbles, or any other game, and won a few half-pence, or got any little money, which I sometimes did, for shaving any one, I used to buy him a little sugar or tobacco, as far as my stock of money would go. He used to say, that he and I never should part; and that when our ship was paid off, as I was as free as himself, or any other man on board, he would instruct me in his business, by which I might gain a good livelihood. This gave me new life and spirits; and my heart burned within me, while I thought the time long till I obtained my freedom. For though my master had not promised it to me, yet, besides the assurances I had received, that he had no right to detain me, he always treated me with the greatest kindness, and reposed in me an unbounded confidence; he even paid attention to my morals, and would never suffer me to deceive him, or tell lies, of which he used to tell me the consequences; and that if I did so, God would not love

4. One of the Channel Islands in the English Channel.
5. The Seven Years' War between England and France began in 1756.

6. The name of a ship.
7. A method of finding a fourth (unknown) number from three given numbers.
8. Took meals.

me. So that, from all this tenderness, I had never once supposed, in all my dreams of freedom, that he would think of detaining me any longer than I wished.

In pursuance of our orders, we sailed from Portsmouth for the Thames, and arrived at Deptford the 10th of December, where we cast anchor just as it was high water. The ship was up about half an hour, when my master ordered the barge to be manned; and all in an instant, without having before given me the least reason to suspect any thing of the matter, he forced me into the barge, saying, I was going to leave him, but he would take care I should not. I was so struck with the unexpectedness of this proceeding, that for some time I did not make a reply, only I made an offer to go for my books and chest of clothes, but he swore I should not move out of his sight, and if I did, he would cut my throat, at the same time taking his hanger.[9] I began, however, to collect myself, and plucking up courage, I told him I was free, and he could not by law serve me so. But this only enraged him the more: and he continued to swear, and said he would soon let me know whether he would or not, and at that instant sprung himself into the barge from the ship, to the astonishment and sorrow of all on board. The tide, rather unluckily for me, had just turned downward, so that we quickly fell down the river along with it, till we came among some outward-bound West Indiamen; for he was resolved to put me on board the first vessel he could get to receive me. The boat's crew, who pulled against their will, became quite faint, different times, and would have gone ashore, but he would not let them. Some of them strove then to cheer me, and told me he could not sell me, and that they would stand by me, which revived me a little, and I still entertained hopes; for, as they pulled along, he asked some vessels to receive me, but they would not. But, just as we had got a little below Gravesend, we came along side of a ship which was going away the next tide for the West Indies. Her name was the Charming Sally. Captain James Doran, and my master went on board, and agreed with him for me; and in a little time I was sent for into the cabin. When I came there, Captain Doran asked me if I knew him. I answered that I did not. "Then," said he, "you are now my slave." I told him my master could not sell me to him, nor to any one else. "Why," said he, "did not your master buy you?" I confessed he did. "But I have served him," said I, "many years, and he has taken all my wages and prize money, for I had only got one sixpence during the war; besides this I have been baptized, and by the laws of the land no man has a right to sell me." And I added that I had heard a lawyer and others at different times tell my master so. They both then said that those people who told me so were not my friends; but I replied, "It was very extraordinary that other people did not know the law as well as they." Upon this, Captain Doran said I talked too much English; and if I did not behave myself well, and be quiet, he had a method on board to make me. I was too well convinced of his power over me to doubt what he said; and my former sufferings in the slave ship presenting themselves to my mind, the recollection of them made me shudder. However, before I retired I told them that, as I could not get any right among men here, I hoped I should hereafter in Heaven; and I immediately left the cabin, filled with resentment and sorrow. The only coat I had with me my master

9. Small sword.

took away him with him, and said, "If your prize money had been £10,000, I had a right to it all, and would have taken it." I had about nine guineas, which, during my long seafaring life, I had scraped together from trifling perquisites and little ventures; and I hid it at that instant, lest my master should take that from me likewise, still hoping that by some means or other I should make my escape to the shore; and indeed some of my old shipmates told me not to despair, for they would get me back again; and that, as soon as they could get their pay, they would immediately come to Portsmouth to me, where the ship was going. But, alas! all my hopes were baffled, and the hour of my deliverance as was yet far off. My master, having soon concluded his bargain with the captain, came out of the cabin, and he and his people got into the boat and put off. I followed them with aching eyes as long as I could, and when they were out of sight I threw myself on the deck, with a heart ready to burst with sorrow and anguish.

From *Chapter V*

* * *

About the middle of May, when the ship was got ready to sail for England, I all the time believing that fate's blackest clouds were gathering over my head, and expecting their bursting would mix me with the dead, Captain Doran sent for me ashore one morning, and I was told by the messenger that my fate was then determined. With trembling steps and fluttering heart, I came to the captain, and found with him one Mr. Robert King, a Quaker, and the first merchant in the place. The captain then told me my former master had sent me there to be sold; but that he had desired him to get me the best master he could, as he told him I was a very deserving boy, which Captain Doran said he found to be true; and if he were to stay in the West Indies, he would be glad to keep me himself; but he could not venture to take me to London, for he was very sure that when I came there I would leave him. I at that instant burst out a crying, and begged much of him to take me to England with him, but all to no purpose. He told me he had got me the very best master in the whole island, with whom I should be as happy as if I were in England, and for that reason he chose to let him have me, though he could sell me to his own brother-in-law for a great deal more money than what he got from this gentleman. Mr. King, my new master, then made a reply, and said the reason he had bought me was on account of my good character; and as he had not the least doubt of my good behavior, I should be very well off with him. He also told me he did not live in the West Indies, but at Philadelphia, where he was going soon; and, as I understood something of the rules of arithmetic, when we got there he would put me to school, and fit me for a clerk. This conversation relieved my mind a little, and I left those gentlemen considerably more at ease in myself than when I came to them; and I was very thankful to Captain Doran, and even to my old master, for the character they had given me. A character which I afterwards found of infinite service to me. I went on board again, and took leave of all my shipmates, and the next day the ship sailed. When she weighed anchor, I went to the waterside and looked at her with a very wishful and aching heart, and followed her with my eyes until she was totally out of sight.

I was so bowed down with grief, that I could not hold up my head for many months; and if my new master had not been kind to me, I believe I should have died under it at last. And, indeed, I soon found that he fully deserved the good character which Captain Doran gave me of him; for he possessed a most amiable disposition and temper, and was very charitable and humane. If any of his slaves behaved amiss he did not beat or use them ill, but parted with them. This made them afraid of disobliging him; and as he treated his slaves better than any other man on the island, so he was better and more faithfully served by them in return. By this kind treatment I did at last endeavor to compose myself; and with fortitude, though moneyless, determined to face whatever fate had decreed for me. Mr. King soon asked me what I could do; and at the same time said he did not mean to treat me as a common slave. I told him I knew something of seamanship, and could shave and dress hair pretty well; and I could refine wines, which I had learned on shipboard, where I had often done it; and that I could write, and understood arithmetic tolerably well, as far as the Rule of Three. He then asked me if I knew any thing of guaging; and, on my answering that I did not, he said one of his clerks should teach me to guage.[1]

Mr. King dealt in all manner of merchandize, and kept from one to six clerks. He loaded many vessels in a year; particularly to Philadelphia, where he was born; and was connected with a great mercantile house in that city. He had, besides, many vessels and droggers,[2] of different sizes, which used to go about the island; and others, to collect rum, sugar, and other goods. I understood pulling and managing those boats very well. And this hard work, which was the first that he set me to, in the sugar seasons used to be my constant employment. I have rowed the boat, and slaved at the oars, from one hour to sixteen in the twenty-four; during which I had fifteen pence sterling per day to live on, though sometimes only ten pence. However, this was considerably more than was allowed to other slaves that used to work often with me, and belonged to other gentlemen on the island. Those poor souls had never more than nine-pence per day, and seldom more than six-pence, from their masters or owners, though they earned them three or four pistareens.[3] For it is a common practice in the West Indies for men to purchase slaves, though they have not plantations themselves, in order to let them out to planters and merchants at so much a piece by the day, and they give what allowance they choose out of this product of their daily work to their slaves, for subsistence; this allowance is often very scanty. My master often gave the owners of the slaves two and a half of these pieces per day, and found the poor fellows in victuals himself, because he thought their owners did not feed them well enough according to the work they did.

* * *

Once, for a few days, I was let out to fit a vessel, and I had no victuals allowed me by either party; at last I told my master of this treatment, and he took me away from it. In many of the estates, on the different islands where I used to be sent for rum or sugar, they would not deliver it to me, or any other negro; he was therefore obliged to send a white man along with me to

1. To measure the depth of a vessel when fully loaded.
2. Slow West Indian vessels that sail along the
coast.
3. These pistareens are of a value of a shilling [Equiano's note].

those places; and then he used to pay him from six to ten pistareens a day. From being thus employed, during the time I served Mr. King, in going about the different estates on the island,[4] I had all the opportunity I could wish for, to see the dreadful usage of the poor men; usage that reconciled me to my situation, and made me bless God for the hands into which I had fallen.

I had the good fortune to please my master in every department in which he employed me; and there was scarcely any part of his business, or household affairs, in which I was not occasionally engaged. I often supplied the place of a clerk, in receiving and delivering cargoes to the ships, in tending stores, and delivering goods. And besides this, I used to shave and dress my master when convenient, and take care of his horse; and when it was necessary, which was very often, I worked likewise on board of different vessels of his. By these means I became very useful to my master, and saved him, as he used to acknowledge, above a hundred pounds a year. Nor did he scruple to say I was of more advantage to him than any of his clerks; though their usual wages in the West Indies are from sixty to a hundred pounds current a year.

I have sometimes heard it asserted that a Negro cannot earn his master the first cost; but nothing can be further from the truth. I suppose nine tenths of the mechanics throughout the West Indies are Negro slaves; and I well know the coopers[5] among them earn two dollars a day, the carpenters the same, and often times more; as also the masons, smiths, and fisherman, etc. And I have known many slaves whose masters would not take a thousand pounds current for them. But surely this assertion refutes itself; for, if it be true, why do the planters and merchants pay such a price for slaves? And, above all, why do those who make this assertion exclaim the most loudly against the abolition of the slave trade? So much are men blinded, and to such inconsistent arguments are they driven by mistaken interest! I grant, indeed, that slaves are sometimes, by half-feeding, half-clothing, overworking and stripes,[6] reduced so low, that they are turned out as unfit for service, and left to perish in the woods, or expire on the dunghill.

My master was several times offered, by different gentlemen, one hundred guineas for me, but he always told them he would not sell me, to my great joy. And I used to double my diligence and care, for fear of getting into the hands of those men who did not allow a valuable slave the common support of life. Many of them even used to find fault with my master for feeding his slaves so well as he did; although I often went hungry, and an Englishman might think my fare very indifferent;[7] but he used to tell them he always would do it, because the slaves thereby looked better and did more work.

While I was thus employed by my master, I was often a witness to cruelties of every kind, which were exercised on my unhappy fellow slaves. I used frequently to have different cargoes of new Negroes in my care for sale; and it was almost a constant practice with our clerks, and other whites, to commit violent depredations on the chastity of the female slaves; and these I was, though with reluctance, obliged to submit to at all times, being unable to help them. When we have had some of these slaves on board my master's vessels, to carry them to other islands, or to America, I have known our mates

4. Equiano remained in the West Indies from 1763 to 1766.
5. Barrel makers.

6. Lashes.
7. Poor, unsatisfactory.

to commit these acts most shamefully, to the disgrace, not of Christians only, but of men. I have even known them to gratify their brutal passion with females not ten years old; and these abominations, some of them practiced to such scandalous excess, that one of our captains discharged the mate and others on that account. And yet in Montserrat[8] I have seen a Negro man staked to the ground, and cut most shockingly, and then his ears cut off bit by bit, because he had been connected with a white woman, who was a common prostitute. As if it were no crime in the whites to rob an innocent African girl of her virtue; but most heinous in a black man only to gratify a passion of nature, where the temptation was offered by one of a different color, though the most abandoned woman of her species.

Another Negro man was half hanged, and then burnt, for attempting to poison a cruel overseer. Thus, by repeated cruelties, are the wretched first urged to despair, and then murdered, because they still retain so much of human nature about them as to wish to put an end to their misery, and retaliate on their tyrants! These overseers are indeed for the most part persons of the worst character of any denomination of men in the West Indies. Unfortunately, many humane gentlemen, but not residing on their estates, are obliged to leave the management of them in the hands of these human butchers, who cut and mangle the slaves in a shocking manner on the most trifling occasions, and altogether treat them in every respect like brutes. They pay no regard to the situation of pregnant women, nor the least attention to the lodging of the field Negroes. Their huts, which ought to be well covered, and the place dry where they take their little repose, are often open sheds, built in damp places; so that when the poor creatures return tired from the toils of the field, they contract many disorders, from being exposed to the damp air in this uncomfortable state, while they are heated, and their pores are open. This neglect certainly conspires with many others to cause a decrease in the births as well as in the lives of the grown Negroes. I can quote many instances of gentlemen who reside on their estates in the West Indies, and then the scene is quite changed; the Negroes are treated with lenity and proper care, by which their lives are prolonged, and their masters profited. To the honor of humanity, I knew several gentlemen who managed their estates in this manner, and they found that benevolence was their true interest. And, among many I could mention in several of the islands, I knew one in Montserrat whose slaves looked remarkably well, and never needed any fresh supplies of Negroes; and there are many other estates, especially in Barbadoes, which, from such judicious treatment, need no fresh stock of Negroes at any time. I have the honor of knowing a most worthy and humane gentleman, who is a native of Barbadoes, and his estates there.[9] This gentleman has written a treatise on the usage of his own slaves. He allows them two hours of refreshment at midday, and many other indulgencies and comforts, particularly in their lodging; and, besides this, he raises more provisions on his estate than they can destroy; so that by these attentions he saves the lives of his Negroes, and keeps them healthy, and as happy as the condition of slavery can admit. I myself, as shall appear in the sequel,[1] managed an estate, where, by those attentions, the Negroes were uncommonly cheerful

8. An island in the West Indies seven miles from Antigua.
9. Two of Equiano's notes identifying these men are omitted.
1. I.e., later.

and healthy, and did more work by half than by the common mode of treatment they usually do. For want,[2] therefore, of such care and attention to the
poor Negroes, and otherwise oppressed as they are, it is no wonder that the
decrease should require 20,000 new Negroes annually, to fill up the vacant
places of the dead.

* * *

From *Chapter VI*

In the preceding chapter I have set before the reader a few of those many
instances of oppression, extortion, and cruelty, which I have been a witness
to in the West Indies; but were I to enumerate them all, the catalog would
be tedious and disgusting. The punishments of the slaves on every trifling
occasion are so frequent, and so well known, together with the different
instruments with which they are tortured, that it cannot any longer afford
novelty to recite them; and they are too shocking to yield delight either to
the writer or the reader. I shall therefore hereafter only mention such as
incidentally befell myself in the course of my adventures.

* * *

Some time in the year 1763, kind Providence seemed to appear rather
more favorable to me. One of my master's vessels, a Bermudas sloop, about
sixty tons burthen, was commanded by one captain Thomas Farmer, an Englishman, a very alert and active man, who gained my master a great deal of
money by his good management in carrying passengers from one island to
another; but very often his sailors used to get drunk and run away from the
vessel, which hindered him in his business very much. This man had taken
a liking to me, and many times begged of my master to let me go a trip with
him as a sailor; but he would tell him he could not spare me, though the
vessel sometimes could not go for want of hands, for sailors were generally
very scarce in the island. However, at last, from necessity or force, my master
was prevailed on, though very reluctantly, to let me go with this captain; but
he gave him great charge to take care that I did not run away, for if I did he
would make him pay for me. This being the case, the captain had for some
time a sharp eye upon me whenever the vessel anchored; and as soon as she
returned I was sent for on shore again. Thus was I slaving, as it were, for
life, sometimes at one thing, and sometimes at another. So that the captain
and I were nearly the most useful men in my master's employment. I also
became so useful to the captain on ship-board, that many times, when he
used to ask for me to go with him, though it should be but for twenty-four
hours, to some of the islands near us, my master would answer he could not
spare me, at which the captain would swear, and would not go the trip, and
tell my master I was better to him on board than any three white men he
had; for they used to behave ill in many respects, particularly in getting
drunk; and then they frequently got the boat stove,[3] so as to hinder the vessel
from coming back as soon as she might have done. This my master knew
very well; and at last, by the captain's constant entreaties, after I had been
several times with him, one day to my great joy, told me the captain would

2. Lack.   3. Put a hole in the boat.

not let him rest, and asked whether I would go aboard as a sailor, or stay on shore and mind the stores, for he could not bear any longer to be plagued in this manner. I was very happy at this proposal, for I immediately thought I might in time stand some chance by being on board to get a little money, or possibly make my escape if I should be used ill. I also expected to get better food, and in greater abundance; for I had oftentimes felt much hunger, though my master treated his slaves, as I have observed, uncommonly well. I therefore, without hesitation, answered him, that I would go and be a sailor if he pleased. Accordingly I was ordered on board directly. Nevertheless, between the vessel and the shore, when she was in port, I had little or no rest, as my master always wished to have me along with him. Indeed he was a very pleasant gentleman, and but for my expectations on ship-board, I should not have thought of leaving him. But the captain liked me also very much, and I was entirely his right hand man. I did all I could to deserve his favor, and in return I received better treatment from him than any other, I believe, ever met with in the West Indies, in my situation.

After I had been sailing for some time with this captain, at length I endeavored to try my luck, and commence merchant. I had but a very small capital to begin with; for one single half bit,[4] which is equal to three pence in England, made up my whole stock. However, I trusted to the Lord to be with me; and at one of our trips to St. Eustatia,[5] a Dutch island, I bought a glass tumbler with my half bit, and when I came to Montserrat, I sold it for a bit, or six pence. Luckily we made several successive trips to St. Eustatia (which was a general mart for the West Indies, about twenty leagues from Montserrat), and in our next, finding my tumbler so profitable, with this one bit I bought two tumblers more; and when I came back, I sold them for two bits, equal to a shilling sterling. When we went again, I bought with these two bits four more of these glasses, which I sold for four bits on our return to Montserrat. And in our next voyage to St. Eustatia, I bought two glasses with one bit, and with the other three I bought a jug of Geneva,[6] nearly about three pints in measure. When we came to Montserrat, I sold the gin for eight bits, and the tumblers for two, so that my capital now amounted in all to a dollar, well husbanded[7] and acquired in the space of a month or six weeks, when I blessed the Lord that I was so rich. As we sailed to different islands, I laid this money out in various things occasionally, and it used to turn out to very good account, especially when we went to Guadaloupe, Grenada, and the rest of the French islands. Thus was I going all about the islands upwards of four years, and ever trading as I went, during which I experienced many instances of ill usage, and have seen many injuries done to other Negroes in our dealings with whites. And, amidst our recreations, when we have been dancing and merry-making, they, without cause, have molested and insulted us. Indeed, I was more than once obliged to look up to God on high, as I had advised the poor fisherman some time before. And I had not been long trading for myself in the manner I have related above, when I experienced the like trial in company with him as follows:—This man, being used to the water, was upon an emergency put on board of us by his master, to work as another hand, on a voyage to Santa Cruz; and at our sailing he had brought

4. In the West Indies, a small silver coin a fraction of the Spanish dollar.
5. St. Eustatius is one of the Leeward Islands in the West Indies.
6. The original name of gin.
7. Managed.

his little all for a venture, which consisted of six bits' worth of limes and oranges in a bag; I had also my whole stock, which was about twelve bits' worth of the same kind of goods, separate in two bags, for we had heard these fruits sold well in that island. When we came there, in some little convenient time, he and I went ashore to sell them; but we had scarcely landed, when we were met by two white men, who presently took our three bags from us. We could not at first guess what they meant to do, and for some time we thought they were jesting with us; but they too soon let us know otherwise, for they took our ventures immediately to a house hard by, and adjoining the fort, while we followed all the way begging of them to give us our fruits, but in vain. They not only refused to return them, but swore at us, and threatened if we did not immediately depart they would flog us well. We told them these three bags were all we were worth in the world, and that we brought them with us to sell when we came from Montserrat, and showed them the vessel. But this was rather against us, as they now saw we were strangers, as well as slaves. They still therefore swore, and desired us to be gone, and even took sticks to beat us; while we, seeing they meant what they said, went off in the greatest confusion and despair. Thus, in the very minute of gaining more by three times than I ever did by any venture in my life before, was I deprived of every farthing I was worth. An unsupportable misfortune! but how to help ourselves we knew not. In our consternation we went to the commanding officer of the fort, and told him how we had been served by his people, but we obtained not the least redress. He answered our complaints only by a volley of imprecations against us, and immediately took a horse-whip, in order to chastise us, so that we were obliged to turn out much faster than we came in. I now, in the agony of distress and indignation, wished that the ire of God in his forked lightning might transfix these cruel oppressors among the dead. Still, however, we persevered; went back again to the house, and begged and besought them again and again for our fruits, till at last some other people that were in the house asked if we would be contented if they kept one bag and gave us the other two. We, seeing no remedy whatever, consented to this; and they, observing one bag to have both kinds of fruit in it, which belonged to my companion, kept that; and the other two, which were mine, they gave us back. As soon as I got them, I ran as fast as I could, and got the first Negro man I could to help me off. My companion, however, stayed a little longer to plead; he told them the bag they had was his, and likewise all that he was worth in the world; but this was of no avail, and he was obliged to return without it. The poor old man wringing his hands, cried bitterly for his loss; and, indeed, he then did look up to God on high, which so moved me in pity for him, that I gave him nearly one-third of my fruits. We then proceeded to the markets to sell them; and Providence was more favorable to us than we could have expected, for we sold our fruits uncommonly well; I got for mine about thirty-seven bits. Such a surprising reverse of fortune in so short a space of time seemed like a dream, and proved no small encouragement for me to trust the Lord in any situation. My captain afterwards frequently used to take my part, and get me my right, when I have been plundered or used ill by these tender Christian depredators; among whom I have shuddered to observe the unceasing blasphemous execrations which are wantonly thrown out by persons of all ages and conditions, not only without occasion, but even as if they were indulgencies and pleasure.

* * *

The reader cannot but judge of the irksomeness of this situation to a mind like mine, in being daily exposed to new hardships and impositions, after having seen many better days, and been, as it were, in a state of freedom and plenty; added to which, every part of the world I had hitherto been in, seemed to me a paradise in comparison to the West Indies. My mind was therefore hourly replete with inventions and thoughts of being freed, and, if possible, by honest and honorable means; for I always remembered the old adage, and I trust it has ever been my ruling principle, that "honesty is the best policy;" and likewise that other golden precept—"To do unto all men as I would they should do unto me." However, as I was from early years a predestinarian, I thought whatever fate had determined must ever come to pass; and, therefore, if ever it were my lot to be freed, nothing could prevent me, although I should at present see no means or hope to obtain my freedom; on the other hand, if it were my fate not to be freed, I never should be so, and all my endeavors for that purpose would be fruitless. In the midst of these thoughts, I therefore looked up with prayers anxiously to God for my liberty; and at the same time used every honest means, and did all that was possible on my part to obtain it. In process of time, I became master of a few pounds, and in a fair way of making more, which my friendly captain knew very well; this occasioned him sometimes to take liberties with me; but whenever he treated me waspishly, I used plainly to tell him my mind, and that I would die before I would be imposed upon as other Negroes were, and that to my life had lost its relish when liberty was gone. This I said, although I foresaw my then well-being or future hopes of freedom (humanly speaking) depended on this man. However, as he could not bear the thoughts of my not sailing with him, he always became mild on my threats. I therefore continued with him; and, from my great attention to his orders and his business, I gained him credit, and through his kindness to me, I at last procured my liberty. While I thus went on, filled with the thoughts of freedom, and resisting oppression as well as I was able, my life hung daily in suspense, particularly in the surfs I have formerly mentioned, as I could not swim. These are extremely violent throughout the West Indies, and I was ever exposed to their howling rage and devouring fury in all the islands. I have seen them strike and toss a boat right up on end, and maim several on board. Once in the Grenada islands, when I and about eight others were pulling a large boat with two puncheons[8] of water in it, a surf struck us, and drove the boat, and all in it, about half a stone's throw, among some trees, and above the high water mark. We were obliged to get all the assistance we could from the nearest estate to mend the boat, and launch it into the water again. At Montserrat, one night, in pressing hard to get off the shore on board, the punt[9] was overset with us four times, the first time I was very near being drowned; however, the jacket I had on kept me up above water a little space of time, when I called on a man near me, who was a good swimmer, and told him I could not swim; he then made haste to me, and, just as I was sinking, he caught hold of me, and brought me to sounding,[1] and then he went and brought the punt also. As soon as we had turned the water out of her, lest we should be used ill for being absent, we attempted again three times more,

8. Large casks.
9. Narrow, flat-bottomed boat.

1. I.e., where one could stand.

and as often the horrid surfs served us as at first; but at last, the fifth time we attempted, we gained our point, at the imminent hazard of our lives. One day also, at Old Road, in Montserrat, our captain, and three men besides myself, were going in a large canoe in quest of rum and sugar, when a single surf tossed the canoe an amazing distance from the water, and some of us, near a stone's throw from each other. Most of us were very much bruised; so that I and many more often said, and really thought, that there was not such another place under the heavens as this. I longed, therefore, much to leave it, and daily wished to see my master's promise performed, of going to Philadelphia.

While we lay in this place, a very cruel thing happened on board our sloop, which filled me with horror; though I found afterwards such practices were frequent. There was a very clever and decent free young mulatto man, who sailed a long time with us; he had a free woman for his wife, by whom he had a child, and she was then living on shore, and all very happy. Our captain and mate, and other people on board, and several elsewhere, even the natives of Bermudas, all knew this young man from a child that he was always free, and no one had ever claimed him as their property. However, as might too often overcomes right in these parts, it happened that a Bermudas captain, whose vessel lay there for a few days in the road, came on board of us, and seeing the mulatto man, whose name was Joseph Clipson, he told him he was not free, and that he had orders from his master to bring him to Bermudas. The poor man could not believe the captain to be in earnest, but he was very soon undeceived, his men laying violent hands on him; and although he showed a certificate of his being born free in St. Kitts, and most people on board knew that he served his time to[2] boat building, and always passed for a free man, yet he was forcibly taken out of our vessel. He then asked to be carried ashore before the Secretary or Magistrates, and these infernal invaders of human rights promised him he should; but instead of that, they carried him on board of the other vessel. And the next day, without giving the poor man any hearing on shore, or suffering him even to see his wife or child, he was carried away, and probably doomed never more in this world to see them again. Nor was this the only instance of this kind of barbarity I was a witness to. I have since often seen in Jamaica and other islands, free men, whom I have known in America, thus villainously trepanned[3] and held in bondage. I have heard of two similar practices even in Philadelphia. And were it not for the benevolence of the Quakers in that city, many of the sable[4] race, who now breathe the air of liberty, would, I believe, be groaning indeed under some planter's chains. These things opened my mind to a new scene of horror, to which I had been before a stranger. Hitherto I had thought slavery only dreadful, but the state of a free negro appeared to me now equally so at least, and in some respects even worse, for they live in constant alarm for their liberty; which is but nominal, for they are universally insulted and plundered, without the possibility of redress; for such is the equity of the West Indian laws, that no free Negro's evidence will be admitted in their courts of justice. In this situation, is it surprising that slaves, when mildly treated, should prefer even the misery of slavery to such a mockery of free-

2. Was apprenticed at.   4. Black.
3. Trapped.

dom? I was now completely disgusted with the West Indies, and thought I never should be entirely free until I had left them.

*　*　*

About the latter end of the year 1764, my master bought a larger sloop, called the Prudence, about seventy or eighty tons, of which my captain had the command. I went with him in this vessel, and we took a load of new slaves for Georgia and Charlestown. My master now left me entirely to the captain, though he still wished me to be with him; but I, who always much wished to lose sight of the West Indies, was not a little rejoiced at the thoughts of seeing any other country. Therefore, relying on the goodness of my captain, I got ready all the little venture I could; and, when the vessel was ready, we sailed, to my great joy. When we got to our destined places, Georgia and Charlestown, I expected I should have an opportunity of selling my little property to advantage. But here, particularly in Charlestown, I met with buyers, white men, who imposed on me as in other places. Notwithstanding, I was resolved to have fortitude, thinking no lot or trial too hard when kind Heaven is the rewarder.

We soon got loaded again, and returned to Montserrat; and there, amongst the rest of the islands, I sold my goods well; and in this manner I continued trading during the year 1764—meeting with various scenes of imposition, as usual. After this, my master fitted out his vessel for Philadelphia, in the year 1765; and during the time we were loading her, and getting ready for the voyage, I worked with redoubled alacrity, from the hope of getting money enough by these voyages to buy my freedom, in time, if it should please God; and also to see the town of Philadelphia, which I had heard a great deal about for some years past. Besides which, I had always longed to prove my master's promise the first day I came to him. In the midst of these elevated ideas, and while I was about getting my little stock of merchandize in readiness, one Sunday my master sent for me to his house. When I came there, I found him and the captain together; and, on my going in, I was struck with astonishment at his telling me he heard that I meant to run away from him when I got to Philadelphia. "And therefore," said he, "I must tell you again, you cost me a great deal of money, no less than forty pounds sterling; and it will not do to lose so much. You are a valuable fellow," continued he, "and I can get any day for you one hundred guineas, from many gentlemen in this island." And then he told me of Captain Doran's brother-in-law, a severe master, who ever wanted to buy me to make me his overseer. My captain also said he could get much more than a hundred guineas for me in Carolina. This I knew to be a fact; for the gentleman that wanted to buy me came off several times on board of us, and spoke to me to live with him, and said he would use me well. When I asked him what work he would put me to, he said, as I was a sailor, he would make me a captain of one of his rice vessels. But I refused; and fearing at the same time, by a sudden turn I saw in the captain's temper, he might mean to sell me, I told the gentleman I would not live with him on any condition, and that I certainly would run away with his vessel: but he said he did not fear that, as he would catch me again, and then he told me how cruelly he would serve me if I should do so. My captain, however, gave him to understand that I knew something of navigation, so he thought better of it; and, to my great joy, he went away. I now told my master,

I did not say I would run away in Philadelphia; neither did I mean it, as he did not use me ill, nor yet the captain; for if they did, I certainly would have made some attempts before now; but as I thought that if it were God's will I ever should be freed, it would be so, and, on the contrary, if it was not His will, it would not happen. So I hoped if ever I were freed, whilst I was used well, it should be by honest means; but as I could not help myself, he must do as he pleased; I could only hope and trust to the God of Heaven; and at that instant my mind was big with inventions, and full of schemes to escape. I then appealed to the captain, whether he ever saw any sign of my making the least attempt to run away, and asked him if I did not always come on board according to the time for which he gave me liberty; and, more particularly, when all our men left us at Guadeloupe, and went on board of the French fleet, and advised me to go with them, whether I might not, and that he could not have got me again. To my no small surprise, and very great joy, the captain confirmed every syllable that I had said, and even more; for he said he had tried different times to see if I would make any attempt of this kind, both at St. Eustatia and in America, and he never found that I made the smallest; but, on the contrary, I always came on board according to his orders; and he did really believe, if I ever meant to run away, that, as I could never have had a better opportunity, I would have done it the night the mate and all the people left our vessel at Guadeloupe. The captain then informed my master, who had been thus imposed on by our mate (though I did not know who was my enemy), the reason the mate had for imposing this lie upon him; which was, because I had acquainted the captain of the provisions the mate had given away or taken out of the vessel. This speech of the captain was like life to the dead to me, and instantly my soul glorified God; and still more so, on hearing my master immediately say that I was a sensible fellow, and he never did intend to use me as a common slave; and that but for the entreaties of the captain, and his character of me, he would not have let me go from the shores about as I had done. That also, in so doing, he thought by carrying one little thing or other to different places to sell, I might make money. That he also intended to encourage me in this, by crediting me with half a puncheon of rum and half a hogshead[5] of sugar at a time; so that, from being careful, I might have money enough, in some time, to purchase my freedom; and, when that was the case, I might depend upon it he would let me have it for forty pounds sterling money, which was only the same price he gave for me. This sound gladdened my poor heart beyond measure; though indeed it was no more than the very idea I had formed in my mind of my master long before, and I immediately made him this reply: "Sir, I always had that very thought of you, indeed I had, and that made me so diligent in serving you." He then gave me a large piece of silver coin, such as I never had seen or had before, and told me to get ready for the voyage, and he would credit me with a tierce[6] of sugar, and another of rum; he also said that he had two amiable sisters in Philadelphia, from whom I might get some necessary things. Upon this my noble captain desired me to go aboard; and, knowing the African metal,[7] he charged me not to say any thing of this matter to any body; and he promised that the lying mate should not go with him

---

5. Large barrel.
6. A third of a barrel.

7. I.e., character.

any more. This was a change indeed: in the same hour to feel the most exquisite pain, and in the turn of a moment the fullest joy. It caused in me such sensations as I was only able to express in my looks; my heart was so overpowered with gratitude, that I could have kissed both of their feet. When I left the room, I immediately went, or rather flew, to the vessel; which being loaded, my master, as good as his word, trusted me with a tierce of rum, and another of sugar, when we sailed, and arrived safe at the elegant town of Philadelphia. I sold my goods here pretty well; and in this charming place I found every thing plentiful and cheap.

While I was in this place, a very extraordinary occurrence befell me. I had been told one evening of a wise woman, a Mrs. Davis, who revealed secrets, foretold events, etc., etc. I put little faith in this story at first, as I could not conceive that any mortal could foresee the future disposals of Providence, nor did I believe in any other revelation than that of the Holy Scriptures; however, I was greatly astonished at seeing this woman in a dream that night, though a person I never before beheld in my life. This made such an impression on me, that I could not get the idea the next day out of my mind, and I then became as anxious to see her as I was before indifferent. Accordingly in the evening, after we left off working, I inquired where she lived, and being directed to her, to my inexpressible surprise, beheld the very woman in the very same dress she appeared to me to wear in the vision. She immediately told me I had dreamed of her the preceding night; related to me many things that had happened with a correctness that astonished me, and finally told me I should not be long a slave. This was the more agreeable news; as I believed it the more readily from her having so faithfully related the past incidents of my life. She said I should be twice in very great danger of my life within eighteen months, which, if I escaped, I should afterwards go on well. So, giving me her blessing, we parted. After staying here sometime till our vessel was loaded, and I had bought in my little traffic, we sailed from this agreeable spot for Montserrat, once more to encounter the raging surfs.

*　*　*

We soon came to Georgia, where we were to complete our landing, and here worse fate than ever attended me; for one Sunday night, as I was with some negroes in their master's yard, in the town of Savannah, it happened that their master, one Doctor Perkins, who was a very severe and cruel man, came in drunk; and not liking to see any strange negroes in his yard, he and a ruffian of a white man, he had in his service, beset me in an instant, and both of them struck me with the first weapons they could get hold of. I cried out as long as I could for help and mercy; but, though I gave a good account of myself, and he knew my captain, who lodged hard by him,[8] it was to no purpose. They beat and mangled me in a shameful manner, leaving me near dead. I lost so much blood from the wounds I received, that I lay quite motionless, and was so benumbed that I could not feel any thing for many hours. Early in the morning, they took me away to the jail. As I did not return to the ship all night, my captain, not knowing where I was, and being uneasy that I did not then make my appearance, made inquiry after me; and having found where I was, immediately came to me. As soon as the good man saw

8. I.e., close by him.

me so cut and mangled, he could not forbear weeping; he soon got me out of jail to his lodgings, and immediately sent for the best doctors in the place, who at first declared it as their opinion that I could not recover. My captain on this went to all the lawyers in the town for their advice, but they told him they could do nothing for me as I was a negro. He then went to Doctor Perkins, the hero who had vanquished me, and menaced him, swearing he would be revenged on him, and challenged him to fight.—But cowardice is ever the companion of cruelty—and the Doctor refused. However, by the skillfullness of one Dr. Brady of that place, I began at last to amend; but, although I was so sore and bad with the wounds I had all over me, that I could not rest in any posture, yet I was in more pain on account of the captain's uneasiness about me, than I otherwise should have been. The worthy man nursed and watched me all the hours of the night; and I was, through his attention and that of the doctor, able to get out of bed in about sixteen or eighteen days. All this time I was very much wanted on board, as I used frequently to go up and down the river for rafts, and other parts of our cargo, and stow them, when the mate was sick or absent. In about four weeks, I was able to go on duty, and in a fortnight after, having got in all our lading, our vessel set sail for Montserrat; and in less than three weeks we arrived there safe towards the end of the year. This ended my adventures in 1764, for I did not leave Montserrat again till the beginning of the following year.

From *Chapter VII*

Every day now brought me nearer my freedom, and I was impatient till we proceeded again to sea, that I might have an opportunity of getting a sum large enough to purchase it. I was not long ungratified; for, in the beginning of the year 1766, my master bought another sloop, named the Nancy, the largest I had ever seen. She was partly laden, and was to proceed to Philadelphia; our captain had his choice of three, and I was well pleased he chose this, which was the largest; for, from his having a large vessel, I had more room, and could carry a larger quantity of goods with me. Accordingly, when we had delivered our old vessel, the Prudence, and completed the lading of the Nancy, having made near three hundred per cent. by four barrels of pork I brought from Charlestown, I laid in as large a cargo as I could, trusting to God's providence to prosper my undertaking. With these views I sailed for Philadelphia. On our passage, when we drew near the land, I was for the first time surprised at the sight of some whales, having never seen any such large sea monsters before; and as we sailed by the land, one morning, I saw a puppy whale close by the vessel; it was about the length of a wherry boat, and it followed us all the day till we got within the Capes.[9] We arrived safe, and in good time at Philadelphia, and I sold my goods there chiefly to the Quakers. They always appeared to be a very honest, discreet sort of people, and never attempted to impose on[1] me; I therefore liked them, and ever after chose to deal with them in preference to any others.

One Sunday morning, while I was here, as I was going to church, I chanced to pass a meetinghouse. The doors being open, and the house full of people,

9. Equiano may be referring to Cape May in southern New Jersey.   1. Cheat.

it excited my curiosity to go in. When I entered the house, to my great surprise, I saw a very tall woman standing in the midst of them, speaking in an audible voice something which I could not understand. Having never seen any thing of this kind before, I stood and stared about me for some time, wondering at this odd scene. As soon as it was over, I took an opportunity to make inquiry about the place and people, when I was informed they were called Quakers. I particularly asked what that woman I saw in the midst of them had said, but none of them were pleased to satisfy me; so I quitted them, and soon after, as I was returning, I came to a church crowded with people; the churchyard was full likewise, and a number of people were even mounted on ladders looking in at the windows. I thought this a strange sight, as I had never seen churches, either in England or the West Indies, crowded in this manner before. I therefore made bold to ask some people the meaning of all this, and they told me the Rev. Mr. George Whitefield was preaching. I had often heard of this gentleman, and had wished to see and hear him; but I never before had an opportunity. I now therefore resolved to gratify myself with the sight, and pressed in amidst the multitude. When I got into the church, I saw this pious man exhorting the people with the greatest fervor and earnestness, and sweating as much as I ever did while in slavery on Montserrat beach. I was very much struck and impressed with this; I thought it strange I had never seen divines exert themselves in this manner before, and was no longer at a loss to account for the thin congregations they preached to.

When we had discharged our cargo here, and were loaded again, we left this fruitful land once more, and set sail for Montserrat. My traffic had hitherto succeeded so well with me, that I thought, by selling my goods when we arrived at Montserrat, I should have enough to purchase my freedom. But as soon as our vessel arrived there, my master came on board, and gave orders for us to go to St. Eustatia, and discharge our cargo there, and from thence proceed for Georgia. I was much disappointed at this; but thinking, as usual, it was of no use to encounter with the decrees of fate, I submitted without repining, and we went to St. Eustatia. After we had discharged our cargo there, we took in a live cargo (as we call a cargo of slaves). Here I sold my goods tolerably well; but, not being able to lay out all my money in this small island to as much advantage as in many other places, I laid out only part, and the remainder I brought away with me net. We sailed from hence for Georgia, and I was glad when we got there, though I had not much reason to like the place from my last adventure in Savannah; but I longed to get back to Montserrat and procure my freedom, which I expected to be able to purchase when I returned. As soon as we arrived here, I waited on my careful doctor, Mr. Brady, to whom I made the most grateful acknowledgments in my power, for his former kindness and attention during my illness.

* * *

When we had unladen the vessel, and I had sold my venture, finding myself master of about forty-seven pounds—I consulted my true friend, the captain, how I should proceed in offering my master the money for my freedom. He told me to come on a certain morning, when he and my master would be at breakfast together. Accordingly, on that morning I went, and met the captain there, as he had appointed. When I went in I made my obeisance to my master, and with my money in my hand, and many fears in my heart, I prayed him to be as good as his offer to me, when he was pleased to promise me my freedom as soon as I could purchase it. This speech seemed to confound him, he began to recoil, and my heart that instant sunk within me. "What," said he, "give you your freedom? Why, where did you get the money? Have you got forty pounds sterling?" "Yes, sir," I answered. "How did you get it?" replied he. I told him, very honestly. The captain then said he knew I got the money honestly, and with much industry, and that I was particularly careful. On which my master replied, I got money much faster than he did; and said he would not have made me the promise he did if he had thought I should have got the money so soon. "Come, come," said my worthy captain, clapping my master on the back, "Come, Robert (which was his name), I think you must let him have his freedom;—you have laid your money out very well; you have received a very good interest for it all this time, and here is now the principal at last. I know Gustavus has earned you more than a hundred a year, and he will save you money, as he will not leave you.—Come, Robert, take the money." My master then said he would not be worse than his promise; and, taking the money, told me to go to the Secretary at the Register Office, and get my manumission[2] drawn up. These words of my master were like a voice from Heaven to me. In an instant all my trepidation was turned into unutterable bliss; and I most reverently bowed myself with gratitude, unable to express my feelings, but by the overflowing of my eyes, and a heart replete with thanks to God, while my true and worthy friend, the captain, congratulated us both with a peculiar degree of heart-felt pleasure. As soon as the first transports of my joy were over, and that I had expressed my thanks to these my worthy friends, in the best manner I was able, I rose with a heart full of affection and reverence, and left the room, in order to obey my master's joyful mandate of going to the Register Office. As I was leaving the house I called to mind the words of the Psalmist, in the 126th Psalm, and like him, "I glorified God in my heart, in whom I trusted." These words had been impressed on my mind from the very day I was forced from Deptford to the present hour, and I now saw them, as I thought, fulfilled and verified. My imagination was all rapture as I flew to the Register Office; and, in this respect, like the apostle Peter[3] (whose deliverance from prison was so sudden and extraordinary, that he thought he was in a vision), I could scarcely believe I was awake. Heavens! who could do justice to my feelings at this moment! Not conquering heroes themselves, in the midst of a triumph—Not the tender mother who has just regained her long lost infant, and presses it to her heart—Not the weary hungry, mariner, at the sight of the desired friendly port—Not the lover, when he once more embraces his beloved mistress, after she has been ravished from his arms! All within my breast was tumult, wildness, and delirium! My feet scarcely touched the ground, for they were winged with joy; and, like Elijah, as he rose to Heaven,[4] they "were with lightning sped as I went on." Every one I met I told of my happiness, and blazed about the virtue of my amiable master and captain.

When I got to the office and acquainted the Register with my errand, he

2. Document declaring his freedom.
3. "Acts xii.9" [Equiano's note]. "And he went out and followed him; and wist not that it was true which was done by the angel; but thought he saw a vision."
4. The Lord takes Elijah into heaven in 2 Kings 2.11.

congratulated me on the occasion, and told me he would draw up my manumission for half price, which was a guinea. I thanked him for his kindness; and, having received it, and paid him, I hastened to my master to get him to sign it, that I might be fully released. Accordingly he signed the manumission that day; so that, before night, I, who had been a slave in the morning, trembling at the will of another, was become my own master, and completely free. I thought this was the happiest day I had ever experienced; and my joy was still heightened by the blessings and prayers of many of the sable race, particularly the aged, to whom my heart had ever been attached with reverence.

*   *   *

As the form of my manumission has something peculiar in it, and expresses the absolute power and dominion one man claims over his fellow, I shall beg leave to present it before my readers at full length:

Montserrat.—To all men unto whom these presents[5] shall come: I, Robert King, of the parish of St. Anthony, in the said island, merchant, send greeting. Know ye, that I, the aforesaid Robert King, for and in consideration of the sum of seventy pounds current money of the said island,[6] to me in hand paid, and to the intent that a negro man slave, named Gustavus Vassa, shall and may become free, having manumitted, emancipated, enfranchised, and set free, and by these presents do manumit, emancipate, enfranchise, and set free, the aforesaid negro man slave, named Gustavus Vassa, for ever; hereby giving, granting, and releasing unto him, the said Gustavus Vassa, all right, title, dominion, sovereignty, and property, which, as lord and master over the aforesaid Gustavus Vassa, I had, or now have, or by any means whatsoever I may or can hereafter possibly have over him, the aforesaid negro, for ever. In witness whereof, I, the above said Robert King, have unto these presents set my hand and seal, this tenth day of July, in the year of our Lord one thousand seven hundred and sixty-six.

ROBERT KING.

Signed, sealed, and delivered in the presence of Terry Legay, Montserrat.

Registered the within manumission at full length, this eleventh day of July, 1766, in liber[7] D.

TERRY LEGAY, Register.

*   *   *

1789

5. The present words; this document.
6. The exchange rate favored the West Indians in this period: forty pounds sterling equaling seventy pounds in "local" currency.
7. Book (Latin).

JUDITH SARGENT MURRAY
1751–1820

Judith Sargent Murray found her most important subject—the independent female mind—in her first published essay, *The Utility of Encouraging a Degree of Self-Complacency, Especially in Female Bosoms*. Writing under the pen name "Constantia," she advises young women that though a "pleasing form is undoubtedly advantageous," mind is much more important. An intellectual woman in a culture that thought of women as men's mental inferiors, a professional writer in an era when almost no one—male or female—made a living by writing, Murray powerfully demonstrated the validity of her own precepts.

She was born and spent much of her life in Gloucester, Massachusetts, a coastal town about forty miles north of Boston. Both her mother, Judith Saunders, and her father, Winthrop Sargent, came from hardworking, seafaring families. The Sargents expressed their independence in many ways. One was in allowing Judith to be tutored by the local clergyman along with her younger brother Winslow in college preparatory subjects like Latin, Greek, and mathematics. Another was in their liberal theology, which questioned the strict Calvinist doctrine of election and damnation. Murray, her parents, and her first husband, John Stevens, whom she married in 1769, knew the teachings of the English Universalist James Relly, which proclaimed that salvation was available to anyone who accepted Jesus Christ. Relly was sure that a rational God would never condemn members of his human flock to hell. The Sargents and Stevens were thus ready to welcome Relly's greatest disciple, John Murray, who had left England and was preaching his way up the eastern seaboard; he came to Gloucester in 1774. The first Universalist church in America was dedicated there in 1780. It was no coincidence that the Universalist church in America was the first to ordain women as ministers. Judith Sargent Murray's later advocacy of cultivating independent, intellectually alert women was totally compatible with her religious position. In 1788, about a year after the death of John Stevens in the West Indies, she married John Murray and her career as a writer began in earnest.

In an increasingly secular world, essays and novels with moral subtexts would make readers into new congregations, and the growing number of magazines like Boston's *Massachusetts Magazine* or *The Gentleman's and Lady's Town and Country Magazine: or, Repository of Instruction and Entertainment*, where Murray's first essay appeared in 1784, would take the place of many pulpits in the years to come. Eighteenth-century readers liked a moral commentary firmly rooted in the Ten Commandments without the trappings of the old theology. But while Murray found her true subject and an audience early on, it was not easy for her to make a living by the pen. In the volatile world of print culture, magazines changed hands frequently and many disappeared without trace, while publishers assumed that contributors would be so grateful to see their name in print that no payment was necessary. Washington Irving was the first American writer to live on income derived solely from his writing.

Murray's most important work and her greatest financial success was a three-volume compilation of her work, published in 1798 as *The Gleaner*. Like many publications of the period, it was financed by subscribers, whose names were listed in the volume. Murray gathered 759 names, among which were Sarah Wentworth Morton and Mercy Otis Warren. She dedicated *The Gleaner* to John and Abigail Adams, who also subscribed. The book, a true miscellany, included two plays, eulogies, and a series of historical essays. Most of it consisted of essays Murray had written for the *Massachusetts Magazine* under the pen name of Mr. Vigilius, who styled himself a "gleaner"—that is, one who picked up bits of ungathered grain after a harvest. Some of these essays told a connected narrative about Mr. Vigilius's adopted daughter, Margaretta; there were also religious essays with Universalist themes; political essays on American foreign and domestic policy (a religious liberal, Murray was a political conservative); and didactic essays in the narrative style of early-eighteenth-century English periodical writing. At the end of the volume Murray "unmasked" Mr. Vigilius and came forward as a woman, explaining that she had hidden her sex because she feared that if she were known to be a woman, her writing would not be taken seriously.

Murray never repeated the financial success of *The Gleaner*; the work itself was not reissued until 1992. Murray seems to have published nothing new from 1796 to 1802, when she offered some poems in a new Boston publication that hoped to take up where the defunct *Massachusetts Magazine* left off. Her major efforts went to the care of her failing and improvident husband. She edited his *Letters and Sketches of Sermons* (1812–13) and his posthumous autobiography (1816). With her work on Murray's behalf completed, she left New England and made a final home with her daughter in Natchez, Mississippi, where she died in 1820.

On the Equality of the Sexes[1]

Part I

That minds are not alike, full well I know,
This truth each day's experience will show.
To heights surprising some great spirits soar,
With inborn strength mysterious depths explore;
Their eager gaze surveys the path of light,   5
Confessed it stood to Newton's[2] piercing sight.
    Deep science, like a bashful maid retires,
And but[3] the *ardent* breast her worth inspires;
By perseverance the coy fair is won,
And Genius, led by Study, wears the crown.   10
    But some there are who wish not to improve,
Who never can the path of knowledge love,
Whose souls almost with the dull body one,
With anxious care each mental pleasure shun.
Weak is the leveled, enervated mind,   15
And but while here to vegetate designed.
The torpid spirit mingling with its clod
Can scarcely boast its origin from God.
Stupidly dull—they move progressing on—
They eat, and drink, and all their work is done,   20
While others, emulous of sweet applause,
Industrious seek for each event a cause,
Tracing the hidden springs whence knowledge flows,
Which nature all in beauteous order shows.
    Yet cannot I their sentiments imbibe   25
Who this distinction to the sex ascribe,
As if a woman's form must needs enroll
A weak, a servile, an inferior soul;
And that the guise of man must still proclaim
Greatness of mind, and him, to be the same.   30

1. The text used here is taken from *The Massachusetts Magazine, or, Monthly Museum of Knowledge and Rational Entertainment*, published in March and April 1790. Both the poem and the essay are by Murray.

2. Sir Isaac Newton (1642–1727), English scientist and philosopher, broke up white light into the colors of the spectrum by means of a prism and likewise recombined the colors.

3. And only.

Yet as the hours revolve fair proofs arise
Which the bright wreath of growing fame supplies,
And in past times some men have *sunk* so *low,*
That female records nothing *less* can show.
But imbecility[4] is still confined,   35
And by the lordly sex to us consigned.
They rob us of the power t'improve,
And then declare we only trifles love.
Yet haste the era when the world shall know
That such distinctions only dwell below.   40
The soul unfettered to no sex confined,
Was for the abodes of cloudless day designed.
   Meantime we emulate their manly fires,
Though erudition all their thoughts inspires,
Yet nature with *equality* imparts,   45
And *noble passions,* swell e'en *female hearts.*

Is it upon mature consideration we adopt the idea that nature is thus partial in her distributions? Is it indeed a fact that she hath yielded to one half of the human species so unquestionable a mental superiority? I know that to both sexes elevated understandings, and the reverse, are common. But, suffer me to ask, in what the minds of females are so notoriously deficient, or unequal? May not the intellectual powers be ranged under these four heads—imagination, reason, memory and judgment? The province of imagination hath long since been surrendered up to us, and we have been crowned undoubted sovereigns of the regions of fancy. Invention is perhaps the most arduous effort of the mind; this branch of imagination hath been particularly ceded to us, and we have been time out of mind invested with that creative faculty. Observe the variety of fashions (here I bar the contemptuous smile) which distinguish and adorn the female world; how continually are they changing, insomuch that they almost render the wise man's assertion problematical, and we are ready to say, *there is something new under the sun.*[5] Now what a playfulness, what an exuberance of fancy, what strength of inventive imagination, doth this continual variation discover?[6] Again, it hath been observed that if the turpitude of the conduct of our sex hath been ever so enormous, so extremely ready are we, that the very first thought presents us with an apology so plausible as to produce our actions even in an amiable light. Another instance of our creative powers is our talent for slander. How ingenious are we at inventive scandal? What a formidable story can we in a moment fabricate merely from the force of a prolific imagination? How many reputations in the fertile brain of a female have been utterly despoiled? How industrious are we at improving a hint? Suspicion[7] how easily do we convert into conviction, and conviction, embellished by the power of eloquence, stalks abroad to the surprise and confusion of unsuspecting innocence. Perhaps it will be asked if I furnish these facts as instances of excellency in our sex. Certainly not; but as proofs of a creative faculty, of a lively imagination. Assuredly great activity of mind is thereby discovered, and was

4. Stupidity.
5. "There is no new thing under the sun" (Ecclesiastes 1.8).

6. Reveal.
7. Imagine. "Improving": making use of.

this activity properly directed what beneficial effects would follow. Is the needle and kitchen sufficient to employ the operations of a soul thus organized? I should conceive not. Nay, it is a truth that those very departments leave the intelligent principle vacant, and at liberty for speculation. Are we deficient in reason? We can only reason from what we know, and if an opportunity of acquiring knowledge hath been denied us, the inferiority of our sex cannot fairly be deduced from thence. Memory, I believe, will be allowed us in common, since every one's experience must testify that a loquacious old woman is as frequently met with as a communicative old man; their subjects are alike drawn from the fund of other times, and the transactions of their youth, or of maturer life, entertain, or perhaps fatigue you, in the evening of their lives. "But our judgment is not so strong—we do not distinguish so well."—Yet it may be questioned, from what doth this superiority in this determining faculty of the soul, proceed? May we not trace its source in the difference of education, and continued advantages? Will it be said that the judgment of a male of two years old is more sage than that of a female's of the same age? I believe the reverse is generally observed to be true. But from that period what partiality! How is the one exalted and the other depressed by the contrary modes of education which are adopted! The one is taught to aspire and the other is early confined and limited. As their years increase the sister must be wholly domesticated, while the brother is led by the hand through all the flowery paths of science. Grant that their minds are by nature equal, yet who shall wonder at the *apparent* superiority, if indeed custom becomes *second nature*; nay if it taketh place of nature, and that it doth the experience of each day will evince. At length arrived at womanhood, the uncultivated fair one feels a void which the employments allotted her are by no means capable of filling. What can she do? To books she may not apply; or if she doth, *to those only of the novel kind*,[8] lest she merit the appellation of a *learned lady*; and what ideas have been affixed to this term, the observation of many can testify. Fashion, scandal, and sometimes what is still more reprehensible are then called in to her relief; and who can say to what lengths the liberties she takes may proceed. Meantime she herself is most unhappy; she feels the want of a cultivated mind. Is she single, she in vain seeks to fill up time from sexual employments or amusements. Is she united to a person whose soul nature made equal to her own, education hath set him so far above her that in those entertainments which are productive of such rational felicity she is not qualified to accompany him. She experiences a mortifying consciousness of inferiority which embitters every enjoyment. Doth the person to whom her adverse fate hath consigned her possess a mind incapable of improvement, she is equally wretched in being so closely connected with an individual whom she cannot but despise. Now was she permitted the same instructors as her brother (with an eye however to their particular departments) for the employment of a rational mind an ample field would be opened. In astronomy she might catch a glimpse of the immensity of the Deity and thence she would form amazing conceptions of the August and supreme Intelligence. In geography she would admire Jehovah in the midst of His benevolence; thus adapting this globe to the various wants and

8. I.e., fiction.

amusements of its inhabitants. In natural philosophy she would adore the infinite majesty of heaven, clothed in condescension[9] and as she traversed the reptile world, she would hail the goodness of a creating God. A mind thus filled would have little room for the trifles with which our sex are, with too much justice, accused of amusing themselves, and they would thus be rendered fit companions for those who should one day wear them as their crown. Fashions, in their variety, would then give place to conjectures, which might perhaps conduce to the improvement of the literary world; and there would be no leisure for slander or detraction. Reputation would not then be blasted, but serious speculations would occupy the lively imaginations of the sex. Unnecessary visits would be precluded, and that custom would only be indulged by way of relaxation, or to answer the demands of consanguinity and friendship. Females would become discreet, their judgments would be invigorated, and their partners for life being circumspectly chosen, an unhappy Hymen[1] would then be as rare as is now the reverse.

Will it be urged that those acquirements would supersede our domestic duties? I answer that every requisite in female economy[2] is easily attained; and, with truth, I can add that when once attained they require no further *mental attention*. Nay, while we are pursuing the needle, or the superintendency of the family, I repeat, that our minds are at full liberty for reflection; that imagination may exert itself in full vigor; and that if a just foundation is early laid, our ideas will then be worthy of rational beings. If we were industrious we might easily find time to arrange them upon paper, or should avocations press too hard for such an indulgence, the hours allotted for conversation would at least become more refined and rational. Should it still be vociferated, "Your domestic employments are sufficient"—I would calmly ask, is it reasonable that a candidate for immortality, for the joys of heaven, an intelligent being, who is to spend an eternity in contemplating the works of Deity, should at present be so degraded as to be allowed no other ideas than those which are suggested by the mechanism of a pudding, or the sewing the seams of a garment? Pity that all such censurers of female improvement do not go one step further and deny their[3] future existence; to be consistent they surely ought.

Yes, ye lordly, ye haughty sex, our souls are by nature *equal* to yours; the same breath of God animates, enlivens, and invigorates us; and that we are not fallen lower than yourselves, let those witness who have greatly towered above the various discouragements by which they have been so heavily oppressed. And though I am unacquainted with the list of celebrated characters on either side, yet from the observations I have made in the contracted circle in which I have moved, I dare confidently believe that from the commencement of time to the present day there hath been as many females, as males, who, by the *mere force of natural powers*, have merited the crown of applause; who, *thus unassisted*, have seized the wreath of fame. I know there are who assert that as the animal powers of the one sex are superior of course their mental faculties also must be stronger; thus attributing strength of mind to the transient organization of this earth born tenement. But if this reasoning is just, man must be content to yield the palm [to] many of the

9. A gracious disregard of its superiority. "Natural philosophy": i.e., natural science.
1. Marriage. In classical mythology the marriage

god is Hymen.
2. Housekeeping.
3. Women's.

brute creation, since by not a few of his brethren of the field he is far surpassed in bodily strength. Moreover, was this argument admitted, it would prove too much, for ocular demonstration evinceth that there are many robust masculine ladies, and effeminate gentlemen. Yet I fancy that Mr. Pope,[4] though clogged with an enervated body, and distinguished by a diminutive stature, could nevertheless lay claim to greatness of soul, and perhaps there are many other instances which might be adduced to combat so unphilosophical an opinion. Do we not often see that when the clay built tabernacle[5] is well nigh dissolved, when it is just ready to mingle with the parent soil, the immortal inhabitant aspires to and even attaineth heights the most sublime and which were before wholly unexplored? Besides, were we to grant that animal strength proved anything, taking into consideration the accustomed impartiality of nature, we should be induced to imagine that she had invested the female mind with superior strength as an equivalent for the bodily powers of man. But waving this however palpable advantage, for *equality only,* we wish to contend.

Part II

I am aware that there are many passages in the sacred oracles which seem to give the advantage to the other sex, but I consider all these as wholly metaphorical. Thus David was a man after God's own heart, yet see him enervated by his licentious passions! Behold him following Uriah[6] to the death and show me wherein could consist the immaculate Being's complacency. Listen to the curses which Job bestoweth upon the day of his nativity,[7] and tell me where is his perfection, where his patience—*literally* it existed not. David and Job were types[8] of Him who was to come; and the superiority of man, as exhibited in scripture, being also emblematical, all arguments deduced from thence of course fall to the ground. The exquisite delicacy of the female mind proclaimeth the exactness of its texture, while its nice[9] sense of honor announceth its innate, its native grandeur. And indeed, in one respect, the preeminence seems to be tacitly allowed us, for after an education which limits and confines, and employments and recreations which naturally tend to enervate the body and debilitate the mind, after we have from early youth been adorned with ribbons and other gewgaws,[1] dressed out like the ancient victims previous to a sacrifice, being taught by the care of our parents in collecting the most showy materials that the ornamenting our exterior ought to be the principal object of our attention; after, I say, fifteen years thus spent, we are introduced into the world amid the united adulation of every beholder. Praise is sweet to the soul; we are immediately intoxicated by large draughts of flattery, which being plentifully administered, is to the pride of our hearts the most acceptable incense. It is expected that with the other sex we should commence immediate war, and that we

4. The English poet Alexander Pope (1688–1744) suffered an early illness that left his body deformed.
5. The body, which houses the soul.
6. When King David lusted after Bathsheba, he contrived to send her husband Uriah into battle to be killed so that David might marry her. See 2 Samuel 11.3–27.
7. Although Job's faith survives many testings, he curses the day he was born (Job 3).
8. Prefigurations. Medieval exegetes argued that Old Testament persons and events took on their full meaning in the New Testament. Job and David are thus, in their sufferings, prefigurations of Jesus.
9. Refined. "Exactness": high finish or quality.
1. Trinkets.

should triumph over the machinations of the most artful. We must be constantly upon our guard; prudence and discretion must be our characteristics, and we must rise superior to, and obtain a complete victory over, those who have been long adding to the native strength of their minds by an unremitted study of men and books, and who have, moreover, conceived from the loose characters which they have seen portrayed in the extensive variety of their reading a most contemptible opinion of the sex. Thus unequal, we are, notwithstanding, forced to the combat, and the infamy which is consequent upon the smallest deviation in our conduct proclaims the high idea which was formed of our native strength; and thus, indirectly at least, is the preference acknowledged to be our due. And if we are allowed an equality of acquirement, let serious studies equally employ our minds and we will bid our souls arise to equal strength. We will meet upon even ground the despot man; we will rush with alacrity to the combat, and, crowned by success, we shall then answer the exalted expectations which are formed. Though sensibility, soft compassion, and gentle commiseration are inmates in the female bosom, yet against every deep laid art, altogether fearless of the event, we will set them in array; for assuredly the wreath of victory will encircle the spotless brow. If we meet an equal, a sensible friend, we will reward him with the hand of amity, and through life we will be assiduous to promote his happiness; but from every deep laid scheme for our ruin, retiring into ourselves, amid the flowery paths of science, we will indulge in all the refined and sentimental pleasures of contemplation. And should it still be urged that the studies thus insisted upon would interfere with our more peculiar department,[2] I must further reply that *early hours* and close application will do wonders; and to her who is from the first dawn of reason taught to fill up time rationally, both the requisites will be easy. I grant that niggard[3] fortune is too generally unfriendly to the mind; and that much of that valuable treasure, time, is necessarily expended upon the wants of the body; but it should be remembered that in embarrassed circumstances our companions have as little leisure for literary improvement as is afforded to us; for most certainly their provident care is at least as requisite as our exertions. Nay, we have even more leisure for sedentary pleasures, as our avocations are more retired, much less laborious, and, as hath been observed, by no means require that avidity of attention which is proper to the employments of the other sex. In high life, or, in other words, where the parties are in possession of affluence, the objection respecting time is wholly obviated, and, of course, falls to the ground. And it may also be repeated that many of those hours which are at present swallowed up in fashion and scandal might be redeemed were we habituated to useful reflections. But in one respect, O ye arbiters of our fate! we confess that the superiority is indubitably yours; you are by nature formed for our protectors; we pretend not to vie with you in bodily strength; upon this point we will never contend for victory. Shield us then, we beseech you, from external evils, and in return *we* will transact *your* domestic affairs. Yes, *your,* for are you not equally interested in those matters with ourselves? Is not the elegancy of neatness as agreeable to your sight as to ours; is not the well favored viand equally delightful to your taste; and doth not your sense

2. I.e., duties belonging more particularly to women.   3. Stingy.

of hearing suffer as much from the discordant sounds prevalent in an ill regulated family produced by the voices of children and many *et ceteras?*

CONSTANTIA.[4]

By way of supplement to the foregoing pages, I subjoin the following extract from a letter, wrote to a friend in the December of 1780.

And now assist me, O thou genius of my sex, while I undertake the arduous task of endeavoring to combat that vulgar, that almost universal error, which hath, it seems, enlisted even Mr. P— under its banners. The superiority of your sex hath, I grant, been time out of mind esteemed a truth incontrovertible; in consequence of which persuasion every plan of education hath been calculated to establish this favorite tenet. Not long since, weak and presuming as I was, I amused myself with selecting some arguments from nature, reason, and experience, against this so generally received idea. I confess that to sacred testimonies[5] I had not recourse. I held them to be merely metaphorical and thus regarding them, I could not persuade myself that there was any propriety in bringing them to decide in this *very important debate.* However, as you, sir, confine yourself entirely to the sacred oracles, I mean to bend the whole of my artillery against those supposed proofs which you have from thence provided, and from which you have formed an entrenchment *apparently* so invulnerable. And first, to begin with our great progenitors;[6] but here, suffer me to premise, that it is for mental strength I mean to contend, for with respect to animal powers, I yield them undisputed to that sex, which enjoys them in common with the lion, the tiger, and many other beasts of prey; therefore your observations respecting the *rib under the arm, at a distance from the head,* etc., etc., in no sort militate against my view.[7] Well, but the woman was first in the transgression. Strange how blind *self love* renders you men. Were you not wholly absorbed in a partial admiration of your own abilities, you would long since have acknowledged the force of what I am now going to urge. It is true some ignoramuses have absurdly enough informed us that the beauteous fair of paradise was seduced from her obedience by a malignant demon *in the guise of a baleful serpent;* but we, who are better informed, know that the fallen spirit presented himself to her view *a shining angel still;* for thus, saith the critics in the Hebrew tongue, ought the word to be rendered.[8] Let us examine her motive—Hark! the seraph declares that she shall attain a perfection of knowledge; for is there aught which is not comprehended under one or other of the terms *good* and *evil.* It doth not appear that she was governed by any one sensual appetite, but merely by a desire of adorning her mind. A laudable ambition fired her soul and a thirst for knowledge impelled the predilection so fatal in its consequences. Adam could not plead the same deception; assuredly he was not deceived; nor ought we to admire his superior strength, or wonder at his sagacity, when we so often confess that example is much more influential than precept. His gentle partner stood before him, a melancholy instance of

---

4. Murray's pen name. "*Et ceteras*": unspecified other things (Latin).
5. The Bible.
6. Ancestors. Here, Adam and Eve.
7. "And the rib, which the Lord God had taken from man, made he a woman, and brought her

unto the man" (Genesis 2.22).
8. The earliest connection with Satan and light is in Isaiah 14.12: "How are thou fallen from heaven, O Lucifer, son of the morning!" *Lucifer* in Latin means "light bearer."

the direful effects of disobedience; he saw her not possessed of that wisdom which she had fondly hoped to obtain, but he beheld the once blooming female disrobed of that innocence which had heretofore rendered her so lovely. To him, then, deception became impossible, as he had proof positive of the fallacy of the argument which the deceiver had suggested. What then could be his inducement to burst the barriers, and to fly directly in the face of that command, which *immediately* from the mouth of deity *he* had received, since, I say, he could not plead that fascinating stimulus, the accumulation of knowledge, as indisputable conviction was so visibly portrayed before him. What mighty cause impelled him to sacrifice myriads of beings yet unborn, and by one impious act, which *he saw* would be productive of such fatal effects, entail undistinguished ruin upon a race of beings which he was yet to produce. Blush, ye vaunters of fortitude, ye boasters of resolution, ye haughty lords of the creation; blush when ye remember that he was influenced by no other motive than a bare pusillanimous attachment to a woman! by sentiments so exquisitely soft that all his sons have from that period, when they have designed to degrade them, described as highly feminine. Thus it should seem that all the arts of the grand deceiver (since means adequate to the purpose are, I conceive, invariably pursued) were requisite to mislead our general mother, while the father of mankind forfeited his own, and relinquished the happiness of posterity, merely in compliance with the blandishments of a female. The subsequent subjection the apostle Paul explains as a figure; after enlarging upon the subject, he adds, "*This is a great mystery; but I speak concerning Christ and the church.*"[9] Now we know with what consummate wisdom the unerring father of eternity hath formed his plans; all the types which he hath displayed he hath permitted *materially* to fail, in the very virtue for which *they* were famed. The reason for this is obvious; we might otherwise mistake his economy and render that honor to the creature which is due only to the creator. I know that Adam was a figure of Him who was to come.[1] The Grace contained in this figure is the reason of my rejoicing, and while I am very far from prostrating before the shadow, I yield joyfully in all things the preeminence to the Second Federal Head.[2] Confiding faith is prefigured by Abraham, yet he exhibits a contrast to affiance when he says of his fair companion, she is my sister.[3] Gentleness was the characteristic of Moses,[4] yet he hesitated not to reply to Jehovah Himself. With unsaintlike tongue he murmured at the waters of strife, and with rash hands he break the Tables[5] which were inscribed by the finger of divinity. David, dignified with the title of the man after God's own heart, and yet how stained was his life. Solomon[6] was celebrated for wisdom, but folly is wrote in legible characters upon his almost every action. Lastly, let us turn our

---

9. Ephesians 5.32.
1. Adam prefigures Jesus.
2. Jesus. Jesus is the "second federal head" because he made a new Covenant of Faith with man after Adam broke God's Covenant of Works. "Federal" comes from the Latin word meaning "compact" or "treaty."
3. When Abraham, the first patriarch and progenitor of the Hebrews, is about to enter Egypt with his wife, he fears for his life and asks her: "Say, I pray thee, thou art my sister: that it may be well with me for thy sake; and my soul shall live because of thee" (Genesis 12.13). "Affiance": plighted faith;

marriage.
4. The lawgiver who led the Israelites out of Egypt: "Now the man Moses was very meek, above all the men which were upon the face of the earth" (Numbers 12.3).
5. Tablets. The Ten Commandments were inscribed on stone, and Moses broke the first tablets (Exodus 32.19).
6. King of Israel (10th century B.C.E.), son of David and Bathsheba, famous for his riches and his wisdom, but a man who worshiped false gods and failed to keep God's commandments (1 Kings 11.1–10).

eyes to man in the aggregate. He is manifested as the figure of strength, but that we may not regard him as any thing more than a figure, his soul is formed in no sort superior, but every way equal to the mind of her who is the emblem of weakness and whom he hails the gentle companion of his better days.

1790, 1995

PHILIP FREENEAU
1752–1832

Philip Freneau had all the advantages that wealth and social position could bestow, and the Freneau household in Manhattan was frequently visited by well-known writers and painters. Philip received a good education at the hands of tutors and at fifteen entered the sophomore class at the College of New Jersey (now Princeton University). There he became fast friends with his roommate, James Madison, a future president, and a classmate, Hugh Henry Brackenridge, who became a successful novelist. In their senior year Freneau and Brackenridge composed an ode on *The Rising Glory of America*, and Brackenridge read the poem at commencement. It establishes early in Freneau's career his recurrent vision of a glorious future in which America would fulfill the collective hope of humankind:

> Paradise anew
> Shall flourish, by no second Adam lost,
> No dangerous tree with deadly fruit shall grow,
> No tempting serpent to allure the soul
> From native innocence. . . . The lion and the lamb
> In mutual friendship linked, shall browse the shrub,
> And timorous deer with softened tigers stray
> O'er mead, or lofty hill, or grassy plain.

For a short time Freneau taught school. He hoped to make a career as a writer, but it was an impractical wish. When he was offered a position as secretary on a plantation in the West Indies in 1776, he sailed to St. Croix and remained there almost three years. It was on that island, where "Sweet orange groves in lonely valleys rise," that Freneau wrote some of his most sensuous lyrics, but as he tells us in *To Sir Toby*, he could not talk of "blossoms" and an "endless spring" forever in a land that abounded in poverty and misery and where the owners grew wealthy on a slave economy. In 1778 he returned home and enlisted as a seaman on a blockade runner; two years later he was captured at sea and imprisoned on the British ship *Scorpion*, anchored in New York harbor. He was treated brutally, and when he was exchanged from the hospital ship *Hunter* his family feared for his life.

Freneau was to spend ten more years of his life at sea, first as a master of a merchant ship in 1784, and again in 1803, but immediately after he regained his health, he moved to Philadelphia to work in the post office, and it was in that city that he gained his reputation as a satirist, journalist, and poet. As editor of the *Freeman's Journal*, Freneau wrote impassioned verse in support of the American Revolution and turned all his rhetorical gifts against anyone thought to be in sympathy with the British monarchy. It was during this period in his life that he became identified as the "Poet of the American Revolution." In 1791, after he returned from duties at sea, Jefferson, as secretary of state, offered him a position as translator in his department, with the understanding that Freneau would have plenty of free time to devote to his newspaper, the *National Gazette*. Like Thomas Paine, Freneau was a strong supporter of the French Revolution, and he had a sharp eye for anyone not sympathetic to the democratic cause. He had a special grudge against Alexander Hamilton, secretary of the treasury, as chief spokesman for the Federalists. President Washington thought it was ironic that "that rascal Freneau" should be employed by his administration when he attacked it so outspokenly.

The *National Gazette* ceased publication in 1793, and after Jefferson resigned his office, Freneau left Philadelphia for good, alternating between ship's captain and newspaper editor in New York and New Jersey. He spent his last years on his New Jersey farm, unable to make it self-supporting and with no hope of further employment. Year after year he sold off the land he inherited from his father and was finally reduced to applying for a pension as a veteran of the American Revolution. He died impoverished and unknown, lost in a blizzard.

Freneau's biographer, Lewis Leary, subtitled his book *A Study in Literary Failure* and began that work by observing that "Philip Freneau failed in almost everything he attempted." Freneau's most sympathetic readers believe that he was born in a time not ripe for poetry and that his genuine lyric gifts were always in conflict with his political pamphleteering. Had he been born fifty years later, perhaps he could have joined Cooper and Irving in a life devoted exclusively to letters. There is no doubt that he did much to pave the way for these later writers. Freneau is not "the father of American poetry" (as his readers, eager for an advocate for a national literary consciousness, liked to call him), but his obsession with the beautiful, transient things of nature and the conflict in his art between the sensuous and the didactic are central to the concerns of American poetry.

Texts used are *The Poems of Philip Freneau* (1902), edited by F. L. Pattee; *The Poems of Freneau* (1929), edited by H. H. Clark; and *The Last Poems of Philip Freneau* (1945), edited by Lewis Leary.

From The House of Night

From *A Vision*

Advertisement——This Poem is founded upon the authority of Scripture, inasmuch as these sacred books assert, that *the last enemy that shall be conquered is Death.*[1] For the purposes of poetry he is here personified, and represented as on his dying bed. The scene is laid at a solitary palace, (the time midnight), which, though before beautiful and joyous, is now become sad and gloomy, as being the abode and receptacle of Death. Its owner, an amiable, majestic youth, who had lately lost a beloved consort,[2] nevertheless with a noble philosophical fortitude and humanity, entertains him in a friendly manner, and by employing Physicians, endeavors to restore him to health, although an enemy; convinced of the excellence and propriety of that divine precept, *If thine enemy hunger, feed him; if he thirst, give him drink.*[3] He nevertheless, as if by a spirit of prophecy, informs this (fictitiously) wicked being of the certainty of his doom, and represents to him in a pathetic manner the vanity of his expectations, either of a reception into the abodes of the just, or continuing longer to make havoc of mankind upon earth. The patient finding his end approaching, composes his epitaph, and orders it to be engraved on his tombstone, hinting to us thereby, that even Death and

1. 1 Corinthians 15.26.
2. Wife and companion.
3. Romans 12.20.

Distress have vanity; and would be remembered with honor after he is no more, although his whole life has been spent in deeds of devastation and murder. He dies at last in the utmost agonies of despair, after agreeing with the avaricious Undertaker to intomb his bones. This reflects upon the inhumanity of those men, who, not to mention an enemy, would scarcely cover a departed friend with a little dust, without certainty of a reward for so doing. The circumstances of his funeral are then recited, and the visionary and fabulous part of the poem disappears. It concludes with a few reflections on the impropriety of a too great attachment to the present life, and incentives to such moral virtue as may assist in conducting us to a better.

1

Trembling I write my dream, and recollect
A fearful vision at the midnight hour;
So late, Death o'er me spread his sable wings,
Painted with fancies of malignant power!

*　*　*

3

Let others draw from smiling skies their theme,
And tell of climes that boast unfading light,   10
I draw a darker scene, replete with gloom,
I sing the horrors of the House of Night.

4

Stranger, believe the truth experience tells,
Poetic dreams are of a finer cast
Than those which o'er the sober brain diffused,   15
Are but a repetition of some action past.

5

Fancy, I own[4] thy power—when sunk in sleep
Thou play'st thy wild delusive part so well
You lift me into immortality,
Depict new heavens, or draw the scenes of hell.   20

6

By some sad means, when Reason holds no sway,
Lonely I roved at midnight o'er a plain
Where murmuring streams and mingling rivers flow,
Far to their springs, or seek the sea again.

7

Sweet vernal May! though then thy woods in bloom   25
Flourished, yet nought of this could Fancy see,
No wild pinks blessed the meads,[5] no green the fields,
And naked seemed to stand each lifeless tree:

*　*　*

4. Acknowledge. "Fancy": imagination.　　　5. Meadows.

11

At last, by chance and guardian fancy led,
I reached a noble dome, raised fair and high,
And saw the light from upper windows flame,
Presage of mirth and hospitality.

12

And by that light around the dome appeared   45
A mournful garden of autumnal hue,
Its lately pleasing flowers all drooping stood
Amidst high weeds that in rank plenty grew.

13

The primrose there, the violet darkly blue,
Daisies and fair narcissus ceased to rise,   50
Gay spotted pinks their charming bloom withdrew,
And polyanthus quenched its thousand dyes.

14

No pleasant fruit or blossom gaily smiled.
Nought but unhappy plants or trees were seen,
The yew, the myrtle, and the church-yard elm,   55
The cypress, with its melancholy green.[6]

15

There cedars dark, the osier, and the pine,
Shorn tamarisks, and weeping willows grew,
The poplar tall, the lotos, and the lime,
And pyracantha did her leaves renew.   60

16

The poppy there, companion to repose,
Displayed her blossoms that began to fall,
And here the purple amaranthus rose
With mint strong-scented, for the funeral.

17

And here and there with laurel shrubs between   65
A tombstone lay, inscribed with strains of woe,
And stanzas sad, throughout the dismal green,
Lamented for the dead that slept below.

18

Peace to this awful dome!—when straight[7] I heard
The voice of men in a secluded room,   70
Much did they talk of death, and much of life,
Of coffins, shrouds, and horrors of a tomb.

6. All the trees and plants mentioned here and in the lines following are identified in mythology with sleep and death.
7. Immediately. "Awful": awesome.

19

Pathetic were their words, and well they aimed
To explain the mystic paths of providence,
Learned were they all, but there remained not I   75
To hear the upshot of their conference.

20

Meantime from an adjoining chamber came
Confuséd murmurings, half distinguished sounds,
And as I nearer drew, disputes arose
Of surgery, and remedies for wounds.   80

* * *

23

Then up three winding stairs my feet were brought
To a high chamber, hung with mourning sad,   90
The unsnuffed candles glared with visage dim,
'Midst grief, in ecstasy of woe run mad.

24

A wide leafed table stood on either side,
Well fraught with phials, half their liquids spent,
And from a couch, behind the curtain's veil,   95
I heard a hollow voice of loud lament.

25

Turning to view the object whence it came,
My frighted eyes a horrid form surveyed;
Fancy, I own thy power—Death on the couch,
With fleshless limbs, at rueful length, was laid.   100

* * *

28

Sad was his countenance, if we can call
That countenance, where only bones were seen   110
And eyes sunk in their sockets, dark and low,
And teeth, that only showed themselves to grin.

29

Reft was his skull of hair, and no fresh bloom
Of cheerful mirth sate[8] on his visage hoar:
Sometimes he raised his head, while deep-drawn groans   115
Were mixed with words that did his fate deplore.

30

Oft did he wish to see the daylight spring,
And often toward the window leaned to hear,
Forerunner of the scarlet-mantled morn,
The early note of wakeful chanticleer.[9]   120

8. Sat.   9. Rooster.

31

Thus he—But at my hand a portly[1] youth
Of comely countenance, began to tell,
"That this was Death upon his dying bed,
"Sullen, morose, and peevish to be well;

32

"Fixed is his doom—the miscreant reigns no more   125
"The tyrant of the dying or the dead;
"This night concludes his all-consuming reign,
"Pour out, ye heav'ns, your vengeance on his head."

*   *   *

47

But now this man of hell toward me turned,   185
And straight, in hideous tone, began to speak,
Long held he sage discourse, but I forebore
To answer him, much less his news to seek.

48

He talked of tombstones and of monuments,
Of equinoctial climes[2] and India shores,   190
He talked of stars that shed their influence,[3]
Fevers and plagues, and all their noxious stores.

*   *   *

50

Much spoke he of the myrtle and the yew,
Of ghosts that nightly walk the church-yard o'er
Of storms that through the wint'ry ocean blow
And dash the well-manned galley on the shore,   200

51

Of broad-mouthed cannons, and the thunderbolt,
Of sieges and convulsions, dearth and fire,
Of poisonous weeds—but seemed to sneer at these
Who by the laurel o'er him did aspire.

52

Then with a hollow voice thus went he on,   205
"Get up, and search, and bring, when found, to me,
"Some cordial, potion, or some pleasant draught,
"Sweet, slumb'rous poppy, or the mild Bohea.[4]

53

"But hark, my pitying friend!—and, if you can,
"Deceive the grim physician at the door—   210

---

1. Dignified.
2. Places on or near the equator.
3. An emanation from the stars. Ancient astrolo-
gers argued that a stream of heavenly fluid affected
human destiny and caused epidemics.
4. Tea.

"Bring half the mountain springs—ah! hither bring
"The cold rock water from the shady bower.

54

"For till this night such thirst did ne'er invade,
"A thirst provoked by heav'n's avenging hand;
"Hence bear me, friends, to quaff, and quaff again   215
"The cool wave bubbling from the yellow sand.

55

"To these dark walls with stately step I came,
"Prepared your drugs and doses to defy;
"Smit with the love of never dying fame,
"I came, alas! to conquer—not to die!"   220

*   *   *

88

Up rushed a band, with compasses and scales
To measure his slim carcass, long and lean—   350
"Be sure," said he, "to frame my coffin strong,
"You, master workman, and your men, I mean:

89

"For if the Devil, so late my trusty friend,
"Should get one hint where I am laid, from you,
"Not with my soul content, he'd seek to find   355
"That moldering mass of bones, my body, too!

90

"Of hardest ebon let the plank be found,
"With clamps and ponderous bars secured around,
"That if the box by Satan should be stormed,
"It may be able for resistance found."   360

*   *   *

125

At distance far approaching to the tomb,
By lamps and lanterns guided through the shade,
A coal-black chariot hurried through the gloom,
Specters attending, in black weeds arrayed,   500

126

Whose woeful forms yet chill my soul with dread,
Each wore a vest in Stygian[5] chambers wove,
Death's kindred all—Death's horses they bestrode,
And galloped fiercely, as the chariot drove.

---

5. Hellish; from the name of the river Styx, over which, in Greek mythology, the souls of the dead must cross.

127

Each horrid face a grisly mask concealed,   505
Their busy eyes shot terror to my soul
As now and then, by the pale lantern's glare,
I saw them for their parted friend condole.

128

Before the hearse Death's chaplain seemed to go,
Who strove to comfort, what he could, the dead;   510
Talked much of Satan, and the land of woe,
And many a chapter from the scriptures read.

129

At last he raised the swelling anthem high,
In dismal numbers seemed he to complain;
The captive tribes that by Euphrates[6] wept,   515
Their song was jovial to his dreary strain.

130

That done, they placed the carcass in the tomb,
To dust and dull oblivion now resigned,
Then turned the chariot toward the House of Night,
Which soon flew off, and left no trace behind.   520

131

But as I stooped to write the appointed[7] verse,
Swifter than thought the airy scene decayed;
Blushing the morn arose, and from the east
With her gay streams of light dispelled the shade.

132

What is this Death, ye deep read sophists,[8] say?—   525
Death is no more than one unceasing change;
New forms arise, while other forms decay,
Yet all is Life throughout creation's range.

133

The towering Alps, the haughty Appenine,
The Andes, wrapt in everlasting snow,   530
The Appalachian and the Ararat[9]
Sooner or later must to ruin go.

134

Hills sink to plains, and man returns to dust,
That dust supports a reptile or a flower;

6. The Euphrates is one of the rivers of paradise (Genesis 2.14) and marked the northern limit of the land promised to the Israelites. Here those Israelites in bondage to the Babylonians weep for the land they have lost. Cf. Psalm 137.
7. Required.
8. Teachers of philosophy.

9. The highest mountain in Turkey. The Alps are mountains in south-central Europe. The Appenine mountains are in Italy. The Andes are in South America. The Appalachians are in eastern North America and run from Newfoundland to Alabama.

Each changeful atom by some other nursed   535
Takes some new form, to perish in an hour.

135

Too nearly joined to sickness, toils, and pains,
(Perhaps for former crimes imprisoned here)
True to itself the immortal soul remains,
And seeks new mansions in the starry sphere.   540

136

When Nature bids thee from the world retire,
With joy thy lodging leave, a fated guest;
In Paradise, the land of thy desire,
Existing always, always to be blest.

1777–78   1779, 1786

On the Emigration to America and Peopling the Western Country

To western woods, and lonely plains,
Palemon[1] from the crowd departs,
Where Nature's wildest genius reigns,
To tame the soil, and plant the arts—
What wonders there shall freedom show,   5
What mighty states successive grow!

From Europe's proud, despotic shores
Hither the stranger takes his way,
And in our new found world explores
A happier soil, a milder sway,   10
Where no proud despot holds him down,
No slaves insult him with a crown.

What charming scenes attract the eye,
On wild Ohio's savage stream!
There Nature reigns, whose works outvie   15
The boldest pattern art can frame;
There ages past have rolled away,
And forests bloomed but to decay.

From these fair plains, these rural seats,
So long concealed, so lately known,   20
The unsocial Indian far retreats,
To make some other clime his own,
Where other streams, less pleasing flow,
And darker forests round him grow.

1. Conventionally, any young man setting out on a journey. Palemon appears in Chaucer's "Knight's Tale,"
an adaptation of Boccaccio's *Teseide*.

Great sire[2] of floods! whose varied wave   25
Through climes and countries takes its way,
To whom creating Nature gave
Ten thousand streams to swell thy sway!
No longer shall *they* useless prove,
Nor idly through the forests rove;   30

Nor longer shall your princely flood
From distant lakes be swelled in vain,
Nor longer through a darksome wood
Advance, unnoticed, to the main,[3]
Far other ends, the heavens decree—   35
And commerce plans new freights for thee.

While virtue warms the generous breast,
There heaven-born freedom shall reside,
Nor shall the voice of war molest,
Nor Europe's all-aspiring pride—   40
There Reason shall new laws devise,
And order from confusion rise.

Forsaking kings and regal state,
With all their pomp and fancied bliss,
The traveler owns,[4] convinced though late,   45
No realm so free, so blessed as this—
The east is half to slaves consigned,
Where kings and priests enchain the mind.

O come the time, and haste the day,
When man shall man no longer crush,   50
When Reason shall enforce her sway,
Nor these fair regions raise our blush,
Where still the *African* complains,
And mourns his yet unbroken chains.

Far brighter scenes a future age,   55
The muse predicts, these states will hail,
Whose genius may the world engage,
Whose deeds may over death prevail,
And happier systems bring to view,
Than all the eastern sages knew.   60

1785

The Wild Honey Suckle

Fair flower, that dost so comely grow,
Hid in this silent, dull retreat,
Untouched thy honeyed blossoms blow,[1]

---

2. Mississippi [Freneau's note].   4. Admits.
3. Ocean.   1. Bloom.

Unseen thy little branches greet:
　No roving foot shall crush thee here,　　　　　　　　　5
　No busy hand provoke a tear.

By Nature's self in white arrayed,
She bade thee shun the vulgar² eye,
And planted here the guardian shade,
And sent soft waters murmuring by;　　　　　　　　　10
　Thus quietly thy summer goes,
　Thy days declining to repose.

Smit with those charms, that must decay,
I grieve to see your future doom;
They died—nor were those flowers more gay,　　　　　15
The flowers that did in Eden bloom;
　Unpitying frosts, and Autumn's power
　Shall leave no vestige of this flower.

From morning suns and evening dews
At first thy little being came:　　　　　　　　　　20
If nothing once, you nothing lose,
For when you die you are the same;
　The space between, is but an hour,
　The frail duration of a flower.

　　　　　　　　　　　　　　　　1786

The Indian Burying Ground

In spite of all the learned have said,
I still my old opinion keep;
The *posture*, that *we* give the dead,
Points out the soul's eternal sleep.

Not so the ancients of these lands—　　　　　　　　5
The Indian, when from life released,
Again is seated¹ with his friends,
And shares again the joyous feast.

His imaged birds, and painted bowl,
And venison, for a journey dressed,　　　　　　　　10
Bespeak the nature of the soul,
Activity, that knows no rest.

His bow, for action ready bent,
And arrows, with a head of stone,
Can only mean that life is spent,　　　　　　　　　15
And not the old ideas gone.

2. Common; unfeeling.
1. The North American Indians bury their dead in a sitting posture; decorating the corpse with wam-
pum, the images of birds, quadrupeds, etc.: And (if that of a warrior) with bows, arrows, tomahawks and other military weapons [Freneau's note].

Thou, stranger, that shalt come this way,
No fraud upon the dead commit—
Observe the swelling turf, and say
They do not *lie*, but here they *sit*.   20

Here still a lofty rock remains,
On which the curious eye may trace
(Now wasted, half, by wearing rains)
The fancies of a ruder race.

Here still an agéd elm aspires,   25
Beneath whose far-projecting shade
(And which the shepherd still admires)
The children of the forest played!

There oft a restless Indian queen
(Pale Sheba,[2] with her braided hair)   30
And many a barbarous form is seen
To chide the man that lingers there.

By midnight moons, o'er moistening dews,
In habit for the chase arrayed,
The hunter still the deer pursues,   35
The hunter and the deer, a shade!

And long shall timorous fancy see
The painted chief, and pointed spear,
And Reason's self shall bow the knee
To shadows and delusions here.   40

1788

To Sir Toby[1]

*A Sugar Planter in the Interior Parts of Jamaica, Near the City of San
Jago de la Vega (Spanish Town), 1784*

> "The motions of his spirit are black as night,
> And his affections dark as Erebus."
> —Shakespeare[2]

If there exists a hell—the case is clear—
Sir Toby's slaves enjoy that portion here:
Here are no blazing brimstone lakes—'tis true;
But kindled rum too often burns as blue;
In which some fiend, whom nature must detest,   5
Steeps Toby's brand, and marks poor Cudjoe's[3] breast.

2. Sheba is the queen who visited Solomon to test
his wisdom (1 Kings 10.1–13).
1. First published in the *Daily Advertiser*, February
1, 1791, titled *The Island Field Negro*. The text
used here is the 1809 version.
2. *The Merchant of Venice* 5.1.79. Freneau has
substituted the word *black* for "dull." "Erebus": in
Greek mythology the region beneath the earth

through which the dead must pass before entering
Hades.
3. "Cudge" or "Cudjoe" was a common name for
a slave. "This passage has a reference to the West
Indian custom (sanctioned by law) of branding a
newly imported slave on the breast, with a red hot
iron, as evidence of the purchaser's property" [Fre-
neau's note].

Here whips on whips excite perpetual fears,
And mingled howlings vibrate on my ears:
Here Nature's plagues abound, to fret and tease,
Snakes, scorpions, despots, lizards, centipedes—   10
No art, no care escapes the busy lash;
All have their dues—and all are paid in cash—
The eternal driver keeps a steady eye
On a black herd, who would his vengeance fly,
But chained, imprisoned, on a burning soil,   15
For the mean avarice of a tyrant toil![4]
The lengthy cart-whip guards this monster's reign—
And cracks, like pistols, from the fields of cane.
    Ye powers! who formed these wretched tribes, relate,
What had they done, to merit such a fate!   20
Why were they brought from Eboe's[5] sultry waste,
To see that plenty which they must not taste—
Food, which they cannot buy, and dare not steal;
Yams and potatoes—many a scanty meal!—
    One, with a gibbet[6] wakes his negro's fears,   25
One to the windmill nails him by the ears;
One keeps his slave in darkened dens, unfed,
One puts the wretch in pickle ere he's dead:
This, from a tree suspends him by the thumbs,
That, from his table grudges even the crumbs!   30
    O'er yond' rough hills a tribe of females go,
Each with her gourd,[7] her infant, and her hoe;
Scorched by a sun that has no mercy here,
Driven by a devil, whom men call overseer—
In chains, twelve wretches to their labors haste;   35
Twice twelve I saw, with iron collars graced!—
    Are such the fruits that spring from vast domains?
Is wealth, thus got, Sir Toby, worth your pains!—
Who would your wealth on terms, like these, possess,
Where all we see is pregnant with distress—   40
Angola's[8] natives scourged by ruffian hands,
And toil's hard product shipped to foreign lands.
    Talk not of blossoms, and your endless spring;
What joy, what smile, can scenes of misery bring?—
Though Nature, here, has every blessing spread,   45
Poor is the laborer—and how meanly fed!—
    Here Stygian[9] paintings light and shade renew,
Pictures of hell, that Virgil's[1] pencil drew:
Here, surly Charons[2] make their annual trip,

---

4. Lines 13–16 were added in 1809.
5. A small Negro kingdom near the river Senegal [Freneau's note].
6. Gallows.
7. Water cup.
8. West African Portuguese colony.
9. Hellish; taken from the river Styx over which, in Greek mythology, souls of the dead must cross.
1. "See *Aeneid,* Book 6th.—and Fenelon's Telem-

achus, Book 18" [Freneau's note]. Aeneas descends to the underworld in the sixth book of the Latin poet Virgil's (70–19 B.C.E.) epic. François de Salignac de la Mothe-Fénelon (1651–1715) was a theologian and the author of *Télémaque* (1699), a didactic romance concerning the son of Ulysses as he searches for his father.
2. In Greek mythology, Charon ferries the souls of the dead over the river Styx to Hades.

And ghosts arrive in every Guinea ship,[3]   50
To find what beasts these western isles afford,
Plutonian[4] scourges, and despotic lords:—
   Here, they, of stuff determined to be free,
Must climb the rude cliffs of the Liguanee;[5]
Beyond the clouds, in sculking haste repair,   55
And hardly safe from brother traitors[6] there.—

1784   1791, 1809

On Mr. Paine's Rights of Man[1]

Thus briefly sketched the sacred rights of man,
How inconsistent with the royal plan!
Which for itself exclusive honor craves,
Where some are masters born, and millions slaves.
With what contempt must every eye look down   5
On that base, childish bauble called a *crown*,
The gilded bait, that lures the crowd, to come,
Bow down their necks, and meet a slavish doom;
The source of half the miseries men endure,
The quack[2] that kills them, while it seems to cure,   10
   Roused by the reason of his manly page,
Once more shall Paine a listening world engage:
From Reason's source, a bold reform he brings,
In raising up *mankind*, he pulls down *kings*,
Who, source of discord, patrons of all wrong,   15
On blood and murder have been fed too long:
Hid from the world, and tutored to be base,
The curse, the scourge, the ruin of our race,
Theirs was the task, a dull designing few,
To shackle beings that they scarcely knew,   20
Who made this globe the residence of slaves,
And built their thrones on systems formed by knaves
—Advance, bright years, to work their final fall,
And haste the period that shall crush them all.
   Who, that has read and scanned the historic page   25
But glows, at every line, with kindling rage,
To see by them the rights of men aspersed,
Freedom restrained, and Nature's law reversed,
Men, ranked with beasts, by monarchs willed away,
And bound young fools, or madmen to obey: 30
Now driven to wars, and now oppressed at home,

3. Slave ship from West Africa.
4. Hellish; in Roman mythology Pluto was the god of the underworld.
5. The mountains northward of the kingdom [Freneau's note].
6. Alluding to the *Independent* negroes in the blue mountains, who, for a stipulated reward, deliver up every fugitive that falls into their hands, to the English Government [Freneau's note].

1. The original title was "To a Republican with Mr. Paine's Rights of Man." Thomas Paine read Edmund Burke's "Reflections on the French Revolution" (1790), a defense of monarchy and an attack on revolution, when he was living in England. In *The Rights of Man* (1791–92) Paine argued for the overthrow of monarchy and the right of the people to govern themselves.
2. One pretending to be a physician.

Compelled in crowds o'er distant seas to roam,
From India's climes the plundered prize to bring
To glad the strumpet, or to glut the king.
  Columbia,[3] hail! immortal be thy reign: 35
Without a king, we till the smiling plain;
Without a king, we trace the unbounded sea,
And traffic round the globe, through each degree;
Each foreign clime our honored flag reveres,
Which asks no monarch, to support the stars: 40
Without a *king*, the laws maintain their sway,
While honor bids each generous heart obey.
Be ours the task the ambitious to restrain,
And this great lesson teach—that kings are vain;
That warring realms to certain ruin haste,   45
That kings subsist by war, and wars are waste:
So shall our nation, formed on Virtue's plan,
Remain the guardian of the Rights of Man,
A vast republic, famed through every clime,
Without a king, to see the end of time.   50

1795

On the Religion of Nature

The power, that gives with liberal hand
  The blessings man enjoys, while here,
And scatters through a smiling land
  Abundant products of the year;
    That power of nature, ever blessed,   5
    Bestowed religion with the rest.

Born with ourselves, her early sway
  Inclines the tender mind to take
The path of right, fair virtue's way
  Its own felicity to make.   10
    This universally extends
    And leads to no mysterious ends.

Religion, such as nature taught,
  With all divine perfection suits;
Had all mankind this system sought   15
    Sophists[1] would cease their vain disputes,
    And from this source would nations know
    All that can make their heaven below.

This deals not curses on mankind,
  Or dooms them to perpetual grief,   20

---

3. The personification of America (from Christopher Columbus).

1. Teachers of philosophy.

If from its aid no joys they find,
   It damns them not for unbelief;
     Upon a more exalted plan
     Creatress nature dealt with man—

Joy to the day, when all agree   25
   On such grand systems to proceed,
From fraud, design, and error free,
   And which to truth and goodness lead:
     Then persecution will retreat
     And man's religion be complete.   30

                                     1815

On Observing a Large Red-Streak Apple

In spite of ice, in spite of snow,
In spite of all the winds that blow,
In spite of hail and biting frost,
Suspended here I see you tossed
You still retain your wonted[1] hold   5
Though days are short and nights are cold.

Amidst this system of decay
How could you have one wish to stay?
If fate or fancy kept you there
They meant you for a solitaire.[2]   10
Were it not better to descend,
Or in the cider mill to end
Than thus to shiver in the storm
And not a leaf to keep you warm—
A moment, then, had buried all,   15
Nor you have doomed so late a fall.

But should the stem to which you cling
Uphold you to another spring,
Another race would round you rise
And view the *stranger* with surprise,   20
And, peeping from the blossoms say
Away, old dotard,[3] get away!

Alas! small pleasure can there be
To dwell, a hermit, on the tree—
Your old companions, all, are gone,   25
Have dropped, and perished, every one;
You only stay to face the blast,
A sad memento of the past.

1. Accustomed.
2. I.e., an isolated example.
3. Feebleminded old person.

Would fate or nature hear my prayer,
I would your bloom of youth repair   30
I would the wrongs of time restrain
And bring your blossom state again:
But fate and nature both say no;
And you, though late must perish too.

What can we say, what can we hope?   35
Ere from the branch I see you drop,
All I can do, all in my power
Will be to watch your parting hour:
When from the branch I see you fall,
A grave we dig a-south the wall.   40
There you shall sleep till from your core,
Of youngsters rises three or four;
These shall salute the coming spring
And red-streaks to perfection bring
When years have brought them to their prime   45
And they shall have their summer's time:
This, this is all you can attain,
And thus, I bid you, live again!

                                                                1822, 1945

To a New England Poet

Though skilled in Latin and in Greek,
And earning fifty cents a week,
Such knowledge, and the income, too,
Should teach you better what to do:
   The meanest drudges, kept in pay,   5
   Can pocket fifty cents a day.

Why stay in such a tasteless land,
Where all must on a level stand,
(Excepting people, at their ease,
Who choose the level where they please:)   10
   See Irving[1] gone to Britain's court
   To people of another sort,
He will return, with wealth and fame,
While Yankees hardly know your name.

Lo! he has kissed a Monarch's—hand!   15
Before a prince I see him stand,
And with the glittering nobles mix,
Forgetting times of seventy-six,[2]

1. Washington Irving (1783–1859) was the first American writer to gain an international reputation; Freneau objects to his success because in works like *Bracebridge Hall* (1822) Irving idealized English country life and often wrote as an American tourist awed by England's past.
2. The American Revolution of 1776.

While you with terror meet the frown
Of Bank Directors of the town,   20
  The home-made nobles of our times,
  Who hate the bard, and spurn his rhymes.

Why pause?—like Irving, haste away,
To England your addresses pay;
And England will reward you well,   25
When you some pompous story tell
  Of British feats, and British arms,
  The maids of honor, and their charms.

Dear bard, I pray you, take the hint,
In England what you write and print,   30
Republished here in shop, or stall,
Will perfectly enchant us all:
  It will assume a different face,
  And post your name at every place,
  From splendid domes of first degree   35
  Where ladies meet, to sip their tea;
  From marble halls, where lawyers plead,
  Or Congress-men talk loud, indeed,
  To huts, where evening clubs appear,
  And 'squires resort—to guzzle Beer.   40

1823, 1945

PHILLIS WHEATLEY
c. 1753–1784

Phillis Wheatley was either nineteen or twenty years old when her *Poems on Various Subjects, Religious and Moral* was published in London in 1773. At the time of its publication she was the object of considerable public attention because, in addition to being a child prodigy, Wheatley was a black slave, born in Africa (probably in present-day Senegal or Gambia) and brought to Boston in 1761. She had been purchased by a wealthy tailor, John Wheatley, for his wife, Susannah, as a companion, and named for the vessel that carried her to our shores. Wheatley was fortunate in her surroundings, for Susannah Wheatley was sympathetic toward this very frail and remarkably intelligent child. In an age in which few white women were given an education, Wheatley was taught to read and write, and in a short time began to read Latin writers. She came to know the Bible well, and three English poets—Milton, Pope, and Gray—touched her deeply and exerted a strong influence on her verse. The Wheatleys moved in a circle of enlightened Boston Christians, and Phillis, as James Levernier has recently shown, was introduced early on to a community that challenged the role of slavery as incompatible with Christian life. Wheatley's poem on the death of the Reverend George Whitefield, the great egalitarian English evangelist who frequently toured New England, made her famous. In June 1773, she arrived in London with her manuscript in the company of the Wheatleys' son Nathaniel. She went to England partly for reasons of health and partly to seek support for her first book. Benjamin Franklin and the lord mayor of London were among those who paid their respects. Her literary gifts, intelligence, and piety were a striking example to her English and American admirers of the triumph of the human spirit over the circumstances of birth. Her poems appeared early in September, and the governor of Massachusetts and John Wheatley and John Hancock were among the eighteen prominent citizens testifying that "under the Disadvantage of serving as a Slave in a Family in this Town," Wheatley "had been examined and thought qualified to write them."

Wheatley did not remain long enough in London to witness their publication; she was called back to Boston with the news that Susannah Wheatley was dying. Early in the fall of 1773 she was manumitted. Susannah Wheatley died in 1774, and John Wheatley, four years later. In that same year, 1778, she married John Peters, a freedman, about whom almost nothing is known other than that the Wheatleys did not like him, that he petitioned for a license to sell liquor in 1784, and that he may have been in debtor's prison when Wheatley died, having endured poverty and the loss of two children in her last years. On her deathbed her third child lay ill beside her and succumbed shortly after Wheatley herself. They were buried together in an unmarked grave. Five years earlier, and only one year after her marriage, a proposal appeared for a second volume of poetry to include thirteen letters and thirty-three poems. The volume was never published, and most of the poems and letters have yet to be found.

Wheatley's poetry was rediscovered in the 1830s by the New England abolitionists, but it is no exaggeration to say that she has never been better understood than at the present. Her recent critics have not only corrected a number of biographical errors but, more important, have provided a context in which her work can be best read and her life understood. This reconsideration shows Wheatley to be a bold and canny spokesperson for her faith and her politics; she early joined the cause of American independence and the abolition of slavery, anticipating her friend the Reverend Samuel Hopkins's complaint that when American Negroes first heard the "sons of liberty" cry for freedom they were shocked by indifference to their own "abject slavery and utter wretchedness." It doesn't take a philosopher, Wheatley told Samson Occom, a Presbyterian minister and Mohegan tribesman, to see that the exercise of slavery cannot be reconciled with a "principle" that God has implanted in every human breast, "Love of Freedom." She was mistaken in thinking that the conservative earl of Dartmouth (William Legge) might be sympathetic to the American cause but correct in reminding him that there could be no justice anywhere if people in authority were deaf to the history of human sorrow:

> Should you, my lord, while you peruse my song,
> Wonder from whence my love of Freedom sprung,
> Whence flow these wishes for the common good,
> By feeling hearts best understood,
> I, young in life, by seeming cruel fate
> Was snatched from Afric's fancied happy seat:
> What pangs excruciating must molest,
> What sorrows labor in my parent's breast?
> Steeled was that soul and by no misery moved
> That from a father seized his babe beloved:
> Such, such my case. And can I then but pray
> Others may never feel tyrannic sway?

With the publication of Wheatley's *Poems*, Henry Louis Gates Jr. has argued, "Wheatley launched two traditions at once—the black American literary tradition *and* the black woman's literary tradition. It is extraordinary that not just one but both of these traditions were founded simultaneously by a black woman—certainly an event unique in the history of literature—it is also ironic that this important fact of common, coterminous literary origin seems to have escaped most scholars."

The text used here for both the poem and the letters is *The Poems of Phillis Wheatley* (1966, rev. 1989) edited by Julian D. Mason. Wheatley's letters retain her spelling.

On Being Brought from Africa to America

'Twas mercy brought me from my pagan land,
Taught my benighted soul to understand
That there's a God, that there's a Savior too:
Once I redemption neither sought nor knew.
Some view our sable[1] race with scornful eye.   5
"Their color is a diabolic dye."
Remember, Christians, Negroes, black as Cain,[2]
May be refined, and join the angelic train.

1773

To Mæcenas[1]

Mæcenas, you, beneath the myrtle shade,
Read o'er what poets sung, and shepherds, played.
What felt those poets but you feel the same?
Does not your soul possess the sacred flame?
Their noble strains your equal genius shares   5
In softer language, and diviner airs.

While Homer paints lo! circumfused[2] in air,
Celestial Gods in moral forms appear;
Swift as they move hear each recess rebound,[3]
Heav'n quakes, earth trembles, and the shores resound.   10
Great Sire of verse, before my mortal eyes,
The lightnings blaze across the vaulted skies,
And, as the thunder shakes the heav'nly plains,
A deep-felt horror thrills through all my veins.
When gentler strains demand thy graceful song,   15
The length'ning line moves languishing along.
When great Patroclus courts Achilles'[4] aid,
The grateful tribute of my tears is paid;

1. Black.
2. Cain slew his brother Abel and was "marked" by God for doing so. This mark has sometimes been taken to be the origin of dark-skinned peoples (Genesis 4.1–15).
1. Gaius Cilnius Mæcenas (d. 8 B.C.E.), Roman aristocrat and statesman most famous as a patron of letters, especially poetry.
2. Enveloped. "Homer": the Greek poet tradition-

ally named as author of the 9th-century B.C.E. epic poems the *Iliad* and the *Odyssey*.
3. I.e., each withdrawal reverberate.
4. In the *Iliad*, the greatest warrior of the Greeks. When in his anger at the leader of the expedition Achilles refuses to fight, his closest friend, Patroclus, goes into battle wearing Achilles' armor and is killed.

Prone on the shore he feels the pangs of love,
And stern Pelides[5] tend'rest passons move.   20

Great Maro's strain in heav'nly numbers flows,
The Nine inspire, and all the bosom glows.
O could I rival thine and Virgil's page,
Or claim the Muses with the Mantuan Sage;[6]
Soon the same beauties should my mind adorn,   25
And the same ardors in my soul should burn:
Then should my song in bolder notes arise,
And all my numbers pleasingly surprize;
But here I sit, and mourn a grov'ling mind,
That fain would mount, and ride upon the wind.   30

Not you, my friend, these plaintive strains become,
Not you, whose bosom is the Muses home;
When they from tow'ring Helicon retire,
They fan in you the bright immortal fire,
But I less happy, cannot raise the song,   35
The fault'ring music dies upon my tongue.

The happier Terence[7] all the choir inspired,
His soul replenished, and his bosom fired;
But say, ye Muses, why this partial grace,
To one alone of Afric's sable[8] race   40
From age to age transmitting thus his name
With the first glory in the rolls of fame?

Thy virtues, great Maecenas! shall be sung
In praise of him, from whom those virtues sprung:
While blooming wreaths around thy temples spread,[9]   45
I'll snatch a laurel from thine honored head,
While you indulgent smile upon the deed.

As long as Thames in streams majestic flows,
Or Naiads[1] in their oozy beds repose,
While Phœbus reigns above the starry train,   50
While bright Aurora purples o'er the main,[2]
So long, great Sir, the muse thy praise shall sing,
So long thy praise shall make Parnassus[3] ring:
Then grant, Maecenas, thy paternal rays,
Hear me propitious, and defend my lays.[4]   55

1773

5. Another name for Achilles (literally, "son of Peleus"), who weeps for Patroclus.
6. The Roman poet Publius Vergilius Maro, or Virgil (70–19 B.C.E.), was born near Mantua. "Numbers": meter. "Muses": in Greek mythology the nine muses were goddesses of learning and the creative arts. They lived on Helicon, one of the two peaks of Mount Parnassus.
7. "He was an *African* by birth" [Wheatley's note]. Terence (c. 190–159 B.C.E.), who came to Rome as a slave from North Africa, gained great fame as a writer of comic plays in Latin.
8. Black.
9. In ancient times victors and heroes were crowned with wreaths of laurel or bay leaves.
1. In classical mythology the nymphs of rivers and lakes. "Thames": England's largest river.
2. Sea. In Roman mythology Aurora was the goddess of the dawn, who goes forth before the sun god, Phoebus Apollo.
3. The home of the nine Muses. See n. 6, above.
4. Songs; poems.

To the Right Honorable William, Earl of Dartmouth,[1] His Majesty's Principal Secretary of State for North America, &c.

Hail, happy day, when, smiling like the morn,
Fair Freedom rose New England to adorn:
The northern clime beneath her genial ray,
Dartmouth, congratulates thy blissful sway:
Elate with hope her race no longer mourns,   5
Each soul expands, each grateful bosom burns,
While in thine hand with pleasure we behold
The silken reins, and Freedom's charms unfold.
Long lost to realms beneath the northern skies
She shines supreme, while hated faction dies: 10
Soon as appeared the Goddess long desired,
Sick at the view, she[2] lanquished and expired;
Thus from the splendors of the morning light
The owl in sadness seeks the caves of night.

No more, America, in mournful strain   } 15
Of wrongs, and grievance unredressed complain, }
No longer shalt thou dread the iron chain,   }
Which wanton Tyranny with lawless hand
Had made, and with it meant t' enslave the land.

Should you, my lord, while you peruse my song,   20
Wonder from whence my love of Freedom sprung,
Whence flow these wishes for the common good,
By feeling hearts alone best understood,
I, young in life, by seeming cruel fate
Was snatch'd from Afric's fancied happy seat: 25
What pangs excruciating must molest,
What sorrows labor in my parent's breast?
Steeled was that soul and by no misery moved
That from a father seized his babe beloved:
Such, such my case. And can I then but pray   30
Others may never feel tyrannic sway?

For favors past, great Sir, our thanks are due,
And thee we ask thy favors to renew,
Since in thy pow'r,[3] as in thy will before,
To sooth the griefs, which thou did'st once deplore.   35
May heav'nly grace the sacred sanction give
To all thy works, and thou forever live
Not only on the wings of fleeting Fame,
Though praise immortal crowns the patriot's name,
But to conduct to heav'ns refulgent fane,[4]   40

---

1. William Legge (1731–1801), second earl of Dartmouth, was appointed secretary in charge of the American colonies in August 1772. Though sympathetic to the Methodist movement in England, he was not sympathetic to the cause of the American Revolution.
2. Faction. "The Goddess": freedom.
3. I.e., since it is in thy power.
4. Shining temple.

May fiery coursers sweep th' ethereal plain,[5]
And bear thee upwards to that blest abode,
Where, like the prophet, thou shalt find thy God.

1773

To the University of Cambridge, in New England[1]

While an intrinsic ardor prompts to write,
The muses promise to assist my pen;
'Twas not long since I left my native shore
The land of errors,[2] and Egyptian gloom:[3]
Father of mercy, 'twas Thy gracious hand   5
Brought me in safety from those dark abodes.

    Students, to you 'tis given to scan the heights
Above, to traverse the ethereal space,
And mark the systems of revolving worlds.
Still more, ye sons of science[4] ye receive   10
The blissful news by messengers from Heav'n,
How Jesus' blood for your redemption flows.
See Him with hands outstretched upon the cross;
Immense compassion in His bosom glows;
He hears revilers, nor resents their scorn: 15
What matchless mercy in the Son of God!
When the whole human race by sin had fall'n,
He deigned to die that they might rise again,
And share with Him in the sublimest skies,
Life without death, and glory without end.   20

    Improve[5] your privileges while they stay,
Ye pupils, and each hour redeem, that bears
Or good or bad report of you to Heav'n.
Let sin, that baneful evil to the soul,
By you be shunned, nor once remit your guard;   25
Suppress the deadly serpent in its egg.
Ye blooming plants of human race divine,
An Ethiop[6] tells you 'tis your greatest foe;
Its transient sweetness turns to endless pain,
And in immense perdition sinks the soul.   30

1767   1773

5. The heavens. "Coursers": steeds; horses.
1. Harvard.
2. I.e., theological errors, because Africa was unconverted.
3. "And Moses stretched forth his hand toward heaven; and there was a thick darkness in all the land of Egypt three days" (Exodus 10.22).
4. Knowledge.
5. Take advantage of.
6. Ethiopian. In Wheatley's time "Ethiopian" was a conventional name for the black peoples of Africa.

On the Death of the
Rev. Mr. George Whitefield,[1] 1770

Hail, happy saint, on thine immortal throne,
Possessed of glory, life, and bliss unknown;
We hear no more the music of thy tongue,
Thy wonted auditories[2] cease to throng.
Thy sermons in unequaled accents flowed,   5
And every bosom with devotion glowed;
Thou didst in strains of eloquence refined
Inflame the heart, and captivate the mind.
Unhappy we the setting sun deplore,
So glorious once, but ah! it shines no more.   10

  Behold the prophet in his towering flight!
He leaves the earth for heav'n's unmeasured height,
And worlds unknown receive him from our sight.
There Whitefield wings with rapid course his way,
And sails to Zion[3] through vast seas of day.   15
Thy prayers, great saint, and thine incessant cries
Have pierced the bosom of thy native skies.
Thou moon hast seen, and all the stars of light,
How he has wrestled with his God by night.
He prayed that grace in every heart might dwell,   20
He longed to see America excel;
He charged[4] its youth that every grace divine
Should with full luster in their conduct shine;
That Savior, which his soul did first receive,
The greatest gift that ev'n a God can give,   25
He freely offered to the numerous throng,
That on his lips with listening pleasure hung.

  "Take Him, ye wretched, for your only good,
Take Him ye starving sinners, for your food;
Ye thirsty, come to this life-giving stream,   30
Ye preachers, take Him for your joyful theme;
Take Him my dear Americans," he said,
"Be your complaints on His kind bosom laid:
Take Him, ye Africans, He longs for you,
Impartial Savior is His title due: 35
Washed in the fountain of redeeming blood,
You shall be sons, and kings, and priests to God."

  Great *Countess*,[5] we Americans revere
Thy name, and mingle in thy grief sincere;

---

1. British clergyman (1714–1770) and follower of John Wesley, the best-known revivalist in the 18th century. He made several visits to America and died in Newburyport, Massachusetts. This was Wheatley's first published poem, and it made her famous.
2. Listeners. "Wonted": accustomed.
3. Here, the heavenly city of God.
4. Exhorted.
5. Selina Shirley Hastings (1707–1791), countess of Huntington, was a strong supporter of George Whitefield and active in Methodist church affairs. Wheatley visited her in England in 1773.

New England deeply feels, the orphans mourn,   40
Their more than father will no more return.

    But, though arrested by the hand of death,
Whitefield no more exerts his laboring breath,
Yet let us view him in the eternal skies,
Let every heart to this bright vision rise;   45
While the tomb safe retains its sacred trust,
Till life divine re-animates his dust.

1770   1770, 1773

Thoughts on the Works of Providence

Arise, my soul, on wings enraptured, rise
To praise the monarch of the earth and skies,
Whose goodness and beneficence appear
As round its center moves the rolling year,
Or when the morning glows with rosy charms,   5
Or the sun slumbers in the ocean's arms:
Of light divine by a rich portion lent
To guide my soul, and favor my intent.
Celestial muse, my arduous flight sustain,
And raise my mind to a seraphic[1] strain!   10

    Adored forever be the God unseen,
Which round the sun revolves this vast machine,
Though to His eye its mass a point appears:
Adored the God that whirls surrounding spheres,
Which first ordained that mighty Sol[2] should reign   15
The peerless monarch of the ethereal train:
Of miles twice forty millions is his height,
And yet his radiance dazzles mortal sight
So far beneath—from him the extended earth
Vigor derives, and every flowery birth: 20
Vast through her orb she moves with easy grace
Around her Phœbus[3] in unbounded space;
True to her course the impetuous storm derides,
Triumphant o'er the winds, and surging tides.

    Almighty, in these wond'rous works of Thine,   25
What Power, what Wisdom, and what Goodness shine!
And are Thy wonders, Lord, by men explored,
And yet creating glory unadored!

    Creation smiles in various beauty gay,
While day to night, and night succeeds to day: 30
That Wisdom, which attends Jehovah's ways,

1. Angelic.
2. The sun.
3. Apollo, the Greek sun god.

Shines most conspicuous in the solar rays:
Without them, destitute of heat and light,
This world would be the reign of endless night:
In their excess how would our race complain,   35
Abhorring life! how hate its lengthened chain!
From air adust⁴ what numerous ills would rise?
What dire contagion taint the burning skies?
What pestilential vapors, fraught with death,
Would rise, and overspread the lands beneath?   40

    Hail, smiling morn, that from the orient main⁵
Ascending dost adorn the heavenly plain!
So rich, so various are thy beauteous dyes,
That spread through all the circuit of the skies,
That, full of thee, my soul in rapture soars,   45
And thy great God, the cause of all adores.

    O'er beings infinite His love extends,
His Wisdom rules them, and His Power defends.
When tasks diurnal⁶ tire the human frame,
The spirits faint, and dim the vital flame,   50
Then too that ever active bounty shines,
Which not infinity of space confines.
The sable veil, that Night in silence draws,
Conceals effects, but shows the Almighty Cause;
Night seals in sleep the wide creation fair,   55
And all is peaceful but the brow of care.
Again, gay Phœbus, as the day before,
Wakes every eye, but what shall wake no more;
Again the face of nature is renewed,
Which still appears harmonious, fair, and good.   60
May grateful strains salute the smiling morn,
Before its beams the eastern hills adorn!

    Shall day to day, and night to night conspire
To show the goodness of the Almighty Sire?
This mental voice shall man regardless hear,   65
And never, never raise the filial prayer?
Today, O hearken, nor your folly mourn
For time misspent, that never will return.

    But see the sons of vegetation rise,
And spread their leafy banners to the skies.   70
All-wise Almighty providence we trace
In trees, and plants, and all the flowery race;
As clear as in the nobler frame of man,
All lovely copies of the Maker's plan.
The power the same that forms a ray of light,   75
That called creation from eternal night.
"Let there be light," He said. From his profound⁷

4. Dried up.
5. Ocean. "Orient": eastern.
6. Daily.

7. Depths. "And God said, Let there be light: and
there was light" (Genesis 1.3).

Old Chaos heard, and trembled at the sound:
Swift as the word, inspired by power divine,
Behold the light around its maker shine,   80
The first fair product of the omnific God,
And now through all His works diffused abroad.

    As reason's powers by day our God disclose,
So we may trace Him in the night's repose:
Say what is sleep? and dreams how passing strange!   85
When action ceases, and ideas range
Licentious and unbounded o'er the plains,
Where Fancy's[8] queen in giddy triumph reigns.
Hear in soft strains the dreaming lover sigh
To a kind fair,[9] or rave in jealousy;   90
On pleasure now, and now on vengeance bent,
The laboring passions struggle for a vent.
What power, O man! thy reason then restores,
So long suspended in nocturnal hours?
What secret hand returns the mental train,   95
And gives improved thine active powers again?
From thee, O man, what gratitude should rise!
And, when from balmy sleep thou op'st thine eyes,
Let thy first thoughts be praises to the skies.
How merciful our God who thus imparts   100
O'erflowing tides of joy to human hearts,
When wants and woes might be our righteous lot,
Our God forgetting, by our God forgot!

    Among the mental powers a question rose,
"What most the image of the Eternal shows?"   105
When thus to Reason (so let Fancy rove)
Her great companion spoke, immortal Love.

    "Say, mighty power, how long shall strife prevail,
And with its murmurs load the whispering gale?
Refer the cause to Recollection's shrine,   110
Who loud proclaims my origin divine,
The cause whence heaven and earth began to be,
And is not man immortalized by me?
Reason let this most causeless strife subside."
Thus Love pronounced, and Reason thus replied.   115

    "Thy birth, celestial queen! 'tis mine to own,
In thee resplendent is the Godhead shown;
Thy words persuade, my soul enraptured feels
Resistless beauty which thy smile reveals."
Ardent she spoke, and, kindling at her charms,   120
She clasped the blooming goddess in her arms.

    Infinite Love wher'er we turn our eyes
Appears: this every creature's wants supplies;

---

8. The imagination in its image-making aspect.   9. Woman.

This most is heard in Nature's constant voice,
This makes the morn, and this the eve rejoice;   125
This bids the fostering rains and dews descend
To nourish all, to serve one general end,
The good of man: yet man ungrateful pays
But little homage, and but little praise.
To Him, whose works arrayed with mercy shine,   130
What songs should rise, how constant, how divine!

1773

To S.M.,[1] a Young African Painter, on Seeing His Works

To show the laboring bosom's deep intent,
And thought in living characters to paint,
When first thy pencil did those beauties give,
And breathing figures learnt from thee to live,
How did those prospects give my soul delight,   5
A new creation rushing on my sight?
Still, wond'rous youth! each noble path pursue,
On deathless glories fix thine ardent view:
Still may the painter's and the poet's fire
To aid thy pencil, and thy verse conspire!   10
And may the charms of each seraphic[2] theme
Conduct thy footsteps to immortal fame!
High to the blissful wonders of the skies
Elate thy soul, and raise thy wishful eyes.
Thrice happy, when exalted to survey   15
That splendid city, crowned with endless day,
Whose twice six gates[3] on radiant hinges ring:
Celestial Salem[4] blooms in endless spring.

    Calm and serene thy moments glide along,
And may the muse inspire each future song!   20
Still, with the sweets of contemplation blest,
May peace with balmy wings your soul invest!
But when these shades of time are chased away,
And darkness ends in everlasting day,
On what seraphic pinions shall we move,   25
And view the landscape in the realms above?
There shall thy tongue in heavenly murmurs flow,
And there my muse with heavenly transport glow:
No more to tell of Damon's[5] tender sighs,
Or rising radiance of Aurora's[6] eyes,   30

1. Scipio Moorhead, a servant to the Reverend
John Moorhead of Boston.
2. Angelic.
3. Heaven, like the city of Jerusalem, is thought to
have had twelve gates (as many gates as tribes of

Israel).
4. Heavenly Jerusalem.
5. In classical mythology Damon pledged his life
for his friend Pythias.
6. The Roman goddess of the dawn.

For nobler themes demand a nobler strain,
And purer language on the ethereal plain.[7]
Cease, gentle muse! the solemn gloom of night
Now seals the fair creation from my sight.

1773

To His Excellency General Washington[1]

Sir. I have taken the freedom to address your Excellency in the enclosed poem, and entreat your acceptance, though I am not insensible of its inaccuracies. Your being appointed by the Grand Continental Congress to be Generalissimo of the armies of North America, together with the fame of your virtues, excite sensations not easy to suppress. Your generosity, therefore, I presume, will pardon the attempt. Wishing your Excellency all possible success in the great cause you are so generously engaged in. I am,
Your Excellency's most obedient humble servant,
Phillis Wheatley

Providence, Oct. 26, 1775.
His Excellency Gen. Washington.

Celestial choir! enthroned in realms of light,
Columbia's[2] scenes of glorious toils I write.
While freedom's cause her anxious breast alarms,
She flashes dreadful in refulgent arms.
See mother earth her offspring's fate bemoan,   5
And nations gaze at scenes before unknown!
See the bright beams of heaven's revolving light
Involved in sorrows and the veil of night!
    The goddess comes, she moves divinely fair,
Olive and laurel[3] binds her golden hair: 10
Wherever shines this native of the skies,
Unnumbered charms and recent graces rise.
    Muse! bow propitious while my pen relates
How pour her armies through a thousand gates,
As when Eolus[4] heaven's fair face deforms,   15
Enwrapped in tempest and a night of storms;
Astonished ocean feels the wild uproar,
The refluent surges beat the sounding shore;
Or thick as leaves in Autumn's golden reign,
Such, and so many, moves the warrior's train.   20
In bright array they seek the work of war,
Where high unfurled the ensign[5] waves in air.
Shall I to Washington their praise recite?
Enough thou know'st them in the fields of fight.

7. In the heavens.
1. This poem was first published in the *Pennsylvania Magazine* when Thomas Paine was editor. After reading it, Washington invited Wheatley to meet him in Cambridge, Massachusetts, in February 1776.
2. This reference to America as "the land Columbus found" is believed to be the first in print.
3. Emblems of victory.
4. Ruler of the winds.
5. Flag or banner.

Thee, first in place and honors—we demand 25
The grace and glory of thy martial band.
Famed for thy valor, for thy virtues more,
Hear every tongue thy guardian aid implore!
  One century scarce performed its destined round,
When Gallic⁶ powers Columbia's fury found; 30
And so may you, whoever dares disgrace
The land of freedom's heaven-defended race!
Fixed are the eyes of nations on the scales,
For in their hopes Columbia's arm prevails.
Anon Britannia droops the pensive head, 35
While round increase the rising hills of dead.
Ah! cruel blindness to Columbia's state!
Lament thy thirst of boundless power too late.
  Proceed, great chief, with virtue on thy side,
Thy every action let the goddess guide. 40
A crown, a mansion, and a throne that shine,
With gold unfading, WASHINGTON! be thine.

1775–76   1776, 1834

Letters

To John Thornton,¹ London

[THE BIBLE MY CHIEF STUDY]

[Boston, April 21, 1772]

Hon'd, Sir

I rec'd your instructive favᵣ² of Feb. 29, for which, return you ten thousand thanks, I did not flatter myself with the tho'ts of your honouring me with an Answer to my letter, I thank you for recommending the Bible to be my chief Study, I find and Acknowledge it the best of Books, it contains an endless treasure of wisdom, and knowledge. O that my eyes were more open'd to see the real worth, and true excellence of the word of truth, my flinty heart Soften'd with the grateful dews of divine grace and the Stubborn will, and affections, bent on God alone their proper object, and the vitiated palate may be corrected to relish heav'nly things. It has pleas'd God to lay me on a bed of Sickness, and I knew not but my deathbed, but he has been graciously pleas'd to restore me in a great measure. I beg your prayers, that I may be made thankful for his paternal corrections, and that I may make a proper use of them to the glory of his grace. I am Still very weak & the Physicians, seem to think there is danger of a consumption.³ And O that when my flesh and my heart fail me God would be my strength and portion for ever, that I might put my whole trust and Confidence in him, who has promis'd never to forsake those who Seek him with the whole heart. You could not, I am

---

6. The French and Indian Wars (1754–63), between France and England, ended the French colonial empire in North America.
1. A London merchant (1720–1790) who was a devout Anglican and lived outside London at Clapham, where a small group of Christians were committed to helping the poor and abolishing slavery. He was a friend of John and Susannah Wheatley and sent them money to be used for work among the American Indians.
2. Favor, i.e., letter.
3. Disease of the lungs.

sure have express greater tenderness and affection for me, than by being a welwisher to my Soul, the friends of Souls bear Some resemblance to the father of Spirits and are made partakers of his divine Nature. I am affraid I have entruded on your patient, but if I had not tho't it ungrateful to omit writing in answer to your favour Should not have troubl'd you, but I can't expect you to answer this,

I am Sir with greatest respect,
your very hum. sert.
Phillis Wheatley

1989

To Arbour Tanner,[1] Newport, Rhode Island

[A SENSE OF THE BEAUTIES AND EXCELLENCE OF THE CRUCIFIED SAVIOUR]

[Boston, May 19, 1772]

Dear Sister

I rec'd your favour of February 6th for which I give you my sincere thanks, I greatly rejoice with you in that realizing view,[2] and I hope experience, of the Saving change which you So emphatically describe. Happy were it for us if we could arrive to that evangelical Repentance, and the true holiness of heart which you mention. Inexpressibly happy Should we be could we have a due Sense of the Beauties and excellence of the Crucified Saviour. In his Crucifixion may be seen marvellous displays of Grace and Love, Sufficient to draw and invite us to the rich and endless treasures of his mercy, let us rejoice in and adore the wonders of God's infinite Love in bringing us from a land Semblant of darkness itself, and where the divine light of revelation (being obscur'd) is as darkness. Here, the knowledge of the true God and eternal life are made manifest; But there, profound ignorance overshadows the Land, Your observation is true, namely, that there was nothing in us to recommend us to God. Many of our fellow creatures are pass'd by, when the bowels[3] of divine love expanded towards us. May this goodness & long Suffering of God lead us to unfeign'd repentance[.]

It gives me very great pleasure to hear of so many of my Nation, Seeking with eagerness the way to true felicity, O may we all meet at length in that happy mansion. I hope the correspondence between us will continue, (my being much indispos'd this winter past was the reason of my not answering yours before now) which correspondence I hope may have the happy effect of improving our mutual friendship. Till we meet in the regions of consummate blessedness, let us endeavor by the assistance of divine grace, to live the life, and we Shall die the death of the Righteous. May this be our happy case and of those who are travelling to the region of Felicity is the earnest request of your affectionate

Friend & hum. Sert.   Phillis Wheatley

1863

---

1. There are more extant Wheatley letters to Arbour (sometimes spelled "Obour") Tanner, a black servant in the family of James Tanner, than to any other person.
2. I.e., to a new realization of Christianity.
3. The seat of compassion.

To John Thornton, London

[THE GIFT OF GOD IS ETERNAL LIFE]

[Boston, December 1, 1773]

Hon'd Sir

It is with great satisfaction, I acquaint you with my experience of the goodness of God in safely conducting my passage over the mighty waters, and returning me in safety to my American Friends.[1] I presume you will Join with them and m[e] in praise to God for so distinguishing a favour, it was amazing Mercy, altogether unmerited by me: and if possible it is augmented by the consideration of the bitter r[e]verse, which is the deserved wages of my evil doings. The Apostle Paul, tells us that the wages of Sin is death.[2] I don't imagine he excepted any sin whatsoever being equally hateful in its nature in the sight of God, who is essential Purity.

Should we not sink hon'd Sir, under this Sentence of Death, pronounced on every Sin, from the comparatively least to the greatest, were not this blessed Co[n]trast annexed to it, "But the Gift of God is eternal Life,["] through Jesus Christ our Lord? It is his Gift. O let us be thankful for it! What a load is taken from the Sinner's Shoulder when he thinks that Jesus has done that work for him which he could never have done, and Suffer'd, that punishment of his imputed Rebellions, for which a long Eternity of Torments could not have made sufficient expiation. O that I could meditate continually on this work of wonde[r] in Deity itself. This, which Kings & Prophets have desir'd to see, & have not See[n]. This, which Angels are continually exploring, yet are not equal to the search,—Millions of Ages shall roll away, and they may try in vain to find out to perfection, the sublime mysteries of Christ's Incarnation. Nor will this desir[e] to look into the deep things of God, cease, in the Breasts of glorified Saints & Angels. It's duration will be coeval with Eternity. This Eternity how dreadf[ul,] how delightful! Delightful to those who have an interest in the Crucifi[ed] Saviour, who has dignified our Nature, by seating it at the Right Hand of the divine Majesty.— They alone who are thus interested have Cause to rejoi[ce] even on the brink of that Bottomless Profound:[3] and I doubt not (without the [lea]st Adulation) that you are one of that happy number. O pray that I may be one also, who Shall Join with you in Songs of praise at the Throne of him, who is no respecter of Persons: being equally the great Maker of all:—Therefor disdain not to be called the Father of Humble Africans and Indians; though despisd on earth on account of our colour, we have this Consolation, if he enables us to deserve it. "That God dwells in the humble & contrite heart." O that I were more & more possess'd of this inestimable blessing; to be directed by the immediate influence of the divine Spirit in my daily walk & Conversation.

Do you, my hon'd Sir, who have abundant Reason to be thankful for the great Share you possess of it, be always mindful in your Closet,[4] of those who want it—of me in particular.—When I first arrivd at home my mistress was so bad as not to be expected to live above two or three days, but through

---

1. Wheatley accompanied John Wheatley to London in the spring of 1773. Upon receiving news of Susannah Wheatley's illness, they left hurriedly, arriving in Boston on September 13.

2. "The wages of sin is death; but the gift of God is eternal life" (Romans 6.23).
3. Eternity.
4. Place of prayer, study.

the goodness of God She is still alive, but remains in a very weak & languishing Condition, She begs a continued interest in your most earnest prayers, that she may be surly prepar'd for that great Change which [She] is likely Soon to undergo; She intreats you, as her Son is Still in England, that you would take all opportun[i]ties to advise & counsel him; She says she is going to leave him & desires you'd be a Spiritual Fath[er] to hi[m]. She will take it very kind. *She thanks you heartily for the kind notice you took of me while in England.* Pleas[e] to give my best Respects to Mrs. & miss Thornton, and masters Henry and Robert who held with me a long conversation on many subjects which Mrs. Drinkwater⁵ knows very well, hope she is in better Health than when I left her. Please to remember me to your whole family & I than[k] them for their kindness to me. begging Still an interest in your best hours

I am Hon'd Sir

most respectfully your Humble Servt.
Phillis Wheatley

I have written to Mrs. Wilberforce⁶ Sometime since Please to give my duty to her; Since writing the above the Rev'd Mr. Moorhead⁷ has made his Exit from this world, in whom we lament the loss of the Zealous Pious & true christian

1989

To Rev. Samson Occom,¹ New London, Connecticut

[THE NATURAL RIGHTS OF NEGROES]

[February 11, 1774]

Rev'd and honor'd Sir,

I have this Day received your obliging kind Epistle, and am greatly satisfied with your Reasons respecting the Negroes, and think highly reasonable what you offer in Vindication of their natural Rights: Those that invade them cannot be insensible that the divine Light is chasing away the thick Darkness² which broods over the Land of Africa; and the Chaos which has reign'd so long, is converting into beautiful Order, and [r]eveals more and more clearly, the glorious Dispensation of civil and religious Liberty, which are so inseparably united, that there is little or no Enjoyment of one without the other: Otherwise, perhaps, the Israelites had been less solicitous for their Freedom from Egyptian slavery; I do not say they would have been contented without it, by no means, for in every human Breast, God has implanted a Principle, which we call Love of Freedom; it is impatient of Oppression, and pants for Deliverance; and by the Leave of our modern Egyptians I will assert, that the same Principle lives in us. God grant Deliverance in his own Way and Time, and get him honour upon all those whose Avarice impels them to

---

5. A mutual friend.
6. Thornton's sister.
7. The Reverend John Moorhead (d. 1773) came to Boston from Scotland in 1730 and was the pastor of a Scotch Presbyterian church near the Wheatley home. Wheatley wrote an elegy on his death and dedicated it to his daughter Mary.
1. A Mohegan Indian (1723–1792) born and living in New London; he was in England from 1766

to 1767. Mason in his edition notes that Occom, an ordained Presbyterian minister and friend of the Wheatleys, suggested to Wheatley that she go to Africa as a missionary, but she rejected the idea. This extract was published in several New England newspapers.
2. "And Moses stretched forth his hand toward heaven; and there was a thick darkness in all the land of Egypt three days" (Exodus 10.22).

countenance and help forward the Calamities of their fellow Creatures. This I desire not for their Hurt, but to convince them of the strange Absurdity of their Conduct whose Words and Actions are so diametrically opposite. How well the Cry for Liberty, and the reverse Disposition for the exercise of oppressive Power over others agree,—I humbly think it does not require the Penetration of a philosopher to determine.

1774, 1989

To John Thornton, London

[THE DEATH OF MRS. WHEATLEY]

[Boston, March 29, 1774]

Much honoured Sir,

I should not so soon have troubled you with the 2d. Letter, but the mournful *Occasion* will sufficiently Apologize. It is the death of Mrs. Wheatley. She has been labouring under a languishing illness for many months past and has at length took her flight from hence to those blissful regions, which need not the light of any, but the Sun of Righteousness. O could you have been present, to See how She long'd to drop the tabernacle of Clay, and to be freed from the cumbrous Shackles of a mortal Body, which had so many Times retarded her desires when Soaring upward. She has often told me how your Letters hav[e] quicken'd her in her spiritual Course: when She has been in darkness of mind they have rais'd and enliven'd her insomuch, that She went on, with chearfuln[ess] and alacrity in the path of her duty. She did truely, *run with patience the race that was Set before her,*[1] and hath, at length obtained the celestial Goal. She is now Sure, that the afflictions of this present time, were not worthy to be compared to the Glory, which is now, revealed in her, Seeing they have wrought out for her, *a far more exceeding and eternal weight of Glory:*[2] This, Sure, is Sufficient encouragement under the bitterest Sufferings, which we can endure.—About half an hour before her Death, She Spoke with a more audible voice, than She had for 3 months before. She calld. her friends & relations around her, and charg'd them not to leave their great work undone till *that* hour, but to fear God, and keep his Commandments. being ask'd if her faith faild her She answer'd, No. Then Spr[ead] out her arms crying come! come quickly! come, come! O pray for an eas[y] and quick Passage! She eagerly longed to depart to be with Christ. She retaind her Senses till the very last moment when "fare well, fare well." with a very low voice, were the last words She utter'd. I sat the whole time by her bed Side, and Saw with Grief and Wonder, the Effects of Sin on the human race. Had not Christ taken away the envenom'd Sting, where had been our hopes? what might we not have fear'd, what might we not have expectd from the dreadful King of Terrors? But *this* is matter of endless praise, to the King eternal immortal, invisible, that, *it is finished.* I hope her Son will be interested in Your Closet duties,[3] & that the prayers which she

1. "Wherefore seeing we also are compassed about with so great a cloud of witnesses, let us lay aside every weight, and the sin which doth so easily beset us, and let us run with patience the race that is set before us" (Hebrews 12.1).

2. "For our light affliction, which is but for a moment, worketh for us a far more exceeding and eternal weight of glory" (2 Corinthians 4.17).
3. I.e., his meditations and prayers.

was continually putting up, & wch. are recorded before God, in the Book of his remembrance for her Son & for me may be answer'd, I can Scarcely think that an Object of so many prayers, will fail of the Blessings implor'd for him ever Since he was born. I intreat the same Interest in your best thoughts for my Self, that her prayers, in my behalf, may be favour'd with an Answer of *Peace*. We received and forwarded your Letter to the rev'd Mr. Occom, but first, took the freedom to peruse it, and am exceeding glad, that you have order'd him to draw immediately for £25. for I really think he is in absolute necessity for that and as much more, he is so loth to run in debt for fear he Shall not be able to repay, that he has not the Least Shelter for his Creatures to defend them from the inclemencies of the weather, and he has lost some already for want of it, His hay is quite as defenceless, thus the former are in a fair way of being lost, and the latter to be wasted; It were to be wished that his *dwelling house* was like the Ark, with appartments, to contain the beasts and their provision; He said Mrs. Wheatley and the rev'd Mr. Moorhead were his best friends in Boston, But alass! they are gone. I trust gone to recieve the rewards promis'd to those, who Offer a Cup of cold water in the name & for the sake of Jesus—They have both been very instrum[ental in meetin]g the wants of that child of God, Mr. Occom—but I fear your pa[tience has been] exhausted, it remains only that we thank you for your kind Letter to my mistress it came above a fortnight after her Death.—Hoping for an interest in your prayers for these [and the] Sanctificiation of this bereaving Providence, I am hon'd Sir with dutiful respect ever your obliged

and devoted Humble Servant   Phillis Wheatley

1989

ROYALL TYLER
1757–1826

The colonial period was by no means conducive to English-speaking theater, let alone drama, and it says something about the theater's strength as an institution that it was able to exist at all. For one thing, settlers were too busy wresting a life from soil to be entertained; more important, both Puritans and Quakers disapproved in principle of what Jonathan in *The Contrast* calls "the devil's drawing-room." Nevertheless, British acting companies occasionally toured the principal cities, amateur theatricals were staged in southern colonies, and college students performed dramatic readings. Even those activities virtually ceased during the Revolution, when Americans were too busy fighting for their new country.

After the Revolution, however, as the theater historian Walter J. Meserve has pointed out, "it became clear that the theatre was to be part of a new nation and that a playwright might even elicit some slight fame and fortune," for a national drama would be part of the search for a cultural identity. Bans against theater were lifted, older acting companies returned, and new ones were formed to occupy the new playhouses. One of the few new playwrights to emerge was Royall Tyler, whose play *The Contrast* was performed in 1787. It was our first English-speaking comedy and an immediate hit.

Tyler was not a dramatist with a mission but an accomplished young man with a flair for letters. He earned degrees simultaneously at Harvard College and Yale College in 1776. He served in the Revolutionary War; he enjoyed playing man about town (in his case, Boston); he paid court to Abigail Adams, John and Abigail's daughter. At length he became a lawyer, and an intelligent and successful one; in his later years, he was both chief justice of the Supreme Court of Vermont and professor of law at the University of Vermont. He also—in the same year *The Contrast* was produced—was a member of the militia that put down Shays's Rebellion, an incident mentioned twice in the play. And he dashed off *The Contrast* in three weeks.

Although its author was an amateur, the play, most readers agree, reads like a polished professional product of the time. It is based, to be sure, on Richard Brinsley Sheridan's famous comedy *The School for Scandal* (1777), which Tyler saw produced in New York in 1787. From Sheridan's play Tyler took the basic story line that contrasts a mean and shallow fashionable demimonde with a world of honest and wholesome sentiment: the latter, of course, triumphs. He repays his debt handsomely in the scene where the comic Jonathan thinks he has witnessed real life in a private home but has actually been watching *The School for Scandal* itself.

What was revolutionary was that Tyler totally Americanized the story. His fashionable New Yorkers ape British modes—most especially the deceitful villain, a young man who runs his life according to Lord Chesterfield's dictates. The hero, Captain Manly, is a model of thoughtful rectitude; a veteran of the Revolution, he may well embody the idea, current at the time, that these officer veterans were America's best hope. His servant Jonathan is one of the first examples of an enduring dramatic type, the comic Yankee: he is the butt of fun because of his ignorance of city ways, but he is also shrewd, honorable, and squarely on the side of homespun good. The critic William L. Hedges notes that Manly and Jonathan embody two American myths— "Publius and Yankee Doodle teamed up to save American virtue from the seductions of British luxury." "Contrasts" run throughout the play.

Tyler continued to write for the rest of his life: other plays, satirical essays, verses, and a picaresque novel, *The Algerine Captive* (1797), one of the first works by an American to be also published in England. None, however, equals *The Contrast*, with its good humor and its brash, sunny nationalism:

> Exult each patriot heart!—this night is shewn
> A piece, which we may fairly call our own.

The new country wanted a national literature, and in Tyler's play got an excellent example of it. Moreover, because social comedy is so topical, we can also read *The Contrast* for a vivid idea of what it was like to be an American when this country was still young.

The Contrast[1]

Prologue

[*Written by a* YOUNG GENTLEMAN *of New York, and Spoken by* MR. WIGNELL]

> Exult each patriot heart!—this night is shewn
> A piece, which we may fairly call our own;
> Where the proud titles of "My Lord! Your Grace!"
> To humble Mr. and plain Sir give place.

---

1. First performed in 1787, it was published in 1790 by Thomas Wignell, which is the source of the text. Wignell, a prominent comic actor and George Washington's favorite comedian, later ran one of the new country's most successful theaters, the Chestnut Street Theatre, in Philadelphia. He played the part of Jonathan in New York.

Our Author pictures not from foreign climes
The fashions, or the follies of the times;
But has confin'd the subject of his work
To the gay scenes—the circles of New York.
On native themes his Muse displays her pow'rs;
If ours the faults, the virtues too are ours.
Why should our thoughts to distant countries roam,
When each refinement may be found at home?
Who travels now to ape the rich or great,
To deck an equipage and roll in state;
To court the graces,[2] or to dance with ease,
Or by hypocrisy to strive to please?
Our free-born ancestors such arts despis'd;
Genuine sincerity alone they priz'd;
Their minds, with honest emulation fir'd.
To solid good—not ornament—aspir'd;
Or, if ambition rous'd a bolder flame,
Stern virtue throve, where indolence was shame.

But modern youths, with imitative sense,
Deem taste in dress the proof of excellence;
And spurn the meanness of your homespun arts,
Since homespun habits would obscure their parts;
Whilst all, which aims at splendor and parade,
Must come from Europe, and be ready made.
Strange! we should thus our native worth disclaim,
And check the progress of our rising fame.
Yet one, whilst imitation bears the sway,
Aspires to nobler heights, and points the way,
Be rous'd, my friends! his bold example view;
Let your own Bards be proud to copy you!
Should rigid critics reprobate our play,
At least the patriotic heart will say,
"Glorious our fall, since in a noble cause.
"The bold attempt alone demands applause."
Still may the wisdom of the Comic Muse
Exalt your merits, or your faults accuse.
But think not, 'tis her aim to be severe;—
We all are mortals, and as mortals err.
If candor pleases, we are truly blest;
Vice trembles, when compell'd to stand confess'd.
Let not light Censure on your faults offend,
Which aims not to expose them, but amend.
Thus does our Author to your candor trust;
Conscious, the free are generous, as just.

---

2. Greek goddesses, personifications of loveliness or grace. "Equipage": coach.

Act First

SCENE 1.

An apartment at CHARLOTTE's.

[CHARLOTTE *and* LETITIA *discovered.*]

LETITIA   And so, Charlotte, you really think the pocket-hoop[3] unbecoming.

CHARLOTTE   No, I don't say so: It may be very becoming to saunter round the house of a rainy day; to visit my grand-mamma, or go to Quakers' meeting: but to swim in a minuet, with the eyes of fifty well-dressed beaux upon me, to trip it in the Mall, or walk on the battery,[4] give me the luxurious, jaunty, flowing, bell-hoop. It would have delighted you to have seen me the last evening, my charming girl! I was dangling o'er the battery with Billy Dimple; a knot of young fellows were upon the platform; as I passed them I faultered with one of the most bewitching false steps you ever saw, and then recovered myself with such a pretty confusion, flirting my hoop to discover a jet black shoe and brilliant buckle. Gad! how my little heart thrilled to hear the confused reptures of—"*Demme,*[5] Jack, what a delicate foot!" "Ha! General, what a well-turn'd—"

LETITIA   Fie! fie! Charlotte [*stopping her mouth*], I protest you are quite a libertine.

CHARLOTTE   Why, my dear little prude, are we not all such libertines? Do you think, when I sat tortured two hours under the hands of my friseur, and an hour more at my toilet,[6] that I had any thoughts of my aunt Susan, or my cousin Betsey? though they are both allowed to be critical judges of dress.

LETITIA   Why, who should we dress to please, but those who are judges of its merits?

CHARLOTTE   Why a creature who does not know *Buffon* from *Souflee*[7]— Man!—my Letitia—Man! for whom we dress, walk, dance, talk, lisp, languish, and smile. Does not the grave Spectator[8] assure us, that even our much bepraised diffidence, modesty, and blushes, are all directed to make ourselves good wives and mothers as fast as we can. Why, I'll undertake with one flirt of this hoop to bring more beaux to my feet in one week, than the grave Maria, and her sentimental circle, can do, by sighing sentiment till their hairs are grey.

LETITIA   Well, I won't argue with you; you always out talk me; let us change the subject. I hear that Mr. Dimple and Maria are soon to be married.

CHARLOTTE   You hear true. I was consulted in the choice of the wedding clothes. She is to be married in a delicate white satin, and has a monstrous pretty brocaded lutestring[9] for the second day. It would have done

3. Hoopskirts became fashionable about 1700; the "pocket hoop," confined to the hips, was smaller than the "bell hoop," mentioned a few lines later.
4. Area at the southernmost tip of Manhattan Island (formerly a Dutch fortification, hence the name). "Beaux": i.e., dandies. "The Mall": fashionable promenade.
5. Affected version of *damn me.*
6. Dressing table, vanity. "Friseur": hairdresser.

7. I.e., soufflé, a puffy dish made with eggs and sauce. "*Buffon*": a pun on Georges Buffon, 18th-century French naturalist, and "bouffant," puffed out, as in a hairdo.
8. A popular periodical written and published by Joseph Addison and Richard Steele, which provided "a wholesome and pleasant regimen" of essays on morals, manners, and literature.
9. A glossy silk.

you good to have seen with what an affected indifference the dear sentimentalist turned over a thousand pretty things, just as if her heart did
not palpitate with her approaching happiness, and at last made her
choice, and arranged her dress with such apathy, as if she did not know
that plain white satin, and a simple blond lace, would shew her clear
skin, and dark hair, to the greatest advantage.

LETITIA   But they say her indifference to dress, and even to the gentleman
himself, is not entirely affected.

CHARLOTTE   How?

LETITIA   It is whispered, that if Maria gives her hand to Mr. Dimple, it will
be without her heart.

CHARLOTTE   Though the giving the heart is one of the last of all laughable
considerations in the marriage of a girl of spirit, yet I should like to hear
what antiquated notions the dear little piece of old fashioned prudery
has got in her head.

LETITIA   Why you know that old Mr. John-Richard-Robert-Jacob-Isaac-
Abraham-Cornelius Van Dumpling, Billy Dimple's father (for he has
thought fit to soften his name, as well as manners, during his English
tour) was the most intimate friend of Maria's father. The old folks, about
a year before Mr. Van Dumpling's death, proposed this match: the young
folks were accordingly introduced, and told they must love one another.
Billy was then a good natured, decent, dressing young fellow, with a little
dash of the coxcomb,[1] such as our young fellows of fortune usually have.
At this time, I really believe she thought she loved him; and had they
then been married, I doubt not, they might have jogged on, to the end
of the chapter, a good kind of a sing-song lack-a-daysaical life, as other
honest married folks do.

CHARLOTTE   Why did they not then marry?

LETITIA   Upon the death of his father, Billy went to England to see the
world, and rub off a little of the patroon rust.[2] During his absence, Maria
like a good girl, to keep herself constant to her *nown*[3] *true-love*, avoided
company, and betook herself, for her amusement, to her books, and her
dear Billy's letters. But, alas! how many ways has the mischievous demon
of inconstancy of stealing into a woman's heart! Her love was destroyed
by the very means she took to support it.

CHARLOTTE   How?—Oh! I have it—some likely young beau found the way
to her study.

LETITIA   Be patient, Charlotte—your head so runs upon beaux.—Why she
read Sir Charles Grandison, Clarissa Harlow, Shenstone, and the Sentimental Journey,[4] and between whiles, as I said, Billy's letters. But as
her taste improved, her love declined. The contrast was so striking
betwixt the good sense of her books, and the flimsiness of her love-letters,
that she discovered she had unthinkingly engaged her hand without her
heart; and then the whole transaction managed by the old folks, now
appeared so unsentimental, and looked so like bargaining for a bale of

1. Conceitedness.
2. I.e., old-fashioned country style or manners.
3. I.e., "own" (probably from a popular song).
4. All sentimental works of the 18th century: *Sir
Charles Grandison* and *Clarissa* (Harlowe) are nov-

els by Samuel Richardson, and *A Sentimental Journey* is by Laurence Sterne. William Shenstone was
a popular poet. Novel reading was then considered
a woman's occupation.

goods, that she found she ought to have rejected, according to every rule of romance, even the man of her choice, if imposed upon her in that manner—Clary Harlow would have scorned such a match.

CHARLOTTE   Well, how was it on Mr. Dimple's return? Did he meet a more favorable reception than his letters?

LETITIA   Much the same. She spoke of him with respect abroad, and with contempt in her closet.[5] She watched his conduct and conversation, and found that he had by traveling acquired the wickedness of Lovelace[6] without his wit, and the politeness of Sir Charles Grandison without his generosity. The ruddy youth who washed his face at the cistern every morning, and swore and looked eternal love and constancy, was now metamorphosed into a flippant, palid, polite beau, who devotes the morning to his toilet, reads a few pages of Chesterfield's letters,[7] and then minces out, to put the infamous principles in practice upon every woman he meets.

CHARLOTTE   But, if she is so apt at conjuring up these sentimental bugbears, why does she not discard him at once?

LETITIA   Why, she thinks her word too sacred to be trifled with. Besides, her father, who has a great respect for the memory of his deceased friend, is ever telling her how he shall renew his years in their union, and repeating the dying injunctions of old Van Dumpling.

CHARLOTTE   A mighty pretty story! And so you would make me believe, that the sensible Maria would give up Dumpling manor, and the all-accomplished Dimple as a husband, for the absurd, ridiculous reason, forsooth, because she despises and abhors him. Just as if a lady could not be privileged to spend a man's fortune, ride in his carriage, be called after his name, and call him her *nown dear lovee* when she wants money, without loving and respecting the great he-creature. Oh! my dear girl, you are a monstrous prude.

LETITIA   I don't say what I would do; I only intimate how I suppose she wishes to act.

CHARLOTTE   No, no, no! A fig for sentiment. If she breaks, or wishes to break, with Mr. Dimple, depend upon it, she has some other man in her eye. A woman rarely discards one lover, until she is sure of another.— Letitia little thinks what a clue I have to Dimple's conduct. The generous man submits to render himself disgusting to Maria, in order that she may leave him at liberty to address me. I must change the subject [*Aside, and rings a bell.*]

[*Enter* SERVANT.]

Frank, order the horses to.—Talking of marriage—did you hear that Sally Bloomsbury is going to be married next week to Mr. Indigo, the rich Carolinian?

LETITIA   Sally Bloomsbury married!—Why, she is not yet in her teens.

CHARLOTTE   I do not know how that is, but, you may depend upon it, 'tis a done affair. I have it from the best authority. There is my aunt Wyerley's Hannah (you know Hannah—though a black, she is a wench that was

5. Private apartment or room.
6. The handsome dashing villain in *Clarissa*.
7. Letters written to his illegitimate son by Philip Stanhope, earl of Chesterfield, on deportment and manners in polite society; published in 1774, they were described by Samuel Johnson as teaching "the morals of a whore and the manners of a dancing master."

never caught in a lie in her life); now Hannah has a brother who courts Sarah, Mrs. Catgut the milliner's girl, and she told Hannah's brother, and Hannah, who, as I said before, is a girl of undoubted veracity, told it directly to me, that Mrs. Catgut was making a new cap for Miss Bloomsbury, which, as it was very dressy, it is very probable is designed for a wedding cap: now, as she is to be married, who can it be to, but to Mr. Indigo? Why, there is no other gentleman that visits at her papa's.

LETITIA Say not a word more, Charlotte. Your intelligence[8] is so direct and well grounded, it is almost a pity that it is not a piece of scandal.

CHARLOTTE Oh! I am the pink of prudence. Though I cannot charge myself with ever having discredited a tea-party by my silence, yet I take care never to report any thing of my acquaintance, especially if it is to their credit,—*discredit*, I mean—until I have searched to the bottom of it. It is true, there is infinite pleasure in this charitable pursuit. Oh! how delicious to go and condole with the friends of some backsliding sister, or to retire with some old dowager or maiden aunt of the family, who love scandal so well, that they cannot forbear gratifying their appetite at the expence of the reputation of their nearest relations! And then to return full fraught with a rich collection of circumstances, to retail to the next circle of our acquaintance under the strongest injunctions of secrecy,—ha, ha, ha!—interlarding the melancholy tale with so many doleful shakes of the head, and more doleful, "Ah! who would have thought it! so amiable, so prudent a young lady, as we all thought her, what a monstrous pity! well, I have nothing to charge myself with; I acted the part of a friend, I warned her of the principles of that rake,[9] I told her what would be the consequence; I told her so, I told her so."—Ha, ha, ha!

LETITIA Ha, ha, ha! Well, but Charlotte, you don't tell me what you think of Miss Bloomsbury's match.

CHARLOTTE Think! why I think it is probable she cried for a plaything, and they have given her a husband. Well, well, well, the puling chit[1] shall not be deprived of her plaything: 'tis only exchanging London dolls for American babies—Apropos, of babies, have you heard what Mrs. Affable's high-flying notions of delicacy have come to?

LETITIA Who, she that was Miss Lovely?

CHARLOTTE The same; she married Bob Affable of Schenectady. Don't you remember?

　　　　[*Enter* SERVANT.]

SERVANT Madam, the carriage is ready.

LETITIA Shall we go to the stores first, or visiting?

CHARLOTTE I should think it rather too early to visit; especially Mrs. Prim: you know she is so particular.

LETITIA Well, but what of Mrs. Affable?

CHARLOTTE Oh, I'll tell you as we go; come, come, let us hasten. I hear Mrs. Catgut has some of the prettiest caps arrived, you ever saw. I shall die if I have not the first sight of them. [*Exeunt.*]

---

8. I.e., news.　　　　　　　　　　　　　　1. Whimpering child or young woman.
9. Or "rakehell," a libertine or dissolute man.

SCENE 2.

A room in VAN ROUGH's *house.*

[MARIA *sitting disconsolate at a Table, with Books, etc.*]

SONG

I

The sun sets in night, and the stars shun the day;
But glory remains when their lights fade away!
Begin, ye tormentors! your threats are in vain,
For the son of Alknomook[2] shall never complain.

II

Remember the arrows he shot from his bow;
Remember your chiefs by his hatchet laid low:
Why so slow?—do you wait till I shrink from the pain?
No—the son of Alknomook will never complain.

III

Remember the wood where in ambush we lay;
And the scalps which we bore from your nation away:
Now the flame rises fast, you exult in my pain;
But the son of Alknomook can never complain.

IV

I go to the land where my father is gone;
His ghost shall rejoice in the fame of his son:
Death comes like a friend, he relieves me from pain;
And thy son, Oh Alknomook! has scorn'd to complain.

There is something in this song which ever calls forth my affections. The manly virtue of courage, that fortitude which steels the heart against the keenest misfortunes, which interweaves the laurel of glory amidst the instruments of torture and death, displays something so noble, so exalted, that in despite of the prejudices of education, I cannot but admire it, even in a savage. The prepossession which our sex is supposed to entertain for the character of a soldier, is, I know, a standing piece of raillery among the wits. A cockade, a lapel'd coat, and a feather,[3] they will tell you, are irresistible by a female heart. Let it be so.—Who is it that considers the helpless situation of our sex, that does not see we each moment stand in need of a protector, and that a brave one too. Formed of the more delicate materials of nature, endowed only with the softer passions, incapable, from our ignorance of the world, to guard against the wiles of mankind, our security for happiness often depends upon their generosity and courage:—Alas! how little of the former do we find. How inconsistent! that man should be leagued to destroy that honor, upon which, solely rests his respect and esteem. Ten thousand temptations allure us, ten thousand passions betray us; yet the smallest deviation

2. An Indian name. The authorship of the song is unknown.

3. I.e., military dress. "Cockade": badge worn on a hat.

from the path of rectitude is followed by the contempt and insult of man, and the more remorseless pity of woman: years of penitence and tears cannot wash away the stain, nor a life of virture obliterate its remembrance. Reputation is the life of woman; yet courage to protect it, is masculine and disgusting; and the only safe asylum a woman of delicacy can find, is in the arms of a man of honor. How naturally then, should we love the brave, and the generous; how gratefully should we bless the arm raised for our protection, when nerv'd by virtue, and directed by honor! Heaven grant that the man with whom I may be connected—may be connected!—Whither has my imagination transported me—whither does it now lead me?—Am I not indissolubly engaged by every obligation of honor, which my own consent, and my father's approbation can give, to a man who can never share my affections, and whom a few days hence, it will be criminal for me to disapprove—to disapprove! would to heaven that were all—to despise. For, can the most frivolous manners, actuated by the most depraved heart, meet, or merit, anything but contempt from every woman of delicacy and sentiment?

       [VAN ROUGH, *without.*] Mary!

MARIA.   Ha, my father's voice—Sir!

       [*Enter* VAN ROUGH.]

VAN ROUGH   What, Mary, always singing doleful ditties, and moping over these plaguy[4] books.

MARIA   I hope, Sir, that it is not criminal to improve my mind with books; or to divert my melancholy with singing at my leisure hours.

VAN ROUGH   Why, I don't know that, child; I don't know that. They us'd to say when I was a young man, that if a woman knew how to make a pudding, and to keep herself out of fire and water, she knew enough for a wife. Now, what good have these books done you? have they not made you melancholy? as you call it. Pray, what right has a girl of your age to be in the dumps? haven't you every thing your heart can wish; ain't you going to be married to a young man of great fortune; ain't you going to have the quit-rent[5] of twenty miles square?

MARIA   One hundredth part of the land, and a lease for life of the heart of a man I could love, would satisfy me.

VAN ROUGH   Pho, pho, pho! child; nonsense, downright nonsense, child. This comes of your reading your story-books; your Charles Grandisons, your Sentimental Journals, and your Robinson Crusoes, and such other trumpery.[6] No, no, no! child, it is money makes the mare go; keep your eye upon the main chance,[7] Mary.

MARIA   Marriage, Sir, is, indeed, a very serious affair.

VAN ROUGH   You are right, child; you are right. I am sure I found it so to my cost.

MARIA   I mean, Sir, that as marriage is a portion for life, and so intimately involves our happiness, we cannot be too considerate in the choice of our companion.

VAN ROUGH   Right, child; very right. A young woman should be very sober when she is making her choice, but when she has once made it, as you have done, I don't see why she should not be as merry as a grig,[8] I am

4. Annoying, irritating.
5. Small fixed rent.
6. Worthless nonsense. *Robinson Crusoe* was pub-

lished by Daniel Defoe in 1719.
7. I.e., the biggest advantage.
8. Lighthearted young person.

sure she has reason enough to be so—Solomon says, that "there is a time to laugh, and a time to weep";[9] now a time for a young woman to laugh is when she has made sure of a good rich husband. Now a time to cry, according to you, Mary, is when she is making choice of him: but, I should think, that a young woman's time to cry was, when she despaired of *getting* one.—Why, there was your mother now; to be sure when I popp'd the question to her, she did look a little silly; but when she had once looked down on her apron-strings, as all modest young women us'd to do, and drawled out ye-s, she was as brisk and as merry as a bee.

MARIA   My honored mother, Sir, had no motive to melancholy; she married the man of her choice.

VAN ROUGH   The man of her choice! And pray, Mary, ain't you going to marry the man of your choice—what trumpery notion is this?—It is these vile books [*throwing them away*]. I'd have you to know, Mary, if you won't make young Van Dumpling the man of *your* choice, you shall marry him as the man of *my* choice.

MARIA   You terrify me, Sir. Indeed, Sir, I am all submission. My will is yours.

VAN ROUGH   Why, that is the way your mother us'd to talk. "My will is yours, my dear Mr. Van Rough, my will is yours": but she took special care to have her own way though for all that.

MARIA   Do not reflect upon my mother's memory, Sir—

VAN ROUGH   Why not, Mary, why not? She kept me from speaking my mind all *her* life, and do you think she shall henpeck me now she is *dead* too? Come, come; don't go to sniveling: be a good girl, and mind the main chance. I'll see you well settled in the world.

MARIA   I do not doubt your love, Sir; and it is my duty to obey you.—I will endeavor to make my duty and inclination go hand in hand.

VAN ROUGH   Well, well, Mary; do you be a good girl, mind the main chance, and never mind inclination.—Why, do you know that I have been down in the cellar this very morning to examine a pipe of Madeira[1] which I purchased the week you were born, and mean to tap on your wedding day.—That pipe cost me fifty pounds sterling. It was well worth sixty pounds; but I over-reached Ben Bulkhead, the supercargo.[2] I'll tell you the whole story. You must know that—

[*Enter* SERVANT.]

SERVANT   Sir, Mr. Transfer, the broker, is below.[*Exit.*]

VAN ROUGH   Well, Mary, I must go.—Remember, and be a good girl, and mind the main chance. [*Exit.*]

MARIA   [*alone*] How deplorable is my situation! How distressing for a daughter to find her heart militating with her filial duty! I know my father loves me tenderly, why then do I reluctantly obey him? Heaven knows! with what reluctance I should oppose the will of a parent, or set an example of filial disobedience; at a parent's command I could wed awkwardness and deformity. Were the heart of my husband good, I would so magnify his good qualities with the eye of conjugal affection, that the defects of his person and manners should be lost in the emanation of

9. "A time to weep, and a time to laugh" (Ecclesiastes 3.4); Ecclesiastes is thought to have been written by Solomon.

1. Big cask of wine.
2. Officer of merchant ship concerned with the voyage's commercial aspects.

his virtues. At a father's command, I could embrace poverty. Were the poor man my husband, I would learn resignation to my lot; I would enliven our frugal meal with good humor, and chase away misfortune from our cottage with a smile. At a father's command, I could almost submit, to what every female heart knows to be the most mortifying, to marry a weak man, and blush at my husband's folly in every company I visited.—But to marry a depraved wretch, whose only virtue is a polished exterior; who is actuated by the unmanly ambition of conquering the defenceless; whose heart, insensible to the emotions of patriotism, dilates at the plaudits of every unthinking girl: whose laurels are the sighs and tears of the miserable victims of his specious behavior.—Can he, who has no regard for the peace and happiness of other families, ever have a due regard for the peace and happiness of his own? Would to heaven that my father were not so hasty in his temper! Surely, if I were to state my reasons for declining this match, he would not compel me to marry a man—whom, though my lips may solemnly promise to honor, I find my heart must ever despise. [*Exit.*]

Act Second

SCENE 1.

CHARLOTTE's *apartment.*

[*Enter* CHARLOTTE *and* LETITIA.]

CHARLOTTE [*at entering*] Betty, take those things out of the carriage and carry them to my chamber; see that you don't tumble[3] them.—My dear, I protest, I think it was the homeliest of the whole. I declare I was almost tempted to return and change it.

LETITIA Why would you take it?

CHARLOTTE Didn't Mrs. Catgut say it was the most fashionable?

LETITIA But, my dear, it will never sit becomingly on you.

CHARLOTTE I know that; but did not you hear Mrs. Catgut say it was fashionable?

LETITIA Did you see that sweet airy cap with the white sprig?

CHARLOTTE Yes, and I longed to take it; but, my dear, what could I do?— Did not Mrs. Catgut say it was the most fashionable; and if I had not taken it, was not that awkward gawky, Sally Slender, ready to purchase it immediately?

LETITIA Did you observe how she tumbled over the things at the next shop, and then went off without purchasing any thing, nor even thanking the poor man for his trouble?—But of all the awkward creatures, did you see Miss Blouze, endeavoring to thrust her unmerciful arm into those small kid gloves?

CHARLOTTE Ha, ha, ha, ha!

LETITIA Then did you take notice, with what an affected warmth of friendship she and Miss Wasp met? when all their acquaintances know how much pleasure they take in abusing each other in every company?

CHARLOTTE Lud![4] Letitia, is that so extraordinary? Why, my dear, I hope

---

3. Rumple, disorder.   4. I.e., Lord.

you are not going to turn sentimentalist.—Scandal, you know, is but amusing ourselves with the faults, foibles, follies, and reputations of our friends;—indeed, I don't know why we should have friends, if we are not at liberty to make use of them. But no person is so ignorant of the world as to suppose, because I amuse myself with a lady's faults, that I am obliged to quarrel with her person, every time we meet; believe me, my dear, we should have very few acquaintances at that rate.

[SERVANT *enters and delivers a letter to* CHARLOTTE, *and exits.*]

CHARLOTTE   You'll excuse me, my dear. [*Opens and reads to herself.*]

LETITIA   Oh, quite excusable.

CHARLOTTE   As I hope to be married, my brother Henry is in the city.

LETITIA   What, your brother, Colonel Manly?

CHARLOTTE   Yes, my dear; the only brother I have in the world.

LETITIA   Was he never in this city?

CHARLOTTE   Never nearer than Harlem Heights,[5] where he lay with his regiment.

LETITIA   What sort of a being is this brother of yours? If he is as chatty, as pretty, as sprightly as you, half the belles in the city will be pulling caps[6] for him.

CHARLOTTE   My brother is the very counterpart and reverse of me: I am gay, he is grave; I am airy, he is solid; I am ever selecting the most pleasing objects for my laughter, he has a tear for every pitiful one. And thus, whilst he is plucking the briars and thorns from the path of the unfortunate, I am strewing on my own path with roses.

LETITIA   My sweet friend, not quite so poetical, and little more particular.

CHARLOTTE   Hands off, Letitia. I feel the rage of simile[7] upon me; I can't talk to you in any other way. My brother has a heart replete with the noblest sentiments, but then, it is like—it is like—Oh! you provoking girl, you have deranged all my ideas—it is like—Oh! I have it—his heart is like an old maiden lady's band-box;[8] it contains many costly things, arranged with the most scrupulous nicety, yet the misfortune is, that they are too delicate, costly, and antiquated, for common use.

LETITIA   By what I can pick out of your flowery description, your brother is no beau.

CHARLOTTE   No, indeed; he makes no pretension to the character. He'd ride, or rather fly, an hundred miles to relieve a distressed object, or to do a gallant act in the service of his country: but, should you drop your fan or bouquet in his presence, it is ten to one that some beau at the farther end of the room would have the honor of presenting it to you, before he had observed that it fell. I'll tell you one of his antiquated, anti-gallant notions.—He said once in my presence, in a room full of company—would you believe it—in a large circle of ladies, that the best evidence a gentleman could give a young lady of his respect and affection, was, to endeavor in a friendly manner to rectify her foibles. I protest I was crimson to the eyes, upon reflecting that I was known as his sister.

LETITIA   Insupportable creature! tell a lady of her faults! If he is so grave, I fear I have no chance of captivating him.

5. Then north of New York City and site of a Revolutionary War battle.
6. I.e., setting their caps.

7. I.e., desire to make poetic comparisons.
8. Cylindrical box for clothes: its lid was held on by a band of ribbon.

CHARLOTTE His conversation is like a rich old fashioned brocade,[9] it will stand alone; every sentence is a sentiment. Now you may judge what a time I had with him in my twelve months' visit to my father. He read me such lectures, out of pure brotherly affection, against the extremes of fashion, dress, flirting, and coquetry, and all the other dear things which he knows I doat upon, that, I protest, his conversation made me as melancholy as if I had been at church; and heaven knows, though I never prayed to go there but on one occasion, yet I would have exchanged his conversation for a psalm and a sermon. Church is rather melancholy, to be sure; but then I can ogle the beaux, and be regaled with "here endeth the first lesson"; but his brotherly *here*, you would think had no end. You captivate him! Why, my dear, he would as soon fall in love with a box of Italian flowers. There is Maria now, if she were not engaged, she might do something.—Oh, how I should like to see that pair of pensorosos[1] together, looking as grave as two sailors' wives of a stormy night, with a flow of sentiment meandering through their conversation like purling streams in modern poetry.

LETITIA Oh! my dear fanciful—

CHARLOTTE Hush! I hear some person coming through the entry.

[*Enter* SERVANT.]

SERVANT Madam, there's a gentleman below who calls himself Colonel Manly; do you chuse to be at home?

CHARLOTTE Shew him in. [*Exit* SERVANT.] Now for a sober face.

[*Enter* COLONEL MANLY.]

MANLY My dear Charlotte, I am happy that I once more enfold you within the arms of fraternal affection. I know you are going to ask (amiable impatience!) how our parents do,—the venerable pair transmit you their blessing by me—they totter on the verge of a well-spent life, and wish only to see their children settled in the world, to depart in peace.

CHARLOTTE I am very happy to hear that they are well. [*Coolly.*] Brother, will you give me leave to introduce you to our uncle's ward, one of my most intimate friends.

MANLY [*saluting* LETITIA] I ought to regard your friends as my own.

CHARLOTTE Come, Letitia, do give us a little dash of your vivacity; my brother is so sentimental, and so grave, that I protest he'll give us the vapors.[2]

MANLY Though sentiment and gravity, I know, are banished the polite world, yet, I hoped, they might find some countenance in the meeting of such near connections as brother and sister.

CHARLOTTE Positively, brother, if you go one step further in this strain, you will set me crying, and that, you know, would spoil my eyes; and then I should never get the husband which our good papa and mamma have so kindly wished me—never be established in the world.

MANLY Forgive me, my sister—I am no enemy to mirth; I love your sprightliness; and I hope it will one day enliven the hours of some worthy man; but when I mention the respectable authors of my existence,—the cherishers and protectors of my helpless infancy, whose hearts glow with

9. Rich stiff fabric.
1. Melancholy, thoughtful people (from the title of John Milton's poem about such a person, "Il Pen-
seroso").
2. I.e., depress us.

such fondness and attachment, that they would willingly lay down their lives for my welfare, you will excuse me, if I am so unfashionable as to speak of them with some degree of respect and reverence.

CHARLOTTE   Well, well, brother; if you won't be gay, we'll not differ; I will be as grave as you wish. [*Affects gravity.*] And so, brother, you have come to the city to exchange some of your commutation notes[3] for a little pleasure.

MANLY   Indeed, you are mistaken; my errand is not of amusement, but business; and as I neither drink nor game, my expences will be so trivial, I shall have no occasion to sell my notes.

CHARLOTTE   Then you won't have occasion to do a very good thing. Why, there was the Vermont General—he came down some time since, sold all his musty notes at one stroke, and then laid the cash out in trinkets for his dear Fanny. I want a dozen pretty things myself; have you got the notes with you?

MANLY   I shall be ever willing to contribute as far as it is in my power, to adorn, or in any way to please my sister; yet, I hope, I shall never be obliged for this, to sell my notes. I may be romantic, but I preserve them as a sacred deposit. Their full amount is justly due to me, but as embarrassments, the natural consequences of a long war, disable my country from supporting its credit, I shall wait with patience until it is rich enough to discharge them. If that is not in my day, they shall be transmitted as an honorable certificate to posterity, that I have humbly imitated our illustrious WASHINGTON, in having exposed my health and life in the service of my country, without reaping any other reward than the glory of conquering in so arduous a contest.

CHARLOTTE   Well said heroics. Why, my dear Henry, you have such a lofty way of saying things, that I protest I almost tremble at the thought of introducing you to the polite circles in the city. The belles would think you were a player[4] run mad, with your head filled with old scraps of tragedy: and, as to the beaux, they might admire, because they would not understand you.—But, however, I must, I believe, venture to introduce you to two or three ladies of my acquaintance.

LETITIA   And that will make him acquainted with thirty or forty beaux.

CHARLOTTE   Oh! brother, you don't know what a fund of happiness you have in store.

MANLY   I fear, sister, I have not refinement sufficient to enjoy it.

CHARLOTTE   Oh! you cannot fail being pleased.

LETITIA   Our ladies are so delicate and dressy.

CHARLOTTE   And our beaux so dressy and delicate.

LETITIA   Our ladies chat and flirt so agreeably.

CHARLOTTE   And our beaux simper and bow so gracefully.

LETITIA   With their hair so trim and neat.

CHARLOTTE   And their faces so soft and sleek.

LETITIA   Their buckles so tonish[5] and bright.

CHARLOTTE   And their hands so slender and white.

LETITIA   I vow, Charlotte, we are quite poetical.

3. Notes given to Continental Army officers after the Revolution, promising payment of a pension when the notes came due; they could be cashed in earlier, for less than the face amount.
4. Actor.
5. Smart, fashionable (from the French *ton*).

CHARLOTTE   And then, brother, the faces of the beaux are of such a lily white hue! None of that horrid robustness of constitution, that vulgar corn-fed glow of health, which can only serve to alarm an unmarried lady with apprehensions, and prove a melancholy memento to a married one, that she can never hope for the happiness of being a widow. I will say this to the credit of our city beaux, that such is the delicacy of their complexion, dress, and address, that, even had I no reliance upon the honor of the dear Adonises,[6] I would trust myself in any possible situation with them, without the least apprehensions of rudeness.

MANLY   Sister Charlotte!

CHARLOTTE   Now, now, now brother [interrupting him], now don't go to spoil my mirth with a dash of your gravity; I am so glad to see you, I am in tip-top spirits. Oh! that you could be with us at a little snug party. There is Billy Simper, Jack Chassé, and Colonel Van Titter, Miss Promonade, and the two Miss Tambours, sometimes make a party, with some other ladies, in a side-box[7] at the play. Everything is conducted with such decorum,—first we bow round to the company in general, then to each one in particular, then we have so many inquiries after each other's health, and we are so happy to meet with each other, and it is so many ages since we last had that pleasure, and, if a married lady is in company, we have such a sweet dissertation upon her son Bobby's chin-cough, then the curtain rises, then our sensibility[8] is all awake, and then by the mere force of apprehension, we torture some harmless expression into a double meaning, which the poor author never dreamt of, and then we have recourse to our fans, and then we blush, and then the gentlemen jog one another, peep under the fan, and make the prettiest remarks; and then we giggle and they simper, and they giggle and we simper, and then the curtain drops, and then for nuts and oranges, and then we bow, and it's pray Ma'am take it, and pray Sir keep it, and oh! not for the world, Sir: and then the curtain rises again, and then we blush, and giggle, and simper, and bow, all over again. Oh! the sentimental charms of a side-box conversation! [All laugh.]

MANLY.   Well, sister, I join heartily with you in the laugh; for, in my opinion, it is as justifiable to laugh at folly, as it is reprehensible to ridicule misfortune.

CHARLOTTE.   Well, but brother, positively, I can't introduce you in these clothes: why, your coat looks as if it were calculated for the vulgar purpose of keeping yourself comfortable.

MANLY.   This coat was my regimental coat in the late war. The public tumults of our state[9] have induced me to buckle on the sword in support of that government which I once fought to establish. I can only say, sister, that there was a time when this coat was respectable, and some people even thought that those men who had endured so many winter campaigns in the service of their country, without bread, clothing, or pay, at

---

6. I.e., handsome youths, named for the beautiful young man beloved by Venus in classical myth. "Address": bearing.
7. Fashionable box seats, near the stage.
8. Responsiveness. "Chin-cough": whooping cough.
9. The young nation's problems, especially the

financial ones, were by no means solved by the Revolution. Manly may be referring specifically to Shays's Rebellion (1787) in Massachusetts. Daniel Shays, a war veteran, led an armed protest against high taxes and the lack of paper money; it was quickly put down by the militia, of which Tyler was at the time a member.

least deserved that the poverty of their appearance should not be ridiculed.

CHARLOTTE.   We agree in opinion entirely, brother, though it would not have done for me to have said it: it is the coat makes the man respectable. In the time of the war, when we were almost frightened to death, why, your coat was respectable, that is, fashionable; now another kind of coat is fashionable, that is, respectable. And pray direct the taylor to make yours the height of the fashion.

MANLY.   Though it is of little consequence to me of what shape my coat is, yet, as to the height of the fashion, there you will please to excuse me, sister. You know my sentiments on that subject. I have often lamented the advantage which the French have over us in the particular. In Paris, the fashions have their dawnings, their routine and declensions,[1] and depend as much upon the caprice of the day as in other countries; but there every lady assumes a right to deviate from the general *ton*, as far as will be of advantage to her own appearance. In America, the cry is, what is the fashion? and we follow it, indiscriminately, because it is so.

CHARLOTTE.   Therefore it is, that when large hoops are in fashion, we often see many a plump girl lost in the immensity of a hoop petticoat, whose want of height and *em-bon-point*[2] would never have been remarked in any other dress. When the high head-dress is the mode, how then do we see a lofty cushion, with a profusion of gauze, feathers, and ribband, supported by a face no bigger than an apple; whilst a broad full-faced lady, who really would have appeared tolerably handsome in a large head-dress, looks with her smart *chapeau*[3] as masculine as a soldier.

MANLY.   But remember, my dear sister, and I wish all my fair country-women would recollect, that the only excuse a young lady can have for going extravagantly into a fashion, is, because it makes her look extravagantly handsome.—Ladies, I must wish you a good morning.

CHARLOTTE   But, brother, you are going to make home with us.

MANLY   Indeed, I cannot. I have seen my uncle, and explained that matter.

CHARLOTTE   Come and dine with us, then. We have a family dinner about half past four o'clock.

MANLY   I am engaged to dine with the Spanish ambassador. I was introduced to him by an old brother officer; and instead of freezing me with a cold card of compliment[4] to dine with him ten days hence, he, with the true old Castilian frankness, in a friendly manner, asked me to dine with him to-day—an honor I could not refuse. Sister, adieu—Madam, your most obedient—[*Exit.*]

CHARLOTTE   I will wait upon you to the door, brother; I have something particular to say to you. [*Exit.*]

LETITIA   [*alone*] What a pair!—She the pink of flirtation, he the essence of everything that is *outré*[5] and gloomy.—I think I have completely deceived Charlotte by my manner of speaking of Mr. Dimple; she's too much the friend of Maria to be confided in. He is certainly rendering himself disagreeable to Maria, in order to break with her and proffer his

1. I.e., pattern and fall.
2. Stoutness. "Want": lack.
3. Hat.

4. Invitation card.
5. Bizarre (French).

hand to me. This is what the delicate fellow hinted in our last conversation. [*Exit.*]

SCENE 2

The Mall.

[*Enter* JESSAMY.]

JESSAMY Positively this Mall is a very pretty place. I hope the city won't ruin it by repairs. To be sure, it won't do to speak of in the same day with Ranelagh or Vauxhall;[6] however, it's a fine place for a young fellow to display his person to advantage. Indeed, nothing is lost here; the girls have taste, and I am very happy to find they have adopted the elegant London fashion of looking back, after a genteel fellow like me has passed them. Ah! who comes here! This, by his awkwardness, must be the Yankee colonel's servant. I'll accost him.

[*Enter* JONATHAN.]

Votre très—humble *serviteur*, Monsieur.[7] I understand Colonel Manly, the Yankee officer, has the honor of your services.

JONATHAN Sir!—

JESSAMY I say, Sir, I understand that Colonel Manly has the honor of having you for a servant.

JONATHAN Servant! Sir, do you take me for a neger,—I am Colonel Manly's waiter.[8]

JESSAMY A true Yankee distinction egad, without a difference. Why, Sir, do you not perform all the offices of a servant? Do you not even blacken his boots?

JONATHAN Yes; I do grease them a bit sometimes; but I am a true blue son of liberty, for all that. Father said I should come as Colonel Manly's waiter to see the world, and all that; but no man shall master me: my father has as good a farm as the colonel.

JESSAMY Well, Sir, we will not quarrel about terms upon the eve of an acquaintance, from which I promise myself so much satisfaction,—therefore *sans cérémonie*[9]—

JONATHAN What?—

JESSAMY I say, I am extremely happy to see Colonel Manly's waiter.

JONATHAN Well, and I vow, too, I am pretty considerably glad to see you— but what the dogs need of all this outlandish lingo? Who may you be, Sir, if I may be so bold?

JESSAMY I have the honor to be Mr. Dimple's servant, or, if you please, waiter. We lodge under the same roof, and should be glad of the honor of your acquaintance.

JONATHAN You a waiter! By the living jingo, you look so topping, I took you for one of the agents to Congress.[1]

JESSAMY The brute has discernment notwithstanding his appearance.— Give me leave to say I wonder then at your familiarity.

JONATHAN Why, as to the matter of that, Mr.—pray, what's your name?

6. London pleasure gardens.
7. Your very humble servant, sir (French).
8. Valet, manservant.

9. Without ceremony (French).
1. Ambassador.

JESSAMY   Jessamy, at your service.

JONATHAN   Why, I swear we don't make any great matter of distinction in our state, between quality and other folks.

JESSAMY   This is, indeed, a leveling principle. I hope, Mr. Jonathan, you have not taken part with the insurgents.

JONATHAN   Why, since General Shays has sneaked off, and given us the bag to hold, I don't care to give my opinion; but you'll promise not to tell—put your ear this way—you won't tell?—I vow, I did think the sturgeons[2] were right.

JESSAMY   I thought, Mr. Jonathan, you Massachusetts men always argued with a gun in your hand.—Why didn't you join them?

JONATHAN   Why, the colonel is one of those folks called the Shin—shin—dang it all, I can't speak them *lignum vitæ* words—you know who I mean—there is a company of them—they wear a China goose at their buttonhole—a kind of gilt thing.[3]—Now the colonel told father and brother,—you must know there are, let me see—there is Elnathan, Silas, and Barnabas, Tabitha—no, no, she's a she—tarnation, now I have it—there's Elnathan, Silas, Barnabas, Jonathan, that's I—seven of us, six went into the wars, and I staid at home to take care of mother. Colonel said that it was burning shame for the true blue Bunker-hill sons of liberty, who had fought Governor Hutchinson, Lord North,[4] and the Devil, to have any hand in kicking up a cursed dust against a government, which we had every mother's son of us a hand in making.

JESSAMY   Bravo!—Well, have you been abroad in the city since your arrival? What have you seen that is curious and entertaining?

JONATHAN   Oh! I have seen a power of fine sights. I went to see two marble-stone men and a leaden horse, that stands out in doors in all weathers; and when I came where they was, one had got no head, and t'other wer'nt there. They said as how the leaden man was a damn'd tory,[5] and that he took wit in his anger and rode off in the time of the troubles.

JESSAMY   But this was not the end of your excursion.

JONATHAN   Oh, no; I went to a place they call Holy Ground. Now I counted this was a place where folks go to meeting,[6] so I put my hymnbook in my pocket, and walked softly and grave as a minister; and when I came there, the dogs a bit of a meeting-house could I see. At last I spied a young gentlewoman standing by one of the seats, which they have here at the doors—I took her to be the deacon's daughter, and she looked so kind, and so obliging, that I thought I would go and ask her the way to lecture, and would you think it—she called me dear, and sweeting, and honey, just as if we were married; by the living jingo, I had a month's mind to buss[7] her.

JESSAMY   Well, but how did it end?

2. Jonathan's awkward mispronunciation of Jessamy's *insurgents*, above; being from Massachusetts, he is on Shays's side.
3. The badge of the Society of the Cincinnati, a Revolutionary officers fraternal group, was a gold eagle. "Lignum vitae": staff of life (Latin, literal trans.); here, the tough wood of a tropical tree recently introduced into New England.
4. Lord Frederick North was prime minister of England from 1770 to 1782. Bunker Hill, then

outside of Boston, was the site of the first engagement in the Revolution. Thomas Hutchinson was British governor of Massachusetts from 1771 to 1774.
5. British loyalist.
6. Church service. "Holy Ground": New York's whorehouse district, apparently so called because Trinity Church owned much of the land.
7. Kiss.

JONATHAN Why, as I was standing talking with her, a parcel of sailor men and boys got round me, the snarl headed curs fell a-kicking and cursing of me at such a tarnal[8] rate, that, I vow, I was glad to take to my heels and split home, right off, tail on end like a stream of chalk.

JESSAMY Why, my dear friend, you are not acquainted with the city; that girl you saw was a—[*Whispers.*]

JONATHAN Mercy on my soul! was that young woman a harlot!—Well, if this is New York Holy Ground, what must the Holy-day Ground be!

JESSAMY Well, you should not judge of the city too rashly. We have a number of elegant fine girls here, that make a man's leisure hours pass very agreeably. I would esteem it an honor to announce[9] you to some of them.—Gad! that announce is a select word; I wonder where I picked it up.

JONATHAN I don't want to know them.

JESSAMY Come, come, my dear friend, I see that I must assume the honor of being the director of your amusements. Nature has given up passions, and youth and opportunity stimulate to gratify them. It is no shame, my dear Blueskin,[1] for a man to amuse himself with a little gallantry.

JONATHAN Girl huntry! I don't altogether understand. I never played at that game. I know how to play hunt the squirrel, but I can't play anything with the girls; I am as good as married.

JESSAMY Vulgar, horrid brute! Married, and above a hundred miles from his wife, and think that an objection to his making love to every woman he meets! He never can have read, no, he never can have been in a room with a volume of the divine Chesterfield.—So you are married?

JONATHAN No, I don't say so; I said I was as good as married, a kind of promise.

JESSAMY As good as married!—

JONATHAN Why, yes; there's Tabitha Wymen, the deacon's daughter, at home, she and I have been courting a great while, and folks say as how we are to be married; and so I broke a piece of money with her when we parted,[2] and she promised not to spark it with Solomon Dyer while I am gone. You wouldn't have me false to my true love, would you?

JESSAMY May be you have another reason for constancy; possibly the young lady has a fortune? Ha! Mr. Jonathan, the solid charms; the chains of love are never so binding as when the links are made of gold.

JONATHAN Why, as to fortune, I must needs say her father is pretty dumb rich; he went representative for our town last year. He will give her—let me see—four times seven is—seven times four—nought and carry one;—he will give her twenty acres of land—somewhat rocky though—a Bible, and a cow.

JESSAMY Twenty acres of rock, a Bible, and a cow! Why, my dear Mr. Jonathan, we have servant maids, or, as you would more elegantly express it, wait'resses, in this city, who collect more in one year from their mistress' cast[3] clothes.

JONATHAN You don't say so!—

---

8. Mild oath (from *eternal*). "Parcel": pack.
9. Present.
1. I.e., Yankee (from the blue of the Revolutionary Army uniform); also, possibly, mulatto.

2. A country custom: a coin was broken by a parting couple, and each kept one of the pieces.
3. I.e., cast-off.

JESSAMY   Yes, and I'll introduce you to one of them. There is a little lump
of flesh and delicacy that lives at next door, wait'ress to Miss Maria; we
often see her on the stoop.

JONATHAN   But are you sure she would be courted by me?

JESSAMY   Never doubt it; remember a faint heart never[4]—blisters of my
tongue—I was going to be guilty of a vile proverb; flat against the authority of Chesterfield.—I say there can be no doubt, that the brilliancy of
your merit will secure you a favorable reception.

JONATHAN   Well, but what must I say to her?

JESSAMY   Say to her! why, my dear friend, though I admire your profound
knowledge on every other subject, yet, you will pardon my saying, that your
want of opportunity has made the female heart escape the poignancy
of your penetration. Say to her!—Why, when a man goes a-courting, and
hopes for success, he must begin with doing, and not saying.

JONATHAN   Well, what must I do?

JESSAMY   Why, when you are introduced you must make five or six elegant
bows.

JONATHAN   Six elegant bows! I understand that; six, you say? Well—

JESSAMY   Then you must press and kiss her hand; then press and kiss, and
so on to her lips and cheeks; then talk as much as you can about hearts,
darts, flames, nectar and ambrosia—the more incoherent the better.

JONATHAN   Well, but suppose she should be angry with I?

JESSAMY   Why, if she should pretend—please to observe, Mr. Jonathan—
if she should pretend to be offended, you must—But I'll tell you how my
master acted in such a case: He was seated by a young lady of eighteen
upon a sofa, plucking with a wanton hand the blooming sweets of youth
and beauty. When the lady thought it necessary to check his ardor, she
called up a frown upon her lovely face, so irresistably alluring, that it
would have warmed the frozen bosom of age: remember, said she, putting
her delicate arm upon his, remember your character and my honor. My
master instantly dropped upon his knees, with eyes swimming with love,
cheeks glowing with desire, and in the gentlest modulation of voice, he
said—My dear Caroline, in a few months our hands will be indissolubly
united at the altar; our hearts I feel are already so—the favors you now
grant as evidence of your affection, are favors indeed; yet when the ceremony is once past, what will now be received with rapture, will then be
attributed to duty.

JONATHAN   Well, and what was the consequence?

JESSAMY   The consequence!—Ah! forgive me, my dear friend, but you New
England gentlemen have such a laudable curiosity of seeing the bottom
of every thing;—why, to the honest, I confess I saw the blooming cherub
of a consequence smiling in its angelic mother's arms, about ten months
afterwards.

JONATHAN   Well, if I follow all your plans, make them six bows, and all
that; shall I have such little cherubim consequences?

JESSAMY   Undoubtedly.—What are you musing upon?

JONATHAN   You say you'll certainly make me acquainted?—Why, I was
thinking then how I should contrive to pass this broken piece of silver—
won't it buy a sugar-dram?[5]

4. I.e., a faint heart never won a fair lady.   5. I.e., a small amount of sugar.

JESSAMY   What is that, the love-token from the deacon's daughter?—You come on bravely. But I must hasten to my master. Adieu, my dear friend.

JONATHAN   Stay, Mr. Jessamy—must I buss her when I am introduced to her?

JESSAMY   I told you, you must kiss her.

JONATHAN   Well, but must I buss her?

JESSAMY   Why, kiss and buss, and buss and kiss, is all one.

JONATHAN   Oh! my dear friend, though you have a profound knowledge of all, a pugnancy[6] of tribulation, you don't know everything. [*Exit.*]

JESSAMY   [*alone*] Well, certainly I improve; my master could not have insinuated himself with more address into the heart of a man he despised.—Now will this blundering dog sicken Jenny with his nauseous pawings, until she flies into my arms for very ease. How sweet will the contrast be, between the blundering Jonathan, and the courtly and accomplished Jessamy.

Act Third

SCENE 1.

DIMPLE'*s room.*

[DIMPLE *discovered at a Toilet,*[7] *reading.*]

DIMPLE   "Women have in general but one object, which is their beauty." Very true, my lord; positively very true. "Nature has hardly formed a woman ugly enough to be insensible to flattery upon her person." Extremely just, my lord; every day's delightful experience confirms this. "If her face is so shocking, that she must, in some degree, be conscious of it, her figure and air, she thinks, make ample amends for it." The sallow Miss Wan is a proof of this.—Upon my telling the distasteful wretch, the other day, that her countenance spoke the pensive language of sentiment, and that Lady Wortley Montague[8] declared, that if the ladies were arrayed in the garb of innocence, the face would be the last part which would be admired as Monsieur Milton expresses it, she grin'd horribly a ghastly smile.[9] "If her figure is deformed, she thinks her face counterbalances it."

[*Enter* JESSAMY *with letters.*]

DIMPLE   Where got you these, Jessamy?

JESSAMY   Sir, the English packet[1] is arrived.

[DIMPLE *opens and reads a letter enclosing notes.*]

"SIR,

"I have drawn bills on you in favor of Messrs. Van Cash and Co. as per margin. I have taken up your note to Col. Piquet, and discharged your debts to my Lord Lurcher and Sir Harry Rook. I herewith enclose you copies of the bills, which I have no doubt will be immediately honored. On failure, I shall empower some lawyer in your country to recover the amounts.

6. Another awkward mispronunciation—of Jessamy's *poignancy,* above.
7. I.e., revealed sitting at a dressing table. He is reading Chesterfield's *Letters.*

8. English poet and letter writer (1689–1762).
9. "Death / Grinned horrible a ghastly smile," *Paradise Lost* 2.845–46, by John Milton (1608–1674).
1. Passenger boat carrying mail and cargo.

"I am, Sir,

"Your most humble servant,

"JOHN HAZARD."

Now, did not my lord expressly say, that it was unbecoming a well-bred man to be in a passion, I confess I should be ruffled. [*Reads.*] "There is no accident so unfortunate, which a wise man may not turn to his advantage; nor any accident so fortunate, which a fool will not turn to his disadvantage." True, my lord: but how advantage can be derived from this, I can't see. Chesterfield himself, who made, however, the worst practice of the most excellent precepts, was never in so embarrassing a situation. I love the person of Charlotte, and it is necessary I should command the fortune of Letitia. As to Maria!—I doubt not by my *sang-froid*[2] behavior I shall compel her to decline the match; but the blame must not fall upon me. A prudent man, as my lord says, should take all the credit of a good action to himself, and throw the discredit of a bad one upon others. I must break with Maria, marry Letitia, and as for Charlotte—why, Charlotte must be a companion to my wife.—Here, Jessamy!

[*Enter* JESSAMY.]

[DIMPLE *folds and seals two letters.*]

DIMPLE   Here, Jessamy, take this letter to my love. [*Gives one.*]

JESSAMY   To which of your honor's loves?—Oh! [*reading*] to Miss Letitia, your honor's rich love.

DIMPLE   And this [*delivers another*] to Miss Charlotte Manly. See that you deliver them privately.

JESSAMY   Yes, your honor. [*Going.*]

DIMPLE   Jessamy, who are these strange lodgers that came to the house last night?

JESSAMY   Why, the master is a Yankee colonel; I have not seen much of him; but the man is the most unpolished animal your honor ever disgraced your eyes by looking upon. I have had one of the most *outré* conversations with him!—He really has a most prodigious effect upon my risibility.

DIMPLE   I ought, according to every rule of Chesterfield, to wait on him[3] and insinuate myself into his good graces.—Jessamy, wait on the colonel with my compliments, and if he is disengaged, I will do myself the honor of paying him my respects.—Some ignorant unpolished boor—

[JESSAMAY *goes off and returns.*]

JESSAMY   Sir, the colonel is gone out, and Jonathan, his servant, says that he is gone to stretch his legs upon the Mall—Stretch his legs! what an indelicacy of diction!

DIMPLE   Very well. Reach me my hat and sword. I'll accost him there, in my way to Letitia's, as by accident; pretend to be struck with his person and address, and endeavor to steal into his confidence. Jessamy, I have no business for you at present. [*Exit.*]

JESSAMY [*taking up the book*]   My master and I obtain our knowledge from the same source;—though, gad! I think myself much the prettier fellow of the two. [*Surveying himself in the glass.*] That was a brilliant thought,

---

2. Cool, unperturbable (French).   3. Pay him a formal call.

to insinuate that I folded my master's letters for him; the folding is so neat, that it does honor to the operator. I once intended to have insinuated that I wrote his letters too; but that was before I saw them; it won't do now! no honor there, positively.—"Nothing looks more vulgar [*reading affectedly*], ordinary, and illiberal, than ugly, uneven, and ragged nails; the ends of which should be kept even and clean, not tipped with black, and cut in small segments of circles"—Segments of circles! surely my lord did not consider that he wrote for the beaux. Segments of circles! what a crabbed term! Now I dare answer, that my master, with all his learning, does not know that this means, according to the present mode, to let the nails grow long, and then cut them off even at top. [*Laughing without*.] Ha! that's Jenny's titter. I protest I despair of ever teaching that girl to laugh; she has something so execrably natural in her laugh, that I declare it absolutely discomposes my nerves. How came she into our house!—[*Calls*.] Jenny!

[*Enter* JENNY.]

JESSAMY   Prythee, Jenny, don't spoil your fine face with laughing.

JENNY   Why, mustn't I laugh, Mr. Jessamy?

JESSAMY   You may smile; but, as my lord says, nothing can authorize a laugh.[4]

JENNY   Well, but I can't help laughing—Have you seen him, Mr. Jessamy? Ha, ha, ha!

JESSAMY   Seen whom?—

JENNY   Why, Jonathan, the New England colonel's servant. Do you know he was at the play last night, and the stupid creature don't know where he has been. He would not go to a play for the world; he thinks it was a show, as he calls it.

JESSAMY   As ignorant and unpolished as he is, do you know, Miss Jenny, that I propose to introduce him to the honor of your acquaintance.

JENNY   Introduce him to me! for what?

JESSAMY   Why, my lovely girl, that you may take him under your protection, as Madam Ramboulliet did young Stanhope; that you may, by your plastic[5] hand, mould this uncouth cub into a gentleman. He is to make love to you.

JENNY   Make love to me!—

JESSAMY   Yes, Mistress Jenny, make love to you; and, I doubt not, when he shall become domesticated in your kitchen, that this boor, under your auspices, will soon become *un aimable petit Jonathan*.[6]

JENNY   I must say, Mr. Jessamy, if he copies after me, he will be vastly monstrously polite.

JESSAMY   Stay here one moment, and I will call him.—Jonathan!—Mr. Jonathan!—[*Calls*.]

JONATHAN   [*within*]   Holla! there—[*Enters*.] You promise to stand by me—six bows you say. [*Bows*.]

JESSAMY   Mrs. Jenny, I have the honor of presenting Mr. Jonathan, Colonel Manly's waiter, to you. I am extremely happy that I have it in my power to make two worthy people acquainted with each other's merit.

JENNY   So Mr. Jonathan, I hear you were at the play last night.

4. "To my mind, there is nothing so illiberal and so ill-bred, as audible laughter"—Chesterfield's *Letters*.

5. Creative.

6. A well-behaved little Jonathan (French).

JONATHAN   At the play! why, did you think I went to the devil's drawing-room!

JENNY   The devil's drawing-room!

JONATHAN   Yes; why ain't cards and dice the devil's device; and the play-house the shop where the devil hangs out the vanities of the world, upon the tenterhooks of temptation. I believe you have not heard how they were acting the old boy one night, and the wicked one came among them sure enough; and went right off in a storm, and carried one quarter of the play-house with him. Oh! no, no, no! you won't catch me at a play-house, I warrant you.

JENNY   Well, Mr. Jonathan, though I don't scruple your veracity, I have some reasons for believing you were there; pray, where were you about six o'clock?

JONATHAN   Why, I went to see one Mr. Morrison, the *hocus pocus* man; they said as how he could eat a café knife.[7]

JENNY   Well, and how did you find the place?

JONATHAN   As I was going about here and there, to and again, to find it, I saw a great croud of folks going into a long entry, that had lantherns over the door; so I asked a man, whether that was not the place where they played *hocus pocus*? He was a very civil kind man, though he did speak like the Hessians,[8] he lifted up his eyes and said—"they play *hocus pocus* tricks enough there, Got knows, mine friend."

JENNY   Well—

JONATHAN   So I went right in, and they shewed me away clean up to the garret, just like a meeting-house gallery. And so I saw a power of topping folks, all sitting round in little cabins,[9] just like father's corncribs;—and then there was such a squeaking with the fiddles, and such a tarnal blaze with the lights, my head was near turned. At last the people that sat near me set up such a hissing—hiss—like so many mad cats; and then they went thump, thump, thump, just like our Peleg threshing wheat, and stampt away, just like the nation;[1] and called out for one Mr. Langolee,— I suppose he helps act the tricks.

JENNY   Well, and what did you do all this time?

JONATHAN.   Gor, I—I liked the fun, and so I thumpt away, and hiss'd as lustily as the best of 'em. One sailor-looking man that sat by me, seeing me stamp, and knowing I was a cute fellow, because I could make a roaring noise, clapt me on the shoulder and said, you are a d—d hearty cock, smite my timbers! I told him so I was, but I thought he need not swear so, and make use of such naughty words.

JESSAMY   The savage!—Well, and did you see the man with his tricks?

JONATHAN   Why, I vow, as I was looking out for him, they lifted up a great green cloth, and let us look right into the next neighbor's house. Have you a good many houses in New York made so in that 'ere way?

JENNY   Not many: but did you see the family?

JONATHAN   Yes, swamp it; I see'd the family.

JENNY   Well, and how did you like them?

---

7. I.e., a restaurant knife: Morrison was evidently not only a conjurer ("*hocus-pocus* man") but also a sword-swallower.
8. Germans, especially from Hesse, had been hired by the British as mercenary troops for the Revolutionary War.
9. I.e., in boxes in the theater.
1. I.e., damnation.

JONATHAN   Why, I vow they were pretty much like other families;—there was a poor, good natured, curse of a husband, and a sad rantipole² of a wife.

JENNY   But did you see no other folks?

JONATHAN   Yes. There was one youngster, they called him Mr. Joseph; he talked as sober and as pious as a minister; but like some ministers that I know, he was a fly tike³ in his heart for all that: He was going to ask a young woman to spark it with him, and—the Lord have mercy on my soul!—she was another man's wife!

JESSAMY   The Wabash!⁴

JENNY   And did you see any more folks?

JONATHAN   Why they came on as thick as mustard. For my part, I thought the house was haunted. There was a soldier fellow, who talked about his row de dow dow, and courted a young woman:⁵ but of all the cute folk I saw, I liked one little fellow—

JENNY   Aye! who was he?

JONATHAN   Why, he had red hair, and a little round plump face like mine, only not altogether so handsome. His name was Darby:—that was his baptizing name, his other name I forgot. Oh! it was, Wig—Wag—Wagall, Darby Wagall;⁶—pray, do you know him?—I should like to take a fling⁷ with him, or a drap of cyder with a pepper-pod in it, to make it warm and comfortable.

JENNY   I can't say I have that pleasure.

JONATHAN   I wish you did, he is a cute fellow. But there was one thing I didn't like in that Mr. Darby; and that was, he was afraid of some of them 'ere shooting irons, such as your troopers wear on training days. Now, I'm a true born Yankee American son of liberty, and I never was afraid of a gun yet in all my life.

JENNY   Well, Mr. Jonathan, you were certainly at the play-house.

JONATHAN   I at the play-house!—Why didn't I see the play then?

JENNY   Why, the people you saw were players.

JONATHAN   Mercy on my soul! did I see the wicked players?—Mayhap that 'ere Darby that I liked so, was the old serpent himself, and had his cloven foot in his pocket. Why, I vow, now I come to think on 't, the candles seemed to burn blue, and I am sure where I sat it smelt tarnally of brimstone.

JESSAMY   Well, Mr. Jonathan, from your account, which I confess is very accurate, you must have been at the play-house.

JONATHAN   Why, I vow I began to smell a rat. When I came away, I went to the man for my money again: you want your money, says he; yes, says I; for what, says he; why, says I, no man shall jocky me out of my money; I paid my money to see sights, and the dogs a bit of a sight have I seen, unless you call listening to people's private business a sight. Why says

2. Unruly, wild person.
3. I.e., artful kid. The "rantipole" wife and the "pious" Joseph had by this time clued in contemporary audiences to the fact that the play Jonathan has taken for real life is Richard Brinsley Sheridan's *The School for Scandal* (1777), which had been performed in New York the previous month— a production that Tyler saw.
4. Perhaps "the scoundrel."

5. As there is no "soldier fellow" in *The School for Scandal*, Jonathan is probably now talking about *The Poor Soldier* (1783), a comic opera played on the same bill as Sheridan's play. "Row de dow dow": noisy disturbance.
6. I.e., Thomas Wignell, one of whose famous parts was Darby in *The Poor Soldier*.
7. Other texts read "sling"—an alcoholic drink.

he, it is the School for Scandalization.—The School for Scandalization—
Oh, ho! no wonder you New York folks are so cute at it, when you go to
school to learn it: and so I jogged off.⁸

JESSAMY My dear Jenny, my master's business drags me from you; would
to heaven I knew no other servitude than to your charms.

JONATHAN Well, but don't go; you won't leave me so.—

JESSAMY Excuse me.—Remember the cash. [*Aside to him, and—Exit.*]

JENNY Mr. Jonathan, won't you please to sit down. Mr. Jessamy tells me
you wanted to have some conversation with me.

[*Having brought forward two chairs, they sit.*]

JONATHAN Ma'am!—

JENNY Sir!—

JONATHAN Ma'am!—

JENNY Pray, how do you like the city, Sir?

JONATHAN Ma'am!—

JENNY I say, Sir, how do you like New York?

JONATHAN Ma'am!—

JENNY The stupid creature! but I must pass some little time with him, if
it is only to endeavor to learn, whether it was his master that made such
an abrupt entrance into our house, and my young mistress's heart, this
morning. [*Aside.*] As you don't seem to like to talk, Mr. Jonathan—do
you sing?

JONATHAN Gor, I—I am glad she asked that, for I forgot what Mr. Jessamy
bid me say, and I dare as well be hanged as act what he bid me do, I'm
so ashamed. [*Aside.*] Yes, Ma'am, I can sing—I can sing Mear, Old Hundred, and Bangor.⁹

JENNY Oh, I don't mean psalm tunes. Have you no little song to please
the ladies; such as Roslin Castle, or the Maid of the Mill?¹

JONATHAN Why, all my tunes go to meeting tunes, save one, and I count
you won't altogether like that 'ere.

JENNY What is it called?

JONATHAN I am sure you have heard folks talk about it, it is called Yankee
Doodle.

JENNY Oh! it is the tune I am fond of; and, if I know anything of my
mistress, she would be glad to dance to it. Pray, sing?

JONATHAN [*sings*]

> Father and I went to camp,—
> Along with Captain Goodwin;
> And there we saw the men and boys,
> As thick as hasty pudding.²
> Yankee Doodle do, etc.
>
> And there we saw a swamping gun,
> Big as log of maple,

8. Trotted off.
9. Popular names for hymn tunes: "Mear" is probably "Meae Animac Amator" (Jesus, lover of my
soul); "Old Hundred" is "All People That on Earth
Do Dwell"; "Bangor" is "Eternal God, We Look to
Thee."
1. Popular songs of the time.
2. Breakfast dish made from Indian corn and
water.

> On a little deuced cart,
> A load for father's cattle.[3]
> >> Yankee Doodle do, etc.
>
> And every time they fired it off,
> It took a horn of powder,
> It made a noise—like father's gun,
> Only a nation louder.
> >> Yankee Doodle do, etc.
>
> There was a man in our town,
> His name was—

No, no, that won't do. Now, if I was with Tabitha Wymen and Jemima Cawley, down at father Chase's, I shouldn't mind singing this all out before them—you would be affronted if I was to sing that, though that's a lucky thought; if you should be affronted, I have something dang'd cute, which Jessamy told me to say to you.

JENNY   Is that all! I assure you I like it of all things.

JONATHAN   No, no; I can sing more, some other time, when you and I are better acquainted, I'll sing the whole of it—no, no—that's a fib—I can't sing but a hundred and ninety verses; our Tabitha at home can sing it all.—   [Sings]

> Marblehead's a rocky place,
> And Cape-Cod is sandy;
> Charleston is burnt down,
> Boston is the dandy.
> >> Yankee Doodle do, etc.

I vow, my own town song has put me into such topping spirits, that I believe I'll begin to do a little, as Jessamy says we must when we go a courting—[Runs and kisses her.] Burning rivers! cooling flames! red hot roses! pignuts! hasty-pudding and ambrosia!

JENNY   What means this freedom! you insulting wretch. [Strikes him.]

JONATHAN   Are you affronted?

JENNY   Affronted ! with what looks shall I express my anger?

JONATHAN   Looks! why, as to the matter of looks, you look as cross as a witch.

JENNY   Have you no feeling for the delicacy of my sex?

JONATHAN   Feeling! Gor, I—I feel the delicacy of your sex pretty smartly [rubbing his cheek], though, I vow, I thought when you city ladies courted and married, and all that, you put feeling out of the question. But I want to know whether you are really affronted, or only pretend to be so? 'Cause, if you are certainly right down affronted, I am at the end of my tether;—Jessamy didn't tell me what to say to you.

JENNY   Pretend to be affronted!

JONATHAN   Aye, aye, if you only pretend, you shall hear how I'll go to work to make cherubim consequences [Runs up to her.]

3. I.e., oxen. "Swamping": big, overwhelming. "Deuced": i.e., damned.

JENNY Begone, you brute!

JONATHAN That looks like mad; but I won't lose my speech. My dearest Jenny—your name is Jenny, I think? My dearest Jenny, though I have the highest esteem for the sweet favors you have just now granted me—Gor, that's a fib though, but Jessamy says it is not wicked to tell lies to the women. [*Aside*.] I say, though I have the highest esteem for the favors you have just now granted me, yet, you will consider, that as soon as the dissolvable knot is tied, they will no longer be favors, but only matters of duty, and matters of course.

JENNY Marry you! you audacious monster! get out of my sight, or rather let me fly from you. [*Exit hastily*.]

JONATHAN Gor! she's gone off in a swinging passion, before I had time to think of consequences. If this is the way with your city ladies, give me the twenty acres of rocks, the Bible, the cow, and Tabitha, and a little peaceable bundling.[4]

SCENE 2.

The Mall.

[*Enter* MANLY.]

MANLY It must be so, Montague! and it is not at all the tribe of Mandevilles[5] shall convince me, that a nation, to become great, must first become dissipated. Luxury is surely the bane of a nation: Luxury! which enervates both soul and body, by opening a thousand new sources of enjoyment, opens, also, a thousand new sources of contention and want: Luxury! which renders a people weak at home, and accessible to bribery, corruption, and force from abroad. When the Grecian states knew no other tools than the axe and the saw, the Grecians were a great, a free, and a happy people. The kings of Greece devoted their lives to the service of their country, and her senators knew no other superiority over their fellow-citizens than a glorious preeminence in danger and virtue. They exhibited to the world a noble spectacle,—a number of independent states united by a similarity of language, sentiment, manners, common interest, and common consent, in one grand mutual league of protection.—And, thus united, long might they have continued the cherishers of arts and sciences, the protectors of the oppressed, the scourge of tyrants, and the safe asylum of liberty: But when foreign gold, and still more pernicious, foreign luxury, had crept among them, they sapped the vitals of their virtue. The virtues of their ancestors were only found in their writings. Envy and suspicion, the vices of little minds, possessed them. The various states engendered jealousies of each other; and, more unfortunately, growing jealous of their great federal council, the Amphictyons,[6] they forgot that their common safety had existed, and would exist, in giving them an honorable extensive prerogative. The common good was lost in the pursuit of private interest; and that people, who, by uniting, might have stood against the world in arms, by dividing, crumbled

4. An old courtship custom, in which a couple occupied the same bed without undressing.
5. Edward Montague and Bernard Mandeville,
18th-century authors of books on the decline of civilizations and the folly of mankind.
6. Religious associations of Greek states.

into ruin;—their name is now only known in the page of the historian, and what they once were, is all we have left to admire. Oh! that America! Oh! that my country, would in this her day, learn the things which belong to her peace!

[*Enter* DIMPLE.]

DIMPLE You are Colonel Manly, I presume?

MANLY At your service, Sir.

DIMPLE My name is Dimple, Sir. I have the honor to be a lodger in the same house with you, and hearing you were in the Mall, came hither to take the liberty of joining you.

MANLY You are very obliging, Sir.

DIMPLE As I understand you are a stranger here, Sir, I have taken the liberty to introduce myself to your acquaintance, as possibly I may have it in my power to point out some things in this city worthy your notice.

MANLY An attention to strangers is worthy a liberal mind, and must ever be gratefully received. But to a soldier, who has no fixed abode, such attentions are particularly pleasing.

DIMPLE Sir, there is no character so respectable as that of a soldier. And, indeed, when we reflect how much we owe to those brave men who have suffered so much in the service of their country, and secured to us those inestimable blessings that we now enjoy, our liberty and independence, they demand every attention which gratitude can pay. For my own part, I never meet an officer, but I embrace him as my friend, nor a private in distress, but I insensibly extend my charity to him.—I have hit the Bumpkin[7] off very tolerably. [*Aside*.]

MANLY Give me your hand, Sir! I do not proffer this hand to everybody; but you steal into my heart. I hope I am as insensible to flattery as most men; but I declare (it may be my weak side), that I never hear the name of soldier mentioned with respect, but I experience a thrill of pleasure, which I never feel on any other occasion.

DIMPLE Will you give me leave, my dear colonel, to confer an obligation on myself, by shewing you some civilities during your stay here, and giving a similar opportunity to some of my friends?

MANLY Sir, I thank you; but I believe my stay in this city will be very short.

DIMPLE I can introduce you to some men of excellent sense, in whose company you will esteem yourself happy; and, by way of amusement, to some fine girls, who will listen to your soft things with pleasure.

MANLY Sir, I should be proud of the honor of being acquainted with those gentlemen;—but, as for the ladies, I don't understand you.

DIMPLE Why, Sir, I need not tell you, that when a young gentleman is alone with a young lady, he must say some soft things to her fair cheek— indeed the lady will expect it. To be sure, there is not much pleasure, when a man of the world and a finished coquette meet, who perfectly know each other; but how delicious is it to excite the emotions of joy, hope, expectation, and delight, in the bosom of a lovely girl, who believes every tittle of what you say to be serious.

MANLY Serious, Sir! In my opinion, the man, who, under pretensions of marriage, can plant thorns in the bosom of an innocent, unsuspecting

7. Rustic.

girl, is more detestable than a common robber, in the same proportion, as private violence is more despicable than open force, and money of less value than happiness.

DIMPLE How he awes me by the superiority of his sentiments. [*Aside.*] As you say, Sir, a gentleman should be cautious how he mentions marriage.

MANLY Cautious, Sir! No person more approves of an intercourse between the sexes than I do. Female conversation softens our manners, whilst our discourse, from the superiority of our literary advantages, improves their minds. But, in our young country, where there is no such thing as gallantry, when a gentleman speaks of love to a lady, whether he mentions marriage, or not, she ought to conclude, either that he meant to insult her, or, that his intentions are the most serious and honorable. How mean, how cruel, is it, by a thousand tender assiduities, to win the affections of an amiable girl, and though you leave her virtue unspotted, to betray her into the appearance of so many tender partialities, that every man of delicacy would suppress his inclination towards her, by supposing her heart engaged! Can any man, for the trivial gratification of his leisure hours, affect the happiness of a whole life! His not having spoken of marriage, may add to his perfidy, but can be no excuse for his conduct.

DIMPLE Sir, I admire your sentiments;—they are mine. The light observations that fell from me, were only a principle of the tongue; they came not from the heart—my practice has ever disapproved these principles.

MANLY I believe you, Sir. I should with reluctance suppose that those pernicious sentiments could find admittance into the heart of a gentleman.

DIMPLE I am now, Sir, going to visit a family, where, if you please, I will have the honor of introducing you. Mr. Manly's ward, Miss Letitia, is a young lady of immense fortune; and his niece, Miss Charlotte Manly is a young lady of great sprightliness and beauty.

MANLY That gentleman, Sir, is my uncle, and Miss Manly is my sister.

DIMPLE The devil she is! [*Aside.*] Miss Manly your sister, Sir? I rejoice to hear it, and feel a double pleasure in being known to you.—Plague on him! I wish he was at Boston again with all my soul. [*Aside.*]

MANLY Come, Sir, will you go?

DIMPLE I will follow you in a moment, Sir. [*Exit* MANLY.]
Plague on it! this is unlucky. A fighting brother is a cursed appendage to a fine girl. Egad! I just stopped in time; had he not discovered himself, in two minutes more I should have told him how well I was with his sister.—Indeed, I cannot see the satisfaction of an intrigue, if one can't have the pleasure of communicating it to our friends. [*Exit.*]

Act Fourth

SCENE 1.

CHARLOTTE's *apartment.*

[CHARLOTTE *leading in* Maria.]

CHARLOTTE This is so kind, my sweet friend, to come to see me at this moment. I declare, if I were going to be married in a few days, as you are, I should scarce have found time to visit my friends.

MARIA   Do you think then that there is an impropriety in it?—How should you dispose of your time?

CHARLOTTE   Why, I should be shut up in my chamber; and my head would so run upon—upon—upon the solemn ceremony that I was to pass through—I declare it would take me above two hours merely to learn that little monosyllable—*Yes*. Ah! my dear, your sentimental imagination does not conceive what that little tiny word implies.

MARIA   Spare me your raillery, my sweet friend; I should love your agreeable vivacity at any other time.

CHARLOTTE   Why this is the very time to amuse you. You grieve me to see you look so unhappy.

MARIA   Have I not reason to look so?

CHARLOTTE   What new grief distresses you?

MARIA   Oh! how sweet it is, when the heart is borne down with misfortune, to recline and repose on the bosom of friendship! Heaven knows, that, although it is improper for a young lady to praise a gentleman, yet I have ever concealed Mr. Dimple's foibles, and spoke of him as of one whose reputation I expected would be linked with mine: but his late conduct towards me, has turned my coolness into contempt. He behaves as if he meant to insult and disgust me; whilst my father, in the last conversation on the subject of our marriage, spoke of it as a matter which laid near his heart, and in which he would not bear contradiction.

CHARLOTTE   This works well: oh! the generous Dimple. I'll endeavor to excite her to discharge him. [*Aside.*] But, my dear friend, your happiness depends on yourself:—Why don't you discard him? Though the match has been of long standing, I would not be forced to make myself miserable: no parent in the world should oblige me to marry the man I did not like.

MARIA   Oh! my dear, you never lived with your parents, and do not know what influence a father's frowns have upon a daughter's heart. Besides, what have I to allege against Mr. Dimple, to justify myself to the world? He carries himself so smoothly, that every one would impute the blame to me, and call me capricious.

CHARLOTTE   And call her capricious! Did ever such an objection start into the heart of woman? For my part, I wish I had fifty lovers to discard, for no other reason, than because I did not fancy them. My dear Maria, you will forgive me; I know your candor and confidence in me; but I have at times, I confess, been led to suppose, that some other gentleman was the cause of your aversion to Mr. Dimple.

MARIA   No, my sweet friend, you may be assured, that though I have seen many gentlemen I could prefer to Mr. Dimple, yet I never saw one that I thought I could give my hand to, until this morning.

CHARLOTTE   This morning!

MARIA   Yes;—one of the strangest accidents in the world. The odious Dimple, after disgusting me with his conversation, had just left me, when a gentleman, who, it seems, boards in the same house with him, saw him coming out of our door, and the houses looking very much alike, he came into our house instead of his lodgings; nor did he discover his mistake until he got into the parlor, where I was: he then bowed so gracefully; made such a genteel apology, and looked so manly and noble!—

CHARLOTTE   I see some folks, though it is so great an impropriety, can praise a gentleman, when he happens to be the man of their fancy. [*Aside.*]

MARIA   I don't know how it was,—I hope he did not think me indelicate—but I asked him, I believe, to sit down, or pointed to a chair. He sat down and instead of having recourse to observations upon the weather, or hackneyed criticisms upon the theater, he entered readily into a conversation worthy a man of sense to speak, and a lady of delicacy and sentiment to hear. He was not strictly handsome, but he spoke the language of sentiment, and his eyes looked tenderness and honor.

CHARLOTTE   Oh! [*eagerly*] you sentimental grave girls, when your hearts are once touched, beat us rattles a bar's length. And so, you are quite in love with this he-angel?

MARIA   In love with him! How can you rattle so, Charlotte? am I not going to be miserable? [*Sighs.*] In love with a gentleman I never saw but one hour in my life, and don't know his name!—No: I only wished that the man I shall marry, may look, and talk, and act, just like him. Besides, my dear, he is a married man.

CHARLOTTE   Why, that was good natured.—He told you so, I suppose, in mere charity, to prevent your falling in love with him?

MARIA   He didn't tell me so [*peevishly*]; he looked as if he was married.

CHARLOTTE   How, my dear, did he look sheepish?

MARIA   I am sure he has a susceptible heart, and the ladies of his acquaintance must be very stupid not to—

CHARLOTTE   Hush! I hear some person coming.

[*Enter* LETITIA.]

LETITIA   My dear Maria, I am happy to see you. Lud! what a pity it is that you purchased your wedding clothes.

MARIA   I think so. [*Sighing.*]

LETITIA   Why, my dear, there is the sweetest parcel of silks come over you ever saw. Nancy Brilliant has a full suit come; she sent over her measure, and it fits her to a hair; it is immensely dressy, and made for a court-hoop. I thought they said the large hoops were going out of fashion.

CHARLOTTE   Did you see the hat?—Is it a fact, that the deep laces round the border is still the fashion?

DIMPLE [*Within*]   Upon my honor, Sir!

MARIA   Ha! Dimple's voice! My dear, I must take leave of you. There are some things necessary to be done at our house.—Can't I go through the other room?

[*Enter* DIMPLE *and* MANLY.]

DIMPLE   Ladies, your most obedient.

CHARLOTTE   Miss Van Rough, shall I present my brother Henry to you? Colonel Manly, Maria,—Miss Van Rough, brother.

MARIA   Her brother! [*Turns and sees* MANLY.] Oh! my heart! The very gentleman I have been praising.

MANLY   The same amiable girl I saw this morning!

CHARLOTTE   Why, you look as if you were acquainted.

MANLY   I unintentionally intruded into this lady's presence this morning, for which she was so good as to promise me her forgiveness.

CHARLOTTE   Oh! ho! is that the case! Have these two penserosos been together? Were they Henry's eyes that looked so tenderly? [*Aside.*] And

so you promised to pardon him? and could you be so good natured?—
have you really forgiven him? I beg you would do it for my sake. [*Whispering loud to* MARIA.] But, my dear, as you are in such haste, it would
be cruel to detain you: I can show you the way through the other room.

MARIA   Spare me, sprightly friend.

MANLY   The lady does not, I hope, intend to deprive us of the pleasure of
her company so soon.

CHARLOTTE   She has only a mantua-maker[8] who waits for her at home.
But, as I am to give my opinion of the dress, I think she cannot go yet.
We were talking of the fashions when you came in; but I suppose the
subject must be changed to something of more importance now.—Mr.
Dimple, will you favor us with an account of the public entertainments?

DIMPLE   Why, really, Miss Manly, you could not have asked me a question
more *mal-apropos.*[9] For my part, I must confess, that to a man who has
traveled, there is nothing that is worthy the name of amusement to be
found in this city.

CHARLOTTE   Except visiting the ladies.

DIMPLE   Pardon me, Madam; that is the avocation of a man of taste. But,
for amusement, I positively know of nothing that can be called so, unless
you dignify with that title the hopping once a fortnight to the sound of
two or three squeaking fiddles, and the clattering of the old tavern windows, or sitting to see the miserable mummers, whom you call actors,
murder comedy, and make a farce of tragedy.

MANLY   Do you never attend the theater, Sir?

DIMPLE   I was tortured there once.

CHARLOTTE   Pray, Mr. Dimple, was it a tragedy or a comedy?

DIMPLE   Faith, Madam, I cannot tell; for I sat with my back to the stage
all the time, admiring a much better actress than any there;—a lady who
played the fine woman to perfection;—though, by the laugh of the horrid
creatures around me, I suppose it was comedy. Yet, on second thoughts,
it might be some hero in a tragedy, dying so comically as to set the whole
house in an uproar.—Colonel, I presume you have been in Europe?

MANLY   Indeed, Sir, I was never ten leagues from the continent.

DIMPLE   Believe me, Colonel, you have an immense pleasure to come; and
when you shall have seen the brilliant exhibitions of Europe, you will
learn to despise the amusements of this country as much as I do.

MANLY   Therefore I do not wish to see them; for I can never esteem that
knowledge valuable, which tends to give me a distaste for my native
country.

DIMPLE   Well, Colonel, though you have not traveled, you have read.

MANLY   I have, a little; and by it have discovered that there is a laudable
partiality, which ignorant, untraveled men entertain for everything that
belongs to their native country. I call it laudable;—it injures no one; adds
to their own happiness; and, when extended, becomes the noble principle
of patriotism. Traveled gentlemen rise superior, in their own opinion, to
this: but, if the contempt which they contract for their country is the
most valuable acquisition of their travels, I am far from thinking that
their time and money are well spent.

---

8. I.e., dressmaker.   9. Inappropriate (French).

MARIA   What noble sentiments!

CHARLOTTE   Let my brother set out from where he will in the fields of conversation, he is sure to end his tour in the temple of gravity.

MANLY   Forgive me, my sister. I love my country; it has its foibles undoubtedly;—some foreigners will with pleasure remark them—but such remarks fall very ungracefully from the lips of her citizens.

DIMPLE   You are perfectly in the right, Colonel—America has her faults.

MANLY   Yes, Sir; and we, her children, should blush for them in private, and endeavor, as individuals, to reform them. But, if our country has its errors in common with other countries, I am proud to say America, I mean the United States, have displayed virtues and achievements which modern nations may admire, but of which they have seldom set us the example.

CHARLOTTE   But, brother, we must introduce you to some of our gay folks, and let you see the city, such as it is. Mr. Dimple is known to almost every family in town;—he will doubtless take a pleasure in introducing you.

DIMPLE   I shall esteem every service I can render your brother an honor.

MANLY   I fear the business I am upon will take up all my time, and my family will be anxious to hear from me.

MARIA   His family! But what is it to me that he is married! [*Aside.*] Pray, how did you leave your lady, Sir?

CHARLOTTE   My brother is not married [*observing her anxiety*]; it is only an odd way he has of expressing himself.—Pray, brother, is this business which you make your continual excuse, a secret?

MANLY   No sister, I came hither to solicit the honorable Congress that a number of my brave old soldiers may be put upon the pension-list, who were, at first, not judged to be so materially wounded as to need the public assistance.—My sister says true: [*To* MARIA.] I call my late soldiers my family.—Those who were not in the field in the late glorious contest, and those who were, have their respective merits; but, I confess, my old brother-soldiers are dearer to me than the former description. Friendships made in adversity are lasting; our countrymen may forget us; but that is no reason why we should forget one another. But I must leave you; my time of engagement approaches.

CHARLOTTE   Well, but brother, if you will go, will you please to conduct my fair friend home? You live in the same street;—I was to have gone with her myself—[*Aside.*] A lucky thought.

MARIA   I am obliged to your sister, Sir, and was just intending to go. [*Going.*]

MANLY   I shall attend her with pleasure.

[*Exit with* MARIA, *followed by* DIMPLE *and* CHARLOTTE.]

MARIA   Now, pray don't betray me to your brother.

CHARLOTTE   [*just as she sees him make a motion to take his leave*]. One word with you, brother, if you please. [*Follows them out.*]

[*Manent* DIMPLE *and* LETITIA.][1]

DIMPLE   You received the billet[2] I sent you, I presume?

---

1. I.e., Dimple and Letitia remain.   2. Letter, note.

LETITIA   Hush!—Yes.

DIMPLE   When shall I pay my respects to you?

LETITIA   At eight I shall be unengaged.

[*Reenter* CHARLOTTE.]

DIMPLE   Did my lovely angel receive my billet? [*To* CHARLOTTE.]

CHARLOTTE   Yes.

DIMPLE   What hour shall I expect with impatience?

CHARLOTTE   At eight I shall be at home, unengaged.

DIMPLE   Unfortunate! I have a horrid engagement of business at that hour.—Can't you finish your visit earlier, and let six be the happy hour?

CHARLOTTE   You know your influence over me. [*Exeunt severally.*]

SCENE 2.

VAN ROUGH's *house.*

[VAN ROUGH, *alone.*]

VAN ROUGH   It cannot possibly be true! The son of my old friend can't have acted so unadvisedly. Seventeen thousand pounds! in bills!—Mr. Transfer must have been mistaken. He always appeared so prudent, and talked so well upon money-matters, and even assured me that he intended to change his dress for a suit of clothes which would not cost so much, and look more substantial, as soon as he married. No, no, no! it can't be; it cannot be.—But, however, I must look out sharp. I did not care what his principles or his actions were, so long as he minded the main chance. Seventeen thousand pounds!—If he had lost it in trade, why the best men may have ill-luck; but to game it away, as Transfer says—why, at this rate, his whole estate may go in one night, and, what is ten times worse, mine into the bargain. No, no; Mary is right. Leave women to look out in these matters; for all they look as if they didn't know a journal from a ledger, when their interest is concerned, they know what's what; they mind the main chance as well as the best of us.—I wonder Mary did not tell me she knew of his spending his money so foolishly. Seventeen thousand pounds! Why, if my daughter was standing up to be married, I would forbid the banns, if I found it was to a man who did not mind the main chance.—Hush! I hear somebody coming. 'Tis Mary's voice: a man with her too! I shouldn't be surprized if this should be the other string to her bow.—Aye, aye, let them alone; women understand the main chance.—Though, i' faith, I'll listen a little. [*Retires into a closet.*]

[MANLY *leading in* MARIA.]

MANLY   I hope you will excuse my speaking upon so important a subject, so abruptly; but the moment I entered your room, you struck me as the lady whom I had long loved in imagination, and never hoped to see.

MARIA   Indeed, Sir, I have been led to hear more upon this subject than I ought.

MANLY   Do you then disapprove my suit, Madam, or the abruptness of my introducing it? If the latter, my peculiar situation, being obliged to leave the city in a few days, will, I hope, be my excuse; if the former, I will retire: for I am sure I would not give a moment's inquietude to her, whom

I could devote my life to please. I am not so indelicate as to seek your immediate approbation; permit me only to be near you, and by a thousand tender assiduities to endeavor to excite a grateful return.

MARIA I have a father, whom I would die to make happy—he will disapprove—

MANLY Do you think me so ungenerous as to seek a place in your esteem without his consent? You must—you ever ought to consider that man as unworthy of you, who seeks an interest in your heart, contrary to a father's approbation. A young lady should reflect, that the loss of a lover may be supplied, but nothing can compensate for the loss of a parent's affection. Yet, why do you suppose your father would disapprove? In our country, the affections are not sacrificed to riches, or family aggrandizement:—should you approve, my family is decent, and my rank honorable.

MARIA You distress me, Sir.

MANLY Then I will sincerely beg your excuse for obtruding so disagreeable a subject and retire. [*Going.*]

MARIA Stay, Sir! Your generosity and good opinion of me deserve a return; but why must I declare what, for these few hours, I have scarce suffered myself to think?—I am—

MANLY What?—

MARIA Engaged, Sir;—and, in a few days, to be married to the gentleman you saw at your sister's.

MANLY Engaged to be married! And have I been basely invading the rights of another? Why have you permitted this—Is this the return for the partiality I declared for you?

MARIA You distress me, Sir. What would you have me to say? You are too generous to wish the truth: ought I to say that I dared not suffer myself to think of my engagement, and that I am going to give my hand without my heart?—Would you have me confess a partiality for you? If so, your triumph is complete; and can be only more so, when days of misery, with the man I cannot love, will make me think of him whom I could prefer.

MANLY [*after a pause*] We are both unhappy; but it is your duty to obey your parent,—mine to obey my honor. Let us, therefore, both follow the path of rectitude; and of this we may be assured, that if we are not happy, we shall, at least deserve to be so. Adieu! I dare not trust myself longer with you. [*Exeunt severally.*[3]]

Act Fifth

SCENE 1.

DIMPLE's *lodgings.*

[JESSAMY *meeting* JONATHAN.]

JESSAMY Well, Mr. Jonathan, what success with the fair?

JONATHAN Why, such a tarnal cross tike[4] you never saw!—You would have

3. Separately.
4. Here, churlish person. "The fair": i.e., the fair sex.

counted she had lived upon crabapples and vinegar for a fortnight. But what the rattle makes you look so tarnation glum?

JESSAMY   I was thinking, Mr. Jonathan, what could be the reason of her carrying herself so coolly to you.

JONATHAN   Coolly, do you call it? Why, I vow, she was fire-hot angry: may be it was because I buss'd her.

JESSAMY   No, no, Mr. Jonathan; there must be some other cause: I never yet knew a lady angry at being kissed.

JONATHAN   Well, if it is not the young woman's bashfulness, I vow I can't conceive why she shou'd n't like me.

JESSAMY   May be it is because you have not the Graces, Mr. Jonathan.

JONATHAN   Grace! Why, does the young woman expect I must be converted before I court her?[5]

JESSAMY   I mean graces of person; for instance, my lord tells us that we must cut off our nails even at top, in small segments of circles;—though you won't understand that—In the next place, you must regulate your laugh.

JONATHAN   Maple-log sieze it! don't I laugh natural?

JESSAMY   That's the very fault, Mr. Jonathan. Besides, you absolutely mis-place it. I was told by a friend of mine that you laughed outright at the play the other night, when you ought only to have tittered.

JONATHAN   Gor! I—what does one go to see fun for if they can't laugh?

JESSAMY   You may laugh;—but you must laugh by rule.

JONATHAN   Swamp it—laugh by rule! Well, I should like that tarnally.

JESSAMY   Why you know, Mr. Jonathan, that to dance, a lady to play with her fan, or a gentleman with his cane, and all other natural motions, are regulated by art. My master has composed an immensely pretty gamut,[6] by which any lady, or gentleman, with a few years' close application, may learn to laugh as gracefully as if they were born and bred to it.

JONATHAN   Mercy on my soul! A gamut for laughing—just like fa, la, sol?

JESSAMY   Yes. It comprises every possible display of jocularity, from an *affetuoso* smile to a *piano* titter, or full chorus *fortissimo*[7] ha, ha, ha! My master employs his leisure-hours in marking out the plays, like a cathe-dral chanting-book,[8] that the ignorant may know where to laugh; and that pit, box, and gallery[9] may keep time together, and not have a snigger in one part of the house, a broad grin in the other, and a d—d grum[1] look in the third. How delightful to see the audience all smile together, then look on their books, then twist their mouths into an agreeable sim-per, then altogether shake the house with a general ha, ha, ha! loud as a full chorus of Handel's, at an Abbey-commemoration.[2]

JONATHAN   Ha, ha, ha! that's dang'd cute, I swear.

JESSAMY   The gentlemen, you see, will laugh the tenor; the ladies will play the counter-tenor; the beaux will squeak the treble; and our jolly friends in the gallery a thorough bass,[3] ho, ho, ho!

5. Jonathan takes "grace" in its religious sense.
6. Full range (of musical notes).
7. Very loud. *"Affetuoso"*: passionate. *"Piano"*: soft. These are all musical terms.
8. I.e., hymnal.
9. I.e. balcony. "Pit": playhouse area nearest the stage.
1. Surly, grim.
2. I.e., in an oratorio by George Frederick Handel (1685–1759), British composer, performed at Westminster Abbey in London.
3. In Baroque music, the bass part.

JONATHAN   Well, can't you let me see that gamut?

JESSAMY   Oh! yes, Mr. Jonathan; here it is. [*Takes out a book.*] Oh! no, this is only a titter with its variations. Ah, here it is. [*Takes out another.*] Now you must know, Mr. Jonathan, this is a piece written by Ben Jonson,[4] which I have set to my master's gamut. The places where you must smile, look grave, or laugh outright, are marked below the line. Now look over me.—"There was a certain man"—now you must smile.

JONATHAN   Well, read it again; I warrant I'll mind my eye.

JESSAMY   "There was a certain man, who had a sad scolding wife,"—now you must laugh.

JONATHAN   Tarnation! That's no laughing matter, though.

JESSAMY   "And she lay sick a-dying";—now you must titter.

JONATHAN   What, snigger when the good woman's a-dying! Gor, I—

JESSAMY   Yes; the notes say you must—"And she asked her husband leave to make a will,"—now you must begin to look grave;—"and her husband said"—

JOHNATHAN   Ay, what did her husband say?—Something dang'd cute, I reckon.

JESSAMY   "And her husband said, you have had your will all your life time, and would you have it after you are dead too?"

JONATHAN   Ho, ho, ho! There the old man was even with her; he was up to the notch—ha, ha, ha!

JESSAMY   But, Mr. Jonathan, you must not laugh so. Why, you ought to have tittered *piano*, and you have laughed *fortissimo*. Look here; you see these marks, A. B. C. and so on; these are the references to the other part of the book. Let us turn to it, and you will see the directions how to manage the muscles. This [*turns over*] was note D you blundered at.— "You must purse the mouth into a smile, then titter, discovering the lower part of the three front upper teeth."

JONATHAN   How! read it again.

JESSAMY   "There was a certain man"—very well!—"who had a sad scolding wife,"—why don't you laugh?

JONATHAN   Now, that scolding wife sticks in my gizzard so pluckily, that I can't laugh for the blood and nowns[5] of me. Let me look grave here, and I'll laugh your belly full where the old creature's a-dying.—

JESSAMY   "And she asked her husband"—[*Bell rings.*] My master's bell! he's returned, I fear—Here, Mr. Jonathan, take this gamut; and, I make no doubt but with a few years' close application, you may be able to smile gracefully. [*Exeunt severally.*]

SCENE 2.

CHARLOTTE'S *apartment.*

[*Enter* MANLY]

MANLY   What, no one at home? How unfortunate to meet the only lady my heart was ever moved by, to find her engaged to another, and con-

---

4. British dramatist (1572–1637).
5. From the oath "God's blood and wounds." "Pluckily" may be a pun to go with "gizzard," for

pluck means not only courage but also the heart, liver, and lungs of a slaughtered animal.

fessing her partiality for me! Yet engaged to a man, who, by her intimation, and his libertine conversation with me, I fear, does not merit her. Aye! there's the sting; for, were I assured that Maria was happy, my heart is not so selfish, but that it would dilate in knowing it, even though it were with another.—But to know she is unhappy!—I must drive these thoughts from me. Charlotte has some books; and this is what I believe she calls her little library. [*Enters a closet.*]

[*Enter* DIMPLE *leading* LETITIA.]

LETITIA And will you pretend to say, now, Mr. Dimple, that you propose to break with Maria? Are not the banns published?[6] Are not the clothes purchased? Are not the friends invited? In short, is it not a done affair?

DIMPLE Believe me, my dear Letitia, I would not marry her.

LETITIA Why have you not broke with her before this, as you all along deluded me by saying you would?

DIMPLE Because I was in hopes she would ere this have broke with me.

LETITIA You could not expect it.

DIMPLE Nay, but be calm a moment; 'twas from my regard to you that I did not discard her.

LETITIA Regard to me!

DIMPLE Yes; I have done everything in my power to break with her, but the foolish girl is so fond of me, that nothing can accomplish it. Besides, how can I offer her my hand, when my heart is indissolubly engaged to you?—

LETITIA There may be reason in this; but why so attentive to Miss Manly?

DIMPLE Attentive to Miss Manly! For heaven's sake, if you have no better opinion of my constancy, pay not so ill a compliment to my taste.

LETITIA Did I not see you whisper her to-day?

DIMPLE Possibly I might—but something of so very trifling a nature, that I have already forgot what it was.

LETITIA I believe, she has not forgot it.

DIMPLE My dear creature, how can you for a moment suppose I should have any serious thoughts of that trifling, gay, flighty coquette, that disagreeable—

[*Enter* CHARLOTTE.]

DIMPLE My dear Miss Manly, I rejoice to see you; there is a charm in your conversation that always marks your entrance into company as fortunate.

LETITIA Where have you been, my dear?

CHARLOTTE Why, I have been about to twenty shops, turning over pretty things, and so have left twenty visits unpaid. I wish you would step into the carriage and whisk round, make my apology, and leave my cards where our friends are not at home; that you know will serve as a visit. Come, do go.

LETITIA So anxious to get me out! but I'll watch you. [*Aside.*] Oh! yes, I'll go; I want a little exercise.—Positively [DIMPLE *offering to accompany her*], Mr. Dimple, you shall not go, why, half my visits are cake and caudle[7] visits; it won't do, you know, for you to go.—

[*Exit, but returns to the door in the back scene and listens.*]

6. I.e., the marriage been publicly announced.
7. Warm ale or wine, mixed with bread, sugar, eggs, and spices.

DIMPLE   This attachment of your brother to Maria is fortunate.

CHARLOTTE   How did you come to the knowledge of it?

DIMPLE   I read it in their eyes.

CHARLOTTE   And I had it from her mouth. It would have amused you to have seen her! She that thought it so great an impropriety to praise a gentleman, that she could not bring out one word in your favor, found a redundancy to praise him.

DIMPLE   I have done everything in my power to assist his passion there: your delicacy, my dearest girl, would be shocked at half the instances of neglect and misbehavior.

CHARLOTTE   I don't know how I should bear neglect; but Mr. Dimple must misbehave himself indeed, to forfeit my good opinion.

DIMPLE   Your good opinion, my angel, is the pride and pleasure of my heart; and if the most respectful tenderness for you and an utter indifference for all your sex besides, can make me worthy of your esteem, I shall richly merit it.

CHARLOTTE   All my sex besides, Mr. Dimple—you forgot your *tête-à-tête*[8] with Letitia.

DIMPLE   How can you, my lovely angel, cast a thought on that insipid, wry-mouthed, ugly creature!

CHARLOTTE   But her fortune may have charms?

DIMPLE   Not to a heart like mine. The man who has been blessed with the good opinion of my Charlotte, must despise the allurements of fortune.

CHARLOTTE   I am satisfied.

DIMPLE   Let us think no more on the odious subject, but devote the present hour to happiness.

CHARLOTTE   Can I be happy, when I see the man I prefer going to be married to another?

DIMPLE   Have I not already satisfied my charming angel that I can never think of marrying the puling Maria. But, even if it were so, could that be any bar to our happiness; for, as the poet sings—

> Love, free as air, at sight of human ties,
> Spreads his light wings, and in a moment flies.[9]

Come then, my charming angel! why delay our bliss! The present moment is ours; the next is in the hand of fate. [*Kissing her.*]

CHARLOTTE   Begone, Sir! By your delusions you had almost lulled my honour asleep.

DIMPLE   Let me lull the demon to sleep again with kisses. [*He struggles with her; she screams.*]
        [*Enter* MANLY.]

MANLY   Turn, villain! and defend yourself.—
        [*Draws.* VAN ROUGH *enters and beats down their swords.*]

VAN ROUGH   Is the devil in you? are you going to murder one another? [*Holding* DIMPLE.]

DIMPLE   Hold him, hold him,—I can command my passion.
        [*Enter* JONATHAN.]

8. Private conversation of two people.
9. "Eloisa to Abelard" (1717), lines 75–76, by Alexander Pope, British poet.

JONATHAN   What are the rattle ails you? Is the old one[1] in you? Let the colonel alone, can't you? I feel chock full of fight,—do you want to kill the colonel?—

MANLY   Be still, Jonathan; the gentleman does not want to hurt me.

JONATHAN   Gor! I—I wish he did; I'd shew him Yankee boys play, pretty quick—Don't you see you have frightened the young woman into the hystrikes[2]

VAN ROUGH   Pray, some of you explain this; what has been the occasion of all this racket?

MANLY   That gentleman can explain it to you; it will be a very diverting story for an intended father-in-law to hear.

VAN ROUGH   How was this matter, Mr. Van Dumpling?

DIMPLE   Sir, upon my honor—all I know is, that I was talking to this young lady, and this gentleman broke in on us, in a very extraordinary manner.

VAN ROUGH   Why, all this is nothing to the purpose: can you explain it, Miss? [To CHARLOTTE.]

[Enter LETITIA through the back scene.][3]

LETITIA   I can explain it to that gentleman's confusion. Though long betrothed to your daughter [to VAN ROUGH], yet allured by my fortune, it seems (with shame do I speak it), he has privately paid his addresses to me. I was drawn in to listen to him by his assuring me that the match was made by his father without his consent, and that he proposed to break with Maria, whether he married me or not. But whatever were his intentions respecting your daughter, Sir, even to me he was false; for he has repeated the same story, with some cruel reflections upon my person, to Miss Manly.

JONATHAN   What a tarnal curse!

LETITIA   Nor is this all, Miss Manly. When he was with me this very morning, he made the same ungenerous reflections upon the weakness of your mind as he has so recently done upon the defects of my person.

JONATHAN   What a tarnal curse and damn too!

DIMPLE   Ha! since I have lost Letitia, I believe I had as good make it up with Maria—Mr. Van Rough, at present I cannot enter into particulars; but, I believe I can explain everything to your satisfaction in private.

VAN ROUGH   There is another matter, Mr. Van Dumpling, which I would have you explain:—pray, Sir, have Messrs. Van Cash and Co. presented you those bills for acceptance?

DIMPLE   The deuce! Has he heard of those bills! Nay, then, all's up with Maria, too; but an affair of this sort can never prejudice me among the ladies; they will rather long to know what the dear creature possesses to make him so agreeable. [Aside.] Sir, you'll hear from me. [To MANLY.]

MANLY   And you from me, Sir.—

DIMPLE   Sir, you wear a sword.—

MANLY   Yes, Sir:—This sword was presented to me by that brave Gallic hero, the Marquis De La Fayette.[4] I have drawn it in the service of my country, and in private life, on the only occasion where a man is justified in drawing his sword, in defence of a lady's honor. I have fought too

---

1. I.e., the devil.
2. Awkward pronunciation of *hysterics*.
3. I.e., from the rear of the acting area.

4. French statesman and general who fought with the Continental Army in 1780 and 1781.

many battles in the service of my country to dread the imputation of cowardice.—Death from a man of honor would be a glory you do not merit; you shall live to bear the insult of man, and the contempt of that sex, whose general smiles afforded you all your happiness.

DIMPLE   You won't meet me, Sir?—Then I'll post you[5] a coward.

MANLY   I'll venture that, Sir.—The reputation of my life does not depend upon the breath of a Mr. Dimple. I would have you to know, however, Sir, that I have a cane to chastise the insolence of a scoundrel, and a sword and the good laws of my country, to protect me from the attempts of an assassin.—

DIMPLE   Mighty well! Very fine, indeed!—ladies and gentlemen, I take my leave, and you will please to observe, in the case of my deportment, the contrast between a gentleman, who has read Chesterfield and received the polish of Europe, and an unpolished, untraveled American. [*Exit.*]
   [*Enter* MARIA.]

MARIA   Is he indeed gone?—

LETITIA   I hope never to return.

VAN ROUGH   I am glad I heard of those bills; though it's plaguy unlucky; I hoped to see Mary married before I died.

MANLY   Will you permit a gentleman, Sir, to offer himself as a suitor to your daughter? Though a stranger to you, he is not altogether so to her, or unknown in this city. You may find a son-in-law of more fortune, but you can never meet with one who is richer in love for her, or respect for you.

VAN ROUGH   Why, Mary, you have not let this gentleman make love to[6] you without my leave?

MANLY   I did not say, Sir—

MARIA   Say, Sir!—I—the gentleman, to be sure, met me accidentally.

VAN ROUGH   Ha, ha, ha! Mark me, Mary; young folks think old folks to be fools; but old folks know young folks to be fools.—Why, I knew all about this affair:—This was only a cunning way I had to bring it about—Hark ye! I was in the closet when you and he were at our house. [*Turns to the company.*] I heard that little baggage say she loved her old father, and would die to make him happy! Oh! how I loved the little baggage!—And you talked very prudently, young man. I have inquired into your character, and find you to be a man of punctuality and mind the main chance. And so, as you love Mary, and Mary loves you, you shall have my consent immediately to be married. I'll settle my fortune on you, and go and live with you the remainder of my life.

MANLY   Sir, I hope—

VAN ROUGH   Come, come, no fine speeches; mind the main chance, young man, and you and I shall always agree.

LETITIA   I sincerely wish you joy [*advancing to* MARIA]; and hope your pardon for my conduct.

MARIA   I thank you for your congratulations, and hope we shall at once forget the wretch who has given us so much disquiet, and the trouble that he has occasioned.

CHARLOTTE   And I, my dear Maria,—how shall I look up to you for for-

5. I.e., denounce you as.   6. I.e., court.

giveness? I, who, in the practice of the meanest arts, have violated the most sacred rights of friendship? I can never forgive myself, or hope charity from the world, but I confess I have much to hope from such a brother! and I am happy that I may soon say, such a sister.—

MARIA   My dear, you distress me; you have all my love.

MANLY   And mine.

CHARLOTTE   If repentance can entitle me to forgiveness, I have already much merit; for I despise the littleness of my past conduct. I now find, that the heart of any worthy man cannot be gained by invidious attacks upon the rights and characters of others;—by countenancing the addresses of a thousand;—or that the finest assemblage of features, the greatest taste in dress, the genteelest address, or the most brilliant wit, cannot eventually secure a coquette from contempt and ridicule.

MANLY   And I have learned that probity, virtue, honor, though they should not have received the polish of Europe, will secure to an honest American the good graces of his fair countrywoman, and, I hope, the applause of THE PUBLIC.

[curtain]

1787, 1790

SARAH WENTWORTH MORTON
1759–1846

Sarah Wentworth Morton was an important voice among the New England women who hoped to help build a specifically national American literature after the Revolution. She was the most socially prominent of them, and her prefaces stress the compatibility of writing with the duties of her "station" in life. A Bostonian by birth, Morton participated in her city's culture and politics as it rebounded from a severe economic depression immediately following the Revolution. From 1790 to 1810, Boston's population nearly doubled, to thirty-three thousand, and the provincial capital became a major city rivaling Philadelphia and New York. Its growing commerce made the city increasingly cosmopolitan. Intellectual life was fostered by social and literary clubs, as well as by weekly magazines and newspapers; the first theater opened in 1794 (with Morton's encouragement); religious diversity increased; and "tea assemblies," where dancing and card playing were acceptable, became fashionable. The old Puritan Boston seemed a remote memory.

Sarah Apthorp was born in Boston on August 29, 1759. She later added her mother's maiden name, Wentworth, at once paying tribute to her mother and asserting her womanly independence. Both parents came from families of successful merchants in Massachusetts and New Hampshire. When she was ten the Apthorps moved to Braintree (now a part of Quincy, Massachusetts) to live on her father's farm. This farming village was famous for its resident political radicals, including John Hancock and John and Abigail Adams. Like Judith Sargent Murray, Morton was determined to educate herself, even though formal schooling was denied to women. Her father's library was extensive, and she had free access to it. John Trumbull, three years her senior and destined to become one of America's chief history painters, provided early guidance of her reading. Throughout her life she socialized with important statesmen and cultural figures.

In 1781, when she was twenty-two, she married Perez Morton, a Harvard graduate trained as a lawyer with a budding reputation as an orator. He later became Massachusetts's attorney general. Though Morton's parents were suspected by Braintree citizens of loyalty to the king (one brother was paymaster to the British forces in Boston, and other brothers served in the royal army and navy), both Sarah and her husband-to-be were devoted to the causes of the American Revolution and personal liberty in general. When he was twenty-five Perez Morton served on the patriot Committee for Correspondence, organizing colonial opposition to the Crown. Sarah's stand for independence is clear from later documents. The cause of abolition was equally dear to her, and she became well known throughout New England as the author of "The African Chief" (1792), familiar then to every schoolchild. Seventy years later Whittier quoted it in *Snow-Bound*, unfortunately confusing its author with Mercy Otis Warren.

Her first known published work appeared in the *Massachusetts Magazine* in July 1789 under the name "Constantia." Since Judith Sargent Murray was already using that pen name, Morton settled on "Philenia," and she appeared in print regularly thereafter. Though best known for short pieces, Morton published three ambitious poems, each over five hundred lines long. The first was "Ouâbi: or the Virtue of Nature, an Indian Tale" (1790), a variation on the captivity narrative; here, a white hunter, Celario, marries the wife of a dying Illinois Indian chief, Ouâbi, and himself becomes the new chieftain. Isaiah Thomas and Ebenezer Andrews published "Ouâbi's Death Song," set to music, three years later, and it was an enormous popular success. Morton's next ambitious undertaking was the first part of a projected American epic, a sweeping panorama filled with Revolutionary heroes and dedicated to the "Citizen-Soldiers" who fought under the banners of "Washington and Freedom." "Beacon Hill, a Local Poem, Historic and Descriptive" (1797) begins with the famous defeat of the patriots at Bunker Hill in Charlestown, Massachusetts, because that defeat in 1775 spurred a great renewal of patriotic fervor and determination. The poem's epic conventions—its heroic couplets, invocation to the Muse of history, roll call of military heroes throughout the colonies, and concluding "Apostrophe to the Progress of Freedom Throughout the World"—attest to Morton's nationalist goals. Disappointed by the lack of public enthusiasm for the multipart project, she never finished it, but she published another long segment, "The Virtues of Society" (1799), as a separate poem.

In 1823 Morton published a collection of short poems and meditative essays, *My Mind and Its Thoughts*. The list of subscribers reads like a who's who of prominent figures, beginning with John Adams, the former president of the United States, who is addressed in several poems in the volume. Though she lived a very socially engaged life, there is something very Poe-like and pensive about its dedicatory lines: "I stood among them, but not of them—/ In a shroud of thoughts, which are not *their* thoughts." Morton's concluding "Apology" has an equally melancholy air, caused, she notes, by the "death of very dear children" and a "series of disappointments." She outlived both her children, and grieved particularly deeply over the death of her son in 1809. Prominent among disappointments must have been a family scandal that indelibly marked her husband's name. She supported her husband unequivocally, but all of Boston was certain that Sarah Morton's sister, Frances Apthorp, had fallen in love with Perez Morton, borne a child whom he denied was his, and poisoned herself. That John Adams and former governor James Bowdoin cleared Perez of accusations made by Sarah Morton's father and brother had little effect. The first American novel, *The Power of Sympathy* (1789) by William Hill Brown, published one year after Frances Apthorp's death, popularized the story.

Morton left her ancestral house in Boston in 1796–97 and moved to the nearby town of Dorchester, residing, for a time, in a house she designed herself. With the publication of *My Mind and Its Thoughts* she apparently stopped writing. After her husband's death in 1837, she returned to the family farm in Braintree to live with her sister until her own death at the age of eighty-seven.

The text used here is from *My Mind and Its Thoughts* (1823).

The African Chief[1]

See how the black ship cleaves the main,[2]
　　High bounding o'er the dark blue wave,
Remurmuring with the groans of pain,
　　Deep freighted with the princely slave!

Did all the gods of Afric sleep,　　　　　　　　　　　　5
　　Forgetful of their guardian love,
When the white tyrants of the deep,
　　Betrayed him in the palmy grove?

A chief of Gambia's[3] golden shore,
　　Whose arm the band of warriors led,　　　　　　　　10
Or more—the lord of generous power,
　　By whom the foodless poor were fed.

Does not the voice of reason cry:
　　Claim the first right that nature gave,
From the red scourge of bondage fly,　　　　　　　　　15
　　Nor deign to live a burdened slave!

Has not his suffering offspring clung,
　　Desponding round his fettered knee;
On his worn shoulder, weeping hung,
　　And urged one effort to be free!　　　　　　　　　　20

His wife by nameless wrongs subdued,
　　His bosom's friend to death resigned,
The flinty pathway drenched in blood,
　　He saw with cold and frenzied mind.

Strong in despair, then sought the plain,　　　　　　　25
　　To heaven was raised his steadfast eye,
Resolved to burst the crushing chain,
　　Or mid the battle's blast to die.

First of his race, he led the band,
　　Guardless of danger, hurling round,　　　　　　　　30

1. Taken in arms, fighting for his freedom, and inhumanly butchered by his conquerors! This affecting event was fully delineated in the various gazettes of that period [Morton's note].
2. Sea.

3. Gambia, in western Africa, bordered on the north, east, and south by Senegal and on the west by the Atlantic, became a British colony in 1843. It became a republic in 1970 and entered into a confederation with Senegal in 1982.

Till by his red avenging hand,
    Full many a despot stained the ground.

When erst Messenia's[4] sons oppressed,
    Flew desperate to the sanguine[5] field,
With iron clothed each injured breast,   35
    And saw the cruel Spartan yield.

Did not the soul to heaven allied,
    With the proud heart as greatly swell,
As when the Roman Decius died,
    Or when the Grecian victim fell?[6]   40

Do later deeds quick rapture raise,
    The boon Batavia's William won,
Paoli's time-enduring praise,
    Or the yet greater Washington![7]

If these exalt thy sacred zeal,   45
    To hate oppression's mad control,
For bleeding Afric learn to feel,
    Whose Chieftain claimed a kindred soul.

Ah, mourn the last disastrous hour,
    Lift the full eye of bootless[8] grief,   50
While victory treads the sultry shore,
    And tears from hope the captive Chief,

While the hard race of pallid hue,
    Unpracticed in the power to feel,
Resign him to the murderous crew,   55
    The horrors of the quivering wheel.[9]

Let sorrow bathe each blushing cheek,
    Bend piteous o'er the tortured slave,
Whose wrongs compassion cannot speak,
    Whose only refuge was the grave.   60

                                                    1792, 1823

4. "The *Messenians* being conquered by the *Spartans,* and agreeably to the custom of the age, the miserable remnant led into slavery, under these circumstances were so inhumanly oppressed, that rising, and united in arms, they seized upon a Spartan fortress and after innumerable injuries, inflicted and reciprocated, finally obtained their freedom" [Morton's note]. Messenia, an ancient territory in southwest Greece, was annexed by Sparta c. 700 B.C.E. to serve as its grainery. The battle of Leuctra in 371 B.C.E. freed Messenia, and Messene was named the capital.
5. Bloody.
6. "Leonidas" [Morton's note]. Leonidas (d. 480 B.C.E.) was king of Sparta. His death was immortalized by Herodotus's account of the battle of Thermopylæ. "Roman Decius": according to leg-

end, there were three early Roman heroes all named Publius Decius Mus—father, son, and grandson—and each sacrificed himself for his country in battle.
7. Morton has three famous revolutionaries in mind here. George Washington (1732–1799), commander in chief of the American Revolutionary forces; King William III (1650–1702) of England, governor in The Netherlands (or "Batavia"), who crossed the English channel in 1688 and was declared king, winning as the "boon" (or prize) the English nation in the Glorious Revolution; and Pasquale Paoli (1725–1807), the liberator of Corsica from the French in 1794.
8. Helpless; unavailing.
9. An instrument of torture.

Ode for Music

*Inscribed to George Washington, upon His Public Entrance in the Town
of Boston, During his Presidency*

The season sheds its mildest ray,
O'er the blue waves the sunbeams play;
The bending harvest clothes the plain,
The bannered vessels cheer the main;[1]
The ruddy ploughboy quits his toil,   5
The pallid miser leaves his spoil.
And grateful paeans hail the festive year,
Which bids Columbia's[2] guiding chief appear.

Hence disappointment's anxious eye,
And pining envy's lingering sigh,   10
Let sorrow from the brow be borne,
And every heart forget to mourn,
While smiles of peace their charms display,
To grace this joy-devoted day;
For the great Washington each lyre be strung,   15
Thy matchless deeds by every bard be sung.

When Freedom raised her drooping head,
And many a suffering hero led;
When every hope to thee resigned,
Were resting on thy glorious mind;   20
How did that breast, to fear unknown,
And feeling for her fate alone—
O'er peril's threatening form the falchion[3] wield,
And tread with dauntless step the endangered field.

Not Decius—patriot dear to fame,   25
Not Cincinnatus' deathless name,—
Not he,[4] who led the Spartan band,
The saviour of a bleeding land—
Could more triumphant worth display,
Nor shine with such unclouded ray.   30
Of age the hope—of youth the leading star—
The eye of peace—the conquering arm of war.

1823

1. Sea.
2. I.e., the United States, derived from Christopher Columbus.
3. Broad-edged sword.
4. Leonidas (d. 480 B.C.E.), king of Sparta, is famous for his defense of the pass of Thermopylae against the Persians. Vastly outnumbered, all the Spartans were slain. "Decius": according to legend, there were three early Roman heroes all named Publius Decius Mus—father, son, and grandson—and each sacrificed himself for his country in battle. "Cincinnatus": legendary Roman hero (c. 500–430 B.C.E.) who was called from his farm to become a military leader. George Washington was frequently compared to him.

Memento

For My Infant, Who Lived But Eighteen Hours

As the pure snow-drop, child of April tears,
    Shook by the rough wind's desolating breath—
Scarce o'er the chilly sod its low head rears,
    And trembling dies upon the parent heath,

So my lost boy, arrayed in fancy's charms,   5
    Just born to mourn—with premature decay
To the cold tyrant stretched his feeble arms,
    And struggling sighed his little life away.

As not in vain the early snow-drop rose,
    Though short its date, and hard the withering gale,   10
Since its pale bloom ethereal balm bestows,
    And cheers with vernal hope the wasted vale.

My perished child, dear pledge of many a pain!
    Torn from this ruffian world, in yon bright sphere,
Joins with awakened voice the cherub train,   15
    And pours his sweet breath on a mother's ear.

Kind dreams of morn his fairy phantom bring,
    And floating tones of ecstasy impart,
Soft as when Seraphs strike the heavenly string
    To charm the settled sorrow of the heart.   20

1823

Lines

Enclosing the Beautiful Ringlets of My Son.

Those hazel ringlets, nature's boon designed,
So oft around my parting fingers twined,
Shorn from their brow of beauty, seem to say,
His praise shall live, bright and unchanged as they.

1823

To Mr. Stuart[1]

Upon Seeing Those Portraits Which Were Painted by Him at Philadelphia, in the Beginning of the Present Century.

Stuart, thy Portraits speak!—with skill divine
Round the light graces flows the waving line;
Expression in its finest utterance lives,

1. Gilbert Stuart (1753–1828) was one of America's finest portrait painters and is now best known for his depictions of George Washington. Born in Rhode Island, he spent much of his life abroad, in England and in Ireland. He returned to America in 1792 and settled first in Philadelphia. In 1805 he went to Boston and spent the remainder of his life there.

And a new language to creation gives.
Each varying trait the gifted artist shows,   5
Wisdom majestic in his bending brows;
The warrior's open front,[2] his eye of fire—
As where the charms of bashful youth retire.
Or patient, plodding, and with wealth content,
The man of commerce counts his cent per cent.   10
'Tis character that breathes, 'tis soul that twines
Round the rich canvas, traced in living lines.
Speaks in the face, as in the form display'd,
Warms in the tint, and mellows in the shade.
Those touching graces, and that front sublime,   15
Thy hand shall rescue from the spoil of time.
Hence the fair victim scorns the threat'ning rage,
And stealing step, of slow advancing age.
Still on her cheek the bright carnation blows,
Her lip's deep blush its breathing sweetness shows,   20
For like the magic wand, thy pencil gives
Its potent charm, and every feature lives.

Even as the powerful eye's transcendant ray
Bends its soft glance and bids the heart obey,
Thy fine perceptions flow, by heaven designed,   25
To reach the thought, and pierce the unfolded mind.
Through its swift course the rapid feeling trace,
And stamp the sovereign passion on the face.

Even one, by no enlivening grace arrayed,
One, born to linger in affliction's shade,   30
Hast thou, kind artist, with attraction dressed,
With all that nature in her soul expressed.[3]

Go on, and may reward thy cares attend;
—The friend of genius must remain thy friend.
Though sordid minds with impious touch presume   35
To blend thy laurel with the cypress gloom,[4]
With tears of grief its shining leaves to fade,
Its fair hope withering in the cheerless shade,
The well-earned meed of liberal praise deny,
And on thy talents gaze with dubious eye.[5]   40

Genius is sorrow's child—to want[6] allied—
Consoled by glory, and sustained by pride.
To souls sublime her richest wreath she owes,
And loves that fame which kindred worth bestows.

1823

2. Forehead; face.
3. Morton sat for three Stuart portraits, the finest of which, unfinished, is in the collection of the Worcester Art Museum in Worcester, Massachusetts. Despite her modesty here, as a young woman Morton was considered a great beauty.
4. The laurel is traditionally associated with victory, the cypress with death.

5. A younger generation of potential clients dismissed Stuart because he was more interested in capturing psychological depth in his portraits than in focusing on clothing and other signs of wealth. Stuart always lived beyond his means, and his debts were the cause of much gossip. "Meed": reward.
6. Poverty.

BRITON HAMMON
fl. 1760

We tend to associate Indian captivity narratives with Puritan colonists in New England, but Briton Hammon's account of his capture and incarceration challenges this preconception. The title page of his *Narrative of the Uncommon Sufferings, and Surprizing Deliverance* (1760) reveals not only that he is "a Negro Man," and thus that Native Americans were quite as willing to capture African Americans if opportunity arose, but also that he was captured in Florida, which indicates that captivity could occur anywhere along the Atlantic coast. However, save for one line on the title page announcing his condition, "Servant to General Winslow, of Marshfield, in New England," Hammon's *Narrative* gives no other clue to his heritage. Published in Boston in 1760, in its day the pamphlet was but another example of the kind of story that since the 1680s had fascinated readers who often lived under the threat of Indian captivity. But for modern readers Hammon's account is not only a geographically atypical example of its genre but also the first known autobiographical text by an African American.

All that we know of Hammon we learn from his *Narrative*. Securing permission from General Winslow to work on a ship bound for Jamaica, presumably under the condition that some of his salary go to his master, he sailed from Plymouth, Massachusetts, in 1747. On the return the ship went aground on a reef off Florida. Ordered ashore, he and several other crewmen were subsequently attacked and captured by Native Americans. After five weeks in captivity, Hammon was rescued by the crew of a Spanish ship and brought to Havana. His troubles were not over, however, for there he was jailed for several years because he refused service on Spanish vessels. Eventually he got aboard an English vessel and was carried to Jamaica and thence to London, where he continued to work in the sea trades. Serendipitously, one day he discovered that he was on the same boat with his old master, General Winslow. After returning with him to Boston, he provided an account of his tribulations (probably at Winslow's suggestion) to a public eager to hear of such adventures.

Along with its details of captivity, Hammon's *Narrative* offers a striking example of life along what historians have come to call the Atlantic Rim, the transatlantic coasts along which thousands of slaves, servants, and common laborers—"hewers of wood and drawers of water," as they were known—expedited the trade on which nations enlarged their treasuries and empires. Hammon's trip to the Caribbean on a coasting vessel to secure "logwood," extended as it was by lengthy imprisonment in Cuba and subsequent work in "the King's service" during what in Europe was called the Seven Years' War, outlines a shadowy world whose parameters are only now being explored by historians. A pioneering example of African American autobiography, Hammon's *Narrative* also marks the beginning of a literature associated with an emergent class consciousness.

Narrative of the Uncommon Sufferings, and Surprizing Deliverance of Briton Hammon, a Negro Man[1]

To the Reader,

As my Capacities and Condition of Life are very low, it cannot be expected that I should make those Remarks on the Sufferings I have met with, or the kind Providence of a good GOD for my Preservation, as one in a higher Station;

---

1. The text is from the first edition of *Narrative of the Uncommon Sufferings, and Surprizing Deliverance of Briton Hammon, a Negro Man* (1760).

but shall leave that to the Reader as he goes along, and so I shall only relate Matters of Fact as they occur to my Mind—

On Monday, 25th Day of *December*, 1747, with the leave of my Master, I went from *Marshfield*,[2] with an Intention to go a Voyage to Sea, and the next Day, the 26th, got to *Plymouth*, where I immediately ship'd myself on board of a Sloop, Capt. *John Howland*, Master, bound to *Jamaica* and the *Bay*.—We sailed from *Plymouth* in a short Time, and after a pleasant Passage of about 30 Days, arrived at *Jamaica*; we was detain'd at *Jamaica* only 5 Days, from whence we sailed for the *Bay*, where we arrived safe in 10 Days. We loaded our Vessel with Logwood, and sailed from the *Bay* the 25th Day of *May* following, and the 15th Day of *June*, we were cast away on *Cape-Florida*, about 5 Leagues from the Shore; being now destitute of every Help, we knew not what to do or what Course to take in this our sad Condition:—The Captain was advised, intreated, and beg'd on, by every Person on board, to heave over but only 20 Ton of the *Wood*, and we should get clear, which if he had done, might have sav'd his Vessel and Cargo, and not only so, but his own Life, as well as the Lives of the Mate and Nine Hands, as I shall presently relate.

After being upon this Reef two Days, the Captain order'd the Boat to be hoisted out, and then ask'd who were willing to tarry on board? The whole Crew was for going on Shore at this Time, but as the Boat would not carry 12 Persons at once, and to prevent any Uneasiness, the Captain, a Passenger, and one Hand tarry'd on board, while the Mate, with Seven Hands besides myself, were order'd to go on Shore in the Boat, which as soon as we had reached, one half were to be Landed, and the other four to return to the Sloop, to fetch the Captain and the others on Shore. The Captain order'd us to take with us our Arms, Ammunition, Provisions and Necessaries for Cooking, as also a Sail to make a Tent of, to shelter us from the Weather; after having left the Sloop we stood towards the Shore, and being within Two Leagues of the same, we espy'd a Number of Canoes, which we at first took to be Rocks, but soon found our Mistake, for we perceiv'd they moved towards us; we presently saw an English Colour hoisted in one of the Canoes, at the Sight of which we were not a little rejoiced, but on our advancing yet nearer, we found them, to our very great Surprize, to be *Indians* of which there were Sixty; being now so near them we could not possibly make our Escape; they soon came up with and boarded us, took away all our Arms[,] Ammunition, and Provision. The whole Number of Canoes (being about Twenty,) then made for the Sloop, except Two which they left to guard us, who order'd us to follow on with them; the Eighteen which made for the Sloop, went so much faster than we that they got on board above Three Hours before we came along side, and had kill'd Captain *Howland*, the Passenger and the other hand; we came to the Larboard side of the Sloop, and they order'd us round to the Starboard, and as we were passing round the Bow, we saw the whole Number of *Indians*, advancing forward and loading their Guns, upon which the Mate said, *"my Lads we are all dead men,"* and before we had got round, they discharged their Small Arms upon us, and kill'd Three of our hands, viz. *Reuben Young of Cape-Cod*, Mate; *Joseph Little* and *Lemuel Doty* of *Plymouth*, upon which I immediately jump'd overboard,

2. Town on the south shore of Massachusetts.

chusing rather to be drowned, than to be kill'd by those barbarous and inhuman Savages. In three or four Minutes after, I heard another Volley which dispatched the other five, viz. *John Nowland*, and *Nathaniel Rich*, both belonging to *Plymouth*, and *Elkanah Collymore*, and *James Webb*, Strangers, and *Moses Newmock*, Molatto. As soon as they had kill'd the whole of the People, one of the Canoes padled after me, and soon came up with me, hawled me into the Canoe, and beat me most terribly with a Cutlass, after that they ty'd me down, then this Canoe stood for the Sloop again and as soon as she came along side, the *Indians* on board the Sloop betook themselves to their Canoes, then set the Vessel on Fire, making a prodigious shouting and hallowing like so many Devils. As soon as the Vessel was burnt down to the Water's edge, the *Indians* stood for the Shore, together with our Boat, on board of which they put 5 hands. After we came to the Shore, they led me to their Hutts, where I expected nothing but immediate Death, and as they spoke broken English, were often telling me, while coming from the Sloop to the Shore, that they intended to roast me alive. But the Providence of God order'd it otherways, for He appeared for my Help, *in this Mount of Difficulty*, and they were better to me then my Fears, and soon unbound me, but set a Guard over me every Night. They kept me with them about five Weeks, during which Time they us'd me pretty well, and gave me boil'd Corn, which was what they often eat themselves. The Way I made my Escape from these Villains was this; A Spanish Schooner arriving there from *St. Augustine*,[3] the Master of which, whose Name was *Romond*, asked the *Indians* to let me go on board his Vessel, which they granted, and the Captain[4] knowing me very well, weigh'd Anchor and carry'd me off to the *Havanna*, and after being there four Days the *Indians* came after me, and insisted on having me again, as I was their Prisoner;—They made Application to the Governor, and demanded me again from him; in answer to which the Governor told them, that as they had put the whole Crew to Death, they should not have me again, and so paid them Ten Dollars for me, adding, that he would not have them kill any Person hereafter, but take as many of them as they could, of those that should be cast away, and bring them to him, for which he would pay them Ten Dollars a-head. At the *Havanna* I lived with the Governor in the Castle about a Twelve-month, where I was walking thro' the Street, I met with a Press-Gang[5] who immediately prest me, and put me into Goal, and with a Number of others I was confin'd till next Morning, when we were all brought out, and ask'd who would go on board the King's Ships, four of which having been lately built, were bound to *Old-Spain*, and on my refusing to serve on board, they put me in a close Dungeon, where I was confin'd *Four Years and seven months*; during which Time I often made application to the Governor, by Persons who came to see the Prisoners, but they never acquainted him with it, nor did he know all this Time what became of me, which was the means of my being confin'd there so long. But kind Providence so order'd it, that after I had been in this Place so long as the Time mention'd above the Captain of a Merchantman, belonging to *Boston*, having sprung a Leak was obliged to put into the *Havanna* to refit, and while he was at Dinner

3. Seaport on the northeast coast of Florida.
4. The Way I came to know this Gentleman was, by his being taken last War by an *English* Privateer, and brought into *Jamaica*, while I was there [Hammon's note].
5. Men charged with finding able-bodied men who were forced to serve the king's navy, particularly in times of war.

at Mrs. *Betty Howard's*, she told the Captain of my deplorable Condition, and said she would be glad, if he could by some means or other relieve me; The Captain told Mrs. *Howard* he would use his best Endeavours for my Relief and Enlargement.

Accordingly, after Dinner, came to the Prison, and ask'd the Keeper if he might see me; upon his Request I was brought out of the Dungeon, and after the Captain had Interrogated me, told me, he would intercede with the Governor for my Relief out of that miserable Place, which he did, and the next Day the Governor sent an Order to release me; I lived with the Governor about a Year after I was delivered from the Dungeon, in which Time I endeavour'd three Times to make my Escape, the last of which proved effectual; the first Time I got on board of Captain *Marsh*, an *English* Twenty Gun Ship, with a Number of others, and lay on board conceal'd that Night; and the next Day the Ship being under sail, I thought myself safe, and so made my Appearance upon Deck, but as soon as we were discovered the Captain ordered the Boat out, and sent us all on Shore—I intreated the Captain to let me, in particular, tarry on board, begging, and crying to him, to commiserate my unhappy Condition, and added, that I had been confin'd almost five Years in a close Dungeon, but the Captain would not hearken to any Intreaties, for fear of having the Governor's Displeasure, and so was obliged to go on Shore.

After being on Shore another Twelve month, I endeavour'd to make my Escape the second Time, by trying to get on board of a Sloop bound to *Jamaica*, and as I was going from the City to the Sloop, was unhappily taken by the Guard, and ordered back to the Castle, and there confined.—However, in a short Time I was set at Liberty, and order'd with a Number of others to carry the[6] *Bishop* from the Castle, thro' the Country, to confirm the old People, baptize Children, &c. for which he receives large Sums of Money.—I was employ'd in this Service about Seven Months, during which Time I lived very well, and then returned to the Castle again, where I had my Liberty to walk about the City, and do Work for my self;—The Beaver, an *English* Man of War then lay in the Harbour, and having been informed by some of the Ship's Crew that she was to sail in a few Days, I had nothing now to do, but to seek an Opportunity how I should make my Escape.

Accordingly one Sunday Night the Lieutenant of the Ship with a Number of the Barge Crew were in a Tavern, and Mrs. *Howard* who had before been a Friend to me, interceded with the Lieutenant to carry me on board: the Lieutenant said he would with all his Heart, and immediately I went on board in the Barge. The next Day the *Spaniards* came along side the *Beaver*, and demanded me again, with a Number of others who had made their Escape from them, and got on board the Ship, but just before I did; but the Captain, who was a true *Englishman*, refus'd them, and said he could not answer it, to deliver up any *Englishmen* under *English* Colours.—In a few Days we set Sail for *Jamaica*, where we arrived safe, after a short and pleasant Passage.

After being at *Jamaica* a short Time we sail'd for *London*, as convoy to a Fleet of Merchantmen, who all arrived safe in the *Downs*,[7] I was turned over to another Ship, the *Arcenceil*, and there remained about a Month. From

6. He is carried (by Way of Respect) in a large Two-arm Chair; the Chair is lin'd with crimson Velvet, and supported by eight Persons [Hammon's note].

7. Southeast coastal area of England, near Dover.

this Ship I went on board the *Sandwich* of 90 Guns; on board the *Sandwich*, I tarry'd 6 Weeks, and then was order'd on board the *Hercules*, Capt. *John Porter*, a 74 Gun Ship, we sail'd on a Cruize, and met with a *French* 84 Gun Ship, and had a very smart Engagement,[8] in which about 70 of our Hands were kill'd and Wounded, the Captain lost his Leg in the Engagement, and I was Wounded in the Head by a small Shot. We should have taken this Ship, if they had not cut away the most of our Rigging; however, in about three Hours after, a 64 Gun Ship, came up with and took her.—I was discharged from the *Hercules* the 12th Day of *May* 1759 (having been on board of that Ship 3 Months) on account of my being disabled in the Arm, and render'd incapable of Service, after being honorably paid the Wages due to me. I was put into the *Greenwich* Hospital where I stay'd and soon recovered.—I then ship'd myself a Cook on board Captain *Martyn*, an arm'd Ship in the King's Service. I was on board this Ship almost Two Months, and after being paid my Wages, was discharg'd in the Month of *October*.—After my discharge from Captain *Martyn*, I was taken sick in *London* of a Fever, and was confin'd about 6 Weeks, where I expended all my Money, and left in very poor Circumstances; and unhappy for me I knew nothing of my *good Master's* being in *London* at this my very difficult Time. After I got well of my sickness, I ship'd myself on board of a large Ship bound to *Guinea*,[9] and being in a publick House one Evening, I overheard a Number of Persons talking about Rigging a Vessel bound to *New-England*, I ask'd them to what Part of *New-England* this Vessel was bound? they told me, to *Boston*; and having ask'd them who was Commander? they told me, Capt. *Watt*; in a few Minutes after this the Mate of the Ship came in, and I ask'd him if Captain *Watt* did not want a Cook, who told me he did, and that the Captain would be in, in a few Minutes; and in about half an Hour the Captain came in, and then I ship'd myself at once, after begging off from the Ship bound to *Guinea*; I work'd on board Captain *Watt's* Ship almost Three Months, before she sail'd, and one Day being at Work in the Hold, I overheard some Persons on board mention the Name of *Winslow*, at the Name of which I was very inquisitive, and having ask'd what *Winslow* they were talking about? They told me it was *General Winslow*; and that he was one of the Passengers, I ask'd them what *General Winslow*? For I never knew *my good Master*, by that Title before; but after enquiring more particularly I found it must be *Master*, and in a few Days Time the Truth was joyfully verify'd by a happy Sight of his Person, which so overcome me, that I could not speak to him for some Time—*My good Master* was exceeding glad to see me, telling me that I was like one arose from the Dead, for he thought I had been Dead a great many Years, having heard nothing of me for almost Thirteen Years.

I think I have not deviated from Truth, in any particular of this my Narrative, and tho' I have omitted a great many Things, yet what is wrote may suffice to convince the Reader, that I have been most grievously afflicted, and yet thro' the Divine Goodness, as miraculously preserved, and delivered out of many Dangers; of which I desire to retain a *grateful Remembrance*, as long as I live in the World.

And now, That in the Providence of that GOD, who delivered his Servant

8. A particular Account of this Engagement, has been Publish'd in the *Boston* News-Papers [Hammon's note].

9. Country on the equatorial coast of West Africa, well known to slaving vessels.

David out of the Paw of the Lion and out of the Paw of the Bear, *I am freed from a* long *and* dreadful Captivity, among worse Savages than they; *And am return'd to my* own Native Land, to Shew how Great Things the Lord hoth done for Me; *I would call upon all Men, and Say*, O Magnifie the Lord with Me, and let us Exalt his Name together!—O that Men would Praise the Lord for His Goodness, and for his Wonderful Works to the Children of Men!

1760

SUSANNA ROWSON
c. 1762–1824

Susanna Haswell Rowson, born in Portsmouth, England, first set foot on American shores when she was about five. Her mother, Susanna Musgrave, died ten days after her birth, and nothing more about her is known. Her father, William Haswell, a British navy lieutenant, left the child behind and went to Boston, Massachusetts, where he was assigned as a revenue officer. After remarrying he sent for his daughter; the family settled in Nantasket, a seaside town of about fifty houses, which Rowson remembered as beautifully set amid "orchards, cornfield, and pasture land." The family's idyllic life there was permanently disrupted when William Haswell's attachment to the Crown became intolerable to their increasingly revolution-minded neighbors. In 1775 the family was sent under guard to nearby Hingham, where they remained for three years until returning to England as part of a prisoner exchange. All their American property was confiscated.

In 1786 Susanna married William Rowson, a hardware merchant and occasional actor and trumpeter whose heavy drinking made it difficult for him to work steadily. It became clear almost at once that Susanna Rowson would have to be a wage earner. She turned to writing and acting, publishing her first novel, *Victoria*, soon after her marriage. She wrote for William Lane's Minerva Press, which published novels— particularly novels by and about women—that were made available through circulating libraries. Also in 1786, she appeared on stage in Brighton with a group of London actors. Two years later, she published *A Trip to Parnassus* (1788), a book of verse observations on the nature of good theater and the obligations of playwrights and actors to create a morally responsible art. Although the book appeared anonymously, Rowson's authorship was known to reviewers. Rowson also began to write song lyrics, a craft she continued for the rest of her life. Before moving to the United States in 1793, she had completed five novels, including *Charlotte: A Tale of Truth* (1791).

In 1793 Rowson and her husband moved to America as actors under contract to Thomas Wignell of Philadelphia. In only two seasons she learned fifty-seven roles. After an outbreak of yellow fever in 1796 closed the Philadelphia theaters, the Rowsons moved to Boston. By this time Rowson had also published another novel, *Trials of the Human Heart* (1795), and a comic opera, *Slaves in Algiers* (1794). Two plays that enunciated strong patriotic sentiments—*The Female Patriot* (1795) and *Americans in England* (1796), later revised as *The Columbian Daughter* (1800)—earned the condemnation of British critics. Most important, she had found an American publisher for *Charlotte: A Tale of Truth*—the Philadelphia entrepreneur Matthew Carey, whose books were among the most widely circulated in the early national period. *Charlotte*, or *Charlotte Temple* as it became known in its third edition, was the first American best-seller, with over two hundred editions published by the end of the nineteenth century. It was far more popular in this country than it had been in England. When we examine existing early American copies, we find a readership cutting across boundaries of class, region, age, religion, and political affiliation. Many people refused to treat the book as fiction and made pilgrimages to New York's Trinity Churchyard, where Charlotte was supposed to be buried. As late as 1903 a resident of the city confessed that "the first tears I ever saw in the eyes of a grown person were shed for her."

Rowson's novel clearly found an audience that preferred fiction to sermons, an audience interested in individual lives, personal emotion, and stories dramatizing the clash of impulse with authority. Besides their intrinsic human interest, these themes had relevance to the politics of an emerging nation that was founded in an act of filial disobedience. As a character, Charlotte served as both a warning and an occasion for sentimental sympathy. The novel combined old-fashioned allegory with new psychological realism.

Unfortunately, Rowson earned almost nothing from the easily pirated editions of her novel, and the need to make money continued, especially as her husband found it increasingly difficult to hold a job. Rowson gave her last theatrical performance in Boston in 1797 and started on a new, successful career as founder-director of an exclusive school for girls in Boston. This endeavor responded to new demands for serious women's education, which would become a dominant feminist motif in the nineteenth century. That the former actress could become a respected teacher, drawing students from the "best" families, points to the extent to which American culture was becoming secularized in the years after the Revolution. In her new career Rowson also wrote textbooks: histories, geographies, spellers, and readers. A popular historical novel, *Reuben and Rachel* (1798)—one of the earliest examples of this genre—combined narrative interest with lessons about United States history from Columbus to the Revolution. Increasingly religious in her later years, Rowson published a biblical "conversation" in 1822, dramatizing family evenings in which the Bible is read and discussed.

After Rowson's death, her executors discovered a manuscript sequel to *Charlotte* called *Charlotte's Daughter: or, Three Orphans*. This appeared posthumously in 1828 and became better known as *Lucy Temple*. Despite its considerable success, neither this book nor any other that Rowson published ever approached the popularity of *Charlotte Temple*. Not until *Uncle Tom's Cabin*—another novel about flight and oppression, also by a woman—did a book achieve such wide circulation in America.

Charlotte: A Tale of Truth[1]

Preface

For the perusal of the young and thoughtless of the fair sex, this Tale of Truth is designed; and I could wish my fair readers to consider it as not merely the effusion of Fancy,[2] but as a reality. The circumstances on which I have founded this novel were related to me some little time since by an old lady who had personally known Charlotte, though she concealed the real names of the characters, and likewise the place where the unfortunate scenes were acted: yet as it was impossible to offer a relation to the public in such an imperfect state, I have thrown over the whole a slight veil of fiction, and substituted names and places according to my own fancy. The principal char-

---

1. The text used here is from a copy owned by the American Antiquarian Society of the first American edition, published in Philadelphia in 1794 for Matthew Carey. *Charlotte: A Tale of Truth* was first published in London in 1791. When the 3rd American edition appeared in 1797, Carey changed the title to *Charlotte Temple*.
2. Imagination.

acters in this little tale are now consigned to the silent tomb: it can therefore hurt the feelings of no one; and may, I flatter myself, be of service to some who are so unfortunate as to have neither friends to advise, or understanding to direct them, through the various and unexpected evils that attend a young and unprotected woman in her first entrance into life.

While the tear of compassion still trembled in my eye for the fate of the unhappy Charlotte, I may have children of my own, said I, to whom this recital may be of use, and if to your own children, said Benevolence, why not to the many daughters of Misfortune who, deprived of natural friends, or spoilt by a mistaken education, are thrown on an unfeeling world without the least power to defend themselves from the snares not only of the other sex, but from the more dangerous arts of the profligate of their own.

Sensible as I am that a novel writer, at a time when such a variety of works are ushered into the world under that name, stands but a poor chance for fame in the annals of literature, but conscious that I wrote with a mind anxious for the happiness of that sex whose morals and conduct have so powerful an influence on mankind in general; and convinced that I have not wrote a line that conveys a wrong idea to the head or a corrupt wish to the heart, I shall rest satisfied in the purity of my own intentions, and if I merit not applause, I feel that I dread not censure.

If the following tale should save one hapless fair one from the errors which ruined poor Charlotte, or rescue from impending misery the heart of one anxious parent, I shall feel a much higher gratification in reflecting on this trifling performance, than could possibly result from the applause which might attend the most elegant finished piece of literature whose tendency might deprave the heart or mislead the understanding.

Chapter I. A Boarding School

"Are you for a walk," said Montraville to his companion, as they arose from table; "are you for a walk? or shall we order the chaise and proceed to Portsmouth?"[3] Belcour preferred the former; and they sauntered out to view the town, and to make remarks on the inhabitants, as they returned from church.

Montraville was a Lieutenant in the army: Belcour was his brother officer: they had been to take leave of their friends previous to their departure for America, and were now returning to Portsmouth, where the troops waited orders for embarkation. They had stopped at Chichester to dine; and knowing they had sufficient time to reach the place of destination before dark, and yet allow them a walk, had resolved, it being Sunday afternoon, to take a survey of the Chichester ladies as they returned from their devotions.

They had gratified their curiosity, and were preparing to return to the inn without honoring any of the belles with particular notice, when Madame Du Pont, at the head of her school, descended from the church. Such an assemblage of youth and innocence naturally attracted the young soldiers: they stopped; and, as the little cavalcade passed, almost involuntarily pulled off their hats. A tall, elegant girl looked at Montraville and blushed: he instantly recollected the features of Charlotte Temple, whom he had once seen and danced with at a ball at Portsmouth. At that time he thought on her only as

---

3. A seaport in the south of England. "Chaise": a light, open horse-drawn carriage.

a very lovely child, she being then only thirteen; but the improvement two years had made in her person, and the blush of recollection which suffused her cheeks as she passed, awakened in his bosom new and pleasing ideas. Vanity led him to think that pleasure at again beholding him might have occasioned the emotion he had witnessed, and the same vanity led him to wish to see her again.

"She is the sweetest girl in the world," said he, as he entered the inn. Belcour stared. "Did you not notice her?" continued Montraville: "she had on a blue bonnet, and with a pair of lovely eyes of the same color, has contrived to make me feel devilish odd about the heart."

"Pho," said Belcour, "a musket ball from our friends, the Americans, may in less than two months make you feel worse."

"I never think of the future," replied Montraville; "but am determined to make the most of the present, and would willingly compound with any kind Familiar[4] who would inform me who the girl is, and how I might be likely to obtain an interview."

But no kind Familiar at that time appearing, and the chaise which they had ordered, driving up to the door, Montraville and his companion were obliged to take leave of Chichester and its fair inhabitant, and proceed on their journey.

But Charlotte had made too great an impression on his mind to be easily eradicated: having therefore spent three whole days in thinking on her and in endeavoring to form some plan for seeing her, he determined to set off for Chichester, and trust to chance either to favor or frustrate his designs. Arriving at the verge of the town, he dismounted, and sending the servant forward with the horses, proceeded toward the place, where, in the midst of an extensive pleasure ground, stood the mansion which contained the lovely Charlotte Temple. Montraville leaned on a broken gate, and looked earnestly at the house. The wall which surrounded it was high, and perhaps the Arguses who guarded the Hesperian fruit within, were more watchful than those famed of old.[5]

" 'Tis a romantic attempt," said he; "and should I even succeed in seeing and conversing with her, it can be productive of no good: I must of necessity leave England in a few days, and probably may never return; why then should I endeavor to engage the affections of this lovely girl, only to leave her a prey to a thousand inquietudes, of which at present she has no idea? I will return to Portsmouth and think no more about her."

The evening now was closed; a serene stillness reigned; and the chaste Queen of Night[6] with her silver crescent faintly illuminated the hemisphere. The mind of Montraveille was hushed into composure by the serenity of the surrounding objects. "I will think on her no more," said he, and turned with an intention to leave the place; but as he turned, he saw the gate which led to the pleasure grounds open, and two women come out, who walked arm-in-arm across the field.

"I will at least see who these are," said he. He overtook them, and giving them the compliments of the evening, begged leave to see them into the

---

4. Acquaintance. "Compound with": bargain with.
5. Any alert or watchful persons, named after the hundred-eyed giant of Greek mythology, Argus. "Hesperian fruit": the golden apples stolen by Her-

cules as one of his labors were guarded by the Hesperides, three young women.
6. The moon.

more frequented parts of the town: but how was he delighted, when, waiting for an answer, he discovered, under the concealment of a large bonnet, the face of Charlotte Temple.

He soon found means to ingratiate himself with her companion, who was a French teacher at the school, and, at parting, slipped a letter he had purposely written, into Charlotte's hand, and five guineas[7] into that of Mademoiselle, who promised she would endeavor to bring her young charge into the field again the next evening.

Chapter II. *Domestic Concerns*

Mr. Temple was the youngest son of a nobleman whose fortune was by no means adequate to the antiquity, grandeur, and I may add, pride of the family. He saw his elder brother made completely wretched by marrying a disagreeable woman, whose fortune helped to prop the sinking dignity of the house; and he beheld his sisters legally prostituted to old, decrepit men, whose titles gave them consequence in the eyes of the world, and whose affluence rendered them splendidly miserable. "I will not sacrifice internal happiness for outward show," said he: "I will seek Content; and, if I find her in a cottage, will embrace her with as much cordiality as I should if seated on a throne."

Mr. Temple possessed a small estate of about five hundred pounds a year; and with that he resolved to preserve independence, to marry where the feelings of his heart should direct him, and to confine his expenses within the limits of his income. He had a heart open to every generous feeling of humanity, and a hand ready to dispense to those who wanted[8] part of the blessings he enjoyed himself.

As he was universally known to be the friend of the unfortunate, his advice and bounty was frequently solicited; nor was it seldom that he sought out indigent merit, and raised it from obscurity, confining his own expenses within a very narrow compass.

"You are a benevolent fellow," said a young officer to him one day; "and I have a great mind to give you a fine subject to exercise the goodness of your heart upon."

"You cannot oblige me more," said Temple, "than to point out any way by which I can be serviceable to my fellow creatures."

"Come along then," said the young man, "we will go and visit a man who is not in so good a lodging as he deserves; and, were it not that he has an angel with him, who comforts and supports him, he must long since have sunk under his misfortunes." The young man's heart was too full to proceed; and Temple, unwilling to irritate his feelings by making further inquiries, followed him in silence, till they arrived at the Fleet prison.[9]

The officer inquired for Captain Eldridge: a person led them up several pair of dirty stairs, and pointing to a door which led to a miserable, small apartment, said that was the Captain's room, and retired.

The officer, whose name was Blakeney, tapped at the door, and was bid

7. A British gold coin, no longer in use, worth one pound one shilling.
8. Lacked.
9. A debtor's prison in London, named for the Fleet River; in this period it was common for people unable to meet their financial obligations to be jailed.

to enter by a voice melodiously soft. He opened the door, and discovered to Temple a scene which rivetted him to the spot with astonishment.

The apartment, though small, and bearing strong marks of poverty, was neat in the extreme. In an arm-chair, his head reclined upon his hand, his eyes fixed on a book which lay open before him, sat an aged man in a Lieutenant's uniform, which, though threadbare, would sooner call a blush of shame into the face of those who could neglect real merit, than cause the hectic[1] of confusion to glow on the cheeks of him who wore it.

Beside him sat a lovely creature busied in painting a fan mount.[2] She was fair as the lily, but sorrow had nipped the rose in her cheek before it was half blown.[3] Her eyes were blue; and her hair, which was light brown, was slightly confined under a plain muslin cap, tied round with a black ribbon; a white linen gown and plain lawn handkerchief[4] composed the remainder of her dress; and in this simple attire, she was more irresistibly charming to such a heart as Temple's, than she would have been, if adorned with all the splendor of a courtly belle.

When they entered, the old man arose from his seat, and shaking Blakeney by the hand with great cordiality, offered Temple his chair; and there being but three in the room, seated himself on the side of his little bed with evident composure.

"This is a strange place," said he to Temple, "to receive visitors of distinction in; but we must fit our feelings to our station. While I am not ashamed to own the cause which brought me here, why should I blush at my situation? Our misfortunes are not our faults; and were it not for that poor girl—"

Here the philosopher was lost in the father. He rose hastily from his seat, and walking toward the window, wiped off a tear which he was afraid would tarnish the cheek of a sailor.

Temple cast his eye on Miss Eldridge: a pellucid drop had stolen from her eyes, and fallen upon a rose she was painting. It blotted and discolored the flower. " 'Tis emblematic,"[5] said he mentally: "the rose of youth and health soon fades when watered by the tear of affliction."

"My friend Blakeney," said he, addressing the old man, "told me I could be of service to you: be so kind then, dear Sir, as to point out some way in which I can relieve the anxiety of your heart and increase the pleasures of my own."

"My good young man," said Eldridge, "you know not what you offer. While deprived of my liberty I cannot be free from anxiety on my own account; but that is a trifling concern; my anxious thoughts extend to one more dear a thousand times than life: I am a poor weak old man, and must expect in a few years to sink into silence and oblivion; but when I am gone, who will protect that fair bud of innocence from the blasts of adversity, or from the cruel hand of insult and dishonor."

"Oh, my father!" cried Miss Eldridge, tenderly taking his hand, "be not anxious on that account; for daily are my prayers offered to heaven that our

1. Flush.
2. A board on which a fan is to be mounted and framed.
3. Bloomed.

4. Probably worn about the neck. "Lawn": a thin cloth woven from either cotton or linen.
5. Symbolic.

lives may terminate at the same instant, and one grave receive us both; for why should I live when deprived of my only friend."

Temple was moved even to tears. "You will both live many years," said he, "and I hope see much happiness. Cheerly, my friend, cheerly; these passing clouds of adversity will serve only to make the sunshine of prosperity more pleasing. But we are losing time: you might ere this have told me who were your creditors, what were their demands, and other particulars necessary to your liberation."

"My story is short," said Mr. Eldridge, "but there are some particulars which will wring my heart barely to remember; yet to one whose offers of friendship appear so open and disinterested, I will relate every circumstance that led to my present, painful situation. But my child," continued he, addressing his daughter, "let me prevail on you to take this opportunity, while my friends are with me, to enjoy the benefit of air and exercise. Go my love; leave me now; to-morrow at your usual hour I will expect you."

Miss Eldridge impressed on his cheek the kiss of filial affection, and obeyed.

Chapter III. Unexpected Misfortunes

"My life," said Mr. Eldridge, "till within these few years was marked by no particular circumstance deserving notice. I early embraced the life of a sailor, and have served my King with unremitted ardor for many years. At the age of twenty-five I married an amiable woman; one son, and the girl who just now left us, were the fruits of our union. My boy had genius and spirit. I straitened my little income to give him a liberal education, but the rapid progress he made in his studies amply compensated for the inconvenience. At the academy where he received his education he commenced an acquaintance with a Mr. Lewis, a young man of affluent fortune: as they grew up their intimacy ripened into friendship, and they became almost inseparable companions.

"George chose the profession of a soldier. I had neither friends or money to procure him a commission, and had wished him to embrace a nautical life: but this was repugnant to his wishes, and I ceased to urge him on the subject.

"The friendship subsisting between Lewis and my son was of such a nature as gave him free access to our family; and so specious[6] was his manner that we hesitated not to state to him all our little difficulties in regard to George's future views. He listened to us with attention, and offered to advance any sum necessary for his first setting out.

"I embraced the offer, and gave him my note for the payment of it, but he would not suffer me to mention any stipulated time, as he said I might do it whenever most convenient to myself. About this time my dear Lucy returned from school, and I soon began to imagine Lewis looked at her with eyes of affection. I gave my child a caution to beware of him, and to look on her mother as her friend. She was unaffectedly artless;[7] and when, as I suspected,

6. Having about it an air of genuineness but deceptive.

7. Without guile.

Lewis made professions of love, she confided in her parents, and assured us her heart was perfectly unbiassed in his favor, and she would cheerfully submit to our direction.

"I took an early opportunity of questioning him concerning his intentions towards my child: he gave an equivocal answer, and I forbade him the house.

"The next day he sent and demanded payment of his money. It was not in my power to comply with the demand. I requested three days to endeavor to raise it, determining in that time to mortgage my half pay, and live on a small annuity which my wife possessed, rather than be under an obligation to so worthless a man: but this short time was not allowed me; for that evening, as I was sitting down to supper, unsuspicious of danger, an officer entered, and tore me from the embraces of my family.

"My wife had been for some time in a declining state of health: ruin at once so unexpected and inevitable was a stroke she was not prepared to bear, and I saw her faint into the arms of our servant, as I left my own habitation for the comfortless walls of a prison. My poor Lucy, distracted with her fears for us both, sunk on the floor and endeavored to detain me by her feeble efforts; but in vain; they forced open her arms; she shrieked, and fell prostrate. But pardon me. The horrors of that night unman me. I cannot proceed."

He rose from his seat, and walked several times across the room: at length, attaining more composure, he cried—"What a mere infant I am! Why, Sir, I never felt thus in the day of battle."

"No," said Temple; "but the truly brave soul is tremblingly alive to the feelings of humanity."

"True," replied the old man (something like satisfaction darting across his features), "and painful as these feelings are, I would not exchange them for that torpor which the stoic mistakes for philosophy. How many exquisite delights should I have passed by unnoticed, but for these keen sensations, this quick sense of happiness or misery? Then let us, my friend, take the cup of life as it is presented to us, tempered by the hand of a wise Providence; be thankful for the good, be patient under the evil, and presume not to inquire why the latter predominates."

"This is true philosophy," said Temple.

" 'Tis the only way to reconcile ourselves to the cross events of life," replied he. "But I forget myself. I will not longer intrude on your patience, but proceed in my melancholy tale.

"The very evening that I was taken to prison, my son arrived from Ireland, where he had been some time with his regiment. From the distracted expressions of his mother and sister, he learnt by whom I had been arrested; and, late as it was, flew on the wings of wounded affection, to the house of his false friend, and earnestly inquired the cause of this cruel conduct. With all the calmness of a cool deliberate villain, he avowed his passion for Lucy; declared her situation in life would not permit him to marry her; but offered to release me immediately, and make any settlement on her, if George would persuade her to live, as he impiously termed it, a life of honor.

"Fired at the insult offered to a man and a soldier, my boy struck the villain, and a challenge[8] ensued. He then went to a coffee house in the neighborhood

8. A demand for a duel.

and wrote a long affectionate letter to me, blaming himself severely for having introduced Lewis into the family, or permitted him to confer an obligation, which had brought inevitable ruin on us all. He begged me, whatever might be the event of the ensuing morning, not to suffer regret or unavailing sorrow for his fate, to increase the anguish of my heart, which he greatly feared was already insupportable.

"This letter was delivered to me early in the morning. It would be vain to attempt describing my feelings on the perusal of it; suffice it to say, that a merciful Providence interposed, and I was for three weeks insensible to miseries almost beyond the strength of human nature to support.

"A fever and strong delirium seized me, and my life was despaired of. At length, nature, overpowered with fatigue, gave way to the salutary power of rest, and a quiet slumber of some hours restored me to reason, though the extreme weakness of my frame prevented my feeling my distress so acutely as I otherways should.

"The first object that struck me on awaking, was Lucy sitting by my bedside; her pale countenance and sable dress prevented my inquiries for poor George: for the letter I had received from him, was the first thing that occurred to my memory. By degrees the rest returned: I recollected being arrested, but could no ways account for being in this apartment, whither they had conveyed me during my illness.

"I was so weak as to be almost unable to speak. I pressed Lucy's hand, and looked earnestly round the apartment in search of another dear object.

"Where is your mother?" said I, faintly.

"The poor girl could not answer: she shook her head in expressive silence; and throwing herself on the bed, folded her arms about me, and burst into tears.

"What! both gone?" said I.

"Both, she replied, endeavoring to restrain her emotions: "but they are happy, no doubt."

Here Mr. Eldridge paused: the recollection of the scene was too painful to permit him to proceed.

Chapter IV. Change of Fortune

"It was some days," continued Mr. Eldridge, recovering himself "before I could venture to inquire the particulars of what had happened during my illness: at length I assumed courage to ask my dear girl how long her mother and brother had been dead: she told me that the morning after my arrest George came home early to inquire after his mother's health, stayed with them but a few minutes, seemed greatly agitated at parting, but gave them strict charge to keep up their spirits, and hope everything would turn out for the best. In about two hours after, as they were sitting at breakfast, and endeavoring to strike out some plan to attain my liberty, they heard a loud rap at the door, which Lucy running to open, she met the bleeding body of her brother, borne in by two men who had lifted him from a litter, on which they had brought him from the place where he fought. Her poor mother, weakened by illness and the struggles of the preceding night, was not able to support this shock; gasping for breath, her looks wild and haggard, she reached the apartment where they had carried her dying son. She knelt by the bedside; and taking his cold hand, 'my poor boy,' said she, 'I will not be parted from thee: husband! son! both at once lost. Father of mercies, spare me!' She fell into a strong convulsion, and expired in about two hours. In the meantime, a surgeon had dressed George's wounds; but they were in such a situation as to bar the smallest hopes of recovery. He never was sensible from the time he was brought home, and died that evening in the arms of his sister.

"Late as it was when this event took place, my affectionate Lucy insisted on coming to me. 'What must he feel,' said she, 'at our apparent neglect, and how shall I inform him of the afflictions with which it has pleased heaven to visit us?'

"She left the care of the dear departed ones to some neighbors who had kindly come in to comfort and assist her; and on entering the house where I was confined, found me in the situation I have mentioned.

"How she supported herself in these trying moments, I know not: heaven, no doubt, was with her; and her anxiety to preserve the life of one parent in some measure abated her affliction for the loss of the other.

"My circumstances were greatly embarrassed,[9] my acquaintance few, and those few utterly unable to assist me. When my wife and son were committed to their kindred earth, my creditors seized my house and furniture, which not being sufficient to discharge all their demands, detainers[1] were lodged against me. No friend stepped forward to my relief; from the grave of her mother, my beloved Lucy followed an almost dying father to this melancholy place.

"Here we have been nearly a year and a half. My half-pay I have given up to satisfy my creditors, and my child supports me by her industry: sometimes by fine needlework, sometimes by painting. She leaves me every night, and goes to a lodging near the bridge; but returns in the morning, to cheer me with her smiles, and bless me by her duteous affection. A lady once offered her an asylum in her family; but she would not leave me. 'We are all the world to each other,' said she. 'I thank God, I have health and spirits to improve the talents with which nature has endowed me; and I trust if I employ them in the support of a beloved parent, I shall not be thought an unprofitable servant.[2] While he lives, I pray for strength to pursue my employment; and when it pleases heaven to take one of us, may it give the survivor resignation to bear the separation as we ought: till then I will never leave him.' "

"But where is this inhuman persecutor?" said Temple.

"He has been abroad ever since," replied the old man; "but he has left orders with his lawyer never to give up the note till the utmost farthing is paid."

"And how much is the amount of your debts in all?" said Temple.

"Five hundred pounds,"[3] he replied.

Temple started: it was more than he expected. "But something must be

---

9. I.e., he was in great financial difficulties.
1. Writs authorizing further detention of a person already in custody.
2. I.e., a useless servant of God. "Improve": make use of.

3. Five hundred pounds was a considerable amount of money in 1791; a clergyman's yearly salary, for example, might well have been less than one-tenth that sum.

done," said he: "that sweet maid must not wear out her life in a prison. I will see you again tomorrow, my friend," said he, shaking Eldridge's hand: "keep up your spirits: light and shade are not more happily blended than are the pleasures and pains of life; and the horrors of the one serve only to increase the splendor of the other."

"You never lost a wife and son," said Eldridge.

"No," replied he, "but I can feel for those that have." Eldridge pressed his hand as they went toward the door, and they parted in silence.

When they got without the walls of the prison, Temple thanked his friend Blakeney for introducing him to so worthy a character; and telling him he had a particular engagement in the city, wished him a good evening.

"And what is to be done for this distressed man," said Temple, as he walked up Ludgate Hill. "Would to heaven I had a fortune that would enable me instantly to discharge his debt: what exquisite transport, to see the expressive eyes of Lucy beaming at once with pleasure for her father's deliverance, and gratitude for her deliverer: but is not my fortune affluence," continued he, "nay superfluous wealth, when compared to the extreme indigence of Eldridge; and what have I done to deserve ease and plenty while a brave worthy officer starves in a prison? Three hundred a year is surely sufficient for all my wants and wishes: at any rate Eldridge must be relieved."

When the heart has will, the hands can soon find means to execute a good action.

Temple was a young man, his feelings warm and impetuous; unacquainted with the world, his heart had not been rendered callous by being convinced of its fraud and hypocrisy. He pitied their sufferings, overlooked their faults, thought every bosom as generous as his own, and would cheerfully have divided his last guinea with an unfortunate fellow creature.

No wonder, then, that such a man (without waiting a moment for the interference of Madam Prudence) should resolve to raise money sufficient for the relief of Eldridge, by mortgaging part of his fortune.

We will not inquire too minutely into the cause which might actuate him in this instance: suffice it to say, he immediately put the plan in execution; and in three days from the time he first saw the unfortunate Lieutenant, he had the superlative felicity of seeing him at liberty, and receiving an ample reward in the tearful eye and half articulated thanks of the grateful Lucy.

"And pray, young man," said his father to him one morning, "what are your designs in visiting thus constantly that old man and his daughter?"

Temple was at a loss for a reply: he had never asked himself the question: he hesitated; and his father continued—

"It was not till within these few days that I heard in what manner your acquaintance first commenced, and cannot suppose anything but attachment to the daughter could carry you such imprudent lengths for the father: it certainly must be her art[4] that drew you in to mortgage part of your fortune."

"Art, Sir!" cried Temple eagerly. "Lucy Eldridge is as free from art as she is from every other error: she is—"

"Everything that is amiable and lovely," said his father, interrupting him

4. Craft; here with a sense of manipulation.

ironically: "no doubt in your opinion she is a pattern of excellence for all her sex to follow; but come, Sir, pray tell me what are your designs towards this paragon. I hope you do not intend to complete your folly by marrying her."

"Were my fortune such as would support her according to her merit, I don't know a woman more formed to insure happiness in the married state."

"Then prithee, my dear lad," said his father, "since your rank and fortune are so much beneath what your *Princess* might expect, be so kind as to turn your eyes on Miss Weatherby; who, having only an estate of three thousand a year, is more upon a level with you, and whose father yesterday solicited the mighty honor of your alliance. I shall leave you to consider on this offer; and pray remember, that your union with Miss Weatherby will put it in your power to be more liberally the friend of Lucy Eldridge."

The old gentleman walked in a stately manner out of the room; and Temple stood almost petrified with astonishment, contempt, and rage.

Chapter V. *Such Things Are*

Miss Weatherby was the only child of a wealthy man, almost idolized by her parents, flattered by her dependants, and never contradicted even by those who called themselves her friends. I cannot give a better description than by the following lines:

> The lovely maid whose form and face
> Nature has decked with ev'ry grace,
> But in whose breast no virtues glow,
> Whose heart ne'er felt another's woe,
> Whose hand ne'er smoothed the bed of pain,
> Or eased the captive's galling chain;
> But like the tulip caught the eye,
> Born just to be admired and die,
> When gone, no one regrets its loss,
> Or scarce remembers that it was.

Such was Miss Weatherby: her form lovely as nature could make it, but her mind uncultivated, her heart unfeeling, her passions impetuous, and her brain almost turned with flattery, dissipation, and pleasure; and such was the girl, whom a partial grandfather left independent mistress of the fortune before mentioned.

She had seen Temple frequently; and fancying she could never be happy without him, nor once imagining he could refuse a girl of her beauty and fortune, she prevailed on her fond father to offer the alliance to the old Earl of D——, Mr. Temple's father.

The Earl had received the offer courteously: he thought it a great match for Henry; and was too fashionable a man to suppose a wife could be any impediment to the friendship he professed for Eldridge and his daughter.

Unfortunately for Temple, he thought quite otherwise: the conversation he had just had with his father, discovered to him the situation of his heart; and he found that the most affluent fortune would bring no increase of happiness unless Lucy Eldridge shared it with him; and the knowledge of the purity of her sentiments, and the integrity of his own heart, made him shudder at the idea his father had started, of marrying a woman for no other reason than because the affluence of her fortune would enable him to injure her by maintaining in splendor the woman to whom his heart was devoted: he therefore resolved to refuse Miss Weatherby, and be the event what it might, offer his heart and hand to Lucy Eldridge.

Full of this determination, he sought his father, declared his resolution, and was commanded never more to appear in his presence. Temple bowed; his heart was too full to permit him to speak; he left the house precipitately, and hastened to relate the cause of his sorrows to his good old friend and his amiable daughter.

In the meantime the Earl, vexed to the soul that such a fortune should be lost, determined to offer himself a candidate for Miss Weatherby's favor.

What wonderful changes are wrought by that reigning power, ambition! The love-sick girl, when first she heard of Temple's refusal, wept, raved, tore her hair, and vowed to found a Protestant nunnery with her fortune; and by commencing abbess, shut herself up from the sight of cruel ungrateful man forever.

Her father was a man of the world: he suffered this first transport to subside, and then very deliberately unfolded to her the offers of the old Earl, expatiated on the many benefits arising from an elevated title, painted in glowing colors the surprise and vexation of Temple when he should see her figuring as a Countess and his mother-in-law, and begged her to consider well before she made any rash vows.

The *distressed* fair one dried her tears, listened patiently, and at length declared she believed the surest method to revenge the slight put on her by the son, would be to accept the father. So said so done, and in a few days she became the Countess D——.

Temple heard the news with emotion: he had lost his father's favor by avowing his passion for Lucy, and he saw now there was no hope of regaining it: "but he shall not make me miserable," said he. "Lucy and I have no ambitious notions: we can live on three hundred a year for some little time, till the mortgage is paid off, and then we shall have sufficient not only for the comforts but many of the little elegancies of life. We will purchase a little cottage, my Lucy," said he, "and thither with your reverend father we will retire; we will forget there are such things as splendor, profusion, and dissipation: we will have some cows, and you shall be queen of the dairy. In a morning, while I look after my garden, you shall take a basket on your arm, and sally forth to feed your poultry; and as they flutter round you in token of humble gratitude, your father shall smoke his pipe in a woodbine alcove, and viewing the serenity of your countenance, feel such real pleasure dilate his own heart, as shall make him forget he had ever been unhappy."

Lucy smiled; and Temple saw it was a smile of approbation. He sought and found a cottage suited to his taste; thither, attended by Love and Hymen, the happy trio retired; where, during many years of uninterrupted felicity, they cast not a wish beyond the little boundaries of their own tenement.[5] Plenty, and her handmaid, Prudence, presided at their board, Hospitality stood at their gate, Peace smiled on each face, Content reigned in each heart, and Love and Health strewed roses on their pillows.

Such were the parents of Charlotte Temple, who was the only pledge of

---

5. Residence. In classical mythology Hymen was the god of marriage.

their mutual love, and who, at the earnest entreaty of a particular friend, was permitted to finish the education her mother had begun, at Madame Du Pont's school, where we first introduced her to the acquaintance of the reader.

Chapter VI. An Intriguing Teacher

Madame Du Pont was a woman every way calculated to take the care of young ladies, had that care entirely devolved on herself; but it was impossible to attend the education of a numerous school without proper assistants; and those assistants were not always the kind of people whose conversation and morals were exactly such as parents of delicacy and refinement would wish a daughter to copy. Among the teachers at Madame Du Pont's school was Mademoiselle La Rue, who added to a pleasing person and insinuating address, a liberal education and the manners of a gentlewoman. She was recommended to the school by a lady whose humanity overstepped the bounds of discretion: for though she knew Miss La Rue had eloped from a convent with a young officer, and, on coming to England, had lived with several different men in open defiance of all moral and religious duties; yet, finding her reduced to the most abject want, and believing the penitence which she professed to be sincere, she took her into her own family, and from thence recommended her to Madame Du Pont, as thinking the situation more suitable for a woman of her abilities. But Mademoiselle possessed too much of the spirit of intrigue to remain long without adventures. At church, where she constantly appeared, her person attracted the attention of a young man who was upon a visit at a gentleman's seat in the neighborhood: she had met him several times clandestinely; and being invited to come out that evening, and eat some fruit and pastry in a summerhouse belonging to the gentleman he was visiting, and requested to bring some of the ladies with her, Charlotte being her favorite, was fixed on to accompany her.

The mind of youth eagerly catches at promised pleasure: pure and innocent by nature, it thinks not of the dangers lurking beneath those pleasures, till too late to avoid them. When Mademoiselle asked Charlotte to go with her she mentioned the gentleman as a relation, and spoke in such high terms of the elegance of his gardens, the sprightliness of his conversation, and the liberality with which he ever entertained his guests, that Charlotte thought only of the pleasure she should enjoy in the visit,—not on the imprudence of going without her governess's knowledge, or of the danger to which she exposed herself in visiting the house of a gay young man of fashion.

Madame Du Pont was gone out for the evening, and the rest of the ladies retired to rest, when Charlotte and the teacher stole out at the back gate, and in crossing the field, were accosted by Montraville, as mentioned in the first chapter.

Charlotte was disappointed in the pleasure she had promised herself from this visit. The levity of the gentlemen and the freedom of their conversation disgusted her. She was astonished at the liberties Mademoiselle permitted them to take; grew thoughtful and uneasy, and heartily wished herself at home again in her own chamber.

Perhaps one cause of that wish might be, an earnest desire to see the contents of the letter which had been put into her hand by Montraville.

Any reader who has the least knowledge of the world, will easily imagine the letter was made up of encomiums on her beauty, and vows of everlasting love and constancy; nor will he be surprised that a heart open to every gentle, generous sentiment, should feel itself warmed by gratitude for a man who professed to feel so much for her; nor is it improbable but her mind might revert to the agreeable person and martial appearance of Montraville.

In affairs of love, a young heart is never in more danger than when attempted by a handsome young soldier. A man of an indifferent appearance, will, when arrayed in a military habit, show to advantage; but when beauty of person, elegance of manner, and an easy method of paying compliments, are united to the scarlet coat, smart cockade, and military sash, ah! well-a-day[6] for the poor girl who gazes on him: she is in imminent danger; but if she listens to him with pleasure, 'tis all over with her, and from that moment she has neither eyes nor ears for any other object.

Now, my dear sober matron (if a sober matron should deign to turn over these pages, before she trusts them to the eye of a darling daughter), let me entreat you not to put on a grave face, and throw down the book in a passion and declare 'tis enough to turn the heads of half the girls in England; I do solemnly protest, my dear madam, I mean no more by what I have here advanced, than to ridicule those romantic girls, who foolishly imagine a red coat and silver epaulet constitute the fine gentleman; and should that fine gentleman make half a dozen fine speeches to them, they will imagine themselves so much in love as to fancy it a meritorious action to jump out of a two pair of stairs window, abandon their friends, and trust entirely to the honor of a man, who perhaps hardly knows the meaning of the word, and if he does, will be too much the modern man of refinement, to practice it in their favor.

Gracious heaven! when I think on the miseries that must rend the heart of a doting parent, when he sees the darling of his age at first seduced from his protection, and afterwards abandoned, by the very wretch whose promises of love decoyed her from the paternal roof—when he sees her poor and wretched, her bosom torn between remorse for her crime and love for her vile betrayer—when fancy paints to me the good old man stooping to raise the weeping penitent, while every tear from her eye is numbered by drops from his bleeding heart, my bosom glows with honest indignation, and I wish for power to extirpate those monsters of seduction from the earth.

Oh my dear girls—for to such only am I writing—listen not to the voice of love, unless sanctioned by paternal approbation: be assured, it is now past the days of romance: no woman can be run away with contrary to her own inclination: then kneel down each morning, and request kind heaven to keep you free from temptation, or, should it please to suffer you to be tried, pray for fortitude to resist the impulse of inclination when it runs counter to the precepts of religion and virtue.

Chapter VII. Natural Sense of Propriety Inherent in the Female Bosom

"I cannot think we have done exactly right in going out this evening, Mademoiselle," said Charlotte, seating herself when she entered her apartment:

6. Alas.

"nay, I am sure it was not right; for I expected to be very happy, but was sadly disappointed."

"It was your own fault, then," replied Mademoiselle: "for I am sure my cousin omitted nothing that could serve to render the evening agreeable."

"True," said Charlotte: "but I thought the gentlemen were very free in their manner: I wonder you would suffer them to behave as they did."

"Prithee, don't be such a foolish little prude," said the artful woman, affecting anger: "I invited you to go in hopes it would divert you, and be an agreeable change of scene; however, if your delicacy was hurt by the behavior of the gentlemen, you need not go again; so there let it rest."

"I do not intend to go again," said Charlotte, gravely taking off her bonnet, and beginning to prepare for bed: "I am sure, if Madame Du Pont knew we had been out tonight, she would be very angry; and it is ten to one but she hears of it by some means or other."

"Nay, Miss," said La Rue, "perhaps your mighty sense of propriety may lead you to tell her yourself: and in order to avoid the censure you would incur, should she hear of it by accident, throw the blame on me: but I confess I deserve it: it will be a very kind return for that partiality which led me to prefer you before any of the rest of the ladies; but perhaps it will give you pleasure," continued she, letting fall some hypocritical tears, "to see me deprived of bread, and for an action which by the most rigid could only be esteemed an inadvertency, lose my place and character, and be driven again into the world, where I have already suffered all the evils attendant on poverty."

This was touching Charlotte in the most vulnerable part: she rose from her seat, and taking Mademoiselle's hand—"You know, my dear La Rue," said she, "I love you too well, to do anything that would injure you in my governess's opinion: I am only sorry we went out this evening."

"I don't believe it, Charlotte," said she, assuming a little vivacity; "for if you had not gone out, you would not have seen the gentleman who met us crossing the field; and I rather think you were pleased with his conversation."

"I had seen him once before," replied Charlotte, "and thought him an agreeable man; and you know one is always pleased to see a person with whom one has passed several cheerful hours. "But," said she pausing, and drawing the letter from her pocket, while a gentle suffusion of vermillion tinged her neck and face, "he gave me this letter; what shall I do with it?"

"Read it, to be sure," returned Mademoiselle.

"I am afraid I ought not," said Charlotte: "my mother has often told me, I should never read a letter given me by a young man, without first giving it to her."

"Lord bless you, my dear girl," cried the teacher smiling, "have you a mind to be in leading strings all your lifetime. Prithee open the letter, read it, and judge for yourself; if you show it your mother, the consequence will be, you will be taken from school, and a strict guard kept over you; so you will stand no chance of ever seeing the smart young officer again."

"I should not like to leave school yet," replied Charlotte, "till I have attained a greater proficiency in my Italian and music. But you can, if you please, Mademoiselle, take the letter back to Montraville, and tell him I wish him well, but cannot, with any propriety, enter into a clandestine correspondence with him." She laid the letter on the table, and began to undress herself.

"Well," said La Rue, "I vow you are an unaccountable girl: have you no curiosity to see the inside now? for my part I could no more let a letter addressed to me lie unopened so long, than I could work miracles: he writes a good hand," continued she, turning the letter, to look at the superscription.

" 'Tis well enough," said Charlotte, drawing it towards her.

"He is a genteel young fellow," said La Rue carelessly, folding up her apron at the same time; "but I think he is marked with the small pox."

"Oh you are greatly mistaken," said Charlotte eagerly; "he has a remarkable clear skin and fine complexion."

"His eyes, if I could judge by what I saw," said La Rue, "are grey and want expression."

"By no means," replied Charlotte; "they are the most expressive eyes I ever saw."

"Well, child, whether they are grey or black is of no consequence: you have determined not to read his letter; so it is likely you will never either see or hear from him again."

Charlotte took up the letter, and Mademoiselle continued—

"He is most probably going to America; and if ever you should hear any account of him, it may possibly be that he is killed; and though he loved you ever so fervently, though his last breath should be spent in a prayer for your happiness, it can be nothing to you: you can feel nothing for the fate of the man, whose letters you will not open, and whose sufferings you will not alleviate, by permitting him to think you would remember him when absent, and pray for his safety."

Charlotte still held the letter in her hand: her heart swelled at the conclusion of Mademoiselle's speech, and a tear dropped upon the wafer[7] that closed it.

"The wafer is not dry yet," said she, "and sure there can be no great harm—" She hesitated. La Rue was silent. "I may read it, Mademoiselle, and return it afterwards."

"Certainly," replied Mademoiselle.

"At any rate I am determined not to answer it," continued Charlotte, as she opened the letter.

Here let me stop to make one remark, and trust me my very heart aches while I write it; but certain I am, that when once a woman has stifled the sense of shame in her own bosom, when once she has lost sight of the basis on which reputation, honor, everything that should be dear to the female heart, rests, she grows hardened in guilt, and will spare no pains to bring down innocence and beauty to the shocking level with herself: and this proceeds from that diabolical spirit of envy, which repines at seeing another in the full possession of that respect and esteem which she can no longer hope to enjoy.

Mademoiselle eyed the unsuspecting Charlotte, as she perused the letter, with a malignant pleasure. She saw that the contents had awakened new emotions in her youthful bosom: she encouraged her hopes, calmed her fears, and before they parted for the night, it was determined that she should meet Montraville the ensuing evening.

---

7. Wax seal.

Chapter VIII. Domestic Pleasures Planned

"I think, my dear," said Mrs. Temple, laying her hand on her husband's arm as they were walking together in the garden, "I think next Wednesday is Charlotte's birthday: now I have formed a little scheme in my own mind, to give her an agreeable surprise; and if you have no objection, we will send for her home on that day." Temple pressed his wife's hand in token of approbation, and she proceeded.—"You know the little alcove at the bottom of the garden, of which Charlotte is so fond? I have an inclination to deck this out in a fanciful manner, and invite all her little friends to partake of a collation of fruit, sweetmeats, and other things suitable to the general taste of young guests; and to make it more pleasing to Charlotte, she shall be mistress of the feast, and entertain her visitors in this alcove. I know she will be delighted; and to complete all, they shall have some music, and finish with a dance."

"A very fine plan, indeed," said Temple, smiling; "and you really suppose I will wink at your indulging the girl in this manner? You will quite spoil her, Lucy; indeed you will."

"She is the only child we have," said Mrs. Temple, the whole tenderness of a mother adding animation to her fine countenance; but it was withal tempered so sweetly with the meek affection and submissive duty of the wife, that as she paused expecting her husband's answer, he gazed at her tenderly, and found he was unable to refuse her request.

"She is a good girl," said Temple.

"She is, indeed," replied the fond mother exultingly, "a grateful, affectionate girl; and I am sure will never lose sight of the duty she owes her parents."

"If she does," said he, "she must forget the example set her by the best of mothers."

Mrs. Temple could not reply; but the delightful sensation that dilated her heart sparkled in her intelligent eyes and heightened the vermillion on her cheeks.

Of all the pleasures of which the human mind is sensible, there is none equal to that which warms and expands the bosom, when listening to commendations bestowed on us by a beloved object, and are conscious of having deserved them.

Ye giddy flutterers in the fantastic round of dissipation, who eagerly seek pleasure in the lofty dome, rich treat, and midnight revel—tell me, ye thoughtless daughters of folly, have ye ever found the phantom you have so long sought with such unremitted assiduity? Has she not always eluded your grasp, and when you have reached your hand to take the cup she extends to her deluded votaries, have you not found the long-expected draught strongly tinctured with the bitter dregs of disappointment? I know you have: I see it in the wan cheek, sunk eye, and air of chagrin, which ever mark the children of dissipation. Pleasure is a vain illusion; she draws you on to a thousand follies, errors, and I may say vices, and then leaves you to deplore your thoughtless credulity.

Look, my dear friends, at yonder lovely Virgin, arrayed in a white robe devoid of ornament; behold the meekness of her countenance, the modesty of her gait; her handmaids are *Humility, Filial Piety, Conjugal Affection, Industry,* and *Benevolence;* her name is *Content;* she holds in her hand the cup of true felicity, and when once you have formed an intimate acquaintance with these her attendants, nay you must admit them as your bosom friends and chief counselors, then, whatever may be your situation in life, the meek eyed Virgin will immediately take up her abode with you.

Is poverty your portion?—she will lighten your labors, preside at your frugal board, and watch your quiet slumbers.

Is your state mediocrity?[8]—she will heighten every blessing you enjoy, by informing you how grateful you should be to that bountiful Providence who might have placed you in the most abject situation; and, by teaching you to weigh your blessings against your deserts, show you how much more you receive than you have a right to expect.

Are you possessed of affluence?—what an inexhaustible fund of happiness will she lay before you! To relieve the distressed, redress the injured, in short, to perform all the good works of peace and mercy.

Content, my dear friends, will blunt even the arrows of adversity, so that they cannot materially harm you. She will dwell in the humblest cottage; she will attend you even to a prison. Her parent is Religion; her sisters, Patience and Hope. She will pass with you through life, smoothing the rough paths and tread to earth those thorns which every one must meet with as they journey onward to the appointed goal. She will soften the pains of sickness, continue with you even in the cold gloomy hour of death, and, cheering you with the smiles of her heaven-born sister, Hope, lead you triumphant to a blissful eternity.

I confess I have rambled strangely from my story: but what of that? If I have been so lucky as to find the road to happiness, why should I be such a niggard[9] as to omit so good an opportunity of pointing out the way to others. The very basis of true peace of mind is a benevolent wish to see all the world as happy as one's self; and from my soul do I pity the selfish churl, who, remembering the little bickerings of anger, envy, and fifty other disagreeables to which frail mortality is subject, would wish to revenge the affront which pride whispers him he has received. For my own part, I can safely declare, there is not a human being in the universe, whose prosperity I should not rejoice in, and to whose happiness I would not contribute to the utmost limit of my power: and may my offences be no more remembered in the day of general retribution, than as from my soul I forgive every offence or injury received from a fellow creature.

Merciful heaven! who would exchange the rapture of such a reflection for all the gaudy tinsel which the world calls pleasure!

But to return.—Content dwelt in Mrs. Temple's bosom, and spread a charming animation over her countenance, as her husband led her in, to lay the plan she had formed (for the celebration of Charlotte's birthday) before Mr. Eldridge.

Chapter IX. We Know Not What a Day May Bring Forth

Various were the sensations which agitated the mind of Charlotte, during the day preceding the evening in which she was to meet Montraville. Several times did she almost resolve to go to her governess, show her the letter, and

8. Only moderately fortunate.　　　　　9. So miserly.

be guided by her advice. But Charlotte had taken one step in the ways of imprudence; and when that is once done, there are always innumerable obstacles to prevent the erring person returning to the path of rectitude. Yet these obstacles, however forcible they may appear in general, exist chiefly in imagination.

Charlotte feared the anger of her governess. She loved her mother, and the very idea of incurring her displeasure gave her the greatest uneasiness. But there was a more forcible reason still remaining: should she show the letter to Madame Du Pont, she must confess the means by which it came into her possession; and what would be the consequence? Mademoiselle would be turned out-of-doors.

"I must not be ungrateful," said she. "La Rue is very kind to me; besides I can, when I see Montraville, inform him of the impropriety of our continuing to see or correspond with each other, and request him to come no more to Chichester."

However prudent Charlotte might be in these resolutions, she certainly did not take a proper method to confirm herself in them. Several times in the course of the day she indulged herself in reading over the letter, and each time she read it, the contents sunk deeper in her heart. As evening drew near she caught herself frequently consulting her watch. "I wish this foolish meeting was over," said she, by way of apology to her own heart, "I wish it was over; for when I have seen him, and convinced him my resolution is not to be shaken, I shall feel my mind much easier."

The appointed hour arrived. Charlotte and Mademoiselle eluded the eye of vigilance; and Montraville, who had waited their coming with impatience, received them with rapturous and unbounded acknowledgments for their condescension:[1] he had wisely brought Belcour with him to entertain Mademoiselle, while he enjoyed an uninterrupted conversation with Charlotte.

Belcour was a man whose character might be comprised in a few words; and as he will make some figure in the ensuing pages, I shall here describe him. He possessed a genteel fortune, and had a liberal education; dissipated, thoughtless, and capricious, he paid little regard to the moral duties, and less to religious ones. Eager in the pursuit of pleasure, he minded not the miseries he inflicted on others, provided his own wishes, however extravagant, were gratified. Self, darling self, was the idol he worshipped, and to that he would have sacrificed the interest and happiness of all mankind. Such was the friend of Montraville. Will not the reader be ready to imagine, that the man who could regard such a character must be actuated by the same feelings, follow the same pursuits, and be equally unworthy with the person to whom he thus gave his confidence?

But Montraville was a different character: generous in his disposition, liberal in his opinions, and goodnatured almost to a fault; yet eager and impetuous in the pursuit of a favorite object, he stayed not to reflect on the consequence which might follow the attainment of his wishes; with a mind ever open to conviction, had he been so fortunate as to possess a friend who would have pointed out the cruelty of endeavoring to gain the heart of an innocent artless girl, when he knew it was utterly impossible for him to marry her, and when the gratification of his passion would be unavoidable infamy

---

1. Graciousness.

and misery to her, and a cause of never-ceasing remorse to himself: had these dreadful consequences been placed before him in a proper light, the humanity of his nature would have urged him to give up the pursuit. But Belcour was not this friend; he rather encouraged the growing passion of Montraville; and being pleased with the vivacity of Mademoiselle, resolved to leave no argument untried which he thought might prevail on her to be the companion of their intended voyage; and he made no doubt but her example, added to the rhetoric of Montraville, would persuade Charlotte to go with them.

Charlotte had, when she went out to meet Montraville, flattered herself that her resolution was not to be shaken, and that, conscious of the impropriety of her conduct in having a clandestine intercourse with a stranger, she would never repeat the indiscretion.

But alas! poor Charlotte, she knew not the deceitfulness of her own heart, or she would have avoided the trial of her stability.

Montraville was tender, eloquent, ardent, and yet respectful. "Shall I not see you once more," said he, "before I leave England? will you not bless me by an assurance, that when we are divided by a vast expanse of sea I shall not be forgotten?"

Charlotte sighed.

"Why that sigh, my dear Charlotte? could I flatter myself that a fear for my safety, or a wish for my welfare occasioned it, how happy would it make me."

"I shall ever wish you well, Montraville," said she; "but we must meet no more."

"Oh say not so, my lovely girl: reflect, that when I leave my native land, perhaps a few short weeks may terminate my existence; the perils of the ocean—the dangers of war—"

"I can hear no more," said Charlotte in a tremulous voice. "I must leave you."

"Say you will see me once again."

"I dare not," said she.

"Only for one half hour tomorrow evening: 'tis my last request. I shall never trouble you again, Charlotte."

"I know not what to say," cried Charlotte, struggling to draw her hands from him: "let me leave you now."

"And you will come tomorrow," said Montraville.

"Perhaps I may," said she.

"Adieu then. I will live upon that hope till we meet again."

He kissed her hand. She sighed an adieu, and catching hold of Mademoiselle's arm, hastily entered the garden gate.

Chapter X. When We Have Excited Curiosity, It Is But an Act of Good Nature to Gratify It

Montraville was the youngest son of a gentleman of fortune, whose family being numerous, he was obliged to bring up his sons to genteel professions, by the exercise of which they might hope to raise themselves into notice.[2]

2. Under English custom the eldest son would inherit his father's estate. Montraville's father would, therefore, try to prepare his other sons for careers suitable to gentlemen because they would be propertyless at his death.

"My daughters," said he, "have been educated like gentlewomen; and should I die before they are settled, they must have some provision made, to place them above the snares and temptations which vice ever holds out to the elegant, accomplished female, when oppressed by the frowns of poverty and the sting of dependence. My boys, with only moderate incomes, when placed in the church, at the bar, or in the field,[3] may exert their talents, make themselves friends, and raise their fortunes on the basis of merit."

When Montraville chose the profession of arms, his father presented him with a commission, and made him a handsome provision for his private purse. "Now, my boy," said he, "go! seek glory in the field of battle. You have received from me all I shall ever have it in my power to bestow. It is certain I have interest[4] to gain you promotion; but be assured that interest shall never be exerted, unless by your future conduct you deserve it. Remember, therefore, your success in life depends entirely on yourself. There is one thing I think it my duty to caution you against; the precipitancy with which young men frequently rush into matrimonial engagements, and by their thoughtlessness draw many a deserving woman into scenes of poverty and distress. A soldier has no business to think of a wife till his rank is such as to place him above the fear of bringing into the world a train of helpless innocents, heirs only to penury and affliction. If, indeed, a woman, whose fortune is sufficient to preserve you in that state of independence I would teach you to prize, should generously bestow herself on a young soldier, whose chief hope of future prosperity depended on his success in the field—if such a woman should offer—every barrier is removed, and I should rejoice in an union which would promise so much felicity. But mark me, boy, if, on the contrary, you rush into a precipitate union with a girl of little or no fortune, take the poor creature from a comfortable home and kind friends, and plunge her into all the evils a narrow income and increasing family can inflict, I will leave you to enjoy the blessed fruits of your rashness; for by all that is sacred, neither my interest or fortune shall ever be exerted in your favor. I am serious," continued he, "therefore imprint this conversation on your memory, and let it influence your future conduct. Your happiness will always be dear to me; and I wish to warn you of a rock on which the peace of many an honest fellow has been wrecked; for believe me, the difficulties and dangers of the longest winter campaign are much easier to be borne, than the pangs that would seize your heart, when you beheld the woman of your choice, the children of your affection, involved in penury and distress, and reflected that it was your own folly and precipitancy had been the prime cause of their sufferings."

As this conversation passed but a few hours before Montraville took leave of his father, it was deeply impressed on his mind. When, therefore, Belcour came with him to the place of assignation with Charlotte, he directed him to inquire of the French woman what were Miss Temple's expectations in regard to fortune.

Mademoiselle informed him that though Charlotte's father possessed a genteel independence, it was by no means probable that he could give his daughter more than a thousand pounds; and in case she did not marry to his liking, it was possible he might not give her a single *sou*;[5] nor did it appear

3. The army.
4. Personal influence. Army officers had to purchase their commissions.

5. A French coin no longer in use and worth about a penny.

the least likely, that Mr. Temple would agree to her union with a young man on the point of embarking for the seat of war.

Montraville therefore concluded it was impossible he should ever marry Charlotte Temple; and what end he proposed to himself by continuing the acquaintance he had commenced with her, he did not at that moment give himself time to inquire.

Chapter XI. Conflict of Love and Duty

Almost a week was now gone, and Charlotte continued every evening to meet Montraville, and in her heart every meeting was resolved to be the last; but alas! when Montraville at parting would earnestly entreat one more interview, that treacherous heart betrayed her; and, forgetful of its resolution, pleaded the cause of the enemy so powerfully, that Charlotte was unable to resist. Another and another meeting succeeded; and so well did Montraville improve each opportunity, that the heedless girl at length confessed no idea could be so painful to her as that of never seeing him again.

"Then we will never be parted," said he.

"Ah, Montraville," replied Charlotte, forcing a smile, "how can it be avoided? My parents would never consent to our union; and even could they be brought to approve it, how should I bear to be separated from my kind, my beloved mother?"

"Then you love your parents more than you do me, Charlotte?"

"I hope I do," said she, blushing and looking down, "I hope my affection for them will ever keep me from infringing the laws of filial duty."

"Well, Charlotte," said Montraville gravely, and letting go her hand, "since that is the case, I find I have deceived myself with fallacious hopes. I had flattered my fond heart, that I was dearer to Charlotte than anything in the world beside. I thought that you would for my sake have braved the dangers of the ocean, that you would, by your affection and smiles, have softened the hardships of war, and, had it been my fate to fall, that your tenderness would cheer the hour of death, and smooth my passage to another world. But farewell, Charlotte! I see you never loved me. I shall now welcome the friendly ball that deprives me of the sense of my misery."

"Oh stay, unkind Montraville," cried she, catching hold of his arm, as he pretended to leave her, "stay, and to calm your fears, I will here protest that was it not for the fear of giving pain to the best of parents, and returning their kindness with ingratitude, I would follow you through every danger, and, in studying to promote your happiness, insure my own. But I cannot break my mother's heart, Montraville; I must not bring the gray hairs of my doting grandfather with sorrow to the grave, or make my beloved father perhaps curse the hour that gave me birth." She covered her face with her hands, and burst into tears.

"All these distressing scenes, my dear Charlotte," cried Montraville, "are merely the chimeras[6] of a disturbed fancy. Your parents might perhaps grieve at first; but when they heard from your own hand that you was with a man of honor, and that it was to insure your felicity by an union with him, to which you feared they would never have given their assent, that you left their protection, they will, be assured, forgive an error which love alone occa-

6. Illusions, imaginary monsters.

sioned, and when we return from America, receive you with open arms and tears of joy."

Belcour and Mademoiselle heard this last speech, and conceiving it a proper time to throw in their advice and persuasions, approached Charlotte, and so well seconded the entreaties of Montraville, that finding Mademoiselle intended going with Belcour, and feeling her own treacherous heart too much inclined to accompany them, the hapless Charlotte, in an evil hour, consented that the next evening they should bring a chaise to the end of the town, and that she would leave her friends, and throw herself entirely on the protection of Montraville. "But should you," said she, looking earnestly at him, her eyes full of tears, "should you, forgetful of your promises, and repenting the engagements you here voluntarily enter into, forsake and leave me on a foreign shore————"

"Judge not so meanly of me," said he. "The moment we reach our place of destination, Hymen shall sanctify our love; and when I shall forget your goodness, may heaven forget me."

"Ah," said Charlotte, leaning on Mademoiselle's arm as they walked up the garden together, "I have forgot all that I ought to have remembered, in consenting to this intended elopement."

"You are a strange girl," said Mademoiselle: "you never know your own mind two minutes at a time. Just now you declared Montraville's happiness was what you prized most in the world; and now I suppose you repent having insured that happiness by agreeing to accompany him abroad."

"Indeed I do repent," replied Charlotte, "from my soul: but while discretion points out the impropriety of my conduct, inclination urges me on to ruin."

"Ruin! fiddlestick!" said Mademoiselle; "am I not going with you? and do I feel any of these qualms?"

"You do not renounce a tender father and mother," said Charlotte.

"But I hazard my dear reputation," replied Mademoiselle, bridling.

"True," replied Charlotte, "but you do not feel what I do." She then bade her good night: but sleep was a stranger to her eyes, and the tear of anguish watered her pillow.

Chapter XII

Nature's last, best gift:
Creature in whom excelled, whatever could
To sight or thought be named!
Holy, divine! good, amiable, and sweet!
How thou art fall'n!—

When Charlotte left her restless bed, her languid eye and pale cheek discovered to Madame Du Pont the little repose she had tasted.

"My dear child," said the affectionate governess, "what is the cause of the languor so apparent in your frame? Are you not well?"

"Yes, my dear Madam, very well," replied Charlotte, attempting to smile, "but I know not how it was; I could not sleep last night, and my spirits are depressed this morning."

"Come cheer up, my love," said the governess; "I believe I have brought a cordial to revive them. I have just received a letter from your good mama, and here is one for yourself."

Charlotte hastily took the letter: it contained these words—

"As tomorrow is the anniversary of the happy day that gave my beloved girl to the anxious wishes of a maternal heart, I have requested your governess to let you come home and spend it with us; and as I know you to be a good affectionate child, and make it your study to improve in those branches of education which you know will give most pleasure to your delighted parents, as a reward for your diligence and attention I have prepared an agreeable surprise for your reception. Your grandfather, eager to embrace the darling of his aged heart, will come in the chaise for you; so hold yourself in readiness to attend him by nine o'clock. Your dear father joins in every tender wish for your health and future felicity, which warms the heart of my dear Charlotte's affectionate mother,   L. TEMPLE."

"Gracious heaven!" cried Charlotte, forgetting where she was, and raising her streaming eyes as in earnest supplication.

Madame Du Pont was surprised. "Why these tears, my love?" said she. "Why this seeming agitation? I thought the letter would have rejoiced, instead of distressing you."

"It does rejoice me," replied Charlotte, endeavoring at composure, "but I was praying for merit to deserve the unremitted attentions of the best of parents."

"You do right," said Madame Du Pont, "to ask the assistance of heaven that you may continue to deserve their love. Continue, my dear Charlotte, in the course you have ever pursued, and you will insure at once their happiness and your own."

"Oh!" cried Charlotte, as her governess left her, "I have forfeited both forever! Yet let me reflect:—the irrevocable step is not yet taken: it is not too late to recede from the brink of a precipice, from which I can only behold the dark abyss of ruin, shame, and remorse!"

She arose from her seat, and flew to the apartment of La Rue. "Oh Mademoiselle!" said she, "I am snatched by a miracle from destruction! This letter has saved me: it has opened my eyes to the folly I was so near committing. I will not go, Mademoiselle; I will not wound the hearts of those dear parents who make my happiness the whole study of their lives."

"Well," said Mademoiselle, "do as you please, Miss; but pray understand that my resolution is taken, and it is not in your power to alter it. I shall meet the gentlemen at the appointed hour, and shall not be surprised at any outrage which Montraville may commit, when he finds himself disappointed. Indeed I should not be astonished, was he to come immediately here, and reproach you for your instability in the hearing of the whole school. And what will be the consequence? You will bear the odium of having formed the resolution of eloping, and every girl of spirit will laugh at your want of fortitude to put it in execution, while prudes and fools will load you with reproach and contempt. You will have lost the confidence of your parents, incurred their anger, and the scoffs of the world; and what fruit do you expect to reap from this piece of heroism (for such no doubt you think it is)? You will have the pleasure to reflect that you have deceived the man who adores you, and whom in your heart you prefer to all other men, and that you are separated from him forever."

This eloquent harangue was given with such volubility, that Charlotte could not find an opportunity to interrupt her, or to offer a single word till the whole was finished, and then found her ideas so confused, that she knew not what to say.

At length she determined that she would go with Mademoiselle to the place of assignation, convince Montraville of the necessity of adhering to the resolution of remaining behind; assure him of her affection, and bid him adieu.

Charlotte formed this plan in her mind, and exulted in the certainty of its success. "How shall I rejoice," said she, "in this triumph of reason over inclination, and, when in the arms of my affectionate parents, lift up my soul in gratitude to heaven as I look back on the dangers I have escaped!"

The hour of assignation arrived. Mademoiselle put what money and valuables she possessed in her pocket, and advised Charlotte to do the same; but she refused. "My resolution is fixed," said she. "I will sacrifice love to duty."

Mademoiselle smiled internally; and they proceeded softly down the back stairs and out of the garden gate. Montraville and Belcour were ready to receive them.

"Now," said Montraville, taking Charlotte in his arms, "you are mine forever."

"No," said she, withdrawing from his embrace, "I am come to take an everlasting farewell."

It would be useless to repeat the conversation that here ensued; suffice it to say, that Montraville used every argument that had formerly been successful, Charlotte's resolution began to waver, and he drew her almost imperceptibly towards the chaise.

"I cannot go," said she; "cease, dear Montraville, to persuade. I must not: religion, duty, forbid."

"Cruel Charlotte," said he, "if you disappoint my ardent hopes, by all that is sacred, this hand shall put a period to my existence. I cannot—will not live without you."

"Alas! my torn heart!" said Charlotte, "how shall I act?"

"Let me direct you," said Montraville, lifting her into the chaise.

"Oh! my dear forsaken parents!" cried Charlotte.

The chaise drove off. She shrieked, and fainted into the arms of her betrayer.

Chapter XIII. Cruel Disappointment

"What pleasure," cried Mr. Eldridge, as he stepped into the chaise to go for his granddaughter, "what pleasure expands the heart of an old man when he beholds the progeny of a beloved child growing up in every virtue that adorned the minds of her parents. I foolishly thought, some few years since, that every sense of joy was buried in the graves of my dear partner and my son; but my Lucy, by her filial affection, soothed my soul to peace, and this dear Charlotte has twined herself round my heart, and opened such new scenes of delight to my view, that I almost forget I have ever been unhappy."

When the chaise stopped, he alighted with the alacrity of youth; so much do the emotions of the soul influence the body.

It was half past eight o'clock; the ladies were assembled in the school room, and Madame Du Pont was preparing to offer the morning sacrifice of prayer and praise, when it was discovered, that Mademoiselle and Charlotte were missing.

"She is busy, no doubt," said the governess, "in preparing Charlotte for her little excursion; but pleasure should never make us forget our duty to our Creator. Go, one of you, and bid them both attend prayers."

The lady who went to summon them, soon returned, and informed the governess that the room was locked, and that she had knocked repeatedly, but obtained no answer.

"Good heaven!" cried Madame Du Pont, "this is very strange:" and turning pale with terror, she went hastily to the door, and ordered it to be forced open. The apartment instantly discovered, that no person had been in it the preceding night, the beds appearing as though just made. The house was instantly a scene of confusion: the garden, the pleasure grounds were searched to no purpose, every apartment rang with the names of Miss Temple and Mademoiselle; but they were too distant to hear; and every face wore the marks of disappointment.

Mr. Eldridge was sitting in the parlor, eagerly expecting his granddaughter to descend, ready equipped for her journey: he heard the confusion that reigned in the house; he heard the name of Charlotte frequently repeated. "What can be the matter?" said he, rising and opening the door: "I fear some accident has befallen my dear girl."

The governess entered. The visible agitation of her countenance discovered that something extraordinary had happened.

"Where is Charlotte?" said he, "Why does not my child come to welcome her doting parent?"

"Be composed, my dear Sir," said Madame Du Pont, "do not frighten yourself unnecessarily. She is not in the house at present; but as Mademoiselle is undoubtedly with her, she will speedily return in safety; and I hope they will both be able to account for this unseasonable absence in such a manner as shall remove our present uneasiness."

"Madam," cried the old man, with an angry look, "has my child been accustomed to go out without leave, with no other company or protector than that French woman? Pardon me, Madam, I mean no reflections on your country, but I never did like Mademoiselle La Rue; I think she was a very improper person to be entrusted with the care of such a girl as Charlotte Temple, or to be suffered to take her from under your immediate protection."

"You wrong me, Mr. Eldridge," replied she, "if you suppose I have ever permitted your granddaughter to go out unless with the other ladies. I would to heaven I could form any probable conjecture concerning her absence this morning, but it is a mystery which her return can alone unravel."

Servants were now dispatched to every place where there was the least hope of hearing any tidings of the fugitives, but in vain. Dreadful were the hours of horrid suspense which Mr. Eldridge passed till twelve o'clock, when that suspense was reduced to a shocking certainty, and every spark of hope which till then they had indulged, was in a moment extinguished.

Mr. Eldridge was preparing, with a heavy heart, to return to his anxiously-expecting children, when Madame Du Pont received the following note without either name or date.

"Miss Temple is well, and wishes to relieve the anxiety of her parents, by letting them know she has voluntarily put herself under the protection of a man whose future study shall be to make her happy. Pursuit is needless; the measures taken to avoid discovery are too effectual to be eluded. When she thinks her friends are reconciled to this precipitate step, they may perhaps be informed of her place of residence. Mademoiselle is with her."

As Madame Du Pont read these cruel lines, she turned pale as ashes, her limbs trembled, and she was forced to call for a glass of water. She loved Charlotte truly; and when she reflected on the innocence and gentleness of her disposition, she concluded that it must have been the advice and machinations of La Rue, which led her to this imprudent action; she recollected her agitation at the receipt of her mother's letter, and saw in it the conflict of her mind.

"Does that letter relate to Charlotte?" said Mr. Eldridge, having waited some time in expectation of Madame Du Pont's speaking.

"It does," said she. "Charlotte is well, but cannot return today."

"Not return, Madam? where is she? who will detain her from her fond, expecting parents?"

"You distract me with these questions, Mr. Eldridge. Indeed I know not where she is, or who has seduced her from her duty."

The whole truth now rushed at once upon Mr. Eldridge's mind. "She has eloped then," said he. "My child is betrayed; the darling, the comfort of my aged heart, is lost. Oh would to heaven I had died but yesterday."

A violent gush of grief in some measure relieved him, and, after several vain attempts, he at length assumed sufficient composure to read the note.

"And how shall I return to my children?" said he: "how approach that mansion, so late the habitation of peace? Alas! my dear Lucy, how will you support these heartrending tidings? or how shall I be enabled to console you, who need so much consolation myself?"

The old man returned to the chaise, but the light step and cheerful countenance were no more; sorrow filled his heart, and guided his motions; he seated himself in the chaise, his venerable head reclined upon his bosom, his hands were folded, his eye fixed on vacancy, and the large drops of sorrow rolled silently down his cheeks. There was a mixture of anguish and resignation depicted in his countenance, as if he would say, henceforth who shall dare to boast his happiness, or even in idea contemplate his treasure, lest, in the very moment his heart is exulting in its own felicity, the object which constitutes that felicity should be torn from him.

Chapter XIV. Maternal Sorrow

Slow and heavy passed the time while the carriage was conveying Mr. Eldridge home; and yet when he came in sight of the house, he wished a longer reprieve from the dreadful task of informing Mr. and Mrs. Temple of their daughter's elopement.

It is easy to judge the anxiety of these affectionate parents when they found the return of their father delayed so much beyond the expected time. They were now met in the dining parlor, and several of the young people who had been invited were already arrived. Each different part of the company was employed in the same manner, looking out at the windows which faced the road. At length the long-expected chaise appeared. Mrs. Temple ran out to receive and welcome her darling: her young companions flocked round the door, each one eager to give her joy on the return of her birthday. The door of the chaise was opened: Charlotte was not there. "Where is my child?" cried Mrs. Temple, in breathless agitation.

Mr. Eldridge could not answer: he took hold of his daughter's hand and led her into the house; and sinking on the first chair he came to, burst into tears, and sobbed aloud.

"She is dead," cried Mrs. Temple. "Oh my dear Charlotte!" and clasping her hands in an agony of distress, fell into strong hysterics.

Mr. Temple, who had stood speechless with surprise and fear, now ventured to inquire if indeed his Charlotte was no more. Mr. Eldridge led him into another apartment; and putting the fatal note into his hand, cried— "Bear it like a Christian," and turned from him, endeavoring to suppress his own too visible emotions.

It would be vain to attempt describing what Mr. Temple felt whilst he hastily ran over the dreadful lines: when he had finished, the paper dropped from his unnerved hand. "Gracious heaven!" said he, "could Charlotte act thus?" Neither tear nor sigh escaped him; and he sat the image of mute sorrow, till roused from his stupor by the repeated shrieks of Mrs. Temple. He rose hastily, and rushing into the apartment where she was, folded his arms about her, and saying—"Let us be patient, my dear Lucy," nature relieved his almost bursting heart by a friendly[7] gush of tears.

Should any one, presuming on his own philosophic temper, look with an eye of contempt on the man who could indulge a woman's weakness, let him remember that man was a father, and he will then pity the misery which wrung those drops from a noble, generous heart.

Mrs. Temple beginning to be a little more composed, but still imagining her child was dead, her husband, gently taking her hand, cried—"You are mistaken, my love. Charlotte is not dead."

"Then she is very ill, else why did she not come? But I will go to her: the chaise is still at the door: let me go instantly to the dear girl. If I was ill, she would fly to attend me, to alleviate my sufferings, and cheer me with her love."

"Be calm, my dearest Lucy, and I will tell you all," said Mr. Temple. "You must not go, indeed you must not; it will be of no use."

"Temple," said she, assuming a look of firmness and composure, "tell me the truth I beseech you. I cannot bear this dreadful suspense. What misfortune has befallen my child? Let me know the worst, and I will endeavor to bear it as I ought."

"Lucy," replied Mr. Temple, "imagine your daughter alive, and in no danger of death: what misfortune would you then dread?"

"There is one misfortune which is worse than death. But I know my child too well to suspect—"

"Be not too confident, Lucy."

"Oh heavens!" said she, "what horrid images do you start: is it possible she should forget—"

"She has forgot us all, my love; she has preferred the love of a stranger to the affectionate protection of her friends."

7. Salutary, comforting.

"Not eloped?" cried she eagerly.

Mr. Temple was silent.

"You cannot contradict it," said she. "I see my fate in those tearful eyes. Oh Charlotte! Charlotte! how ill have you requited our tenderness! But, Father of Mercies," continued she, sinking on her knees, and raising her streaming eyes and clasped hands to heaven, "this once vouchsafe to hear a fond, a distracted mother's prayer. Oh let Thy bounteous Providence watch over and protect the dear thoughtless girl, save her from the miseries which I fear will be her portion, and oh! of Thine infinite mercy, make her not a mother, lest she should one day feel what I now suffer."

The last words faltered on her tongue, and she fell fainting into the arms of her husband, who had involuntarily dropped on his knees beside her.

A mother's anguish, when disappointed in her tenderest hopes, none but a mother can conceive. Yet, my dear young readers, I would have you read this scene with attention, and reflect that you may yourselves one day be mothers. Oh my friends, as you value your eternal happiness, wound not, by thoughtless ingratitude, the peace of the mother who bore you: remember the tenderness, the care, the unremitting anxiety with which she has attended to all your wants and wishes from earliest infancy to the present day; behold the mild ray of affectionate applause that beams from her eye on the performance of your duty: listen to her reproofs with silent attention; they proceed from a heart anxious for your future felicity: you must love her; nature, all-powerful nature, has planted the seeds of filial affection in your bosoms.

Then once more read over the sorrows of poor Mrs. Temple, and remember, the mother whom you so dearly love and venerate will feel the same, when you, forgetful of the respect due to your Maker and yourself, forsake the paths of virtue for those of vice and folly.

Chapter XV. Embarkation

It was with the utmost difficulty that the united efforts of Mademoiselle and Montraville could support Charlotte's spirits during their short ride from Chichester to Portsmouth, where a boat waited to take them immediately on board the ship in which they were to embark for America.

As soon as she became tolerably composed, she entreated pen and ink to write to her parents. This she did in the most affecting, artless manner, entreating their pardon and blessing, and describing the dreadful situation of her mind, the conflict she suffered in endeavoring to conquer this unfortunate attachment, and concluded with saying her only hope of future comfort consisted in the (perhaps delusive) idea she indulged, of being once more folded in their protecting arms, and hearing the words of peace and pardon from their lips.

The tears streamed incessantly while she was writing, and she was frequently obliged to lay down her pen: but when the task was completed, and she had committed the letter to the care of Montraville to be sent to the post office, she became more calm, and indulging the delightful hope of soon receiving an answer that would seal her pardon, she in some measure assumed her usual cheerfulness.

But Montraville knew too well the consequences that must unavoidably ensue should this letter reach Mr. Temple: he therefore wisely resolved to walk on the deck, tear it in pieces, and commit the fragments to the care of Neptune,[8] who might or might not, as it suited his convenience, convey them on shore.

All Charlotte's hopes and wishes were now concentrated in one, namely that the fleet might be detained at Spithead till she could receive a letter from her friends: but in this she was disappointed, for the second morning after she went on board, the signal was made, the fleet weighed anchor, and in a few hours (the wind being favorable) they bid adieu to the white cliffs of Albion.[9]

In the meantime every inquiry that could be thought of was made by Mr. and Mrs. Temple; for many days did they indulge the fond hope that she was merely gone off to be married, and that when the indissoluble knot was once tied, she would return with the partner she had chosen, and entreat their blessing and forgiveness.

"And shall we not forgive her?" said Mr. Temple.

"Forgive her!" exclaimed the mother. "Oh yes, whatever be our errors, is she not our child? and though bowed to the earth even with shame and remorse, is it not our duty to raise the poor penitent, and whisper peace and comfort to her desponding soul? Would she but return, with rapture would I fold her to my heart, and bury every remembrance of her faults in the dear embrace."

But still day after day passed on, and Charlotte did not appear, nor were any tidings to be heard of her: yet each rising morning was welcomed by some new hope—the evening brought with it disappointment. At length hope was no more; despair usurped her place; and the mansion which was once the mansion of peace, became the habitation of pale, dejected melancholy.

The cheerful smile that was wont[1] to adorn the face of Mrs. Temple was fled, and had it not been for the support of unaffected piety, and a consciousness of having ever set before her child the fairest example, she must have sunk under this heavy affliction.

"Since," said she, "the severest scrutiny cannot charge me with any breach of duty to have deserved this severe chastisement, I will bow before the Power who inflicts it with humble resignation to His will; nor shall the duty of a wife be totally absorbed in the feelings of the mother; I will endeavor to appear more cheerful, and by appearing in some measure to have conquered my own sorrow, alleviate the sufferings of my husband, and rouse him from that torpor into which this misfortune has plunged him. My father too demands my care and attention: I must not, by a selfish indulgence of my own grief, forget the interest those two dear objects take in my happiness or misery: I will wear a smile on my face, though the thorn rankles in my heart; and if by so doing, I in the smallest degree contribute to restore their peace of mind, I shall be amply rewarded for the pain the concealment of my own feelings may occasion."

Thus argued this excellent woman: and in the execution of so laudable a resolution we shall leave her, to follow the fortunes of the hapless victim of imprudence and evil counsellors.

---

8. In Roman mythology Neptune is the god of the sea.

9. England.

1. Accustomed.

Chapter XVI. Necessary Digression

On board of the ship in which Charlotte and Mademoiselle were embarked was an officer of large unencumbered fortune and elevated rank, and whom I shall call Crayton.

He was one of those men, who, having traveled in their youth, pretend to have contracted a peculiar fondness for everything foreign, and to hold in contempt the productions of their own country; and this affected partiality extended even to the women.

With him, therefore, the blushing modesty and unaffected simplicity of Charlotte passed unnoticed; but the forward pertness of La Rue, the freedom of her conversation, the elegance of her person, mixed with a certain engaging *je ne sais quoi*,[2] perfectly enchanted him.

The reader no doubt has already developed the character of La Rue: designing, artful, and selfish, she had accepted the devoirs[3] of Belcour because she was heartily weary of the retired life she led at the school, wished to be released from what she deemed a slavery, and to return to that vortex of folly and dissipation which had once plunged her into the deepest misery; but her plan she flattered herself was now better formed: she resolved to put herself under the protection of no man till she had first secured a settlement; but the clandestine manner in which she left Madame Du Pont's prevented her putting this plan in execution, though Belcour solemnly protested he would make her a handsome settlement the moment they arrived at Portsmouth. This he afterwards contrived to evade by a pretended hurry of business; La Rue readily conceiving he never meant to fulfil his promise, determined to change her battery, and attack the heart of Colonel Crayton. She soon discovered the partiality he entertained for her nation; and having imposed on him a feigned tale of distress, representing Belcour as a villain who had seduced her from her friends under promise of marriage, and afterwards betrayed her, pretending great remorse for the errors she had committed, and declaring whatever her affection for Belcour might have been, it was now entirely extinguished, and she wished for nothing more than an opportunity to leave a course of life which her soul abhorred; but she had no friends to apply to, they had all renounced her, and guilt and misery would undoubtedly be her future portion through life.

Crayton was possessed of many amiable qualities, though the peculiar trait in his character, which we have already mentioned, in a great measure threw a shade over them. He was beloved for his humanity and benevolence by all who knew him, but he was easy and unsuspicious himself, and became a dupe to the artifice of others.

He was, when very young, united to an amiable Parisian lady, and perhaps it was his affection for her that laid the foundation for the partiality he ever retained for the whole nation. He had by her one daughter, who entered into the world but a few hours before her mother left it. This lady was universally beloved and admired, being endowed with all the virtues of her mother, without the weakness of the father: she was married to Major Beauchamp, and was at this time in the same fleet with her father, attending her husband to New York.

2. Indescribable something (French; literally, "I don't know what"). 　　3. Courteous attentions.

Crayton was melted by the affected contrition and distress of La Rue: he would converse with her for hours, read to her, play cards with her, listen to all her complaints, and promise to protect her to the utmost of his power. La Rue easily saw his character; her sole aim was to awaken a passion in his bosom that might turn out to her advantage, and in this aim she was but too successful, for before the voyage was finished, the infatuated Colonel gave her from under his hand a promise of marriage on their arrival at New York, under forfeiture of five thousand pounds.

And how did our poor Charlotte pass her time during a tedious and tempestuous passage? Naturally delicate, the fatigue and sickness which she endured rendered her so weak as to be almost entirely confined to her bed: yet the kindness and attention of Montraville in some measure contributed to alleviate her sufferings, and the hope of hearing from her friends soon after her arrival, kept up her spirits, and cheered many a gloomy hour.

But during the voyage a great revolution took place not only in the fortune of La Rue but in the bosom of Belcour: whilst in pursuit of his amour with Mademoiselle, he had attended little to the interesting, inobtrusive charms of Charlotte, but when, cloyed by possession, and disgusted with the art and dissimulation of one, he beheld the simplicity and gentleness of the other, the contrast became too striking not to fill him at once with surprise and admiration. He frequently conversed with Charlotte; he found her sensible, well informed, but diffident and unassuming. The languor which the fatigue of her body and perturbation of her mind spread over her delicate features served only in his opinion to render her more lovely: he knew that Montraville did not design to marry her, and he formed a resolution to endeavor to gain her himself whenever Montraville should leave her.

Let not the reader imagine Belcour's designs were honorable. Alas! when once a woman has forgot the respect due to herself, by yielding to the solicitations of illicit love, they lose all their consequence, even in the eyes of the man whose art has betrayed them, and for whose sake they have sacrificed every valuable consideration:

> The heedless Fair, who stoops to guilty joys,
> A man may pity—but he must despise.

Nay, every libertine will think he has a right to insult her with his licentious passion; and should the unhappy creature shrink from the insolent overture, he will sneeringly taunt her with pretence of modesty.

Chapter XVII. A Wedding

On the day before their arrival at New York, after dinner, Crayton arose from his seat, and placing himself by Mademoiselle, thus addressed the company—

"As we are now nearly arrived at our destined port, I think it but my duty to inform you, my friends, that this lady" (taking her hand), "has placed herself under my protection. I have seen and severely felt the anguish of her heart, and through every shade which cruelty or malice may throw over her, can discover the most amiable qualities. I thought it but necessary to mention my esteem for her before our disembarkation, as it is my fixed resolution, the morning after we land, to give her an undoubted title to my favor and protection by honorably uniting my fate to hers. I would wish every gentleman here therefore to remember that her honor henceforth is mine, and," continued he, looking at Belcour, "should any man presume to speak in the least disrespectfully of her, I shall not hesitate to pronounce him a scoundrel."

Belcour cast at him a smile of contempt, and bowing profoundly low, wished Mademoiselle much joy in the proposed union; and assuring the Colonel that he need not be in the least apprehensive of any one throwing the least odium on the character of his lady, shook him by the hand with ridiculous gravity, and left the cabin.

The truth was, he was glad to be rid of La Rue, and so he was but freed from her, he cared not who fell a victim to her infamous arts.

The inexperienced Charlotte was astonished at what she heard. She thought La Rue had, like herself, only been urged by the force of her attachment to Belcour, to quit her friends, and follow him to the seat of war: how wonderful then, that she should resolve to marry another man. It was certainly extremely wrong. It was indelicate. She mentioned her thoughts to Montraville. He laughed at her simplicity, called her a little idiot, and patting her on the cheek, said she knew nothing of the world. "If the world sanctifies such things, 'tis a very bad world I think," said Charlotte. "Why I always understood they were to have been married when they arrived at New York. I am sure Mademoiselle told me Belcour promised to marry her."

"Well, and suppose he did?"

"Why, he should be obliged to keep his word I think."

"Well, but I suppose he has changed his mind," said Montraville, "and then you know the case is altered."

Charlotte looked at him attentively for a moment. A full sense of her own situation rushed upon her mind. She burst into tears, and remained silent. Montraville too well understood the cause of her tears. He kissed her cheek, and bidding her not make herself uneasy, unable to bear the silent but keen remonstrance, hastily left her.

The next morning by sunrise they found themselves at anchor before the city of New York. A boat was ordered to convey the ladies on shore. Crayton accompanied them; and they were shown to a house of public entertainment. Scarcely were they seated when the door opened, and the Colonel found himself in the arms of his daughter, who had landed a few minutes before him. The first transport of meeting subsided, Crayton introduced his daughter to Mademoiselle La Rue, as an old friend of her mother's (for the artful French woman had really made it appear to the credulous Colonel that she was in the same convent with his first wife, and, though much younger, had received many tokens of her esteem and regard).

"If, Mademoiselle," said Mrs. Beauchamp, "you were the friend of my mother, you must be worthy the esteem of all good hearts."

"Mademoiselle will soon honor our family," said Crayton, "by supplying the place that valuable woman filled: and as you are married, my dear, I think you will not blame—"

"Hush, my dear Sir," replied Mrs. Beauchamp: "I know my duty too well to scrutinize your conduct. Be assured, my dear father, your happiness is mine. I shall rejoice in it, and sincerely love the person who contributes to it. But tell me," continued she, turning to Charlotte, "who is this lovely girl? Is she your sister, Mademoiselle?"

A blush, deep as the glow of the carnation, suffused the cheeks of Charlotte.

"It is a young lady," replied the Colonel, "who came in the same vessel with us from England." He then drew his daughter aside, and told her in a whisper, Charlotte was the mistress of Montraville.

"What a pity!" said Mrs. Beauchamp softly (casting a most compassionate glance at her.) "But surely her mind is not depraved. The goodness of her heart is depicted in her ingenuous countenance."

Charlotte caught the word pity. "And am I already fallen so low?" said she. A sigh escaped her, and a tear was ready to start, but Montraville appeared, and she checked the rising emotion. Mademoiselle went with the Colonel and his daughter to another apartment. Charlotte remained with Montraville and Belcour. The next morning the Colonel performed his promise, and La Rue became in due form Mrs. Crayton, exulted in her own good fortune, and dared to look with an eye of contempt on the unfortunate but far less guilty Charlotte.

Chapter XVIII. *Reflections*

"And am I indeed fallen so low," said Charlotte, "as to be only pitied? Will the voice of approbation no more meet my ear? and shall I never again possess a friend, whose face will wear a smile of joy whenever I approach? Alas! how thoughtless, how dreadfully imprudent have I been! I know not which is most painful to endure, the sneer of contempt, or the glance of compassion, which is depicted in the various countenances of my own sex: they are both equally humiliating. Ah! my dear parents, could you now see the child of your affections, the daughter whom you so dearly loved, a poor solitary being, without society, here wearing out her heavy hours in deep regret and anguish of heart, no kind friend of her own sex to whom she can unbosom her griefs, no beloved mother, no woman of character will appear in my company, and low as your Charlotte is fallen, she cannot associate with infamy."

These were the painful reflections which occupied the mind of Charlotte. Montraville had placed her in a small house a few miles from New York: he gave her one female attendant, and supplied her with what money she wanted; but business and pleasure so entirely occupied his time, that he had little to devote to the woman, whom he had brought from all her connections, and robbed of innocence. Sometimes, indeed, he would steal out at the close of evening, and pass a few hours with her; and then so much was she attached to him, that all her sorrows were forgotten while blessed with his society: she would enjoy a walk by moonlight, or sit by him in a little arbor at the bottom of the garden, and play on the harp, accompanying it with her plaintive, harmonious voice. But often, very often, did he promise to renew his visits, and, forgetful of his promise, leave her to mourn her disappointment. What painful hours of expectation would she pass! She would sit at a window which looked toward a field he used to cross, counting the minutes, and straining her eyes to catch the first glimpse of his person, till blinded with tears of disappointment, she would lean her head on her hands, and give free vent to her sorrows: then catching at some new hope, she would again renew her watchful position, till the shades of evening enveloped every object in a dusky cloud: she would then renew her complaints, and, with a heart bursting with disappointed love and wounded sensibility, retire to a bed which remorse had strewed with thorns, and court in vain that comforter of weary nature (who seldom visits the unhappy) to come and steep her senses in oblivion.

Who can form an adequate idea of the sorrow that preyed upon the mind of Charlotte? The wife, whose breast glows with affection to her husband, and who in return meets only indifference, can but faintly conceive her anguish. Dreadfully painful is the situation of such a woman, but she has many comforts of which our poor Charlotte was deprived. The duteous, faithful wife, though treated with indifference, has one solid pleasure within her own bosom, she can reflect that she has not deserved neglect—that she has ever fulfilled the duties of her station with the strictest exactness; she may hope, by constant assiduity and unremitted attention, to recall her wanderer, and be doubly happy in his returning affection; she knows he cannot leave her to unite himself to another: he cannot cast her out to poverty and contempt; she looks around her, and sees the smile of friendly welcome, or the tear of affectionate consolation, on the face of every person whom she favors with her esteem; and from all these circumstances she gathers comfort: but the poor girl by thoughtless passion led astray, who, in parting with her honor, has forfeited the esteem of the very man to whom she has sacrificed everything dear and valuable in life, feels his indifference in the fruit of her own folly, and laments her want of power to recall his lost affection; she knows there is no tie but honor, and that, in a man who has been guilty of seduction, is but very feeble: he may leave her in a moment to shame and want; he may marry and forsake her forever; and should he, she has no redress, no friendly, soothing companion to pour into her wounded mind the balm of consolation, no benevolent hand to lead her back to the path of rectitude; she has disgraced her friends, forfeited the good opinion of the world, and undone herself; she feels herself a poor solitary being in the midst of surrounding multitudes; shame bows her to the earth, remorse tears her distracted mind, and guilt, poverty, and disease close the dreadful scene: she sinks unnoticed to oblivion. The finger of contempt may point out to some passing daughter of youthful mirth, the humble bed where lies this frail sister of mortality; and will she, in the unbounded gaiety of her heart, exult in her own unblemished fame, and triumph over the silent ashes of the dead? Oh no! has she a heart of sensibility, she will stop, and thus address the unhappy victim of folly—

"Thou had'st thy faults, but sure thy sufferings have expiated them: thy errors brought thee to an early grave; but thou wert a fellow creature—thou hast been unhappy—then be those errors forgotten."

Then, as she stoops to pluck the noxious weed from off the sod, a tear will fall, and consecrate the spot to Charity.

Forever honored be the sacred drop of humanity; the angel of mercy shall record its source, and the soul from whence it sprang shall be immortal.

My dear Madam, contract not your brow into a frown of disapprobation. I mean not to extenuate the faults of those unhappy women who fall victims to guilt and folly; but surely, when we reflect how many errors we are ourselves subject to, how many secret faults lie hid in the recesses of our hearts, which we should blush to have brought into open day (and yet those faults require the lenity and pity of a benevolent judge, or awful would be our prospect of futurity) I say, my dear Madam, when we consider this, we surely may pity the faults of others.

Believe me, many an unfortunate female, who has once strayed into the thorny paths of vice, would gladly return to virtue, was any generous friend to endeavor to raise and reassure her; but alas! it cannot be, you say; the world would deride and scoff. Then let me tell you, Madam, 'tis a very unfeeling world, and does not deserve half the blessings which a bountiful Providence showers upon it.

Oh, Thou benevolent giver of all good! how shall we erring mortals dare to look up to Thy mercy in the great day of retribution, if we now uncharitably refuse to overlook the errors, or alleviate the miseries, of our fellow creatures.

Chapter XIX. *A Mistake Discovered*

Julia Franklin was the only child of a man of large property, who, at the age of eighteen, left her independent mistress of an unencumbered income of seven hundred a year;[4] she was a girl of a lively disposition, and humane, susceptible heart: she resided in New York with an uncle, who loved her too well, and had too high an opinion of her prudence, to scrutinize her actions so much as would have been necessary with many young ladies, who were not blest with her discretion: she was, at the time Montraville arrived at New York, the life of society, and the universal toast. Montraville was introduced to her by the following accident.

One night when he was upon guard, a dreadful fire broke out near Mr. Franklin's house, which, in a few hours, reduced that and several others to ashes; fortunately no lives were lost, and, by the assiduity of the soldiers, much valuable property was saved from the flames. In the midst of the confusion an old gentleman came up to Montraville, and, putting a small box into his hands, cried—"Keep it, my good Sir, till I come to you again;" and then rushing again into the thickest of the crowd, Montraville saw him no more. He waited till the fire was quite extinguished and the mob dispersed; but in vain: the old gentleman did not appear to claim his property; and Montraville, fearing to make any inquiry, lest he should meet with impostors who might lay claim, without any legal right to the box, carried it to his lodgings, and locked it up. He naturally imagined that the person who committed it to his care knew him, and would, in a day or two, reclaim it; but several weeks passed on, and no inquiry being made, he began to be uneasy, and resolved to examine the contents of the box, and if they were, as he supposed, valuable, to spare no pains to discover, and restore them to the owner. Upon opening it, he found it contained jewels to a large amount, about two hundred pounds in money, and a miniature picture set for a bracelet. On examining the picture, he thought he had somewhere seen features very like it, but could not recollect where. A few days after, being at a public assembly, he saw Miss Franklin, and the likeness was too evident to be mistaken. He inquired among his brother officers if any of them knew her, and found one who was upon terms of intimacy in the family: "then introduce me to her immediately," said he, "for I am certain I can inform her of something which will give her peculiar pleasure."

He was immediately introduced, found she was the owner of the jewels,

4. An income of seven hundred pounds a year free of debt.

and was invited to breakfast the next morning in order to their restoration. This whole evening Montraville was honored with Julia's hand; the lively sallies of her wit, the elegance of her manner, powerfully charmed him: he forgot Charlotte, and indulged himself in saying everything that was polite and tender to Julia. But on retiring, recollection returned. "What am I about?" said he: "though I cannot marry Charlotte, I cannot be villain enough to forsake her, nor must I dare to trifle with the heart of Julia Franklin. I will return this box," said he, "which has been the source of so much uneasiness already, and in the evening pay a visit to my poor melancholy Charlotte, and endeavor to forget this fascinating Julia."

He arose, dressed himself, and taking the picture out, "I will reserve this from the rest," said he, "and by presenting it to her when she thinks it is lost, enhance the value of the obligation." He repaired to Mr. Franklin's, and found Julia in the breakfast parlor alone.

"How happy am I, Madam," said he, "that being the fortunate instrument of saving these jewels has been the means of procuring me the acquaintance of so amiable a lady. There are the jewels and money all safe."

"But where is the picture, Sir?" said Julia.

"Here, Madam. I would not willingly part with it."

"It is the portrait of my mother," said she, taking it from him: " 'tis all that remains." She pressed it to her lips, and a tear trembled in her eyes. Montraville glanced his eye on her gray night gown[5] and black ribbon, and his own feelings prevented a reply.

Julia Franklin was the very reverse of Charlotte Temple: she was tall, elegantly shaped, and possessed much of the air and manner of a woman of fashion; her complexion was a clear brown, enlivened with the glow of health, her eyes, full, black, and sparkling, darted their intelligent glances through long silken lashes; her hair was shining brown, and her features regular and striking; there was an air of innocent gaiety that played about her countenance, where good humor sat triumphant.

"I have been mistaken," said Montraville. "I imagined I loved Charlotte: but alas! I am now too late convinced my attachment to her was merely the impulse of the moment. I fear I have not only entailed lasting misery on that poor girl, but also thrown a barrier in the way of my own happiness, which it will be impossible to surmount. I feel I love Julia Franklin with ardor and sincerity; yet, when in her presence, I am sensible of my own inability to offfer a heart worthy her acceptance, and remain silent."

Full of these painful thoughts, Montraville walked out to see Charlotte: she saw him approach, and ran out to meet him: she banished from her countenance the air of discontent which ever appeared when he was absent, and met him with a smile of joy.

"I thought you had forgot me, Montraville," said she, "and was very unhappy."

"I shall never forget you, Charlotte," he replied, pressing her hand.

The uncommon gravity of his countenance, and the brevity of his reply, alarmed her.

"You are not well," said she; "your hand is hot; your eyes are heavy; you are very ill."

---

5. Dressing gown.

"I am a villain," said he mentally, as he turned from her to hide his emotions.

"But come," continued she tenderly, "you shall go to bed, and I will sit by, and watch you; you will be better when you have slept."

Montraville was glad to retire, and by pretending sleep, hide the agitation of his mind from her penetrating eye. Charlotte watched by him till a late hour, and then, lying softly down by his side, sunk into a profound sleep, from whence she awoke not till late the next morning.

Chapter XX

Virtue never appears so amiable as when reaching forth her hand
to raise a fallen sister.
                                          CHAPTER OF ACCIDENTS.[6]

When Charlotte awoke, she missed Montraville; but thinking he might have arisen early to enjoy the beauties of the morning, she was preparing to follow him, when casting her eye on the table, she saw a note, and opening it hastily, found these words—

"My dear Charlotte must not be surprised, if she does not see me again for some time: unavoidable business will prevent me that pleasure: be assured I am quite well this morning; and what your fond imagination magnified into illness, was nothing more than fatigue, which a few hours rest has entirely removed. Make yourself happy, and be certain of the unalterable friendship of   MONTRAVILLE."

"Friendship!" said Charlotte emphatically, as she finished the note, "is it come to this at last? Alas! poor, forsaken Charlotte, thy doom is now but too apparent. Montraville is no longer interested in thy happiness; and shame, remorse, and disappointed love will henceforth be thy only attendants."

Though these were the ideas that involuntarily rushed upon the mind of Charlotte as she perused the fatal note, yet after a few hours had elapsed, the siren[7] Hope again took possession of her bosom, and she flattered herself she could, on a second perusal, discover an air of tenderness in the few lines he had left, which at first had escaped her notice.

"He certainly cannot be so base as to leave me," said she, "and in styling himself my friend does he not promise to protect me. I will not torment myself with these causeless fears; I will place a confidence in his honor; and sure he will not be so unjust as to abuse it."

Just as she had by this manner of reasoning brought her mind to some tolerable degree of composure, she was surprised by a visit from Belcour. The dejection visible in Charlotte's countenance, her swollen eyes and neglected attire, at once told him she was unhappy: he made no doubt but Montraville had, by his coldness, alarmed her suspicions, and was resolved, if possible, to rouse her to jealousy, urge her to reproach him, and by that means occasion a breach between them. "If I can once convince her that she has a rival," said he, "she will listen to my passion if it is only to revenge his slights." Belcour knew but little of the female heart; and what he did

6. Rowson's quotation is from Sophia Lee's play *The Chapter of Accidents* (1782), 2.5: "Virtue never looks so lovely as when she stretches out her hand to the fallen."

7. Temptress. In Greek mythology the sirens lured sailors to destruction by their singing.

know was only of those of loose and dissolute lives. He had no idea that a woman might fall a victim to imprudence, and yet retain so strong a sense of honor, as to reject with horror and contempt every solicitation to a second fault. He never imagined that a gentle, generous female heart, once tenderly attached, when treated with unkindness might break, but would never harbor a thought of revenge.

His visit was not long, but before he went he fixed a scorpion in the heart of Charlotte, whose venom embittered every future hour of her life.

We will now return for a moment to Colonel Crayton. He had been three months married, and in that little time had discovered that the conduct of his lady was not so prudent as it ought to have been: but remonstrance was vain; her temper was violent; and to the Colonel's great misfortune he had conceived a sincere affection for her: she saw her own power, and, with the art of a Circe,[8] made every action appear to him in what light she pleased: his acquaintance laughed at his blindness, his friends pitied his infatuation, his amiable daughter, Mrs. Beauchamp, in secret deplored the loss of her father's affection, and grieved that he should be so entirely swayed by an artful, and, she much feared, infamous woman.

Mrs. Beauchamp was mild and engaging; she loved not the hurry and bustle of a city, and had prevailed on her husband to take a house a few miles from New York. Chance led her into the same neighborhood with Charlotte; their houses stood within a short space of each other, and their gardens joined: she had not been long in her new habitation before the figure of Charlotte struck her; she recollected her interesting features; she saw the melancholy so conspicuous in her countenance, and her heart bled at the reflection, that perhaps deprived of honor, friends, all that was valuable in life, she was doomed to linger out a wretched existence in a strange land, and sink brokenhearted into an untimely grave. "Would to heaven I could snatch her from so hard a fate," said she; "but the merciless world has barred the doors of compassion against a poor weak girl, who, perhaps, had she one kind friend to raise and reassure her, would gladly return to peace and virtue; nay, even the woman who dares to pity, and endeavor to recall a wandering sister, incurs the sneer of contempt and ridicule, for an action in which even angels are said to rejoice."

The longer Mrs. Beauchamp was a witness to the solitary life Charlotte led the more she wished to speak to her, and often as she saw her cheeks wet with the tears of anguish, she would say—"Dear sufferer, how gladly would I pour into your heart the balm of consolation, were it not for the fear of derision."

But an accident soon happened which made her resolve to brave even the scoffs of the world, rather than not enjoy the heavenly satisfaction of comforting a desponding fellow creature.

Mrs. Beauchamp was an early riser. She was one morning walking in the garden, leaning on her husband's arm, when the sound of a harp attracted their notice: they listened attentively, and heard a soft melodious voice distinctly sing the following stanzas:

> Thou glorious orb, supremely bright,
> Just rising from the sea,

8. An enchantress. In Homer's *Odyssey* (8th century B.C.E.), Circe is a goddess whose powerful magic turns men into beasts.

To cheer all nature with thy light,
   What are thy beams to me?
In vain thy glories bid me rise,
   To hail the new-born day,
Alas! my morning sacrifice
   Is still to weep and pray.
For what are nature's charms combined,
   To one, whose weary breast
Can neither peace nor comfort find,
   Nor friend whereon to rest?
Oh! never! never! whilst I live
   Can my heart's anguish cease:
Come, friendly death, thy mandate give,
   And let me be at peace.

" 'Tis poor Charlotte!" said Mrs. Beauchamp, the pellucid drop of human-ity stealing down her cheek.

Captain Beauchamp was alarmed at her emotion. "What Charlotte?" said he; "do you know her?"

In the accent of a pitying angel did she disclose to her husband Charlotte's unhappy situation, and the frequent wish she had formed of being service-able to her. "I fear," continued she, "the poor girl has been basely betrayed; and if I thought you would not blame me, I would pay her a visit, offer her my friendship, and endeavor to restore to her heart that peace she seems to have lost, and so pathetically laments. Who knows, my dear," laying her hand affectionately on his arm, "who knows but she has left some kind, affection-ate parents to lament her errors, and would she return, they might with rapture receive the poor penitent, and wash away her faults in tears of joy. Oh! what a glorious reflection would it be for me could I be the happy instru-ment of restoring her. Her heart may not be depraved, Beauchamp."

"Exalted woman!" cried Beauchamp, embracing her, "how dost thou rise every moment in my esteem. Follow the impulse of thy generous heart, my Emily. Let prudes and fools censure if they dare, and blame a sensibility they never felt; I will exultingly tell them that the heart that is truly virtuous is ever inclined to pity and forgive the errors of its fellow creatures."

A beam of exulting joy played round the animated countenance of Mrs. Beauchamp, at these encomiums bestowed on her by a beloved husband, the most delightful sensations pervaded her heart, and, having breakfasted, she prepared to visit Charlotte.

Chapter XXI

Teach Me to feel another's Woe;
   To hide the Fault I see;
That Mercy I to others show,
   That Mercy show to me.
                     Pope.[9]

When Mrs. Beauchamp was dressed, she began to feel embarrassed at the thought of beginning an acquaintance with Charlotte, and was distressed how to make the first visit. "I cannot go without some introduction," said

---

9. The quotation is from Alexander Pope's *The Universal Prayer* (1738), lines 37–40.

she, "it will look so like impertinent curiosity." At length recollecting herself, she stepped into the garden, and gathering a few fine cucumbers, took them in her hand by way of apology for her visit.

A glow of conscious shame vermillioned Charlotte's face as Mrs. Beauchamp entered.

"You will pardon me, Madam," said she, "for not having before paid my respects to so amiable a neighbor; but we English[1] people always keep up that reserve which is the characteristic of our nation wherever we go. I have taken the liberty to bring you a few cucumbers, for I observed you had none in your garden."

Charlotte, though naturally polite and well-bred, was so confused she could hardly speak. Her kind visitor endeavored to relieve her by not noticing her embarrassment. "I am come, Madam," continued she, "to request you will spend the day with me. I shall be alone; and, as we are both strangers in this country, we may hereafter be extremely happy in each other's friendship."

"Your friendship, Madam," said Charlotte blushing, "is an honor to all who are favored with it. Little as I have seen of this part of the world, I am no stranger to Mrs. Beauchamp's goodness of heart and known humanity: but my friendship—" She paused, glanced her eye upon her own visible situation, and, spite of her endeavors to suppress them, burst into tears.

Mrs. Beauchamp guessed the source from whence those tears flowed. "You seem unhappy, Madam," said she: "shall I be thought worthy your confidence? will you entrust me with the cause of your sorrow, and rest on my assurances to exert my utmost power to serve you." Charlotte returned a look of gratitude, but could not speak, and Mrs. Beauchamp continued—"My heart was interested in your behalf the first moment I saw you, and I only lament I had not made earlier overtures towards an acquaintance; but I flatter myself you will henceforth consider me as your friend."

"Oh Madam!" cried Charlotte, "I have forfeited the good opinion of all my friends; I have forsaken them, and undone myself."

"Come, come, my dear," said Mrs. Beauchamp, "you must not indulge these gloomy thoughts: you are not I hope so miserable as you imagine yourself: endeavor to be composed, and let me be favored with your company at dinner, when, if you can bring yourself to think me your friend, and repose a confidence in me, I am ready to convince you it shall not be abused." She then arose, and bade her good morning.

At the dining hour Charlotte repaired to Mrs. Beauchamp's, and during dinner assumed as composed an aspect as possible; but when the cloth was removed,[2] she summoned all her resolution and determined to make Mrs. Beauchamp acquainted with every circumstance preceding her unfortunate elopement, and the earnest desire she had to quit a way of life so repugnant to her feelings.

With the benignant aspect of an angel of mercy did Mrs. Beauchamp listen to the artless tale: she was shocked to the soul to find how large a share La Rue had in the seduction of this amiable girl, and a tear fell, when she reflected so vile a woman was now the wife of her father. When Charlotte

1. The action of the novel takes place before the Revolution.

2. After the meal is finished the tablecloth would be removed.

had finished, she gave her a little time to collect her scattered spirits, and then asked her if she had never written to her friends.

"Oh yes, Madam," said she, "frequently: but I have broke their hearts: they are either dead or have cast me off forever, for I have never received a single line from them."

"I rather suspect," said Mrs. Beauchamp, "they have never had your letters: but suppose you were to hear from them, and they were willing to receive you, would you then leave this cruel Montraville, and return to them?"

"Would I!" said Charlotte, clasping her hands; "would not the poor sailor, tossed on a tempestuous ocean, threatened every moment with death, gladly return to the shore he had left to trust to its deceitful calmness? Oh, my dear Madam, I would return, though to do it I were obliged to walk barefoot over a burning desert, and beg a scanty pittance of each traveler to support my existence. I would endure it all cheerfully, could I but once more see my dear, blessed mother, hear her pronounce my pardon, and bless me before I died; but alas! I shall never see her more; she has blotted the ungrateful Charlotte from her remembrance, and I shall sink to the grave loaded with her's and my father's curse."

Mrs. Beauchamp endeavored to sooth her. "You shall write to them again," said she, "and I will see that the letter is sent by the first packet that sails for England; in the meantime keep up your spirits, and hope everything, by daring to deserve it."

She then turned the conversation, and Charlotte having taken a cup of tea, wished her benevolent friend a good evening.

Chapter XXII. *Sorrows of the Heart*

When Charlotte got home she endeavored to collect her thoughts, and took up a pen in order to address those dear parents, whom, spite of her errors, she still loved with the utmost tenderness, but vain was every effort to write with the least coherence; her tears fell so fast they almost blinded her; and as she proceeded to describe her unhappy situation, she became so agitated that she was obliged to give over the attempt and retire to bed, where, overcome with the fatigue her mind had undergone, she fell into a slumber which greatly refreshed her, and she arose in the morning with spirits more adequate to the painful task she had to perform, and, after several attempts, at length concluded the following letter to her mother—

TO MRS. TEMPLE.

New York.

"Will my once kind, my ever beloved mother, deign to receive a letter from her guilty, but repentant child? or has she, justly incensed at my ingratitude, driven the unhappy Charlotte from her remembrance? Alas! thou much injured mother! shouldst thou even disown me, I dare not complain, because I know I have deserved it: but yet, believe me, guilty as I am, and cruelly as I have disappointed the hopes of the fondest parents, that ever girl had, even in the moment when, forgetful of my duty, I fled from you and happiness, even then I loved you most, and my heart bled at the thought of what you would suffer. Oh! never, never! whilst I have existence, will the agony of that moment be erased from my memory. It seemed like the separation of soul and body. What can I plead in excuse for my conduct? alas! nothing! That I loved my seducer is but too true! yet powerful as that passion is when operating in a young heart glowing with sensibility, it never would have conquered my affection to you, my beloved parents, had I not been encouraged, nay, urged to take the fatally imprudent step, by one of my own sex, who, under the mask of friendship, drew me on to ruin. Yet think not your Charlotte was so lost as to voluntarily rush into a life of infamy; no, my dear mother, deceived by the specious appearance of my betrayer, and every suspicion lulled asleep by the most solemn promises of marriage, I thought not those promises would so easily be forgotten. I never once reflected that the man who could stoop to seduction, would not hesitate to forsake the wretched object of his passion, whenever his capricious heart grew weary of her tenderness. When we arrived at this place, I vainly expected him to fulfil his engagements, but was at last fatally convinced he had never intended to make me his wife, or if he had once thought of it, his mind was now altered. I scorned to claim from his humanity what I could not obtain from his love: I was conscious of having forfeited the only gem that could render me respectable in the eye of the world. I locked my sorrows in my own bosom, and bore my injuries in silence. But how shall I proceed? This man, this cruel Montraville, for whom I sacrificed honor, happiness, and the love of my friends, no longer looks on me with affection, but scorns the credulous girl whom his art has made miserable. Could you see me, my dear parents, without society, without friends, stung with remorse, and (I feel the burning blush of shame die my cheeks while I write it) tortured with the pangs of disappointed love; cut to the soul by the indifference of him, who, having deprived me of every other comfort, no longer thinks it worth his while to sooth the heart where he has planted the thorn of never-ceasing regret. My daily employment is to think of you and weep, to pray for your happiness and deplore my own folly: my nights are scarce more happy, for if by chance I close my weary eyes, and hope some small forgetfulness of sorrow, some little time to pass in sweet oblivion, fancy, still waking, wafts me home to you: I see your beloved forms, I kneel and hear the blessed words of peace and pardon. Ecstatic joy pervades my soul; I reach my arms to catch your dear embraces; the motion chases the illusive dream; I wake to real misery. At other times I see my father angry and frowning, point to horrid caves, where, on the cold damp ground, in the agonies of death, I see my dear mother and my revered grandfather. I strive to raise you; you push me from you, and shrieking cry—'Charlotte, thou hast murdered me!' Horror and despair tear every tortured nerve; I start, and leave my restless bed, weary and unrefreshed.

"Shocking as these reflections are, I have yet one more dreadful than the rest. Mother, my dear mother! do not let me quite break your heart when I tell you, in a few months I shall bring into the world an innocent witness of my guilt. Oh my bleeding heart, I shall bring a poor little helpless creature, heir to infamy and shame.

"This alone has urged me once more to address you, to interest you in behalf of this poor unborn, and beg you to extend your protection to the child of your lost Charlotte; for my own part I have wrote so often, so frequently have pleaded for forgiveness, and entreated to be received once more beneath the paternal roof, that having received no answer, not even one line, I much fear you have cast me from you forever.

"But sure you cannot refuse to protect my innocent infant: it partakes not of its mother's guilt. Oh my father, oh beloved mother, now do I feel the anguish I inflicted on your hearts recoiling with double force upon my own.

"If my child should be a girl (which heaven forbid) tell her the unhappy fate of her mother, and teach her to avoid my errors; if a boy, teach him to lament my miseries, but tell him not who inflicted them, lest in wishing to revenge his mother's injuries, he should wound the peace of his father.

"And now, dear friends of my soul, kind guardians of my infancy, farewell. I feel I never more must hope to see you; the anguish of my heart strikes at the strings of life, and in a short time I shall be at rest. Oh could I but receive your blessing and forgiveness before I died, it would smooth my passage to the peaceful grave, and be a blessed foretaste of a happy eternity. I beseech you, curse me not, my adored parents, but let a tear of pity and pardon fall to the memory of your lost   CHARLOTTE."

Chapter XXIII. A Man May Smile, and Smile, and Be a Villain

While Charlotte was enjoying some small degree of comfort in the consoling friendship of Mrs. Beauchamp, Montraville was advancing rapidly in his affection towards Miss Franklin. Julia was an amiable girl; she saw only the fair side of his character; she possessed an independent fortune, and resolved to be happy with the man of her heart, though his rank and fortune were by no means so exalted as she had a right to expect; she saw the passion which Montraville struggled to conceal; she wondered at his timidity, but imagined the distance fortune had placed between them occasioned his backwardness, and made every advance which strict prudence and a becoming modesty would permit. Montraville saw with pleasure he was not indifferent[3] to her, but a spark of honor which animated his bosom would not suffer him to take advantage of her partiality. He was well acquainted with Charlotte's situation, and he thought there would be a double cruelty in forsaking her at such a time; and to marry Miss Franklin, while honor, humanity, every sacred law, obliged him still to protect and support Charlotte, was a baseness which his soul shuddered at.

He communicated his uneasiness to Belcour: it was the very thing this pretended friend had wished. "And do you really," said he, laughing, "hesitate at marrying the lovely Julia, and becoming master of her fortune, because a little foolish, fond girl chose to leave her friends, and run away with you to America? Dear Montraville, act more like a man of sense; this whining, pining Charlotte, who occasions you so much uneasiness, would have eloped with somebody else if she had not with you."

"Would to heaven," said Montraville, "I had never seen her; my regard for her was but the momentary passion of desire, but I feel I shall love and revere

3. Of no consequence, unimportant.

Julia Franklin as long as I live; yet to leave poor Charlotte in her present situation would be cruel beyond description."

"Oh my good sentimental friend," said Belcour, "do you imagine nobody has a right to provide for the brat but yourself?"

Montraville started. "Sure," said he, "you cannot mean to insinuate that Charlotte is false."

"I don't insinuate it," said Belcour, "I know it."

Montraville turned pale as ashes. "Then there is no faith in woman," said he.

"While I thought you attached to her," said Belcour with an air of indifference, "I never wished to make you uneasy by mentioning her perfidy, but as I know you love and are beloved by Miss Franklin, I was determined not to let these foolish scruples of honor step between you and happiness, or your tenderness for the peace of a perfidious girl prevent your uniting yourself to a woman of honor."

"Good heavens!" said Montraville, "what poignant reflections does a man endure who sees a lovely woman plunged in infamy, and is conscious he was her first seducer; but are you certain of what you say, Belcour?"

"So far," replied he, "that I myself have received advances from her which I would not take advantage of out of regard to you: but hang it, think no more about her. I dined at Franklin's today, and Julia bid me seek and bring you to tea: so come along, my lad, make good use of opportunity, and seize the gifts of fortune while they are within your reach."

Montraville was too much agitated to pass a happy evening even in the company of Julia Franklin. He determined to visit Charlotte early the next morning, tax her with her falsehood, and take an everlasting leave of her; but when the morning came, he was commanded on duty,[4] and for six weeks was prevented from putting his design in execution. At length he found an hour to spare, and walked out to spend it with Charlotte: it was near four o'clock in the afternoon when he arrived at her cottage; she was not in the parlor, and without calling the servant he walked upstairs, thinking to find her in her bed room. He opened the door, and the first object that met his eyes was Charlotte asleep on the bed, and Belcour by her side.

"Death and distraction," said he, stamping, "this is too much. Rise, villain, and defend yourself." Belcour sprang from the bed. The noise awoke Charlotte; terrified at the furious appearance of Montraville, and seeing Belcour with him in the chamber, she caught hold of his arm as he stood by the bedside, and eagerly asked what was the matter.

"Treacherous, infamous girl," said he, "can you ask? How came he here?" pointing to Belcour.

"As heaven is my witness," replied she weeping, "I do not know. I have not seen him for these three weeks."

"Then you confess he sometimes visits you?"

"He came sometimes by your desire."

" 'Tis false; I never desired him to come, and you know I did not: but mark me, Charlotte, from this instant our connection is at an end. Let Belcour, or any other of your favored lovers, take you and provide for you; I have done with you forever."

---

4. Recalled to his army post and prevented from leaving.

He was then going to leave her; but starting wildly from the bed, she threw herself on her knees before him, protesting her innocence and entreating him not to leave her. "Oh Montraville," said she, "kill me, for pity's sake kill me, but do not doubt my fidelity. Do not leave me in this horrid situation; for the sake of your unborn child, oh! spurn not the wretched mother from you."

"Charlotte," said he, with a firm voice, "I shall take care that neither you nor your child want anything in the approaching painful hour; but we meet no more." He then endeavored to raise her from the ground; but in vain; she clung about his knees, entreating him to believe her innocent, and conjuring Belcour to clear up the dreadful mystery.

Belcour cast on Montraville a smile of contempt: it irritated him almost to madness; he broke from the feeble arms of the distressed girl; she shrieked and fell prostrate on the floor.

Montraville instantly left the house and returned hastily to the city.

Chapter XXIV. Mystery Developed

Unfortunately for Charlotte, about three weeks before this unhappy *rencontre*, Captain Beauchamp, being ordered to Rhode Island, his lady[5] had accompanied him, so that Charlotte was deprived of her friendly advice and consoling society. The afternoon on which Montraville had visited her she had found herself languid and fatigued, and after making a very slight dinner had lain down to endeavor to recruit her exhausted spirits, and, contrary to her expectations, had fallen asleep. She had not long been lain down, when Belcour arrived, for he took every opportunity of visiting her, and striving to awaken her resentment against Montraville. He inquired of the servant where her mistress was, and being told she was asleep, took up a book to amuse himself: having sat a few minutes, he by chance cast his eyes towards the road, and saw Montraville approaching; he instantly conceived the diabolical scheme of ruining the unhappy Charlotte in his opinion forever; he therefore stole softly up stairs, and laying himself by her side with the greatest precaution, for fear she should awake, was in that situation discovered by his credulous friend.

When Montraville spurned the weeping Charlotte from him, and left her almost distracted with terror and despair, Belcour raised her from the floor, and leading her downstairs, assumed the part of a tender, consoling friend. She listened to the arguments he advanced with apparent composure; but this was only the calm of a moment: the remembrance of Montraville's recent cruelty again rushed upon her mind: she pushed him from her with some violence, and crying—"Leave me, Sir, I beseech you leave me, for much I fear you have been the cause of my fidelity being suspected; go, leave me to the accumulated miseries my own imprudence has brought upon me."

She then left him with precipitation, and retiring to her own apartment, threw herself on the bed, and gave vent to an agony of grief which it is impossible to describe.

It now occurred to Belcour that she might possibly write to Montraville, and endeavor to convince him of her innocence: he was well aware of her pathetic remonstrances, and, sensible of the tenderness of Montraville's heart, resolved to prevent any letters ever reaching him: he therefore called the servant, and, by the powerful persuasion of a bribe, prevailed with her to promise whatever letters her mistress might write should be sent to him. He then left a polite, tender note for Charlotte, and returned to New York. His first business was to seek Montraville, and endeavor to convince him that what had happened would ultimately tend to his happiness: he found him in his apartment, solitary, pensive, and wrapped in disagreeable reflections.

"Why how now, whining, pining lover?" said he, clapping him on the shoulder. Montraville started; a momentary flush of resentment crossed his cheek, but instantly gave place to a death-like paleness, occasioned by painful remembrance—remembrance awakened by that monitor, whom, though we may in vain endeavor, we can never entirely silence.

"Belcour," said he, "you have injured me in a tender point."

"Prithee, Jack," replied Belcour, "do not make a serious matter of it: how could I refuse the girl's advances? and thank heaven she is not your wife."

"True," said Montraville; "but she was innocent when I first knew her. It was I seduced her, Belcour. Had it not been for me, she had still been virtuous and happy in the affection and protection of her family."

"Pshaw," replied Belcour, laughing, "if you had not taken advantage of her easy nature, some other would, and where is the difference, pray?"

"I wish I had never seen her," cried he passionately, and starting from his seat. "Oh that cursed French woman," added he with vehemence, "had it not been for her, I might have been happy———" He paused.

"With Julia Franklin," said Belcour. The name, like a sudden spark of electric fire, seemed for a moment to suspend his faculties—for a moment he was transfixed; but recovering, he caught Belcour's hand, and cried—"Stop! stop! I beseech you, name not the lovely Julia and the wretched Montraville in the same breath. I am a seducer, a mean, ungenerous seducer of unsuspecting innocence. I dare not hope that purity like hers would stoop to unite itself with black, premeditated guilt: yet by heavens I swear, Belcour, I thought I loved the lost, abandoned Charlotte till I saw Julia—I thought I never could forsake her; but the heart is deceitful, and I now can plainly discriminate between the impulse of a youthful passion, and the pure flame of disinterested affection."

At that instant Julia Franklin passed the window, leaning on her uncle's arm. She curtseyed as she passed, and, with the bewitching smile of modest cheerfulness, cried—"Do you bury yourselves in the house this fine evening, gents?" There was something in the voice! the manner! the look! that was altogether irresistible. "Perhaps she wishes my company," said Montraville mentally, as he snatched up his hat: "if I thought she loved me, I would confess my errors, and trust to her generosity to pity and pardon me." He soon overtook her, and offering her his arm, they sauntered to pleasant but unfrequented walks. Belcour drew Mr. Franklin on one side and entered into a political discourse: they walked faster than the young people, and Belcour by some means contrived entirely to lose sight of them. It was a fine evening in the beginning of autumn; the last remains of daylight faintly streaked the western sky, while the moon, with pale and virgin lustre in the room of gorgeous gold and purple, ornamented the canopy of heaven with silver, fleecy clouds, which now and then half hid her lovely face, and, by partly concealing, heightened every beauty; the zephyrs[6] whispered softly through the trees, which now began to shed their leafy honors; a solemn silence reigned: and to a happy mind an evening such as this would give serenity, and calm, unruffled pleasure; but to Montraville, while it soothed the turbulence of his passions, it brought increase of melancholy reflections. Julia was leaning on his arm: he took her hand in his, and pressing it tenderly, sighed deeply, but continued silent. Julia was embarrassed; she wished to break a silence so unaccountable, but was unable; she loved Montraville, she saw he was unhappy, and wished to know the cause of his uneasiness, but that innate modesty, which nature has implanted in the female breast, prevented her inquiring. "I am bad company, Miss Franklin," said he, at last recollecting himself; "but I have met with something today that has greatly distressed me, and I cannot shake off the disagreeable impression it has made on my mind."

"I am sorry," she replied, "that you have any cause of inquietude. I am sure if you were as happy as you deserve, and as all your friends wish you—" She hesitated. "And might I," replied he with some animation, "presume to rank the amiable Julia in that number?"

"Certainly," said she, "the service you have rendered me, the knowledge of your worth, all combine to make me esteem you."

"Esteem, my lovely Julia," said he passionately, "is but a poor cold word. I would if I dared, if I thought I merited your attention—but no, I must not—honor forbids. I am beneath your notice, Julia, I am miserable and cannot hope to be otherwise."

"Alas!" said Julia, "I pity you."

"Oh thou condescending charmer," said he, "how that sweet word cheers my sad heart. Indeed if you knew all, you would pity; but at the same time I fear you would despise me."

Just then they were again joined by Mr. Franklin and Belcour. It had interrupted an interesting discourse. They found it impossible to converse on indifferent subjects, and proceeded home in silence. At Mr. Franklin's door Montraville again pressed Julia's hand, and faintly articulating "good night," retired to his lodgings dispirited and wretched, from a consciousness that he deserved not the affection, with which he plainly saw he was honored.

Chapter XXV. Reception of a Letter

"And where now is our poor Charlotte?" said Mr. Temple one evening, as the cold blasts of autumn whistled rudely over the heath, and the yellow appearance of the distant wood, spoke the near approach of winter. In vain the cheerful fire blazed on the hearth, in vain was he surrounded by all the comforts of life; the parent was still alive in his heart, and when he thought that perhaps his once darling child was ere this exposed to all the miseries of want in a distant land, without a friend to sooth and comfort her, without the benignant look of compassion to cheer, or the angelic voice of pity to pour the balm of consolation on her wounded heart; when he thought of this, his whole soul dissolved in tenderness; and while he wiped the tear of

6. Gentle western winds.

anguish from the eye of his patient, uncomplaining Lucy, he struggled to suppress the sympathizing drop that started in his own.

"Oh, my poor girl," said Mrs. Temple, "how must she be altered, else surely she would have relieved our agonizing minds by one line to say she lived— to say she had not quite forgot the parents who almost idolized her."

"Gracious heaven," said Mr. Temple, starting from his seat, "who would wish to be a father, to experience the agonizing pangs inflicted on a parent's heart by the ingratitude of a child?" Mrs. Temple wept: her father took her hand; he would have said, "be comforted my child," but the words died on his tongue. The sad silence that ensued was interrupted by a loud rap at the door. In a moment a servant entered with a letter in his hand.

Mrs. Temple took it from him: she cast her eyes upon the superscription; she knew the writing. " 'Tis Charlotte," said she, eagerly breaking the seal, "she has not quite forgot us." But before she had half gone through the contents, a sudden sickness seized her; she grew cold and giddy, and putting it into her husband's hand, she cried—"Read it: I cannot." Mr. Temple attempted to read it aloud, but frequently paused to give vent to his tears. "My poor deluded child," said he, when he had finished.

"Oh, shall we not forgive the dear penitent?" said Mrs. Temple. "We must, we will, my love; she is willing to return, and 'tis our duty to receive her."

"Father of Mercy," said Mr. Eldridge, raising his clasped hands, "let me but live once more to see the dear wanderer restored to her afflicted parents, and take me from this world of sorrow whenever it seemeth best to Thy wisdom."

"Yes, we will receive her," said Mr. Temple; "we will endeavor to heal her wounded spirit, and speak peace and comfort to her agitated soul. I will write to her to return immediately."

"Oh!" said Mrs. Temple, "I would if possible fly to her, support and cheer the dear sufferer in the approaching hour of distress, and tell her how nearly penitence is allied to virtue. Cannot we go and conduct her home, my love?" continued she, laying her hand on his arm. "My father will surely forgive our absence if we go to bring home his darling."

"You cannot go, my Lucy," said Mr. Temple: "the delicacy of your frame would but poorly sustain the fatigue of a long voyage; but I will go and bring the gentle penitent to your arms. We may still see many years of happiness."

The struggle in the bosom of Mrs. Temple between maternal and conjugal tenderness was long and painful. At length the former triumphed, and she consented that her husband should set forward to New York by the first opportunity. She wrote to her Charlotte in the tenderest, most consoling manner, and looked forward to the happy hour when she should again embrace her, with the most animated hope.

Chapter XXVI. What Might Be Expected

In the meantime the passion Montraville had conceived for Julia Franklin daily increased, and he saw evidently how much he was beloved by that amiable girl: he was likewise strongly prepossessed with an idea of Charlotte's perfidy. What wonder then if he gave himself up to the delightful sensation which pervaded his bosom; and finding no obstacle arise to oppose his happiness, he solicited and obtained the hand of Julia. A few days before his marriage he thus addressed Belcour:

"Though Charlotte, by her abandoned conduct, has thrown herself from my protection, I still hold myself bound to support her till relieved from her present condition, and also to provide for the child. I do not intend to see her again, but I will place a sum of money in your hands, which will amply supply her with every convenience; but should she require more, let her have it, and I will see it repaid. I wish I could prevail on the poor deluded girl to return to her friends: she was an only child, and I make no doubt but that they would joyfully receive her; it would shock me greatly to see her henceforth leading a life of infamy, as I should always accuse myself of being the primary cause of all her errors. If she should choose to remain under your protection, be kind to her, Belcour, I conjure you. Let not satiety prompt you to treat her in such a manner, as may drive her to actions which necessity might urge her to, while her better reason disapproved them: she shall never want a friend while I live, but I never more desire to behold her; her presence would be always painful to me, and a glance from her eye would call the blush of conscious guilt into my cheek.

"I will write a letter to her, which you may deliver when I am gone, as I shall go to St. Eustatia[7] the day after my union with Julia, who will accompany me."

Belcour promised to fulfill the request of his friend, though nothing was farther from his intentions, than the least design of delivering the letter, or making Charlotte acquainted with the provision Montraville had made for her; he was bent on the complete ruin of the unhappy girl, and supposed, by reducing her to an entire dependence on him, to bring her by degrees to consent to gratify his ungenerous passion.

The evening before the day appointed for the nuptials of Montraville and Julia, the former retired early to his apartment; and ruminating on the past scenes of his life, suffered the keenest remorse in the remembrance of Charlotte's seduction. "Poor girl," said he, "I will at least write and bid her adieu; I will too endeavor to awaken that love of virtue in her bosom which her unfortunate attachment to me has extinguished." He took up the pen and began to write, but words were denied him. How could he address the woman whom he had seduced, and whom, though he thought unworthy his tenderness, he was about to bid adieu forever? How should he tell her that he was going to abjure her, to enter into the most indissoluble ties with another, and that he could not even own the infant which she bore as his child? Several letters were begun and destroyed: at length he completed the following:

To CHARLOTTE.

"Though I have taken up my pen to address you, my poor injured girl, I feel I am inadequate to the task; yet, however painful the endeavor, I could not resolve upon leaving you forever without one kind line to bid you adieu, to tell you how my heart bleeds at the remembrance of what you was, before you saw the hated Montraville. Even now imagination paints the scene, when, torn by contending passions, when, struggling between love and duty, you fainted in my arms, and I lifted you into the chaise: I see the agony of your mind, when, recovering, you found yourself on the road to Portsmouth:

---

7. St. Eustatius, one of the Leeward Islands in the West Indies.

but how, my gentle girl, how could you, when so justly impressed with the value of virtue, how could you, when loving as I thought you loved me, yield to the solicitations of Belcour?

"Oh Charlotte, conscience tells me it was I, villain that I am, who first taught you the allurements of guilty pleasure; it was I who dragged you from the calm repose which innocence and virtue ever enjoy; and can I, dare I tell you, it was not love prompted to the horrid deed? No, thou dear, fallen angel, believe your repentant Montraville, when he tells you the man who truly loves will never betray the object of his affection. Adieu, Charlotte: could you still find charms in a life of unoffending innocence, return to your parents; you shall never want the means of support both for yourself and child. Oh! Gracious heaven! may that child be entirely free from the vices of its father and the weakness of its mother.

"Tomorrow—but no, I cannot tell you what tomorrow will produce; Belcour will inform you: he also has cash for you, which I beg you will ask for whenever you may want it. Once more adieu: believe me could I hear you was returned to your friends, and enjoying that tranquillity of which I have robbed you, I should be as completely happy as even you, in your fondest hours, could wish me, but till then a gloom will obscure the brightest prospects of

MONTRAVILLE."

After he had sealed this letter he threw himself on the bed, and enjoyed a few hours repose. Early in the morning Belcour tapped at his door: he arose hastily, and prepared to meet his Julia at the altar.

"This is the letter to Charlotte," said he, giving it to Belcour: "take it to her when we are gone to Eustatia; and I conjure you, my dear friend, not to use any sophistical arguments to prevent her return to virtue; but should she incline that way, encourage her in the thought, and assist her to put her design in execution."

Chapter XXVII

Pensive she mourn'd, and hung her languid head,
Like a fair lily overcharg'd with dew.

Charlotte had now been left almost three months a prey to her own melancholy reflections—sad companions indeed; nor did any one break in upon her solitude but Belcour, who once or twice called to inquire after her health, and tell her he had in vain endeavored to bring Montraville to hear reason; and once, but only once, was her mind cheered by the receipt of an affectionate letter from Mrs. Beauchamp. Often had she wrote to her perfidious seducer, and with the most persuasive eloquence endeavored to convince him of her innocence; but these letters were never suffered to reach the hands of Montraville, or they must, though on the very eve of marriage, have prevented his deserting the wretched girl. Real anguish of heart had in a great measure faded her charms, her cheeks were pale from want of rest, and her eyes, by frequent, indeed almost continued weeping, were sunk and heavy. Sometimes a gleam of hope would play about her heart when she thought of her parents—"They cannot surely," she would say, "refuse to forgive me; or should they deny their pardon to me, they will not hate my innocent infant on account of its mother's errors." How often did the poor mourner wish for the consoling presence of the benevolent Mrs. Beauchamp.

"If she were here," she would cry, "she would certainly comfort me, and sooth the distraction of my soul."

She was sitting one afternoon, wrapped in these melancholy reflexions, when she was interrupted by the entrance of Belcour. Great as the alteration was which incessant sorrow had made on her person, she was still interesting, still charming; and the unhallowed flame, which had urged Belcour to plant dissension between her and Montraville, still raged in his bosom: he was determined, if possible, to make her his mistress; nay, he had even conceived the diabolical scheme of taking her to New York, and making her appear in every public place where it was likely she should meet Montraville, that he might be a witness to his unmanly triumph.

When he entered the room where Charlotte was sitting, he assumed the look of tender, consolatory friendship. "And how does my lovely Charlotte?" said he, taking her hand: "I fear you are not so well as I could wish."

"I am not well, Mr. Belcour," said she, "very far from it; but the pains and infirmities of the body I could easily bear, nay, submit to them with patience, were they not aggravated by the most insupportable anguish of my mind."

"You are not happy, Charlotte," said he, with a look of well-dissembled sorrow.

"Alas!" replied she mournfully, shaking her head, "how can I be happy, deserted and forsaken as I am, without a friend of my own sex to whom I can unburthen my full heart, nay, my fidelity suspected by the very man for whom I have sacrificed everything valuable in life, for whom I have made myself a poor despised creature, an outcast from society, an object only of contempt and pity."

"You think too meanly of yourself, Miss Temple: there is no one who would dare to treat you with contempt: all who have the pleasure of knowing you must admire and esteem. You are lonely here, my dear girl; give me leave to conduct you to New York, where the agreeable society of some ladies, to whom I will introduce you, will dispell these sad thoughts, and I shall again see returning cheerfulness animate those lovely features."

"Oh never! never!" cried Charlotte, emphatically: "the virtuous part of my sex will scorn me, and I will never associate with infamy. No, Belcour, here let me hide my shame and sorrow, here let me spend my few remaining days in obscurity, unknown and unpitied, here let me die unlamented, and my name sink to oblivion." Here her tears stopped her utterance. Belcour was awed to silence: he dared not interrupt her; and after a moment's pause she proceeded—"I once had conceived the thought of going to New York to seek out the still dear, though cruel, ungenerous Montraville, to throw myself at his feet, and entreat his compassion; heaven knows, not for myself; if I am no longer beloved, I will not be indebted to his pity to redress my injuries, but I would have knelt and entreated him not to forsake my poor unborn—" She could say no more; a crimson glow rushed over her cheeks, and covering her face with her hands, she sobbed aloud.

Something like humanity was awakened in Belcour's breast by this pathetic speech: he arose and walked towards the window; but the selfish passion which had taken possession of his heart, soon stifled these finer emotions; and he thought if Charlotte was once convinced she had no longer any dependence on Montraville, she would more readily throw herself on his protection. Determined, therefore, to inform her of all that had happened, he again resumed his seat; and finding she began to be more composed, inquired if she had ever heard from Montraville since the unfortunate *rencontre* in her bed chamber.

"Ah no," said she. "I fear I shall never hear from him again."

"I am greatly of your opinion," said Belcour, "for he has been for some time past greatly attached—"

At the word "attached" a death-like paleness overspread the countenance of Charlotte, but she applied to some hartshorn[8] which stood beside her, and Belcour proceeded.

"He has been for some time past greatly attached to one Miss Franklin, a pleasing lively girl, with a large fortune."

"She may be richer, may be handsomer," cried Charlotte, "but cannot love him so well. Oh may she beware of his art, and not trust him too far as I have done."

"He addresses her publicly," said he, "and it was rumored they were to be married before he sailed for Eustatia, whither his company is ordered."

"Belcour," said Charlotte, seizing his hand, and gazing at him earnestly, while her pale lips trembled with convulsive agony, "tell me, and tell me truly, I beseech you, do you think he can be such a villain as to marry another woman, and leave me to die with want and misery in a strange land: tell me what you think; I can bear it very well; I will not shrink from this heaviest stroke of fate; I have deserved my afflictions, and I will endeavor to bear them as I ought."

"I fear," said Belcour, "he can be that villain."

"Perhaps," cried she, eagerly interrupting him, "perhaps he is married already: come, let me know the worst," continued she with an affected look of composure: "you need not be afraid, I shall not send the fortunate lady a bowl of poison."

"Well then, my dear girl," said he, deceived by her appearance, "they were married on Thursday, and yesterday morning they sailed for Eustatia."

"Married—gone—say you?" cried she in a distracted accent, "what without a last farewell, without one thought on my unhappy situation! Oh Montraville, may God forgive your perfidy." She shrieked, and Belcour sprang forward just in time to prevent her falling to the floor.

Alarming faintings now succeeded each other, and she was conveyed to her bed, from whence she earnestly prayed she might never more arise. Belcour stayed with her that night, and in the morning found her in a high fever. The fits she had been seized with had greatly terrified him; and confined as she now was to a bed of sickness, she was no longer an object of desire: it is true for several days he went constantly to see her, but her pale, emaciated appearance disgusted him: his visits became less frequent; he forgot the solemn charge given him by Montraville; he even forgot the money entrusted to his care; and, the burning blush of indignation and shame tinges my cheek while I write it, this disgrace to humanity and manhood at length forgot even the injured Charlotte; and, attracted by the blooming health of a farmer's daughter, whom he had seen in his frequent excursions to the country, he

8. Smelling salts; an inhalant to relieve faintness.

left the unhappy girl to sink unnoticed to the grave, a prey to sickness, grief, and penury; while he, having triumphed over the virtue of the artless cottager,[9] rioted in all the intemperance of luxury and lawless pleasure.

Chapter XXVIII. A Trifling Retrospect

"Bless my heart," cries my young, volatile reader, "I shall never have patience to get through these volumes, there are so many ahs! and ohs! so much fainting, tears, and distress, I am sick to death of the subject." My dear, cheerful, innocent girl, for innocent I will suppose you to be, or you would acutely feel the woes of Charlotte, did conscience say, thus might it have been with me, had not Providence interposed to snatch me from destruction: therefore, my lively, innocent girl, I must request your patience: I am writing a tale of truth: I mean to write it to the heart: but if perchance the heart is rendered impenetrable by unbounded prosperity, or a continuance in vice, I expect not my tale to please, nay, I even expect it will be thrown by with disgust. But softly, gentle fair one; I pray you throw it not aside till you have perused the whole; mayhap you may find something therein to repay you for the trouble. Methinks I see a sarcastic smile sit on your countenance.—"And what," cry you, "does the conceited[1] author suppose we can glean from these pages, if Charlotte is held up as an object of terror, to prevent us from falling into guilty errors? Does not La Rue triumph in her shame, and by adding art to guilt, obtain the affection of a worthy man, and rise to a station where she is beheld with respect, and cheerfully received into all companies. What then is the moral you would inculcate? Would you wish us to think that a deviation from virtue, if covered by art and hypocrisy, is not an object of detestation, but on the contrary shall raise us to fame and honor? while the hapless girl who falls a victim to her too great sensibility, shall be loaded with ignominy and shame?" No, my fair querist,[2] I mean no such thing. Remember the endeavors of the wicked are often suffered to prosper, that in the end their fall may be attended with more bitterness of heart; while the cup of affliction is poured out for wise and salutary ends, and they who are compelled to drain it even to the bitter dregs, often find comfort at the bottom; the tear of penitence blots their offences from the book of fate, and they rise from the heavy, painful trial, purified and fit for a mansion in the kingdom of eternity.

Yes, my young friends, the tear of compassion shall fall for the fate of Charlotte, while the name of La Rue shall be detested and despised. For Charlotte, the soul melts with sympathy; for La Rue, it feels nothing but horror and contempt. But perhaps your gay hearts would rather follow the fortunate Mrs. Crayton through the scenes of pleasure and dissipation in which she was engaged, than listen to the complaints and miseries of Charlotte. I will for once oblige you; I will for once follow her to midnight revels, balls, and scenes of gaiety, for in such was she constantly engaged.

I have said her person was lovely; let us add that she was surrounded by splendor and affluence, and he must know but little of the world who can wonder (however faulty such a woman's conduct) at her being followed by the men, and her company courted by the women: in short Mrs. Crayton

9. Naive country dweller.
1. Deluded.

2. Questioner.

was the universal favorite: she set the fashions, she was toasted by all the gentlemen, and copied by all the ladies.

Colonel Crayton was a domestic man. Could he be happy with such a woman? impossible! Remonstrance was vain: he might as well have preached to the winds, as endeavor to persuade her from any action, however ridiculous, on which she had set her mind: in short, after a little ineffectual struggle, he gave up the attempt, and left her to follow the bent of her own inclinations: what those were, I think the reader must have seen enough of her character to form a just idea. Among the number who paid their devotions at her shrine, she singled one, a young ensign of mean birth, indifferent education,[3] and weak intellects. How such a man came into the army, we hardly know to account for, and how he afterwards rose to posts of honor is likewise strange and wonderful. But fortune is blind, and so are those too frequently who have the power of dispensing her favors: else why do we see fools and knaves at the very top of the wheel, while patient merit sinks to the extreme of the opposite abyss. But we may form a thousand conjectures on this subject, and yet never hit on the right. Let us therefore endeavor to deserve her smiles, and whether we succeed or not, we shall feel more innate satisfaction, than thousands of those who bask in the sunshine of her favor unworthily. But to return to Mrs. Crayton: this young man, whom I shall distinguish by the name of Corydon,[4] was the reigning favorite of her heart. He escorted her to the play, danced with her at every ball, and when indisposition prevented her going out, it was he alone who was permitted to cheer the gloomy solitude to which she was obliged to confine herself. Did she ever think of poor Charlotte?—if she did, my dear Miss, it was only to laugh at the poor girl's want of spirit in consenting to be moped up[5] in the country, while Montraville was enjoying all the pleasures of a gay, dissipated city. When she heard of his marriage, she smiling said, so there's an end of Madam Charlotte's hopes. I wonder who will take her now, or what will become of the little affected prude?

But as you have led to the subject, I think we may as well return to the distressed Charlotte, and not, like the unfeeling Mrs. Crayton, shut our hearts to the call of humanity.

Chapter XXIX. We Go Forward Again

The strength of Charlotte's constitution combatted against her disorder, and she began slowly to recover, though she still labored under a violent depression of spirits: how must that depression be increased, when, upon examining her little store, she found herself reduced to one solitary guinea, and that during her illness the attendance of an apothecary and nurse, together with many other unavoidable expences, had involved her in debt, from which she saw no method of extricating herself. As to the faint hope which she had entertained of hearing from and being relieved by her parents, it now entirely forsook her, for it was above four months since her letter was dispatched, and she had received no answer: she therefore imagined that her conduct had either entirely alienated their affection from her, or broken their hearts, and she must never more hope to receive their blessing.

3. I.e., he did not attend good schools and his social class is low.
4. A name conventionally given to a shepherd in pastoral poetry.
5. Dejected.

Never did any human being wish for death with greater fervency or with juster cause; yet she had too just a sense of the duties of the Christian religion to attempt to put a period to her own existence.[6] "I have but to be patient a little longer," she would cry, "and nature, fatigued and fainting, will throw off this heavy load of mortality, and I shall be released from all my sufferings."

It was one cold stormy day in the latter end of December, as Charlotte sat by a handful of fire, the low state of her finances not allowing her to replenish her stock of fuel, and prudence teaching her to be careful of what she had, when she was surprised by the entrance of a farmer's wife, who, without much ceremony, seated herself, and began this curious harangue.

"I'm come to see if as how you can pay your rent, because as how we hear Captain Montable[7] is gone away, and it's fifty to one if he b'ant killed afore he comes back again; an then, Miss, or Ma'am, or whatever you may be, as I was saying to my husband, where are we to look for our money."

This was a stroke altogether unexpected by Charlotte: she knew so little of the ways of the world that she had never bestowed a thought on the payment for the rent of the house; she knew indeed that she owed a good deal, but this was never reckoned among the others: she was thunderstruck; she hardly knew what answer to make, yet it was absolutely necessary that she should say something; and judging of the gentleness of every female disposition by her own, she thought the best way to interest the woman in her favor would be to tell her candidly to what a situation she was reduced, and how little probability there was of her ever paying anybody.

Alas poor Charlotte, how confined was her knowledge of human nature, or she would have been convinced that the only way to insure the friendship and assistance of your surrounding acquaintance is to convince them you do not require it, for when once the petrifying aspect of distress and penury appear, whose qualities, like Medusa's head, can change to stone all that look upon it; when once this Gorgon[8] claims acquaintance with us, the phantom of friendship, that before courted our notice, will vanish into unsubstantial air, and the whole world before us appear a barren waste. Pardon me, ye dear spirits of benevolence, whose benign smiles and cheerful-giving hand have strewed sweet flowers on many a thorny path through which my wayward fate forced me to pass; think not, that, in condemning the unfeeling texture of the human heart, I forget the spring from whence flow all the comforts I enjoy: oh no! I look up to you as to bright constellations, gathering new splendors from the surrounding darkness; but ah! whilst I adore the benignant rays that cheered and illumined my heart, I mourn that their influence cannot extend to all the sons and daughters of affliction.

"Indeed, Madam," said poor Charlotte in a tremulous accent, "I am at a loss what to do. Montraville placed me here, and promised to defray all my expenses: but he has forgot his promise, he has forsaken me, and I have no friend who has either power or will to relieve me. Let me hope, as you see my unhappy situation, your charity—"

"Charity," cried the woman impatiently interrupting her, "charity indeed: why, Mistress, charity begins at home, and I have seven children at home, *honest, lawful* children, and it is my duty to keep them; and do you think I will give away my property to a nasty, impudent hussy, to maintain her and

---

6. I.e., kill herself. "A period": a stop.
7. A mispronunciation of "Montraville."
8. In classical mythology there were three Gor-

gons, including Medusa, who had snakes for hair; anyone who looked at them was turned to stone.

her bastard; an I was saying to my husband the other day what will this world come to; honest women are nothing now-a-days, while the harlotings are set up for fine ladies, and look upon us no more nor the dirt they walk upon: but let me tell you, my fine spoken Ma'am, I must have my money; so seeing as how you can't pay it, why you must troop, and leave all your fine gimcracks and fal der ralls[9] behind you. I don't ask for no more nor my right, and nobody shall dare for to go for to hinder me of it."

"Oh heavens," cried Charlotte, clasping her hands, "what will become of me?"

"Come on ye!" retorted the unfeeling wretch: "why, go to the barracks and work for a morsel of bread; wash and mend the soldiers' clothes, and cook their victuals, and not expect to live in idleness on honest people's means. Oh I wish I could see the day when all such cattle were obliged to work hard and eat little; it's only what they deserve."

"Father of Mercy," cried Charlotte, "I acknowledge Thy correction just; but prepare me, I beseech thee, for the portion of misery Thou may'st please to lay upon me."

"Well," said the woman, "I shall go and tell my husband as how you can't pay; and so d'ye see, Ma'am, get ready to be packing away this very night, for you should not stay another night in this house, though I was sure you would lay in the street."

Charlotte bowed her head in silence; but the anguish of her heart was too great to permit her to articulate a single word.

Chapter XXX

And what is friendship but a name,
A charm that lulls to sleep,
A shade that follows wealth and fame,
But leaves the wretch to weep.

When Charlotte was left to herself, she began to think what course she must take, or to whom she could apply, to prevent her perishing for want, or perhaps that very night falling a victim to the inclemency of the season. After many perplexed thoughts, she at last determined to set out for New York, and inquire out Mrs. Crayton, from whom she had no doubt but she should obtain immediate relief as soon as her distress was made known; she had no sooner formed this resolution than she resolved immediately to put it in execution: she therefore wrote the following little billet[1] to Mrs. Crayton, thinking if she should have company with her it would be better to send it in than to request to see her.

To Mrs. Crayton.

"Madam,

"When we left our native land, that dear, happy land which now contains all that is dear to the wretched Charlotte, our prospects were the same; we both, pardon me, Madam, if I say, we both too easily followed the impulse of our treacherous hearts, and trusted our happiness on a tempestuous

9. More commonly "folderols" or "falderals": trin- 1. Short letter.
kets. "Troop": be off. "Gimcracks": knickknacks.

ocean, where mine has been wrecked and lost forever; you have been more fortunate—you are united to a man of honor and humanity, united by the most sacred ties, respected, esteemed, and admired, and surrounded by innumerable blessings of which I am bereaved, enjoying those pleasures which have fled my bosom never to return; alas! sorrow and deep regret have taken their place. Behold me, Madam, a poor forsaken wanderer, who has nowhere to lay her weary head, wherewith to supply the wants of nature, or to shield her from the inclemency of the weather. To you I sue, to you I look for pity and relief. I ask not to be received as an intimate or an equal; only for charity's sweet sake receive me into your hospitable mansion, allot me the meanest apartment in it, and let me breath out my soul in prayers for your happiness; I cannot, I feel I cannot long bear up under the accumulated woes that pour in upon me; but oh! my dear Madam, for the love of heaven suffer me not to expire in the street; and when I am at peace, as soon I shall be, extend your compassion to my helpless offspring, should it please heaven that it should survive its unhappy mother. A gleam of joy breaks in on my benighted soul while I reflect that you cannot, will not refuse your protection to the heartbroken.   CHARLOTTE."

When Charlotte had finished this letter, late as it was in the afternoon, and though the snow began to fall very fast, she tied up a few necessaries which she had prepared against her expected confinement, and terrified lest she should be again exposed to the insults of her barbarous landlady, more dreadful to her wounded spirit than either storm or darkness, she set forward for New York.

It may be asked by those, who, in a work of this kind, love to cavil at every trifling omission, whether Charlotte did not possess any valuable of which she could have disposed, and by that means have supported herself till Mrs. Beauchamp's return, when she would have been certain of receiving every tender attention which compassion and friendship could dictate: but let me entreat these wise, penetrating gentlemen to reflect, that when Charlotte left England, it was in such haste that there was no time to purchase anything more than what was wanted for immediate use on the voyage, and after her arrival at New York, Montraville's affection soon began to decline, so that her whole wardrobe consisted of only necessaries, and as to baubles, with which fond lovers often load their mistresses, she possessed not one, except a plain gold locket of small value, which contained a lock of her mother's hair, and which the greatest extremity of want could not have forced her to part with.

I hope, Sir, your prejudices are now removed in regard to the probability of my story? Oh, they are. Well then, with your leave, I will proceed.

The distance from the house which our suffering heroine occupied, to New York, was not very great, yet the snow fell so fast, and the cold so intense, that, being unable from her situation to walk quick, she found herself almost sinking with cold and fatigue before she reached the town; her garments, which were merely suitable to the summer season, being an undress robe[2] of plain white muslin, were wet through, and a thin black cloak and bonnet, very improper habiliments for such a climate, but poorly

2. An everyday dress.

defended her from the cold. In this situation she reached the city, and inquired of a foot soldier whom she met, the way to Colonel Crayton's.

"Bless you, my sweet lady," said the soldier with a voice and look of compassion, "I will show you the way with all my heart; but if you are going to make a petition to Madam Crayton it is all to no purpose I assure you: if you please I will conduct you to Mr. Franklin's; though Miss Julia is married and gone now, yet the old gentleman is very good."

"Julia Franklin," said Charlotte; "is she not married to Montraville?"

"Yes," replied the soldier, "and may God bless them, for a better officer never lived, he is so good to us all; and as to Miss Julia, all the poor folk almost worshipped her."

"Gracious heaven," cried Charlotte, "is Montraville unjust then to none but me?"

The soldier now showed her Colonel Crayton's door, and, with a beating heart, she knocked for admission.

Chapter XXXI. Subject Continued

When the door was opened, Charlotte, in a voice rendered scarcely articulate, through cold and the extreme agitation of her mind, demanded whether Mrs. Crayton was at home. The servant hesitated: he knew that his lady was engaged at a game of picquet[3] with her dear Corydon, nor could he think she would like to be disturbed by a person whose appearance spoke her of so little consequence as Charlotte; yet there was something in her countenance that rather interested him in her favor, and he said his lady was engaged, but if she had any particular message he would deliver it.

"Take up this letter," said Charlotte: "tell her the unhappy writer of it waits in her hall for an answer."

The tremulous accent, the tearful eye, must have moved any heart not composed of adamant. The man took the letter from the poor suppliant, and hastily ascended the stair case.

"A letter, Madam," said he, presenting it to his lady: "an immediate answer is required."

Mrs. Crayton glanced her eye carelessly over the contents. "What stuff is this," cried she haughtily, "have not I told you a thousand times that I will not be plagued with beggars, and petitions from people one knows nothing about? Go tell the woman I can't do any thing in it. I'm sorry, but one can't relieve everybody."

The servant bowed, and heavily returned with this chilling message to Charlotte.

"Surely," said she, "Mrs. Crayton has not read my letter. Go, my good friend, pray go back to her; tell her it is Charlotte Temple who requests beneath her hospitable roof to find shelter from the inclemency of the season."

"Prithee, don't plague me, man," cried Mrs. Crayton impatiently, as the servant advanced something in behalf of the unhappy girl. "I tell you I don't know her."

3. A game of cards for two.

"Not know me," cried Charlotte, rushing into the room (for she had followed the man upstairs), "not know me, not remember the ruined Charlotte Temple, who, but for you, perhaps might still have been innocent, still have been happy. Oh! La Rue, this is beyond everything I could have believed possible."

"Upon my honor, Miss," replied the unfeeling woman with the utmost effrontery, "this is a most unaccountable address: it is beyond my comprehension. John," continued she, turning to the servant, "the young woman is certainly out of her senses: do pray take her away, she terrifies me to death."

"Oh God," cried Charlotte, clasping her hands in an agony, "this is too much; what will become of me? but I will not leave you; they shall not tear me from you; here on my knees I conjure you to save me from perishing in the streets; if you really have forgot me, oh for charity's sweet sake this night let me be sheltered from the winter's piercing cold."

The kneeling figure of Charlotte in her affecting situation might have moved the heart of a stoic to compassion; but Mrs. Crayton remained inflexible. In vain did Charlotte recount the time they had known each other at Chichester, in vain mention their being in the same ship, in vain were the names of Montraville and Belcour mentioned. Mrs. Crayton could only say she was sorry for her imprudence, but could not think of having her own reputation endangered by encouraging a woman of that kind in her own house, besides she did not know what trouble and expense she might bring upon her husband by giving shelter to a woman in her situation.

"I can at least die here," said Charlotte, "I feel I cannot long survive this dreadful conflict. Father of Mercy, here let me finish my existence." Her agonizing sensations overpowered her, and she fell senseless on the floor.

"Take her away," said Mrs. Crayton, "she will really frighten me into hysterics; take her away I say this instant."

"And where must I take the poor creature?" said the servant with a voice and look of compassion.

"Anywhere," cried she hastily, "only don't let me ever see her again. I declare she has flurried me so I shan't be myself again this fortnight."

John, assisted by his fellow-servant, raised and carried her downstairs. "Poor soul," said he, "you shall not lay in the street this night. I have a bed and a poor little hovel, where my wife and her little ones rest them, but they shall watch tonight, and you shall be sheltered from danger." They placed her in a chair; and the benevolent man, assisted by one of his comrades, carried her to the place where his wife and children lived. A surgeon was sent for: he bled her,[4] she gave signs of returning life, and before the dawn gave birth to a female infant. After this event she lay for some hours in a kind of stupor; and if at any time she spoke, it was with a quickness and incoherence that plainly evinced the total deprivation of her reason.

Chapter XXXII. Reasons Why and Wherefore

The reader of sensibility may perhaps be astonished to find Mrs. Crayton could so positively deny any knowledge of Charlotte; it is therefore but just that her conduct should in some measure be accounted for. She had ever

4. Drawing blood was a common 18th-century procedure to remedy illness.

been fully sensible of the superiority of Charlotte's sense and virtue; she was conscious that she had never swerved from rectitude, had it not been for her bad precepts and worse example. These were things as yet unknown to her husband, and she wished not to have that part of her conduct exposed to him, as she had great reason to fear she had already lost considerable part of that power she once maintained over him. She trembled whilst Charlotte was in the house, lest the Colonel should return; she perfectly well remembered how much he seemed interested in her favor whilst on their passage from England, and made no doubt, but, should he see her in her present distress, he would offer her an asylum, and protect her to the utmost of his power. In that case she feared the unguarded nature of Charlotte might discover to the Colonel the part she had taken in the unhappy girl's elopement, and she well knew the contrast between her own and Charlotte's conduct would make the former appear in no very respectable light. Had she reflected properly, she would have afforded the poor girl protection; and by enjoining her silence, ensured it by acts of repeated kindness; but vice in general blinds its votaries, and they discover their real characters to the world when they are most studious to preserve appearances.

Just so it happened with Mrs. Crayton: her servants made no scruple of mentioning the cruel conduct of their lady to a poor distressed lunatic who claimed her protection; everyone joined in reprobating her inhumanity; nay even Corydon thought she might at least have ordered her to be taken care of, but he dare not even hint it to her, for he lived but in her smiles, and drew from her lavish fondness large sums to support an extravagance to which the state of his own finances was very inadequate; it cannot therefore be supposed that he wished Mrs. Crayton to be very liberal in her bounty to the afflicted suppliant; yet vice had not so entirely seared over his heart, but the sorrows of Charlotte could find a vulnerable part.

Charlotte had now been three days with her humane preservers, but she was totally insensible of everything: she raved incessantly for Montraville and her father: she was not conscious of being a mother, nor took the least notice of her child except to ask whose it was, and why it was not carried to its parents.

"Oh," said she one day, starting up on hearing the infant cry, "why, why will you keep that child here; I am sure you would not if you knew how hard it was for a mother to be parted from her infant: it is like tearing the cords of life asunder. Oh could you see the horrid sight which I now behold— there—there stands my dear mother, her poor bosom bleeding at every vein, her gentle, affectionate heart torn in a thousand pieces, and all for the loss of a ruined, ungrateful child. Save me—save me—from her frown. I dare not—indeed I dare not speak to her."

Such were the dreadful images that haunted her distracted mind, and nature was sinking fast under the dreadful malady which medicine had no power to remove. The surgeon who attended her was a humane man; he exerted his utmost abilities to save her, but he saw she was in want of many necessaries and comforts, which the poverty of her hospitable host rendered him unable to provide: he therefore determined to make her situation known to some of the officers' ladies, and endeavor to make a collection for her relief.

When he returned home, after making this resolution, he found a message from Mrs. Beauchamp, who had just arrived from Rhode Island, requesting he would call and see one of her children, who was very unwell. "I do not know," said he, as he was hastening to obey the summons, "I do not know a woman to whom I could apply with more hope of success than Mrs. Beauchamp. I will endeavor to interest her in this poor girl's behalf; she wants the soothing balm of friendly consolation: we may perhaps save her; we will try at least."

"And where is she," cried Mrs. Beauchamp when he had prescribed something for the child, and told his little pathetic tale, "where is she, Sir? we will go to her immediately. Heaven forbid that I should be deaf to the calls of humanity. Come we will go this instant." Then seizing the doctor's arm, they sought the habitation that contained the dying Charlotte.

Chapter XXXIII. Which People Void of Feeling Need Not Read.

When Mrs. Beauchamp entered the apartment of the poor sufferer, she started back with horror. On a wretched bed, without hangings and but poorly supplied with covering, lay the emaciated figure of what still retained the semblance of a lovely woman, though sickness had so altered her features that Mrs. Beauchamp had not the least recollection of her person. In one corner of the room stood a woman washing, and, shivering over a small fire, two healthy but half naked children; the infant was asleep beside its mother, and, on a chair by the bedside, stood a porringer and wooden spoon, containing a little gruel, and a tea cup with about two spoonfulls of wine in it. Mrs. Beauchamp had never before beheld such a scene of poverty; she shuddered involuntarily, and exclaiming—"heaven preserve us!" leaned on the back of a chair ready to sink to the earth. The doctor repented having so precipitately brought her into this affecting scene; but there was no time for apologies: Charlotte caught the sound of her voice, and starting almost out of bed, exclaimed—"Angel of peace and mercy, art thou come to deliver me? Oh, I know you are, for whenever you was near me I felt eased of half my sorrows; but you don't know me, nor can I, with all the recollection I am mistress of, remember your name just now, but I know that benevolent countenance, and the softness of that voice which has so often comforted the wretched Charlotte."

Mrs. Beauchamp had, during the time Charlotte was speaking, seated herself on the bed and taken one of her hands; she looked at her attentively, and at the name of Charlotte she perfectly conceived the whole shocking affair. A faint sickness came over her. "Gracious heaven," said she, "is this possible?" and bursting into tears, she reclined the burning head of Charlotte on her own bosom; and folding her arms about her, wept over her in silence. "Oh," said Charlotte, "you are very good to weep thus for me: it is a long time since I shed a tear for myself: my head and heart are both on fire, but these tears of yours seem to cool and refresh it. Oh now I remember you said you would send a letter to my poor father: do you think he ever received it? or perhaps you have brought me an answer: why don't you speak, Madam? Does he say I may go home? Well he is very good; I shall soon be ready."

She then made an effort to get out of bed; but being prevented, her frenzy again returned, and she raved with the greatest wildness and incoherence. Mrs. Beauchamp, finding it was impossible for her to be removed, contented herself with ordering the apartment to be made more comfortable, and procuring a proper nurse for both mother and child; and having learned the particulars of Charlotte's fruitless application to Mrs. Crayton from honest John, she amply rewarded him for his benevolence, and returned home with a heart oppressed with many painful sensations, but yet rendered easy by the reflection that she had performed her duty towards a distressed fellow creature.

Early the next morning she again visited Charlotte, and found her tolerably composed; she called her by name, thanked her for her goodness, and when her child was brought to her, pressed it in her arms, wept over it, and called it the offspring of disobedience. Mrs. Beauchamp was delighted to see her so much amended, and began to hope she might recover, and, spite of her former errors, become an useful and respectable member of society; but the arrival of the doctor put an end to these delusive hopes: he said nature was making her last effort, and a few hours would most probably consign the unhappy girl to her kindred dust.

Being asked how she found herself, she replied—"Why better, much better, doctor. I hope now I have but little more to suffer. I had last night a few hours sleep, and when I awoke recovered the full power of recollection. I am quite sensible of my weakness; I feel I have but little longer to combat with the shafts of affliction. I have an humble confidence in the mercy of Him who died to save the world, and trust that my sufferings in this state of mortality, joined to my unfeigned repentance, through His mercy, have blotted my offences from the sight of my offended maker. I have but one care—my poor infant! Father of Mercy," continued she, raising her eyes, "of Thy infinite goodness, grant that the sins of the parent be not visited on the unoffending child. May those who taught me to despise Thy laws be forgiven; lay not my offences to their charge, I beseech Thee; and oh! shower the choicest of Thy blessings on those whose pity has soothed the afflicted heart, and made easy even the bed of pain and sickness."

She was exhausted by this fervent address to the throne of mercy, and though her lips still moved her voice became inarticulate: she lay for some time as it were in a doze, and then recovering, faintly pressed Mrs. Beauchamp's hand, and requested that a clergyman might be sent for.

On his arrival she joined fervently in the pious office,[5] frequently mentioning her ingratitude to her parents as what lay most heavy at her heart. When she had performed the last solemn duty, and was preparing to lie down, a little bustle on the outside door occasioned Mrs. Beauchamp to open it, and inquire the cause. A man in appearance about forty, presented himself, and asked for Mrs. Beauchamp.

"That is my name, Sir," said she.

"Oh then, my dear Madam," cried he, "tell me where I may find my poor, ruined, but repentant child."

Mrs. Beauchamp was surprised and affected; she knew not what to say; she foresaw the agony this interview would occasion Mr. Temple, who had just arrived in search of his Charlotte, and yet was sensible that the pardon and blessing of her father would soften even the agonies of death to the daughter.

5. Last rites.

She hesitated. "Tell me, Madam," cried he wildly, "tell me, I beseech thee, does she live? shall I see my darling once again? Perhaps she is in this house. Lead, lead me to her, that I may bless her, and then lie down and die."

The ardent manner in which he uttered these words occasioned him to raise his voice. It caught the ear of Charlotte: she knew the beloved sound: and uttering a loud shriek, she sprang forward as Mr. Temple entered the room. "My adored father." "My long lost child." Nature could support no more, and they both sunk lifeless[6] into the arms of the attendants.

Charlotte was again put into bed, and a few moments restored Mr. Temple: but to describe the agony of his sufferings is past the power of any one, who, though they may readily conceive, cannot delineate the dreadful scene. Every eye gave testimony of what each heart felt—but all were silent.

When Charlotte recovered, she found herself supported in her father's arms. She cast on him a most expressive look, but was unable to speak. A reviving cordial was administered. She then asked, in a low voice, for her child: it was brought to her: she put it in her father's arms. "Protect her," said she, "and bless your dying—"

Unable to finish the sentence, she sunk back on her pillow: her countenance was serenely composed; she regarded her father as he pressed the infant to his breast with a steadfast look; a sudden beam of joy passed across her languid features, she raised her eyes to heaven—and then closed them forever.

Chapter XXXIV. *Retribution*

In the meantime Montraville having received orders to return to New York, arrived, and having still some remains of compassionate tenderness for the woman whom he regarded as brought to shame by himself, he went out in search of Belcour, to inquire whether she was safe, and whether the child lived. He found him immersed in dissipation, and could gain no other intelligence than that Charlotte had left him, and that he knew not what was become of her.

"I cannot believe it possible," said Montraville, "that a mind once so pure as Charlotte Temple's, should so suddenly become the mansion of vice. Beware, Belcour," continued he, "beware if you have dared to behave either unjust or dishonorably to that poor girl, your life shall pay the forfeit:—I will revenge her cause."

He immediately went into the country, to the house where he had left Charlotte. It was desolate. After much inquiry he at length found the servant girl who had lived with her. From her he learned the misery Charlotte had endured from the complicated evils of illness, poverty, and a broken heart, and that she had set out on foot for New York, on a cold winter's evening; but she could inform him no further.

Tortured almost to madness by this shocking account, he returned to the city, but, before he reached it, the evening was drawing to a close. In entering the town he was obliged to pass several little huts, the residence of poor women who supported themselves by washing the clothes of the officers and soldiers. It was nearly dark: he heard from a neighboring steeple a solemn

6. Unconscious.

toll that seemed to say some poor mortal was going to their last mansion: the sound struck on the heart of Montraville, and he involuntarily stopped, when, from one of the houses, he saw the appearance of a funeral. Almost unknowing what he did, he followed at a small distance; and as they let the coffin into the grave, he inquired of a soldier who stood by, and had just brushed off a tear that did honor to his heart, who it was that was just buried. "An[7] please your honor," said the man, " 'tis a poor girl that was brought from her friends by a cruel man, who left her when she was big with child, and married another." Montraville stood motionless, and the man proceeded—"I met her myself not a fortnight since one night all wet and cold in the streets; she went to Madam Crayton's, but she would not take her in, and so the poor thing went raving mad." Montraville could bear no more; he struck his hands against his forehead with violence; and exclaiming "poor murdered Charlotte!" ran with precipitation towards the place where they were heaping the earth on her remains. "Hold, hold, one moment," said he. "Close not the grave of the injured Charlotte Temple till I have taken vengeance on her murderer."

"Rash young man," said Mr. Temple, "who art thou that thus disturbest the last mournful rites of the dead, and rudely breakest in upon the grief of an afflicted father."

"If thou art the father of Charlotte Temple," said he, gazing at him with mingled horror and amazement—"if thou art her father—I am Montraville." Then falling on his knees, he continued—"Here is my bosom. I bare it to receive the stroke I merit. Strike—strike now, and save me from the misery of reflection."

"Alas!" said Mr. Temple, "if thou wert the seducer of my child, thy own reflections be thy punishment. I wrest not the power from the hand of omnipotence. Look on that little heap of earth, there hast thou buried the only joy of a fond father. Look at it often; and may thy heart feel such true sorrow as shall merit the mercy of heaven." He turned from him; and Montraville starting up from the ground, where he had thrown himself, and at that instant remembering the perfidy of Belcour, flew like lightning to his lodgings. Belcour was intoxicated; Montraville impetuous: they fought, and the sword of the latter entered the heart of his adversary. He fell, and expired almost instantly. Montraville had received a slight wound; and overcome with the agitation of his mind and loss of blood, was carried in a state of insensibility to his distracted wife. A dangerous illness and obstinate delirium ensued, during which he raved incessantly for Charlotte: but a strong constitution, and the tender assiduities of Julia, in time overcame the disorder. He recovered; but to the end of his life was subject to severe fits of melancholy, and while he remained at New York frequently retired to the churchyard, where he would weep over the grave, and regret the untimely fate of the lovely Charlotte Temple.

Chapter XXXV. Conclusion

Shortly after the interment of his daughter, Mr. Temple, with his dear little charge and her nurse, set forward for England. It would be impossible

7. If it.

to do justice to the meeting scene between him, his Lucy, and her aged father. Every heart of sensibility can easily conceive their feelings. After the first tumult of grief was subsided, Mrs. Temple gave up the chief of her time to her grandchild, and as she grew up and improved, began to almost fancy she again possessed her Charlotte.

It was about ten years after these painful events, that Mr. and Mrs. Temple, having buried their father, were obliged to come to London on particular business, and brought the little Lucy with them. They had been walking one evening, when on their return they found a poor wretch sitting on the steps of the door. She attempted to rise as they approached, but from extreme weakness was unable, and after several fruitless efforts fell back in a fit. Mr. Temple was not one of those men who stand to consider whether by assisting an object in distress they shall not inconvenience themselves, but instigated by the impulse of a noble feeling heart, immediately ordered her to be carried into the house, and proper restoratives applied.

She soon recovered; and fixing her eyes on Mrs. Temple, cried—"You know not, Madam, what you do; you know not whom you are relieving, or you would curse me in the bitterness of your heart. Come not near me, Madam, I shall contaminate you. I am the viper that stung your peace. I am the woman who turned the poor Charlotte out to perish in the street. Heaven have mercy! I see her now," continued she looking at Lucy; "such, such was the fair bud of innocence that my vile arts blasted ere it was half blown."

It was in vain that Mr. and Mrs. Temple entreated her to be composed and to take some refreshment. She only drank half a glass of wine; and then told them that she had been separated from her husband seven years, the chief of which she had passed in riot, dissipation, and vice, till, overtaken by poverty and sickness, she had been reduced to part with every valuable, and thought only of ending her life in a prison; when a benevolent friend paid her debts and released her; but that her illness increasing, she had no possible means of supporting herself, and her friends were weary of relieving her. "I have fasted," said she, "two days, and last night lay my aching head on the cold pavement: indeed it was but just that I should experience those miseries myself which I had unfeelingly inflicted on others."

Greatly as Mr. Temple had reason to detest Mrs. Crayton, he could not behold her in this distress without some emotions of pity. He gave her shelter that night beneath his hospitable roof, and the next day got her admission into an hospital; where having lingered a few weeks, she died, a striking example that vice, however prosperous in the beginning, in the end leads only to misery and shame.

F I N I S.

1791

CHARLES BROCKDEN BROWN
1771–1810

As Susanna Rowson's *Charlotte: A Tale of Truth* indicates, the emergence of early American fiction in the 1790s owed much to the reading public's interest in the culture of sentiment. Of equal concern, however, was the vexed and ambiguous situation of women in the new republic. Widely viewed as repositories of virtue whose attention to the domestic sphere guaranteed the success of the nation's new political experiment, women quickly began to chafe (as Abigail Adams's letters to her husband indicate) at the intellectual and emotional restrictions such views of them entailed. Moreover, with its emphasis on the individual's capacity for self-improvement, republican ideology itself implied an enlarged role for women, one that protofeminists like Judith Sargent Murray, among others, began to explore. Influenced in part by British author Mary Wollstonecraft's *Vindication of the Rights of Woman* (1792), these writers argued that truly republican marriages required women to be treated as men's equals. The emergent province of fiction provided an imaginative space that was useful for testing, celebrating, and sometimes rejecting this and other radical implications of revolutionary ideology.

No one better understood the usefulness of fiction for gauging the emotional depths of men and women than Charles Brockden Brown. Influenced by the gothic tradition in fiction as exemplified by the work of such English writers as William Godwin (Wollstonecraft's husband), Brown used its conventions to probe his generation's often uncritical embrace of Enlightenment principles. For him, the sentimental plot was just a starting point for very different kinds of explorations. His fiction overturned readers' Enlightenment faith in the rationality of human behavior and indicated that the emotional and obsessive, as much as the logical, were touchstones to character. Brown thus began to explore a rich vein in American fiction that Poe, Melville, and Hawthorne subsequently mined with great success.

Raised by Quaker parents in Philadelphia, one of the new nation's largest and most significant cultural centers, Brown prepared for a career in law. But as the time approached for him to strike out on his own, he gravitated instead to the world of belles-lettres. He might well have succeeded in Philadelphia, which by the 1790s— it was home to important publishers, including Mathew Carey—had become a place where a writer could aspire to the emergent profession of authorship. But Brown opted instead for New York City, where in the 1790s he met and befriended, among others, the Hartford Wit and future president of Yale, Timothy Dwight; lexicographer Noah Webster; and Elihu Hubbard Smith, who in 1793 published the first anthology of American poetry. A bona fide member of the nascent American republic of letters, Brown read widely in English literature and, beginning in 1798, published seven important novels in the gothic mode, produced in a mere four years.

The first of these, *Wieland,* is the best known. It was followed by *Ormond* (1799), in which the main character, a freethinker recently returned from the Continent, tries the virtue of Constantia, an epitome of republican womanhood. In *Edgar Huntly* (1799), the novelist capitalized on the public's continuing interest in tales of Indian captivity and the wilderness generally, even as he teased readers, as in *Wieland,* with a rational explanation—in this case, sleepwalking—of the strange behavior of one of his central characters. Brown turned to his home city for the setting of *Arthur Mervyn* (1799–1800), whose melodramatic plot, centered on a Godwinian character, has as its background Philadelphia's yellow fever outbreak of 1793. With *Clara Howard* and *Jane Talbot,* both published in 1801, Brown concluded his remarkably fecund career as a novelist.

Although his novels were reissued in a uniform edition after his death in 1827, in his own lifetime Brown had a difficult time making a living through writing fiction alone. To augment his income he involved himself in other publishing ventures. Over the course of a decade, for example, he founded and edited *The Monthly Magazine and American Review* (1799–1800), *The Literary Magazine and American Register* (1803–07), and the *American Register, or General Repository of History, Politics, and Science* (1807–10), all of which provided outlets for his varied talents and ambitions. He contributed many essays to these and other journals, his most important effort being "Alcuin," a lengthy dialogue on women's rights that shows Wollstonecraft's influence, which appeared in the *Philadelphia Weekly Magazine* in 1798. His pamphlet *An Address to the Government of the United States on the Cession of Louisiana to the French* (1803) helped sway public opinion toward the purchase of the Louisiana Territory; and his translation of C. F. Volney's *A View of the Soil and Climate of the United States of America* (1804), with his own commentary, introduced this important thinker to many Americans.

Although he is sometimes termed America's first professional author, Brown did not enjoy the kind of success available to his immediate successors, Washington Irving and James Fenimore Cooper, primarily because the technological infrastructure for the rapid printing and widespread distribution of such work was not yet fully developed. His significance thus resides in his ability to identify those topics—like the limits of rationality and the role of the senses in epistemology—that were of growing interest to the American readership and in his willingness to explore the implications of republican ideology on gender relations.

By turns sensational and sentimental, *Wieland; or, The Transformation*, which also catered to the public interest in criminality and insanity, examines and discards the Enlightenment's belief in human reason and reliance on the evidence of one's senses. The novel centers on Clara Wieland, who narrates the story in the form of a long letter; Theodore Wieland, whose reason gives way under the power of religious enthusiasm; Henry Pleyel, a family friend whom Clara loves and who believes only in what his senses register; and Carwin, a sharper whose sudden appearance disrupts these lives and those of other members of the family. In the chapter from *Wieland* printed here, Clara is in her room, planning to read in the manuscript journal of her father, who in her youth had died a mysterious death. She is surprised to hear noise in her closet, where earlier she thought she heard some ruffians plotting against her. Having recently had a nightmare in which her brother urged her on to what would be her destruction, she cannot help thinking that it is her brother who is in the closet. Instead of running from danger, as a mysterious voice (heard once before by her) instructs her, and as the reader might expect, Clara tempts fate by commanding whoever is hidden to emerge, thus inviting the violence about which she has fantasized. Her discovery that it is Carwin who is in her closet only makes her confusion, and the novel's mystery, greater. In Clara's discussion of how she has gotten into her confused state, and thus to where her imagination has run away from her logic, Brown leads the reader to the kinds of questions that occupied him in all his major fiction. If the senses are not to be trusted, what evidence can the reason use to understand reality? If fear and fantasy easily sway reason, how can a nation based on belief and reason survive?

Wieland; or, The Transformation: An American Tale[1]

Chapter IX

My brother had received a new book from Germany. It was a tragedy, and the first attempt of a Saxon poet, of whom my brother had been taught to

---

1. The text used here is from the Bicentennial Edition of *The Novels and Related Works of Charles Brockden Brown* (1977), edited by Sydney Krause, S. W. Reid, et al.

entertain the highest expectations. The exploits of Zisca, the Bohemian hero, were woven into a dramatic series and connection. According to German custom, it was minute and diffuse, and dictated by an adventurous and lawless fancy. It was a chain of audacious acts, and unheard-of disasters. The moated fortress, and the thicket; the ambush and the battle; and the conflict of headlong passions, were pourtrayed in wild numbers, and with terrific energy. An afternoon was set apart to rehearse this performance. The language was familiar to all of us but Carwin, whose company, therefore, was tacitly dispensed with.

The morning previous to this intended rehearsal, I spent at home. My mind was occupied with reflections relative to my own situation. The sentiment which lived with chief energy in my heart, was connected with the image of Pleyel. In the midst of my anguish, I had not been destitute of consolation. His late deportment had given spring to my hopes. Was not the hour at hand, which should render me the happiest of human creatures? He suspected that I looked with favorable eyes upon Carwin. Hence arose disquietudes, which he struggled in vain to conceal. He loved me, but was hopeless that his love would be compensated. Is it not time, said I, to rectify this error? But by what means is this to be effected? It can only be done by a change of deportment in me; but how must I demean myself for this purpose?

I must not speak. Neither eyes, nor lips, must impart the information. He must not be assured that my heart is his, previous to the tender of his own; but he must be convinced that it has not been given to another; he must be supplied with space whereon to build a doubt as to the true state of my affections; he must be prompted to avow himself. The line of delicate propriety; how hard it is, not to fall short, and not to overleap it!

This afternoon we shall meet at the temple.[2] We shall not separate till late. It will be his province to accompany me home. The airy expanse is without a speck. This breeze is usually stedfast, and its promise of a bland and cloudless evening, may be trusted. The moon will rise at eleven, and at that hour, we shall wind along this bank. Possibly that hour may decide my fate. If suitable encouragement be given, Pleyel will reveal his soul to me; and I, ere I reach this threshold, will be made the happiest of beings. And is this good to be mine? Add wings to thy speed, sweet evening; and thou, moon, I charge thee, shroud thy beams at the moment when my Pleyel whispers love. I would not for the world, that the burning blushes, and the mounting raptures of that moment, should be visible.

But what encouragement is wanting? I must be regardful of insurmountable limits. Yet when minds are imbued with a genuine sympathy, are not words and looks superfluous? Are not motion and touch sufficient to impart feelings such as mine? Has he not eyed me at moments, when the pressure of his hand has thrown me into tumults, and was it possible that he mistook the impetuosities of love, for the eloquence of indignation?

But the hastening evening will decide. Would it were come! And yet I shudder at its near approach. An interview that must thus terminate, is surely

2. A roofed structure on a hill over the Wieland estate that the family used for literature readings, plays, and music. Their father had built it for his religious devotions, and it was there that he met a strange death by burning.

to be wished for by me; and yet it is not without its terrors. Would to heaven it were come and gone!

I feel no reluctance, my friends to be thus explicit. Time was, when these emotions would be hidden with immeasurable solicitude, from every human eye. Alas! these airy and fleeting impulses of shame are gone. My scruples were preposterous and criminal. They are bred in all hearts, by a perverse and vicious education, and they would still have maintained their place in my heart, had not my portion been set in misery. My errors have taught me thus much wisdom; that those sentiments which we ought not to disclose, it is criminal to harbour.

It was proposed to begin the rehearsal at four o'clock; I counted the minutes as they passed; their flight was at once too rapid and too slow; my sensations were of an excruciating kind; I could taste no food, nor apply to any task, nor enjoy a moment's repose: when the hour arrived, I hastened to my brother's.

Pleyel was not there. He had not yet come. On ordinary occasions, he was eminent for punctuality. He had testified great eagerness to share in the pleasures of this rehearsal. He was to divide the task with my brother, and, in tasks like these, he always engaged with peculiar zeal. His elocution was less sweet than sonorous; and, therefore, better adapted than the melliflu-ences of his friend, to the outrageous vehemence of this drama.

What could detain him? Perhaps he lingered through forgetfulness. Yet this was incredible. Never had his memory been known to fail upon even more trivial occasions. Not less impossible was it, that the scheme had lost its attractions, and that he staid, because his coming would afford him no gratification. But why should we expect him to adhere to the minute?

An half hour elapsed, but Pleyel was still at a distance. Perhaps he had misunderstood the hour which had been proposed. Perhaps he had con-ceived that to-morrow, and not to-day, had been selected for this purpose: but no. A review of preceding circumstances demonstrated that such mis-apprehension was impossible; for he had himself proposed this day, and this hour. This day, his attention would not otherwise be occupied; but to-morrow, an indispensible engagement was foreseen, by which all his time would be engrossed: his detention, therefore, must be owing to some unfore-seen and extraordinary event. Our conjectures were vague, tumultuous, and sometimes fearful. His sickness and his death might possibly have detained him.

Tortured with suspense, we sat gazing at each other, and at the path which led from the road. Every horseman that passed was, for a moment, imagined to be him. Hour succeeded hour, and the sun, gradually declining, at length, disappeared. Every signal of his coming proved fallacious, and our hopes were at length dismissed. His absence affected my friends in no insupport-able degree. They should be obliged, they said, to defer this undertaking till the morrow; and, perhaps, their impatient curiosity would compel them to dispense entirely with his presence. No doubt, some harmless occurrence had diverted him from his purpose; and they trusted that they should receive a satisfactory account of him in the morning.

It may be supposed that this disappointment affected me in a very different manner. I turned aside my head to conceal my tears. I fled into solitude, to give vent to my reproaches, without interruption or restraint. My heart was ready to burst with indignation and grief. Pleyel was not the only object of my keen but unjust upbraiding. Deeply did I execrate my own folly. Thus fallen into ruins was the gay fabric which I had reared! Thus had my golden vision melted into air!

How fondly did I dream that Pleyel was a lover! If he were, would he have suffered any obstacle to hinder his coming? Blind and infatuated man! I exclaimed. Thou sportest with happiness. The good that is offered thee, thou hast the insolence and folly to refuse. Well, I will henceforth intrust my felicity to no one's keeping but my own.

The first agonies of this disappointment would not allow me to be reasonable or just. Every ground on which I had built the persuasion that Pleyel was not unimpressed in my favor, appeared to vanish. It seemed as if I had been misled into this opinion, by the most palpable illusions.

I made some trifling excuse, and returned, much earlier than I expected, to my own house. I retired early to my chamber, without designing to sleep. I placed myself at a window, and gave the reins to reflection.

The hateful and degrading impulses which had lately controuled me were, in some degree, removed. New dejection succeeded, but was now produced by contemplating my late behaviour. Surely that passion is worthy to be abhorred which obscures our understanding, and urges us to the commission of injustice. What right had I to expect his attendance? Had I not demeaned myself like one indifferent to his happiness, and as having bestowed my regards upon another? His absence might be prompted by the love which I considered his absence as a proof that he wanted. He came not because the sight of me, the spectacle of my coldness or aversion, contributed to his despair. Why should I prolong, by hypocrisy or silence, his misery as well as my own? Why not deal with him explicitly, and assure him of the truth?

You will hardly believe that, in obedience to this suggestion, I rose for the purpose of ordering a light, that I might instantly make this confession in a letter. A second thought shewed me the rashness of this scheme, and I wondered by what infirmity of mind I could be betrayed into a momentary approbation of it. I saw with the utmost clearness that a confession like that would be the most remediless and unpardonable outrage upon the dignity of my sex, and utterly unworthy of that passion which controuled me.

I resumed my seat and my musing. To account for the absence of Pleyel became once more the scope of my conjectures. How many incidents might occur to raise an insuperable impediment in his way? When I was a child, a scheme of pleasure, in which he and his sister were parties, had been, in like manner, frustrated by his absence; but his absence, in that instance, had been occasioned by his falling from a boat into the river, in consequence of which he had run the most imminent hazard of being drowned. Here was a second disappointment endured by the same persons, and produced by his failure. Might it not originate in the same cause? Had he not designed to cross the river that morning to make some necessary purchases in Jersey? He had preconcerted to return to his own house to dinner; but, perhaps, some disaster had befallen him. Experience had taught me the insecurity of a canoe, and that was the only kind of boat which Pleyel used: I was, likewise, actuated by an hereditary dread of water. These circumstances combined to bestow considerable plausibility on this conjecture; but the consternation with which I began to be seized was allayed by reflecting, that if this disaster had happened my brother would have received the speediest information of it. The consolation which this idea imparted was ravished from me by a new thought. This disaster might have happened, and his family not be apprized of it. The first intelligence of his fate may be communicated by the livid corpse which the tide may cast, many days hence, upon the shore.

Thus was I distressed by opposite conjectures: thus was I tormented by phantoms of my own creation. It was not always thus. I cannot ascertain the date when my mind became the victim of this imbecility; perhaps it was coeval with the inroad of a fatal passion; a passion that will never rank me in the number of its eulogists; it was alone sufficient to the extermination of my peace: it was itself a plenteous source of calamity, and needed not the concurrence of other evils to take away the attractions of existence, and dig for me an untimely grave.

The state of my mind naturally introduced a train of reflections upon the dangers and cares which inevitably beset an human being. By no violent transition was I led to ponder on the turbulent life and mysterious end of my father. I cherished, with the utmost veneration, the memory of this man, and every relique connected with his fate was preserved with the most scrupulous care. Among these was to be numbered a manuscript, containing memoirs of his own life. The narrative was by no means recommended by its eloquence; but neither did all its value flow from my relationship to the author. Its stile had an unaffected and picturesque simplicity. The great variety and circumstantial display of the incidents, together with their intrinsic importance, as descriptive of human manners and passions, made it the most useful book in my collection. It was late; but being sensible of no inclination to sleep, I resolved to betake myself to the perusal of it.

To do this it was requisite to procure a light. The girl had long since retired to her chamber: it was therefore proper to wait upon myself. A lamp, and the means of lighting it, were only to be found in the kitchen. Thither I resolved forthwith to repair; but the light was of use merely to enable me to read the book. I knew the shelf and the spot where it stood. Whether I took down the book, or prepared the lamp, in the first place, appeared to be a matter of no moment. The latter was preferred, and, leaving my seat, I approached the closet in which, as I mentioned formerly, my books and papers were deposited.

Suddenly the remembrance of what had lately passed in this closet occurred. Whether midnight was approaching, or had passed, I knew not. I was, as then, alone, and defenceless. The wind was in that direction in which, aided by the deathlike repose of nature, it brought to me the murmur of the water-fall. This was mingled with that solemn and enchanting sound, which a breeze produces among the leaves of pines. The words of that mysterious dialogue, their fearful import, and the wild excess to which I was transported by my terrors, filled my imagination anew. My steps faultered, and I stood a moment to recover myself.

I prevailed on myself at length to move towards the closet. I touched the lock, but my fingers were powerless; I was visited afresh by unconquerable apprehensions. A sort of belief darted into my mind, that some being was concealed within, whose purposes were evil. I began to contend with these fears, when it occurred to me that I might, without impropriety, go for a lamp previously to opening the closet. I receded a few steps; but before I reached my chamber door my thoughts took a new direction. Motion seemed to produce a mechanical influence upon me. I was ashamed of my weakness. Besides, what aid could be afforded me by a lamp?

My fears had pictured to themselves no precise object. It would be difficult to depict, in words, the ingredients and hues of that phantom which haunted me. An hand invisible and of preternatural strength, lifted by human passions, and selecting my life for its aim, were parts of this terrific image. All places were alike accessible to this foe, or if his empire were restricted by local bounds, those bounds were utterly inscrutable by me. But had I not been told by some one in league with this enemy, that every place but the recess in the bank was exempt from danger?

I returned to the closet, and once more put my hand upon the lock. O! may my ears lose their sensibility, ere they be again assailed by a shriek so terrible! Not merely my understanding was subdued by the sound: it acted on my nerves like an edge of steel. It appeared to cut asunder the fibres of my brain, and rack every joint with agony.

The cry, loud and piercing as it was, was nevertheless human. No articulation was ever more distinct. The breath which accompanied it did not fan my hair, yet did every circumstance combine to persuade me that the lips which uttered it touched my very shoulder.

"Hold! Hold!" were the words of this tremendous prohibition, in whose tone the whole soul seemed to be rapt up, and every energy converted into eagerness and terror.

Shuddering, I dashed myself against the wall, and by the same involuntary impulse, turned my face backward to examine the mysterious monitor. The moon-light streamed into each window, and every corner of the room was conspicuous, and yet I beheld nothing!

The interval was too brief to be artificially measured, between the utterance of these words, and my scrutiny directed to the quarter whence they came. Yet if a human being had been there, could he fail to have been visible? Which of my senses was the prey of a fatal illusion? The shock which the sound produced was still felt in every part of my frame. The sound, therefore, could not but be a genuine commotion. But that I had heard it, was not more true than that the being who uttered it was stationed at my right ear; yet my attendant was invisible.

I cannot describe the state of my thoughts at that moment. Surprize had mastered my faculties. My frame shook, and the vital current was congealed. I was conscious only to the vehemence of my sensations. This condition could not be lasting. Like a tide, which suddenly mounts to an overwhelming height, and then gradually subsides, my confusion slowly gave place to order, and my tumults to a calm. I was able to deliberate and move. I resumed my feet, and advanced into the midst of the room. Upward, and behind, and on each side, I threw penetrating glances. I was not satisfied with one examination. He that hitherto refused to be seen, might change his purpose, and on the next survey be clearly distinguishable.

Solitude imposes least restraint upon the fancy. Dark is less fertile of images than the feeble lustre of the moon. I was alone, and the walls were chequered by shadowy forms. As the moon passed behind a cloud and emerged, these shadows seemed to be endowed with life, and to move. The apartment was open to the breeze, and the curtain was occasionally blown from its ordinary position. This motion was not unaccompanied with sound. I failed not to snatch a look, and to listen when this motion and this sound occurred. My belief that my monitor was posted near, was strong, and instantly converted these appearances to tokens of his presence, and yet I could discern nothing.

When my thoughts were at length permitted to revert to the past, the first idea that occurred was the resemblance between the words of the voice which I had just heard, and those which had terminated my dream in the summer-house. There are means by which we are able to distinguish a substance from a shadow, a reality from the phantom of a dream. The pit, my brother beckoning me forward, the seizure of my arm, and the voice behind, were surely imaginary. That these incidents were fashioned in my sleep, is supported by the same indubitable evidence that compels me to believe myself awake at present; yet the words and the voice were the same. Then, by some inexplicable contrivance, I was aware of the danger, while my actions and sensations were those of one wholly unacquainted with it. Now, was it not equally true that my actions and persuasions were at war? Had not the belief, that evil lurked in the closet, gained admittance, and had not my actions betokened an unwarrantable security? To obviate the effects of my infatuation, the same means had been used.

In my dream, he that tempted to me to my destruction, was my brother. Death was ambushed in my path. From what evil was I now rescued? What minister or implement of ill was shut up in this recess? Who was it whose suffocating grasp I was to feel, should I dare to enter it? What monstrous conception is this? my brother!

No; protection, and not injury is his province. Strange and terrible chimera! Yet it would not be suddenly dismissed. It was surely no vulgar agency that gave this form to my fears. He to whom all parts of time are equally present, whom no contingency approaches, was the author of that spell which now seized upon me. Life was dear to me. No consideration was present that enjoined me to relinquish it. Sacred duty combined with every spontaneous sentiment to endear to me my being. Should I not shudder when my being was endangered? But what emotion should possess me when the arm lifted against me was Wieland's?

Ideas exist in our minds that can be accounted for by no established laws. Why did I dream that my brother was my foe? Why but because an omen of my fate was ordained to be communicated? Yet what salutary end did it serve? Did it arm me with caution to elude, or fortitude to bear the evils to which I was reserved? My present thoughts were, no doubt, indebted for their hue to the similitude existing between these incidents and those of my dream. Surely it was phrenzy that dictated my deed. That a ruffian was hidden in the closet, was an idea, the genuine tendency of which was to urge me to flight. Such had been the effect formerly produced. Had my mind been simply occupied with this thought at present, no doubt, the same impulse would have been experienced; but now it was my brother whom I was irresistibly persuaded to regard as the contriver of that ill of which I had been forewarned. This persuasion did not extenuate my fears or my danger. Why then did I again approach the closet and withdraw the bolt? My resolution was instantly conceived, and executed without faultering.

The door was formed of light materials. The lock, of simple structure, easily forewent its hold. It opened into the room, and commonly moved upon its hinges, after being unfastened, without any effort of mine. This effort, however, was bestowed upon the present occasion. It was my purpose to open it with quickness, but the exertion which I made was ineffectual. It refused to open.

At another time, this circumstance would not have looked with a face of mystery. I should have supposed some casual obstruction, and repeated my efforts to surmount it. But now my mind was accessible to no conjecture but one. The door was hindered from opening by human force. Surely, here was new cause for affright. This was confirmation proper to decide my conduct. Now was all ground of hesitation taken away. What could be supposed but that I deserted the chamber and the house? that I at least endeavoured no longer to withdraw the door?

Have I not said that my actions were dictated by phrenzy? My reason had forborne, for a time, to suggest or to sway my resolves. I reiterated my endeavours. I exerted all my force to overcome the obstacle, but in vain. The strength that was exerted to keep it shut, was superior to mine.

A casual observer might, perhaps, applaud the audaciousness of this conduct. Whence, but from an habitual defiance of danger, could my perseverance arise? I have already assigned, as distinctly as I am able, the cause of it. The frantic conception that my brother was within, that the resistance made to my design was exerted by him, had rooted itself in my mind. You will comprehend the height of this infatuation, when I tell you, that, finding all my exertions vain, I betook myself to exclamations. Surely I was utterly bereft of understanding.

Now had I arrived at the crisis of my fate. "O! hinder not the door to open," I exclaimed, in a tone that had less of fear than of grief in it. "I know you well. Come forth, but harm me not. I beseech you come forth."

I had taken my hand from the lock, and removed to a small distance from the door. I had scarcely uttered these words, when the door swung upon its hinges, and displayed to my view the interior of the closet. Whoever was within, was shrouded in darkness. A few seconds passed without interruption of the silence. I knew not what to expect or to fear. My eyes would not stray from the recess. Presently, a deep sigh was heard. The quarter from which it came heightened the eagerness of my gaze. Some one approached from the farther end. I quickly perceived the outlines of a human figure. Its steps were irresolute and slow. I recoiled as it advanced.

By coming at length within the verge of the room, his form was clearly distinguishable. I had prefigured to myself a very different personage. The face that presented itself was the last that I should desire to meet at an hour, and in a place like this. My wonder was stifled by my fears. Assassins had lurked in this recess. Some divine voice warned me of danger, that at this moment awaited me. I had spurned the intimation, and challenged my adversary.

I recalled the mysterious countenance and dubious character of Carwin. What motive but atrocious ones could guide his steps hither? I was alone. My habit suited the hour, and the place, and the warmth of the season. All succour was remote. He had placed himself between me and the door. My frame shook with the vehemence of my apprehensions.

Yet I was not wholly lost to myself: I vigilantly marked his demeanor. His looks were grave, but not without perturbation. What species of inquietude it betrayed, the light was not strong enough to enable me to discover. He stood still; but his eyes wandered from one object to another. When these powerful organs were fixed upon me, I shrunk into myself. At length, he broke silence. Earnestness, and not embarrassment, was in his tone. He advanced close to me while he spoke.

"What voice was that which lately addressed you?"

He paused for an answer; but observing my trepidation, he resumed, with undiminished solemnity: "Be not terrified. Whoever he was, he hast done you an important service. I need not ask you if it were the voice of a companion. That sound was beyond the compass of human organs. The knowledge that enabled him to tell you who was in the closet, was obtained by incomprehensible means.

"You knew that Carwin was there. Were you not apprized of his intents? The same power could impart the one as well as the other. Yet, knowing these, you persisted. Audacious girl! But, perhaps, you confided in his guardianship. Your confidence was just. With succour like this at hand you may safely defy me.

"He is my eternal foe; the baffler of my best concerted schemes. Twice have you been saved by his accursed interposition. But for him I should long ere now have borne away the spoils of your honor."

He looked at me with greater stedfastness than before. I became every moment more anxious for my safety. It was with difficulty I stammered out an entreaty that he would instantly depart, or suffer me to do so. He paid no regard to my request, but proceeded in a more impassioned manner.

"What is it you fear? Have I not told you, you are safe? Has not one in whom you more reasonably place trust assured you of it? Even if I execute my purpose, what injury is done? Your prejudices will call it by that name, but it merits it not.

"I was impelled by a sentiment that does you honor; a sentiment, that would sanctify my deed; but, whatever it be, you are safe. Be this chimera still worshipped; I will do nothing to pollute it." Here he stopped.

The accents and gestures of this man left me drained of all courage. Surely, on no other occasion should I have been thus pusillanimous. My state I regarded as a hopeless one. I was wholly at the mercy of this being. Whichever way I turned my eyes, I saw no avenue by which I might escape. The resources of my personal strength, my ingenuity, and my eloquence, I estimated at nothing. The dignity of virtue, and the force of truth, I had been accustomed to celebrate; and had frequently vaunted of the conquests which I should make with their assistance.

I used to suppose that certain evils could never befall a being in possession of a sound mind; that true virtue supplies us with energy which vice can never resist; that it was always in our power to obstruct, by his own death, the designs of an enemy who aimed at less than our life. How was it that a sentiment like despair had now invaded me, and that I trusted to the protection of chance, or to the pity of my persecutor?

His words imparted some notion of the injury which he had meditated. He talked of obstacles that had risen in his way. He had relinquished his design. These sources supplied me with slender consolation. There was no security but in his absence. When I looked at myself, when I reflected on the hour and the place, I was overpowered by horror and dejection.

He was silent, useful, and inattentive to my situation, yet made no motion to depart. I was silent in my turn. What could I say? I was confident that reason in this contest would be impotent. I must owe my safety to his own suggestions. Whatever purpose brought him hither, he had changed it. Why then did he remain? His resolutions might fluctuate, and the pause of a few minutes restore to him his first resolutions.

Yet was not this the man whom we had treated with unwearied kindness? Whose society was endeared to us by his intellectual elevation and accomplishments.? Who had a thousand times expatiated on the usefulness and beauty of virtue? Why should such a one be dreaded? If I could have forgotten the circumstances in which our interview had taken place, I might have treated his words as jests. Presently, he resumed:

"Fear me not: the space that severs us in small, and all visible succour is distant. You believe yourself completely in my power; that you stand upon the brink of ruin. Such are your groundless fears. I cannot lift a finger to hurt you. Easier it would be to stop the moon in her course than to injure you. The power that protects you would crumble my sinews, and reduce me to a heap of ashes in a moment, if I were to harbour a thought hostile to your safety.

"Thus are appearances at length solved. Little did I expect that they originated hence. What a portion is assigned to you? Scanned by the eyes of this intelligence, your path will be without pits to swallow, or snares to entangle you. Environed by the arms of this protection, all artifices will be frustrated, and all malice repelled."

Here succeeded a new pause. I was still observant of every gesture and look. The tranquil solemnity that had lately possessed his countenance gave way to a new expression. All now was trepidation and anxiety.

"I must be gone," said he in a faltering accent. "Why do I linger here? I will not ask your forgiveness. I see that your terrors are invincible. Your pardon will be extorted by fear, and not dictated by compassion. I must fly from you forever. He that could plot against your honor, must expect from you and your friends persecution and death. I must doom myself to endless exile."

Saying this, he hastily left the room. I listened while he descended the stairs, and, unbolting the outer door, went forth. I did not follow him with my eyes, as the moon-light would have enabled me to do. Relieved by his absence, and exhausted by the conflict of my fears, I threw myself on a chair, and resigned myself to those bewildering ideas which incidents like these could not fail to produce.

1798

Selected Bibliographies

For study of American literature to 1820, the best handbook is Clarence Gohdes and Sanford E. Marovitz's *Bibliographical Guide to the Literature of the U.S.A.* (1984), 5th ed. Lists of significant works for the present volume of *The Norton Anthology of American Literature* are given under such useful categories as "American studies or American civilization," "American history: general tools," "American history: special studies," "Selected histories of ideas in the U.S.," "Psychology," "Philosophy," "Religion in the U.S.," "Chief general bibliographies of American literature," "Chief general histories and selected critical discussions of American literature," and "Studies of the 17th and 18th centuries." The fourth edition (1976) contained a useful section on "Arts other than literature." In *American Literature: A Study and Research Guide* (1976), Lewis Leary with John Auchard duplicates some of the categories in Gohdes's book, but the pithy evaluations of the works he mentions are very helpful; Leary also provides an interesting "History of the Study and Teaching of American Literature." Relatively few items on this period are listed in Robert C. Schweik and Dieter Riesner's *Reference Sources in English and American Literature: An Annotated Bibliography* (1977), but those few are helpfully annotated. The 1998 *Encyclopedia of the Novel*, ed. Paul Schellinger et al., includes essays on the novel in colonial America and the early United States: William J. Scheick on the eighteenth century and Joseph Alkana on 1800–1850. A basic reference book is Phillip Leninger's 1995 updating of James D. Hart's *Oxford Companion to American Literature*, 6th ed.

LITERATURE TO 1700

Few major studies address the great body of writings produced in various European languages, or codified in Native American ones, in the century following first contact; those that do concern themselves more with matters of context than with patterns of language. For the basic outline of European expansion westward, Samuel Eliot Morison's *The European Discovery of America* (1971–74), 2 vols., is useful. For North America, David Beers Quinn's thorough *North America from Earliest Discovery to First Settlements* (1977) and his *England and the Discovery of America, 1481–1620* (1973) give detailed narrative and analysis, as does Gary Nash's *Red, White, and Black: The People of Early America* (1974). Edmundo O'Gorman's insightful *The Invention of America* (1961) shifts the discussion away from the geographical discoveries of Renaissance Europe and toward

the cultural responses that those discoveries called forth, a theme followed out as well in J. H. Elliot's brief *The Old World and the New, 1492–1650* (1970) and in Stephen Greenblatt's *Marvelous Possessions: The Wonder of the New World* (1991). Roy Harvey Pearce's *Savagism and Civilization: A Study of the Indian and the American Mind* (1953; 1988) goes from 1609 to the mid-nineteenth-century and serves as an indispensable starting point for the literary impact of the Native American on "the American mind." In a related vein, Alfred W. Crosby traces the biological exchanges between the hemispheres in his influential *The Columbian Exchange: Biological and Cultural Consequences of 1492* (1972), while Carl O. Sauer takes up the question of how the Caribbean was altered after 1492 in *The Early Spanish Main* (1966). A similar project is carried out for New England in William

Cronon's excellent *Changes in the Land: Indians, Colonists, and the Ecology of New England* (1983); for the South, see Timothy Silver, *A New Face on the Countryside: Indians, Colonists, and Slaves in the South Atlantic Forests, 1500–1800* (1990).

Among books that deal with the verbal shape of the early documents, William Carlos Williams's *In the American Grain* (1925) gives brief but evocative guidance. Howard Mumford Jones places early American culture in the context of Renaissance Europe in *O Strange New World: American Culture, the Formative Years* (1964). In *The Machine in the Garden: Technology and the Pastoral Ideal in America* (1964), Leo Marx offers insightful readings of some Renaissance texts (such as Shakespeare's *The Tempest*) that reflect on the new lands suddenly opened to the Old World; responses to the New World (and a reading, again, of *The Tempest*) are considered in Eric Cheyfitz's *The Poetics of Imperialism: Translation and Colonization from "The Tempest" to "Tarzan"* (1991). A feminist perspective guides Annette Kolodny's *The Lay of the Land; Metaphor as Experience and History in American Life and Letters* (1975), and the opening chapters of Richard Drinnon's *Facing West: The Metaphysics of Indian-Hating and Empire-Building* (1980) offer a psychohistorical perspective. William C. Spengemann argues for the centrality of early American texts in the transformation of Western writing generally in *The Adventurous Muse: The Poetics of American Fiction, 1789–1900* (1977), John Seelye offers ingenious readings of many early texts in *Prophetic Waters: The River in Early American Life and Literature* (1977), and Wayne Franklin gives attention to sixteenth-century works in *Discoveries, Explorers, Settlers: The Diligent Writers of Early America* (1979). Gordon Sayre's *"Les Sauvages Américains": Representations of Native Americans in French and English Colonial Literature* (1997) offers fresh comparative readings of English and French texts and the codes they developed for depicting encounters with Native American peoples. No generally inclusive bibliography of the literary texts of the period is available, although Joseph Sabin's massive *Biblioteca Americana: A Dictionary of Books Relating to America, from its Discovery to the Present Time* (1868–1936), 29 vols., is invaluable. Among anthologies, the most useful are David Beers Quinn's *New American World: A Documentary History of North America to 1612* (1979), 5 vols., and the modern editions of Richard Hakluyt's collection of 1598–1600, *The Principall Navigations, Voyages, Traffiques, & Discoveries of the English Nation* (1903–05), 12 vols., and Samuel Purchas's 1625 sequel to it, *Hakluytus Posthumus or Purchas His Pilgrimes* (1905–07), 20 vols. The Hakluyt volumes also were reprinted in the Everyman's Library, 8 vols. (1907). A companion series to Quinn's is John

H. Parry and Robert G. Keith, *New Iberian World: A Documentary History of the Discovery and Settlement of Latin America to the Early 17th Century* (1984), 5 vols.

Although we tend to favor recent criticism, some of the best critical writing on early American literature is the earliest. Even though its biographical details are not always reliable, Moses Coit Tyler's monumental study *A History of American Literature during the Colonial Period, 1607–1765,* (1878; rev. ed. 1897), 2 vols., remains a fundamental document of the field, notable especially for its broadly inclusive definition of literature. It is not attentive, however, to writings in languages other than English. The same point is largely true of Myra Jehlen's useful essay "The Literature of Colonization," in *The Cambridge History of American Literature* (1994), vol. 1, edited by Sacvan Bercovitch. Some coverage of Dutch colonial culture is provided by Ellis L. Raesly's *Portrait of New Netherland* (1945); it can be supplemented by Donna Merwick's case studies *Possessing Albany, 1630–1710, The Dutch and English Experiences* (1990) and *Death of A Notary: Conquest and Change in Colonial New York* (1999). Henry C. Murphy's *Anthology of New Netherland* (1865) remains the single best source of translated texts (with biographical sketches) of three seventeenth-century writers. German immigrant experience and writings from the seventeenth century are briefly treated in Henry A. Pochmann's *German Culture in America, 1600–1900, Philosophical and Literary Influences* (1957). John J. Stoudt's *Pennsylvania German Poetry, 1685–1830* (1955), surveys one form of expression in depth. The texts and introductory materials and notes in the following volumes of the *Original Narratives of Early American History* series remain useful for non-English (and in some cases English) writers: *Narratives of New Netherland, 1609–1664* (1909), edited by J. Franklin Jameson; *Journal of Jasper Danckaerts* (1913), edited by Jameson and Bartlett Burleigh James; *Narratives of Early Pennsylvania, West New Jersey, and Delaware, 1630–1707* (1912), edited by Albert Cook Myers; *The Spanish Explorers in the Southern United States, 1528–1543* (1907), edited by Frederick W. Hodge; *Spanish Exploration in the Southwest, 1542–1706* (1916), edited by Herbert Eugene Bolton; and *Early Narratives of the Northwest, 1634–1699* (1917), edited by Louise P. Kellogg.

The classic study of the Puritans remains Perry Miller's *The New England Mind: The Seventeenth Century* (1939) and *The New England Mind: From Colony to Province* (1953). Useful essays by Miller are included in *Errand into the Wilderness* ("The Marrow of Puritan Divinity" and "From Edwards to Emerson" are especially important) (1956). Miller and Thomas H. Johnson edited the anthology *The Puritans: A Sourcebook of Their Writings* in 1938 (rev. ed., 1963), which contains useful introductions. A valuable collection is *Seventeenth-Century American Poetry* (1968), compiled by Harrison T. Meserole. Peter White edited *Puritan Poets and Poetics* in 1985. Patricia Caldwell discusses Puritan "relations" (accounts of conversions or spiritual autobiographies) in *The Puritan Conversion Narrative* (1983). Other books of general interest are Edmund S. Morgan's *Visible Saints: The History of a Puritan Idea* (1963), Kenneth B. Murdock's *Literature and Theology in Colonial New England* (1949), and Larzer Ziff's *Puritans in America: New Culture in a New World* (1973). On Puritan historians, see Peter Gay's *Loss of Mastery* (1966) and David Levin's *In Defense of Historical Literature* (1967). Sacvan Bercovich edited a useful collection of essays on the Puritans in *The American Puritan Imagination: Essays in Revaluation* (1974); it contains a good selected bibliography. Another useful revaluation of Puritans that brings together some hard-to-come-by essays is Michael McGiffert's *Puritanism and the American Experience* (1969). Some of the best accounts of the intellectual and cultural life of the seventeenth century are to be found in the biographies of writers included in this anthology. One important study of a writer not included is Edmund Morgan's life of Ezra Stiles, *The Gentle Puritan* (1962).

Fifteen American Authors before 1900: Bibliographic Essays on Research and Criticism (1971, rev. 1984), edited by Robert A. Rees and Earl N. Harbert, contains discursive chapters on the scholarship and criticism that had appeared up to that date on three authors in this period: Edwards, Franklin, and Taylor. *American Prose to 1820: A Guide to Information Sources* (1979), edited by Donald Yannella and John H. Roch, provides a helpful description of primary works and secondary sources. Writers like Anne Bradstreet and Edward Taylor are included because they wrote prose as well as poetry.

Bartolomé de las Casas
The most important of Casas's many writings, his *General History of the Indies*, was finished by 1561, but did not see publication until the late nineteenth century. Among more recent editions in Spanish, that edited by Agustín Millares Carlo and published in Mexico City (1951) is useful. An abridged translation by Andrée M. Collard (1971) makes part of it readily available in English. Casas's most influential text, the *Brevissima relación*, is well rendered in Herma Briffault's translation, *The Devastation of the Indies: A Brief Account* (1974; 1992). Stafford Poole has translated as *In Defense of the Indians* (1992) a long major manuscript treatise written by Casas in the early 1550s. Studies of Casas include Lewis Hanke's *Bartolomé de las Casas: An Interpretation of His Life and Writings* (1951) and Henry Raup Wagner and Helen Rand Par-

ish's *The Life and Writings of Bartolomé de las Casa* (1967).

William Bradford
Samuel Eliot Morison's edition of *Of Plymouth Plantation* (1952) is the standard edition of Bradford's history, and his life of Bradford in *The Dictionary of American Biography* (1933) is useful. For a discussion of Puritan historians, see Kenneth B. Murdock's *Literature and Theology in Colonial New England* (1949) and David Levin's "William Bradford: The Value of Puritan Historiography," in E. H. Emerson's *Major Writers of Early American Literature* (1972).

Anne Bradstreet
The standard edition is now Jeannine Hensley's *The Works of Anne Bradstreet* (1967), with an introduction by Adrienne Rich. Students interested in textual variants will want to consult *The Complete Works* (1981), edited by J. R. McElrath Jr. and Allen P. Robb. Useful critical discussions may be found in Josephine K. Piercy's *Anne Bradstreet* (1965), Elizabeth W. White's *Anne Bradstreet: The Tenth Muse* (1971), Ann Stanford's *Anne Bradstreet: The Worldly Puritan* (1974), and Rosamond Rosenmeier's *Anne Bradstreet* (1991). Jeffrey Hammond's *Sinful Self, Saintly Self* (1993) is useful on Wigglesworth and Taylor as well as Bradstreet.

Samuel de Champlain
The standard (bilingual) edition is *The Works of Samuel de Champlain* (1922–36), 6 vols., edited by H. P. Biggar and others. A useful one-volume English version, edited by W. L. Grant in the *Original Narratives of Early American History* series, is *Voyages of Samuel de Champlain, 1604–1618* (1907). Samuel Eliot Morison's biography, *Samuel de Champlain: Father of New France* (1972), is useful.

Christopher Columbus
Cecil Jane's *Select Documents Illustrating the Four Voyages of Columbus* (1930–33; 1988) is the best bilingual edition of various writings. It does not include the "journal" of the first voyage, which survives only in summaries and unreliable transcriptions by others. The best text of that problematic work is Oliver Dunn and James E. Kelley's bilingual *The Diario of Christopher Columbus's First Voyage to America, 1492–93* (1989); on the problems associated with this text (and others), see David Heninge's *In Search of Columbus: The Sources for the First Voyage* (1991). Biographies include Samuel Eliot Morison's now somewhat dated *Admiral of the Ocean Sea* (1942) and Kirkpatrick Sale's contentious *The Conquest of Paradise: Christopher Columbus and the Columbian Legacy* (1990). James Axtell's *After Columbus* (1988) and *Beyond 1492* (1992) offer excellent and broad coverage of key topics.

Bernal Díaz del Castillo
A complete translation of Díaz del Castillo's *The True Story of the Conquest of New Spain* was published by Λ. P. Maudlslay, (1908–16), 5 vols. This has been reissued in a one-volume abridgment (1956;1970); a newer abridged translation was undertaken by J. M. Cohen, *The Conquest of New Spain* (1963). An excellent Native American record of the conquest, originally assembled by Miguel Leon-Portilla in Spanish, was translated by Lysander Kemp as *The Broken Spears* (1962). An intriguing collection of early Spanish letters is James Lockhart and Enrique Otte's *Letters and People of the Spanish Indies: Sixteenth Century* (1976). Guidance on the complex issues associated with the fall of the Aztec Empire can be found in R. C. Padden's *The Hummingbird and the Hawk: Conquest and Sovereignty in the Valley of Mexico: 1503–1541* (1967) and in Serge Gruzinski's *The Conquest of Mexico: The Incorporation of Indian Societies into the Western World, 16th–18th Centuries* (1993), translated by Eileen Corrigan.

Garcilaso de la Vega
Harold V. Livermore translated and edited *The Royal Commentaries of the Incas and General History of Peru* (1966), 2 vols. *The Florida of the Inca* is available in a translation by John Varner and Jeannette Varner (1951) and that of Charmion Shelby, printed as the second volume of *The De Soto Chronicles: The Expedition of Hernando de Soto to North America in 1539–1543* (1993), edited by Lawrence A. Clayton, Vernon James Knight Jr., and Edward C. Moore. John Varner's study *El Inca: The Life and Times of Garcilaso de la Vega* (1968) is useful for biographical and historical backgrounds and for its bibliography.

Thomas Harriot
Muriel Rukeyser's *The Traces of Thomas Harriot* (1971) is an innovative biography. John W. Shirley's edited volume *Thomas Harriot, Renaissance Scientist* (1974) collects a number of modern studies. David Beers Quinn includes Harriot among his topics in *England and the Discovery of America, 1481–1620* (1974) and gives the best text of Harriot's *A Brief and True Report of the New Found Land of Virginia* in *The Roanoke Voyages, 1584–1590*, 2 vols. (1955; 1991). The collaborative edition of that work illustrated with engravings based on John White's drawings and watercolors has been reprinted (1972).

Iroquois Creation Stories
First published in 1851, Lewis Henry Morgan's *League of the Iroquois* (1972, with an introduction by William Fenton) remains useful as an introduction to things Iroquoian. Daniel K. Richter's *The Ordeal of the Longhouse: The Peoples of the Iroquois League in the Era of European Colonization* (1992) covers the basic elements of Iroquois language, culture, and history and begins with an overview of Iroquois cosmogonic myths that builds on the work of William Fenton, whose "This Island, the World on the Turtle's Back," *Journal of American Folklore*, 75 (1962), is a rich analysis of Iroquois mythology. For the most detailed versions of the stories themselves, consult J. N. B. Hewitt's "Iroquoian Cosmology," part I, Bureau of American Ethnology, *Annual Report, 1899–1900* (1903) and "Iroquoian Cosmology," part II, Bureau of American Ethnology, *Annual Report, 1925–26* (1928) as well as Seneca ethnologist Arthur C. Parker's *Seneca Myths and Folk Tales*, Buffalo Historical Society Publications No. 27 (1923). In addition to these scholarly accounts, Edmund Wilson's meditation on the Iroquois, *Apologies to the Iroquois* (1960), remains fascinating. See also the contemporary Abenaki poet and story-teller Joseph Bruchac's *New Voices from the Longhouse: An Anthology of Contemporary Iroquois Writing* (1989). W. G. Spittal's *Iroquois Women: An Anthology* (1992) and *Extending the Rafters: Interdisciplinary Approaches to Iroquoian Studies*, edited by Michael Foster, Jack Campisi, and Marianne Mithun (1984) are useful. Recent studies of interest include Scott Michaelsen's "Ely Parker and Amerindian Voices in Ethnography," *American Literary History*, 8 (1996); Douglas Boyce's " 'As the Wind Scatters the Smoke': The Tuscaroras in the Eighteenth Century," in *Beyond the Covenant Chain: The Iroquois and Their Neighbors in Indian North America, 1600–1800* (1987), edited by Daniel Richter and James Merrell; David Landy's "Tuscarora among the Iroquois," in *Handbook of North American Indians* (1978), vol. 15, edited by Bruce Trigger; Russell Judkins's "David Cusick's *Ancient History of the Six Nations*: A Neglected Classic," in his *Iroquois Studies: A Guide to Documentary and Ethnographic Resources from Western New York and the Genesee Valley* (1987).

Native American Oral Literature
As Fr. Walter Ong cogently stated, "Writing is a technology that alters thought." It is therefore useful to consult such texts on orality in general as Ong's *Orality and Literacy: The Technologizing of the Word* (1982), Deborah Tannen's *Spoken and Written Language: Exploring Orality and Literacy* (1982), and Eric Havelock's *The Muse Learns to Write* (1986). Richard Bauman's edited *Verbal Art as Performance* (1984) includes contributions from a variety of disciplines, and Barre Toelken's *The Dynamics of Folklore* (rev. ed. 1996) is an excellent recent survey of oral materials by someone specifically interested in Native American expression. Bruce Rosenberg's *Folklore and Literature: Rival Siblings* (1991) makes the case for his title. Jay Miller's *Oral Literature* (1991) is also worth consulting.

Still indispensable introductions to mythography or ethnopoetics—terms for indicating the questions at issue when attempting to turn an oral performance into a written text—are Dell Hymes's "In Vain I Tried to Tell You": Essays in Native American Ethnopoetics (1981) and Dennis Tedlock's The Spoken Word and the Work of Interpretation (1983). Karl Kroeber's Traditional Literatures of the American Indians: Texts and Interpretations (1981) contains fine critiques by Dell Hymes, Dennis Tedlock, and Barre Toelken of, respectively, Northwest Coast, Zuni, and Navajo narratives. Kroeber's Artistry in Native American Myths (1998) reprints a wide range of stories with detailed commentaries and notes. Toelken transcribes another tale by the Navajo storyteller Yellowman in "Life and Death in the Navajo Coyote Tales," in Recovering the Word: Essays on Native American Literatures (1987), edited by Brian Swann and Arnold Krupat. Swann's edited On the Translation of Native American Literatures (1992) contains several fine essays. Krupat edited New Voices in Native American Literary Criticism (1993), which contains work on oral narrative both in English and in native languages. A wide range of fine translations from many oral traditions can be found in Brian Swann's edited Coming to Light: Contemporary Translations of the Native Literatures of North America (1994). Some of the many more recent collections of the oral literature of specific cultures are Stories That Make the World: Oral Literature of the Indian Peoples of the Inland Northwest (1995), edited by Rodney Frey; The White Deer and Other Stories Told by the Lenape (1995), edited by John Bierhorst; Haa Kusteeyi, Our Culture: Tlingit Life Stories (1994), edited by Nora Marks Dauenhauer and Richard Dauenhauer; and Haboo: Native American Stories from Puget Sound (1988), edited by Vi Hilbert.

Native American Trickster Tales
Daniel G. Brinton was the first to use the term trickster, in his Myths of the New World (1868), and his collection and commentaries are still of some interest. Paul Radin's The Trickster: A Study in American Indian Mythology (1956; rpt. 1972) with commentaries by Karl Kerényi and C. G. Jung contains much useful information, although Radin's psychological interpretations have not worn well. Mac Linscott Ricketts's "The Native American Indian Trickster," History of Religions (1965), and Barbara Babcock-Abraham's " 'A Tolerated Margin of Mess': The Trickster and His Tales Reconsidered," Journal of the Folklore Institute (1975), are learned and theoretically sophisticated. See also Andrew Wiget's "His Life in His Tail: The Native American Trickster and the Literature of Possibility," in Redefining American Literary History (1990), edited by A. LaVonne Brown Ruoff and Jerry W. Ward. For Hopi Coyote tales see Ekkehart Malotki and Michael Lomatuway'ma's edited Hopi

Coyote Tales/Instutuwutsi (1978). For northwestern Coyote tales there are Jarold Ramsey's edited Coyote Was Going There: Indian Literature of the Oregon Country (1977) and William Bright's A Coyote Reader (1993), an omnibus collection of Coyote tales, poems, and stories that also provides a good deal of information about Canis latrans, "barking dog," or Coyote. Some of Bright's analyses of Karuk (northwestern California) trickster material are "The Travels of Coyote, a Karok Myth," Kroeber Anthropological Society Papers (1954); "Coyote's Journey," American Indian Culture and Research Journal (1980); and "Coyote Gives Acorn and Salmon to Humans," in Coyote Stories II (1980), edited by Martha Kendall. Commentary—and stories—by a traditional storyteller appears in Judy Trejo's "Coyote Tales: a Paiute Commentary," Journal of American Folklore (1974).

Dennis Tedlock offers translations of some Zuni trickster tales in Finding the Center: Narrative Poetry of the Zuni Indians (1972; rpt. 1978). For other Navajo Coyote tales see Karl Luckert's edited Coyoteway: A Navajo Healing Ceremony (1979). The most recent version of Barre Toelken's Navajo Coyote story can be found in Coming to Light: Contemporary Translations of the Native Literatures of North America (1994), edited by Brian Swann. Toelken's "Life and Death in the Navajo Coyote Tales," in Recovering the Word: Essays on Native American Literature (1987), edited by Swann and Arnold Krupat, tells of his discovery of a level of meaning in Navajo Coyote tales relating to witchcraft. Thomas Parkhill's " 'Of Glooscap's Birth, and of His Brother Malsum, the Wolf': The Story of Charles Godfrey Leland's 'Purely American Creation,' " in American Indian Culture and Research Journal (1992), is a study of a lesser known trickster tradition.

For Koasati and other Southeast cultures, see John R. Swanton's Koasati Texts (1910) and Myths and Tales of the Southeastern Indians (1929). More recently, there is George Lankford's edited Native American Southeastern Legends: Tales from the Natchez, Caddo, Biloxi, Chickasaw and Other Nations (1987).

For Okanagan material there is a new edition of Coyote Stories (1990) edited by Jay Miller. Alanna K. Brown published "The Evolution of Mourning Dove's Coyote Stories," in Studies in American Indian Literatures (1992). For older, ethnographic material, see Folk-Tales of Salishan and Sahaptin Tribes (1917), edited by Franz Boas, and Eileen Yanan's edited Coyote and the Colville (1971). Mattina published a prose version of a trickster tale narrated by Peter Seymour, "Bluejay and His Brother-in-Law Wolf," in Coming to Light (1994), edited by Swann. Harry Robinson, a contemporary Okanagan storyteller, narrates some traditional trickster tales in "Red English," which were printed in verse format in

Write It on Your Heart: The Epic World of an Okanagan Storyteller (1989) and *Nature Power: In the Spirit of an Okanagan Storyteller* (1992), both edited by Wendy Wickwire.

A recent overview is William J. Hynes and William Doty's edited *Mythical Trickster Figures: Contours, Contexts, and Criticisms* (1993). For Ikto, Iya, and other Lakota trickster materials, see James R. Walker's *Lakota Belief and Ritual* (1980), edited by Elaine Jahner and Raymond DeMallie, and Walker's *Lakota Myth* (1983), edited by Jahner. William Powers's *Oglala Religion* (1977) is useful for background material. Raymond DeMallie and Douglas Park's *Sioux Indian Religion: Tradition and Innovation* (1987) specifically treats the Deloria Ikto story, as does Julian Rice's *Lakota Storytelling: Black Elk, Ella Deloria, and Frank Fools Crow* (1989). Karl Kroeber's *Artistry in Native American Myths* (1998) analyzes a Lakota Stone Boy story, in which it is Stone Boy, the Lakota culture hero, rather than Ikto, who tricks and defeats Iya.

Cotton Mather

Kenneth Silverman's *The Life and Times of Cotton Mather* (1984) supersedes earlier biographies like that of Barrett Wendell (1891), but the introduction to Kenneth B. Murdock's *Selections from Cotton Mather* (1926) is still useful. In addition to Silverman's biography, interested students will want to read David Levin's *Cotton Mather: The Young Life of the Lord's Remembrancer* (1978) and Robert Middlekauff's *The Mathers: Three Generations of Puritan Intellectuals* (1971). Sacvan Bercovich has written about Mather in *Major Writers of Early American Literature* (1972), edited by E. H. Emerson, and in his influential book *The Puritan Origins of the American Self* (1975).

Thomas Morton

The introduction to Charles Francis Adams's edition of *New English Canaan* (1883) answers a number of questions about the life of this enigmatic figure, but the interested student will also want to read *Thomas Morton* (1969) by Donald F. Connors.

Álvar Núñez Cabeza de Vaca

An excellent colloquial translation of *La Relación* is Cyclone Covey's *Cabeza de Vaca's Adventures in the Unknown Interior of America* (1961; 1983). This relies on studies of Cabeza de Vaca's itinerary by Cleve Hallenbeck, *Álvar Núñez Cabeza de Vaca: The Journey and Route of the First European to Cross the Continent of North America, 1534–1536* (1940; 1971) and Carl O. Sauer's *Sixteenth-Century North America* (1971). Two translations of *La Relación* are *The Account: Álvar Núñez Cabeza de Vaca's Relación* (1993), translated by Martin A. Favata and José Fernández; and *Castaways: The Narrative of Álvar Núñez Cabeza de Vaca*, ed. Enrique Pupo-Walker (1993), translated by Frances M.

López-Morillas. Morris Bishop's *The Odyssey of Cabeza de Vaca* (1933) treats the whole of the life, including the later South American episodes. Cabeza de Vaca's Río de la Plata narrative, *Commentarios* (1555), was translated by Luis L. Dominguez in *The Conquest of the River Plate* (1891). A fictional account of Estevánico, the Moorish slave who was one of the four survivors of the Cabeza de Vaca party, is offered in Daniel Panger's *Black Ulysses* (1982). Interesting later notes on Cabeza de Vaca and Estevánico are to be found in the various narratives of the Coronado expedition collected in George Parker Winship and Frederick Webb Hodge's *The Journey of Francisco Vázquez de Coronado, 1540–1542* (1933; 1990).

Francis Daniel Pastorius

Marion D. Learned's *The Life of Francis Daniel Pastorius* (1908) is a full-length biography. It is supplemented by chapter 3 of Samuel W. Pennypacker's *The Settlement of Germantown* (1899). Oswald Seidensticker offers a bibliography of the works of Pastorius in *The First Century of German Printing in America, 1728–1830* (1893). The English poetry of Pastorius, most of it left in a manuscript called "The Bee-Hive," is sampled in Harrison T. Meserole's *Seventeenth-Century American Poetry* (1968). John Stoudt's *Pennsylvania German Poetry, 1685–1830* (1955) give the fullest treatment of Pastorius's verse.

Pima Stories of the Beginning of the World

Ruth M. Underhill's studies in the 1930s and 1940s of the Akimel O'odham (Pima) (and their close relatives the Tohono O'odham [Papago]) are useful for the student who would like to learn more about the history and culture of these Southwestern desert peoples. Her *Singing for Power: The Song Magic of the Papago Indians of Southern Arizona* (1938, 1973, 1993) is still valuable, as is her *Rainhouse and Ocean: Speeches for the Papago Year* (1979). Dean Saxton and Lucille Saxton's *Legends and Lore of the Papago and Pima Indians* (1973) offers some creation stories in both English translation and the original language. Somewhat more specialized, but of great importance, are Donald M. Bahr's *Pima and Papago Ritual Oratory: A Study of Three Texts* (1975, 1988) and his book (with Juan Smith, William Smith Allison, and Julian Hayden) *The Short Swift Time of Gods on Earth: the Hohokam Chronicles* (1994), a collection of thirty-six Pima narratives. Bahr's *Oriole Songs* (1994) is a collection, with extended commentaries, of one variety of Pima "dream songs" still being sung today. For an individual's view of her people, see Underhill's *Maria Chona: The Autobiography of a Papago Woman*, which was reprinted as *Papago Woman* (1979). A specifically Pima autobiography is that of Anna Moore Shaw, *A Pima Past* (1974), which details the customs of the Pima.

Mary Rowlandson
Richard Slotkin's *Regeneration through Violence* (1973) contains a useful discussion of Rowlandson's captivity. See also R. H. Pearce's "The Significance of the Captivity Narrative," *American Literature* 19 (1947). Neal Salisbury's edition (1997) of the *Narrative* has a fine introduction.

Samuel Sewall
The Diary of Samuel Sewall, 1674–1729 (1973), edited by M. Halsey Thomas, is now the standard edition and preferred over that published by the Massachusetts Historical Society from 1878 to 1882. Thomas's edition includes *The Selling of Joseph*, but the introduction and commentary in Sidney Kaplan's edition (1969) is valuable for what it tells us about slavery in New England. Ola E. Winslow has written a succinct biography (1964).

John Smith
A definitive edition of Smith's many writings is *The Complete Works of Captain John Smith* (1986), edited by Philip Barbour in 3 vols. The best single book on Smith is Everett H. Emerson's *Captain John Smith* (1971), but for a more expansive treatment of Smith's life the student can turn to Bradford Smith's *Captain John Smith, His Life and Legend* (1953) and Philip L. Barbour's *The Three Worlds of Captain John Smith* (1964). A useful descriptive bibliography can be found in *American Prose in 1820* (1979), edited by Donald Yanella and John H. Roche.

Jacob Steendam
The single best source for Steendam's poetry remains Henry C. Murphy's *Anthology of New Netherland* (1865), which also provides a biographical sketch based on Murphy's *Jacob Steendam: Noch Vaster* (1861). William Loring Andrews's *Jacob Steendam: The First Poet in New Netherland* (1908) is also of interest.

Edward Taylor
The standard edition *The Poems of Edward Taylor* (1960) is by Donald E. Stanford. Taylor's *Diary* (1964) was edited by Francis Murphy and his *Christographia* sermons (1962) and *Treatise Concerning the Lord's Supper* (1966) by Norman S. Grabo, who has also written the best critical biography (1961, rev. 1988). Thomas M. and Virginia L. Davis edited *The Minor Poetry* with an informative introduction (1981). Thomas Davis also published *A Reading of Edward Taylor* (1992). Important critical studies include William J. Scheick's *The Will and the Word* (1974), Karen E. Rowe's *Saint and Singer*

(1986), and Jeffrey Hammond's *Sinful Self, Saintly Self* (1993).

Adriaen Van der Donck
The first English translation of *A Description of New Netherland* was published by Jeremiah Johnson in the *Collections of the New York Historical Society* (1841). This is reprinted, with a biographical and critical introduction, by Thomas F. O'Donnell (1968). The other work on the Dutch province credited to Van der Donck, *The Representation of New Netherland*, is available in a translation by Henry C. Murphy (revised by A. Clinton Crowell) in *Narratives of New Netherland* (1909), edited by J. Franklin Jameson. Background on the patroon system and the Dutch West India Company is provided by S. G. Nissenson's *The Patroon's Domain* (1937).

Michael Wigglesworth
Kenneth B. Murdock's edition of *The Day of Doom* (1929) includes a valuable introduction. Wigglesworth's *Diary* was edited by Edmund S. Morgan (1970). The standard life is Richard Crowder's *No Featherbed to Heaven* (1962). Jeffrey Hammond looks at Wigglesworth poetry in *Sinful Self, Saintly Self* (1993).

Roger Williams
There are a number of distinguished studies of Williams, but the best of these are Perry Miller's *Roger Williams: His Contribution to the American Tradition* (1953), Ola E. Winslow's *Roger Williams* (1957), Edmund S. Morgan's *Roger Williams: The Church and the State* (1967), and Henry Chupack's *Roger Williams* (1969). *The Complete Writings of Roger Williams* (1963) includes a valuable essay by Perry Miller as an introduction to vol. 7.

John Winthrop
The standard edition of *The Journal* is that edited by Richard S. Dunn, James Savage, and Laetitia Yeandle (1996). It contains a valuable introduction by Dunn. Dunn and Yeandle prepared an abridged and modernized edition of *The Journal* (1966). *The Winthrop Papers, 1498–1654* (1929–) is a multivolume series in progress published under the auspices of the Massachusetts Historical Society, Boston. Richard S. Dunn's *Puritans and Yankees: The Winthrop Dynasty of New England* (1962) and Edmund S. Morgan's *The Puritan Dilemma: The Story of John Winthrop* (1958) are among the best critical and biographical studies. For a more sympathetic account of Mrs. Hutchinson see Philip F. Gura's *A Glimpse of Sion's Glory* (1984).

AMERICAN LITERATURE 1700–1820

The first volume of Sacvan Bercovitch's *The Cambridge History of American Literature* (1994) offers a rich introduction to the literature of this period. David S. Shields contributes "British-American Belles Lettres," Michael T. Gilmore adds "The Literature of the Revolutionary and Early National Periods," and Robert Ferguson provides an overview to religious and philosophical matters in "The American Enlightenment, 1750–1820" (also issued as a separate volume in 1997). Shields has emerged as the most astute commentator on the complexity of eighteenth-century transatlantic literary relations. See his *Civil Tongues and Polite Letters in America* (1997), in which, among other topics, he treats the significance of club and manuscript culture, and *Oracles of Empire: Poetry, Politics, and Commerce in British America, 1690–1750* (1990). Hugh Amory and David D. Hall's edited *A History of the Boook in America Volume I* (2000) recounts the history of print culture during this period; see especially the contribution of James N. Green on Franklin. The early American novel is treated fully in Cathy S. Davidson's *Revolution and the World* (1986); and drama, in Jeffrey H. Richards's *Theater Enough* (1991), supplemented by Walter J. Meserve's *An Emerging Entertainment* (1977). Richards also edited a useful selection in *Early America Drama* (1997). Michael Warner's *Letters of the Republic* (1990) discusses the relation of literature to the emergence of the public sphere. Good overviews of the religious history of the period, and particularly of the pervasive influence of the Great Awakening, are Alan Heimert's *Religion and the American Mind* (1966), Jon Butler's *Awash in a Sea of Faith* (1990), and Richard Crawford's *Seasons of Grace* (1991). The significance of print culture to Edwards and the revivals is detailed in Frank Lambert's *Inventing the Great Awakening* (1999). Julie Ellison's *Cato's Tears and the Making of Anglo-American Emotion* (1999) and Julia A. Stern's *The Plight of Feeling* (1997) treat the importance of sentiment as a moral and philosophical category. Older but still useful works that provide overviews of literature and the arts in this period include Emory Elliot's *Revolutionary Writers* (1982), Kenneth Silverman's *A Cultural History of the American Revolution* (1976), Michael Kammen's *A Season of Youth* (1978), and Russel B. Nye's *The Cultural Life of the New Nation* (1960). Henry F. May's *The American Enlightenment* (1976) provides a similar service for philosophical issues. Women's evolving roles in the new republic are treated in Mary Beth Norton's *Liberty's Daughters* (1980) and *Founding Mothers and Fathers* (1996) and Linda Kerbert's *Women of the Republic* (1980). A good introduction to African American authors of the Atlantic Rim is Vincent Caretta's *Unchained Voices* (1996). Finally, those who seek to understand the immense significance of republican discourse in the new nation are urged to consult Gordon Wood's magisterial *The Creation of the American Republic* (1969).

John Adams and Abigail Adams

The best biography of John Adams is the two-volume study by Page Smith (1962). More recently, see John Ferling's *John Adams: A Life* (1992). A challenging critical biography is Joseph J. Ellis's *Passionate Sage: The Character and Legacy of John Adams* (1993). The best biography of Abigail Adams is Lynne Withey's *Dearest Friend* (1981). A recent biography is David McCullough's *John Adams* (2001). Paul C. Nagel has written a useful study of *The Adams Women* (1987). Earlier editions of the letters written between John and Abigail Adams have been superseded by the *Adams Family Correspondence* (1963), a two-volume collection edited by Lyman H. Butterfield.

Charles Brockden Brown

Sydney J. Krause et al. edited Brown's *Novels and Related Works* (1977–87) in a modern edition. In the past few decades, this novelist has had the benefit of many astute commentarics that view him as central to the development of the early American novel. Among these are Norman Grabo's *The Coincidental Art of Charles Brockden Brown* (1981), Steven Watts's *The Romance of Real Life* (1994), and Bill Christophersen's *The Apparition in the Glass* (1993). The best biography remains Harry R. Warfel's *Charles Brockden Brown* (1949). Cathy S. Davidson's section on Brown in her *Revolution and the Word* (1986) places him against emergent contemporary women novelists.

William Byrd

Byrd's prose works are available in an edition edited by Louis B. Wright (1966). *The Secret Diary of William Byrd of Westover, 1709–1712* (1941) was edited by Louis B. Wright and Marion Tinling. *Another Secret Diary of William Byrd of Westover, 1739–1741*, edited by M. H. Woodfin and M. Tinling, appeared in 1942. Byrd's *London Diary* (1958) was edited by Louis B. Wright and Marion Tinling. A provocative study is Kenneth A. Lockridge's *The Diary, and Life, of William Byrd II of Virginia, 1674–1744* (1987). A useful critical essay is Lewis P. Simpson's "William Byrd and the South," *Early American Literature* 7 (1972).

J. Hector St. John de Crèvecoeur

Sketches of Eighteenth Century America, More Letters of St. John de Crèvecoeur. (1925) was edited by H. L. Bourdin and co-workers. *Eighteenth Century Travels in Pennsylvania and New*

York (1962) was edited by P. G. Adams. The best biographies are by Thomas Philbrick (1970) and Gay Wilson Allen and Roger Asselineau (1987).

Jonathan Edwards

Yale University Press is in the process of publishing a complete edition of the works of Jonathan Edwards. Some of the editors of this project have issued *A Jonathan Edwards Reader* (1995), the best single-volume collection of Edwards's writings. Also useful are two recent collections of essays: Nathan O. Hatch and Harry S. Stout's edited *Jonathan Edwards and the American Experience* (1988) and Stephen J. Stein's edited *Jonathan Edwards's Writings* (1996). David Levin's *Jonathan Edwards: A Profile* (1969) includes Samuel Hopkins's *Life and Character of the Late Rev. Mr. Jonathan Edwards* (1765). Perry Miller's *Jonathan Edwards* (1949) and essays included in *Errand into the Wilderness* (1956) are indispensable. Daniel B. Shea Jr. includes a discussion of the *Personal Narrative* in his *Spiritual Autobiography in Early America* (1968). Richard Bushman's "Jonathan Edwards as a Great Man" appeared in *Soundings* 52 (1969), and Patricia J. Tracy considers the implications of his career in *Jonathan Edwards, Pastor* (1980). Barbara B. Oberg and Harry S. Stout edited *Benjamin Franklin, Jonathan Edwards, and the Representation of American Culture* (1993).

Olaudah Equiano

The Interesting Narrative was edited by Werner Sollors in a Norton Critical Edition in 2001. Sidney Kaplan in *The Black Presence in the Era of the American Revolution, 1770–1800* (1973) discusses the American publication of Equiano's *Narrative*. Vincent Carretta assembles the evidence concerning Equiano's birth in "Olaudah Equiano or Gustavus Vassa: New Light on an Eighteenth-Century Question of Identity," *Slavery and Abolition* (1999).

The Federalist

A very useful introduction to *The Federalist* papers is found in Benjamin Fletcher Wright's edition of 1961.

Benjamin Franklin

The Papers of Benjamin Franklin are being published by Yale University Press, which in 2002 brought out Edmund S. Morgan's biography, *Benjamin Franklin*. A good selection of Franklin's writings may be found in *Benjamin Franklin: Representative Selection* (1936), edited by F. L. Mott and C. L. Jorgensen. The standard biography is by Carl Van Doren (1938). Useful critical studies include Bruce I. Granger's *Benjamin Franklin, an American Man of Letters* (1964), Robert Middlekauff's *Benjamin Franklin and His Enemies* (1996), and Alfred O. Aldridge's *Benjamin Franklin and Nature's God* (1967). See also David Levin's "The Autobiography of Benjamin Franklin: The Puritan Experimenter in Life and Art," *Yale Review* 53 (1964). A famous unfavorable response to Franklin can be found in D. H. Lawrence's *Studies in Classic American Literature* (1923). Franklin's early years are discussed in A. B. Tourtellot's *Benjamin Franklin: The Boston Years* (1977). Francis Jennings wrote *Benjamin Franklin, Politician* (1996), and Nian-Sheng Huang surveys two hundred years of American response to Franklin in *Benjamin Franklin in America* (1994).

Philip Freneau

The standard edition of *The Poems of Philip Freneau* is that of F. L. Pattee, 3 vols. (1902–07). Lewis Leary, who edited *The Last Poems of Philip Freneau* (1945), wrote the best biography, *That Rascal Freneau: A Study in Literary Failure* (1941). A very useful introduction to Freneau can be found in Harry H. Clark's edition of *Philip Freneau: Representative Selections* (1929). Richard C. Vitzhum offers a study of Freneau's lyrics in *Land and Sea* (1978).

James Grainger

Very little has been written about Grainger. See Thomas W. Krise's headnote to his reprint of *The Sugar Cane* in *Caribbeana: An Anthology of English Literature of the West Indies, 1657–1777* (1999) and David Shields's discussion in *Oracles of Empire* (1990), where he also treats literature about the American staple colonies more generally.

Briton Hammon

The best discussion of Hammon is John Sekora's in "Red, White, and Black: Indian Captives, Colonial Printers, and the Early African-American Narrative," in *A Mixed Race* (1993), edited by Frank Shuffelton. Also see Vincent Carretta's *Unchained Voices* (1996).

Thomas Jefferson

Princeton University Press is currently engaged in publishing the *Papers of Thomas Jefferson*. The best biography is Dumas Malone's six-volume *Jefferson and His Time* (1948–81). Malone's article on Jefferson in *The Dictionary of American Biography* (1933) is very helpful. Useful critical studies include M. D. Peterson's *Thomas Jefferson and the New Nation* (1970), Garry Wills's *Inventing America: Jefferson's Declaration of Independence* (1978), and Pauline Maier's *American Scripture* (1997). Fawn Brodie published a controversial biography in 1974. Jefferson's Monticello is the subject of a distinguished study by William Howard Adams (1983). Joseph J. Ellis's *American Sphinx: The Character of Thomas Jefferson* is an important addition to Jefferson biography (1997) and Jay Fliegelman's *Declaring Independence* (1993) to the critical literature.

Sarah Kemble Knight

A useful biographical sketch by Sidney Gunn can be found in *The Dictionary of American Biography* (1933). G. P. Winship's edition of the *Private Journal* (1920) contains Theodore

Dwight's original introduction to the first edition (1825).

Sara Wentworth Morton

My Mind and Its Thoughts, in Sketches, Fragments, and Essays is available in a facsimile reprint with an introduction by W. K. Bottorff (1975). The standard life remains Emily Pendleton and Milton Ellis's *Philenia: The Life and Works of Sarah Wentworth Morton, 1759–1846* (1931).

Judith Sargent Murray

A modern reprint of *The Gleaner* is available with an introduction by Nina Baym (1992). *Selected Writings* (1995), edited by Sharon M. Harris, offers useful commentary on Murray's work. The standard life remains Vena Bernadette Field's *Constantia: A Study of the Life and Work of Judith Sargent Murray, 1751–1820* (1931).

Samson Occom

The published writings of Samson Occom are *A Short Narrative of My Life,* composed in 1768 but first published in Berndt Peyer's *The Elders Wrote: An Anthology of Early Prose by North American Indians, 1768–1931* (1982); *A Sermon Preached at the Execution of Moses Paul, an Indian* (1772); and *A Choice Collection of Hymns and Spiritual Songs, Intended for the Edification of Sincere Christians of All Denominations* (1774). After his death, Occom's account of the Montauks among whom he had lived and worked was published as "An Account of the Montauk Indians, on Long-Island," *Collections of the Massachusetts Historical Society* 10 (1809). Harold Blodgett's *Samson Occom,* Dartmouth College Manuscript Series No. 3 (1935), is dated, but full of useful biographical information; Blodgett also reprints most of Occom's extant letters. Preceding Blodgett's study was Leon Burr Richardson's *An Indian Preacher in England,* Dartmouth College Manuscript Series No. 2 (1933), which offers documents relating to Occom's fund-raising trip to England. Peyer's "Samson Occom, Mohegan Missionary of the 18th Century," *American Indian Quarterly* 6 (1982), offers a brief biographical account of Occom. "Christian Indians: Samson Occom and William Apes," in David Murray's *Forked Tongues: Speech, Writing and Representation in North American Indian Texts* (1991) is a fine consideration of Occom, and Michael Elliott's " 'This Indian Bait': Samson Occom and the Voice of Liminality," *Early American Literature* 29 (1994), is a sophisticated study. Laurie Weinstein's "Samson Occom: A Charismatic Eighteenth-Century Mohegan Leader" in her *Enduring Traditions: The Native Peoples of New England* (1994) is useful, along with Bernd Peyer's *The Tutor'd Mind: Indian Missionary-Writers in Antebellum America* (1997). Laura J. Murray's *To Do Good to My Indian Brethren:*

The Writings of Joseph Johnson, 1751–1776 (1998), an edition of the writing of a Mohegan who also attended Eleazar Wheelock's Indian school and who married Tabitha, the daughter of Samson Occom, has much useful information. See Colin Calloway's *The World Turned Upside Down: Indian Voices from Early America* (1994).

Thomas Paine

Moncure D. Conway, who edited *The Writings of Thomas Paine,* 4 vols. (1894–96), wrote the best life of Paine (1892). H. H. Clark's *Thomas Paine: Representative Selections* (1944) contains a very helpful introduction. Crane Brinton's entry in *The Dictionary of American Biography* (1933) is justly admired. Cecil Kenyon's "Where Paine Went Wrong," *American Political Science Review* 45 (1951), is a challenging critical assessment, as is Eric Foner's *Tom Paine and Revolutionary America* (1976). More recent biographies are by David F. Hawke (1974) and John Keane (1995).

Susanna Rowson

Rowson has profited from the current interest in women writers, and, in general, the most recent criticism of her work is the best. Patricia L. Parker's *Susanna Rowson* (1986) offers an excellent survey of Rowson's fiction as well as her work for the stage and gives the fullest account of her life. Blythe Forcey provides valuable insights on the development of the novel in her essay "*Charlotte Temple* and the End of Epistolarity," *American Literature* 63 (1991). Cathy N. Davidson (1986) and Ann Douglas (1991) give useful critical interpretations of *Charlotte Temple* in the introductions to their respective editions of the novel.

Moses Bon Sàam

Very little is known about Sàam. In *Caribbeana* (1999) Thomas W. Krise reprints Sàam's speech and discusses issues of provenance. Also see Wylie Sypher's *Guinea's Captive Kings* (1942).

Annis Boudinot Stockton

Carla Mulford's *Only for the Eye of a Friend: The Poems of Annis Boudinot Stockton* (1995) collects all of Stockton's poems and provides a thorough introduction to her life and work. Alfred Hoyt Bill and Constance M. Greiff provide a good account of Stockton's household in *A House Called Morven* (1978). Another important example of women's writing left in manuscript is *Milcah Martha Moore's Book* (1997), edited by Catherine La Courreye Blecki and Karin A. Wulf. The fullest treatment of manuscript culture in the eighteenth-century colonies is David Shields's *Civil Tongues and Polite Letters in British America* (1997). On the place of women in late-eighteenth-century American society, see Linda Kerber's *Women of the Republic* (1986) and Mary Beth Norton's *Liberty's Daughters* (1980).

Royall Tyler

In *Early American Drama* (1997), Jeffrey Richards reprints *The Contrast* as well as several other plays that establish Tyler's context. Marius Peladeau collected *The Verse of Royall Tyler* (1968). Donald Cook (1970) edited Tyler's novel *The Algerine Captive*. G. Thomas Tanselle provides his biography in *Royall Tyler* (1967).

Phillis Wheatley

The best edition of the poems is that edited by Julian D. Mason (1966, rev. 1989). Shirley Graham's *The Story of Phillis Wheatley* (1969) and William G. Allen's *Wheatley, Banneker, and Horton* (1970) are useful critical biographies. William H. Robinson edited *Critical Essays* (1982).

John Woolman

The standard edition is *The Journal and Major Essays of John Woolman* (1971), edited by Phillips P. Moulton. Amelia M. Gummere's edition of the journal (1927) contains a useful introduction. See also Daniel B. Shea Jr.'s *Spiritual Autobiography in Early America* (1968).

PERMISSIONS ACKNOWLEDGMENTS

John Adams and Abigail Adams: from volume I of THE ADAMS PAPERS: ADAMS FAMILY CORRESPONDENCE, edited by L. H. Butterfield. Cambridge, Mass.: The Belknap Press of Harvard University Press. Copyright © 1963 by the Massachusetts Historical Society. Reprinted by permission of the publisher.

William Bradford: from OF PLYMOUTH PLANTATION 1620–1647 by William Bradford, edited by Samuel Eliot Morison. Copyright 1952 by Samuel Eliot Morison and renewed 1980 by Emily M. Beck. Used by permission of Alfred A. Knopf, a division of Random House, Inc.

William Bright: "Coyote Establishes Fishing Taboos" from A COYOTE READER by William Bright. Copyright © 1992 The Regents of the University of California. Reprinted by permission of The Regents of the University of California and the University of California Press.

William Byrd: from THE PROSE WORKS OF WILLIAM BYRD OF WESTOVER, edited by Louis B. Wright. Cambridge, Mass.: Harvard University Press. Copyright © 1966 by the President and Fellows of Harvard College. Reprinted by permission of the publisher.

Bartolomé de Las Casas: from THE DEVASTATION OF THE INDIES: A BRIEF ACCOUNT by Bartolomé de Las Casas. English translation copyright © 1974 by The Crossroad Publishing Company. Reprinted by permission of The Continuum Publishing Company.

Bernal Díaz Del Castillo: from THE CONQUEST OF NEW SPAIN (pp. 92–94,214–19, 278–83, 387–88, 404–13) by Bernal Díaz, translated by J. M. Cohen (Penguin Classics, 1963). Copyright © J. M. Cohen, 1963. Reproduced by permission of Penguin Books Ltd.

Samuel de Champlain: from THE WORKS OF SAMUEL DE CHAMPLAIN (H. P. Biggar, General Editor), Vol. 1 and Vol. 3, trans. and edited by H. H. Langton and W. S. Ganong. Reprinted by permission of the Champlain Society.

Christopher Columbus: Letters from SELECT DOCUMENTS ILLUSTRATING THE FOUR VOYAGES OF COLUMBUS, translated and edited by Cecil Jane, published by the Hakluyt Society, London. Reprinted by permission of David Higham Associates Ltd.

Jonathan Edwards: from THE GREAT AWAKENING, Vol. 4 of THE WORKS OF JONATHAN EDWARDS, edited by C. C. Goen. Copyright © 1972 by Yale University. From TYPOLOGICAL WRITINGS, Vol. 11 of THE WORKS OF JONATHAN EDWARDS, edited by Wallace E. Anderson. Copyright © 1993 by Yale University. From LETTERS AND PERSONAL WRITINGS, Vol. 16 of THE WORKS OF JONATHAN EDWARDS. Copyright © 1998 by Yale University. Reprinted by permission of Yale University Press.

Thomas Jefferson: from NOTES ON THE STATE OF VIRGINIA by Thomas Jefferson. Edited, with an introduction and notes by William Peden. Copyright © 1955 by The University of North Carolina Press, renewed 1982 by William Peden. Used by permission of the publisher.

Arnold Krupat: Native American Trickster Tales, from NEW VOICES IN NATIVE AMERICAN LITERARY CRITICISM, edited by Arnold Krupat. Copyright © 1993 by the Smithsonian Institution. Reprinted by permission of the publisher.

Samson Occom: "A Short Narrative of My Life," by Samson Occom, from THE ELDERS WROTE: AN ANTHOLOGY OF EARLY PROSE BY NORTH AMERICAN INDIANS 1768–1931, edited by Berndt Peyer. Copyright © Dietrich Reimer Verlag, Berlin. Reprinted by permission of Dietrich Reimer Verlag and the Dartmouth College Library.

Paul Radin: "The Winnebago Trickster Cycle" from THE TRICKSTER: A STUDY IN INDIAN MYTHOLOGY by Paul Radin. Reprinted by permission of the publisher, Routledge.

John Smith: from THE COMPLETE WORKS OF CAPTAIN JOHN SMITH, 1580–1631, edited by Philip L. Barbour, with a foreword by Thad W. Tate. Copyright © 1986 by The University of North Carolina Press. Used by permission of the publisher.

Brian Swann: "Coyote, Skunk and Prairie Dog" from COMING TO LIGHT by Brian Swann. Copyright © 1995 by Brian Swann. Used by permission of Random House, Inc.

Edward Taylor: from *Preparatory Meditations* (Prologue, 8, 16, 22, 38, 42, First Series; 26, Second Series); from *God's Determinations* ("The Preface," "The Soul's Groan to Christ for Succor," "Christ's Reply," "The Joy of Church Fellowship Rightly Attended"); "Upon Wedlock and Death of Children," "Let By Rain," "Upon a Wasp, Chilled with Cold," "Huswifery," and "A Fig for Thee, Oh! Death!" from THE POEMS OF EDWARD TAYLOR, edited by Donald E. Stanford. Copyright © 1960, renewed 1988 by Donald E. Stanford. Published by Yale University Press in 1960; reissued by University of North Carolina Press in 1989. Reprinted by permission of Don D. Stanford. "Psalm Two (First Version)" from EDWARD TAYLOR'S MINOR POETRY, edited by Thomas M. and Virginia L. Davis. Copyright © 1981 by G. K. Hall & Company. Reprinted by permission of The Gale Group.

Álvar Núñez Cabeza de Vaca: excerpts from CABEZA DE VACA'S ADVENTURES IN THE UNKNOWN INTERIOR OF AMERICA, trans. by Cyclone Covey. Copyright © 1961 by Macmillan Publishing Company. Reprinted by permission of Simon & Schuster, Inc.

Garcilaso de la Vega: from "La Florida" by Garcilaso de la Vega, trans. by Charmion Shelby, from THE DE SOTO CHRONICLES, vol. 2. Copyright © 1993 by The University of Alabama Press. Reprinted by permission of the publisher, The University of Alabama Press.

Phillis Wheatley: from THE POEMS OF PHILLIS WHEATLEY, edited and with an introduction by Julian D. Mason Jr. Copyright © 1966 and renewed 1989 by The University of North Carolina Press. Used by permission of the publisher.

John Winthrop: from JOURNAL OF JOHN WINTHROP, edited by Richard S. Dunn, James Savage, and Laetitia Yeandle. Cambridge, Mass.: Harvard University Press. Copyright © 1996 by the President and Fellows of Harvard College. Reprinted by permission of the publisher.

John Woolman: excerpts from THE JOURNAL AND MAJOR ESSAYS OF JOHN WOOLMAN, edited by Phillips P. Moulton, 1971. Reprinted by permission of Friends United Press, Richmond, IN 47374.

Index